T0136996

Lecture Notes in Computer Science 12888

More information about this subseries at http://www.springer.com/series/7412

Yuxin Peng · Shi-Min Hu ·
Moncef Gabbouj · Kun Zhou ·
Michael Elad · Kun Xu (Eds.)

Image
and Graphics

11th International Conference, ICIG 2021
Haikou, China, August 6–8, 2021
Proceedings, Part I

 Springer

Editors
Yuxin Peng
Peking University
Beijing, China

Shi-Min Hu
Tsinghua University
Beijing, China

Moncef Gabbouj
Tampere University
Tampere, Finland

Kun Zhou
Zhejiang University
Hangzhou, China

Michael Elad
Technion – Israel Institute of Technology
Haifa, Israel

Kun Xu
Tsinghua University
Beijing, China

ISSN 0302-9743   ISSN 1611-3349   (electronic)
Lecture Notes in Computer Science
ISBN 978-3-030-87354-7   ISBN 978-3-030-87355-4   (eBook)
https://doi.org/10.1007/978-3-030-87355-4

LNCS Sublibrary: SL6 – Image Processing, Computer Vision, Pattern Recognition, and Graphics

This Springer imprint is published by the registered company Springer Nature Switzerland AG
The registered company address is: Gewerbestrasse 11, 6330 Cham, Switzerland

Preface

These are the proceedings of the 11th International Conference on Image and Graphics (ICIG 2021), which was supposed to be held in Haikou, China, during August 6–8, 2021, but was postponed due to COVID-19.

The China Society of Image and Graphics (CSIG) has hosted the series of ICIG conferences since 2000. ICIG is the biennial conference organized by the CSIG that focuses on innovative technologies of image, video, and graphics processing and fosters innovation, entrepreneurship, and networking. This time, the conference was organized by Hainan University. Details about the past conferences are as follows:

Conference	Place	Date	Submitted	Proceeding
First (ICIG 2000)	Tianjin, China	August 16–18	220	156
Second (ICIG 2002)	Hefei, China	August 15–18	280	166
Third (ICIG 2004)	Hong Kong, China	December 17–19	460	140
4th (ICIG 2007)	Chengdu, China	August 22–24	525	184
5th (ICIG 2009)	Xi'an, China	September 20–23	362	179
6th (ICIG 2011)	Hefei, China	August 12–15	329	183
7th (ICIG 2013)	Qingdao, China	July 26–28	346	181
8th (ICIG 2015)	Tianjin, China	August 13–16	345	170
9th (ICIG 2017)	Shanghai, China	September 13–15	370	172
10th (ICIG 2019)	Shanghai, China	August 23–25	384	183

For ICIG 2021, 421 submissions were received and 198 papers were accepted. To ease the search of a required paper in these proceedings, the accepted papers have been arranged into different sections according to their topic.

We sincerely thank all the contributors, who came from around the world to present their advanced work at this event. We would also like to thank all the reviewers, who carefully reviewed all submissions and made their valuable comments for improving the accepted papers. The proceedings could not have been produced without the invaluable efforts of the members of the Organizing Committee, and a number of active members of CSIG.

August 2021

Yuxin Peng
Shi-Min Hu
Moncef Gabbouj
Kun Zhou
Michael Elad
Kun Xu

Organization

Organizing Committee

General Chairs

Yaonan Wang   Hunan University, China
Laurence T. Yang   Hainan University, China
Ming Lin   University of Maryland at College Park, USA

Technical Program Chairs

Yuxin Peng   Peking University, China
Shi-Min Hu   Tsinghua University, China
Moncef Gabbouj   TUT, Finland
Kun Zhou   Zhejiang University, China

Organizing Committee Chairs

Mingming Cheng   Nankai University, China
Zhaohui Wang   Hainan University, China
Faouzi Alaya Cheikh   NTNU, Norway

Sponsorship Chairs

Rongrong Ji   Xiamen University, China
Yafeng Deng   Qihoo 360 Technology Co., Ltd., China

Finance Chair

Jing Dong   Institute of Automation, CAS, China

Special Session Chairs

Ioan Tabus   Tampere University, Finland
Jian Cheng   Institute of Automation, CAS, China

Award Chairs

Yirong Wu   Aerospace Information Research Institute, CAS, China
Ridha Hamila   Qatar University, Qatar
Jieqing Feng   Zhejiang University, China

Publicity Chairs

Sid Ahmed Fezza   INTTIC, Algeria
Zhi Jin   Sun Yat-sen University, China
Jimin Xiao   Xi'an Jiaotong-Liverpool University, China

Exhibits Chairs

Jinjian Wu	Xidian University, China
Drahansky Martin	Brno University of Technology, Czech Republic
Dong Wang	Dalian University of Technology, China

Publication Chairs

Michael Elad	Israel Institute of Technology, Israel
Kun Xu	Tsinghua University, China

Oversea Liaison Chairs

Yubing Tong	University of Pennsylvania, USA
Azeddine Beghdadi	University Sorbonne Paris Nord, France

Local Chair

Xiaozhang Liu	Hainan University, China

Tutorial Chairs

Hongkai Xiong	Shanghai Jiao Tong University, China
Yo-Sung Ho	GIST, South Korea
Zhanchuan Cai	MUST, Macau, China

Workshop Chairs

Yunchao Wei	UTS, Australia
Joaquín Olivares	University of Cordoba, Spain
Cheng Deng	Xidian University, China

Symposium Chairs

Chia-wen Lin	Tsing Hua University, Taiwan, China
Frederic Dufaux	CNRS, France

Website Chair

Zhenwei Shi	Beihang University, China

Area Chairs

Weihong Deng	Meina Kan	Huimin Lu	Hang Su
Jing Dong	Weiyao Lin	Wanli Ouyang	Hao Su
Hu Han	Risheng Liu	Jinshan Pan	Nannan Wang
Gao Huang	Jiaying Liu	Houwen Peng	Shuhui Wang
Di Huang	Si Liu	Xi Peng	Yunhai Wang
Xu Jia	Zhilei Liu	Boxin Shi	Xinchao Wang

Limin Wang
Dong Wang
Yunhai Wang
Yingcai Wu

Baoyuan Wu
Yong Xia
Guisong Xia
Junchi Yan

Shiqi Yu
Shanshan Zhang
Xi Sheryl Zhang
Xiaoyu Zhang

Liang Zheng
Xiaobin Zhu
Chao Zuo

Additional Reviewers

Haoran Bai
Xiaoyu Bai
Zhidong Bai
Bingkun Bao
Daniel Barath
Chunjuan Bo
Jintong Cai
Zewei Cai
Zhanchuan Cai
Anqi Cao
Jian Cao
Jianhui Chang
Di Chen
Han Chen
Hao Chen
Jinsong Chen
Shuaijun Chen
Wenting Chen
Xiaojun Chen
Xin Chen
Xiu Chen
Yang Chen
Yuanyuan Chen
Yuqing Chen
Zhibo Chen
Zhihua Chen
De Cheng
Yu Cheng
Zhanglin Cheng
Xiangtong Chu
Yang Cong
Hengfei Cui
Yutao Cui
Zhaopeng Cui
Enyan Dai
Ju Dai
Congyue Deng
Dazhen Deng

Jiajun Deng
Weijian Deng
Shangzhe Di
Jian Ding
Hao Du
Heming Du
Peiqi Duan
Yuping Duan
Jiahao Fan
Yao Fan
Yongxian Fan
Zejia Fan
Zhenfeng Fan
Sheng Fang
Xianyong Fang
Jieqing Feng
Qianjin Feng
Xiaomei Feng
Zunlei Feng
Chenping Fu
Jiahui Fu
Xueyang Fu
Jingru Gan
Difei Gao
Guangshuai Gao
Jiaxin Gao
Jun Gao
Ruochen Gao
Shang Gao
Ziteng Gao
Zhang Ge
Yuanbiao Gou
Heng Guo
Jie Guo
Senhui Guo
Xuyang Guo
Yingkai guo
Chunrui Han

Songfang Han
Xinzhe Han
Yahong Han
Yizeng Han
Zheng Han
Zhenjun Han
Shuai Hao
You Hao
Zhongkai Hao
Xiangyang He
Richang Hong
Yuchen Hong
Chenping Hou
JieBo Hou
Yunzhong Hou
Yuxuan Hou
Donghui Hu
Fuyuan Hu
Lanqing Hu
Peng Hu
Qingyong Hu
Ruimin Hu
Shishuai Hu
Yang Hu
Zhenzhen Hu
Yan Hu
Bao Hua
Haofeng Huang
Jun Huang
Shaofei Huang
Yan Huang
Zhenghua Huang
Zhenyu Huang
Xiaopeng Ji
Haozhe Jia
Mengxi Jia
Muwei Jian
Xinrui Jiang

Zeren Jiang
Zhiying Jiang
Lianwen Jin
Zhuochen Jin
Yongcheng Jing
Meina Kan
Yongzhen Ke
Jianhuang Lai
Nan Lai
Xing Lan
Hyeongmin Lee
Baohua Li
Boyun Li
Fenghai Li
Guozhang Li
Han Li
Hangyu Li
Hongjun Li
Jiaji Li
Ping Li
Ruihuang Li
Shuang Li
Wenbin Li
Wenhao Li
Yi Li
Yifan Li
Yixuan Li
Yunfan Li
Zekun Li
Zhuoshi Li
Zhuoxiao Li
Hao Liang
Min Liang
Zhifang Liang
Xin Liao
Zehui Liao
Yijie Lin
Chang Liu

Chenglin Liu
Hao Liu
Jie Liu
Jinyuan Liu
Liu Liu
Min Liu
Minghua Liu
Pengbo Liu
Qingshan Liu
Risheng Liu
Ruijun Liu
Shiguang Liu
Shuaiqi Liu
Si Liu
Wenyu Liu
Xuan Liu
Xuejing Liu
Yaohua Liu
Yaqi Liu
Yiguang Liu
Yipeng Liu
Yong Liu
Yu Liu
Yuchi Liu
Yunan Liu
Zhenguang Liu
Zimo Liu
Yang Long
Hongtao Lu
Hu Lu
Kaiyue Lu
Linpeng Lu
Tao Lu
Bin Luo
Weiqi Luo
Kai Lv
Youwei Lyu
Huimin Ma
Lizhuang Ma
Long Ma
Tengyu Ma
Xiaorui Ma
Xinzhu Ma
Yuhao Ma
Qirong Mao
Shitong Mao

Yongwei Miao
Weidong Min
Zhou Ning
Xuesong Niu
Weihua Ou
Xuran Pan
Guansong Pang
Bo Peng
Sida Peng
Xi Peng
Zhaobo Qi
Jiaming Qian
Rui Qian
Zhenxing Qian
Qingyang Wu
Jiayan Qiu
Xinkuan Qiu
Zelin Qiu
Zhong Qu
Wenqi Ren
Tushar Sandhan
Hanbo Sang
Nong Sang
Cai Shang
Shuai Shao
Zhiwen Shao
Chunhua Shen
Linlin Shen
Qian Shen
Yuefan Shen
Shurong Sheng
Haichao Shi
Jun Shi
Yongjie Shi
Zhenghao Shi
Zhenwei Shi
Shizhan Liu
Jaskirat Singh
Guoxian Song
Sijie Song
Bowen Sun
Haomiao Sun
Jiande Sun
Jianing Sun
Shitong Sun
Xiaoxiao Sun

Bin Tan
Haoteng Tang
Hong Tang
Shixiang Tang
Jun Tao
Zhou Tao
Yadong Teng
Zhan Tong
Jun Tu
Kurban Ubul
Thomas Verelst
Fang Wan
Renjie Wan
Beibei Wang
Bowen Wang
Ce Wang
Chengyu Wang
Di Wang
Dong Wang
Feipeng Wang
Fudong Wang
Guodong Wang
Hanli Wang
Hanzi Wang
Hongyu Wang
Hu Wang
Huiqun Wang
Jinwei Wang
Kaili Wang
Kangkan Wang
Kunfeng Wang
Lijun Wang
Longguang Wang
Mei Wang
Meng Wang
Min Wang
Qiang Wang
Runzhong Wang
Shengjin Wang
Shuhui Wang
Shujun Wang
Tao Wang
Dongsheng Wang
Wei Wang
Weizheng Wang
Wenbin Wang

Xiaoxing Wang
Xingce Wang
Xinhao Wang
Xueping Wang
Xun Wang
Yifan Wang
Yingqian Wang
Yongfang Wang
Yuehuan Wang
Zhengyi Wang
Zhihui Wang
Ziming Wang
Hongyuan Wang
Jinjia Wang
Jie Wei
Xiushen Wei
Ziyu Wei
Weifan Guan
Ying Wen
Di Weng
Shuchen Weng
Zhi Weng
Wenhua Qian
Kan Wu
Runmin Wu
Yawen Wu
Yicheng Wu
Zhongke Wu
Zizhao Wu
Zhuofan Xia
Fanbo Xiang
Tao Xiang
Wei Xiang
Wenzhao Xiang
Qinjie Xiao
Jingwei Xin
Xiaomeng Xin
Bowen Xu
Fang Xu
Jia Xu
Qian Xu
Shibiao Xu
Mingliang Xue
Xiangyang Xue
Xinwei Xue
Zhe Xue

Zhenfeng Xue	Wei Yin	Jiawan Zhang	Yifan Zhang
Ziyu Xue	Yongkai Yin	Jie Zhang	Zhanqiu Zhang
Xuejuan Wu	Zhaoxia Yin	Jing Zhang	Zhexi Zhang
Bin Yan	Zhenfei Yin	Junxing Zhang	Ziwei Zhang
Xin Yan	Chengyang Ying	Kaihua Zhang	Jie Zhao
Bangbang Yang	Di You	Pengyu Zhang	Tianxiang Zhao
Hongyu Yang	Baosheng Yu	Pingping Zhang	Wenda Zhao
Mouxing Yang	Hongyuan Yu	Runnan Zhang	Yan Zhao
Qisen Yang	Nenghai Yu	Shaoxiong Zhang	Qian Zheng
Shuo Yang	Zhenxun Yuan	Shizhou Zhang	Weishi Zheng
Xue Yang	Yuzhang Hu	Songyang Zhang	Chengju Zhou
Yiding Yang	Jiabei Zeng	Xiaoshuai Zhang	Chu Zhou
Yifang Yang	Geng Zhan	Xinfeng Zhang	Dawei Zhou
Yuansheng Yao	Yinwei Zhan	Xinpeng Zhang	Guijing Zhu
Yue Yao	Bohua Zhang	Xinyu Zhang	Jianqing Zhu
Jingwen Ye	Boyuan Zhang	Yanan Zhang	Mingrui Zhu
Shuainan Ye	Cuicui Zhang	Yanfu Zhang	Zijian Zhu
Yiwen Ye	Jialin Zhang	Yanhao Zhang	Yunzhi Zhuge
Zhichao Ye	Jianguo Zhang	Yaru Zhang	Junbao Zhuo

Contents – Part I

Object Detection and Recognition

Low-Level and Physics-Based Vision

Contents – Part II

Face, Gesture, and Body Pose

Contents – Part III

Computational Photography

Computer Graphics and Visualization

Motion and Tracking

Video Analysis and Understanding

Object Detection and Recognition

L2-CVAEGAN: Feature Aligned Generative Networks for Zero-Shot Learning

Jinhui Liu[✉] and Peng Zhao

School of Computer Science and Technology, Anhui University, Hefei, China
liujinhui-ahu@foxmail.com

Abstract. Many generative methods in zero-shot learning (ZSL) and generalized zero-shot learning (GZSL) perform data augmentation by random distribution. This naive strategy ignores the visual divergences of different classes, which will result in excessive differences between generated and real samples. In this work, random vectors sample from the real visual distribution encoded by the encoder. Therefore, the generated samples are more close to real-world samples. Additionally, the instances generated by GAN and VAE are not in the uniform numerical range, which causes the inconsistency of domain distributions. We perform domain alignment on visual features through L2 normalization. This strategy narrows variance between real and generated visual features. For fine-grained datasets, we set attribute, Word2Vec and Glove as the class-embedding vector of generative models. This natural way of semantic combination adds more potential information to each class. We name the proposed approach as L2-CVAEGAN, and conduct extensive experiments on several benchmark datasets. Compared with existing methods, these simple strategies lead to significant promotions. The comprehensive experiments of ZSL and GZSL prove the effectiveness of L2-CVAEGAN.

Keywords: Zero-shot learning · Generative adversarial networks · Domain alignment

1 Introduction

Deep learning is developing rapidly in computer vision. However, image recognition relies on the abundance of supervised instances. As a matter of fact, there are countless novel classes (unseen classes) required to be recognized in practical scenarios, but it is impossible to fetch various annotated samples. As we all know, humans are excellent at recognizing new objects that never saw before. Zero-shot learning (ZSL) focuses on the extreme case where training samples are absent. The concept of zero-shot learning was proposed by Palatucci and Hinton and attracted growing attentions [8,15,25].

The goal of conventional zero-shot learning [10,18] is to identify objects that have not emerged in training. Generalized zero-shot learning (GZSL) is a more realistic problem. It means that test images come from both seen and

© Springer Nature Switzerland AG 2021
Y. Peng et al. (Eds.): ICIG 2021, LNCS 12888, pp. 3–15, 2021.
https://doi.org/10.1007/978-3-030-87355-4_1

unseen classes. A straightforward strategy is Attribute-based method, which uses attribute to separate diverse classes. However, the visual features of identical classes possess plenty of inter-class divergences, which will arouse domain shift problem [5]. Embedding-based methods project visual features to attribute space. Different classes are clustered as fixed points in low-dimensional seman tic space, overlooking the variance in instances. It will give birth to the hubness problem [9]. Besides, if the manifold space composed of visual space and semantic space is inconsistent, it will bring about semantic gap problem [26].

To alleviate these issues, a few approaches based on generation emerged. Generative methods transform [13, 22, 27–30] the ZSL to a supervised classification problem by synthesizing pseudo training samples. However, these methods sample from Gaussian distribution to form arbitrary domain, but ignore the underlying visual distribution. Meanwhile, the numerical values of features generated by different models are inconsistent. We propose the feature domain alignment to mitigate this problem. The main contributions of this paper are summarized below.

- We propose the L2-CVAEGAN that leverages CVAE and CGAN to generate more realistic visual features, and we evaluate our model under ZSL and GZSL settings.
- The parameters of visual distributions obtained by the encoder are reparameterized to infer random variables. The random variables come from real distribution instead of Gaussian distribution.
- This model aligns domain distribution of visual features through L2 normalization, which can minimize the numerical difference between generated and real features.
- Our method assembles attributes and word vectors to form new auxiliary class embedding. We conduct extensive experiments on four widely used datasets. Experiment results consistently demonstrate satisfactory performance through the above modules.

The rest of this paper is organized as follows. We review related works of zero-shot learning and generative models in Sect. 2. In Sect. 3, we introduce the model L2-CVAEGAN and display relevant algorithm. The experiments of L2-CVAEGAN are discussed in Sect. 4. In the end, we summarize this paper with a discussion of future research in Sect. 5.

2   Related Work

2.1   Zero-Shot Learning

As one of the pioneering approaches, DAP [7] captures the relationship between image-label pairs by the combination of attributes. ConSE [14], ALE [21], SJE [1], Latem [25], ESZSL [19] learn a fixed mapping between images and semantics, and use different rank compatibility functions to identify corresponding labels. DeVISE [4] and SYNC [2] detect a deep embedding relationship between image and semantic by feature extraction backbone.

Unlike to learn a liner projection between visual and semantic space, our methods try to capture the latent relationship by deep networks to remedy the limitation of lacking visual information.

2.2 Generative Models

In recent years, generative methods have received tremendous concentration. The Variational Autoencoder (VAE) comprises an encoder and a decoder. CVAE [12] leveraged the attribute as the class embedding to learn the underlying probability distribution of image features. The Generating Adversarial Network (GAN) includes a generator and a discriminator, which can capture any distributions by a min-max game. The f-CLSWGAN [23] optimized the Wasserstein divergence to prevent mode collapse. The cycle-CLSWGAN [3] exerts regressor network and cycle consistency loss to promote the generation of WGAN.

Indeed, the joint structure is the dominant approach in Generation-based methods. CADA-VAE [20] utilizes cross-domain and alignment constraints to align the distribution between semantic and visual modality. GDAN [6] applies the regressor network and cycle consistency constraint to generate visual features similar to corresponding class prototype. The f-VAEGAN-D2 [24] combines WGAN and two discriminators, improve the interpretability of generated images by semantic retrieval. Our model uses the merits of GAN and VAE to execute data augmentation, and we leverage the feature domain alignment module to regularize sample numerical range.

3 Methodology

In this section, we formally describe the zero-shot learning and generalized zero-shot learning, give an overview of our proposed model, and introduce each component.

3.1 Setup

The class set in zero-shot learning can be split into disjoint seen subsets Y_U and unseen subsets Y_S, which can be represented as $(Y_U \cap Y_S = \emptyset)$. Let $D_S = \left\{ (x_i, y_i, c_i)|_{i=1}^{N_S} \right\}$, where $x_i \in X_S$ represents d-dimensional visual features obtained by CNN, $y_i \in Y_S$ represents label of x_i, and $c_i \in C$ are k dimensional class embedding vectors, which means we can choose attributes or word vectors flexibly. Furthermore, the auxiliary training set can be described as $D_U = \left\{ (y_i, c_i)|_{i=1}^{N_U} \right\}$, which means we just know the class label and class-embedding of unseen classes, while visual images are absent. That is to say, the goal of zero-shot learning is to learn a classifier $f_{ZSL} : x \rightarrow y_U$, which needs to predict unseen classes. In generalized zero-shot learning, both seen classes and unseen classes are likely to be predicted, and the learned classifier becomes $f_{GZSL} : x \rightarrow y_U \cup y_S$.

3.2   Model Overview

Previous methods do not consider the numerical range of visual features generated by different models. The VAE and GAN in our model synthesize more discriminative visual samples simultaneously. In addition, we align the feature domain distribution to ensure the consistency of generated features. Our model achieves stable training and better results through these measures. The proposed generative model L2-CVAEGAN is illustrated in Fig. 1, and the detailed process is in the following paragraph.

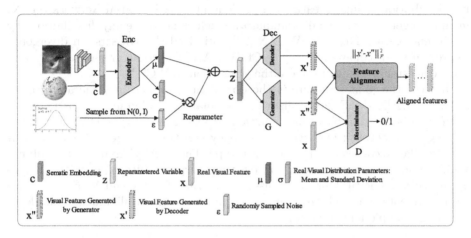

Fig. 1. The network architecture of L2-CVAEGAN model. The entire framework of the network consists of a visual distribution encoder (Enc) to get real domain distribution, a noise decoder (Dec) as well as a feature generator (G) to execute feature augmentation, a real/fake discriminator (D) to distinguish fake sample from real ones, and a feature domain alignment module to align the visual features synthesized by Dec and G.

Firstly, the visual features x and semantic embeddings c (attributes or word vectors) of seen classes are input into the network. Subsequently, the encoder network maps visual features to the latent space, and gets domain distribution parameters μ and σ. Then a noise vector ε is sampled from the Gaussian distribution and employs the reparameter technology $z = \sigma^* \varepsilon + \mu$ to crop a random variable z. After that, the random variable z and attribute are concatenated to train the generator and decoder. Finally, the generator and decoder can synthesize images of specified classes.

3.3   Our Proposed Method

The Regularization and Reconstruction Loss. Conditional Variational Autoencoder (CVAE) wants to maximize the generated sample probability through max $\log\left(p_\theta(x|z,c)\right)$, and the decomposed formulation is:

$$L_{L2-CVAE} = KL\left(q_\varphi(z|x,c)\|p_\theta(z|c)\right) - \mathbf{E}\left[\log p_\theta(x|z,c)\right] \qquad (1)$$

In Eq. (1), the $q_\varphi(z|x,c)$ desires to gain the distribution of underlying variable z through image x and the semantic c. The $p_\theta(x|z,c)$ aims to generate images x at a given latent distribution and class embedding. Above distributions can be seen as encoder and decoder. Besides, θ and φ are corresponding parameters.

The first term denotes the Kullback-Leibler divergence between $q_\varphi(z|x,c)$ and $p_\theta(z|c)$. We name this term as the distribution regularization L_{reg}, where the $p_\theta(z|c)$ is treated as a Gaussian distribution. The second term stands for the reconstruction loss of images, and the $E[\sim]$ denotes the expectation of this term. We use L_{rec} to symbolize this reconstruction loss, which indicates the mean square error (MSE) between real and generated images.

Generator and Discriminator Loss. CGAN consists of a generator $G(x|z,c)$ and a discriminator $D(x;c)$, and α, λ are the parameters of the generator and the discriminator respectively. The $G(x|z,c)$ inputs a class embedding vector and random sampled noise, output a generated image. The $D(x;c)$ inputs a pair of samples and outputs a discriminant value. The random variables in our model come from the encoder, rather than directly sample from Gaussian distribution, which can be represented as $z = Enc(x_s, c)$, and the objective function of CGAN is:

$$L_{CGAN} = E_{p_{data}(x)}[\log(D(x,c))] + E_{p_z(z)}[\log(1 - D(G(Enc(x_s,c),c)))] \quad (2)$$

When the generator or discriminator needs to be optimized, the other module remains fixed. The objective function $V(D,G)$ can be minimized or maximized, which can be formulated as,

$$\min_G \max_D V(D,G) = \min_G \max_D L_{CGAN} \quad (3)$$

Feature Domain Distribution Alignment Loss. Existing joint approaches use GAN and VAE to synthesize new image features, but overlook that the parameters of different generative models are not shared. The synthetic samples from the joint model no longer follow the unified visual distribution. Synthetic data from multiple domains will bring difficulties to the training of classifiers.

To avoid the divergence of domain distribution, this work proposes the feature domain distribution alignment loss, which aligns the visual features generated by VAE and GAN. The real and generated image features are aligned uniformly in terms of L2 normalization, which can be written as:

$$L_{ALN} = L2(G(z,c), Dec(z,c)) = \sum_{i=1}^{N} \left(\|x'_{i1} - x'_{i2}\|_F^2 + \sum_{j=1}^{2} \|x'_{ij} - x_i\|_F^2 \right) \quad (4)$$

Among them, i represents the i-th class that needs to be generated, and j represents the j-th generation module (generator or decoder). Therefore, x'_i represents the image generated for the i-th class, and x'_{ij} is images of i-th class generated by the j-th generation module. Besides, $\|\sim\|_F^2$ represents the difference between different visual features.

By minimizing the numerical difference between visual features, the range of feature domain can be aligned, and generated features are more close to real features.

Overall Objective of L2-CVAEGAN. We describe the above regularization loss, reconstruction loss, the loss of GAN, and feature alignment loss. As well, we get the overall objective function:

$$L_{L2-CVAEGAN} = L_{rec} + L_{reg} + L_{CGAN} + L_{ALN} \qquad (5)$$

The training processes of our L2-CVAEGAN are as follows: we first train the CVAE using Eq. (1), then we train the GAN in an adversarial way by Eq. (3). After then, we execute the feature alignment through Eq. (4).

Algorithm 1 describes the overall optimization procedure of L2-CVAEGAN. We will introduce the implementation details in the experiment.

Algorithm 1: The optimization of L2-CVAEGAN

Input: Seen class datasets $D_s = \{(x_i, y_i, c_i)\}_{i=1}^{N_S}$, iterator number: N_{iter}
Output: Learned parameters $\varphi, \theta, \alpha, \lambda$ of L2-CVAEGAN
1. Randomly initialize $\varphi, \theta, \alpha, \lambda$
2. **For** iter=1: N_{iter} **Do**
3. Sample x_i, y_i, c_i from D_s
4. Use encoder $q_\varphi(x_i, c_i)$ to get μ and σ
5. Sample $\mathcal{E}$ from N(0,I), reparameterize $\mathcal{E}$ by $z = \sigma^* \varepsilon + \mu$
6. Use decoder $p_\theta(z_i, c_i)$ to get x_i'
7. Compute the reconstruction loss L_{rec} and regularization loss L_{reg}
8. Use generator $G(z_i, c_i)$ to get x_i''
9. Use discriminator $D(x_i, c_i)$ to get the feature is real or fake
10. Compute the GAN loss L_{CGAN}
11. Compute the feature domain alignment loss L_{ALN}
12. g $\leftarrow \nabla(L_{rec} + L_{reg} + L_{CGAN} + L_{ALN})$
13. Update parameters through gradient descent optimization
14. **End For**
15. Use decoder and generator to generate unseen class feature
Return $\varphi, \theta, \alpha, \lambda$

Once the generative model has been trained, it can generate samples for any class. The generated visual features and labels become the training set (x', y_U) to train the classifier. In the prediction, the images of unseen classes are delivered to the optimized classifier, and the labels can be output.

3.4 Evaluation Protocol

There are two typically used evaluation protocols for zero-shot classification: Average Per-class Top-1 Accuracy (Top-1 Accuracy) and Mean Average Precision (mAP). We employ the mAP as the benchmark to evaluate the performance of our model, which can assess the overall accuracy and alleviate the class imbalance.

In the more realistic generalized zero-shot learning, the prediction result can be evaluated by the Harmonic Mean (H) [26], which is:

$$H = \frac{2 \times ACC_S \times ACC_U}{ACC_S + ACC_U} \times 100\% \tag{6}$$

where ACC_S is the accuracy of seen classes, as well ACC_U expresses the accuracy of unseen classes. This protocol can achieve a fair metric accuracy.

4 Experiments

In this part, we validate our L2-CVAEGAN in zero-shot learning and generalized zero-shot learning. In detail, we present the benchmark datasets, compare with other competing models, visualize and analyze results. In the end, we test the effect of generalized zero-shot learning and semantic combinations.

4.1 Settings

DataSets. The widely used datasets in zero-shot learning include Animals with Attributes (AwA) [15], Animals with Attributes 2 (AWA2) [26], Caltech UCSD Birds 200-2011 (CUB) [22] and SUN Attribute dataset (SUN) [16]. Statistics for each dataset are presented in Table 1.

Table 1. Statistics for different zero-shot learning datasets.

Dataset	#seen classes	#unseen classes	#images	#attribute dimension	#grain
CUB	150	50	11788	312	fine
SUN	645	72	14340	102	coarse
AWA	40	10	30475	85	coarse
AWA2	40	10	37322	85	coarse

CUB is a fine-grained bird dataset, which contains 11788 images from 200 classes. SUN is a scenery dataset with 717 classes of scenes and 14340 images. AWA dataset has 30475 images from 50 animal classes, which is a coarse-grained dataset, but is restricted to be downloaded. Xian et al. proposed the AWA2 dataset, which possesses 37322 images from 50 classes.

Visual Features. In ZSL and GZSL settings, we evaluate our model on CUB, AWA, AWA2, and SUN datasets by the splits of [26]. All images are rescaled to 224×224 pixels, then fed into the pre-trained ResNet-101 to obtain 2048-dim CNN features for each dataset.

Semantic Representations. We leverage two types of semantics: attribute and word vector. The word vectors used in zero-shot learning mainly include Word2Vec [11] and Glove [17], which are extracted from Wikipedia articles. In the fine-grained dataset CUB, we combine word vectors with attributes to form new auxiliary class-embeddings. In other datasets, we use attribute as the side information of each class.

Implementation Details. We set the epoch of VAE and GAN to 25 and 10. The VAE and GAN are trained by mini-batch gradient descent with Adam optimizer. All models have the dropout of 0.8 to reduce the risk of over-fitting. We set the batch size to 64 for all datasets. We use a traditional KNN classifier to test the model effects.

4.2   Comparing with Different Methods

To evaluate the effect of L2-CVAEGAN in zero-shot learning, we carry on comparisons of our model with others. The performance of L2-CVAEGAN is compared with 12 works. We provide results of zero-shot learning in Table 2.

We observe that L2-CVAEGAN achieves preferable performance than other methods in most zero-shot learning tasks. The average accuracy achieved 1.3% and 0.9% promotion than state-of-the-art in AWA2 and SUN. Compared with other generative models, when random noise comes from real visual features, the generated samples are more helpful for the classifier.

Table 2. Zero-shot learning accuracy for different methods in widely used datasets.

Type	Method	CUB	AWA	AWA2	SUN
Traditional methods	DAP	40.0%	44.1%	46.1%	39.9%
	CONSE	34.3%	45.6%	44.5%	38.8%
	ALE	54.9%	59.9%	62.5%	58.1%
	SJE	53.9%	65.6%	61.9%	53.7%
	ESZSL	53.9%	58.2%	58.6%	54.5%
	SAE	28.6%	47.4%	50.2%	37.4%
	SYNC	54.4%	54.0%	46.6%	56.3%
Deep learning methods	DeViSE	52.0%	54. 2%	59. 7%	56. 5%
	GDAN	46.4%	50.2%	49.1%	52.5%
	CADA-VAE	54.8%	57.7%	61.6%	60.0%
	F-CLSWGAN	**55.8%**	63.7%	64.2%	60.1%
	CVAE	54.3%	62.1%	64.6%	60.2%
Our methods	w/o VAE	47.7%	55.0%	59.5%	53.7%
	w/o Align	53.0%	63.0%	61.9%	60.5%
	L2-CVAEGAN	55.7%	**67.2%**	**66.0%**	**61.4%**

However, the accuracy of CUB is not the highest, which is because the fine-grained data set has more subjective components only through semantic attribute annotation, so it is necessary to supplement different dimensional features at the attribute level. In the following, we combine different types of CUB semantics, increase the representation ability of category information, and prove the effect of semantic combination through experiments.

In our methods, the first line (w/o VAE) denotes the effect of L2-CGAN. The second line (w/o Align) indicates CVAEGAN without alignment. The last line (L2-CVAEGAN) is the result of our proposed method. We found that the discrimination mechanism and feature alignment are beneficial to promote the prediction.

Generally speaking, L2-CVAEGAN can generate unseen class images effectively and achieve accurate classification.

4.3 Visualization and Analyzing

We display the confusion matrix to display the prediction effects of different categories in the AWA data set in Fig. 2.

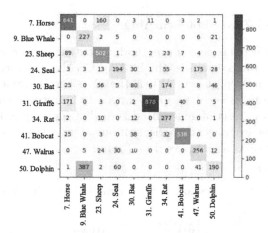

Fig. 2. The confusion matrix of prediction result in the AWA dataset. The x-axis is the true label of each category, and the y-axis is the label predicted by the classifier.

After comparison, we find that most samples are correct, but a few of seals are predicted to walrus. Besides, some bats are predicted to rats, and a lot of dolphins are predicted to be blue whales. Blue whale, walrus, seal, and dolphin, bat and rat are close in shape or environment, which increases prediction difficulty.

For convenient display of the prediction effect, we visualize the original unseen class samples and the generated samples of AWA by t-SNE. The visualization is illustrated in Fig. 3.

 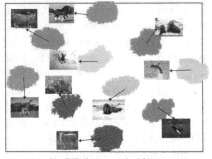

(a) t-SNE of real visual features   (b) t-SNE of generated visual features

Fig. 3. The t-SNE presentation of real (a) and generated (b) sample points for unseen classes in the AWA dataset.

We empirically found that a few real samples will map to the neighbors of other classes, while the pseudo visual features generated make the intra-class distance smaller and the inter-class distance bigger. This seemingly simple manner can help the classifier to recognize a similar category more easily.

4.4   Generalized Zero-Shot Learning

To point out the effectiveness of our method, we extend our model to generalized zero-shot learning. In other words, the L2-CVAEGAN generates visual features of both seen and unseen classes. When the classifier is trained, unseen class samples and remaining seen class samples need to be recognized.

The evaluation criteria of generalized zero-shot learning is Harmonic Mean (H) in Eq. (6). The accuracy comparison of our approach and seven generalized zero-shot learning tasks are displayed in Table 3.

Table 3. Results of different methods under generalized zero-shot learning settings(%).

Method	CUB			AWA			AWA2			SUN		
	U	S	H	U	S	H	U	S	H	U	S	H
ALE	23.7	62.8	34.4	16.8	76.1	27.5	14.0	81.8	23.9	21.8	33.1	26.3
IAP	0.2	72.8	4.1	0.9	87.6	1.8	0.2	72.8	0.4	1.0	37.8	1.8
SJE	23.5	52.9	33.6	11.3	74.6	19.6	8.0	73.9	14.4	14.7	30.5	19.8
ESZSL	12.6	63.8	21.0	6.6	75.6	12.1	5.9	77.8	11.0	11.0	27.9	15.8
SYNC	11.5	70.9	19.8	8.9	87.3	16.2	10.0	90.5	18.0	7.9	43.3	13.4
SAE	7.8	54.0	13.6	–	–	–	1.1	82.2	2.2	8.8	18.0	11.8
DEVISE	23.8	53.0	32.8	13.4	68.7	22.4	17.1	74.7	27.8	16.9	27.4	20.9
Ours	25.6	53.7	**34.7**	34.3	83.2	**48.5**	36.0	87.4	**51.0**	21.5	36.6	**27.1**

We find that our method surpasses most traditional generalized zero-shot learning methods via the Harmonic Mean benchmark. Compared with these traditional GZSL methods, our method achieves state-of-the-art on CUB, AWA, AWA2 and SUN datasets, which also proves the effectiveness of our method in GZSL settings.

4.5 Effect of Semantic Combination

For fine-grained birds dataset CUB, using attribute as class embedding alone cannot describe all aspects of each class prototype. Therefore, we utilize word vectors and attributes in CUB, and combine each other.

This way of semantic combination gets rid of manually searching for specific potential information. At the same time, this method can increase the diversity of semantic descriptions, instead of relying on existing different attribute features, so that the model can learn a richer class level representation.The experiment was carried out under identical settings, and the results are reported in Table 4.

Table 4. Results of semantic combination.

Type	Dimension	mAP (%)
Glove	300	12.18
Word2Vec	300	12.35
Word2Vec+Glove	300+300	18.01
Attribute	312	32.93
Attribute+Glove	312+300	34.48
Attribute+Word2Vec	312+300	**40.82**

In terms of experiments, we found that it is not favorable for using Glove and Word2Vec only to generate unseen class images. While the combination of Glove and Word2Vec can achieve a small promotion. After combined with attributes, the effect of classification can be greatly improved. Compared with only using the attribute, the combination of Glove, Word2Vec reached 2.55% to 8.09% promotion, respectively.

5 Conclusion

In this paper, a promising Generation-based method is proposed. Besides, the real feature distribution and feature domain alignment are used to generate visual images. As well, the semantic combinations are used to magnify the diversity of class descriptions. Future extensions of our method include few-shot learning (FSL) and more accurate generative framework.

Acknowledgements. This work was supported by the Natural Science Foundation of Anhui Province (2008085MF219, 1908085MF188, 1908085MF182), and the Key Research and Development Program of Anhui Province (1804d08020309).

References

1. Akata, Z., Reed, S.E., Walter, D., Lee, H., Schiele, B.: Evaluation of output embeddings for fine-grained image classification. In: IEEE Conference on Computer Vision and Pattern Recognition, pp. 2927–2936 (2015)
2. Changpinyo, S., Chao, W., Gong, B., Sha, F.: Synthesized classifiers for zero-shot learning. In: 2016 IEEE Conference on Computer Vision and Pattern Recognition, pp. 5327–5336 (2016)
3. Felix, R., Vijay Kumar, B.G., Reid, I., Carneiro, G.: Multi-modal cycle-consistent generalized zero-shot learning. In: Ferrari, V., Hebert, M., Sminchisescu, C., Weiss, Y. (eds.) ECCV 2018. LNCS, vol. 11210, pp. 21–37. Springer, Cham (2018). https://doi.org/10.1007/978-3-030-01231-1_2
4. Frome, A., et al.: Devise: a deep visual-semantic embedding model. In: Advances in Neural Information Processing Systems 26: 27th Annual Conference on Neural Information Processing Systems, pp. 2121–2129 (2013)
5. Fu, Y., Hospedales, T.M., Xiang, T., Fu, Z., Gong, S.: Transductive multi-view embedding for zero-shot recognition and annotation. In: Fleet, D., Pajdla, T., Schiele, B., Tuytelaars, T. (eds.) ECCV 2014. LNCS, vol. 8690, pp. 584–599. Springer, Cham (2014). https://doi.org/10.1007/978-3-319-10605-2_38
6. Huang, H., Wang, C., Yu, P.S., Wang, C.D.: Generative dual adversarial network for generalized zero-shot learning. In: IEEE Conference on Computer Vision and Pattern Recognition, pp. 801–810 (2019)
7. Lampert, C.H., Nickisch, H., Harmeling, S.: Learning to detect unseen object classes by between-class attribute transfer. In: 2009 IEEE Computer Society Conference on Computer Vision and Pattern Recognition, pp. 951–958 (2009)
8. Larochelle, H., Erhan, D., Bengio, Y.: Zero-data learning of new tasks. In: Proceedings of the Conference on Artificial Intelligence, pp. 646–651 (2008)
9. Lazaridou, A., Dinu, G., Baroni, M.: Hubness and pollution: Delving into cross-space mapping for zero-shot learning. In: Proceedings of the 7th International Joint Conference on Natural Language Processing, pp. 270–280 (2015)
10. Liu, Z., Li, Y., Yao, L., Wang, X., Long, G.: Task aligned generative meta-learning for zero-shot learning. In: Thirty-Fifth AAAI Conference on Artificial Intelligence, AAAI 2021, Thirty-Third Conference on Innovative Applications of Artificial Intelligence, IAAI 2021, The Eleventh Symposium on Educational Advances in Artificial Intelligence, EAAI 2021, Virtual Event, 2–9 February 2021, pp. 8723–8731 (2021)
11. Mikolov, T., Sutskever, I., Kai, C., Corrado, G., Dean, J.: Distributed representations of words and phrases and their compositionality. In: Advances in Neural Information Processing Systems 26: 27th Annual Conference on Neural Information Processing Systems, pp. 3111–3119 (2013)
12. Mishra, A., Reddy, M., Mittal, A., Murthy, H.A.: A generative model for zero shot learning using conditional variational autoencoders. In: 2018 IEEE Conference on Computer Vision and Pattern Recognition Workshops, pp. 2188–2196. IEEE Computer Society (2017)
13. Mishra, A., Pandey, A., Murthy, H.A.: Zero-shot learning for action recognition using synthesized features. Neurocomputing **390**, 117–130 (2020)
14. Norouzi, M., et al.: Zero-shot learning by convex combination of semantic embeddings. In: 2nd International Conference on Learning Representations (2014)
15. Palatucci, M., Pomerleau, D., Hinton, G.E., Mitchell, T.M.: Zero-shot learning with semantic output codes. In: Advances in Neural Information Processing Systems 22: 23rd Annual Conference on Neural Information Processing Systems, pp. 1410–1418. Curran Associates, Inc. (2009)

16. Patterson, G., Hays, J.: Sun attribute database: Discovering, annotating, and recognizing scene attributes. In: 2012 IEEE Conference on Computer Vision and Pattern Recognition, pp. 2751–2758 (2012)
17. Pennington, J., Socher, R., Manning, C.: Glove: Global vectors for word representation. In: Proceedings of the 2014 Conference on Empirical Methods in Natural Language Processing, pp. 1532–1543 (2014)
18. Qin, P., Wang, X., Chen, W., Zhang, C., Xu, W., Wang, W.Y.: Generative adversarial zero-shot relational learning for knowledge graphs. In: The Thirty-Fourth AAAI Conference on Artificial Intelligence, pp. 8673–8680 (2020)
19. Romera-Paredes, B., Torr, P.H.S.: An embarrassingly simple approach to zero-shot learning. In: Proceedings of the 32nd International Conference on Machine Learning, vol. 37, pp. 2152–2161 (2015)
20. Schonfeld, E., Ebrahimi, S., Sinha, S., Darrell, T., Akata, Z.: Generalized zero- and few-shot learning via aligned variational autoencoders. In: IEEE Conference on Computer Vision and Pattern Recognition, pp. 8247–8255 (2019)
21. Socher, R., Ganjoo, M., Manning, C.D., Ng, A.Y.: Zero-shot learning through cross-modal transfer. In: Annual Conference on Neural Information Processing Systems 2013, pp. 935–943 (2013)
22. Welinder, P.: Caltech-UCSD birds 200. California Institute of Technology (2010)
23. Xian, Y., Lorenz, T., Schiele, B., Akata, Z.: Feature generating networks for zero-shot learning. In: 2018 IEEE Conference on Computer Vision and Pattern Recognition, pp. 5542–5551 (2018)
24. Xian, Y., Sharma, S., Schiele, B., Akata, Z.: F-VAEGAN-D2: a feature generating framework for any-shot learning. In: IEEE Conference on Computer Vision and Pattern Recognition, pp. 10275–10284 (2019)
25. Xian, Y., Akata, Z., Sharma, G., Nguyen, Q.N., Hein, M., Schiele, B.: Latent embeddings for zero-shot classification. In: 2016 IEEE Conference on Computer Vision and Pattern Recognition, pp. 69–77 (2016)
26. Xian, Y., Schiele, B., Akata, Z.: Zero-shot learning - the good, the bad and the ugly. In: 2017 IEEE Conference on Computer Vision and Pattern Recognition, pp. 3077–3086 (2017)
27. Xing, N., Liu, Y., Zhu, H., Wang, J., Han, J.: Zero-shot learning via discriminative dual semantic auto-encoder. IEEE Access 9, 733–742 (2021)
28. Xu, T., Zhao, Y., Liu, X.: Dual generative network with discriminative information for generalized zero-shot learning. Complexity 2021, 6656797:1–6656797:11 (2021)
29. Zhang, Z., Li, Y., Yang, J., Li, Y., Gao, M.: Cross-layer autoencoder for zero-shot learning. IEEE Access 7, 167584–167592 (2019)
30. Zhong, F., Chen, Z., Zhang, Y., Xia, F.: Zero- and few-shot learning for diseases recognition of citrus aurantium l. using conditional adversarial autoencoders. Comput. Electron. Agric. 179, 105828 (2020)

HQ-Trans: A High-Quality Screening Based Image Translation Framework for Unsupervised Cross-Domain Pedestrian Detection

Gelin Shen[1], Zhi-Ri Tang[2(✉)], Peng Shen[1], and Yang Yu[1(✉)]

[1] College of Intelligence Science and Technology, National University of Defense Technology, Changsha, China
[2] School of Microelectronics, Wuhan University, Wuhan, China

Abstract. Pedestrian detection plays an important role in the research of computer vision, which has been used in many areas. Pedestrian detection is mainly to classify and locate pedestrians in a given input image, whose performance greatly depends on the number of annotations. When faced with unlabeled scenes in the target domain, the performance of a detector is severely degraded. Based on the above, an unsupervised image translation framework is adopted to generate an intermediate domain between the source and the target domains, which can effectively improve the cross-domain pedestrian detection performance. However, due to the instability of the translation network, some unsatisfactory images might be generated in the newly generated intermediate domain. Therefore, we propose a new method to process these unsatisfactory images. First, a blind image quality assessment framework is adopted on the original dataset, which aims to select relatively high-quality images as the training set for the translation framework and remove relatively low-quality images. Second, the image quality assessment framework is also adopted on the newly generated domain, which retain relatively high-quality generated images and replace the low-quality images with the corresponding images in the source domain. Finally, a new mixed domain, which is obtained from the above process, is applied to cross-domain pedestrian detection. The experimental results show that the proposed method can help to achieve good performance. Compared with some latest works, the proposed method can also achieve state-of-the-art performance under miss rate metrics.

Keywords: Unsupervised pedestrian detection · Image translation · Image quality assessment · Intermediate domain

1 Introduction

Pedestrian detection technology has been widely used in practical applications. The main goal of pedestrian detection is to classify and locate pedestrians, whose

© Springer Nature Switzerland AG 2021
Y. Peng et al. (Eds.): ICIG 2021, LNCS 12888, pp. 16–27, 2021.
https://doi.org/10.1007/978-3-030-87355-4_2

performance largely depends on the number of annotations. Due to differences including instance density, scene, resolution and others between source and target domains, a well-trained model will face serious performance degradation in the target domain [21, 26, 29]. For this reason, unsupervised cross-domain pedestrian detection framework needs to be developed.

To our knowledge, it can be achieved from the perspective of minimizing the difference between the images in the source and target domains. The image translation framework, which can generate a set of target-like images based on source domain, can be adopted to generate an intermediate domain between the source and target domains [35]. Although it is a feasible way, the stability of image translation framework is usually poor, which may lead a bad translation result and even a worse cross-domain detection performance.

In this work, a new framework named HQ-Trans, which is a high-quality screen based image translation framework, is proposed for unsupervised cross-domain pedestrian detection. Our contributions can be summarized as follows:

1) A blind image assessment framework is adopted to filter low-quality images in original source and target domains before the training of image translation framework, which can help the translation framework to learn from better and higher-quality images;
2) After generation of the intermediate domain, the image quality assessment framework is adopted to screen the low-quality generated images, which can help to obtain training images with higher-quality in the intermediate domain;
3) Experimental results on two benchmark pedestrian detection datasets show that our method can help to improve the unsupervised detection performance. Comparisons with some state-of-the-art works also show the efficiency of the proposed HQ-Trans.

2 Related Work

2.1 Image Translation

Conditional GAN (CGAN) [18] is one of the earliest methods used in image translation, and is used in pixel-to-pixel to learn the mapping between domains. However, as a supervised framework, paired images are required during training. In practical applications, a large number of paired datasets are often difficult to obtain. Therefore, some unsupervised image translation frameworks have been proposed recently, including CycleGAN [35] and UNIT [14]. However, the above works cannot explain the multi-modality of image translation. A single image in one domain can be translated to a diverse output image in another domain by BicycleGAN [36], while MUNIT [11] and DRIT [12] encode the content and attributes of global images. Besides the above image-level translation without considering object instances. InstaGAN [20] was presented to solve instance-level translation, and furthermore, Detection-based Unsupervised Image Translation (DUNIT) [2], which extracted representations for global images and local instances, and then merged them into a public representation to generate translated images.

2.2   Object Detection

Traditional object detection relies on pre-defined anchors of different sizes and proportions to obtain the height and width of the target instances. Anchor-based detectors can be divided into two main types: two-stage and one-stage. Representative studies of two-stage detectors are Faster R-CNN [23] and R-FCN [5], which generate candidate bounding boxes for the targets and then give the classification results. In one-stage detectors, such as YOLO [22], it does not generate candidates for the targets, thereby increasing the processing speed of the entire system.

In addition to the above-mentioned anchor-based detectors, some new types of anchor-free detectors have been proposed in recent years, such as Corner-Net [8], FSAF [34], and FCOS [27]. In addition, CSP [16] also proposed a detection head, which can predict the center point and scale from the feature map extracted by the deep convolutional neural network (CNN) directly [30,31].

2.3   Unsupervised Pedestrian Detection

In 2014, X. Zeng et al. [32] proposed a pedestrian detection classifier for specific scenes, X. Wang et al. [28] also proposed another pedestrian detection framework for specific scenarios, which consists of four steps and weights the samples. L. Liu et al. [13] proposed a deep domain adaptation method for unsupervised pedestrian detection in 2016. In 2017, T. Adel et al. [1] proposed a loose covariate offset hypothesis for UDA, which proposed a general generative modeling method. Faster R-CNN was also modified into a domain adaptive version by Y. Chen et al. [3] in 2018. A. Roychowdhury et al. [24] proposed an automatic adaptation of the detection framework to the target domain in 2019. As a new technology, GAN has been used for image-level domain bridging in some recent studies. H.K. Hsu et al. [10] applied GAN to generate a new domain between the source domain and the target domain.

3   Method

We consider introducing image generation technology to perform scene translation, where an intermediate domain is generated from the source data with the style characteristics of the target domain. Due to the similarity of style features, it can improve the cross-domain detection performance to a certain extent. To help to avoid the influence from instability of translation framework, it is considered to process the datasets appropriately before and after image translation, mainly using a blind image quality assessment (IQA) framework to improve the quality of the images in the intermediate domain. An overview of the proposed framework is shown in Fig. 1.

3.1   The First Screening

Firstly, a blind IQA framework named NIQE [19] is applied to score the images of the source and target domains in the original datasets. The relatively low-quality images are removed and the scene translation framework is trained using

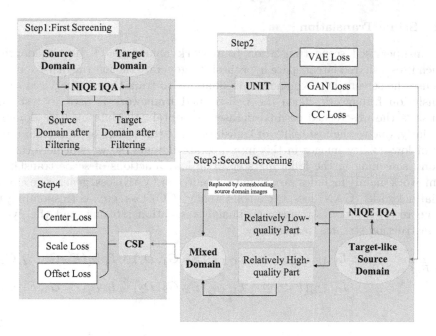

Fig. 1. An overview of the proposed framework.

relatively high-quality images. If the number of remaining high-quality images is too few, it is not conducive to extracting effective features. On the other hand, the number of high-quality images should not be too large, otherwise the screening method will have no obvious effect.

NIQE is a classic no-reference IQA framework that only needs to evaluate the deviation of the statistical information in the image. It is a "completely blind" IQA framework, which is suitable for giving scores to images and reducing the impact of low-quality images. The lower the NIQE score, the higher the image quality. The NIQE index is described by the distance between the multivariate gaussian model (MVG) fitting of a simple but highly regular natural scene statistics (NSS) model in the natural and the distorted images:

$$D(\mu_1, \mu_2, \sigma_1, \sigma_2) = ((\mu_1 - \mu_2)^T (\frac{\sigma_1 + \sigma_2}{2})^{-1} (\mu_1 - \mu_2))^{\frac{1}{2}} \tag{1}$$

Through the processing of scoring and screening the original datasets, the quality of the images in the intermediate domain can be improved, which helps reduce the negative effects caused by the instability of the translation framework, and is conducive to achieving stable and effective cross-domain detection results.

3.2   Scene Translation

An unsupervised scene translation framework named UNIT [14] is adopted, which uses a shared latent space hypothesis to generate the intermediate domain. We use the screened source and target domains to train the unsupervised scene translation framework. Then the well-trained framework is used to test and translate the unscreened original datasets to obtain the intermediate domain. Similarly, due to the instability of translation network, there are a certain number of low-quality images in this intermediate domain, so we will perform the second screening in the following step. The loss functions of scene translation framework mainly includes variational autoencoder (VAE) loss, generative adversarial networks (GAN) loss, cycle consistency (CC) loss, etc., corresponding to image reconstruction streams, the image translation streams, and the cycle-reconstruction streams, respectively:

$$\min_{E_1,E_2,G_1,G_2} \max_{D_1,D_2} L_{VAE_1}(E_1,G_1) + L_{GAN_1}(E_1,G_1,D_1) + L_{CC_1}(E_1,G_1,E_2,G_2)$$

$$L_{VAE_2}(E_2,G_2) + L_{GAN_2}(E_2,G_2,D_2) + L_{CC_2}(E_2,G_2,E_1,G_1)$$

$$(2)$$

3.3   The Second Screening

For the generated intermediate domain, due to the inevitable low-quality images generated by the instability of the translation network, we use NIQE again to filter the datasets by scene. The difference is that for the subsequent detection steps, we should maintain the amount of the datasets is the same as the original datasets, so that it is convenient to effectively show the improvement on detection performance using the proposed method. First, we replace the low-quality images eliminated by the screening with the corresponding images in the original datasets, and then combine them with the high-quality generated images in the intermediate domain to form a mixed domain for cross-domain pedestrian detection in the next step. Based on the above steps, the mixed domain not only has the style characteristics of the target domain, but also has clear content characteristics, including pedestrians, backgrounds, and roads, of the source domain, which can help to improve the detection accuracy under the unsupervised cross-domain settings.

3.4   Pedestrian Detector

Finally, we use the CSP detector as backbone to evaluate the performance of our proposed method for unsupervised cross-domain pedestrian detection. The CSP detector is a kind of novel anchor-free detector, which needs no preset anchors and gives detection results based on center and scale prediction. CSP detector uses a set of detection heads to seek the center and scale of targets, whose loss function consists of center classification, scale regression, and offset regression losses, denoted as L_{center}, L_{scale}, and L_{offset}, respectively. The loss function is:

$$L = \lambda_c L_{center} + \lambda_s L_{scale} + \lambda_o L_{offset} \tag{3}$$

where λ_c, λ_s, and λ_o represent the weights of L_{center}, L_{scale}, and L_{offset}, respectively.

4 Experiments

4.1 Experiment Settings

Implement Details. RTX 2080Ti GPU is applied as experiment platform and ResNet-50 [9] is chosen as the backbone of the detection network with batch size equaling to 1. For the training of Citypersons [33], training image size is set as $240 * 480$, the initial learning rate is set to $2 * 10^{-4}$. For the training of Caltech [7], training image size is set as $240 * 320$, the initial learning rate is set to $1 * 10^{-4}$. λ_c, λ_s, and λ_o are set as 0.01, 1, and 0.1, respectively.

Datasets. We choose Caltech [7] and CityPersons [33], which are two benchmark pedestrian detection datasets, to evaluate the performance of the proposed method. The Caltech dataset was mainly shot on a small car, which contains about 10 h of 30 Hz video, marked with about 350,000 rectangular boxes and 2300 pedestrians. The CityPersons dataset is a new set of high-quality pedestrian detection dataset with bounding box annotations provided on the Cityscapes [4] dataset. Evaluations follow standard Caltech metrics [7], which is log-average miss rate over false positive per image in $[10^{-2}, 10^0]$ (denoted as MR^{-2}).

4.2 Experimental Results and Analysis

We compare the images translated from the dataset after the first screening with the images directly translated from the original dataset, denoted as Filtered-Once dataset, UNIT-Only dataset, respectively, as shown in Fig. 2. It can be seen that the images in Filtered-Once dataset are better.

But at the same time, there are some low-quality images in the images obtained by the translation of the datasets after the first screening. To this end, a statistical distribution of the generated images is given, where Fig. 3 shows the histogram generated after scoring the quality of the datasets using IQA. Figure 3(a) is the quality distribution diagram of a scene under CityPersons in the intermediate domain before secondary screening, while Fig. 3(b) is only used the quality distribution map in the same scene of the intermediate domain generated by translation framework. It can be seen that when using translation framework directly, the quality scores are mainly concentrated between 12 and 14. In the images generated by translation after a screening, the quality distribution is more scattered, and the number of images, whose scores are below 12,

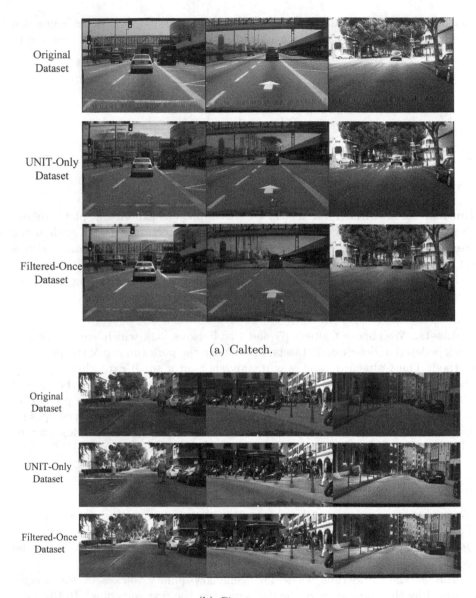

(a) Caltech.

(b) Citypersons.

Fig. 2. Some samples of the datasets in various situations: (a) Caltech dataset, (b) Citypersons dataset, in (a), the sky of the first two images in the UNIT-Only dataset is distorted compared to the original image, the road surface of the third image has water-like distortion. The effect is relatively better in the corresponding Filtered-Once dataset. In (b), the color distortions of the road surface, the bottom of the pillars, etc. appear in the UNIT-Only dataset, and they are displayed in red, while no obvious color distortion can be seen in the corresponding Filtered-Once dataset. (Color figure online)

is obviously increased, which means that the number of high-quality images has increased significantly. However, the number of images, whose scores are higher than 14, has also increased, that is, the number of low-quality images has also increased. This also proves the necessity of secondary screening. We replace the low-quality image in the intermediate domain with the corresponding original images, while retaining the improved high-quality images in the intermediate domain.

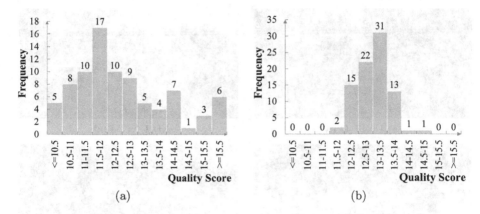

(a)   (b)

Fig. 3. Histogram of the quality of the dataset. (a) High-Quality. (b) With translation framework directly. "Quality Score" represents the scoring of the dataset using NIQE, and "Frequency" represents the number of images in the score segment.

The cross-domain detection results are shown in Table 1, where "Original" indicates the cross-domain results without any changes, "UNIT-Only" indicates the results training from intermediate domain generated by translation framework directly, "HQ-Trans" indicates the results using the proposed method, and "Oracle" indicates the supervised detection results using CSP detector. It can be seen that HQ-Trans can help to improve the unsupervised detection performance under both experimental settings, where the lowest miss rates among the three are marked in bold in the table.

Furthermore, we qualitatively compare the cross-domain detection results in Fig. 4, where the green boxes represent the correctly detected pedestrians, the yellow boxes indicate the invalid detection results, and the red boxes indicate the missed pedestrians. It can be seen that HQ-Trans can help to give more correct detection boxes and reduce the number of invalid and missed boxes effectively.

4.3 Comparisons with Other Works

To compare with state-of-the-art works, five works, including ACF [6], Adapted FasterRCNN [33], ALFNet [17], PRNet [25], and APGAN [15], which have unsupervised cross-domain detection performance from Citypersons to Caltech are

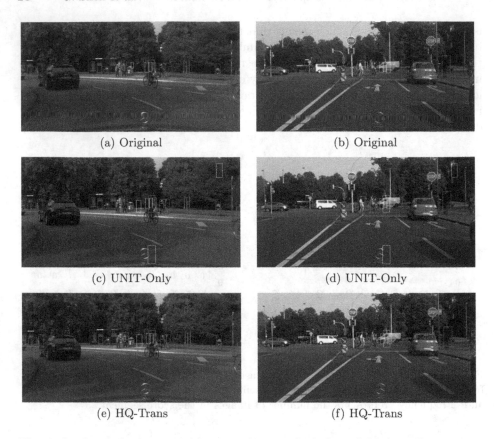

(a) Original

(b) Original

(c) UNIT-Only

(d) UNIT-Only

(e) HQ-Trans

(f) HQ-Trans

Fig. 4. Qualitatively comparisons among three methods from Caltech to Citypersons. Compared with Original, UNIT-Only has improved the detection performance to a certain extent, but produced additional redundant detection results on the other hand, which shows that the instability of UNIT has a certain negative effect on the detection performance. In HQ-Trans, there are more correct detection results and fewer redundant detection results. (Color figure online)

Table 1. Unsupervised cross-domain detection performance from Caltech to Citypersons and from Citypersons to Caltech. The best experiment results are shown in bold.

Caltech —> Citypersons		Citypersons —> Caltech	
Training datasets	$MR^{-2}(\%)$	Training datasets	$MR^{-2}(\%)$
Original	55.94	Original	19.13
UNIT-Only	55.34	UNIT-Only	11.55
HQ-Trans	**52.50**	HQ-Trans	**10.69**
Oracle	23.28	Oracle	8.04

introduced, where the comparisons are shown in Table 2. While compared with other frameworks in miss rate, HQ-Trans can succeed ACF by about 40–41%, Adapted FasterRCNN by about 10–11%, ALFNet by about 14–15%, PRNet by about 7–8%, and APGAN by about 9–10%. From the above results, it can be seen that the proposed HQ-Trans can achieve state-of-the-art unsupervised cross-domain pedestrian detection performance.

Table 2. Unsupervised cross-domain detection performance and comparisons with state-of-the-art works from Citypersons to Caltech. The best experiment results are shown in bold.

Citypersons —> Caltech							
Method	ACF [6]	Adapted FasterRCNN [33]	ALFNet [17]	PRNet [25]	APGAN [15]	Ours	Oracle
MR^(−2)(%)	51.28	21.18	25.0	18.3	20.5	**10.69**	8.04

5 Conclusion

Based on the introduction of the image translation framework to unsupervised cross-domain pedestrian detection, this paper proposed a new framework named HQ-Trans aiming to improve the image quality of the intermediate domain, and then improve the performance of cross-domain detection. The data processing operation is carried out by scoring and screening using the blind image quality assessment framework. Experimental results on two benchmark datasets prove that our proposed HQ-Trans can help to improve the cross-domain pedestrian detection performance effectively. Furthermore, compared with some other latest works, HQ-Trans can also succeed them by no less than 7% in miss rate, which shows our method has the state-of-the-art performance. In the future, there are also some methods that can be further improved: 1. Fuse the image quality assessment into image translation directly, rather than give scores before and after translation; 2. Adopt image quality assessment framework to generate high-quality pedestrians in source data, aiming to improve generalization ability of well-trained models.

Acknowledgement. This work was supported by the National Natural Science Foundation of China (62006239).

References

1. Adel, T., Zhao, H., Wong, A.: Unsupervised domain adaptation with a relaxed covariate shift assumption. In: Proceedings of the AAAI Conference on Artificial Intelligence, vol. 31 (2017)
2. Bhattacharjee, D., Kim, S., Vizier, G., Salzmann, M.: Dunit: detection-based unsupervised image-to-image translation. In: 2020 IEEE/CVF Conference on CVPR (2020)

3. Chen, Y., Li, W., Sakaridis, C., Dai, D., Gool, L.V.: Domain adaptive faster R-CNN for object detection in the wild. In: 2018 IEEE/CVF Conference on CVPR (2018)
4. Cordts, M., Omran, M., Ramos, S., Rehfeld, T., Schiele, B.: The cityscapes dataset for semantic urban scene understanding. In: 2016 IEEE Conference on CVPR (2016)
5. Dai, J., Li, Y., He, K., Sun, J.: R-FCN. object detection via region based fully convolutional networks. Curran Associates Inc. (2016)
6. Dollar, P., Appel, R., Belongie, S., Perona, P.: Fast feature pyramids for object detection. IEEE Trans. PAMI **36**(8), 1532–1545 (2014)
7. Dollar, P., Wojek, C., Schiele, B., Perona, P.: Pedestrian detection: a benchmark. In: Proceedings of Conference on CVPR, pp. 304–311 (2009)
8. Duan, K., Bai, S., Xie, L., Qi, H., Huang, Q., Tian, Q.: Centernet: keypoint triplets for object detection. In: ICCV (2019)
9. He, K., Zhang, X., Ren, S., Jian, S.: Deep residual learning for image recognition. In: IEEE Conference on CVPR (2016)
10. Hsu, H.K., Yao, C., Tsai, Y.H., Hung, W.C., Yang, M.H.: Progressive domain adaptation for object detection. In: 2020 IEEE WACV (2020)
11. Huang, X., Liu, M.-Y., Belongie, S., Kautz, J.: Multimodal unsupervised image-to-image translation. In: Ferrari, V., Hebert, M., Sminchisescu, C., Weiss, Y. (eds.) ECCV 2018. LNCS, vol. 11207, pp. 179–196. Springer, Cham (2018). https://doi.org/10.1007/978-3-030-01219-9_11
12. Lee, H.Y., Tseng, H.Y., Huang, J.B., Singh, M.K., Yang, M.H.: Diverse image-to-image translation via disentangled representations (2018)
13. Liu, L., Lin, W., Wu, L., Yu, Y., Yang, M.Y.: Unsupervised deep domain adaptation for pedestrian detection. In: Hua, G., Jégou, H. (eds.) ECCV 2016. LNCS, vol. 9914, pp. 676–691. Springer, Cham (2016). https://doi.org/10.1007/978-3-319-48881-3_48
14. Liu, M.Y., Breuel, T., Kautz, J.: Unsupervised image-to-image translation networks (2017)
15. Liu, S., Guo, H., Hu, J.G., Zhao, X., Tang, M.: A novel data augmentation scheme for pedestrian detection with attribute preserving GAN. Neurocomputing **401**, 123–132 (2020)
16. Liu, W., Liao, S., Ren, W., Hu, W., Yu, Y.: High-level semantic feature detection: a new perspective for pedestrian detection. In: 2019 IEEE/CVF Conference on CVPR (2020)
17. Liu, W., Liao, S., Hu, W., Liang, X., Chen, X.: Learning efficient single-stage pedestrian detectors by asymptotic localization fitting. In: Proceedings of the ECCV, pp. 618–634 (2018)
18. Mirza, M., Osindero, S.: Conditional generative adversarial nets. Computer Science, pp. 2672–2680 (2014)
19. Mittal, A., Soundararajan, R., Bovik, A.C.: Making a 'completely blind' image quality analyzer. IEEE Signal Process. Lett. **20**(3), 209–212 (2013)
20. Mo, S., Cho, M., Shin, J.: Instagan: instance-aware image-to-image translation (2018)
21. Qwu, E., Tang, Z., Xiong, P., Wei, C.F., Song, A., Zhu, L.: ROpenPose: a rapider OpenPose model for astronaut operation attitude detection. IEEE (2021)
22. Redmon, J., Divvala, S., Girshick, R., Farhadi, A.: You only look once: unified, real-time object detection. In: CVPR (2016)

23. Ren, S., He, K., Girshick, R., Jian, S.: Faster R-CNN: towards real-time object detection with region proposal networks. IEEE Trans. Pattern Anal. Mach. Intell. **39**(6), 1137–1149 (2015)
24. Roychowdhury, A., Chakrabarty, P., Singh, A., Jin, S.Y., Learned-Miller, E.: Automatic adaptation of object detectors to new domains using self-training. In: 2019 IEEE/CVF Conference on CVPR (2019)
25. Song, X., Zhao, K., Chu, W.-S., Zhang, H., Guo, J.: Progressive refinement network for occluded pedestrian detection. In: Vedaldi, A., Bischof, H., Brox, T., Frahm, J.-M. (eds.) ECCV 2020. LNCS, vol. 12368, pp. 32–48. Springer, Cham (2020). https://doi.org/10.1007/978-3-030-58592-1_3
26. Tang, Z., et al.: A multilayer neural network merging image preprocessing and pattern recognition by integrating diffusion and drift memristors. IEEE (2020)
27. Tian, Z., Shen, C., Chen, H., He, T.: FCOS: fully convolutional one-stage object detection. In: 2019 IEEE/CVF ICCV (2020)
28. Wang, X., Meng, W., Li, W.: Scene-specific pedestrian detection for static video surveillance. IEEE Trans. Pattern Anal. Mach. Intell. **36**(2), 361–74 (2014)
29. Wu, E.Q., et al.: Detecting fatigue status of pilots based on deep learning network using EEG signals. IEEE (2020)
30. Wu, E.Q., et al.: Nonparametric Bayesian prior inducing deep network for automatic detection of cognitive status. IEEE (2020)
31. Wu, E.Q., et al.: Nonparametric hierarchical hidden semi-Markov model for brain fatigue behavior detection of pilots during flight. IEEE (2021)
32. Zeng, X., Ouyang, W., Wang, M., Wang, X.: Deep learning of scene-specific classifier for pedestrian detection. In: Fleet, D., Pajdla, T., Schiele, B., Tuytelaars, T. (eds.) ECCV 2014. LNCS, vol. 8691, pp. 472–487. Springer, Cham (2014). https://doi.org/10.1007/978-3-319-10578-9_31
33. Zhang, S., Benenson, R., Schiele, B.: Citypersons: a diverse dataset for pedestrian detection. In: 2017 IEEE Conference on CVPR (2017)
34. Zhu, C., He, Y., Savvides, M.: Feature selective anchor-free module for single-shot object detection. In: 2019 IEEE/CVF Conference on CVPR (2019)
35. Zhu, J.Y., Park, T., Isola, P., Efros, A.A.: Unpaired image-to-image translation using cycle-consistent adversarial networks. IEEE (2017)
36. Zhu, J.Y., Zhang, R., Pathak, D., Darrell, T., Shechtman, E.: Toward multimodal image-to-image translation (2017)

FER-YOLO: Detection and Classification Based on Facial Expressions

Hui Ma[1]($^{(\boxtimes)}$) (iD), Turgay Celik[1,2] (iD), and Hengchao Li[1] (iD)

[1] Southwest Jiaotong University, Chengdu 610031, China
[2] University of the Witwatersrand, Johannesburg 2000, South Africa

Abstract. Due to the wide application prospect and market value of emotion recognition, it has become an important research topic in today's society. Among them, facial expression recognition (FER) plays an important role in expressing human emotional information. Generally, the FER classification process includes face pre-processing (face detection, alignment, etc.), which adds extra workload. To this end, detection and classification are carried out simultaneously in this paper. We first manually annotated the RAF-DB dataset. We then designed an end-to-end FER network with better performance and applied it to facial expressions called FER-YOLO. FER-YOLO is built on the basis of YOLOv3. We combine the squeeze-and-excitation (SE) module with the backbone network and assign a certain weight to each feature channel so that FER-YOLO can focus on learning prominent facial features. We also discussed the performance changes caused by the lightweight enhanced feature extraction networks. Experimental results show that the proposed FER-YOLO network is 3.03% mAP higher than YOLOv3 on the RAF-DB dataset.

Keywords: Emotion recognition · Facial Expression Recognition (FER) · Detection · Convolutional Neural Network (CNN)

1 Introduction

Emotion recognition is a popular research topic in computer vision and pattern recognition. With the development of artificial intelligence and deep learning technology, as well as the widespread application of emotion recognition in the fields of emotion computing [1], human-computer interaction [2], auxiliary medical [3], intelligent monitoring and security, entertainment industry [4], remote education [5], emotional state analysis [6] and other fields have attracted the attention of many researchers. Emotions play an active and important role in daily human communication. It can be expressed by detecting physiological signals such as breathing, heart rhythm, and body temperature and by detecting emotional behaviors such as facial expressions, language, and posture.

Southwest Jiaotong University.

Among them, facial expressions contain rich human emotion information. Emotional changes in human hearts will lead to different degrees of changes in facial expressions, indicating the daily emotions of human beings as well as subtle and complex emotional changes. In addition, emotional recognition based on facial expression recognition [7–9] is simple, and facial expression images are easy to capture.

The research and development of facial expression recognition can accelerate the advancement of research and technological development in machine vision, human-computer interaction, psychology, etc., and help demonstrate and analyze new interdisciplinary theories and methods. Facial expression recognition methods are divided into traditional methods and deep learning-based methods. The traditional FER method includes three steps: pre-processing (detection, alignment, etc.), feature extraction, and face image classification. Unlike traditional FER, deep learning-based methods allow end-to-end learning directly from the input image, reducing reliance on pre-processing and the cost of manually extracting features. Because deep neural networks' automatic learning has the advantage of discrimination, the FER method based on deep learning is better than the traditional FER method [10–12]. GPU computing technology development further promotes facial expression recognition based on deep learning to become the mainstream of today's research. There are also many research achievements in facial expression recognition based on deep learning.

Zou et al. [7] improved the convolutional neural network by using batch regularization, ReLU activation function, and Dropout technology. Singh et al. [8] studied the static images based on CNN in the cases of pre-processing and without pre-processing, respectively. Mohan et al. [10] proposed a FER-net network, which first automatically learns facial image features through the FER-net network and then recognizes them through the Softmax classifier. Xie et al. [11] designed two CNNs to extract local features and global features of the face images and obtain rich face information by fusing the two features to complete the classification.

The above-mentioned facial expression recognition method based on deep learning separately completes face image detection and classification tasks independently. With the rapid development of object detection technology based on deep learning, it is possible to simultaneously complete detection and classification tasks. In 2015, Redmon et al. [13] proposed YOLO (You Only Look Once), which was the first one-stage detector. Later, YOLOv2(YOLO9000) [14], YOLOv3 [15], and YOLOv4 [16] were extended on the basis of YOLO. Yolo divided the image into different regions and simultaneously predicted each region's bounding box and possibilities. To improve accuracy, YOLOv2 first modified the pre-trained classification network's resolution to 448×448 and then removed the fully connected layer (to obtain more spatial information) and used anchor boxes to predict bounding boxes. YOLOv3 introduces the FPN structure to realize multi-scale prediction. The backbone feature extraction network uses a better classification network, Darknet53, and the classification loss function uses Binary Cross-entropy Loss instead of Softmax. YOLOv4 has been improved on the basis of YOLOv3, mainly by changing the backbone feature extraction network Darknet53 into CSPDarknet53 and enhancing the feature extraction network using SPP and PANET structures as well as data augmentation techniques. In 2016, Liu et al. [17] proposed the SSD model. SSD adopts the structure of the pyramidal feature hierarchy and introduces the prior box, which has the advantage of mean Average Precision (mAP) compared with YOLO. In 2017, Lin et al. [18] proposed RetinaNet. RetinaNet alleviates the problem of data imbalance by introducing a focal loss function.

Although the above one-stage object detection methods have achieved excellent results in many fields, they are rarely used in FER tasks to the best of our knowledge. In this paper, we have applied FER tasks based on one-stage object detection methods. First, we manually annotated the RAF-DB dataset. Then based on YOLOV3, the SE [19] module is combined with the Backbone module to improve the ability to enhance the feature extraction network. We also discussed the performance changes caused by the lightweight enhanced feature networks.

2   Methodology

2.1   Model Architecture

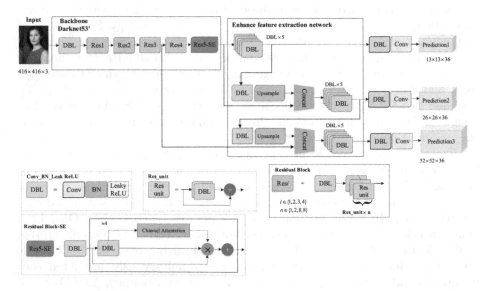

Fig. 1. The architecture of FER-YOLO, which includes the backbone network (red dashed line), enhance feature extraction network (blue dashed line) and result prediction. (Color figure online)

In this paper, the FER-YOLO network model architecture based on FER is shown in Fig. 1. The backbone feature extraction network uses Darknet-53' with the fully connected layer removed. Enhance feature extraction network fuses three scales feature maps. In order to improve the performance of the feature extraction network, the SE module is introduced into the Res5 residual block (Res5-SE). Res5-SE aims to extract more useful information from the deep features of the backbone network. Compared with datasets dedicated to object detection, although the facial expression dataset has a single characteristic, it still contains many environmental backgrounds. In the facial expression recognition task, pre-processing is usually carried out to remove the image background and reduce the difficulty of recognition. Unlike other general facial expression recognition methods, FER-YOLO input data does not have any pre-processing steps. Our input data contains a lot of background information and the size of the input image is $416 \times 416 \times 3$.

Finally, output the prediction results corresponding to the three feature layers, and the shape of the output layer is $13 \times 13 \times 36$, $26 \times 26 \times 36$ and $52 \times 52 \times 36$. $36 = 3 \times (7 + 4 + 1)$, where, 3 is the three prior boxes, 7 is the number of expression categories, 4 is the parameters of x, y, w, and h, and 1 is the detection of objects.

2.2   Channel Attention

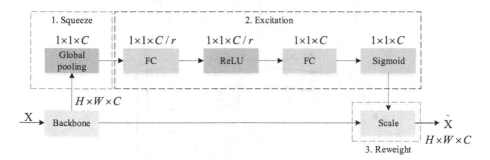

Fig. 2. FER-YOLO channel attention, including squeeze module (red dotted line), excitation module (blue dotted line) and reweight module (green dotted line). (Color figure online)

In order to enable the FER-YOLO network to learn more discriminative features and improve accuracy, this paper uses the channel attention mechanism to recalibrate the depth feature maps extracted by the backbone network. Equivalent to input enhanced feature extraction network information is more discriminant.

As shown in Fig. 2, FER-YOLO channel attention consists of the squeeze module (red dotted line), the excitation module (blue dotted line), and the reweight module (green dotted line). The squeezing operation compresses each feature channel of the output U ($U \in R^{W \times H \times C}$) of the backbone through the global average pooling layer to obtain a $1 \times 1 \times C$ real number sequence. The excitation module is composed of two fully connected layers, in which the scaling parameter r is used to reduce the number of channels and thus reduce the amount of calculation. Empirically, here we set it to 4. After the channel attention, the input and output shapes are the same, but each position's value has been re-corrected.

2.3   Depth-Wise Separable Convolution

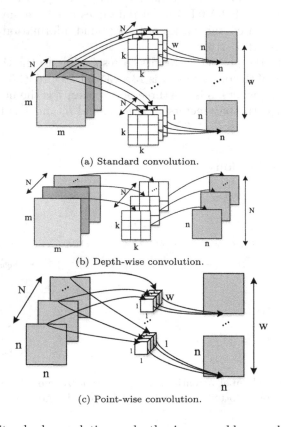

(a) Standard convolution.

(b) Depth-wise convolution.

(c) Point-wise convolution.

Fig. 3. Standard convolution vs depth-wise separable convolution (a)

In 2012, Mamalet et al. [20] first proposed depth-wise separable convolution. Depth-wise separable convolution (DSC) consists of depth-wise convolution (DW) and point-wise convolution (PW). The standard convolution (SC) operation is that all channels in the corresponding image region are considered simultaneously. Different from the standard convolutional network, the convolution kernel is first divided into single channels. The convolution operation is performed on each channel without changing the depth of the input feature image. In this way, the output feature map with the same number of channels as the input feature map is obtained. However, this operation independently performs convolution operations on each channel of the input layer, and there is no information exchange between channels. Therefore, 1×1 convolution is needed to increase the information exchange between channels. The separation of channels and regions can accelerate the training process, and the trained model has fewer parameters and faster speed, which is suitable for lightweight models.

As shown in Fig. 3, given the input feature maps size is $m \times m \times N$, and the kernel size is $m \times k \times k \times N \times w$, and the stride is 1, the parameters (P) of standard convolution is:

$$P(SC) = k \times k \times N \times w \tag{1}$$

And the floating point operations ($FLOPs$) is:

$$FLOPs(SC) = m \times m \times k \times k \times N \times w \tag{2}$$

For the depth-wise separable convolution, the number of parameters and FLOPs are:

$$P(DSC) = P(DW) + P(PW) = k \times k \times N + N \times w \tag{3}$$

$$FLOPs(DSC) = FLOPs(DW) + FLOPs(PW)$$
$$= m \times m \times k \times k \times N + m \times m \times N \times w \tag{4}$$

$$F_P = \frac{P(DSC)}{P(SC)} = \frac{1}{w} + \frac{1}{k^2} \tag{5}$$

$$F_{FLOPs} = \frac{FLOPs(DSC)}{FLOPs(SC))} = \frac{1}{w} + \frac{1}{k^2} \tag{6}$$

It can be seen from Eq. (6) and Eq. (5) that the depth-wise separable convolution has advantages in terms of the number of parameters and the FLOPs.

3   Experimental Results and Analysis

3.1   Implementation Details

Our experiment is implemented by using the PyTorch framework on a workstation computer with the following specifications: Intel(R) Core(TM) i9-9980XE CPU @ 3.00GHz, 125 GB RAM, and GeForce RTX 2080 Ti.

1) *Facial expression dataset:* The experiment in this paper is based on the RAF-DB dataset [21], which is an unconstrained large-scale facial expression recognition dataset of various sizes. For end-to-end experiment, we manually annotated them. It is worth pointing out that we did not perform any pre-processing such as face alignment. The RAF-DB dataset contains 12,271 training images and 3,068 test images. The details are shown in Table 1.

Table 1. The sample statistics of RAF-DB dataset.

Facial Expression Categories						
Angry	Disgust	Fear	Happy	Sad	Surprise	Neutral
training						
705	717	281	4,772	1,982	1,290	2,524
testing						
162	160	74	1,185	478	329	680

2) *Parameter settings:* We use the Adam optimization method for all models, with 16 bacth-size samples for end-to-end training. To be fair, we train all network models for 160 epochs and set the initial learning rate to 0.001, which is multiplied by 0.9 times every 5 epochs. During the training process, we initialize the FER-YOLO model network's parameters with the weights of DarkNet53 pre-trained on the COCO dataset. It is worth pointing out that all models in this paper only initialize the backbone network's weights.

3.2   Ablation Experiments

We conducted experiments on the FER-YOLO network model and its deformation. The test results on the test set are shown in Table 2. FER-YOLO* indicates that FER-YOLO removes the first feature fusion channel, which is the prediction result of $52 \times 52 \times 36$. In the same way, YOLOv3* represents YOLOv3 removes the first feature fusion channel. FER-YOLO-L means that the depth-wise separable convolution replaces the standard convolution in the enhanced feature extraction network in FER-YOLO, thereby lightweight FER-YOLO. Similarly, YOLOv3*-L, YOLOv3-L, and FER-YOLO*-L represents the lightweight of YOLOv3*, YOLOv3, and FER-YOLO*, respectively.

Table 2. Ablation experiments for FER-YOLO and some of its deformation. Legend: "Angry" (Ang); "Disgust" (Dis); "Fear" (Fea); "Happy" (Hap); "Neutral" (Neu); "Sad" (Sad) and "Surprise" (Sur)

Method	Ang	Dis	Fea	Hap	Neu	Sad	Sur	mAP(%)	Param(M)
FER-YOLO*	65.71	36.31	54.48	93.14	76.22	81.22	82.81	69.98	61.56
YOLOv3*	77.16	45.43	50.37	92.01	76.73	86.00	83.74	73.06	46.91
FER-YOLO*-L	75.85	51.26	46.94	93.79	77.42	83.19	83.84	73.19	60.51
YOLOv3*-L	80.15	49.92	47.78	94.23	75.99	**87.52**	83.83	74.20	**44.81**
YOLOv3-L	**80.79**	46.66	55.34	93.86	77.98	85.19	83.48	74.76	45.07
FER-YOLO-L	77.55	51.82	54.75	92.96	**78.62**	84.72	84.93	75.05	47.17
FER-YOLO	80.41	**52.44**	**61.04**	**94.48**	76.46	84.47	**88.06**	**76.77**	63.65

We use depth-wise separable convolution instead of standard convolution in the enhanced feature extraction network to explore these two different convolutions' impact on network performance. From the theoretical analysis of Sect. 2 B, it can be seen that compared to standard convolution, depth-wise separable convolution can indeed greatly reduce model parameters. From the experimental results in Table 2, it can be seen that the depth-wise separable convolution reduces the network model parameters used in this paper by approximately 15M. For different network structures, the depth-wise separable convolution replaces the standard convolution, and mAP may not be improved. And our experimental results show that in the RAF-DB dataset, a small receptive field has a large impact on mAP. If the small receptive field is removed, the network will miss small face images, and the mAP of the FER-YOLO network will be reduced from 76.77% to 69.98%.

Figure 4 shows the detection results of the FER-YOLO network model on the RAF-DB test dataset. The corresponding categories and scores are the prediction results and confidence scores of the detected images, respectively. We can see that the FER-YOLO network model can successfully detect facial expressions in images with complex backgrounds and accurately locate and predict them.

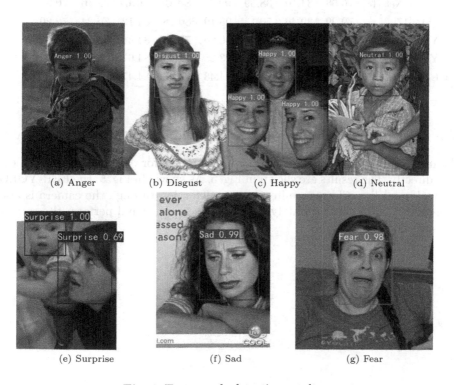

(a) Anger   (b) Disgust   (c) Happy   (d) Neutral

(e) Surprise   (f) Sad   (g) Fear

Fig. 4. Test sample detection results.

3.3   Comparisons with State-of the Art Methods

In Table 3, we compare the FER-YOLO network model with one-shot object detection state-of-the-art methods. Black bold font represents the best result.

The results show that our proposed FER-YOLO network model is better than the one-shot object detection model considered in this paper. Compared with YOLOv4 and YOLOv3, mAP has increased by 3.13% and 3.03%, respectively. The Average precision (AP) of the FER-YOLO network model in the categories of "Angry", "Disgust", "Fear" and "Surprise" is higher than the other one-shot object detection methods listed in the paper. The AP values of "Happy", "Neutral", and "Sad" are lower than the highest RetinaNet by 0.1%, 7.62%, and 2.14%, respectively.

Table 3. Comparisons with one-shot object detection state-of the art methods. Legend: "Angry" (Ang); "Disgust" (Dis); "Fear" (Fea); "Happy" (Hap); "Neutral" (Neu); "Sad" (Sad) and "Surprise" (Sur)

Method	Ang	Dis	Fea	Hap	Neu	Sad	Sur	mAP(%)
RetinaNet [18]	76.58	34.10	38.59	**94.58**	**84.08**	**86.61**	82.16	70.96
SSD [17]	79.99	39.46	50.13	95.19	80.28	84.12	76.24	72.20
YOLOv4 [16]	79.95	42.19	60.39	90.86	79.08	84.34	82.70	73.64
YOLOv3 [15]	79.07	45.55	57.38	93.28	71.69	84.67	84.51	73.74
FER-YOLO	**80.41**	**52.44**	**61.04**	94.48	76.46	84.47	**88.06**	**76.77**

3.4   Real-Time Facial Expression Detection via Camera

We use the real-time camera to read the face image for detection and classification directly. The results are shown in Fig. 5. As shown in Fig. 5, the FER-YOLO network model's performance in real-time detection through the camera is also prominent, which can accurately locate the face image and perform the correct classification.

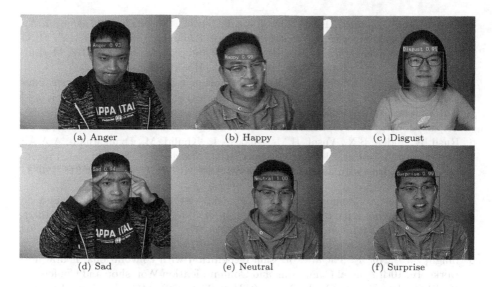

(a) Anger (b) Happy (c) Disgust

(d) Sad (e) Neutral (f) Surprise

Fig. 5. Detected facial expressions via real-time camera.

4 Conclusion

In this paper, we design a FER-YOLO network model for facial expression recognition. This model's backbone is combined with the SE module to improve the performance of the enhanced feature extraction network. Experiments were performed on the manually annotated RAF-DB dataset. The experimental results show that FER-YOLO achieves better results compared with other one-shot object detection methods. It provides a reference for one-shot object detection methods based on expression recognition.

Acknowledgements. This work was supported by Sichuan Provincial Science and Technology Projects (2019JDJQ0023).

References

1. Poria, S., Cambria, E., Bajpai, R., Hussain, A.: A review of affective computing: from unimodal analysis to multimodal fusion. Inf. Fusion **37**, 98–125 (2017)
2. Spezialetti, M., Placidi, G., Rossi, S.: Emotion recognition for human-robot interaction: recent advances and future perspectives. Front. Robot. AI **7**, 145–155 (2020)
3. Joesph, C., Rajeswari, A., Premalatha, B., Balapriya, C.: Implementation of physiological signal based emotion recognition algorithm. In: IEEE 36th International Conference on Data Engineering (ICDE) 2020, Dallas, TX, USA, pp. 2075–2079 (2020). https://doi.org/10.1109/ICDE48307.2020.9153878

4. Cosentino, S., Randria, E.I.S., Lin, J.-Y., Pellegrini, T., Sessa, S., Takanishi, A.: Group emotion recognition strategies for entertainment robots. In: IEEE/RSJ International Conference on Intelligent Robots and Systems (IROS) 2018, Madrid, Spain, pp. 813–818 (2018). https://doi.org/10.1109/IROS.2018.8593503

5. Li, G., Wang, Y.: Research on Learner's emotion recognition for intelligent education system. In: IEEE 3rd Advanced Information Technology, Electronic and Automation Control Conference (IAEAC), Chongqing, China, pp. 754–758 (2018). https://doi.org/10.1109/IAEAC.2018.8577590

6. Rusli, N., Sidek, S.N., Yusof, H.M., Ishak, N.I., Khalid, M., Dzulkarnain, A.A.A.: Implementation of wavelet analysis on thermal images for affective states recognition of children with autism spectrum disorder. IEEE Access **8**, 120818–120834 (2020)

7. Zou, J., Cao, X., Zhang, S., Ge, B.: A facial expression recognition based on improved convolutional neural network. In: IEEE International Conference of Intelligent Applied Systems on Engineering (ICIASE), Fuzhou, China, pp. 301–304 (2019). https://doi.org/10.1109/ICIASE45644.2019.9074074

8. Singh, S., Nasoz, F.: Facial expression recognition with convolutional neural networks. In: 10th Annual Computing and Communication Workshop and Conference (CCWC), Las Vegas, NV, USA, pp. 0324–0328 (2020). https://doi.org/10.1109/CCWC47524.2020.9031283

9. Ma, H., Celik, T., Li, H.-C.: Lightweight attention convolutional neural network through network slimming for robust facial expression recognition. Signal Image Video Process. 1863–1711 (2021)

10. Mohan, K., Seal, A., Krejcar, O., Yazidi, A.: FER-net: facial expression recognition using deep neural net. Neural Comput. Appl. **33**(15), 9125–9136 (2021). https://doi.org/10.1007/s00521-020-05676-y

11. Xie, S., Hu, H.: Facial expression recognition using hierarchical features with deep comprehensive multipatches aggregation convolutional neural networks. IEEE Trans. Multimedia **21**(1), 211–220 (2019)

12. Ma, H., Celik, T.: FER-Net: facial expression recognition using densely connected convolutional network. Electron. Lett. **55**(4), 184–186 (2019)

13. Redmon, J., Divvala, S., Girshick, R., Farhadi, A.: You only look once: unified, real-time object detection. In: IEEE Conference on Computer Vision and Pattern Recognition (CVPR), Las Vegas, NV, USA, pp. 779–788 (2016). https://doi.org/10.1109/CVPR.2016.91

14. Redmon, J., Farhadi, A.: YOLO9000: better, faster, stronger. In: IEEE Conference on Computer Vision and Pattern Recognition (CVPR), Honolulu, HI, USA, pp. 6517–6525 (2017). https://doi.org/10.1109/CVPR.2017.690

15. Joseph, R., Ali, F.: YOLOv3: An Incremental Improvement. arXiv:1804.02767 (2018)

16. Bochkovskiy, A., Wang, C.-Y., Liao, H.-Y.M.: YOLOv4: Optimal Speed and Accuracy of Object Detection. arXiv:2004.10934 (2020)

17. Liu, W., et al.: SSD: single shot MultiBox detector. In: Leibe, B., Matas, J., Sebe, N., Welling, M. (eds.) ECCV 2016. LNCS, vol. 9905, pp. 21–37. Springer, Cham (2016). https://doi.org/10.1007/978-3-319-46448-0_2

18. Lin, T.-Y., Goyal, P., Girshick, R., He, K., Dollár, P.: Focal loss for dense object detection. IEEE Trans. Pattern Anal. Mach. Intell. **422**, 318–327 (2020). https://doi.org/10.1109/TPAMI.2018.2858826

19. Hu, J., Shen, L., Albanie, S., Sun, G., Wu, E.: Squeeze-and-excitation networks. IEEE Trans. Pattern Anal. Mach. Intell. **428**, 2011–2023 (2020)

20. Mamalet, F., Garcia, C.: Simplifying ConvNets for fast learning. In: International Conference on Artificial Neural Networks (ICANN 2012), Lausanne, Switzerland, pp. 58–65 (2012). https://doi.org/10.1007/978-3-642-33266-1_8
21. Li, S., Deng, W., Du, J.: Reliable crowdsourcing and deep locality-preserving learning for expression recognition in the wild. In: IEEE Conference on Computer Vision and Pattern Recognition (CVPR), Honolulu, HI, USA, pp. 2584–2593 (2017). https://doi.org/10.1109/CVPR.2017.277

MSC-Fuse: An Unsupervised Multi-scale Convolutional Fusion Framework for Infrared and Visible Image

Guo-Yang Chen, Xiao-Jun Wu$^{(\boxtimes)}$, Hui Li, and Tian-Yang Xu

Jiangsu Provincial Engineering Laboratory of Pattern Recognition and Computational Intelligence, Jiangnan University, Wuxi 214122, Jiangsu, China

Abstract. Lacking the labeled data, how to establish an unsupervised learning method is essential for the infrared and visible image fusion task. As such, this article introduces a novel unsupervised learning fusion framework. Our proposed framework consists of three components: encoder, fusion layer, and decoder, respectively. Firstly, an encoder is designed to extract salient features from multiple source images. With the multi-scale convolution modules, the encoder can produce more useful features. Then these features are fused at the fusion layer. Finally, the decoder reconstructs the fused features to generate the fused image. To achieve the unsupervised training of the network, a no-reference quality metric and a pixel-level function are utilized to calculate the loss function. Experimental results show that compared with other fusion methods, our proposed method can achieve better performance in both objective and subjective assessments.

Keywords: Image fusion · Infrared image · Multi-scale convolution · Unsupervised learning

1 Introduction

Image fusion is the process of integrating the salient features of two or more source images into one image to enhance perception [1]. Visible images and infrared images have a very close relationship. Visible images have much texture information, which can reflect the real environment of the target and correspond to the human visual system. However, the performance of visible light sensors for target detection will be reduced under varying illumination or bad weather conditions. Infrared images produced by infrared sensors reflect the thermal radiation of objects. Meanwhile, the infrared sensors can work in all-weather conditions and highlight the target object according to the difference of radiation information under complex backgrounds [2]. Unfortunately, infrared images always have low resolution and poor texture information. Therefore, if the complementary information in infrared and visible images is fused in a reasonable way, the fused images with richer information can be obtained.

© Springer Nature Switzerland AG 2021
Y. Peng et al. (Eds.): ICIG 2021, LNCS 12888, pp. 40–51, 2021.
https://doi.org/10.1007/978-3-030-87355-4_4

Traditional image fusion algorithms are mainly based on multi-scale transformation [3–5] and sparse representation [6–8]. These methods generally feature manual design with much effort, high computational complexity, and low efficiency. In recent years, deep learning has played a crucial role in many computer vision tasks [9–11]. It is also gradually applied in the field of image fusion, which have solved the above problems to a certain extent. In [12], Liu et al. proposed a CNN based method for multi-focus image fusion. They used pairs of clear images and blurred images to train the network to produce a binary classifier that would determine whether a pixel was focused or not. This algorithm skillfully transforms the multi-focus image fusion problem into a classification problem.

However, the above method is not suitable for infrared and visible image fusion tasks due to the lack of ground-truth. In [13], Li et al. used a pre-trained VGG network to extract multi-layer deep features, and then these features were fused by constructing the weight map. After that, they proposed an auto-encoder network called DenseFuse [14]. DenseFuse trained the network with the COCO dataset [15] to achieve features extraction and reconstruction. Song et al. [16] proposed a multi-scale DenseNet (MSDNet), in which a multi-scale mechanism was added and achieved better performance. These methods have achieved good results in infrared and visible fusion missions. The main drawbacks are that they are not end-to-end methods and some still rely on pre-trained models.

In [17], Prabhakar proposed an unsupervised approach named DeepFuse. DeepFuse also provides an end-to-end solution. The main drawback of DeepFuse is that the network structure is too simple to adequately extract image features. Based on DeepFuse, we develop an unsupervised multi-scale convolution fusion framework (MSC-Fuse) for fusing infrared and visible images. The contributions of our work include the following aspects:

1) We proposed a unsupervised end-to-end deep learning framework. All the parameters in the model are closely related to the fusion task. It can effectively fuse the infrared image and the visible image without any labeled data.
2) We design a multi-scale convolution module to improve the ability of network feature extraction. The features of different scales in the source images can be extracted effectively.
3) We construct a robust mixed loss function that consists of a no-reference metric and a pixel loss. Experiments show that the loss function can effectively constrain the model.

The rest sections of this paper are organized as follows. In Sect. 2, the proposed fusion framework will be presented in detail. And in Sect. 3, we show the experimental results and make a discussion. Finally, we summarize this article in Sect. 4.

2 Proposed Fusion Method

The past few years have witnessed the great success of convolutional neural networks (CNNs) in many visual tasks. It is also the foundation of our approach.

In this section, we will give an elaborate introduction of our proposed method. The images discussed below are all grayscale ones.

2.1 Network Architecture

The MSC-Net architecture is illustrated in Fig. 1.

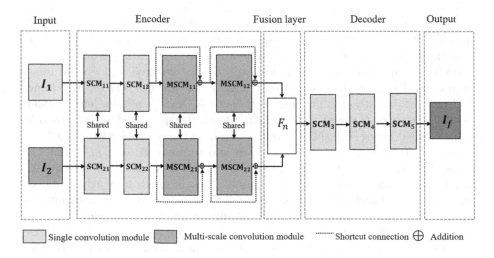

Fig. 1. The architecture of the proposed method.

Encoder. Let I_1 denote the visible image and I_2 denote the infrared image, respectively. The encoder is a weight sharing siamese network. There are two advantages to using a siamese network. It can reduce the number of parameters while generating the same type of features so that it is convenient for the subsequent fusion work. For the source image I_1, I_1 passes through two single convolution modules (SCM_{11}, SCM_{12}) which extract low-level features and two multi-scale convolution modules ($MSCM_{11}$, $MSCM_{12}$) which extract high-level features. Besides, we use the shortcut connection between each MSC module, which is beneficial to network optimization. The feature extraction process of I_2 is similar to that of I_1.

Fusion Layer. At the fusion layer, the feature maps obtained by encoder are combined. The process of feature fusion can be formulated by Eq. 1. ϕ_1^n and ϕ_2^n denote the feature maps extracted by the encoder network. F_n denotes the fused features. n is the channel of the feature maps.

$$F_n = average(\phi_1^n + \phi_2^n). \tag{1}$$

Decoder. The decoder network is composed of three single convolution modules (SCM_3, SCM_4, SCM_5) and its purpose is to reconstruct the target image. The fused features pass through the decoder network and output a fused image, eventually.

2.2   The Basic Convolution Blocks

The schematic diagram of basic convolution modules is shown in Fig. 2. The network contains two kinds of basic convolution modules.

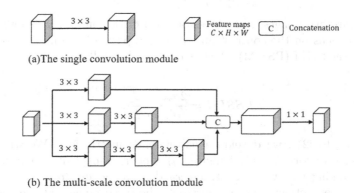

(a)The single convolution module

(b) The multi-scale convolution module

Fig. 2. Basic convolution modules.

One is the single convolution module (SCM) that contains only one convolution layer with 3×3 filters, represented in Fig. 2(a). Another is the multi-scale convolution module (MSCM) which is more complex. The purpose of this module is to obtain multi-scale information and enrich the acquired features, represented in Fig. 2(b). The common way to obtain multi-scale features is to use the different sizes of convolution kernels such as 3×3, 5×5, and 7×7. It is pointed out in [18] that the receptive field of a 5×5 convolutional layer is equal to a stack of two 3×3 convolutional layers. Similarly, a 7×7 convolution layer can be replaced by a stack of three 3×3 convolutional layers. In this way, the same receptive field characteristics can be obtained with fewer parameters. In Fig. 2(b), we can see that the MSCM has three branches. Each branch has a different number of 3×3 convolution layers to obtain features of different scales. Then these features are concatenated to form a more robust representation. The final 1×1 convolution layer is used to compress the number of channels in the feature maps.

2.3   Loss Function

The loss function is the key to train CNNs. Our purpose is to achieve an unsupervised learning process. The total loss function is shown in Eq. 2 and is made up of two parts, L_{PSSIM} and L_{Pixel}. The α is used to control trade-off between the two terms.

$$L_{Total} = \alpha L_{PSSIM} + L_{Pixel}. \tag{2}$$

First, we introduce SSIM loss function briefly. SSIM means structural similarity index measure [19]. Because the image produced by using SSIM as the loss function is more consistent with the human visual system, it is widely used in the image reconstruction task [20]. SSIM is defined as follows:

$$SSIM = \frac{2\mu_x\mu_y + C_1}{\mu_x^2 + \mu_y^2 + C_1} \cdot \frac{2\sigma_{xy} + C_2}{\sigma_x^2 + \sigma_y^2 + C_2} \tag{3}$$

where x, y are two images, σ denotes standard deviation and μ denotes means. We want to focus on the contrast and structure parts of the image, so we only use part of the SSIM (PSSIM) which is described as follows:

$$PSSIM = \frac{2\sigma_{xy} + C_2}{\sigma_x^2 + \sigma_y^2}. \tag{4}$$

According to [21], we develop a no-reference metric loss. We will use the source images to form an ideal image (y). Let x_k represent a pair of images from the training set, $k = \{1,2\}$. x_1, x_2 denote the infrared image and the visible image respectively and y_f represents the fused image. The image can be decomposed into three components: contrast(c), structure(s) and luminance(l). The formula is described as follows:

$$x_k = ||x_k - \mu_k||_2 \cdot \frac{x_k - \mu_k}{||x_k - \mu_k||_2} + \mu_k, \tag{5}$$

$$c_k = ||x_k - \mu_k||_2, \tag{6}$$

$$s_k = \frac{x_k - \mu_k}{||x_k - \mu_k||_2}, \tag{7}$$

$$l_k = \mu_k, \tag{8}$$

where c_k denotes the contrast part of the image, s_k denotes the structure part of the image and μ_k is the average pixel values of x_k, namely the luminance part. $||\cdot||_2$ is the l_2 norm. For the contrast part of this pair of images, we will select the part with the highest contrast. Higher contrast means more salient information about the source image.

$$c = max(c_k). \tag{9}$$

For the structure part and the luminance part, we take the weighted strategy through the l_1 norm. The definition is given as follows:

$$\omega_k = \frac{||x_k||_1}{\sum_{k=1}^{2}||x_k||_1}, \tag{10}$$

$$s = \sum_{k=1}^{2}\omega_k s_k, \tag{11}$$

$$l = average(\sum_{k=1}^{2}\omega_k x_k), \tag{12}$$

where $||\cdot||_1$ is the l_1 norm.

The image we need is described as:

$$y = c \cdot s + l. \tag{13}$$

After getting the ideal image y, the final L_{PSSIM} is calculated as follows:

$$L_{PSSIM} = 1 - PSSIM(y, y_f) \tag{14}$$

Furthermore, to get more refined fusion results and retain the detailed information of visible images better, a pixel loss function L_{Pixel} is added. The definition of L_{Pixel} is given as follows:

$$L_{Pixel} = ||y_f - x_2||_1 \tag{15}$$

where x_2 denotes the visible image, y_f represents the fused image.

3   Experimental Results

3.1   Experimental Environment and Parameter Setting

Our network was implemented on PyTorch and trained on a PC with Intel i7-6850K 3.6 GHz CPU. The Graphics Processing Unit(GPU) is NVIDIA TITAN XP GPU. The learning rate was set as 1e-4, and weight decay was set as 1e-4. Furthermore, the batch size was set as 32, and the total epochs were set as 128, respectively.

TNO [22] is a dataset that is widely used for infrared and visible image fusion tasks. All data in the dataset are corrected and registered. We selected 15 pairs of images as the training dataset. Some of them in the dataset are shown in Fig. 3(a). We cropped these images as data augment according to a sliding window of 64 × 64 with a step length of 20. Finally, more than 10000 pairs of patches were generated. We chose 10,000 patches as our training dataset. We use 21 pairs of infrared and visible images which were collected from [22] and [23] as our test images. Some of these images are shown in Fig. 3(b).

(a) Some samples of the TNO dataset.   (b) Four pairs of test images.

Fig. 3. The dataset.

Six objective quality metrics are used to evaluate the fused images performance, including: entropy (En) [24], standard deviation (SD) [25], spatial frequency(SF) [26], visual information fidelity (VIF) [27], mutual information (MI) [28], and Qabf [29].

3.2   Ablation Study

In this part, we discuss the effect of L_{Pixel} and different values of α in the loss function on the experimental results. We will choose a pairs of images "bunker" to illustrate it, which are shown in Fig. 4. Red boxes are used to mark some regions to show the main difference between each fused image.

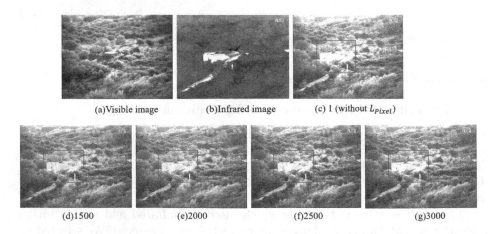

(a)Visible image   (b)Infrared image   (c) 1 (without L_{pixel})

(d)1500   (e)2000   (f)2500   (g)3000

Fig. 4. Experiment on "bunker" images. (Color figure online)

First, we only use the L_{P_SSIM} function to train the network, and the fusion result is shown in Fig. 4 (c). The thermal information of the target object in the fused image is significant, but some edge information and texture information are lost. Then we use two loss functions to train the network. Because the two kinds of loss functions have different orders of magnitude, the parameter α is required for balance. We set the α to 1500, 2000, 2500, and 3000, respectively. The experimental results are shown in Fig. 4 (d–g). It can be seen that with the increase of α, the brightness information in the fused image becomes more and more significant, but the details become blurred.

Table 1 shows the objective evaluation metrics of ablation study on 21 test images. The best values are in red and the second-best values are in blue. Q_{abf} is a metric that measures edge information. We can find that in several experiments where pixel loss is added, Q_{abf} has increased to varying degrees. When the α is 2000, the optimal number of objective evaluation metrics takes up the largest proportion. Combining subjective assessment and objective assessment, we choose the experimental results of $\alpha = 2000$ in subsequent experiments.

Table 1. The metrics values with different loss function and different α

α	En [24]	SD [25]	SF [26]	VIF [27]	MI [28]	Qabf [29]
without $L_{pixel}(\alpha = 1)$	6.8659	83.4349	23.2161	0.8417	13.7913	0.4747
1500	6.8604	80.7508	23.1797	0.7934	13.7208	0.4881
2000	6.8918	82.7193	24.8076	0.8841	13.7837	0.4789
2500	6.8767	83.9751	22.8068	0.8148	13.7534	0.4863
3000	6.8766	84.4559	22.8351	0.8160	13.7533	0.4839

3.3   Compared with Other Methods

We choose 9 representative methods to compare with our methods, which include discrete cosine harmonic wavelet transform (DCHWT) [30], joint sparse representation model with saliency detection (JSRSD) [31], gradient transfer and total variation minimization method (GTF) [32], convolutional sparse representation (CSR) [33], VGG based and the multi-layer fusion method (VGGML) [13], Deep-Fuse [17], DenseFuse [14], FusionGAN [34] and a general image fusion framework (IFCNN) [35].

To begin with, we select 2 representative pairs of images, "Street" and "Man" from test images to analyze them from the visual perspective, which are shown in Fig. 5 and Fig. 6, respectively. We use two different color boxes to mark some regions of the fused images. The image regions in the red boxes mainly focus on salient features, while the image regions in the yellow boxes mainly focus on details and texture information.

From Fig. 5, we can see that the visible image is darker but has more detail. The resolution of the infrared image is low, but the thermal information of the targets is abundant. The fused images generated by DCHWT and JSRSD methods contain a lot of noise information, which are not friendly to the human visual

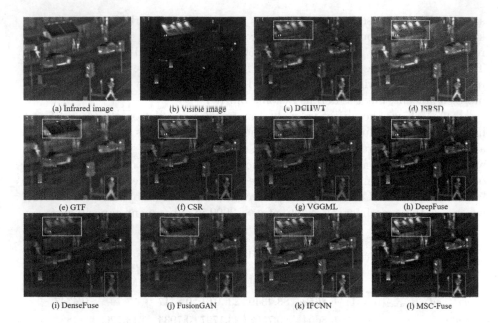

Fig. 5. Experiment on "street" images. (a) Infrared image; (b) Visible image; (c) DCHWT; (d) JSRSD; (e) GTF; (f) CSR; (g) VGGML; (h) DeepFuse; (i) DenseFuse; (j) FusionGan; (k) IFCNN; (l) MSC-Fuse. (Color figure online)

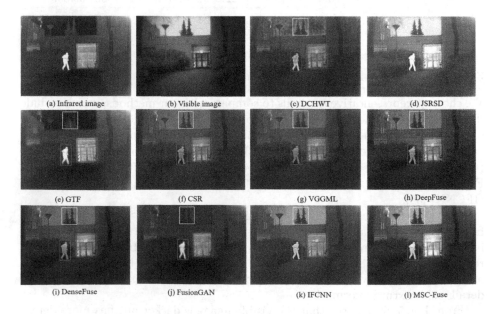

Fig. 6. Experiment on "man" images. (a) Infrared image; (b) Visible image; (c) DCHWT; (d) JSRSD; (e) GTF; (f) CSR; (g) VGGML; (h) DeepFuse; (i) DenseFuse; (j) FusionGan; (k) IFCNN; (l) MSC-Fuse. (Color figure online)

system. As for DenseFuse, CSR, and VGGML, the fused images of these methods are smooth and unclear, and the thermal information of the infrared image is not well preserved. The FusionGan result seems to lose some details(yellow box). Compared with IFCNN, the fused image produced by our method has better contrast. The DeepFuse result is similar to our result, but our method is better at extracting salient features (red boxes). This indicates that the multi-scale structure can extract the features more effectively.

In Fig. 6, the visible image has high resolution and can provide environmental information. The infrared image highlights the high thermal target. Therefore, the ideal fused image should contain the high brightness part of the infrared image and well retain the environmental information of the visible image. To sum up, our method highlights the thermal targets of the infrared image and well preserves the details of the visible image, thus achieving better visual effects compared with other methods. Next, we will evaluate the results of all fusion algorithms by calculating the six objective metrics.

The average values of objective evaluation metrics of 21 fused images through different fusion methods are shown in Table 2. We represent the optimal results of each evaluation index in red and the second in blue. As can be seen from Table 2, out of the six metrics, our method achieves the best results on four of them. This result shows that compared with other methods, our method has more detail information and feature information. From the subjective evaluation and objective analysis, we can see that our method is very effective for the fusion of infrared and visible images.

Table 2. The average values of quality metrics for 21 test images.

Methods	En [24]	SD [25]	SF [26]	VIF [27]	MI [28]	Q_{abf} [29]
DCHWT [30]	6.5678	64.9789	20.7040	0.5056	13.1355	0.4659
JSRSD [31]	6.6979	79.0872	32.3554	0.6691	13.3959	0.3259
GTF [32]	6.6353	67.6260	19.4198	0.4136	13.2707	0.4247
CSR [33]	6.2587	50.7437	19.2429	0.3922	12.5174	0.5348
VGGML [13]	6.1819	48.1385	13.4113	0.2949	12.3639	0.3677
DeepFuse [17]	6.6664	65.3599	23.1797	0.7653	13.3329	0.4674
DenseFuse [14]	6.7247	66.0013	18.7059	0.6601	13.4493	0.4009
IFCNN [35]	6.5955	66.8758	23.9414	0.5903	13.1909	0.5033
FusionGAN [34]	6.3629	54.3575	11.9606	0.4535	12.7257	0.2183
MSC-Fuse	6.8918	82.7193	24.8076	0.8841	13.7837	0.4789

4   Conclusions

In this paper, we present a novel end-to-end fusion framework MSC-Fuse for the fusion of visible and infrared image. We introduce multi-scale convolution modules to enhance the feature extraction capability of the network, which is proved to be very useful in our experiments. In particular, our network adopts a no-reference metric and l_1 loss as the loss function to accomplish unsupervised learning. This solves the difficulty of having no labeled data for the visible and infrared image fusion task. The experimental results demonstrate that MSC-Fuse can effectively fuse the significant information of infrared and visible images. In future, we will apply our method for video fusion.

References

1. Li, S., Kang, X., Fang, L., Hu, J., Yin, H.: Pixel-level image fusion: a survey of the state of the art. Inf. Fusion **33**, 100–112 (2017)
2. Ma, J., Ma, Y., Li, C.: Infrared and visible image fusion methods and applications: a survey. Inf. Fusion **33**, 153–178 (2019)
3. Ben, H.A., Yun, H., Hamid, K., Alan, W.: A multiscale approach to pixel-level image fusion. Integr. Comput. Aided Eng. **12**(2), 135–146 (2005)
4. Bulanon, D.M., Burks, T.F., Alchanatis, V.: Image fusion of visible and thermal images for fruit detection. Biosys. Eng. **103**(1), 12–22 (2009)
5. Ming, Z., Ji-Gang, S., Wei, L., Li-Qiang, G.: Multiple multifocus color image fusion using quaternion curvelet transform. Opt. Precis. Eng. **21**(10), 2671–2678 (2013)
6. Yang, B., Li, S.: Multifocus image fusion and restoration with sparse representation. IEEE Trans. Instrum. Meas. **59**(4), 884–892 (2010)
7. Zhang, Q., Fu, Y., Li, H., Zou, J.: Dictionary learning method for joint sparse representation-based image fusion. Opt. Eng. **52**(5), 7006 (2013)
8. Li, H., Wu, X.-J.: Multi-focus image fusion using dictionary learning and low-rank representation. In: Zhao, Y., Kong, X., Taubman, D. (eds.) ICIG 2017. LNCS, vol. 10666, pp. 675–686. Springer, Cham (2017). https://doi.org/10.1007/978-3-319-71607-7_59
9. Li, B., Wu, W., Wang, Q., Zhang, F., Yan, J.: Siamrpn++: evolution of siamese visual tracking with very deep networks. In: Proceedings of the IEEE Conference on Computer Vision and Pattern Recognition (CVPR) (2019)
10. Peng, S., Jiang, W., Pi, H., Li, X., Bao, H., Zhou, X.: Deep snake for real-time instance segmentation. In: Proceedings of the IEEE Conference on Computer Vision and Pattern Recognition (CVPR) (2020)
11. Yang, C., Xu, Y., Shi, J., Dai, B., Zhou, B.: Temporal pyramid network for action recognition. In: Proceedings of the IEEE Conference on Computer Vision and Pattern Recognition (CVPR) (2020)
12. Liu, Y., Chen, X., Peng, H., Wang, Z.: Multi-focus image fusion with a deep convolutional neural network. Inf. Fusion **36**, 191–207 (2017)
13. Li, H., Wu, X.J., Kittler, J.: Infrared and Visible Image Fusion using a Deep Learning Framework. In: 2018 24th International Conference on Pattern Recognition (ICPR), pp. 2705–2710. IEEE (2018)
14. Li, H., Wu, X.J.: Densefuse: a fusion approach to infrared and visible images. IEEE Trans. Image Process. **28**(5), 2614–2623 (2019)
15. Lin, T.Y., Maire, M., Belongie, S., Hays, J., Zitnick, C.L.: Microsoft coco: common objects in context (2014)
16. Song, X., Wu, X.-J., Li, H.: MSDNet for medical image fusion. In: Zhao, Y., Barnes, N., Chen, B., Westermann, R., Kong, X., Lin, C. (eds.) ICIG 2019. LNCS, vol. 11902, pp. 278–288. Springer, Cham (2019). https://doi.org/10.1007/978-3-030-34110-7_24

17. Ram Prabhakar, K., Sai Srikar, V., Venkatesh Babu, R.: Deepfuse: a deep unsu-pervised approach for exposure fusion with extreme exposure image pairs. In: Pro-ceedings of the IEEE International Conference on Computer Vision, pp. 4714–4722 (2017)
18. Simonyan, K., Zisserman, A.: Very deep convolutional networks for large-scale image recognition. Computer Science (2014)
19. Wang, Z.: Image quality assessment: from error visibility to structural similarity. IEEE Trans. Image Process. **13**(4), 600–612 (2004)
20. Zhao, H., Gallo, O., Frosio, I., Kautz, J.: Loss functions for image restoration with neural networks. IEEE Trans. Comput. Imaging **3**(1), 47–57 (2017)
21. Ma, K., Zeng, K., Wang, Z.: Perceptual quality assessment for multi-exposure image fusion. IEEE Trans. Image Process. **24**(11), 3345 (2015)
22. Toet, A.: TNO Image Fusion Dataset (2014)
23. Ma, J., Zhou, Z., Wang, B., Zong, H.: Infrared and visible image fusion based on visual saliency map and weighted least square optimization. Infrared Phys. Technol. **82**, 8–17 (2017)
24. Roberts, J.W., Van Aardt, J.A., Ahmed, F.B.: Assessment of image fusion pro-cedures using entropy, image quality, and multispectral classification. J. Appl. Remote Sens. **2**(1), 023522 (2008)
25. Rao, Y.J.: In-fibre bragg grating sensors. Meas. Sci. Technol. **8**(4), 355 (1997)
26. Li, S., Yang, B.: Multifocus image fusion using region segmentation and spatial frequency. Image Vis. Comput. **26**(7), 971–979 (2008)
27. Han, Y., Cai, Y., Cao, Y., Xu, X.: A new image fusion performance metric based on visual information fidelity. Inf. Fusion **14**(2), 127–135 (2013)
28. Peng, H., Long, F., Ding, C.: Feature selection based on mutual information: crite-ria of max-dependency, max-relevance, and min-redundancy. IEEE Trans. Pattern Anal. Mach. Intell. **8**, 1226–1238 (2005)
29. Xydeas, C.S., Pv, V.: Objective image fusion performance measure. Mil. Tech. Cour. **56**(4), 181–193 (2000)
30. Shreyamsha Kumar, B.K.: Multifocus and multispectral image fusion based on pixel significance using discrete cosine harmonic wavelet transform. SIViP **7**(6), 1125–1143 (2012). https://doi.org/10.1007/s11760-012-0361-x
31. Liu, C.H., Qi, Y., Ding, W.: Infrared and visible image fusion method based on saliency detection in sparse domain. Infrared Phys. Technol. **83**, 94–102 (2017)
32. Ma, J., Chen, C., Li, C., Huang, J.: Infrared and visible image fusion via gradient transfer and total variation minimization. Inf. Fusion **31**, 100–109 (2016)
33. Liu, Y., Chen, X., Ward, R.K., Wang, Z.J.: Image fusion with convolutional sparse representation. IEEE Signal Process. Lett. **23**(12), 1882–1886 (2016)
34. Ma, J., Yu, W., Liang, P., Li, C., Jiang, J.: FusionGAN: a generative adversarial network for infrared and visible image fusion. Inf. Fusion **48**, 11–26 (2019)
35. Zhang, Y., Liu, Y., Sun, P., Yan, H., Zhao, X., Zhang, L.: IFCNN: a general image fusion framework based on convolutional neural network. Inf. Fusion **54**, 99–118 (2020)

Relation-Aware Reasoning with Graph Convolutional Network

Lei Zhou[1], Yang Liu[1], Xiao Bai[1(✉)], Xiang Wang[1], Chen Wang[1],
Liang Zhang[1], and Lin Gu[2,3]

[1] School of Computer Science and Engineering, State Key Laboratory
of Software Development Environment, Jiangxi Research Institute,
Beihang University, Beijing, China
baixiao@buaa.edu.cn
[2] RIKEN AIP, Tokyo, Japan
[3] The University of Tokyo, Tokyo, Japan

Abstract. Semantic dependencies among objects are crucial for the recognition system to enhance performance. However, utilizing object-object relationships is a non-trivial task as objects are of various scales and locations, leading to irregular relationships. In this paper, we present a novel visual reasoning framework that incorporates both semantic and spatial relationships to improve the recognition system. We at first construct a knowledge graph to represent the co-occurrence frequency and relative position among categories. Based on this knowledge graph, we are able to enhance the original regional features by a Graph Convolutional Network (GCN) that encodes the high-level semantic contexts. Experiments show that our framework manages to outperform the baselines and state-of-the-art on different backbones in terms of both per-instance and per-class classification accuracy.

Keywords: Visual reasoning · Object-object relationship · Knowledge graph · Graph Convolutional Network

1 Introduction

When recognizing the objects, human can instinctively gain richer information from both spatial and semantic relationships in the scene. It has been demonstrated that modeling object-object relationships could help both conventional methods [9,26] and deep convolutional neural networks [13,21,24,28,29,32,33]. However, such modelling is non-trivial because objects are often of various scales and locations, leading to irregular relationships [12].

In this paper, we present a novel knowledge graph based reasoning framework to help recognize objects. To exploit both semantic and spatial object-object relationships to help reasoning, we represent the regional features, that

---

L. Zhou and Y. Liu—Equal contribution.

© Springer Nature Switzerland AG 2021
Y. Peng et al. (Eds.): ICIG 2021, LNCS 12888, pp. 52–64, 2021.
https://doi.org/10.1007/978-3-030-87355-4_5

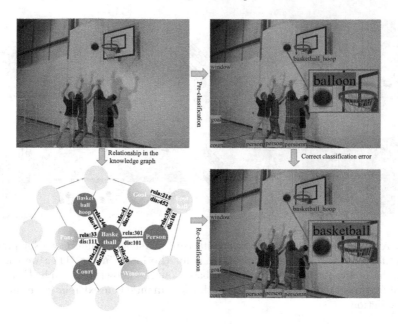

Fig. 1. An example on how knowledge graph helps reasoning. Existing recognition model such as ResNet-50 would recognize the "basketball" as a "balloon", while human can easily recognize from the relation of "basketball hoop" and the "court". Here, we propose a relation-aware reasoning framework to exploit the knowledge graph to mimic humans' prior knowledge.

are extracted by baseline CNNs, as graph node that represents individual category. The edges are defined on the co-occurrence frequency and relative position relation of different objects. Based on this knowledge graph, we are able to train a graph convolutional network (GCN) [16] to enhance the regional features with the reasoning information. Let us take Fig. 1 as an example, since the "basketball" is small and unclear, the baseline ResNet-50 [11] tends to recognize it as a "balloon". If only the semantic relationships are considered, the ball may also be recognized as a "football" since there is a "goal" in this image. With both semantic and spatial relationships encoded in the knowledge graph, our reasoning method easily corrects the baseline's recognition to be "basketball" as it is closer to the "basketball hoop" and "court" than "goal".

There are two main challenges in semantic context reasoning. First, the object-object relationships are irregular due to various size and locations, thus making it challenging to accommodate these irregular relations into a regular end-to-end network architecture. Some existing methods simply utilized the relationships for pre-processing or post-processing steps [8,9,23]. Here, we propose to use GCN to encode these complex and irregular relations. Since the relationships are represented as graph, we could update the regional features through the nodes propagation in GCN. In addition, through end-to-end training, we are able to automatically learn the shared weights between different regions.

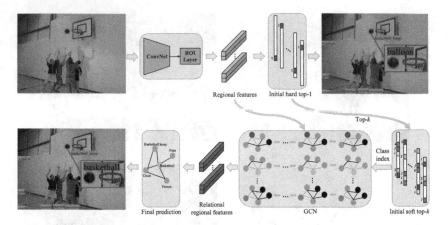

Fig. 2. An overview of our network architecture. First a baseline ConvNet produces regional features and soft initial predictions for the input image. Then we construct the graphs of the regional features with based on the knowledge graph. Finally, the regional features are updated by GCN with the semantic context relation to make the final prediction.

Secondly, since ADE [31] and Visual Genome (VG) [17] datasets both have more than 3,000 categories, it is difficult to directly build such large knowledge graph with limited GPU memory. From the knowledge graph in Fig. 1, we find that relativity between two objects is positively related with their co-occurrence frequency while negatively with their distance. Based on this [9], we propose a novel filtering mechanism to address the large knowledge graph problem. Specifically, during the GCN propagation, we first choose the top-n related classes for each region depend on the rank of co-occurrence frequency. Then for each of the top-n classes, we choose its top-m nearby regions to update the regional features. The proposed filtering mechanism not only reduces the memory requirement of the model, but also ignores the irrelevant regions during relational features update.

As shown in Fig. 2, our proposed framework consists of two key components. On the top row, a baseline ConvNet generates the convolutional features and initial predictions of each region. The bottom row is the core component of proposed framework where a multi-layers GCN is used for regional features update. The regional features are regarded as nodes of graph. The relationships between nodes are from the knowledge graph that accounts for both co-occurrence frequency and distance relation. Then we use the features enhanced with semantic contexts relationships to produce the final prediction. Note that the GCN may fail to update the useful relationships if the initial prediction is wrong. To solve this problem, we use a soft classification strategy in the initial prediction stage that we simultaneously update the regional feature on top-k estimated classes. With this strategy, the class that wrongly predicted initially, could not fit the correct nodes of knowledge graph, thus making its classification decrease afterwards. On the contrary, the correct initial prediction would benefit from the reasonable relationships and see its confidence increased.

In summary, the main contributions of this paper are: (1) We propose a novel end-to-end framework to exploit the object-object relationships to help reasoning. We build a knowledge graph to represent both semantic and spatial relationships. Finally, we use the GCN to update the regional features with this relation. (2) We present a soft initial prediction strategy that are robust to wrongly initial estimation from baseline. We further design a novel filtering strategy to solve the large knowledge graph problem. (3) Experimental results on different public datasets show the effectiveness of our framework. Our method outperforms state-of-the-art on different backbones on the task of region classification.

2 Related Works

2.1 Knowledge Graph Based Methods

Knowledge graphs are popular in computer vision. Marino *et al.* [22] proposed a model that reasoned different types of relationships between class labels by propagating information in a knowledge graph for image classification. Li *et al.* [20] proposed a method based on Graph Neural Networks for situation recognition, which can efficiently capture joint dependencies between roles using neural networks defined on a graph. Several works [15,18,27] used knowledge graph to solve the challenging task of zero-shot recognition. Yang *et al.* [29] proposed a visual semantic navigation framework which dynamically updated manually defined knowledge graphs and incorporates semantic knowledge to better generalize to unseen scenarios.

2.2 Relational Reasoning

Object-object relationships have been explored in many conventional visual methods before the age of deep learning. Divvala *et al.* [5] proposed an object detection method which utilized the co-occurrence relationship to re-score the detected objects. Some similar works [8,23] also used object-object relationships to re-score objects in the post-processing step for object detection. Spatial relationships between objects have also been exploited to help improve image segmentation [9,10]. The semantic relationships are also found useful for the computer vision tasks, such as image retrieval [14], image caption [7], and object localization [25]. With the great success of deep neural networks, extensive deep leaning based methods [2,3,12,15,18,19,22,27,30] also take advantage of the object-object relationships.

Among these methods, relation-aware reasoning has been studied extensively. Chen *et al.* [1] proposed a spatial memory network (SMN) for object detection, where a spatial memory is used to store previously detected objects. Then this memory is fed back into ConvNet to extract context information beneficial for the follow-up detection. A problem of SMN is that it learns object-object relationships from a single image. Therefore, SMN cannot take advantage of many commonsense object-object relationships. The subsequent work [2] used two graphs to respectively represent semantic and spatial relations between classes and regions before passing information among them. However, the iterative update strategy is very time consuming. Based on the attention module, Hu et al. proposed relation networks [12] in which relational features are obtained by exploiting the spatial locality in the input image. However, it encountered the same drawback as SMN that the relationships are from a single image. Most recently, Xu et al. [28] proposed a global reasoning network to enhance the regional feature by propagating over a global semantic pool with location relationship and attribute similarity.

Here, we present a novel knowledge graph based reasoning framework, where a commonsense knowledge graph containing both semantic and spatial relationships is built to improve recognizing relational objects. The main difference with existing works [2,28] lies in two aspects. First, we exploit the spatial distance to help measure the relevance between objects. This also serves as filtering mechanics to reduce the size of knowledge graph. Moreover, our framework incorporates the knowledge graph into a GCN architecture to learn and propagate the semantic and spatial relationships.

3   Proposed Framework

3.1   Knowledge Graph Construction

The goal of building knowledge graph for visual reasoning is to extract commonsense semantic and spatial relationships among different object categories. Here, we measure the semantic relationship with their co-occurrence frequency. In the meantime, we gauge the spatial relationship by the Euclidean distance among objects.

In this paper, we build the knowledge graph over all object categories in the dataset (not limited to those appearing the image). Each object category is represented as a node in the graph. We then traverse the training set and count the co-occurrence frequency of different object categories. The edges between nodes denote the occurrence times of object-object relationships. When the graph of specific image is used for updating regional features, the distances between object regions are added to the edges. In order to avoid the scale difference of objects in different images, we compute the spatial distance between the centers of regions in specific image as the relative distance of different object categories. An example of the knowledge graph is shown in Fig. 1.

3.2   GCN for Visual Reasoning

The proposed visual reasoning framework comprises of three key components: 1) initial soft classification; 2) regional features update and 3) reclassification.

Initial Soft Classification. The network input is an image with rectangular regions. We at first use a backbone ConvNet, such as ResNet-50, to give the initial predictions for each region. As shown in Fig. 2, we represent the regional features as the nodes of the graph, and the object-object relationships as the edges between the nodes. With the initial prediction, the relationships of different regions can be obtained from the knowledge graph. However, if the initial prediction is wrong, the corresponding regional feature would not be updated with the correct relationships. To solve this problem, we use a soft classification strategy in the initial prediction stage. The predicted classes with the top-k scores for each region are respectively used for the update of regional features. Under this strategy, knowledge graph could not update the wrong classes, thus would decrease their final confidence. On the contrary, the correct one would benefit from the reasonable relationships and get its final confidence improved.

Update of Regional Feature. Our core idea is to incorporate the complex and irregular object-object relationships into the regional features. Here, we encode the irregular relationship with Graph Convolutional Network (GCN) [16]. With the knowledge graph structure representation, the irregular relationships can be propagated between different nodes. We initialise each node based on the soft initial classification and then perform relationship propagation to compute a knowledge based regional feature that is passed as another feature vector to the policy function.

The GCNs are the extension of the Convolution Neural Networks to graph structures, where the goal is to learn a function representation for a given graph $G = \{V, E\}$. The input to each node v is a feature vector x_v. The inputs of all nodes can be summarized as a matrix $X = [x_1, \ldots, x_N] \in R^{N \times M}$, where N is the number of nodes, and M denotes the dimension of the input feature. The graph structure is represented as an adjacency matrix A. We perform raw-wise normalization on A and obtain $\widehat{A}$, where $\widehat{A} = A + I_N$ is the adjacency matrix with added self-connections, I_N is the identity matrix. The GCN outputs a node-level representation $Z = [z_1, \ldots, z_N] \in R^{N \times M}$. Let $f(\cdot)$ denote the ReLU activation function, we have

$$H^{(l+1)} = f(\widehat{A} H^{(l)} W^{(l)}) \tag{1}$$

with $H^{(0)} = X$ and $H^{(L)} = Z$, where $W^{(l)}$ is the parameter for the l-th layer and L is the number of GCN layers.

In the proposed framework, each region of the input image is regarded as the node in the graph. Since the knowledge graph is usually large in practice, its computation may take ages. Based on the observation [9] that the affinity of two objects is positively related with their co-occurrence frequency and negative with their distance, we propose a novel filtering mechanism to solve the large knowledge graph problem.

Let $X = [x_1, \ldots, x_N] \in R^{N \times M}$ denotes the feature matrix of input regions, N is the number of regions in the input image, M is the dimension of regional feature, $A \in R^{N \times N}$ is the relationship matrix where A_{ij} is the co-occurrence times of the i-th category and the j-th category in the training set, $D \in R^{N \times N}$

is the distance matrix where D_{ij} is the spatial distance between the center of the i-th region and the j-th region. We first choose the top-n related classes for each region depending on the rank of co-occurrence frequency, the index is denoted as $r_i \in R^n$ for the i-th region. Then for each of the top-n classes, we use its top-m near regions to update the regional feature, the index is denoted as $d_{r_i} \in R^m$ for class r_i. A' and D' are the raw-wise normalization of A and D, respectively. $\widehat{A'} = A' + I_N$ is the relationship matrix with added self-connections, and I_N is the identity matrix. Then the update of the i-th regional feature can be computed as

$$x_i^{(l+1)} = f(\sum_{r_i} \sum_{d_{r_i}} D'_{id_{r_i}} \widehat{A'}_{ir_i} X^{(l)} W^{(l)}) \qquad (2)$$

where $x_i^{(0)} = x_i$ and $X^{(0)} = X$, $W^{(l)}$ is the parameter for the l-th layer of GCN layers. We use a three layers GCN [16] in the experiments.

Our filtering mechanism not only reduces the memory requirement, but also removes the irrelevant regions during relationship propagation.

Reclassification. With the GCN, correct initial prediction can benefit from the relationship propagation while the wrongly predicted classes would be discarded. After the update by GCN, we use a fully connected layer and softmax on the enhanced regional features to give the final predictions.

Since the updated regional features are fusion of relative objects, the reclassification results should include the relative objects information. Based on the rank of co-occurrence time for each category y_i (annotated label), we first compute a relational probability vector $\mathbf{p}^i$ in which

$$p_j^i = \frac{exp(t_j^i)}{\sum_{j=1}^n exp(t_j^i)} \; j = 1, 2, \ldots, n \qquad (3)$$

where t_j^i is the co-occurrence time of category y_i and y_j in the knowledge graph.

Then we employ the cross entropy loss as our objective function

$$\mathcal{L} = -\frac{1}{N} \sum_{i=1}^N \sum_{j=1}^n \tau(y_i = j) \log p_j^i \qquad (4)$$

where $\tau(\cdot)$ is the indicator function.

3.3   Implementation Details

Our baseline for region classification is based on maskrcnn-benchmark. As the ground truth boxes are used as the RoIs, the region proposal branch and bounding box regression branch are removed. ResNet-50 and ResNet-101 pre-trained on ImageNet [4] are used as our backbone respectively and images are resized to shorter size with 800 pixels during training and testing. For each RoI, features are cropped from the *conv4* stage's (stride is 16) feature map, resized to

Table 1. Results on ADE test and VG test (%).

Dataset	Method	Backbone	Per-instance		Per-class	
			AP	AC	AP	AC
ADE	Baseline	ResNet-50	67.8	67.8	38.4	33.9
		ResNet-101	68.5	68.5	39.2	34.5
	Iterative [2]	ResNet-50	69.7	69.7	39.8	35.2
		Resnet-101	71.1	71.2	41.5	36.8
	Ours	ResNet-50	**71.2**	**71.2**	**40.5**	**36.2**
		ResNet-101	**73.0**	**73.0**	**43.2**	**38.5**
VG	Baseline	ResNet-50	50.2	50.4	18.3	13.2
		ResNet-101	50.8	51.1	19.0	13.8
	Iterative [2]	Resnet-50	51.2	51.5	19.2	14.0
		ResNet-101	53.0	53.2	20.5	15.4
	Ours	ResNet-50	**53.4**	**53.8**	**20.5**	**15.6**
		ResNet-101	**54.6**	**54.9**	**21.8**	**16.3**

7×7 with a 2×2 maxpooling layer. Then the features are used for the baseline classification.

All the models apply stochastic gradient descent with momentum to optimize the parameters. Our learning rate schedule is the same as [2]: 5e-4 for the first 280K iterations, and reduced to 5e-5 between 280K and 320K iterations for ADE; and the numbers are 320K/560K for VG. The batch size is set to 1 during training. No augmentation is used for both training and testing.

4   Experiments

4.1   Datasets and Evaluation

We conducted experiments on ADE [31] and VG [17] with different backbones compared. We validate the effectiveness of our framework in regional classification task as [2], where the goal was to assign labels to designated regions denoted by rectangular bounding boxes. For both training and testing, we used the provided ground-truth locations. Since ADE is a segmentation dataset, we converted the segmentation masks to bounding boxes. For object classes (e.g. "person"), each instance was created with a separate box. Parts (e.g. "head") and sub-parts (e.g. "nose") were also included. For VG, the boxes provided in the dataset were directly used.

Both classification accuracy (AC) and average precision (AP) [6] were adopted for evaluation. Since all regions are fixed with known labels, it is not necessary to set a region overlap threshold for AP. Results can be aggregated in two ways. The first way ("per-class") computes metrics separately for each class in the set, and takes the mean. Since the final scores are all taken from a calibrated soft-max output, a second way ("per-instance") computes metrics

Table 2. Left: Comparison of baseline with fully connected layers added (%). Right: Comparison of soft initial classification and hard initial classification (%).

Dataset	Method	Per-instance		Per-class		Method	Per-instance		Per-class	
		AP	AC	AP	AC		AP	AC	AP	AC
ADE	Baseline	67.8	67.8	38.4	33.9	Baseline	67.8	67.8	38.4	33.9
	+3fc	67.9	67.9	37.6	33.2	Ours (Hard)	68.5	68.5	38.9	34.6
	Ours	71.2	71.2	40.5	36.8	Ours (Soft)	71.2	71.2	40.5	36.8
VG	Baseline	50.2	50.4	18.3	13.2	Baseline	50.2	50.4	18.3	13.2
	+3fc	50.5	50.7	18.5	13.3	Ours (Hard)	50.8	51.2	18.5	13.3
	Ours	53.4	53.8	20.5	15.6	Ours (Soft)	53.4	53.8	20.5	15.6

Table 3. Left: Results with different GCN layers (%). Right: Importance of semantic and spatial relationships (%).

Dataset	Method	Per-instance		Per-class		Method	Per-instance		Per-class	
		AP	AC	AP	AC		AP	AC	AP	AC
ADE	Baseline	67.8	67.8	38.4	33.9	Baseline	67.8	67.8	38.4	33.9
	1 layer	70.5	70.5	39.6	35.5	Ours (Spatial)	68.2	68.2	38.9	34.6
	2 layers	70.9	70.9	39.9	36.0	Ours (Semantic)	69.5	69.6	39.5	35.2
	3 layers	71.2	71.2	40.5	36.8	Ours (Full)	71.2	71.2	40.5	36.8
VG	Baseline	50.2	50.4	18.3	13.2	Baseline	50.2	50.4	18.3	13.2
	1 layer	52.8	52.9	19.8	14.9	Ours (Spatial)	51.3	51.8	18.8	13.6
	2 layers	53.0	53.2	20.1	15.2	Ours (Semantic)	52.6	52.8	19.7	14.8
	3 layers	53.4	53.8	20.5	15.6	Ours (Full)	53.4	53.8	20.5	15.6

simultaneously for all classes. Intuitively, "per-class" assigns more weights to instances from rare classes.

4.2   Experimental Results

The experimental results on ADE and VG are given in Table 1. The parameters (k, n, m) were set as $(100, 40, 15)$. We verified our framework on different backbones including ResNet-50 and ResNet-101 [11]. As can be seen, our reasoning framework outperforms all the baselines on both ADE and VG datasets. On ADE with ResNet-101 as the backbone, our method achieves 4.5% increase for per-instance AP and AC. For per-class evaluation, the AP and AC also increase by 4.0%. Compared with the state-of-the-art method Iterative [2], our method also shows significant improvement. For VG dataset, our method achieves better performance on all backbones and outperforms state-of-the-art. In addition, our framework achieves higher per-instance metric gains than per-class ones because the rare classes have less relationships in the knowledge graph. To better demonstrate the effectiveness of our framework, we show in Fig. 3 some qualitative results.

4.3   Ablation Study

We conducted thorough ablative analysis on our framework. Due to the space limitation, we only show results with ResNet-50 as the backbone. The parameters

Fig. 3. Examples from the ADE test set. We highlight the bounding boxes of regions by red color, where the predictions of baseline are wrong and are corrected by our framework. In these examples, our method gives the correct predictions for "easel" and "shelf" which are difficult to recognize without the help from object-object relationships. Our method has shown strong capability to recognize small objects, such as "windows", "handle", "sconce", "remote control", and "blade". The examples of "person" and "refrigerator" and "towel" in the bottom row show that our reasoning framework can also help to recognize the occluded objects or missing regions. Especially in middle image of third row, Iterative [2] fail to recognize the "remote control", but our method successfully corrects it with the co-occurrence relationship of "remote control" and "night table".

$(k,\ n,\ m)$ were all set as $(100, 40, 15)$. Ablation studies were designed on four aspects.

Firstly, to validate that the improvement is from the object-object relationships rather than more parameters or depths, we conducted experiment by adding 3 fully connected layers on baseline instead of GCN. As can be seen in Table 2 (Left), a deeper 3fc only leads to slight improvement. This indicates that the object-object relationships play an important role in the reasoning process.

Then, we show the effectiveness of our proposed soft initial classification strategy. We conducted experiment on our framework with hard initial classification which only uses the top-1 score corresponded prediction for feature update. Table 2 (Right) shows the comparison of soft initial classification and hard initial classification. It can be seen that hard initial classification can only lead to slight improvement, even cause a decrease in some cases.

Thirdly, we report the performance of our framework with different numbers of GCN layers. As shown in Table 3 (Left), we updated the regional features respectively with one layer, two layers and three layers GCN. The results show that our method achieves slight improvement with deeper GCN.

We finally verified the effectiveness of semantic and spatial relationships respectively. The results are shown in Table 3 (Right). We can see that removing semantic relationships decreases performance heavily, whereas removing spatial relationships only causes slight decrease. Compared with the full framework, they both result in worse performance.

5   Conclusion

In this paper, we propose a novel relation-aware reasoning framework. We at first extract both semantic and spatial relationships between objects to construct a knowledge graph. Then we encode them with a GCN to enhance the regional features. Our framework achieves significant improvement on both ADE and VG datasets over different backbones. In addition, our method demonstrates strong reasoning capability especially for small regions and occluded objects which are hard examples for the state-of-the-art CNNs.

Acknowledgement. This work was supported by the National Natural Science Foundation of China project no. 61772057, Beijing Natural Science Foundation (4202039), the support funding Jiangxi Research Institute of Beihang University. Supported by the Academic Excellence Foundation of BUAA for PhD Students.

References

1. Chen, X., Gupta, A.: Spatial memory for context reasoning in object detection. In: ICCV (2017)
2. Chen, X., Li, L.J., Fei-Fei, L., Gupta, A.: Iterative visual reasoning beyond convolutions. In: CVPR (2018)
3. Chen, Y., Rohrbach, M., et al.: Graph-based global reasoning networks. In: CVPR (2019)

4. Deng, J., Dong, W., Socher, R., Li, L.J., Li, K., Fei-Fei, L.: Imagenet: a large-scale hierarchical image database. In: CVPR (2009)
5. Divvala, S.K., Hoiem, D., Hays, J.H., Efros, A.A., Hebert, M.: An empirical study of context in object detection. In: CVPR (2009)
6. Everingham, M., Van Gool, L., Williams, C.K., Winn, J., Zisserman, A.: The pascal visual object classes (VOC) challenge. IJCV **88**(2), 303–338 (2010)
7. Fang, H., Gupta, S., et al.: From captions to visual concepts and back. In: CVPR (2015)
8. Felzenszwalb, P.F., Girshick, R.B., McAllester, D., Ramanan, D.: Object detection with discriminatively trained part-based models. TPAMI **32**(9), 1627–1645 (2009)
9. Galleguillos, C., Rabinovich, A., Belongie, S.: Object categorization using co-occurrence, location and appearance. In: CVPR (2008)
10. Gould, S., Rodgers, J., Cohen, D., Elidan, G., Koller, D.: Multi-class segmentation with relative location prior. IJCV **80**(3), 300–316 (2008)
11. He, K., Zhang, X., Ren, S., Sun, J.: Deep residual learning for image recognition. In: CVPR (2016)
12. Hu, H., Gu, J., Zhang, Z., Dai, J., Wei, Y.: Relation networks for object detection. In: CVPR (2018)
13. Jiang, C., Xu, H., Liang, X., Lin, L.: Hybrid knowledge routed modules for large-scale object detection. In: NeurIPS (2018)
14. Johnson, J., Krishna, R., Stark, M., Li, L.J., Shamma, D., Bernstein, M., Fei-Fei, L.: Image retrieval using scene graphs. In: CVPR (2015)
15. Kampffmeyer, M., Chen, Y., et al.: Rethinking knowledge graph propagation for zero-shot learning. In: CVPR (2019)
16. Kipf, T.N., Welling, M.: Semi-supervised classification with graph convolutional networks. In: ICLR (2017)
17. Krishna, R., Zhu, Y., et al.: Visual genome: connecting language and vision using crowdsourced dense image annotations. IJCV **123**(1), 32–73 (2017)
18. Lee, C.W., Fang, W., Yeh, C.K., Frank Wang, Y.C.: Multi-label zero-shot learning with structured knowledge graphs. In: CVPR (2018)
19. Li, L., Gan, Z., Cheng, Y., Liu, J.: Relation-aware graph attention network for visual question answering. In: ICCV (2019)
20. Li, R., Tapaswi, M., Liao, R., Jia, J., Urtasun, R., Fidler, S.: Situation recognition with graph neural networks. In: ICCV (2017)
21. Liu, Y., et al.: Goal-oriented gaze estimation for zero-shot learning. In: CVPR (2021)
22. Marino, K., Salakhutdinov, R., Gupta, A.: The more you know: using knowledge graphs for image classification. In: CVPR (2017)
23. Mottaghi, R., Chen, X., et al.: The role of context for object detection and semantic segmentation in the wild. In: CVPR (2014)
24. Ning, X., Gong, K., Li, W., Zhang, L., Bai, X., Tian, S.: Feature refinement and filter network for person re-identification. TCSVT (2020)
25. Sadeghi, M.A., Farhadi, A.: Recognition using visual phrases. In: CVPR (2011)
26. Torralba, A., Murphy, K.P., Freeman, W.T., Rubin, M.A.: Context-based vision system for place and object recognition. In: ICCV (2003)
27. Wang, X., Ye, Y., Gupta, A.: Zero-shot recognition via semantic embeddings and knowledge graphs. In: CVPR (2018)
28. Xu, H., Jiang, C., Liang, X., Lin, L., Li, Z.: Reasoning-RCNN: unifying adaptive global reasoning into large-scale object detection. In: CVPR (2019)
29. Yang, W., Wang, X., Farhadi, A., Gupta, A., Mottaghi, R.: Visual semantic navigation using scene priors. In: ICLR (2019)

30. Yao, T., Pan, Y., Li, Y., Mei, T.: Exploring visual relationship for image captioning. In: ECCV (2018)
31. Zhou, B., Zhao, H., Puig, X., Fidler, S., Barriuso, A., Torralba, A.: Scene parsing through ADE20K dataset. In: CVPR (2017)
32. Zhou, L., Bai, X., Liu, X., Zhou, J., Hancock, E.R.: Learning binary code for fast nearest subspace search. Pattern Recognit. **98**, 107040 (2020)
33. Zhou, L., Dai, X., Liu, X., Zhou, J., Hancock, E.R., et al.: Latent distribution preserving deep subspace clustering. In: IJCAI (2019)

Feature Separation GAN for Cross View Gait Recognition

Chongdong Huang[1], Yonghong Song[2(✉)], and Yuanlin Zhang[2]

[1] School of Software Engineering, Xi'an Jiaotong University, Xi'an, China
huang22112211@stu.xjtu.edu.cn
[2] Institute of Artificial Intelligence and Robotics, Xi'an Jiaotong University, Xi'an, China
{songyh,ylzhangxian}@mail.xjtu.edu.cn

Abstract. Gait information can be collected by a long-distance camera. But the relative angle between the subject and the camera changes, resulting in a cross-view gait recognition problem. This paper proposes a view transformation model method based on feature separation generate adversarial networks. Based on the GAN model, this method separates the features of the input data as an additional discriminant basis. On the premise of building a single model, it can convert image to any angle as needed. In order to make the images generated by GAN more realistic, the proposed method separates view and dress information from the identity data and encodes them. The discriminator is also optimized by adding the conditional codes as an additional basis, so that the generator can generate the corresponding image more realistically based on the encoded information image. In addition, the proposed method also adds a constraint to increase the inter-class variation of subjects and reduce their intra-class distance. Thus, the synthesized image retains more feature information of original subject. The proposed method achieves a great generating effect and improves the performance of cross-view gait recognition.

Keywords: Gait recognition · Generative adversarial network · View transform · Feature separation

1 Introduction

Gait is a kind of behavioral biometric feature. Unlike other biometric modalities such as fingerprint, face or iris, it can be obtained at a long distance without any active interaction with people. As a new biometric feature, gait is inconspicuous, difficult to hide and pretend, and is more suitable for long-distance human body recognition than other biometric modalities.

However, there are many factors that affect gait recognition performance, such as changes in walking direction [1], various perspectives, different carrying bags [2] and changes of dressing [3]. In practical applications, the subject may walk in different paths under a stationary camera, which has a negative effect on the accuracy of recognition and causes a problem of gait recognition in cross-view.

Y. Peng et al. (Eds.): ICIG 2021, LNCS 12888, pp. 65–76, 2021.
https://doi.org/10.1007/978-3-030-87355-4_6

In order to solve the problem of cross view gait recognition, most existing methods are based on constructing models to extract view invariant features [4] or eliminate interference caused by perspective changes. In early research, gait recognition algorithm extracts static or dynamic features related to gait from the silhouette sequence, and dimension reduction processes or matches the features [5, 6]. Larger angle of view changes will result in a nonlinear correlation between gait features at different angles of view. To address the problem of perspective changes, early researchers mainly focused on anthropometry and spatial mapping based on human body models method [7] project gait information from different angles into a common subspace independent of perspective for recognition by learning projection. In addition to the method based on learning projection, there are also methods for identifying gait information from one view angle to another angle. The model proposed by Makihara et al. [8] is the earliest method to transform the gait information by constructing a view transform model (VTM) to solve the cross-view problem. On this basis, many subsequent improvements have been made. However, in the case where the viewing angle's variation is large, this method needs to construct multiple VTMs for transformation to ensure that a large amount of view information is contained. This paper proposes a method of constructing a multi-view conversion model by separating the target features of GAN to solve the cross-view gait recognition problem.

The rest of this paper is organized as follows. Section 2 discusses related works and Sect. 3 presents the proposed method. Section 4 presents the experiments and evaluation. Section 5 gives the conclusion.

2   Related Work

2.1   Generative Adversarial Networks

Generative adversarial networks (GAN) [9] have received extensive attention and research since it was proposed. GAN is structurally inspired by the zero-sum game in game theory. It sets the participating players as a generator G and a discriminator D. The purpose of the generator is to learn and capture the potential distribution of real data samples as much as possible and generate new data samples. The discriminator tries to correctly determine whether the input data comes from real data or from the generator. In order to win the game, the two players need to be continuously optimized to improve their own generating ability and discriminating ability. This learning optimization process is a minimum and maximum game problem, the purpose is to find a Nash equilibrium between D and G. Thus, the generator can estimate the distribution of data samples as real as possible. Chen et al. proposed a model named Info-GAN [10] which optimized G through information regularization by using the additional latent code. And DR-GAN [11] designs the generative model of disentangled representation based on the idea of latent code. This paper proposes a method which is adapted from DR -GAN and applies to cross view gait recognition.

2.2   Generative Method for Gait Recognition

The methods for gait recognition based on deep learning are divided into discriminant methods and generative methods. Generative method of gait recognition transforms the gait features input in one state to another state before matching or feature extraction. Taking cross view gait recognition as an example, generative method first encodes the gait features in various perspectives through an encoder. Then through a feature transformation network, the encoded features are transformed to a typical perspective or a probe set angle. Finally, the transformed features are reconstructed by the decoder. Feng et al. [12] proposed the use of posture-based long-term and short-term memory modules to sequence thermal maps of human joints. For the traditional generative method, the angle of the gait sequence needs to be estimated in advance, and for each pair of angles, a model needs to be trained separately for recognition. Yu et al. [13] proposed a unified model based on a multi-layer autoencoder for gait recognition. The model uses gait energy images as its input data and reconstruction object of each layer in the multi-layer auto encoder. They also proposed a method for generating an adversarial network based on gait [14], which can alleviate the impact of covariates such as perspective and clothing on recognition performance. It also verified that the generated adversarial network can already be used to effectively fit the sample distribution in gait recognition.

2.3 Gait Energy Image

Gait energy image [15] is one of the most commonly used features in gait recognition. It is produced by averagely synthesizing the silhouette map of the gait sequence in one walking cycle. GEI(Gait Energy Image) contains body contour information of the subject, and the pixel value in GEI represents the probability of the subject occupying the pixel position when walking [16]. The experiment uses GEI as its input and output of the model, and achieves the purpose of recognition by processing the information contained in GEI.

3 Proposed Method

3.1 Network Structure

The proposed model is inspired by the one in [11] which is named as Disentangled Representation Learning GAN(DR-GAN). The model in [11] is proposed to deal with pose-invariant face recognition. This paper adapts it to deal with the view, clothing and carrying condition challenges in gait recognition. The proposed method aims to generate a GEI in arbitrary angles when there is just a specific view GEI as input. The framework of the proposed method is illustrated in Fig. 1 which consists of a generator G, a discriminator D and an identity constraint A.

A gait image x in one view is input into generator G as a source image. Every gait image has its original state and target state. Generator G learns a feature representation for a gait image and an eigenvector $f(x)$ is generated by encoder. Meanwhile a pose code c and a dress code s are designed according to the target state. Decoder in G takes $f(x)$, c and s as its input and generates a corresponding target gait image $\tilde{x}$. Thus, the source gait image can be transformed to an arbitrary target state. And discriminator D learns to distinguish whether the input image is real and which state it is in, constraint A learns to promote the generated image inter-class variations.

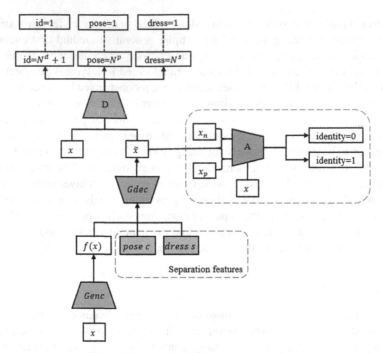

Fig. 1. Framework of the proposed method.

3.2 Separation Features

In order to improve the authenticity of the generated image, this method designs feature codes based on feature separation. Feature coding is designed according to the common attributes of the data set. In cross-view gait recognition, the subject's identity information is the most important basis for recognition. The change of pose angle is the main factor affecting the recognition accuracy. The subject's dress state also interferes with the recognition effect. Therefore, gait data can separate two major features from identity information: pose angle and dress state. Given a real image x with label $y = \{y^d, y^p, y^s\}$ as input, where y^d represents the label for identity, y^p for pose and y^s for dress. The discriminator D is a multi-task CNN consisting of three parts: $D = [D^d, D^p, D^s].D^d \in \mathbb{R}^{N^d+1}$ is for identity classification with Nd as the total number of subjects in the training set and the additional dimension is for the fake class. $D^P \in \mathbb{R}^{N^P}$ is for view classification with Np as the total number of pose views. And $D^S \in \mathbb{R}^{N^s}$ is for dress state classification just like D^P. When a real gait image x is input into D, D aims to classify its identity, pose and dress state. When the input is a synthetic gait image from the generator $\tilde{x}$, D tries to classify $\tilde{x}$ as fake with the following objective:

$$\tilde{x} = G(x, c, s) \tag{1}$$

$$Loss_D(G, D, x, y, \tilde{x}) = E_{x,y \sim p_d(x,y)} \left[\log D_{y^d}^d(x) + \log D_{y^p}^p(x) + \log D_{y^s}^s(x) \right]$$
$$+ E_{\tilde{x} \sim p_{\tilde{x}}(\tilde{x})} \left[\log D_{N^d+1}^d(G(\tilde{x})) \right] \tag{2}$$

Where D_i^d, D_i^p and D_i^s are the i th element in D^d, D^P and D^s. The first term maximizes the probability that x is classified as a true identity and state. For generated image, the second term maximizes the probability that $\tilde{x}$ is classified as a fake class.

3.3 Constraint Block

The constraint A is inspired by [17, 18] which has a same struct like D but it is a binary classify. According to an input image x, a positive image x_p which has the same identity with x and a negative image x_n which has not will be chose from database. Additionally, x_p and x_n are under input image's target condition code c and s. The source image x will be combined with $\tilde{x}$, x_p, and x_n into three groups and input into the constraint A. And A learns to discriminate whether the two images have same identity or not by using the following objective:

$$
\begin{aligned}
Loss_A\left(A, I_p, I_n, I_g\right) &= E_{I_p \sim p_p(I_p)}[\log A(I_p)] \\
&+ E_{I_n \sim p_n(I_n)}[\log(1 - A(I_n))] + E_{I_g \sim p_g(I_g)}[\log(1 - A(I_g))]
\end{aligned}
\tag{3}
$$

Where $I_p = \left(x, x_p\right)$, $I_n = (x, x_n)$ and $I_g = (x, \tilde{x})$.

3.4 Generator Optimizing

G is composed of an encoder G_{enc} and a decoder G_{dec}. G_{enc} aims to learn the feature representation of the input image. The feature representation $f(x)$ is obtained after the source image x is encoded by G_{enc}. Then $f(x)$ is used as the input of G_{dec} together with c and s, where c and s are one-hot vector with the target pose y^c being 1 and the target dress state y^t being 1. G_{dec} aims to synthesize a gait image with the input condition vector. The goal of G is to make the synthesized image $\tilde{x}$ reach the given condition. In which case, it can fool D and A to classify $\tilde{x}$ to the domain of source image x, which can be denoted as:

$$
Loss_G^D(\tilde{x}, y) = E_{\tilde{x}, y \sim p_{\tilde{d}}(\tilde{x}, y)}\left[\log D_{y^d}^d(\tilde{x}) + \log D_{y^c}^p(\tilde{x}) + \log D_{y^t}^s(\tilde{x})\right]
\tag{4}
$$

$$
Loss_G^A(A, I_g) = E_{I_g \sim p_g(I_g)}\left[\log A(I_g)\right]
\tag{5}
$$

$$
Loss_G = Loss_G^D + Loss_G^A
\tag{6}
$$

During the adversarial training, D, A and G alternatively improve their own learning ability. D tries to discriminate the synthesized image and classifies the source image to the proper labels by its feature representation. And A learns to distinguish which input pair is associated and which is not. With D and A improve their discrimination about input data, G strives for generating a more realistic image to fool D and A into treating it as real. The pose code c and dress state s which are kept separate from $f(x)$ are input into G_{dec}. Thus, the representation $f(x)$ can preserve as much identity information as possible without pose and dress interference.

4 Experiment Result

4.1 Data Set

CASIA-B gait database [16] is adopted for evaluating the proposed method in this experiment. The dataset was created by the Institute of Automation, Chinese Academy of Sciences in 2005. It has 124 subjects, including 31 females and 93 males, with 11 angles and 3 dress states for each subject. The subject has a total of 10 sequences, including 6 sequences that are normally worn denoting as NM01-NM06, 2 sequences that carry bags denoting as BG01-BG02, and 2 sequences that wear coats denoting as CL01-CL02. All the angles of each sequence are between 0° and 180° at 18° intervals. And the database has provided the corresponding GEI [15] for each sequence which can be used in this experiment. The size of input image is 64x64. Among the 124 subjects, the first 62 subjects (ID001-ID062) are used as training data. Therefore, the parameters of training can be set as $Nd = 62, Np = 11, Ns = 3$.

4.2 Implementation Details

The implementation details of this method are shown in Table 1,2, G_{enc}, D and A contain batch normalization layer and leaky rectified linear unit between layer 2 and layer 4 after each convolutional layer. In layer 5, G_{enc} and D have the same struct like layer 4 but A just has a *sigmod* activation function after convolutional layer. G_{dec} contains batch normalization layer and rectified linear unit between layer 1 and layer 4 after convolutional layer but in layer 5 using a *tanh* activation function.

Table 1. The implementation details of G_{enc}, D and A

G_{enc}, D and A			
Layer	Filter	Stride	Numbers of filter
Conv1	4×4	2	64
Conv2	4×4	2	128
Conv3	4×4	2	256
Conv4	4×4	2	512
Conv5	4×4	$2(G_{enc}, D)/4(A)$	$1024(G_{enc}, D)/1(A)$
AvgPool (G_{enc}, D only)	2×2	1	1024

The implementation of G and D is modified from [11]. And the design of A is adapted from [14] which named domain discriminator. The model is trained using Adam [19] with a learning rate of 0.0001 and all weights are initialized from a zero-centered normal distribution with a standard deviation of 0.02. The batch size is set to be 64 and training epoch is set to be 400. As the training strategy of traditional GAN, this model is also alternatively optimizing generator G, discriminator D and constraint A. But D and A will be update after G has optimized four times because discriminator has strong supervisions thanks to the additional class labels.

Table 2. The implementation details of G_{dec}

Layer	Filter	Stride	Numbers of filter
Conv1	4×4	2	512
Conv2	4×4	2	256
Conv3	4×4	2	128
Conv4	4×4	2	64
Conv5	4×4	2	1

G_{dec}

4.3 Experimental Result

In order to assess the impact of changes in perspective on gait recognition, this experiment evaluates the recognition effect between any two perspectives in three states (NM, BG, CL).

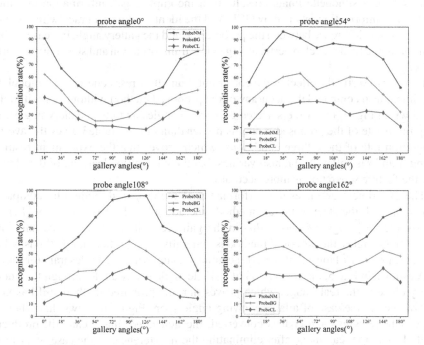

Fig. 2. Recognition rate of three conditions under four probe angles

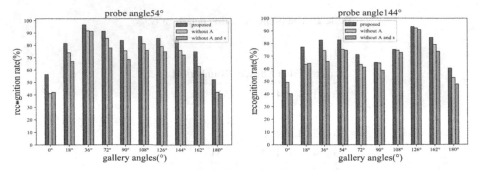

Fig. 3. The comparison of the effect of constraint A and dress code s on the model.

The test data set is composed of the walking sequences of the rest 62 subjects, and is divided into Gallery and Probe, where Gallery contains NM01-NM04, and Probe consists of (NM05-NM06, BG01-BG02, CL01-CL02) according to the status. Figure 2 shows that the recognition rate in the case of NM is much higher than that of BG and CL. This is because carrying bags and wearing coats significantly change the shape of the subject's silhouette image, resulting in incomplete gait information and more interference information retained by GEI. And the identification accuracy will gradually decrease as the difference between the probe angle and the gallery angle increases. Thus, it is a challenge for a model to perform large view transformation and state normalization perfectly.

In order to verify the effect of the constraint A and the dress code s on the model, the experiment also compared the accuracy of the proposed method without s or without A. As shown in Fig. 3, under the selected two probe angles and other gallery angles, the recognition rate of the proposed model is higher than others. Table3 gives the average recognition rate of these three conditions, which proves that the experiment result of adding A and s is better. And it also verifies that the recognition learning of the identity after the feature separation is more accurate.

The experiment evaluates the performance of the proposed method by comparing the results with the state-of-the-art methods including SPAE [13], gaitGAN [14] and gaitGANv2 [20]. Figure 4 shows that in the gait recognition of any probe angle and other gallery angles, the proposed method is generally superior to other methods, which solves the problem of low identification accuracy in large viewing angles transformation.

As shown in Fig. 5, the conversion of a single angle to any angle through this model is very close to the real image, which proves that the proposed method still has good performance in the case of a large viewing angle span. Figure 6 shows that when the image with carryings and coat is converted, the generated image can still produce a result close to the real image after eliminating the interference. In the case of 11 probe angles and 11 gallery angles, the experiment obtained a total of 121 sets of cross-view identity recognition accuracy and the average accuracy, as shown in Table 4. Compared with other gait recognition methods, as shown in Table 5, the average accuracy of this method is higher than others.

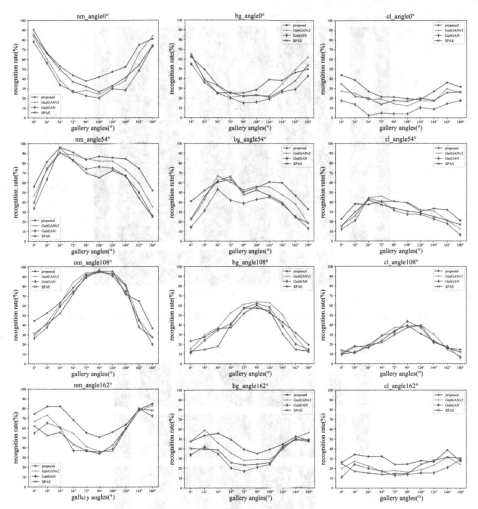

Fig. 4. The comparation of the proposed method and other methods in recognition rate. Each row represents a probe angle and each column represents a different state (NM, BG, CL).

Table 3. Average recognition rate of model in three conditions

		Probe view(nm05–06)				
		36	72	108	144	180
model	Without A and s	68.78	65.56	66.80	67.30	50.87
	Without A	72.48	68.04	70.00	71.19	56.38
	proposed	79.34	73.67	73.05	73.08	59.91

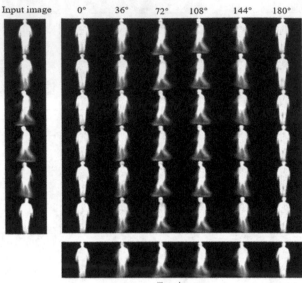

Fig. 5. The comparison between the synthetic image and real image at 6 angles.

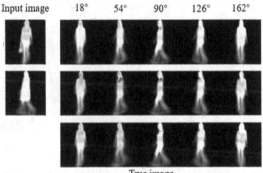

Fig. 6. The comparison between the synthetic image generated by the model, which the input images have clothing interference, and the real image at other 5 angles.

Table 4. Recognition rate of state NM in 11 gallery and probe views

		Probe view(nm05-nm06)										
		0	18	36	54	72	90	108	126	144	162	180
Gallery view(nm01-nm04)	0	100.0	89.39	68.56	56.26	43.76	43.56	44.51	50.00	58.71	74.62	81.25
	18	90.53	100.0	94.70	81.44	56.82	51.14	52.65	63.26	77.08	82.20	81.44
	36	66.86	96.02	99.24	96.59	74.43	65.72	63.26	74.24	82.58	82.39	71.21
	54	53.22	74.24	96.02	99.43	89.58	81.44	78.98	77.27	82.77	68.37	54.92

(*continued*)

Table 4. (*continued*)

	0	18	36	54	72	90	108	126	144	162	180
Probe view(nm05-nm06)											
72	43.56	60.61	72.16	91.29	99.24	97.73	92.61	85.98	71.02	55.30	40.91
90	37.88	53.79	61.74	83.71	97.92	98.11	95.83	82.58	64.77	50.95	38.83
108	41.67	51.89	63.83	87.12	96.02	97.73	99.05	93.37	75.00	56.06	41.86
126	47.16	51.33	68.18	85.61	82.95	82.58	96.02	100.0	93.37	63.64	44.51
144	52.08	65.91	71.02	84.47	66.86	63.64	71.97	92.99	97.54	78.98	58.52
162	74.62	78.79	83.52	74.62	52.46	54.36	64.96	67.23	84.66	97.92	89.77
180	80.87	70.45	57.77	52.08	32.95	33.90	36.74	49.05	60.23	85.04	100.0

Table 5. The average identification accuracy of each method.

Method	PLSTM[12]	ViDP[6]	SPAE	gaitGAN	gaitGANv2	Proposed
Average accuracy	59.5%	63.2%	63.9%	62.8%	68.87%	72.33%

5 Conclusion

In this paper, a gait recognition method FSGAN based on generative adversarial networks is proposed. Pose code and state code are added by separating features. The discriminator is redesigned and a constraint is added to optimize the generated image. The view transformation model constructed by FSGAN can convert gait images from any angle to any angle. It can also eliminate the interference of clothing and carrying without the need to estimate the subject's angle, clothing and carrying conditions in advance. Experimental results show that the model can achieve a great view transformation effect and retain the subject's identity information, and the recognition rate has been further improved. The feature separation idea of the proposed method can also be modified and optimized according to other common characteristics of the input data, and can be applied in other computer vision fields.

References

1. Kusakunniran, W., Wu, Q., Li, H., Zhang, J.: Multiple views gait recognition using view transformation model based on optimized gait energy image. In: ICCV Workshops, pp. 1058–1064 (2009)
2. Makihara, Y., Suzuki, A., Muramatsu, D., Li, X., Yagi, Y.: Joint intensity and spatial metric learning for robust gait recognition. In: CVPR, pp. 5705–5715 (2017)
3. Singh, S., Biswas, K.: Biometric gait recognition with carrying and clothing variants. In: ICPRMI, pp. 446–451 (2009)
4. Johnson, A.Y., Bobick, A.F.: A multi-view method for gait recognition using static body parameters. In: 3rd International Conference on Audio and Video Based Biometric Person Authentication, pp. 301–311 (2001)
5. Bashir, K., Xiang, T., Gong, S.: Cross-view gait recognition using correlation strength. In: BMVC (2010)

6. Hu, M., Wang, Y., Zhang, Z., Little, J.J., Huang, D.: View-invariant discriminative projection for multi-view gait-based human identification. IEEE TIFS **8**(12), 2034–2045 (2013)
7. Kusakunniran, W., Wu, Q., Li, H., Zhang, J.: Recognizing gaits across views through correlated motion co-clustering. IEEE Trans. Image Process. **23**(2), 696–709 (2014)
8. Makihara, Y., Sagawa, R., Mukaigawa, Y., Echigo, T., Yagi, Y.: Gait recognition using a view transformation model in the frequency domain. In: Leonardis, A., Bischof, H., Pinz, A. (eds.) ECCV 2006. LNCS, vol. 3953, pp. 151–163. Springer, Heidelberg (2006). https://doi.org/10.1007/11744078_12
9. Goodfellow, I., et al.: Generative adversarial nets. In: NIPS (2014)
10. Chen, X., Duan, Y., Houthooft, R., Schulman, J., Sutskever, I., Abbeel, P.: InfoGAN: interpretable representation learning by information maximizing generative adversarial nets. In: NIPS (2016)
11. Tran, L., Yin, X., Liu, X.: Disentangled representation learning GAN for pose-invariant face recognition. In: CVPR, pp. 1283–1292 (2017)
12. Feng, Y., Li, Y., Luo, J.: Learning effective gait features using LSTM. In: International Conference on Pattern Recognition, pp. 325–330 (2017)
13. Yu, S., Chen, H., Wang, Q., Shen, L., Huang, Y.: Invariant feature extraction for gait recognition using only one uniform model. Neurocomputing **239**, 81–93 (2017)
14. Yu, S., Chen, H., Garcia Reyes, E.B., Poh, N.: Gaitgan: Invariant gait feature extraction using generative adversarial networks. In: CVPR Workshops, pp. 532–539 (2017)
15. Han, J., Bhanu, B.: Individual recognition using gait energy image. IEEE TPAMI **28**(2), 316–322 (2006)
16. Yu, S., Tan, D., Tan, T.: A framework for evaluating the effect of view angle, clothing and carrying condition on gait recognition. In: ICPR, pp. 441–444 (2006)
17. Yoo, D., Kim, N., Park, S., Paek, A.S., Kweon, I.S.: Pixel-level domain transfer. arXiv:CoRR **1603**, 07442 (2016)
18. Deng, W., Zheng, L., Kang, G., Yang, Y., Ye, Q., Jiao, J.: Imageimage domain adaptation with preserved self-similarity and domaindissimilarity for person reidentification. In: CVPR, pp. 994–1003 (2018)
19. Kingma, D.P., Ba, J.: Adam: a method for stochastic optimization. arXiv preprint arXiv:1412.6980 (2014)
20. Yu, S., et al.: Gaitganv2: invariant gait feature extraction using generative adversarial networks. Pattern Recogn. **87**, 179–189 (2019)

Global Feature Polishing Network for Glass-Like Object Detection

Minyu Zhu, Xiuqi Xu, Jinhao Yu, Shuhan Chen[✉], Jian Wang, Xuelong Hu, and Jinrong Zhu

School of Information Engineering, Yangzhou University, Yangzhou, China
shchen@yzu.edu.cn

Abstract. Glass object detection aims to detect and segment glass-like objects in an input image. Compared with other binary segmentation tasks, the transparent property of glass brings great challenges to glass object detection. This requires the model to capture more richer image global semantics and local detail information. In this work, we propose a novel global feature polishing network for glass object detection. We first design a global perception module for coarse localization by embedding a self-attention block on top of the backbone. Then we propose a global feature polishing module to establish long-distance semantic dependence between different pixels and a multi-scale refinement module to combine multi-level side-output features, which can well explore the missing object parts and also refine the false detection in previous layers. In addition, we build a challenging Window dataset for comprehensive evaluation and further research. Experimental results demonstrate that the proposed method performs favorably against state-of-the-art methods without any pre-processing and post-processing.

Keywords: Glass object detection · Global feature polishing · Multi-scale refinement

1 Introduction

Researches on glass object detection has gradually emerged in recent years. Both as a binary segmentation task, salient object detection (SOD) [1–7,15,23,24,30] have developed rapidly in recent years, but the field of glass object detection (GOD) [8,28,29] has not received much attention. Generally, glass usually reflects objects or refracts light as shown in Fig. 1, which makes it difficult for SOD methods to accurately locate the glass-like object. This means that the model needs to capture richer global semantics and local detail information.

In this paper, we propose a Global Feature Polishing Network (GFPN) which incorporates multi-scale residual block into refinement process and makes full use of the side-output features to capture useful semantic information as much as possible. Specifically, it starts with a Global Perception Module (GP) expanding

---

M. Zhu and X. Xu—Equal contribution.

© Springer Nature Switzerland AG 2021
Y. Peng et al. (Eds.): ICIG 2021, LNCS 12888, pp. 77–88, 2021.
https://doi.org/10.1007/978-3-030-87355-4_7

Fig. 1. The refraction and transmission properties of the glass-like object make it difficult to be distinguished and segmented even by our human eyes, as illustrated in this figure(from left to right are input images and corresponding ground truth).

the receptive field by stacking self-attention blocks to find the coarse location of the glass object. Then, we propose a Global Feature Polishing Module (GFP) to establish long-distance semantic dependence between different pixels and a multi-scale refinement correction module to combine multi-level side-output features in a prediction-to-feature fusion strategy, which can further optimize the quality of the input features. Through this feature enhancement operation, the fuzzy boundary of coarse positioning can be effectively fixed, which means that the optimized input features can be better fused in the refinement step. Finally, we further propose Multi-scale Refinement Module (MSR) to merge multi-level features with top-down guidance to alleviate the dilution problem. In addition, to evaluate the effectiveness of our proposed network, we comb through a challenging glass detection dataset called Window, which includes 4,419 large glass images of various categories.

In summary, the contributions of this paper can be summarized as follows:

1) We first propose GP to capture richer semantic information for accurate initial location of glass.
2) We propose MSR to refine the initial prediction in a multi-scale manner with top-down guidance.
3) We propose GFP to enhance side-output features for better detection, which establishes the long-distance dependency between semantic correlative pixels.
4) We build a challenging GOD dataset called Window with 4,419 glass images in diverse scenes. Extensive experiments show the state-of-the-art performance of the proposed model.

2   Related Work

Salient Object Detection. Early methods predicted the saliency map using a bottom-up pattern by the hand-craft feature, such as contrast [12], boundary background [19,20], center prior [13] and so on. More details are introduced in [16–18]. In this review, we mainly focus on the latest deep models in recent years. Among them, multi-scale feature fusion is a common way to combine the complementary. Hou *et al.* [6] introduced short connections to the skip-layer structures within the HED [22] architecture. Wu *et al.* [11] proposed a novel cascaded partial decoder framework which directly utilize generated saliency map to refine the features of backbone. Wei *et al.* [9] aggregated multi-level features and selects complementary components from embedded features before fusion to avoid the introduction of too much redundant information. Deng *et al.* [10] learned the residual between the intermediate saliency prediction and the ground truth Wu *et al.* [7] proposed a Stacked Cross Refinement Network which aims to simultaneously refine multi-level features of salient object detection and edge detection by stacking cross refinement unit.

Shadow Detection. Hu *et al.* [26] developed a direction-aware attention mechanism by introducing attention weights when aggregating spatial context features. Zhu *et al.* [27] developed a Bidirectional Feature Pyramid Network (BFPN), which iteratively combined and detailed context features by deploying two series of RAR modules. Khan *et al.* [25] trained two networks to detect shadow regions and boundaries respectively, and input the detection results into the conditional random field to optimize the image results.

Glass Object Detection. However, the segmentation method mentioned above may not be applicable to the glass object detection task, because the glass area generally occupies a large space in the input image, rather than one or more significant objects. In general, glass images do not have the same strong differences as those between shaded and unshaded areas. The transparent glass will completely reveal the objects behind it, making it difficult to detect and precisely divide the glass. In the early years, the traditional methods were mostly based on the physical and optical properties of glass or material properties. Recently, the convolutional neural network(CNNs) begin to show its superiority in the glass detection task. Yang *et al.* [8] proposed a segmentation method based on multi-layer background contrast feature for detection. Lin *et al.* [29] inferred potential areas of glass by establishing relationships between some objects inside the glass and those outside. Mei *et al.* [28] explored rich contextual clues for robust glass detection using a new large field context feature integration module. All of these approaches miss an important point: they do not make full and effective use of the extracted features. As a result, the shape of the glass is not very ideal and the edge of the detected glass is rough and inaccurate, where there even exist cases of false detection and missed detection.

3 Proposed Framework

3.1 Overview

As mentioned above, glass are different from ordinary conspicuous objects. Due to their unique optical properties, glass objects usually have specular reflection effect and perspective effect, which can not be distinguished directly even by human eyes. In the human visual system, when the target appears within the line of sight, people will first locate the target subject in space, and then observe the details of other parts. In view of this, we propose our network based on Feature Pyramid Network (FPN) [32], a classic U-Net [30] structure. As shown

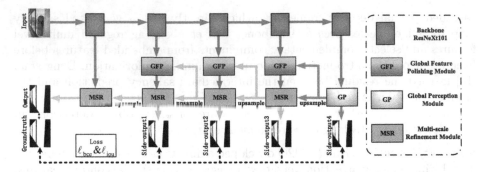

Fig. 2. Pipeline of proposed structure. We use ground truth as side-outputs to supervise until network learning the feature of the input image. The purple block marks the trunk of ResneXt-101. On the basis of side-output supervision, results are further refined to output the final salient graph. The dotted line section gives the monitoring flow (Color figure online).

in Fig. 2, we implement the network function through a two-stage strategy. The GP guided by the self-attention mechanism and the MSR are respectively used for the initial coarse positioning and the progressive edge details. Starting with GP to locate glass object roughly, we apply GFP to capture the long distance dependencies of the pixels between the input feature and the salient image. The MSR is then used for refining coarse positioning image progressively with multi-scale top-down guidance. Details of the modules mentioned above are described in the following subsections.

3.2 Global Perception Module

Long-range dependencies methods such as self-attention [35], which can capture useful contextual information to benefit visual understanding problems. Among them, Cheng *et al.* [31] proposed a strip-pooling for scene parsing based on spatial pooling, which can effectively capture the characteristics of long and narrow targets. Unlike traditional spatial pooling that collects contextual information from a fixed square area, strip-pooling uses a long and narrow pooling kernel to enable the network to extract local and global information more efficiently. In addition, the strip-pooling has better resolution for regular narrow objects.

Inspired by the above work, we insert several strip-pooling modules on the top layer of the backbone in a stacked manner to construct a self-attention global perception module. With the help of this self-attention mechanism-based module, the ability of capturing the boundary information of long and narrow objects is significantly improved. It's worth pointing out that this structure is embedded at the top of the network from the bottom to the top link, so it further enhances the network's feature representation capability and expands the network's receptive field while effectively saving the computational complexity of the network. After passing through the GSP module, the network will output the initial coarse positioning of the glass. The details of this rough edge will be further improved in the module described below.

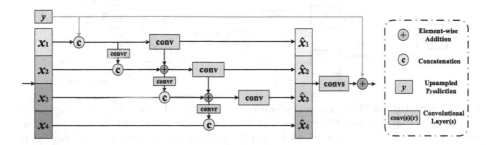

Fig. 3. Structure of MSR module. The red block is the input after splitting the channel. The first input will be concatenated with the side-output from the upper layer and the rest of the input will then be then concatenated with the output of previous part, followed by a step by step fusion, and finally the splicing of each slice part for output (Color figure online).

3.3 Multi-scale Refinement Module

After obtained the initial coarse localization map, we need to remedy the missing object parts and fix the false detection by integrating multi-level convolutional features. As we know, different layers of deep CNNs learn different scale features. Shallow layers capture low-level structure information while deep layers capture high-level semantic information. We try to fully integrate their complementary information in an efficient manner to get a better feature representation. In general, there are two basic requirements for seamless aggregation: high-level semantic information should be fully preserved, while noisy distractions in shallow layers should be filtered out as much as possible. Following these two criterion, we design an efficient guided refinement module in a prediction to feature fusion manner.

As can be seen in Fig. 3, the input side-output with channel C is first equally split into g groups, each of which consists of $\frac{C}{g}$ channel feature maps. Then, the upper side-output is used as a guidance to be concatenated with the $\frac{C}{g}$ channel feature maps within each group to achieve $(\frac{C}{g} + 1)$ channel. In all branches except the last branch, we embed convolution after the concatenated feature map to further increase the receptive field. In addition, starting from the second branch, we use the output of the previous branch as a guidance to concatenate with the input feature map of the current branch to further preserve the feature information in the current branch. Among them, g is set to 4 in this paper, then the output feature of the k-th branch can be expressed as:

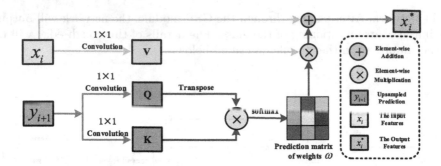

Fig. 4. Structure of GFP. The red block is the upsampled prediction, and the yellow one is the input feature. We generate a dense attention map with $H \times W$ weights, which is then multiplied by the input pixel by pixel for feature polishing (Color figure online).

$$\hat{x}_k^i = \begin{cases} Conv_k(Cat(x_k^i, y^{i+1})), k = 1 \\ Conv_k(\hat{x}_{k-1}^i + Cat(x_k^i, Conv_k(\hat{x}_{k-1}^i))), 1 < k < 4 \\ Cat(x_k^i, \hat{x}_{k-1}^i), k = 4 \end{cases} \qquad (1)$$

where $\hat{x}_k^i$ and x_k^i represent the input and output features of the i-th branch respectively; $Conv_k$ represent the obvious features that are concatenated in the k-th branch; Cat represent the concatenation operation; y^{i+1} represent the side-output prediction map from the upper layer.

Then, the features with $C + g$ channel channels obtained by concatenating the outputs of all branches are sent to several convolutional layers to acquire a refined residual, which will be added to the deep side-output to get the result of layer i. The above process can be expressed as:

$$y^i = y^{i+1} + Convs(\hat{x}^i) \qquad (2)$$

In our model, the multi-level features are fed into our MSR progressively for residual refinement,which doesn't need upsample features with multiple channels for concatenation, thus can be more efficient.

3.4   Global Feature Polishing Module

Glass objects usually have continuous and regular boundaries, but in the process of full convolutional neural network (FCN) [23] upsampling, the mapping relationship between pixels will be gradually diluted, making it impossible to retain the dependence relationship between long-distance pixels, eventually leading to missing and false detection of the boundary. In order to solve this problem, we propose the GFP module to obtain long-distance dependencies between different pixels. The details are shown in Fig. 4.

Firstly, the side-output y obtained in the previous layer will be put into two 1×1 convolutional layers to obtain two new feature maps $\{Q, K\} \in R^{C \times N}$, and then perform matrix multiplication between the matrices Q and K. After softmax activation, the weights of the prediction image are given. The above process can be expressed as:

$$\sigma_{j,i} = \frac{\exp(\omega_{i,j})}{\sum_{i=1}^{N} \exp(\omega_{i,j})}, \omega_{i,j} = (K_j)^T \cdot Q_i \tag{3}$$

$\sigma_{j,i}$ represents the dependency between position i and position j in the image. Generally, the feature representations of two positions with stronger correlation are more similar.

Then, we feed the feature map x of the current layer into another 1×1 convolutional layer to generate a new feature map $V \in R^{C \times N}$, and then perform matrix multiplication on ω and V. The above calculation process can be expressed by the following formula:

$$x_i^* = \alpha \sum_{i=1}^{N} (\sigma_{j,i} V_i) + x_j \tag{4}$$

In this paper, we initialize the scale parameter α to 0, which is gradually assigned more weights during the training process.

The traditional Non-local module only relies on input features to explore the inner self-attention, while our GFP introduces confident semantic information in deep layer to guide the network to capture the long-distance pixel semantic correlation, which effectively improves the feature representation and benefits for the subsequent refinement, thus results in more accurate detection.

4 Experiments

4.1 Experimental Setup

Datasets. We perform extensive experiments on the following two datasets: GDD [28] and Window. **GDD** [28] is the first large-scale benchmark specifically for glass detection proposed by Mei *et al.* which contains 3,916 glass images. **Window** is a noval dataset that we have sorted out on the basis of Trans10K proposed by Xie *et al.* [21]. A total of 4,419 glass pictures were screened out and added to Window, mainly including windows, glass walls, glass doors and other transparent materials at different angles. All images in Window are selected from complex real-world scenarios that have large variations such as scale, viewpoint, contrast, occlusion, category and transparency. We trained our network on GDD, and tested it on both the Window and GDD.

Evaluation Metrics. Four widely used metrics are adopt for thorough evaluation, which are F-measure (F_β) [14], E-measure ($E\varphi$) [1], S-measure ($S\alpha$) [3], and MAE (M). The threshold value of F in this paper is adaptive, which is twice of the mean value. Only the maximum F_β and $E\varphi$ are reported here to show the best performance a model can achieve. Higher values of F_β, $E\varphi$, $S\alpha$, indicate better performance, while it is opposite for M.

Implementation Details. All the experiments are implemented in PyTorch with an NVIDIA TITAN Xp GPU and Intel i7-6700K CPU 4.0 GHz processor. Pre-trained ResNeXt-101 [2] on ImageNet is used as backbone. We apply data augmentation like random flipping and multi-scale input images to alleviate over-fitting risk. All the images are resized into 352 × 352 both for training and testing. The training set is the same as GDNet [28]. To obtain high quality regional segmentation and clear boundaries, We define a hybrid loss as the sum of IOU loss [34] and BCE loss [33]. The hyper-parameters are set as follows: initial learning rate is set to 0.0005 which is decreased by 10 after 25 epochs, the batch size is set to 10 and the maximum epoch is 50.

Image   GT   Ours   GDNet   DSC   BDRAR   CPD   SCRN   R³Net   F³Net

Fig. 5. Visual comparison. From left to right: input image, ground truth (GT), our method, GDNet [28], DSC [6], BDRAR [27], CPD [11], SCRN [7], R³Net [10], F³Net[9].

Table 1. Quantitative results. Training set is the same as GDNet [28]. The best result is highlighted in bold. ↑ and ↓ indicate higher and lower is better performance.

Methods	Backbone	GDD				Window			
		$E\varphi \uparrow$	$S\alpha \uparrow$	$F_\beta \uparrow$	$M \downarrow$	$E\varphi \uparrow$	$S\alpha \uparrow$	$F_\beta \uparrow$	$M \downarrow$
CPD [11]	ResNet50	0.628	0.831	0.900	0.077	0.577	0.776	0.779	0.136
SCRN [7]	ResNet50	0.610	0.821	0.892	0.086	0.587	0.781	0.778	0.141
F³Net [9]	ResNet50	0.638	0.824	0.908	0.079	0.620	**0.796**	0.803	0.120
DSC [6]	ResNeXt101	0.597	0.743	0.844	0.125	0.546	0.723	0.741	0.168
BDRAR [27]	ResNeXt101	0.636	0.784	0.887	0.094	**0.641**	0.782	0.806	0.115
R³Nct [10]	ResNeXt101	0.501	0.661	0.772	0.194	0.420	0.595	0.654	0.288
GDNet [28]	ResNeXt101	0.632	0.836	0.918	**0.063**	0.618	**0.796**	0.806	0.115
Ours	ResNeXt101	**0.641**	**0.840**	**0.920**	**0.063**	0.626	**0.796**	**0.811**	**0.113**

4.2 Comparisons with SOTAs

Quantitative Evaluation. Our proposed network is compared with 7 state-of-the-art methods [6,7,9–11,27,28]. Table 1 shows the detailed experimental results. As can be seen that our proposed network significantly outperforms other methods on GOD datasets, in specific, we achieved 0.47% improvement over the second method in term of E_φ and $S\alpha$. For the Window, we also obtained best evaluation scores except E-measure. Although additional CRF post-processing are applied in several methods(4rd, 5th, 6th and 7th row), we are still comparable with it in $S\alpha$.

Visual Comparison. Figure 5 shows a visual comparison of the results of our method with the other state-of-the-art methods [6,7,9–11,27,28] on the GOD. It's intuitive to see that existing methods perform poorly when glass occupies a large part of the image. As shown by the two shadow detection methods (5th and 6th column), the effective shadow detection methods are difficult to accurately segment the object edge. As for the boundary awareness algorithm SCRN, the boundary supervision does not work in this task. When the object is glass rather than a significant object (3th and 4th row), most of the SOD methods listed in the figure have errors in the object positioning. The results show that after the glass object can be accurately located, there is still a part of the object boundary predicted by the network is distorted and fuzzy. In contrast, our method has achieved impressive results, which shows that the proposed module is effective.

4.3 Ablation Analysis

In this section, we focus on the performance improvement of the proposed GFP. Therefore, we set the baseline to a network without the GFP loaded.

Table 2. Ablation experimental results on GDD. NL stands for Non-local module.

Methods	GDD			
	$E\varphi \uparrow$	$S\alpha \uparrow$	$F_\beta \uparrow$	$M \downarrow$
Baseline	0.630	0.814	0.891	0.078
Baseline + Nl [35]	0.632	0.821	0.901	0.075
Baseline + GFP	**0.637**	**0.824**	**0.906**	**0.073**

In order to prove that the proposed global feature polishing module has more obvious advantages than the classic self-attention module, we try to separately integrate the two modules into the baseline for comparison. It can be seen from the results in Table 2 that GFP has significantly improved various performance indicators, especially S-measure, which is 1.2% higher than the baseline. But when we replaced the proposed GFP with Non-local [35] module, the performance dropped significantly, where S-measure dropped from 0.824 to 0.821, and there were also 0.7% and 0.5% decline in term of $E\varphi$ and F_β. This shows that optimizing the input features of each layer can significantly improve the performance of the final output. In particular, our proposed method of applying side-output weights to input features enables the network to integrate its own structural information to optimize the input. Compared with the traditional self-attention structure, the long-distance dependence relationship between pixels collected by our proposed global feature polishing module is utilized by the network in a more efficient manner. In other words, our proposed GFP greatly improves the network's ability to extract spatial structure features, which is beneficial to current glass detection tasks.

5 Conclusion

Glass object detection is a challenging object detection task as the optical properties of glass make it difficult to be accurately segmented from the background. In this paper, we propose an efficient network for GOD with multi-scale top-down guidance. By stacking several self-attention blocks on the top of the backbone in a recurrent manner, the glass object can be located more accurately. Subsequently, the long distance dependence between pixels is explored by the GFP for feature polishing. Furthermore, such coarse prediction is refined progressively by fusing with side-output features in a multi-scale guided manner. As a result, the missing parts and false detection can by well remedied. Experimental results on GDD and Window show the effectiveness of the proposed method.

Acknowledgement. Supported by the Natural Science Foundation of China (No. 61802336 No. 61806175 No. 62073322), Jiangsu Province 7th Projects for Summit Talents in Six Main Industries, Electronic Information Industry (DZXX-149, No.110), Yangzhou University "Qinglan Project".

References

1. Fan, D., Gong, C., Cao, Y., Ren, B., Cheng, M., Borji, A.: Enhanced-alignment measure for binary foreground map evaluation. In: IJCAI, pp. 698–704 (2018)
2. He, K., Zhang, X., Ren, S., Sun, J.: Deep residual learning for image recognition. In: IEEE CVPR, pp. 770–778 (2016)
3. Fan, D., Cheng, M., Liu, Y., Li, T., Borji, A.: Structure-measure: a new way to evaluate foreground maps. In: IEEE ICCV, pp. 4548–4557 (2017)
4. Zhang, P., Wang, D., Lu, II., Wang, H., Ruan, X.: Amulet: aggregating multi-level convolutional features for salient object detection. In: IEEE CVPR, pp. 202–211 (2017)
5. Zhao, J., Liu, J., Fan, D., Cao, Y., Yang, J., Cheng, M.: Edge guidance network for salient object detection. In: IEEE ICCV (2019)
6. Hou, Q., Cheng, M., Hu, X., Borji, A., Tu, Z., Torr, P.H.S.: Deeply supervised salient object detection with short connections. In: IEEE TPAMI, vol. 41, no. 4, pp. 815–828 (2019)
7. Wu, Z., Su, L., Huang, Q.: Stacked cross refinement network for edge-aware salient object detection. In: IEEE ICCV, pp. 7264–7273 (2019)
8. Yang, X., Mei, H., Xu, K., Wei, X., Yin, B., Lau, R.W.H.: Where is my mirror? In: IEEE ICCV (2019)
9. Wei, J., Wang, S., Huang, Q.: F3Net: fusion. Feedback and focus for salient object detection. In: AAAI (2020)
10. Deng, Z., et al.: R3Net: Recurrent residual refinement network for saliency detection. In: IJCAI, pp. 684–690 (2018)
11. Wu, Z., Su, L., Huang, Q.: Cascaded partial decoder for fast and accurate salient object detection. In: IEEE CVPR, pp. 3907–3916 (2019)
12. Cheng, M., Mitra, N.J., Huang, X., Torr, P.H.S., Hu, S.: Global contrast based salient region detection. IEEE TPAMI **37**(3), 569–582 (2015)
13. Klein, D.A., Frintrop, S.: Center-surround divergence of feature statistics for salient object detection. In: IEEE ICCV, pp. 2214–2219 (2011)
14. Ran, M., Zelnikmanor, L., Tal, A.: How to evaluate foreground maps. In: IEEE CVPR, pp. 248–255 (2014)
15. Chen, S., Tan, X., Wang, B., Hu, X.: Reverse attention for salient object detection. In: ECCV, pp. 234–250 (2018)
16. Borji, A., Cheng, M.-M., Hou, Q., Jiang, H., Li, J.: Salient object detection: a survey. Comput. Visual Media **5**(2), 117–150 (2019). https://doi.org/10.1007/s41095-019-0149-9
17. Borji, A., Cheng, M., Jiang, H., Li, J.: Salient object detection: a benchmark. IEEE TIP **24**(12), 5706–5722 (2015)
18. Fan, D., Cheng, M., Liu, J., Gao, S., Hou, Q., Borji, A.: Salient objects in clutter: bringing salient object detection to the foreground. In: ECCV, pp. 186–202 (2018)
19. Yang, C., Zhang, L., Lu, H., Ruan, X., Yang, M.: Saliency detection via graph-based manifold ranking. In: IEEE CVPR, pp. 3166–3173 (2013)
20. Zhu, W., Liang, S., Wei, Y., Sun, J.: Saliency optimization from robust background detection. In: IEEE CVPR, pp. 2814–2821 (2014)
21. Xie, E., Wang, W., Wang, W., Ding, M., Shen, C., Luo, P.: Segmenting transparent objects in the wild. In: Vedaldi, A., Bischof, H., Brox, T., Frahm, J.-M. (eds.) ECCV 2020. LNCS, vol. 12358, pp. 696–711. Springer, Cham (2020). https://doi.org/10.1007/978-3-030-58601-0_41

22. Xie, S., Tu Z.: Holistically-nested edge detection. In: IEEE CVPR, pp. 1395–1403 (2015)
23. Long, J., Shelhamer, E., Darrell, T.: Fully convolutional networks for semantic segmentation. In: IEEE CVPR, pp. 3431–3440 (2015)
24. Qin, X., Zhang, Z., Huang, C., Gao, C., Dehghan, M., Jagersand, M.: BASNet: boundary-aware salient object detection. In: IEEE CVPR, pp. 7479–7489 (2019)
25. Khan, O.II., Bonnamoun, M, Sohel, F.: Automatic feature learning for robust shadow detection. In: IEEE CVPR, pp. 1939–1946 (2014)
26. Xiaowei, H., ChiWing, F., Zhu, L., Qin, J., Heng, P.A.: Direction-aware spatial context features for shadow detection and removal. In: IEEE CVPR (2018)
27. Zhu, L., et al: Bidirectional feature pyramid network with recurrent attention residual modules for shadow detection. In: ECCV (2018)
28. Mei, H., Yang, X., Wang, Y., Liu, Y., Lau, R.W.H.: Don't hit me! Glass detection in real-world scenes. In: IEEE CVPR, pp. 3684–3693 (2020)
29. Lin, J., Wang, G., Lau, R.W.H.: Progressive mirror detection. In: IEEE CVPR, pp. 3694–3702 (2020)
30. Zhou, Z., Rahman Siddiquee, M.M., Tajbakhsh, N., Liang, J.: UNet++: a nested U-Net architecture for medical image segmentation. In: Stoyanov, D., et al. (eds.) DLMIA/ML-CDS -2018. LNCS, vol. 11045, pp. 3–11. Springer, Cham (2018). https://doi.org/10.1007/978-3-030-00889-5_1
31. Hou, Q., Zhang, L., Cheng, M.M., Feng, J.: Rethinking spatial pooling for scene parsing. In: IEEE CVPR (2020)
32. Lin, T., Dollar, P., Girshick, R., He, K., Hariharan, B., Belongie, S.: Feature pyramid networks for object detection. In: IEEE CVPR, pp. 936–944 (2017)
33. de Boer, P.-T., Kroese, D.P., Mannor, S., Rubinstein, R.Y.: A tutorial on the cross-entropy method. Ann. OR **134**(1), 19–67 (2005). https://doi.org/10.1007/s10479-005-5724-z
34. Mattyus, G., Luo, W., Urtasun, R.: DeepRoadMapper: extracting road topology from aerial images. In: IEEE ICCV (2017). 10.1109
35. Wang, X., Girshick, R., Gupta, A., He, K.: Non-local neural networks. In: IEEE CVPR, pp. 7794–7803 (2018)

Imitating What You Need: An Adaptive Framework for Detector Distillation

Ruoyu Sun[iD] and Hongkai Xiong[✉][iD]

Shanghai Jiao Tong University, 800 Dongchuan Road, Shanghai, China
{sunruoyu1,xionghongkai}@sjtu.edu.cn

Abstract. Object detection models with favorable performances usually suffer from high computational costs. Knowledge distillation, a simple model compression method, aims at training a light-weight student network by transferring knowledge from a cumbersome teacher model. In this paper, we investigate different components of typical two-stage and single-stage detector in details, and propose a detector distillation framework that adaptively transfers knowledge from teacher to student according to task specific priors. The knowledge is transferred adaptively at three levels, *i.e.*, feature backbone, classification head, and bounding box regression head, according to which model performs more reasonably. Furthermore, considering that it would introduce optimization dilemma when minimizing distillation loss and detection loss simultaneously, we propose a distillation decay strategy to help improve model generalization via gradually reducing the distillation penalty. Experiments on widely used detection benchmarks demonstrate the effectiveness of our method. Particularly, taking Faster R-CNN as an example, we achieve an accuracy of 39.4% with Resnet-50 on MS COCO 2017 dataset, which surpasses its baseline 37.5% by 1.9% points, and even better than the teacher model with 39.3% mAP.

Keywords: Object detection · Knowledge distillation · Gaussian masking · Adaptive regularization

1 Introduction

Object detection is a fundamental and challenging problem in computer vision. Typical detection models, varying from single-stage [17,19,23] to two-stage [5,6, 20], achieves significant improvement in performances. However, these detectors are usually equipped with cumbersome models and suffer expensive computation cost. Hence, designing light-weight neural networks with high performance has attracted much attention in real-world applications.

Knowledge Distillation (KD), introduced by Hinton [11], has received much attention due to its simplicity and efficiency. The distilled knowledge is defined as soft label outputs from a large teacher model, which contain structural information among different classes. Following KD, many methods are proposed to either utilize softmax outputs [4,16] or mimic the feature layer of teacher models

© Springer Nature Switzerland AG 2021
Y. Peng et al. (Eds.): ICIG 2021, LNCS 12888, pp. 89–101, 2021.
https://doi.org/10.1007/978-3-030-87355-4_8

[21,27,28]. However, detection requires reliable localization in addition to classification, while the interleaved relationships among various modules in detector make it difficult to transfer knowledge directly.

To address the above issues, this paper proposes an adaptive distillation framework for typical object detectors, of which we deliberately design specific distillation strategy for each module according to their intrinsic properties. The highlight is that what we want to borrow from the teacher model is its generalization ability. In particular, our method adaptively mimics responses of teacher model in three aspects: 1) At feature backbone level, we highlight foreground regions by Gaussian masking operation for feature distillation. 2) At classification level, benefiting from a region proposal sharing mechanism, teacher model outputs soft labels within regions that student provides. 3) At bounding box regression level, regressed bounding box locations from teacher model's regression head are used as extra regressed targets for student model.

In addition, minimizing distillation loss and original training loss simultaneously would introduce optimization dilemma, where the optimal state suitable for distillation may not be acceptable for detection. To solve this issue, we further propose a distillation decay strategy to improve student's generalization via gradually reducing distillation penalty. In this way, the distillation term can be treated as regularization to help student model converge to a better optimization point.

To sum up, this paper makes following contributions:

- We propose an adaptive distillation framework for object detection, which transfers knowledge from teacher to student according to task specific priors. This is achieved by imitating knowledge at three levels, *i.e.*, feature backbone, classification head, and bounding box regression head, according to which model performs more reasonably.
- We propose a distillation decay strategy to gradually reduce teacher's interference to student, and help improve model generalization.

2   Related Works

2.1   Object Detection

Current CNN-based object detectors mainly include single-stage, two-stage and anchor-free detectors, where the former two are well-developed. Single-stage object detectors such as YOLO [19] directly perform object classification and bounding box regression on the feature maps. RetinaNet [14] proposes focal loss to mitigate the unbalanced positive and negative samples. Two-stage detectors [2,5,6,9,20] treat detection as a coarse-to-fine process via firstly generating candidate regions of interests and followed by a region refinement procedure. In particular, Faster R-CNN [20] introduces Region Proposal Network (RPN) to produce region proposals.

2.2 Knowledge Distillation

In order to accelerate network training, various model compression strategies have been proposed, such as weight quantization [7, 26, 29], network pruning [8, 18, 24], and low-rank factorization [12, 22]. However, these methods either change network structure or contains large complexity, even hurting performance significantly.

Knowledge distillation is proposed to transfer knowledge from a high performance teacher model to a compact student model, aiming at improving latter's performance. It is first proposed by Hinton *et al.* [11] on image classification models, utilizing teacher's class probability vectors as soft labels to guide student's training. Hint learning [21] distills a deeper and thinner student model by imitating both soft outputs and intermediate feature representations of teacher model. Similar works are presented in [4, 16, 28].

In detection domains, knowledge distillation also shows its potential. Wang *et al.* [25] only distill backbone features within local regions near object. Chen *et al.* [1] distill two-stage detectors on all components including task heads. Li *et al.* [13] transfer knowledge from both positive and negative proposals on high-level features and corresponding task heads. However, these methods either have accuracy limited by redundant selected background features or suffer from drowning background proposals. Misguidance may also be provided when confronting proposals teacher model performs poorly on.

In summary, current distillation frameworks either lack specific design for detectors or fail to effectively select the most informative parts for distillation. Different from these works, our adaptive distillation method designs specific distillation strategy for each module according to their intrinsic properties and utilizes distillation decay strategy to further improve generalization.

3 Method

3.1 Network Overview

In this section, we describe our proposed adaptive distillation framework in detail. Without losing generality, we take the typical two-stage object detector Faster R-CNN [20] for instance, and the whole framework is shown in Fig. 1. Our proposed distillation method effects mainly on three parts: distillation of feature backbone, classification head, and bounding box regression head, respectively. We adaptively transfer knowledge from teacher to student model with different imitation strategies.

Based on responses of each components: 1) For backbone features, the foreground regions are modeled by a two-dimensional Gaussian mask inside ground truth bounding boxes to enhance objects while suppressing backgrounds. 2) For classification head, by region proposal sharing, teacher model utilizes student's positive samples to outputs soft labels and student's classification head is supervised by both one-hot labels and soft ones. 3) For bounding box regression head, a selective distillation scheme takes regressed bounding box locations from teacher

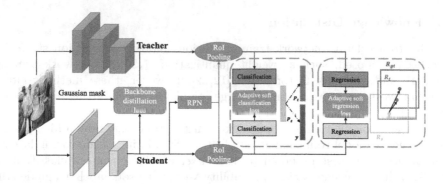

Fig. 1. Overview of the proposed task adaptive distillation framework. The proposed distillation method consists of three modules. Blue parts remain unchanged during distillation, while yellow parts are adaptively supervised by the teacher (Color figure online).

model as extra regressed targets to guide student model. As such, regression targets are progressively approaching to ground truths, which is more robust for bounding box regression. Each component would be elaborated as follows.

3.2 Backbone Features

For CNN-based detectors, the performance gain mainly credits to better backbone features. However, previous work [25] has found that directly imitating features at all locations would not promote the performance much. The reason is that it is the foreground regions that counts for a successful detector. Since drowning background regions usually occupy the majority area of a feature map, merely perform distillation at all the locations would inevitably introduce large amount of noise from those uncared negative regions. To address this issue, we introduce a Gaussian mask to highlight the centric foreground pixels and suppress those boundary regions around the objects.

Specifically, given a bounding box B of an object, with size of $w \times h$ and centered at (x_0, y_0), the two-dimensional Gaussian mask is defined as:

$$M = \begin{cases} e^{-\frac{(x-x_0)^2}{\sigma_x^2(w/2)^2} - \frac{(y-y_0)^2}{\sigma_y^2(h/2)^2}}, & (x,y) \in B \\ 0, & \text{otherwise} \end{cases} \tag{1}$$

where σ_x^2 and σ_y^2 are decay factors along the two directions, and we set $\sigma_x^2 = \sigma_y^2$ for simplicity. The mask is only effective within ground truth bounding boxes and equals to zero everywhere else. In particular, when several Gaussian masks overlap over a single pixel (x, y), the mask value is simply set as point-wise maximum. Figure 2 illustrates two images, as well as their corresponding Gaussian masks.

With the delicately designed Gaussian mask, the backbone features are distilled via minimizing the following loss:

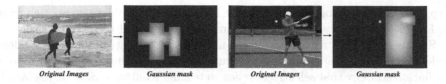

Original Images   Gaussian mask   Original Images   Gaussian mask

Fig. 2. An illustration of the generated Gaussian masks over samples from MS COCO [15] dataset.

$$L_{bk} = \frac{1}{2N_a} \sum_{i=1}^{W} \sum_{j=1}^{H} \sum_{c=1}^{C} M^{ijc} (F_s^{ijc} - F_t^{ijc})^2, \tag{2}$$

where $N_a = \sum_{i=1}^{W} \sum_{j=1}^{H} \sum_{c=1}^{C} M^{ijc}$, W, H, C are the width, height, and channels of the feature map, F_s^{ijc} and F_t^{ijc} denote the backbone features of student and teacher models, respectively.

3.3 Classification Head

Knowledge distillation is widely used in classification tasks [11,21,28], where soft labels provide structural information among different categories. However, directly transferring soft labels in a detection system is not applicable: First, background regions occupy the majority of proposals, which introduce a large amount of noise to their structural information; Second, proposals output by two models are inevitably different, which makes them not comparable for knowledge distillation.

Our method effectively address the above issues: 1) We only focus on positive samples which are beneficial when modeling inter-class structural priors and neglect negative ones. 2) We share student's RPN proposals to teacher model, and use its corresponding outputs as soft labels. Specifically, given N region proposals from student RPN's output, we compute soft labels of N_p positive samples over teacher model $\{y_t^i\}_{i=1}^{N_p} \in \mathbb{R}^{C'}$, where C' denotes the number of classes. Accompanying with all the N proposals and their ground truth labels $\{y^j\}_{j=1}^{N} \in \mathbb{R}^{C'}$, total loss for classification head is reformulated as

$$L_{cls} = \sum_{j=1}^{N} L_{CE}(y_s^j, y^j) + \beta_1 \sum_{i=1}^{N_p} L_{BCE}(y_s^i, y_t^i), \tag{3}$$

where L_{CE} and L_{BCE} denote cross-entropy and binary cross-entropy, respectively. y_s is prediction of student model, and β_1 is a balancing factor that controls the two loss terms.

3.4 Bounding Box Regression Head

Regression head in detectors adjusts locations and sizes of candidate region proposals. For bounding box regression distillation, we expect teacher model's output to offer a reasonable mild target for student model to regress, relieving the forced abrupt regression targets from current proposal to ground truth.

However, teacher's regression output may provide wrong guidance for student model and even contradicts to ground truth's direction. Therefore, we propose a distillation strategy that selectively relies on teacher's outputs. Similar to classification head distillation, student's positive proposals are shared to teacher model. Specifically, given N_p positive region proposals from student's RPN output, we denote $\{r_p^i\}_{i=1}^{N_p}$, $\{r_t^i\}_{i=1}^{N_p}$, $\{r_s^i\}_{i=1}^{N_p}$, $\{r_{gt}^i\}_{i=1}^{N_p}$ as proposal locations before regression, teacher's regression output, student's regression output, and corresponding ground truth, respectively. We first calculate IoU (Intersection-Over-Union) between r_p^i and r_{gt}^i, and IoU between r_t^i and r_{gt}^i. If $IoU(r_t^i, r_{gt}^i) > IoU(r_p^i, r_{gt}^i)$, it indicates that teacher's regression output is a reliable indicator to provide correct guidance for student. Otherwise, this proposal is abandoned in distillation. The final regression loss is formulated as follows:

$$L_{reg} = \sum_{j=1}^{N} L(r_s^j, r_{gt}^j) + \beta_2 \sum_{i=1}^{N_p} L_{dist}(r_s^i, r_t^i, r_{gt}^i), \tag{4}$$

where L is $L1$ loss defined as $L1$ distance between two vectors, β_2 is a balance factor, and L_{dist} is the selective distillation loss:

$$L_{dist}(r_s^i, r_t^i, r_{gt}^i) = \begin{cases} L(r_s^i, r_t^i) & \text{if } IoU(r_t^i, r_{gt}^i) > IoU(r_p^i, r_{gt}^i) \\ 0. & \text{otherwise} \end{cases} \tag{5}$$

Integrating the above three distillation terms produces our overall training targets of the student model, which can be formulated as:

$$L = \lambda L_{bk} + L_{cls} + L_{reg} + L_{rpn}, \tag{6}$$

where λ is the balance parameter for backbone distillation and L_{rpn} is the RPN training loss in two-stage detector as described in [20].

3.5   Adaptive Distillation Decay

The overall loss function in Eq. (6) simultaneously minimizes distillation loss and detection loss. It formulates a multi-task learning issue and makes training process hard to converge. To solve this issue, we propose a distillation decay strategy to help improve model generalization via gradually reducing distillation penalty, hoping that the model focuses more on detection task in the training process. This is achieved by introducing a time decay variable $\gamma(t)$, which decreases to 0 as the training proceeds. In our implementation, we simply set $\gamma(t) = 1 - t/T$ at the tth training iteration, where T is the total training iterations. The time decay variable is imposed to balance parameters β_1, β_2, and λ in Eq. (3), Eq. (4), Eq. (6) to control the intensity of distillation loss, $i.e.$,

$$\tilde{\beta}_1 = \gamma(t)\beta_1, \quad \tilde{\beta}_2 = \gamma(t)\beta_2, \quad \tilde{\lambda} = \gamma(t)\lambda. \tag{7}$$

4 Experiments

In this section, we evaluate our adaptive distillation framework for object detection, providing extensive designed evaluation and making comparison with previous works.

4.1 Experimental Setup

Datasets and Evaluation Metrics. We evaluate our approach on two widely used detection datasets: 1) PASCAL VOC 2007 [3], containing totally 9,963 images of 20 object classes, of which 5,011 images are included in *trainval* and the rest 4,952 in *test*; 2) Microsoft COCO 2017 [15], a large scale dataset that contains over 135k images spanning 80 categories, of which over 120k images are used for *train* and around 5k for *val*. Following the default settings, for PASCAL VOC, we choose the *trainval* split for training and the *test* split for test, while for MS COCO, we choose the *train* split for training and the *val* split for test. For performance evaluation, the average precision(AP) is used. We report the COCO style (AP [0.5:0.95]) detection accuracy for MS COCO, and PASCAL style (AP [0.5]) accuracy for PASCAL VOC.

Baseline Models. We evaluate our method based on both two-stage and single-stage detection frameworks. For two-stage detectors, we choose widely used Faster R-CNN [20] detector and for single-stage detectors, RetinaNet [14] is selected. Since there are no RPN layers for RetinaNet and anchors generated by teacher and student are exactly the same, we directly utilize positive anchors for task heads' distillation. Other operations and parameters are the same with those in two-stage detectors. Resnet [10] series networks are used as backbones of detectors, depending on their model sizes. For ease of narration, if Resnet-101 is used as teacher model and Resnet-50 as student, the distilled model is simply denoted as R-101-50.

Implementation Details. All experiments are performed on NVIDIA Tesla V100 8 GPUs with parallel acceleration. With Stochastic Gradient Descend (SGD) as optimization method, we set batch size to 16, allocating 2 images per GPU. The Gaussian parameters σ_x^2 and σ_y^2 in Eq. (1) are set to 2. The balance factors β_1, β_2, and λ are set to 10, 3, 0.6, respectively, via diagnosing the initial loss of each branch and ensuring that all losses are within the same scale. We find that these parameters are robust in our method, and do not affect the results too much as long as they are in similar scale. Unless specified, all experiments choose 1x schedule for training 12 epochs. The resolutions for images in COCO and PASCAL VOC are set as (1333,800) and (1000,600), respectively, following traditional implementation of each dataset.

Table 1. Effects of various distillation modules on PASCAL VOC 2007.

Student R-50	✓						
Teacher R-101							✓
Backbone?		✓			✓	✓	
Classification Head?			✓		✓	✓	
Regression Head?				✓	✓	✓	
Distillation Decay?						✓	
mAP (%)	70.0	72.8	73.2	73.4	73.8	**74.5**	74.3

Table 2. Hyperparameter analysis of Gaussian mask's variances on PASCAL VOC 2007. 'Rectangle' denotes using rectangle mask while 'All features' denotes distilling the whole feature map.

$\sigma_x^2 = \sigma_y^2$	1	2	4	Rectangle	All features
mAP	72.7	**72.8**	72.7	72.4	72.1

4.2 Ablation Study

Component Analysis. We first conduct experiments to understand how each distillation module contributes to the final performance, as well as the robustness of our method to different parameters. Without loss of generality, all experiments in this section are based on PASCAL VOC 2007 with Resnet-101 as teacher and Resnet-50 as student, which produces accuracy of 74.3% and 70.0%, respectively.

As shown in Table 1, different distillation components includes 1) backbone with Gaussian masking, 2) classification head, 3) regression head, 4) distillation decay. From the table we make following observations:

- *Backbone Distillation:* The backbone distillation brings about 2.8% mAP gain. The results demonstrates that our masking strategy enables student model to learn highlighted foreground information.
- *Classification and Regression Head Distillation:* The independent distillation strategies on classification head and regression head improve the student model by 3.2% and 3.4% points, respectively. It indicates that classification head distillation can provide effective soft labels, while regression head offers correct guidance.
- *Combination:* Combination of the above three distillation targets achieves better results, which brings about another 0.4% points gain compared with the best single distillation module. The combination strategy obtains marginal improvement compared with the individual components, partially due to the difficulty of joint optimization.
- *Distillation Decay:* The distillation decay strategy can further improve the results from 73.8% to 74.5%. This demonstrates effectiveness of the proposed distillation decay strategy. In this way, teacher model can be treated as a guider that leads student to a better optimization point gradually, which improves its generalization ability.

Table 3. Per category evaluation results on PASCAL VOC 2007.

Network	mAP	aero	bike	bird	boat	bott.	bus	car	cat	chai.	cow	tabl.	dog	hors.	mbike	pern	plnt	sheep	sofa	train	tv
R-101	74.3	73.3	83.6	78.2	60.2	61.5	75.5	84.6	85.7	58.6	80.1	61.1	85.7	82.5	80.0	82.9	50.2	74.7	72.0	81.1	75.2
R-50	70.0	67.1	79.1	73.9	56.3	54.4	74.9	81.5	82.7	51.7	76.4	53.2	82.3	81.4	75.7	80.5	45.0	71.9	64.0	77.7	70.9
R-101-50	74.5	74.0	82.4	75.7	60.9	62.0	79.9	84.7	86.1	58.2	80.3	64.0	84.7	83.7	81.0	83.2	51.2	77.9	70.2	78.3	72.1

Table 4. Evaluation results for different teacher and student models for Faster R-CNN on MS COCO 2017.

Network	Model info	mAP	AP50	AP75	APs	APm	APl
R-152	76.5M/10.8 fps	41.3	61.9	45.1	24.2	45.8	53.3
R-101	60.9M/11.9 fps	39.3	60.0	42.7	22.8	43.7	51.0
R-152-101		**41.8**	**61.8**	**45.5**	**23.6**	**46.1**	**54.5**
R-50	41.8M/13.6 fps	37.5	58.3	40.8	21.8	40.9	48.5
R-101-50		39.4	59.8	43.0	22.5	43.5	52.0
R-152-50		40.2	60.4	43.9	23.4	44.3	53.1
R-152-101-50		**40.6**	**60.9**	**44.2**	**23.4**	**44.5**	**53.2**

Table 5. Distillation results of RetinaNet on MS COCO 2017, together with the model size and inference speed.

Network	Model info	mAP	AP50	AP75	APs	APm	APl
Retina-101	57.1M/10.9 fps	38.6	57.6	41.3	22.2	42.5	51.0
Retina-50	38.0M/12.1 fps	36.4	55.5	38.6	20.3	40.0	47.9
Retina-101-50		**38.6**	**57.8**	**41.2**	**21.9**	**42.1**	**50.9**

Hyperparameter of Gaussian Mask. We now investigate the influence of Gaussian mask for detection performance. For simplicity, we fixed $\sigma_x^2 = \sigma_y^2 = k$ and jointly change the two parameters. In principle, with larger k, Gaussian mask becomes more scattered, while with smaller k, the mask will concentrate more on center of the box. As an extreme condition, when $\sigma_x^2 = \sigma_y^2 = +\infty$, Gaussian mask degrades to a rectangle mask. To verify the effectiveness of Gaussian mask, we take experiments on rectangle mask and the whole feature map without any masking operation. The results are shown in Table 2, where we find that the performance is relatively robust to Gaussian mask and it is much better than simply using rectangle mask or the whole feature maps for distillation.

4.3 Experimental Results

PASCAL VOC. The detection results by category on PASCAL VOC are shown in Table 3. Our distillation model R-101-50 achieves a significant boost for each category, and brings 4.5% overall gain (from 70.0% to 74.5%) compared to student model, which demonstrates superior performance of our proposed distillation framework.

Table 6. Comparison with previous distillation methods for detectors on VOC 2007.

	Network	Mimic [13]	FGFI [25]	Ours
Teacher	R-101	74.3	74.4	74.3
Student	R-50	70.0	69.1	70.0
Distilled	R-101-50	72.7	72.0	**74.5**
Improvement	–	+2.7	+2.9	**+4.5**

MS COCO. Table 4 and Table 5 show overall distillation performances on COCO dataset for Faster R-CNN [20] and RetinaNet [14], respectively. As shown, R-101-50 exceeds its teacher R-101 and R-152-101 also surpasses R-152. Specifically, R-152-50 (40.2%) even exceeds R-101 (39.3%) by a large margin. The reason for the gap between R-152-50 and its teacher R-152 is the large differences in structures and features between them. The progressive distillation approach R-152-101-50 brings R-50 closer to R-152. In detail, R-101 is firstly utilized as teacher model to distill R-50, obtaining R-101-50. Then we use R-152 as teacher model to further distill R-101-50, resulting R-152-101-50 which achieves a further mAP gain compared to R-152-50. It is worth mentioning that although R-50 contains much less layers than those of R-152 (almost 1/3), our R-152-101-50 still has a comparable result to the R-152. Similarly, distillation on single-stage RetinaNet also obtains outstanding performance. Retina-101 improves Retina-50 by 2.2% mAP and shows equal performance with its teacher Retina-101. The experiment results demonstrate significant performance improvement brought by our distillation framework.

Compression and Acceleration. To better illustrate compression and acceleration effect of knowledge distillation in object detection, we provide parameters amount and inference speed of each model in Table 4 and Table 5. The two metrics are shown in 'model info' column, where 'M' and 'fps' denote 'million(s)' and 'frames per second', respectively. According to the results, our distillation framework effectively lightens network sizes and increases their inference speed. For Faster R-CNN, the distillation models (*e.g.*, R-101-50, R-152-50) are much faster, while offering comparable or better performance against their teacher models. For RetinaNet, Retina-101-50 compresses Retina-101 by about 68% with 1.2 fps gain, while its performance remains comparable to Retina-101.

4.4   Comparison with Previous Distillation Methods

To further explore effectiveness of the proposed distillation framework in object detection, we present comparative results between our method with previous works [13, 25]. Since the devil is in experimental details, the results of teacher and student models may differ in our implementation. We simply re-implement results of [13] which distills all proposals, while for method in [25], we refer to results in the original paper. From Table 6, we make following observations:

Mimic [13] improves R-50 from 70.0% to 72.7% with 2.7% mAP gain, while FGFI [25] offers a little better result with 2.9% mAP gain. Apparently, our approach outperforms these distillation methods on absolute performance with a prominent mAP gain of 4.5%. The significant advantage of our method mainly comes from three aspects: 1) The Gaussian mask effectively suppresses the undesirable background noise while retaining informative foregrounds; 2) Adaptive distillation for task heads provides suitable guide for student model; 3) Distillation decay strategy helps model's optimization.

5   Conclusion

In this paper, we proposed an adaptive distillation framework for typical object detectors. The key contribution is that we deliberately design different imitating schemes according to the property of each distilled target. Based on the responses, we are able to successfully select crucial part of teacher's feature maps, classification structural priors, and bounding box regression results as supervision for distillation. Besides, a distillation decay strategy is deployed to help improve model generalization via gradually reducing the distillation penalty. Experiments conducted on widely used detection benchmarks demonstrate the effectiveness of the proposed method.

References

1. Chen, G., Choi, W., Yu, X., Han, T., Chandraker, M.: Learning efficient object detection models with knowledge distillation. In: Advances in Neural Information Processing Systems, pp. 742–751 (2017)
2. Dai, J., Li, Y., He, K., Sun, J.: R-FCN: object detection via region-based fully convolutional networks. In: Advances in Neural Information Processing Systems, pp. 379–387 (2016)
3. Everingham, M., Van Cool, L., Williams, C.K., Winn, J., Zisserman, A.: The pascal visual object classes (VOC) challenge. Int. J. Comput. Vis. 88(2), 303–338 (2010)
4. Fukuda, T., Suzuki, M., Kurata, G., Thomas, S., Cui, J., Ramabhadran, B.: Efficient knowledge distillation from an ensemble of teachers. In: Interspeech, pp. 3697–3701 (2017)
5. Girshick, R.: Fast R-CNN. In: Proceedings of the IEEE International Conference on Computer Vision, pp. 1440–1448 (2015)
6. Girshick, R., Donahue, J., Darrell, T., Malik, J.: Rich feature hierarchies for accurate object detection and semantic segmentation. In: Proceedings of the IEEE Conference on Computer Vision and Pattern Recognition, pp. 580–587 (2014)
7. Han, S., Mao, H., Dally, W.J.: A deep neural network compression pipeline: pruning, quantization, Huffman encoding. arXiv preprint arXiv:1510.00149 (2015)
8. Han, S., Pool, J., Tran, J., Dally, W.: Learning both weights and connections for efficient neural network. In: Advances in Neural Information Processing Systems, pp. 1135–1143 (2015)
9. He, K., Zhang, X., Ren, S., Sun, J.: Spatial pyramid pooling in deep convolutional networks for visual recognition. IEEE Trans. Pattern Anal. Mach. Intell. 37(9), 1904–1916 (2015)

10. He, K., Zhang, X., Ren, S., Sun, J.: Deep residual learning for image recognition. In: Proceedings of the IEEE Conference on Computer Vision and Pattern Recognition, pp. 770–778 (2016)
11. Hinton, G., Vinyals, O., Dean, J.: Distilling the knowledge in a neural network. arXiv preprint arXiv:1503.02531 (2015)
12. Kim, Y.D., Park, E., Yoo, S., Choi, T., Yang, L., Shin, D.: Compression of deep convolutional neural networks for fast and low power mobile applications. arXiv preprint arXiv:1511.06530 (2015)
13. Li, Q., Jin, S., Yan, J.: Mimicking very efficient network for object detection. In: Proceedings of the IEEE Conference on Computer Vision and Pattern Recognition, pp. 6356–6364 (2017)
14. Lin, T.Y., Goyal, P., Girshick, R., He, K., Dollár, P.: Focal loss for dense object detection. In: Proceedings of the IEEE International Conference on Computer Vision, pp. 2980–2988 (2017)
15. Lin, T.Y., et al.: Microsoft COCO: common objects in context. In: Fleet, D., Pajdla, T., Schiele, B., Tuytelaars, T. (eds.) ECCV 2014. LNCS, vol. 8693, pp. 740–755. Springer, Cham (2014). https://doi.org/10.1007/978-3-319-10602-1_48
16. Liu, P., Liu, W., Ma, H., Mei, T., Seok, M.: KTAN: knowledge transfer adversarial network. In: Association for the Advance of Artificial Intelligence (2019)
17. Liu, W., et al.: SSD: single shot MultiBox detector. In: Leibe, B., Matas, J., Sebe, N., Welling, M. (eds.) ECCV 2016. LNCS, vol. 9905, pp. 21–37. Springer, Cham (2016). https://doi.org/10.1007/978-3-319-46448-0_2
18. Park, J., et al.: Faster CNNs with direct sparse convolutions and guided pruning. arXiv preprint arXiv:1608.01409 (2016)
19. Redmon, J., Divvala, S., Girshick, R., Farhadi, A.: You only look once: unified, real-time object detection. In: Proceedings of the IEEE Conference on Computer Vision and Pattern Recognition, pp. 779–788 (2016)
20. Ren, S., He, K., Girshick, R., Sun, J.: Faster R-CNN: towards real-time object detection with region proposal networks. In: Advances in Neural Information Processing Systems, pp. 91–99 (2015)
21. Romero, A., Ballas, N., Kahou, S.E., Chassang, A., Gatta, C., Bengio, Y.: FitNets: hints for thin deep nets. In: International Conference on Learning Representations (2015)
22. Sainath, T.N., Kingsbury, B., Sindhwani, V., Arisoy, E., Ramabhadran, B.: Low-rank matrix factorization for deep neural network training with high-dimensional output targets. In: 2013 IEEE International Conference on Acoustics, Speech and Signal Processing, pp. 6655–6659. IEEE (2013)
23. Sermanet, P., Eigen, D., Zhang, X., Mathieu, M., Fergus, R., LeCun, Y.: OverFeat: integrated recognition, localization and detection using convolutional networks. arXiv preprint arXiv:1312.6229 (2013)
24. Tung, F., Mori, G.: Deep neural network compression by in-parallel pruning-quantization. IEEE Trans. Pattern Anal. Mach. Intell. **42**(3), 568–579 (2018)
25. Wang, T., Yuan, L., Zhang, X., Feng, J.: Distilling object detectors with fine-grained feature imitation. In: Proceedings of the IEEE Conference on Computer Vision and Pattern Recognition, pp. 4933–4942 (2019)
26. Wu, J., Leng, C., Wang, Y., Hu, Q., Cheng, J.: Quantized convolutional neural networks for mobile devices. In: Proceedings of the IEEE Conference on Computer Vision and Pattern Recognition, pp. 4820–4828 (2016)
27. Yim, J., Joo, D., Bae, J., Kim, J.: A gift from knowledge distillation: fast optimization, network minimization and transfer learning. In: Proceedings of the IEEE Conference on Computer Vision and Pattern Recognition, pp. 4133–4141 (2017)

28. Zagoruyko, S., Komodakis, N.: Paying more attention to attention: improving the performance of convolutional neural networks via attention transfer. In International Conference on Learning Representations (2017)

29. Zhou, A., Yao, A., Guo, Y., Xu, L., Chen, Y.: Incremental network quantization: towards lossless CNNs with low-precision weights. arXiv preprint arXiv:1702.03044 (2017)

Fine-Grained Classification of Neutrophils with Hybrid Loss

Qingtao Zhu[1], Danwei Lu[1], Tao Zhang[1], Junjun Yin[2], and Jian Yang[1(✉)]

[1] Department of Electronic Engineering, Tsinghua University,
Beijing 100084, China
yangjian_ee@tsinghua.edu.cn
[2] School of Computer and Communication Engineering, University of Science
and Technology, Beijing 100083, China

Abstract. Acute leukemia is a malignant clonal disease of hematopoietic stem cells, which is usually diagnosed by morphological examination of bone marrow cells. However, the morphological examination usually relies on the subjective inference of cell morphology experts and is labor-intensive. With the development of computer vision, automatic classification and counting of blood cells is increasingly popular, which greatly improves work efficiency. Within this context, we here propose a novel method for neutrophil classification, which is based on deep neural network. In brief, it first crops the single cells from the large images, and then makes use of the loss functions designed for face recognition and weakly-supervised fine-grained visual classification. With the hybrid loss, the trained network can focus on nucleus areas, extract features with inter-class differences and intra-class compactness. Experiments show that the proposed method can obtain higher overall accuracy. Data is available at https://github.com/stevenxmy/subAML-dataset.git.

Keywords: Acute leukemia · Fine-grained classification · Neural network

1 Introduction

Leukemia is a highly heterogeneous tumor with malignant hyperplasia of hematopoietic tissue or clonal hyperplasia of lymphoid tissue, which has high morbidity and fatality rate. Early haematological diagnosis of acute leukemia is crucial for the patients. Comprehensive haematological diagnostics are usually combined with complex inspection such as blood routine, bone marrow cell morphological examination and cytogenetic analysis. Particularly, morphological evaluation of leukocytes from peripheral blood or bone marrow samples is one of the most basic and important methods. During the hamatological diagnostics, trained human examiners observe bone marrow smears under microscopes, check whether there are abnormal cells and count different types of nucleated cells, the proportion of which depicts the pathological trend.

© Springer Nature Switzerland AG 2021
Y. Peng et al. (Eds.): ICIG 2021, LNCS 12888, pp. 102–113, 2021.
https://doi.org/10.1007/978-3-030-87355-4_9

The specific process of hamatological diagnostics is shown in Fig. 1. First, bone marrow smears are generated by bone marrow aspiration. Next, the cytochemical staining was performed by the Wright-Giemsa staining analysis technique. Then, morphological analysis and classification of bone marrow cells are conducted under oil immersion lens. Finally, preliminary diagnoses of the type of acute leukemia are made according to the French-American-British classification standard [1]. However, it takes quite a long time to cultivate an expert in cell morphology, and the cell examination is time-consuming and laborious.

Fig. 1. Diagram of the human examination of cell morphology

With the advancement of computer vision technologies and pattern recognition algorithms, emphasis is laid on automatic recognition of bone marrow cell types, which can reduce the burden on experts and improve work efficiency. A feasible solution is to make use of artificially designed feature extractions combined with feature selection and classifiers. Gurcan et al. [15] extracted chromaticity, morphology and texture features, and used SVM for classification. In recent years, deep learning has demonstrated outstanding performance in various fields of computer vision, such as image detection, segmentation, and recognition. Researchers have focused on the bone marrow cell classification based on deep neural networks. Christian et al. [11] used the ResNext network to classify 18,365 blood cell smear images of 200 patients collected by the Munich University Hospital Laboratory from 2014 to 2017. The blood cells are divided into 15 categories, while a few classes only contain dozens of images. It is not surprising that the precision and sensitivity of partial sub-categories obtained by such a generic classification network structure are very low. Hong et al. [6] made use of the deep neural network to classify the bone marrow cells based on 3000 marrow smear samples collected by Sir Run Run Shaw Hospital affiliated to Zhejiang University School of Medicine between 2016 and 2018. However, the sensitivity of certain types of cells such as myelocytes and promyelocytes are poor. In conclusion, although the classification of main blood cell types has been widely developed, the fine-grained classification of sub-categories, which is crucial for hamatological diagnostics, has not been well analyzed.

In recent years, face recognition and fine-grained visual classification(FGVC) have been increasingly popular. The common challenging problems of face recognition and FGVC are the large inter-class similarity and intra-class variability [12]. Researchers have focused on the loss functions to train deep neural networks for feature extraction, which greatly improve the performance of the networks. The morphological classification of blood cells is similar to the above tasks to a certain extent. However, there have been few research on white blood cell classification taking the algorithms of face recognition and FGVC into consideration, which may contribute to the precise classification of sub-categories of blood cells.

To address the gap above, we propose a pipeline similar to the face recognition which involves the steps of detection and classification. The feature pyramid network is applied to detect single cells. The backbone of EfficientNet [16] is adopted. A hybrid loss function containing the clustering component and diversity component is also designed to reinforce the inter-class difference and intra-class compactness, which borrows the idea of the loss functions designed for face recognition and weakly-supervised FGVC.

The contributions are summarized as follows:

- An half-automatic cell detection pipeline is designed to generate the actual single-cell images.
- The backbone of EfficientNet is adopted to enhance the feature extraction and save the memory.
- A hybrid loss for classification is designed by combining the center loss and diversity loss.
- Data cleaning and augmentation is done for part of the Munich AML Morphology Dataset [11] which is open source.

2   Related Work

2.1   Generic Object Detection

Generic object detection refers to the task of determining whether there are certain types of objects in the scene, and return the locations if the targets exist [9]. Traditional target detection algorithms mainly include preprocessing, window sliding, feature extraction, feature selection, feature classification and post-processing. The generic object detection algorithms based on deep learning are divided into two groups: two-stage methods with region proposal stage and object recognition stage, and single-stage methods without candidate boxes. Girshick et al. [14] proposed the classic dual-stage object detection method Faster R-CNN, which gained state-of-the-art results on PASCAL VOC 2007. Redmon et al. [13] implemented feature extraction, bounding box classification and regression in a branchless deep convolutional network, which effectively improved the low efficiency of Faster R-CNN. Recently, numerous studies on dual-stage and single-stage methods have been conducted, such as FPN [7] and YOLOv4 [2], the accuracy and speed of which are much better.

2.2   Fined-Grained Visual Classification

Fined-grained visual classification(FGVC) refers to the task of classifying sub-categories of a certain category such as vehicles, birds and flowers, which draws considerable attention. Types of research approach on FGVC can be divided into two groups: strongly-supervised algorithms and weakly-supervised algorithms. Wei et al. [18] proposed an end-to-end model which localized parts and selected descriptors for FGVC of birds, which made use of strong supervision annotations. Chang et al. [3] proposed the mutual-channel loss with a discriminality component and a diversity component to force the channel maps of each class to be discriminative and mutually exclusive.

2.3 Face Recognition

Three basic steps are included in robust face recognition system: face detection, feature extraction and face recognition. With the development of deep learning, the second and third steps are usually merged in deep neural network. Different from generic object classification, there are numerous identities which may also change irregularly in total number. Therefore, feature embeddings and similarity measures are combined to recognize identities without fine-tuning the model frequently. Discriminative feature embeddings are usually extracted by training with particular losses such as center loss [19], CosFace [17] and ArcFace [4]. Cosine similarity and euclidean distance are usually adopted as the similarity measures.

3 Methods

3.1 Single Cell Detection

Although the common two-stage detection network Faster R-CNN has designed multiple sizes of anchor boxes and multiple aspect ratios, it has not solved the problem of low resolution of deep feature maps, which leads to the poor performance of small target detection. We adopt the idea of Feature Pyramid Network (FPN) [7] and combines multi-scale feature map information for detection. First, the proposal bounding boxes are generated through the region proposal network. After that, the coarse screening and preliminary anchor box regression are performed. Finally, the bounding boxes of different scales are finely selected while coordinates are revised by the fully connected network. The inference of FPN is depicted in Fig. 2(a). Specifically, due to the small scale variation range of blood cells, compared with generic object detetion, only three output scales are used as the final prediction to reduce the false alarm rate.

However, the locations of the bounding boxes may not have been annotated. The strategy of active learning is adopted. We first annotated part of the bounding boxes, then fine-tuned FPN for detection with the pretrained MS COCO [8] weights. After that, the inference results of the bounding boxes are manually revised, in case of the missed targets or the bad boxes. If the dataset is quite large, the revision work can be done in an iterative way, and the detection model can be updated for several times. Finally, the single-cell images are cropped from the original images. The diagram of the annotation work is depicted in Fig. 2(b).

3.2 EfficientNet Backbone

Tan et al. [16] made use of neural architecture search to design a baseline network EfficientNet-B0, and scale it up to build a series of models called EfficientNets.

The MBConv module in EfficientNet includes the squeeze-and-excitation [5] block to automatically recalibrates the channel-wise feature responses. In the squeeze-and-excitation block, the weights of the channels in feature maps are redistributed by global average pooling layer, fully connected layer and pointwise product layer. The channel attention blocks mentioned above contribute to the excellent feature extraction capabilities of the network.

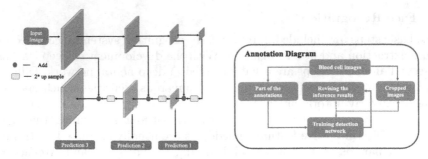

(a) Inference of Feature Pyramid Net-   (b) Diagram of bounding box annota-
work   tion

Fig. 2. FPN structure and half-automatic annotations

3.3   Loss Functions

Clustering Component. We adopt the center loss [19] as clustering component to improve the intra-class compactness.

The traditional softmax loss function is presented as follow.

$$\mathcal{L}_{softmax} = -\sum_{i=1}^{n} log \frac{e^{W_{y_i}^T x_i + b_{y_i}}}{\sum_{j=1}^{m} e^{W_j^T x_i + b_j}} \tag{1}$$

In Eq. 1, n denotes the batch size of input data, while m denotes the number
of class. $x_i \in \mathbb{R}^d$ denotes the ith extracted feature of the mini-batch. $W \in \mathbb{R}^{d \times m}$
and $b \in \mathbb{R}^d$ denotes the weight and bias in the fully connected layer. Suppose
the ith input belongs to class y_i, then the softmax loss is calculated as Eq. 1.
However, the softmax loss mainly focuses on the inter-class differences. With the
center loss [19] formulated in Eq. 2, the intra-class differences are minimized and
the discriminative power of the convolutional neural network is improved.

$$\mathcal{L}_{center} = \frac{1}{2} \sum_{i=1}^{m} ||x_i - c_{y_i}||^2 \tag{2}$$

On each mini-batch, the center of features are computed once and the parameters of the center loss are updated. Scalar α is used to avoid perturbations
caused by bad annotations. The gradients of $\mathcal{L}_{center}$ and the updating step is
depicted as follow. c_{y_i} denotes the center of the feature embeddings extracted by
the network. The centers of the embedding features are only updated when the
predictions are correct.

$$\frac{\partial \mathcal{L}_{center}}{\partial x_i} = x_i - c_{y_i} \tag{3}$$

$$\Delta c_j = \frac{\sum_{i=1}^{m} \delta(y_i = j) \cdot (c_j - x_i)}{1 + \sum_{i=1}^{m} \delta(y_j = j)} \tag{4}$$

Diversity Component. The diversity component is presented as follow. W and H denote the width and height of the extracted feature map $\boldsymbol{F}$, which has ξ channels. Different from the diversity loss in mutual-channel loss [3], we take all feature channels into consideration instead of manually splitting the channels into m groups, where m denotes the number of classes. Therefore, the number of hyperparameters is reduced.

$$\mathcal{L}_{div} = -\sum_{k=1}^{WH} \max_{j=1,2,\dots,\xi} \left[\frac{e^{F_{j,k}}}{\sum_{k'=1}^{WH} e^{F_{j,k'}}} \right] \tag{5}$$

The diversity loss aims to reinforce the attention on different areas of the images, which may be crucial for the fine-grained classification of cells.

Hybrid Loss. The hybrid loss adopted in our approach is presented in Eq. 6. Considering the problem of convergence and the bad samples, the center loss and diversity loss are combined with the softmax loss. α and β are the hyperparameters which controls the proportion of $\mathcal{L}_{softmax}$, $\mathcal{L}_{center}$ and $\mathcal{L}_{div}$.

$$\mathcal{L}_{hybrid} = \mathcal{L}_{softmax} + \alpha \cdot \mathcal{L}_{center} + \beta \cdot \mathcal{L}_{div} \tag{6}$$

4 Experiments

4.1 Implementation Details

Datasets. As given in Table 1, we employ the subset of the Munich AML Morphology Dataset called Sub-AML Dataset which contains myelocytes in different stages as our training data and conduct comparison with other approaches. Additionally, promyelocyte (PMO) and myelocyte (MYB) cells are combined into the PMOMYB class, since many cells in these two classes are much alike. Although it is claimed that the Munich AML Morphology Dataset only contains single-cell images, there are still images containing more than one cell, as depicted in Fig. 3(a). Please note that the metamyelocyte class is removed because of the low proportion. There are 8484 segmented neutrophils in the original dataset, while some should be considered as band neutrophils, as depicted in Fig. 3(b). To best of our knowledge, data imbalance is unfriendly to network training. We apply Gaussian blur, average blur, random jittering in HSV space, rotation and flipping to alleviate data imbalance. To avoid data leaking, single-cell cropped images augmented from the same images can not be included in both training and validation folds. Finally, the Sub-AML Dataset contains 11655 PMOMYB cells, 13760 band neutrophils (NGB) and 11976 segmented neutrophils (NGS). The precision and sensitivity of different categories gained by the method in [11] are also depicted in Table 1.

NGB_0086   NGS_1039   NGS_0080_cropped   NGS_0237_cropped

(a) Images containing more   (b) Suspected annotations
than one cell

Fig. 3. Multi-cell images and suspected annotations

Table 1. The subset of Munich AML Morphology Dataset

Class	Precision	Sensitivity	Images	Chosen	No.	Final No.
Erythroblast	0.75	0.87	78			
Lymphocyte (typical)	0.96	0.95	3937			
Lymphocyte (atypical)	0.20	0.07	11			
Monoblast	0.52	0.58	26			
Monocyte	0.90	0.90	1789			
Myeloblast	0.94	0.94	3268			
Promyelocyte (bilobled)	0.45	0.41	18			
Smudge cell	0.53	0.77	15			
Eosinophil	0.95	0.95	424			
Basophil	0.48	0.82	79			
Promyelocyte	**0.63**	**0.54**	**70**	√	111	11655
Myelocyte	**0.46**	**0.43**	**42**	√		
Metamyelocyte	0.07	0.13	15			
Neutrophil (band)	**0.25**	**0.59**	**109**	√	344	13760
Neutrophil (segmented)	**0.99**	**0.96**	**8484**	√	1996	11976

Experimental Settings. As mentioned in Sect. 3.1, single cells are detected by FPN and cropped from the 400 × 400 images in the Munich AML Morphology Dataset with a half-automatic pipeline. Single-cell images are then resized to 224 × 224. We set the batch size to 32 and train models on one NVIDIA RTX 2080TI GPU. The training process is finished at 60 epochs in Pytorch 1.4.0. Momentum is set to 0.9 and weight decay is set to 5e−4. The learning rate starts from 0.0005 and is divided by 10 at 30, 48 epochs. Additionally, 5-fold cross-validation is used to evaluate the methods. The accuracy of fold-k is denoted as 'acc$k$'.

4.2   Ablation Study

Performance Metrics. We calculate accuracy as the comparison metric, which represents the ratio of correct predictions among the total samples.

Center Loss. We explore the proportion of center loss on the Sub-AML Dataset with the backbone of EfficientNet-B0. As depicted in Table 2, the center loss is effective for improving classification accuracy. The best value of α observed in our experiments is 0.5. We also compare center loss with classic margin based losses such as ArcFace and CosFace, and the selection of hyperparameters refers to [4] and [17], in which scaling parameter is set to 64 and margin parameters are set to 0.5 and 0.35. However, the performance of the ArcFace and CosFace is bad, which may due to the small number of classes.

Table 2. Verification results of different α

Backbone	Loss Function	α	acc1	acc2	acc3	acc4	acc5	Average acc
Efficient-B0	Center	0.0	96.27%	95.24%	95.87%	95.04%	96.29%	95.74%
Efficient-B0	Center	0.1	96.50%	**96.04%**	96.10%	95.05%	96.27%	96.00%
Efficient-B0	Center	0.3	**96.77%**	94.96%	96.73%	**95.88%**	95.97%	96.06%
Efficient-B0	Center	0.5	96.14%	95.66%	96.73%	95.37%	96.65%	**96.11%**
Efficient-B0	Center	0.7	96.52%	95.00%	96.69%	94.24%	96.90%	95.87%
Efficient-B0	Center	0.9	96.38%	95.07%	**96.85%**	94.87%	**96.93%**	96.01%
Efficient-B0	ArcFace	/	94.22%	92.31%	94.10%	93.90%	94.24%	93.75%
Efficient-B0	CosFace	/	93.99%	92.75%	93.02%	93.07%	93.15%	93.20%

Since the dimension of the feature embedding is high, we adopt the t-SNE visualization tool [10], which can retain the local structure of the extracted data and reveal important global structure.

As depicted in Fig. 4, points with three colors which refer to the three classes show local clustering. Additionally, the similarity between NGB and NGS cells leads to the overlaps on the borders. To put it in a nutshell, the center loss successfully enhances the intra-class compactness of the testing data as well as the inter-class discrimination.

Diversity Loss. We explore the proportion of diversity loss on the Sub-AML Dataset with the backbone of EfficientNet-B0. As depicted in Table 3, the best value of β varies in each fold, and the diversity loss does work under certain hyperparameters. On average, the best value of β observed in our experiments is 0.05, while the weight of center loss is set to 0. The overall accuracy is not improved with only diversity loss. However, there is much difference on the attention maps of the extracted features. In Fig. 5, more emphasis is laid on nucleus areas. It is obvious that the attention areas of the features extracted by the neural network trained with diversity loss are sometimes more abundant.

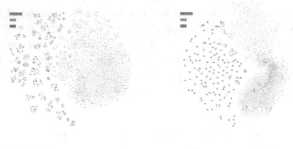

(a) Without center loss   (b) With center loss

Fig. 4. T-SNE visualization of the feature embeddings

Table 3. Vertification results of different β

Backbone	β	acc1	acc2	acc3	acc4	acc5	Average acc
Efficient-B0	0.0	96.27%	95.24%	95.87%	95.04%	96.29%	95.74%
Efficient-B0	0.00005	96.29%	94.83%	95.58%	**95.21%**	96.29%	95.64%
Efficient-B0	0.0005	**96.47%**	**95.36%**	95.53%	94.20%	96.24%	95.56%
Efficient-B0	0.005	95.83%	95.10%	95.51%	95.15%	**96.33%**	95.58%
Efficient-B0	0.05	96.06%	95.29%	95.77%	95.03%	96.14%	95.66%
Efficient-B0	0.5	96.14%	95.19%	**96.26%**	94.75%	95.98%	95.66%

4.3 Evaluation Results

We train EfficientNet-B0 model with hybrid loss of different hyperparameters. Since the datasets of blood cell morphology are very few, we only compare our work with other CNN-based methods on Sub-AML Dataset, such as ResNext-101, VGG-16, ResNet-18, ResNet-50 and DenseNet-121, as depicted in Table 4. The performance of mutual-channel loss is also evaluated. Our method achieves the best accuracy among all the methods listed, while the backbone of Efficient-B0 has the smallest FLOPs [16]. Take fold-1 for instance, the best accuracy on test set is achieved at epoch 14. The curves of loss and accuracy are depicted in Fig. 6(a) and 6(b), while the confusion matrix of our method is depicted in Fig. 6(c). The convergence of our method is fast. With the data cleaning and augmentation work, the accuracy of the sub-category, especially NGB, have been significantly improved, compared with the results in [11]. Additionally, even though the diversity loss is not effective separately, the hybrid loss obviously contributes to the improvement of overall accuracy.

(a) Original image   (b) Without diversity loss   (c) With diversity loss

Fig. 5. Original single-cell image and the attention map of the extracted features

Table 4. Vertification performance of different methods on Sub-AML Dataset

Method	(α, β)	acc1	acc2	acc3	acc4	acc5	Average acc
Proposed	(0.5, 0.0005)	**96.57%**	**96.10%**	**96.71%**	**95.97%**	**96.86%**	**96.44%**
Mutual-channel loss	/	95.96%	95.92%	95.88%	95.14 %	96.18%	95.82%
Efficient-B0	/	96.27%	95.24%	95.87%	95.04%	96.29%	95.74%
ResNet-18	/	93.62%	91.93%	93.54%	94.49%	94.20%	93.56%
ResNet-50	/	94.97%	93.75%	94.77%	94.97%	94.62%	94.83%
ResNext-101	/	96.38%	95.49%	95.97%	94.77%	96.29%	95.78%
VGG-16	/	94.26%	93.29%	93.96%	93.98%	95.44%	94.19%
DenseNet-121	/	95.84%	95.27%	95.95%	94.96%	96.11%	95.63%

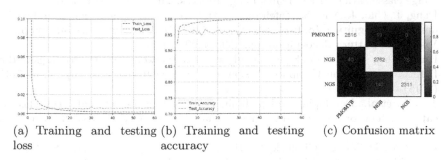

(a) Training and testing loss   (b) Training and testing accuracy   (c) Confusion matrix

Fig. 6. The curves and confusion matrix of fold-1

5   Conclusions

Automatic morphology examination of blood cells is a promising field, since it can save much labor. There have already exist a few studies which focus on rough classification of five types of blood cells. However, little research lays emphasis on fine-grained classification of the sub-categories, which is more difficult.

In this paper, we borrow the idea from the pipeline of face recognition, and propose half-automatic bounding box annotation method and resize the images which contain only one cell to a fixed size. Hybrid loss function is designed to gain better performance on the fine-grained classification of the neutrophils in adjacent stages. Clustering component reinforces the compactive distribution of the feature embeddings of the blood cells belonging to the same class, which also contributes to the inter-class discrimination. Diversity component reinforces the broad receptive field of the network, which helps to discover important local features. From the comprehensive experiments done on the Sub-AML Dataset, we demonstrate that the method proposed outperforms the popular deep neural network based methods. With the increasing blood smear data, combined with rough classification techniques, our fine-grained classification of sub-categories may greatly contribute to the improvement of the overall accuracy of automatic blood cell fine classification in the future, which is crucial for the diagnosis of leukemia.

Acknowledgements. We thank Christian Matek and Antje for the morphologcial dataset of leukocytes.

References

1. Bennett, J.M., et al.: Proposals for the classification of the acute leukaemias French-American-British (fab) co-operative group. Br. J. Haematol. **33**(4), 451–458 (1976)
2. Bochkovskiy, A., Wang, C.Y., Liao, H.Y.M.: YOLOv4: optimal speed and accuracy of object detection. arXiv preprint arXiv:2004.10934 (2020)
3. Chang, D., et al.: The devil is in the channels: mutual-channel loss for fine-grained image classification. IEEE Trans. Image Process. **29**, 4683–4695 (2020)
4. Deng, J., Guo, J., Xue, N., Zafeiriou, S.: ArcFace: additive angular margin loss for deep face recognition. In: Proceedings of the IEEE/CVF Conference on Computer Vision and Pattern Recognition, pp. 4690–4699 (2019)
5. Hu, J., Shen, L., Sun, G.: Squeeze-and-excitation networks. In: Proceedings of the IEEE Conference on Computer Vision and Pattern Recognition, pp. 7132–7141 (2018)
6. Jin, H., et al.: Developing and preliminary validating an automatic cell classification system for bone marrow smears: a pilot study. J. Med. Syst. **44**(10), 1–10 (2020)
7. Lin, T.Y., Dollár, P., Girshick, R., He, K., Hariharan, B., Belongie, S.: Feature pyramid networks for object detection. In: Proceedings of the IEEE Conference on Computer Vision and Pattern Recognition, pp. 2117–2125 (2017)
8. Lin, T.Y., et al.: Microsoft COCO: common objects in context. In: Fleet, D., Pajdla, T., Schiele, B., Tuytelaars, T. (eds.) ECCV 2014. LNCS, vol. 8693, pp. 740–755. Springer, Cham (2014). https://doi.org/10.1007/978-3-319-10602-1_48
9. Liu, L., et al.: Deep learning for generic object detection: a survey. Int. J. Comput. Vis. **128**(2), 261–318 (2020)
10. Van der Maaten, L., Hinton, G.: Visualizing data using t-SNE. J. Mach. Learn. Res. **9**(11) (2008)
11. Matek, C., Schwarz, S., Spiekermann, K., Marr, C.: Human-level recognition of blast cells in acute myeloid leukaemia with convolutional neural networks. Nat. Mach. Intell. **1**(11), 538–544 (2019)
12. Qiu, C., Zhou, W.: A survey of recent advances in CNN-based fine-grained visual categorization. In: 2020 IEEE 20th International Conference on Communication Technology (ICCT), pp. 1377–1384. IEEE (2020)

13. Redmon, J., Divvala, S., Girshick, R., Farhadi, A.: You only look once: unified, real-time object detection. In: Proceedings of the IEEE Conference on Computer Vision and Pattern Recognition, pp. 779–788 (2016)
14. Ren, S., He, K., Girshick, R., Sun, J.: Faster R-CNN: towards real-time object detection with region proposal networks (2016)
15. Sarrafzadeh, O., Rabbani, H., Talebi, A., Banaem, H.U.: Selection of the best features for leukocytes classification in blood smear microscopic images. In: Medical Imaging 2014: Digital Pathology, vol. 9041, p. 90410P. International Society for Optics and Photonics (2014)
16. Tan, M., Le, Q.: EfficientNet: rethinking model scaling for convolutional neural networks. In: International Conference on Machine Learning, pp. 6105–6114. PMLR (2019)
17. Wang, H., et al.: CosFace: large margin cosine loss for deep face recognition. In: Proceedings of the IEEE Conference on Computer Vision and Pattern Recognition, pp. 5265–5274 (2018)
18. Wei, X.S., Xie, C.W., Wu, J., Shen, C.: Mask-CNN: localizing parts and selecting descriptors for fine-grained bird species categorization. Pattern Recogn. **76**, 704–714 (2018)
19. Wen, Y., Zhang, K., Li, Z., Qiao, Yu.: A discriminative feature learning approach for deep face recognition. In: Leibe, B., Matas, J., Sebe, N., Welling, M. (eds.) ECCV 2016. LNCS, vol. 9911, pp. 499–515. Springer, Cham (2016). https://doi.org/10.1007/978-3-319-46478-7_31

Open-Set Product Authentication Based on Deep Texture Verification

Sudao Cai[1,2], Lin Zhao[1,2], and Changsheng Chen[1,2(✉)] (iD)

[1] The Guangdong Key Laboratory of Intelligent Information Processing,
Shenzhen Key Laboratory of Media Security, Shenzhen University,
Shenzhen 518060, China
cschen@szu.edu.cn
[2] The Shenzhen Institute of Artificial Intelligence and Robotics for Society,
Shenzhen 518129, China

Abstract. The authenticity of consumer products has a significant impact on the economic and social issues of countries around the world. Due to the recent advancements in machine learning, there emerges some authentication techniques, in a close-set setting, based on texture features extracted from the product surfaces. However, the existing techniques have suffered from the problem of low accuracies or inability to deal with unknown classes in open-set authentication. In this work, we build an anti-counterfeiting system that works for consumer products in an open-set scenario. Different from other anti-counterfeiting methods, this work considers the problem of product authentication as a simple texture verification process. It allows the authentication being conducted under both close-set and open-set scenarios by a distance comparison operation with some customized metrics in the embedding space. We evaluate our system with two state-of-the-art texture databases. Experimental results show that the proposed system achieves 89.91% open-set authentication accuracy for a feature of 256 dimensions in the Outex texture database.

Keywords: Texture · Authentication · Deep metric learning

1 Introduction

Product counterfeiting has become an unprecedented problem for the global trade. Especially, the luxurious brands have suffered from economic loss amount to over 30 billion dollars during 2018 and 2020 [1]. Among all counterfeiting goods, leather products (e.g., footwear, clothing and bag) have dominated the counterfeit market. Leathers of the luxury brands are important company assets, which are usually manufactured by proprietary process and are protected by patent.

This work was supported in part by Guangdong Basic and Applied Basic Research Foundation (Grant 2020A1515010563, 2019B151502001), National Science Foundation of China (Grant 62072313), and Shenzhen R&D Program (Grant JCYJ2018030512 4550725, 20200813110043002, JCYJ20200109105008228).

© Springer Nature Switzerland AG 2021
Y. Peng et al. (Eds.): ICIG 2021, LNCS 12888, pp. 114–125, 2021.
https://doi.org/10.1007/978-3-030-87355-4_10

To authenticate the leather products, there are some recent attempts by exploiting machine vision and deep learning-based technologies in inspecting the unique texture of the leather surface. As demonstrated in [20], it is possible to generate useful and compact features from texture image to authenticate highly similar objects. Moreover, the discriminative of the data-driven features has improved a lot with the advancement of deep learning-based technology. Sharma et al. [16] proposed to authenticate leather texture with an online database and a microscopy. The captured images of the leather products are compared against those stored online with deep texture features. The extracted features are classified according to the predefined classes of leathers. A correct classification result indicates the authenticity of the product. However, the technique in [16] has not considered an important scenario where a new class of leather (unknown to not encountered during training) is introduced into the market. In such scenario, the deep learning model needs to be updated (i.e., retrained); otherwise, the classification (class label prediction) and authentication performances will be degraded seriously. As shown in [15], a generic handcrafted feature (e.g., Local Binary Pattern [11] and Local Ternary Pattern [18]) based scheme is evaluated under both the close-set and open-set texture classification setups. The error rates for the samples from some unknown classes have raised significantly from less than 10% (the close-set scenario) to more than 40% (the open-set scenario).

However, the performance of the data-driven features usually depends on the uniformity between the training and testing data. The open-set authentication (for unknown classes) has not considered in [16] while it remains a difficult task in the exploitation of [15]. The performance for samples from unknown classes is unguaranteed in the existing works. In order to work with samples from classes that were not observed during training, various research have been conducted in the field of zero-shot learning. Nevertheless, the existing zero-shot classification approaches [8,19] usually exploit the semantic properties of the objects (zebra, horse, panda, etc.) to allow extension towards unknown classes. This is not practical in the problem of texture classification since the property of textures is abstract and not well-defined.

In this work, a deep learning-based texture authentication framework is proposed to fight against counterfeiting leather products under open-set scenarios. To allow generalization towards unknown textures (such as, new leather pattern in fashion products), our system reformulates the texture authentication setup in [16] into a verification setup. In other words, [16] determines the authenticity of a texture image by correctness of the classification result, while the proposed scheme achieves such decision by comparing the questioned texture image with a referenced one in the feature embedding space. In system enrollment, a set of compact feature of a reference (authentic) texture image is extracted with deep learning network and stored off-line in a barcode to serve as the reference feature. In the verification process, the texture image under inspection goes through the same feature extraction network, and the resulting feature vector will be compared to the one decoded from the barcode label. In the feature level comparison, a state-of-the-art metric learning framework is adopted with a margin loss [21] designed by jointly considering the performances of both the known and unknown classes. Thus, a texture feature comparator is generalizable under open-set scenario, which involves training with some texture images from the existing (known) classes, and testing with those from the new (unknown) classes. Experiments are conducted in two state-of-the-art texture image datasets with a large number of texture classes. Experimental results demonstrate that the proposed system achieves 89.91% open-set authentication accuracy for a compact feature of 256 dimensions in a subset of data in Outex database [10] (a practical texture database with variation in illumination, resolution and rotation). The results show a promising application prospect in a practical product authentication scenario.

The contributions of this work can be summarized as follow.

1. We reformulate the problem of product authentication with a simple texture verification setting by a distance comparison operation to allow the authentication being conducted under both close-set and open-set scenarios in the embedding space;
2. We introduce a Siamese network with margin loss into our authentication framework to generate a texture feature embedding that separates the known classes by a constant distance and potentially keeps the unknown classes apart by a safety margin;
3. We evaluate the different metric learning schemes in the experiment with two state-of-the-art texture databases, and demonstrate that the proposed authentication framework is of good generalization performance under open-set scenario.

The remaining of this paper is organized as follows. Section 2 introduces the proposed product authentication framework based on Siamese network with margin loss. Section 3 evaluates the proposed framework under two state-of-the-art texture databases. Section 4 concludes this paper.

2   The Proposed Texture Authentication Framework

Figure 1 depicts the system diagram of the proposed open-set texture authentication scheme with possible application on leathers. In the production process, the texture features of different leather samples are extracted by a pre-trained deep network. The extracted features are then encoded into 2D barcode labels which serve as off-line reference features. It should be noted that the 2D barcode pattern can be designed flexibly according to the shape and size of the leather samples [3]. The leather labels are then attached (in an undetachable manner) to the corresponding products which distributed through various channels. For a customer, one can initiate an authentication request by scanning the barcode label and capturing the leather sample simultaneously (in a single image). The texture features will then be extracted by the pre-trained deep network (same as the one used in label production) from the leather sample, as well as by decoding the barcode label. The two sets of texture features are then compared in the feature embedding space, and their similarity determines the authenticity of the products.

Fig. 1. The system diagram of the proposed scheme.

It is worth mentioning that the proposed framework is different from that outlined in [16]. The authentication of the proposed scheme is achieved by a similarity comparison between the texture features extracted from the leather and the reference feature decoded from the barcode, while [16] classifies the leather sample under inspection into different leather types, and determine its authenticity by the correctness of classification result. In other words, the proposed scheme authenticates the product by verification, which leads to a better generalization performance under open-set scenario [17]. Meanwhile, re-training is required for the model proposed in [16], otherwise the leathers of samples from new classes will be misclassified to the existing classes.

Given that the authentication decision is achieved by comparing two sets of texture features extracted from a texture image and stored in a barcode, our feature extraction network should be designed with feature comparison in mind. As shown in Fig. 2, a generic Siamese convolution neural network architecture is utilized in training an efficient feature extractor for our framework. During the training process, the paired samples are employed to train the model which extracts the texture feature of the paired samples x_i, x_i and determines whether the samples are from the same texture class by the corresponding distances

$$d_{ij} = d\Big(\phi(x_i), \phi(x_j)\Big), \tag{1}$$

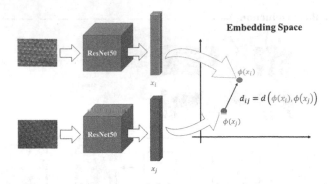

Fig. 2. The Siamese convolutional neural network architecture.

where $\phi(\cdot)$ maps the texture features to the embedding space, and $d(\cdot, \cdot)$ evaluates the distance of a pair of features in the embedding space. It is worth mentioning that the Siamese network not only generates features in an embedding space to classify different textures, it also leads to the following advantages. First, discriminative features can be generated by comparing paired samples from both same and different classes, instead of merely fitting the label of each sample. Second, a customized loss function can be designed to shape the embedding space according to the requirement of the application. For example, an embedding space with a fixed distance between different classes is desirable for our case, since the authentication decision is made by a hard threshold operation on the distance between two sets of features.

Therefore, the margin loss [21], with explicit intra-class and inter-class distances requirement, is adopted in our authentication framework. The margin loss introduces a trainable threshold β and a hyper-parameter α as the distance and the margin between positive and negative pairs into the standard triple loss. Formally, the margin loss of a sample pair is defined in [21] as

$$\mathcal{L}_m = (1 - y_{ij})[(\beta + \alpha) - d_{ij}]_+ + y_{ij}[d_{ij} - (\beta - \alpha)]_+ \tag{2}$$

where i, j denote the index of the input samples, $y_{ij} = 1$ indicates a pair of sample is from the same class while $y_{ij} = 0$ means otherwise, β is a trainable parameter ranged from 0.6 to 1.2, α is a hyper-parameter set as 0.2 according to [21], and d_{ij} evaluates the Euclidean distance between the pair of sample. For a sample pair from the same class ($y_{ij} = 1$), the loss reduces to $[d_{ij} - (\beta - \alpha)]_+$. Therefore, the training process minimizes the loss by generating a feature embedding with *small intra-class distances*. For a sample pair from different classes ($y_{ij} = 0$), the loss becomes $[(\beta + \alpha) - d_{ij}]_+$. Thus, the loss can be minimized by generating a feature embedding with *large inter-class distances*.

From Eq. (2), we can see that the design of margin loss is suitable for our authentication setting which consist of both known and unknown classes. First, a trainable threshold β is employed to limit the spread of samples from the same classes, i.e., $d_{ij} < \beta - \alpha$. As shown in Fig. 3 (a) and (b), such design facilitates our

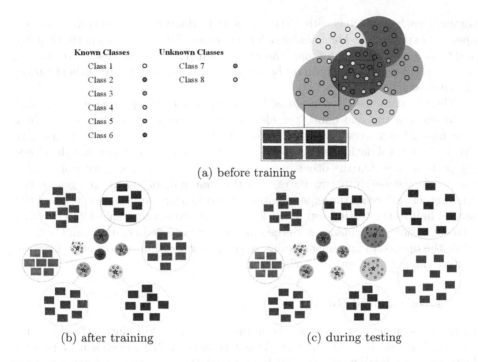

Known Classes | Unknown Classes
Class 1 ○ | Class 7 ◉
Class 2 ● | Class 8 ○
Class 3 ◉
Class 4 ○
Class 5 ○
Class 6 ●

(a) before training

(b) after training   (c) during testing

Fig. 3. Illustration of the feature embedding of the proposed methods (viewed better in color). (a) Original feature embedding of the known texture classes. (b) Feature embedding of the known texture classes after training. (c) Feature embedding of the known and unknown texture classes in testing.

authentication process by thresholding the distances between texture features extracted from the leather and decoded from the barcode. Second, the hyperparameter α sets a margin for the feature embeddings in the hyperspace between different classes, i.e., $d_{ij} > \beta + \alpha$. As shown in Fig. 3 (c), this potentially adds a safety margin for authenticating samples under the open-set scenario where the samples from unknown classes have not been seen in the training process.

3   Datasets and Experimental Results

3.1   Texture Datasets

To evaluate the performance of the proposed scheme, a large collection of product texture images is needed. According to our survey, Oulu Texture (Outex) database [10] and Amsterdam Library of Textures (ALOT) [2] are two high quality texture image datasets that could be adopted in our experiment. The Outex database contains 320 different texture classes collected under 3 illumination conditions and 9 rotation angles. It is one of the largest collections of texture image that available in the public domain. Specifically, the canvas class, which consists of the largest number (46) of texture types, is suitable to our application scenario of product authentication. On the other hand, ALOT is a texture image database of 250 classes rough textures, each of which is with 100 samples. Both datasets are also suitable to our open-set experiment which requires a large number of texture types in the training and testing sets. Although there is no leather texture image in these two datasets, they can still serve as preliminary benchmark for different texture authentication algorithms.

The two databases are employed in both close-set and open-set experimental protocols. On the one hand, the close-set experiment considers the first half (the first 23 out of 46 types) of canvas textures from the Outex dataset. A five-fold cross validation is then performed on these samples to obtain the close-set performance. On the other hand, the open-set experiment protocol divides the whole dataset into two parts, i.e., the first half of canvas images as the training set (following the experiments of metric learning approaches [6]), and the second half as the testing set. Thus, the close-set experiment shows the baseline authentication performance with the same texture classes in training and testing, while the open-set experiment evaluates the generalization performance towards texture images from unknown classes.

3.2   Experimental Results

In the experiment, we compare the authentication performances of traditional handcrafted features (such as, local binary pattern (LBP)), deep learning-based features (e.g., ResNet [4] with 50 layers) and the deep metric learning-based schemes (including Softmax [22], ProxyNCA [7] and Margin [21] loss). To allow a fair comparison under limited off-line storage capacity (in a 2D barcode), the feature dimension of LBP and the last fully-connected (FC) layer in the deep networks are reduced to the dimensions of 128 and 256. More specifically, the LBP feature vectors (of 11564 dimension with the default parameters) are fed into the principal component analysis (PCA) process which reduces the feature to 2048, 256 and 128 dimensions, respectively. Given that the data capacity of a high-capacity 2D barcode is around 500 bytes [23], the chosen feature dimensions is practical.

For the close-set experiments, the extracted features are utilized in machine learning-based classifiers with different setups. For LBP and ResNet50, the texture authentication process is regarded as a classification task. During the training process, the classifiers are trained in a supervised fashion with predetermined texture classes. The testing samples are then classified according to the similarity with the given texture classes. On the other hand, the metric learning-based approaches consider the texture authentication process as a verification task. Paired samples are required in the training process to facilitate the learning of similarities between positive pairs (from the same classes) and differences between negative pairs (from different classes). The similarity threshold between known classes can be determined by the distribution of the training samples. According to the three-sigma rule [12], the threshold is computed as $T_k = \mu_d + 3\bar{\sigma}_k \approx 0.5$, where μ_k and $\bar{\sigma}_k$ are the mean and mean standard deviation for the intra-class distance for the known classes.

For the open-set experiment, only the metric learning-based approaches are applicable since both LBP and ResNet50 works in a classification setup, which does not involve unknown texture classes and undefined number of classes. The metric learning-based approaches work in the same manner as in the close-set experiment. They determine the authenticity of the texture by comparing the questioned texture (be it known or unknown) feature with the reference one. If the distance between the compared features is smaller than the predefined threshold, the questioned texture passes the authentication. To allow a better performance, the inter-class threshold is different from the threshold used for authenticating known classes, T_k. It is computed as $T_u = \beta + \alpha - T_k$, where $\beta + \alpha$ is the minimum distance between samples from two different classes according to Eq. (2), T_k is the three-sigma intra-class distance for known classes. Thus, T_u is a minimum intra-class distance for the unknown classes. According to our experiment, $\alpha = 0.2$ is a hyper-parameter to tradeoff authentication performances between the known and unknown classes, $\beta \approx 1.0$ is obtained from the training process. Therefore, $T_u \approx 1 + 0.2 - 0.5 = 0.7$.

In the implementation, we use ResNet50 as the backbone of our Siamese feature extraction network due to its success in recent state-of-the-art approaches [14]. Parameters of batch normalization (BN) layers in the backbones are frozen during training. To accommodate the samples to the network input size, each image is cropped into patches of size 224×224 pixels. The samples are augmented with random cropping, rotation strategies. The Outex (canvas class) dataset and ALOT dataset are trained for 100 and 150 epochs, respectively, until the loss converges. The ADAM optimizer with a fixed learning rate of 10^{-5}, and the SPC-2 sampling strategy [6] are employed. Our implementation is based on Pytorch 1.5.0 and runs on Nvidia Tesla V100 32 GB GPU.

To allow a better understanding of the experimental performances under a product authentication setup, we employ four patch-level performance metrics.

- $mAcc_k$: mean authentication accuracy for each known class.
- $mFAR_{kk}$: mean false acceptance rate between two known classes.
- $mAcc_u$: mean authentication accuracy for each known class.
- $mFAR_{uk}$: mean false acceptance rate between known and unknown classes, with the known class as the reference.

The above metrics focus on the practical product authentication scenarios. The mean authentication accuracies $mAcc_k$ and $mAcc_u$ measure the accuracies of a user authenticates an authentic product in a close-set and open-set experiment, respectively. The mean false acceptance rates $mFAR_{kk}$ and $mFAR_{uk}$ measure the probability that a counterfeit texture is accepted by our authentication system. It indicates the security level against the attacks where different textures are employed to fool the authentication system. At this moment, the false rejection rate (the probability that a genuine texture is rejected) is not considered in our experiment, since a user can always re-initiate the authentication process. The system is practical as long as the authentication accuracies ($mAcc_k$ and $mAcc_u$) are high and false acceptance rates ($mFAR_{kk}$ and $mFAR_{uk}$) are low. It should be noted that the proposed metrics are different from the commonly used ones in the area of metric learning, e.g., Recall@K and normalized mutual information (NMI) which focus on clustering and information retrieval performance [9].

Table 1. Patch-level performance comparisons of different texture authentication schemes under both close-set and open-set experimental protocols. $T_k = 0.5$ for known classes, $T_u = 0.7$ for unknown classes

Schemes	Outex_Canvas				ALOT			
	Close-set		Open-set		Close-set		Open-set	
	mAcc$_k$	mFAR$_{kk}$	mAcc$_u$	mFAR$_{uk}$	mAcc$_k$	mFAR$_{kk}$	mAcc$_u$	mFAR$_{uk}$
LBP (11564D) + SVM	98.75 ± 0.21%	1.25 ± 0.21%	n/a	n/a	91.95 ± 0.35%	8.05 ± 0.35%	n/a	n/a
LBP+PCA (2048D) + SVM	90.25 ± 0.21%	9.75 ± 0.21%	n/a	n/a	78.70 ± 0.58%	21.30 ± 0.58%	n/a	n/a
LBP+PCA (256D) + SVM	87.35 ± 0.07%	12.65 ± 0.07%	n/a	n/a	72.80 ± 0.75%	27.20 ± 0.75%	n/a	n/a
LBP+PCA (128D) + SVM	85.85 ± 0.49%	14.15 ± 0.49%	n/a	n/a	69.40 ± 0.62%	30.60 ± 0.62%	n/a	n/a
ResNet50 (2048D)	99.64 ± 0.29%	0.36 ± 0.29%	n/a	n/a	98.03 ± 0.22%	1.97 ± 0.22%	n/a	n/a
ResNet50 (256D)	99.18 ± 0.33%	0.82 ± 0.33%	n/a	n/a	97.43 ± 0.18%	2.57 ± 0.18%	n/a	n/a
ResNet50 (128D)	98.49 ± 0.35%	1.51 ± 0.35%	n/a	n/a	95.73 ± 0.31%	4.27 ± 0.31%	n/a	n/a
Softmax (256D)	95.52%	0.00%	70.85%	0.08%	99.80%	0.00%	90.28%	0.02%
Softmax (128D)	95.14%	0.00%	67.79%	0.04%	94.24%	0.00%	90.25%	0.03%
ProxyNCA (256D)	100.00%	0.00%	70.82%	2.04%	100.00%	0.00%	85.93%	0.17%
ProxyNCA (128D)	100.00%	0.00%	59.47%	1.61%	100.00%	0.00%	82.48%	0.27%
Margin (256D)	96.78%	0.00%	89.91%	0.07%	96.47%	0.00%	97.03%	0.05%
Margin (128D)	96.51%	0.00%	72.73%	0.05%	95.96%	0.00%	96.35%	0.02%

According to the results in Table 1, the traditional handcrafted feature, LBP performances poorly after dimension reduction by PCA. From the default setting (uniform LBP with radius 8 pixels and 8 sampling points) with 11564D to a practical setting with 128D, the mAcc$_k$ of LBP drops by more than 13% and 20% for Outex and ALOT databases, respectively. This is because PCA is not task specific [13] and may not be optimized for such heavy reduction on feature dimension. By employing data-driven feature extraction and fully-connected layers in ResNet50, the performance degradation during dimension reduction is alleviated. Less than 3% performance loss has been observed by reducing the feature dimension from 2048D to 128D.

Among different metric learning schemes, ProxyNCA works the best under close-set scenario. It is due to the similarity between the metric loss calculation and our authentication setting. ProxyNCA loss assigns a single proxy for each class, associates each data point with a proxy, and encourages the positive pairs to be close and negative pairs to be further than a distance [5]. This is similar to our authentication scheme by comparing query texture images with the reference ones (proxies). However, the margin loss is more suitable for the open-set scenario. Though the authentication accuracy is 72.73% in the Outex dataset for feature dimension of 128D, the accuracy can be significantly improved by doubling the feature dimension (as shown in the case of 256D). It maintains a margin between different classes in the embedding space, such that distances between the positive pairs are kept within a normalized threshold and distances between negative pairs are pushed further away with a safe margin. The safe margin will be especially useful for unknown classes whose distribution may not

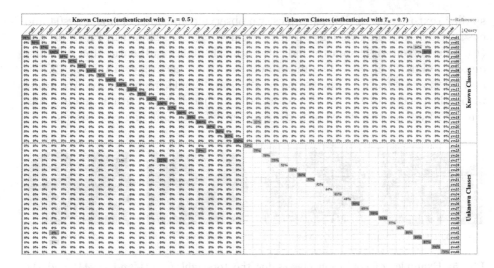

Fig. 4. Confusion matrix for both known and unknown classes, including authentication accuracies of different classes (shown along the diagonal line) and false acceptance rates between different pairs of classes (shown in the off-diagonal cells). The results in black and blue fonts are generated with the thresholds for known and unknown classes ($T_k = 0.5$ and $T_u = 0.7$), respectively. The green and red shadings indicate results with high accuracies and high error rates for the diagonal and off-diagonal elements, respectively. (Color figure online)

be as compact as the known classes in the embedding space. To improve the performance of Softmax and ProxyNCA schemes, a margin $\alpha = 0.2$ is also added to the threshold in open-set experiments.

To further evaluate the performance of the metric learning scheme based on margin loss, we show the confusion matrix for both known and unknown classes. For instance, the results in top-left quarter of Fig. 4 show the authentication performance within known classes. The first column considers the cases where the first type of texture (cvs01) is used as the verification target, while different textures (e.g., cvs01 to cvs23) are employed as queries. The performance metric in each cell indicates the probability of accepting the query from corresponding row. Therefore, the metrics along the diagonal direction indicates the probability of successful authentication within each texture, while the off-diagonal elements imply the probability of confusions between two different textures. It should be noted that the confusion matrix is not symmetric. For two cells at symmetric positions w.r.t. the diagonal line, different textures have been assigned as the reference and query. Secondly, according to the proposed metric learning scheme in open-set and close-set conditions, different authentication thresholds (i.e., $T_k = 0.5, T_u = 0.7$) have been employed for the known and unknown classes.

The top-left quarter of Fig. 4 shows satisfactory authentication performance within known classes. About 97% mAcc$_k$ is achieved as highlighted in the green cells. The top-right and bottom-left quarters show some confusions between those similar texture classes. For examples, we observe confusions between cvs04 and cvs44 which are some visually similar texture images as shown in Fig. 5 (a) and (b). The bottom-right quarter indicates a much higher authentication difficulty among unknown classes. The mean authentication accuracy $mAcc_u$ is 72.73% and 89.91% for feature dimensions of 128D and 256D, respectively. According to our inspection of the cvs33 texture, the authentication error is mainly contributed by large variations of texture under different imaging resolutions.

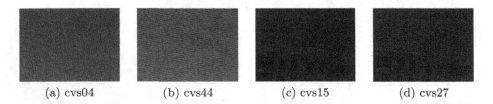

| (a) cvs04 | (b) cvs44 | (c) cvs15 | (d) cvs27 |

Fig. 5. Examples of confusion classes for the top-right (cvs04 and cvs44) and the bottom-left (cvs15 and cvs27) quarters.

4   Conclusion

In this work, we build an anti-counterfeiting system that works for consumer products in an open-set scenario with a texture verification setting. By incorporating a customized metric in the embedding space, we allow the authentication being conducted under both close-set and open-set scenarios by a simple distance comparison operation. Experimental results demonstrate that the proposed system achieves 89.91% open-set authentication accuracy for a feature of 256 dimensions in the Outex texture database. The results show a promising application prospect in a practical product authentication scenario.

In the future, we will collect a texture image dataset of different leathers by mobile imaging devices to evaluate the authentication performance under a practical setting. Moreover, we will also investigate more sophisticated distance metrics in the embedding space to exploit the prior knowledge of the training samples, such as resolution, illumination, distance.

References

1. Global Brand Counterfeiting Report, 2018. Research and Market Technical Report No. 4438394, December 2017
2. Burghouts, G.J., Geusebroek, J.M.: Material-specific adaptation of color invariant features. Pattern Recogn. Lett. **30**(3), 306–313 (2009)
3. Chen, C., Zhou, B., Mow, W.H.: RA code: a robust and aesthetic code for resolution-constrained applications. IEEE Trans. Circ. Syst. Video Technol. **28**(11), 3300–3312 (2018)
4. He, K., Zhang, X., Ren, S., Sun, J.: Deep residual learning for image recognition. In: Proceedings of IEEE Conference on Computer Vision and Pattern Recognition, pp. 770–778 (2016)

5. Kim, S., Kim, D., Cho, M., Kwak, S.: Proxy anchor loss for deep metric learning. In: Proceedings of IEEE Conference on Computer Vision and Pattern Recognition, pp. 3238–3247 (2020)
6. Li, X., Yu, L., Fu, C.W., Fang, M., Heng, P.A.: Revisiting metric learning for few-shot image classification. Neurocomputing **406**, 49–58 (2020)
7. Movshovitz-Attias, Y., Toshev, A., Leung, T.K., Ioffe, S., Singh, S.: No fuss distance metric learning using proxies. In: Proceedings of IEEE Conference on Computer Vision and Pattern Recognition, pp. 360–368 (2017)
8. Norouzi, M., et al.: Zero-shot learning by convex combination of semantic embeddings. arXiv preprint arXiv:1312.5650 (2013)
9. Oh Song, H., Xiang, Y., Jegelka, S., Savarese, S.: Deep metric learning via lifted structured feature embedding. In: Proceedings of IEEE Conference on Computer Vision and Pattern Recognition, pp. 4004–4012 (2016)
10. Ojala, T., Maenpaa, T., Pietikainen, M., Viertola, J., Kyllonen, J., Huovinen, S.: Outex: new framework for empirical evaluation of texture analysis algorithms. In: Object Recognition Supported by User Interaction for Service Robots, vol. 1, pp. 701–706. IEEE (2002)
11. Ojala, T., Pietikainen, M., Maenpaa, T.: Multiresolution gray-scale and rotation invariant texture classification with local binary patterns. IEEE Trans. Pattern Anal. Mach. Intell. **24**(7), 971–987 (2002)
12. Pukelsheim, F.: The three sigma rule. Am. Stat. **48**(2), 88–91 (1994)
13. Qian, Q., Shang, L., Sun, B., Hu, J., Li, H., Jin, R.: SoftTriple loss: deep metric learning without triplet sampling. In: Proceedings of IEEE Conference on Computer Vision and Pattern Recognition, pp. 6450–6458 (2019)
14. Sanakoyeu, A., Tschernezki, V., Buchler, U., Ommer, B.: Divide and conquer the embedding space for metric learning. In: Proceedings of IEEE Conference on Computer Vision and Pattern Recognition, pp. 471–480 (2019)
15. Schraml, R., Debiasi, L., Kauba, C., Uhl, A.: On the feasibility of classification-based product package authentication. In: IEEE Workshop on International Forensics and Security (WIFS), pp. 1–6 (2017)
16. Sharma, A., Srinivasan, V., Kanchan, V., Subramanian, L.: The fake vs real goods problem: microscopy and machine learning to the rescue. In: Proceedings of the 23rd ACM SIGKDD International Conference on Knowledge Discovery and Data Mining, pp. 2011–2019 (2017)
17. Sun, Y., Wang, X., Tang, X.: Hybrid deep learning for face verification. IEEE Trans. Pattern Anal. Mach. Intell. **38**(10), 1997–2009 (2015)
18. Tan, X., Triggs, B.: Enhanced local texture feature sets for face recognition under difficult lighting conditions. IEEE Trans. Image Process. **19**(6), 1635–1650 (2010)
19. Wang, X., Ye, Y., Gupta, A.: Zero-shot recognition via semantic embeddings and knowledge graphs. In: Proceedings of the IEEE Conference on Computer Vision and Pattern Recognition, pp. 6857–6866 (2018)
20. Wong, C.W., Wu, M.: Counterfeit detection based on unclonable feature of paper using mobile camera. IEEE Trans. Inf. Forensics Secur. **12**(8), 1885–1899 (2017)
21. Wu, C.Y., Manmatha, R., Smola, A.J., Krahenbuhl, P.: Sampling matters in deep embedding learning. In: Proceedings of IEEE Conference on Computer Vision and Pattern Recognition, pp. 2840–2848 (2017)
22. Zhai, A., Wu, H.Y.: Classification is a strong baseline for deep metric learning. In: Proceedings of the British Machine Vision Conference (BMVC) (2019)
23. Zhang, L., Chen, C., Mow, W.H.: Accurate modeling and efficient estimation of the print-capture channel with application in barcoding. IEEE Trans. Image Process. **28**(1), 464–478 (2018)

Moving Object Detection Based on Self-adaptive Contour Extraction

Xin Shi[1,2], Tao Xue[1,2,3], and Xueqing Zhao[1,2,3]($\boxtimes$)

[1] School of Computer Science, Xi'an Polytechnic University, Xi'an, Shaanxi, China
[2] Shaanxi Key Laboratory of Clothing Intelligence, School of Computer Science,
Xi'an Polytechnic University, Xi'an 710048, China
[3] National and Local Joint Engineering Research Center for Advanced Networking
and Intelligent Information Service, Xi'an Polytechnic University,
Xi'an 710048, China
zhaoxueqing@xpu.edu.cn

Abstract. Object detection of moving targets requires both accuracy and real-time performance. In this paper, we propose a contour extraction prior to convolutional neural network to extract more salient features and use region proposal network to generate candidate regions. Afterwards, the feature maps and proposal regions are inputed to ROI pooling layer followed with some fully connected layers to classify objects and regress bounding box. Simulation experiments show that our method is effective in improving detection accuracy by testing on the dataset with 11 categories of moving targets.

Keywords: Moving object detection · Contour extraction · Region proposal network

1 Introduction

As one of the core problems in the field of computer vision, object detection refers to the process of identifying the regions of interest, determining their categories and locating their positions [1–3]. The object detection tasks can be decomposed into two subproblems towards multiple objects; namely, objects' locating and objects' classifying [4,5]. Due to the different exteriors, shapes and postures, the interference of illumination and shades, object detection is always one of the most challenging problems in the field of computer vision. Deep learning methods, represented by neural networks [6,7], have achieved excellent performance in the field of object recognition recently, which attracts more and more researchers to devote to improving neural networks and building new computing models to deal with the problem.

Supported by the National Natural Science Foundation of China under Grant No.61806160 and Shaanxi Association for Science and Technology of Colleges and Universities Youth Talent Development Program, No. 20190112 and the Youth Innovation Team of Shaanxi Universities.

© Springer Nature Switzerland AG 2021
Y. Peng et al. (Eds.): ICIG 2021, LNCS 12888, pp. 126–135, 2021.
https://doi.org/10.1007/978-3-030-87355-4_11

The proposal of convolutional based neural network named AlexNet [8] in 2012 has successfully demonstrated the effectiveness and potential of deep learning in the field of computer vision. Afterwards, an increasing number of deep neural networks have emerged and promoted the development of computer vision rapidly. In terms of object detection tasks, current algorithms and networks can be classified into two categories, the two-stage algorithms and the one-stage algorithms. The former ones require the generation of region proposal prior to the object detection, RCNN [9], Fast-RCNN [10] and Faster-RCNN [11] are some of the typical representations of them, these algorithms achieve relatively better accuracy. The latter ones are represented by SSD [12], RetinaNet [13] and YOLO series [14], which implement objects' locating and classifying directly in a single network so that they are capable of improving efficiency.

With regard to dynamic objects' detection in video series, it not only requires for the accuracy and precision of detection, but also expects a better capability in terms of real-time performance. However, either current one-stage algorithms or two-stage algorithms, their abilities of striking a balance between efficiency and accuracy are still less than satisfactory. Therefore, in this paper, we attempt to integrate contour extraction into deep learning based object detection neural networks with an expectation of enabling the application on dynamic objects' detection. Specifically, we extract contour information prior to the convolutional neural network (CNN for short) so as to acquire more distinct and salient feature maps. Besides, we substitute region proposal network (RPN for short) [11] for selective search (SS for short) to generate region proposal which greatly improves the generation speed of bounding box. Literature reviews have demonstrated that the replacement of RPN network has increased the speed of region proposal generation from 2 s to 10 milliseconds, which enables the requirement of end-to-end object detection. Experiment results in this paper further show that, our method effectively improves the accuracy of moving object detection in video series.

The rest of paper is organized as follows. The framework and technical details of our method are introduced in Sect. 2. Experiments and discussions are presented in Sect. 3. Lastly, Sect. 4 gives the conclusion of this paper.

2 Methods

In this section, we firstly introduce the network architecture of our method, followed by some core implementation technical details.

2.1 Framework Description

Features are always the most important factors of computer vision tasks either in traditional methods or in deep learning based methods. The more salient and distinct the features are extracted, the more accurate the task is achieved. Hence, in our method, we firstly extract the contours of input images because the contour information ignores the effect of background as well as some noise interference inside the object, which is capable of protruding objects to some extent. Afterwards, the contour images are inputed to convolution neural network to generate feature maps; then comes to the RPN network to estimate and generate region proposals. ROI pooling receives the feature maps as well as the region proposals to convert proposals of different dimensions to outputs with fixed length with the purpose of adapting to successive fully connected layers. The last step composes of two branches, one is to predict the final bounding box of the objects, the other is the classification of objects. The overall flowchart of our method is illustrated as Fig. 1, the technical details of contour extraction and the main idea RPN network are introduced later.

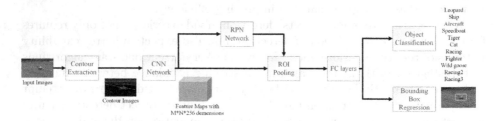

Fig. 1. The overall flowchart of the method in this paper.

2.2 Contour Extraction

Before inputting source images to deep neural network, we firstly carry on a pre-processing to the images by extracting their contour information.

As one of the most dominant edge detection algorithms, Canny [15] has been widely used with the help of its better signal to noise ratio and detection accuracy. However, some parameters in Canny require manual setting, such as variance of Gaussian filter and the two thresholds of binarization, which results in a poor adaptability and difficulty in practical application. Therefore, to improve the adaptability of Canny, we substitute self-adaptive smoothing filter for Gaussian filter and use Otsu [16] algorithm to generate the low and high threshold according to the distribution of gray-scale pixels automatically. In this way, the noises and some pseudo edges are eliminated so that the contours can be extracted with no artificial intervention. The flowchart of the self-adaptive contour extraction process is shown in Fig. 2.

To be more precise, the basic idea of self-adaptive filter lies in the iterative convolution between original image and a small average weighted template, the weighted coefficients of each pixel are changed adaptively during each iteration. The filtered image $f^{(n+1)}(x,y)$ after n iterations is defined as Eq. (1),

$$f^{(n+1)}(x,y) = \frac{\sum_{i=-1}^{+1}\sum_{j=-1}^{+1} f^{(n)}(x+i,y+j)w^{(n)}(x+i,y+j)}{\sum_{i=-1}^{+1}\sum_{j=-1}^{+1} w^{(n)}(x+i,y+j)} \qquad (1)$$

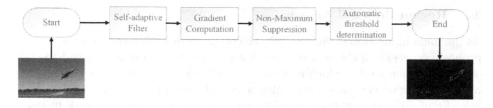

Fig. 2. The flowchart of the self-adaptive contour extraction.

where $w^{(n)}$ is the weighted coefficients in the nth iteration of each pixel defined as Eq. (2),

$$w^{(n)}(x,y) = exp[-\frac{G_x^2(x,y) + G_y^2(x,y)}{2k^2}]$$ (2)

$G_x^2(x,y)$ and $G_y^2(x,y)$ are gradient components as shown in Eq. (3) and Eq. (4) respectively. k is a parameter to determine the size of convolutional template which is set to be 10 in this paper.

$$G_x(x,y) = \frac{1}{2}[f(x+1,y) - f(x,y)]$$ (3)

$$G_y(x,y) = \frac{1}{2}[f(x,y+1) - f(x,y)]$$ (4)

In terms of the threshold selection, the threshold is determined as the one which enables the maximum between-cluster variance of foreground and background. The between-cluster variance is defined as Eq. (5),

$$\sigma_B^2 = \frac{[m_G P_1(k) - m(k)]^2}{P_1(k)[1 - P_1(k)]}$$ (5)

where m_G is the average grayscale of the image defined as Eq. (6), L is the largest grayscale and p_i refers to the probability of grayscale i. $m(k)$ is the average grayscale from grayscale 0 to k, as shown in Eq. (7). $P_1(k)$ is the probability that a pixel is in the range of 0 and k, as shown in Eq. (8),

$$m_G = \sum_{i=0}^{L-1} ip_i$$ (6)

$$m(k) = \sum_{i=0}^{k} ip_i$$ (7)

$$P_1(k) = \sum_{i=0}^{k} p_i$$ (8)

The value of k which enables σ_B^2 to be maximized is selected as the optimal high threshold T_H in Canny and the low threshold T_L is accordingly set to be $\frac{1}{2}k$.

2.3   Region Proposal Network

As the main innovation of Fast-RCNN, the proposal of RPN integrates the region proposal process into the neural network architecture and realizes an end-to-end object detection model, which increases the detection efficiency by reducing the redundant region generation and integrating all computations onto GPUs. The purpose of RPN is to extract proposal regions through neural network instead of the traditional selective search based methods [17]. The input of RPN is the feature map extracted from original images by backbone convolution neural networks such as VGG16 [18], the output of RPN can be used to determine possible region proposal. The basic idea of RPN can be summarized as follows.

After feature extracting though some convolution and pooling layers, a feature map with the dimension of $M \times N \times 256$ is acquired, which is taken as the input of RPN network. To better fuse the neighborhood information so as to make the features more robust, a 3×3 convolution is applied to the feature maps.

As the feature maps are extracted through convolution and pooling, it is not hard to comprehend that each point on the feature map can be mapped to a region on original image, by adding some parameters and restrictions, RPN determines k kinds of mapping for each point on feature maps and renamed points on feature maps as anchors. Therefore, two branches are followed after the 3×3 convolution layer where each branch is a fully connected layer (FC layer for short) with different output dimensions. The first branch is used to determine whether the mapped region from anchors to original image contains object or not, the output is a vector with the size of $M \times N \times 2k$ and is further reshaped into (M, N, k, 2) where the last dimension contains two numbers to show the scores with or without object. The second branch is used to determine the offset from anchors on feature map to original image, for any possibility of k kinds of mappings, it has 4 coordinates which are center coordinates (x, y) and the height-width size of the rectangular mapping (h, w). Therefore, the output of the second branch is a vector with the size of $M \times N \times 4k$.

To sum up, the output of the RPN network is two vectors with the dimension of (M, N, k, 2) and (M, N, k, 4), respectively, which also means that for each feature map with the size of $M \times N$, RPN generates $M \times N \times k$ proposal regions primarily. This is still a large amount of proposal regions which is not only computational resources consuming but also inefficient. Therefore, a proposal layer is attached to further screen the candidate regions. It firstly sorts the k candidate proposal regions according to their scores of having objects and selects the top k' with highest scores. Secondly, it maps the k' anchors to original image and compares with the ground truth by using non-maximum suppression [19] to determine the final region proposal results of RPN network.

3   Simulation Experiments

3.1   Dataset and Environmental Settings

We construct the dataset with 8650 images by extracting frames from 11 video series with moving object, the size of each image is 640×320 pixels, Fig. 3 shows some examples of dataset.

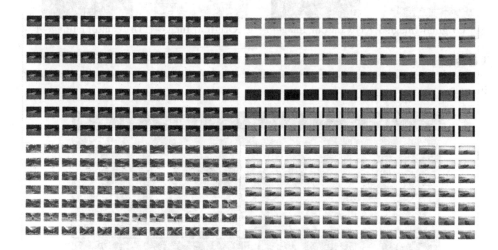

Fig. 3. Examples of the dataset.

Our experiments are executed on the basis of Window 10 operation system with Intel(R) Core(TM) i5-6500 CPU with 4 GB RAM. The program is written in MATLAB under MATLAB R2018a. The parameters of the simulation experiments are shown in Table 1.

Table 1. The parameter settings in simulation experiments.

Parameter names	Parameter values
Mini BatchSize	5
Initial LearnRate	0.001
MaxEpochs	100
Verbose frequency	200

3.2   Results and Analysis

Figure 4 shows some examples after contour extraction, it is obviously that the objects in extracted images are salient and distinct.

(a) Original Image-1 (b) Contour Image-1 (c) Original Image-2 (d) Contour Image-2

(e) Original Image-3 (f) Contour Image-3 (g) Original Image-4 (h) Contour Image-4

Fig. 4. Some examples of original images and results after contour extraction. (a)(c)(e)(f) are examples of original images, (b)(d)(f)(h) are corresponding contour images.

Fig. 5. Examples of the object detection results.

Figure 5 is the video screenshot of the testing videos, it can be seen that the moving targets have been detected and recognized successfully.

To validate the effectiveness of our method, we further compare it with Faster-RCNN on the dataset with 11 categories in terms of detection accuracy which is defined as F1-score in Eq. (9),

$$F1 - score = \frac{2 * P * R}{P + R} \tag{9}$$

where P means precision rate defined as $P = TP/(TP + FP)$ and R represents recall rate defined as $R = TP/(TP + FN)$. TP, FP, FN show the relationship between predicted result and real result are true-positive, false-positive and false-negative, respectively. Table 2 illustrates the comparison results of our method and Faster-RCNN. It can be seen that the F1-scores of different categories increase by an average of 2 percent, the average accuracy rate is about 88.08% with some categories exceeding 90%. To further analyze the relationship between the content of videos and detection accuracy, we find that the accuracy rate is inversely proportional to the moving speed of objects. For example, the videos with slow moving objects such as cat and wild goose reach the higher accuracy while videos with leopard and speedboat get relatively lower accuracy.

Table 2. The $F1 - score$ comparison results of our method and Faster-RCNN in terms of 11 categories.

Category name	Result of faster-RCNN (%)	Result of our method (%)
Leopard	81.75	84.66
Ship	86.79	89.45
Aircraft	87.23	89.26
Speedboat	82.75	85.57
Tiger	83.81	86.66
Cat	89.45	91.64
Racing	87.67	89.47
Fighter	87.83	90.71
Wild goose	86.68	90.39
Racing2	85.44	88.57
Racing3	87.16	90.20

Moreover, we shuffle the dataset for ten times and divide the training and testing set in a ratio of 8:2 to further make the comparison between our method and Faster-RCNN in terms of average F1-scores, Fig. 6 shows the comparison results. The average accuracy of our method is about 2.5 percents higher than that of Faster-RCNN, which validates that our method is effective for the accuracy improvement.

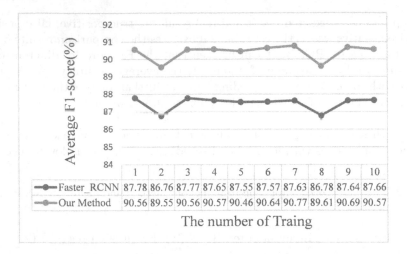

The number of Traing

	1	2	3	4	5	6	7	8	9	10
Faster_RCNN	87.78	86.76	87.77	87.65	87.55	87.57	87.63	86.78	87.64	87.66
Our Method	90.56	89.55	90.56	90.57	90.46	90.64	90.77	89.61	90.69	90.57

Fig. 6. The comparison results of average F1-score between our method and Faster-RCNN for 10 iterations of training.

4   Conclusion

To balance between efficiency and accuracy of moving object detection, in this paper, we integrate contour extraction into deep learning based object detection neural network. Specifically, we extract contour information prior to the feature map generation of convolutional neural network (CNN for short) so as to acquire more distinct and salient feature maps. Besides, we use RPN network to generate region proposal which enables the requirement of end-to-end object detection. The simulation experiments show that our method increases the average F1-score by 2.5% than that of Faster-RCNN in terms of moving object detection by testing on the dataset with 11 categories. Our future work will concentrate on the improving the detection accuracy of fast moving objects and high resolution videos.

References

1. Borji, A., Cheng, M.-M., Hou, Q., Jiang, H., Li, J.: Salient object detection: a survey. Comput. Visual Media **5**(2), 117–150 (2019). https://doi.org/10.1007/s41095-019-0149-9
2. Xiao, Y., et al.: A review of object detection based on deep learning. Multimedia Tools Appl. **79**(33), 23729–23791 (2020). https://doi.org/10.1007/s11042-020-08976-6
3. arXiv:1905.05055. https://arxiv.org/abs/1905.05055. Accessed 16 May 2019
4. Everingham, M., Eslami, S., Gool, L.V., et al.: The pascal visual object classes challenge: a retrospective. Int. J. Comput. Vis. **111**(1), 98–136 (2015)
5. Redmon, J., et al.: You only look once: unified, real-time object detection. In: Computer Vision & Pattern Recognition IEEE (2016)

6. Rawat, W., Wang, Z.: Deep convolutional neural networks for image classification: a comprehensive review. Neural Comput. **29**(9), 2352–2449 (2017)
7. Gu, J., et al.: Recent advances in convolutional neural networks. Pattern Recogn. **77**, 354–377 (2015)
8. Krizhevsky, A., Sutskever, I., Hinton, G. E.: ImageNet classification with deep convolutional neural networks. In: Advances in Neural Information Processing Systems, 1097–1105(2012)
9. Girshick, R., Donahue, J., Darrell, T., Malik, J.: Rich feature hierarchies for accurate object detection and semantic segmentation, In: IEEE Conference on Computer Vision and Pattern Recognition (CVPR), Columbus, OH, USA, pp. 580–587 (2014)
10. Girshick, R. : Fast R-CNN. In: Computer Science (2015)
11. Ren, S., He, K., Girshick, R., et al.: Faster R-CNN: towards real-time object detection with region proposal networks. IEEE Trans. Pattern Anal. Mach. Intell. **39**(6), 1137–1149 (2017)
12. Liu, W., et al.: SSD: single shot MultiBox detector. In: Leibe, B., Matas, J., Sebe, N., Welling, M. (eds.) ECCV 2016. LNCS, vol. 9905, pp. 21–37. Springer, Cham (2016). https://doi.org/10.1007/978-3-319-46448-0_2
13. Lin, T.Y., Goyal, P., Girshick, R., et al.: Focal loss for dense object detection. IEEE Trans. Pattern Anal. Mach. Intell. **42**(2), 318–327 (2017)
14. Redmon, J., Farhadi, A.: YOLOv3: an incremental improvement. arXiv e-prints(2018)
15. Canny, J.: A computational approach to edge detection. IEEE Trans. Pattern Anal. Mach. Intell. (PAMI) **8**(6), 679–698 (1986)
16. Otsu, N.: A thresholding selection method from gray-level histogram. IEEE Trans. Syst. Man Cybern. **9**(1), 62–66 (2007)
17. Syed, H.: Selective search for object recognition. Int. J. Comput. Vis. **104**(2), 154–171 (2013)
18. Simonyan, K., Zisserman A.: Very deep convolutional networks for large-scale image recognition. Computer Science (2014)
19. Neubeck, A., Gool, L. V.: Efficient non-maximum suppression. In: International Conference on Pattern Recognition, Hong Kong, pp. 850–855. IEEE Computer Society (2006)

Small Infrared Aerial Target Detection Using Spatial and Temporal Cues

Liangchao Guo, Wenlong Zhang, Xiaoliang Sun[✉], Zi Wang, and Yang Shang

National University of Defense Technology, Changsha, China
alexander_sxl@nudt.edu.cn

Abstract. Due to rapidly relative motion between target and infrared imaging platform, clutter background, etc., robust small infrared aerial target detection is still an open problem. A novel small infrared aerial target detection method using spatial and temporal cues is proposed in this paper. First, using spatial cues, we take target candidate detection as a binary classification problem. Target candidates in each single frame are detected via interesting pixel detection and a trained LightGBM model. Then, using temporal cues, we model the local smoothness and global continuous characteristic of the target trajectory as short-strict and long-loose constraints. The trajectory constraints within image sequence are used in detecting the true small infrared aerial targets from numerical target candidates. Experiment results on the public dataset SIATD show that the proposed method performs better than other existing methods in detecting small infrared aerial target and shows great robustness toward clutter backgrounds.

Keywords: Aerial · Small infrared target detection · Spatial and temporal cues · Trajectory constraint · LightGBM

1 Introduction

Infrared detection has advantages of all-day and all-weather operation, high resolution, etc. Thus, infrared detection system has been widely used in air platform early warning, guidance, etc. [1]. Due to the rapidly relative motion and clutter backgrounds, small aerial target detection is still an open problem for the airborne infrared detection system.

Existing infrared detection methods can be categorized into single frame based methods and multiple successive frames based methods. Single frame based methods detect the small infrared target mainly using the differences between the target and background. The small infrared target is often modeled as a spot target of isotropic distribution and this kind method is easy to be implemented and efficiently. However, cues provided by a single frame may be inadequate for robust small infrared target detection. The temporal cues contained in multiple successive frames are important to robust small infrared target detection [1]. Multiple successive frames based methods boost the performance of small target detection by associating multiple image data. However, the adoption of the temporal cues increases the computational complexity. And such existing methods have

© Springer Nature Switzerland AG 2021
Y. Peng et al. (Eds.): ICIG 2021, LNCS 12888, pp. 136–147, 2021.
https://doi.org/10.1007/978-3-030-87355-4_12

trouble in detecting small aerial targets for airborne infrared detecting systems focused in this paper.

Existing works have demonstrated that temporal cues play an important role in robust small infrared target detection, especially for complex cases. For the targets, we find that the true targets exhibit continuous and smooth long trajectories while the clutter does not. Based on the facts, this paper tackles the problem of small infrared aerial target detection by using spatial and temporal cues. The proposed method firstly detects the target candidates from each frame using interesting pixel selection and a trained highly efficient gradient boosting decision tree (LightGBM) [2] model. Then based on the short-strict and long-loose constraints, the true targets are detected from numerical target candidates by trajectory segment growth and merging. Experimental results indicate that our method can detect the small infrared aerial targets robustly and achieves superior performance than other existing methods.

2 Related Works

Most related works to this paper are summarized in this section. As mentioned above, existing small infrared target detection methods can be classified into single frame and multiple frames based methods.

2.1 Single Frame Based Methods

Single frame based methods detect the small infrared targets from a single image. They are mainly using the difference between the target and the background.

Moradi et al. [3] modeled the spot target using the point spread function of the imaging system. Such a method is simple and efficient. However, it performs poorly under clutter backgrounds. Based on the remote imaging and infrared imaging characteristics, researchers modeled the background as approximately common or uniform components. Compared to the background, the small target has a small spatial spread. The small target is detected by subtracting the estimated background. Gao et al. [4] modeled the background using Infrared Patch-Image (IPI) reconstruction. Xue et al. [5] introduced multiple sparse constraints in reconstruction. These methods usually work well only when the background satisfies the assumption of large space expansion, and the background modeling takes a lot of time. Zhao et al. [6] extract spatial size and contrast information of small infrared targets in the max-tree and min-tree and proposed a novel detection method based on multiple morphological profiles. The method suffers a high false alarm rate for clutter backgrounds.

For CNN-related methods, Dai et al. [7] preserved and highlighted the small target feature by exploiting a bottom-up attentional modulation integrating the low-level features into the high-level features of deeper layers. And the authors of [8] constructed a Generative Adversarial Networks (GAN), upon U-Net, to learn the features of small infrared targets and directly predict the intensity of targets.

2.2 Multiple Frames Abased Methods

Single frame based methods have trouble in detecting small infrared targets under clutter backgrounds. Multiple frames based methods introduce temporal cues in target detecting via association between successive frames.

Marco et al. [9] proposed a generalized likelihood ratio test based method for small target detection in sea background. [10] adopted passion distribution in energy accumulation for small infrared target detection. Single pixel association methods are sensitive to clutter backgrounds or isolated spot noise. Li et al. [11] enhanced the small infrared target via saliency analysis based on motion and appearance. The spatio-temporal tensor model is adopted to model the background in [12, 13]. The multiple subspace learning is adopted to modify [14] in [15]. Such methods cannot handle rapidly changing backgrounds well. In addition, the methods are often complex and cannot meet the needs of real-time applications.

Most of existing exploration works are single frame based methods. Temporal cues have not been adopted in the mentioned works. Although the performance of related works has been improved, they have difficulties in detecting small infrared aerial targets under clutter backgrounds.

3 Small Infrared Aerial Target Detection using Spatial and Temporal Cues

The proposed method firstly detects target candidates from each frame using a trained LightGBM model. Then the trajectory candidates are generated by linking the target candidates within successive frames. The true trajectories that meet the short-strict and long-loose constraints are detected finally.

3.1 Target Candidate Detection for Each Frame

Due to remote imaging, the small aerial targets are presented as spot targets in the image. And, the spot targets may brighter or darker than their surroundings. This paper takes the target candidate detection for each frame as a binary classification problem. For each interesting pixel, we extract features in the local region centered on it. Then the trained LightGBM model takes the features as input and determines the pixel is a target candidate or not.

Interesting Pixel Detection. The small infrared targets only correspond to s small part of pixels in the images. In order to detect the small infrared target efficiently, we extract the interesting pixels which are more likely to be the target from the image and enter the following process. As mention above, the small infrared aerial target focused in this paper is often presented as a spot target. It may brighter or darker than its neighbors. This paper adopts positive and negative median filter to detect interesting pixels, as shown in Eq. (1).

$$Label(x, y) = \begin{cases} 1, & I(x, y) > (k_1 + median((x, y)))|I(x, y) < (median((x, y)) + k_2) \\ 0, & otherwise \end{cases}$$

$$(1)$$

For the input image I, $Label(x, y)=1$ indicates the pixel (x, y) is an interesting pixel and $Label(x, y)=0$ denotes not. $median((x, y))$ calculates the median value in a local region of certain size centered on (x, y). We set the parameters $k_1 = 15$ to select the brighter targets and $k_2 = -20$ to select the darker targets.

Feature Extraction and Learning. This paper adopts LightGBM [2] in target candidate detection. This paper extracts features for each interesting pixel in the local region which is as rectangle centered on it and computes 7 features from the local region, including kurtosis γ_2, skew S_k, entropy H, mean μ, variance σ^2, maximum v_{max} and minimum v_{min}. Let $L_{R_1 \times R_2}(x, y)$ denotes the local rectangle region centered on the pixel (x, y) of size $R_1 \times R_2$. We flat the region into vector $V=\{v_0, v_1, ..., v_{N-1}\}_{N=R_1 \times R_2}$. The definitions of the 7 features are as Eq. (2) shows. $p(.)$ denotes the probability of the intensity value and it can be inferred from the intensity histogram of the input image.

$$
\begin{aligned}
\text{kurtosis}: \gamma_2 &= \frac{\mu_4}{\sigma^4} - 3 & \text{variance}: \sigma^2 &= \frac{1}{N}\sum_{v_i \in V}(v_i - \mu) \\
\text{skew}: S_k &= \frac{\mu_3}{\sigma^3} & \text{maximum}: v_{max} &= \max_{v_i \in V}(v_i) \\
\text{entropy}: H(V) &= -\sum_{v_i \in V} p(v_i)\log p(v_i) & \text{minimum}: v_{min} &= \min_{v_i \in V}(v_i) \\
\text{mean}: \mu &= \frac{1}{N}\sum_{v_i \in V} v_i
\end{aligned}
\tag{2}
$$

In the training dataset, the small infrared aerial targets are annotated. We take the pixels within the regions centered on the label positions of size 3×3 as positive samples. The remaining pixels in the images can be taken as negative samples. The 7 dimension feature vector by multi-scale processing strategy is calculated for each sample to train the LightGBM model.

3.2 Target Detection Using Trajectory Constraints

The target candidates in each frame have been detected as mentioned above. We use the homograph transform to model the inter-frame movement in this paper. The registration between successive frames is built by SURF [16] feature point extraction and matching. Then we remap the target candidates in each frame to the coordinate of the first frame within the time window.

We intend to detect the true targets whose trajectories obey the short-strict and long-loose constraints. In the captured image sequence, the true target form a continuous and smooth long trajectory. The long trajectory can be used to distinguish targets from back- grounds robustly. This paper models the target's movement as a piecewise uniform motion. We impose the strict constraint, uniform motion, on the trajectory in a small time interval to eliminate the interference of noise as much as possible. On the contrary, we impose the relax constraint on the trajectory in a long time range to extend the length of the trajectory as much as possible. The trajectory synthetizing and validation include trajectory segment growth and merging. They are detailed as the following.

Trajectory Segment Growth with Short-Strict Constraint. Trajectory segment growth links the target candidates in the current frame to the existing trajectory segments properly. This paper models the target movement as uniform motion, i.e. under the short-strict constraint, in a small time interval. We set the small time interval is 3 successive frames in this paper. Trajectory segments are growing under the short-strict constraint. Given the existing trajectory segment set $\{T^i\}_M$ and the target candidate set $\{c_j^t\}_N$ in the current frame t.

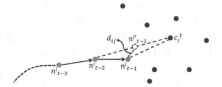

Fig. 1. Trajectory segment growth with short-strict constraint.

As shown in Fig. 1, we take a sample trajectory segment $T^i = \{\cdots, n_{t-3}^i, n_{t-2}^i, n_{t-1}^i\}$ to detail the implementation of trajectory segment growth. n_{t-1}^i is the detected target in the last frame $(t-1)$. Under the uniform motion constraint in the small time interval, we define the cost of linking c_j^t to T^i. The link involves n_{t-2}^i, n_{t-1}^i and c_j^t. Using n_{t-2}^i and c_j^t, we get the ideal middle point $n_{t-1}^{i'}$ under the uniform motion constraint. d_{ij} is the Euclidean distance between n_{t-1}^i and $n_{t-1}^{i'}$. The cost $C(i,j)$ of the link is defined as Eq. (3).

$$C(i,j) = \frac{d_{ij}}{\left\| n_{t-2}^i - n_{t-1}^i \right\|_2} = \frac{\left\| n_{t-2}^i + c_j^t - 2n_{t-1}^i \right\|_2}{2 \times \left\| n_{t-2}^i - n_{t-1}^i \right\|_2} \tag{3}$$

The smaller the $C(i,j)$ is, the more the link is met with the short-strict constraint. The cost matrix C contains all possible links' cost values. We define the binary linking matrix A_1 in Eq. (4).

$$A_1(i,j) = \begin{cases} 1, & C(i,j) \le \sigma_1 \\ 0, & C(i,j) > \sigma_1 \end{cases} \tag{4}$$

σ_1 is the cost threshold and is set 0.2. We also restrict the absolute velocity value of the target. The restriction for the target candidates c_j^{t-1} and c_j^t in successive frames is defined as Eq. (5). σ_2, a velocity threshold, is set 10.

$$CoV\left(c_j^{t-1}, c_j^t\right) = \begin{cases} 1, & \left\| n_{t-2}^i - n_{t-1}^i \right\|_2 \le \sigma_2 \\ 0, & \left\| n_{t-2}^i - n_{t-1}^i \right\|_2 > \sigma_2 \end{cases} \tag{5}$$

For an existing trajectory segment, if more than one target candidate meet Eq. (3–4), we link the trajectory segment to each target candidate and record every new link as a new trajectory segment. In order to find new target, we also link the target candidates $\left\{c_j^t\right\}_N$ in the current frame t and the candidates $\left\{c_j^{t-1}\right\}_{N'}$ in the last frame $(t-1)$ under Eq. (5) to form new trajectory segments.

Trajectory Segment Merging with Long-Loose Constraint. Due to noise interference or clutter background, it results in that the true target trajectory is divided into sev-eral segments. Trajectory segment merging intends to link the trajectory segments which correspond to the same target. The merging is performed according to the similarity between trajectory segments. Figure 2 presents three track segment pairs with different relative positions. Comparing to the segments in Fig. 2(a, c), the segments in Fig. 2(b) are more likely to corresponding to the same target.

This paper summarizes the features of the track segments which are correspond-ing to the same target as follows: (a) The track segments do not overlap in time. (b) The extension of the track segments is close to each other. (c) The velocity values of different track segments are close to each other. We take two track segments and as samples to detail the definition of the similarity measure, as shown in Fig. 3.

Fig. 2. Track segment pairs with different relative positions. (The dot line represents the extension of the track segment.)

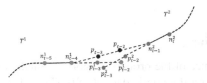

Fig. 3. Similarity measure for trajectory segment merging

T^1 and T^2 do not overlap in time. T^1 ends at frame $(t-4)$ and T^2 starts at frame $(t-1)$. According to the uniform motion constraint, we extend T^1 and T^2 to frame $(t-3)$ and $(t-2)$. The extended target positions are $\left\{p_{t-3}^1, p_{t-2}^1\right\}$ and $\left\{p_{t-3}^2, p_{t-2}^2\right\}$. If T^1 and T^2 belong to the same target trajectory, we link n_{t-4}^1 and n_{t-1}^2. Under the uniform motion constraint, the interpolated target positions are $\left\{p_{t-3}, p_{t-2}\right\}$ as shown in Fig. 5. This paper uses the distances between extended target positions and the interpolated target positions to define the similarity measure $s\left(T^1, T^2\right)$ between T^1 and T^2 as Eq. (6).

$$s\left(T^1, T^2\right) = \frac{(t-1) - (t-4) - 1}{\sum\limits_{k=t-3}^{t-2} \left(\left\|p_k^1 - p_k\right\|_2 + \left\|p_k^2 - p_k\right\|_2\right)} \tag{6}$$

The above is a detail description of the similarity definition of two trajectory segments T^1 and T^2 with a time interval 2. For other cases, the similarity is calculated similar to the above definition. The similarity matrix $S=[s(T^i, T^j)]_{M \times M}$ is a symmetric matrix ($S(i,j) = S(j,i)$) with zero diagonal elements ($S(i,i) = 0$). We get the binary link matrix A_2 as Eq. (7).

$$A_2(i,j) = \begin{cases} 1, S(i,j) \geq \sigma_3 \\ 0, S(i,j) < \sigma_3 \end{cases} \tag{7}$$

Where $\sigma_3 = 0.1$ is a set threshold. The parameter corresponds to the degree of relaxation of the long-loose constraint. Considering the continuous of the target movement, we give priority to merging long trajectory segments. We sort the trajectory segments according to their lengths in a descend order, i.e. the first row A_2 in corresponding to the longest trajectory segment in $\{T^i\}_M$.

We delete the trajectory segment without growth or merging in last 5 frames from the list.

After trajectory segment growth and merging, we detect small aerial infrared target according to the length of the trajectory. The length threshold σ_5 is defined as Eq. (8).

$$\sigma_5 = \lfloor \mu \times L \rfloor \tag{8}$$

Where μ is a constant. L is the length of the time window. If the length of a trajectory is larger than σ_5, the corresponded target candidates are detected as true targets. The target can be detected continuously through the trajectory segment growth. We assume that there is at most one target in a position at the same time. Thus for the crossed trajectory segments, we keep the longest trajectory and eliminate others.

4   Experiments

4.1   Experimental Settings

To validate the performance of the proposed algorithm qualitatively and quantitatively, we conduct experiments on the public datasets SIATD [17]. We perform comparisons between our method with representative existing methods, including single frame based methods (RIPT [18], MLCM [19], AGADM [20]) and multiple frames based method (TIPI [21]). For the compared methods, we use the implementations released by the authors and default parameter settings suggested in their papers. For the proposed method, the parameters are set as follows: local region size $R_1 \times R_2$: 3×3, 7×7, 11×11, 15×15, length percentage μ: 0.15, and time window length L: 20. For conveniently, we denote our target candidate detection algorithm as "Med-LGBM" and the whole method as "Proposed".

We appoint that the target is correctly detected if the detection locates in the 3-pixel neighborhood of the ground truth in the experiments within this paper.

4.2   Target Detection from Image Sequence

In this section, we conduct experiments of small infrared aerial target detection from image sequences in the SIATD dataset. The proposed method firstly detects target candidates from each single frame via interesting pixels detection and a trained LightGBM

Table 1. Target candidate detection on the testing subset of SIATD dataset.

Algorithm	Recall	Precision	$F_\beta - measure$	Average number of target candidate per frame
Inter-frame differencing	0.73	0.30	0.43	3.96
Med-LGBM	0.74	0.84	0.79	0.87

model as described in Sect. 3.1. For successive frames, a simple commonly used target candidate detection method is inter-frame differencing and thresholding. We compare the simple method with the proposed target candidate detection method on the testing subset of the SIATD dataset. For the inter-frame differencing based method, we perform inter-frame registration as described in Sect. 3.2. And the threshold is determined adaptively via Otsu [22]. The LightGBM model trained on the training subset of the SIATD dataset. The results are presented in Table 1.

The results in Table 1 show that the proposed target candidate detection method achieves higher recall and precision than the inter-frame differencing based method. It is about 0.87 target candidates on average detected by the proposed method which makes the following trajectory growth and merging as efficient as possible. It should be noted that there are at most 3 true targets in each frame and the target may move out of view in SIATD. Thus the average number of target candidate per frame of Med-LGBM is less than 1. The low average number indicates the high precision of the proposed target candidate detection method to some extent.

This paper detects the true targets from target candidates using trajectory constraints. The short-strict and long-loose constraints described in Sect. 3.2 make the proposed method enable to track long target trajectories. We present two detected trajectories within two sample image sequences from SIATD in Fig. 4. It can be seen from Fig. 4 that the targets' trajectories are tortuous but smooth and continuous. The proposed method detects them correctly.

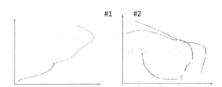

Fig. 4. The detected trajectories for two sample image sequences form SATD dataset.

We train the LightGBM model using the training subset in SIATD. For fairness, we only reported the results on the testing subset in this section. Figure 5 shows sample detection results from the SIATD dataset.

We note that only the correct detections are labeled for the compared methods. Due to too many false alarms detected by some compared methods (e.g. the $2^{nd}-th$ row in Fig. 5), this paper don't labeled the false detections for clearly. However, there are not much false detection outputted by our method and we labeled them in presented

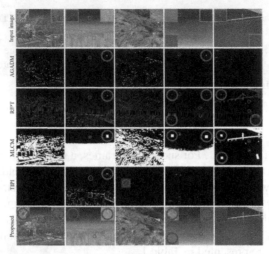

Fig. 5. Sample detection results of AGADM, RIPT, MLCM, TIPI and the proposed method. (The detected target are labeled by "O" and the true targets are labeled by "□".)

results. The results in Fig. 5 show that existing algorithms have trouble in detecting the small infrared aerial targets, especially for targets under clutter backgrounds. Clutter backgrounds bring great difficulties for AGADM, RIPT and MLCM. False targets are detected in the clutter background area as shown in Fig. 5. TIPI has trouble in modeling.

the quick changing of the background. Strong edges bring false detections as shown in the 3rd row in Fig. 5. While the proposed method detects the targets correctly and performs better than other algorithms. As shown in the 2nd column in Fig. 5, a darker target locates in the building region. The proposed method detects it correctly while others not.

For quantitative evaluation, the quantitative evaluations of each algorithm on the testing subset are reported in Table 2, including results of each scene type and the whole testing subset.

Table 2. Quantitative evaluation of AGADM, RIPT, MLCM, TIPI and the proposed method on the testing subset of SATD. (**P** for precision, **R** for recall and **F** for $F_\beta - measure$.)

		Up looking	Head up looking	Down looking (Vegetation)	Down looking (Water)	Down looking (Building)	Whole
AGADM	P	0.14	0.14	0.03	0.01	0.01	0.01
	R	0.33	0.33	0.18	0.07	0.05	0.02
	F	0.20	0.20	0.06	0.02	0.02	0.01
RIPT	P	0.33	0.33	0.26	0.32	0.30	0.30
	R	0.79	0.79	0.63	0.78	0.74	0.75
	F	0.47	0.47	0.38	0.46	0.44	0.43

(continued)

Table 2. (*continued*)

		Up looking	Head up looking	Down looking (Vegetation)	Down looking (Water)	Down looking (Building)	Whole
MLCM	P	0.26	0.26	0.14	0.13	0.13	0.05
	R	0.61	0.61	0.33	0.33	0.33	0.13
	F	0.36	0.36	0.20	0.19	0.20	0.08
TIPI	P	0.03	0.01	0.01	0.01	0.00	0.01
	R	0.37	0.02	0.01	0.01	0.00	0.08
	F	0.07	0.01	0.01	0.01	0.00	0.02
Med-LGBM	P	0.54	0.42	0.87	0.50	0.68	0.68
	R	0.87	0.85	0.72	0.88	0.59	0.76
	F	0.67	0.56	**0.79**	0.64	0.64	0.72
Proposed	P	0.95	0.76	0.99	0.93	0.98	0.92
	R	0.66	0.65	0.60	0.69	0.57	0.63
	F	**0.78**	**0.72**	0.75	**0.79**	**0.72**	**0.75**

As mentioned above, clutter backgrounds bring great challenges for existing single frame based methods. AGADM, RIPT and MLCM achieve lower precisions than the proposed method. The cluttered degrees of the backgrounds within the Down looking scene are higher than that within the Up looking scene generally. The performances of the compared methods decrease with the increase of the cluttered degree as shown in Table 2. Our target candidate detection method Med-LGBM achieves better performance than them. LightGBM is a learning based method. Its performance heavily depends on the training data. We reported the results for each scene type separately and the whole testing subset in Table 2. The results on the whole testing subset are similar to those on different scene types. It indicates that Med-LGBM can deal with a variety of complex scenes.

TIPI cannot handle quick changing clutter background well and achieves poor performance on SIATD dataset a shown in Table 2. By introducing the short-strict and long-loose trajectory constraints, the proposed method achieves superior performance than other existing algorithms in detecting small infrared aerial targets as shown in Table 2.

The results in Table 2 indicate that the precision is improved greatly from Med-LGBM to Proposed by introducing trajectory constraints. The false detections are removed effectively. The clutter within the background cannot form a smooth and continuous trajectory as the true target does. However, as Table 2 shows, the recall is decreased from Med-LGBM to Proposed. It means that some correct detected targets are removed wrongly in trajectory growth and merging. We analyzed the experimental results and found that most of the removed correct detected target candidates are isolated detected targets. There is no detected target close to them in the previous and the subsequent frames. So they cannot form valid trajectory segments and are removed from the final detection.

5   Conclusions

This paper tackles the challenge of small infrared aerial target detection. According to the characteristics of continuity and smoothness of target trajectory, a novel small infrared aerial target detection method using spatial and temporal cues is proposed in this paper. For the target candidate detection from each single frame, using the spatial cues, this paper treats it as a binary classification problem. We use interesting pixel detection and a trained LightGBM model to detect target candidates. For the temporal cues, we adopt the piecewise uniform motion model to approximate the target movement. The true targets are detected from the target candidates using the short-strict and long-loose constraints. The constraints are used in trajectory segment growth and merging. Experiments on the publicly available dataset SIATD indicate that the proposed method achieves better performance than other existing methods.

Acknowledgments. This work is funded by Postgraduate Scientific Research Innovation Project of Hunan Province (project number: CX20200088), Postgraduate Scientific Research Innovation Project of Hunan Province (project number: CX20200024), Postgraduate Scientific Research Innovation Project of Hunan Province (project number: CX20200025) and the National Natural Science Foundation of China (Grant No. 62003357).

References

1. Sun, X., Liu, X., Tang, Z.: Real-time visual enhancement for infrared small dim targets in video. Infrared. Phys. Tech. 83, 217–226 (2017)
2. Ke, G., Meng, Q., Finley, T.: LightGBM: a highly efficient gradient boosting decision tree. In: 31st Annual Conference on Neural Information Processing Systems (NIPS), vol. 30. Neural Information Processing Systems (Nips), 10010 North Torrey Pines Rd, La Jolla, California 92037 USA (2017)
3. Moradi, S., Moallem, P., Sabahi, M.F.: A false-alarm aware methodology to develop robust and efficient multi-scale infrared small target detection algorithm. INFRARED. PHYS. TECHN 89, 387–397(2018).
4. Gao, C., Meng, D., Yang, Y.: Infrared patch-image model for small target detection in a single image. IEEE TIP **22**(12), 4996–5009 (2013)
5. Xue, W., Qi, J., Shao, G., Xiao, Z.: Low-rank approximation and multiple sparse constraints modeling for infrared low-flying fixed-wing UAV detection. IEEE. J-Stars **99**, 1 (2021)
6. Zhao, M., Li, L., Li, W., Li, L.: Infrared small-target detection based on multiple morphological profiles. IEEE. TGRS 1–15 (2020)
7. Dai, Y., Wu, Y., Zhou, F., Barnard, K.: Attentional local contrast networks for infrared small target detection. IEEE. TGRS 1–12 (2021)
8. Zhao, B., Wang, C., Fu, Q., Han, Z.: A novel pattern for infrared small target detection with generative adversarial network. IEEE. TGRS 1–12 (2020)
9. Rodriguez-Blanco, M., Golikov, V.: Multiframe GLRT-based adaptive detection of multipixel targets on a sea surface. IEEE. J-STARS **9**(12), 5506–5512 (2016)

10. Fan, X., Xu, Z., Zhang, J.: Dim small target detection based on high-order cumulant of motion estimation. Infrared. Phys. Tech. **99**, 86–101 (2019)
11. Li, Y., Tan, Y., Li, H., Li, T., Tian, J.: Biologically inspired multilevel approach for multiple moving targets detection from airborne forward-looking infrared sequences. J. Opt. Soc. Am. A **31**(4), 734–744 (2014)
12. Zhu, H., Liu, S., Deng, L., Li, Y., Xiao, F.: Infrared small target detection via low-rank tensor completion with top-hat regularization. IEEE. TGRS **58**(2), 1004–1016 (2020)
13. Liu, H.K., Zhang, L., Huang, H.: Small target detection in infrared videos based on spatio-temporal tensor model. IEEE. TGRS **58**(12), 8689–8700 (2020)
14. Sun, Y., Yang, J., Li, M., An, W.: Infrared small target detection via spatial-temporal infrared patch-tensor model and weighted schatten p-norm minimization. Infrared. Phys. Tech. **102**, 103050 (2019)
15. Sun, Y., Yang, J., An, W.: Infrared dim and small target detection via multiple subspace learning and spatial-temporal patch-tensor model. IEEE. TGRS **99**, 1–16 (2020)
16. Bay, H., Tuytelaars, T., Van Gool, L.: SURF: speeded up robust features. Comput. Vis. Image Understand. **110**(3), 346–359 (2008)
17. SIATD download. https://small-infrared-aerial-target-detection.grand-challenge.org/Download/. Accessed 04 Nov 2021
18. Dai, Y., Wu, Y.: Reweighted infrared patch-tensor model with both nonlocal and local priors for single-frame small target detection. IEEE. J-STARS **10**(8), 3752–3767 (2017)
19. Yao, S., Chang, Y., Qin, X.: A coarse-to-fine method for infrared small target detection. IEEE. GRSL **16**(2), 256–260 (2019)
20. Wang, G., Zhang, T., Wei, L., Sang, N.: Efficient method for multiscale small target detection from a natural scene. Optical Eng. **35**(3), 761–768 (1996)
21. Gao, C., Wang, L., Xiao, Y., Zhao, Q.: Infrared small-dim target detection based on Markov random field guided noise modeling. Pattern. Recognit **76**, 463–475 (2018)
22. Otsu, N.: A threshold selection method from gray-level histograms. IEEE. T. Syst. Man. CY-S **9**(1), 62–66 (1979)

Boundary Information Aggregation and Adaptive Keypoint Combination Enhanced Object Detection

Ping Zhao[1], Dongsheng Yao[2]($\boxtimes$), Lijun Sun[1]($\boxtimes$), Jiaqi Fan[1], Panyue Chen[1], and Zhihua Wei[1]

[1] Tongji University, Shanghai, China
{zhaoping,sunlijun,1930795,chenpanyue,zhihua_wei}@tongji.edu.cn
[2] Shanghai Police College, Shanghai, China

Abstract. Keypoint-based methods achieve increasing attention and competitive performance in the field of object detection. In this paper, we propose a new keypoint-based object detection method in order to better locate center keypoints of objects and adaptively combine keypoints to obtain more accurate bounding boxes. Specifically, to better locate center keypoints of objects, we aggregate boundary information by adding the center pooling operation to the original center keypoints prediction branch. The boundary information is the location of object boundary which is more easier to predict than object center. Furthermore, to obtain more accurate bounding boxes, we propose an adaptive keypoint combination algorithm to map all keypoints back to the original image so that the keypoints are combined with less localization errors. Experiments have demonstrated the effectiveness of the our proposed methods.

Keywords: Object detection · Keypoint prediction

1 Introduction

Object detection is a challenging task in computer vision. Keypoint-based object detection methods have achieved increasing attention in the last few years. They regard object detection as a keypoint combination problem. I.e. Detecting different keypoints firstly, then combining keypoints to obtain the final bounding box. In keypoint-based methods, predicting the center keypoint accurately is an important factor to improve the detection performance. However, the widely used center keypoint prediction method focuses on geometric centers of objects, which may fail to contain discriminative information of objects. Take the pedestrian as an example, the geometric center of a pedestrian is usually the middle of the human body. However, the face contains more discriminative information of a pedestrian. Besides, keypoint-based object detection methods predict keypoints instead of bounding boxes, so they need a well-designed combination

© Springer Nature Switzerland AG 2021
Y. Peng et al. (Eds.): ICIG 2021, LNCS 12888, pp. 148–159, 2021.
https://doi.org/10.1007/978-3-030-87355-4_13

algorithm to obtain bounding boxes from keypoints. However, existing combination algorithms are carried out on the feature maps which are usually smaller than the original image, so the location of keypoints is not accurate enough.

Therefore, in this paper, we focus on the following two problems in keypoint-based methods: (1) how to better locate center keypoints and (2) how to adaptively combine keypoints. To better locate center keypoints, we use object boundary information which is the location of object boundary. Specifically, we add an extra center pooling [2] operation to the original center keypoints prediction algorithm. The center pooling operation extracts boundary information of the object, which ensures that the predicted center keypoint contains more discriminative information of the object. Besides, to adaptively combine keypoints, we map all keypoints back to the original image and carry out all operations on the original image so that the keypoint locations are more accurate.

Based on the above two mechanisms, we design a new object detection network, namely BANet (i.e. Network with Boundary information aggregation and Adaptive keypoint combination). Given an input image, our BANet predicts four extreme keypoints (i.e. the extremely top, bottom, left, and right points of an object) and a center keypoint of the object, an adaptive keypoints combination algorithm is then used to combine the predicted keypoints and obtain the final bounding box of the object.

The previous study, ExtremeNet has similar procedure of object detection with our BANet. However, ExtremeNet directly takes the geometric center of an object as the center keypoint, which may not contains the discriminative information of the object. Besides, ExtremeNet combines keypoints based on small-size feature maps, which ignores the combination error caused by the keypoints offsets from feature maps to original images. In comparison, our BANet improves the above two problems at the same time.

Contributions of the proposed BANet can be summaried as follows. First, we make use of object boundary information by adding the center pooling operation to the original center keypoints prediction algorithm for better center keypoint prediction. Second, we propose a new keypoints combination algorithm to adaptively combine different keypoints, so as to improve the accuracy of bounding box prediction. Experiments have demonstrated the effectiveness of our BANet.

2   Related Works

Deep learning based object detection can be roughly divided into two categories according to their network structure: two-stage approaches and one-stage approaches.

Two-stage approaches decompose object detection task into two stages: extracting Region of Interests (RoIs), classifying and regressing RoIs.

R-CNN [5] uses an selective search method [20] to locate the ROIs in the input image. Then, each ROI is adjusted to a fixed size image and input into a CNN model trained on ImageNet to extract features. Finally, the linear SVM classifier is used to predict the target category. Later, SPP [6] and Fast RCNN [4] improve

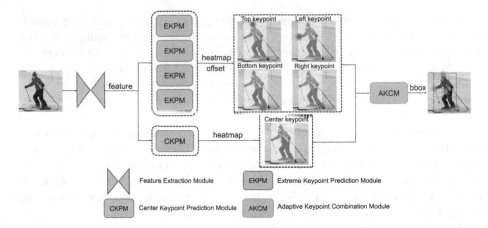

Fig. 1. Our network architecture. An image is first sent to the feature extraction module, then the output features are sent to the detection head composed of four extreme keypoint prediction modules to obtain extreme keypoint heatmaps and offsets, one center keypoint prediction module in parallel to obtain center keypoint heatmap. By combining these heatmaps and offsets, we can obtain the candidate bounding boxes.

R-CNN by designing a special pooling layer that pools each region from feature maps instead. Faster RCNN [17] proposes Region Proposal Network (RPN) to replace selective search method, so that the object detection network can be trained in an end-to-end manner. RPN generate RoIs by regressing anchor boxes. Later, anchor boxes are widely used in many object detection tasks. R-FCN [1] further improves the efficiency of Faster-RCNN by replacing the fully connected prediction head with a fully convolutional prediction head. Many following methods are mainly improved on the network details.

One-stage approaches remove the RoI extracting step and directly get bounding box in a single network.

SSD [11] classifies and regresses by densely placing anchor boxes on multi-scale feature maps. YOLO [15] divides grid on image and makes coordinate prediction directly. DSSD [3] proposes a structure similar to hourglass network to fuse features of different scales. At this time, there is a big performance gap between one-stage approaches and two-stage approaches. The emergence of RetinaNet [9] solves this problem. It proposes FocalLoss to deal unbalanced positive and negative samples. This loss can be well applied to other networks. CornerNet [8] is a completely different one-stage approach. It predicts the positions of different keypoints and combines them instead of getting the bounding box directly. Therefore, CornerNet can be regarded as a bottom-up method. ExtremeNet [23] is similar to CornerNet, but it detects four extreme points instead of two corners.

3   Methods

Preliminaries: Extreme-Points-Based Bounding Box Representation
In the field of object detection, an object is detected using a bounding box, which is usually represent using two points, i.e. the top left point of the bounding box, $(x^{(tl)}, y^{(tl)})$, and the bottom right point of the bounding box, $(x^{(br)}, y^{(br)})$. Instead of using such traditional bounding box representation, in this study, we use four extreme points [14] to represent an object, i.e. the extremely top point of the object, $(x^{(t)}, y^{(t)})$, the extremely left point of the object, $(x^{(l)}, y^{(l)})$, the extremely bottom point of the object, $(x^{(b)}, y^{(b)})$, and the extremely right point of the object, $(x^{(r)}, y^{(r)})$. Obviously, these four extreme points can completely represent the object (by using $(x^{(l)}, y^{(t)}, x^{(r)}, y^{(b)})$) that represented by the traditional bounding box. Compared with the traditional bounding box representation, extreme-points-based bounding box representation has four more values, which bring in more information. In addition, extreme-points-based bounding box representation is easier to obtain than the traditional bounding box representation. When annotating the traditional bounding box, we need to accurately locate up-left corner point $(x^{(tl)}, y^{(tl)})$ and bottom-right corner point $(x^{(br)}, y^{(br)})$ of the box. This process usually requires multiple adjustments.

3.1   Overview of BANet

As shown in Fig. 1, our network consists of four modules, including (a) the feature extraction module, (b) the extreme keypoint prediction module, (c) the center keypoint prediction module, and (d) the adaptive keypoint combination module.

Given an input image I, the feature extraction module extract features $X \in \mathbb{R}^{C \times H \times W}$, where C denotes the number of channels; $H \times W$ denotes the size of the feature maps. Then, based on such features X, four extreme keypoint prediction modules are parallelly used to predict four different extreme keypoint heatmaps, $Y_t, Y_b, Y_l, Y_r \in \mathbb{R}^{M \times H \times W}$, where M denotes object categories, and offsets, $O_t, O_b, O_l, O_r \in \mathbb{R}^{2 \times H \times W}$. The center keypoint prediction module uses the extracted features X to predict the center keypoint heatmaps $Y_c \in \mathbb{R}^{M \times H \times W}$. Then, by combining these heatmaps and offsets, the adaptive keypoint combination module obtains the candidate bounding boxes. After getting all candidate bounding boxes, Non-maximum suppression (NMS) is used to determine the final bounding box of the object.

Feature Extraction Module: The feature extraction module is implemented based on the hourglass network [8, 13].

Center Keypoint Prediction Module: As shown in Fig. 2 (a), the center keypoint prediction module uses a boundary information aggregation module followed by a single convolution to predict heatmaps. The boundary information aggregation module consists of a center pooling branch and a single convolution residual connection. Details will be discussed in Sect. 3.3.

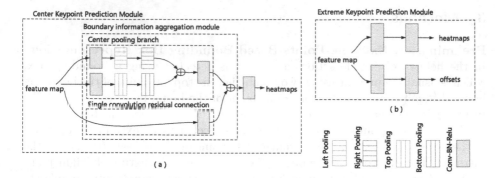

Fig. 2. Center keypoint prediction module (a) uses a boundary information aggregation module followed by a single convolution to predict heatmaps, and two convolutions to predict offsets, while extreme keypoint prediction module (b) uses two parallel double convolutions to predict heatmaps and offsets respectively. Boundary information aggregation module consists of a center pooling branch and a single convolution residual connection.

Extreme Keypoint Prediction Module: As shown in Fig. 2 (b), the extreme keypoint prediction module uses two parallel double convolution branches to predict heatmaps and offsets of extreme keypoints. Our network uses four extreme keypoint prediction modules to predict four extreme keypoints respectively.

Adaptive Keypoint Combination Module: The adaptive keypoint combination module is used to combine different keypoints and get candidate bounding boxes. By using keypoint heatmaps and offsets, the process can be finished accurately on original image. The detailed algorithm will be discussed in Sect. 3.4.

3.2   Boundary Information Aggregation

To better locate center keypoints, we aggregate object boundary information inside the center keypoint prediction module. As mentioned above, directly using the geometric center of the object as the predicted center keypoint may hamper the performance of object detection. Therefore, to predict the center with more discriminative information of the object, we design a module named Boundary Information Aggregation (BIA) to aggregate boundary information of objects. As Fig. 2 shows, the BIA module contains two parallel branches: a center pooling branch and a simple convolution residual connection.

The center pooling [2] branch is composed of pooling operations in four directions, *i.e.* the left pooling, the right pooling, the bottom pooling, and the top pooling. Given an input feature map $x \in \mathbb{R}^{H \times W}$, let $x_{i,:} \in \mathbb{R}^{1 \times W}$ denote the vector of activation scores of the i-th row of the feature map. Then, after the left pooling, we can obtain the following vector of activation scores.

$$Pool_{\text{left}}(x_{i,:}) = [\max_{j=1,\dots,W} x_{ij}, \max_{j=2,\dots,W} x_{ij}, \dots, \max_{j=W} x_{ij}] \tag{1}$$

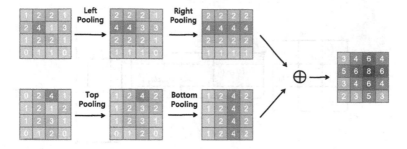

Fig. 3. Example of the center pooling operation. The input feature maps are trained to be sensitive to the left and right boundary (top) and the upper and lower boundary (bottom) respectively, after center pooling, we can aggregate boundary information and get the feature map which is sensitive to the object center.

Similarly, we can obtain the following vector of activation scores after the right pooling.

$$Pool_{\text{right}}(x_{i,:}) = [\max_{j=1} x_{ij}, \max_{j=1,2} x_{ij}, \ldots, \max_{j=1,\ldots,W} x_{ij}] \tag{2}$$

Let $x_{:,j} \in \mathbb{R}^{H \times 1}$ denote the vector of activation scores of the j-th column of the feature map. Then, after the top pooling, we can obtain the following vector of activation scores.

$$Pool_{\text{top}}(x_{:,j}) = [\max_{i=1,\ldots,H} x_{ij}, \max_{i=2,\ldots,H} x_{ij}, \ldots, \max_{i=H} x_{ij}] \tag{3}$$

Similarly, we can obtain the following vector of activation scores after the bottom pooling.

$$Pool_{\text{bottom}}(x_{:,j}) = [\max_{i=1} x_{ij}, \max_{i=1,2} x_{ij}, \ldots, \max_{i=1,\ldots,H} x_{ij}] \tag{4}$$

In order to determine whether a location in the feature map is a center keypoint, we need to find the maximum value in its both horizontal and vertical directions and add them together, as shown in Fig. 3. These maximum values correspond to the boundaries of the object in four directions.

However, there are usually many objects in an image, one possible case is that the maximum value of one object in the horizontal direction and the maximum value of another object in the vertical direction are added in a meaningless position after center pooling, that means not even the values of center keypoint are enhanced. Simply using the output of center pooling to predict center keypoint may be harmful, so we add an additional branch which contains a single convolution to represent the feature map before center pooling. We add these two outputs to obtain the final output.

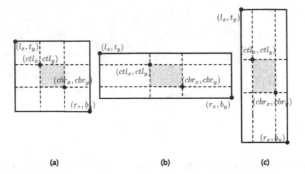

Fig. 4. Some typical central regions. The central region lies in the center of the candidate box (grey part), its length and width are adaptive according to the length and width of the candidate bounding box respectively.

3.3   Adaptive Keypoint Combination

Directly combines keypoints based on the feature map (here we can also call it heatmap) may bring in error, because the feature map is smaller (usually with the size of 128×128) than the size of the original image (usually with the size of 511×511). *I.e.* a pixel of a feature map corresponds to 4×4 pixels of the original image. Therefore, the location of keypoints on feature maps are not accurate. Based on such observation, we propose an adaptive keypoint combination algorithm worked on original images by using keypoint offset information.

The process of our algorithm is as follows: (1) Five keypoint sets, C (center keypoint set), T (top keypoint set), L (left keypoint set), B (bottom keypoint set), and R (right keypoint set), are extracted from the predicted five keypoint heatmaps. These keypoints correspond to the positions whose values are greater than the pre-defined threshold τ_p; (2) Keypoints in C, T, L, B and R are mapped back to the original image according to their offsets. For example, if the size of feature map and original image are 128×128 and 511×511 respectively, and one keypoint locate at (k_x, k_y) on heatmap has offset (o_x, o_y), after mapping, its coordinates on original image are $(4(k_x + o_x), 4(k_y + o_y))$. Note that in our model, we don't predict offsets for center keypoints, their offsets are always 0.5. After this step, we can get five new keypoint sets on original image, $C_m, T_m, L_m,$ B_m and R_m; (3) Let (l, t, r, b) represents a combination by selecting four points from T_m, L_m, B_m and R_m respectively. Candidate boxes $bbox(l_x, t_y, r_x, b_y)$ are obtained by enumerating all combinations of (l, t, r, b); (4) For each candidate box $bbox(l_x, t_y, r_x, b_y)$, defines a central region. As long as a center keypoint c from C_m falls in this region, the candidate bounding box $bbox(l_x, t_y, r_x, b_y)$ is accepted. If there are many center keypoints fall in this region, we will choose the center keypoint with the largest value on heatmap. The score of $bbox(l_x, t_y, r_x, b_y)$ is the sum of the values of the four extreme keypoints and the chosen center keypoint.

We can find that how to define central region can significantly affect the detection results. A small central region means the prediction of center keypoint must be more accurate, which leads to low recall rate and high accuracy, Similarly, a large central region leads to high recall rate and low accuracy. To deal with this trade-off, our definition is: (1) The central region is a rectangle lying in the center of the candidate box; (2) Its height and width are adaptive according to the height and width of the candidate bounding box respectively. Let (ctl_x, ctl_y) and (cbr_x, cbr_y) donate the top-left and bottom-right corners respectively, to obey the first defination, we have:

$$\begin{cases} ctl_x + cbr_x = l_x + r_x \\ ctl_y + cbr_y = t_y + b_y \end{cases} \tag{5}$$

To obey the second defination, we have:

$$\begin{cases} cbr_x - ctl_x = (r_x - l_x) * \left(\frac{6}{r_x - l_x + 18} + \frac{1}{6} \right) \\ cbr_y - ctl_y = (b_y - t_y) * \left(\frac{6}{b_y - t_y + 18} + \frac{1}{6} \right) \end{cases} \tag{6}$$

Figure 4 shows some typical central regions. As we can see, when $r_x - l_x \to \infty$, we have:

$$cbr_x - ctl_x = \frac{1}{6} (r_x - l_x) \tag{7}$$

When $r_x - l_x \to 0$, we have:

$$cbr_x - ctl_x = \frac{1}{2} (r_x - l_x) \tag{8}$$

4   Experiments

We conducted experiments on the popular MSCOCO datasets [10]. In order to prove the competitiveness of our model, we compared it with many different one-stage methods. Furthermore, to prove the effectiveness of the proposed methods, we conducted ablation study and error analysis.

Implementation Details: In real implementation, the feature extraction module was implemented based on the hourglass network [8,13]. During training, the resolution of input image was adjusted to 511×511, and the resolution of output feature map was 128×128. The whole network was optimized by adam optimizer with an initial learning rate of 2.5e−4, learning rate decreased with the number of iterations. In addition, parameters of the hourglass network (*i.e.* the feature extraction module) were preloaded from the official pre-trained CornerNet [8].

Dataset and Evaluation Metrics: We evaluated the proposed model based on the MS COCO dataset [10]. There are 80 kinds of object bounding box annotations in MS COCO dataset. The training process of the model was based on the train2017 dataset, the test and ablation experiments were based on the val2017 dataset. The main evaluation criteria were average precision of fixed recall threshold (AP) and average recall of fixed box number (AR).

Table 1. Comparisons with other one-stage object detectors.

Method	Backbone	AP	AP_{50}	AP_{75}	AP_S	AP_M	AP_L	AR_1	AR_{10}	AR_{100}	AR_S	AR_M	AR_L
YOLOv2 [16]	DarkNet-19	21.6	44.0	19.2	5.0	22.4	35.5	20.7	31.6	33.3	9.8	36.5	54.4
DSOD300 [18]	DS/64-192-48-1	29.3	47.3	30.6	9.4	31.5	47.0	27.3	40.7	43.0	16.7	47.1	65.0
GRP-DSOD320 [19]	DS/64-192-48-1	30.0	47.9	31.8	10.9	33.6	46.3	28.0	42.1	44.5	18.8	49.1	65.0
SSD513 [11]	ResNet-101	31.2	50.4	33.3	10.2	34.5	49.8	28.3	42.1	44.4	17.6	49.2	65.8
DSSD513 [3]	ResNet-101	33.2	53.3	35.2	13.0	35.4	51.1	28.9	43.5	46.2	21.8	49.1	66.4
RefineDet512 [22]	ResNet-101	36.4	57.5	39.5	16.6	39.9	51.4	–	–	–	–	–	–
RetinaNet800 [9]	ResNet-101	39.1	59.1	42.3	21.8	42.7	50.2	–	–	–	–	–	–
ExtremeNet511 [23]	Hourglass-104	40.3	55.1	43.7	21.6	44.0	56.1	32.0	50.2	53.1	30.7	57.8	69.9
CornerNet511 [8]	Hourglass-104	40.6	56.4	43.2	19.1	42.8	54.3	35.3	54.7	59.4	37.4	62.4	77.2
BANet	Hourglass-104	40.7	56.5	43.6	22.4	44.9	55.8	32.5	52.1	55.4	31.5	60.2	74.8

Table 2. Ablation study and error analysis. Here bia means boundary information aggregation, akc means adaptive keypoint combination, gt ex means using ground truth extreme keypoints, gt ct means using ground truth center keypoints.

Method	AP	AP_{50}	AP_{75}	AP_S	AP_M	AP_L	AR_1	AR_{10}	AR_{100}	AR_S	AR_M	AR_L
BANet	40.7	**56.5**	43.6	**22.4**	**44.9**	55.8	**32.5**	**52.1**	**55.4**	31.5	**60.2**	**74.8**
BANet without bia	39.4	55.2	42.0	21.7	42.6	54.1	31.8	51.2	54.9	**31.7**	59.2	73.8
BANet without akc	**41.0**	56.2	**44.2**	21.9	44.8	**56.9**	32.2	51.1	54.1	31.3	58.6	72.0
BANet without bia & akc	39.9	54.6	42.9	20.8	43.7	54.0	31.6	49.8	52.8	30.5	57.5	69.0
BANet without bia + gt ex	52.9	66.1	56.7	34.7	60.2	64.3	36.4	56.0	58.2	39.3	65.3	68.2
BANet + gt ex	**54.0**	**67.5**	**57.7**	**35.6**	**61.1**	**67.1**	**36.9**	**57.1**	**59.5**	**40.7**	**66.3**	**71.1**
BANet without bia + gt ct	50.7	64.1	56.0	26.9	55.7	70.0	36.7	55.1	57.2	32.1	62.5	77.4
BANet + gt ct	**51.3**	**64.8**	**56.7**	**27.3**	56.1	71.5	**36.9**	55.7	57.7	**32.3**	62.8	**78.8**

4.1 Comparisons with Other One-Stage Object Detectors

Table 1 showed the comparison with several popular one-stage object detectors on the MS COCO val2017 dataset. Compared with the baseline ExtremeNet [23], the proposed BANet achieved a comparative improvement. BANet reported a testing AP of 40.7%, an improvement of 0.4% over 40.3%, and a test AR_{100} of 55.4%, an improvement of 2.3% over 53.1%, achieved by ExtremeNet under the same setting. Moreover, BANet surpassed CornerNet [8] in AP. CornerNet used associative embeddings to help combine different keypoints, while BANet used a pure geometric method. These results firmly demonstrate the effectiveness of BANet.

4.2 Ablation Study and Error Analyse

Boundary Information Aggregation: After adding boundary information aggregation module, our network reached 41.0%AP and 54.1%AR, which was 1.1% and 1.3% higher than the baseline. This proved the effectiveness of our proposed module. See Table 2 for more details. We can find that boundary information aggregation had the greatest improvement on large objects, it was because keypoint-based methods were very strict in detecting large objects. In their postprocessing, no matter large objects, medium objects and small objects, the object

Fig. 5. Visualization of detection results. Images showed detected extreme keypoints heatmaps (left), center keypoint heatmaps (middle), and detection results (right) respectively.

center only occupied a pixel on the feature map, so for large objects, its location should be more accurate.

Adaptive Keypoint Combination: Results were shown in Table 2. We can see that the adaptive keypoint combination algorithm had little change in AP, but because of the use of offset information and the definition of central region, the model greatly exceeded baseline in AR, especially for large objects, which indicated that combination algorithms on feature maps were very strict in detecting the center keypoint of large objects. After changing, the acceptable region of candidate boxes had been expanded, especially large objects, so their recall rates had been greatly improved.

Error Analysis: In order to further analyze the influence of boundary information aggregation on different parts of the whole model, we used ground truth extreme keypoint heatmaps and ground truth center keypoint heatmap to replace the corresponding predicted heatmaps, and compared the gap of the other part. The specific comparative information was shown in Table 2.

Discussions: Through the experimental results, we can get the following two conclusions: (1) After adding boundary information aggregation, the model had a great improvement in the prediction of center keypoints. This further shows that proposed module can obtain boundary information and locate center keypoints more accurately. (2) Without modifying other parts of the model, boundary information aggregation also slightly improved the prediction performance of extreme keypoints, which showed that the model paid more attention to the training of extreme keypoints (the proportion of loss was larger) due to the reduction of the difficulty of center keypoint prediction.

4.3 Visualization of Detection Results

Images in Fig. 5 visualized detected heatmaps and final results. In order to show the detected keypoints, we added a mask to the original image and highlight different categories of keypoints with different colors on the heatmaps. These qualitative results proved that our network can find keypoints and combine them to obtain the final bounding boxes accurately.

5 Conclusions

In this paper, we have proposed a new keypoint-based object detection network, namely BANet. Specifically, we propose the boundary information aggregation algorithm to achieve better center keypoint location. Besides, we propose the adaptive keypoint combination algorithm to obtain more accurate keypoints combination. Experiments have demonstrated the effectiveness of our BANet.

References

1. Dai, J., Li, Y., He, K., Sun, J.: R-FCN: object detection via region-based fully convolutional networks. arXiv preprint arXiv:1605.06409 (2016)
2. Duan, K., Bai, S., Xie, L., Qi, H., Huang, Q., Tian, Q.: CenterNet: keypoint triplets for object detection. In: Proceedings of the IEEE/CVF International Conference on Computer Vision, pp. 6569–6578 (2019)
3. Fu, C.Y., Liu, W., Ranga, A., Tyagi, A., Berg, A.C.: DSSD: deconvolutional single shot detector. arXiv preprint arXiv:1701.06659 (2017)
4. Girshick, R.: Fast R-CNN. In: Proceedings of the IEEE International Conference on Computer Vision, pp. 1440–1448 (2015)
5. Girshick, R., Donahue, J., Darrell, T., Malik, J.: Rich feature hierarchies for accurate object detection and semantic segmentation. In: Proceedings of the IEEE Conference on Computer Vision and Pattern Recognition, pp. 580–587 (2014)
6. He, K., Zhang, X., Ren, S., Sun, J.: Spatial pyramid pooling in deep convolutional networks for visual recognition. IEEE Trans. Pattern Anal. Mach. Intell. **37**(9), 1904–1916 (2015)

7. Jiao, L., et al.: A survey of deep learning-based object detection. IEEE Access **7**, 128837–128868 (2019)

8. Law, H., Deng, J.: CornerNet: detecting objects as paired keypoints. In: Proceedings of the European Conference on Computer Vision (ECCV), pp. 734–750 (2018)

9. Lin, T.Y., Goyal, P., Girshick, R., He, K., Dollár, P.: Focal loss for dense object detection. In: Proceedings of the IEEE International Conference on Computer Vision, pp. 2980–2988 (2017)

10. Lin, T.Y., et al.: Microsoft COCO: common objects in context. In: Fleet, D., Pajdla, T., Schiele, B., Tuytelaars, T. (eds.) ECCV 2014. LNCS, vol. 8693, pp. 740–755. Springer, Cham (2014). https://doi.org/10.1007/978-3-319-10602-1_48

11. Liu, W., et al.: SSD: single shot MultiBox detector. In: Leibe, B., Matas, J., Sebe, N., Welling, M. (eds.) ECCV 2016. LNCS, vol. 9905, pp. 21–37. Springer, Cham (2016). https://doi.org/10.1007/978-3-319-46448-0_2

12. Newell, A., Huang, Z., Deng, J.: Associative embedding: end-to-end learning for joint detection and grouping. arXiv preprint arXiv:1611.05424 (2016)

13. Newell, A., Yang, K., Deng, J.: Stacked hourglass networks for human pose estimation. In: Leibe, B., Matas, J., Sebe, N., Welling, M. (eds.) ECCV 2016. LNCS, vol. 9912, pp. 483–499. Springer, Cham (2016). https://doi.org/10.1007/978-3-319-46484-8_29

14. Papadopoulos, D.P., Uijlings, J.R., Keller, F., Ferrari, V.: Extreme clicking for efficient object annotation. In: Proceedings of the IEEE International Conference on Computer Vision, pp. 4930–4939 (2017)

15. Redmon, J., Divvala, S., Girshick, R., Farhadi, A.: You only look once: unified, real-time object detection. In: Proceedings of the IEEE Conference on Computer Vision and Pattern Recognition, pp. 779–788 (2016)

16. Redmon, J., Farhadi, A.: YOLO9000: better, faster, stronger. In: Proceedings of the IEEE Conference on Computer Vision and Pattern Recognition, pp. 7263–7271 (2017)

17. Ren, S., He, K., Girshick, R., Sun, J.: Faster R-CNN: towards real-time object detection with region proposal networks. arXiv preprint arXiv:1506.01497 (2015)

18. Shen, Z., Liu, Z., Li, J., Jiang, Y.G., Chen, Y., Xue, X.: DSOD: learning deeply supervised object detectors from scratch. In: Proceedings of the IEEE International Conference on Computer Vision, pp. 1919–1927 (2017)

19. Shen, Z., et al.: Learning object detectors from scratch with gated recurrent feature pyramids. arXiv preprint arXiv:1712.00886 (2017)

20. Uijlings, J.R., Van De Sande, K.E., Gevers, T., Smeulders, A.W.: Selective search for object recognition. Int. J. Comput. Vis. **104**(2), 154–171 (2013)

21. Xiao, B., Wu, H., Wei, Y.: Simple baselines for human pose estimation and tracking. In: Proceedings of the European Conference on Computer Vision (ECCV), pp. 466–481 (2018)

22. Zhang, S., Wen, L., Bian, X., Lei, Z., Li, S.Z.: Single-shot refinement neural network for object detection. In: Proceedings of the IEEE Conference on Computer Vision and Pattern Recognition, pp. 4203–4212 (2018)

23. Zhou, X., Zhuo, J., Krahenbuhl, P.: Bottom-up object detection by grouping extreme and center points. In: Proceedings of the IEEE/CVF Conference on Computer Vision and Pattern Recognition, pp. 850–859 (2019)

24. Zou, Z., Shi, Z., Guo, Y., Ye, J.: Object detection in 20 years: a survey. arXiv preprint arXiv:1905.05055 (2019)

Accurate Oriented Instance Segmentation in Aerial Images

ZhenRong Zhang and Jun Du[✉]

University of Science and Technology of China, Hefei, China
zzr666@mail.ustc.edu.cn, jundu@ustc.edu.cn

Abstract. The dominant instance segmentation methods first detect the object with an axis-aligned box, then predict the foreground mask on each proposal. While in aerial images, methods detecting objects with axis-aligned boxes are unsuitable, since the orientation of objects is arbitrary. What's more, the RoI pooling step existed in these systems results in the loss of spatial details due to the feature warping and resizing, which will degrade the segmentation quality, especially for large elongated objects. In this paper, we propose a novel accurate oriented instance segmentation method, named Rotated Blend Mask R-CNN. We perform mask prediction in oriented bounding boxes and predict the final mask by combining instance-level information with lower-level fine-granularity information. The proposed method is evaluated on the iSAID dataset, and competitive outcomes show that our model achieves state-of-the-art. Code will be made available at https://github.com/ZZR8066/RotatedBlendMaskRCNN

Keywords: Aerial images · Oriented instance segmentation

1 Introduction

Instance segmentation in aerial images is important as it can be applied in many areas, such as precision agriculture, security, military reconnaissance, etc. Instance segmentation aims at predicting category labels of all objects of interest and localizing them in pixel-level masks. Recently, many powerful instance segmentation systems [1–3] have been proposed, but most of them are researched on natural scene datasets, such as MSCOCO [4], PASCAL-VOC [5], Cityscapes [6] etc. Compared with the above datasets, objects in aerial images occur in high density, arbitrary orientation, large ratios, and huge scale variation. Most of the recent aerial images datasets focus on object detection [7,8], few datasets [9] provide annotations for instance segmentation and typically focus on a single object category annotation. A large-scale Instance Segmentation in Aerial Images Dataset (iSAID) [10], which is far more comprehensive and suitable for real-world applications in aerial scenes, was proposed just recently. Due to the above reasons, instance segmentation in aerial images has not been well researched.

© Springer Nature Switzerland AG 2021
Y. Peng et al. (Eds.): ICIG 2021, LNCS 12888, pp. 160–170, 2021.
https://doi.org/10.1007/978-3-030-87355-4_14

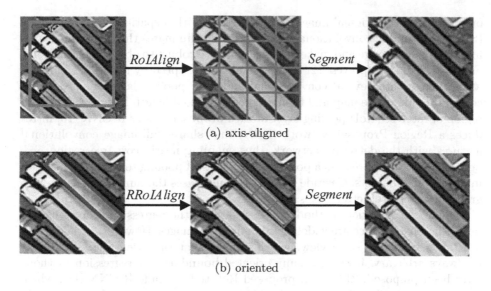

(a) axis-aligned

(b) oriented

Fig. 1. The comparison between axis-aligned and oriented instance segmentation.

In this study, we take a full consideration on the aforementioned situation and propose a novel accurate oriented instance segmentation method, named Rotated Blend Mask R-CNN, which is based on the representative two-stage instance segmentation method Mask R-CNN [1]. Our method mainly consists of two parts, a detection network and a segmentation network. Specifically, in order to eliminate the ambiguity of axis-aligned boxes in densely packed objects, we achieve oriented bounding box regression in the detection network, which will generate more accurate mask prediction as shown in Fig. 1(b). As for the segmentation network, similar to [11], we improved mask prediction by effectively combining instance-level information with lower-level fine-granularity information, and we find that it can well process the situation for large elongate objects which are densely surrounded by objects of other categories.

The main contributions of our work are summarized as follows:

– We present a novel oriented instance segmentation method which predicts accurate instance masks based on oriented bounding boxes.
– Furthermore, we merge top-level coarse instance information with lower-level fine-granularity for describing the instance information within their best capacities.

2   Relate Work

2.1   Object Detection

The R-CNN [12] is a milestone for object detection method, many following methods [13–15] are based on it. SPPnet [13] removes crop/warp and other operations on the original image and replaces it with a spatial pyramid pooling (SPP) layer on the convolutional features, which eliminates the requirement of a fixed-size input image and makes the system more robust to object deformations. Fast R-CNN [14] improves [12] training and testing speed by first processing the whole image with several convolutional and max pooling layers to produce a convolutional feature map and then extracting a fixed-length feature vector by a region of interest (RoI) pooling layer of each proposal. Faster R-CNN [15] introduces a Region Proposal Network (RPN) that shares full-image convolutional features with the detection network, thus enabling nearly cost-free region proposals. R-FCN [16] presents a position-sensitive RoI pooling to learn the location information of objects. Cascade R-CNN [17] increases the number of R-CNN to gradually generate better boxes.

The above detection methods are designed for the regression of axis-aligned bounding boxes, which are widely used in natural images. However, aerial images are taken from bird's-eye view, which implies that the orientation of objects is always arbitrary. Recently, many oriented bounding box regression methods have been proposed. Zhu et al. proposed Rotated Cascade R-CNN [18], which estimates the outline of the object in the first stage and regresses four vertices in the second stage. [19] proposed Adaptive Period Embedding (APE) to address the angular periodicity. Jian et al. proposed the RoI Transformer [20], which learns the spatial transformation parameters from the feature maps of axis-align RoIs and decodes them to generate oriented RoIs.

2.2 Instance Segmentation

He et al. proposed Mask R-CNN [1] which extends Faster R-CNN by adding a Fully Convolutional Network (FCN) [21] for predicting an object mask in parallel with the existing branch for bounding box recognition. The path aggregation network (PANet) [2], which won the COCO 2017 Challenge Instance Segmentation task, improves Mask R-CNN by bottom-up path augmentation, adaptive feature pooling and fully connected fusion. In order to calibrate the misalignment between the mask quality and the predicted score, the Mask Scoring R-CNN [3] proposed network block takes the instance feature and the corresponding predicted mask together to regress the mask IoU.

However, an underlying drawback in the above methods is that the RoI pooling step loses spatial details due to feature warping and resizing. Such distortion and fixed-size representation degrades the segmentation accuracy, especially for large objects. To address this issue, YOLACT [22] and YOLACT++ [23] accomplish this by breaking instance segmentation into two parallel subtasks, generating a set of prototype masks and predicting per-instance mask coefficient respectively, and producing instance masks by linearly combining the prototypes with the mask coefficients. Different from YOLACT, BlendMask [11], which outperforms Mask R-CNN in both mask AP and inference efficiency, merges top-level coarse instance information with lower-level fine-granularity to generate the final mask prediction.

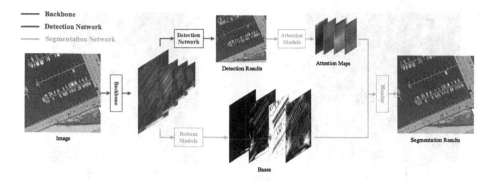

Fig. 2. The Rotated Blend Mask R-CNN architecture.

3   Method

In this section, we will present details of our proposed method, Rotated Blend Mask R-CNN, which is based on Mask R-CNN [1]. As shown in Fig. 2, the backbone is first applied to the input image to extract features that are used for the following detection and segmentation network. The detection network generates the oriented proposals, and the segmentation network will do the mask prediction of each proposal. Next we will elaborate on the above two networks respectively.

3.1   Detection Network

We detect objects in oriented boxes instead of axis-aligned boxes due to the orientation of densely packed objects as shown in Fig. 1. The detection network is illustrated in Fig. 3. We first obtain axis-aligned proposals from RPN [15], then for each proposal the RoIAlign [1] extracts a fixed-length feature vector from the feature map. Each feature vector is fed into a sequence of fully connected (FC) layers and outputs a five-dimensional vector t for each proposal. More specifically [20], each vector t consists of $(t_x, t_y, t_w, t_h, t_\theta)$ which are parameters of spatial transformation from axis-aligned boxes to oriented boxes and corresponding regression targets are:

$$
\begin{aligned}
t_x^* &= \tfrac{1}{w_r}\big((x^* - x_r)\cos\theta_r + (y^* - y_r)\sin\theta_r\big), \\
t_y^* &= \tfrac{1}{h_r}\big((y^* - y_r)\cos\theta_r - (x^* - x_r)\sin\theta_r\big), \\
t_w^* &= \log \tfrac{w^*}{w_r}, \quad t_h^* = \log \tfrac{h^*}{h_r}, \\
t_\theta^* &= \tfrac{1}{2\pi}\big((\theta^* - \theta_r)\bmod 2\pi\big),
\end{aligned}
\tag{1}
$$

where $(x_r, y_r, w_r, h_r, \theta_r)$ is a stacked vector for representing location, width, height and orientation of an oriented proposal and $(x^*, y^*, w^*, h^*, \theta^*)$ is the ground truth parameters of an oriented bounding box. The corresponding oriented proposals can be obtained by decoding the vector t. The Rotated RoIAlign

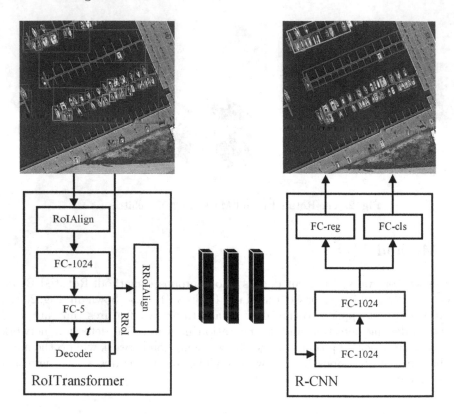

Fig. 3. The detection network.

(RRoIAlign) [18] is used to extract a fixed-length feature vector of each corresponding oriented proposal to maintain the rotation invariance. The final R-CNN stage fine-tunes oriented proposals and outputs D detection results $\mathbf{P}$. The regression targets of R-CNN are the same as Eq. (1). We use the Smooth L1 loss [12] function for the regression loss.

3.2   Segmentation Network

As shown in Fig. 2, the segmentation network is composed of three parts, a bottom module, an attention module and a blender. The bottom module aims at predicting the score maps containing semantic information with lower-level fine-granularity. The attention module predicts the attention maps in the instance-level of each oriented proposal. The blender module is used to merge the scores with attentions to generate the final mask predictions.

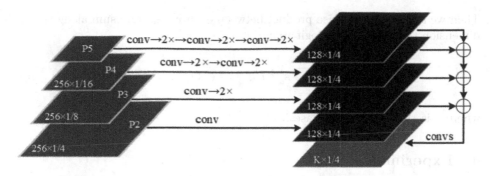

Fig. 4. The bottom module. Each conv is the convolution stage, and 2× is the upsampling stage.

Bottom Module. Figure 4 illustrates our bottom module in detail. We first obtain multi-level features {P2, P3, P4, P5} from the backbone, then perform upsampling stages for each level to yield the feature map at 1/4 scale. Each upsampling stage [24] consists of 3 × 3 convolution, group norm, ReLU, and 2× bilinear upsampling. The element-wise summation is applied to fused multi-level features. The final four convolution stages and the 1 × 1 convolution layer are used to generate score maps which are called bases [11], **B**. **B** has a shape of $N \times K \times \frac{H}{s} \times \frac{W}{s}$, where N is the batch size, K is the number of bases, $H \times W$ is the input size and s is the output stride of score map, here s is 4.

Attention Module. After obtaining the oriented proposals from detection network, we use RRoIAlign to extract a fixed-size feature map of each oriented proposal, then predict attention maps **A** using an FCN [1,21]. Specifically, FCN has a shape of KM^2 dimensional output for each proposal, which encodes instance-level information into K maps with a resolution of $M \times M$.

Blender. The inputs of the blender module [11] contain bases **B**, attention maps **A** and oriented proposals **P** from the detection network. We first use RRoIAlign to extract a fixed-size $R \times R$ feature map r_d for each proposal p_d from bases **B**.

$$\mathbf{r}_d = \mathrm{RRoIAlign}_{R \times R}(\mathbf{B}, \mathbf{p}_d), \quad \forall d \in \{1 \ldots D\}. \tag{2}$$

Then we use the bilinear interpolation to resize attention maps $\mathbf{a}_d$ from $M \times M$ to $R \times R$ to ensure the sizes of $\mathbf{a}_d$ and $\mathbf{r}_d$ are the same.

$$\mathbf{a}'_d = \mathrm{interpolate}_{M \times M \to R \times R}(\mathbf{a}_d), \quad \forall d \in \{1 \ldots D\}. \tag{3}$$

$\mathbf{a}'_d$ is first normalized with softmax function along the K dimension to make it a set of score maps $\mathbf{s}_d$.

$$\mathbf{s}_d = \mathrm{softmax}(\mathbf{a}'_d), \quad \forall d \in \{1 \ldots D\}. \tag{4}$$

Then we apply element-wise product between each $\mathbf{r}_d$, $\mathbf{s}_d$, and sum along the K dimension to get the mask logit $\mathbf{m}_d$:

$$\mathbf{m}_d = \sum_{k=1}^{K} \mathbf{s}_d^k \circ \mathbf{r}_d^k, \quad \forall d \in \{1 \ldots D\} \tag{5}$$

where k is the index of the bases.

4 Experiments

4.1 Datasets

iSAID [10] is a large-scale dataset for instance segmentation in aerial images, which contains 2806 aerial images from different sensors and platforms and comprises 655,451 annotated instances of 15 categories. Images with large resolutions (*e.g.* 4000 pixels in width) are commonly present in iSAID, it is necessary to crop the image and detect the objects in the cropped images. There are densely packed oriented objects such as large vehicles, small vehicles, and large elongated objects like harbors, which make segment objects in aerial images challenging.

It is worth to note that the detection network of our system performs oriented boxes regression, however, iSAID dataset does not provide the ground truth parameters of the oriented box $(x^*, y^*, w^*, h^*, \theta^*)$. Here, we use the smallest oriented bounding box of the instance mask as the regression target.

4.2 Implementation Details

The backbone of our detector is ResNet-50 [25] pre-trained on ImageNet [26]. The number of FPN channels is set to 256. Our network is trained with SGD, where the batchsize is 2 and the initial learning rate is set to 0.00125, which is then divided by 10 at $\frac{2}{3}$ and $\frac{8}{9}$ of the entire training. Due to the limited memory, we crop images to 800×800 with the stride of 200 for training and testing. The model is trained and tested at a single scale. By default, we train our model with training set and evaluate it on validation and testing set. Since our detection boxes are oriented, quadrilateral non-maximum suppression with the threshold of 0.3 is used during evaluation. As some configurable parameters of our segmentation network have been comprehensively researched in [11], unless otherwise stated, we take $K = 4$, $M = 28$, $R = 56$ as default.

4.3 Ablation Study

To have a fair comparison, we conduct ablation experiments based on mmdetection [27] framework to evaluate the effect of each component on the validation set of iSAID. The model is not modified except the component being tested.

Table 1. Instance segmentation results using mask mAP on iSAID validation set. Note that ADN means the axis-aligned detection network.

Detection		Segmentation		mAP
ADN	Ours	FCN	Ours	
✓		✓		33.5
	✓	✓		34.0
✓			✓	33.9
	✓		✓	34.4

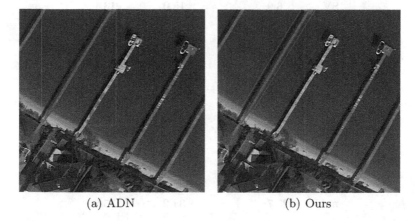

(a) ADN   (b) Ours

Fig. 5. The detection network comparison between ADN and ours. Both are using FCN as segmentation network. (Color figure online)

The Effect of Detection Network. When detecting densely packed oriented objects in aerial images, axis-aligned proposals often contain other instances, which will finally affect the instance segmentation results as shown in Fig. 1. Moreover, the oriented boxes generally contain much less background than the axis-aligned boxes as shown in Fig. 5, which makes the given resolution will be used much more efficiently. To evaluate whether the proposed detection network can handle well the above situation, we conduct ablation experiments as shown in Table 1. No matter what segmentation network is used, when the oriented detection network is used instead of the axis-aligned detection network, the performance will be improved to a certain extent. We also show the comparison in Fig. 5, where in ADN the mask prediction (red part) is not only on the target object, but also on another instance area in the detection result (green box). The background and other objects can be well removed when applying our proposed detection network, which will improve the accuracy of instance segmentation.

Table 2. Class-wise instance segmentation results on iSAID test set. Note that short names are used to define categories: BD-Baseball diamond, GTF-Ground field track, SV-Small vehicle, LV-Large vehicle TC-Tennis court, BC-Basketball court, SC-Storage tank, SBF-Soccer-ball field, RA-Roundabout, SP-Swimming pool, and HC-Helicopter.

Method	Mask R-CNN [10]	PANet [10]	Ours
Plane	37.7	39.2	40.0
BD	42.5	45.5	51.6
Bridge	13.0	15.1	17.3
GTF	23.6	29.3	27.7
SV	6.9	15.0	13.1
LV	7.4	28.8	**29.6**
Ship	26.6	45.9	44.5
TC	54.9	74.1	74.8
BC	34.6	47.4	48.7
ST	28.0	29.6	34.3
SBF	20.8	33.9	33.7
RA	35.9	36.9	41.2
Harbor	22.5	26.3	**30.4**
SP	25.1	36.1	13.1
HC	5.3	9.5	14.9
mAP	25.7	34.2	35.8

The Effect of Segmentation Network. To evaluate the performance of our segmentation network, we conduct ablation experiments with the same axis-aligned boxes regression method [15] as the detection network. The comparison results are shown in Table 1 and visualized in Fig. 6, from which we can see FCN can hardly provide a convincing mask prediction of large elongated objects (e.g. harbor), especially when they are surrounded by many other category objects (e.g. ship). This is because the features of the harbor and ships are confused in the top-level feature map, which eventually leads to poor prediction results (red part) as shown in Fig. 6(a). However, we use the bottom module to generate score maps, then merge scores with top-levels feature to supplement fine-granularity information about the harbor, accordingly our model can obtain a more accurate result as shown in Fig. 6(b).

4.4   Comparison with State-of-the-Art Methods

We compare our method with other state-of-the-art methods. In order to form a fair comparison, we use a heavier backbone (ResNet-101-FPN) which is the same as original Mask R-CNN [1] and PANet [2]. The comparison experiments are based on mmdetection framework [27]. Compared with other instance segmentation methods in aerial images, our model can well process objects in arbitrary orientation (e.g. large vehicle) and large elongated objects (e.g. harbor) as shown in Table 2.

(a) FCN   (b) Ours

Fig. 6. The segmentation network comparison between FCN and ours. Both are using ADN as detection network. (Color figure online)

5   Conclusion

Instance segmentation in aerial images is a challenging task. In this study, we take a full consideration on the arbitrariness of the orientation. A novel method named Rotated Blend Mask R-CNN is proposed which can well segment instances in aerial images. Compared with methods using axis-aligned boxes, applying oriented bounding boxes can well remove the other instances and background. Besides, we improve the segmentation network by merging top-level coarse instance information with lower-level fine-granularity. Our ablation study proves the effectiveness of each module. The proposed method outperform Mask R-CNN and PANet to a certain extent. In the future, we will explore a more efficient and accurate method for segmenting objects in aerial images.

Acknowledgement. This work was supported by the Youtu Lab of Tencent.

References

1. He, K., Gkioxari, G., Dollár, P., Girshick, R.B.: Mask R-CNN. CoRR, vol. abs/1703.06870 (2017)
2. Liu, S., Qi, L., Qin, H., Shi, J., Jia, J.: Path aggregation network for instance segmentation. CoRR, vol. abs/1803.01534 (2018)

3. Huang, Z., Huang, L., Gong, Y., Huang, C., Wang, X.: Mask scoring R-CNN. CoRR, vol. abs/1903.00241 (2019)
4. Lin, T.-Y., et al.: Microsoft COCO: Common objects in context (2014)
5. Everingham, M., Van Gool, L., Williams, C., Winn, J., Zisserman, A.: The pascal visual object classes (VOC) challenge. Int. J. Comput. Vis. **88**, 303–338 (2010)
6. Cordts, M., et al.: The cityscapes dataset for semantic urban scene understanding. CoRR, vol. abs/1604.01685 (2016)
7. Xia, G.-S., et al.: DOTA: a large-scale dataset for object detection in aerial images. CoRR, vol. abs/1711.10398 (2017)
8. Liu, Z., Wang, H., Weng, L., Yang, Y.: Ship rotated bounding box space for ship extraction from high-resolution optical satellite images with complex backgrounds. IEEE Geosci. Remote Sens. Lett. **13**(8), 1074–1078 (2016)
9. Weir, N., et al.: SpaceNet MVOI: a multi-view overhead imagery dataset. CoRR, vol. abs/1903.12239 (2019)
10. Zamir, S.W., et al.: iSAID: a large-scale dataset for instance segmentation in aerial images. CoRR, vol. abs/1905.12886 (2019)
11. Chen, H., Sun, K., Tian, Z., Shen, C., Huang, Y., Yan, Y.: BlendMask: top-down meets bottom-up for instance segmentation (2020)
12. Girshick, R.B., Donahue, J., Darrell, T., Malik, J.: Rich feature hierarchies for accurate object detection and semantic segmentation. CoRR, vol. abs/1311.2524 (2013)
13. He, K., Zhang, X., Ren, S., Sun, J.: Spatial pyramid pooling in deep convolutional networks for visual recognition. CoRR, vol. abs/1406.4729 (2014)
14. Girshick, R.B.: Fast R-CNN. CoRR, vol. abs/1504.08083 (2015)
15. Ren, S., He, K., Girshick, R.B., Sun, J.: Faster R-CNN: towards real-time object detection with region proposal networks. CoRR, vol. abs/1506.01497 (2015)
16. Dai, J., Li, Y., He, K., Sun, J.: R-FCN: object detection via region-based fully convolutional networks. CoRR, vol. abs/1605.06409 (2016)
17. Cai, Z., Vasconcelos, N.: Cascade R-CNN: delving into high quality object detection. CoRR, vol. abs/1712.00726 (2017)
18. Zhu, Y., Ma, C., Jun, D.: Rotated cascade R-CNN: a shape robust detector with coordinate regression. Pattern Recogn. **96**, 106964 (2019)
19. Zhu, Y., Wu, X., Du, J.: Adaptive period embedding for representing oriented objects in aerial images. CoRR, vol. abs/1906.09447 (2019)
20. Ding, J., Xue, N., Long, Y., Xia, G.-S., Lu, O.: Learning ROI transformer for detecting oriented objects in aerial images. CoRR, vol. abs/1812.00155 (2018)
21. Long, J., Shelhamer, E., Darrell, T.: Fully convolutional networks for semantic segmentation. CoRR, vol. abs/1411.4038 (2014)
22. Bolya, D., Zhou, C., Xiao, F., Lee, Y.J.: YOLACT: real-time instance segmentation. CoRR, vol. abs/1904.02689 (2019)
23. Bolya, D., Zhou, C., Xiao, F., Lee, Y.: Yolact++: Better real-time instance segmentation (2019)
24. Kirillov, A., Girshick, R., He, K., Dollar, P.: Panoptic feature pyramid networks, pp. 6392–6401 (2019)
25. He, K., Zhang, X., Ren, S., Sun, J.: Deep residual learning for image recognition, pp. 770–778 (2016)
26. Deng, J., Dong, W., Socher, R., Li, L.-J., Li, K., Li, F.F.: ImageNet: a large-scale hierarchical image database, pp. 248–255 (2009)
27. Chen, K., et al.: MMDetection: open MMLab detection toolbox and benchmark. arXiv preprint arXiv:1906.07155 (2019)

Six-Channel Image Representation
for Cross-Domain Object Detection

Tianxiao Zhang[1], Wenchi Ma[1], and Guanghui Wang[2(✉)]

[1] Department of Electrical Engineering and Computer Science, University of Kansas,
Lawrence, KS 66045, USA
[2] Department of Computer Science, Ryerson University,
Toronto, ON M5B 2K3, Canada
wangcs@ryerson.ca

Abstract. Most deep learning models are data-driven and the excellent performance is highly dependent on the abundant and diverse datasets. However, it is very hard to obtain and label the datasets of some specific scenes or applications. If we train the detector using the data from one domain, it cannot perform well on the data from another domain due to domain shift, which is one of the big challenges of most object detection models. To address this issue, some image-to-image translation techniques have been employed to generate some fake data of some specific scenes to train the models. With the advent of Generative Adversarial Networks (GANs), we could realize unsupervised image-to-image translation in both directions from a source to a target domain and from the target to the source domain. In this study, we report a new approach to making use of the generated images. We propose to concatenate the original 3-channel images and their corresponding GAN-generated fake images to form 6-channel representations of the dataset, hoping to address the domain shift problem while exploiting the success of available detection models. The idea of augmented data representation may inspire further study on object detection and other applications.

Keywords: Object detection · Domain shift · Unsupervised image-to-image translation

1 Introduction

Computer vision has progressed rapidly with deep learning techniques and more advanced and accurate models for object detection, image classification, image segmentation, pose estimation, and tracking emerging almost every day [31, 42, 49]. Even though computer vision enters a new era with deep learning, there are still plenty of problems unsolved and domain shift is one of them. Albeit CNN models are dominating the computer vision, their performances often become inferior when testing some unseen data or data from a different domain, which is denoted as domain shift. Since most deep learning models are data-driven and

© Springer Nature Switzerland AG 2021
Y. Peng et al. (Eds.): ICIG 2021, LNCS 12888, pp. 171–184, 2021.
https://doi.org/10.1007/978-3-030-87355-4_15

the high-accurate performance is mostly guaranteed by the enormous amount of various data, domain shift often exists when there are not enough labeled specific data but we have to test those kinds of data in the testing set. For instance, although we only detect cars on the roads, training the models on day scenes cannot guarantee an effective detection of cars in the night scenes. We might have to utilize enough datasets from night scenes to train the models, nonetheless, sometimes the datasets from some specific scenes are rare or unlabeled, which makes it even more difficult to mitigate the domain shift effect.

To mitigate the situation where some kinds of training data are none or rare, The image-to-image translation that could translate images from one domain to another is highly desirable. Fortunately, with the advent of Generative Adversarial Networks (GANs) [15], Some researchers aim to generate some fake datasets in specific scenes using GAN models to overcome the lack of data. With some unpaired image-to-image translation GAN models (i.e., CycleGAN [52]), it can not only translate images from the source domain to target domain, but also translate images from target domain to source domain, and the entire process does not require any paired images, which make it ideal for real-world applications.

The GAN models for image-to-image translation can generate the corresponding fake images of the target domain from the original images of the source domain in the training dataset, and we can utilize the GAN-generated images to train object detection models and test on images of target domain [2]. Since we expect to solve cross-domain object detection problems, after pre-processing the data and generating the fake images with image-to-image translation models, the generated data has to be fed into the object detection models to train the model and the trained model could demonstrate its effectiveness through testing the data from the target domain. Employing GAN-generated fake images to train the detection models to guarantee the domain of the training data and testing data being the same illustrated the effectiveness of the approach and the detection performance was boosted for the scenario where the training data for the detection models is from one domain while the testing data is in another domain [2].

Instead of simply utilizing the fake images to train the model, we propose to solve the problem from a new perspective by concatenating the original images and their corresponding GAN-translated fake images to form new 6-channel representations. For instance, if we only have source domain images but we intend to test our model on unlabeled images in the target domain, what we did was training the image-to-image translation model with source domain data and target domain data. And then we could employ the trained image translation model to generate the corresponding fake images. Since some image-to-image translation models [52] could translate images in both directions, we are able to acquire the corresponding fake data for the data from both the source domain and target domain. Thus, both training images and testing images would be augmented into 6-channel representations by concatenating the RGB three channels of the original images with those from the corresponding fake images. Then we can train and test the detection models using available detection models, the only difference is the dimension of the kernel of the CNN models for detection in the first layer becomes 6 instead of 3. The process of training and testing the proposed method is depicted in Fig. 1.

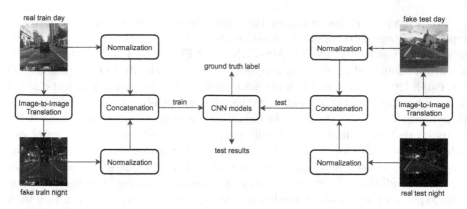

Fig. 1. The flow chart of the proposed 6-channel image augmentation approach for training and testing CNN-based detection models.

2 Related Work

Image-to-image translation is a popular topic in computer vision [43,44]. With the advent of Generative Adversarial Networks [15], it could be mainly categorized as supervised image-to-image translation and unsupervised image-to-image translation [1]. The supervised image-to-image translation models such as pix2pix [20] and BicycleGAN [54], require image pairs from two or more domains (i.e., the exact same image scenes from day and night), which are extremely expensive and unrealistic to be acquired in the real world. Perhaps the quality of the translated images is sometimes beyond expectations, they are not ideal for real-world applications.

The unsupervised image-to-image translation models can be divided as cycle consistency based models (i.e., CycleGAN [52], DiscoGAN [22], DualGAN [46]) which introduce cycle consistency losses, autocncoder based models (i.e., UNIT [29]) combined with autoencoder [23], and recent disentangled representation models (i.e., MUNIT [18], DIRT [25]). Since the unsupervised image-to-image translation models only require image sets from two or more domains and do not necessitate any paired images which are arduous to collect and annotate, they are often leveraged to generate some fake data in the target domain and applied to other computer vision tasks such as object detection and image classification. Among those unsupervised image-to-image translation models, CycleGAN [52] is frequently utilized as the image-mapping model to generate some fake data to be employed in some cross-domain problems [2,19].

Object detection addresses the problem that detects the semantic instances on digital images or videos. The fundamental purpose of object detection is to classify the objects shown on the images or videos and simultaneously locate those objects by coordinates [32]. The applications of object detection are in various fields such as medical image analysis [33], self-driving car, pose estimation, segmentation, etc.

From the perspective of stages, the object detectors are categorized into two types: one-stage detectors and two-stage detectors. For two-stage object detectors such as Faster R-CNN [37], MS-CNN [4], R-FCN [8], FPN [26], these models are often comprised of a region proposal network as the first stage that selects the candidate anchors which have high probabilities to contain objects and a detection network as the second stage that classify the objects to be contained by these candidates and further do the bounding box regression for these candidates to refine their coordinates and finally output the results. For one-stage object detectors like SSD [30], YOLOv1-v4 [3,34–36], RetinaNet [27], these detectors often directly classify and regress the pre-defined anchor boxes instead of choosing some candidates. Thus the two-stage models often outperform the one-stage counterparts while one-stage models frequently have a faster inference rate than two-stage approaches.

Due to the various sizes and shapes of the objects, some models [26,27,30,48] design anchor boxes on different levels of feature maps (the pixels on lower level feature maps have a small receptive field and the pixels on higher-level feature maps have large receptive field) so that the anchors on lower level features are responsible for the relative small objects and the anchors on higher-level features are in charge of detecting relatively large objects. The middle-sized objects are perhaps recognized by the middle-level feature maps.

The aforementioned detection models are anchor-based that we have to design pre-defined anchor boxes for these models. In recent years, some anchor-free models [10,24,39,50,51] are attracting great attention for their excellent performance without any pre-defined anchor boxes. Some of them are even dominating the accuracy on COCO benchmark [28]. Since a large amount of anchors has to be generated for some anchor-based models and most of them are useless because no object is contained in the majority of anchors, anchor-free models might predominate in the designs of object detectors in the future. Recently, the transformer [40] is applied successfully to object detection [5], which is an anchor-free model with attention mechanisms.

Nonetheless, many problems have not been well solved in this field, especially in cross-domain object detection. Since modern object detectors are based on deep learning techniques and deep learning is data-driven so that the performance of modern object detectors is highly dependent on how many annotated data can be employed as the training set. Cross-domain issues arise when there are not enough labeled training data that have the same domain as the testing data, or the dataset is diverse or composed of various datasets of different domains in both training and testing data.

Domain Adaptive Faster R-CNN [6] explores the cross-domain object detection problem based on Faster R-CNN. By utilizing Gradient Reverse Layer (GRL) [12] in an adversarial training manner which is similar to Generative Adversarial Networks (GAN)[15], this paper proposes an image-level adaptation component and an instance-level adaptation component which augment the Faster R-CNN structure to realize domain adaptation. In addition, a consistent regularizer between those two components is to alleviate the effects of the domain shift between different dataset such as KITTI [13], Cityscapes [7], Foggy Cityscapes [38], and SIM10K [21].

Universal object detection by domain attention [41] addresses the universal object detection of various datasets by attention mechanism [40]. The universal object detection is arduous to realize since the object detection datasets are diverse and there exists a domain shift between them. The paper [17] proposes a domain adaption module which is comprised of a universal SE adapter bank and a new domain-attention mechanism to realize universal object detection. [19] deals with cross-domain object detection that instance-level annotations are accessible in the source domain while only image-level labels are available in the target domain. The authors exploit an unpaired image-to-image translation model (CycleGAN [52]) to generate fake data in the target domain to fine-tune the trained model which is trained on the data in the source domain. Finally, the model is fine-tuned again on the detected results of the testing data (pseudo-labeling) to make the model even better.

The study [2] utilizes CycleGAN [52] as the image-to-image translation model to translate the images in both directions. The model trained on the fake data in the target domain has better performance than that trained on the original data in the source domain on testing the test data from the target domain. The dataset we employ in this paper is from [2] and we follow exactly the same pre-processing procedure to prepare the dataset. In the following, we will discuss our proposal that utilizes concatenated image pairs (real images and corresponding fake images) to train the detection model and compare it to the corresponding approach from [2].

3   Proposed Approach

The framework of our proposed method is depicted in Fig. 1. In our implementation, we employ CycleGAN for image-to-image translation, which is trained with the data from the source domain (i.e., day images) and the data from the target domain (i.e., night images). First, the fake data (target domain) is generated from the original data (source domain) via the trained image-to-image translation model (i.e., generating the fake night images from the real day images). Then, the real and fake images are normalized and concatenated (i.e., concatenating two 3-channel images to form a 6-channel representation of the image). Finally, the concatenated images are exploited to train the CNN models. During the stage of test, the test data is processed in a similar way as the training data to form concatenated images and sent to the trained CNN model for detection.

3.1   Image-to-Image Translation

To realize the cross-domain object detection, we have to collect and annotate the data in the target domain to train the model. While it is difficult to acquire the annotated data in the target domain, image-to-image translation models provide an option to generate fake data in the target domain.

Fig. 2. Several samples of original-day images (1st row) and their corresponding GAN-generated fake-night images (2nd row).

Fig. 3. Several samples of original-night images (1st row) and their corresponding GAN-generated fake-day images (2nd row).

In our experiment, we employed an unpaired image-to-image translation model: CycleGAN [52]. CycleGAN is an unsupervised image-to-image translation that only requires images from two different domains (without any image-level or instance-level annotations) to train the model. Furthermore, unpaired translation illustrates that the images from two domains do not need to be paired which is extremely demanding to be obtained. Last but not least, the locations and sizes of the objects on the images should be the same after the image-to-image translation so that any image-level labels and instance-level annotations of the original images can be utilized directly on the translated images. This property is extraordinarily significant since most CNN models are data-driven and the annotations of the images are indispensable to successfully train the supervised CNN models (i.e., most object detection models). Unpaired image-to-image translation models such as CycleGAN [52] can translate the images in two directions without changing the key properties of the objects on the images. Thus the annotations such as coordinates and class labels of the objects on the original images can be smoothly exploited in the fake translated images. As manually annotating the images is significantly expensive, by image-to-image translation, the translated images would automatically have the same labels as their original counterparts, which to some extent makes manually annotating images unnecessary.

3.2   CNN Models

In Fig. 1, the CNN model can be any CNN-based object detection model, where the dimension of the convolutional kernel in the first layer is changed from 3 to 6. In our implementation, we employ Faster R-CNN [37] for detection, and we use ResNet-101 [16] as the backbone network for the detection model.

Faster R-CNN is a classic two-stage anchor-based object detector that is comprised of Region Proposal Network (RPN) and detection network. Since it is an anchor-based model, we have to design some pre-defined anchor boxes on the feature maps. Typically, 9 anchors with 3 different sizes and 3 different aspect ratios are designed to act as the pre-defined anchor boxes on each location of the feature maps. The objective of RPN is to select some region proposals with a high probability of containing objects from the pre-defined anchors and further refine their coordinates. Each pre-defined anchor would be associated with a score indicating the probability of that anchor box containing an object. Only the anchor boxes with associated scores higher than some threshold can be selected as region proposals and those region proposals are further refined by RPN and later fed into the detection network.

The purpose of the detection network is to receive the region proposals selected and refined by RPN and finally do the classification for each rectangle proposal and bounding box regression to improve the coordinates of the box proposals. Since the region proposals may have various sizes and shapes, more accurately, the number of elements each proposal has might be varying. To guarantee the region proposals are fed into the fully connected layers effectively (the fully connected layer needs the length of input data fixed), the ROI pooling layer is adopted to ensure the size of the input of each proposal to the detection network is fixed. The detection network is simply from Fast R-CNN [14] that is to classify the object which might be contained by each region proposal and simultaneously refine the coordinates of the rectangle boxes. The output of the Faster R-CNN network is the class of the object each proposal might include and the coordinates of the bounding box for each refined proposal.

4   Experiments

In this section, the datasets and the experimental methodology and parameter settings are elaborated. We conducted some of the experiments from [2] for comparison.

4.1   Datasets

We employ the same dataset as [2] in our experiments. The original datasets are from BDD100K [47] which is a large-scale diverse dataset for driving scenes. Since the dataset is extremely large and contains high-resolution images and various scenarios on the road and the weather conditions (sunny, rainy, foggy, etc.) [2], the authors only choose the clear or partly cloudy day and night images to demonstrate the domain shift from day to night [2]. In addition, all selected images are cropped to 256 × 256 pixels with proper adjustment. There are a total 12,000 images left and processed (6,000 day images and 6,000 night images). After that, the images are randomly sampled and divided into four sets: train-day, train-night, test-day, and test-night, each of the sets contains 3,000 256 × 256 images. We harness the set of train-day and train-night to train the CycleGAN model and utilized the trained GAN model to generate fake train-night (from train-day), fake train-day (from train-night), fake test-night (from test-day), and fake test-day (from test-night). Now we have a total of 12,000 real images (3,000 for each set) and 12,000 fake images (3,000 for each set). Then we can concatenate the real images and their corresponding fake images to generate 6-channel representations that would be fed into the Faster R-CNN object detector. After choosing and processing the images, the car is the only object on the image to be detected. Some samples of real images and their corresponding GAN-generated fake counterparts are illustrated in Fig. 2 and Fig. 3.

4.2 Experimental Evaluations

Faster R-CNN model is implemented in Python [45] with Pytorch 1.0.0 and CycleGAN is implemented in Python [53] with PyTorch 1.4.0. All experiments are executed with CUDA 9.1.85 and cuDNN 7 on a single NVIDIA TITAN XP GPU with a memory of 12 GB.

The metric we employed is mean Average Precision (mAP) from PASCAL VOC [11], which is the same metric employed in [2]. Since the car is the only object to be detected, the mAP is equivalent to AP in this dataset since mAP calculating the mean AP for all classes.

For CycleGAN, the parameters are default values in [53]. For Faster R-CNN, similarly to [2], we utilize pre-trained ResNet-101 [16] on ImageNet [9] as our backbone network. We select the initial learning rates from 0.001 to 0.00001 and the experiments are implemented separately for those chosen initial learning rates, but we do not utilize them all for each experiment since our experiments demonstrate that the higher the learning rate we selected from above, the better the results would be. In each 5 epoch, the learning rate decays as 0.1 of the previous learning rate. The training process would be executed 20 to 30 epochs, but the results indicate that the Faster R-CNN model converges relatively early on the dataset. Training every 5 epochs, we record the testing results on test data, but we would report the best one for each experiment. The model parameters are the same for 6-channel experiments and 3-channel experiments, except for 6-channel experiments, the kernel dimension of the first layer of the Faster R-CNN model is 6 instead of 3. And we just concatenate each kernel by itself to create 6-dimension kernels in the first layer of ResNet-101 backbone for 6-channel experiments. While for 3-channel experiments, we simply exploit the original ResNet-101 backbone as our initial training parameters.

4.3 Experimental Results

First, we implemented the training and testing of the original 3-channel Faster R-CNN model which is illustrated in Table 1. The test set is test-night data which is fixed. With different training sets, the detection results on test night are varying.

Table 1. 3-channel detection

Train set	mAP
Train-day (3,000 images)	0.777
Fake train-night (3,000 images)	0.893
Train-night (3,000 images)	0.933
Train-day + train-night (6,000 images)	0.941

From Table 1 we can see that, for testing the test-night set, the model trained on the fake-train night set is much better than that trained on the original train-day set, which corresponds to the results from [2]. These experimental results indicate that if the annotated day images are the only available training data while the test set contains only night images, we could leverage fake night images generated by the image-to-image translation models to train the CNN model. The results are excellent when the model is trained on the train-night set (without domain shift), indicating the domain shift is the most significant influence on the performance of the CNN model in this experiment.

Then we conduct the experiments for our proposed 6-channel Faster R-CNN model which is shown in Table 2. The test data is comprised of test-night images concatenated with corresponding translated fake test-day images. The training sets in Table 2 have 6 channels. For instance, train-day in the table indicates train-day images concatenated with corresponding fake train-night images, and train-day plus train-night in the table represents train-day images concatenated with corresponding fake train-night images plus train-night images concatenated with corresponding fake train-day images.

Table 2. 6-channel detection

Train set	mAP
Train-day (3,000 6-channel representations)	0.830
Train-night (3,000 6-channel representations)	0.931
Train-day + train-night (6,000 6-channel representations)	0.938

From Table 1 and Table 2, it is noticeable that even though the model trained on train-day images concatenated with fake train-night images (6-channel) has a better result with AP 0.830 than that just training on train-day (3-channel) with AP 0.777, it is worse than the model only trained on fake train-night (3-channel) with AP 0.893.

To demonstrate if the 6-channel approach can improve the detection results in the situation where the training set and testing set do not have domain shift, we also performed the experiment that trains the model on train-night set (3-channel) and tests it on test night set. From Table 1, the average precision is 0.933, which is pretty high since there is no domain shift between the training data and testing data. Accordingly, we did the corresponding 6-channel experiment which trains on train-night set concatenated with fake train-day set and tests it on test-night images concatenated with fake test-day images. From Table 2, the average precision of this 6-channel model is almost the same as its corresponding 3-channel model.

We increase the size of the training data by training the model with the train-day set plus the train-night set and testing it on test-night data. From Table 1 and Table 2, the result of 6-channel model also performs similar to its 3-channel counterpart. More experimental results are shown in Table 3, which are from the original 3-channel models. To remove the effect of domain shift, the training set and the testing set do not have domain shift (they are all day images or night images). From Table 3, it is obvious that the "quality" shift influences the performance of the models. For instance, the model trained on the original train-day (or train-night) set has better performance on the original test-day (or test-night) set than the GAN-generated fake day (or night) images. Similarly, the model which is trained on GAN-generated fake train-day (or fake train-night) set performs better on the GAN-generated fake test-day (or fake test-night) set than the original test-day (or test-night) set.

Table 3. 3-channel extra experiments

Train set	Test set	mAP
Train-day	Test-day	0.945
	Fake test-day	0.789
Fake train-day	Fake test-day	0.914
	Test-day	0.903
Train-night	Test-night	0.932
	Fake test-night	0.859
Fake train-night	Fake test-night	0.924
	Test-night	0.868

5   Conclusion

The study has evaluated a 6-channel approach to address the domain-shift issue by incorporating the generated fake images using image-to-image translation.

However, we have not achieved the expected results. One possible reason is the quality of the generated images is inferior compared to the original images, especially the fake day images generated from the data of night scenes, as illustrated in Fig. 2 and Fig. 3. If we merely concatenate the original high-quality images with their inferior counterparts, the model may treat the low-quality fake image channels as some kind of "noise", and thus, the model could hardly learn more useful information from the concatenated 6-channel representations. Another possible reason is that the domain shift issue may still exist in the combined 6-channel representations, which prevents the model from extracting useful information from the concatenated representations. Moreover, the dataset we used in the experiments only has limited samples, which are insufficient to train the model. We hope the idea of augmented data representation can inspire more further investigations and applications.

References

1. Alotaibi, A.: Deep generative adversarial networks for image-to-image translation: a review. Symmetry **12**(10), 1705 (2020)
2. Arruda, V.F., et al.: Cross-domain car detection using unsupervised image-to-image translation: from day to night. In: 2019 International Joint Conference on Neural Networks (IJCNN), pp. 1–8. IEEE (2019)
3. Bochkovskiy, A., Wang, C.Y., Liao, H.Y.M.: Yolov4: optimal speed and accuracy of object detection. arXiv preprint arXiv:2004.10934 (2020)
4. Cai, Z., Fan, Q., Feris, R.S., Vasconcelos, N.: A unified multi-scale deep convolutional neural network for fast object detection. In: Leibe, B., Matas, J., Sebe, N., Welling, M. (eds.) ECCV 2016, Part IV. LNCS, vol. 9908, pp. 354–370. Springer, Cham (2016). https://doi.org/10.1007/978-3-319-46493-0_22
5. Carion, N., Massa, F., Synnaeve, G., Usunier, N., Kirillov, A., Zagoruyko, S.: End-to-end object detection with transformers. arXiv preprint arXiv:2005.12872 (2020)
6. Chen, Y., Li, W., Sakaridis, C., Dai, D., Van Gool, L.: Domain adaptive faster R-CNN for object detection in the wild. In: Proceedings of the IEEE Conference on Computer Vision and Pattern Recognition, pp. 3339–3348 (2018)
7. Cordts, M., et al.: The cityscapes dataset for semantic urban scene understanding. In: Proceedings of the IEEE Conference on Computer Vision and Pattern Recognition, pp. 3213–3223 (2016)
8. Dai, J., Li, Y., He, K., Sun, J.: R-FCN: object detection via region-based fully convolutional networks. arXiv preprint arXiv:1605.06409 (2016)
9. Deng, J., Dong, W., Socher, R., Li, L.J., Li, K., Fei-Fei, L.: ImageNet: a large-scale hierarchical image database. In: 2009 IEEE Conference on Computer Vision and Pattern Recognition, pp. 248–255. IEEE (2009)
10. Duan, K., Bai, S., Xie, L., Qi, H., Huang, Q., Tian, Q.: Centernet: keypoint triplets for object detection. In: Proceedings of the IEEE International Conference on Computer Vision, pp. 6569–6578 (2019)
11. Everingham, M., Eslami, S.A., Van Gool, L., Williams, C.K., Winn, J., Zisserman, A.: The pascal visual object classes challenge: a retrospective. Int. J. Comput. Vis. **111**(1), 98–136 (2015)
12. Ganin, Y., Lempitsky, V.: Unsupervised domain adaptation by backpropagation. In: International Conference on Machine Learning, pp. 1180–1189. PMLR (2015)

13. Geiger, A., Lenz, P., Stiller, C., Urtasun, R.: Vision meets robotics: the KITTI dataset. Int. J. Robot. Res. **32**(11), 1231–1237 (2013)
14. Girshick, R.: Fast R-CNN. In: Proceedings of the IEEE International Conference on Computer Vision, pp. 1440–1448 (2015)
15. Goodfellow, I., et al.: Generative adversarial nets. In: Advances in Neural Information Processing Systems, pp. 2672–2680 (2014)
16. He, K., Zhang, X., Ren, S., Sun, J.: Deep residual learning for image recognition. In: Proceedings of the IEEE Conference on Computer Vision and Pattern Recognition, pp. 770–778 (2016)
17. Hu, J., Shen, L., Sun, G.: Squeeze-and-excitation networks. In: Proceedings of the IEEE Conference on Computer Vision and Pattern Recognition, pp. 7132–7141 (2018)
18. Huang, X., Liu, M.-Y., Belongie, S., Kautz, J.: Multimodal unsupervised image-to-image translation. In: Ferrari, V., Hebert, M., Sminchisescu, C., Weiss, Y. (eds.) ECCV 2018, Part III. LNCS, vol. 11207, pp. 179–196. Springer, Cham (2018). https://doi.org/10.1007/978-3-030-01219-9_11
19. Inoue, N., Furuta, R., Yamasaki, T., Aizawa, K.: Cross-domain weakly-supervised object detection through progressive domain adaptation. In: Proceedings of the IEEE Conference on Computer Vision and Pattern Recognition, pp. 5001–5009 (2018)
20. Isola, P., Zhu, J.Y., Zhou, T., Efros, A.A.: Image-to-image translation with conditional adversarial networks. In: Proceedings of the IEEE Conference on Computer Vision and Pattern Recognition, pp. 1125–1134 (2017)
21. Johnson-Roberson, M., Barto, C., Mehta, R., Sridhar, S.N., Rosaen, K., Vasudevan, R.: Driving in the matrix: can virtual worlds replace human-generated annotations for real world tasks? arXiv preprint arXiv:1610.01983 (2016)
22. Kim, T., Cha, M., Kim, H., Lee, J.K., Kim, J.: Learning to discover cross-domain relations with generative adversarial networks. arXiv preprint arXiv:1703.05192 (2017)
23. Kingma, D.P., Welling, M.: Auto-encoding variational bayes. arXiv preprint arXiv:1312.6114 (2013)
24. Law, H., Deng, J.: Cornernet: detecting objects as paired keypoints. In: Proceedings of the European Conference on Computer Vision (ECCV), pp. 734–750 (2018)
25. Lee, H.Y., Tseng, H.Y., Huang, J.B., Singh, M., Yang, M.H.: Diverse image-to-image translation via disentangled representations. In: Proceedings of the European Conference on computer vision (ECCV), pp. 35–51 (2018)
26. Lin, T.Y., Dollár, P., Girshick, R., He, K., Hariharan, B., Belongie, S.: Feature pyramid networks for object detection. In: Proceedings of the IEEE Conference on Computer Vision and Pattern Recognition, pp. 2117–2125 (2017)
27. Lin, T.Y., Goyal, P., Girshick, R., He, K., Dollár, P.: Focal loss for dense object detection. In: Proceedings of the IEEE International Conference on Computer Vision, pp. 2980–2988 (2017)
28. Lin, T.-Y., et al.: Microsoft COCO: common objects in context. In: Fleet, D., Pajdla, T., Schiele, B., Tuytelaars, T. (eds.) ECCV 2014, Part V. LNCS, vol. 8693, pp. 740–755. Springer, Cham (2014). https://doi.org/10.1007/978-3-319-10602-1_48
29. Liu, M.Y., Breuel, T., Kautz, J.: Unsupervised image-to-image translation networks. In: Advances in Neural Information Processing Systems, pp. 700–708 (2017)
30. Liu, W., et al.: SSD: single shot multibox detector. In: Leibe, B., Matas, J., Sebe, N., Welling, M. (eds.) ECCV 2016, Part I. LNCS, vol. 9905, pp. 21–37. Springer, Cham (2016). https://doi.org/10.1007/978-3-319-46448-0_2

31. Ma, W., Li, K., Wang, G.: Location-aware box reasoning for anchor-based single-shot object detection. IEEE Access **8**, 129300–129309 (2020)
32. Ma, W., Wu, Y., Cen, F., Wang, G.: MDFN: multi-scale deep feature learning network for object detection. Pattern Recognit. **100**, 107149 (2020)
33. Mo, X., Tao, K., Wang, Q., Wang, G.: An efficient approach for polyps detection in endoscopic videos based on faster R-CNN. In: 2018 24th International Conference on Pattern Recognition (ICPR), pp. 3929–3934. IEEE (2018)
34. Redmon, J., Divvala, S., Girshick, R., Farhadi, A.: You only look once: unified, real-time object detection. In: Proceedings of the IEEE Conference on Computer Vision and Pattern Recognition, pp. 779–788 (2016)
35. Redmon, J., Farhadi, A.: Yolo9000: better, faster, stronger. In: Proceedings of the IEEE Conference on Computer Vision and Pattern Recognition, pp. 7263–7271 (2017)
36. Redmon, J., Farhadi, A.: Yolov3: an incremental improvement. arXiv preprint arXiv:1804.02767 (2018)
37. Ren, S., He, K., Girshick, R., Sun, J.: Faster R-CNN: towards real-time object detection with region proposal networks. IEEE Trans. Pattern Anal. Mach. Intell. **39**(6), 1137–1149 (2016)
38. Sakaridis, C., Dai, D., Van Gool, L.: Semantic foggy scene understanding with synthetic data. Int. J. Comput. Vis. **126**(9), 973–992 (2018)
39. Tian, Z., Shen, C., Chen, H., He, T.: Fcos: fully convolutional one-stage object detection. In: Proceedings of the IEEE International Conference on Computer Vision, pp. 9627–9636 (2019)
40. Vaswani, A., et al.: Attention is all you need. In: Advances in Neural Information Processing Systems, pp. 5998–6008 (2017)
41. Wang, X., Cai, Z., Gao, D., Vasconcelos, N.: Towards universal object detection by domain attention. In: Proceedings of the IEEE Conference on Computer Vision and Pattern Recognition, pp. 7289–7298 (2019)
42. Wu, Y., Zhang, Z., Wang, G.: Unsupervised deep feature transfer for low resolution image classification. In: Proceedings of the IEEE International Conference on Computer Vision Workshops (2019)
43. Xu, W., Keshmiri, S., Wang, G.: Stacked wasserstein autoencoder. Neurocomputing **363**, 195–204 (2019)
44. Xu, W., Shawn, K., Wang, G.: Toward learning a unified many-to-many mapping for diverse image translation. Pattern Recognit. **93**, 570–580 (2019)
45. Yang, J., Lu, J., Batra, D., Parikh, D.: A faster Pytorch implementation of faster R-CNN (2017). https://github.com/jwyang/faster-rcnn.pytorch
46. Yi, Z., Zhang, H., Tan, P., Gong, M.: DualGAN: unsupervised dual learning for image-to-image translation. In: Proceedings of the IEEE International Conference on Computer Vision, pp. 2849–2857 (2017)
47. Yu, F., et al.: Bdd100k: a diverse driving video database with scalable annotation tooling. arXiv preprint arXiv:1805.04687 2(5), 6 (2018)
48. Zhang, S., Wen, L., Bian, X., Lei, Z., Li, S.Z.: Single-shot refinement neural network for object detection. In: Proceedings of the IEEE Conference on Computer Vision and Pattern Recognition, pp. 4203–4212 (2018)
49. Zhang, X., Zhang, T., Yang, Y., Wang, Z., Wang, G.: Real-time golf ball detection and tracking based on convolutional neural networks. In: 2020 IEEE International Conference on Systems, Man, and Cybernetics (SMC), pp. 2808–2813. IEEE (2020)
50. Zhou, X., Zhuo, J., Krahenbuhl, P.: Bottom-up object detection by grouping extreme and center points. In: Proceedings of the IEEE Conference on Computer Vision and Pattern Recognition, pp. 850–859 (2019)

51. Zhu, C., He, Y., Savvides, M.: Feature selective anchor-free module for single-shot object detection. In: Proceedings of the IEEE Conference on Computer Vision and Pattern Recognition, pp. 840–849 (2019)
52. Zhu, J.Y., Park, T., Isola, P., Efros, A.A.: Unpaired image-to-image translation using cycle-consistent adversarial networks. In: Proceedings of the IEEE International Conference on Computer Vision, pp. 2223–2232 (2017)
53. Zhu, J.Y., Park, T., Wang, T.: CycleGAN and pix2pix in Pytorch (2020). https://github.com/junyanz/pytorch-CycleGAN-and-pix2pix
54. Zhu, J.Y., et al.: Toward multimodal image-to-image translation. In: Advances in Neural Information Processing Systems, pp. 465–476 (2017)

Skeleton-Aware Network for Aircraft Landmark Detection

Yuntong Ye[1,2], Yi Chang[2], Yi Li[1], and Luxin Yan[1(✉)]

[1] National Key Laboratory of Science and Technology on Multi-spectral Information Processing, School of Artificial Intelligence and Automation, Huazhong University of Science and Technology, Wuhan, China
{yuntongye,li_yi,yanluxin}@hust.edu.cn

[2] AI Center, Pengcheng Lab, Shenzhen, China
yichang@hust.edu.cn

Abstract. The landmark detection has been widely investigated for the human pose with rapid progress in recent years. In this work, we aim at dealing with a new problem: *aircraft landmark detection in the wild*. We have a key observation: the aircraft is a rigid object with global structural relationships between local landmarks. This motivates us to progressively learn the global geometrical structure and local landmark localization in a coarse-to-fine guidance manner. In this paper, we propose a simple yet effective skeleton-aware landmark detection (SALD) network, including one stream for exploiting the coarse global skeleton structure and one stream for the precise local landmarks localization. The global skeleton structure models the aircraft "images" into skeleton "lines", in which the multiple skeletons of the holistic aircraft and the parts are explicitly extracted to serve as the geometrical structure constraints for landmarks. Then, the local landmark localization precisely detects the key "points" with the guidance of skeleton "lines". Consequently, the progressive strategy of "extracting lines from images, detecting points with lines" significantly eases the landmark detection task by decomposing the task into the simpler coarse-to-fine sub-tasks, thus further improving the detection performance. Extensive experimental results show the superiority of proposed method compared to state-of-the-arts.

Keywords: Aircraft · Landmark detection · Convolutional neural network · Skeleton

1 Introduction

Landmark detection refers to the task of locating keypoints in the given images. In aircraft landmark detection these keypoints are predefined at aircraft endpoints and joints such as head, tip and stabilizer, as shown in Fig. 1 (a). The aircraft landmark detection serves as an important prior work for applications like aircraft fine-grained classification [1–3], and aircraft detection [4,5]. In this paper, we focus on the problem of single aircraft landmark detection.

© Springer Nature Switzerland AG 2021
Y. Peng et al. (Eds.): ICIG 2021, LNCS 12888, pp. 185–197, 2021.
https://doi.org/10.1007/978-3-030-87355-4_16

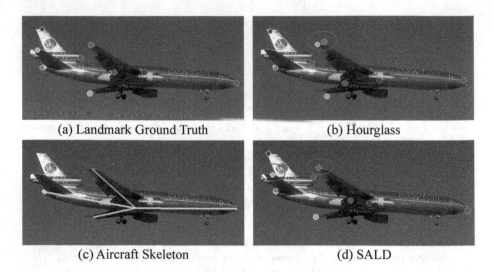

(a) Landmark Ground Truth   (b) Hourglass

(c) Aircraft Skeleton   (d) SALD

Fig. 1. Illustration of the proposed skeleton-aware landmark detection (SALD). (a) Landmark ground truth. (b) Hourglass [16] wrongly detects the right tip on the right stabilizer due to the similarity of local features in aircraft. (c) The skeletons model the coarse global geometrical structure of the aircraft. (d) With the guidance of the aircraft structure, SALD predicts the precise landmark locations in a progressive coarse-to-fine manner. The right stabilizer landmark is located near the end point of the stabilizer part, with a correct semantic and geometrical relationship with the structure.

There are few researchers devoted to aircraft landmark detection in the wild despite its importance. In remote sensing images, the landmarks of aircraft aerial view images are detected by effective convolutional neural networks (CNN) and utilized by the following aircraft type recognition and detection tasks. The focus is on the landmark utilization rather than the detection. For instance, Zhao et al. [2] proposed a six-layer model based on vanilla CNN [25] to regress the aircraft landmarks and perform landmark template matching to recognize the aircraft type. Zhou et al. [13] predicted aircraft keypoints via convolutions and designed attention mechanism on the keypoints to enhance the features for detection. In this paper, detecting the aircraft landmarks in the wild is more challenging due to the vastly different appearances in variable viewpoints.

Related to the aircraft landmark detection problem, the 2D human landmark detection has achieved rapid progress in recent years [7,9,11,20,22,24]. To alleviate the problems of the occlusion and variable viewpoints in human body, the landmark relationships are studied to guide landmark detection [7,12,15,17], which improves the robustness and accuracy. However, the landmark relationships in the deformable human body mostly lie in the local body parts, and are modelled in an implicit manner. Chen et al. [12] trained a landmark distribution discriminator in an adversarial to make the predicted landmarks distribute naturally like the real ones. Ke et al. [15] connected landmarks in the same body part and designed a structure-aware loss to preserve the structure layout. Tang

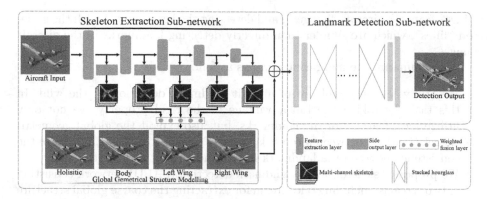

Fig. 2. Overview of the proposed skeleton-aware landmark detection (SALD) method. Our network consists of a skeleton extraction sub-network for modelling the coarse global aircraft structure and a landmark detection sub-network for precisely locating landmarks with the structure guidance. The framework decompose the landmark detection into the two simpler sub-tasks in a progressive coarse-to-fine manner, which eases the learning procedure and improves the detection performance.

et al. [7] classified the landmarks into five groups and jointly learned the shared features for the landmarks without explicit constraints. In this paper, we focus on the landmark detection for the aircraft with the rigid property, in which the landmark relationships are not only lie in the local parts, but also exist in the global geometrical distributions for all the landmarks. This motivates us to explicitly model the global aircraft structure, which serves as the coarse guidance to provide the structure cues and ease the precise local landmark detection task. Consequently, the aircraft landmark detection task is decomposed into the progressive coarse-to-fine learning of two simpler sub-tasks: extracting the coarse global structure from the image, and locating the precise local landmarks with the guidance of structure. As illustrated in Fig. 1, compared with Hourglass [16] which wrongly detects the right stabilizer on the similar right tip (Fig. 1 (b)), the aircraft skeletons serve as the global structure (Fig. 1 (c)), and guide the correct local landmarks localization on the right stabilizer (Fig. 1 (d)).

To this end, we propose a skeleton-aware landmark detection (SALD) network consisting of a structure extraction stream for explicitly modelling the geometrical structure via the hierarchical aircraft skeletons, and a landmark detection stream for locating the landmarks with the guidance of aircraft skeletons, as shown in Fig. 2. Specifically, the hierarchical skeletons have multiple channels including the holistic skeleton channels for all the landmarks, and part skeleton channels for the aircraft parts, such as the wings and aircraft body. The skeletons provide the global relationships among the landmarks in geometrics and semantics. With the guidance of the global understanding for aircraft structure, the precise local landmark localization is performed to achieve the coherency between landmark distributions and the structure. Consequently, the two streams in SALD progressively focus on the sub-task of extracting skeleton "lines" from the aircraft "images", and detecting the key "points" with the skeleton "lines", which are simpler than directly detecting landmarks in the aircraft images.

We summarize the main contributions as follows:

– We study the new problem of aircraft landmark detection in the wild. In this task, by taking the full advantage of the rigid property, we not only utilize local features of the landmarks, but also exploit the global geometrical relationships between aircraft landmarks, which consequently achieve the consistency between the landmark layout and aircraft structure.
– We propose a skeleton-aware landmark detection (SALD) network consisting of two streams, including one stream for extracting the coarse global structure from the image, and one stream for locating the precise local landmarks with the guidance of structure. The framework decomposes the landmark detection task into two simpler sub-tasks in a progressive coarse-to-fine manner, which eases the learning procedure, thus further improves the performance of landmark detection.
– Extensive quantitative and qualitative evaluations on the aircraft datasets show that SALD performs favorably against the state-of-the-art methods, which demonstrates the effectiveness of the skeleton guidance for aircraft landmark detection.

2   Skeleton-Aware Landmark Detection Network

2.1   Global Geometrical Structure

Skeleton Structure. To model the global geometrical structure of the rigid aircraft, we intuitively resort to the aircraft skeleton as the representations which is an important graphics description with intrinsic relationships to the landmark, and possess strong constraints with the landmarks in both geometrics and semantics. For instance, the aircraft tip should distribute on the wing, and the precise location should be near the endpoint of the wing skeletons. To fully exploit the skeletons as the global geometrical structure, we propose the hierarchical multi-channel skeletons to present the structure of both holistic aircraft and the parts, including the including holistic channel, body channel, left wing channel and right wing channel as shown in Fig. 2. Specifically, the holistic channel encodes the geometrical relationships for all the landmarks from a global viewpoint, while the skeletons of aircraft parts in the other channels provide explicit guidances for locating landmarks near the corresponding parts. We obtain the skeleton labels by connecting the head, tail and wing tip landmarks with aircraft center point which is calculated as the average coordinate of the leading and trailing edge flaps. The label generating procedure dose not require additional manual work.

Skeleton Extraction. To extract the aircraft skeletons, we introduce a hierarchical deep-supervised network for the skeleton extraction sub-network which generates high quality skeletons by fully utilizing the multi-scale spatial information in aircraft images. Specifically, the multi-channel skeletons are side outputted at different scales of the network, which are deeply supervised during training by the ground truth skeletons connected by the landmarks, as shown in Fig. 2. Then the multi-scale side outputs are fused together through a weighted fuse layer to generate the final multi-channel skeletons. Denoting X as the given aircraft image, we extract the multi-channel skeletons $\hat{L}$ by the skeleton extraction sub-network G, which is formulated as:

$$\hat{L} = G(X; W, w_G), \tag{1}$$

where w_G, W denote the parameters of the side output layers and feature extraction layers. For each side output of the skeletons $\hat{L}^c$, we impose cross-entropy loss function, which is defined as:

$$
\begin{aligned}
Loss^c_{ske} = &- \sum_{j \in L^c_+} \log \Pr(\hat{L}^c_j = 1 | X; W, w^c_G) \\
&- \alpha_c \sum_{j \in L^c_-} \log \Pr(\hat{L}^c_j = 0 | X; w^c_G),
\end{aligned}
\tag{2}
$$

where the function $\Pr(\cdot)$ is computed by the output of sigmoid function on activation value at pixel j. w^c_G denotes the parameters of c-th side output layer. α_c denotes the balance weights corresponding the ratio of skeleton pixels. The final loss for the skeleton extraction sub-network is defined as:

$$Loss_{ske} = \sum_c^C \gamma_c Loss^c_{ske}, \tag{3}$$

where C is the total number of the side output layers, while γ_c denotes the balance weights. The extracted hierarchical skeletons represent the coarse global aircraft structures are then utilized for precise localization.

2.2   Local Landmark Localization

After obtaining the coarse global aircraft structure represented by the hierarchical skeletons, we perform the precise landmark localization under the explicit guidance of the aircraft geometrics and landmark relationships. Specifically, we feed the concatenation of the aircraft image and the hierarchical skeletons to stacked Hourglass [16], in which up and down sampling processes are repeated with intermediate conjunction and supervision to learn features across all the scales. During training, the skeleton channels indicate the corresponding localization of the aircraft parts. Taking an example, the left wing channel skeleton explicitly represents the structure of the wing. With the guidance of the left wing channel skeleton, the left leading and trailing edge flap should be detected

Table 1. Effectiveness of the global skeleton structure. L and $\hat{L}$ refer to the ground truth and extracted skeletons. Y and $\hat{Y}$ refer to the ground-truth and predicted landmarks. $-$ refers to the average Euler distances. The small deviation in the second and third columns justify the accuracy of the skeleton extraction, while the last two columns show that with the skeleton guidance, the landmarks are more related to the skeleton structures. The detection performances are improved in terms of the PCKh, which demonstrates the effectiveness of the skeleton guidance, and further illustrate the accuracy of the skeleton extraction.

Landmarks	$L-Y$	$\hat{L}-Y$	$\hat{L}-\hat{Y}$ w/o Guidance	$\hat{L}-\hat{Y}$ w/ Guidance
Head	0	1.23	2.42	1.91
Wing tip	0	4.46	11.02	9.74
Leading edge flap	6.39	6.55	8.52	6.72
Trailing edge flap	6.07	6.96	11.36	8.20
PCKh	100	100	86.17	87.57

near the endpoint of the left wing skeleton, while the left tip should be located near the other endpoint, which is possible to shift onto the right wing or the stabilizers due to the similar local features without the global skeleton guidance. Learning both global geometrical structure from the skeletons and local features from the aircraft appearances in the images, the detection sub-network regresses landmark heatmaps $\hat{Y}$ in which the location of highest value is determined as the final prediction. MSE loss is imposed on the heatmaps, which is defined by:

$$Loss_{land} = \sum_{i}^{N} \|\hat{Y}^i - Y^i\|_2, \tag{4}$$

where $\hat{Y}^i$ denotes the heatmap for the i-th landmark. Denoting β as the balance weight, the full objective is given by:

$$Loss = Loss_{ske} + \beta Loss_{land}. \tag{5}$$

2.3   Effectiveness of the Global Skeleton Structure

Accuracy of the Skeleton Extraction. The extracted skeleton should possess the strong relationships with the aircraft landmarks in both geometrics and semantics. Wrong skeletons will do harm to the landmark detection, even though the structure extraction task is coarse compared with the precise localization. To illustrate the accuracy of the skeleton extraction, we calculate the average Euler distances between landmarks and skeletons in the 256×256 aircraft images in the dataset. The small distances indicate the strong geometrical relationships between the skeletons and landmarks. The first three columns in Table 1 show that compared to the ground-truth skeletons which have the strongest relationships with the landmarks, the extracted skeletons by SALD deviate from the

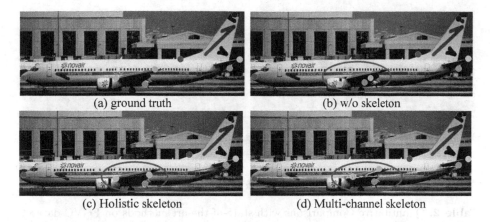

Fig. 3. The superiority of multi-channel skeleton guidance. (a) The landmark ground truth. (b) Without skeleton guidance, the detected left tip shifts onto the wing. (c) The holistic skeleton provides a provides a rough structure information of the aircraft, which corrects the location of the left edge flap landmarks. (d) The multi-channel skeleton models the structure more explicitly, in which the left wing structure is further represented, thus obtaining better performance.

ground-truth in a small extent, but still holds the strong relationships with the ground-truth landmarks in terms of the small distance, which can help the landmark detection sub-network to locate the landmarks with the coarse global understanding.

Effectiveness of the Skeleton Guidance. The last two columns in Table 1 illustrates the effectiveness of skeleton guidance. Compared with the results in which no global geometrical constraint is imposed as shown in the fourth column, our extracted skeleton guides the detector to locate the landmarks near the corresponding part, enforcing the landmark layout to be consistent with the structure. The distances between landmarks and the aircraft structure in the fifth column become smaller when the skeleton constraint is imposed, and consequently improve the accuracy of landmark detection in terms of the quantitative evaluation method PCKh, thus justifying the effectiveness of skeleton guidance and further illustrating the accuracy of the skeleton extraction.

To further show the superiority of the multi-channel skeleton guidance, we perform the comparison between the landmark detection results with no skeleton guidance, with only holistic skeleton guidance, and with multi-channel skeleton guidance in Fig. 3. Without the skeleton guidance, the local features of left wings are not discriminative enough, the landmarks on the left wing shift from the correct location. The holistic skeleton provides a rough structure of the aircraft, which guides the detector to locate the leading and trailing edge flaps at the joints of left wing and aircraft body. The multi-channel skeletons model both the holistic and part structures as more explicit cues to distinguish the left

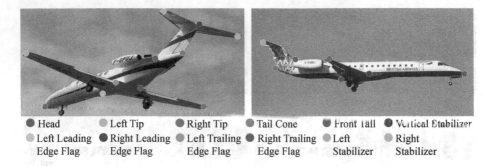

Head   Left Tip   Right Tip   Tail Cone   Front Tail   Vertical Stabilizer

Left Leading   Right Leading   Left Trailing   Right Trailing   Left   Right

Edge Flag   Edge Flag   Edge Flag   Edge Flag   Stabilizer   Stabilizer

Fig. 4. Illustration of the landmark labelling on the ALDW dataset.

Table 2. Quantitative Comparisons with state-of-the-art methods on FGVC dataset. SALD outperforms the competing methods, especially in landmarks on the wings whose structure is explicitly modelled by the multi-channel skeleton.

Methods	Head & tail cone	Leading edge flap	Wing tip	Trailing edge flap	Horizontal stabilizer	Vertical stabilizer	PCKh
Hourglass [16]	96.60	79.55	82.30	72.93	83.13	87.95	86.17
DAN [8]	97.46	80.52	80.82	79.49	83.80	88.22	86.78
PoseAtten [21]	97.27	81.87	77.05	78.54	**86.40**	89.29	87.16
PyraNet [19]	97.15	82.69	77.59	81.14	85.06	88.69	87.17
CU-Net [18]	97.54	80.43	78.29	80.75	84.38	88.28	87.14
SALD	**97.98**	**82.89**	**83.47**	**82.55**	85.74	**89.37**	**87.57**

wing and the body via additional body and left wing channel, and consequently further improving the detection performance on left tip.

2.4 Implementation Detail

SALD is implemented using Tensorflow framework on a RTX 2080Ti GPU. The input images are resized to 256×256 and random flip is applied for augmentation. The skeleton balance weights α_c are 186, 113, 45 and 51 for skeletons of holistic, body, left wing and right wing, which are the average ratio of skeleton pixels in ground truth. γ_c and β are set as 1. We respectively train the two sub-networks for 200 epochs with initial learning rate 0.001, decay rate 0.99 and decay step 5000. Then we fine-tune the two sub-networks together with learning rate 0.0001 for 50 epochs. For the optimizer, the RMSprop is adopted with batch size 6.

3 Experiments

Dataset. Since there exist few datasets for the task, we apply a new dataset for aircraft landmark detection in the wild (ALWD), in which we annotate 7819 (6245 for training and 1574 for testing) aircraft images from the FGVC [26]

GT   Hourglass   SALD

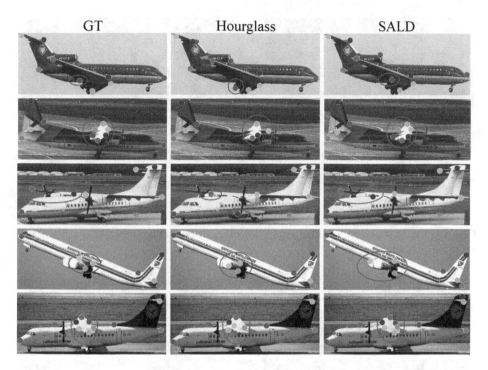

Fig. 5. Visualization of landmark detection results on ALDW dataset. Under the global geometrical skeleton guidance, SALD predicts more accurate landmarks whose layout is consistent with the aircraft structure.

dataset and Google search. For each aircraft, we annotate the location and visibility of 12 aircraft landmarks, whose locations are defined on the joints or endpoints of the head, wings and stabilizers as illustrated in Fig. 4.

Experiment Settings. We select five state-of-the-art human landmark detection methods: Hourglass [16], DAN [8], PoseAtten [21], PyraNet [19] and CU-Net [18] and fine-tune them on ALDW for comparison, in which PCKh [7,21,24] is utilized for quantitative assessment. The codes of our methods will be released in the homepage of the author.

Evaluation on ALDW Dataset. The results in Table 2 show that SALD outperforms the competing methods. Especially, SALD achieves significantly better performance in landmarks on the wings whose structures are explicitly modelled by the multi-channel skeletons, demonstrating the effectiveness of the skeleton guidance. The qualitative comparison is shown in Fig. 5. The feature extracted by Hourglass is not discriminative enough due to similarity of the aircraft parts, resulting in the landmark shifts. SALD generates structure-consistent results which distribute near the aircraft skeletons in a reasonable layout.

Fig. 6. Visualization results of landmark detection in real scene. The SALD still obtains accurate predictions.

Fig. 7. Effectiveness of the skeleton guidance. The skeletons provide geometrical constraints for the consistency between landmark layout and aircraft structure.

Evaluation in Real Scene. We also test SALD on the aircraft images collected from Google. The qualitative results in Fig. 6 show that we still obtain accurate predictions. By recognizing the main structure of the aircraft in the real scene as the guidance for the precise landmark detection, SALD achieves the coherency between landmarks and structure, thus performing well in the real scene.

Ablation Study. We perform ablation study on the effectiveness of the multichannel skeleton guidance quantitatively and qualitatively. Figure 7 shows that with the geometrical constraints of the skeletons, the detector achieves the consistency with aircraft structure, and consequently obtains significant improvement of detection accuracy. Table 3 further illustrates the effect of each channel. Compared with the first row, the other rows show the improvements brought by each skeleton channel. Especially, compared with the second row, the fourth and fifth rows show the wing channel brings more improvement in the landmarks

Table 3. Ablation study on the effectiveness of different skeleton channel. * refers to guiding detection with ground truth skeletons.

Holistic	Body	Left Wing	Right wing	Head	Wing	Stabilizer	PCKh
				97.95	80.23	84.32	86.17
✓				97.94	82.25	84.44	86.42
✓	✓			97.95	82.38	84.43	86.63
✓		✓		97.97	82.87	84.43	86.61
✓			✓	97.97	82.53	85.46	86.72
✓	✓	✓	✓	**97.98**	**83.03**	**86.13**	**87.57**
✓*	✓*	✓*	✓*	98.12	85.37	88.77	88.84

on the wing, demonstrating the specific contribution of the wing channel skeleton in guiding their corresponding landmarks. The landmark detection with all skeleton channel guidance achieves the best performance. In the last row, the performance of landmark detection is the best with the guidance of ground truth skeleton, which further demonstrates the effectiveness of the skeleton guidance.

4   Conclusions

In this paper, we have studied the new problem of aircraft landmark detection in the wild by utilizing the rigid property to progressively learn global structure extraction and local landmark localization in a coarse-to-fine manner. Specifically, we propose a skeleton-aware aircraft landmark (SALD) method consisting of two streams, including one stream for modelling the coarse aircraft structure by extracting the hierarchical skeletons, and one stream for detecting the precise landmark localization with the guidance of the global skeleton structures. Consequently, the landmark detection is decomposed into two simpler sub-tasks. By the global guidance for local landmark detection, SALD achieves the consistency between landmark layout and aircraft structure, which improves the accuracy and the robustness of aircraft landmark detection. Extensive experiments show that SALD outperforms state-of-the-art landmark detection methods.

Acknowledgement. This work was supported by This work was supported by National Natural Science Foundation of China under Grant No. 61971460, China Postdoctoral Science Foundation under Grant 2020M672748, National Postdoctoral Program for Innovative Talents BX20200173, the Open Research Fund of the National Key Laboratory of Science and Technology on Multispectral Information Processing under Grants 6142113200304 and Industrial Technology Development Program grant JCKY2018204B068.

References

1. Fu, K., Dai, W., Zhang, Y., Wang, Z., Yan, M., Sun, X.: MultiCAM: multiple class activation mapping for aircraft recognition in remote sensing images. Remote Sens. **11**(5), 544–553 (2019)
2. Zhao, A., et al.: Aircraft recognition based on landmark detection in remote sensing images, IEEE Geosci. Remote Sens. Lett. **14**(8), 1413–1417 (2017)
3. Zuo, J., Xu, G., Fu, K., Sun, X., Sun, H.: Aircraft type recognition based on segmentation with deep convolutional neural networks. IEEE Geosci. Remote Sens. Lett. **15**(2), 282–286 (2018)
4. Yang, Y., Zhang, Y., Bi, F., Shi, H., Xie, Y.: M-FCN: effective fully convolutional network-based airplane detection framework. IEEE Geosci. Remote Sens. Lett. **14**(8), 1293–1297 (2017)
5. Qiu, S., Wen, G., Deng, Z., Fan, Y., Hui, B.: Automatic and Fast PCM generation for occluded object detection in high-resolution remote sensing images. IEEE Geosci. Remote Sens. Lett. **14**(10), 1730–1734 (2017)
6. Zou, X., Zhong, S., Yan, L., Zhao, X., Zhou, J., Wu, Y.: Learning robust facial landmark detection via hierarchical structured ensemble. In: ICCV, pp. 141–150 (2019)
7. Tang, W., Wu, Y.: Does learning specific features for related parts help human pose estimation? In: CVPR, pp. 1107–1116 (2019)
8. Kowalski, M., Naruniec, J., Trzcinski, T.: Deep alignment network: a convolutional neural network for robust face alignment. In: CVPR Workshop, pp. 88–97 (2017)
9. Qiu, Z., Qiu, K., Fu, J., Fu, D.: Learning recurrent structure-guided attention network for multi-person pose estimation. In: ICME, pp. 418–423 (2019)
10. Zhou, L., Chen, Y., Wang, J., Tang, M., Lu, H.: Bi-directional message passing based ScaNet for human pose estimation. In: ICME, pp. 1048–1053 (2019)
11. Zhu, M., Shi, D.: Deep geometry embedding networks for robust facial landmark detection. In: ICME, pp. 1222–1227 (2019)
12. Chen, Y., Shen, C., Wei, X., Liu, L., Yang, J.: Adversarial PoseNet: a structure-aware convolutional network for human pose estimation. In: ICCV, pp. 1221–1230 (2017)
13. Zhou, M., Zou, Z., Shi, Z., Zeng, W., Gui, J.: Local attention networks for occluded airplane detection in remote sensing images. IEEE Geosci. Remote Sens. Lett. **3**(17), 381–385 (2020)
14. Liu, Z., Yan, S., Luo, P., Wang, X., Tang, X.: Fashion landmark detection in the wild. In: Leibe, B., Matas, J., Sebe, N., Welling, M. (eds.) ECCV 2016. LNCS, vol. 9906, pp. 229–245. Springer, Cham (2016). https://doi.org/10.1007/978-3-319-46475-6_15
15. Ke, L., Chang, M.-C., Qi, H., Lyu, S.: Multi-scale structure-aware network for human pose estimation. In: Ferrari, V., Hebert, M., Sminchisescu, C., Weiss, Y. (eds.) ECCV 2018. LNCS, vol. 11206, pp. 731–746. Springer, Cham (2018). https://doi.org/10.1007/978-3-030-01216-8_44
16. Newell, A., Yang, K., Deng, J.: Stacked hourglass networks for human pose estimation. In: Leibe, B., Matas, J., Sebe, N., Welling, M. (eds.) ECCV 2016. LNCS, vol. 9912, pp. 483–499. Springer, Cham (2016). https://doi.org/10.1007/978-3-319-46484-8_29
17. Tang, W., Yu, P., Wu, Y.: Deeply learned compositional models for human pose estimation. In: Ferrari, V., Hebert, M., Sminchisescu, C., Weiss, Y. (eds.) ECCV 2018. LNCS, vol. 11207, pp. 197–214. Springer, Cham (2018). https://doi.org/10.1007/978-3-030-01219-9_12

18. Tang, Z., Peng, X., Geng, S., Wu, L., Zhang, S., Metaxas, D.: Quantized densely connected u-nets for efficient landmark localization. In: Ferrari, V., Hebert, M., Sminchisescu, C., Weiss, Y. (eds.) ECCV 2018. LNCS, vol. 11207, pp. 348–364. Springer, Cham (2018). https://doi.org/10.1007/978-3-030-01219-9_21
19. Yang, W., Li, S., Ouyang, W., Li, H., Wang, X.: Learning feature pyramids for human pose estimation. In: ICCV, pp. 1281–1290 (2017)
20. Chandran, P., Bradley, D., Gross, M., Beeler, T.: Attention-driven cropping for very high resolution facial landmark detection. In: ICCV, pp. 5861–5870 (2020)
21. Chu, X., Yang, W., Ouyang, W., Ma, C., Yuille, A., Wang, X.: Multi-context attention for human pose estimation. In: CVPR, pp. 1831–1840 (2017)
22. Zhang F., Zhu, X., Dai H., Ye, M., Ce, Z.: Multi-context attention for human pose estimation. In: CVPR, pp. 7093–7102 (2020)
23. Xie, S., Tu, Z.: Holistically-nested edge detection. In: CVPR, pp. 1395–1403 (2015)
24. Ke, W., Chen, J., Jiao, J., Zhao, G., Ye, Q.: SRN: side-output residual network for object symmetry detection in the wild. In: CVPR, pp. 1068–1076 (2017)
25. Wu, Y., Hassner, T., Kim, K., Medioni, G., Natarajan, P.: Facial landmark detection with tweaked convolutional neural networks. IEEE Trans. Pattern Anal. Mach. Intell. **40**(12), 3067–3074 (2017)
26. Maji, S., Rahtu, E., Kannala, J., Blaschko, M., Vedaldi, A.: Fine-grained visual classification of aircraft. arXiv preprint arXiv:1306.5151 (2013)

Efficient Spectral Pyramid and Spectral-Spatial Feature Interactive Hyperspectral Image Classification

Jun Wu[1,2], Huimin Wang[1], Xingliang Zhu[1], Meng Wang[1], Jian Yang[1], Wenting Luo[1], and Lei Qu[1(✉)]

[1] School of Electronics and Information Engineering, AnHui University,
111 Jiulong Road, Hefei 230601, China
qulei@ahu.edu.cn
[2] The 38th Research Institute of China Electronics Technology Group Corporation,
199 Xiangzhang Avenue, Hefei 230601, China

Abstract. Deep-learning frameworks have been widely used in the hyperspectral image (HSI) classification and have demonstrated promising performance. In this paper, we propose a novel HSI classification method with a deeper network and fewer parameters. Two novel modules named the efficient spectral pyramid (ESP), and improved spectral-spatial feature interactive (SSI) are designed to improving the SS3FCN, which is proposed in our previous work. Specifically, the ESP module composed of the dilated convolution is utilised to increase the spectral receptive field and make up the lost spectral information. In addition, the improved SSI module is leveraged to reduce trainable parameters and strengthen spectral features. Finally, the advancement of the proposed method is experimentally proved on three representative HSI data sets, and the effectiveness of these two novel modules are verified with ablation experiments.

Keywords: Hyperspectral image classification · Spectral-spatial exploration · Dilated convolution · Residual connection

1 Introduction

Hyperspectral imaging technology, which captures rich information in both spectral and spatial dimensions, has advantages for the recognition of different substances in the observed scene. Recently, the success of hyperspectral image (HSI)

J. Wu and H. Wang—Contributed equally to this work.

This research was funded by the National Natural Science Foundation of China (61871411 and 61901003), the Anhui Provincial Natural Science Foundation (1908085QF255), and The University Synergy Innovation Program of Anhui Province (GXXT-2019-008). And the authors acknowledge the High-performance Computing Platform of Anhui University for providing computing resources.

© Springer Nature Switzerland AG 2021
Y. Peng et al. (Eds.): ICIG 2021, LNCS 12888, pp. 198–209, 2021.
https://doi.org/10.1007/978-3-030-87355-4_17

classification has made this technique widely applied in various fields, such as scene recognition [1], environmental surveillance [2,3], astronomy [4], and chemical imaging [5]. Although there are many significant breakthroughs in the past few years, HSI classification is still a challenging task because of the characteristic spectral-spatial relation and the limited amount of labelled pixels.

HSI is characterised by a large amount of high spectral dimension. However, when the training data is insufficient, redundancy spectral bands can produce the Hughes phenomenon, which seriously affects the classification results of HSI [6]. In response to this problem, many traditional dimensionality reduction methods are introduced to extract primary spectral features and reduce redundancy bands, such as the principal component analysis (PCA) [7], linear discriminant analysis (LDA) [8] and independent component analysis (ICA) [9]. On the other hand, the specific physical properties of the spectrum, which play the most major role in HSI classification, could be destroyed when using a simple and crude manner to reduce the spectral bands [10]. The destruction and missing of the spectral information directly lead to the decline of classification accuracy.

With the maturity of deep-learning theory and methods, the convolutional neural networks (CNN) have become a mainstream trend in image processing and have achieved great performance in HSI classification [11–13]. In the early stage, some researchers utilised 1D-CNN [11] to analyse and study unique spectral features for classification. Then, the spatial information was found to be complementary to spectral-based methods, and hence, 2D-CNN [12] was often designed as a branch for 1D-CNN to improve classification accuracy. Soon after, researchers found that the feature extracted from two independently branches [14] ignored the correlation between the spectral and spatial features. Therefore, the 3D-CNN was proposed to jointly extract spectral-spatial features and had achieved a breakthrough in the HSI classification [15].

Recently, most 3D-CNN-based methods are found to be optimistic in their framework design [16]. Nevertheless, the 3D convolution kernel may significantly increase the number of trainable parameters, which could easily lead to the overfitting of accuracy and the wasting of computation time [17]. On the other side, the limited number of training samples in HSI also make it difficult to train a deeper 3D network for better classification accuracy [18]. To address above concerns, we propose an Effective Spatial extraction based Interacted Network (ESI-Net) by considering the interaction between spectral and spatial features. The main contributions of this paper can be concluded in three aspects:

1) We propose a novel interaction-based Fully Convolutional Networks (FCN) which allows the information interaction between the spectral branch and the spectral-spatial branch network in the transmission of feature maps.
2) An Efficient Spectral Pyramid (ESP) module is applied to reduce the spectral information loss and retain the global and local spectrum characteristics under different receptive fields in the process of dimensionality reduction.
3) An improved Spectral-Spatial feature Interaction (SSI) module is conducted to reduce the number of trainable parameters and strengthen the extraction of spectral features. Specifically, we replace the traditional 3D convolution in

SSI with a novel Spectral-spatial Separated Convolution (SSC) block, which divides an original 3D kernel into a 1D spectral extraction kernel followed by a 2D spatial extraction kernel.

2   Related Works

In this section, we briefly introduce some related works which inspired our ESI-Net. As we summarised before, CNN-based frameworks have shown their promising performance in HSI classification [19,20], and the crucial issue is how to make full use of the spectral and spatial information of HSI.

To solve this issue, some two-branch networks via the fusion of one 1D-CNN branch and one 2D-CNN branch were proposed to aggregate spectral and spatial features at the end of each branch [14]. Moreover in our previous work [21], we introduced a novel two-branch network to exploit the spectral-spatial information by combining 1D- and 3D-CNN. These methods generally ignored the correlation and excitation between two separate branches. In ESI-Net, we try to make consideration of the information interaction between different branches of the multi-branch network.

Another solution is to jointly extract deep spectral-spatial information with 3D-CNN [15]. In [20], a 3D-CNN was proposed to choose effective channels and reduce the redundancy in spectral bands. Although frameworks via 3D-CNN have achieved significant performance improvements, it makes the learnable parameters increase significantly, which limiting the depth and feature representation capabilities of the network [22]. Inspired by recent 3D separable convolution [23], we introduce the SSC module to reduce the calculation and take account of the characteristics of HSI.

In image semantic segmentation and target detection, dilated convolution was widely used to reduce spatial resolution and information loss after reducing the image resolution [24]. In [25], an spatial pyramid convolution module was introduced to retain detailed spatial information in the segmentation task. In [26], the pyramid dilated convolution is integrated into the bottom of ResNet to increase the receptive field of the original network. Our proposed ESP module is partly inspired by these works but more suitable for the dimensionality reduction of spectrum in HSI classification.

3   Proposed Network

The architecture of the proposed ESI-Net is shown in Fig. 1. There are three key components: The backbone ESI-Net, The ESP module, and The improved SSI module.

3.1   Effective Spatial Extraction Based Interacted Network

In our previous work SS3FCN [21], the convolution operation strides are utilised to reduce the spectral redundancy, which could lose useful spectral information.

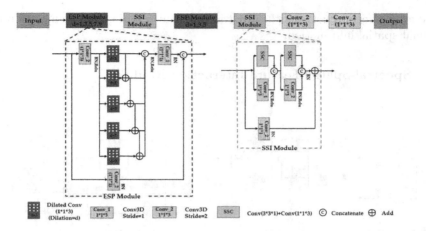

Fig. 1. Overview of our ESI-Net. ESP represents the efficient spectral pyramid module; SSI represents the spectral-spatial feature interaction module; SSC represents the spectral-spatial separation convolution.

Therefore, in the ESI-Net, we propose an ESP module to reduce the redundant spectral bands while retaining the global and local spectral characteristics under different receiving fields. Additionally, the SS3FCN does not fully consider the information interaction between the spectral and spatial branches in the SSI module. Therefore, we improve the SSI module by replacing the 3D-CNN block with a novel SSC block which will be detailed in Sect. 3.3. With the SSC block, the cross-correlation between the two branches could be established to enhance the representation ability of features, and the amount of trainable parameters will be reduced accordingly.

3.2   Efficient Spectral Pyramid Module

Recently, the HSI classification method based on deep learning usually adopts convolution with strides and pooling operations to reduce redundant spectral bands. Although the Hughes phenomenon is effectively avoided, it could induce the destruction and loss of spectral information, which will affect the classification accuracy [10].

Inspired by [25], we introduce an efficient spectral pyramid module to preserve global and local spectral features under different receiving fields. The ESP module utilises a pyramid structure to extract multi-scale spectral features and avoid the destruction of spectral characteristics. As shown in Fig. 1, the original image block is imported into the 1D convolution with strides to remove redundant spectral information. Then the extracted features are sent to the $1 \times 1 \times 3$ convolution with different dilation rates to preserve the global and local features of the spectrum. Finally, the $1 \times 1 \times 1$ convolution is added after the concatenate layer to reduce the number of feature maps output. Moreover, we also add a residual connection between the input and output feature maps to maintain the original spatial information.

3.3 Spectral-Spatial Feature Interaction Module

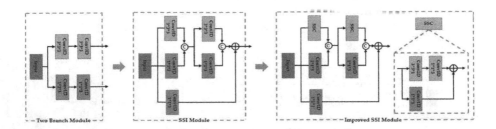

Fig. 2. Comparison of Two branch module, SSI module and Improved SSI module.

Recent research has demonstrated that two-branches architecture is beneficial for the HSI classification. However, researchers pay their attention to the design of each branch for a better spectral (or spatial) feature expression and ignore the interaction between two branches. For example, in Fig. 2, the classical two branch module and our previously proposed SSI module extract the spectral and spatial features separately in each branch. The 1D and 3D convolution extract spectral and spectral-spatial information, respectively. In contrast, in the improved SSI module, we replace the 3D convolution with an SSC block which is composed of a separable convolution [23] and a residual connection.

Take advantage of this new structure, the spatial information is added to the spectral feature with the residual connection. Moreover, the original $3 \times 3 \times 3$ convolution kernel is replaced by a combination of $3 \times 3 \times 1$ and $1 \times 1 \times 3$ convolution. Therefore, the number of trainable parameters could be effectively reduced, and the training data limitation could be accordingly mitigated [27]. In addition, the additional ReLU between 2D and 1D convolution has doubled the number of nonlinearities and increase the complexity of the representable function. Meanwhile, the separate extraction of spectral and spatial features is more consistent with the characteristics of HSI.

4   Experiment Setup

In this section, in order to verify the effectiveness of our method, three widely used hyperspectral datasets are utilised in the experimental setup. We leverage the same data partitioning strategy as [21] to avoiding the information leakage problem, and each fold is repeated three times to reduce the influence of randomness.

4.1   Experimental Datasets

Salinas Valley: The Salinas data is taken by the Airborne Visual Infrared Imaging Spectrometer (AVIRIS) imaging spectrometer, an image of the Salinas Valley in California, USA. The data encompasses 512×217 pixels with a spatial resolution of 3.7 miles per pixel. Each HSI has 204 spectral bands and 16 land cover classes.

Pavia University: The Pavia University data set is acquired by ROSIS sensors. The data encompasses 610×340 pixels, and the spatial resolution is 1.3 miles per pixel. Due to the influence of noise, only 103 bands are used for classification experiments, including 9 types of ground objects.

Indian Paines: The Indian Pines dataset is captured by the Airborne Visual Infrared Imaging Spectrometer (AVIRIS) in the Pine Agricultural Area of the United States. The data resolution consists of 145×145 pixels and the spatial resolution of 20 miles per pixel. Each HSI includes 220 spectral bands and 16 types of ground features.

4.2   Competing Methods

We compare the ESI-Net method with other state-of-the-art methods based on no information leakage, such as 3DCNN [28], VHIS [16], DA-VHIS [29], SS3FCN [21]. The 3DCNN network is based on 3D CNN. Both VHIS and DA-VHIS utilise 1-D networks. SS3FCN proposed two-branch network.

4.3   Parameter Setting

In order to objectively evaluate the experimental results, three indicators are utilised to evaluate the performance of each competing method, including the overall accuracy (OA), average accuracy (AA) and Kappa coefficient, a larger value indicates a better classification performance. The deep learning framework is Keras 2.3.1, and the programming language is Python 3.6. The optimisation algorithm is Adam ($beta\_1 = 0.9$, $beta\_2 = 0.999$, epsilon $= 1 \times 10^{-8}$), the initial learning rate is set to 0.01, and the batch size is set to 64.

5   Classification Result

Table 1 shows the experimental results on the Salinas Valley dataset. From Table 1, we can draw the following conclusions. The OA & AA achieved by our proposed ESI-Net is significantly better than the 3DCNN [28], VHIS [16], DA-VHIS [29] and SS3FCN [21]. The OA & AA by ESI-Net increase from 64.20% & 64.70% to 83.31% & 89.28%, compared with that by VHIS methods. The ESI-Net also improves OA & AA & Kappa by 5.79%, 10.04%, 0.082% compared with DA-VHIS. In addition, compared with SS3FCN, the ESI-Net achieves 1.99% & 3.15% better performance than SS3FCN in terms of OA and AA.

Table 2 demonstrates the experimental results on the Pavia University dataset. From Table 2 we can find that, compared to VHIS, SS3FCN, and DA-VHIS, the OA and AA obtained by our proposed ESI-Net are significantly

Table 1. Classification results for the Salinas Valley dataset (%).

Class	Comparing method				
	3DCNN	VHIS	DA-VHIS	SS3FCN	ESI-Net
C1	**96.49**	85.91	97.36	92.36	96.05 ± 4.66
C2	75.15	73.88	94.71	92.58	**98.01 ± 3.96**
C3	30.90	33.72	49.95	66.35	**85.55 ± 18.35**
C4	61.61	65.92	79.62	98.13	**98.55 ± 0.95**
C5	52	46.42	64.3	95.63	**96.51 ± 2.13**
C6	79.21	79.63	79.89	99.30	**99.56 ± 0.35**
C7	76.81	73.59	79.62	**99.43**	99.35 ± 0.34
C8	**74.84**	72.16	74.54	69.27	69.66 ± 24.71
C9	78.14	71.87	96.10	**99.67**	99.58 ± 0.87
C10	85.69	73.11	**87.28**	84.07	79.33 ± 15.24
C11	71.56	72.51	73.08	85.31	**91.34 ± 14.80**
C12	76.49	71.06	**98.25**	97.98	97.97 ± 3.93
C13	80.86	75.80	97.67	**98.45**	97.86 ± 3.02
C14	62.15	72.04	88.07	87.32	**92.38 ± 5.05**
C15	61.8	45.03	**62.92**	52.31	54.50 ± 28.05
C16	33	22.54	45.39	59.97	**72.32 ± 31.02**
OA	69.72	64.20	77.52	81.32	**83.31 ± 3.15**
AA	69.09	64.70	79.24	86.13	**89.28 ± 2.80**
Kappa	/	/	0.749	/	**0.813 ± 0.03**

improved. The ESI-Net improves OA & AA by 13.15% & 20.59% compared with 3DCNN. The OA & AA by ESI-Net increase from 73.26% & 62.08% to 83.22% & 80.72%, compared with that by VHIS methods. The ESI-Net also improves OA & AA by 3.33% & 4.12% & compared with SS3FCN.

Table 2. Classification results for the Pavia University dataset (%).

Class	Comparing method				
	3DCNN	VHIS	DA-VHIS	SS3FCN	ESI-Net
C1	90.66	93.40	93.42	**97.48**	96.37 ± 0.87
C2	81.85	86.20	86.52	90.86	**91.51 ± 2.04**
C3	41.92	47.58	46.88	58.75	**59.47 ± 6.45**
C4	93.02	86.89	92.21	84.81	**93.14 ± 1.25**
C5	59.79	59.81	59.74	**94.82**	93.06 ± 4.92
C6	25.20	27.14	27.68	23.59	**35.63 ± 6.76**
C7	0.00	0.00	0.00	61.61	**77.39 ± 5.17**
C8	70.18	7.84	78.32	88.84	**90.26 ± 1.95**
C9	79.03	79.27	79.6	88.68	**92.14 ± 2.83**
OA	70.07	73.26	73.84	79.89	**83.22 ± 3.28**
AA	60.18	62.08	62.71	76.60	**80.72 ± 3.76**
Kappa	/	/	0.631	/	**0.768 ± 0.04**

In Table 3, we show the classification results of all competing methods on the Indian Pines dataset. The Indian Pines dataset is affected by the serious imbalance of the pixel number in each class, resulting in lower classification accuracy than other datasets. It can be seen that our proposed method obtains the best classification performance compared with other methods. The OA & AA by ESI-Net increase from 71.47% & 62.08% to 72.41% & 60.65%, compared with that by SS3FCN.

The overall classification results from three datasets have proved that our proposed ESI-Net is effective and advanced for the HSI classification task.

Table 3. Classification results for the Indian Pines dataset (%).

Class	Comparing method				
	3DCNN	VHIS	DA-VHIS	SS3FCN	ESI-Net
C1	5.00	17.68	15.89	**40.40**	31.30 ± 24.91
C2	33.70	56.89	70.41	**77.89**	75.94 ± 5.62
C3	28.30	51.55	61.44	60.74	**62.23 ± 10.81**
C4	17.88	36.27	**42.28**	11.80	23.79 ± 14.63
C5	51.32	69.02	**73.02**	67.50	72.20 ± 6.99
C6	60.18	92.35	92.13	91.95	**93.09 ± 1.69**
C7	0.00	0.00	0.00	**20.14**	0.74 ± 1.74
C8	65.99	86.95	86.44	81.71	**92.77 ± 7.21**
C9	1.67	19.55	21.28	31.67	**61.91 ± 45.11**
C10	53.06	60.05	67.47	**78.15**	72.59 ± 8.24
C11	54.27	**74.05**	65.24	69.32	67.07 ± 7.88
C12	23.20	43.71	**49.56**	40.81	45.92 ± 9.90
C13	65.87	94.15	96.01	93.77	**97.24 ± 2.16**
C14	77.01	91.18	92.68	91.77	**97.43 ± 2.46**
C15	37.95	43.39	**52.79**	37.93	35.09 ± 7.03
C16	37.94	45.04	44.78	75.19	**75.24 ± 14.73**
OA	48.89	67.11	69.49	71.47	**72.41 ± 2.31**
AA	38.33	55.11	58.15	60.65	62.94 ± 3.04
Kappa	/	/	0.65	/	68.39 ± 2.68

6   Ablation Analysis

In order to further verify the effectiveness of each proposed module, we also conducted ablation experiments on three databases.

6.1   Impact of the ESP Module

To evaluate the effectiveness of the ESP module, we constructed another ESI′ method. It has the same network stages, parameter settings and network configuration as the ESI-Net but removing the ESP module. The results on three datasets are shown in Fig. 3. We multiply the Kappa value by a factor of 100 to obtain a uniform scale denoted as K×100. It can be seen from Fig. 3 that after the ESP module is removed, the indicators of ESI-Net on the three datasets have decreased to varying degrees. This demonstrates that the ESP Module has a greater impact on classification accuracy.

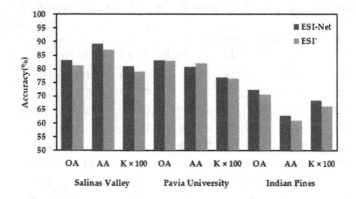

Fig. 3. Impact of the ESP module.

6.2   Impact of the Improved SSI Module

In order to reflect the effectiveness of the improved SSI module, we constructed the ESI″ method, which replaces the SSC block with $3 \times 3 \times 3$ convolution. At the same time, we compare the SS3FCN method in Table 4. From Table 4, we can have two observations. Firstly, the ESI-Net obtains better indicators than the ESI″, which demonstrate the effectiveness of the improved SSI module. Secondly, the difference between the ESI″ and SS3FCN is that the ESI″ take advantage of the ESP module, and thus, the indicators of ESI″ are better than the SS3FCN. This observation reflects the effectiveness of the proposed ESP module on the other aspect.

In addition, we also verified the advantages of the improved SSI module in computational complexity. The FLOPs indicator in Table 4 represents the total amount of network trainable parameters. The ESI-Net has the least number of parameters on the Salinas Valley and Pavia University datasets. This experimental result proves that our method could effectively reduce the amount of algorithm parameters.

Table 4. The impact of the improved SSI module on OA & AA & Kappa (%) & FLOPS (MB).

Method	Salinas valley				Pavia university				Indian pines			
	OA	AA	Kappa	FLOPs	OA	AA	Kappa	FLOPs	OA	AA	Kappa	FLOPs
ESI-Net	**83.31**	**89.28**	**0.813**	9.3	**83.22**	**80.72**	**0.768**	**3.2**	**72.41**	**62.94**	**0.684**	9.3
ESI''	83.15	89.07	0.811	15.2	82.78	80.46	0.762	5.3	71.66	61.49	0.675	15.2
SS3FCN	81.32	86.13	/	15.7	79.89	76.6	/	15.7	71.47	60.65	/	**9.1**

7 Conclusions

In order to improve our previous work and achieving more accurate classification results, we designed two novel modules to solve two corresponding issues in our previously proposed HSI classification method. Specifically, the ESP module was proposed to solve the problem of spectral information distortion, and the improved SSI module is designed to leverage the interaction information between the spectral and spatial branches, as well as reduce the number of trainable parameters. Through a series of experiments, we had verified the effectiveness of these two modules. In future work, We will jointly consider the issue of information leakage and spectrum information loss to obtain better classification accuracy.

References

1. Xiaoqiang, L., Li, X., Mou, L.: Semi-supervised multitask learning for scene recognition. IEEE Trans. Cybern. **45**(9), 1967–1976 (2014)
2. Plaza, A., et al.: Recent advances in techniques for hyperspectral image processing. Remote Sens. Environ. **113**, S110–S122 (2009)
3. Sankey, T., Donager, J., McVay, J., Sankey, J.B.: UAV lidar and hyperspectral fusion for forest monitoring in the southwestern USA. Remote Sens. Environ. **195**, 30–43 (2017)
4. Keith Hege, E., O'Connell, D., Johnson, W., Basty, S., Dereniak, E.L.: Hyperspectral imaging for astronomy and space surveillance. In: Imaging Spectrometry IX, vol. 5159, pp. 380–391. International Society for Optics and Photonics (2004)
5. Gowen, A.A., O'Donnell, C.P., Cullen, P.J., Downey, G., Frias, J.M.: Hyperspectral imaging-an emerging process analytical tool for food quality and safety control. Trends Food Sci. Technol. **18**(12), 590–598 (2007)
6. Hughes, G.: On the mean accuracy of statistical pattern recognizers. IEEE Trans. Inf. Theory **14**(1), 55–63 (1968)
7. Licciardi, G., Marpu, P.R., Chanussot, J., Benediktsson, J.A.: Linear versus non-linear PCA for the classification of hyperspectral data based on the extended morphological profiles. IEEE Geosci. Remote Sens. Lett. **9**(3), 447–451 (2011)
8. Bandos, T.V., Bruzzone, L., Camps-Valls, G.: Classification of hyperspectral images with regularized linear discriminant analysis. IEEE Trans. Geosci. Remote Sens. **47**(3), 862–873 (2009)
9. Villa, A., Benediktsson, J.A., Chanussot, J., Jutten, C.: Hyperspectral image classification with independent component discriminant analysis. IEEE Trans. Geosci. Remote Sensi. **49**(12), 4865–4876 (2011)

10. Rasti, B., et al.: Feature extraction for hyperspectral imagery: the evolution from shallow to deep: overview and toolbox. IEEE Geosci. Remote Sens. Mag. **8**(4), 60–88 (2020)
11. Li, W., Guodong, W., Zhang, F., Qian, D.: Hyperspectral image classification using deep pixel-pair features. IEEE Trans. Geosci. Remote Sens. **55**(2), 844–853 (2016)
12. Liu, B., Xuchu, Yu., Zhang, P., Tan, X., Anzhu, Yu., Xue, Z.: A semi-supervised convolutional neural network for hyperspectral image classification. Remote Sens. Lett. **8**(9), 839–848 (2017)
13. Yang, X., Ye, Y., Li, X., Lau, R.Y.K., Zhang, X., Huang, X.: Hyperspectral image classification with deep learning models. IEEE Trans. Geosci. Remote Sens. **56**(9), 5408–5423 (2018)
14. Ma, W., Yang, Q., Yue, W., Zhao, W., Zhang, X.: Double-branch multi-attention mechanism network for hyperspectral image classification. Remote Sens. **11**(11), 1307 (2019)
15. Pan, B., Xia, X., Shi, Z., Zhang, N., Luo, H., Lan, X.: DSSNET: a simple dilated semantic segmentation network for hyperspectral imagery classification. IEEE Geosci. Remote Sens. Lett. **17**(11), 1968–1972 (2020)
16. Nalepa, J., Myller, M., Kawulok, M.: Validating hyperspectral image segmentation. IEEE Geosci. Remote Sens. Lett. **16**(8), 1264–1268 (2019)
17. Dang, L., Pang, P., Lee, J.: Depth-wise separable convolution neural network with residual connection for hyperspectral image classification. Remote Sens. **12**(20), 3408 (2020)
18. Liu, Y., Gao, L., Xiao, C., Ying, Q., Zheng, K., Marinoni, A.: Hyperspectral image classification based on a shuffled group convolutional neural network with transfer learning. Remote Sens. **12**(11), 1780 (2020)
19. Lee, H., Kwon, H.: Going deeper with contextual CNN for hyperspectral image classification. IEEE Trans. Image Process. **26**(10), 4843–4855 (2017)
20. Wang, C., Ma, N., Ming, Y., Wang, Q., Xia, J.: Classification of hyperspectral imagery with a 3D convolutional neural network and JM distance. Adv. Space Res. **64**(4), 886–899 (2019)
21. Zou, L., Zhu, X., Changfeng, W., Liu, Y., Lei, Q.: Spectral-spatial exploration for hyperspectral image classification via the fusion of fully convolutional networks. IEEE J. Sel. Top. Appl. Earth Obser. Remote Sens. **13**, 659–674 (2020)
22. Xue, Y., Zeng, D., Chen, F., Wang, Y., Zhang, Z.: A new dataset and deep residual spectral spatial network for hyperspectral image classification. Symmetry **12**(4), 561 (2020)
23. Tran, D., Wang, H., Torresani, L., Ray, J., LeCun, Y., Paluri, M.: A closer look at spatiotemporal convolutions for action recognition. In Proceedings of the IEEE Conference on Computer Vision and Pattern Recognition, pp. 6450–6459 (2018)
24. Wang, P., et al.: Understanding convolution for semantic segmentation. In: 2018 IEEE winter conference on applications of computer vision (WACV), pp. 1451–1460. IEEE (2018)
25. Mehta, S., Rastegari, M., Caspi, A., Shapiro, L., Hajishirzi, H.: ESPNet: efficient spatial pyramid of dilated convolutions for semantic segmentation. In: Ferrari, V., Hebert, M., Sminchisescu, C., Weiss, Y. (eds.) ECCV 2018. LNCS, vol. 11214, pp. 561–580. Springer, Cham (2018). https://doi.org/10.1007/978-3-030-01249-6_34
26. Zhenyu, L., et al.: The classification of gliomas based on a pyramid dilated convolution ResNet model. Pattern Recogn. Lett. **133**, 173–179 (2020)
27. Pan, B., Shi, Z., Xia, X.: MugNet: deep learning for hyperspectral image classification using limited samples. ISPRS J. Photogramm. Remote Sens. **145**, 108–119 (2018)

28. Gao, Q., Lim, S., Jia, X.: Hyperspectral image classification using convolutional neural networks and multiple feature learning. Remote Sens. **10**(2), 299 (2018)
29. Nalepa, J., Myller, M., Kawulok, M.: Training-and test-time data augmentation for hyperspectral image segmentation. IEEE Geosci. Remote Sens. Lett. **17**(2), 292–296 (2019)

Semi-supervised Cloud Edge Collaborative Power Transmission Line Insulator Anomaly Detection Framework

Yanqing Yang[1], Jianxu Mao[1], Hui Zhang[1(✉)], Yurong Chen[1], Hang Zhong[1], Zhihong Huang[2], and Yaonan Wang[1]

[1] National Engineering Laboratory of Robot Visual Perception and Control Technology, Hunan University, Changsha, Hunan, China
[2] State Grid Hunan Electric Power Corporation Limited Research Institute, Changsha, Hunan, China

Abstract. The widely deployed power transmission line expedites developing the age of electricity. Thus, it is necessary to maintain a power system with a great quantity of manpower and material resources, especially for crucial equipment, such as insulator string. However, the current main inspection method relies on artificial with the problem of time-consuming and labor-intensive. There is a trend of utilizing deep learning techniques on unmanned aerial vehicles (UAVs) to accomplish the inspection task, but its development is restricted by the limitation of energy. In this paper, we propose a semi-supervised cloud edge collaborative insulator string anomaly detection framework. Specifically, an anchor-free object detector is deployed on the edge device for locating the insulator. On the cloud side, we propose a generative insulator defect detection model based on the autoencoder (AE) with a generator-discriminator pattern. Particularly, we introduce the variational memory encoder-decoder architecture to model defect-free insulator data distribution. Furthermore, the adversarial strategy is employed to regularize the generated data space with input data space. In the end, the anomaly can be detected if its data space is an outlier of training defect-free distribution. Comprehensive experiments demonstrate that our method can effectively reduce the computational load, meanwhile archiving superior performance, including accuracy (0.968) and recall (0.985), for defect recognition using a standard insulator data set.

Keywords: Insulator detection · Defect recognition · Autoencoder

1 Introduction

The transmission line connects power plants, substations, and users to form a transmission grid and a distribution network, and its status greatly influences the safety and reliable operation of the whole power system. Accordingly, the condition monitoring for transmission lines has always been the focus of attention,

© Springer Nature Switzerland AG 2021
Y. Peng et al. (Eds.): ICIG 2021, LNCS 12888, pp. 210–221, 2021.
https://doi.org/10.1007/978-3-030-87355-4_18

especially for the main component such as the insulator string. Insulator plays a conductor insulation and mechanical support function in the power transmission task, yet vulnerable due to the long-term exposure in the external environment. And a plenty of fact proof that insulator failure is the main reason causing the electrical accidents [1]. Moreover, it is challenging to screen the status of insulators, since deployed on high-voltage lines with strong currents. The traditional manual inspection method is cumbersome and inefficient, which need to blackout first, and then the staff members are supposed to climb to the position of insulator for checking its condition [1]. Thus, researchers and developers make a lot of effort on designing techniques of insulator string anomaly detection tasks.

Last few years, appreciating the maturity of Micro-Electro-Mechanical Systems (MEMS) techniques, people have witnessed unprecedented developments of the unmanned aerial vehicles (UAVs) field [2,3]. UAVs equipped with cameras can obtain a large amount of insulator image data, however, the lack of automatic status monitoring of insulator string methods brings a heavy burden workload of the developers. It is impractical to manually identifying defective insulators from such an enormous data source. In this case, a series of methods have been proposed for insulator detection and fault recognition, and they can be generally divided into two categories: (1) traditional image processing-based techniques [4,5]; (2) deep learning-based [6,7] algorithms. The former methods commonly make use of factors like color, shape, and texture features to analyze the insulator string, but limited by the sensitivity to the complex background and hard to get a trade-off between the detection speed and accuracy [1]. On the other hand, deep learning is an overwhelming technique on industrial of things [8,9]. There are many works that utilize deep convolutional neural networks (DCNNs) to inspect the equipment condition of the transmission line. Such as Zhao et al. [10] represent the insulator status by applying a multi-patch CNN feature extraction method, and [6] proposes a cascading DCNN for the defect recognition tasks.

It is a trend to deploy those algorithms on UAVs to realize real-time power transmission line condition screening, yet is hindered because of two main reasons. Firstly, the methods mentioned above [6] require high computational costs, and the accuracy of detection methods can not be guaranteed, so that the real-time video is needed to transmitted from UAVs to the local server to ensuring, which causes much energy wasting. In addition, the *data island* phenomenon that is the small-scale, inaccessible, inconsistent, and of poor quality fine-annotated data, hampers the deployment of those mentioned deep learning models in practical applications scenarios.

In this paper, we propose a novel cloud edge collaborative intelligence method for insulator string defect-recognition to mitigate those challenges, as Fig. 1 shown. Specifically, the whole framework is divided into two parts. In edge devices (UAVs), we locate the insulator with an anchor-free object detector, which only needs labels of the location of insulator but fault part. It is simple and inexpensive to prepare large-scale training data. When the insulator is detected, the image will be transported to the cloud server and predicted by the

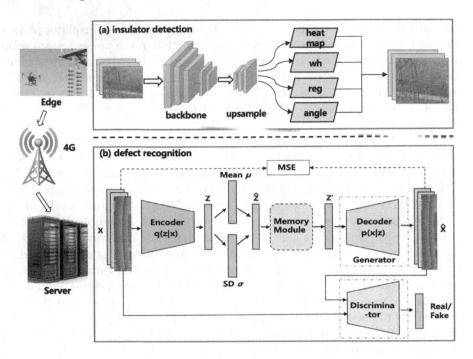

Fig. 1. The proposed cloud edge collaboration framework includes two parts: (a) insulator detection (b) defect recognition. The solid line is the forward propaganda and the dashed line represents the back propaganda.

defect recognition network following. The main contributions of this work are the following:

1) We deploy an anchor-free object detector to locate the insulator on the UAVs. We improve the CenterNet [13] with an extra angle regression, for reducing the energy consumption and predicting the insulator string with the oriented bounding box, respectively.

2) To address the scarcity of faulty insulator data, a generative insulator defect detection model based on the autoencoder with a generator-discriminator pattern is proposed. Particularly, we introduce the variational memory encoder-decoder architecture to model defect-free insulator data distribution. It mitigates the overly-smooth problem of traditional variational autoencoder (VAE). Furthermore, the adversarial strategy is employed to regularize the generated data space with input data space.

The remainder of this paper is structured as follows. Section 2 presents the related work about insulator anomaly detection using CNNs. Section 3 introduces the proposed architecture of the cloud edge collaborative network. Section 4 presents the results of the experiments and provides comparisons to other work. Finally, the conclusions are demonstrates in Sect. 5.

2   Related Work

The availability of large-scale data sets and the high performance of GPU have enabled deep learning to develop rapidly, which powers many computer vision filed. Likewise, the application of deep learning methods for condition monitoring of transmission line equipment is gaining momentum. The most common method for insulator condition screening usually extracts the insulator string from the complex background first and then identifies the defect location. There are many works [7,14] adopt the representative deep convolutional network such as Fast-RCNN and Faster-RCNN to locate the insulators, but it is hard to realize real-time inspection due to their complicated calculation. [9] et al. detect the insulator string from coarse to fine with traditional method and CNN respectively, and then take advantage of the segmentation result in the previous step to identify the defect position. A cascading architecture is utilized in [6,16], which deploy different CNN for the insulator location and defect-recognition task, and both works contain a crop operation between two different networks.

The generative anomaly detection models attract lots of attention, it only needs normal samples, which alleviate the bottleneck of scarce defective insulator images. Thus, those methods avoid being over-fitting problem under the few-shot learning. For example, Kang et al. [15] integrate a deep material classifier and a deep denoising autoencoder together into a multitask learning framework and only need normal insulator samples for training a defect detection network. Deep autoencoder [22,23] is basically consisted of an encoder that able to extract the high-dimensional representation of input images, and a decoder to reconstruct the encoded data. The autoencoder(AE) technique has been extensively used now for anomaly detection in the unsupervised setting. But there exists a problem that it may perform too "well", that leading to a "great" reconstruction of anomalies. Exiting VAEs-based work [17], however, are observed can only learn an ambiguous model, which exists the same issues like the standard AE, due to the lack of constraints. Furthermore, MemAE [18][19] is introduced to alleviate this problem based on the reconstruction of the most relevant item of the input in the memory module to enlarge the difference of the normal sample and novelty. Yet it ignores the local feature learning and is limited by the capability of storage, the *over-smooth* [20] problem is arisen by utilizing the mean square loss function with averaging effect. The adversarial autoencoder networks [25,26] blends the autoencoder architecture with the adversarial loss concept introduced by GAN [24]. Inspired by these works, we convert the insulator defect detection to an unsupervised anomaly detection problem, and an implicate-explicate combined generative insulator defect detection model based on the autoencoder with an adversarial pattern is introduced.

3   Method

The whole framework consist of two phases: insulator detection on the edge device and defect recognition on cloud, and they are supposed to be processed separately. In the following, we will introduce an anchor-free oriented insulators detector and reconstruction-based defect detection network, respectively.

3.1 Insulator Detection on the Edge Device

For the purpose of reducing energy consumption, we introduce the CenterNet [13] which is a simpler and efficient anchor-free keypoint-based detector compared with corresponding bounding box-based detectors. The common object detection algorithm heavily relies on the time-consuming post-grouping process, which is not suitable for deployment on the edge device. Moreover, it is observed that the aspect ratios of insulator string are mostly larger than general objects, which may be even larger than 20. The larger aspect ratios lead to a bad performance in the fault detection task because the predicted regions contain much meaningless background information. In this paper, we extend Zhou's work [13] to the oriented insulator string detection task.

Specifically, our network use the Deep Layer Aggregation (DLA) [31] as backbone, whose parameters are less than ResNet50. Feature maps for prediction are fused from multi-layer of backbone network. We build it on a U-shaped architecture, whose size is 4 times smaller than the input image. The progressively combination of shallow and deep layer provides a comprehensive fine and coarse granularity information. In particular, given a RGB image as input $I \in R^{W \times H \times 3}$, where W and H represents the width and height, respectively, the output feature map $X \in R^{\frac{W}{4} \times \frac{H}{4} \times C}$ (C denotes the channel) is then fed into our four branch heads: heatmap ($H \in R^{\frac{W}{4} \times \frac{H}{4} \times 1}$), offset ($O \in R^{\frac{W}{4} \times \frac{H}{4} \times 2}$), box-parameter ($B \in R^{\frac{W}{4} \times \frac{H}{4} \times 2}$), and angle map ($A \in R^{\frac{W}{4} \times \frac{H}{4} \times 1}$).

The grand truth is denoted as (x, y, w, h, α), where x, y denotes the centers' coordinates and w, h, α is the weight, height, and angle. Following, we use the focal loss to train the heatmap:

$$L_H = -\frac{1}{N} \sum_i \begin{cases} (1 - H_i)^\alpha log(H_i) & if \hat{H}_i = 1 \\ (1 - \hat{H}_i)^\beta H_i^\alpha log(1 - H_i) & otherwise, \end{cases} \tag{1}$$

where $\hat{H}_i$ refer to the Ground Truth and H_i is predicted heatmap values, α and β are the hyper-parameters. The offset between the scaled center point and the predicted is:

$$o = (\frac{x}{4} - \frac{\hat{x}}{4}, \frac{y}{4} - \frac{\hat{y}}{4}). \tag{2}$$

And the offset is trained by minimizing a smooth $L1$ Loss:

$$L_O = \frac{1}{N} \sum_i Smooth_{L_1}(o_i - \hat{o}_i). \tag{3}$$

Likewise, the box parameters $b_i = [w_i, h_i]$ and angle α_i are trained with offset o_i using smooth $L1$ Loss, which denotes as L_B and L_A, respectively. Finally, the network is optimized by the sum of L_H, L_O, L_B, and L_A.

3.2   Defect Recognition on the Cloud Server

In this paper, we propose an adversarial Variational memory autoencoder network. Opposite of object detection-based anomaly detection methods, this paper utilizes an implicit method based on Variational autoencoder (VAE) architecture to model normal data distribution. It can alleviate the dilemma of defining encompasses of a real-world high-diversity outlier, owing to the abnormal insulator sample is hard and costly to collect. In the following part, we firstly provide the structure of Variational autoencoder architecture; then we introduce memory module architecture; in the end, we will give the whole framework process combining Variational memory autoencoder and discriminator and the corresponding loss functions.

Variational Memory Autoencoder consists of three components: (i) the encoder network for learning a meaningful latent representation of the input normal data on its manifold space; (ii) the Variational part for learning a data generating distribution, and the memory module which given random samples from latent space distribution, it can retrieve the most homogeneous item; (iii) the decoder network for reconstructing the item from the memory module. In the training phase, the parameter of the network only trained on normal data. In the inference stage, the memory module is fixed. Therefore, the normal samples can be reconstructed well with its homogeneous memory item while the defective insulator string leads to a high reconstruction error due to it has to retrieve the most relevant normal item.

The objective of the encoder is to learn an approximation to the posterior distribution $p(z|x)$ of defect-free data, however, it is cumbersome and intractable to analytically approach, due to the high computationally expensive sampling of Markov Chain Monte Carlo (MCMC) methods. Alternatively, the Variational autoencoder approximates the posterior distribution $p(z|x)$ as a family of possible distribution $p(z)$ which is able to be generated by our controllable data, such as Gaussian distribution, Poisson, binomial, etc. In this paper, we follow the work [17] which uses the Gaussian distribution $p(z) = Normal(0,1)$. So that, we maneuver the approximation of $p(z|x)$ as $p(z)$. In our task, only given the normal samples, the encoder network models its probability distribution $p(z|x)$:

$$p(z|x) = \frac{p(x|z)p(z)}{p(x)} = \frac{p(x|z)p(z)}{\sum_z p(x|z)p(z)}. \tag{4}$$

In the second stage, it concludes two modules: variational function and memory table. The variational function taken the mean and standard deviations of the latent embedding feature of the current input image from the encoder forms data generating distribution $p(z|x)$. Essentially, the variational parameter is independent of each other, therefore, we can multiply together to give a joint probability:

$$p(z|x) \approx p(z) = \prod_{i=1}^{N} p_i(z_i). \tag{5}$$

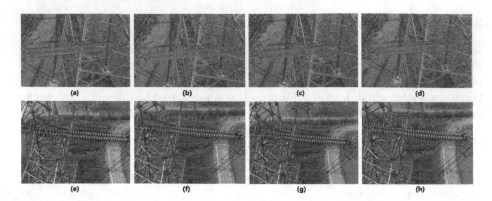

Fig. 2. Insulator string detection results comparison

We employ Kullback-Leibler (KL) divergence to measure their similarity:

$$KL(p(z)||p(z|x)) = \mathbb{E}_{z\sim p}logp(z) - \mathbb{E}_{z\sim p}logp(z|x)$$
$$= \mathbb{E}_{z\sim p}logp(z) - \mathbb{E}_{z\sim p}logp(z,x) + logp(x). \tag{6}$$

Through minimize KL divergence, we achieve approximation $p(z|x)$ as $p(z)$. The new feature vector $\hat{z}$ is sampled from the "learned" latent space $p(z|x)$, which is feed into our memory module and stored at the memory slots matrix $M = \{m_1, m_2, ..., m_i, ..., m_N\} \in \mathbb{R}^{N \times F}$, where N means the number of memory slots and F represents dimension of every latent feature that is memorized. Simultaneously, the similarity coefficients W_i is denoted as cosine distance between input $\hat{z}$ and the memory item m_i as:

$$W_i = \frac{\hat{z} \cdot m_i^T}{||\hat{z}|| \cdot ||m_i||}. \tag{7}$$

In the end, following [18], the final embedding feature z' is retrieved and feed into decoder with soft address method with the similarity coefficients W_i:

$$z' = \sum_{i=1}^{N} \frac{exp(W_i)}{\sum_{i=1}^{N} exp(W_i)} m_i. \tag{8}$$

$$L_D = logD(x) + log(1 - D(G(z'))) \tag{9}$$

The decoder network $p(x|z')$ learns to reconstruct the input space distribution given latent representation distribution. The architecture of decoder is symmetrical with encoder network. In the sum, the loss function of variational memory autoencoder (L_{VMAE}) consists two parts, reconstruction loss and KL:

$$L_{VMAE} = MSE(x, \hat{x}) + KL(p(z)||p(z|x)), \tag{10}$$

where MSE is the mean square error between input and reconstructed images.

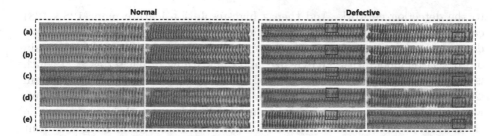

Fig. 3. The comparison of reconstruction normal insulator (left), defective insulator (right) of our method and other baselines. (a) input samples (b) reconstruction of AE (c) reconstruction of MemAE [18] (d) reconstruction of Variational AE [17] (e) reconstruction of our proposed method (Color figure online)

Adversarial Discriminator. Moreover, autoencoder is inherently blurry, inspired by the Ganomaly [27], we introduce the discriminator to improve the reconstruction image quality and senses. The objective of the discriminator network is to classify the input x and the reconstructed $\hat{x}$ as real or fake, respectively. The discriminator is constructed by multi-layer perception neural networks. In addition, the decoder network in this paper is treated as a generator, which reconstructs an image from the latent space in order to interfere with the judgment of the discriminator network. The discriminator can be trained by minimizing the loss function as: where D denotes the discriminator function, G represents the generator function. x means the input image and z' is the output of the variational memory autoencoder. Furthermore, the generator is adversarial trained by maximizing the second part of the discriminator loss function:

$$L_G = log(1 - D(G(z'))). \tag{11}$$

4 Experiments

Our method for insulator string detection and defect recognition are evaluated in this section independently. The data set we used comes from [6], which includes 600 high resolution normal insulator string images and 248 images with bunch-drop defect. The dataset are captured by an UAV with a DJI M200 camera. All positive samples includes one or more anomaly-free insulators. Negative cases are defective insulator images. Besides, the experiment is conducted based on the configuration as: Intel Core i7-7600, and GTX 1080 GPU with 8-GB memory.

4.1 Implementation Detail

For the insulator detection experiment, the fully convolutional upsampling version of DLA is utilized to obtain an informative feature map. Following the work in [13], the original convolution at each upsampling layer is replaced by 3×3 deformable convolution. The input image is resized to 512×512 before sending to the detection network. And then a high-resolution feature map (128 × 128) can be acquired. Moreover, a series of data augmentation such as cropping, random flip, and scaling is used to increase the robustness of our model. We train our detection model with 8 batch-size, and the learning rate is set as 2e–4 which is supposed to drop 10 times at 90 and 120 epochs. In addition, we use Adam [29] to optimize the objective function. For the defect recognition experiment, we cropping and rotating the inspection bounding box, which is predicated on the normal insulator data set, to a horizontal level. And then resizing the result to 68 × 500 before feeding into the autoencoder network. Meanwhile, we build an encoder network with ResNet50, and the decoder is symmetrical to the encoder. The memory size N of the memory module is set as 1000. And we train with batch-size 8 and learning rate 10e–4 for every 500 epochs. Furthermore, we still utilize Adam as the optimizer in this experiment.

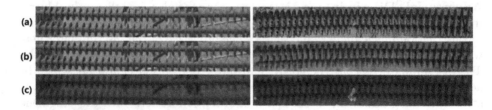

Fig. 4. The discrepancy between input samples and reconstruction result of our method in normal sample (left) and defective sample (right) (a) input samples (b) reconstruction result (c) the discrepancy. (Color figure online)

4.2   Experiment Results

Figure 2 gives the insulator detection results using different methods. (a), (e) indicate the manual label, and the middle two columns are predicted by the CenterNet-ResNet18 and CenterNet-ResNet50 respectively. We yield the best performance utilizing the CenterNet-Dla34 as (d) and (h) shown, which locate the insulator string with high accuracy. Besides, the precision, recall, F1 score, parameter, and testing speed comparison are reported at Table 1. The first three rows are tested with anchor-based detection methods, and the remaining models are all based on CenterNet. From the reported results, we can see that under the high inference speed, our framework achieves superior precision and recall.

Figure 3 compares the reconstruction images generated by different methods, and for better visualization, we enclose the defective area by red lines. The standard AE "generalize" so well on both normal and defective image as (b) represent, thus it can not recognize the abnormal data according to the difference of reconstruction error. Moreover, the generalization capability of MAE is unsatisfied, which means it may only perform well on trained data. The VAEs learn the generating distribution of training data so that it is able to reconstruct a more normal-like image. But as shown in (d), the reconstruction images are too

Table 1. Detection performance for different methods.

Method	Precision	Recall	F1	Parameter	Testing speed
Faster R-CNN [7]	0.791	0.573	0.665	138M	180 ms/image
ILN-VGG16 [6]	0.904	0.966	0.934	136M	115 ms/image
Cascaded DNN [30]	0.882	0.861	0.871	–	387 ms/image
CenterNet-ResNet18	0.876	0.571	0.691	14.91M	34 ms/image
CenterNet-ResNet50	0.910	0.455	0.607	31.16M	48 ms/image
CenterNet-DLA34 (ours)	**0.946**	**0.864**	**0.903**	20.32 M	52 ms/image

Table 2. The performance of our model compared with the SOTA methods.

Method	Precision	Recall	F1
Autoencoder	0.410	0.516	0.457
Memory autoencoder [18]	0.512	0.677	0.583
Ganomaly [27]	0.509	0.903	0.651
Variational autoencoder [17]	0.704	0.954	0.810
Ours	**0.968**	**0.985**	**0.9769**

blurry to distinguish the defect region. The bottom row (e) indicates the output of our proposed model, which efficiently mitigates the issues mentioned above. Besides, the absent piece of defect insulator has been 'patched' after reconstruction. In this case, the faulty insulator is able to get a higher reconstruction error compared with the normal insulator.

Figure 4 shows the discrepancy between the input image and reconstruction image. The first column represents the normal insulator, and the second column is the defective insulator with a bunch-drop fault. The defective region is highlighted with bright color, and the normal part maintains a dark blue color as (c) shown. From the discrepancy result, we can easily locate the fault. Table 2 compare the value of precision, recall, and F1 score between four methods with our proposed model. The standard autoencoder without any constraints gets the lowest precision and recall score. Besides, simply appending the memory module and variation process achieve no significant improvement. The precision of Ganomaly can not meet the detection requirement. It shows that our method yields the best performance with the result of 0.9688, 0.9853, and 0.9769 respectively which is highlighted in bold in Table 2.

5   Conclusion

In this paper, a cloud edge collaborative insulator string anomaly detection framework is proposed. We depart the defect inspection task into two independent procedures: (1) insulator detection; (2) defect recognition. The former step is carried out by improving an anchor-free detector called CenterNet, which is able to alleviate the calculation burden of the edge device. Moreover, we introduce an adversarial autoencoder model with a variation process and memory module for defect recognition. The experiment results proof that the proposed framework can achieve state-of-the-art performance on abnormal detection. In further work, we will explore the knowledge distillation methods on edge devices to prune the network and anomaly detection generative model on the cloud side.

Acknowledgment. This work was supported in part by the National Natural Science Foundation of China under Grants 62027810, 61733004, National Key RD Program of China under Grant 2020YFB1712600, and the Hunan Provincial Natural Science Foundation of China under Grant 2020JJ5090, 2018GK2022, 2017XK2102, and China Postdoctoral Science Foundation under Grant BX20200122 and 2020M682555.

References

1. Han, J., et al.: A method of insulator faults detection in aerial images for high-voltage transmission lines inspection. Appl. Sci. **9**(10), 2009 (2019)
2. Zhong, H., Miao, Z., Wang, Y., et al.: A practical visual servo control for aerial manipulation using a spherical projection model. IEEE Trans. Ind. Electron. **67**(12), 10564–10574 (2019)
3. Zhong, H., Wang, Y., et al.: Circumnavigation of a moving target in 3D by multi-agent systems with collision avoidance: an orthogonal vector fields-based approach. Int. J. Control Autom. Syst. **17**(1), 212–224 (2019)
4. Tiantian, Y., et al.: Feature fusion based insulator detection for aerial inspection. In: 2017 36th Chinese Control Conference (CCC), pp. 10972–10977. IEEE (2017)
5. Liao, S., An, J.: A robust insulator detection algorithm based on local features and spatial orders for aerial images. IEEE Geosci. Remote Sens. Lett. **12**(5), 963–967 (2014)
6. Tao, X., Zhang, D., Wang, Z., et al.: Detection of power line insulator defects using aerial images analyzed with convolutional neural networks. IEEE Trans. Syst. Man Cybern. Syst. **50**(4), 1486–1498 (2018)
7. Ren, S., He, K., Girshick, R., et al.: Faster R-CNN: towards real-time object detection with region proposal networks. IEEE Trans. Pattern Anal. Mach. Intell. **39**(6), 1137–1149 (2016)
8. Liu, D., Zeng, X., Wang, Y.: Edge-computing-driven autonomous ubiquitous internet of things in electricity: architecture and challenges. In: 2019 IEEE 3rd Conference on Energy Internet and Energy System Integration (EI2), pp. 456–461. IEEE (2019)
9. Song, C., et al.: A cloud edge collaborative intelligence method of insulator string defect detection for power IIoT. IEEE Internet Things J. **8**(9), 7510–7520 (2020)
10. Zhao, Z., Xu, G., Qi, Y., et al.: Multi-patch deep features for power line insulator status classification from aerial images. In: 2016 International Joint Conference on Neural Networks (IJCNN), pp. 3187–3194. IEEE (2016)
11. Wang, W., Wang, Y., Han, J., et al.: Recognition and drop-off detection of insulator based on aerial image. In: 2016 9th International Symposium on Computational Intelligence and Design (ISCID), vol. 1, pp. 162–167. IEEE (2016)
12. Zhai, Y., Chen, R., Yang, Q., et al.: Insulator fault detection based on spatial morphological features of aerial images. IEEE Access **6**, 35316–35326 (2018)

13. Zhou, X., Wang, D., Krähenbühl, P.: Objects as points. arXiv preprint arXiv:1904.07850 (2019)
14. Ma, L., Xu, C., Zuo, G., et al.: Detection method of insulator based on faster R-CNN. In: 2017 IEEE 7th Annual International Conference on CYBER Technology in Automation, Control, and Intelligent Systems (CYBER), pp. 1410–1414. IEEE (2017)
15. Kang, G., Gao, S., Yu, L., et al.: Deep architecture for high-speed railway insulator surface defect detection: denoising autoencoder with multitask learning. IEEE Trans. Instrum. Meas. **68**(8), 2679–2690 (2018)
16. Ling, Z., Qiu, R.C., Jin, Z., et al.: An accurate and real-time self-blast glass insulator location method based on faster R-CNN and U-net with aerial images. arXiv preprint arXiv:1801.05143 (2018)
17. Kingma, D.P., Welling, M.: Auto-encoding variational bayes. arXiv preprint arXiv:1312.6114 (2013)
18. Gong, D., Liu, L., Le, V., et al.: Memorizing normality to detect anomaly: memory-augmented deep autoencoder for unsupervised anomaly detection. In: Proceedings of the IEEE/CVF International Conference on Computer Vision, pp. 1705–1714 (2019)
19. Chen, Y., Zhang, H., Wang, Y., et al.: MAMA net: multi-scale attention memory autoencoder network for anomaly detection. IEEE Trans. Med. Imaging **40**(3), 1032–1041 (2020)
20. Zhao, H., Gallo, O., Frosio, I., et al.: Loss functions for image restoration with neural networks. IEEE Trans. Comput. Imaging **3**(1), 47–57 (2016)
21. Wang, X., Du, Y., Lin, S., Cui, P., Shen, Y., Yang, Y.: Advae: a self-adversarial variational autoencoder with gaussian anomaly prior knowledge for anomaly detection. Knowl.-Based Syst. **190**, 105187 (2020)
22. Zhou, C., Paffenroth, R.C.: Anomaly detection with robust deep autoencoders. In: Proceedings of the 23rd ACM SIGKDD International Conference on Knowledge Discovery and Data Mining, pp. 665–674 (2017)
23. Chen, J., Sathe, S., Aggarwal, C., Turaga, D.: Outlier detection with autoencoder ensembles. In: Proceedings of the 2017 SIAM International Conference on Data Mining, pp. 90–98. SIAM (2017)
24. Goodfellow, I., et al.: Generative adversarial nets. In: Advances in Neural Information Processing Systems, pp. 2672–2680 (2014)
25. Makhzani, A., Shlens, J., Jaitly, N., et al.: Adversarial autoencoders. arXiv preprint arXiv:1511.05644 (2015)
26. Chen, Y.: Graph-embedding Enhanced Attention Adversarial Autoencoder. University of Pittsburgh (2020)
27. Akcay, S., Atapour-Abarghouei, A., Breckon, T.P.: GANomaly: semi-supervised anomaly detection via adversarial training. In: Jawahar, C.V., Li, H., Mori, G., Schindler, K. (eds.) ACCV 2018. LNCS, vol. 11363, pp. 622–637. Springer, Cham (2019). https://doi.org/10.1007/978-3-030-20893-6_39
28. Donahue, J., Krahenbuhl, P., Darrell, T.: Adversarial feature learning. In: International Conference on Learning Representations (ICLR) (2016)
29. Kingma, D.P., Ba, J.: Adam: a method for stochastic optimization. ICLR (2014)
30. Chen, J., Liu, Z., Wang, H., Núñez, A., Han, Z.: Automatic defect detection of fasteners on the catenary support device using deep convolutional neural network. IEEE Trans. Instrum. Meas. **67**(2), 257–269 (2018)
31. Yu, F., Wang, D., Shelhamer, F.: Darrell. Deep layer aggregation. In: CVPR (2018)

Illumination-Enhanced Crowd Counting Based on IC-Net in Low Lighting Conditions

Haoyu Zhao[1] , Weidong Min[2,3]( ) , and Yi Zou[1]

[1] School of Information Engineering, Nanchang University, Nanchang 330031, China
[2] School of Software, Nanchang University, Nanchang 330047, China
minweidong@ncu.edu.cn
[3] Jiangxi Key Laboratory of Smart City, Nanchang 330047, China

Abstract. The low lighting in some extreme conditions always affect the accuracy of the crowd counting and other vision tasks. The existing methods mainly rely on the generalization ability of deep-learning model to count the crowd number. But in extremely low lighting conditions, these methods are not efficient. To alleviate this issue, this paper proposes a novel approach, named Illumination-aware Cascading Network (IC-Net). The IC-Net can handle the low lighting conditions and generate a high-quality crowd density map. It contains two submodules, i.e., the Illumination Fusion Module and the Feature Cascading Module. The Illumination Fusion Module can fuse the low-illumination feature and the illumination enhanced feature to highlight the missing feature in darkness. The Feature Cascading Module is a cascading model and used to further express the illumination feature. It can generate the high-quality density map. In addition, a new dataset is collected, named Low Light Scenes Crowd (LLSC) dataset, which all come from extremely low illumination conditions. Experimental results on LLSC and benchmark show that the proposed method outperforms the existing state-of-the art methods in such extreme conditions.

Keywords: Crowd counting · Low lighting conditions · Deep learning

1 Introduction

Crowd counting, applied to many domains, such as security systems, urban planning, and video surveillance, is an interesting and useful technology [1,2]. It aims to count the number of people in an area [3–5]. With the development of deep learning, CNN-based methods achieve the amazing performance on many tasks, including crowd counting. [6] firstly proposed multi-column network to handle

Supported by the National Natural Science Foundation of China (Grant No. 62076117 and No. 61762061), the Natural Science Foundation of Jiangxi Province, China (Grant No. 20161ACB20004) and Jiangxi Key Laboratory of Smart City (Grant No. 20192BCD40002).

Y. Peng et al. (Eds.): ICIG 2021, LNCS 12888, pp. 222–234, 2021.
https://doi.org/10.1007/978-3-030-87355-4_19

this issue. [7,8] mainly relied on the generalization capability of the deep-learning model. Following the train-and-test pattern, these models can get some good performance on benchmarks. But such power has its limits, especially facing the extreme conditions, such as low lighting, perspective distortion, and dense crowd.

In addition, illumination feature is very significant to vision tasks. So, the deep-learning methods is hard to use in low lighting environment. Several work had been done to solve this issue in many domains. [9] proposed a deep neural network for low lighting field restoration. [10] proposed an illumination recovery model to transform severe varying illumination to slight illumination. [11] introduced an illumination-aware Faster R-CNN for object detection. To solve the crowd counting task in low lighting scenes, [12] proposed a deep spatial regression model to handle the appearance variations and the illumination various problems. [13] combined the audio information as auxiliary feature for crowd counting in low lighting environments. But audio feature has limitations when in large and open place. Thus, the existing crowd counting methods cannot directly be used in low lighting scenes.

In order to alleviate such problem, this paper proposes a novel and end-to-end approach, named Illumination-aware Cascading Network (IC-Net). It contains two submodules, i.e., the Illumination Fusion Module and the Feature Cascading Module. The Illumination Fusion Module can fuse the low-illumination feature and the illumination enhanced feature to highlight the missing feature in darkness. The Feature Cascading Module is a cascading model and used to further express the illumination feature. It can generate the high-quality density map. Due to lacking such challenging dataset, this work collects a new dataset, named Low Light Scenes Crowd (LLSC) dataset. The images come from extremely low illumination conditions in outdoor and indoor. The experiments based on the self-collected dataset and benchmark show that the proposed approach outperforms the existing methods.

The main contributions of this study are summarized as follows:

1. This work proposes a novel IC-Net for crowd counting, which can handle the low lighting conditions and generate a high-quality crowd density map.
2. To fuse the illumination feature, the Illumination Fusion Module and the Feature Cascading Module are proposed. They can highlight the missing illumination information in darkness and further express the CNN feature.
3. A new dataset which contains multiple scenes in low lighting conditions is proposed. The IC-Net can get good performances on self-collected dataset and benchmark.

2   Related Work

Crowd counting has significant applications in people's daily life. Many excellent methods based on deep-learning approach have been proposed to solve this problem. Some work also tried to solve this issue in extreme conditions, such as apparent perspective distortion, dense crowd, and illumination variations.

2.1   Crowd Counting Based on Deep Learning

Existing methods mainly based on deep-learning structure [14,15] to solve the crowd counting. Zhang et al. [6] proposed a simple but effective Multi-column Convolutional Neural Network (MCNN) to estimate the crowd density map. Zeng et al. [16] proposed an improved multi-scale CNN. Different from the multi-column network, Wu et al. [17] present a featured channel enhancement block for crowd counting. Cao et al. [18] introduced an encoder decoder approach to extract multi-scale features and generates high-resolution density maps. In addition, considering the scale variation problem, [19–21] proposed novel network structures with structured features and fixed small receptive fields. [22–24] tried to use map-estimation networks to count the highly dense crowds in images. Some work also tried to solve the over-fitting for crowd counting. Such as Shi et al. [25] designed a new learning strategy to produce generalizable features by the means of deep negative correlation learning.

2.2   Crowd Counting Methods for Low Lighting Scenes

Due to the importance of illumination feature to vision-based tasks, some researchers also explored some methods to count the crowd in low lighting scenes. Hu et al. [13] introduced a novel task of audiovisual crowd counting, in which visual and auditory information are integrated for counting purposes. Wu et al. [26] proposed an adaptive scenario discovery framework for counting crowds with varying densities, which can deal different environments. Zhao et al. [27] designed a depth embedding module as add-ons into existing networks, which aims to solve the scale and illumination variety. Some work also built new benchmark for crowd counting. Wang et al. [28] collected a large-scale dataset which contains many low lighting scenes. It can also improve the train-test pattern models' accuracy.

According to the above analyses, most of existing methods for crowd counting are based on deep-learning structure. And they mainly relied on the generalization capability of convolutional neural network. When facing some extreme conditions, such as low lighting scene, these methods would not get the satisfactory results. In spite of some work, such as [13] tried to use extra audio information to assist the vision feature. The audio feature has limitations in large and open place.

By contrast, this work proposes an illumination enhanced method for crowd counting. To the best of our knowledge, this is the first study which directly improves the illumination feature in low lighting scenes for crowd counting. And a challenging dataset is also collected to show the efficiency of the proposed model.

3   The Proposed IC-Net for Crowd Counting

To solve the crowd counting issue in extremely low lighting conditions, this paper proposes a novel approach, named Illumination-aware Cascading Network (IC-Net), as the Fig. 1 shows. The IC-Net is an end-to-end training structure which

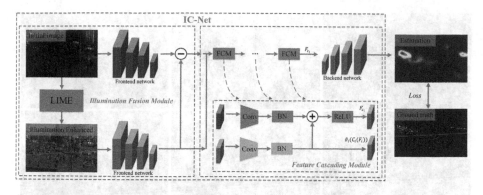

Fig. 1. The crowd counting based on Illumination-aware Cascading Network (IC-Net).

contains two submodules, i.e., the Illumination Fusion Module and the Feature Cascading Module. It can handle the low lighting conditions and generate a high-quality crowd density map. The input crowd image is converted to the density map by [6]. The density map is used to estimate the crowd number.

3.1 Illumination Fusion Module (IFM)

The structure of the IFM is shown in Fig. 1. The input crowd image is taken in low lighting conditions. The image often suffers from low visibility and the crowd is hidden in the darkness. The poor illumination quality will significantly degenerate the performance of many computer vision tasks [10], including crowd counting. Due to lack of enough vision information, it is difficult for convolutional neural network to handle such images. To get the hidden information about the crowd, the initial image is dealt with LIME [29]. LIME belongs to Retinex-based category, which aims to enhance a low light image by estimating its illumination map.

As the Fig. 2 shows, the LIME has a good performance in the outdoor and indoor scenes. The top-left corner in red box is the illumination enhanced images, which have significant increases in brightness. To prove the improvement of illumination can indeed increase the accuracy of the model, this work also conducted related experiments, which can be found in Experiments.

After getting the illumination enhanced operation, IFM puts the low lighting image and the illumination enhanced image into the frontend network at the same time. The frontend network is constructed with convolution, ReLU, and Max-Pooling operations. It is used to get the initial image feature $F_{low-illumination}$ and $F_{enhanced-illumination}$. The enhanced image feature contains more detailed information than the low illumination feature. Such as the people in dark environments would not be detected. When convolutional neural network does the convolution operation, these features will be lost.

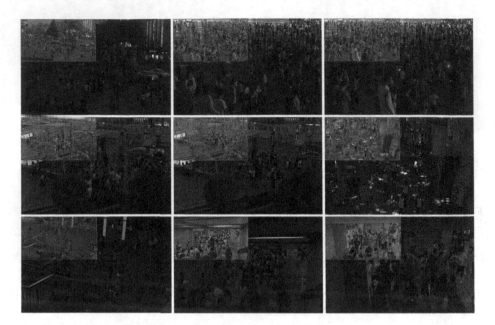

Fig. 2. The illumination enhanced results using LIME.

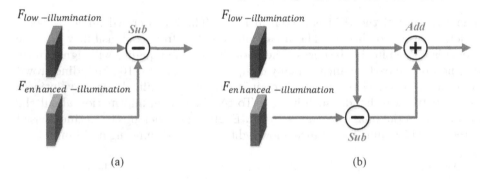

$F_{low-illumination}$

Sub

$F_{enhanced-illumination}$

$F_{low-illumination}$

Add

$F_{enhanced-illumination}$

Sub

(a)   (b)

Fig. 3. Two different solutions to fuse the illumination features.

To highlight the missing illumination information in the original image feature, this work tries to fuse the two illumination features $F_{low-illumination}$ and $F_{enhanced-illumination}$. As the Fig. 3 shows, two different solutions are considered. The solution (a) and (b) can be described as Eq. (1) and Eq. (2).

$$F_f = sub(F_{low-illumination}, F_{enhanced-illumination}) \qquad (1)$$

$$F_f = add(sub(F_{enhanced-illumination}, F_{low-illumination}), F_{low-illumination}) \qquad (2)$$

The $sub()$ operation is used to do the subtraction between the corresponding features. The $add()$ operation is used to do the addition between the corresponding features. F_f is the fused image feature. To get the difference between the low-illumination and the enhanced illumination images, $sub()$ operation can get such difference. The $add()$ operation tries to supplement the original information of the image. In the experiment, the solution (a) is found having better performance. This work analyzes that the overlay of the supplement feature and the original feature will bring some interferences.

3.2 Feature Cascading Module (FCM)

After the IFM, the fused image feature F_f and the illumination-enhanced feature F_i are integrated by several FCMs. F_i donates the $F_{enhanced-illumination}$. The structure of the FCM can be seen in Fig. 1. This module is a cascading model and is used to further combine the illumination feature and the image feature adaptively. The two features are dealt with convolution (C_f and C_i) and batch normalization (ϑ_f and ϑ_i) operations. The batch normalization can accelerate the network learning rate. Then, the two output features are dealt with $add()$ and ReLU operations. The whole process can be described as Eq. (3).

$$F_{c_i} = ReLU(add(\vartheta_f(C_f(F_f)), \vartheta_i(C_i(F_i)))) \tag{3}$$

The F_{c_i} donates the output feature of i module. This work set six FCMs to extract the image. In the final FCM, the feature $\vartheta_i(C_i(F_i))$ doesn't enter into the backend network. The output feature F_c can be got by Eq. (4).

$$F_c = \sum_{i=1}^{n} F_{c_i}, (n = 6) \tag{4}$$

To get the final estimation results, the feature F_c is sent into backend network to recover the size of the feature. In addition, the Mean square loss function is used to train the model. The estimation density map $\hat{M}_e$ and the ground truth density map c can be calculated with Eq. (5).

$$loss = \sum(M_g - \hat{M}_e)^2 \tag{5}$$

4   Experiments

The IC-Net for crowd counting is implemented under the Windows 10 and Pytorch 1.4.0 experimental environment. The hardware environments are Inter Xeon E-2136 3.3 GHz and Quadro P5000.

4.1   Evaluation Metrics

The two standard evaluation metrics to test the IC-Net is used, i.e., Mean Absolute Error (MAE) and the Root Mean Squared Error (RMSE) [30,31]. They are defined as Eq. (6) and Eq. (7).

$$MAE = \frac{1}{N} \sum_{i=1}^{N} |y_i - \hat{y}_i| \tag{6}$$

$$RMSE = \sqrt{\frac{1}{N} \sum_{i=1}^{N} (y_i - \hat{y}_i)^2} \tag{7}$$

The parameter N represents the total number of the test images, y_i is the ground-truth number of people inside the whole i image and $\hat{y}_i$ is the estimated number of people.

4.2   Models' Performances with the Illumination Enhanced Image

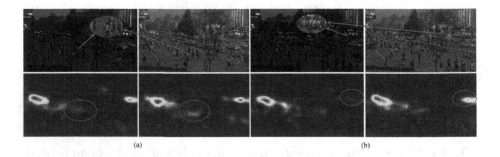

(a)   (b)

Fig. 4. The different experimental results of the darkness and the brightness.

The Importance of Illumination Information. As the Fig. 4 shows, two scenes (a) and (b) are tested. The first and the third columns are initial low lighting images, the second and the fourth columns are illumination enhanced images. The second row is the corresponding density map results generated by CANNet [8] for each image. The people in low lighting images are almost invisible. Such as the areas with red oval in the first row, these people are easily ignored by the convolutional neural network. The illumination enhanced images recover such detailed information. The images in the second row show that the people can be detected in illumination enhanced image. But they cannot be detected in low lighting image. This result explains the importance of the illumination for the vision tasks, including crowd counting.

Model Performances on Extended Datasets. In order to test the influence of the illumination enhanced images, this work tests the CANNet, CSRNet [7] and the MSR-FAN [32] on the ShanghaiTech dataset [6]. ShanghaiTech dataset includes part A and part B. Part A has 482 images and part B has 716 images. The two parts are divided into training data and testing data. This work directly improves the brightness of the images in Par A and Part B. The illumination enhanced images and the initial images are put together to train the model.

Table 1. The training results on extended datasets.

Methods	Part A		Part B	
	MAE	RMSE	MAE	RMSE
The initial images				
CSRNet [7]	68.2	115.0	10.6	16.0
CANNet [8]	62.3	100.0	7.8	12.2
MSR-FAN [32]	**59.9**	**94.6**	**7.6**	**11.3**
The illumination enhanced images and the initial images				
CSRNet [7]	67.3	113.6	9.2	15.3
CANNet [8]	60.6	100.2	7.1	12.3
MSR-FAN [32]	**57.1**	**98.1**	**6.0**	**11.1**

The Table 1 shows that the performance of these model all gets better results when extended the dataset with illumination enhanced images. The CANNet gets the MAE with 62.3 in the initial dataset and gets the MAE with 60.6 in the extended dataset. The MSR-FAN boosts 2.8 in MAE. The structures of these networks have not changed, but the performances of the networks have improved. This work assumes that the illumination enhanced images in extended dataset bring some neglected feature for network training step.

The Performances of IC-Net in Different Datasets. To test the IC-Net in extremely low lighting conditions, this work collected a new dataset, named Low Light Scenes Crowd (LLSC) dataset. It contains 780 images and they all come from DISCO dataset [13]. The DISCO dataset contains 1,935 images and the corresponding audio clips, and 170,270 annotated instances. These images include many kinds of scenes and conditions. This work chooses all the low lighting images from the DISCO and the audio clips are useless in this work. In these scenes, the illumination information is weak and some people are invisible, which are difficult to count. So, the LLSC is a challenging dataset.

To verify the impact of the model, some state-of-the-art methods are also tested on DISCO dataset. This paper compared with MCNN [6], AudioCSRNet [13], CANNet, and CSRNet. AudioCSRNet is also a novel method which tried to combine audio feature to assist the crowd counting task.

The Table 2 shows the experimental results on LLSC dataset and DISCO dataset. The IC-Net gets the MAE with 20.50 and RMSE with 29.08, which is the best model on LLSC. The AudioCSRNet gets the MAE with 21.46 and RMSE with 29.43 on LLSC. On the DISCO dataset, the IC-Net can get the MAE with 13.01 and RMSE with 26.98. The AudioCSRNet gets the MAE with 13.34 and RMSE with 27.20, which is lower than IC-Net. Except the low lighting images, the DISCO contains many bright scenes which can be handled by network. The LIME would not improve such images' illumination. The two same images are sent into IC-Net and get the final density map. Due to the help of audio feature, the AudioCSRNet performs better than MCNN, CANNet and the CSRNet. It can illustrate that the illumination feature can indeed help deep-learning model to get higher accuracy.

Table 2. The experimental results on the LLSC and DISCO datasets.

Methods	LLSC dataset		DISCO dataset	
	MAE	RMSE	MAE	RMSE
MCNN [6]	68.30	71.08	42.89	66.36
CSRNet [7]	26.81	35.72	17.66	33.35
CANNet [8]	24.08	31.98	15.12	29.85
AudioCSRNet [13]	21.46	29.43	13.34	27.20
Ours	**20.50**	**29.08**	**13.01**	**26.98**

Except from the comparison on the benchmarks, the visualized results between AudioCSRNet and the IC-Net on several images in LLSC are also introduced in Fig. 5. The first line is the initial images, the second line is the illumination-enhanced images, the third line is the ground truth, the fourth line is the results of AudioCSRNet, and the fifth line is the results of IC-Net. The 'gt' donates the ground truth number of the crowd. The 'es' donates the estimation number of the crowd. It can be found that the IC-Net has a good performance.

4.3   Ablation Studies

Considering that different structures of network have different performances [33–35], this work does some ablation studies to prove the efficiency of the IC-Net. In IFM, two different solutions, as the Fig. 3 shows, come forward to fuse the illumination features. To get the best accuracy of IC-Net, the two solutions, $IC_{(a)}$ and $IC_{(b)}$, are tested on the LLSC.

From the Table 3, it can be seen that the $IC_{(a)}$ performs better than $IC_{(b)}$. So, the solution (a) in Fig. 3 is employed in IC-Net to fuse the illumination features.

Table 3. The results tested on LLSC of two solutions.

Methods	MAE	RMSE
$IC_{(a)}$	**20.50**	**29.08**
$IC_{(b)}$	23.46	31.53

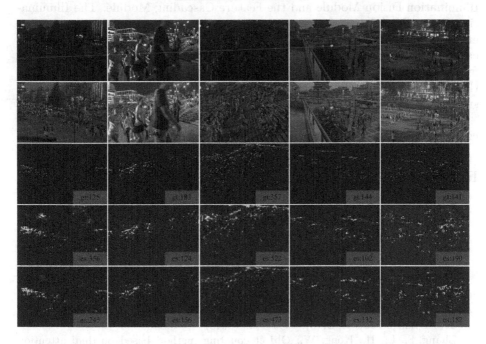

Fig. 5. Visualized results of the AudioCSRNet and IC-Net on several images in LLSC.

In addition, IC-Net contains several FCMs. To find the best number of the FCM, this work also tests the $IC_{(3)}$, $IC_{(4)}$, $IC_{(6)}$, and $IC_{(7)}$ on LLSC dataset. $IC_{(6)}$ donates that six FCMs are employed in IC-Net. From the Table 4, it can be found that the $IC_{(6)}$ performs best. So, the number of the FCM are set as six in IC-Net.

Table 4. The performances of IC-Net with different number of FCMs.

Methods	$IC_{(3)}$	$IC_{(4)}$	$IC_{(6)}$	$IC_{(7)}$
MAE	25.53	22.98	**20.50**	24.08
RMSE	34.93	33.61	**29.08**	35.36

5   Conclusion

In this work, a novel approach named Illumination-aware Cascading Network (IC-Net) is proposed. The IC-Net can handle the low lighting conditions and generate a high-quality crowd density map. It contains two submodules, i.e., the Illumination Fusion Module and the Feature Cascading Module. The Illumination Fusion Module can fuse the low-illumination feature and the illumination enhanced feature to highlight the missing feature in darkness. The Feature Cascading Module is a cascading model and used to further express the illumination feature. It can generate the high-quality density map. Experimental results show that the proposed method outperforms the existing state-of-the art methods in such extreme conditions.

In the future, more work will be done to improve the accuracy of the crowd counting model in extreme conditions.

References

1. Liu, Y., Wen, Q., Chen, H., et al.: Crowd counting via cross-stage refinement networks. IEEE Trans. Image Process. **29**, 6800–6812 (2020)
2. Gao, J., Wang, Q., Li, X.: PCC Net: perspective crowd counting via spatial convolutional network. IEEE Trans. Circ. Syst. Video Technol. **30**(10), 3486–3498 (2019)
3. Sindagi, V., Patel, V.: A survey of recent advances in CNN-based single image crowd counting and density estimation. Pattern Recogn. Lett. **107**, 3–16 (2018)
4. Huang, S., Xi, L., Zhang, Z.: Body structure aware deep crowd counting. IEEE Trans. Image Process. **27**(3), 1049–1059 (2018)
5. Zhang, S., Li, H., Kong, W.: Object counting method based on dual attention network. IET Image Process. **14**(8), 1621–1627 (2020)
6. Zhang Y., Zhou D., Chen S., et al.: Single-image crowd counting via multi-column convolutional neural network. In: Proceedings of IEEE Conference Computer Vision and Pattern Recognition (CVPR), Las Vegas, pp. 589–597. IEEE Xplore (2016)
7. Li Y., Zhang X., Chen D.: CSRNet: dilated convolutional neural networks for understanding the highly congested scenes. In: Proceedings of IEEE Conference on Computer Vision and Pattern Recognition (CVPR), pp. 1091–1100. IEEE Xplore, Utah (2018)
8. Liu, W., Salzmann, M., Fua, P.: Context-aware crowd counting. In: Proceedings of IEEE Conference on Computer Vision and Pattern Recognition (CVPR), Long Beach, pp. 5094–5103. IEEE Xplore (2019)
9. Lamba, M., Rachavarapu, K., Mitra, K.: Harnessing multi-view perspective of light fields for low-light imaging. IEEE Trans. Image Process. **30**, 1501–1513 (2021)
10. Hui, C., Yu, J., We, F., et al.: Face illumination recovery for the deep learning feature under severe illumination variations. Pattern Recogn. **111**, (2021). https://doi.org/10.1016/j.patcog.2020.107724
11. Li, C., Song, D., Tong, R., et al.: Illumination-aware faster R-CNN for robust multispectral pedestrian detection. Pattern Recogn. **85**, 161–171 (2019)
12. Yao, H., Han, K., Wan, W., et al.: Deep spatial regression model for image crowd counting. arXiv:1710.09757 (2017)

13. Hu, D., Mou, L., Wang, Q., et al.: Ambient sound helps: audiovisual crowd counting in extreme conditions. arXiv:2005.07097 (2020)
14. Yang, H., Liu, L., Min, W., et al.: Driver yawning detection based on subtle facial action recognition. IEEE Trans. Multimedia **23**, 572–583 (2021)
15. Wang, Q., Min, W., He, D., et al.: Discriminative fine-grained network for vehicle reidentification using two-stage re-ranking. Sci. China Inf. Sci. **63**(11), 1–12 (2020)
16. Zeng, L., Xu, X., Cai, B., et al.: Multi-scale convolutional neural networks for crowd counting. In: Proceedings of IEEE International Conference on Image Processing (ICIP), Beijing, pp. 465–469. IEEE Xplore (2017)
17. Wu, X., Kong, S., Zheng, Y., et al.: Feature channel enhancement for crowd counting. IET Image Process. **14**(11), 2376–2382 (2020)
18. Cao, X., Wang, Z., Zhao, Y., Su, F.: Scale aggregation network for accurate and efficient crowd counting. In: Ferrari, V., Hebert, M., Sminchisescu, C., Weiss, Y. (eds.) ECCV 2018. LNCS, vol. 11209, pp. 757–773. Springer, Cham (2018). https://doi.org/10.1007/978-3-030-01228-1_45
19. Liu, L., Qiu, Z., Li, G., et al.: Crowd counting with deep structured scale integration network. In: Proceedings of IEEE International Conference on Computer Vision (ICCV), Seoul, pp. 1774–1783. IEEE Xplore (2019)
20. Qiu, Z., Liu, L., Li, G., et al.: Crowd counting via multi-view scale aggregation networks. In: Proceedings of IEEE International Conference on Multimedia and Expo (ICME), Shanghai, pp. 1498–1503. IEEE Xplore (2019)
21. Zhang, L., Shi, M., Chen, Q.: Crowd counting via scale-adaptive convolutional neural network. In: Proceedings of IEEE Winter Conference on Applications of Computer Vision (WACV), Lake Tahoe, pp. 1113–1121. IEEE Xplore (2018)
22. Lokesh, B., Srinivas, S., Venkatesh, R.: CrowdNet: a deep convolutional network for dense crowd counting. In: ACM International Conference on Multimedia, Amsterdam, pp. 640–644. ACM (2016)
23. Sam, D., Surya, S., Babu, R.: Switching convolutional neural network for crowd counting. In: Proceedings of IEEE Conference on Computer Vision and Pattern Recognition (CVPR), Honolulu, pp. 4031–4039, IEEE Xplore (2017)
24. Li, H., Zhang, S.H., Kong, W.: Crowd counting using a self-attention multi-scale cascaded network. IET Comput. Vis. **13**(6), 556–561 (2019)
25. Shi, Z., Le, Z., Cao, X., et al.: Crowd counting with deep negative correlation learning. In: Proceedings of IEEE Conference on Computer Vision and Pattern Recognition (CVPR), Salt Lake City, pp. 5382–5390. IEEE Xplore (2018)
26. Wu, X., Zheng, Y., Ye, H., et al.: Counting crowds with varying densities via adaptive scenario discovery framework. Neurocomputing **397**, 127–138 (2020)
27. Zhao, M., Zhang, C., Zhang, J., et al.: Scale-aware crowd counting via depth-embedded convolutional neural networks. IEEE Trans. Circ. Syst. Video Technol. **30**(10), 3651–3662 (2020)
28. Wang, Q., Gao, J., Lin, W., et al.: NWPU-crowd: a large-scale benchmark for crowd counting and localization. IEEE Trans. Pattern Anal. Mach. Intell. **43**(6), 2141–2149 (2020)
29. Guo, X., Li, Y., Ling, H.: LIME: low-light image enhancement via illumination map estimation. IEEE Trans. Image Process. **26**(2), 982–993 (2017)
30. Xiong, F., Shi, X., Yeung, D.: Spatiotemporal modeling for crowd counting in videos. In: Proceedings of IEEE International Conference on Computer Vision (ICCV), Venice, pp. 5161–5169. IEEE Xplore (2017)
31. Zhang, C., Li, H., Wang, X., et al.: Cross-scene crowd counting via deep convolutional neural networks. In: Proceedings of IEEE Conference on Computer Vision and Pattern Recognition (CVPR), Boston, pp. 833–841. IEEE Xplore (2015)

32. Zhao H., Min W., Wei X., et al.: MSR-FAN: multi-scale residual feature-aware network for crowd counting. IET Image Process. 1–10 (2021). https://doi.org/10.1049/ipr2.12175

33. Shami, M., Maqbool, S., Sajid, H., et al.: People counting in dense crowd images using sparse head detections. IEEE Trans. Circ. Syst. Video Technol. 29(9), 2627–2636 (2019)

34. Zhang, Y., Chang, F., Wang, M., et al.: Auxiliary learning for crowd counting via count-net. Neurocomputing 273, 190–198 (2018)

35. Wang, L., Yin, B., Guo, A., et al.: Skip-connection convolutional neural network for still image crowd counting. Appl. Intell. 48, 3360–3371 (2018)

An Open-Source Library of 2D-GMM-HMM Based on Kaldi Toolkit and Its Application to Handwritten Chinese Character Recognition

Jiefeng Ma[1], Zirui Wang[2], and Jun Du[1(✉)]

[1] University of Science and Technology of China, Hefei, China
jfma@mail.ustc.edu.cn, jundu@ustc.edu.cn
[2] Chongqing University of Posts and Telecommunications, Chongqing, China
wangzr@cqupt.edu.cn

Abstract. As an open source toolkit based on 1D-HMM framework, Kaldi toolkit is widely used in many signal processing tasks. However, when dealing with complex spatial structures, e.g. in image related tasks, 2D-HMM is more suitable since it allows free transition between hidden states in both horizontal and vertical directions. Although 2D-HMM framework has been proposed for years, there is still a lack of efficient open source toolkit for further research due to its complexity. In this paper we present a highly efficient code library of 2D-GMM-HMM based on Kaldi toolkit with implementation details. As a demonstration of its effectiveness, we apply 2D-GMM-HMM to handwritten Chinese character recognition (HCCR) task. The experiments on a 50-class HCCR task have proved that the 2D-GMM-HMM system has obvious advantages over the 1D-GMM-HMM system in terms of recognition accuracy and modeling precision. Moreover, the visual analysis shows that 2D-GMM-HMM can well segment the Chinese characters into basic components such as radicals via the hidden states in both horizontal and vertical directions while 1D-GMM-HMM can only conduct the segmentation in the horizontal direction. The project code of 2D-GMM-HMM library and its recipe on HCCR is publicly available at https://github.com/jfma-USTC/2DHMM.

Keywords: Hidden Markov model · Open source library · Kaldi toolkit · Handwritten Chinese character recognition

1 Introduction

As a generalization of Markov process, hidden Markov model (HMM) was first proposed in 1960s [1]. Because of its intuitive description of sequential modeling in time domain, HMM has achieved great success in many fields, e.g., automatic speech recognition (ASR) task [2], computational biology [3], protein structure prediction [4].

© Springer Nature Switzerland AG 2021
Y. Peng et al. (Eds.): ICIG 2021, LNCS 12888, pp. 235–244, 2021.
https://doi.org/10.1007/978-3-030-87355-4_20

However, the conventional one-dimensional HMM (1D-HMM) for sequential modeling can not well handle the problem of modeling complex spatial structures, e.g., optical character recognition and semantic segmentation in the field of computer vision. In order to solve the problem of dimension mismatch, many scholars have tried to extend one-dimensional HMM to two-dimensional HMM (2D-HMM) since the 1990s. Some researchers proposed pseudo two-dimensional hidden Markov model (P2DHMM) [5] to simulate two-dimensional situation by adding super states, which is essentially the same as one-dimensional HMM with the constraints on the hidden state transition matrix. Nefian et al. took this state structure one step further in [6] by introducing the Embedded HMM (EHMM). Although the image in EHMM is scanned in a 2D manner where each observation block retains two indices, the vertical transitions among states in different superstates are still missing. The first 2D-HMM framework based on Markov random field [7] was proposed in 1998. Under the third-order Markov hypothesis, it introduced a complete formula derivation for training and testing. However, due to the complexity of the model, only the experiment on a small-scale handwritten digit database was conducted. Then, a second-order 2D-HMM framework [8] was presented in 2003, which achieved a good balance between model complexity and system performance. After that, the same framework was applied to several tasks including image classification [9] and image segmentation [10].

Unfortunately, previous works on 2D-HMM did not provide runnable source code, and no convincing visualization results of segmentation via the hidden states were given for analysing why 2D-HMM could outperform 1D-HMM by a large margin in image-related tasks. In this study, we propose an open source library of 2D-HMM with Gaussian mixture model as the output distribution (2D-GMM-HMM) based on Kaldi [11] which is a toolkit of 1D-HMM widely used for sequential modeling tasks such as speech recognition [12] and speech synthesis [13]. As a demonstration of its effectiveness, we apply 2D-GMM-HMM to handwritten Chinese character recognition (HCCR) task. The experiments on 50-class HCCR task show that the 2D-GMM-HMM system has obvious advantages over the 1D-GMM-HMM system in terms of recognition accuracy and modeling precision. Moreover, the visual analysis shows that 2D-GMM-HMM can well segment the Chinese characters into basic components such as radicals via the hidden states in both horizontal and vertical directions while 1D-GMM-HMM can only conduct the segmentation in the horizontal direction.

2 Implement of 2D-HMM Based on Kaldi

2.1 Mathematical Formulation

As shown in Fig. 1, an image is cut into grids of K rows and L columns, and the hidden state set of N_r rows and N_c columns is used to describe the hidden state distribution of 2D-HMM. The hidden state set can be formulated as $\mathbf{S} = \{s_{m,n}\}, 1 \leq m \leq N_r, 1 \leq n \leq N_c$, which contains all possible hidden states that may appear in a 2D-HMM system. And the observation set can be formulated

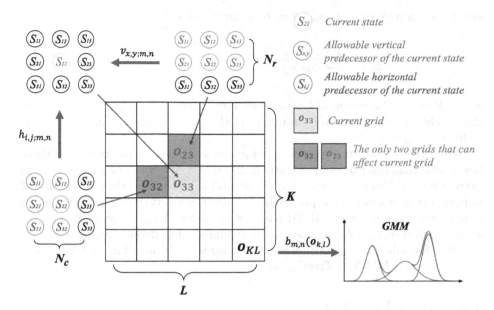

Fig. 1. 2D-GMM-HMM system.

as $\mathbf{O} = \{o_{k,l}\}, 1 \leq k \leq K, 1 \leq l \leq L$ with each grid corresponding to a hidden variable $\mathbf{Q} = \{q_{k,l}\}, 1 \leq k \leq K, 1 \leq l \leq L$.

In addition, a second-order Markov hypothesis is applied to reduce the computational complexity, which means the hidden state corresponding to the current grid is only affected by the hidden state of the upper grid and the left grid. Under this assumption, the state transition can be separated into vertical state transitions $\mathbf{V}$ and horizontal state transitions $\mathbf{H}$ as in (1).

$$\begin{aligned}
\mathbf{V} =& \{v_{x,y;m,n} = P\left(q_{k,l} = s_{m,n} | q_{k-1,l} = s_{x,y}\right) : \\
& 1 \leq x \leq N_r, 1 \leq y \leq N_c\} \\
\mathbf{H} =& \{h_{i,j;m,n} = P\left(q_{k,l} = s_{m,n} | q_{k,l-1} = s_{i,j}\right) : \\
& 1 \leq i \leq N_r, 1 \leq j \leq N_c\}
\end{aligned} \tag{1}$$

The initial probability can also be separated into horizontal and vertical parts, respectively. Initial horizontal probability distribution can be formulated as $\mathbf{\Pi}_h = \{\pi_{h;m,n}\}$, where $\pi_{h;m,n}$ means the probability of each hidden state appearing in the first column. And initial vertical probability distribution can be formulated as $\mathbf{\Pi}_v = \{\pi_{v;m,n}\}$, where $\{\pi_{v;m,n}\}$ means the probability of each hidden state appearing in the first row.

When using Gaussian mixture model (GMM) to describe the emitting probability $\mathbf{B} = \{b_{m,n}(o_{k,l})\}$, the likelihood of a given observation block $o_{k,l}$ being generated by a given state $s_{m,n}$ can be formulated as (2)

$$b_{m,n}\left(o_{k,l}\right) = \sum_{g=1}^{G_s} \frac{c_{m,n}^{(g)}}{[2\pi]^{\frac{V}{2}} \Sigma^{\frac{1}{2}}} \cdot e^{-\frac{\left(o_{k,l}-\mu_{m,n}^{(g)}\right)\Sigma_{m,n}^{(g)-1}\left(o_{k,l}-\mu_{m,n}^{(g)}\right)^{T}}{2}} \tag{2}$$

where V is the dimension of feature vector $o_{k,l}$, and $c_{m,n}^{(g)}$, $\mu_{m,n}^{(g)}$, and $\Sigma_{m,n}^{(g)}$ are the weight, the mean, and the covariance of the g-th Gaussian component in the PDF of $s_{m,n}$, respectively.

After the explicit mathematical definition has been given, there are three key issues that need to be addressed in 2D-HMM system. The first is how to extract features from a given image, the second is how to find the optimal model parameters to maximize the probability of observation variables, and the last is how to use the well-trained HMM parameters to get the most probable label of an unlabelled image. We will describe implementation details in next sections. Detailed formulation of algorithm for above issues can be found in *APPENDIX B* of [8] and the *LEARNING* section of [14].

2.2   Feature Extraction

As shown in Fig. 2, an image is first divided into L frames using a $F_h \times F_w$ sliding window from left to right, with a frame shift of F_r pixels. In each frame, a smaller sliding window of size $F_p \times F_w$ is used to scan from top to bottom with a window shift of F_d pixels. After using the task specific feature extraction method, each grid can be represented by a feature vector $o_{k,l}$. If F_p is set to the same value as F_h, the number of rows K in the grids will be reduced to 1 and that is the feature extraction method used in 1D-HMM. The implementation details will be discussed in Sect. 3.2

2.3   Training Process

Assume that there are C classes in total, we use a separate 2D-HMM for each class, and the parameter set can be formulated as $\boldsymbol{\Theta} = \{\theta^c : c = 1, 2, \ldots, C\}$. When we get labelled images of class c from the training set $\mathbf{X}_{tr}^c$, we can use the Algorithm 1 to find the optimal 2D-HMM parameters for every θ^c.

Note that step 5 use the decoding method in *APPENDIX B* of [8] and step 6 use the *Decision-Directed* learning in [7].

2.4   Testing Process

For every unlabelled image T_i from test set $\mathbf{X}_{ts}$, we need to find the most probable label $\hat{C}_i$ of it, which can be formulated as Eq. 3, and the general idea of the test algorithm is listed in Algorithm 2.

$$\hat{C}_i = \arg\max_c \left\{ \max_{m,n} \ln\left[P\left(q_{K,L} = s_{m,n}, O_i|\theta^c\right)\right] \right\} \tag{3}$$

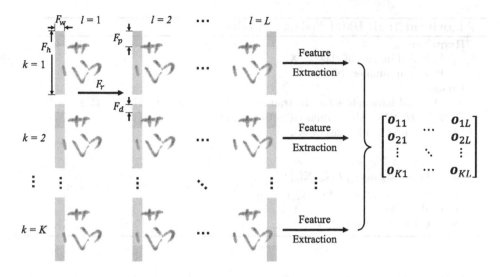

Fig. 2. Feature extraction method in 2D-HMM.

2.5   Implementation Details with Kaldi

We implement a complete codebase for 2D-HMM framework as shown in Fig. 3.
The main differences between our work and the original 1D-HMM system in
Kaldi are annotated with red boxes. For the feature extraction part, we use
Perl scripts to integrate executable programs written in C++. For the training and test parts, we design two new classes named *TransitionModel_2D* and
HmmTopology_2D in Kaldi. *TransitionModel_2D* is used to describe transition
matrix in both vertical and horizontal directions. And *HmmTopology_2D* is used
to describe 2D-HMM topology including the shape and initial transition probabilities of hidden states map. All functions of 1D-HMM used in Kaldi is rewritten
as member functions of two classes. We use the decoding algorithm described
in [14] instead of WFST [15] used in Kaldi, since the transition between hidden
states in 2D-HMM is nonlinear and hard to be integrated with WFST framework.

3   Experiments

3.1   Task Description

Due to the variety of Chinese characters and the great differences in writing
styles, handwritten recognition for Chinese character has always been a challenging problem [16]. According to the type of data acquisition, handwriting
recognition can be divided into online and offline. For offline handwritten Chinese character recognition task, we need to analyze and classify a group of gray
images containing Chinese characters.

Algorithm 1: 2D HMM Training Algorithm

Require:
    Labelled images of class c, $\mathbf{X}_{tr}^c$,
    Iteration number, $\mathbf{N}_0$;
Ensure:
    Optimal parameters for the training set, $\hat{\theta}^c = \{\hat{\boldsymbol{\Pi}}_h^c, \hat{\boldsymbol{\Pi}}_v^c, \hat{\mathbf{H}}^c, \hat{\mathbf{V}}^c, \hat{\mathbf{B}}^c\}$;
1: $\boldsymbol{\Pi}_{h1}^c, \boldsymbol{\Pi}_{v1}^c, \mathbf{H}_1^c, \mathbf{V}_1^c \leftarrow$ random initialisation
2: $\mathbf{B}_1^c \leftarrow$ first ten images of $\mathbf{X}_{tr}^c$
3: $i \leftarrow 1$;
4: **while** $i < \mathbf{N}_0$ **do**
5:    $\hat{\mathbf{Q}}_i \leftarrow \arg\max_{\mathbf{Q}} P(\mathbf{Q}, \mathbf{X}_{tr}^c | \theta_i^c)$
6:    $\theta_{i+1}^c \leftarrow \arg\max_{\theta^c} P(\theta^c | \hat{\mathbf{Q}}_i)$
7: **end while**
8: **return** $\hat{\theta}^c = \theta_{N_0}^c$;

Different from sound-based writing systems such as Greek and Hebrew, Chinese characters are mainly logographic and consist of basic radicals. It is natural to decompose Chinese characters to radicals and spatial structures then use these knowledge for character recognition. In previous works, CNN-based models [17,18] treat each Chinese character as a whole without considering inner sub-structures. [20] adopts 1D-HMM framework for handwritten Chinese text recognition, but only one-dimensional alignment results in horizontal direction can be obtained. Contrarily, the 2D-HMM method can provide segmentation results in both horizontal and vertical directions, with each radical modeled by one or several hidden states.

3.2   Experimental Setup

We conduct our experiments on 50-class Chinese characters randomly selected from the HWDB-1.0 and HWDB-1.1 databases [19] released by Institute of Automation, Chinese Academy of Sciences. For each character class, there are 650 samples for training and 65 samples for testing in average.

The feature extraction method in 1D-GMM-HMM system is basically the same as [20]. Firstly, the image is processed by Otsu binarization, and then the height of the image is normalized to 60 pixels while the aspect ratio remains unchanged. Then, an 80×40 rectangular sliding window is used to scan the whole image from left to right along the center line of Chinese characters with a frame shift of 3 pixels. And a 256-dimensional feature vector is extracted for each frame [21,22]. Finally, PCA transformation is adopted to obtain a compressed 50-dimensional feature vector fed to the training and testing process. In 2D-GMM-HMM system, a 40×40 sliding window is used to scan from top to bottom in each frame with a window shift of 5 pixels. The dimension of feature vector is correspondingly reduced from 256 to 128, while the feature dimension after PCA remains 50.

Algorithm 2: 2D HMM Test Algorithm

Require:
  Unlabelled image, $T_i \in \mathbf{X}_{ts}$,
  2D-HMM parameters, $\boldsymbol{\Theta} = \{\theta^c : c = 1, 2, \ldots, C\}$;
Ensure:
  The most probable label, $\hat{C}_i$;
  1: $C_{best} \leftarrow 1$
  2: $P_{max} \leftarrow -\infty$
  3: $c \leftarrow 1$
  4: **while** $c \leq C$ **do**
  5:   $p_i^c = \max_{m,n} \ln [P(q_{K,L} = s_{m,n}, O_i|\theta^c)]$
  6:   **if** $p_i^c > P_{max}$ **then**
  7:     $P_{max} = p_i^c$
  8:     $C_{best} = c$
  9:   **end if**
 10: **end while**
 11: **return** $\hat{C}_i = C_{best}$;

After feature extraction, the 1D-GMM-HMM and 2D-GMM-HMM systems are trained with iteration times set to 40 and the number of Gaussian kernels per hidden state set to 50 in average. And the system performance are compared under the character error rate (*CER*) criterion.

Table 1. CER comparison of 1D-GMM-HMM and 2D-GMM-HMM systems with different number of hidden states

Methods	N_r	N_c	CER
1D-GMM-HMM	1	3	16.19%
	1	5	14.39%
2D-GMM-HMM	1	3	13.87%
	1	5	11.02%
	3	3	10.06%
	7	7	7.15%

N_r means the row number of hidden states
N_c means the column number of hidden states

3.3 Result Analysis

The results of 50 classes Chinese handwritten character recognition with different hidden states in both system are shown in Table 1. We can observe that under the same number of hidden states (1×3 and 1×5), the 2D-GMM-HMM system has a large *CER* reduction of 2.85% in average over 1D-GMM-HMM system. When we increase the number of hidden states to 3×3 and 7×7, the *CER* can be further reduced by 4.33% and 7.24%.

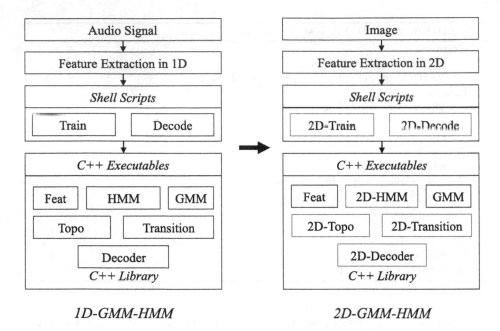

Fig. 3. Code framework comparison between 1D-GMM-HMM and 2D-GMM-HMM system with Kaldi.

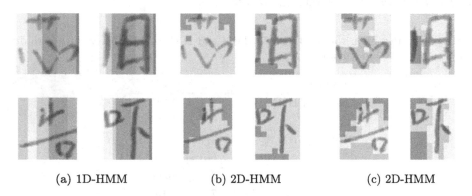

(a) 1D-HMM   (b) 2D-HMM   (c) 2D-HMM

Fig. 4. Hidden state alignment visualization results. (a) 1D-HMM with 5 hidden states, (b) 2D-HMM with 2 hidden states, (c) 2D-HMM with 4 hidden states

Furthermore, we compare the hidden state alignment results of the two systems. From the visualization results in Fig. 4 with different colors representing different hidden states, we can observe that 1D-HMM system can only generate one-dimensional alignments from left to right, while 2D-HMM system is more suitable to capture the complex structure of Chinese radicals due to the flexibility of hidden state transitions in both vertical and horizontal directions. As the increase of hidden states number, the 2D-HMM framework can get better alignment results from simple separation of background and foreground to explicit segmentation of Chinese characters on radical level.

4 Conclusion

In this paper, we present a highly efficient code library of 2D-GMM-HMM based on Kaldi toolkit with detailed implementation. The experiments on 50-class HCCR task show that 2D-GMM-HMM system has obvious advantages over 1D-GMM-HMM system in both recognition accuracy and modeling precision. We will introduce the new framework of 2D-DNN-HMM using deep neural network to model state posterior probability instead of generative model like GMM in the future. The code is released in Github at https://github.com/jfma-USTC/2DHMM, hope this code library can provide convenience for researchers handling many other image related tasks.

Acknowledgment. This work was supported by the Youtu Lab of Tencent.

References

1. Baum, L.E., Petrie, T.: Statistical inference for probabilistic functions of finite state Markov chains. Ann. Mathe. Stat. **37**(6), 1554–1563 (1966)
2. Varga, A.P., Moore, R.K.: Hidden markov model decomposition of speech and noise. In: International Conference on Acoustics, Speech, and Signal Processing (2002)
3. Eddy, S.R.: Hidden Markov models. Curr. Opin. Struct. Biol. **6**(3), 361–5 (1996)
4. Krogh, A., Larsson, B., Heijne, G.V., Sonnhammer, E.L.: Predicting transmembrane protein topology with a hidden Markov model: application to complete genomes. J. Mol. Biol. **305**(3), 567–580 (2001)
5. Bippus, R., Margner, V.: Script recognition using inhomogeneous P2DHMM and hierarchical search space reduction, pp. 773–776 (1999)
6. Nefian, A., Nefian, A.: An embedded hmm-based approach for face detection and recognition. In: 1999 IEEE International Conference on Acoustics, Speech, and Signal Processing, vol. 6, pp. 3553–3556, Los Alamitos, CA, USA. IEEE Computer Society, March 1999
7. Park, H.S., Lee, S.W.: A truly 2-D hidden Markov model for off-line handwritten character recognition. Pattern Recogn. **31**, 1849–1864 (1998)
8. Othman, H., Aboulnasr, T.: A separable low complexity 2D HMM with application to face recognition. IEEE Trans. Pattern Anal. Mach. Intell. **25**(10), 1229–1238 (2003)
9. Ma, X., Schonfeld, D., Khokhar, A.: A general two-dimensional hidden Markov model and its application in image classification. In: 2007 IEEE International Conference on Image Processing, vol. 6, pp. VI - 41–VI - 44 (2007)
10. Baumgartner, J., Flesia, A.G., Gimenez, J., Pucheta, J.: A new approach to image segmentation with two-dimensional hidden Markov models. In: 2013 BRICS Congress on Computational Intelligence and 11th Brazilian Congress on Computational Intelligence, pp. 213–222 (2013)

11. Povey, D., et al.. The Kaldi speech recognition toolkit. In: IEEE 2011 Workshop on Automatic Speech Recognition and Understanding. IEEE Signal Processing Society, December 2011. IEEE Catalog No.: CFP11SRW-USB

12. Ghahremani, P., BabaAli, D. Povey, K. Riedhammer, Trmal, J., Khudanpur, S.: A pitch extraction algorithm tuned for automatic speech recognition. In: 2014 IEEE International Conference on Acoustics, Speech and Signal Processing (ICASSP), pp. 2494–2498 (2014)

13. Hayashi, T., et al.: ESPnet-TTS: unified, reproducible, and integratable open source end-to-end text-to-speech toolkit. In: 2020 IEEE International Conference on Acoustics, Speech and Signal Processing (ICASSP), pp. 7654–7658 (2020)

14. Othman, H., Aboulnasr, T.: A simplified second-order hmm with application to face recognition. In: ISCAS 2001. The 2001 IEEE International Symposium on Circuits and Systems (Cat. No. 01CH37196), vol. 2, pp. 161–164 (2001)

15. Mohri, M., Pereira, F., Riley, M.: Weighted finite-state transducers in speech recognition. Comput. Speech Lang. **16**, 69–88 (2002)

16. Dai, R.-W., Liu, C.-L., Xiao, B.-H.: Chinese character recognition: history, status and prospects. Front. Comput. Sci. China **1**, 126–136 (2007)

17. Cireşan, D., Meier, U.: Multi-column deep neural networks for offline handwritten Chinese character classification. In: 2015 International Joint Conference on Neural Networks (IJCNN), pp. 1–6 (2015)

18. Zhong, Z., Zhang, X.Y., Yin, F.,Liu, C.L.: Handwritten Chinese character recognition with spatial transformer and deep residual networks. In: 2016 23rd International Conference on Pattern Recognition (ICPR), pp. 3440–3445 (2016)

19. Liu, C.L., Yin, F., Wang, D.H., Wang, Q.F.: CASIA online and offline Chinese handwriting databases. In: International Conference on Document Analysis & Recognition (2011)

20. Wang, Z.-R., Jun, D., Wang, W.-C., et al.: A comprehensive study of hybrid neural network hidden Markov model for offline handwritten Chinese text recognition. Int. J. Doc. Anal. Recogn. **21**(4), 241–251 (2018)

21. Liu, C.-L.: Normalization-cooperated gradient feature extraction for handwritten character recognition. IEEE Trans. Pattern Anal. Mach. Intell. **29**(8), 1465–1469 (2007)

22. Bai, Z.L., Huo, Q.: A study on the use of 8-directional features for online handwritten Chinese character recognition. In: 8th International Conference on Document Analysis & Recognition (2006)

Automatic Leaf Diseases Detection System Based on Multi-stage Recognition

Songyun Deng[1], Lekai Cheng[1], Wenlin Li[2], Wei Sun[1], Yaonan Wang[1], and Qiaokang Liang[1(✉)]

[1] College of Electrical and Information Engineering, Hunan University, Changsha 410082, China
qiaokang@hnu.edu.cn
[2] DUT-RU International School of Information Science & Engineering, Dalian University of Technology, Dalian 116620, China

Abstract. The problem of plant diseases is an important issue affecting the growth of world food. However, the existing technology still has many defects in the automatic detection of plant diseases. These defects are mainly concentrated in three aspects: lack of dataset, no algorithm suitable for large range detection and lack of systems used on agricultural production. In this paper, we have made the following contributions to these shortcomings. First, we proposed a multi-stage system which could not only do the plant species classification but also do the disease classification at the same time. Besides, this approach could also reduce the dependence of the model on dataset to some extent. Second, an improved network proposed by us could perform fast calculations while maintaining accuracy. Third, we have realized the function of real-time leaf disease recognition on the embedded platform, which would provide ideas for the plant diseases detection of a wide range.

Keywords: Multi-stage recognition · SEI-ResNet · Embedded platform

1 Introduction

Plant diseases have always been a significant obstacle in agricultural production and gardening fields. In general, the traditional manual methods that people used to detect plant diseases are complicated and subjective [1]. Besides, due to the manual detection methods which require many steps and take a long time, it cannot be applied to the detection of plant diseases in a large range [2]. Today, advances in computer science and technology make it possible for machine vision recognition technology to replace naked eye identification to some extent [3]. It's the reason that plant diseases recognition is an important research task in machine vision field.

Supported by organization x.

Among the organs of plants, leaves are considered as one of the important organs for confirming plant categories [4]. Therefore, in recent years, there were a great number of researches on leaf diseases recognition based on machine vision technologies. These methods can be divided into two categories. The first one is the traditional image processing technique which mainly contains the pattern recognition method based on statistical method, pattern recognition method based on structure and fuzzy pattern recognition method in image classification field [5]. However, these traditional methods require experienced people to use them well and can be limited by the influence of environment, which means that traditional technique is not a perfect solution to automatic identification on leaf diseases [6,7]. The second one is the image processing technique based on machine learning technology. This approach is considered as a more valuable method than traditional methods in leaf diseases detection [3].

In this paper, we propose a solution for automatic identification of leaf diseases including two steps: cropping and classification. In the first step, YOLOv4-Tiny [8] is used to determine the position of leaves and remove redundant background. On the second step, a changed network architecture is used to classify species of plants and categories of leaf diseases. What's more, this classification network was designed for efficient computing speed. Finally, the algorithm is deployed to an embedded platform, and this system can identify leaf diseases in real time.

2   Related Work

The image classification technology based on deep learning has developed rapidly since 2012, which made the automated identification of large-scale leaf diseases possible [9]. In the field of automatic image recognition on leaf diseases, most research focused on the PlantVillage dataset [6,10]. Mohanty et al. [11] tested the performance of some classical network models in the PlantVillage dataset and found that the inception module got the best score in this dataset. Besides, Anjaneya [12] used the methods of transfer learning and discriminant learning to research the performance of ResNet34 and ResNet50 on PlantVillage. The result is that only four epochs were needed to achieve 98% accuracy on this dataset.

The scarcity of dataset made it difficult to implement the automatic leaf diseases identification system. Moreover, using ordinary network models to detect leaf diseases in the natural environment was of difficulty when the training of these models only relied on PlantVillage [13]. For the implementation of this system, Udutalapally et al. [14] set up a fully automatic monitoring and irrigation agricultural equipment on the field. This test lasted for 3 months and completed the task relatively successfully. However, the network structure used on equipment was relatively unitary. It couldn't finish the identification task of complex disease species. In the improvement of the identification method, Brahimi et al. [15] proposed a Teacher/Student Network based on transfer learning to fix this flaw, while Lee et al. [4] used attention-based RNN model to solve this problem. On the other hand, Bi et al. [16] used the Wasserstein way based on gradient punishment with the Label Smooth Regularization(LSR) method to improve classification accuracy.

3   Network Construction Scheme:YOLOv4-Tiny + SEI-ResNet

Our solution is mainly used to solve two difficulties: the scarcity of dataset and the difficulty in implementation of this system. Therefore, we propose a multi-stage recognition scheme, and its specific process is shown in Fig. 1.

3.1   YOLOv4-Tiny: A Fast Method to Remove Redundant Background

The step to remove the unnecessary background needs to be positioned quickly and accurately. However, traditional image segmentation technology is difficult to indicate good results in complex backgrounds, and the image processing speed of image segmentation technology based on deep learning is slower than that of image detection technology. Moreover, the error tolerance rate of image segmentation technology is worse than that of image detection technology. Therefore, image detection technology is the best way to remove redundant background.

| Original Image | Class 1
Positioning and Cropping
(YOLOv4-tiny) | Class 2
Classification
(SEI-ResNet) |

Fig. 1. Process of Identification. Our scheme is divided into two steps: the removal of redundant background and the image classification.

On the other hand, YOLOv4-tiny has a faster computing speed compared to the same period of other networks. It can achieve detection speed close to 375fps on 1080ti graphics card while maintaining high positioning accuracy [8].

3.2   SEI-ResNet

In order to enable the network to be deployed in embedded devices for real-time detection, by referring to the speed test of different networks on Jetson Nano [17], the detection speed needs to be significantly higher than ResNet50 and the accuracy should be close to it.

Therefore, we propose an improved CNN model based on Inception module, ResNet and SE-Net [18]: SEI-ResNet. Its overview figure is shown in Fig. 2.

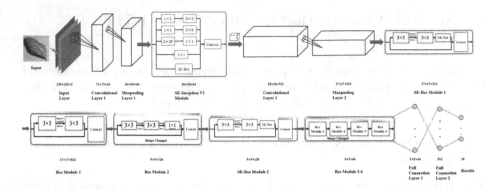

Fig. 2. Overview of SEI-ResNet. It mainly includes six parts: Convolutional Layer, Maxpooling Layer, SE-Inception V1 Module, SE-Res Module, Res Module and Full Connection Layer.

At the front end of this network, we combined SE Module and Inception Module to develop the SE-Inception V1 Module. This type of module is considered to have multi-stage feature extraction capabilities and have good robustness for the extraction of complex features [19]. Besides, SE-Res Module has similar functions in this network. Nevertheless, the powerful feature extraction capabilities as these modules have, too many of which may greatly increase the fragmentation of network operations. Moreover, different channel width may increase the memory access cost (MAC) [20]. Thus, in this network, we used as many "balanced" convolutions (equal channel width) as possible and used as few modules as possible, which may increase the degree of fragmentation.

On the other hand, since the number of layers in the model does not exceed 30, which is less than that of ResNet34, some overfitting methods like Dropout, Batch-Normalization [21] still need to be used in the network. In detail, its structure can be shown on Table 1.

3.3   Network Training

Training for YOLOv4-Tiny. Since the role of YOLOv4-tiny is mainly to locate the position of the leaf, pictures that can only show the local part of the leaf will not be able to be positioned. Therefore, all images of corn and the squash leaf images cannot be used to train. We manually annotate the remaining 33 categories of images, each category is labeled with 50 images. Finally, a total of 1650 images can be used for training. In these images, 70% of them are used for training and the remaining 30% are used for validation. The details of the train environment are shown on Table 2. Moreover, the loss of the model no longer drops significantly after 21000 iterations, and this indication is the termination condition of training.

Table 1. Details of the SEI-ResNet

Network number	Network type	Number of feature maps	Kernel size	Padding size	Step size	Additional operating
Input	Input layer	3	–	–	–	–
C-1	Convolution	64	13	2	3	BatchNorm2d
MP-2	Maxpooling	64	3	0	2	–
SE-In-3	Convolution	128	1, 3, 5	0, 1, 2	1	BatchNorm2d
	Maxpooling		3	1	1	BatchNorm2d
	SE-Net		–	–	–	BatchNorm2d
C-4	Convolution	512	6	2	2	BatchNorm2d
MP-5	Maxpooling	512	2	0	1	–
SE-Res-6	Convolution	512	3	0	1	BatchNorm2d
	SE-Net		–	–	–	BatchNorm2d
Res-7	Convolution	512	3	0	1	BatchNorm2d
Res-8	Convolution	128	1, 3	0	1	BatchNorm2d
SE-Res-9	Convolution	128	3	0	1	BatchNorm2d
	SE-Net		–	–	–	BatchNorm2d
Res-10	Convolution	128	3	0	1	BatchNorm2d
Res-11	Convolution	64	1, 3	0	1	BatchNorm2d
Res-12	Convolution	64	3	0	1	BatchNorm2d
Res-13	Convolution	64	3	0	1	BatchNorm2d
F-14	Fully Connected	Number of Neurons: 1600	–	–	–	BatchNorm1d and Dropout
F-15	Fully Connected	Number of Neurons: 512	–	–	–	–
Output	Output Layer	Number of Categories: 38	–	–	–	–

Table 2. Details of the train environment

Train environment		
Type	Configuration (YOLOv4-tiny)	Configuration (SEI-ResNet)
System	Windows10	Ubuntu 18.04.5 LTS
CPU	Intel(R) Core(TM) i5-8300H CPU@2.30 GHZ	Intel(R) Core(TM) i9-10920X CPU@ 3.50 GHz
GPU	NVIDIA GeForce GTX 1050 (4G)	NVIDIA GeForce RTX 3090 (24G)
CUDA	10.2	11.1
Cudnn	7.6.5	8.0.3
Pytorch	1.8.1	1.7
Python	3.8.5	3.8.5
Train parameters		
Type	Value (YOLOv4-tiny)	Value (SEI-ResNet)
Batch	32	16
Momentum	0.9	–
Decay	0.0005	0.05
Epoch	21000	33
Learning Rate	0–100: 0.001	0.0002 StepLR (Size = 3)
	100–10000: 0.0001	
	10000–21000: 0.00001	

Training for SEI-ResNet. It's necessary for SEI-ResNet to train all images. On the contrary, 80% of these images are trained while 20% of them are used to validate. In order to prevent the model from overfitting, when the accuracy of the validation set exceeds 99.4%, the model will stop training. On the other hand, the Adam optimizer and an optimization algorithm that decreases the learning rate with epoch (StepLR) [22] are used to train the model. Besides, the other training details are recorded in Table 2.

In terms of image preprocessing, preventing overfitting of the model is the primary goal. In this step, online learning of images is used for pictures in every epoch, and its process is shown in Fig. 3.

Fig. 3. Process of online learning. During image training, each image must be processed by the 4 steps: Resize, Center Crop, Random Horizontal Flip and Random Crop

4   Experimental Results

4.1   Automatic Leaf Diseases Detection(ALDD) Network Positioning Test

In the field of deep learning, there are many methods to evaluate the quality of a model. In this condition, our model just needs to judge whether there are leaves in the target area. Hence, this model can be considered a two-class classification model, and a discriminant table can be indicated on Table. 3.

Table 3. Matrix for leaves detection

	Leaves (in the forecast)	Non-leaves (in the forecast)
Leaves (in fact)	TP	FN
Non-leaves (in fact)	FP	TN

In this table, TP indicates that there are actually leaves in the target area, and the predicted result is also the same; TN indicates that there are actually no leaves and no leaves are predicted; FP means that there are actually no leaves, but the predicted is the opposite; FN means that there are leaves in reality, but this result is not predicted. Based on these conditions, the formula of Recall and Precision can be demonstrated.

$$Recall = \frac{TP}{TP + FN} \tag{1}$$

$$Precision = \frac{TP}{TP + FP} \tag{2}$$

By using the formula (1) and (2), in the validation set containing 330 images, the value of *Recall* is 100% and that of *Precision* is 98.82%. Thus, combining these two values according to the sequence of sample confidence, the average precision (AP) curve can be shown in Fig. 4.

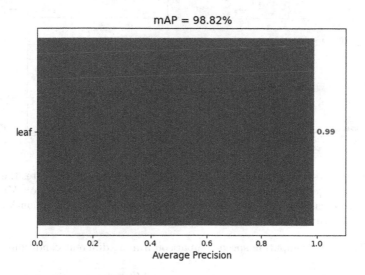

Fig. 4. AP Curve. Because this model only needs to detect one category, AP is the best indicator to evaluate the effect of the precision of the model, and the mean average precision (mAP) is the area under the curve, which can demonstrate the overall precision of this model [3].

4.2 ALDD Network Ablation Test

The effectiveness of the residual structure, SE Module and Inception V1 Module have been proven in many networks [18,19]. However, the effect of these structures used in SEI-ResNet is still undefined. By comparing the differences between these structures and ordinary convolutional structures, their effects in the network can be verified.

In this test, the training process and training duration of the model were used as indicators to evaluate the effectiveness of these structures. Specifically, the kernel size of the ordinary convolutional structure is set as 3, the stride is set to 1, and the padding is 1. Besides, parameters such as learning rate and Decay were set to the same value and the hardware environment was also kept consistent with Table 2 in this test. Moreover, the iteration termination condition was set when the accuracy of the verification set exceeded 99.4%. Figure 5 shows the result of ablation test on SE-Inception V1 module, which indicates the effects on SE Module, Inception V1 Module and SE-Inception V1

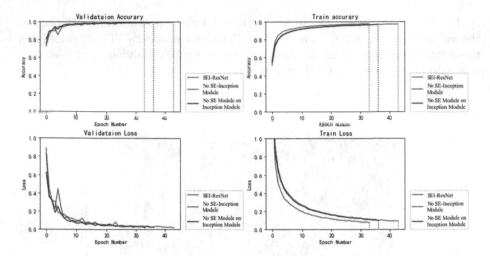

Fig. 5. Ablation Test on SE-Inception V1 Module. The red curve indicates the training process that convolution structure is used to replace the SE-Inception V1 Module while the purple curve shows that the training process that SE-Inception V1 Module is replaced with Inception V1 Module. (Color figure online)

Table 4. Computing speed comparison among different conditions

Model type	Mean training time (s)
No SE-inception module	192.58
No SE module on inception module	213.78
SEI-ResNet	216.56

Module. On the other hand, Table 4 indicates the computing speed comparison among the three conditions.

From the result, it's clear that the Inception V1 Module is a structure that takes a long time to compute and the ability of SE-Inception V1 Module to improve the learning efficiency of models is stronger than other structures. It indicates the necessity of using the SE-Inception V1 Module at the front end of this network. Besides, due to the time-consuming nature of this structure, it was only used once in the network. On the other hand, SE Module can slightly improve the learning performance of the model with almost no additional time. That's the reason that this structure was used repeatedly in residual structures.

4.3   ALDD Network Classification Test

Computing speed and computing efficiency are the two key points for evaluating the performance of classification models. In order for the automatic identification system to have a wide range of leaf disease identification capability, the system needs to have the function of real-time identification. This function has a high demand for model speed. Thus, comparing mainstream networks in a single learning time of PlantVillage, the Table. 5 can be listed.

Table 5. Computing speed comparison among different networks

Model type	Mean training time (s)
DesNet101	640.28
ResNet34	234.76
ResNet50	323.94
SEI-ResNet	**216.56**
VGG16	444.54
SqueezeNet1.1	142.62

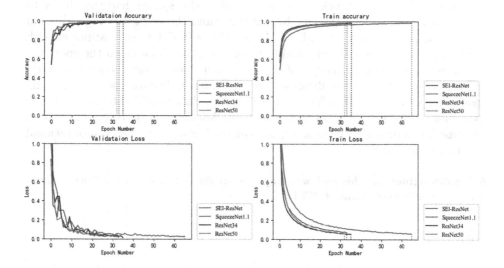

Fig. 6. Accuracy and loss curve for 4 networks.

By selecting the top 4 (short time) networks to compare their training curves, it's clear that there is only one epoch between the SEI-ResNet and the ResNet50 in Fig. 6. However, although ResNet50 exceeds SEI-ResNet by one epoch in training efficiency, its computational speed is 49.58% slower than SEI-ResNet, which means that SEI-ResNet has better overall performance than mainstream classification networks.

4.4   ALDD System Test

All algorithms are finally put into the embedded platform for testing after being trained. For the embedded platform, because of the cost-effective performance,

Jetson Nano was selected as our test platform. What's more, the system on Jetson Nano is Ubuntu 18.04 LTS, and the development environment on this platform is Python3.7 with the OpenCV3.4.6, Pytorch1.4 and CUDA10.

After converting the model to TensorRT for acceleration, the recognition speed of our ALDD System can reach 15.32fps. Compared with the test done by Nvidia [17], our system is closer to the speed of SSD, ResNet18, and it surpasses classic networks such as Inception V4 and VGG19.

5   Conclusion

In this paper, we proposed a multi-stage detection algorithm in leaf diseases recognition field. This algorithm has three main contributions. First, it made up for the defect that the general target detection algorithm needed to confirm the location and category of the target at the same time. Second, the core network (SEI-ResNet) proposed by us in this system had better performance than mainstream classification networks as a whole. Third, this system had the ability to automatically detect leaf diseases in real time, and the recognition speed could reach 15.32fps on Jetson Nano. Even though the lack of data set was not enough to provide the system with the ability to detect plant diseases on the spot, the improvement in the performance of the algorithm showed that the system would be capable of real-time identification of a wide range of leaf diseases after getting enough data to learn. In the future, we will collect data provided by plant disease specialists and use these data to conduct small-scale tests by using our system on some farms or orchards. Besides, we will further optimize the computational cost of this architecture.

Acknowledgments. This work was supported by the National Natural Science Foundation of China under Grant 62073129.

References

1. Nalini, S., et al.: Paddy leaf disease detection using an optimized deep neural network. Comput. Mater. Continua **68**, 1117–1128 (2021)
2. Buja, I., et al.: Advances in plant disease detection and monitoring: from traditional assays to in-field diagnostics. Sensors **21**, 2129 (2021)
3. Liu, J., Wang, X.: Plant diseases and pests detection based on deep learning: a review. Plant Meth. **17**, 22 (2021)
4. Lee, S.H., Chan, C.S., Mayo, S.J., Remagnino, P.: How deep learning extracts and learns leaf features for plant classification. Pattern Recogn. **71**, 1–13 (2017)
5. Wallace, T.P., Mitchell, O.R., Fukunaga, K.: Three-dimensional shape analysis using local shape descriptors. IEEE Trans. Pattern Anal. Mach. Intell. PAMI **3**, 310–323 (1981)
6. Boulent, J., Foucher, S., Théau, J., St-Charles, P.-L.: Convolutional neural networks for the automatic identification of plant diseases. Front. Plant Sci. **10**, 941 (2019)

7. Tsaftaris, S.A., Minervini, M., Scharr, H.: Machine learning for plant phenotyping needs image processing. Trends Plant Sci. **21**, 989–991 (2016)
8. Darknet: Open Source Neural Networks. https://github.com/AlexeyAB/darknet. Accessed 10 Apr 2021
9. Krizhevsky, A., Sutskever, I., Hinton, G.E.: ImageNet classification with deep convolutional neural networks. Commun. ACM **60**, 84–90 (2017)
10. PlantVillage-Dataset: Open data set on plant leaf diseases. https://github.com/spMohanty/PlantVillage-Dataset. Accessed 10 Feb 2021
11. Mohanty, S.P., Hughes, D.P., Salathé, M.: Using deep learning for image-based plant disease detection. Front. Plant Sci. **7**, 1419 (2016)
12. Anjaneya: Plant disease detection from images. arXiv pre-print arXiv:2003.05379 (2020)
13. Ferentinos, K.P.: Deep learning models for plant disease detection and diagnosis. Comput. Electron. Agricult. **145**, 311–318 (2018)
14. Udutalapally, V., Mohanty, S.P., Pallagani, V., Khandelwal, V.: sCrop: a novel device for sustainable automatic disease prediction, crop selection, and irrigation in Internet-of-Agro-things for smart agriculture. IEEE Sens. J. (2020)
15. Brahimi, M., Mahmoudi, S., Boukhalfa, K., Moussaoui, A.: Deep interpretable architecture for plant diseases classification. In: 2019 Signal Processing Algorithms, Architectures, Arrangements, and Applications, pp. 111–116 (2019). IEEE
16. Bi, L., Hu, G.: Improving image-based plant disease classification with generative adversarial network under limited training set. Front. Plant Sci. **11** (2020)
17. Jetson Nano: Deep learning inference benchmarks. https://developer.nvidia.com/embedded/jetson-nano-dl-inference-benchmarks. Accessed 4 Mar 2021
18. Hu, J., Shen, L., Sun, G.: Squeeze-and-excitation networks. In: 2018 IEEE Conference on Computer Vision and Pattern Recognition, CVPR 2018, Salt Lake City, UT, USA, 18–23 June 2018, pp. 7132–7141 (2018). https://doi.org/10.1109/cvpr.2018.00745
19. Xie, S., Girshick, R., Dollar, P., Tu, Z., He, K.: Aggregated residual transformations for deep neural networks. In: 2017 IEEE Conference on Computer Vision and Pattern Recognition, CVPR 2017, Honolulu, HI, USA, 21–26 July 2017, pp. 5987–5995 (2017). https://doi.org/10.1109/CVPR.2017.634
20. Ma, N., Zhang, X., Zheng, H.-T., Sun, J.: ShuffleNet V2: practical guidelines for efficient CNN architecture design. In: Ferrari, V., Hebert, M., Sminchisescu, C., Weiss, Y. (eds.) Computer Vision – ECCV 2018. LNCS, vol. 11218, pp. 122–138. Springer, Cham (2018). https://doi.org/10.1007/978-3-030-01264-9_8
21. Goodfellow, I., Bengio, Y., Couville, A.: Deep Learning, 1st edn. MIT Press, Cambridge (2016)
22. Loshchilov, I., Hutter, F.: SGDR: stochastic gradient descent with warm restarts. arXiv pre-print arXiv:1608.03983 (2017)

Aerial Image Object Detection Based on Superpixel-Related Patch

Jiehua Lin[✉], Yan Zhao, Shigang Wang, Meimei Chen, Hongbo Lin, and Zhihong Qian

Jilin University, Changchun, China
linjh20@mails.jlu.edu.cn, {zhao_y,wangsg,chenmm, hblin}@jlu.edu.cn

Abstract. Aerial image object detection and recognition has attracted increasing attention in recent years. Many excellent detectors have been proposed. However, due to the high-resolution of aerial images, these detectors are difficult to directly apply to aerial images. In order to solve the problem of hard processing caused by high resolution, it is generally to resize the high-resolution images into low-resolution images or cut the high-resolution images into small image patches. Cutting high-resolution aerial images into small image patches without overlap may cut an object into multiple parts which may lose the integrity of the object and causes one object to be detected as multiple objects. We design a new baseline to cut high-resolution aerial images into small image patches by using superpixel. Firstly, we use pixel-related GMM (Gaussian mixture model) to segment the high-resolution aerial images into superpixel images. Then we utilize superpixel label to cut high-resolution aerial images into low-resolution image patches with integrity of the object. Finally, we use YOLOv5 with CSL (Circular Smooth Label) to detect oriented objects. Our method effectively preserves the integrity of the object and improves the AP (Average Precision) of the object detection. This baseline can be applied not only to object detection, but also to aerial image segmentation, classification and so on. Experiments on the UCAS-AOD dataset show the effectiveness of the proposed method.

Keywords: Superpixel · Object detection · Aerial image · YOLOv5

1 Introduction

In recent years, with the development of deep learning, object detection has been improved rapidly. Many object detection methods with good performance based on deep learning have been proposed. Although these object detection methods have achieved remarkable results in natural scene images, they cannot be directly applied to aerial image object detection because of the differences between aerial images and natural scene images. Aerial image has the characteristics of dense object, arbitrary orientation and high resolution. In order to solve the problems of dense objects and arbitrary directions, researchers have proposed some oriented object detection methods such as

Y. Peng et al. (Eds.): ICIG 2021, LNCS 12888, pp. 256–268, 2021.
https://doi.org/10.1007/978-3-030-87355-4_22

CSL (circular smooth label) [1], BBAVectors [2] and ROI transformer [3]. Because the resolution of remote sensing image is very high, if the detector is applied to the original image, it will consume a lot of hardware resources, so researchers generally have two ways to apply the detector. One is to resize high-resolution aerial image into low-resolution image for object detection, but it cannot extract enough features resulting in inaccurate detection. The other is to cut the aerial image into small image patches for object detection, and then merge image patches into a high-resolution aerial image. This may cut a whole object into multiple parts, which results in an object being detected as multiple objects. If there is overlap areas when cutting into small image patches, it will cause great information redundancy and resource consumption.

In this paper, we aim to find a new way to transform high-resolution image into low-resolution image for object detection, which can preserve the integrity of the object, retain more information, and avoid information redundancy. Superpixel will be a small area composed of adjacent pixels with similar characteristics such as color, brightness, texture, etc. And pixels belonging to the same object will be assigned the same superpixel label. Therefore, we propose a new baseline for high-resolution aerial image object detection. Specifically, we use the pixel-related GMM (Gaussian mixture model) superpixel segmentation method to pre-process the high-resolution aerial image, and then cut the high-resolution aerial image into low-resolution image patches according to the result of superpixel segmentation. When cutting, we keep all the pixels of one object in one superpixel at the edge area to ensure the integrity of the object, and there is no overlapping area between image patches. Finally, we take the image patches as input for object detection. YOLOv5 object detection algorithm has good performance in speed and detection performance. But because the aerial image object has arbitrary orientation, and YOLOv5 can only detect the object in the horizontal orientation, we cannot directly use YOLOv5 to detect objects. Therefore, we adopt the YOLOv5 detector combined with CSL as object detector, which introduces the angle variable to control the orientation in the representation of the bounding box of the object.

The rest of this paper is structured as follows: Sect. 2 introduces the related work about our method including the superpixel segmentation and oriented object detection. In Sect. 3, we briefly describe the proposed method. The results of the proposed method are provided in Sect. 4. At last, we conclude the whole work in Sect. 5.

2 Related Work

2.1 Superpixel Segmentation

The concept of superpixel is an image segmentation technology proposed and developed by Ren and Malik [9]. It refers to irregular pixel blocks with a certain visual significance composed of adjacent pixels with similar texture, color, brightness and other characteristics. Superpixel uses the similarity between pixels to group pixels, and uses a small number of superpixels instead of a large number of pixels to express image features, and it has been widely used in image segmentation, pose estimation, object tracking, object recognition and other computer vision applications. SLIC [10] converts the colorful image into a 5-dimensional feature vector of the color and XY coordinates in the

CIELAB color space, and then constructs a distance metric for the 5-dimensional feature vector, and performs local clustering of image pixels to generate superpixels. Zhihua Ban [11] proposed a pixel-related Gaussian mixture model (GMM) to segment images into superpixels. GMM is a weighted sum of Gaussian functions. Each function corresponds to a superpixel to set the label for pixels into superpixels. SpixelFCN [12] uses an encoding-decoding full convolutional network to implement an end-to-end superpixel prediction network.

2.2 Oriented Object Detection

The difference between the oriented object detector and the horizontal object detector is that the oriented object detector relies on oriented bounding boxes (OBB), and the horizontal object detector uses horizontal bounding boxes (HBB). The horizontal object detector is mainly classified into two-stage and single-stage object detectors. RCNN [4] is a typical two-stage object detection network. It first uses convolutional neural network to extract features, then uses region proposal network (RPN) to get the proposals and performs ROIpool on the region of interest (ROI), and finally classifies objects and regresses the bounding box of the proposal. Typical single-stage object detectors are YOLO [5], RetinaNet [6], CenterNet [7], etc. Compared with the two-stage object detector, the single-stage object detector directly predicts the bounding box of the object, and its speed is faster than the two-stage detector. Most of the current oriented object detector is extended from the horizontal object detector, and the angle variable is introduced to control the orientation in the representation of the object's bounding box. For example, R2CNN [8] uses a two-stage Faster RCNN architecture, first obtains the horizontal bounding box (HBB) proposals through the RPN network, then uses multi-scale pooling (ROIPooling) for each proposal, and finally predicts the orientation and obtains the oriented object bounding box (OBB). Based on RetinaNet, CSL [1] introduces a classification method to predict the orientation of the object to obtain an oriented bounding box (OBB) when regressing the bounding box. BBAVectors uses a U-shaped network based on CenterNet to generate heatmaps and obtain the center point position of the object, and then regress to a box boundary-aware vectors (BBAVectors) to obtain an oriented bounding box to achieve the result of oriented object detection.

3 Method

The framework of our proposed method is shown in the Fig. 1. The method we proposed is divided into the following steps. First, we use the GMM-based superpixel segmentation algorithm to segment the high-resolution aerial image, and then use the superpixel segmentation results to cut the high-resolution aerial image into small image patches. In this process, the pixels belonging to one superpixel at the edge area of the patch will be reserved. The start position of the next image patch is the end position of the superpixel at the edge of the previous image patch. In this way, cutting the high-resolution aerial image into small image patches not only avoid one object being cut into multiply parts, and there is no redundant information between patches. Then we use YOLOv5 [13] combined with CSL bounding representation to detect oriented objects.

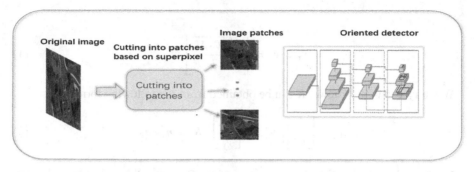

Fig. 1. Framework of our proposed method

3.1 Cutting Aerial Image into Image Patches Based on Superpixel

Superpixel segmentation aggregates some pixels with similar characteristics to form a larger "element" that is more representative. And this new element will serve as the basic unit of the latter image processing. The pixels in the same superpixel generally belong to the same object, which can effectively separate the object from the background, and has strong integrity.

SLIC converts the colorful image into a 5-dimensional feature vector which contains color and XY coordinates in the CIELAB color space, and then constructs a distance metric for the 5-dimensional feature vector, and performs local clustering of image pixels to generate superpixels. Assuming that the image has N pixels and is to be segmented into K superpixels, then the size of each superpixel is N/K. The distance between super pixels is $S = \sqrt{N/K}$ (the side length of super pixels under regular conditions). The specific steps are as follows: First, it distributes the centers of K superpixels to the pixel points of the image and fine-tunes the position of the seed. The center of the superpixel is moved to the point with the smallest gradient among the 9 points in the 3 × 3 range, to avoid superpixels falling on noise or boundaries. Then, two matrix **LABEL** and **DIS** are initialized, which are respectively used to store the superpixel label each pixel belonging to and the distance between the pixel to the center of the superpixel it belongs to. And the distance between each pixel within 2S and the center of the superpixel is calculated. If the distance from the point to the center of the superpixel x is less than the distance from the point to the center of the superpixel it originally belongs to, then the point belongs to the superpixel x. Furthermore, the **DIS** matrix and **LABEL** matrix are updated. Finally, the above steps are iterated to obtain the minimum cost function, that is, the sum of the distances from the pixel to the center of its corresponding super pixel.

The main idea of superpixel segmentation based on GMM is to use Gaussian distribution to relate pixels. The main procedure of the algorithm is as follows: let I represent the input image, W and H represent the width and height of the image, $i \in V \overset{\text{def}}{=} \{0, 1, ..., N - 1\}$ (N is the number of pixels in the image), (x_i, y_i) represent the position of the ith pixel, and c_i represent gray value of the pixel (the color image is the RGB value) of the ith pixel, $z_i = (x_i, y_i, c_i)$ represent pixel i. Let v_x and v_y denote the width and height of the superpixels, K is the number of super pixels. When K is known, v_x and v_y can be obtained as follow.

$$v_x = v_y = \left\lfloor \sqrt{\frac{W \cdot H}{K}} \right\rfloor. \tag{1}$$

When v_x and v_y are known, K can be obtained from the following formula:

$$n_x = \left\lfloor \frac{W}{v_x} \right\rfloor, \ n_y = \left\lfloor \frac{H}{v_y} \right\rfloor, \ K = n_x \cdot n_y. \tag{2}$$

Let $\theta_k = \left\{ \hat{u}_k, \hat{\Sigma}_k \right\}$ denote the parameters of the Gaussian distribution model corresponding to the k-th superpixel, and I_k is used to denote the area where the kth superpixel is distributed (this area is initially limited to an area with width of 3 v_x and height of 3 v_y), Where $\hat{u}_k$ represents the mean value vector and $\hat{\Sigma}_k$ represents the covariance matrix. Then the Gaussian distribution probability density function corresponding to a superpixel can be expressed by

$$p(z, \theta) = \frac{1}{(2\pi)^{D/2}\sqrt{\det(\Sigma)}} exp\left\{ -\frac{1}{2}(z - u)^T \Sigma^{-1}(z - u) \right\}. \tag{3}$$

where D represents the number of elements in the pixel vector z. The K_i is used to represent the label of the pixel in the area where the kth superpixel is distributed. Let L_i denote the random variable of the superpixel label of pixel i, the pixel-related Gaussian mixture model can be expressed by

$$P_i(z) = \sum_{k \in K_i} P_r(L_i = k)p(z; \theta_k), \ \forall i \in V. \tag{4}$$

where $P_r(L_i = k)$ represents the probability that the superpixel label of pixel i is k, which is represented by P_i and defined as a constant, so (4) can be simplified to:

$$P_i(z) = P_i \sum_{k \in K_i} P(z; \theta_k), \ \forall i \in V. \tag{5}$$

When parameter set $\theta_k = \left\{ \hat{u}_k, \hat{\Sigma}_k \right\}$ is determined, the label L_i of pixel i is determined by

$$L_i = arg_k \max_{k \in K_i} \frac{p(z_i; \theta_k)}{\Sigma_{k \in K_i} p(z_i; \theta_k)} \tag{6}$$

If labels L_i of each pixel i is determined. The parameter set θ can be obtained by maximum likelihood estimation:

$$f(\theta) = \sum_{i \in V} ln p_i(z_i)$$
$$= \sum_{i \in V} ln P_i + \sum_{i \in V} ln \sum_{k \in K_i} p(z_i; \theta k). \tag{7}$$

where $\sum_{i \in v} ln P_i$ is a constant, and maximizing $f(\theta)$ is equivalent to maximizing

$$L(\theta) = \sum_{i \in V} \ln \sum_{k \in K_i} p(z_i; \theta_k) = \sum_{i \in V} \ln \sum_{k \in K_i} R_{i,k} \frac{p(z_i; \theta_k)}{R_{i,k}}$$

$$\geq \sum_{i \in V} \sum_{k \in K_i} R_{i,k} \ln \frac{p(z_i; \theta_k)}{R_{i,k}} \tag{8}$$

After initializing parameter set θ, R and θ are iterative updated using the EM algorithm to obtain its best estimate. Until EM algorithm converges, the result of super pixel segmentation is obtained.

We preprocess the high-resolution aerial image by using superpixel segmentation method, and retain the super pixel segmentation results. Let I denote the high-resolution aerial image, W and H represent the width and height of the origin high-resolution aerial image. Let (x_i, y_i) represent the position of the ith pixel, where $x_i \in \{1, 2, ..., W\}$, $y_i \in \{1, 2, ..., H\}$. We use matric **SP** denote the superpixel label of each pixel obtained by the superpixel segmentation algorithm. Let L_i represent the superpixel label of pixel i, as shown in the following formula:

$$L_i = SP(x_i, y_i) \tag{9}$$

Take the first image patch (starting from the upper left corner of the image) as an example to illustrate our method based on the superpixel to cut high-resolution aerial image into image patches. We initialize the width and height of the image patch as w and h, and the starting position of each row and column of the patch is 0. We use superpixel labels to cut the high-resolution aerial image into image patches. We use the vector *flag1* to save the superpixel label of pixels (*when* x_i = w in each row of the image), as shown in the following formula:

$$flag1(i) = SP(w, i), i \in \{1, 2, ..., h\} \tag{10}$$

Let $i \in \{1, 2, ..., h\}$, find the pixel i with the largest x_i which superpixel label is *flag1(i)* in the ith row, and record the value of x_i in the vector *flag_x*, and save it in *flag_w*, and record the maximum value of x_i in *flag_w* as *x_max*.

We use vector *flag2* to save the superpixel label of each column of the image when $y_i = h$, as shown in the following formula:

$$flag2(j) = SP(j, h), j \in \{1, 2, ..., x\_max\} \tag{11}$$

Let $j \in \{1, 2, ..., x\_max\}$, find the pixel j with the largest y_j whose superpixel label is *flag2(j)* in the jth column, and record its y_j value in the vector *flag_y*, and save it in *flag_h*, and record the maximum value of y_j in *flag_y* as *y_max*.

At this time, the width and height of image patch become *x_max* and *y_max*. And we record the position of pixels the image patch, which should take from each row and each column of the original high-resolution aerial image. Same as the above steps, the row starting position of the second patch is the value stored in the *flag_x* vector, and the column starting position is the value stored in *flag_y*. This is to avoid information redundancy. The width and height of the image patch are initialized as w and h, and the second image patch can be obtained according to the above steps until all the image patches are obtained.

The Fig. 2 is an example of using our method to cut high-resolution aerial image into image patches, in which the resolution of the aerial image is 1280 × 659 and image patches are taken with the width of 640 and height of 659. We only take the first patch as example. In Fig. 2 (a), we directly cut the high-resolution aerial image into image patches without superpixel segmentation. The two cars in the bottom right corner of the patch are cut into two parts. And Fig. 2 (b) is the result of cutting the high-resolution aerial image into image patches based the proposed method. We use the red dots to show the edge positions, which is obtained using superpixel labels to expand the edges of patch. The horizontal coordinate of each row of red dots is the value stored in the vector *flag_w*, and the largest value is *x_max*.

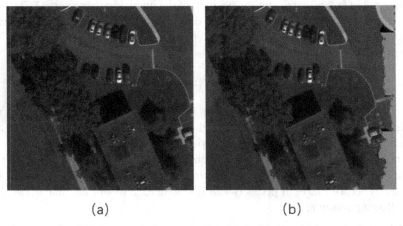

(a)   (b)

Fig. 2. An example of the low-resolution patch. The result of cutting high-resolution aerial image into image patches without superpixel is shown in (a). The result of cutting high-resolution aerial image into image patches with surperpixel is shown in (b). (Color figure online)

3.2 Oriented Object Detection Based on YOLOv5

The object detector based on neural network generally consists of the following parts: Input, Backbone, Neck, Prediction. Input is the input terminal, which is generally an image or image batches. Backbone performs feature extraction on the input data. Neck realizes the extraction of multi-scale features. Prediction uses the extracted features to predict the location of the objects and the object category.

The network framework of YOLOv5 is shown in Fig. 3.

YOLOv5 has the advantages of fast detection and high accuracy. However, it is based on horizontal bounding boxes (HBB). We use a combination of CSL and YOLOv5 [14] to realize oriented object detection.

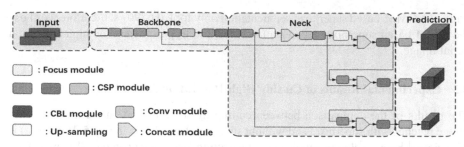

Fig. 3. The network framework of YOLOv5

4 Experiments

4.1 Dateset

We use the UCAS_AOD [15] dataset for experiments. UCAS_AOD is annotated by the Pattern Recognition and Intelligent System Development Laboratory of the University of Chinese Academy of Sciences, and it contains two types of objects and background negative samples. The resolution of aerial images ranges from 1280 × 659 to 1372 × 972, and the number of samples is given in Table 1. For this dataset, we cut the high-resolution aerial image into 2 image patches in the horizontal direction. All experiments are implemented on a desktop machine equipped with an Intel(R) Core (TM) i5-8600k CPU @ 3.60 GHz and 16.0 GB RAM.

Table 1. UCAS_AOD dataset

	Plane image	Plane sample	Car image	Car sample	negative
Version1	600	3591	310	4475	492
Version2	400	3891	200	2639	408
Total	1000	7482	510	7114	910

4.2 Superpixel Segmentation Comparison Experiments

For SLIC and GMM-based superpixel segmentation algorithms, we have done comparative experiments, and the experimental results are shown in Fig. 4. Where, (a) is the original aerial high-resolution image for super pixel segmentation, (b) is a partial enlarged image of aerial image, (c) is the result image of SLIC superpixel segmentation, (d) is a partial enlargement of the result image of SLIC superpixel segmentation, (e) is the result of GMM-based super pixel segmentation, and (f) is a partial enlarged image of GMM-based superpixel segmentation. It can be intuitively observed from the segmentation result image and the partial enlarged image that the superpixel segmentation based on GMM is better than SLIC in preserving the integrity of the object. In addition, the SLIC algorithm took 15.2200 s on the image with the resolution of 1280 × 659, while the GMM-based superpixel segmentation only took 0.67967 s, therefore we chose the GMM-based superpixel segmentation algorithm to pre-process the high-resolution aerial image.

4.3 Experimental Results of Cutting High-Resolution Aerial Image

The results of the comparison between cutting the high-resolution aerial image into image patches with superpixel and without superpixel are shown in Fig. 5. Where, (a) is the original high resolution aerial image for cutting into image patches, (b) and (c) are image patches obtained by cutting the high-resolution aerial image into image patches based on superpixels, (d) and (e) are image patches obtained by cutting high-resolution aerial image into image patches without superpixels. It can be clearly seen that when the high-resolution aerial image is directly cut into patches, the car circled in red in the original high-resolution image is cut into two parts, and our method avoids the car from being cut into two parts and retains the integrity of the whole object.

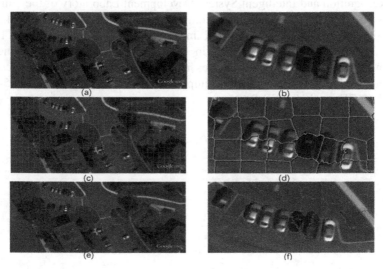

Fig. 4. Superpixel segmentation comparison experiments. (a) is the original aerial high-resolution image for super pixel segmentation, (b) is a partial enlarged image of aerial image, (c) is the result image of SLIC super-pixel segmentation, (d) is a partial enlargement of the result image of SLIC super-pixel segmentation, (e) is the result of GMM-based super pixel segmentation, and (f) is a partial enlarged image of GMM-based superpixel segmentation.

4.4 Oriented Object Detection

We first cut the UCAS_AOD dataset into low-resolution image patches, and then randomly divide it into a training set and a testing set at a ratio of 9:1. And then, we use YOLOv5 network combined with CSL to realize oriented object detection. The object detection AP (Average Precision) and mAP (mean Average Precision) of two methods

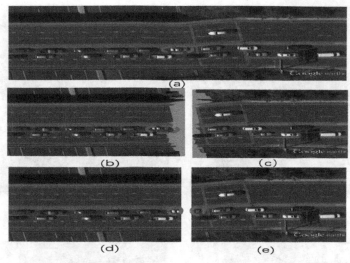

Fig. 5. Comparison between using superpixel-based cutting high resolution aerial image into image patches and direct cutting, (a) is the original high resolution aerial image for cutting into image patches, (b) and (c) are image patches obtained by cutting the high-resolution aerial image into image patches based on superpixels, (d) and (e) are image patches obtained by cutting high-resolution aerial image into image patches without superpixels. (Color figure online)

to cut high- resolution aerial image to small image patches are shows in Table 2. As shown in Table 2, our method improved by 0.223% in car category AP and improved by 0.071% in plane category AP compared with cutting high-resolution aerial image into image patches without suerpixel. Our method has improved on the mAP by 0.147%. And the oriented object detection results of cutting high- resolution into image patches with superpixel or not are shown in Fig. 6. Figure 6 (a) is the result of detection in patches cutting from high-resolution aerial image without superpixel and Fig. 6 (b) is the result of detection in patches cutting from high-resolution aerial image based on superpixel. As shown in Fig. 6 (a) and Fig. 6 (b), the detection performance at the edge area of cutting has been improved by our method. If cutting the high-resolution aerial image into image patches without superpixel, the objects in the edge area will be cut into multiple parts which will not be detected in the following object detection. Cutting high-resolution image into image patches by our method can preserve the integrity of objects in the edge area that is helpful for the detector to detect the object correctly.

Table 2. The object detection mAP of two cutting methods

	AP of CAR	AP of PLANE	mAP
Our method	44.137%	45.047%	44.591%
Without superpixel	43.914%	44.976%	44.444%

(a)   (b)

Fig. 6. Comparison of object detection in patches between using superpixel-based cutting high resolution aerial image into image patches and direct cutting, (a) are the results of object detection in patches from cutting high-resolution aerial image into images patches directly, and (b) are the results of object detection in patches from cutting high-resolution aerial image into images patches based on superpixel.

5 Conclusion

In this paper, we propose a new baseline for object detection in high-resolution aerial image. In general, the resolution of remote sensing image is very high. Therefore, if the detector is applied to the original image, it will consume a lot of hardware resources. Cutting the high-resolution aerial image into image patches can be divided into two cases. In the case of no overlapping areas between patches, the object located at the edge area of the patches will be cut into multiple parts, causing the detector to fail to accurately detect these objects. In the case of overlapping areas between patches, this will lead to a lot of information redundancy and consume a lot of resources. Compared to the previous cutting method, our proposed cutting method based on superpixel will not cut a whole object into multiple parts and cause information redundancy, and improves the performance of detector.

Acknowledgment. This work is supported by the National Natural Science Foundation of China (No. 61631009, No. 61771220).

References

1. Yang, X., Yan, J.: Arbitrary-oriented object detection with circular smooth label. In: Vedaldi, A., Bischof, H., Brox, T., Frahm, J.-M. (eds.) ECCV 2020. LNCS, vol. 12353, pp. 677–694. Springer, Cham (2020). https://doi.org/10.1007/978-3-030-58598-3_40
2. Yi, J., Wu, P., Liu, B., et al.: Oriented object detection in aerial images with box boundary-aware vectors. In: Proceedings of the IEEE/CVF Winter Conference on Applications of Computer Vision, pp. 2150–2159 (2021)
3. Ding, J., Xue, N., Long, Y., Xia, G.S., Lu, Q.K.: Learning ROI transformer for oriented object detection in aerial images. In: 2019 IEEE/CVF Conference on Computer Vision and Pattern Recognition (CVPR), Long Beach, CA, USA, pp. 2844–2853 (2019)
4. Girshick, R., Donahue, J., Darrell, T., Malik, J.: Rich feature hierarchies for accurate object detection and semantic segmentation. In: 2014 IEEE Conference on Computer Vision and Pattern Recognition, Columbus, OH, USA, pp. 580–587 (2014)
5. Redmon, J., Farhadi, A.: YOLOv3: an Incremental Improvement. In: IEEE Conference on Computer Vision and Pattern Recognition, pp. 1–6 (2018)
6. Lin, T.Y., Goyal, P., Girshick, R., He, K., Dollár, P.: Focal loss for dense object detection. In: Proceedings of the IEEE International Conference on Computer Vision, pp. 2980–2988 (2017)
7. Duan, K., Bai, S., Xie, L., Qi, H., Huang, Q., Tian, Q.: Centernet: Keypoint triplets for object detection. In: Proceedings of the IEEE International Conference on Computer Vision, pp. 6569–6578 (2019)
8. Jiang, Y., et al.: R2CNN: rotational region CNN for orientation robust scene text detection. arXiv preprint. arXiv:1706.09579 (2017)
9. Ren, X., Malik, J.: Learning a classification model for segmentation. In: Proceedings ICCV, pp. 10–17 (2003)
10. Achanta, R., Shaji, A., Smith, K., Lucchi, A., Fua, P., Süsstrunk, S.: SLIC superpixels compared to state-of-the-art superpixel methods. In: IEEE Trans. Pattern Anal. Mach. Intell. 34, 2274–2282 (2012)

11. Ban, Z., Liu, J. Cao, L.: Superpixel segmentation using Gaussian mixture model. IEEE Trans. Image Process. 27(8), 4105–4117 (2018)
12. Yang, F., Sun, Q., Jin, H., Zhou, Z.: Superpixel segmentation with fully convolutional networks. In: 2020 IEEE/CVF Conference on Computer Vision and Pattern Recognition (CVPR), Seattle, WA, USA, pp. 13961–13970 (2020)
13. Ultralytics.: yolov5. https://github.com/ultralytics/yolov5
14. YOLOv5_DOTA_OBB. https://github.com/hukaixuan19970627/YOLOv5_DOTA_OBB
15. Zhu, H., Chen, X., Dai, W., Fu, K., Ye, Q., Jiao, J.. Orientation robust object detection in aerial images using deep convolutional neural network. In: 2015 IEEE International Conference on Image Processing (ICIP), Quebec City, QC, Canada, pp. 3735–3739 (2015)

AROA: Attention Refinement One-Stage Anchor-Free Detector for Objects in Remote Sensing Imagery

Xu He[1], Shiping Ma[1], Linyuan He[1,2(✉)], Fei Zhang[1], Xulun Liu[1], and Le Ru[1]

[1] Aeronautics Engineering College, Air Force Engineering University, Xi'an 710038, China
[2] Unbanned system Research Institute, Northwestern Polytechnical University, Xi'an 710072, China

Abstract. Object detection in remote sensing images is a typical computer vision application, which has broad requirements in practice. Recently, attention mechanisms have been widely utilized in a diverse range of visual tasks such as object detection and semantic segmentation. Aimed at the characteristics of remote sensing objects such as rotation variations and inter-class similarity, a question we ask is, what kind of attention mechanism do we really need? In this article, we propose a novel attention refinement one-stage anchor-free object detector (AROA) that leverages attention mechanisms to refine the performance of remote sensing object detection in a one-stage anchor-free network framework. Specifically, we first design an asymmetric spatial self-attention (AS^2A) mechanism to capture rich long-range spatial contexts and eliminate the rotate distortion. Then, to solve the issue of inter-class similarity and boost the multiclass identification capability, we propose a channel attention mechanism, named chain-connected channel attention (C^3A), which connects the adjacent attention blocks like a chain and dramatically mines the channel relationships. In addition, we also introduce an IoU-wise module (IM) to strengthen the correlation between localization and classification branches and filter out the detected boxes with low positioning quality. Extensive experimental results on the DOTA and NWPU VHR-10 datasets demonstrate the effectiveness of the proposed AROA.

Keywords: Object detection · Remote sensing images · Attention mechanisms · Anchor-free · One-stage

1 Introduction

With the fast-paced development of unmanned aerial vehicles (UAVs) and remote sensing technology, remote sensing image analysis has been increasingly applied in fields such as land surveying, environmental monitoring, and emergency relief. Object detection in remote sensing images is regarded as a high-level computer vision task which is purposed to pinpoint the targets in a remote sensing image. Due to the characteristics of remote sensing targets such as complex backgrounds, sparse texture, multiple scales, and variations of orientations, remote sensing object detection remains a challenging and significant research issue.

© Springer Nature Switzerland AG 2021
Y. Peng et al. (Eds.): ICIG 2021, LNCS 12888, pp. 269–279, 2021.
https://doi.org/10.1007/978-3-030-87355-4_23

In recent years, due to outstanding learning ability, the most advanced detection models have been developed by deep convolutional neural networks (DCNNs). Two-stage and one-stage are two basic research paradigms for remote sensing object detection. Two-stage detectors [1,2] resolve the task of object detection in two steps. The first step is to generate numerous region proposals as candidate regions of the objects. The second step is to extract the features of each region proposal from the backbone network and feed the features into the classifier and regressor for classification and position fine adjustment. Despite the two-stage detectors being effective and accurate, the computational cost is fairly high because of the complex traversal process of the region proposals. Compared with two-stage detectors, one-stage detectors [3–6] directly predict the classification and localization in a simple pipeline, which is more computationally efficient. Nevertheless, anchor-based one-stage detectors that rely on anchors mechanism would result in complicated computations related to anchor boxes. Therefore, research on one-stage anchor-free detectors that emancipate the model from massive computations on anchors has drawn much attention in recent years. To the best of our knowledge, many scholars have begun to design one-stage anchor-free detectors [7–17] used in remote sensing images. For instance, X-LineNet [7] detected the oriented aircraft in remote sensing images by predicting a pair of middle lines segments inside each bounding box. Combined with CornerNet [5] and CenterNet [18], Chen *et al.* [8] utilized an end-to-end fully convolutional network (FCN) to identity the targets according to the predicted corners, center, and angle of the ship. Shi *et al.* [17] transformed the vehicle detection task into the multitask learning issue of center keypoint and morphological sizes. These methods illustrated significant advantages for applying one-stage anchor-free detectors to extract remote sensing targets. Nevertheless, due to the cluttered arrangement, rotation variations, and inter-class similarity, conventional one-stage anchor-free detectors cannot be applicable to remote sensing object detection task directly.

Similar to the selective mechanism of human visual attention system, the attention in computer vision attends to the discriminative and valuable feature representation and restrain the information useless. Concretely, non-local neural network [19] (NLNN) is the most classical mechanism of spatial self-attention, which can capture long-range spatial contexts in order to obtain rich semantic information. Some works have made several attempts to incorporate NLNN in remote sensing object detection task. Li *et al.* [10] designed a cross-layer attention to obtain the non-local correlation between small objects. Wang *et al.* [11] inserted the NLNN block into the feature pyramid network to provide the richer spatial association information. However, the above-mentioned NLNN attention has serious rotate distortion, leading to performance degradation for multi-orientation remote sensing objects. Therefore, inspired by the asymmetric convolution, we proposed a novel asymmetric spatial self-attention (AS^{2}A) which strengthens the input of the NLNN with a 3×3 square convolution and two asymmetric central skeleton parts of the square convolution, i.e., 1×3 convolution and 3×1 convolution. AS^{2}A can be exploited to capture rich long-range spatial contexts and enhance the rotational robustness. Beyond spatial attention, squeeze and excitation network [20] (SENet), which can be served as the pioneer of channel attention for classification task, adaptively assign the attention weights of different channels. Wu *et al.* [12] made use

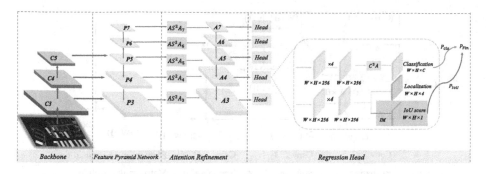

Fig. 1. The architecture of the proposed AROA, where C3, C4 and C5 represent the feature maps of the backbone network. P3 to P7 and A3 to A7 denote the feature levels of feature pyramid network (FPN) used for subsequent attention refinement and regression head, respectively. The shared regression head consists of three branches: classification, localization, and IoU score prediction, respectively. W, H, and C indicate the height, weight, and channel of the feature map, respectively.

of the SENet to enhance the small target capture capability. Zhang *et al.* [13] proposed a selective concatenation module to fuse the low- and high-level features by the SENet attention mechanism. However, as far as we know, these methods only integrate a single SE block into the network, which lacks of the adequate representation ability to identify different categories of targets with similar appearance. To solve this problem, we design a chain-connected channel attention (C^3A) to connect the multiple adjacent SE blocks for learning the deep channel relationships and discriminating the multiclass remote sensing objects with inter-class similarity. In addition, to filter out the low-quality detection boxes in densely arranged remote sensing objects, we propose an IoU-wise module (IM) to predict the Intersection-over-Union (IoU) for each detected box and the final bounding box confidence is set as the harmonic mean of the predicted IoU score and classification score. This can dramatically pull down the box probability as long as the localization or classification score has a rather small probability, so as to remove the low-quality bounding box. The experimental results have shown that the proposed attention mechanisms and IoU-wise module effectively improve the multiclass object detection performance.

2 Methodology

Figure 1 illustrates the architecture of our method. Based by FCOS [6], we implement a one-stage anchor-free detector as a fundamental framework. The input remote sensing images utilize a backbone network to extract features to FPN, and a shared regression head is used to perform the classification, localization, and IoU score prediction tasks. In this letter, the proposed AS^2A is employed behind the FPN for refining the feature representations of each level and the C^3A is merged before the final classification branch to boost the classification performance. Moreover, IM can be formulated as the harmonic mean of classification and localization confidences for the final non-maximum suppression post-processing and average precise computational.

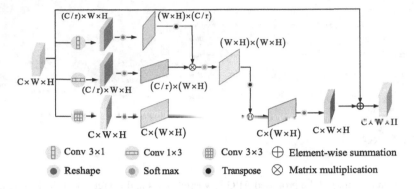

Fig. 2. Details of the position-wise spatial attention module inspired by [19]. C, W, H denote the channel, width, and height dimensions of the feature maps, respectively.

2.1 Asymmetric Spatial Self-attention

Observation shows that the targets in remote sensing images usually has a complicated background and multi-orientation patterns. Therefore, to obtain the long-range valuable context information and eliminate the rotate distortion, our method incorporates the asymmetric convolution which enhances the central cross section of square convolution in the input of the non-local network. As shown in Fig. 2, on the one hand, we first feed the given pyramid feature maps $P \in \mathbb{R}^{C \times W \times H}$ into two convolution units with the kernels of 1×3 and 3×1, resulting in two feature maps $P^{3 \times 1}, P^{3 \times 1} \in \mathbb{R}^{C/r \times W \times H}$, where r is set to 4 in our method. Next, $P^{3 \times 1}$ and $P^{3 \times 1}$ are reshaped to $\mathbb{R}^{(C/r) \times (W \times H)}$. In addition, $P^{3 \times 1}$ follows the operation of transpose, which results in $P^{3 \times 1} \in \mathbb{R}^{(W \times H) \times (C/r)}$. Then, we multiply the two feature maps and perform an operation of softmax on the calculated position-wise matrix to obtain the spatial attention maps $M \in \mathbb{R}^{(W \times H) \times (W \times H)}$:

$$m_{i,j} = \frac{\exp(P_i^{1 \times 3} \cdot P_j^{3 \times 1})}{\sum_{i=1}^{W \times H} \exp(P_i^{1 \times 3} \cdot P_j^{3 \times 1})} \tag{1}$$

where $m_{i,j}$ assesses the effect of the ith position on the jth position. On the other hand, we feed the pyramid feature maps P into a 3×3 convolution unit to obtain a feature map $P^{3 \times 3}$ of the same shape and reshape it to $\mathbb{R}^{C \times (W \times H)}$. Then, we multiply $P^{3 \times 3}$ by the transpose of spatial attention map M and reshape the output feature maps F to $\mathbb{R}^{C \times W \times H}$. Finally, we obtain the final output feature maps O by an element-wise summation operation between F and given feature map P as follows:

$$O_j = \delta F_j + P_j = \delta \sum_{i=0}^{W \times H} (m_{j,i} P_i^{3 \times 3}) + P_j \tag{2}$$

where δ is initialized to 0 and learnable to balance the weights between the features that traverse all positions and original features. Thus, the asymmetric spatial self-attention mechanisms adaptively enhance the long-range correlation of the spatial contexts and eliminate the rotate distortion, thus improving the representation capability for the subsequent per-pixel classification and regression.

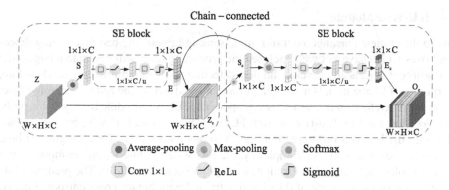

Fig. 3. Diagram of the proposed C^3A. In the first SE block, we use average pooling to squeeze the feature and max-pooling in the second SE block.

2.2 Chain-Connected Channel Attention

For reducing the effect of inter-class similarity in the multiclass remote sensing objects, it is necessary to adaptively rescale features across channels and boost the feature representation capability for classification task. Based on SENet, we design a chain-connected channel attention to learn the channel relationships and enhance category discrimination. For one SE attention block, we first squeeze the given feature maps $Z \in \mathbb{R}^{W \times H \times C}$ by a squeezer $s : S = s(Z)$, where $S \in \mathbb{R}^{1 \times 1 \times C}$ is the output vector and s is the squeeze operation, e.g., average pooling and max-pooling. Then, we feed the output S into an exciter $e : E = e(S, u) = \sigma(conv_1\rho(conv_2 S))$, where $E \in \mathbb{R}^{1 \times 1 \times C}$ is the output of the excitation operation, u denotes the scaling factor of channels and is set to 4 in our method, ρ is a ReLU function, σ is a sigmoid function, and $conv_1$ and $conv_2$ indicate 1×1 convolution layers to rescale the channel number. Next, we can obtain the final output feature maps $U \in \mathbb{R}^{W \times H \times C}$ of one attention block by a fuser $f : U = f(E, Z) = (E \otimes Z) \oplus Z$, where $\otimes$ represents element-wise multiplication and $\oplus$ denotes the element-wise summation operation. In addition, to deeply mine the channel relationships, we connect the adjacent attention blocks like a chain by a connector $c : c(\alpha S, \beta \hat{E}) = softmax(\alpha S, \beta \hat{E})$, where $\hat{E}$ denotes the output vector of the exciter in the previous attention block, α and β are learnable parameters. Finally, we can obtain the final chain channel attention optimized output feature map $O_c \in \mathbb{R}^{W \times H \times C}$ as follows:

$$O_c = f(E_c, Z_c) = f((e(c(\alpha S_c, \beta \hat{E}), u), Z_c) \tag{3}$$

where O_c, Z_c, E_c, and S_c represent the feature maps and vectors used in the final attention block for the classification prediction. Figure 3 illustrates a two attention block connected structure. In our method, we adopt a triple attention blocks-connected pattern for best performance.

2.3 IoU-Wise Module

Due to the cluttered arrangement of remote sensing targets, the bad positioning detection boxes which have not well enclosed the grounding truth will generate a larger IoU with adjacent objects and severely hinders detection precision improvement. Therefore, the quality of localization is also an important index affecting the remote sensing object detection. Therefore, in this article, we propose an IoU-wise module to tackle this problem. As shown in Fig. 1, different from FCOS, we design an IoU wise branch, in parallel with the localization regression branch to predict the IoU of each regressed box. To reduce the computational complexity, the IoU-wise module is only composed of a 1×1 convolution, batch normalization, and sigmoid activation layer. The predicted IoU score P_{IoU} falls in the range of 0 to 1 and is trained with binary cross entropy. Finally, we can obtain the final prediction confidence P_{Fin} for the NMS and AP computational processes as follows:

$$P_{Fin} = 2/(\frac{1}{P_{IoU}} + \frac{1}{P_{Cls}}) \tag{4}$$

where P_{Cls} represents the classification score. Therefore, IM will filter out the low-quality boxes and retain the detection boxes with high IoU score and classification score.

3 Experiments and Result Analysis

3.1 Datesets

In this article, we conduct experiments on two remote sensing datasets: DOTA [21] and NWPU VHR-10 [22].

DOTA. Comprised of 15 categories targets, it has 1,411 images and 188,282 instances annotated with horizontal and oriented bounding boxes. In our experiments, only the annotations of the horizontal bounding boxes are utilized. In addition, the validation, test, and training images have corresponding ratios of 1/6, 1/3, and 1/2. Each image has a size within 800×800 to $4,000 \times 4,000$ pixels.

NWPU VHR-10. These images contain 10 geospatial object classes, having 3,775 target instances. 715 RGB images and 85 sharpened color infrared images are included. Among them, 715 RGB images were collected from Google Earth with spatial resolutions ranging from 0.5 m to 2 m, while 85 pan-sharpened infrared images with a spatial resolution of 0.08 m were collected from Vaihingen data. These object instances were manually labelled with horizontal borders by experts.

3.2 Experimental Details

In the experiments, ResNet-100, which is initialized with the weights pretrained on ImageNet, is used as the backbone network. We use stochastic gradient descent (SGD) to optimize the network and set the initial learning rate to 0.001. The learning rate is reduced by a factor of 1.8 every 20k iterations. In addition, the weight

Table 1. Comparisons on DOTA with the State-of-the-Art Detectors. We choose the threshold of IoU which is 0.5 during calculating AP

Method	Pl	Bd	Br	Gft	Sv	Lv	Sh	Tc	Bc	St	Sbf	Ra	Ha	Sp	He	mAP	FPS
SSD [3]	76.84	57.26	27.09	30.73	23.96	56.91	41.73	80.83	37.53	36.01	33.85	32.98	63.19	29.89	20.48	43.25	15.65
Faster R-CNN [1]	75.23	56.07	39.94	33.71	26.29	47.43	29.64	81.24	27.01	31.56	28.50	32.10	53.10	45.73	35.04	42.84	7.13
CornerNet [5]	87.33	66.23	34.32	52.98	65.93	72.11	74.02	88.93	72.53	74.02	41.77	55.23	50.98	54.18	24.99	61.09	1.13
FCOS [6]	88.53	68.21	34.78	58.33	65.98	74.22	76.34	88.34	74.18	76.59	44.88	57.23	52.90	57.92	23.01	62.76	16.85
P-RSDet [14]	89.02	73.65	47.33	72.03	70.58	73.71	72.76	90.82	80.12	81.32	59.45	57.87	60.79	65.21	52.59	69.82	12.78
CAD-Net [15]	87.80	82.40	49.40	**73.50**	71.10	63.50	76.70	90.90	79.20	73.30	48.44	60.93	62.08	67.02	62.23	69.90	6.82
RetinaNet [4]	88.92	67.67	33.55	56.83	66.11	73.28	75.24	90.87	73.95	75.07	43.77	56.72	51.05	55.86	21.46	62.02	7.34
IENet [16]	80.20	64.54	39.82	32.07	49.71	65.01	52.58	81.45	44.06	78.51	46.54	56.73	64.40	64.24	36.75	57.14	**17.05**
O²-DNet [17]	89.91	82.14	47.33	67.21	71.32	74.03	78.62	90.76	82.23	81.36	60.93	60.17	58.21	66.98	61.03	71.04	15.28
SCRDet [2]	**90.18**	81.88	55.30	73.29	72.09	77.55	78.06	**90.91**	82.44	86.39	64.53	63.45	75.77	78.21	60.11	75.35	5.37
SAOA	88.33	**82.73**	**56.02**	71.58	**72.98**	**77.59**	78.29	88.63	**83.33**	**86.61**	**65.93**	**63.52**	**76.03**	**78.43**	**61.33**	**75.41**	15.65

The abbreviations are defined as: Pl: Plane, Bd: Baseball diamond, Br: Bridge, Gft: Ground field track, Sv: Small vehicle, Lv: Large vehicle, Sh:Ship, Tc: Tennis court, Bc: Basketball court, St: Storage tank, Sbf: Soccer-ball field, Ra: Roundabout, Ha: Harbor, Sp: Swimming pool, and He: Helicopter.

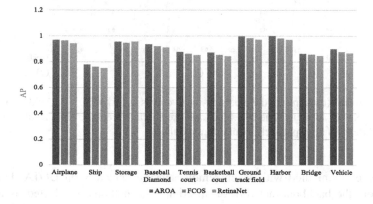

Fig. 4. Detection results of three one-stage detectors on NWPU VHR-10.

decay and momentum are set as 0.0001 and 0.9, respectively. The experiments are conducted in PyTorch1.1 using an NVIDIA GeForce RTX 2080 Ti 11 GB and CPUE52603v4@2.20 GHz CPU. We randomly divide the training and testing sets of NWPU VHR-10 according to the rate of 7:3. Additionally, we use the batch sizes of 10 for DOTA and 12 for the NWPU VHR-10 dataset. In our model, we set the vital parameters $\gamma = \mu = 4$ for best performance.

3.3 Experimental Results and Analysis

In this article, three frequently-used evaluation metrics, the average precision (AP) and the mean average precision (mAP), are adopted to evaluate the accuracy of the detectors in our experiments. In addition, we use a common metric, frames per second (FPS), to measure the speed of object detection.

Comparing with State-of-the-Art Detectors. To verify the effectiveness of our AROA, we compare it with several state-of-the-art detectors. As shown in Table 1,

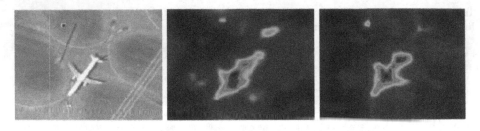

Fig. 5. Visualization of attention map of the AS^2A (middle) and C^3A (right).

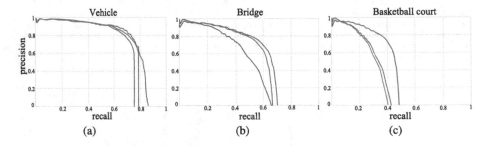

Fig. 6. (a), (b), and (c) represent the precision-recall curves at IoU = $\{0.5, 0.75, 0.9\}$ for vehicle, bridge, and basketball court. The red, blue, and green curves represent the results of AROA, FCOS, and RetinaNet, respectively. (Color figure online)

we compare our method with seven remote sensing detectors on DOTA. For a fair comparison, the backbone network of all compared methods is selected as ResNet-100 and the input image size of all methods is resized to a fixed scale (800 × 800). We also utilize data augmentation to enlarge the datasets such as flipping, rotation, and so on. The proposed AROA achieves 75.41% in mAP at a relatively fast speed with 15.65 FPS, outperforming all reported anchor-based detectors (SSD, Faster R-CNN, RetinaNet, CAD-Net, and SCRDet). It is about five as fast at almost the same accuracy compared with SCRDet, which manifests the high accuracy and efficiency of our method. In addition, Fig. 4 shows the detection results of FCOS, RetinaNet, and our AROA on NWPU VHR-10. The AP values of ten class objects on the proposed AROA are all higher than the other two one-stage detectors, which also demonstrates the advantage of our method for remote sensing object detection. Meanwhile, we perform the comparison experiments on three multi-orientation, high inter-class similarity, and low-discernibility targets (vehicle, basketball court, and bridge). Figure 6 shows the precision-recall curves of AROA, FCOS and RetineNet. We can see that our AROA achieves better performance than FCOS and RetinaNet. Moreover, it is remarkable that with a stricter IoU threshold, AROA takes a larger improvement over FCOS and RetinaNet, which indicates that AROA can locate the objects more accurately. As shown in Fig. 5, we present the partial attention maps of the AS^2A and the C^3A. We observe that the AS^2A effectively enhances the object information, especially for the orientation information. Meanwhile, the C^3A improves the classification ability by generating more discriminative feature maps.

Fig. 7. The green, red, and yellow bounding boxes represent the true positives, false positives, and true negatives, respectively (Color figure online)

Table 2. Ablation study of the proposed AROA on NWPU VHR-10.

Setting	mAP	FPS
Baseline	89.21%	17.13
Baseline + C^3A	90.36%	16.98
Baseline + AS^2A	90.79%	16.71
Baseline + IM	90.56%	16.89
Baseline + C^3A + IM	92.91%	16.61
Baseline + C^3A + AS^2A	92.12%	15.83
Baseline + AS^2A + IM	92.65%	16.04
AROA	93.45%	15.65

Ablation Study. We perform an ablation study to study the effects of the proposed AS^2A, C^3A and IM over the NWPU VHR-10 dataset. Eight network models are trained for the ablation study. First, **Baseline:** The basic network structure in FCOS does not include the centerness branch. Next, three network models which add the components of AS^2A, C^3A, and IM, respectively. Then, **AROA:** The full implementation of the proposed AROA architecture in Fig. 1. In addition, three network models which equip with paired components are included to verify the complementarity of the three proposed modules. As shown in Table 2, the Baseline model can only achieve mAP of 89.21% at 17.13 FPS. After adding AS^2A, C^3A and IM to the Baseline model sequentially, the mAP is improved by 1.15%, 1.58%, and 1.35%, respectively. The same situation occurs in three models with different paired components, which illustrates that three improvement modules are complementary. Finally, the proposed AROA that combines the AS^2A, C^3A and IM achieves a 4.24% mAP improvement compared to the Baseline model, pushing the mAP to 93.45% with a relatively little additional computational cost (a decrease of 1.48 FPS). As shown in Fig. 7, some targets that are not detected or imprecisely located with the **Baseline** (the first row) are accurately detected with our **AROA** (the second row).

4 Conclusion

In this article, the challenge issues of complicated background, rotation variations, and interclass similarity are identified in remote sensing object detection. Aimed at these problems, we presents a novel attention refinement one-stage anchor-free detector. The core components contain asymmetric spatial self-attention and chain-connected channel attention which are designed to refine spatial and channel feature expression. Moreover, an IoU-wise module is proposed to strengthen the correlation between localization and classification for accurate object detection. Extensive experiments demonstrate the superiority of our method for object detection in remote sensing images. In future work, we will design more auxiliary modules to achieve the detection of oriented targets in remote sensing images.

Acknowledgment. This work was supported in part by the National Natural Science Foundation of China under Grant 61701524, 62006245 and in part by the China Postdoctoral Science Foundation under Grant 2019M653742. Thanks to the anonymous reviewers for their valuable suggestions.

References

1. Ren, S., He, K., Girshick, R., Sun, J.: Faster R-CNN: towards real-time object detection with region proposal networks. IEEE Trans. Pattern Anal. Mach. Intell. **2015**, 91–99 (2015)
2. Yang, X., et al.: SCRDet: towards more robust detection for small, cluttered and rotated objects. In: Proceedings of the IEEE International Conference on Computer Vision, pp. 8232–8241 (2019)
3. Liu, W., et al.: SSD: Single Shot MultiBox Detector. In: Leibe, B., Matas, J., Sebe, N., Welling, M. (eds.) ECCV 2016. LNCS, vol. 9905, pp. 21–37. Springer, Cham (2016). https://doi.org/10.1007/978-3-319-46448-0_2
4. Lin, T.-Y., Goyal, P., Girshick, R., He, K., Dollár, P.: Focal loss for dense object detection. In: Proceedings of the IEEE International Conference on Computer Vision, pp. 2980–2988 (2017)
5. Law, H., Deng, J.: CornerNet: detecting objects as paired keypoints. In: Proceedings of the European Conference on Computer Vision, pp. 734–750 (2018)
6. Tian, Z., Shen, C., Chen, H., He, T.: FCOS: fully convolutional one-stage object detection. In: Proceedings of the IEEE/CVF International Conference on Computer Vision, pp. 9627–9636 (2019)
7. Wei, H., Zhang, Y., Wang, B., Yang, Y., Li, H., Wang, H.: X-LineNet: detecting aircraft in remote sensing images by a pair of intersecting line segments. IEEE Trans. Geosci. Remote Sens. **9**(2), 1645–1659 (2020)
8. Chen, J., Xie, F., Lu, Y., Jiang, Z.: Finding arbitrary-oriented ships from remote sensing images using corner detection. IEEE Geosci. Remote Sens. Lett. **17**(10), 1712–1716 (2019)
9. Shi, F., Zhang, T., Zhang, T.: Orientation-aware vehicle detection in aerial images via an anchor-free object detection approach. IEEE Trans. Geosci. Remote Sens. **59**(6), 5221–5233 (2020)

10. Li, Y., Huang, Q., Pei, X., Chen, Y., Jiao, L., Shang, R.: Cross-layer attention network for small object detection in remote sensing imagery. IEEE J. Sel. Top. Appl. Earth Observ. Remote Sens. 14, 2148–2161 (2020)

11. Wang, J., Wang, Y., Wu, Y., Zhang, K., Wang, Q.: FRPNet: a feature-reflowing pyramid network for object detection of remote sensing images. IEEE Geosci. Remote Sens. Lett. (2020)

12. Wu, Y., Zhang, K., Wang, J., Wang, Y., Wang, Q., Li, Q.: CDD-Net: a context-driven detection network for multiclass object detection. IEEE Geosci. and Remote Sens. Lett. (2020)

13. Zhang, X., Wang, G., Zhu, P., Zhang, T., Li, C., Jiao, L.: GRS-Det: an anchor-free rotation ship detector based on Gaussian-mask in remote sensing images. IEEE Trans. Geosci. Remote Sens. **59**(4), 3518–3531 (2020)

14. Zhou, L., Wei, H., Li, H., Zhao, W., Zhang, Y., Zhang, Y.: Arbitrary-oriented object detection in remote sensing images based on polar coordinates. IEEE Access **8**, 223373–223384 (2020)

15. Zhang, G., Lu, S., Zhang, W.: CAD-Net: a context-aware detection network for objects in remote sensing imagery. IEEE Trans. Geosci. Remote Sens. **57**(12), 10015–10024 (2019)

16. Lin, Y., Feng, P., Guan, J.: IENet: interacting embranchment one stage anchor free detector for orientation aerial object detection (2019). arXiv:1912.00969

17. Wei, H., Zhang, Y., Chang, Z., Li, H., Wang, H., Sun, X.: Oriented objects as pairs of middle lines. ISPRS-J. Photogramm. Remote Sens. **169**, 268–279 (2020)

18. Zhou, X., Wang, D., Krähenbühl, P.: Objects as points (2019). arXiv:1904.07850

19. Wang, X., Girshick, R., Gupta, A., He, K.: Non-local neural networks. In: Proceedings of the IEEE Conference on Computer Vision and Pattern Recognition, pp. 7794–7803 (2018)

20. Hu, J., Shen, L., Sun, G.: Squeeze-and-excitation networks. In: Proceedings of the IEEE Conference on Computer Vision and Pattern Recognition, pp. 7132–7141 (2018)

21. Xia, G., et al.: DOTA: a large-scale dataset for object detection in aerial images. In: Proceedings of the IEEE Conference on Computer Vision and Pattern Recognition, pp. 3974–3983 (2018)

22. Cheng, G., Han, J.: A survey on object detection in optical remote sensing images. ISPRS-J. Photogramm. Remote Sens. **117**, 11–28 (2016)

Human-Object Interaction Detection Based on Multi-scale Attention Fusion

Qianling Wu and Yongzhao Zhan[✉]

School of Computer Science and Telecommunication Engineering, Jiangsu University,
Zhenjiang, China
yzzhan@ujs.edu.cn

Abstract. Human-object interaction detection is one of the key issues of scene understanding. It has widespread applications in advanced computer vision technology. However, due to the diversity of human postures, the uncertainty of the shape and size in objects, as well as the complexity of the relationship between people and objects. It is very challenging to detect the interaction relationship between people and objects. To solve this problem, this paper proposes a multi-scale attention fusion method to adapt to people and objects of different sizes and shapes. This method increases the range of attention which can more accurately judge the relationships between people and objects. Besides, we further propose a weighting mechanism to better characterize the interaction between people and close objects and express people's intention of interaction. We evaluated the proposed method on HICO-DET and V-COCO datasets, which has verified its effectiveness and flexibility as well as has achieved a certain improvement in accuracy.

Keywords: Interaction detection · Multi-Scale attention fusion

1 Introduction

Human-object interaction detection which promoted the ability of machines to understand the visual world has made tremendous progress. It is applied in many fields, such as security monitoring, service robots, sports training and image retrieval. In some cases, action recognition [1] is considered to be similar to human-object interaction detection. However, there are substantial differences between them. Action recognition, which mainly focuses on the simple classification of individual instance actions in images [2] or video clips [3], is not sufficient to describe complex visual scenes in the real world because of not consider the type of interaction between them. In contrast, human-object relationship detection provides a more specific and comprehensive description of the objective context for human activities.

Generally speaking, human-object detection first performs object detection to identify humans and objects in the images. Then we can infer the predicates in the triple group of <human, predicate, object> which is based on the detected people and objects. Finally, we can obtain the relationship between people and objects. However, there may

© Springer Nature Switzerland AG 2021
Y. Peng et al. (Eds.): ICIG 2021, LNCS 12888, pp. 280–292, 2021.
https://doi.org/10.1007/978-3-030-87355-4_24

be multiple interaction possibilities between people and the same object. These complex and diverse scenes have brought major challenges to the detection of human-object interaction relationships.

The main task of human-object interaction detection is to obtain high-level semantic information of entities from complex semantic scenes. Specifically, due to differences in human-object instances and contexts, the visual patterns in the same human-object interaction category may be very different. In addition, since many interactions involve subtle movements of certain body parts, the appearance deviations between different categories are small. In response to these problems, although some existing methods have also made some progress, there are some shortcomings. The recently proposed methods ICAN [4] and TIN [5] both use attention mechanisms, but neither took into account the shape and size of the object nor the influence of the distance between people and objects on the detection of interaction.

To cope with the above challenges, this paper proposes a multi-scale attention fusion method, which is based on the different shapes and sizes of people and objects in images. This method introduces multi-scale attention. After obtaining the features of people and objects, this multi-scale attention is used to obtain the attention range of people and objects with different sizes and shapes which increases the receptive field. In the final interaction fusion, we increase the weight of the object, which emphasizes the interaction between people and close objects. The main contributions of this paper are as follows:

(1) Considering that the shape and size of people and objects in the image have a certain influence on the judgment of the interaction relationship, multi-scale attention is proposed to obtain different attention ranges and improve the accuracy of interaction relationship detection.
(2) We propose a weighting mechanism that emphasizes the interaction between people and objects that close to people and can better express the intention of interaction.
(3) Compared with recent relative methods, our approach achieves superior performance on both V-COCO and HICO-DET benchmarks.

2   Related Work

Object Detection.   In recent years, due to the development of deep convolutional neural networks, significant progress has been made in the field of object detection. Generally speaking, object detection methods can be divided into single-stage [6–9] and two-stage [10–13]. Usually, two-stage object detection methods first generate candidate object proposal boxes and then classify and regress these proposals in the second stage. The single-stage object detection methods directly classify and regress the default anchor box at each position. Two-stage methods are generally more accurate, while single-stage methods are relatively faster.

The first step in human and object interaction detection is to correctly detect people and objects. Recently, some object detection frameworks such as R-CNN [14], Faster R-CNN [10], YOLO [6], feature pyramid network [15] and SSD [7] models can robustly detect multi-scale targets in images. We use a pre-trained Fast R-CNN model to detect people and objects. In addition, we take advantage of the idea of a Faster R-CNN region proposal network, then we extend it to interaction detection to infer whether there is interaction in a human-object combination.

Attention. Attention has been extensive used in image captioning [31, 32, 39, 40], fine-grained classification [33], pose estimation [34], action recognition [2, 16] and human-object interaction tasks [17, 18]. The attention mechanism helped to highlight the global and local key areas in the image. In recent years, methods based on end-to-end trainable attention have been proposed to improve the performance of action recognition [19] or image classification [21]. However, these methods were designed for image-level classification tasks. Our work is based on the latest developments in attention technology and then we extend it to instance-level human-object recognition tasks, which can adapt to the difference in the size of objects in the image.

Human-Object Interaction. Among the existing human-object interaction detection methods, [21] was the first method to explore the problem of visual semantic role labeling, which located people and objects and detected the interaction between them. [22] introduced a human-centered approach, which extended the Faster R-CNN framework and added a branch to learn the interaction-specific density map at the target location. Qi et al. [23] proposed a method that treats HOI as a graph structure optimization problem by graph convolutional neural networks. Chao et al. [24] established a multi-stream network that is based on human-object regions of interest and paired interaction branches. The input of multi-stream architecture is a pre-trained detector (FPN [15]) which predicted the bounding box of the original image. Subsequent researches have extended the above-mentioned multi-stream architecture, such as the introduction of instance-centric attention [4], gesture information [5], appearance features based on context awareness [25] and deep context attention. Liang et al. [26] proposed a human-object interaction detection model, which used vision, space and graphics. They made use of graph convolution to simulate the interaction between pairs. Xu et al. [27] proposed a new region proposal network for human-object interaction detection tasks, which applied human visual cues to find objects.

3   Methods

In this section, we elaborate on the proposed multi-scale attention fusion mechanism for human-object interaction detection. The overall framework is illustrated in Fig. 1. We outline the details of each part in Sect. 3.1, then we describe our multi-scale attention fusion method in detail in Sect. 3.2.

3.1   Framework

In the traditional human-object interaction detection [4, 5], the range of attention was the same. However, people and objects have different shapes and sizes. Therefore, they should have different attention ranges, which can better characterize the interaction between people and objects. To solve this problem, we propose a multi-scale attention fusion. To accomplish interaction detection, we first perform object detection and pose estimation to obtain human features, object features, spatial maps and human pose maps. Then human features and object features are sent to the multi-scale attention to locate the key area of interaction between people and objects, which can extract more fine-grained attention features. Finally, the attention features and appearance features of people and objects are embedded, then which are sent to the human stream and the object stream respectively. After obtaining the features, we use the interactive network to filter the human-object pair which does not have interaction first. Then the classification network combines the output of the interactive network to obtain the final interactive detection result. The interactive network and the classification network share the weight in the above process. The interactive network mainly suppresses non-interactive pairs based on visual appearance, spatial location and human posture. It also suppresses pairs of humans and objects that do not have interactive behaviors, which can reduce the resource consumption of interactive relationship detection and classification. The classification network mainly combines the non-interaction suppression of the interactive network, and then it uses a method based on a multi-scale attention fusion mechanism to classify the results of human and object interaction detection. Our overall framework is shown in Fig. 1.

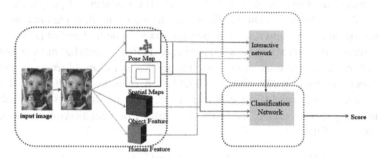

Fig. 1. Our overall network framework.

Object Detection and Pose Estimation. The prerequisite for the judgment of the human-object relationship is to know the location of the human and the object instance first. Therefore, we must detect the human instance and the object instance in the image first. The object detector used in this paper is Faster R-CNN and combines with the use of ResNet50-FPN as a feature extraction network to obtain feature maps of people and objects. In addition to convolutional features, we also extract a set of geometric features to encode the spatial configuration of each person and object instance. We start with the two binary masks proposed by people and objects, and capture the spatial configuration of the object level in their joint space, as in [4, 25]. In addition, we obtain fine-grained spatial information of humans and objects through pose maps with predicted poses. Given the joint box of each person and their counterparts, we use pose estimation [28, 29] to estimate the 17 key points of humans. Then we link the key points with lines of different gray values ranging from 0.15 to 0.95 to represent different body parts, which can implicitly encode pose features.

Interactive Network. The interactive network is mainly based on visual appearance, spatial location and human posture information to determine whether it is an interactive pair. It is composed of a human stream, object stream and spatial posture stream. The spatial posture stream is comprised of spatial graphs and posture graphs. Human stream and object stream consists of residual blocks, global average pooling layer, fully connected layer and Sigmoid function to obtain human, object and context features. The spatial posture stream including a convolutional layer, a max-pooling layer and a fully connected layer represents the positional relationship between people and objects in space and can predict actions based on people's postures. The outputs of the three streams are merged, and then we use two fully connected layers to perform the interactive discrimination. Finally, non-interaction suppression is used to determine whether there is an interaction between the human and the object, which can filter out the pairs that do not have interaction.

Classification Network. The classification network is mainly to obtain the result of the final interaction relationship detection. Figure 2 shows the classification network. It consists of pairwise stream, human stream and object stream. The human stream and object stream here are identical to those in the interactive network. The pairwise stream uses the channel attention mechanism to highlight the key areas of people and objects, which can obtain attention features. Then the channel attention features are used to encode the spatial layout between the bounding boxes of people and objects.

In real scenes, the interaction between people and close objects has more possibilities. To better characterize the interaction between people and close objects, we propose a human-object weighting mechanism for interaction relationship detection. The main idea is to increase the weight of the object score when the human stream, the object stream and the pairwise stream are fused. The interaction relationship detection final score is shown as follows:

$$S(h, o) = S_{sp} \times \left(S_h + \left(1 + (IoU(h, o))^2 \right) \times S_o \right) \tag{1}$$

where S_o is the output score of the object stream, S_h is the output score of the human stream and S_{sp} is the output score of the pairwise stream. IoU represents the relation between human and object, which is the ratio of the intersection and union of the "predicted bounding box" and the "ground truth bounding box".

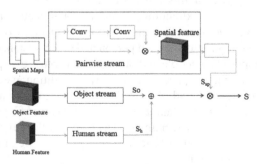

Fig. 2. Classification network

3.2 Multi-scale Attention Fusion Mechanism

In the previous detection of the interaction relationship between people and objects, the attention mechanism usually uses 1×1 convolution to locate the key areas of people and objects. However, it has some problems. For instance, for some relatively large objects, the range of the extracted attention features is relatively small. So the range of the receptive field mapped to the image is relatively limited and some important areas that affect the detection result of the interaction relationship may be ignored, which causes the result of the interaction relationship detection inaccurate. Therefore, we propose a multi-scale attention fusion in human stream and object stream. It will use a 1×1, a 1×3 and a 3×1 convolution to label the key areas of people and objects. Then, at the feature fusion stage, the attention features of different scales are fused with appearance features to obtain the multi-scale attention fusion features. The features of multi-scale attention fusion can be expressed as the following:

$$att\_o = (((head\_phi \odot fc1) \odot head\_g) \odot head\_h) \qquad (2)$$

where head_h denotes features from the 3×1 convolution, head_g denotes feature from the 1×3 convolution, head_phi denotes features from the 1×1 convolution, fc1 denotes appearance feature of the object and $\odot$ represents Hadamard product.

This multi-scale attention fusion can flexibly adapt to the shape and size of the object bounding box, which can improve the accuracy of the interaction relationship detection between people and objects. As shown in Fig. 3, the upper branch uses the pooling layer, the residual blocks, the global average pooling layer and the fully connected layer to extract the appearance features of humans and objects. The following branch uses three different convolutions to achieve the features based on the multi-scale attention fusion. Then the appearance feature and the features from the three convolutions are merged. After that, the final attention feature is obtained through 1×1 convolution and the fully connected layer. Finally, the obtained attention feature and the appearance feature are connected to acquire the final feature.

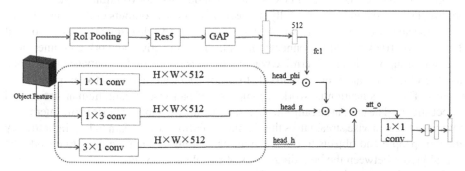

Fig. 3. Multi-scale attention fusion mechanism

4 Experimental

In this section, we first introduce the datasets and metrics, then give the implementation details of the framework. Next, we will make a quantitative and qualitative comparison with the most advanced methods. After that, we report our HOI test results. Finally, we conduct an ablation study to verify the effectiveness of the components in our framework.

4.1 Datasets and Metrics

We use two datasets HICO-DET [34] and V-COCO [21] for the detection of the human-object interaction relationship. HICO-DET [34] contains 47,776 images (38,118 in the training set and 9,658 in the test set), 600 human-object categories on 80 object categories and 117 verbs. Meanwhile, it provides more than 150k annotated instances of human-objects pairs. V-COCO [21] provides 10,346 images (2,533 images for training, 2,867 images for verification and 4,946 images for testing) and 16,199 human examples. Each person has an annotation for 29 action categories (5 of which have no matching objects).

Metrics. We use the role mean average precision [21] to measure performance. That is, when referring to the ground-truth label, and the IoU of the bounding box of the human and the object are greater than 0.5, the prediction is positive, and the HOI classification result is accurate.

4.2 Implementation Details

We use Faster R-CNN as the object detection framework and ResNet-50-FPN as the feature extractor. Using RMPE [28] and CrowdPose [29] as a pose estimator, each human pose consists of 17 key points. Then we link the key points with lines of different gray values ranging from 0.15 to 0.95 to represent different body parts. The size of the pose map is 64×64. The interactive network mainly contains three streams: human stream, object stream and spatial pose stream. Human stream and object stream are composed of residual blocks, a global average pooling layer, two 1024-size fully connected layers and a Sigmoid function. The spatial pose stream includes two convolutional layers, a max-pooling layer and two 1024-size fully connected layers. The outputs of the three streams are connected through a post-fusion strategy and interactive discrimination is performed through two 1024-size fully connected layers. The interactive network combines non-interaction suppression to determine whether there is an interaction between the human and the object. It can filter out pairs that do not have interaction between people and objects. The classification network is composed of pairwise stream, human stream and object stream. The human stream and object stream are the same as those in the interactive network. The pairwise stream uses the channel attention mechanism to highlight the key areas of people and objects to obtain attention features, which are used to encode the spatial layout between the bounding boxes of people and objects.

We conduct experiments on two datasets for a fair comparison, setting the initial learning rate to 0.001, weight decay to 0.0001 and momentum to 0.9. We use the stochastic gradient descent algorithm in the experiment. For V-COCO datasets, we set the human threshold to 0.6 and the object threshold to 0.4. For HICO-DET datasets, we set the human threshold to 0.8 and the object threshold to 0.3.

4.3 Results and Comparisons

We compare our method with the latest method on two datasets. Table 1 and Table 2 show our quantitative results on V-COCO and HICO-DET datasets respectively. From Table 1, we can see that on V-COCO datasets, the AP_{role} of our method is best and is 1.05 higher than the AP_{role} of the HBP method.

Table 1. Performance comparison on V-COCO test set.

Methods	AP_{role}
Interact [22]	40.0
GPNN [23]	44.0
ICAN [4]	45.3
TIN [5]	47.8
Cascade [36]	48.9
HBP [35]	49.05
Our method	50.1

From Table 2 we can see that the AP_{role} obtained from the default Object and the known Object on HICO-DET datasets has also been improved in most cases. Therefore, it can be said that our method based on a multi-scale attention fusion has a certain degree of feasibility and a certain degree of improvement in accuracy on both HICO-DET and V-COCO datasets.

Table 2. Performance comparison on HICO-DET test set.

Methods	Default object			Known object		
	Full	Rare	Non-rare	Full	Rare	Non-rare
Interact [22]	9.94	7.16	10.77	–	–	–
GPNN [23]	13.11	9.34	14.23	–	–	–
ICAN [4]	14.84	10.45	16.15	16.26	11.33	17.73
TIN [5]	17.22	13.51	18.32	19.38	15.38	20.57
PMFNet [37]	17.46	15.65	18.00	20.34	17.47	21.20
Wang.et [38]	19.56	12.79	21.58	22.05	15.77	23.92
Our method	19.90	14.67	21.35	22.30	15.80	24.50

Figure 4 shows our visualization results on HICO-DET. Figure 5 shows the visualization results on V-COCO. The test results prove that our method is reasonable and satisfactory.

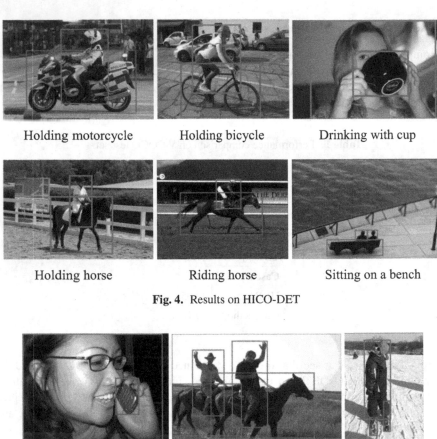

Fig. 4. Results on HICO-DET

Fig. 5. Results on V-COCO

4.4 Ablation Studies

In this part, we implement several experiments to prove the effectiveness of every part of our method on V-COCO and HICO-DET datasets. Results are shown in Table 3 and Table 4.

Multi-Scale Attention Fusion Mechanism. The multi-scale attention fusion uses a 1 × 1, a 1 × 3 and a 3 × 1 convolution to locate the key areas of people and objects. Then when in the feature fusion stage, the features of different scales are dot-multiplied, which can obtain the finally multi-scale attention fusion feature. This part can flexibly adapt to the shape and size of the object, thereby improving the accuracy of interaction detection between people and objects.

Fusion. The interaction between people and close objects is more possible. If the distance between the object and the human is closer, the weight of the object should be greater. To better express people's intention of interaction and characterize the interaction between people and close objects, we also propose a method of fusion that is based on a weighting mechanism. From Table 4, we can see that our method gets the best performance.

Table 3. Ablation study on V-COCO datasets

Components	AP_{role}
Baseline	47.8
Multi-scale attention	49.6
Our method	50.1

Table 4. Ablation study on HICO-DET datasets

Methods	Default object			Known object		
	Full	Rare	Non-rare	Full	Rare	Non-rare
Baseline	17.22	13.51	18.32	19.38	15.38	20.57
Attention	19.78	14.21	20.82	21.54	15.47	23.20
Our method	19.90	14.67	21.35	22.30	15.80	24.50

5 Conclusions

In this paper, we propose a multi-scale attention fusion method for human-object interaction detection. Our main idea is that for people and objects of different sizes in the image, we use different convolutions to adapt to different people and objects, which can increase the range of attention, and more accurately determine the interaction between people and objects. Meanwhile, the interaction between people and close objects has more possibilities. To better characterize the interaction between people and close objects, we propose a weighting mechanism. It can better express people's intention of interaction and improve the accuracy of interaction relationship detection. We verify the effectiveness of the method on two datasets and achieved excellent performance. In the future, we will study the interaction detection of the relationship between people and objects in the video.

Acknowledgments. This work was supported by the National Natural Science Foundation of China (No. 61672268).

References

1. Tian, Y., Ruan, Q., An, G., et al.: Action recognition using local consistent group sparse coding with spatio-temporal structure. In: Proceedings of the 24th ACM International Conference on Multimedia, pp. 317–321 (2016)
2. Gkioxari, G., Girshick, R., Malik, J.: Contextual action recognition with r* cnn. In: Proceedings of the IEEE International Conference on Computer Vision, pp. 1080–1088 (2015)
3. Xu, B., Ye, H., Zheng, Y., et al.: Dense dilated network for few shot action recognition. In: Proceedings of the ACM on International Conference on Multimedia Retrieval, pp. 379–387 (2018)
4. Gao, C., Zou, Y., Huang, J.B.: ican: Instance-centric attention network for human-object interaction detection. arXiv preprint arXiv:1808.10437 (2018)
5. Li, Y.L., Zhou, S., Huang, X., et al.: Transferable interactiveness knowledge for human-object interaction detection. In: Proceedings of the IEEE/CVF Conference on Computer Vision and Pattern Recognition, pp. 3585–3594 (2019)
6. Redmon, J., Divvala, S., Girshick, R., et al.: You only look once: unified, real-time object detection. In: Proceedings of the IEEE Conference on Computer Vision and Pattern Recognition, pp. 779–788 (2016)
7. Liu, W., Anguelov, D., Erhan, D., et al.: SSD: Single shot multibox detector. In: European Conference on Computer Vision, pp. 21–37. Springer, Cham (2016). https://doi.org/10.1007/978-3-319-46448-0_2
8. Li, Y., Qi, H., Dai, J., et al.: Fully convolutional instance-aware semantic segmentation. In: Proceedings of the IEEE Conference on Computer Vision and Pattern Recognition, pp. 2359–2367 (2017)
9. Law, H., Deng, J.: Cornernet: detecting objects as paired keypoints. In: Proceedings of the European Conference on Computer Vision (ECCV), pp. 734–750 (2018)
10. Ren, S., He, K., Girshick, R., et al.: Faster R-CNN: towards real-time object detection with region proposal networks. arXiv preprint arXiv:1506.01497 (2015)
11. He, K., Gkioxari, G., Dollár, P., et al.: Mask R-CNN. In: Proceedings of the IEEE International Conference on Computer Vision, pp. 2961–2969 (2017)
12. Chen, K., Pang, J., Wang, J., et al.: Hybrid task cascade for instance segmentation. In: Proceedings of the IEEE/CVF Conference on Computer Vision and Pattern Recognition, pp. 4974–4983 (2019)
13. Cai, Z., Vasconcelos, N.: Cascade R-CNN: high quality object detection and instance segmentation. IEEE Trans. Pattern Anal. Mach. Intell. **43**, 1483–1498 (2019)
14. Girshick, R., Donahue, J., Darrell, T., et al.: Rich feature hierarchies for accurate object detection and semantic segmentation. In: Proceedings of the IEEE Conference on Computer Vision and Pattern Recognition, pp. 580–587 (2014)
15. Lin, T.Y., Dollár, P., Girshick, R., et al.: Feature pyramid networks for object detection. In: Proceedings of the IEEE Conference on Computer Vision and Pattern Recognition, pp. 2117–2125 (2017)

16. Chéron, G., Laptev, I., Schmid, C.: P-CNN: pose-based cnn features for action recognition. In: Proceedings of the IEEE International Conference on Computer Vision, pp. 3218–3226 (2015)

17. Lu, C., Krishna, R., Bernstein, M., Fei-Fei, L.: Visual relationship detection with language priors. In: Leibe, B., Matas, J., Sebe, N., Welling, M. (eds.) ECCV 2016. LNCS, vol. 9905, pp. 852–869. Springer, Cham (2016). https://doi.org/10.1007/978-3-319-46448-0_51

18. Mallya, A., Lazebnik, S.: Learning models for actions and person-object interactions with transfer to question answering. In: European Conference on Computer Vision, pp. 414–428. Springer, Cham (2016). https://doi.org/10.1007/978-3-319-46448-0_25

19. Girdhar, R., Ramanan, D.: Attentional pooling for action recognition. arXiv preprint arXiv: 1711.01467 (2017)

20. Jetley, S., Lord, N.A., Lee, N., et al.: Learn to pay attention. arXiv preprint arXiv:1804.02391 (2018)

21. Gupta, S., Malik, J.: Visual semantic role labeling. arXiv preprint arXiv:1505.04474 (2015)

22. Gkioxari, G., Girshick, R., Dollár, P., et al.: Detecting and recognizing human-object interactions. In: Proceedings of the IEEE Conference on Computer Vision and Pattern Recognition, pp. 8359–8367 (2018)

23. Qi, S., Wang, W., Jia, B., Shen, J., Zhu, S.-C.: Learning human-object interactions by graph parsing neural networks. In: Ferrari, V., Hebert, M., Sminchisescu, C., Weiss, Y. (eds.) ECCV 2018. LNCS, vol. 11213, pp. 407–423. Springer, Cham (2018). https://doi.org/10.1007/978-3-030-01240-3_25

24. Chao, Y.W., Liu, Y., Liu, X., et al.: Learning to detect human-object interactions. In: 2018 IEEE Winter Conference on Applications of Computer Vision (WACV), pp. 381–389. IEEE (2018)

25. Wang, T., Anwer, R.M., Khan, M.H., et al.: Deep contextual attention for human-object interaction detection. In: Proceedings of the IEEE/CVF International Conference on Computer Vision, pp. 5694–5702 (2019)

26. Liang, Z., Liu, J., Guan, Y., et al.: Visual-semantic graph attention networks for human-object interaction detection. arXiv e-prints: arXiv: 2001.02302 (2020)

27. Xu, B., Li, J., Wong, Y., et al.: Interact as you intend: intention-driven human-object interaction detection. IEEE Trans. Multimedia 22(6), 1423–1432 (2019)

28. Fang, H.S., Xie, S., Tai, Y.W., et al.: RMPE: regional multi-person pose estimation. In: Proceedings of the IEEE International Conference on Computer Vision, pp. 2334–2343 (2017)

29. Li, J., Wang, C., Zhu, H., et al.: Crowdpose: efficient crowded scenes pose estimation and a new benchmark. In: Proceedings of the IEEE/CVF Conference on Computer Vision and Pattern Recognition, pp. 10863–10872 (2019)

30. Xu, K., Ba, J., Kiros, R., et al.: Show, attend and tell: neural image caption generation with visual attention. In: International Conference on Machine Learning. PMLR, pp. 2048–2057 (2015)

31. You, Q., Jin, H., Wang, Z., et al.: Image captioning with semantic attention. In: Proceedings of the IEEE Conference on Computer Vision and Pattern Recognition, pp. 4651–4659 (2016)

32. Ji, Z., Fu, Y., Guo, J., et al.: Stacked semantics-guided attention model for fine-grained zero-shot learning. In: Advances in Neural Information Processing Systems, pp. 5995–6004 (2018)

33. Chu, X., Yang, W., Ouyang, W., et al.: Multi-context attention for human pose estimation. In: Proceedings of the IEEE Conference on Computer Vision and Pattern Recognition, pp. 1831–1840 (2017)

34. Chao, Y.W., Wang, Z., He, Y., et al.: Hico: A benchmark for recognizing human-object interactions in images. In: Proceedings of the IEEE International Conference on Computer Vision, pp. 1017–1025 (2015)

35. Kuang, H., Zheng, Z., Liu, X., et al.: A human-object interaction detection method inspired by human body part information. In: 2020 12th International Conference on Measuring Technology and Mechatronics Automation (ICMTMA), pp. 342–346. IEEE (2020)
36. Zhou, T., Wang, W., Qi, S., et al.: Cascaded human-object interaction recognition. In: Proceedings of the IEEE/CVF Conference on Computer Vision and Pattern Recognition, pp. 4263–4272 (2020)
37. Wan, B., Zhou, D., Liu, Y., et al.: Pose-aware multi-level feature network for human object interaction detection. In: Proceedings of the IEEE/CVF International Conference on Computer Vision, pp. 9469–9478 (2019)
38. Wang, T., Yang, T., Danelljan, M., et al.: Learning human-object interaction detection using interaction points. In: Proceedings of the IEEE/CVF Conference on Computer Vision and Pattern Recognition, pp. 4116–4125 (2020)
39. Zhao, W., Lu, H., Wang, D.: Multisensor image fusion and enhancement in spectral total variation domain. IEEE Trans. Multimedia **20**(4), 866–879 (2017)
40. Lan, R., Sun, L., Liu, Z., et al.: MADNet: a fast and lightweight network for single-image super resolution. IEEE Trans. Cybern. **51**, 1443–1453 (2020)

Progressive Fusion Network for Safety Protection Detection

Futian Wang⑩, Lugang Wang⑩, Jin Tang⑩, and Chenglong Li$^{(\boxtimes)}$⑩

Anhui University, Hefei 230601, China
`lcl1314@foxmail.com`

Abstract. In recent years, it leads to the occurrence of many accidents and huge economic losses, because the construction personnel do not wear safety protective equipment normatively. Therefore, safety protection detection becomes an important problem in the computer vision community. It is a challenging problem because the targets are usually very small, the background is usually very complex at construction site image. To solve these problems, we propose a progressive fusion network PFNet. In PFNet, we use a progressive fusion module to enrich semantic information and a feature enhancement module to enhance detailed information in feature learning. Therefore, we can obtain effective features for safety protection detection. To provide an evaluation platform, we create an image dataset, with 5430 images and careful annotations for safety protection detection. PFNet achieves detection accuracy of 63.7% mAP in our dataset, which is 3.6% higher than the baseline method. PFNet also achieves great detection performance on other datasets.

Keywords: Object detection · Safety protection detection · Progressive fusion · Feature enhancement

1 Introduction

With the continuous expansion of the scale of engineering construction, safety accidents of construction projects often occur. Safety accidents not only affect normal production but also bring enormous impact on people's lives and property safety. And a large part of the reason for the occurrence of safety accidents is people's unsafe behaviors. If the construction personnel can wear safety protective equipment, the probability of accidents can reduce to a minimum. Therefore, it is particularly important to supervise the safety protective equipment of workers.

In recent years, deep learning becomes one of the hot research directions of scholars. Many experts propose a series of deep learning object detection algorithms, such as YOLO [20], SSD [15], Faster R-CNN [22], Cascade R-CNN [1], etc. Safety protection detection based on deep learning aims to realize intelligent supervision of construction personnel and find people's unsafe behaviors, such as not wearing safety protective equipment. Once defects are found, people can make adjustments to greatly improve the safety of the construction site.

© Springer Nature Switzerland AG 2021
Y. Peng et al. (Eds.): ICIG 2021, LNCS 12888, pp. 293–304, 2021.
https://doi.org/10.1007/978-3-030-87355-4_25

As a subtask of object detection, safety protection detection has many challenges. Firstly, the environment of the construction site is very complex, there are lots of construction equipment, buildings, trees, and so on. It causes target occlusion and illumination change. Secondly, because the construction site is large and the shooting is usually far away from the construction site, there are many small targets. These difficulties also exist in general object detection. Different from general object detection, safety protection detection also identifies the normal and abnormal of safety protective equipment. There are many similarities between some classes, such as the normal and abnormal wearing of safety helmet. This situation can easily lead to misclassification in the detection task. Therefore, safety protection detection has a very high detection difficulty.

In order to solve these problems, we propose a progressive fusion network for better feature extraction, as shown in Fig. 1. Firstly, we progressively fuse features of two identical backbones at each stage to obtain features with richer semantic information. Then, we fuse the features of different networks to enhance the detailed information, which is more conducive to the detection of safety protective equipment.

The main contributions of this paper are as follows:

- We create a dataset and call it PSPD. We label the normal and abnormal wearing of safety protective equipment in PSPD. The dataset covers a variety of real-world challenges, such as complex background, small targets, illumination change, occlusion and small differences between different classes. PSPD will be made available to the public.
- We propose a progressive fusion network for safety protection detection, named PFNet. It uses two backbones to extract features and fuses features from different networks. Experimental results show that PFNet can improve the detection performance greatly. The detection accuracy of PFNet is 63.7% mAP on PSPD, which is 3.6% higher than the baseline and higher than some existing advanced detection algorithms. We also conduct experiments on other datasets and obtain great detection results.

2   Related Work

According to the relevance of our work, we review the relevant work from three research directions: object detection, safety protection detection and feature fusion.

2.1   Object Detection

Object detection is an important task in computer vision. Before 2014, the most effective method of object detection is the Deformable Part Model [5]. However, the detection performance of DPM is far inferior to the deep learning methods in recent years.

Since AlexNet [7] shows great results in image classification, various deep learning methods are used in visual tasks. At present, object detection methods are divided into one-stage detectors and two-stage detectors. The one-stage detectors aim to directly classify the predefined anchors and further refine them without generating the suggested steps. There are mainly algorithms such as YOLO [20], SSD [15], RetinaNet [13], CornerNet [9] and FSAF [28]. The two-stage detectors detect objects by generating region suggestions and the region classifier. The two-stage detectors includes Faster R-CNN [22], R-FCN [2], FPN [12], Cascade R-CNN [1], SNIPER [23], TridentNet [10], and so on. In general, the accuracy of the two-stage detector is higher, while the speed of the one-stage detector is faster.

2.2   Safety Protection Detection

Due to the occurrence of safety accidents, people are gradually concerned about the safety protection detection. Long et al. [17] propose a new detection method based on SSD [15] to detect the safety helmet of substation personnel, but the detection accuracy is only 78.3% AP. Marco Di Benedetto et al. [3] create a virtual dataset of safety protective equipment and use Faster R-CNN [22] for training. However, the detection accuracy of virtual data much higher than actual data and the detection performance in real complex scenes is not good. Fatih Can Ksafetyurnaz et al. [8] create a dataset of tools. It includes two types of safety protective equipment: helmet and gloves. Faster R-CNN [22], Cascade R-CNN [1] and other algorithms are used to detect the dataset, Cascade R-CNN [1] with the highest detection accuracy achieves 33.4% mAP.

2.3   Feature Fusion

For object detection, feature fusion is an important means to improve performance. Low-level features have higher resolution and contain more location information. High-level features have much semantic information.

Through top-down connection and horizontal connection, FPN [12] fuses the adjacent features of the backbone to construct the feature pyramid. It enhances the expression of shallow features and significantly improves detection performance. On the basis of FPN [12], PANet [14] performs one more feature fusion from the bottom to the top to further enhance the fusion information of FPN [12]. It has good performance on detection and segmentation. Golnaz Ghiasi et al. [6] create a new feature pyramid structure called NAS-FPN. Unlike the previous method of designing feature fusion, it uses the neural architecture search [29] to select the optimal model architecture in a given search space. It fuses features across a range by top-down and bottom-up connections. Recently, Qiao et al. [19] propose the Recursive Feature Pyramid in DetectoRS. It adds the additional feedback of the feature pyramid network into the backbone network and achieves great detection accuracy.

3 Progressive Fusion Network

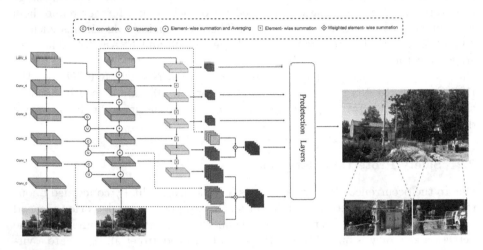

Fig. 1. Illustration of the PFNet architecture, including a progressive fusion module and a feature enhancement module.

3.1 Overal Architecture

In this work, we propose a progressive fusion network PFNet, as shown in Fig. 1. Firstly, we propose a progressive fusion module to extract features with more semantic information. The progressive fusion module fuses the adjacent high-level and low-level features of two backbones. Then we use the second backbone to extract the fused features and obtain rich semantic information. The feature fusion method we used can also reduce the noise in the features. But the features have less detailed information due to lower resolution. Therefore, we design a feature enhancement module to increase more detailed information. We perform the feature pyramid operation on the features from the second backbone. Then the features from the two backbones and the feature pyramid are fused for enriching detailed information.

3.2 Backbone

In PFNet, we use DetNet59 [11] as our backbone. It designs new bottlenecks using dilated convolution [25]. The dilated convolution can increase the range of the receptive field while the feature map is unchanged. Therefore, DetNet59 [11] is more powerful at locating large targets and finding small targets, and it can be well applied in object detection. During training, the classification loss function in the network is CrossEntropyLoss, and the bounding box regression loss function is SmoothL1Loss.

3.3   Progressive Fusion Module

Firstly, we propose a progressive fusion module based on CBNet [16]. We believe that the feature fusion method of direct element-wise summation introduces lots of noise when training complex data. It is not conducive to detect small targets. Therefore, we propose a progressive fusion module to better extract features.

As shown in Fig. 1, the progressive fusion module consists of two identical backbones and they have the same input. We fuse the high-level features of the first backbone with the adjacent low-level features of the second backbone. In detail, the input for each stage of the second backbone is the fusion of the features of the previous stage with the adjacent higher-level features of the first backbone. In this way, we gradually introduce the high-level information in the first backbone into the second backbone. Finally, we obtain the features with rich semantic information. The method of feature fusion is the element-wise summation and averaging. This method can not only ensure the increase of useful information and the averaging operation can also avoid the introduction of excessive noise. Adjacent higher-level and lower-level features are less different, and feature fusion between them allows for the better introduction of higher-level information. And the subsequent convolution operation can reduce the information difference caused by the feature fusion of different layers. The fusion method can be described as:

$$F_2^i = G_i \left[\frac{F_2^{i-1} + C(F_1^i)}{2} \right] \tag{1}$$

where F_1^i refers to the output of the i-th stage in the first backbone and F_2^{i-1} is the output of the $i-1$-th stage in the second backbone. C consists of 1×1 convolution, batch normalization and upsampling. In this way, we can change the size and channels of the features for subsequent fusion. G_i is the i-th stage in the second backbone.

3.4   Feature Enhancement Module

After progressive fusion, we obtain the features containing rich semantic information, but the low resolution of the features leads to insufficient detailed information. Therefore, we design a feature enhancement module to enhance the detailed information.

Firstly, we use FPN [12] to obtain features with different resolutions. Then we do feature enhancement on them to enhance the detailed information.

As shown in Fig. 1, it can be seen that PFNet consists of three parts from left to right: the first backbone, the second backbone and the feature pyramid. Relatively speaking, high-level semantic information gradually increases while shallow detailed information gradually decreases. So we can integrate the features from multiple networks to further enhance the detailed information. The feature enhancement method is to fuse the same level features of different networks. Using features at the same level can ensure that the differences between features are small and can better enhance detailed information. The feature enhancement method is as follows:

$$F_2 = P_2 + \alpha \times F_{12} + F_{22} \qquad (2)$$

$$F_3 = P_3 + \beta \times F_{13} \qquad (3)$$

where F_{12} and F_{13} are the output features of the second and third stages In the first backbone. In the second backbone, F_{22} is the input of the third stage. And P_2 and P_3 are the features in FPN. In this paper, $\alpha = \beta = 0.3$.

We only perform feature enhancement on the second and third layers. This is because higher features are used to detect large targets and adding too much detailed information will affect the detection effect. That is worth mentioning that the feature enhancement just performs the addition operation on the features of the same size and adds almost no computation.

4   Dataset

To provide an evaluation platform, we create a dataset and call it PSPD in this paper. This section introduces the details of PSPD, including dataset collection, annotation and statistics.

4.1   Data Collection

The images in PSPD are high-resolution images taken at the construction sites and cover various scene changes such as weather changes, day and night alternations and seasonal changes. They can effectively reflect the actual complex situation of the construction site.

4.2   Data Annotation

In the actual construction process, if construction personnel can wear safety helmet, work clothes and safety belt normatively, it can make the incidence of construction accidents greatly reduced. Therefore, we label them in detail and divide them into six classes in our dataset.

For safety helmet, we label three classes: standard wearing(aqm), without safety helmet (aqmqs), and nonstandard (aqmyc). Aqmyc refers to the helmet strap that does not lace-ups correctly and this situation also has safety hazards. For work clothes, it is divided into wearing standard (gzf) and nonstandard (gzfyc). After discussing with the relevant staff, if the construction personnel have naked arms, their clothes are labeled as nonstandard. Besides, we label the safety belt (aqd) of the construction personnel at height.

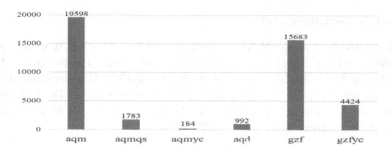

Fig. 2. The number of instances each class in PSPD.

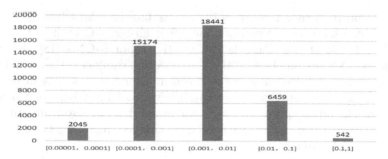

Fig. 3. The number of instances in the proportion of the image.

4.3 Data Statistics

After filtering the data, we obtain 5430 images and 42661 target instances. Then we divide the training set and test set according to the ratio of 9:1. The dataset is shot in real construction scenes. So there are numerous targets of standardized wearing of safety helmet and work clothes, the number of aqmqs, aqmyc and aqd is relatively small. As shown in Fig. 2.

The distribution of pixel size about the images is inconsistent, and the size of most images ranges from 480 × 640 to 14272 × 3968. Therefore we make statistics on the proportion of the targets in the image, as shown in Fig. 3. Then, we use relative size to distinguish between large and small targets, because the small target is less than one hundredth of the image. We find that small targets account for about 83% of PSPD.

The characteristics of our dataset are that it completely conforms to the actual construction scene, the classes are more detailed, the proportion of small targets is relatively high, the background is very complex and the difference between different classes is small. Therefore, this dataset has high research value and is of great help to practical engineering applications.

5   Experimental Results

In this section, we present the experimental results of PFNet on PSPD, PASCAL VOC [4] and SHWD. SHWD is a dataset for safety helmet detection.

5.1   Implementation Details

We re-implement Cascade RCNN [1] with the FPN [12] as our baseline and the
backbone is DetNet59 [11]. For the PSPD dataset, we set the image size to 600
× 800 during training and 1000 × 1000 during testing. Our experiments train
and test on an NVIDIA Titan XP GPU and develop with PyTorch 0.3.0. The
learning rate is initialized to 0.001, and learning rate decay is set to 0.1. In
addition, the batchsize is set to 1 on PSPD.

5.2   Results

In order to prove the effectiveness of PFNet, we use the most advanced detectors
to carry out a series of experiments, including Faster R-CNN [22], R-FCN [2],
YOLOV3 [21], SSD [15], Cascade R-CNN [1], Libra R-CNN [18], ATSS [27],
Dynamic R-CNN [26] and FCOS [24]. The detection results are shown in Table 1.
It can be seen that PFNet achieves a detection accuracy of 63.73% mAP, which
is higher than many existing advanced algorithms. PFNet has good detection
performance for aqm, aqmyc and aqd. It can prove that our algorithm can extract
more effective features and achieve good detection for small targets and different
classes with high similarity.

Table 1. Detection accuracy comparisons in terms of mAP percentage on the PSPD
test set.

Methods	aqm	aqmqs	aqmyc	aqd	gzf	gzfyc	mAP
Faster R-CNN [22]	62.10	31.80	38.72	25.21	78.40	73.70	51.66
SSD512 [15]	80.88	38.63	30.07	43.67	76.09	69.96	56.55
RFCN [2]	79.50	40.02	26.07	43.65	82.90	79.56	58.62
YOLOV3 [21]	92.38	54.68	11.91	42.42	85.26	76.32	60.50
Libra R-CNN [18]	84.90	41.40	11.30	68.80	83.80	78.90	61.52
ATSS [27]	88.60	44.10	7.400	52.10	83.90	76.50	58.77
Dynamic R-CNN [26]	81.00	39.90	26.20	50.40	83.70	77.30	59.75
FCOS [24]	89.50	43.70	10.20	54.50	85.30	77.30	60.08
Cascade R-CNN [1] w FPN [12]	80.66	43.33	39.95	43.64	78.70	74.69	60.16
PFNet	80.62	44.25	42.32	55.00	83.21	76.96	63.73

Moreover, we conduct experiments on PASCAL VOC [4] and SHWD. For
PASCAL VOC, we reduce the image to 500 × 500 during training and 600 × 600
during testing. For SHWD, the image size is set to 600 × 600. The experimental
results are shown in Table 2. Compared with the baseline, the detection accuracy
of PFNet improves 0.64% mAP and 1.65% mAP respectively. Therefore, PFNet
achieves great detection performance on these datasets.

Table 2. Comparison between PFNet and Baseline on PASCAL VOC and SHWD.

Methods	Dataset	mAP	Hat	Person
Baseline	PASCAL VOC	79.64	–	–
	SHWD	83.13	88.07	78.19
PFNet	PASCAL VOC	80.28	–	–
	SHWD	84.78	89.35	80.22

5.3 Ablation Study

Since PFNet consists of two components, we need to verify the impact of each component on the final performance.

Progressive Fusion Module. As shown in Table 3, to demonstrate the effectiveness of the progressive fusion module, we conduct a set of experiments. On the one hand, we add this module to the baseline and compare it with the baseline. It can be seen that the detection accuracy of the algorithm is 61.74%mAP, which is 1.6% higher than the baseline. On the other hand, we prove the effectiveness of the feature fusion method in the progressive fusion module. In addition to the method we used, we also try the fusion methods of concat, element-wise summation and max operation. They obtain 58.77%, 60.60% and 60.20% mAP respectively, which are lower than our method. It concludes that our method can increase the useful information effectively and has better detection performance.

Table 3. Ablation study. PFM is the progressive fusion module and FEM is the feature enhancement module.

Methods	aqm	aqmqs	aqmyc	aqd	gzf	gzfyc	mAP
Baseline	80.66	43.33	39.95	43.64	78.70	74.69	60.16
+PFM (max)	80.85	44.94	27.89	49.90	78.87	75.66	60.20
+PFM (concat)	80.63	41.36	33.17	42.91	78.87	75.66	58.77
+PFM (element-wise summation)	80.76	47.73	30.81	50.15	79.16	74.97	60.60
+PFM (ours)	80.67	49.77	30.76	54.17	79.08	75.96	61.74
+PFM + FEM ($\alpha, \beta = 1$)	80.86	44.37	35.22	53.39	83.23	76.60	62.28
+PFM + FEM (ours)	80.62	44.25	42.32	55.00	83.21	76.96	63.73

Feature Enhancement Module. We use the baseline with the progressive fusion module to verify the effectiveness of the feature enhancement module. We use the directly element-wise summation to fuse the features from different networks and obtained 62.28% mAP. It improves 0.54% compared with the original. Therefore, a good detection effect can be obtained by fusing the features of different networks. Finally, we fuse the different features in the weighted method and obtain 63.73% mAP, which is 2% higher than the method with the progressive fusion module. Therefore, it can be proved that the feature enhancement module can better enhance detailed information by fusing the features.

Fig. 4. Detection results on PSPD. The green box is aqm, the black box is aqmqs, the sky blue box is gzf, the purple box is gzfyc, and the red box is aqd. (Color figure online)

6   Conclusion

In this paper, we propose a dataset PSPD and a progressive fusion network PFNet for safety protection detection. PSPD includes lots of images of construction personnel taken at the construction site, and we label the safety protective equipment of the construction personnel. It can be used as an evaluation platform for safety protection detection. PFNet includes a progressive fusion module and a feature enhancement module. These modules can enrich semantic and detailed information in feature learning and achieve great detection performance on multiple datasets.

Acknowledgment. This work was supported by University Synergy Innovation Program of Anhui Province (No. GXXT-2019-007), the National Natural Science Foundation of China (No. 62076003), Anhui Provincial Natural Science Foundation (No. 1908085MF206).

References

1. Cai, Z., Vasconcelos, N.: Cascade R-CNN: delving into high quality object detection. In: Proceedings of the IEEE Conference on Computer Vision and Pattern Recognition, pp. 6154–6162 (2018)
2. Dai, J., Li, Y., He, K., Sun, J.: R-FCN: object detection via region-based fully convolutional networks. arXiv preprint arXiv:1605.06409 (2016)
3. Di Benedetto, M., Carrara, F., Meloni, E., Amato, G., Falchi, F., Gennaro, C.: Learning accurate personal protective equipment detection from virtual worlds. Multimedia Tools Appl. **80**(15), 23241–23253 (2020). https://doi.org/10.1007/s11042-020-09597-9
4. Everingham, M., Van Gool, L., Williams, C.K., Winn, J., Zisserman, A.: The pascal visual object classes (VOC) challenge. Int. J. Comput. Vis. **88**(2), 303–338 (2010)
5. Felzenszwalb, P., McAllester, D., Ramanan, D.: A discriminatively trained, multi-scale, deformable part model. In: 2008 IEEE Conference on Computer Vision and Pattern Recognition, pp. 1–8. IEEE (2008)
6. Ghiasi, G., Lin, T.Y., Le, Q.V.: NAS-FPN: learning scalable feature pyramid architecture for object detection. In: Proceedings of the IEEE/CVF Conference on Computer Vision and Pattern Recognition, pp. 7036–7045 (2019)
7. Krizhevsky, A., Sutskever, I., Hinton, G.E.: ImageNet classification with deep convolutional neural networks. In: Advances in Neural Information Processing Systems, vol. 25, pp. 1097–1105 (2012)
8. Kurnaz, F.C., Hocaoğlu, B., Yılmaz, M.K., Sülo, İ, Kalkan, S.: ALET (Automated Labeling of Equipment and Tools): a dataset for tool detection and human worker safety detection. In: Bartoli, A., Fusiello, A. (eds.) ECCV 2020. LNCS, vol. 12538, pp. 371–386. Springer, Cham (2020). https://doi.org/10.1007/978-3-030-66823-5_22
9. Law, H., Deng, J.: CornerNet: detecting objects as paired keypoints. In: Proceedings of the European Conference on Computer Vision (ECCV), pp. 734–750 (2018)
10. Li, Y., Chen, Y., Wang, N., Zhang, Z.: Scale-aware trident networks for object detection. In: Proceedings of the IEEE/CVF International Conference on Computer Vision, pp. 6054–6063 (2019)
11. Li, Z., Peng, C., Yu, G., Zhang, X., Deng, Y., Sun, J.: DetNet: a backbone network for object detection. arXiv preprint arXiv:1804.06215 (2018)
12. Lin, T.Y., Dollár, P., Girshick, R., He, K., Hariharan, B., Belongie, S.: Feature pyramid networks for object detection. In: Proceedings of the IEEE Conference on Computer Vision and Pattern Recognition, pp. 2117–2125 (2017)
13. Lin, T.Y., Goyal, P., Girshick, R., He, K., Dollár, P.: Focal loss for dense object detection. In: Proceedings of the IEEE International Conference on Computer Vision, pp. 2980–2988 (2017)
14. Liu, S., Qi, L., Qin, H., Shi, J., Jia, J.: Path aggregation network for instance segmentation. In: Proceedings of the IEEE Conference on Computer Vision and Pattern Recognition, pp. 8759–8768 (2018)
15. Liu, W., et al.: SSD: single shot MultiBox detector. In: Leibe, B., Matas, J., Sebe, N., Welling, M. (eds.) ECCV 2016. LNCS, vol. 9905, pp. 21–37. Springer, Cham (2016). https://doi.org/10.1007/978-3-319-46448-0_2
16. Liu, Y., et al.: CBNet: a novel composite backbone network architecture for object detection. In: Proceedings of the AAAI Conference on Artificial Intelligence, vol. 34, pp. 11653–11660 (2020)

17. Long, X., Cui, W., Zheng, Z.: Safety helmet wearing detection based on deep learning. In: 2019 IEEE 3rd Information Technology, Networking, Electronic and Automation Control Conference (ITNEC), pp. 2495–2499. IEEE (2019)

18. Pang, J., Chen, K., Shi, J., Feng, H., Ouyang, W., Lin, D.: Libra R-CNN: towards balanced learning for object detection. In: Proceedings of the IEEE/CVF Conference on Computer Vision and Pattern Recognition, pp. 821–830 (2019)

19. Qiao, S., Chen, L.C., Yuille, A.: DetectoRS: detecting objects with recursive feature pyramid and switchable atrous convolution. arXiv preprint arXiv:2006.02334 (2020)

20. Redmon, J., Divvala, S., Girshick, R., Farhadi, A.: You only look once: unified, real-time object detection. In: Proceedings of the IEEE Conference on Computer Vision and Pattern Recognition, pp. 779–788 (2016)

21. Redmon, J., Farhadi, A.: YOLOv3: an incremental improvement. arXiv preprint arXiv:1804.02767 (2018)

22. Ren, S., He, K., Girshick, R., Sun, J.: Faster R-CNN: towards real-time object detection with region proposal networks. arXiv preprint arXiv:1506.01497 (2015)

23. Singh, B., Najibi, M., Davis, L.S.: SNIPER: efficient multi-scale training. arXiv preprint arXiv:1805.09300 (2018)

24. Tian, Z., Shen, C., Chen, H., He, T.: FCOS: fully convolutional one-stage object detection. In: Proceedings of the IEEE/CVF International Conference on Computer Vision, pp. 9627–9636 (2019)

25. Yu, F., Koltun, V.: Multi-scale context aggregation by dilated convolutions. arXiv preprint arXiv:1511.07122 (2015)

26. Zhang, H., Chang, H., Ma, B., Wang, N., Chen, X.: Dynamic R-CNN: towards high quality object detection via dynamic training. In: Vedaldi, A., Bischof, H., Brox, T., Frahm, J.-M. (eds.) ECCV 2020. LNCS, vol. 12360, pp. 260–275. Springer, Cham (2020). https://doi.org/10.1007/978-3-030-58555-6_16

27. Zhang, S., Chi, C., Yao, Y., Lei, Z., Li, S.Z.: Bridging the gap between anchor-based and anchor-free detection via adaptive training sample selection. In: Proceedings of the IEEE/CVF Conference on Computer Vision and Pattern Recognition, pp. 9759–9768 (2020)

28. Zhu, C., He, Y., Savvides, M.: Feature selective anchor-free module for single-shot object detection. In: Proceedings of the IEEE/CVF Conference on Computer Vision and Pattern Recognition, pp. 840–849 (2019)

29. Zoph, B., Le, Q.V.: Neural architecture search with reinforcement learning. arXiv preprint arXiv:1611.01578 (2016)

A Densely Connected Neural Network Based on SSD for Multiscale SAR Ship Detection

Jialong Guo[1,2], Ling Wan[2,3], Lei Ma[2,3], and Zongli Jiang[1(✉)]

[1] Beijing University of Technology, Beijing 100124, China
jiangzl@bjut.edu.cn
[2] Institute of Automation, Chinese Academy of Sciences, Beijing 100190, China
wanling15@mails.ucas.ac.cn, lei.ma@ia.ac.cn
[3] University of Chinese Academy of Sciences, Beijing 100039, China

Abstract. Synthetic Aperture Radar (SAR) ship detection plays an increasingly important role in marine applications. With the development of deep learning methods, many object detection algorithms based on deep neural networks have emerged. However, these methods only obtain detection scores from a high-level convolutional feature map, ignoring the multiscale characteristic of objects. To solve the above problem, this paper proposes a densely connected neural network based on SSD. Theoretically, the high-level convolutional feature maps contain more semantic information, while the low-level convolutional feature maps collect the detailed features of the image. Thus, we combine the high- and low- level feature maps by adding dense connections to SSD, achieving the multiscale and multiscene SAR ship detection. In addition, considering the characteristics of SAR images, we discard the image augmentation strategy and use K-means clustering to design the multiscale candidate bounding boxes, improving the object detection accuracy. Finally, experiments carried out on SAR Ship Detection Dataset (SSDD) verify that the proposed method achieves satisfactory performance on multiscale and multiscene SAR ship detection.

Keywords: SAR · Ship detection · Densely connected neural network · SSD

1 Introduction

Synthetic Aperture Radar (SAR), as an active sensor, has the ability to monitor targets in all-time and all-weather conditions, playing an important role in the civil and military fields. Recently, with the development of SAR sensors, such as TerraSAR-X, Sentinel-1 and Gaofen-3, SAR ship detection receives increasing attentions in various applications, including maritime management, fishery management and battlefield environmental perception [13].

The conventional approaches for SAR ship detection can be divided into three types, including statistical theory-based methods [1,8], template matching-based

© Springer Nature Switzerland AG 2021
Y. Peng et al. (Eds.): ICIG 2021, LNCS 12888, pp. 305–314, 2021.
https://doi.org/10.1007/978-3-030-87355-4_26

methods [12, 20] and polarization information-based methods [2, 6]. Among them, the statistical theory methods based on constant false alarm rate (CFAR) are the most commonly used methods, which determine the detection threshold based on the pre-established clutter statistical model. However, these models are susceptible to ocean currents, climate and other factors, and thus their application scenarios are limited [11]. Template matching is another common method. Through artificially designed multiple templates, corresponding to different features such as length, width, area, contour and texture, perform a sliding search on the image to obtain the detection result. However, these methods consume a lot of manpower to establish a comprehensive template library, and often rely on expert experience, resulting in poor generalization ability. In particular, window sliding in SAR images takes a long time, which brings challenges to real-time performance.

In recent years, with the development of deep learning methods, many object detection algorithms based on deep neural networks have emerged, which can overcome the shortcomings of traditional methods to a certain extent. The deep learning-based object detection methods can be roughly divided into two main categories: (1) two-stage detection algorithms, which first generate candidate proposals and then carry out classification and refined location. Common two-stage methods include R-CNN [9], Fast R-CNN [10], Faster R-CNN [19] and their improved versions. (2) one-stage detection algorithms, which discard the region proposal stage, and directly predict the bounding boxes and corresponding classes using a single convolutional network. Typical one-stage algorithms include You Only Look Once (Yolo) v1–v3 [16–18], Single Shot MultiBox Detector (SSD) [15] and their improved versions [7, 14]. Generally, the two-stage methods are more accurate in bounding box prediction, whereas the one-stage approaches are faster and easier to train.

For SAR ship detection, to improve the efficiency and accuracy of detection, researchers input the origin SAR images into the model and realize the end-to-end ship detection through the automatic feature extraction ability of networks. Chen et al. [4] proposed an FPN mode that uses the anchor boxes obtained by SSD-Kmeans clustering to identify small ship targets under complex backgrounds. Chang et al. [3] adopted YOLOv2 to detect ships in SAR images and reduced the computational expenses. Zhang et al. [21] proposed a Grid Convolutional Neural Network to solve real-time detection problems. In addition, the attention mechanism is usually adopted to enhance the salient features and suppress the redundant information. For example, Zhao et al. [22] introduced a dilated attention block to enhance the feature extraction ability of the detectors. Du et al. [5] combined the saliency information into the model to make the detector pay more attention to the target areas. However, these methods only obtain detection scores from a high-level convolutional feature map, which ignore the multiscale characteristic of objects, resulting in limitations in processing multiscale SAR ship detection. Theoretically, the high-level convolutional feature maps contain more semantic information, while the low-level convolutional feature maps collect the detailed features of the image. Therefore, it is reasonable to perform SAR ship detection by combining the information of different layers.

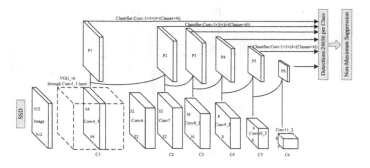

Fig. 1. Architecture of our proposed model.

To solve the above problem, this paper proposes a densely connected neural network based on SSD, realizing SAR ship detection in multiscale and multiscene conditions. Because the feature maps at different scales contain different spatial and semantic information, we combine the high- and low-level feature maps by adding dense connections to SSD, achieving the multiscale and multiscene SAR ship detection. Besides, taking into account the characteristics of SAR images, we discard the image augmentation strategy to improve the adaptability of the model. In addition, we carry out K-means clustering on the length and width of the real targets to design the multiscale candidate bounding boxes, improving the object detection accuracy. Experiments carried out on SAR Ship Detection Dataset (SSDD) verify that the proposed method achieves satisfactory performance on multiscale and multiscene SAR ship detection.

2   Methodology

In deep convolutional neural networks, feature maps at different convolutional layers have different spatial resolutions and semantic information. Generally, the low-level feature maps have higher resolution and contain rich spatial information, while the high-level feature maps have lower resolution and contain more semantic information. Thus, detecting SAR ships only from high- or low- level convolutional feature maps may ignore the multiscale characteristic of objects, resulting in limitations in practical application of SAR ship detection. Therefore, this paper proposes a densely connected neural network based on SSD, realizing SAR ship detection in multiscale and multiscene conditions. The architecture of our proposed model is shown in Fig. 1.

2.1   Densely Connected Feature Extraction Network

In our proposed method, VGG16 with 512×512 input image size is selected as the basic network. To ensure that the ships are not distorted from resizing, for image slices with the size less than 512, we fill in gray before inputting the image to the network. As show in Fig. 1, we take the feature map of conv4_3

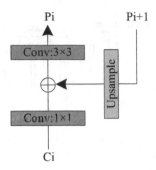

Fig. 2. Architecture of dense connection.

in the VGG16 network structure as the first initial feature layer C_1. Next, we perform maximum pooling and dilated convolution to obtain the second initial feature layer C_2. Then, the third to the sixth initial feature layers (C_3 to C_6) are successively obtained, using the same convolution operation as the SSD. Finally, a total of six initial feature layers (C_1–C_6) are obtained as the input for subsequent dense connections.

In order to make low-level feature maps contain more semantic information, we densely connect the feature maps from high to low, as shown in Fig. 2. Specifically, the initial feature map P_{i+1} is resized to the same size as C_i by upsampling. The initial feature map C_i passes through 1×1 convolution to fuse the current initial layer features, and then the up-sampled feature layer P_{i+1} is merged into C_i. Finally, in order to reduce the aliasing effect of upsampling, a 3×3 convolution is added to each merged feature layer to generate the final synthesized feature layer. Because there is no higher feature layer than C_6, we do not do any processing on the feature layer with the coarsest resolution. The above process can be summarized as:

$$\begin{cases} P_i = Conv_{3\times3} \left[\sum_{j=i+1}^{5} Upsample(P_j) + Conv_{1\times1}(C_i) \right] \\ P_6 = C_6 \end{cases} \tag{1}$$

2.2 Multiscale Bounding Box Design

In the SSD, the aspect ratio of the candidate bounding box at each scale is set to 2 and 3. To set the aspect ratio of the candidate bounding box for the SSDD dataset used in this paper, we carry out K-means clustering on the length and width of the real targets in the training set. With seven randomly initialized clustering centers, the clustering result is shown in Fig. 3, where the abscissa is the width of the target and the ordinate is the height of the target. We can see that most of the ratios are in the range of 1–3. Therefore, it is reasonable to set the aspect ratio of the candidate bounding box to (2.0, 3.0).

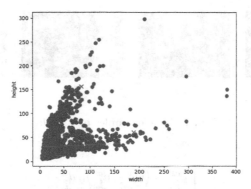

Fig. 3. Clustering result.

In addition, traditional object detection algorithms usually perform image augmentation processing on the input images, including image flipping, random zooming, and changing color gamut. However, the imaging method of SAR sensors is different from the optical sensors, and the imaging results in different angles are quite different. Therefore, in the experiments of this paper, we do not use image augmentation strategies for training.

2.3   Training

For the training process, we need to match a set of default boxes to the ground truth boxes. For each ground truth box, we match it with the best overlapped default box and the default boxes with the Jaccard overlap greater than a predefined threshold (e.g. 0.5). For the default boxes that do not match, we select some of them as negative samples according to the confidence loss, making the ratio to matching is 3:1.

Let $x_{ij}^p = \{1, 0\}$ be the indicator for matching the i-th default box to the j-th ground truth box of the category p, and $\sum_i x_{ij}^p \geq 1$. We establish the loss function by combining the localization loss (loc) and the confidence loss (conf).

$$L(x, c, l, g) = \frac{1}{N}\left(L_{\text{conf}}(x, c) + \alpha L_{loc}(x, l, g)\right) \qquad (2)$$

where N is the number of matched default boxes. If $N = 0$, the loss is set to 0.

The localization loss is the smooth L_1 loss between the predicted box (l) and the ground truth box (g).

$$L_{loc}(x, l, g) = \sum_{i \in Pos}^{N} \sum_{m \in \{cx, cy, w, h\}} x_{ij}^k \text{smooth}_{\text{L1}}\left(l_i^m - \hat{g}_j^m\right) \qquad (3)$$

310   J. Guo et al.

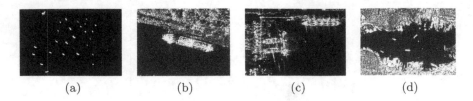

(a)   (b)   (c)   (d)

Fig. 4. Some examples of SSDD.

$$\begin{cases} \hat{g}_j^{cx} = \left(g_j^{cx} - d_i^{cx}\right)/d_i^w \\ \hat{g}_j^{cy} = \left(g_j^{cy} - d_i^{cy}\right)/d_i^h \\ \hat{g}_j^w = \log\left(\frac{g_j^w}{d_i^w}\right) \\ \hat{g}_j^h = \log\left(\frac{g_j^h}{d_i^h}\right) \end{cases} \tag{4}$$

The confidence loss is defined by the softmax loss over multiple classes confidences.

$$L_{\text{conf}}(x,c) = -\sum_{i\in\text{Pos}}^{N} x_{ij}^p \log\left(\hat{c}_i^p\right) - \sum_{i\in\text{Neg}} \log\left(\hat{c}_i^0\right) \tag{5}$$

$$\hat{c}_i^p = \frac{\exp\left(c_i^p\right)}{\sum_p \exp\left(c_i^p\right)} \tag{6}$$

3 Experiments

3.1 Dataset

In this paper, we use SSDD to verify the effectiveness of our proposed method. The SSDD contains SAR ships in different image resolutions, polarization modes, sensors and environments. The details of SSDD are presented in Table 1. The SSDD has 1160 image slices and 2456 ship instances in total, and Fig. 4 provides some examples. Besides, we randomly divide the SSDD into three parts: 928 training images and 232 test images.

Table 1. The details of SSDD.

Sensors	RadarSat-2, TerraSAR-X, Sentinel-1
Polarization	HH, VV, VH, HV
Resolution	1 m–15 m
Location	Yantai, China, Visakhapatnam, India
Position	Inshore, offshore

3.2 Experiments Setup

All experiments are implemented in the Pytorch framework and executed on the NVIDIA 1080Ti GPU. The architecture in Fig. 1 is trained end to end. By convention, the pre-trained VGGNet on the ImageNet dataset is used to initialize the model. In addition, we adopt synchronized SGD with a weight decay of 0.0005 and a momentum of 0.9 to train the model. The number of training iterations is set to 50 epochs, where the VGGNet weights are frozen for the first 20 epochs and the entire network is trained for the next 30 epochs. The initial learning rate is set to 0.0005 and then it decreases by 10 times every 20k.

To quantitative evaluate the performance of the proposed method, three criteria are used, including precision, Recall and F1-score.

3.3 Experimental Results

Our Model *vs* SSD. As can be observed from the results in Fig. 5, the proposed method performs better than original SSD. For small ships in the offshore scenes, the original SSD have more missed ships, but our method can accurately detect the small ships, since our network is able to learn more semantic information from top feature map. For the ships in coastal ports, our method gets better performance in complex scenes. The results reveal that our approach is practical for multiscale and multiscene SAR ship detection and achieves a better performance than the original SSD.

Our Model *vs* State-of-the-Art Methods. To illustrate the detection performance of the proposed method, several versions of Faster RCNN and SSD are applied to SSDD, and the experimental results are listed in Table 2. We can find that SSD with data augment has poor detection performance. After removing the data augment, the precision and recall values are increased. In addition, thanks to the dense connection, our method improves the precision value by 5% and increases the F1-score from 84.94% to 88.21%, comparing with the original SSD. Comparing to Faster RCNN, the precision of our proposed method increases from 87.28% to 91.05%. The results show that the detection performance has been improved by densely connected neural network, and delete data augmentation can effectively improve the ship detection performance for SAR images.

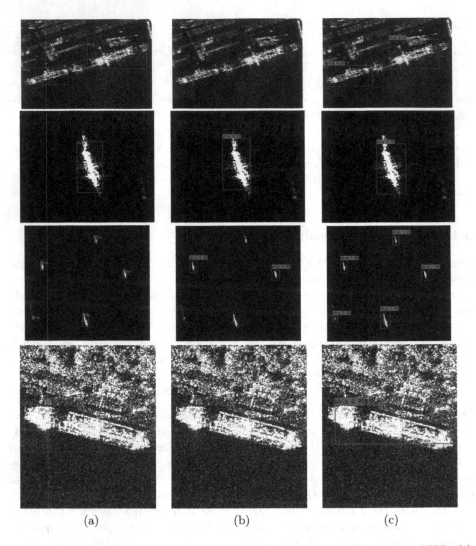

        (a)   (b)   (c)

Fig. 5. Some detection results on the test set: (a) ground truth; (b) results of SSD; (c) results of our model.

Table 2. Evaluation indices of different methods.

Method	Backbone	Precision(%)	Recall(%)	F1(%)	Augmentation
Faster RCNN	VGGNet	85.15	81.16	83.11	Yes
Faster RCNN	VGGNet	87.28	84.12	85.67	No
SSD512	VGGNet	84.36	79.82	82.03	Yes
SSD512	VGGNet	86.71	83.25	84.94	No
SSD512+Densely	VGGNet	88.61	82.41	85.40	Yes
SSD512+Densely	VGGNet	91.05	85.56	88.21	No

4   Conclusions

In this paper, we propose a densely connected neural network based on SSD, realizing SAR ship detection in multiscale and multiscene conditions. Theoretically, the high-level convolutional feature maps contain more semantic information, while the low-level convolutional feature maps collect the detailed features of the image. Thus, we combine the high- and low- level feature maps by adding dense connections to SSD, achieving the multiscale and multiscene SAR ship detection. In addition, considering the characteristics of SAR images, we discard the image augmentation strategy and use K-means clustering to design the multiscale candidate bounding boxes, improving the object detection accuracy. Finally, experiments carried out on SAR Ship Detection Dataset (SSDD) verify that the proposed method achieves satisfactory performance on multiscale and multiscene SAR ship detection.

References

1. An, W., Xie, C., Yuan, X.: An improved iterative censoring scheme for CFAR ship detection with SAR imagery. IEEE Trans. Geosci. Remote Sens. **52**(8), 4585–4595 (2014)
2. Brekke, C., Anfinsen, S.N.: Ship detection in ice-infested waters based on dual-polarization SAR imagery. IEEE Geosci. Remote Sens. Lett. **8**(3), 391–395 (2011)
3. Chang, Y.L., Anagaw, A., Chang, L., Wang, Y.C., Hsiao, C.Y., Lee, W.H.: Ship detection based on YOLOv2 for SAR imagery. Remote Sens. **11**(7), 786 (2019)
4. Chen, P., Li, Y., Zhou, H., Liu, B., Liu, P.: Detection of small ship objects using anchor boxes cluster and feature pyramid network model for SAR imagery. J. Marine Sci. Eng. **8**(2), 112 (2020)
5. Du, L., Li, L., Wei, D., Mao, J.: Saliency-guided single shot multibox detector for target detection in SAR images. IEEE Trans. Geosci. Remote Sens. **58**(5), 3366–3376 (2020)
6. Fan, Q., Chen, F., Cheng, M., Wang, C., Li, J.: A modified framework for ship detection from compact polarization SAR image. In: IGARSS 2018–2018 IEEE International Geoscience and Remote Sensing Symposium, pp. 3539–3542 (2018)
7. Fu, C.Y., Liu, W., Ranga, A., Tyagi, A., Berg, A.C.: DSSD: deconvolutional single shot detector. arXiv preprint arXiv:1701.06659 (2017)
8. Gao, G.: A Parzen-window-kernel-based CFAR algorithm for ship detection in SAR images. IEEE Geosci. Remote Sens. Lett. **8**(3), 557–561 (2011)
9. Girshick, R., Donahue, J., Darrell, T., Malik, J.: Rich feature hierarchies for accurate object detection and semantic segmentation. In: 2014 IEEE Conference on Computer Vision and Pattern Recognition, pp. 580–587 (2014)
10. Girshick, R.: Fast R-CNN. In: Proceedings of the IEEE International Conference on Computer Vision (ICCV), December 2015
11. Hou, B., Chen, X., Jiao, L.: Multilayer CFAR detection of ship targets in very high resolution SAR images. IEEE Geosci. Remote Sens. Lett. **12**(4), 811–815 (2015)
12. Jiang, S., Chao, W., Bo, Z., Hong, Z.: Ship detection based on feature confidence for high resolution SAR images. In: 2012 IEEE International Geoscience and Remote Sensing Symposium (IGARSS) (2012)

13. Jiao, J., et al.: A densely connected end-to-end neural network for multiscale and multiscene SAR ship detection. IEEE Access **6**, 20881–20892 (2018)
14. Li, Z., Zhou, F.: FSSD: feature fusion single shot multibox detector. arXiv preprint arXiv:1712.00960 (2017)
15. Liu, W., et al.: SSD: single shot multibox detector. In: Leibe, B., Matas, J., Sebe, N., Welling, M. (eds.) ECCV 2016. LNCS, vol. 9905, pp. 21–37. Springer, Cham (2016). https://doi.org/10.1007/978-3-319-46448-0_2
16. Redmon, J., Divvala, S., Girshick, R., Farhadi, A.: You only look once: unified, real-time object detection. In: Proceedings of the IEEE Conference on Computer Vision and Pattern Recognition, pp. 779–788 (2016)
17. Redmon, J., Farhadi, A.: YOLO9000: better, faster, stronger. In: Proceedings of the IEEE Conference on Computer Vision and Pattern Recognition, pp. 7263–7271 (2017)
18. Redmon, J., Farhadi, A.: YOLOv3: an incremental improvement. arXiv preprint arXiv:1804.02767 (2018)
19. Ren, S., He, K., Girshick, R., Sun, J.: Faster R-CNN: towards real-time object detection with region proposal networks. IEEE Trans. Pattern Anal. Mach. Intell. **39**(6), 1137–1149 (2017)
20. Wang, S., Wang, M., Yang, S., Jiao, L.: New hierarchical saliency filtering for fast ship detection in high-resolution SAR images. IEEE Trans. Geosci. Remote Sens. **55**(1), 351–362 (2017)
21. Zhang, T., Zhang, X.: High-speed ship detection in SAR images based on a grid convolutional neural network. Remote Sens. **11**(10), 1206 (2019)
22. Zhao, Y., Zhao, L., Li, C., Kuang, G.: Pyramid attention dilated network for aircraft detection in SAR images. IEEE Geosci. Remote Sens. Lett. **18**(4), 662–666 (2021)

Multi-level Features Selection Network Based on Multi-attention for Salient Object Detection

Jianyi Ren[1,2], Zheng Wang[1,2(✉)], and Meijun Sun[1,3]

[1] College of Intelligence and Computing, Tianjin University, Tianjin, China
wzheng@tju.edu.cn
[2] Tianjin Key Lab of Machine Learning, Tianjin, China
[3] Tianjin Key Lab Cognit Comp and Applicat, Tianjin, China

Abstract. Both the attention mechanism and Salient Object Detection aim to locate the most obvious regions in an image. However, common algorithms focus on micro attention but neglect the similarity in the macro perspective. Besides, they also ignore the differences among multi-scale information. To tackle these problems, we propose MFS-Net that progressive select features to predict salient regions. First, we design the Pyramid Attention module that integrates channel and spatial attention to extract semantic information for multi-scale high-level features and design the Self-Interaction Attention module to extract detailed information for multi-scale low-level features. Besides, to refine the saliency edge, we propose the Semantic-Detail Attention module which exploits high-level features to guide low-level features in a macro-attention manner. Finally, we selectively integrate global context information by the Interaction-Fusion Attention module, aiming to learn the relationship among different salient regions and alleviate the dilution effect of features. Experimental results on six benchmark datasets demonstrate that the proposed method performs well compared with 20 state-of-the-art methods.

Keywords: Salient object detection · Attention mechanism · Multi-scale features

1 Introduction

Salient Object Detection aims to locate the most obvious regions in an image. As a preprocessing step, it has been widely applied in various computer vision fields, such as object detection [18] and semantic segmentation [16]. Earlier SOD algorithms mainly used traditional methods to generate saliency maps, which rely on heuristic priors. However, these hand-crafted features are of great difficulty to capture the semantic information contained in images, thus they fail to yield satisfactory results for images with complex scenarios.

Recently, with the development of deep learning, salient object detection has made prominent progress. Due to the powerful capability to extract low-level information and high-level information at the same time [28], CNNs have

© Springer Nature Switzerland AG 2021
Y. Peng et al. (Eds.): ICIG 2021, LNCS 12888, pp. 315–326, 2021.
https://doi.org/10.1007/978-3-030-87355-4_27

Fig. 1. Motivating examples for the proposed MFS-Net. (a) Image. (b) Low-level feature. (c) High-level feature. (d) Features extracted after SIA. (e) Features extracted after PA. (f) Features extracted after SDA. (g) Features extracted after IFA. (h) Saliency result. (i) Groung truth. (j) The boundary of (i). (k) The boundary of (h).

emerged as an important trend for SOD. Besides, the attention mechanism plays a more and more crucial role in saliency object detection. The goal of the SOD is to allocate attention to the most obvious regions in the image, and the attention mechanism focuses on local saliency information. From this perspective, the attention mechanism provides a feasible solution for SOD. Wang et al. [13] integrate the attention mechanism into the saliency object detection, which has achieved superior performance. Zhang et al. [30] propose an attention-guided model to promote the wide application of attention mechanisms in salient object detection, in which the attention mechanism makes a critical difference.

Despite CNNs and attention mechanisms have achieved excellent performance in salient object detection, there are still the following major challenges: (1) In most cases, the attention mechanism uses micro attention to generate features, such as channel and spatial attention [30]. For salient object detection which is essentially similar to the attention mechanism, they neglect the similarity in the macro perspective. (2) Many saliency studies have revealed that multi-scale features are essential for SOD [28]. Specifically, high-level features have rich semantic information (Fig. 1 (c)), and low-level features contain abundant details (Fig. 1 (b)). However, previous methods simply fuse them which ignores their different contributions. (3) Early algorithms comprehensively utilize contextual information to extract features [7,31], whereas not all contextual information contributes to the final saliency mapping. As a result, the feature extracted is incomplete while background noise is integrated.

To deal with the problem, we propose MFS-Net that selects features at multiply levels. MFS-Net emphasizes the combination of micro and macro attention mechanisms to generate saliency maps in a supervised way. In order to extract high-level semantic features and low-level detail features, we respectively propose a Pyramid Attention module (PA) and a Self-Interaction Attention module (SIA) taking advantage of the micro attention mechanism, such as the spatial and channel attention mechanism. Considering the different contributions of multi-scale features, we propose the Semantic-Detail Attention module (SDA). This module employs the macro attention mechanism to encourage high-level features to guide low-level features to suppress the background response of the original features (Fig. 1 (f)). Besides, the Interaction-Fusion Attention module (IFA) inherits the feature-enhancing ability of attention mechanisms from a macro perspective and fuse multi-scale global context information to avoid irrelevant noise caused by traditional fusion methods (Fig. 1 (g)).

In short, our contributions can be summarized as follows:

(1) In order to achieve salient object detection, we propose MFS-Net including PA, SIA, SDA and IFA modules. The PA module and the SIA module utilize the attention mechanism to extract high-level and low-level features respectively. Then the extracted semantic information guides the detailed information to suppress irrelevant background by the SDA module. Finally, the IFA module selectively integrates global context information to improve the integrity of the saliency map.
(2) Compared with 20 start-of-art SOD methods on 6 public benchmark datasets, the proposed method MFS-Net achieves remarkable performance in both quantitative and qualitative evaluation.

2   Related Works

In this section, we introduce related works from two aspects. Firstly, we review several representative salient object detection methods, and then we describe the application of attention mechanisms in various visual fields.

2.1   Salient Object Detection

Earlier saliency methods are mainly based on hand-crafted priors to estimate saliency objects, such as color contrast [3], background prior [20]. In recent years, due to the CNNs-based saliency models allow flexible feature utilization and equip powerful end-to-end capabilities, deep learning has emerged as a promising alternative for SOD.

Zhao et al. [31] proposed to use fully connected CNN to integrate global context information for saliency detection; Li et al. [7] extract multi-scale information from images of different resolutions to estimate saliency; Hu et al. [6] concatenate multi-layer features for saliency detection; Zhang et al. [26] build a directional message-passing model to better integrate multi-scale features.

The above researches demonstrate that the extraction of effective features plays a crucial role in generating a complete saliency map. Therefore, the proposed MFS-Net selectively integrates multi-scale information to generate low-level saliency feature maps guided by high-level semantic information.

2.2   Attention Mechanism

The essence of the attention mechanism is to locate obvious information and suppress useless information, which is mainly divided into spatial attention and channel attention. Attention mechanisms have been proven to be beneficial in visual tasks, such as image classification [13] and image subtitles [1].

Chen et al. [1] propose a SCA-CNN network that combines spatial and channel attention for image captioning; Li et al. [8] focus on the global context to guide target detection by using the attention mechanism; Liu et al. [10] construct

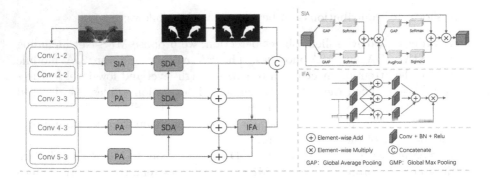

Fig. 2. Overall framework of the proposed model.

a pixel-level contextual attention model to pay attention to the information context position of each pixel; Zhang et al. [30] build a progressive attention model which sequentially generates attention features for saliency detection through the channel and spatial attention mechanisms.

The above studies demonstrate that the attention mechanism is of great help in SOD. However, most of the attention mechanisms only consider attention based on channels and spaces, named micro attention. For SOD, they ignore macro attention which is attention guidance at the feature level. On the contrary, MFS-Net proceeds with both the micro and macro aspects, which integrate global and pixel-level attention guidance, fusing the feature extraction capabilities of multi-scale information and the feature enhancement capabilities of the attention mechanism.

3   Method

In this section, we illuminate how each component made up and elucidate its effect on saliency detection. The overall architecture is illustrated in Fig. 2.

3.1   Pyramid Attention Module

In the feature extraction module, convolution operations of different levels correspond to features extraction of different levels, which directly affects the expression force of the model. For each convolutional layer containing deep semantic information, combining multi-scale information can produce more robust feature expressions. Therefore, in order to better extract the semantic information in the high-level features, we propose the Pyramid Attention module. But if we integrate multi-scale features without distinction, resulting in information redundancy and even performance degradation. Consequently, it is necessary to filtrate multi-scale information.

From Fig. 1, we can observe that the high-level feature map is rough, in which key parts may be weakened but some places that are not worthy of attention are

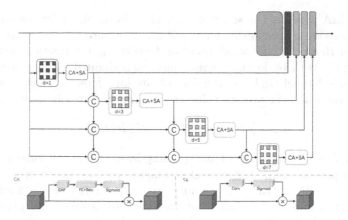

Fig. 3. Detailed structure of pyramid attention module.

given more attention. So, channel attention helps to allocate more attention to channels that show high response to salient regions. Given feature map $f^{h \times w \times c}$, we apply channel attention to generate the saliency map:

$$CA = \delta[FC(\theta(FC(GAP(f))))] \cdot f \qquad (1)$$

Where GAP refers to the global average pooling layer, FC is the full connected layer, θ donates Relu function and δ represents the sigmoid operation.

The contribution of each area in the feature maps diverse a lot. We prefer to highlight salient objects rather than consider all areas equally, so we use spatial attention to pay more attention to salient regions. For increasing the receptive field and obtaining global information, we adopted the method of [4], exploiting various convolution operations whose kernels respectively are $1 \times k$, $k \times 1$ and $k \times k$ to capture features, and then apply the sigmoid function to map the feature map to $[0, 1]$ for normalization. Ultimately, the attention weight is multiplied by the original feature map to obtain the saliency map.

In the PA module, as shown in Fig. 3, given the feature map, we concatenate 4 dilated convolutional layers with dilated rates of 1, 3, 5, and 7 respectively which are combined with channel attention and spatial attention to get filtered multi-scale feature maps. Eventually, we concatenate them with the input feature map to obtain a feature map containing semantic information.

3.2   Self-interaction Attention Module

Natural images usually contain complex details. From Fig. 1, the saliency map of low-level features comprises a lot of details, some of which are beneficial for SOD but others are counterproductive. In order to extract the detailed information thoroughly from the low-level features, we propose the Self-Interaction Attention module.

In the SIA module, the score of each pixel is obtained by comparing with all other positions. Specifically, for the shallow feature $f_l^{h \times w \times c}$, it is necessary to highlight those channels which focus on foreground information and suppress other channels with background noise since each channel focuses on a different feature. Each channel can be regarded as a boundary detector, so we calculate the maximum value and the average value at the same time to obtain soft attention:

$$f_s = [\sigma(GAP(f_l)) + \sigma(GMP(f_l))] \cdot f_l \qquad (2)$$

Where GMP refers to the global max-pooling layer, σ donates softmax function. GMP only pays attention to the most significant part and GAP treats all pixels equally which will inevitably merge noise, so we train f_s to make a soft choice.

In addition, in order to ensure that the attention score of each pixel is calculated both locally and globally, we add two items for global and local information extraction (Fig. 2 (upper right)). The global item is the same as the structure described above where the softmax function is combined with global average pooling of the spatial average matrix. For local item, we use local average pooling to figure out the local information similarity where a 2×2 pooling layer is applied to obtain the attention score of each local pixel.

$$f_o = [\sigma(GAP(f_s)) + \delta(AvP(f_s))] \cdot f_s \qquad (3)$$

Considering that local information should be independent of each other, we use the sigmoid function when calculating local attention.

3.3   Semantic-Detail Attention Module

Due to multiple downsampling, high-lever features have a lot of semantic information, but they lose a lot of detailed information. At the same time, the low-level features retain rich details and background noise on account of the limitation of the receptive field. In order to refine the details of semantic features and suppress the background noise of detail features, we propose the Semantic-Detail Attention module.

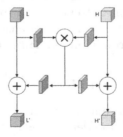

Fig. 4. Detailed structure of semantic-detail attention module.

The attention mechanism in the SDA is diverse from mentioned above. Instead of normalizing the features among [0, 1], it directly adopts the cross-guidance of attention using different feature maps on the macro level (Fig. 4). The module first applies element multiplication operation to merge the semantic feature f_h and the detailed feature f_l to extract the common feature f_c. Then the common feature f_c is combined with the previous features f_h and f_l by element addition operation respectively and the combined features f_h' and f_l' after macro attention are obtained. This attention fusion algorithm can effectively avoid the *pollution* caused by background noise. We cascade multiple SDA modules in series to make the semantic features and detailed features fully merged. Finally, the boundary of the high-level feature is sharpened and the background noise of the low-level feature is suppressed.

3.4 Interaction-Fusion Attention Module

In the process of feature transmission, some of the information will be diluted inevitably, which leads to incomplete extraction of effective features. Most methods comprehensively utilize global context information to extract features, but not all global context information contributes to the final saliency mapping. Unselected fusion will result in excessive background noise. Therefore, we propose the Interaction-Fusion Attention module.

As shown in Fig. 2 (middle right), the input of the IFA module comes from the salient feature maps after the feature filtrated at different resolutions. These feature maps are adjusted to an appropriate resolution through convolution layer, batchnorm and relu. During the process of interaction-fusion, different feature maps are fused through element addition operations to generate three feature maps that incorporate global context information. After that, we make use of the attention strategy to train three branches and obtain soft attention. Finally, for suppressing those unnecessary background noises, we utilize the macro attention mechanism to match the original features with the features filtered by the IFA module. Through the Interaction-Fusion Attention selection strategy, we can suppress those worthless background noises and integrate the filtered global context information.

3.5 Loss

We introduce the consistency enhancement loss (CEL) [12]:

$$L = \frac{|FP + FN|}{|FP + 2TP + FN|} \tag{4}$$

Where TP, FP and FN represent true-positive, false-positive and false-negative, respectively. $FP+FN$ refers to the difference between the union and intersection of the predicted map and the ground truth, while $FP + 2TP + FN$ represents the sum of the union and the intersection.

Table 1. Performance comparison with 20 methods over 6 datasets. The best three results are shown in red, blue, and green.

Methods	DUT-OMRON			PASCAL-S			DUTS-TE			ECSSD			HKU-IS			SOD		
	MAE	E-m	F-m	MAE	E-m	F-m	MAE	E-m	F-m	MAE	E-m	F-m	MAE	E-m	F-m	MAE	E-m	F-m
WSS (2017 CVPR)	0.110	0.729	0.602	0.139	0.740	0.715	0.100	0.745	0.653	0.104	0.805	0.823	0.079	0.818	0.821	0.169	0.663	0.725
SBF (2017 ICCV)	0.108	0.763	0.608	0.131	0.778	0.695	0.107	0.763	0.622	0.088	0.850	0.809	0.075	0.855	0.801	0.156	0.734	0.711
UCF (2017 ICCV)	0.120	0.760	0.621	0.115	0.811	0.726	0.112	0.775	0.631	0.069	0.890	0.844	0.062	0.886	0.823	0.164	0.742	0.695
NLDF (2017 CVPR)	0.080	0.798	0.684	0.098	0.844	0.769	0.065	0.851	0.738	0.063	0.900	0.878	0.048	0.914	0.873	0.123	0.782	0.788
AMU (2017 ICCV)	0.098	0.793	0.647	0.100	0.837	0.737	0.068	0.817	0.870	0.060	0.990	0.908	0.047	0.959	0.788	0.141	0.786	0.752
FSN (2017 ICCV)	0.066	0.844	0.706	0.093	0.853	0.766	0.066	0.861	0.729	0.053	0.924	0.872	0.044	0.928	0.858	0.126	0.809	0.772
C2S (2018 ECCV)	0.072	0.824	0.682	0.081	0.872	0.762	0.062	0.863	0.717	0.053	0.919	0.865	0.046	0.921	0.853	0.123	0.789	0.761
BDMP (2018 CVPR)	0.064	0.831	0.692	0.074	0.876	0.758	0.049	0.883	0.745	0.045	0.927	0.868	0.039	0.930	0.871	0.106	0.803	0.761
PAGRN (2018 CVPR)	0.071	0.772	0.711	0.089	0.834	0.798	0.056	0.842	0.783	0.061	0.893	0.894	0.047	0.898	0.886	0.145	0.708	0.770
PICA (2018 CVPR)	0.068	0.833	0.710	0.078	0.869	0.789	0.054	0.872	0.749	0.046	0.923	0.885	0.042	0.921	0.870	0.101	0.800	0.788
MWS (2019 CVPR)	0.109	0.729	0.609	0.133	0.735	0.713	0.091	0.743	0.684	0.096	0.791	0.840	0.084	0.787	0.814	0.166	0.660	0.734
CAPSAL (2019 CVPR)	0.104	0.669	0.563	0.075	0.871	0.810	0.062	0.846	0.743	0.082	0.843	0.819	0.055	0.885	0.843	0.147	0.698	0.688
HRS (2019 ICCV)	0.065	0.772	0.690	0.079	0.847	0.804	0.050	0.853	0.788	0.052	0.916	0.905	0.042	0.912	0.886	0.134	0.724	0.728
deepCRF (2019 ICCV)	0.057	0.838	0.738	0.082	0.852	0.790	0.059	0.854	0.744	0.049	0.921	0.896	0.039	0.925	0.881	0.121	0.776	0.785
PAGE (2019 CVPR)	0.062	0.849	0.736	0.076	0.878	0.806	0.052	0.883	0.777	0.042	0.936	0.906	0.037	0.934	0.882	0.110	0.801	0.796
TDBU (2019 CVPR)	0.061	0.867	0.739	0.071	0.883	0.775	0.048	0.892	0.766	0.041	0.937	0.880	0.038	0.933	0.878	0.104	0.821	0.767
CSNet (2020 ECCV)	0.081	0.801	0.675	0.103	0.815	0.723	0.074	0.820	0.687	0.065	0.886	0.844	0.059	0.883	0.840	0.136	0.742	0.731
SS (2020 CVPR)	0.068	0.840	0.703	0.092	0.854	0.774	0.062	0.865	0.742	0.059	0.911	0.870	0.047	0.923	0.860	0.129	0.771	0.758
EDNS (2020 ECCV)	0.076	0.811	0.682	0.094	0.837	0.790	0.065	0.851	0.735	0.068	0.894	0.872	0.046	0.918	0.873	0.142	0.754	0.776
GateNet (2020 ECCV)	0.061	0.840	0.723	0.068	0.886	0.797	0.045	0.893	0.783	0.041	0.932	0.896	0.036	0.933	0.889	-	-	-
Ours	0.067	0.815	0.718	0.072	0.885	0.805	0.048	0.897	0.790	0.043	0.936	0.897	0.037	0.939	0.881	0.102	0.815	0.794

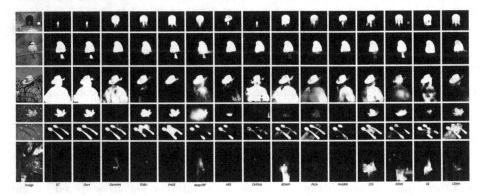

Fig. 5. Qualitative comparison of the proposed model with other methods.

4   Experiments

4.1   Datasets

We evaluate the proposed model on six public saliency detection benchmark datasets: ECSSD, DUT-OMRON, HKU-IS, PASCAL-S, DUTS and SOD, which are human-labeled with pixel-wise ground truth for quantitative evaluations.

4.2   Evaluation Criteria

To quantitatively evaluate the effectiveness of our proposed model, we adopt precision-recall (PR) curves, F-measure (Fm) score, Mean Absolute Error (MAE), and mean E-measure (Em) score as our performance measures.

4.3   Implementation Details

Following most existing state-of-the-art methods, we use DUTS-TR as our training dataset. We deploy VGG-16 trained on ImageNet as our backbone. During the training stage, we crop the image to a size of 224×224. Besides, we exploit random cropping and random rotation operations for data enhancement to avoid overfitting. The entire model is trained end-to-end and applies the poly strategy, where the variable is set to 0.9. To ensure model convergence, our model was trained on NVIDIA GTX 1080 Ti GPU with a batshsize of 8.

4.4   Performance Comparison

We compare the proposed MFS-Net against 20 recent SOD algorithms: WSS [14], SBF [23], UCF [29], NLDF [11], AMU [28], FSN [2], C2S [9], BDMP [26], PAGRN [30], PICA [10], MWS [22], CAPSAL [27], HRS [21], deepCRF [19], PAGE [17], TDBU [15], CSNet [5], SS [25], EDNS [24] and GateNet [32]. For fair, all the saliency maps of the above methods are provided by the authors or predicted through codes published by them.

Quantitative Comparison. In order to fully compare our proposed model with the above models, the experimental results under different metrics are listed in Table 1. It can be seen from the results that our method exhibits excellent performance, which proves the effectiveness of the proposed model. Besides, Fig. 6 shows the PR curve of the above algorithm on 6 datasets. The results reveal that our method is the most prominent in most cases, indicating that our model is highly competitive.

Qualitative Evaluation. To further illustrate the advantages of the proposed method, we provide some visual examples of different methods. Some representative examples are shown in Fig. 5. These examples reflect various scenarios, including small objects (1st row), foreground disturbance (2nd row), large salient object (3rd row), low contrast between salient object and image background (4th row), multiple salient objects (5th row) and no salient object (6th row). Compared with other methods, the saliency maps produced by our method are more complete and more accurate.

Table 2. Ablation study for different modules on the ECSSD dataset.

Baseline	SIA	PA	SDA	IFA	MAE
✓					0.071
✓	✓				0.056
✓	✓	✓			0.049
✓	✓	✓	✓		0.045
✓	✓	✓	✓	✓	0.043

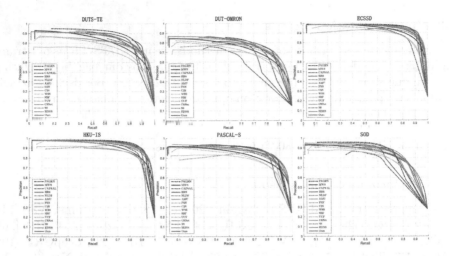

Fig. 6. Precision-Recall curves on 6 common saliency datasets.

4.5   Ablation Study

To illustrate the effectiveness of each module designed in the proposed model, we conduct the ablation study. The ablation experiments are applied on the ECSSD dataset and VGG-16 is adopted as the backbone. As shown in Table 2, the proposed model containing all components (i.e. PA, SIA, SDA and IFA) achieves the best performance, which demonstrates the necessity of each component for the proposed model to obtain the best saliency detection results.

We adopt the model which only uses high-level features after up-sampling as the baseline model, then we add each module progressively. First, we concatenate high-level features and low-feature after the SIA module which largely improves the baseline from 0.071 to 0.056 in terms of MAE. Furthermore, we add PA and get a decline of 31% in MAE compared with the basic model. On this basis, the MAE score is improved by 37% after adding SDA to both high-level features and low-level features. Finally, the combination of IFA achieves the best result.

5   Conclusion

In this paper, we propose the MFS-Net to achieve salient object detection. Taking into account the characteristics of multi-scale features, we design the PA and SIA modules to extract high-level and low-level features respectively. For refining the saliency edge, we introduce the SDA module which exploits the attention mechanism to boost detailed features guided by semantic features. Finally, we introduce the filtered global context information to alleviate the dilution effect of features. Extensive experiments on 6 datasets validate that the proposed model outperforms 20 state-of-the-art methods under different evaluation metrics.

References

1. Chen, L., et al.: SCA-CNN: spatial and channel-wise attention in convolutional networks for image captioning. In: Proceedings of the IEEE Conference on Computer Vision and Pattern Recognition, pp. 5659–5667 (2017)
2. Chen, X., Zheng, A., Li, J., Lu, F.: Look, perceive and segment: finding the salient objects in images via two-stream fixation-semantic CNNs. In: Proceedings of the IEEE International Conference on Computer Vision, pp. 1050–1058 (2017)
3. Cheng, M.M., Mitra, N.J., Huang, X., Torr, P.H., Hu, S.M.: Global contrast based salient region detection. IEEE Trans. Pattern Anal. Mach. Intell. **37**(3), 569–582 (2014)
4. Ding, X., Guo, Y., Ding, G., Han, J.: ACNet: strengthening the kernel skeletons for powerful cnn via asymmetric convolution blocks. In: Proceedings of the IEEE International Conference on Computer Vision, pp. 1911–1920 (2019)
5. Gao, S.H., Tan, Y.Q., Cheng, M.M., Lu, C., Chen, Y., Yan, S.: Highly efficient salient object detection with 100k parameters. arXiv preprint arXiv:2003.05643 (2020)
6. Hu, X., Zhu, L., Qin, J., Fu, C.W., Heng, P.A.: Recurrently aggregating deep features for salient object detection. In: Thirty-Second AAAI Conference on Artificial Intelligence (2018)
7. Li, G., Yu, Y.: Visual saliency based on multiscale deep features. In: Proceedings of the IEEE Conference on Computer Vision and Pattern Recognition, pp. 5455–5463 (2015)
8. Li, J., et al.: Attentive contexts for object detection. IEEE Trans. Multimed. **19**(5), 944–954 (2016)
9. Li, X., Yang, F., Cheng, H., Liu, W., Shen, D.: Contour knowledge transfer for salient object detection. In: Ferrari, V., Hebert, M., Sminchisescu, C., Weiss, Y. (eds.) ECCV 2018. LNCS, vol. 11219, pp. 370–385. Springer, Cham (2018). https://doi.org/10.1007/978-3-030-01267-0_22
10. Liu, N., Han, J., Yang, M.H.: PiCANet: learning pixel-wise contextual attention for saliency detection. In: Proceedings of the IEEE Conference on Computer Vision and Pattern Recognition, pp. 3089–3098 (2018)
11. Luo, Z., Mishra, A., Achkar, A., Eichel, J., Li, S., Jodoin, P.M.: Non-local deep features for salient object detection. In: Proceedings of the IEEE Conference on Computer Vision and Pattern Recognition, pp. 6609–6617 (2017)
12. Pang, Y., Zhao, X., Zhang, L., Lu, H.: Multi-scale interactive network for salient object detection. In: Proceedings of the IEEE/CVF Conference on Computer Vision and Pattern Recognition, pp. 9413–9422 (2020)
13. Wang, F., et al.: Residual attention network for image classification. In: Proceedings of the IEEE Conference on Computer Vision and Pattern Recognition, pp. 3156–3164 (2017)
14. Wang, L., eLearning to detect salient objects with image-level supervision. In: Proceedings of the IEEE Conference on Computer Vision and Pattern Recognition, pp. 136–145 (2017)
15. Wang, W., Shen, J., Cheng, M.M., Shao, L.: An iterative and cooperative top-down and bottom-up inference network for salient object detection. In: Proceedings of the IEEE Conference on Computer Vision and Pattern Recognition, pp. 5968–5977 (2019)
16. Wang, W., Shen, J., Porikli, F.: Saliency-aware geodesic video object segmentation. In: Proceedings of the IEEE Conference on Computer Vision and Pattern Recognition, pp. 3395–3402 (2015)

17. Wang, W., Zhao, S., Shen, J., Hoi, S.C., Borji, A.: Salient object detection with pyramid attention and salient edges. In: Proceedings of the IEEE Conference on Computer Vision and Pattern Recognition, pp. 1448–1457 (2019)
18. Xu, K., et al.: Show, attend and tell: neural image caption generation with visual attention. In: International Conference on Machine Learning, pp. 2048–2057 (2015)
19. Xu, Y., et al.: Structured modeling of joint deep feature and prediction refinement for salient object detection. In: Proceedings of the IEEE International Conference on Computer Vision, pp. 3789–3798 (2019)
20. Yang, C., Zhang, L., Lu, H., Ruan, X., Yang, M.H.: Saliency detection via graph-based manifold ranking. In: Proceedings of the IEEE Conference on Computer Vision and Pattern Recognition, pp. 3166–3173 (2013)
21. Zeng, Y., Zhang, P., Zhang, J., Lin, Z., Lu, H.: Towards high-resolution salient object detection. In: Proceedings of the IEEE International Conference on Computer Vision, pp. 7234–7243 (2019)
22. Zeng, Y., Zhuge, Y., Lu, H., Zhang, L., Qian, M., Yu, Y.: Multi-source weak supervision for saliency detection. In: Proceedings of the IEEE Conference on Computer Vision and Pattern Recognition, pp. 6074–6083 (2019)
23. Zhang, D., Han, J., Zhang, Y.: Supervision by fusion: towards unsupervised learning of deep salient object detector. In: Proceedings of the IEEE International Conference on Computer Vision, pp. 4048–4056 (2017)
24. Zhang, J., Xie, J., Barnes, N.: Learning noise-aware encoder-decoder from noisy labels by alternating back-propagation for saliency detection. arXiv preprint arXiv:2007.12211 (2020)
25. Zhang, J., Yu, X., Li, A., Song, P., Liu, B., Dai, Y.: Weakly-supervised salient object detection via scribble annotations. In: Proceedings of the IEEE/CVF Conference on Computer Vision and Pattern Recognition, pp. 12546–12555 (2020)
26. Zhang, L., Dai, J., Lu, H., He, Y., Wang, G.: A bi-directional message passing model for salient object detection. In: Proceedings of the IEEE Conference on Computer Vision and Pattern Recognition, pp. 1741–1750 (2018)
27. Zhang, L., Zhang, J., Lin, Z., Lu, H., He, Y.: CapSal: leveraging captioning to boost semantics for salient object detection. In: Proceedings of the IEEE Conference on Computer Vision and Pattern Recognition, pp. 6024–6033 (2019)
28. Zhang, P., Wang, D., Lu, H., Wang, H., Ruan, X.: Amulet: aggregating multi-level convolutional features for salient object detection. In: Proceedings of the IEEE International Conference on Computer Vision, pp. 202–211 (2017)
29. Zhang, P., Wang, D., Lu, H., Wang, H., Yin, B.: Learning uncertain convolutional features for accurate saliency detection. In: Proceedings of the IEEE International Conference on Computer Vision, pp. 212–221 (2017)
30. Zhang, X., Wang, T., Qi, J., Lu, H., Wang, G.: Progressive attention guided recurrent network for salient object detection. In: Proceedings of the IEEE Conference on Computer Vision and Pattern Recognition, pp. 714–722 (2018)
31. Zhao, R., Ouyang, W., Li, H., Wang, X.: Saliency detection by multi-context deep learning. In: Proceedings of the IEEE Conference on Computer Vision and Pattern Recognition, pp. 1265–1274 (2015)
32. Zhao, X., Pang, Y., Zhang, L., Lu, H., Zhang, L.: Suppress and balance: a simple gated network for salient object detection. arXiv preprint arXiv:2007.08074 (2020)

Learning Disentangled Representation for Fine-Grained Visual Categorization

Wenjie Dang[1], Shuiwang Li[2] , Qijun Zhao[1,2(✉)], and Fang Liu[3]

[1] National Key Laboratory of Fundamental Science on Synthetic Vision,
Sichuan University, Chengdu, China
qjzhao@scu.edu.cn
[2] College of Computer Science, Sichuan University, Chengdu, China
[3] School of Information Science and Technology, Tibet University, Lhasa, China
liu1221@utibet.edu.cn

Abstract. Fine-grained visual categorization (FGVC) that aims to recognize objects from subcategories with very subtle differences remains a challenging task due to the large intra-class and small inter-class variation caused by, e.g., deformation, occlusion, illumination, background clutter, etc. A great deal of recent work tackles this problem by forcing the network to focus on partial discriminable features using attention mechanisms or part-based methods. However, these methods neglect the point that the network may learn to discriminate objects from identity-unrelated features, for instance, when backgrounds are discriminable in training samples, degrading the network's generalization ability. In this paper, for the first time, we use disentangled representation learning to disentangle the fine-grained visual feature into two parts: the identity-related feature and the identity-unrelated feature. Only the identity-related feature is used for the final classification. Since identity-unrelated information is neglected in classification, intra-class variation is reduced while inter-class variation is amplified through the disentanglement, improving the classification performance as a result. Experimental results on three standard fine-grained visual categorization datasets, i.e., CUB-200-2011 (CUB), Stanford Cars (CAR) and FGVC-Aircraft (AIR), demonstrate the effectiveness of our method and show that we achieve state-of-the-art performance on the benchmarks.

Keywords: Fine-grained visual categorization · Disentangled representation learning · Adversarial learning

1 Introduction

The tasks of fine-grained visual categorization (FGVC) are to classify object categories that are similar in appearance and subtle in differences, e.g., bird species [19], car models [8], aircraft [12] and retail commodity [20], etc. Such tasks are more challenging than generic object classification. For one thing, true

© Springer Nature Switzerland AG 2021
Y. Peng et al. (Eds.): ICIG 2021, LNCS 12888, pp. 327–339, 2021.
https://doi.org/10.1007/978-3-030-87355-4_28

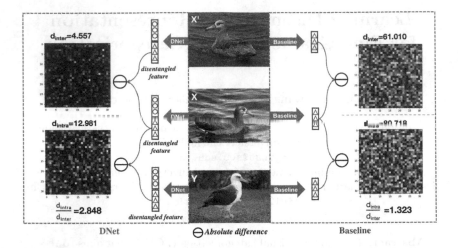

Fig. 1. Feature comparison between the proposed DNet and the Baseline. The former uses disentangle representation learning to get disentangled identity-related features for classification, whereas the latter does not. X and X' are of the same class label but Y is a different class. The heat maps show the absolute differences between the feature pairs while d_{inter} and d_{intra} denote the Euclidian distances between the feature pairs. $\frac{d_{intra}}{d_{inter}}$ represents the ratio of inter-class distance to intra-class distance. Note that the ratio of inter-class distance to intra-class distance of the DNet is significantly larger than that of the Baseline.

discriminative information is much less due to the subtlety of inter-class differences. For another, annotated training data is very deficient due to the difficulties of data collection. Benefiting from the progress of deep learning, the recognition performance of FGVC has been significantly improved in the past years [2,5,6,11]. A great deal of recent work tackles this problem by forcing the network to focus on partial discriminative features using attention mechanisms or part-based methods. For instance, Fu et al. [4] proposed a reinforced attention proposal network to learn discriminative region attention and region-based feature representation at multiple scales. Sun et al. [17] proposed an attention-based convolutional neural network that first learns multiple attention region features of each input image through the one-squeeze multi-excitation (OSME) module and then applies a multi-attention multi-class constraint in a metric learning framework. Zheng et al. [26] proposed a part learning approach by using a channel grouping network to generate multiple parts by clustering and then classified these parts features to predict the categories of input images. To avoid costly annotations of parts or key areas for training some researchers used weakly supervised methods or tried to explicitly constraint the model to locate discriminative regions. For instance, Peng et al. [15] proposed the object part attention model (OPAM) for weakly supervised fine-grained image classification, in which part-level attention is exploited to select discriminative parts of objects and an object spatial constraint is used to ensure selected parts highly representative. Yang et al. [23] proposed a self-supervision mechanism to localize informative regions without the need for part annotations. Chen et al. [2] proposed a destruction and construction learning method to learn discriminative regions and features by first partitioning the input image into local regions, then shuffling them by a region confusion mechanism, and finally restoring the original spatial layout of local regions through a region alignment network.

All of the methods just mentioned intend to learn a model which is able to locate the discriminative information for fine-grained visual categorization, and either explicitly or implicitly guide the model with information such as part annotations, part-based constraints, and attention mechanisms. However, these methods neglect the point that the network may learn to discriminate objects from identity-unrelated features, for instance, when backgrounds are discriminative in training samples, degrading the network's generalization ability. In this paper, for the first time, we use disentangled representation learning to disentangle the fine-grained visual feature into two parts: the identity-related feature and the identity-unrelated feature. Only the identity-related feature is used for the final classification. Since the identity-unrelated information is neglected in classification, intra-class variation is reduced while inter-class variation is amplified through the disentanglement, improving the classification performance as a result. We visualize the pair-wise absolute differences of the features for classification of three images X, X' and Y, as shown in Fig. 1. X and X' are of the same class label which is different from the label of Y. Obviously, regarding our DNet, the identity-related features of X and X' are visually more similar than those of X and Y. And, quantitatively, the ratio of inter-class distance to intra-class distance of the DNet is significantly larger than that of the Baseline as well in these examples. It suggests the effectiveness of disentangled representation learning in reducing intra-class variation while amplifying inter-class variation for fine-grained visual categorization.

The contributions of this paper can be summarized as follows,

- We propose for the first time to use disentangled representation learning for fine-grained visual categorization, and we propose a disentanglement network (DNet) that combines two strategies for training.
- We evaluate the proposed method on three benchmarks for fine-grained visual categorization. Experimental results demonstrate the effectiveness of the proposed method and show that the proposed DNet achieves state-of-the-art performance.

The remainder of this paper is organized as follows: We review the related work in Sect. 2. In Sect. 3, we will elaborate on our methods. Experimental results are presented and analyzed in Sect. 4, and the paper is finally concluded in Sect. 5

2   Related Work

2.1   Fine-Grained Visual Categorization

There have been a variety of methods designed to distinguish fine-grained categories. Strong supervised fine-grained classification uses additional manual annotation information such as bounding box or part annotation. It can reduce the clutter of background and improve the accuracy of classification. And it has certain interpretability. The frameworks of early works [1,24] are similar to detection, which select regions and classify the pose-normalized objects. They use bounding- box/part annotations during the training and inference phase. Although this setting makes fine-grained classification more useful in practice, it is very expensive to obtain annotation information and has poor universality. Therefore, the research of fine-grained image classification is gradually replaced by weak supervision. This paper will mainly consider the last setting, where bounding-box/part annotations are not needed either at the training or inference phase.

In order to learn without fine-grained annotations, Xiao et al. [22] proposed a two-level attention algorithm, which uses the selective search algorithm [18] to detect and extract the foreground image from the original image to reduce the interference of the background and get the candidate region with local discrimination. Lin et al. [10] proposed the Bilinear CNN model, which used high-order images to capture the relationship between feature channels, and achieved 84.1% classification accuracy on CUB-200-2011. And Bilinear CNN has done a lot of work towards improvement and simplification in the later related research. Later, in order to obtain local feature information better-attention mechanism was introduced into fine-grained image classification. Fu et al. [4] develop a recurrent attention module to recursively learn discriminative region attention and region-based feature representation at multiple scales in a mutually reinforced way. Chen et al. [2] deconstructed and re-constructed input images to find discriminative regions and features. Zheng et al. [27] proposed a trilinear attention sampling network to learn features from different details.Vgg-16/Vgg-19, ResNet, DenseDet, and GoogleNet are often used as backbone networks for fine-grained classification, among which ResNet-50 is the one most used. In this paper, we also use ResNet-50 as the backbone to construct our DNet model.

2.2   Disentangled Representations

The disentangled representation is a kind of distributed feature representation that could separate the latent codes into disjoint explanatory factors. It can be used to learn not only representations that each factor corresponds to a single interpretable factor of variation in data sets of which the interpretable latent factors are not too many for applications such as image and video generation, but also representations of merely coarse interpretability in data sets of which the interpretable latent factors are too many or too hard to be correctly separated for applications such as image recognition and classification. There are two popular strategies in learning disentangled representations for image recognition and classification. One strategy is to use a pair of images to guide the representation learning from a generative perspective. It requires that the generated image decoded from a swapped representation, which is obtained by swapping the identity-unrelated factors of the two disentangled representations, should be close to the input image with the same identity-unrelated factors so that the identity-related factors are an invariant representation for recognition and classification. The other strategy is to use a single image to guide the representation learning from a discriminative perspective, in which methods of adversarial learning are usually used to squeeze out identity-unrelated factors from the latent codes. For instance, Zhang et al. [25] use an encoder-decoder network to disentangle the appearance feature and gait feature of the human body in the walking videos. Gait features are extracted by a similarity loss between two videos from the same person. DrNet [3] disentangles content and pose vectors with a two-encoders architecture, which removes content information in the pose vector by generative adversarial training. Peng et al. [14] proposes a pose independent feature representation method to find a rich embedding layer to encode identity-related features and identity-unrelated features. A new feature reconstruction metric is proposed to learn how to disentangle the features.

However, the first strategy does not work well in the case where the identity-unrelated factors are too complicated to encode. In especially the fine-grained birds' categorization concerted here, the backgrounds of a pair of images could be so different that the identity-unrelated factors of the two images may not even intersect semantically. So it is very hard to encode the identity-unrelated factors by which a swapped representation can be decoded validly. Therefore, in this paper, we adopt the first strategy to learn disentangling feature representation and decompose the depth feature into two parts: identity-related feature and identity-unrelated feature. They are then decoded under the constraints of minimizing the reconstruction error. And the Euclidian distance between the identity-related features of the image pair is minimized as usual to learn an invariant representation for classification. Since the swapping strick is abandoned in the adjusted first strategy, the identity-unrelated factors in the disentangled representations are learned with very weak constraints. To make up this, we use the second strategy to purposefully guide the learning of the identity-unrelated factors in an adversarial manner.

3   Method

In this section, we propose a disentanglement network (DNet) for fine-grained visual categorization, as shown in Fig. 2. It combines two strategies of disentangled representation learning to disentangle identity-related and identity-unrelated components in the feature obtained by ResNet-50. Our DNet consists of a backbone network, two encoders E_1 and E_2, two classifiers C_{noid} and C_{id}, and one decoder D, in which two subnetworks could be identified, i.e., the single sample adversarial learning subnetwork and the paired samples disentanglement subnetwork, as shown in Fig. 3.

The former aims to train the encoder E_1 using adversarial learning with a single sample so that it outputs identity-unrelated feature only, corresponding to the first strategy of disentangled representation learning mentioned in Sect. 2.2, while the latter aims to jointly train both the encoders E_1 and E_2, the decoder D and the classifier C_{id} using a pair of samples of the same categorical label,

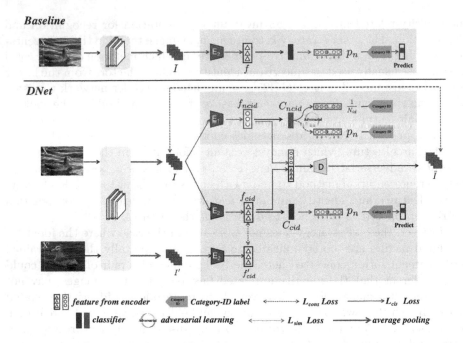

Fig. 2. Overview of the proposed DNet and the Baseline model. Note that the backbones of the two models are both ResNet-50. Also note that the disentangled representation learning is used in our DNet but not used in the Baseline.

corresponding to the second strategy of disentangled representation learning. Note that during inference time, only the backbone, the encoder E_2, and the classifier C_{id} are needed. Our DNet is trained in two stages sequentially, which will be discussed in detail in the following.

3.1 The Single-Sample Adversarial Learning Subnetwork (SSALNet)

This subnetwork will be trained first. Given a sample X, let's denote by $I = B(X)$ the feature map obtained by compositing the ResNet-50 network and the average pooling layer. The encoder E_1 and the classifier C_{ncid} are trained with adversarial learning by alternately performing the following two steps. In the first step, the encoder E_1 is fixed, the classifier C_{ncid} is trained to minimize the following cross-entropy loss:

$$L_{adv1} = -\sum_{j=1}^{N_{id}} p[j] \log(softmax(C_{ncid}(f_{ncid}))[j]), \qquad (1)$$

where N_{id} is the number of classes, p is the one-hot label corresponding to the input X, $p[j]$ denotes the jth entry of p, $f_{ncid} = E_1(I)$ represents the output

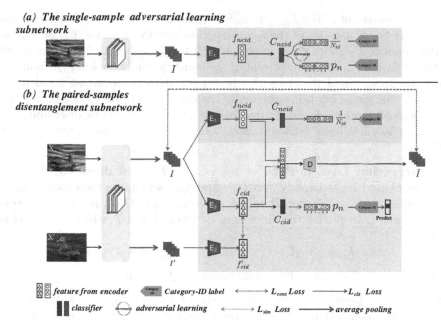

Fig. 3. Overview of the two subnetworks of the proposed DNet. (a) and (b) show, respectively, the single-sample adversarial learning subnetwork and the paired-samples disentanglement subnetwork.

codes of the encoder E_1 with I as input, $softmax(\cdot)$ indicates the softmax function. In the second step, we update the encoder E_1 with the classifier C_{ncid} being fixed. The way to ensure that the feature f_{ncid} has lost all information about identity is that it produces the same prediction for all classes after being sent into the classifier C_{ncid} [28]. One way to impose this constraint is to assign the probability of each id label to be $\frac{1}{N_{id}}$ in the softmax cross-entropy loss. The problem of this loss is that it would still backward gradient for updating parameters even if it reaches the minimum, so the Euclidean distance is used instead in [28], which is also utilized here. Thus, with fixed C_{ncid}, E_1 is trained with the following loss:

$$L_{adv2} = \sum_{j=1}^{N_{id}} \|softmax(C_{ncid}(f_{ncid}))[j] - \frac{1}{N_{id}}\|_2^2. \qquad (2)$$

3.2 The Paired-Samples Disentanglement Subnetwork (PSDNet)

If the SSALNet is well trained, the encoder E_1 tends to output identity-unrelated features. Then, given two samples X and X' of the same class label, the PSDNet is trained to learn the final disentangled representation and the classifier C_{cid} for fine-grained visual categorization under four losses, i.e., the L_{adv2} loss, the reconstruction loss, the classification loss and the identity similarity loss. Hopefully,

under the constraint of the L_{adv2} loss, E_1 should repel identity-related information, under the constraint of the reconstruction loss the features f_{cid} outputted
by the encoder E_2 should be complementary to f_{ncid}, hence f_{cid} are basically
identity-related; under the constraint of the identity similarity loss, f_{cid} and f'_{cid}
should be similar and therefore E_2 are supposed to be invariant to identity-
unrelated changes of input images; under the constraint of the classification loss,
the E_2 should produce discriminative feature and C_{cid} should be discriminative.
The L_{adv2} loss has been defined in Sect. 3.1, the rest three losses are described
as follows.

Reconstruction Loss. In PSDNet, the feature I is first disentangled by the
encoders E_1 and E_2 separately into f_{ncid} and f_{cid}, which are then concatenated
and decoded by the decoder D to get a reconstructed feature $\tilde{I}$. The reconstruction loss is to punish the differences between $\tilde{I}$ and I, which is defined as
follow,

$$L_{rcons} = \|\tilde{I} - I\|_2^2 = \|D(\{f_{ncid}, f_{cid}\}) - I\|_2^2, \tag{3}$$

where $\{f_{ncid}, f_{cid}\}$ denotes the concatenation of f_{ncid} and f_{cid}.

Classification Loss. Only the identity-related feature f_{cid} is used for classification. The classification loss is just the cross-entropy loss as usually defined,
i.e.,

$$L_{cls} = -\sum_{j=1}^{N_{id}} p[j] \log(softmax(C_{cid}(f_{cid}))[j]). \tag{4}$$

Identity Similarity Loss. Since the input images X and X' are of the same
class label, ideally the two identity-related features f_{cid} and f'_{cid} corresponding
to X and X', respectively, should be identical for the purpose of classification.
Note that the backbone is shared by X and X'. So the identity similarity loss is
used to punish the differences between f_{cid} and f'_{cid}, which is defined by

$$L_{Idsim} = \|f_{cid} - f'_{cid}\|_2^2. \tag{5}$$

The overall loss L_{PSDNet} for training the PSDNet is:

$$L_{PSDNet} = \alpha L_{adv2} + \beta L_{rcons} + \gamma L_{cls} + \theta L_{Idsim} \tag{6}$$

where α, β, γ and θ are coefficients to balance these losses.

4   Experiments

We evaluate the performance of our proposed DNet on three standard fine-
grained object recognition datasets: CUB-200-2011 (CUB) [19], Stanford Cars
(CAR) [8] and FGVC-Aircraft (AIR) [12]. We do not use any bounding box/part
annotations in all our experiments. The category label of the image is the only
annotation used for training.

4.1   Implementation Details

The input images are resized to a fixed size of 512-512 and randomly cropped into 448-448. Random rotation and random horizontal flip are applied for data augmentation. The average pooling layer connected to the backbone ResNet maps an output of the backbone to a feature of size $2048 \times 1 \times 1$. The encoders E_1, E_2 both consist of 1024 convolution kernels of size 1×1. The classifiers C_{ncid} and C_{cid} are both a fully connected layer that maps a 1024 dimensional vector to a N_{id} dimensional one. The decoder D consists of 2048 convolution kernels of size 1×1. f_{ncid} and f_{cid} are feature vectors of dimensions 1024. In addition, in view of that the bird images in the CUB-200-2011 dataset have very large variations in birds' posture, age, shooting angle and etc., we manually annotate these images into two classes, i.e., the normal and the extremal classes. The former are images of normal birds' posture, age, shooting angle and etc. while the latter corresponds to extremal cases. In the training phase, X' is selected from those normal images only in this dataset.

Table 1. Comparison of the proposed DNet with state-of-the-art methods on CUB-200-2011 (CUB) [19], Stanford Cars (CAR) [8] and FGVC-Aircraft (AIR) [12]. The best results are in bold. Note that our DNet outperforms all of the competing methods.

Method	Accuracy (%)		
	CUB-200-2011	Stanford Cars	FGVC-Aircraft
M-CNN (+BBox) (PR, 2018) [21]	84.2%	-	-
HS-net (+BBox) (CVPR, 2017) [9]	87.5%	-	-
IB-CNN (CVPR, 2017) [7]	84.2%	90.9%	87.3%
MA-CNN (ICCV, 2017) [26]	86.5%	92.8%	89.9%
NTS-net (ECCV, 2018) [23]	87.5%	93.9%	91.4%
DCL (CVPR, 2019) [2]	87.8%	94.5%	**93.0%**
TASN (CVPR, 2019) [27]	87.9%	93.8%	-
Bi-modal PMA (IEEE TIP, 2020) [16]	87.5%	93.1%	90.8%
Cross-X (CVPR, 2020) [11]	87.7%	94.6%	92.6%
CIN (AAAI, 2020) [5]	88.1%	94.1%	92.6%
ACNet (CVPR, 2020) [6]	88.1%	94.6%	92.4%
Baseline	84.0%	92.4%	89.7%
DNet	**88.3%**	**95.0%**	92.7%

Baseline and DNet are both trained for 200 epochs to obtain stable accuracies, and learning rates decay by a factor of 10 for every 40 epochs. We set $\alpha=1$, $\gamma = 1$, $\theta = 10$ for all experiments reported in this paper. It is worth mentioning that we use dynamic adjustment to train the reconstruction loss. From epoch 1 to 60, β is set to 1 and from epoch 60 to 200 it is set to 0.1.

4.2 Performance Comparison

The results on CUB-200-2011, Stanford Cars, and FGVC-Aircraft are presented
in Table 1. Considering that some of the compared methods use image-level
labels or bounding box annotations, the information of extra annotations is
also presented in parentheses for direct comparisons. As can be seen, our DNet
significantly outperforms the Baseline on the three benchmarks, having gains
of 4.3%, 2.6% and 3.0%, respectively, on CUB-200-2011, Stanford Cars, and
FGVC-Aircraft, justifying the effectiveness of the proposed method. Moreover,
DNet surpasses state-of-the-art methods on CUB-200-2011 and Stanford Cars
and is also very competitive on FGVC-Aircraft. Considering the simple structures of the encoders and decoder used in DNet, it suggests that disentangled
representation learning is promising in improving the performance of fine-grained
visual categorization.

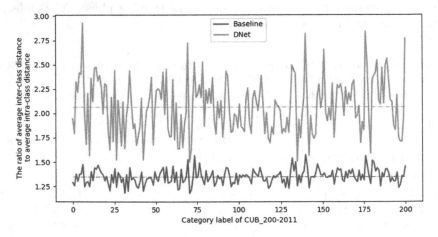

Fig. 4. Ratios of average inter-class distance to average intra-class distance of Our
DNet and the Baseline model on CUB-200-2011 test data, computed in the one-vs-rest
manner.

4.3 Ablation Study

We conduct ablation studies on CUB-200-2011 dataset to validate that the proposed DNet is effective in reducing inter-class variation meanwhile amplifying
intra-class variation. We evaluate inter-class and intra-class distances of feature
vectors of Baseline and DNet on the test data of CUB-200-2011. Since the number of inter-class distances is a big combinatorial number for CUB-200-2011
which has 200 categories, it is not suitable to use class distance matrices for
evaluation. In view of that a multi-class classification can be splitted into multiple binary classification problems using the one-vs-rest method [13], we use this
method to reduce the large amount of inter-class distances into 200 average inter-
class distances, which is equal to the number of average intra-class distances. In

doing this, we obtain 200 ratios of average inter-class distance to average intra-class distance for each model. By plotting these ratios, we can visually compare different models' performance in reducing inter-class variation meanwhile amplifying intra-class variation. Figure 4 shows the 200 ratios of average inter-class distance to average intra-class distance of the Baseline and our DNet, respectively. The average ratio of each model, specifically 2.07 and 1.35, is plotted as a dash line in corresponding color. As can be seen, our DNet is significantly better than the Baseline, justifying the effectiveness of the proposed method in reducing inter-class variation meanwhile amplifying intra-class variation.

5 Conclusion

We proposed the network DNet that uses disentangled representation learning to extract feature representation for FGVC. As far as we know, this is the first time to utilize feature disentanglement to solve the tasks of FGVC. In view of the difficulties in disentangling features of images with complicated backgrounds, we combined two strategies to train the DNet. Experimental results show that the proposed method achieves state-of-the-art performance. Considering the simple structures of the encoders and decoder used in DNet, we believe that disentangled representation learning is promising for FGVC.

Acknowledgments. This research is supported by the Science and Technology Department of Tibet (Grant No. XZ202102YD0018C).

References

1. Branson, S., Beijbom, O., Belongie, S.: Efficient large-scale structured learning. In: Proceedings of the IEEE Conference on Computer Vision and Pattern Recognition, pp. 1806–1813 (2013)
2. Chen, Y., Bai, Y., Zhang, W., Mei, T.: Destruction and construction learning for fine-grained image recognition. In: Proceedings of the IEEE/CVF Conference on Computer Vision and Pattern Recognition, pp. 5157–5166 (2019)
3. Denton, E., Birodkar, V.: Unsupervised learning of disentangled representations from video. arXiv preprint arXiv:1705.10915 (2017)
4. Fu, J., Zheng, H., Mei, T.: Look closer to see better: Recurrent attention convolutional neural network for fine-grained image recognition. In: Proceedings of the IEEE Conference on Computer Vision and Pattern Recognition, pp. 4438–4446 (2017)
5. Gao, Y., Han, X., Wang, X., Huang, W., Scott, M.: Channel interaction networks for fine-grained image categorization. In: Proceedings of the AAAI Conference on Artificial Intelligence, vol. 34, pp. 10818–10825 (2020)
6. Ji, R., et al.: Attention convolutional binary neural tree for fine-grained visual categorization. In: Proceedings of the IEEE/CVF Conference on Computer Vision and Pattern Recognition, pp. 10468–10477 (2020)
7. Kong, S., Fowlkes, C.: Low-rank bilinear pooling for fine-grained classification. In: Proceedings of the IEEE Conference on Computer Vision and Pattern Recognition, pp. 365–374 (2017)

8. Krause, J., Stark, M., Deng, J., Fei-Fei, L.: 3D object representations for fine-grained categorization. In: Proceedings of the IEEE International Conference on Computer Vision Workshops, pp. 554–561 (2013)
9. Lam, M., Mahasseni, B., Todorovic, S.: Fine-grained recognition as HSnet search for informative image parts. In: Proceedings of the IEEE Conference on Computer Vision and Pattern Recognition, pp. 2520–2529 (2017)
10. Lin, T.Y., RoyChowdhury, A., Maji, S.: Bilinear CNN models for fine-grained visual recognition. In: Proceedings of the IEEE International Conference on Computer Vision, pp. 1449–1457 (2015)
11. Luo, W., et al.: Cross-x learning for fine-grained visual categorization. In: Proceedings of the IEEE/CVF International Conference on Computer Vision, pp. 8242–8251 (2019)
12. Maji, S., Rahtu, E., Kannala, J., Blaschko, M., Vedaldi, A.: Fine-grained visual classification of aircraft. arXiv preprint arXiv:1306.5151 (2013)
13. Murphy, K.P.: Machine Learning: A Probabilistic Perspective (2012)
14. Peng, X., Yu, X., Sohn, K., Metaxas, D.N., Chandraker, M.: Reconstruction-based disentanglement for pose-invariant face recognition. In: Proceedings of the IEEE International Conference on Computer Vision, pp. 1623–1632 (2017)
15. Peng, Y., He, X., Zhao, J.: Object-part attention model for fine-grained image classification. IEEE Trans. Image Process. **27**(3), 1487–1500 (2017)
16. Song, K., Wei, X.S., Shu, X., Song, R.J., Lu, J.: Bi-modal progressive mask attention for fine-grained recognition. IEEE Trans. Image Process. **29**, 7006–7018 (2020)
17. Sun, M., Yuan, Y., Zhou, F., Ding, E.: Multi-attention multi-class constraint for fine-grained image recognition. In: Ferrari, V., Hebert, M., Sminchisescu, C., Weiss, Y. (eds.) ECCV 2018. LNCS, vol. 11220, pp. 834–850. Springer, Cham (2018). https://doi.org/10.1007/978-3-030-01270-0_49
18. Uijlings, J.R., Van De Sande, K.E., Gevers, T., Smeulders, A.W.: Selective search for object recognition. Int. J. Comput. Vision **104**(2), 154–171 (2013)
19. Wah, C., Branson, S., Welinder, P., Perona, P., Belongie, S.: The Caltech-UCSD Birds-200-2011 dataset (2011)
20. Wei, X.S., Cui, Q., Yang, L., Wang, P., Liu, L.: RPC: a large-scale retail product checkout dataset. arXiv preprint arXiv:1901.07249 (2019)
21. Wei, X.S., Xie, C.W., Wu, J., Shen, C.: Mask-CNN: localizing parts and selecting descriptors for fine-grained bird species categorization. Pattern Recogn. **76**, 704–714 (2018)
22. Xiao, T., Xu, Y., Yang, K., Zhang, J., Peng, Y., Zhang, Z.: The application of two-level attention models in deep convolutional neural network for fine-grained image classification. In: Proceedings of the IEEE Conference on Computer Vision and Pattern Recognition, pp. 842–850 (2015)
23. Yang, Z., Luo, T., Wang, D., Hu, Z., Gao, J., Wang, L.: Learning to navigate for fine-grained classification. In: Ferrari, V., Hebert, M., Sminchisescu, C., Weiss, Y. (eds.) Computer Vision – ECCV 2018. LNCS, vol. 11218, pp. 438–454. Springer, Cham (2018). https://doi.org/10.1007/978-3-030-01264-9_26
24. Zhang, N., Donahue, J., Girshick, R., Darrell, T.: Part-based R-CNNs for fine-grained category detection. In: Fleet, D., Pajdla, T., Schiele, B., Tuytelaars, T. (eds.) ECCV 2014. LNCS, vol. 8689, pp. 834–849. Springer, Cham (2014). https://doi.org/10.1007/978-3-319-10590-1_54
25. Zhang, Z., et al.: Gait recognition via disentangled representation learning. In: Proceedings of the IEEE/CVF Conference on Computer Vision and Pattern Recognition, pp. 4710–4719 (2019)

26. Zheng, H., Fu, J., Mei, T., Luo, J.: Learning multi-attention convolutional neural network for fine-grained image recognition. In: Proceedings of the IEEE International Conference on Computer Vision, pp. 5209–5217 (2017)
27. Zheng, H., Fu, J., Zha, Z.J., Luo, J.: Looking for the devil in the details: Learning trilinear attention sampling network for fine-grained image recognition. In: Proceedings of the IEEE/CVF Conference on Computer Vision and Pattern Recognition, pp. 5012–5021 (2019)
28. Zhou, H., Liu, Y., Liu, Z., Luo, P., Wang, X.: Talking face generation by adversarially disentangled audio-visual representation. In: Proceedings of the AAAI Conference on Artificial Intelligence, vol. 33, pp. 9299–9306 (2019)

Timeception Single Shot Action Detector: A Single-Stage Method for Temporal Action Detection

Xiaoqiu Chen, Miao Ma$^{(\boxtimes)}$, Zhuoyu Tian, and Jie Ren

School of Computer Science, Shaanxi Normal University, Xi'an 710119, China
mmthp@snnu.edu.cn

Abstract. Temporal action detection is used to detect the start and end times and classify the potentially specific actions in a video. Prior studies in temporal action detection perform weak because they can not fully understand the whole input video's temporal structure and context information, and fail to adapt to the diversity of action time span. We propose a novel Timeception Single Shot Action Detector (TC-SSAD) to solve the problems mentioned above. In detail, we leverage the multiple Timeception layers to generate multi-scale feature sequences, where each Timeception layer uses depthwise-separable temporal convolution with multi-scale convolution kernels to capture the diversity of time spans. Besides, we use the super-event modules to learn the entire input video's temporal structure and contextual information. The experimental results on THUMOS14 dataset show that when IoU threshold is 0.5, our method achieves 38.2% and 44.3% mAP on Two-stream features and Two-stream i3D features respectively, which is better than Decouple-SSAD network based method by 2.4% and 0.6%. Our method on Activitynet-1.3 dataset achieves 20.4% mAP, which is better than Decouple-SSAD network based method by 0.61% as far as Two-stream features on concerned.

Keywords: Temporal action detection · Multi-scale convolution kernel · Super-event module · Temporal structure and context

1 Introduction

With the development of the Internet and the proliferation of personal smart mobile devices, people are generating, storing and using large amounts of video [1, 2]. Most videos are long untrimmed videos, which often contain multiple action instances and have more interference from background and irrelevant actions. Action detection is detecting action instances in long videos, including the start and end times corresponding to action instances and action categories. Action detection is more practical, and its progress can promote a large number of related tasks from real-time applications, such as extracting highlights from sports videos, to automatic video subtitles and other higher-level tasks [3].

Like the object detection task, the common temporal action detection methods can be divided into two-stage and single-stage. The Two-stage method uses sliding windows or

© Springer Nature Switzerland AG 2021
Y. Peng et al. (Eds.): ICIG 2021, LNCS 12888, pp. 340–354, 2021.
https://doi.org/10.1007/978-3-030-87355-4_29

some specific methods (sliding window or action probability curve) to generate proposals and then classifies these action proposals. First of all, the common sliding window method can only produce short proposals no larger than the predefined window size [4]. Second, because the two-stage detection method train action proposal generation and classification separately, the time boundary of action proposals before classification has been fixed. The indirect optimization strategy can not get the optimal solution[5]. At the same time, the single-stage method ignores the action proposal generation and directly predict the time boundary and categories confidence of actions. This type of method encapsulates two subtasks of localization and classification into a single network but ignores the characteristics of each subtask. Since the single-stage methods share the same feature map when predicting the action category and coordinate offset values, this coupling characteristic may affect the accuracy of each task. Therefore, Decouple-SSAD [5] network introduces parallel classification and localization units through deconvolution operation to decouple two subtasks.

The diversity of time spans of action segments in videos is one of the main reasons for the poor performance of current action detection methods. The traditional single-stage action detection methods shorten the length of the feature sequence and increase the receptive field of each temporal position in feature sequences by stacking multiple 1D temporal convolutional layers, thereby predicting the coordinate offsets and categories confidence of the action proposals. These 1D temporal convolutional layers usually use convolution kernels with a fixed scale. Therefore, the receptive fields corresponding to each temporal position in the generated feature map sequence are fixed. Therefore, these methods cannot adapt well to the diversity of the time spans of action segments.

Compared with the spatial contextual information of pictures in object detection, the temporal structure and contextual information of the video may be more important for obtaining accurate time boundaries and classification results [3]. The single-stage methods cannot effectively use the temporal contextual information of action proposals due to the characteristics of generation and classification action proposals at the same time. To solve these problems, we propose TC-SSAD, a Decouple-SSAD based network. The main contributions of this paper are:

(1) In this paper, we use Timeception layer with multi-scale convolution kernel to construct the backbone network, which is used to obtain multi-scale feature sequences. Instead of using 1D temporal convolution layer with a fixed kernel size, the multi-scale convolution kernel can better capture the diversity of action segments during a period.
(2) We also introduce a super-event module to model the whole input video's temporal structure and context information. This module obtains the super-event representation, which can effectively enhance the performance of action detection.

2   Related Work

2.1   Temporal Action Proposal Generation

Temporal action detection can be decomposed into two sub-tasks: action proposal generation and classification. High-quality action proposals are essential to enhance the effectiveness of action detection task.

The methods for generating temporal action proposals can be divided into two major categories: the first type of methods formulates it as a binary classification problem on sliding windows. Among them, SCNN-prop [6] trains a C3D network [7] for action proposal generation. TURN [8] builds video units in a pyramid manner and improves the recall rate of action proposal generation through temporal boundary regression. The second type of methods uses the Temporal Action Grouping (TAG) [9, 10] algorithm to aggregate consecutive high scoring intervals as action proposals based on Snippet-level action scores. For example, Boundary Sensitive Network (BSN) [11] generates action proposals based on three sets of actions curves, but this kind method based on action scores may be omitted dense and short actions due to the difficulty in distinguishing very close start and end peaks in the action score curves.

2.2 Temporal Action Detection

S-CNN [6] solved this problem by constructing a proposal generation network, a classification network, and a localization network based on 3D convolution. CDC [12] uses convolution-deconvolution operations on the basis of C3D network to predict the actions of frame-level granularity. Inspired by the Faster R-CNN [13] algorithm, R-C3D [14] extended the Faster R-CNN framework to the field of action detection, showed its versatility on different datasets. On the basis of R-C3D, TAL-Net [3] has researched and improved how to deal with the diversity of action time spans and how to use temporal contextual information, obtained state-of-the-art performance on THUMOS14 dataset [15].

The single-stage SSAD [16] network skips the process of generating action proposals and uses traditional 1D temporal convolutional layers to directly perform boundary regression and classification on multiple generated action proposals. Similarly, SS-TAD [17] uses reinforcement learning to train the RNN structure, which is end-to-end and directly performs action detection.

3   Methodology

3.1   Overview of TC-SSAD

Figure 1 presents TC-SSAD, a single stage action detection network based on Decouple-SSAD [5].

First, Two-stream i3D network [18] is used to encode the frame sequence corresponding to a long video into 1D feature sequence. The generated feature sequence goes through two traditional 1D temporal convolutional layers and a maximum pooling layer to reduce the time dimension. After that, the feature sequence is sent to a multi-unit network to generate multi-scale feature sequences. Multi-unit network consists of three parts: backbone unit, classification and localization unit. The backbone unit is composed of multiple Timeception layers [19] and super-event modules [20] in a cascade manner. Furthermore, parallel classification and localization units are constructed from the deep feature sequences of the backbone unit through deconvolution operations and the fusion of the prevIoUs layer feature sequences. The two parallel units focus on the

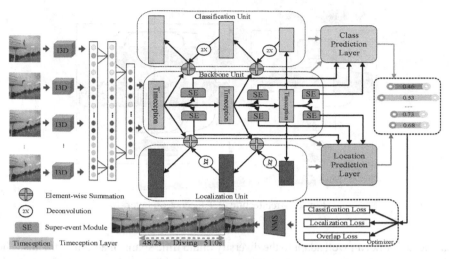

Fig. 1. Overview of TC-SSAD

task of action category confidence generation and coordinate regression, respectively. In addition, in order to learn the temporal structure and contextual information of the entire input video, multi-scale features generated by each Timeception layer of the backbone unit passes the super-event module to obtain the super-event representation, the learned super-event representation is fused with the multi-scale feature sequences generated by two parallel units to obtain the final feature expressions. A series of multi-scale feature sequences generated by three units pass the classification prediction layer and the localization prediction layer to predict categories confidence and coordinate offsets values corresponding to the action proposals. Classification loss, regression loss, and overlap loss are used to optimize different units during the training phase. Post-processing and non-maximum suppress (NMS) are performed on the generated action instances during testing phase to obtain the final results.

3.2 Backbone Unit

The backbone unit of TC-SSAD consists of Timeception layers and the corresponding super-event modules in a cascade manner.

Timeception Layer. For input feature F, hypothesis the feature dimension of F is $d_m = \mathbb{R}^{\{T \times L \times L \times C\}}$, where T is the temporal dimension, L is spatial dimension, C is the number of channels. Figure 2 presents the multi-scale feature sequences of the backbone unit are obtained by the Timeception layers through the following steps:

Firstly, the input features are divided into some groups according to channels to reduce the dependency and complexity between channels. The feature dimension of each group is $g_m = \mathbb{R}^{\{T \times L \times L \times C/N\}}$. Then, each group uses a temporal convolution module to convolve the obtained feature sequences. Specially, each group is further divided into 5 units, and the middle 3 units use depthwise-separable temporal convolution with multi-scale convolution kernels to reduce the amount of network parameters while ensuring

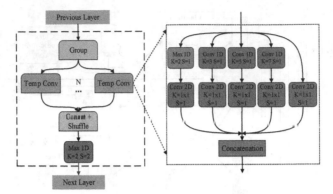

Fig. 2. Architecture of Timeception layer

that the network can well adapt to the diversity of the time spans of action segments. The leftmost unit only uses maximum pooling with kernel size $K = 2$ and stride $S = 1$. A 2D convolution with kernel size after each unit is used to enhance the non-linear expression ability of this Timeception layer. Last, the output of the 5 units through concatenation operation to obtain the final output feature sequences of this group. Finally, for the output features of each group, first perform shuffle operations on these features to exchange information between different channels to ensure the randomness of the channels when the next Timeception layer performs grouping operations. We concat the output features of each group and then go through the maximum pooling layer with kernel size $K = 2$ and stride $S = 2$ to get the final output features of this layer. Specifically, after each Timeception layer, the time dimension of feature sequence is reduced to 1/2, and the number of channels is increased to 1.25 times. For the features input the backbone unit, after three Timeception layers, feature sequences of 3 different scales are finally generated for subsequent processing.

Super-Event Module. As shown in Fig. 3 super-event representation is obtained by the temporal structure filters in the super-event module by learning the soft attention weights of each type of action. Temporal structure filters capture temporal context in videos by paying attention to the frame information of some temporal positions and representing the variable length input video features as fixed length feature vectors.

For the feature sequence with time dimension T, each temporal structure filter can be determined by the following formula:

$$\hat{x}_n = \frac{(T - 1) \cdot (\tanh(x_n) + 1)}{2}$$

$$\hat{\gamma}_n = \exp(1 - 2 \cdot |\tanh(\gamma_n)|)$$

$$F[t, n] = \frac{1}{Z_n \pi \hat{\gamma}_n} \left(\frac{\left(t - \hat{x}_n \right)}{\hat{\gamma}_n} \right)^2 \tag{1}$$

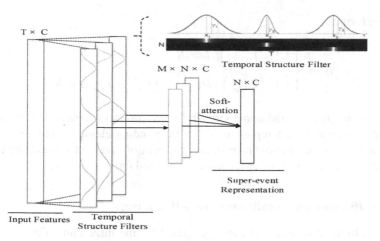

Fig. 3. Architecture of super-events module

where $t \in \{1, ..., T\}$, $n \in \{1, ..., N\}$, two parameters x_n and γ_n are used to control the center and width of the Cauchy distribution, Z_n is a normalization constant, In particular, for each super-event module, only two parameters x_n and γ_n need to be learned.

Because the number of action categories is much larger than the number of temporal structure filters. In order to use a fixed number of temporal structure filters to represent multiple types of actions, it is necessary to combine the temporal structure filter and soft attention mechanism to obtain the final super-event representation, as shown in the following formula:

$$S_C = \sum_m^M A_{c,m} \cdot \sum_t^T F_m[t] \cdot v_t$$

$$A_{c,m} = \frac{\exp(W_{c,m})}{\sum_k^M \exp(W_{c,k})}$$

$$(2)$$

where S_c is the finally obtained super-event representation, M is the number of temporal structure filters, V_t represents the video features, that is, the output of the Timeception layer, $A_{c,m}$ represents the soft attention weight corresponding to each temporal structure filter. The subscript C represents the number of video action categories.

3.3 Classification and Localization Units

Like the backbone unit, each parallel unit contains three kinds of multi-scale feature sequences. Each type feature sequences are obtained by averaging the corresponding deeper feature sequences in the backbone unit through deconvolution operation with shallow feature sequences. The specific decoupling process can be expressed by the following formula:

$$f_k^L = \begin{cases} C\left(f_n^f\right), & \text{if } L = N_f \\ C\left(S\left(C\left(f_n^f\right), D\left(f_k^{L+1}\right)\right)\right), & \text{if } 1 \leq L < N_f \end{cases} \tag{3}$$

where C represents the traditional temporal convolution operation, D represents the deconvolution operation, S represents the corresponding element addition and fusion operation, N_f is the number of layers of the Timeception layer in the backbone unit, and L is used to indicate which layer is currently operated on.

3.4 Classification and Localization Prediction Layers

For the multi-scale feature sequences generated by the three units. First, a series of anchors with different basic scale B_S and aspect ratio R_S are predefined for each temporal position of the feature sequence.

For a series of predefined anchors obtained above, we send the corresponding feature sequence to the classification and localization prediction layer to generate the prediction result vector $V_{pred} = (S_{cls}, S_{over}, \Delta_c, \Delta_W)$, where S_{cls} and S_{over} are categories confidence and overlapping confidence, Δ_c and Δ_W are predicted centre and width coordinate offset values. It is worth noting that for the classification unit, we generate the result vectors through a multi-class prediction layer because it focuses on classification tasks. The localization unit focuses on localization tasks, and we generate the result vectors through a binary classification prediction layer. For each predefined anchor, the final prediction results can be obtained by the following formula:

$$\begin{aligned} \varphi_C &= \mu_C + \alpha_1 \mu_W \cdot \Delta_C \\ \varphi_W &= \mu_W \cdot \exp(\alpha_2 \cdot \Delta_W) \end{aligned} \tag{4}$$

where μ_c and μ_w are the predefined center point and width, respectively. The parameters α_1 and α_2 are used to control the degree of influence of the predicted value on the result. φ_c and φ_w are final predicted results.

3.5 Loss Function

Training TC-SSAD networks is a multi-task optimization problem. The final loss function is:

$$L = L_{cls} + \lambda L_{reg} + \beta L_{over} \tag{5}$$

where L_{cls}, L_{reg}, L_{over} are classification loss function, localization loss function and overlap loss function. For the multi-classification tasks in this paper, we use the common softmax loss function. We use the Smooth L1 loss function to measure the degree of error between the predicted coordinate values and the true values. Finally, we use the mean square error loss function to measure the overlap between the predicted action proposals and the real annotations.

4 Experiments

4.1 Datasets and Evaluation Metrics

THUMOS14 Dataset [15]. The dataset contains videos from 20 sports action classes, with a total duration of more than 24 h. We use the validation set to train the model and evaluate it on the test set. The validation and test sets contain 200 and 213 untrimmed videos with temporal annotations. The average duration of each video is more than 3 min and contains more than 15 action instances, which makes the dataset particularly challenging.

ActicityNet-1.3 Dataset [21]. The dataset contains 19994 videos, each video contains about 1.5 action instances, about 36% of which are background clips, and there are 200 kinds of actions in total. The whole data set is divided into training set, verification set and test set according to the ratio of 2:1:1, and the test set is not open for competition, so most researches test the model performance on the validation set.

Evaluation Metrics. In this paper, the public evaluation code is used to evaluate the experimental results. We use mean Average Precision (mAP) as the main evaluation metrics. For the predicted action proposals, we only mark the result as correct if the prediction category is correct and the intersection ratio with ground truth is greater than the specified IoU threshold.

4.2 Implementation Details

For THUMOS14 [15] and ActivityNet-1.3 [21] datasets we set batch size is 24; the learning rate for the first 38 epochs to 0.0001 and the learning rate for the last 3 epochs to 0.00001. Adaptive moment estimation (Adam) algorithm is used to optimize the network, and Xavier algorithm randomly initializes network parameters before training. In the test phase, we use non-maximum suppression (NMS) to remove redundant prediction results (NMS threshold is 0.2). For the Timeception layers, we set groups equal to 4. The weight of classification loss is 1, and the weight of location loss and overlap loss is 10. For THUNOS14 dataset, we set $Bs = \{1/16, 1/8, 1/4\}$, $Rs = \{0.5, 0.75, 1, 1.5, 2\}$; For ActivityNet-1.3 dataset, we set $Bs = \{1/16, 1/12, 1/8, 1/6, 1/4\}$, $Rs = \{0.15, 0.25, 0.5, 0.75, 1, 1.5, 2, 3\}$. For two datasets, the convolution kernel size $K = \{3, 5, 7\}$ and the number of temporal structure filters $N = 3$ are used in the following experiments. Due to the large scale of ActicityNet-1.3 dataset, we did not specifically extract its features but directly used the Two-stream features provided by BSN [11].

4.3 Experimental Results

Results of THUMOS14 Dataset. When using a single GTX TITANX GPU, the training time of the verification set composed of 200 videos on the THUMOS14 dataset is about 102 min, and the test time is about 4 min. The experimental results of THUMOS14 dataset [15] are shown in Table 1.

Table 1. Experimental results of THUMOS14 dataset.

Method	Feature	Model	mAP(%)@IoU = 0.5		
			Spatial	Temporal	Fuse
Decouple-SSAD [5]	Bn-Inception	Decouple-SSAD(512)	22.1	33.1	35.8
	Inception_V3	Decouple-SSAD(512)	**30.7**	**44.2**	**43.7**
TC-SSAD	Bn-Inception	DS + TC(512)	23.9	35.1	36.6
	Bn-Inception	DS + TC + SE(512)	23.3	36.9	38.2
	i3D	DS + TC(512)	32.5	35.6	38.2
	i3D	DS + TC + SE(512)	33.1	**41.1**	42.3
	i3D	DS + TC + SE(1024)	**36.4**	41.0	**44.3**

In the feature column, "Bn-Inception" and "Inception_V3" are the original Two-stream feature extraction backbone networks, while Two-Stream i3D network [25] is the feature extraction network used in this paper. In the model column, "Decouple-SSAD" indicates the method adopted in [5], "DS" indicates the use of parallel decoupling units, "TC" indicates the use of Timeception layers, "SE" indicates whether to use the super-event modules, and the bracket is the window size when extract feature. As can be seen from the table, the highest mAP value obtained by our method is 44.3%.

Effectiveness of Timeception Layer and Super-Event Module. In order to verify the validity of the Timeception layers and the super-event modules in our model. First, we use the same features for experiments. The results of the first four rows of Table 1 show that when using only the Timeception layers, there is some improvement over Decouple-SSAD. Spatial and Temporal features increased by 1.8% and 2.0%, respectively, and the result after fusion increased by 0.8%. Besides, when the super-event module is added, the performance is improved significantly, and the fused mAP is increased from 35.8% to 38.2%.

Impact of Different Features on Results. Because a traditional Two-stream network uses 2D convolution, it cannot capture the temporal dependency between frames. As with Decouple-SSAD, we first extract the Two-stream i3D features with 512-frame window size. Based on these features, only the Timeception layers can be used to achieve the same effect after the original super-event representation was added. The results illustrate the effectiveness of i3D network for spatiotemporal modelling.

In addition, we further expanded the window to 1024 frames (about 34 s in duration), and we found that the network's performance was further improved, from 42.3% to 44.3%. We suspect that this is mainly because the long video contains the richer temporal structure and contextual information, and the super-event modules can effectively learn the temporal structure and contextual information in these input videos to further enhance network performance.

Per-class AP. We compared the AP values of each action category after fusion between our method and Decouple-SSAD at IoU = 0.5. The results are shown in Fig. 4 Our method shows good detection performance on two different video features. Through the analysis of "basketball dunk", "billiards" and other categories of video, we find that the duration of these categories of action is very different, and our method performs well in these categories of video.

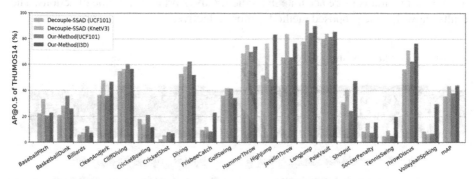

Fig. 4. Comparison of per-class Average Precision and mAP with overlap threshold 0.5 in THUMOS14 test set.

Results of ActivityNet-1.3 Dataset. We also make a comparative experiment on Activitynet-1.3 dataset [21]. During the experiment, we all used the Two-stream features provided by BSN [11]. The results of mAP and average mAP (0.5:0.05:0.95) when IoU = {0.5,0.75,0.95} after fusion are shown in Table 2.

Table 2. Experimental results of activityNet-1.3 dataset.

Method	Feature	Model	mAP(%)@IoU			
			0.5	0.75	0.95	AVG
Decouple-SSAD [5]	Two-stream	Decouple-SSAD	33.15	19.99	1.78	19.81
TC-SSAD	Two-stream	DS + TC	**34.11**	20.17	**2.47**	20.41
	Two-stream	DS + TC + SE	33.61	**20.71**	2.32	**20.42**

Table 2 shows that the average mAP is still 0.61% higher than that of Decouple-SSAD in ActivityNet-1.3 dataset. In particular, we find that the results are not effectively improved after using super-event modules, and the results under some thresholds are still reduced. This is because ActivityNet-1.3 dataset contains 200 types of actions, and each video contains only about 1.5 action instances. Most of the action instances occupy more than half of the whole video. In this case, there is no rich temporal structure and context information to learn.

4.4 Visualization of Temporal Action Detection Results

In Fig. 5 The temporal action detection results of THUMOS14 dataset are visualized. Each row contains the predicted start and ends time and category of the action, and the sampled frame image is used at the top to display the content of the video. As shown in Fig. 5, Our method is more accurate in predicting the start and end time of actions. The results show that the proposed method is more effective.

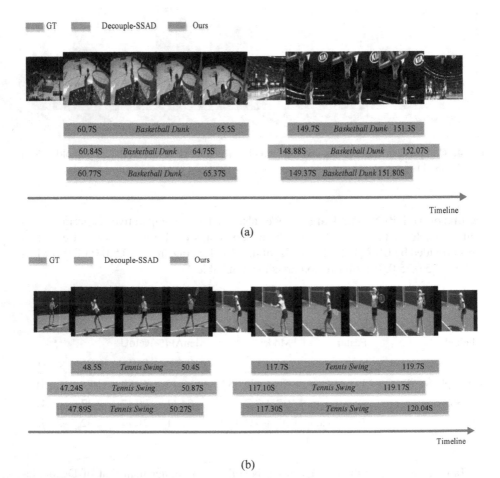

(a)

(b)

Fig. 5. Qualitative visualization of TC-SSAD model predictive action instances. (a) Detection results after fusion under UCF101 pre-trained Two-stream features; (b) Detection results after fusion under Kinetics pre-trained Two-stream features, where we use Two-Stream i3D network [18].

4.5 Comparison with State-of-the-Art Methods

The performance comparison between TC-SSAD and current mainstream methods on ActivityNet-1.3 dataset [21] is shown in Table 3. It is not difficult to find that TC-SSAD does not perform well on ActivityNet-1.3 dataset.

Table 3. Comparison of mAP under different IoU thresholds with state-of-the-art methods in ActivityNet-1.3 dataset.

Methods	mAP(%)@IoU			
	0.5	0.75	0.95	Average
Singh *et al.* [22]	26.01	15.22	2.61	14.62
CDC [12]	45.30	26.00	0.20	23.80
TAG-D [9]	39.12	23.48	5.49	23.98
BSN [11]	52.50	33.53	8.85	33.72
GTAN [23]	**52.61**	**34.14**	**8.91**	**34.31**
TC-SSAD	33.61	20.71	2.32	20.42

The first reason is that the action time span of ActivityNet-1.3 dataset changes too much. Some action instances almost occupy the whole video time, while some action instances only take less than 1 s. Using the anchor of preset scale can not capture the actions with too many time spans; Second, due to large scale of ActicityNet-1.3 dataset, we directly use the two-stream feature provided by [11] instead of the sliding window method in Decouple-SSAD for feature extraction. The length of all video feature sequences provided is 100. After multi-layer backbone unit, the length of feature sequence is gradually shortened. Therefore, the receptive field of each time sequence position of the feature sequence output by the deep network layer corresponding to the original video will be too large, resulting in a significant decrease in the sensitivity to some short-term actions, especially for the case of original video with a long time.

For THUMOS14 dataset, Table 4 lists the mAP values of two-stage and single-stage methods under different IoU thresholds. In terms of mAP value, our method is superior to most mainstream temporal action detection methods on THUMOS14 dataset.

Table 4. Comparison of mAP under different IoU thresholds with state-of-the-art methods in THUMOS14 dataset.

Two-stage action detection					
Methods	mAP(%)@IoU				
	0.1	0.2	0.3	0.4	0.5
SCNN [6]	47.7	43.5	36.3	28.7	19.0
SST [24]	–	–	37.8	–	23.0

(continued)

Table 4. (*continued*)

Two-stage action detection					
Methods	mAP(%)@IoU				
	0.1	0.2	0.3	0.4	0.5
CDC [12]	–	–	40.1	29.4	23.3
TURN [8]	54.0	50.9	44.1	34.9	25.6
R-C3D [14]	54.5	51.5	44.8	35.6	28.9
SSN [10]	66.0	59.4	51.9	41.0	29.8
BSN [11]	–	–	53.5	45.0	36.9
TAL-Net [3]	59.8	57.1	53.2	48.5	42.8
P-GCN [25]	**69.5**	**67.8**	**63.6**	**57.8**	**49.1**
Single-stage action detection					
SMS [26]	51.0	45.2	36.5	27.8	17.8
SSAD [16]	50.1	47.8	43.0	35.0	24.6
SS-TAD [17]	–	–	45.7	–	29.2
GTAN [23]	69.1	63.7	57.8	47.2	38.8
Decouple-SSAD [5]	66.4	65.1	60.9	53.4	43.7
TC-SSAD	**69.1**	**67.0**	**63.0**	**55.0**	**44.3**

5 Conclusion

In this paper, we propose a single-stage temporal action detection network TC-SSAD. By cascading the Timeception layer and super-event module, and the network can better adapt to the diversity of action time span in the video and effectively use the temporal structure and context information of the whole input video. The experimental results show that the mAP of TC-SSAD in THUMOS14 datasets is 44.3%, which is 2.4% higher than Decouple-SSAD network. In ActivityNet-1.3 dataset, the average mAP is 20.4%, better than the Decouple-SSAD network 0.61%.

However, the current research is still far from practical applications. In future work, we should consider how to improve the detection accuracy of these difficult action categories, how to build a lightweight end-to-end network and combine it with other video tasks such as video description.

Acknowledgements. This work was supported by National Natural Science Foundation of China (61877038, 61501287, 61902229) and Fundamental Research Funds for the Central Universities (No. TD2020044Y, No. GK201703058, No. GK202103084).

References

1. Ren, J., Yuan, L., Nurmi, P., et al.: Camel: Smart, adaptive energy optimization for mobile web interactions. In: Proceedings of the IEEE INFOCOM Conference on Computer Communications, pp. 119–128 (2020)

2. Qin, Q., Ren, J., Yu, J., et al.: To compress, or not to compress: characterizing deep learning model compression for embedded inference. In: 2018 IEEE International Conference on Parallel & Distributed Processing with Applications, Ubiquitous Computing & Communications, Big Data & Cloud Computing, Social Computing & Networking, Sustainable Computing & Communications (ISPA/IUCC/BDCloud/SocialCom/SustainCom), pp. 729–736 (2018)

3. Y.-W., Chao, S., Vijayanarasimhan, B., et al.: Rethinking the faster R-CNN architecture for temporal action localization. In: Proceedings of the IEEE Conference on Computer Vision and Pattern Recognition, pp. 1130–1139 (2018)

4. Wang, J., Jiang, W., Ma, L., et al.: Bidirectional attentive fusion with context gating for dense video captioning. In: Proceedings of the IEEE Conference on Computer Vision and Pattern Recognition, pp. 7190–7198 (2018)

5. Huang, Y., Dai, Q., Lu, Y.: Decoupling localization and classification in single shot temporal action detection. In: 2019 IEEE International Conference on Multimedia and Expo (ICME), pp. 1288–1293 (2019)

6. Shou, Z., Wang, D., Chang, S.F.: Temporal action localization in untrimmed videos via multi-stage cnns. In: Proceedings of the IEEE Conference on Computer Vision and Pattern Recognition, pp. 1049–1058 (2016)

7. Tran, D., Bourdev, L., Fergus, R., et al.: Learning spatiotemporal features with 3D convolutional networks. In: Proceedings of the IEEE international conference on computer vision, pp. 4489–4497 (2015)

8. Gao, J., Yang, Z., Chen, K., et al.: Turn tap: temporal unit regression network for temporal action proposals. In: Proceedings of the IEEE international conference on computer vision, pp. 3628–3636 (2017)

9. Xiong, Y., Zhao, Y., Wang, L., et al.: A pursuit of temporal accuracy in general activity detection. arXiv preprint arXiv:1703.02716 (2017)

10. Zhao, Y., Xiong, Y., Wang, L., et al.: Temporal action detection with structured segment networks. In: Proceedings of the IEEE International Conference on Computer Vision, pp. 2914–2923 (2017)

11. Lin, T., Zhao, X., Su, H., Wang, C., Yang, M.: BSN: boundary sensitive network for temporal action proposal generation. In: Ferrari, V., Hebert, M., Sminchisescu, C., Weiss, Y. (eds.) ECCV 2018. LNCS, vol. 11208, pp. 3–21. Springer, Cham (2018). https://doi.org/10.1007/978-3-030-01225-0_1

12. Shou, Z., Chan, J., Zareian, A., et al.: CDC: convolutional-de-convolutional networks for precise temporal action localization in untrimmed videos. In: Proceedings of the IEEE Conference on Computer Vision and Pattern Recognition, pp. 5734–5743 (2017)

13. Ren, S., He, K., Girshick, R., et al.: Faster R-CNN: towards real-time object detection with region proposal networks. IEEE Trans. Pattern Anal. Mach. Intell. **39**(6), 1137–1149 (2016)

14. Xu, H., Das, A., Saenko, K.: R-c3d: region convolutional 3D network for temporal activity detection. In: Proceedings of the IEEE international conference on computer vision, pp. 5783–5792 (2017)

15. Idrees, H., Zamir, A.R., Jiang, Y.G., et al.: The THUMOS challenge on action recognition for videos "in the wild". Comput. Vis. Image Understand. **155**, 1–23 (2017)

16. Lin, T., Zhao, X., Shou, Z.: Single shot temporal action detection. In: Proceedings of the 25th ACM international conference on Multimedia, pp. 988–996 (2017)

17. Buch, S., Escorcia, V., Ghanem, B., et al.: End-to-end, single-stream temporal action detection in untrimmed videos. In: Procedings of the British Machine Vision Conference 2017. British Machine Vision Association, pp. 1–12 (2017)

18. Carreira, J., Zisserman, A.: Quo vadis, action recognition? A new model and the kinetics dataset. In: proceedings of the IEEE Conference on Computer Vision and Pattern Recognition, pp. 6299–6308 (2017)

19. Hussein, N., Gavves, E., Smeulders, A.W.M.: Timeception for complex action recognition. In: Proceedings of the IEEE Conference on Computer Vision and Pattern Recognition, pp. 254–263 (2019)
20. Piergiovanni, A.J., Ryoo, M.S.: Learning latent super-events to detect multiple activities in videos. In: Proceedings of the IEEE Conference on Computer Vision and Pattern Recognition, pp. 5304–5313 (2018)
21. Heilbron, F.C., Escorcia, V., Ghanem, B., et al.: Activitynet: a large-scale video benchmark for human activity understanding. In: Proceedings of the ieee conference on computer vision and pattern recognition, pp. 961–970 (2015)
22. Singh, B., Marks, T.K., Jones, M., et al.: A multi-stream bi-directional recurrent neural network for fine-grained action detection. In: Proceedings of the IEEE conference on computer vision and pattern recognition, pp. 1961–1970 (2016)
23. Long, F., Yao, T., Qiu, Z., et al.: Gaussian temporal awareness networks for action localization. In: Proceedings of the IEEE Conference on Computer Vision and Pattern Recognition, pp. 344–353 (2019)
24. Buch, S., Escorcia, V., Shen, C., et al.: Sst: single-stream temporal action proposals. In: Proceedings of the IEEE conference on Computer Vision and Pattern Recognition, pp. 2911–2920 (2017)
25. Zeng, R., Huang, W., Tan, M., et al.: Graph convolutional networks for temporal action localization. In: Proceedings of the IEEE International Conference on Computer Vision, pp. 7094–7103 (2019)
26. Yuan, Z., Stroud, J.C., Lu, T., et al.: Temporal action localization by structured maximal sums. In: Proceedings of the IEEE Conference on Computer Vision and Pattern Recognition, pp. 3684–3692 (2017)

LLNet: A Lightweight Lane Line Detection Network

Lu Zhang[1,2,3], Bin Kong[1,3(✉)], and Can Wang[1,3]

[1] Institute of Intelligent Machines, Chinese Academy of Sciences, Hefei 230031, China
iszhang@mail.ustc.edu.cn, {bkong,cwang}@iim.ac.cn
[2] University of Science and Technology of China, Hefei 230026, China
[3] The Key Laboratory of Biomimetic Sensing and Advanced Robot Technology,
Hefei 230031, China

Abstract. The lane line detection methods based on semantic segmentation networks have achieved remarkable results in recent years. However, the semantic segmentation networks are aimed at the pixel level. These methods have a large amount of computation, which can reduce the real-time performance. To reduce the calculation, we propose a Lightweight Lane line detection Network (LLNet). A new sub-layer is established. We also adopt a jumping structure between two sub-layers to enhance the supervisory role of ground truth. Furthermore, we adopt two branches, including instance segmentation and embeddable branch. The combination of two branches can filter out the wrongly detected pixels and further improve the accuracy of detection. Experimental results in the Tusimple dataset show that the detection accuracy of the proposed network is comparable with LaneNet. Meanwhile, it has good real-time performance, and the processing time of a single image is 10.285 ms, which is about one-half of LaneNet.

Keywords: Lane detection · Lightweight · CNN · Real-time

1 Introduction

Lane line is the sign of the road division area in the traffic system, and it is the guarantee of orderly driving of vehicles [1]. Consequently, a rapid and accurate method of lane line detection is very important to improve the safety of autonomous vehicles [2,3].

Many factors in road driving can bring great challenges to the task of lane line detection (see Fig. 1). Methods of lane line detection are primarily divided into based on the traditional image processing and deep learning [4]. The lane lines can be identified by extracting the color and texture information based on the method of traditional image processing [5,6]. Those methods must manually extract the characteristics of lane lines. It is very difficult to deal with all sorts of practical situations, so most methods are limited to a specific application environment. In recent years, an increasing number of people are applying deep

© Springer Nature Switzerland AG 2021
Y. Peng et al. (Eds.): ICIG 2021, LNCS 12888, pp. 355–369, 2021.
https://doi.org/10.1007/978-3-030-87355-4_30

(a) Scenario with cars blocked   (b) Scenario with shadow of trees   (c) Scenario with curved road

(d) Scenario with sloping road   (e) Scenario with damaged   (f) Scenario with shadow of bridge

Fig. 1. Difficult scenarios for detection (examples in TuSimple dataset).

learning to lane line detection [7,8]. Compared with traditional methods, deep learning can automatically extract features of lane lines from training data. Meanwhile, it has good robustness and generalizable capacity [9]. On the basis of the above analysis, a light lane detection network (LLNet) is proposed. LLNet can enhance the accuracy and real-time performance of lane line detection. In summary, the contribution of this article can be summarized as follows:

1) We propose a new sub-layer to reduce the calculation. Furthermore, a jump structure is adopted between the two sub-layers to form a dense block. As a result, each layer in the dense block will have a direct impact on the gradient of the ultimate loss function, which may strengthen the supervisory role of ground truth.

2) We propose a Lightweight Lane line detection Network (LLNet). LLNet can reduce the parameter count and save training time. The biggest runtime gap between LLNet and LaneNet [10] is that LLNet could run one times faster, and LLNet takes 10.285 ms to process a single image.

3) The decoder of LLNet divides the final layer into the instance segmentation and the embeddable branch. Two branches are multiplied by the element-wise multiplication, which can filter out the wrong pixels and obtain more precise pixels that belong to the certain lane lines.

The remainder of this paper is organized as follows. Section 2 reviews the related works. Section 3 introduces the proposed network. Section 4 reports the experiments and results. Section 5 concludes our work and briefly discusses the possible future work.

2   Related Works

Correct lane detection can allow autonomous vehicles to make further decisions and judgements about their positions and status. In general, methods for lane line detection can be divided into two types, which are based on traditional image processing and deep learning.

Traditional image processing methods rely on the detection of image characteristics, such as color, texture and edge characteristics. Kang et al. [11] extracted the edge features of lane lines by using a Sobel operator. The dynamic programming algorithm was used for lane line detection. Suddamalla et al. [12] combined pixel intensity with boundary information, and used the adaptive threshold algorithm to detect lane lines. Cela et al. [13] proposed an unsupervised adaptive classifier to detect lane lines. However, this method was not strong enough and had erratic effects under major changes in shadows and lighting. Since the methods of traditional image processing involve too many constraints, such as the color or shape of the lane line.

Over the past few years, deep learning has developed rapidly in the field of computer vision and is one of the hottest areas of research. ResNet [14], UNet [15] and ERFNet [16] continually enhance the performance of the convolutional neuronal network (CNN) in deep learning. Kim et al. [17] proposed a method for lane line and vehicle detection based on CNNs. It also ran at the frame rate that is required by the system in real time. Literature [18] proposed a novel method to address the issue of lane occlusion detection (SCNN). Davy et al. [10] considered the lane line detection to be an image segmentation problem. The binary segmentation and embeddable branch were combined to derive one category for each pixel to enhance the detection accuracy of the lane line. Qiao et al. [19] proposed the Line-CNN, which can handle with infinite number of lanes and also can acquire the categories of lanes. Literature [20] adopted the self-attention mechanism and made use of the simple structure of lane lines to predict the credibility of lane lines in the horizontal and vertical directions of images. Lu et al. [21] proposed a fast and robust method for lane line detection combining semantic segmentation network and optical flow estimation network. However, this method not only improved running speed, it also reduced accuracy. Ron et al. [22] proposed LaneDraw based on full binary segmentation pixel embedding self-grouping clustering. This method eliminated the curve fitting process, reduced post-processing complexity and reached a detection speed of 35 fps.

Above all, the methods for lane line detection based on deep learning take advantage of the powerful automatic feature extraction capability of CNNs, which can extract useful features from large amounts of data. Therefore, this paper proposes a novel lane line detection network based on deep learning. The network proposed can distinguish the pixels belong to the lane line or background, the categorical attributes of each lane line can also be obtained. Details are provided in Sect. 3.

3   Method

In order to reduce the computational load, this paper constructs sub-layer (see Sect. 3.1). Then, the layer is used to design LLNet (see Sect. 3.2). Different from LaneNet which combines binary segmentation with embeddable branch, LLNet combines embeddable and instance segmentation branch, which can use the category of lane line to complement the embeddable branch.

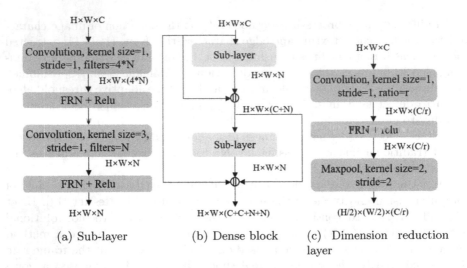

(a) Sub-layer   (b) Dense block   (c) Dimension reduction layer

Fig. 2. The composition of sub-layer, dense block and dimension reduction layer. H represents the height of input, W represents the width of input, C represents the channel of input, r represents the ratio of output channel.

3.1 Sub-layer

The current methods for lane line detection employs a semantic segmentation network. However, the number of parameters in those methods is very large, which will increase the training time. As a result, there is a need to reduce the number of parameters while improving identification accuracy. Inspired by ResNet, this paper proposes the sub-layer. Figure 2a is the composition of the sub-layer. Among them, H represents the height of input, W represents the width of input, C represents the channel of input.

The sub-layer uses the 1×1 convolution group to increase the number of channels and obtain more features. Then, a 3×3 convolution group is used to fuse the features of each channel and reduce the number of channels to the original dimension. Therefore, the sub-layer can reduce the computed amount, but also integrates the characteristics of each channel. Filter response normalization (FRN) is proposed by [23]. FRN solves the problem of mini-batch size while ensuring that the performance is better than that of the BN layer. Therefore, this paper chooses FRN for data normalization.

In order to further strengthen the transmission of the features of each layer, we construct a dense block by the inspiration of Densenet [24]. Its structure is shown in Fig. 2b. Dense block consists of two sub-layers. The parallel jump structure serves to link the characteristics of the upper sub-layer to those of the next sub-layer. This enables us to use several layers of information to make predictions. And the entrance for each layer comes from all the previous layers in the block. This structure enables each layer to directly affect the gradient of the ultimate loss function. Each layer is affected by the original input signal,

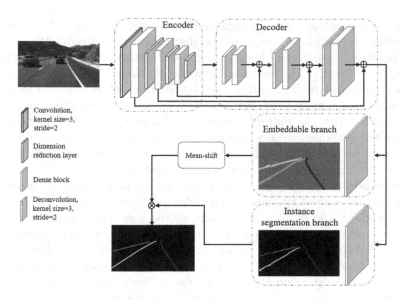

Fig. 3. The architecture of the LLNet proposed by this article.

which can strengthen the supervisory role of categorization of information. And this type of dense connection can produce the regulating effect and reduce over-fitting.

This type of dense connection will increase the dimension of the channel, and therefore the computing load of the network. Therefore, we adopt the dimension reduction layer to reduce the dimension of the channel. Figure 2c is the composition of the dimension reduction layer. The dimension reduction layer comprises a 1×1 convolution group and a max-pool operation. 1×1 convolution group is used to reduce the number of channels, thereby reducing the computational effort. And, r represents the ratio of output channel and is set to 0.5. The kernel size of max-pool is 2, and the stride is 2. Therefore, by entering the characteristic of $H \times W \times C$, we are able to obtain the characteristic of $H/2 \times W/2 \times C/r$. In this way, the adoption of the dimension reduction layer can not only reduce the number of channels, but also maintain the most representative features.

3.2   Architecture of LLNet

This article proposes LLNet based on the sub-layer, dimension reduction layer and dense block designed in Sect. 3.1 to reduce the computation, as shown in Fig. 3. LLNet is composed of encoder-decoder structure. The network has 20 layers. Among them, layers 1 to 10 are encoder, and the rest is decoder layers. Inspired by LaneNet, the 20th layer of decoder is split into the instance segmentation and the embeddable branch. LanNet uses binary segmentation branch, which can only distinguish the background and lane lines. LaneNet strongly relies on the result of embeddable branch, which can be handled by the cluster algorithm. Instance segmentation branch can not only distinguish the background and lane lines, but also distinguish the category for each lane line. Therefore, we choose the instance segmentation branch to replace the binary segmentation branch. The instance segmentation branch is designed to get the category for each lane line, and the embeddable branch is designed to get the location characteristics of each lane line. The instance segmentation map can be complemented with the embeddable map to obtain a more precise lane line. In this way, the lane line category information obtained by the instance segmentation branch can be used to guide the subsequent cluster operation, so as to more accurately distinguish the lane lines with different ids.

The decoder of LLNet uses the deconvolution operation to make the network scale up to the size of the input image. As the feature map of the last layer in the encoder is too small, many details will be lost. Thus, inspired by UNet, this paper integrates the features of the encoder with the decoder. Consequently, these features may contain rich global information. First of all, the deconvolution is performed on the features of the last layer in the encoder. Afterwards, the result of the deconvolution is fed to the dense block. The results obtained at that moment are fused with the features of the 9th layer in the encoder. And so forth, the results of the 16th layer and the 6th layer are fused, and the results of the 19th layer and the 3rd layer are fused. Such a fusion operation allows the final feature to retain both global information and local details. We can make full use of the features extracted in the encoder to compensate for the missing details by the deconvolution.

Assume that the resolution of the input image is H × W and the initial channel of LLNet is N. The category number for the instance segmentation branch is N_{ins}, and the category number for the embeddable branch is N_{emb}. The detailed configuration of each layer of LLNet is shown in Table 1.

3.3　Loss Function

The loss function reflects the degree to which the network has fitted the data. The smaller the loss function value is, the better the robustness of the network is. Since the instance segmentation branch is to get the category of path lines, it belongs to the image classification. Therefore, this article uses the weighted cross-entropy loss feature to train the instance segmentation branch. The calculation equation of the loss function is shown in Eq. 1.

$$l_{ins} = \frac{1}{n} \sum_{i=1}^{n} -[w_i \cdot y_i \cdot \log(p_i)] \tag{1}$$

Therein, n is the number of pixels, y_i is the category of the i-th pixel, p_i is the category prediction probability of the pixel i, w_i stands for weight information of the pixel i.

The result of the embeddable branch requires a cluster operation to retrieve the lane lines. This process requires the category of lane lines. Therefore, we need to ensure the minimum distance between pixels belonging to the same lane

Table 1. The detailed configuration of each layer of LLNet.

	Layer	Type	Output
Encoder	1	Convolution	[H/2, W/2, N × 2]
	2–3	Dense block	[H/2, W/2, N × 6]
	4	Dimension reduction layer	[H/4, W/4, N × 3]
	5–6	Dense block	[H/4, W/4, N × 8]
	7	Dimension reduction layer	[H/8, W/8, N × 4]
	8–9	Dense block	[H/8, W/8, N × 10]
	10	Dimension reduction layer	[H/16, W/16, N × 5]
Decoder	11	Deconvolution	[H/8, W/8, N × 4]
	12–13	Dense block	[H/8, W/8, N × 10]
	14	Deconvolution	[H/4, W/4, N × 3]
	15–16	Dense block	[H/4, W/4, N × 8]
	17	Deconvolution	[H/2, W/2, N × 2]
	28-19	Dense block	[H/2, W/2, N × 6]
	20	Instance branch	[H, W, N_{ins}]
	20	Embeddable branch	[H, W, N_{emb}]

line and the maximum distance between pixels belonging to different lane lines. Thus, the calculation equation for the embeddable branch of the loss function is shown in Eq. 2.

$$l_{emb} = \min\{\sum_{i=1}^{N}\sum_{k=1}^{M_i}(||p_{ik} - \mu_i||)^2\} + \max\{\sum_{i=1,j=1,i\neq j}^{N}\sum_{k=1}^{M_i}(||p_{ik} - \mu_j||)^2\} \quad (2)$$

Among them, N expresses the number of lane lines, M_i is the number of pixels which belong to lane line i, μ_i represents the average value of pixels for lane line i, p_{ik} represents the k-th pixel for lane line i, μ_j represents the average value of pixels which belong to lane line j, $||x||$ represents the euclidean distance.

The calculation formula of the final loss function is as follows:

$$l_{total} = l_{ins} + l_{emb} \quad (3)$$

3.4   Cluster Module

We can gain two maps by the instance segmentation and embeddable branch. Then, like LaneNet, the embeddable map will be processed by the cluster module, which consists of a mean-shift algorithm. The purpose of the cluster module is to cluster the pixels to different lane lines. Meanwhile, the results of cluster module and instance segmentation map are multiplied by the element-wise multiplication. In the process of the element-wise multiplication, when the pixels that one branch is certain but the other is uncertain, we serve those pixels as

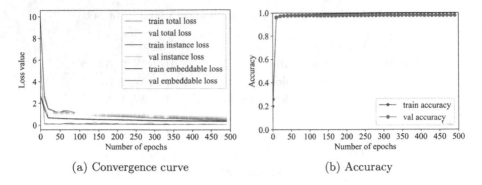

(a) Convergence curve   (b) Accuracy

Fig. 4. Convergence curve of the loss function and accuracy in the training.

the background. In this way, we can filter out the wrong pixels and obtain more precise pixels that belong to lane lines.

4   Experiments and Results

4.1   Datasets and Metric

Tusimple dataset [25] has severe lane wear. And the continuous segment of the lane lines is shortened. The image resolution is 720×1280. We employ the 3626 annotated images for training and the remaining 2782 images for testing.
In TuSimple dataset, the metric of LLNet includes accuracy ($Acc = \sum \frac{N_c}{T_c}$), false positive rate ($FPR = \sum \frac{N_{wp}}{N_p}$)) and false negative rate ($FNR = \sum \frac{N_{mp}}{N_{gt}}$)). Among them, N_c represents the number of correct points predicted of lane lines, and T_c is the number of correct points of lane lines in ground truth. N_{wp} represents the number of points wrongly predicted, and N_p represents the number of points predicted. N_{mp} represents the number of points that were not predicted. N_{gt} means the number of points in ground truth.

4.2   Implementation Details

The experiments for lane line detection are implemented on a computer equipped with an Intel Core i7-9700K CPU with 64 GB RAM and one GeForce GTX 2080ti GPU. The dataset is randomly divided into a training set (3263 images) and a verification set (363 images). During training, epoch is 500 and batch size is 4. To increase the speed of the network, we resized the images of the dataset to 256×512. The initial rate is set to 0.001 with a "poly" learning rate strategy. Since the dataset has a maximum of six lane lines annotated, the final dimension of the instance segmentation branch is 6. We set 4 as the output dimension of the embeddable branch.

4.3 Convergence Analysis of LLNet

Figure 4 shows the convergence curve of the loss function and the accuracy in the training. From Fig. 4a, the curves of train loss and val loss tend to converge with the increase of epochs. And the difference between train loss and the val loss is very small. At the same time, it can be seen from Fig. 4b that, with the increase of epochs, the training accuracy and val accuracy will gradually reach the peak and eventually become stable. Therefore, LLNet is a better network, and there is no over-fitting or under-fitting.

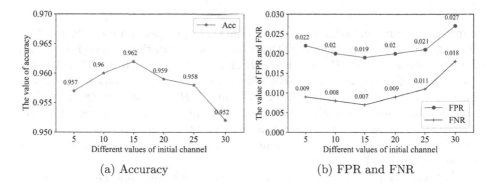

(a) Accuracy   (b) FPR and FNR

Fig. 5. The accuracy, FPR and FNR with different values of initial channel.

Table 2. Results of ablation experiment.

Binary	Instance	Embeddable	Acc	FPR	FNR
	✓		0.921	0.051	0.049
✓		✓	0.951	0.025	0.019
	✓	✓	**0.962**	**0.019**	**0.007**

4.4 Ablation Experiments

The initial channel value of the network directly affects the channel value of each subsequent layer. Therefore, to compare the effects on LLNet by employing different initial channel values, we set the initial channel values as 5, 10, 15, 20, 25, and 30 (see Fig. 5). The results in Fig. 5 show that when the initial channel number is 15, LLNet achieves the optimal performance. Thus, the following experiments adopt 15 as the initial channel value. LaneNet [10] is divided into binary segmentation and embeddable branch. The binary segmentation branch marks the pixels which belong to the lane or background. However, this article adopts the instance segmentation branch, which can not only distinguish the pixels belong to the background or the lane, but also obtain the category of each lane line. In order to verify the effectiveness of the combination of the instance

Table 3. Running time of each branch and cluster module. Here "-" means without value.

Binary	Instance	Embeddable	Time (ms)		
			Inference	Cluster	Total
✓			7.011	-	7.011
✓		✓	7.029	4.681	11.710
	✓		6.827	-	6.827
	✓	✓	7.158	3.127	10.285

segmentation and embeddable branch, ablation experiments are conducted (see Table 2). From Table 2, when only the instance segmentation branch is selected, the Acc decreases by 0.041, and the FPR and FNR increase by 0.032 and 0.042, respectively. Thus, when the embeddable and instance segmentation branch are selected, the Acc decreases by 0.011, FPR and FNR increase by 0.006 and 0.012, respectively. Thus, integrating the embeddable and the instance segmentation branch can achieve better detection accuracy. That's because the category of lane line through the instance segmentation branch can complement the results of the embeddable branch.

Further, Table 3 shows the running time of each branch and cluster module. When only the binary segmentation branch or the instance segmentation branch is selected, the inference time is 7.011 ms and 6.827 ms, respectively. When the two branches are combined with the embeddable branch, the inference time is 7.029 ms and 7.158 ms, and the cluster time is 4.681 ms and 3.127 ms, respectively. The lane line category information that can be obtained by the instance segmentation branch and the result of the embeddable branch are mutually make up. It can reduce the time of the cluster module by using this approach.

Figure 6 shows the visual results of the integrating binary or instance segmentation branch with embeddable branch in different scenarios. From Fig. 6, the binary segmentation branch recognizes many wrong pixels. And, the results of combing the embeddable with binary segmentation branch have many miscellaneous pixels, which are wrongly detected lane lines. However, these wrong pixels can be eliminated by the instance segmentation branch. Thus, the validity of instance segmentation branch is further verified.

4.5   Comparison with State of the Art Methods

We compare LLNet with Cascaded CNN [26], LaneNet [10], literature [21], Lane-Draw [22], Line-CNN [19], and PolyLaneNet [27]. Table 3 reports the comparison results of different methods in TuSimple dataset. From Table 4, our method has achieved better performance in Acc, FPR, and FNR, except for LaneNet. Because LaneNet adopts ENet as the baseline model, ENet itself has a very good feature extraction performance. Acc of LaneNet is slightly higher than LLNet, but FPR and FNR are much higher than LLNet. This phenomenon indicates

	Embeddable branch	Segmentation branch	Combination of two branches	Ground truth	Input image

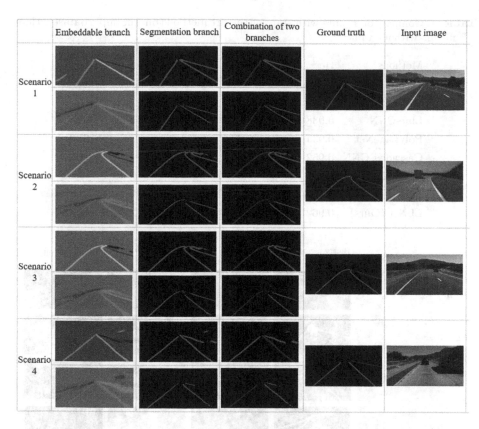

Fig. 6. Detection results of lane lines with different strategies under four scenarios. For each scenario, the combing embeddable with binary segmentation branch is on the top, the combing embeddable with instance segmentation branch is on the bottom.

wrong and missing detection exist in LaneNet. In this article, the instance segmentation branch can be complementary to embeddable branch to reduce the probability of wrong detection. Moreover, the processing time of LLNet is 10.285 ms, including inference time and cluster time. Although the processing time of PolyLaneNet is 8.696 ms, its Acc is decreased by 0.028 than LLNet, and the rate of wrong and missing detection are also very high. Cascaded CNN adopts REFNet as the baseline. ERFNet is a semantic segmentation network and has a better performance in cityscapes datasets [28]. However, the Acc of LLNet is higher than Cascaded CNN. Thus, LLNet still has a better performance. In Fig. 1, we show some images to explain the challenges in lane line detection. Thus, LLNet and LaneNet are adopted to deal with these challenging images. Visual results adopting LaneNet and LLNet are shown in Fig. 7 and Fig. 8. From Fig. 7, the embeddable and binary segmentation branch in these

Table 4. Comparison results with state-of-the-art methods on TuSimple dataset. Here "-" means without value.

Methods	Acc	FPR	FNR	Time cost (ms)		
				Inference	Cluster	Total
LaneDraw	0.928	-	-	28.571	-	28.571
Line-CNN	0.938	0.041	0.019	68.000	-	68.000
PolyLaneNet	0.934	0.094	0.093	8.696	-	**8.696**
Cascaded CNN	0.952	0.119	0.062	16.969	-	16.969
Lu et al.	0.960	0.033	0.046	-	-	-
LaneNet	**0.964**	0.078	0.024	12.400	6.60	19.000
LLNet (Ours)	0.962	**0.019**	**0.007**	**7.158**	**3.127**	10.285

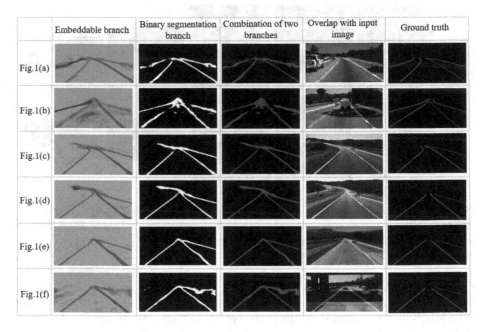

Fig. 7. Visual results of LaneNet in the scenarios shown in Fig. 1.

scenario have many wrong detections, respectively. And, the lane lines also have many wrongly detected pixels by combining embeddable with binary segmentation branch. However, the combination of the two branches can remove the pixels which are wrongly detected as shown in Fig. 8. Furthermore, LLNet can improve the accuracy of detection.

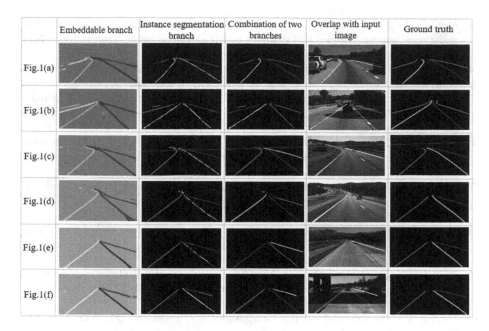

	Embeddable branch	Instance segmentation branch	Combination of two branches	Overlap with input image	Ground truth
Fig.1(a)					
Fig.1(b)					
Fig.1(c)					
Fig.1(d)					
Fig.1(e)					
Fig.1(f)					

Fig. 8. Visual results of LLNet in the scenarios shown in Fig. 1.

5 Conclusion

In this article, a lightweight lane line detection network is proposed. In the network, sub-layer can not only reduce the computation, but also integrate the characteristics of each channel. The dense block directly affects the final result, and strengthens the supervisory role of categorization of information. Furthermore, we employ two branches in the last layer of our network, including embeddable and instance segmentation branch. Since single branch will wrong detect some pixels belonging to background. The results of the two branches can be complementary to filter out the wrong pixels and obtain more precise pixels that belong to lane lines. The experiments show that our network can achieve a comparable accuracy. The *Acc* is slightly 0.002 lower than LaneNet, but the running time of LaneNet is twice as much as our network. Although our network got a good performance, it still has some work we need to do in the future. Our network adopts cluster module for post-processing, and increases time consumption. Thus, how to reduce the time consumption is our next step for work.

References

1. Hillel, A.B., Lerner, R., Levi, D., Raz, G.: Recent progress in road and lane detection: a survey. Mach. Vis. Appl. **25**(3), 727–745 (2014)
2. Yenikaya, S., Yenikaya, G., Düven, E.: Keeping the vehicle on the road: a survey on on-road lane detection systems. ACM Comput. Surv. (CSUR) **46**(1), 1–43 (2013)

3. McCall, J.C., Trivedi, M.M.: Video-based lane estimation and tracking for driver assistance: survey, system, and evaluation. IEEE Trans. Intell. Transp. Syst. **7**(1), 20–37 (2006)

4. Ye, Y.Y., Hao, X.L., Chen, H.J.: Lane detection method based on lane structural analysis and CNNs. IET Intell. Transp. Syst. **12**(6), 513–520 (2018)

5. Satzoda, R.K., Sathyanarayana, S., Srikanthan, T., Sathyanarayana, S.: Hierarchical additive Hough transform for lane detection. IEEE Embedded Syst. Lett. **2**(2), 23–26 (2010)

6. Aminuddin, N.S., Ibrahim, M.M., Ali, N.M., Radzi, S.A., Saad, W.H.M., Darsono, A.M.: A new approach to highway lane detection by using Hough transform technique. J. Inf. Commun. Technol. **16**(2), 244–260 (2017)

7. Li, J., Mei, X., Prokhorov, D., Tao, D.: Deep neural network for structural prediction and lane detection in traffic scene. IEEE Trans. Neural Netw. Learn. Syst. **28**(3), 690–703 (2016)

8. Kim, J., Kim, J., Jang, G.-J., Lee, M.: Fast learning method for convolutional neural networks using extreme learning machine and its application to lane detection. Neural Netw. **87**, 109–121 (2017)

9. Zou, Q., Jiang, H., Dai, Q., Yue, Y., Chen, L., Wang, Q.: Robust lane detection from continuous driving scenes using deep neural networks. IEEE Trans. Veh. Technol. **69**(1), 41–54 (2019)

10. Neven, D., De Brabandere, B., Georgoulis, S., Proesmans, M., Van Gool, L.: Towards end-to-end lane detection: an instance segmentation approach. In 2018 IEEE Intelligent Vehicles Symposium (IV), pp. 286–291. IEEE (2018)

11. Kang, D.-J., Jung, M.-H.: Road lane segmentation using dynamic programming for active safety vehicles. Pattern Recogn. Lett. **24**(16), 3177–3185 (2003)

12. Suddamalla, U., Kundu, S., Farkade, S., Das, A.: A novel algorithm of lane detection addressing varied scenarios of curved and dashed lanemarks. In: 2015 International Conference on Image Processing Theory, Tools and Applications (IPTA), pp. 87–92. IEEE (2015)

13. Cela, A.F., Bergasa, L.M., Sanchez, F.L., Herrera, M.A.: Lanes detection based on unsupervised and adaptive classifier. In: 2013 Fifth International Conference on Computational Intelligence, Communication Systems and Networks, pp. 228–233. IEEE (2013)

14. He, K., Zhang, X., Ren, S., Sun, J.: Deep residual learning for image recognition. In: Proceedings of the IEEE Conference on Computer Vision and Pattern Recognition, pp. 770–778 (2016)

15. Ronneberger, O., Fischer, P., Brox, T.: U-net: convolutional networks for biomedical image segmentation. In: Navab, N., Hornegger, J., Wells, W.M., Frangi, A.F. (eds.) MICCAI 2015. LNCS, vol. 9351, pp. 234–241. Springer, Cham (2015). https://doi.org/10.1007/978-3-319-24574-4_28

16. Romera, E., Alvarez, J.M., Bergasa, L.M., Arroyo, R.: ERFNet: efficient residual factorized convnet for real-time semantic segmentation. IEEE Trans. Intell. Transp. Syst. **19**(1), 263–272 (2017)

17. Kim, J., Lee, M.: Robust lane detection based on convolutional neural network and random sample consensus. In: Loo, C.K., Yap, K.S., Wong, K.W., Teoh, A., Huang, K. (eds.) ICONIP 2014. LNCS, vol. 8834, pp. 454–461. Springer, Cham (2014). https://doi.org/10.1007/978-3-319-12637-1_57

18. Pan, X., Shi, J., Luo, P., Wang, X., Tang, X.: Spatial as deep: spatial CNN for traffic scene understanding. In: Proceedings of the AAAI Conference on Artificial Intelligence, vol. 32 (2018)

19. Qiao, D., Wu, X., Wang, T.: A lane recognition based on line-CNN network. In: 2020 Asia-Pacific Conference on Image Processing, Electronics and Computers (IPEC), pp. 96–100. IEEE (2020)
20. Lee, M., Lee, J., Lee, D., Kim, W., Hwang, S., Lee, S.: Robust lane detection via expanded self attention. arXiv preprint arXiv:2102.07037 (2021)
21. Sheng, L., Luo, Z., Gao, F., Liu, M., Chang, K.H., Piao, C.: A fast and robust lane detection method based on semantic segmentation and optical flow estimation. Sensors **21**(2), 400 (2021)
22. Ren, K., Hou, H., Li, S., Yue, T.: LaneDraw: cascaded lane and its bifurcation detection with nested fusion. Sci. China Technol. Sci., pp. 1–12 (2021)
23. Singh, S., Krishnan, S.: Filter response normalization layer: Eliminating batch dependence in the training of deep neural networks. In: Proceedings of the IEEE/CVF Conference on Computer Vision and Pattern Recognition, pp. 11237–11246 (2020)
24. Huang, G., Liu, Z., Van Der Maaten, L., Weinberger, K.Q.: Densely connected convolutional networks. In: Proceedings of the IEEE Conference on Computer Vision and Pattern Recognition, pp. 4700–4708 (2017)
25. Tusimple dataset. https://github.com/TuSimple/tusimple-benchmark/wiki/
26. Pizzati, F., Allodi, M., Barrera, A., García, F.: Lane detection and classification using cascaded CNNs. In: Moreno-Díaz, R., Pichler, F., Quesada-Arencibia, A. (eds.) EUROCAST 2019. LNCS, vol. 12014, pp. 95–103. Springer, Cham (2020). https://doi.org/10.1007/978-3-030-45096-0_12
27. Tabelini, L., Berriel, R., Paixao, T.M., Badue, C., De Souza, A.F., Oliveira-Santos, T.: PolylaneNet: lane estimation via deep polynomial regression. arXiv preprint arXiv:2004.10924 (2020)
28. Cordts, M., et al.: The cityscapes dataset for semantic urban scene understanding. In: Proceedings of the IEEE Conference on Computer Vision and Pattern Recognition, pp. 3213–3223 (2016)

Two-Stage Polishing Network
for Camouflaged Object Detection

Xuan Jiang[1,2], Zhe Wu[3], Yajie Zhang[1,2], Li Su[1,2(✉)], and Qingming Huang[1,2,3]

[1] University of Chinese Academy of Sciences, Beijing, China
{jiangxuan20,zhangyajie19,suli,qmhuang}@ucas.ac.cn
[2] Key Laboratory of Big Data Mining and Knowledge Management,
Chinese Academy of Sciences, Beijing, China
[3] Peng Cheng Laboratory, Shenzhen, China
wuzhe02@pcl.ac.cn

Abstract. Due to the needs of medical and military fields, Camouflaged Object Detection (COD) becomes one of important branches of object detection. It has gradually gained people's attention in recent years. How to correctly locate camouflaged objects accurately segment them are the main problems in this field. The COD task is far different from SOD because of the more complex background with similar colors and textures. Therefore it is more challenging. At present, there are still few existing methods, and lacks targeted method for the edge detection problem. In this paper, we propose a novel **Two-Stage Polishing Network** (TSPNet). This network consists of Front Feature Fusion Module (FFFM) and Polishing Module (PM). FFFM adopts Cross-modal Feature Aggregation and Global and Local Feature Aggregation to capture global context information and detail local information simultaneously. Meanwhile, PM uses edge truth map as supervision imformation to further study the object edge features. The experiments was conducted on three available datasets and the result shows that the proposed framework outperforms state-of-the-arts. Besides, TSPNet is compact with 50% model size saving than existed COD models.

Keywords: Camouflaged object detection · Two-stage polishing network · Feature aggregation · Channel-wise attention

1 Introduction

As people's expectations for intelligent life tend to be more diverse, object detection tasks are also developing in different directions and deriving many important topics. Especially, camouflaged object detection (COD) is concerned with the separation of objects that blend into the environment. These blending phenomena are called camouflage. Camouflage is ubiquitous in human life and nature, especially in animals. In the process of hunting or avoiding natural enemies, many animals would change their body color, shape and movement. In this way,

© Springer Nature Switzerland AG 2021
Y. Peng et al. (Eds.): ICIG 2021, LNCS 12888, pp. 370–380, 2021.
https://doi.org/10.1007/978-3-030-87355-4_31

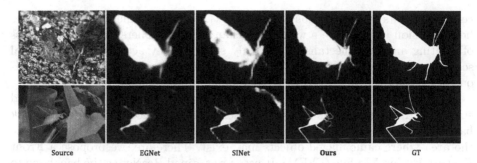

Source   EGNet   SINet   Ours   GT

Fig. 1. Illustration of camouflage object detection. As the figure shows, it is not easy to identify the butterfly and the katydid in image. They are blend into their surroundings. These similarities make detection difficult.

they can reduce the difference between themselves and the surroundings and improve their survival ability. These camouflaged strategies are usually implemented based on fuzzing the judgment of the observer [22].

Biological studies have shown that the human vision system (HVS) is most sensitive to large blocky areas and color features, and it perceives objects mainly by observing the contrast between objects and their background [12, 16, 24]. Thus for camouflaged objects, HVS can be difficult to recognize them due to their low contrast with the background.

However, distinguishing camouflaged objects from backgrounds is necessary in some cases. Besides that camouflaged objects can provide technical support for animal protection, in the military realm [26, 28], a detection of camouflaged object on the battlefield could also be a game-changer. Many passive camouflaged phenomena in life are also important. In medicine [23], small changes in background tissues could mean some kinds of disease. Therefore, it is challenging but significant to study COD in depth.

Recently, deep convolutional network (CNN) has been widely applied in various computer vision tasks due to its powerful feature representation ability. Researchers also begin to utilize CNN to construct models for COD. Fan et al. [5] layered the extracted features. Then these features of different layers are fused, enhanced, or aggregated to help to obtain positioning and edge information, so as to achieve accurate detection of camouflaged objects. Yan et al. divided the MirrorNet [27] into original image segmentation stream and mirror segmentation image stream. It is designed to find the visual difference between the original image and the flipped image. In this way, the network can locate the camouflage objects better. Although these methods are proposed according to the attributes of the camouflaged object, there is still room for improvement in their performance in edge processing (Fig. 1).

Inspired by the cheetah's predation process [10], we proposed the Two-Stage Polishing Network (TSPNet). Cheetahs are better able to distinguish camouflage colors due to its much more abundant S cones [1,6]. Meanwhile, they have a larger field of vision and can see a wider area than humans. Therefore, in the process of hunting animals, cheetahs will roughly select a prey according to the visual scanning of the environment. Then they would choose specific hunting methods on the basis of the characteristics and whereabouts of the prey.

Get inspired, TSPNet can be roughly divided into two stages: positioning and specific segmentation. This Network is a self-attention encoder-decoder Network based on ResNet [8] and UNET [19]. The purpose of the first stage is to locate the area where camouflaged objects may exist. Therefore, we propose a **Front Feature Fusion Module (FFFM)**. It uses pre-trained ResNet as the backbone to extract the features of different levels effectively. In the second stage, due to the similar characteristics between camouflaged objects and background, we design a **Polishing Module (PM)**. PM pays more attention to the objects' boundaries. It introduces the boundary truth map as the supervision information to explore the differences between the objects and the background. And at the same time, it can further refines the features extracted from the FFFM. In Pursuit of the balance between performance and efficiency, we also design a **Channel Attention (CA) Module**. This attention module can guide the network to focus on the camouflaged region and retaining valid features. The experiments show that the proposed network has yielded promising results.

2   Proposed Method

In this part, we first illustrate the Two-Stage Polishing network (TSPNet) proposed for detecting camouflaged objects. Then we elaborate on the **Front Feature Fusion Module (FFFM)** and **Polishing Module (PM)** designed in the network. Finally, we will provide the specific setup of the network and show the effectiveness of the network.

2.1   Overview

The Two-Stage Polishing Network in this paper has two stages. The first stage follows the encoder-decoder structure and takes Resnet-50 as the backbone for feature extraction. This stage is used to recognize and localize camouflaged objects and generate coarse mapping. In the second stage, we design a parallel decoder structure, which adopts the edge truth map as supervision information to promote the network to focus on the edge of the objects and optimize the features from the first stage.

2.2   Front Feature Fusion Module

Front Feature Fusion Module (FFFM) is designed for coarse-grained camou-flaged mapping. We adopt pre-trained ResNet-50 as the backbone of the encoder to enhance the generalization ability and computational efficiency of the model. Meanwhile, to identify the camouflaged objects in images accurately, we make

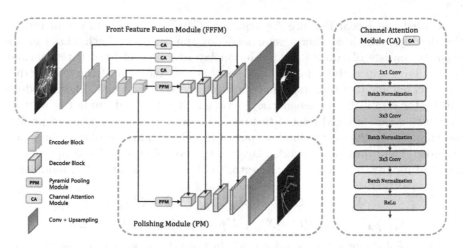

Fig. 2. Architecture of the proposed camouflaged object detection network: TSPNet.

full use of each layer and combine the global and the local information. Furthermore, the attention mechanism could be applied to improve performance with limited computational complexity increasing. As a result, we propose the following three modules.

Channel Attention. In CNN, different channels respond to different semantics, features of diverse levels contain different degrees of details and context information. Despite the deeper convolutional layers have a wider receptive field, many details are missing in the feature extraction of the encoder. On the contrary, shallow layers maintain more details, while redundant information is kept. Therefore, a **C**hannel **A**ttention (CA) module is applied on each output of encoder layer. It aims to extract effective information, denoted as $X_{Attn}^i = Attention(X_{En}^i); i = 2, 3, 4, 5$. After CA, the input channel number of each decoder is decreased to 32 and the parameter number is also reduced. As a result, a smaller size model can be obtained to accelerate the reasoning speed.

CA module consists of four layers: a 1×1 convolutional layer used to reduce the number of channels to 32, two 3×3 convolutional layers and a ReLu activation function. Each convolutional layer is followed with batch normalization.

Global and Local Feature Aggregation. According to the work [31], deeper features in CNN usually contain global context information. These features are suitable to locate salient areas. While the shallow features contain more spatial details and are able to detect the boundary. For camouflaged object, the object and the environment have similar appearances such as color and texture, and the global features contain these common information. Therefore, the aggregation of global and local features can guide the network to learn more discriminant features and to locate the objects.

Global and **L**ocal **F**eature **A**ggregation (GLFA) module is implemented in the decoder, which is almost symmetric to the encoder. Each phase of the decoder consists of two 3×3 convolution layers, followed by a batch normalization layer and a ReLu function. Meanwhile, we introduced the cSE module and sSE module [20] to obtain more accurate detection results. These modules can better establish the dependency between channels and guide the network to focus on camouflaged related features. Moreover, We use a pyramid pooling module (PPM) [29] on the final output of the CA module to obtain the global features. The input of a decoder layer is the combination of the upsampling result of its previous stage and the output of the corresponding CA module:

$$X_{GLFA}^5 = GLFA(Cat(X_{Attn}^5, PPM(X_{Attn}^5)))$$
$$X_{GLFA}^i = GLFA(Cat(X_{Attn}^i, Upsample(X_{GLFA}^{i+1}))); i = 2, 3, 4$$

where $GLFA$ denotes the decoder block in the GLFA (shown in Fig. 2), $Cat()$ denotes concatenation, $Upsample()$ denotes upsampling, X_{Attn}^i denotes the output of the i-th block after channel-wise attention, X_{GLFA}^i denotes the output of the i-th decoder stage in the GLFA module. Thereby the decoder could learn comprehensive semantic information. Furthermore, we construct a prediction module to obtain the final result, which contains a 3×3 convolution layer, a ELU activation function and an additional 1×1 convolution layer.

2.3 Polishing Module

The COD task is very challenging because of the high similarity between the objects and the environment. Therefore, the purpose of the polishing module is to further distinguish the camouflaged objects from the background via utilizing the edge information. Since the object features have been extracted in the previous stage, we introduce the edge truth map as the supervision information in this stage. It is designed to make the model pay more attention to the difference of the edge region. The edge truth map can be computed directly from the ground truth, so there does not need for extra annotations.

The **P**olishing **M**odule (PM) uses the same decoder structure as the GLFA Module and forms a parallel one-to-one relationship with it. With the upsampled output of the previous layer, the polishing decoder layers also use the features extracted by corresponding layers in FFFM as input. Similarly, the result of PPM is fed into the first layer of PM. Therefore, PM can constrain the process of feature extraction in FFFM by further utilizing its ouput while extracting edge features. Features in the entire network can be reconstructed in a more comprehensive way and achieve the purpose of refining the feature map finally.

As we get the predictions from both decoders, the training loss of TPSNet is calculated by the sum of these two parts. We use the binary cross-entropy loss and the total loss function is:

$$L_{total} = L_{BCE}^C(pred\_c, GT) + L_{BCE}^E(pred\_e, GT\_edge)$$

where L_{total} denotes the total loss. L_{BCE}^{C} denotes the loss of FFFM, and L_{BCE}^{E} is the loss between the prediction of PM $pred\_e$ and the edge truth map GT_edge.

2.4 Implementation Details

TSPNet is implemented in PyTorch and uses NVIDIA TITAN RTX for both training and test. The pretrained ResNet-50 is employed to initialize the backbone parameters. We use SGD with 0.9 momentum and 5e-4 weight decay to optimize the network. During the whole training process, there are 50 epochs and the learning rate is reduced from the initial 1e-2 to 1e-3 after 30 epochs. The batch size is set as 32, and the images are resized to 352×352 for both training and testing sessions. The average inference time is 0.2 s (Fig. 3).

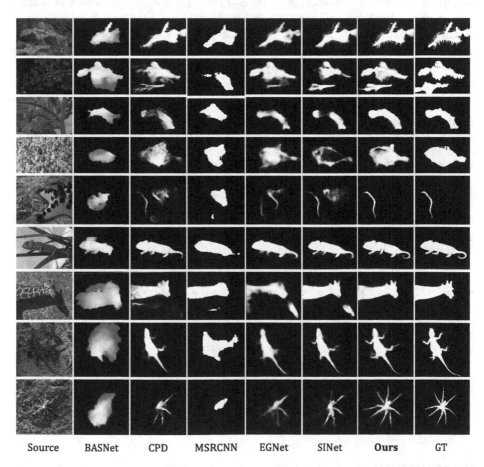

| Source | BASNet | CPD | MSRCNN | EGNet | SINet | **Ours** | GT |

Fig. 3. Prediction results comparison of typical deep learning benchmark and latest COD models on the COD10K dataset.

3 Experiment

3.1 Experimental Settings

Four evaluation metrics are adopted in experiment: (i) MAE (Mean Absolute Error, M) [17]: MAE is commonly used in saliency detection, which can comprehensively evaluate the pixel-level accuracy between the predicted image and the ground truth. (ii) S-measure (S_α) [3]: S-measure is designed to measure the structural similarity of non-binary foreground maps, which is suitable to judge if the camouflaged object is segmented from the background correctly. (iii) Weighted F-Measure (F_β^ω) [15]: Considering the ignoring of false-positive detection property in F-Measure and pixel dependency, weighted F-Measure can achieve a more accurate evaluation result. (iv) E-Measure (E_m) [4]: E-Measure considers not only the matching of pixel-level information, but also the statistics of image-level information. It can evaluate the overall and local accuracy at the same time. Following the setting of previous works, the default training data from CAMO and COD10K and extra data is used as our training set (24240 images in total). Three widely-used datasets are used for experimental evaluation:

Table 1. Quantitative evaluation results on three datasets. The Anet-SRM [11] model and the MirrorNet [27] model (both trained only on CAMO) do not have open source code, so it is not possible to show their performance results on other datasets. (The evaluation of S_α, E_m, F_β^ω are the higher the better and M is the lower the better.)

BASELINE	CHAMELEON				CAMO-Test				COD10K-Test			
	$S_\alpha \uparrow$	$E_m \uparrow$	$F_\beta^\omega \uparrow$	$M \downarrow$	$S_\alpha \uparrow$	$E_m \uparrow$	$F_\beta^\omega \uparrow$	$M \downarrow$	$S_\alpha \uparrow$	$E_m \uparrow$	$F_\beta^\omega \uparrow$	$M \downarrow$
2017 FPN [13]	0.794	0.783	0.590	0.075	0.684	0.677	0.483	0.131	0.697	0.691	0.411	0.075
2017 MaskRCNN [7]	0.643	0.778	0.518	0.099	0.574	0.715	0.430	0.151	0.613	0.748	0.402	0.080
2017 PSPNet [29]	0.773	0.758	0.555	0.085	0.663	0.659	0.455	0.139	0.678	0.680	0.377	0.080
2018 UNet++ [32]	0.695	0.762	0.501	0.094	0.599	0.653	0.392	0.149	0.623	0.672	0.350	0.086
2018 PiCANet [14]	0.769	0.749	0.536	0.085	0.609	0.584	0.356	0.156	0.649	0.643	0.322	0.090
2019 MSRCNN [9]	0.637	0.686	0.443	0.091	0.617	0.669	0.454	0.133	0.641	0.706	0.419	0.073
2019 BASNet [18]	0.687	0.721	0.474	0.118	0.618	0.661	0.413	0.159	0.634	0.678	0.365	0.105
2019 PFANet [29]	0.679	0.648	0.378	0.144	0.659	0.622	0.391	0.172	0.636	0.618	0.286	0.128
2019 CPD [25]	0.863	0.866	0.706	0.052	0.726	0.729	0.550	0.115	0.747	0.770	0.508	0.059
2019 HTC [2]	0.517	0.489	0.204	0.129	0.476	0.442	0.174	0.172	0.548	0.520	0.221	0.088
2019 EGNet [30]	0.848	0.870	0.702	0.050	0.732	0.768	0.583	0.104	0.737	0.779	0.509	0.056
2019 Anet-SRM [11]	–	–	–	–	0.682	0.685	0.484	0.126	–	–	–	–
2020 SINet [5]	0.869	0.891	0.740	0.044	**0.751**	0.771	0.606	0.100	0.771	0.806	0.551	0.051
2020 MirrorNet [27]	–	–	–	–	0.741	**0.804**	0.652	0.100	–	–	–	–
Ours	**0.882**	**0.906**	**0.770**	**0.032**	0.746	0.768	**0.672**	**0.098**	**0.793**	**0.831**	**0.602**	**0.043**

CHAMELEON [21]. Images in Chameleon are obtained through Google image search using the keyword "camouflaged Animal". This dataset contains only 76 images, each of which was manually annotated with object-level ground-truths.

CAMO [11]. CAMO has both categories of naturally camouflaged objects and artificially camouflaged objects. It totally consists of 2500 images, and 2000 of them are split for the training set and the other 500 images are used as the testing set.

COD10K [5]. COD10K is currently the largest dataset for COD. It covers 78 categories of camouflaged objects and contains a total of 10,000 images (6,000 for training and 4,000 for test). In addition to object-level labels, this dataset is also marked with category and instance-level labels.

Since there are a few deep-learning-based COD models at present, this paper follows the experimental setup of SINet [5] and compares TSPNet with 12 deep learning benchmark models [2, 7, 9, 11, 13, 14, 18, 25, 29–32]. In addition, the recent COD models, SINet and MirrorNet (both using public data), are also compared. This aims to verify the performance of TSPNet in COD tasks comprehensively.

3.2 Results and Data Analysis

As shown in Table 1, the proposed method outperforms existing methods in almost all evaluation metrics and datasets. We also test the validity of the proposed methods by two ablation experiments on the COD10K dataset:

Table 2. Ablation study on different architectures and losses: En-De: Encoder-Decoder in FFFM, 1×1 conv: 1×1 convolution layer, L_{abl_e}: loss function of using common ground truth instead of edge truth map in L_{total}.

Dataset	Setting	$S_\alpha \uparrow$	$E_m \uparrow$	$F_\beta^\omega \uparrow$	$M \downarrow$
CHAMELEON	En-De+1x1conv+PM+L_{total}	0.873	0.895	0.746	0.036
	En-De+CA+PM+L_{abl_e}	0.872	0.890	0.739	0.036
	En-De+CA+PM+L_{total}	**0.882**	**0.906**	**0.770**	**0.032**
CAMO-Test	En-De+1x1conv+PM+L_{total}	0.746	0.768	0.611	0.099
	En-De+CA+PM+L_{abl_e}	0.743	0.755	0.600	0.104
	En-De+CA+PM+L_{total}	**0.746**	**0.768**	**0.672**	**0.098**
COD10K-Test	En-De+1x1conv+PM+L_{total}	0.789	0.825	0.602	0.043
	En-De+CA+PM+L_{abl_e}	0.785	0.812	0.587	0.046
	En-De+CA+PM+L_{total}	**0.793**	**0.831**	**0.602**	**0.043**

The Effectiveness of the CA. As shown in the first row of Table 2, TSPNet with CA module performs better than only use an 1×1 convolution layer with batch nomalization. It indicates that the attention mechanism can indeed reduce the model size and retain the effective information to the maximum extent.

The Effectiveness of Using Edeg Truth Map. The loss function in this study can be defined as:

$$L_{abl\_e} = L_{BCE}^{C}(pred\_c, GT) + L_{BCE}^{abl\_E}(pred\_e, GT)$$

The edge truth map in L_{BCE}^{E} is changed to common ground truth. As shown in the second row of Table 2, the performance of not using the edge truth map as extra supervision information is lower than using it. The result shows the effectiveness of using the edge information to explore differences between camouflaged objects and the background. To this end, TSPNet can further improve the accuracy of camouflaged detection.

4   Conclusion

In order to precisely detect camouflaged objects from the complex background, we propose a Two-Stage Polishing network (TSPNet) in this paper. This network includes two modules: the Front Feature Fusion Module and the Polishing Module. The first module aims to identify and locate camouflaged objects in images by using both large-scale and detailed information. The second module further uses the location information and features of different levels to segment the camouflaged objects. We also designed Channel Attention module to guide the network to reduce redundant information and retain effective information. As a result, the detection accuracy of camouflaged objects can be ensured while the number of parameters in the model greatly reduces. Experiments conducted on three widely-used datasets show that the proposed method can achieve better results compared with current COD models.

Acknowledgments. This work was supported in part by the National Key R&D Program of China under Grant 2018AAA0102003, in part by National Natural Science Foundation of China: 61472389, 61931008.

References

1. Ahnelt, P., Schubert, C., Kübber Heiss, A., Anger, E.: Adaptive design in retinal cone topographies of the cheetah and other felids. Investigative Ophthalmol. Vis. Sci., 195 (2005)
2. Chen, K., et al.: Hybrid task cascade for instance segmentation. In: Proceedings of the IEEE/CVF Conference on Computer Vision and Pattern Recognition, pp. 4974–4983 (2019)
3. Fan, D.P., Cheng, M.M., Liu, Y., Li, T., Borji, A.: Structure-measure: a new way to evaluate foreground maps, pp. 4548–4557 (2017)
4. Fan, D.P., Gong, C., Cao, Y., Ren, B., Cheng, M.M., Borji, A.: Enhanced-alignment measure for binary foreground map evaluation, pp. 698–704 (2018)
5. Fan, D.P., Ji, G.P., Sun, G., Cheng, M.M., Shen, J., Shao, L.: Camouflaged object detection. In: IEEE Conference on Computer Vision and Pattern Recognition (CVPR) (2020)

6. Hauzman, E., Bonci, D.M., Ventura, D.F.: Retinal topographic maps: a glimpse into the animals' visual world. Sensory Nervous Syst., 101–126 (2018)
7. He, K., Gkioxari, G., Dollár, P., Girshick, R.: Mask R-CNN. In: Proceedings of the IEEE International Conference on Computer Vision, pp. 2961–2969 (2017)
8. He, K., Zhang, X., Ren, S., Sun, J.: Deep residual learning for image recognition. In: Proceedings of the IEEE Conference on Computer Vision and Pattern Recognition, pp. 770–778 (2016)
9. Huang, Z., Huang, L., Gong, Y., Huang, C., Wang, X.: Mask scoring R-CNN. In: Proceedings of the IEEE/CVF Conference on Computer Vision and Pattern Recognition, pp. 6409–6418 (2019)
10. Lazareva, O.F., Shimizu, T., Wasserman, E.A.: How Animals See the World: Comparative Behavior, Biology, and Evolution of Vision. Oxford University Press (2012)
11. Le, T.N., Nguyen, T.V., Nie, Z., Tran, M.T., Sugimoto, A.: Anabranch network for camouflaged object segmentation. J. Comput. Vis. Image Understanding **184**, 45–56 (2019)
12. Lin, C.J., Chang, C.C., Lee, Y.H.: Evaluating camouflage design using eye movement data. Appl. Ergon. **45**(3), 714–723 (2014)
13. Lin, T.Y., Dollár, P., Girshick, R., He, K., Hariharan, B., Belongie, S.: Feature pyramid networks for object detection. In: Proceedings of the IEEE Conference on Computer Vision and Pattern Recognition, pp. 2117–2125 (2017)
14. Liu, N., Han, J., Yang, M.H.: PicaNet: learning pixel-wise contextual attention for saliency detection. In: Proceedings of the IEEE Conference on Computer Vision and Pattern Recognition, pp. 3089–3098 (2018)
15. Margolin, R., Zelnik-Manor, L., Tal, A.: How to evaluate foreground maps? pp. 248–255 (2014)
16. Neider, M.B., Zelinsky, G.J.: Searching for camouflaged targets: effects of target-background similarity on visual search. Vision. Res. **46**(14), 2217–2235 (2006)
17. Perazzi, F., Krähenbühl, P., Pritch, Y., Hornung, A.: Saliency filters: contrast based filtering for salient region detection, pp. 733–740 (2012)
18. Qin, X., Zhang, Z., Huang, C., Gao, C., Dehghan, M., Jagersand, M.: BasNet: boundary-aware salient object detection. In: Proceedings of the IEEE/CVF Conference on Computer Vision and Pattern Recognition, pp. 7479–7489 (2019)
19. Ronneberger, O., Fischer, P., Brox, T.: U-net: convolutional networks for biomedical image segmentation. In: Navab, N., Hornegger, J., Wells, W.M., Frangi, A.F. (eds.) MICCAI 2015. LNCS, vol. 9351, pp. 234–241. Springer, Cham (2015). https://doi.org/10.1007/978-3-319-24574-4_28
20. Roy, A.G., Navab, N., Wachinger, C.: Concurrent spatial and channel 'squeeze & excitation' in fully convolutional networks. In: Frangi, A.F., Schnabel, J.A., Davatzikos, C., Alberola-López, C., Fichtinger, G. (eds.) MICCAI 2018. LNCS, vol. 11070, pp. 421–429. Springer, Cham (2018). https://doi.org/10.1007/978-3-030-00928-1_48
21. Skurowski, P., Abdulameer, H., Błaszczyk, J., Depta, T., Kornacki, A., Kozieł, P.: Animal camouflage analysis: chameleon database. Unpublished Manuscript (2018)
22. Stevens, M., Merilaita, S.: Animal camouflage: current issues and new perspectives. Philosophical Trans. Roy. Soc. B Biolog. Sci. **364**(1516), 423–427 (2009)
23. Taghanaki, S.A., Abhishek, K., Cohen, J.P., Cohen-Adad, J., Hamarneh, G.: Deep semantic segmentation of natural and medical images: a review. Artif. Intell. Rev. **54**(1), 137–178 (2021)

24. Tong, Y., Konik, H., Cheikh, F., Tremeau, A.: Full reference image quality assessment based on saliency map analysis. J. Imaging Sci. Technol. **54**(3), 30503–1 (2010)
25. Wu, Z., Su, L., Huang, Q.: Cascaded partial decoder for fast and accurate salient object detection. In: Proceedings of the IEEE/CVF Conference on Computer Vision and Pattern Recognition, pp. 3907–3916 (2019)
26. Xue, F., Xu, S., Luo, Y.T., Jia, W.: Design of digital camouflage by recursive overlapping of pattern templates. Neurocomputing **172**, 262–270 (2016)
27. Yan, J., Le, T.N., Nguyen, K.D., Tran, M.T., Do, T.T., Nguyen, T.V.: MirrorNet: bio-inspired camouflaged object segmentation. IEEE Access (2021)
28. Zhang, X., Zhu, C., Wang, S., Liu, Y., Ye, M.: A Bayesian approach to camouflaged moving object detection. IEEE Trans. Circuits Syst. Video Technol. **27**(9), 2001–2013 (2016)
29. Zhao, H., Shi, J., Qi, X., Wang, X., Jia, J.: Pyramid scene parsing network. In: Proceedings of the IEEE Conference on Computer Vision and Pattern Recognition, pp. 2881–2890 (2017)
30. Zhao, J.X., Liu, J.J., Fan, D.P., Cao, Y., Yang, J., Cheng, M.M.: EGNET: edge guidance network for salient object detection. In: Proceedings of the IEEE/CVF International Conference on Computer Vision, pp. 8779–8788 (2019)
31. Zhao, T., Wu, X.: Pyramid feature attention network for saliency detection. In: Proceedings of the IEEE/CVF Conference on Computer Vision and Pattern Recognition, pp. 3085–3094 (2019)
32. Zhou, Z., Rahman Siddiquee, M.M., Tajbakhsh, N., Liang, J.: UNet++: a nested U-net architecture for medical image segmentation. In: Stoyanov, D., et al. (eds.) DLMIA/ML-CDS -2018. LNCS, vol. 11045, pp. 3–11. Springer, Cham (2018). https://doi.org/10.1007/978-3-030-00889-5_1

Towards More Powerful Multi-column Convolutional Network for Crowd Counting

Jiabin Zhang[1,2], Qi Chu[1,2], Weihai Li[1,2(✉)], Bin Liu[1,2], Weiming Zhang[1,2], and Nenghai Yu[1,2]

[1] School of Cyberspace Security, University of Science and Technology of China, Hefei, China
munian@mail.ustc.edu.cn, whli@ustc.edu.cn
[2] Key Laboratory of Electromagnetic Space Information, Chinese Academy of Science, Hefei, China

Abstract. Scale variation has always been one of the most challenging problems for crowd counting. By using multi-column convolutions with different receptive fields to deal with different scales in the scene, the multi-column convolutional networks have achieved good performance. However, there is still great potential waiting to be explored for multi-column convolutional networks. To this end, we propose to design a multi-column neural network that can more effectively adapt to scene scale variations automatically, by applying Neural Architecture Search technology. First, we combine Progressive Neural Architecture Search scheme with crowd counting to construct our Progressive Multi-column Architecture Serach (PMAS) framework. Furthermore, to reduce the bias caused by the weight-share scheme, which is widely adopted in efficient Neural Architecture Search, we propose a novel pre-architecture-based weight-share scheme. Experiments on several challenging datasets demonstrate the effectiveness of our method.

Keywords: Crowd counting · Neural architecture search · Multi-column convolutional network

1 Introduction

Crowd counting is one of the most important tasks of crowd scene understanding and has attracted the interest of many researchers due to its practical applications, such as traffic monitoring, crowd flows analysis and other public safety field. One of the most challenging difficulties of crowd counting is the extreme variations in the size of people in the scene, as shown in Fig. 1. To obtain multi-scale features that encode different scale information, previous works [1–3] attempt to design their network as a multi-column form. However, [4–6] pointed out that different columns of these architectures tend to generate similar features, which contraries to the intention of the multi-column architecture design. In other words, there are huge redundant parameters among columns. To solve

© Springer Nature Switzerland AG 2021
Y. Peng et al. (Eds.): ICIG 2021, LNCS 12888, pp. 381–392, 2021.
https://doi.org/10.1007/978-3-030-87355-4_32

Fig. 1. Examples from ShanghaiTech Part A dataset [1]. The extreme scale variation caused by perspective distortion is one of the most challenging difficulties for crowd counting.

this problem, McML [4] proposed a novel training strategy, which uses an auxiliary network to estimate the mutual information among columns. The estimated mutual information measures the correlation between features learned by different columns, so the learning target is to minimize counting errors and mutual information between columns, which achieved by an iterative and mutual learning scheme. But what if we improve the multi-column architecture from the architecture itself? In other words, we want to design a multi-column architecture that can learn richer multi-scale features easier and each column can learn the real characteristics of scenes of different scales. And with the development of Neural Architecture Search (NAS) [8–10,18,19], we can design the ideal network in an automatic and learnable way.

In this paper, we develop a novel Progressive Multi-column Architecture Search (PMAS) framework. First, we develop a Progressive Multi-column Architecture Search framework with a novel multi-column search space and multi-target search scheme. Furthermore, inspired by previous works [9,10,13–16], we propose a novel weight-share strategy, pre-architecture-based weight-share. The proposed strategy can improve the search result without increasing the cost of the search process. The proposed framework is illustrated in Fig. 2.

The main contributions of this paper include:

1. A novel, NAS-based framework to improve the multi-column architecture performance in crowd counting.
2. A novel weight-share strategy that achieves better search result than previous weight-share strategy.

2   Related Work

2.1   Density Map Estimation-Based Crowd Counting

There are mainly three types of approaches in previous literature on crowd counting: detection-based methods [21,22], regression-based methods [23,24] and density map estimation-based methods [1–6,12,17]. In recent years, density map estimation-based methods are dominant in related research, a lot of novel methods are proposed: MCNN [1] proposed to learn multi-scale features by multi-column network for the first time. But CSRNet [5] criticized that the multi-column architecture in MCNN cannot effectively learn different feature representations for different scale, and then designed a deeper single-column network. McML [4] turned back to multi-column architecture again, they started with the discovery that there are lots of redundancy in the learned parameters in different columns of the multi-column architecture, and proposed mutual learning scheme assisted by a mutual information estimation network to reduce the redundancy.

Our work is inspired by McML [4], but we focus on the multi-column architecture itself.

2.2 Neural Architecture Search

In the past, because it would cost hundreds or thousands of GPU hours [13,18,19], the research and application of NAS progressed slowly. But since ENAS [12] adopted the weight-share scheme, such efficient NAS [9,10] only needs to cost a few GPU hours to complete the search, which brings great convenience. With the rapid development of efficient NAS technology, the application of NAS has expanded from classification to other fields of deep learning. When talking about the design and application of a NAS algorithm, three points are mainly considered:

Search Space. Existing methods can be categorized into searching the macro space [13,19], which performs a global search and the search result is just the network itself, the micro space [8–10], which presets the network to be constructed by several cells, typically regular-cell and reduction-cell, and the search is performed on the cell. The search space of our framework belongs to the macro space, which means when the search is completed, we can directly get the searched network.

Search Algorithm. It is the key to designing an efficient and effective NAS framework. So far, various search strategies based on different theories are proposed, such as: evolutionary algorithm based [13], reinforcement learning based [10,18,19], gradient-based [20], and the method we adopt: performance predictor based [8,9].

Search Target. It is task-specific, for example, in classification, the accuracy rate may be adopted as the search target [9,10,13,18,19]; In detection, mean Average Precision (mAP) may be the search target [20]. As for crowd counting, one of the most intuitive idea is taking Mean Absolute Error (MAE) as the search target, but we additionally proposed using the weighted sum of MAE and Multi-scale Structural SIMilarity (MSSIM) as the search target, and experiments demonstrate that it performs better than only MAE used.

3   Progressive Multi-column Architecture Search

In this section, we present the proposed Progressive Multi-column Architecture Search framework, as shown in Fig. 2. The definition of our search space is intro-

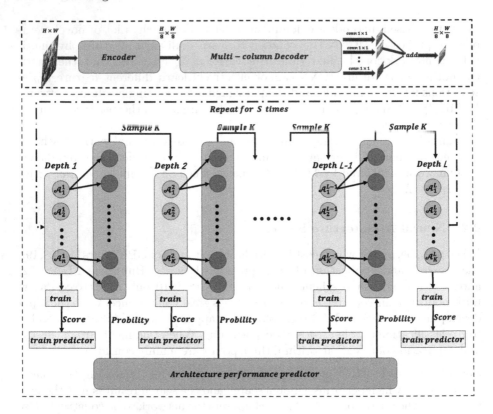

Fig. 2. An illustration of our Progressive Multi-column Architecture Search framework. *Top*: The paradigm of the multi-column network. The encoder is the first ten layers of VGG-16 [9], and the decoder is searched by algorithm. *Bottom*: The sample → train → predict → sample circulation search progress, and we repeat it for S times then select the top-5 to train from scratch. The blue circle nodes represent network architectures, $\mathcal{A}_j^i$ represents the j-th network sampled for depth i, the search space for depth i + 1 is derived by stacking convolutional layers on $\mathcal{A}_1^i$ to $\mathcal{A}_K^i$. More details on Algorithm 1 (Color figure online)

duced in Sect. 3.1. Then the search target is defined in Sect. 3.2. The search algorithm and the overview of the framework is described in Sect. 3.3.

3.1 Multi-column Decoder Search Space

Similar to CSRNet [5], all networks in our search space are constructed by a front-end encoder and a back-end decoder. Regarding the front-end, we adapt the first ten layers of VGG-16 network [7] and only use 3×3 kernels, as settings in CSRNet. The search process on the back-end decoder, which has maximum depth L and maximum number of columns K. Six operations are allowed when constructing a back-end decoder, and we identify them with the numbers {0, 1, 2, 3, 4, 5}:

- 0 : identity mapping;
- 1 : 3 × 3 convolution;
- 2 : 3 × 3 dilated convolution with rate 2;
- 3 : 3 × 3 dilated convolution with rate 4;
- 4 : 5 × 5 depth-wise separable convolution;
- 5 : 7 × 7 depth-wise separable convolution;

There have been three down-sampling in the front-end encoder [5], so all operations above used in back-end decoder will preserve the spatial size of the feature maps.

Then, we can encode a back-end decoder into a numerical matrix, which has maximum column L and maximum row K, corresponding to the maximum depth and maximum number of columns. In our experiments, the counting baseline is constructed as described in McML [4], we treat the four configurations of back-end in CSRNet [6] as four columns, and we discard the column with mixed dilation rate.

It is worth noting that in most previous NAS literature, the minimum unit during the search process is a single convolution, which may not be suitable in our multi-column search. The intention of the multi-column architecture is that different columns deal with different scales, and they are complementary and cooperating. But taking a single convolution as the minimum unit weakens the correlation among columns and cannot explicitly meet the above requirements. So, we take the K convolutions in the same depth l as the minimum search unit, in which way, the expansion of network and weight-share will not process on a single convolution, but K convolutions in the same depth.

3.2   Multi-objective Search

Typically, the so-called search target is the metric that evaluates how a network performs on the target-task. Mean Absolute Error (MAE) is widely used in crowd counting:

$$MAE = \frac{1}{N} \sum_{i=1}^{N} |C_i - C_i^{gt}| \tag{1}$$

Here N is the number of images in test-set, C_i is the estimated count and C_i^{gt} is the ground truth count of the i-th image.

In addition to MAE, there are many other metrics to evaluate the quality of estimated density map, such as PSNR, SSIM and so on. In these metrics, Multi-scale Structural Similarity (MS-SSIM) [11] is easy to implement and can effectively measure the similarity between the estimated density map and the ground truth one. Here we use the ameliorated Dilated MS-SSIM [12]:

$$DMS \cdot SSIM(X_0, Y_0) = \prod_{i=0}^{m-1} \{SSIM(X_i, Y_i)\}^{\alpha_i} \tag{2}$$

Where X_0 is the estimated density map and Y_0 is the corresponding ground truth, and X_i, Y_i is the corresponding features in i-th level of DMS-SSIM network, which is a dilated convolutional neural network with fixed Gaussian kernel,

α^i is the importance weight of $SSIM(X_i, Y_i)$. For more details, we recommend to refer to [12].

Finally, our search target can be formulated as:

$$score = MAE + \gamma \frac{1}{N} \sum_{i=1}^{N} [1 - DMS \cdot SSIM(C_i, C_i^{gt})] \tag{3}$$

Here, γ is the importance weight of the mean DMS · SSIM on the test-set. It is worth noting that the lower the score, the better the network performance.

3.3 Efficient Progressive Multi-column Architecture Search Algorithm

Algorithm 1 shows the pseudocode, and Fig. 2 illustrates the whole search process.

Our search algorithm incorporates the core idea of PNAS [8] and the improved version EPNAS [9], there are two key points:

First, a progressive and sequential searching process. This means our search starts with the simplest situation, for example, the networks that are constructed by one convolutional layer, and expands the depth and complexity of networks by stacking convolutional layers or blocks behind the former ones.

Second, network performance predictor. It is a neural network trained to learn the mapping from network structure to performance on the target task [8,9]. If the network performance predictor has a good prediction of the performance of networks in search space, we can just simply give networks that are predicted good higher probability to be sampled in next stage, and constrain the number of networks to be sampled in each stage. In this way, we can control the search cost without missing good networks.

But there are still some deficiencies in Algorithm 1. The reasonableness of pruning the search space lies in the assumption that the predictor has a good prediction of the performance of the networks. But in the initial stage, without sufficient training, the predictor cannot predict well. Following EPNAS [9], we adopted a temperature-driven sampling procedure, in which the sampling probability π_i of architecture i is amended to $\pi_i^{1/\tau} / \sum_j \pi_j^{1/\tau}$ with temperature τ decaying quickly to 1 as the search iterations increases. In this way, the sampling is likely random at beginning, and we trust more the prediction results of the predictor as it gets more training. More details will be introduced in Sect. 5.

4   Pre-architecture-Based Weight-Share

Weight-share scheme is key to conducting an efficient Neural Architecture Search. This method was proposed in ENAS [10], but similar idea 'weight inheritance' first appeared in [13], and the core of these two methods is "share whenever possible", in other words, as long as the two networks have the same shape in a certain convolutional layer, the weights of this layer will share or inherit.

Algorithm 1. Efficient Progressive Multi-Column Architecture Search

---

Input: K(max columns), L(max depth), N(numbers of arch sampled each time),
S(times the search repeats), P(the performance predictor),
$\mathcal{A}_1$(all possible arch that depth of back-end equal 1), trainSet, valSet.

1: **for** s=1:S **do**
2:     **for** l=1:L **do**
3:         **if** l==1 **then**
4:             weight-share($\mathcal{A}_1$)   ▷ Loads weight that saved before when s is not 1
5:             train($\mathcal{A}_1$,trainSet)   ▷ Train all depth-1 arch one epoch on trainSet
6:             save-weight($\mathcal{A}_1$)   ▷ Save network weights
7:             MAE,MSSIM=eval($\mathcal{A}_1$,valSet)   ▷ Evaluate performance on valSet
8:             Calculate score according formula(3)
9:             train(P,$\mathcal{A}_1$,score) ▷ Train predictor with input-label pairs (arch, score)
10:         **end if**
11:         **if** l>1 **then**
12:             $\mathcal{A}_l$=create-all-arch($\mathcal{A}_{l-1}$)   ▷ Expand $depth_l$ search space based on
    $depth_{l-1}$ sampled architectures
13:             $\mathcal{P}$=inference($\mathcal{A}_l$)   ▷ Predictor infers score of all architectures in the
    $depth_l$ search space
14:             π=SoftMax($-\mathcal{P}$)   ▷ Calculate sample probability distribution, higher
    score, lower probability
15:             $\hat{\mathcal{A}}_l$=sample(pi,N,$\mathcal{A}_l$)   ▷ Sample N architectures from the $depth_l$ search
    space
16:             weight-share($\hat{\mathcal{A}}_l$)   ▷ Loads weights according to weight-share strategy
17:             train($\hat{\mathcal{A}}_l$,trainSet)   ▷ Train sampled networks one epoch on trainSet
18:             save-weight($\hat{\mathcal{A}}_l$)   ▷ Save network weights
19:             MAE,MSSIM=eval($\hat{\mathcal{A}}_l$,valSet)   ▷ Evaluate performance
20:             Calculate score according formula(3)
21:             train(P,$\hat{\mathcal{A}}_l$,score)   ▷ Train predictor
22:         **end if**
23:     **end for**
24: **end for**
25: Get top-5 architectures during the whole search space.

There is no doubt that weight-share can greatly speed up the search process. But recently, some works [14–16] indicated that weight-share scheme may degrade the performance because it may degenerate search-evaluation correlation, for example, architectures with a better validation performance during the search phase may perform worse in final evaluation. Specific causes of this phenomenon are not clear, but it is obvious that the weights shared from one network may not be suitable for another network, and the latter may perform worse because of this. So, we can alleviate this negative impact of weight-share by decreasing the amount of sharing. The proposed pre-architecture-based weight-share scheme is illustrated in Fig. 3. If and only if the two networks have the same structure from the 1-th layer to the i-th layer, and the $(i + 1)$-th layer is inconsistent, there is a sharing of convolution weights from the 1-th layer to the i-th layer between the two networks. The intention of the proposed method is

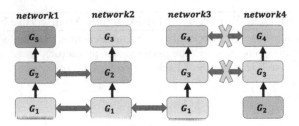

Fig. 3. An illustration of our pre-architecture-based weight-share scheme. G_i denotes index of convolutional layer type.

to strengthen the correlation among convolutional layers and thus alleviate the degraded search.

5   Experiments

We perform search on ShanghaiTech Part A dataset [1], and then train the searched model on other dataset [1,17] to demonstrate the robustness of our searched model.

5.1   Evaluation Metrics

We use mean absolute error (MAE) and mean square error (MSE) to evaluate the performance. MAE is defined as formula 1, and MSE is defined as:

$$MSE = \sqrt{\frac{1}{N}\sum_{i=1}^{N}(C_i - C_i^{gt})^2} \tag{4}$$

These two metrics indicate the accuracy and robustness of the model. We also calculate Structural Similarity (SSIM) to evaluate the quality of estimated density map.

Table 1. Estimation errors on ShanghaiTech, UCF_CC_50 datasets.

Method	ShanghaiTech A		ShanghaiTech B		UCF_CC_50	
	MAE	MSE	MAE	MSE	MAE	MSE
MCNN [1]	110.2	173.2	26.4	41.3	377.6	509.1
ic-CNN [3]	72.5	118.2	13.6	21.1	291.4	349.4
CSRNet [7]	68.2	115.0	10.6	16.0	266.1	397.5
SANet [5]	67.0	104.5	8.4	13.6	258.4	334.9
McML [6]	59.1	104.3	8.1	10.6	246.1	367.7
Counting baseline	64.8	106.9	9.3	15.3	252.3	343.6
Best searched	61.2	98.3	8.1	13.0	246.6	351.2

Table 2. Ablation study results on ShanghaiTech Part A dataset.

Configurations		Performance	
		Top-5 mean MAE	Best model MAE
Weight-share scheme	Share-as-possible	64.01 ± 1.10	62.21
	Pre-architecture-based	63.30 ± 0.52	62.65
Search target	MAE	63.30 ± 0.52	62.65
	MSSIM	63.67 ± 0.87	62.26
	MAE+MSSIM	62.91 ± 1.35	61.19
vs. random search	Random search	64.65 ± 0.98	63.46
	Our full method	62.91 ± 1.35	61.19

Table 3. Comparison with other multi-column networks in Shanghai Part A dataset.

Method	SSIM among columns	SSIM between ET& GT
MCNN [1]	0.71	0.55
CSRNet [7]	0.84	0.71
ic-CNN [3]	0.72	0.68
McML [6]	0.70	0.82
Our best searched	0.60	0.76

5.2 Implementation Details

In architecture search experiments, the maximum column number is 3, and the maximum depth is 8. During the search, except for $depth_1$ in each stage, 25 architectures are sampled at each sampling step, and these sampled networks are trained with MSSIM loss [12] and Adam optimizer with learning rate 1e-5 for one epoch. As for the predictor, we implement it as a fully-connection network with two hidden layers. To deal with architecture with arbitrary columns and depth, we encode all possible permutations in a single convolutional layer (in the case 3 columns and 6 candidate-operations, there are $6^3 - 1 = 216$ for a single layer) as 100-dims vectors in a hash-embedding way, and save them as a lookup-table. Then, 8 embeddings of 8 layers are concatenated as a 800-dims vector, which is inputted into the predictor. For training the predictor, we use L2 loss and learning rate 1e-3. The whole search progress and training the searched networks from scratch cost approximately 24 TITAN Xp GPU hours.

5.3 Ablation Study

Effectiveness of Pre-architecture-Based Weight-Share. The result is shown in Table 2. Besides the best architectures searched by two weight-share schemes, which are somewhat random, we also calculate the mean MAE of the searched top-5 architectures, which can indicate the overall performance of the architecture

input		
Front-end encoder (fine-tuned from VGG-16)		
Searched back-end multi-column decoder		
Conv3-256-1	Conv3-256-4	Conv7-256-1
Conv3-256-2	Conv7-256-1	Conv3-256-4
Conv5-256-1	Conv5-256-1	Conv3-256-2
Conv5-128-1	Conv3-128-4	Conv5-128-1
Conv5-128-1	Conv5-64-1	Conv3-128-1
Conv5-64-1	Conv5-32-1	Conv3-64-4
Conv1-1-1	Conv1-1-1	Conv3-64-1
		Conv5-32-1
		Conv1-1-1
output		

$$\begin{bmatrix} 1 & 2 & 4 & 4 & 4 & 4 & 0 & 0 \\ 3 & 5 & 4 & 3 & 0 & 4 & 0 & 4 \\ 5 & 3 & 2 & 4 & 1 & 3 & 1 & 4 \end{bmatrix}$$

Fig. 4. The best architecture found by our progressive multi-column architecture search.

cluster and better reflect the ability of the search algorithm. As shown in Table 2, because our pre-architecture-based weight-share scheme strengthens the correlation between adjacent convolutional layers and the weights are shared in a more reasonable way, so it can improve the search result in a great margin.

Effectiveness of Multi-objective Search. As shown in Table 2, the result of taking MAE or MSSIM alone as search target are similar, and the combination of these two makes it possible to evaluate the performance of a candidate network during the search process from a more comprehensive metric, so that we can search for better architecture cluster.

Effectiveness of the Whole Search Framework. Previous works [14,15] has pointed out that the excellent performance shown by many NAS literature may be attributed to the design of the search space, and has nothing to do with the search algorithm. To validate the effectiveness of our search framework, we set up a random search baseline as the control. As a fair comparison, we constrain the random search costs the same GPU hours as our other search experiments, we randomly sample 1000 architectures from the search space, and train them for 1 epoch, then select the top-5 architectures and train them from scratch. The result is shown in Table 2. Our search framework outperforms the random search baseline by a great margin, and it indicates that our search framework can search excellent networks in the huge search space effectively.

5.4 Performance and Comparison

The best architecture we searched is shown in Fig. 4. Besides ShanghaiTech Part A, we also train the searched network on other public datasets, the result and comparison with other multi-column architectures are shown in Table 1 and Table 3. Notably, without complex training scheme, our searched architecture is comparable with the state-of-the-art multi-column architecture not only in extremely crowd scenes (Shanghai Part A), but also in relatively sparse scenes (Shanghai Part B) and small datasets (UCF_CC_50). Besides, we evaluate the similarity among columns as McML [4] in Shanghai Part A dataset. We can observe that our searched architecture obtains lower SSIM among columns and higher SSIM between estimated density map and ground truth than other multi-column networks. Lower SSIM among columns indicates that different columns of our searched architecture adapt well to different scale in the regular end-to-end training manner. Higher SSIM between estimated density map and ground truth indicates the success of the MSSIM metric in our multi-objective search target, and our model can generate density map with higher quality.

6   Conclusion

In this paper, we integrate the Progressive Neural Architecture Search framework with multi-column architecture, and develop a novel Progressive Multi-column Architecture Search framework towards crowd counting task. To get a more powerful multi-column network, we not only construct special search space, but propose multi-objective search, which improve the search result and estimated density map of searched model. Besides, to deal with flaws of the weight-share scheme, we propose a novel pre-architecture-based weight-share scheme, and the experiments demonstrate its effectiveness. Finally, our searched model achieves comparable performance with the state-of-the-art multi-column architecture without a complex train scheme.

References

1. Zhang, Y., Zhou, D., Chen, S., Gao, S., Ma, Y.: Single-image crowd counting via multi-column convolutional neural network. In: 2016 IEEE Conference on Computer Vision and Pattern Recognition, pp. 589–597. IEEE (2016)
2. Cheng, Z.-Q., Li, J.-X., Dai, Q., Wu, X., Hauptmann, A.: Learning spatial awareness to improve crowd counting. In: 2019 IEEE/CVF International Conference on Computer Vision, pp. 6152–6161. IEEE (2019)
3. Ranjan, V., Le, H.M., Hoai, M.: Iterative crowd counting. In: Proceedings of the European Conference on Computer Vision, pp. 270–285. IEEE (2018)
4. Cheng, Z.-Q., Li, J.-X., Dai, Q., Wu, X., He, J.-Y., Hauptmann, A.G.: Improving the learning of multi-column convolutional neural network for crowd counting. In: Proceedings of the 27th ACM International Conference on Multimedia, pp. 1897–1906. ACM (2019)
5. Li, Y., Zhang, X., Chen, D.: CSRNet: dilated convolutional neural networks for understanding the highly congested scenes. In: 2018 IEEE/CVF Conference on Computer Vision and Pattern Recognition, pp. 1091–1100. IEEE (2018)
6. Wang, Z., Xiao, Z., Xie, K., Qiu, Q., Zhen, X., Cao, X.: In defense of single-column networks for crowd counting. In BMVC, p. 78 (2018)
7. Simonyan, K., Zisserman, A.: Very deep convolutional networks for large-scale image recognition. In: International Conference on Learning Representations (2015)

8. Liu, C., et al.: Progressive neural architecture search. In: Ferrari, V., Hebert, M., Sminchisescu, C., Weiss, Y. (eds.) ECCV 2018. LNCS, vol. 11205, pp. 19–35. Springer, Cham (2018). https://doi.org/10.1007/978-3-030-01246-5_2

9. Perez-Rua, J.-M., Baccouche, M., Pateux, S.: Efficient progressive neural architecture search. In: BMVC, p. 150 (2018)

10. Pham, H., Guan, M.Y., Zoph, B., Le, Q.V., Dean, J.: Efficient neural architecture search via parameters sharing. In: International Conference on Machine Learning, pp. 4092–4101 (2018)

11. Wang, Z., Simoncelli, E.P., Bovik, A.C.: Multiscale structural similarity for image quality assessment. In: The Thrity-Seventh Asilomar Conference on Signals, Systems & Computers, vol. 2, pp. 1398–1402 (2003)

12. Liu, L., Qiu, Z., Li, G., Liu, S., Ouyang, W., Lin, L.: Crowd counting with deep structured scale integration network. In: 2019 IEEE/CVF International Conference on Computer Vision (ICCV), pp. 1774–1783 (2019)

13. Real, E., et al.: Large-scale evolution of image classifiers. In: ICML 2017 Proceedings of the 34th International Conference on Machine Learning, vol. 70, pp. 2902–2911 (2017)

14. Yu, K., Sciuto, C., Jaggi, M., Musat, C.,Salzmann, M.: Evaluating the search phase of neural architecture search. In: Eighth International Conference on Learning Representations (2020)

15. Bender, G., et al.: Can weight sharing outperform random architecture search? An investigation with Tu-NAS. In: 2020 IEEE/CVF Conference on Computer Vision and Pattern Recognition (CVPR), pp. 14323–14332. IEEE (2020)

16. Li, G., Qian, G., Delgadillo, I.C., Muller, M., Thabet, A., Ghanem, B.: SGAS: sequential greedy architecture search. In: 2020 IEEE/CVF Conference on Computer Vision and Pattern Recognition (CVPR), pp. 1620–1630. IEEE (2020)

17. Idrees, H., Saleemi, I., Seibert, C., Shah, M.: Multi-source multi-scale counting in extremely dense crowd images. In: 2013 IEEE Conference on Computer Vision and Pattern Recognition, pp. 2547–2554. IEEE (2013)

18. Zoph, B., Vasudevan, V., Shlens, J., Le, Q. V.: Learning transferable architectures for scalable image recognition. In: 2018 IEEE/CVF Conference on Computer Vision and Pattern Recognition, pp. 8697–8710. IEEE (2018)

19. Zoph, B., Le, Q.V.: Neural architecture search with reinforcement learning. In: ICLR (2016)

20. Ghiasi, G., Lin, T.-Y., Le, Q.V.: NAS-FPN: learning scalable feature pyramid architecture for object detection. In: 2019 IEEE/CVF Conference on Computer Vision and Pattern Recognition (CVPR), pp. 7036–7045. IEEE (2019)

21. Brostow, G.J., Cipolla, R.: Unsupervised Bayesian detection of independent motion in crowds. In: 2006 IEEE Computer Society Conference on Computer Vision and Pat-tern Recognition, vol. 1, pp. 594–601. IEEE (2016)

22. Lin, S.-F., Chen, J.-Y., Chao, H.-X.: Estimation of number of people in crowded scenes using perspective transformation. Syst. Man Cybern. **31**(6), 645–654 (2001)

23. Chan, A.B., Vasconcelos, N.: Counting people with low-level features and Bayesian regression. IEEE Trans. Image Process. **21**(4), 2160–2177 (2012)

24. Chen, K., Gong, S., Xiang, T., Loy, C.C.: Cumulative attribute space for age and crowd density estimation. In: 2013 IEEE Conference on Computer Vision and Pattern Recognition, pp. 2467–2474. IEEE (2013)

Hole Detection with Texture-Suppression on Wooden Plate Surfaces

Xiaojie An, Xiaohua Xie, and Xiang Chen$^{(\boxtimes)}$

Sun Yat-sen University, Guangzhou, China
anxj@mail2.sysu.edu.cn, {xiexiaoh6,chenxiang}@mail.sysu.edu.cn

Abstract. We devote to the detection of holes on the surface of household panels. Due to the wide variety of furniture panel patterns, the most critical problem is to eliminate the interference of the texture attached to the panel surface. Because of the disadvantage of noise-sensitive in traditional detection methods, we design a typical network that makes full use of multi-level features to extract the edge of the hole and propose a new circle fitting method to obtain the hole. To verify the effectiveness of our network, we constructed a new database called "HoleEdge". Our method perfectly merge the shallow local features and deep semantic features to obtain the mask by taking the intersection and get the final edge map, which can eliminate the texture interference while retaining the edge information to the maximum extent. The experiments show that our proposed architecture benefits hole detection with better performance and outperform the current state-of-the-art hole edge detection methods by a large margin on our data sets. It's F-measure can reach 0.808.

Keywords: Edge detection · Plate surface · Round holes · Super resolution · Deep learning

1 Introduction

With the increasing complexity and diversity of home panel products, automatic hole detection on industrial production lines has become a new hot spot for research. And the interference of complex textures becomes a new challenge for hole detection. The existing hole detection methods can be roughly divided into statistical methods and edge detection methods.

On the one hand, the statistical methods use iterations to find the best-fitting set of points in a least squares [1] sense or the best-fitting circle with hough transform [2,6,7] to detect hole. This is usually a nonlinear problem, which will make it difficult to guarantee the convergence and efficiency of the algorithm if the initial values are not chosen appropriately.

On the other hand, the edge detection methods [11,12,15–18] employs an edge detector and uses edge information to infer locations and radius values of holes. This way can greatly improve the efficiency of hole detection, but the interference of complex textures on edge extraction leads to poor final edge map.

© Springer Nature Switzerland AG 2021
Y. Peng et al. (Eds.): ICIG 2021, LNCS 12888, pp. 393–404, 2021.
https://doi.org/10.1007/978-3-030-87355-4_33

Thus, this paper proposes an efficient hole detection algorithm based on texture-suppression which belongs to the edge detection method. The proposed method improve the efficiency of hole detection and guarantees the detection accuracy. The main contributions of this paper are as follows:

(1) Hole edge extraction. Inspired by [20], a new fusion method is designed for hole edge extraction. The main advantage of our method is texture elimination by extracting the low-level features and the high-level features ot the network separately and using their intersection as the mask features. Then the mask features and stage1–5 fusion layer features are fused to obtain the final edge map.
(2) Circle fit. Based on the edge map obtained by the network, a new circle fitting method is proposed to make full use of the location information and circle center coordinate information provided by the edge species for fine fitting of the holes.
(3) Hole database. To validate our method, we constructed a hole database called "HoleEdge". And propose a data preprocessing method, i.e., using fine-tuned EDSR [19] (Enhanced Deep Residual Networks for Single Image Super-Resolution) to reconstruct the images of HoleEdge to improve their quality. It has significant benefits in terms of improving resolution of the predicted edges and obtain finer edge map.

2   Related Work

This work is mainly related to hole detection with complex textures. To illuminate this area, we examined some advanced studies as following.

2.1   Statistical Methods

The statistical methods use iterations to find the best-fitting set of points in a least squares (LS) sense or the best-fitting circle with hough transform (HT) to detect hole. The LS-based methods [3–5] minimizes the sum of squares of the differences between the sample points and the fitted results, and can detect reference holes well under good environmental conditions. However, large differences in data points will lead to inaccurate detection results. The HT-based methods, the core of which is a voting process, estimate parameters through clustering in the parameter space, and it has been widely used in the detection of straight lines, circles, etc. [8,9]. However, the storage requirements and computation time hinder the use of such methods. Therefore, the probabilistic Hough transform is presented in [6] for improve the speed of Hough transform computation by polling instead of voting. And the randomized Hough transform (RHT) is presented in [7]. The RHT-based methods, in which data points are selected randomly and mapped to an circle, reduce the computational complexity, computing time, and the influence of noise [10]. Yet, false detection results often occur when severe environmental disturbances and too much noise exist.

2.2 Edge Detection Methods

In edge detection methods, Sobel operator and the canny edge detection algorithm in [11] directly uses the pixel gradient value to determine the edge pixels, which is simple and fast, but the calculation direction is too single to obtain high detection accuracy. Furthermore, the Berkeley Segmentation Benchmark [13] was used in [12]. Their work show that even if low-level features such as color, luminance and gradient can be learned simultaneously, it is still difficult to achieve robust detection for particular scenes.

With the development of convolutional neural networks [14] (CNN), DeepEdge [15] used a top-down structure with target-level features for contour prediction, successfully demonstrating that convolutional neural networks can be applied to low-level vision tasks. Further, S. Xie et al. proposed Holistically-Nested Edge Detection (HED) [16], which significantly improves the effectiveness and speed of edge detection by converting pixel-by-pixel edge classification to image-to-image edge prediction using Fully convolutional networks for semantic segmentation (FCN) [17]. However, due to the low resolution of the high-level convolutional features with strong semantic information, the overall resolution of the predicted edges is reduced. To better utilize the information of the convolutional features in each layer, Y. Liu et al. proposed Richer Convolutional Features for Edge Detection (RCF) [18], which further fuses the convolutional features of each network layer to obtain richer semantic information and improve the edge detection, but the overall resolution of the predicted edges is still not high enough due to the poor quality of the hole database acquired by the sampled conventional cameras.

These methods have deficiencies such as too low resolution, serious interference by texture and edge breakage, and incomplete detection of edges, etc. We propose to make improvements in anti-texture interference to further improve the model detection accuracy.

Table 1. Percentage of each sample in the database.

Sample name	Sample size	Proportion
BaiFuDiao	45	14.8%
BeiMeiHuTao	40	13.3%
BeiOuFengMu	24	7.9%
kingblue	45	14.8%
LiuJinYingTao	45	14.8%
MiLeYingTao	12	3.9%
MoKaHuTao	45	14.8%
NuoSiHuTao	12	3.9%
SuXiangTong	12	3.9%
TuoSiKaNa	24	7.9%
Summation	304	100%

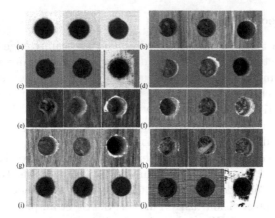

Fig. 1. Example diagram of various classes of samples. Their types in (a)–(j) are BaiFuDiao, BeiMeiHuTao, BeiOuFengMu, kingblue, LiuJinYingTao, MiLeYingTao, MoKaHuTao, NuoSiHuTao, SuXiangTong, TuoSiKaNa.

3   HoleEdge Database

This section mainly introduces the composition of the HoleEdge database and the corresponding preprocessing process.

3.1   Image Collection

A decorative sheet manufacturing company usually own several production lines and produce various kinds of decorative sheets with different colors and textures. It is realistic to add some cameras on production lines to obtain images for hole detection. The industrial digital camera LA-CM-08K-08A-00-R was used for collection of hole images. A total of 304 images of panels from 10 categories were collected according to different patterns and textures. Some samples are shown in Fig. 1 and the percentage of each category is shown in Table 1.

3.2   Database Annotation

The results of four different volunteers are averaged to obtain the final center coordinates and radius for label making. The label was drawing by single pixel on an all-black image with the same resolution as hole images. (binary map: 1 for edges, 0 for non-edges).

4   Proposed Methods

4.1   Network Architecture

Motivated by RCF, we propose a new fusion strategy and construct a Multilayer Features with Texture Suppression (MFTS) network, which is combined texture suppression and a convolutional feature extraction network that can effectively

suppress texture information with more prominent edge details. The whole network consists of input and output layers, five convolutional blocks (stages) and
three fusion modules as shown in Fig. 2. The structures of stage1 stage4 and
stage5 are shown in Fig. 3. Compared with the RCF, our network have differences as following:

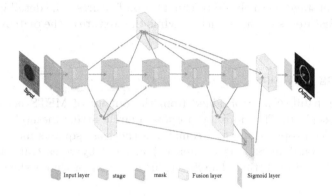

Fig. 2. The structure of MFTS network.

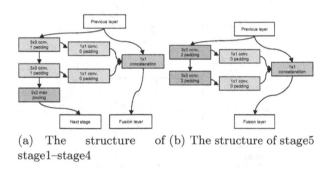

(a) The   structure   of (b) The structure of stage5
stage1–stage4

Fig. 3. The structures of stages

Reduce Redundancy. Remove the convolutional layers conv3-3, conv4-3, and
conv5-3 from the stage3, stage4, and stage5 parts of the RCF network. Since our
target-identifying hole edges is relatively clear, it does not require much deeper
network to complete the basic task of extracting round hole edge features, so
removing unnecessary convolutional layers can reduce the network redundancy
while alleviating the problem of low resolution of deep feature maps and excessive loss of location information brought by deeper networks, and improve the
resolution of subsequent fused features.

Texture Suppression. Get the fusion layers of the first three stages are taken as
the low-level fusion features, and the fusion layers of the last two stages are taken
as the high-level fusion features. The intersection of the two is taken as the mask
features using the pixel-by-pixel comparison method. The purpose of this design
is to fully combine the overall information of the edges in the high level features

and the detailed information of the edges in the low level features. The operation of taking intersection is effective to getting out of the interference of texture and obtain more detailed and pure edge features without losing the integrity.

Final Fusion. Superimpose the mask features with the original fusion features obtained from stage1-5 to obtain the final fusion features. The detail information of the edge features is further enriched, while the texture of the plate is effectively suppressed.

4.2   Fitting Methods

The edge probability map obtained from the output of MFTS network is too rough to recognized. Therefore, we propose a circle fitting method to refine the edge map. The proposed method combining the least squares method and the Ransac [25] (Random Sample Consensus) method by researching the related methods [24] on circle fitting. The flow chart of the algorithm is shown in Fig. 4.

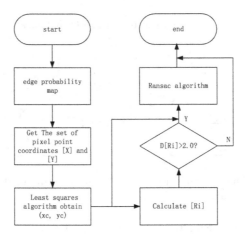

Fig. 4. The flow chart of the Fitting method. (x_c, y_c) is the possible circle center coordinates, and the set of all possible radius R_i is calculated using these coordinates and (x_i, y_i) in the pixel point coordinate set [X] and [Y]. $D[R_i]$ is the variance of R_i. In our experiments, we found that when $D[R_i]$ is greater than 2.0, it indicates that there may be bad data in R_i, which will greatly affect the accuracy of the circle fitting. Therefore we take 2.0 as our threshold value.

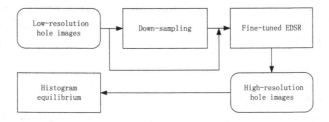

Fig. 5. Data preprocessing framework.

4.3   Data Pre-processing

To obtain higher resolution edge features and suppress texture features, we use a combination of super-resolution and histogram equalization to pre-process the images. The operation process is shown in Fig. 5.

Database Super-Resolution. We combine super-resolution techniques to reconstruct the hole images with the help of EDSR(Enhanced Deep Residual Networks for Single Image Super-Resolution) for improving their quality and thus enhance the detail information of edges.

(1) The hole images were down-sampled by bicubic (bi-triple interpolation). Their Scales was cut down by a factor of 2, 3 and 4 respectively to obtain low-resolution images.
(2) The original hole images were used as high-resolution data, and the data obtained from (1) is used as low-resolution data. They are fed into the EDSR (Enhanced Deep Residual Networks for Single Image Super-Resolution) network for training, and the model parameters are fine-tuned for adapting to the hole images.
(3) Super-resolution reconstruction of the original hole images using the trained EDSR model. The resolution of the reconstructed images is increased by a factor of 4, resulting in a clearer edge and higher quality hole dataset. However, the texture features of the plates are also enhanced, so histogram equalization for the texture features is required subsequently. Examples of some samples have reconstructed are shown in Fig. 6.

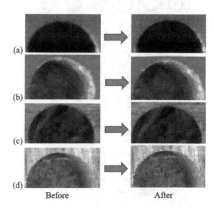

Fig. 6. Example of EDSR super-resolution database. Group (a) super-resolution from 84 * 84 to 336 * 336. Group (b) super-resolution from 136 * 136 to 544 * 544. Group (c) super-resolution from 170 * 170 to 680 * 680. Group (d) super-resolution from 256 * 256 to 1024 * 1024.

Histogram Equalization. The reconstructed hole database is enhanced in edge details, but also amplifies the effect of texture features on edge feature extraction. Therefore, we want to blur out the texture features as much as possible while preserving the edge features to the maximum extent. Inspired by [21], we use the adaptive histogram equalization to suppress the texture features of hole images.

5   Experiments

5.1   Model Training

Parameter Configuration. Due to the limited number of samples, we used migration learning in the training of MFTS. We use the VGG16 [23] model, which performs well on the publicly available dataset ImageNet [22], as a pre-training model to initialize the corresponding parameters in each convolutional layer. The small-batch stochastic gradient descent (StochasticGradientDescent, SGD) is used uniformly throughout the training process, and 10 images are randomly sampled for small batches in each iteration. For the other SGD hyperparameters, the global learning rate is set to 1e-8, and the learning rate is reduced to 0.1 after every 10k iterations. The learning momentum is 0.9, and the weight decay is 0.0002.

Data Enhancement. The reconstructed hole images are randomly flipped horizontally, flipped vertically and cropped with a crop factor of 0.8 (i.e., the size of the cropped image is 0.8 times the initial image) to expand the hole database by 5 times.

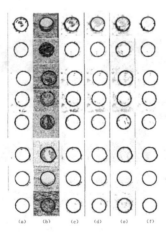

(a)   (b)   (c)   (d)   (e)   (f)

Fig. 7. The visualization of MFTS. (a)∼(f)shows the features map of The last stage in the network, the fusion layer of the first 3 stages - low-level fusion features, the fusion layer of the last two stages - high-level fusion features, the intersection of high and low-level fusion features - mask features, the direct fusion of the original fusion features of stages 1∼5, and the final fusion features obtained by superimposing mask and original fusion layers in turn.

Visualization. To more intuitively verify the effectiveness of our proposed fusion module for suppressing texture for complex textures on panel surfaces, we randomly selected samples from the training set for visualization. Visualize some key layer output feature maps, as shown in Fig. 7. It indicated that compared with RCF, our methods can effectively suppress the texture of the plate while strengthening the edge information.

5.2 Model Validation

In the model accuracy validation, the model with stable convergence when epoch is 39 is selected for hole edge extraction. We use two different accuracy evaluation methods to validate the model:

(1) The widely used edge detection accuracy evaluation method proposed by [2] in computer image processing, hereafter referred to as the threshold method.
(2) Our own constructed circle-fitting method, hereafter referred to as the fitting method.

Thresholding Method. There are two common judgment modes: dataset-scale optimal ODS and image-scale optimal OIS. It is also necessary to set matching thresholds, which are used as the basis for classifying edge pixels. This is done by calculating the pixel distance between each edge pixel in the round hole label and the corresponding position in the edge probability map. Then the edge pixel is correctly predicted if it is within the matching threshold distance, and incorrectly predicted if it is beyond the threshold. Further, the accuracy P and recall R are calculated based on the statistics of the edge pixels.

Fitting Method. The fitting method first needs to extract a set of pixel points for edge probability map to obtain a single-pixel edge map. The center coordinates and radius of the fitted circle are compared with label to calculate its mean square error value. Finally, the threshold range of the mean square error is set according to the actual situation, so that the round holes below the threshold range as correctly recognized. At last, the percentage of correctly identified round holes in the overall sample is used as the model performance evaluation criterion.

Table 2. The values of F-measure under different methods.

Method	ODS	OIS	AP
HED	0.505	0.505	0.506
RCF	0.687	0.737	0.412
MFTS	**0.807**	**0.808**	**0.856**

5.3   Model Evaluation

Thresholding Method. To cross-sectionally evaluate the effectiveness of our network model for hole detection on plate surfaces with complex textures, we use an accuracy assessment method consistent with the more advanced HED and RCF networks in related studies. And evaluate the performance of the three on our HoleEdge, as shown in Table 2. The experimental results further validate the excellent performance of the MFTS network for round hole detection on plate surfaces with complex textures.

The F-measure [26] is defined by follows:

$$F = PR/(\alpha * R + (1 - \alpha) * P) \tag{1}$$

We set to α as 0.5 in our experiments, which is commonly referred to as the F1-score. It has a maximum value of 1 and a minimum value of 0. The higher the value, the better the model. As can be seen from Table 2, the F1-score of MFTS on the round hole dataset is about 30% points higher than the HED and 12% points higher than the RCF, and the average accuracy is also nearly doubled, which greatly improves the efficiency and accuracy of round hole recognition.

Fitting Method. It is experimentally verified that the fitted circle basically coincides with the real hole edge when $MSE <= 2.0$, which can achieve the purpose of accurate identification of round holes. Under this criterion, the accuracy rate of round hole recognition can reach 96%. Some of the final detection results are shown in Fig. 8.

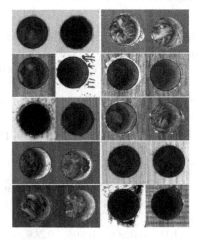

Fig. 8. Some of the final detection results

6   Conclusion

We presented a novel MFTS architecture for hole detection with complex textures on the surface of the plate. The special fusion structure that focus on the texture suppression was used to obtain enhanced edge features. The intersection of the shallow features and the depth features which rendered from multilevel are fused with original fusion features and then fed to the Sigmoid layer. The MFTS structure design is inspired by the double cascade structure of deep learning. And our method can be very effective in suppressing the surface texture information of plates and thus obtain high quality round hole edges, which makes it promising to be applied to other computer vision tasks. Application of the proposed network architecture to other domains (e.g. salient object detection and semantic segmentation) is also well worth exploring. And we construct a round hole edge database called "HoleEdge" for the validation of our model effectiveness. The database covers dozens of panel samples with a total of 304 original sample images. We hope that the scale, accuracy, diversity and hierarchical structure of HoleEdge can offer unparalleled opportunities to researchers in the computer vision community and beyond.

Acknowledgments. The work was supported in part by the State's Key Project of Research and Development Plan under Grants (2019YFE0196400), in part by the Guangdong R&D Project in Key Areas under Grant (2019B010156004), in part by the Guangdong Provincial Special Fund For Modern Agriculture Industry Technology Innovation Teams under Grant (2021KJ122), and in part by XG Intelligent Co. Ltd.

References

1. Aldrich, J.: Doing least squares: perspectives from Gauss and Yule. Int. Stat. Rev. **66**(1), 61–81 (1998)
2. Ballard, D.H.: Generalizing the Hough transform to detect arbitrary shapes. Pattern Recogn. **13**(2), 111–122 (1981)
3. Liu, D., Wang, Y., Tang, Z., et al.: A robust circle detection algorithm based on top-down least-square fitting analysis. Comput. Electr. Eng. **40**(4), 1415–1428 (2014)
4. Kanatani, K., et al.: Hyper least squares fitting of circles and ellipses. Comput. Stat. Data Anal. **55**(6), 2197–2208 (2011)
5. Ma, Z., Ho, K.C., Yang, L.: Solutions and comparison of maximum likelihood and full-least-squares estimations for circle fitting. In: 2009 IEEE International Conference on Acoustics, Speech and Signal Processing, pp. 3257–3260 (2009)
6. Shaked, D., Yaron, O., Kiryati, N.: Deriving stopping rules for the probabilistic Hough transform by sequential analysis. Comput. Vis. Image Underst. **63**(3), 512–526 (1996)
7. Xu, L., Oja, E., Kultanen, P.: A new curve detection method: Randomized Hough transform (RHT). Pattern Recogn. Lett. **5**(11), 331–338 (1990)
8. Cicconet, M., Geiger, D., Werman, M.: Complex-valued Hough transforms for circles. In: 2015 IEEE International Conference on Image Processing (ICIP), pp. 2801–2804 (2015)

9. Manzanera, A., Nguyen, T.P., Xu, X.: Line and circle detection using dense one-to-one Hough transforms on greyscale images. EURASIP J. Image Video Process. **2016**(1), 1–18 (2016). https://doi.org/10.1186/s13640-016-0149-y

10. Chiu, S.H., Liaw, J.J., Lin, K.H.: A fast randomized Hough transform for circle/circular arc recognition. Int. J. Pattern Recogn. Artif. Intell. **24**(3), 457–474 (2010)

11. Canny, J.: A computational approach to edge detection. IEEE Trans. Pattern Anal. Mach. Intell. **8**(6), 679–698 (1986)

12. Martin, D.R., Fowlkes, C.C., Malik, J.: Learning to detect natural image boundaries using local brightness, color, and texture cues. IEEE Trans. Pattern Anal. Mach. Intell. **26**(5), 530–549 (2004)

13. Berkeley Segmentation and Boundary Detection Benchmark and Dataset. http://www.cs.berkeley.edu/projects/vision/grouping/segbench

14. LeCun, Y., Boser, B. E., Denker, J. S., et al.: Handwritten digit recognition with a back-propagation network. In: NIPS, pp. 396–404 (1989)

15. Bertasius, G., Shi, J., Torresani, L.: DeepEdge: a multi-scale bifurcated deep network for top-down contour detection. In: CVPR, Boston, MA, USA, pp. 4380–4389 (2015)

16. Xie, S., Tu, Z.: Holistically-nested edge detection. In: IEEE International Conference on Computer Vision (ICCV), Santiago, pp. 1395–1403 (2015)

17. Long, J., Shelhamer, E., Darrell, T.: Fully convolutional networks for semantic segmentation. In: CVPR, Boston, MA, pp. 3431–3440 (2015)

18. Liu, Y., Cheng, M., Hu, X., et al.: Richer convolutional features for edge detection. In: CVPR, Honolulu, HI, pp. 5872–5881 (2017)

19. Lim, B., Son, S., Kim, H., et al.: Enhanced deep residual networks for single image super-resolution. In: IEEE Conference on Computer Vision and Pattern Recognition Workshops (CVPRW), Honolulu, HI, USA, pp. 1132–1140 (2017)

20. He, J., Zhang, S., Yang, M., et al.: BDCN: bi-directional cascade network for perceptual edge detection. In: IEEE/CVF Conference on Computer Vision and Pattern Recognition (CVPR), 2019 (2020)

21. Soman, P.: Low contrast satellite image restoration based on adaptive histogram equalization and discrete wavelet transform. In: International Conference on Communication and Signal Processing (ICCSP), Melmaruvathur, India, pp. 0402–0406 (2016)

22. Deng, J., Dong, W., Socher, R., et al.: ImageNet: a large-scale hierarchical image database. In: IEEE Conference on Computer Vision and Pattern Recognition, Miami, FL, USA, pp. 248–255 (2009)

23. Simonyan, K., Zisserman, A.: Very deep convolutional networks for large-scale image recognition. Computer Science (2014)

24. Umbach, D., Jones, K.N.: A few methods for fitting circles to data. IEEE Trans. Instrum. Measure. **52**(6), 1881–1885 (2003)

25. Fischler, M.A., Bolles, R.C.: Random sample consensus: a paradigm for model fitting with applications to image analysis and automated cartography. Commun. ACM **24**(6), 381–395 (1981)

26. Van Rijsbergen, C.J.: Information retrieval. Department of Computer Science, University of Glasgow (1979)

Multi-scale Attention-Based Feature Pyramid Networks for Object Detection

Xiaodong Zhao[1,2], Junliang Chen[1,2], Minmin Liu[1,2], Kai Ye[1,2],
and Linlin Shen[1,2(✉)]

[1] Computer Vision Institute, School of Computer Science and Software Engineering,
Shenzhen University, Shenzhen, China
{zhaoxiaodong2020,chenjunliang2016,liuminmin2020,
yekai2020}@email.szu.edu.cn, llshen@szu.edu.cn
[2] Guangdong Key Laboratory of Intelligent Information Processing, Shenzhen
University, Shenzhen 518060, China

Abstract. Feature pyramid network (FPN) is widely used for multi-scale object detection. While lots of FPN based methods have been proposed to improve detection performance, there exists semantic difference between cross-scale features. Therefore, simple connections bring spatial or channel information loss, while excessive connections bring extra parameters and inference cost. Besides, the fusion of too many features may lead to the information decay and feature aliasing. To deal with the above problems, we propose the Multi-scale Attention-based Feature Pyramid Networks (MAFPN), to fully exploit spatial and channel information and generate a better feature representation for each level from multi-scale features. Taking scale, spatial and channel information into consideration at the same time, MAFPN can process multi-scale input more comprehensively than most conventional methods. The experimental results show that our MAFPN can improve the detection performance of both two-stage and one-stage detectors with an acceptable increase of inference cost.

Keywords: Object detection · Feature Pyramid Network

1 Introduction

Object detection is a fundamental task in computer vision. However, it is challenging to recognize and locate various objects with a wide range of scales in object detection. To address this issue, a simple but effective way is to utilize multi-level features. Features of higher levels have stronger semantic information with lower resolution, while the lower-level features with higher resolutions contains more accurate localization information. Therefore, higher-level features are more beneficial for large-object detection and lower-level features are more suitable for small-object detection. The pyramidal architectures, which represent an image with multi-scale feature layers, are widely used by most modern object detectors [14, 20, 22, 24, 26].

© Springer Nature Switzerland AG 2021
Y. Peng et al. (Eds.): ICIG 2021, LNCS 12888, pp. 405–417, 2021.
https://doi.org/10.1007/978-3-030-87355-4_34

Feature Pyramid Network (FPN) [13] is one of the representative pyramidal architectures in object detection. It takes multi-scale features from a backbone network as input and utilizes top-down and lateral connections to combine two adjacent layers from different levels in backbone. High-level features are upsampled and added to the low-level ones to generate new features. After aggregating features in a top-down pathway, the low-level features are semantically enhanced.

Although FPN is simple and effective for many detectors, it can be further improved. Path Aggregation Network (PANet) [16] creates a bottom-up pathway on the base of FPN. It strengthens the entire feature hierarchy with accurate localization information existing in low-level features. Different from PANet that integrates multi-level features by using lateral connections, Balanced Feature Pyramid (BFP) [18] uses the same deeply integrated balanced semantic features to enhance the multi-level features. Another way to generate multi-scale feature representations is NAS-FPN [4]. It designs the search space that covers all possible cross-scale connections with Neural Architecture Search (NAS) algorithm. Recent works [10,11] explore better connections or operations of aggregating multi-scale features to generate a pyramidal architecture.

However, there is a common problem among these methods, i.e., the imbalance of network complexity and detection performance. Simple connections and fusions such as PANet cannot fully exploit spatial and channel information, while excessive connections such as NAS-FPN bring extra parameters and inference cost. Besides, the fusion of too many features may cause information decay and feature aliasing.

To address above problems, we propose an architecture, named Multi-scale Attention-based Feature Pyramid Networks (MAFPN), to make full use of spatial and channel information and generate a better feature representation for each level from multi-scale features. MAFPN can improve the detection performance of both single-stage and two-stage detectors with only a reasonable increase of inference cost.

In this paper, we make the following contributions:

- We propose the Multi-scale Attention-based Feature Pyramid Networks (MAFPN), to generate the feature for each level by merging features from multiple scales.
- Integrated with MAFPN, FreeAnchor achieves state-of-the-art performance of 49.3% AP on COCO dataset.
- The experimental results show that our proposed framework can be widely applied to one-stage and two-stage object detectors to improve the detection performance.

2   Related Work

2.1   Object Detectors

Object detectors based on deep convolution network are generally divided into two categories: two-stage detectors and one-stage ones.

Two-Stage Detectors. R-CNN [6] adopts selective search algorithm to generate region of interest (RoI), and then extracts features with a convolutional neural network to refine these proposals. To improve the speed of training and inference, SPPNet [8] generates region features with spatial pyramid pooling, while RoI pooling is first used in Fast R-CNN [5]. Faster R-CNN [20] proposes a region proposal network (RPN) and develops an end-to-end trainable framework, which promotes the performance and efficiency of detectors significantly. To reduce spatial and channel information loss and deal with scale-invariance, feature pyramid network (FPN) [13] is used to make predictions at different pyramid levels according to the scales of region proposals. RoI Align [7] addresses the misalignment between the RoI and the features extracted in RoI pooling. Cai et al. proposes Cascade R-CNN [1], which is a multi-stage framework based on Faster R-CNN. Cascade R-CNN achieves higher detection performance.

One-Stage Detectors. Contrary to two-stage detectors, one-stage detectors usually generate prediction results of classification and regression directly with multi-scale input features. Single Shot Multi-Box Detector (SSD) [17] make predictions based on dense anchors on multi-scale features. RetinaNet [14] introduces the focal loss function to address the imbalance problem of easy and hard examples, which has better performance than Faster R-CNN [20] and comparable performance with most two-stage detectors. Anchor-free detectors [22,24] generate object recognition and location results by per-pixel prediction. To avoid object ambiguity, each pixel is only related to single object. Many methods have been proposed in both anchor-based and anchor-free detectors to deal with the problem of information loss and improve detection performance.

2.2   Multi-scale Feature Augmentation

Many researchers are exploring methods to make better use of the spatial and channel information in multi-scale features. We can divide these methods into two categories: methods fusing features from partial scales (partial connections for short) and methods fusing features from all scales (full connections for short).

Partial Connections. FPN [13] introduces lateral connection to merge features from adjacent scales in a top-down path. PANet [16] brings an additional bottom-up path on the basis of FPN to shorten the information path and enhance features of each level. NAS-FPN [4] designs a search space that covers all possible cross-scale connections to discover a better architecture for pyramidal representations with neural architecture search (NAS) algorithm. These methods can enhance original features using features from other scales, but only obtain limited information.

Full Connections. Another way to integrate multi-level features is to gather and fuse features from multiple levels, then scatter the fused features to each level. Kong et al. [11] gathers multi-level features and then use global attention for further refinement. After that, the local reconfiguration module is used to further capture local information and generate the feature for each level. Balanced Feature Pyramid (BFP) [18] gathers features to the middle level and element-wisely average them. Then a non-local module [23] is used to refine the integrated features. Finally the refined features are scatter to each level and element-wisely summed up with the original input features.

Based on the methods above, we focus on making full use of channel and spatial information of features from FPN [13] to reduce the information loss due to the decrease of channels and spatial resolutions, and further improve the features after feature integration.

3   Method

3.1   Overview

Figure 1 shows the overview of our Multi-scale Attention-based Feature Pyramid Networks. Features at level l from the vanilla FPN [13] are denoted as P_l. The number of total levels is denoted as L. To integrate features from different levels, we first resize the multi-scale features $\{P_2, P_3, P_4, P_5, P_6\}$ to an intermediate size. Then we concatenate all resized multi-scale features and pass them to the feature refinement block (FRB) to obtain a fused feature. The fused features are scattered to each level and enhanced through bottom-up feature augmentation. Finally, a shared residual block (ResBlock) is applied on the enhanced features to generate the final output at each level.

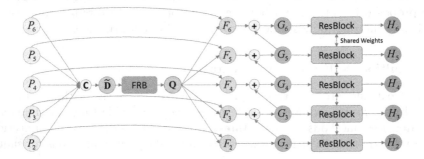

Fig. 1. Overview of the multi-scale attention-based feature pyramid network.

3.2   Feature Gathering

To aggregate features from all levels, we first resize the features $\{P_2, P_3, P_4, P_5, P_6\}$ to an intermediate size. Here we resize them to the size of P_4, with interpolation and max-pooling. The features after resizing are denoted as $\{\mathbf{D}_2, \ldots, \mathbf{D}_6\}$. After gathering the multi-level features to the same level, we first concatenate them as:

$$\tilde{\mathbf{D}} = [\mathbf{D}_2, \ldots, \mathbf{D}_6] \qquad (1)$$

where $\tilde{\mathbf{D}} \in \mathbb{R}^{LC \times H \times W}$, H and W denote the height and width of P_4, respectively.

3.3   Feature Refinement Block

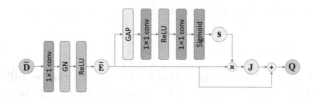

Fig. 2. The architecture of feature refinement block.

We notice that the simple fusion of all-scale features is easy to produce redundant information, so the gathered features $\tilde{\mathbf{D}}$ can be further refined to be more discriminative. In order to exploit global information to selectively augment informative features and suppress useless ones, we propose the feature refinement block (FRB), as shown in Fig. 2.

To reduce the number of channels and obtain initial features, we first apply a convolutional block, which includes a 3×3 convolutional layer followed by group normalization and a ReLU activation. The initial features $\tilde{\mathbf{E}} \in \mathbb{R}^{C \times H \times W}$ is calculated by:

$$\tilde{\mathbf{E}} = f_{conv\_block}(\tilde{\mathbf{D}}) \qquad (2)$$

where f_{conv_block} denotes the convolutional block.

To properly select features from different channels, we first generate the weight of each channel. The global information can be obtained by using a global average pooling (GAP) layer. The result after GAP is denoted as $\mathbf{x}$. The c'-th channel of $\mathbf{x}$ can be calculated by the following formula:

$$x_{c'} = \frac{1}{HW} \sum_{i=1}^{H} \sum_{j=1}^{W} \tilde{E}_{c',i,j} \qquad (3)$$

Then we generate the weight of each channel by using two 1×1 convolutional layers followed by the sigmoid function:

$$\mathbf{s} = \sigma(f_{conv}(\delta(f_{conv}(\mathbf{x})))) \qquad (4)$$

where f_{conv} denotes a 1×1 convolutional layer, δ is the ReLU function and σ is the sigmoid function.

After that, we rescale the features of each channel by channel-wise multiplication of the weights $\mathbf{s}$ and $\tilde{\mathbf{E}}$. The output after rescaling is denoted as $\mathbf{J}$. The c'-th channel of $\mathbf{J}$ is generated as:

$$\mathbf{J}_{c'} = s_{c'} \otimes \tilde{\mathbf{E}}_{c'} \tag{5}$$

where $\otimes$ denotes channel-wise multiplication.

To avoid losing the details of the initial features, the output features $\mathbf{Q}$ are generated through a element-wise summation of the initial features $\tilde{\mathbf{E}}$ and the rescaled features $\mathbf{J}$:

$$\mathbf{Q} = \tilde{\mathbf{E}} \oplus \mathbf{J} \tag{6}$$

where $\oplus$ denotes element-wise summation.

3.4 Feature Scattering

After feature refinement block, the cross-scale features can be fully fused. The fused features $\mathbf{Q}$ are then scattered to the corresponding level via resizing. However, the fused features loss the spatial details during feature gathering, due to the decrease of resolution.

To address this problem, at each level, the resized features is enhanced by summing up with the original input features. For the l-th level, the output features F_l can be computed as:

$$F_l = Resize(\mathbf{Q}) \oplus P_l \tag{7}$$

where $Resize$ denotes the resizing function.

3.5 Bottom-Up Feature Enhancement

We notice that features at high levels have strong response to the entire objects, while the ones at low levels are more likely to be activated by local texture and patterns. As the local details are very important to locate the objects, it is necessary to build a bottom-up path to propagate local information from low levels and enhance the features at high levels.

To achieve this goal, we proposal the bottom-up feature enhancement (BFE) module. The output features of BFE of all levels are denoted as $\{G_2, G_3, G_4, G_5, G_6\}$.

As shown in Fig. 3, bottom-up feature enhancement (BFE) is applied in a bottom-up path, $\{G_2, G_3, G_4, G_5, G_6\}$ are generated in sequence. From F_2 to F_6, the resolution is gradually reduced by a factor 2. G_2 is equal to F_2 without any processing.

At the i-th level, we first use max-pooling with stride 2 to down-sample G_{i-1}. G_i is generated by element-wisely summing up F_i with the down-sampled features from the lower level. The features of next level G_{i+1} is generated in the same way. The iterative process terminates when G_i approaches F_6. Generally, the features of the i-th level G_i can be calculated by the following function:

Fig. 3. The architecture of bottom-up feature enhancement.

Fig. 4. The architecture of residual block.

$$G_i = \begin{cases} F_i & i = 2 \\ DownSample(G_{i-1}) + F_i & i > 2 \end{cases} \tag{8}$$

where $i \in \{2, 3, 4, 5, 6\}$.

3.6 Residual Block

We finally generate the output features $\mathbf{H}_i$ of the i-th level by passing $\mathbf{G}$ to a shared residual block (ResBlock), as shown in Fig. 4. It consists of a 3×3 convolutional layer, a 1×1 convolutional layer and 3×3 convolutional layer in order. Each convolutional layer is followed by group normalization and ReLU activation. The final output features $\mathbf{H}_i$ of the i-th level is generated as:

$$\mathbf{H}_i = ResBlock(\mathbf{G}_i) \tag{9}$$

where $i \in \{2, 3, 4, 5, 6\}$.

4 Experiment

4.1 Dataset and Evaluation Metrics

Our experiments are conducted on COCO [15] dataset. We train our models with the data in train-2017 split containing around 115k images, and evaluate the performance of ablation studies on val-2017 split with about 5k images. Main results are reported on the test-dev split (20k images without available public annotations). We report all the results in the standard COCO-style average precision (AP).

4.2 Experimental Settings

For fair comparisons, we conduct our experiments on MMDetection [2] platform in PyTorch [19] framework. If not specified, all the settings are the default settings in MMDetection.

Training Settings. Unless specified, ResNet-50 [9] is used as our default backbone network, and Faster R-CNN [20] with FPN as our default object detector.

Table 1. Ablation studies on component effectiveness on COCO val-2017. "FRB", "BFE" and "ResBlock" denote feature refinement block, bottom-up feature enhancement and residual block respectively.

FRB	BFE	ResBlock	AP	AP_{50}	AP_{75}	AP_S	AP_M	AP_L
			36.0	56.4	38.8	18.5	39.8	50.3
✓			36.3	56.9	39.0	18.7	40.0	50.3
✓	✓		36.8	57.6	39.6	18.7	40.4	51.2
✓	✓	✓	**37.7**	**58.4**	**40.6**	**20.0**	**41.1**	**51.9**

Table 2. Ablation studies on stacking MAFPN on COCO val-2017. "×n" denotes the repeat times of MAFPN.

	AP	AP_{50}	AP_{75}
Baseline	35.6	55.8	38.3
MAFPN			
×1	37.7 [+2.1]	58.4	40.6
×2	38.4 [+2.8]	58.7	41.3
×3	38.3 [+2.7]	58.1	41.2
×4	38.5 [+2.9]	58.6	41.7

Table 3. The effectiveness of different gathering levels on COCO val-2017.

Gathering level	AP	AP_{50}	AP_{75}
P6	38.0	58.3	40.8
P4	38.4	58.7	41.3
P2	38.5	58.5	41.6

The backbone networks are initialized with the weight of the models pretrained on ImageNet [3]. Specifically, our network is trained with stochastic gradient descent (SGD) optimizer for 12 epochs with an initial learning rate of 0.02 and a mini-batch of 16 images. The learning rate is reduced by a factor of 10 after epoch 8 and 11, respectively. Due to memory limitation, the resolution of the input images is set to 640 × 640 and the batch size (16 by default) will be adjusted with a linearly scaled learning rate. Momentum and weight decay are set to 0.9 and $1e^{-4}$, respectively.

Inference Settings. The inference settings are as follows if not specified. We first select the top 1000 confidence predictions from each prediction layer and use a confidence threshold of 0.05 to filter out the predictions with low confidence for each class. Then, we apply non-maximum suppression (NMS) to the filtered predictions for each class separately with a threshold of 0.5. Finally, we adopt the predictions with top 100 confidences for each image as the final results.

4.3   Ablation Studies

The Effectiveness of Each Component. We analyze whether each component of our model is effective for improvement of detection performance. The results are listed in Table 1. We gradually add feature refinement block (FRB), bottom-up feature enhancement (BFE) and residual block (ResBlock)

Table 4. Comparisons with other pyramidal architectures on COCO val-2017. The number in "[]" denotes the relative improvement over the baseline.

	AP	AP_{50}	AP_{75}	AP_S	AP_M	AP_L	Params(M)	FLOPs(G)
FPN (baseline)	35.6	55.8	38.3	18.3	39.1	48.7	41.53	91.41
BFP	36.7	57.6	39.1	19.4	40.2	50.9	41.79	91.83
PANET	35.9	56.1	38.7	18.1	39.5	50.3	45.07	101.32
BiFPN	36.7	55.7	39.6	19.6	39.8	49.7	62.93	198.43
NAS-FPN	38.1	56.7	40.8	19.6	41.9	52.3	**68.17**	**265.37**
MAFPN(Ours)	**38.4 [+2.8]**	**58.7**	**41.3**	**20.5**	**41.8**	**53.1**	50.19	185.87

Table 5. Application in one-stage and two-stage detectors on COCO val-2017. The number in [] is the relative improvement over the original detector.

	MAFPN	AP	AP_{50}	AP_{75}	AP_S	AP_M	AP_L
One-stage							
RetinaNet		34.3	52.9	36.4	17.1	38.1	48.2
RetinaNet	✓	**36.3 [+2.0]**	**55.4**	**38.5**	**19.1**	**40.4**	**50.5**
Free Anchor		36.3	54.6	38.5	18.2	39.1	50.6
Free Anchor	✓	**38.7 [+2.4]**	**57.6**	**41.1**	**19.8**	**42.0**	**54.2**
RepPoints		35.9	56.1	38.4	17.6	40.4	49.6
RepPoints	✓	**37.5 [+1.6]**	**57.4**	**40.3**	**18.9**	**42.2**	**52.3**
two-stage							
Mask R-CNN		36.4	56.4	39.5	18.3	40.1	50.1
Mask R-CNN	✓	**39.2 [+2.8]**	**59.0**	**42.7**	**20.4**	**42.9**	**54.6**
Cascade R-CNN		38.3	56.1	41.5	19.4	41.6	53.8
Cascade R-CNN	✓	**40.6 [+2.3]**	**58.7**	**43.7**	**21.2**	**44.2**	**56.5**

on ResNet-50 FPN Faster R-CNN baseline. Feature refinement block improves the box AP from 36.0% to 36.3%. When combined with FRB and BFE, the AP is improved from 36.3% to 36.8%. When all the modules are used, the AP is further improved to 37.7%. To sum up, our ablation studies show that FRB, BFE and ResBlock can effectively boost the detection performance.

The Effectiveness of Stacking MAFPN. In this section, we analyze the effectiveness of stacking MAFPN architectures. As shown in Table 2, stacking more MAFPN bring better detection performance. However, stacking too many MAFPN architectures only increases a little in AP, but brings a large number of parameters. Therefore, stacking MAFPN for 2 times in the detector can obtain a better performance with acceptable inference cost. Unless specified, the stacking number of MAFPN is 2 in the following experiments.

The Effectiveness of Different Gathering Levels. In this section, we analyze the effectiveness of different gathering levels of MAFPN. As shown in

Table 3, the performances under all metrics increase when the gathering level decreases (from P6 to P2). The results show that the level with the largest scale (P2) can keep the most information with the least loss. However, it brings a large increase of inference cost if we gather multi-scale features to the level with the largest resolution. Taking into all factors into consideration, we finally choose P4 as the gathering level.

4.4   Comparisons with Other Pyramid Architectures

In this section, we compare the performance of our MAFPN with other closely related FPNs, such as FPN [13], BFP [18] and PANet [16]. We use ResNet-50 FPN Faster R-CNN as the baseline. As shown in Table 4, BFP [18], PANet [16], BiFPN [21] and NAS-FPN [4] get 1.1% , 0.3%, 1.1% and 2.5% improvement in AP respectively. Our MAFPN achieves 2.8% improvements in AP, with fewer parameters and FLOPs than NAS-FPN.

Table 6. Comparisons with state-of-the-art methods on COCO *test-dev* under single-model and single-scale settings.

Method	Backbone	AP	AP_{50}	AP_{75}	AP_S	AP_M	AP_L
Two-stage methods							
Faster R-CNN w/ FPN [13]	ResNet-101	36.2	59.1	39.0	18.2	39.0	48.2
Mask R-CNN [7]	ResNet-101	38.2	60.3	41.7	20.1	41.1	50.2
Mask R-CNN [7]	ResNeXt-101	39.8	62.3	43.4	22.1	43.2	51.2
Cascade R-CNN [1]	ResNet-101	42.8	62.1	46.3	23.7	45.5	55.2
One-stage methods							
RetinaNet [14]	ResNet-101	39.1	59.1	42.3	21.8	42.7	50.2
RetinaNet [14]	ResNeXt-101	40.8	61.1	44.1	24.1	44.2	51.2
FreeAnchor [26]	ResNet-101	43.1	62.2	46.4	24.5	46.1	54.8
FreeAnchor [26]	ResNeXt-101	44.9	64.3	48.5	26.8	48.3	55.9
FCOS [22]	ResNet-101	41.5	60.7	45.0	24.4	44.8	51.6
FCOS [22]	ResNeXt-101	44.7	64.1	48.4	27.6	47.5	55.6
ATSS [25]	ResNet-101	43.6	62.1	47.4	26.1	47.0	53.6
ATSS [25]	ResNet-101-DCN	46.3	64.7	50.4	27.7	49.8	58.4
ATSS [25]	ResNeXt-101-DCN	47.7	66.6	52.1	29.3	50.8	59.7
GFL [12]	ResNet-101	45.0	63.7	48.9	27.2	48.8	54.5
GFL [12]	ResNet-101-DCN	47.3	66.3	51.4	28.0	51.1	59.2
GFL [12]	ResNeXt-101-DCN	48.2	67.4	52.6	29.2	51.7	60.2
FreeAnchor w/ MAFPN	ResNeXt-101-DCN	**49.3**	**69.3**	**53.4**	**31.1**	**52.6**	**61.7**

4.5   Application in One-Stage and Two-Stage Detectors

In this section, we conduct experiments to evaluate the effectiveness of our model in one-stage detectors, including anchor-based or anchor-free detectors such as FreeAnchor [26] and RepPoints [24], and two-stage detectors such as Cascade R-CNN [1].

As shown in the first group of Table 5, when combined with our method, the one-stage detectors can get an obvious improvement in AP. MAFPN can provide improvement of 2.0%, 2.4% and 1.6% in AP for RetinaNet, Free Anchor and RepPoints, respectively.

Besides, MAFPN can also improve the detection performance of two-stage detectors. The second group in Table 5 shows the results of MAFPN applied in two-stage detectors. When combined with MAFPN, Mask R-CNN [7] and Cascade R-CNN [1] get improvement of 2.8% and 2.3% in AP, respectively.

4.6 Comparisons with State-of-the-Art Methods

In this section, we compare the performance of MAFPN with state-of-the-art methods under single-model single-scale settings on COCO test-dev split. We use FreeAnchor as our detector and adopt 2× learning schedule with scale-jitter for training. As shown in Table 6, the combination of our MAFPN and ResNeXt-101-DCN backbone achieves as high as 49.3%, which surpasses the AP of all other competitors.

5   Conclusion

In this paper, we propose the Multi-scale Attention-based Feature Pyramid Networks (MAFPN) for object detection, to address the problem of different semantics of the cross-scale features. Our method fuses multi-scale features with the feature refinement block (FRB) and reproduce the features for each level with bottom-up feature enhancement (BFE) and residual block (ResBlock). Our experiments show that MAFPN achieves state-of-the-art performance on COCO dataset. Besides, MAFPN can be widely applied in both one-stage and two-stage detectors to boost their performances.

Acknowledgments. This work was supported by National Natural Science Foundation of China under Grant 91959108

References

1. Cai, Z., Vasconcelos, N.: Cascade R-CNN: delving into high quality object detection. In: Proceedings of the IEEE Conference on Computer Vision and Pattern Recognition, pp. 6154–6162 (2018)
2. Chen, K., et al.: MMDetection: Open MMLab detection toolbox and benchmark. arXiv preprint arXiv:1906.07155 (2019)
3. Deng, J., Dong, W., Socher, R., Li, L.J., Li, K., Fei-Fei, L.: ImageNet: a large-scale hierarchical image database. In: 2009 IEEE Conference on Computer Vision and Pattern Recognition, pp. 248–255. IEEE (2009)
4. Ghiasi, G., Lin, T.Y., Le, Q.V.: NAS-FPN: learning scalable feature pyramid architecture for object detection. In: Proceedings of the IEEE/CVF Conference on Computer Vision and Pattern Recognition, pp. 7036–7045 (2019)
5. Girshick, R.: Fast R-CNN. In: Proceedings of the IEEE International Conference on Computer Vision, pp. 1440–1448 (2015

6. Girshick, R., Donahue, J., Darrell, T., Malik, J.: Rich feature hierarchies for accurate object detection and semantic segmentation. In: Proceedings of the IEEE Conference on Computer Vision and Pattern Recognition, pp. 580–587 (2014)
7. He, K., Gkioxari, G., Dollár, P., Girshick, R.: Mask R-CNN. In: Proceedings of the IEEE International Conference on Computer Vision, pp. 2961–2969 (2017)
8. He, K., Zhang, X., Ren, S., Sun, J.: Spatial pyramid pooling in deep convolutional networks for visual recognition. IEEE Trans. Pattern Anal. Mach. Intell. 37(9), 1904–1916 (2015)
9. He, K., Zhang, X., Ren, S., Sun, J.: Deep residual learning for image recognition. In: Proceedings of the IEEE Conference on Computer Vision and Pattern Recognition, pp. 770–778 (2016)
10. Kim, S.W., Kook, H.K., Sun, J.Y., Kang, M.C., Ko, S.J.: Parallel feature pyramid network for object detection. In: Proceedings of the European Conference on Computer Vision (ECCV), pp. 234–250 (2018)
11. Kong, T., Sun, F., Tan, C., Liu, H., Huang, W.: Deep feature pyramid reconfiguration for object detection. In: Proceedings of the European Conference on Computer Vision (ECCV), pp. 169–185 (2018)
12. Li, X., et al.: Generalized focal loss: learning qualified and distributed bounding boxes for dense object detection. In: Advances in Neural Information Processing Systems 33: Annual Conference on Neural Information Processing Systems 2020, NeurIPS 2020, 6–12 December 2020, virtual (2020)
13. Lin, T.Y., Dollár, P., Girshick, R., He, K., Hariharan, B., Belongie, S.: Feature pyramid networks for object detection. In: Proceedings of the IEEE Conference on Computer Vision and Pattern Recognition, pp. 2117–2125 (2017)
14. Lin, T.Y., Goyal, P., Girshick, R., He, K., Dollár, P.: Focal loss for dense object detection. In: Proceedings of the IEEE International Conference on Computer Vision, pp. 2980–2988 (2017)
15. Lin, T.-Y., et al.: Microsoft COCO: common objects in context. In: Fleet, D., Pajdla, T., Schiele, B., Tuytelaars, T. (eds.) ECCV 2014. LNCS, vol. 8693, pp. 740–755. Springer, Cham (2014). https://doi.org/10.1007/978-3-319-10602-1_48
16. Liu, S., Qi, L., Qin, H., Shi, J., Jia, J.: Path aggregation network for instance segmentation. In: Proceedings of the IEEE Conference on Computer Vision and Pattern Recognition, pp. 8759–8768 (2018)
17. Liu, W., et al.: SSD: single shot MultiBox detector. In: Leibe, B., Matas, J., Sebe, N., Welling, M. (eds.) ECCV 2016. LNCS, vol. 9905, pp. 21–37. Springer, Cham (2016). https://doi.org/10.1007/978-3-319-46448-0_2
18. Pang, J., Chen, K., Shi, J., Feng, H., Ouyang, W., Lin, D.: Libra R-CNN: towards balanced learning for object detection. In: Proceedings of the IEEE/CVF Conference on Computer Vision and Pattern Recognition, pp. 821–830 (2019)
19. Paszke, A., et al.: PyTorch: an imperative style, high-performance deep learning library. arXiv preprint arXiv:1912.01703 (2019)
20. Ren, S., He, K., Girshick, R., Sun, J.: Faster R-CNN: towards real-time object detection with region proposal networks. IEEE Trans. Pattern Anal. Mach. Intell. 39(6), 1137–1149 (2016)
21. Tan, M., Pang, R., Le, Q.V.: EfficientDET: scalable and efficient object detection. In: Proceedings of the IEEE/CVF Conference on Computer Vision and Pattern Recognition, pp. 10781–10790 (2020)
22. Tian, Z., Shen, C., Chen, H., He, T.: FCOS: fully convolutional one-stage object detection. In: Proceedings of the IEEE/CVF International Conference on Computer Vision, pp. 9627–9636 (2019)

23. Wang, X., Girshick, R., Gupta, A., He, K.: Non-local neural networks. In: Proceedings of the IEEE Conference on Computer Vision and Pattern Recognition, pp. 7794–7803 (2018)
24. Yang, Z., Liu, S., Hu, H., Wang, L., Lin, S.: RepPoints: point set representation for object detection. In: Proceedings of the IEEE/CVF International Conference on Computer Vision, pp. 9657–9666 (2019)
25. Zhang, S., Chi, C., Yao, Y., Lei, Z., Li, S.Z.: Bridging the gap between anchor-based and anchor-free detection via adaptive training sample selection. In: Proceedings of the IEEE/CVF Conference on Computer Vision and Pattern Recognition, pp. 9759–9768 (2020)
26. Zhang, X., Wan, F., Liu, C., Ji, R., Ye, Q.: FreeAnchor: learning to match anchors for visual object detection. In: Neural Information Processing Systems (2019)

A Similarity Constraint Divergent Activation Method for Weakly Supervised Object Detection in Remote Sensing Images

Mengmeng Zhu, Shouhong Wan$^{(\boxtimes)}$, Peiquan Jin, and Jian Xu

University of Science and Technology of China, No.96, JinZhai Road, Hefei
230026, People's Republic of China
{zhumeng,xxxujian}@mail.ustc.edu.cn, {wansh,jpq}@ustc.edu.cn

Abstract. With the development of remote sensing technology and object detection technology, many fully-supervised convolutional neural networks (CNN) methods based on object labeling information such as bounding box have achieved good results in remote sensing image object detection. However, due to the wide detection range of remote sensing images, diversity of objects, and the complexity of background, it is very difficult to manually label large-scale remote sensing images. Therefore, in recent years, more and more attention has been paid to the weakly supervision method using only image-level labels in object detection. Class activation mapping (CAM) method based on weakly supervision works well for object detection in natural scene images, but it has the problem when it is used in remote sensing images: a large number of small objects are lost. In this paper, we propose an object detection method for remote sensing image based on similarity constraint divergent activation (SCDA). The divergent activation (DA) module in SCDA improves the response intensity of the low response regions in the shallow layer feature map. According to the similarity between the objects, the similarity constraint module (SCM) is used to further improve the feature distribution and suppress background noise. By fusing DA and SCM, the missed rate of small objects can be reduced. Comprehensive experiments and comparisons with state-of-the-art methods on WSADD and DIOR data sets demonstrate the superiority of our proposed method.

Keywords: Object detection · Weakly supervised · Remote sensing image · Divergent activation · Similarity constraint

1 Introduction

With the rapid development of remote sensing technology, more and more high-quality remote sensing images with high spatial resolution and rich objects are emerging, which provide sufficient data and analysis conditions for the research of remote sensing image in various fields. And remote sensing image object detection has practical application scenarios and values in both civil and military fields.

© Springer Nature Switzerland AG 2021
Y. Peng et al. (Eds.): ICIG 2021, LNCS 12888, pp. 418–430, 2021.
https://doi.org/10.1007/978-3-030-87355-4_35

Here are many object detection algorithms proposed for remote sensing images, which are mainly divided into machine learning algorithm based on hand-crafted features and deep learning algorithm based on convolution neural network (CNN). Although hand-crafted features, such as Histogram of Oriented Gradient (HOG) [3], Scale-Invariant Feature Transform (SIFT) [5] and Bag of Words (BOW) [7] have achieved some results, their object detection effect is not good enough because they cannot express the high-level semantic information of the objects. CNN can not only describe the low-level features of the objects, but also express the high-level semantic information of the objects, so it has achieved good results in the field of natural scene target detection. Inspired by the deep learning technology in natural scenes, Cao et al. [1] And Yao et al. [13] introduced R-CNN and Faster-RCNN into remote sensing image object detection.

However, most of the existing deep learning methods that perform well require training data labeling the position information of objects. And if the location information of objects is labeled manually, the construction of large-scale image dataset is a huge workload and greatly increases the human cost of the dataset. As a result, Weakly Supervised Object Detection (WSOD) has received increasing attention. WSOD refers to the use of image-level labels in a given image to learn the location of objects, so it does not require expensive object bounding box labels for training.

It is a challenging task for object detection only using the image-level labels to learn a deep model. And some pioneer works have been proposed to achieve WSOD in natural scene. For example, a weakly supervised learning algorithm based on Class Activation Map (CAM) [16] is proposed to realize target detection. Next, adversarial erasing methods [2, 6, 10, 15] pursue learning full object extent by erasing the discriminative regions. The divergent activation method [9, 12, 14] designs multiple parallel branches or introduces attention modules to drive the network to locate the complete object region.

However, when these methods are applied to remote sensing images, there will be some problems with a large number of small objects, such as inaccurate positioning and object loss. Active Region Corrected (ARC) method [11] can effectively solve the problem of inaccurate positioning of objects by combining shallow feature positioning maps. And structure-preserving activation (SPA) method [8] extracts the structure preserving ability of features, so as to achieve accurate object location. But these methods cannot solve the problem of small object loss. This is because these missed objects may exist in the shallow layer of the network, but their responsiveness is insufficient, which results in the loss of features when they are transmitted backwards, and results in the loss of objects when they are last located.

Therefore, this paper introduces the divergent activation (DA) module and designed similarity constraint module (SCM) on the basis of ARC, and proposes an object detection method for remote sensing image based on similarity constraint divergent activation (SCDA). The idea is to enhance the response intensity of the low response region and the non-response region in the shallow layer network feature map by using DA module [12], and to enhance the intensity of similar features in the high response region and suppress background noise through SCM. It uses SCDA to improve the feature distribution in the shallow layer feature map and to solve the problem of large number of small object loss.

Our contributions are summarized as: 1) We propose a simple and effective SCDA method to improve the feature distribution in the shallow layer feature map to focus on more small object regions. 2) We experiment our method on two datasets, and compared with state-of-the-art methods based on CAM, precision and recall method have significant improvement.

2 Related Work

Weakly supervised object detection (WSOD) aims to detect the object with only image-level labels training data. Zhou et al. [16] proposed a weakly supervised learning algorithm based on Class Activation Map (CAM) to achieve object detection. They add a global average pooling layer and a full connection layer to the convolution neural network, and combine the weights of the final convolution layer features and the full connection layer to generate a CAM for the localization purpose. Wei et al. [10] proposed a method of adversarial erasing to locate a complete object. On this basis, Zhang et al. [15] propose an end-to-end network based on Adversarial Complementary Learning (ACoL), which uses two parallel classifiers with dynamic erasing and adversarial learning to discover complementary object regions more effectively. Xue et al. [12] proposed the Divergent Activation Network (DANet), which enlarges the difference of each dimension by increasing the dimension of the deep feature map, thereby increasing the response intensity of the unresponsive region and the weakly response region, and ultimately locating the complete object region. And structure-preserving activation (SPA) method [8] extracts the structure preserving ability of features by proposing a self-correlation map generating (SCG) module, so as to achieve accurate object location.

However, when these methods are applied to remote sensing images, there will be some problems with a large number of small objects, such as inaccurate positioning and object loss. We proposed an Active Region Corrected (ARC) [11] method, which can effectively solve the problem of inaccurate positioning of objects by combining shallow feature positioning maps, but it cannot solve the problem of object loss. This is because these missed objects may exist in the shallow layer of the network, but their responsiveness is insufficient, which results in the loss of features when they are transmitted backwards, and results in the loss of objects when they are last located.

3 Proposed Method

3.1 Framework

Because there are a large number of small objects in remote sensing images, it is not suitable to use a deeper network. We use ResNet34 as the basic network, and use a similarity constraint divergent activation (SCDA) framework on the basis of the ARC [11] network. As shown in Fig. 1, since the third-layer features of ResNet34 contain certain semantic information and also do not contain too much noise, the DA module and the similarity constraint module (SCM) are embedded in the third layer of ResNet34. First, through the DA module, the dimension of the network extracted shallow layer features is increased by 1×1 convolution. By activating the shallow layer feature map, the

DA module increases the response intensity of the low-response region, and activates the non-response region to increase the response intensity of the region, thereby increasing the number of response regions. Then, the output of the DA module is merged as the input of SCM. The SCM builds a similarity matrix to improve the response intensity of similar regions, suppress the response intensity of background noise regions, and improve feature distribution.

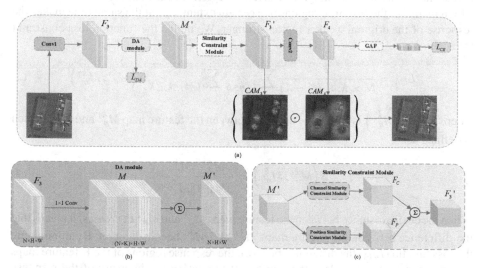

Fig. 1. The framework of the proposed SCDA approach. (a) We use ResNet34 as the basic network and use SCDA approach improve the feature distribution in the shallow feature map. (b) Illustration of the DA module. (c) Similarity constraint module completes feature fusion by summing the output of the channel similarity constraint module and position similarity constraint module.

In addition, we use divergent activation loss (L_{DA}) and classification loss (L_{CE}) to cooperate to drive the model to detect more objects in the training phase. The total loss of SCDA training is defined as:

$$L = L_{CE} + \lambda L_{DA} \tag{1}$$

where L_{CE} uses cross-entropy loss in two-class classification, and uses marge loss in multi-label classification. L_{DA} is the divergent activation loss in DA module, and we will introduce it in detail in next section. λ is a regularization factor to balance the two items.

3.2 Divergent Activation Module

The DA module increases the size of the shallow layer feature map to K times the original size, and expands the cosine distance between the corresponding K feature maps in each group to activate the regions and form more activation regions.

We denote the feature map output by the third layer network as $F_3 \in R^{N \times H \times W}$. As shown in Fig. 1, we use 1×1 convolution to increase the dimension of the feature map

F_3 from N × H × W to (N × K) × H × W. We denote the feature map obtained by 1 × 1 convolution as $M \in R^{(N \times K) \times H \times W}$. For clarity of description, we use M_n^k to represent each channel of the feature map M, where $k \in \{1, 2, \ldots, K\}$, $n \in \{1, 2, \ldots, N\}$.

In the initial stage, for each group of K feature maps M_n^k, they are equal, such as $M_n^1 = M_n^2 = \ldots = M_n^K$, where $n \in \{1, 2, \ldots, N\}$. In order to find more activation regions, we use the cosine distance between each feature map as a function loss constraint, so that during the network training, the activation regions in each feature map are different, which increases the response regions to a certain extent, and at the same time makes the response of the original weaker region stronger. We define the function loss constraint as:

$$L_{DA} = \frac{2}{N \times K \times (K-1)} \sum_{1 \le n \le N} \sum_{1 \le k_1 \le k_2 \le K} S\left(M_n^{k_1}, M_n^{k_2}\right) \qquad (2)$$

where $S\left(M_n^{k_1}, M_n^{k_2}\right)$ is the cosine distance between the feature map $M_n^{k_1}$ and $M_n^{k_2}$, which is defined as:

$$S\left(M_n^{k_1}, M_n^{k_2}\right) = \frac{M_n^{k_1} \cdot M_n^{k_2}}{\|M_n^{k_1}\| \|M_n^{k_2}\|} \qquad (3)$$

When the cosine distance between the feature maps $M_n^{k_1}$ and $M_n^{k_2}$ decreases, it means that the difference between the feature maps $M_n^{k_1}$ and $M_n^{k_2}$ becomes larger. By minimizing the loss function L_{DA}, the difference between the response regions of the K feature maps are enlarged, so as to achieve the purpose of increasing the intensity of the response region and increasing the number of response regions.

Finally, we sum each feature map M_n^k in the n-th group to obtain the fused feature map M_n' by sum module. The sum module is defined as:

$$M_n' = \frac{1}{K} \sum_{k=1}^K M_n^k \qquad (4)$$

where $n \in \{1, 2, \ldots, N\}$, M_n' corresponds to the n-th channel of the feature map F_3 output by the third layer network. The N feature maps M_n' are spliced to obtain the final output feature map $M' \in R^{N \times H \times W}$ of DA module.

3.3 Similarity Constraint Module

Through the DA module, more response regions are activated in the feature map output by the convolution neural network. However, when DA module is divergent activating, it mainly enlarges the cosine distance between the feature maps, without considering the feature of the object regions. Therefore, we use the similarity constraint module (SCM) to further modify the output of the DA module, suppress the response intensity of non-object regions, and improve the response intensity of object regions.

As shown in Fig. 1(c), the SCM is composed of the channel similarity constraint module (CSCM) and the position similarity constraint module (PSCM). The CSCM constructs a channel similarity matrix based on the feature map output by the DA module, and measures the feature similarity of regions on each channel by using the dependency relationship between channel mappings. The PSCM measures the similarity of features in different locations by building a location similarity matrix. Through two different similarity constraints, the background noise in image is further removed and the response intensity of the object regions is improved.

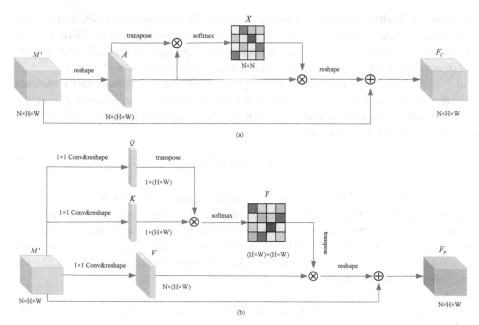

Fig. 2. Detail implementation of two different SCM. (a) CSCM aims to enhance features through the similarity between channels. (b) PSCM aims to enhance features through the similarity between positions.

Channel Similarity Constraint Module. We denote the feature map output by the DA module as $M' \in R^{N \times H \times W}$. The specific process of the channel similarity constraint module (CSCM) is shown in Fig. 2(a). First, we convert the dimension of feature map M to $N \times (H \times W)$, and denote it as matrix A. Then we use matrix A to calculate the similarity between each channel, and construct a channel similarity matrix X to measure the degree of correlation between different channels. The calculation formula of the channel similarity matrix X is as:

$$X = softmax\left(AA^{T}\right) \qquad (5)$$

where $X \in R^{N \times N}$. Through the channel similarity matrix X, we use the similarity between the feature map channels to update the feature map matrix A. Then multiply the result obtained by the scale parameter α, and convert its dimension to $N \times H \times W$. Finally, the result is added to the feature map M' to obtain the channel feature map F_C, which is output by the CSCM. We define the calculation formula of the channel feature map F_C as:

$$F_C = reshape(\alpha XA) + M'$$ (6)

where $F_C \in R^{N \times H \times W}$.

Position Similarity Constraint Module. The specific process of the position similarity constraint module (PSCM) is shown in Fig. 2(b). First, we use three different 1×1 convolutions to perform a convolution operation on the feature map M', and reshape the dimension of the results to obtain three different feature matrices $Q, K \in R^{1 \times (H \times W)}$ and $V \in R^{N \times (H \times W)}$. Then, we use matrix Q and K to calculate the similarity between different positions, and construct a position similarity matrix Y to measure the degree of association of features at different positions. The calculation formula of the position similarity matrix Y is defined as:

$$Y = softmax\left(Q^T K\right)$$ (7)

where $Y \in R^{(H \times W) \times (H \times W)}$. Through the position similarity matrix Y, we update the feature map matrix V by using the correlation degree of the features at different positions of the feature map. Then multiply the result obtained by the scale parameter number β, and convert its dimension to $N \times H \times W$. Finally, the result is added to the feature map M' to obtain the position feature map F_P, which is output by the PSCM. We define the calculation formula of the position feature map F_P as:

$$F_P = reshape\left(\beta VY^T\right) + M'$$ (8)

where $F_P \in R^{N \times H \times W}$.

4 Experiments

4.1 Data Sets and Experimental Settings

Datasets. In order to evaluate the effectiveness of the weakly supervised object detection algorithm based on similarity constraint divergent activation (SCDA), we conducted verification experiments on the data sets WSADD and DIOR respectively. WSADD (Weakly Supervised Airplane Detection Dataset, WSADD) is an object detection dataset independently constructed by our laboratory. The data set has 700 remote sensing images in total, including 400 images containing the aircraft as the positive samples and the other 300 images, which are the background images mainly composed of the airstrip and apron, as the negative samples. In the training phase, we use 600 remote sensing images of 300 aircraft and 300 background images as the training set. In the test phase, 100 aircraft remote sensing images are used as the test set, which contains 308 aircraft. DIOR dataset [4] is a public remote sensing image target detection dataset, which contains 20 categories and 23463 remote sensing images. In the experiment, because there are too few dam images in the DIOR dataset, we removed the dam category. Therefore, the Dior data set we used has only 19 categories and 23287 remote sensing images, including 11725 images in the training set and 11562 images in the test set. Since in the DIOR dataset, many large objects do not have the problem of the objects with a small proportion of the image or a large number. So, for large objects, such as expressway service area, we directly use deep positioning maps to locate these objects. While for small objects with problems, we use the proposed methods to locate such objects as airplane, baseball field, basketball court, chimney, ship, tennis court, vehicle, and so on.

Metrics. For WSADD dataset, there are only two categories, so we use precision rate and recall rate to evaluate the performance of the model. They are defined as:

$$Precision = \frac{TP}{TP + FP} \tag{9}$$

$$Recall = \frac{TP}{TP + FN} \tag{10}$$

where TP, FP, and FN represent the number of true positives, false positives, and false negatives respectively in the detection results where IoU > 0.5 is setting to evaluate the results as positive detection. If the recall rate is higher, it means that the correct object accounts for a larger proportion of all objects. And if the precision rate is higher, it means that the correct test results account for a larger proportion of all test results. For DIOR dataset, we choose mean average precision (*mAP*) as evaluation criteria where IoU > 0.3 is setting to evaluate the results as positive detection. The *mAP* is defined as:

$$AP = \sum\nolimits_{k=1}^{N} \max_{\tilde{k} \geq k} P\left(\tilde{k}\right) \times (r(k) - r(k-1)) \tag{11}$$

$$mAP = \frac{1}{C} \sum\nolimits_{i=1}^{C} AP_i \tag{12}$$

where N is the number of detection results, $P\left(\tilde{k}\right)$ is the precision rate of the top $\tilde{k}$ detection results, $r(k)$ is the recall rate of the top k detection results, and C is the number of categories of the dataset.

Experimental Environment. The experiments are conducted in Ubuntu 16.04 operation system. The CPU is Intel Core i7–7700. Memory is 32GB. The graphics card is GeForce GTX 1080 Ti. The program is coded by Python with the Pytorch deep learning framework.

4.2 Experimental Results and Comparisons

In order to verify the effectiveness of the method in this paper, it is compared with the four algorithms of CAM [16], DANet [12], ACoL [15] and SPA [8], which are outstanding in natural scenes, and with the ARC [11] algorithm which is suitable for remote sensing scenes.

The detection results of the data set WSADD are shown in Table 1. It can be seen from the table that the CAM, DANet, ACoL, and SPA methods that achieve good results in natural scenes can hardly complete the positioning effect. This shows that the method applicable in natural scenes is not suitable for the remote sensing scenes with a large number of small objects. The ARC method has a significant improvement in precision and recall compared with the method in natural scenes. However, it still cannot solve the problem of the loss of a large number of objects with a small proportion of images in remote sensing images. Compared with the ARC method, our method increases the precision rate from 0.65 to 0.80 and the recall rate from 0.81 to 0.91 after adding the DA module and the similarity constraint module (SCM). This shows that our method effectively alleviates the problem of the loss of a large number of objects with a small proportion of images in remote sensing images.

Table 1. The detection precision and recall of representative methods on WSADD test set

Method	TP	FP	FN	Precision	Recall
CAM [16]	33	167	275	0.17	0.11
DANet [12]	23	160	285	0.13	0.07
ACol [15]	23	153	285	0.13	0.07
SPA [8]	119	206	189	0.39	0.38
ARC [11]	251	137	27	0.65	0.81
Ours	280	70	28	**0.80**	**0.91**

Table 2. Object classes in the DIOR data set

C1	C2	C3	C4	C5	C6	C7
Airplane	Airport	Baseball field	Basketball count	Bridge	Chimney	Dam
C8	C9	C10	C11	C12	C13	C14
Expressway service area	Expressway toll station	Golf field	Ground track field	Harbor	Overpass	Ship
C15	C16	C17	C18	C19	C20	
Stadium	Storage tank	Tennis court	Train Station	Vehicle	Wind mil	

The object categories of the DIOR data set are shown in Table 2. And the detection results of the DIOR data set are shown in Table 3. Because our method is proposed for a large number of small objects in remote sensing images, it can be seen from the table that compared with ACR, the SCDA method improves more in small object categories, such as airplanes and tennis courts, but it basically does not improve in large object categories. Overall, compared to ARC, SCDA has a 1.22% improvement in mAP. And compared to SPA, SCDA has a 1.15% improvement in mAP.

Table 3. Detection average precision (%) of representative methods on the proposed DIOR test set. The entries with the best APs for each object category are bold-faced. We only show 9 categories in which the results are quite different.

Method	C1	C3	C4	C8	C16	C17	C19	C20	mAP
CAM [16]	2.94	17.92	18.20	**26.44**	1.19	7.05	1.74	9.78	18.78
DANet [12]	1.33	13.56	17.95	25.84	0.56	5.85	1.11	3.08	17.37
ACol [15]	0.15	2.38	0.00	7.82	0.63	2.27	0.17	0.27	5.89
SPA [8]	10.68	**28.28**	18.13	25.11	**7.36**	13.05	5.15	11.42	20.93
ARC [11]	13.52	19.04	18.28	**26.44**	5.39	17.48	5.68	14.41	20.86
Ours	**18.03**	24.06	**23.46**	24.82	7.08	**25.56**	**6.45**	**18.77**	**22.08**

4.3 Analysis of Components

In this section, the contributions of the two key components in our proposed method including DA module and Similarity Constraint Module (SCM) are further evaluated. To this end, we conducted a series of experiments on the WSADD dataset to verify the effectiveness of the DA module and SCM, and to determine the hyper-parameters K and λ when using the DA module.

Table 4. Effect of DA module and SCM.

Method	TP	FP	FN	Precision	Recall
baseline	251	137	57	0.65	0.81
baseline + CSCM	239	130	69	0.65	0.78
baseline + PSCM	243	126	65	0.66	0.79
baseline + CSCM + PSCM	245	110	63	0.69	0.80
baseline + DA	**284**	183	**24**	0.61	**0.92**
baseline + CSCM + PSCM + DA	280	**70**	28	**0.80**	0.91

Similarity Constraint Module. In order to verify whether the shallow layer feature maps that have not passed the DA module can improve the response strength of similar targets through the similarity constraint module (SCM), we remove the DA module from the basic network and only verify the effect of the SCM. The experimental results on the data set WSADD are shown in Table 4. From Table 4, it can be seen that both the CSCM and the PSCM can improve the precision rate, but the effect is not obvious enough. This shows that in the shallow layer feature map, the features are scattered and sparse. Only paying attention to the similarity of position or channel features between feature maps cannot improve the response strength of similar features. After combining the two similarities, the precision rate has increased significantly, indicating that the combination of

Table 5. Effect of the hyper-parameters K and λ

Method	TP	FP	FN	Precision	Recall
Ours without DA	245	110	63	0.69	0.80
$K = 4, \lambda = 0.01$	260	86	48	0.75	0.84
$K = 4, \lambda = 0.05$	272	82	36	0.77	0.88
$K = 4, \lambda = 0.1$	**280**	**70**	**28**	**0.80**	**0.91**
$K = 4, \lambda = 0.5$	273	88	35	0.76	0.89
$K = 8, \lambda = 0.1$	271	94	37	0.74	0.88
$K = 16, \lambda = 0.1$	279	98	31	0.73	0.90

the two similarities can better improve the feature distribution and increase the response strength of similar features.

DA Module. In the DA module, we need to explore whether different K values will affect network performance. Similarly, in the network training segment, the loss function L_{DA} is constrained by the hyper-parameter λ. So, we need to analyze the impact of different λ on network performance. We design a comparative experiment on the WSADD data set to discuss the role of two hyper-parameters in the DA module. The experimental results are shown in Table 5. From Table 5, we can see that when the hyper-parameters K and λ are small, the DA module activation strength is weaker, and it cannot effectively activate more regions and improve the response strength of the region. When the value of K and λ is too large, such as $K = 16$ and $\lambda = 0.5$, the DA module has a strong activation intensity, but the activation regions contain more noise, which causes the false accuracy and recall rate to drop to zero. When the values of K and λ are moderate, such as $K = 4$, $\lambda = 0.1$, the DA module activation intensity is moderate at this time, and the precision and recall rates are improved. This shows that when the DA module activation intensity is moderate, it can effectively activate more regions and improve the response intensity of the region without increasing too much background noise.

Through Table 4, we can also see that it is difficult to improve the performance of the model using only the DA module or SCM. Using only the DA module can detect more objects, but it will also cause more error-detection. And just using the SCM can reduce error-detection, but it will also cause some objects to be undetected. Our proposed SCDA model uses both the DA module and the SCM to detect more targets without increasing the error detection rate.

5   Conclusion

In this article, we consider that there are a large number of small objects in remote sensing images. In order to better identify small objects in remote sensing images based on WSOD, we propose a similarity constraint divergent activation (SCDA) method to activate the response regions of small objects. SCDA uses the DA module to obtain more response regions in the shallow layer feature map, and then removes noise through the SCM, which can better detect the small objects in remote sensing images. Experiments on WSADD and DIOR have proved that this method can solve the problem of remote sensing image object loss to a certain extent when weakly supervised learning is transferred to remote sensing scenes.

References

1. Cao, Y., Niu, X., Dou, Y.: Region-based convolutional neural networks for object detection in very high resolution remote sensing images. In: 2016 12th International Conference on Natural Computation, Fuzzy Systems and Knowledge Discovery (ICNC-FSKD), pp. 548–554. IEEE (2016)
2. Choe, J., Shim, H.: Attention-based dropout layer for weakly supervised object localization. In: Proceedings of the IEEE/CVF Conference on Computer Vision and Pattern Recognition, pp. 2219–2228 (2019)
3. Dalal, N., Triggs, B.: Histograms of oriented gradients for human detection. In: 2005 IEEE Computer Society Conference on Computer Vision and Pattern Recognition (CVPR 2005), vol. 1, pp. 886–893. IEEE (2005)
4. Li, K., Wan, G., Cheng, G., Meng, L., Han, J.: Object detection in optical remote sensing images: a survey and a new benchmark. ISPRS J. Photogramm. Remote. Sens. **159**, 296–307 (2020)
5. Lindeberg, T.: Scale invariant feature transform. Scholarpedia **7**(5), 10491 (2012)
6. Mai, J., Yang, M., Luo, W.: Erasing integrated learning: a simple yet effective approach for weakly supervised object localization. In: Proceedings of the IEEE/CVF Conference on Computer Vision and Pattern Recognition, pp. 8766–8775 (2020)
7. Nowak, E., Jurie, F., Triggs, B.: Sampling strategies for bag-of-features image classification. In: European Conference on Computer Vision, pp. 490–503. Springer, Cham (2006). https://doi.org/10.1007/11744085_38
8. Pan, X., et al.: Unveiling the potential of structure-preserving for weakly supervised object localization. arXiv preprint arXiv:2103.04523 (2021)
9. Singh, K.K., Lee, Y.J.: Hide-and-seek: forcing a network to be meticulous for weakly-supervised object and action localization. In: 2017 IEEE international conference on computer vision (ICCV), pp. 3544–3553. IEEE (2017)
10. Wei, Y., Feng, J., Liang, X., Cheng, M.M., Zhao, Y., Yan, S.: Object region mining with adversarial erasing: a simple classification to semantic segmentation approach. In: Proceedings of the IEEE Conference on Computer Vision and Pattern Recognition, pp. 1568–1576 (2017)
11. Xu, J., Wan, S., Jin, P., Tian, Q.: An active region corrected method for weakly supervised aircraft detection in remote sensing images. In: Eleventh International Conference on Digital Image Processing (ICDIP 2019), vol. 11179, p. 111792H. International Society for Optics and Photonics (2019)
12. Xue, H., Liu, C., Wan, F., Jiao, J., Ji, X., Ye, Q.: Danet: divergent activation for weakly supervised object localization. In: Proceedings of the IEEE/CVF International Conference on Computer Vision, pp. 6589–6598 (2019)
13. Yao, Y., Jiang, Z., Zhang, H., Zhao, D., Cai, B.: Ship detection in optical remote sensing images based on deep convolutional neural networks. J. Appl. Remote Sens. **11**(4), 042611 (2017)
14. Yun, S., Han, D., Oh, S.J., Chun, S., Choe, J., Yoo, Y.: Cutmix: regularization strategy to train strong classifiers with localizable features. In: Proceedings of the IEEE/CVF International Conference on Computer Vision, pp. 6023–6032 (2019)

15. Zhang, X., Wei, Y., Feng, J., Yang, Y., Huang, T.S.: Adversarial complementary learning for weakly supervised object localization. In: Proceedings of the IEEE Conference on Computer Vision and Pattern Recognition, pp. 1325–1334 (2018)
16. Zhou, B., Khosla, A., Lapedriza, A., Oliva, A., Torralba, A.: Learning deep features for discriminative localization. In: Proceedings of the IEEE Conference on Computer Vision and Pattern Recognition, pp. 2921–2929 (2016)

GSCAM: Global Spatial Coordinate Attention Module for Fine-Grained Image Recognition

Haojie Guo, Zhe Guo[✉], and Zhaojun Pan

School of Electronics and Information, Northwestern Polytechnical University, Xi'an, People's Republic of China
guozhe@nwpu.edu.cn

Abstract. Fine-grained image recognition is more difficult than conventional image classification tasks. Previous advanced network models require a large number of complex structure design and preliminary training. In this paper, a novel attention mechanism: Global Spatial Coordinate Attention Module (GSCAM) is proposed. This structure inherits the advantages of widely used SE channel attention and CBAM spatial attention, uses two 1D features for spatial position coding, and parallels global attention convergence blocks to extract context features, which can obtain the spatial location information and global context feature information of the region of interest of the image, so as to accurately locate the distinguishable region in the image. We apply this module to the mainstream classification network (ResNet50, ResNeXt50) pre-trained by ImageNet. Under the condition that the original network increases a very small number of parameters and computational cost, the accuracy of fine-grained image recognition is close to the SOTA level in different benchmark datasets, and there is no need to design the network structure from scratch, which is simple and fast.

Keywords: Fine-grained image recognition · Attention mechanisms · Convolutional neural network

1 Introduction

Fine-grained image recognition (FGIR) is a challenging visual classification task, which aims to identify subcategories of targets in some specific scenes, such as different categories of flowers and birds. Compared with the common object classification tasks, due to its high similarity between subclasses and low difference between categories, FGIR is more difficult, as it shows the characteristics of small inter-class differences and large inner-class differences [1]. So far, among the existing fine-grained image recognition solutions, the most effective way is to extract fine-grained semantic features of the local distinguishable regions in the image, or firstly locate the objects in the image, and then classify them. In the past, these fine-grained image recognition methods use complex network structure, a large number of training skills and rely on the information of the object anchor frame in the image. As a result, these network models need to be trained from scratch, which costs large amount of GPU computation.

© Springer Nature Switzerland AG 2021
Y. Peng et al. (Eds.): ICIG 2021, LNCS 12888, pp. 431–442, 2021.
https://doi.org/10.1007/978-3-030-87355-4_36

The existing classification networks [2, 3] have achieved high Top-1 and Top-5 accuracy in conventional different scene datasets ImageNet. According to the pre-trained model of these networks on ImageNet, we can easily transfer to the classification tasks of other datasets. After Fine-tune training, the training time and computational consumption are greatly reduced, and a higher recognition rate can be obtained at the same time. However, this method is only suitable for classification tasks on the dataset which is similar to ImageNet, and the effect is not ideal for FGIR.

Attention mechanism has been widely used to improve the performance of modern deep neural networks. At present, the most popular attention mechanism is Squeeze-and-Excitation (SE) attention [4], which can achieve significant performance improvement by modeling features at the channel level. However, this method only focuses on channel information and ignores the importance of spatial location information. The Convolutional Block Attention Module (CBAM) [5] add spatial attention, but require manual design of complex operations such as pooling, MLP. In order to solve the above problems, this paper designs a novel Global Spatial Coordinate Attention Module (GSCAM) attention mechanism, which can capture the location information and global context feature of local divisible regions in fine-grained images. In the pre-trained network model on ImageNet, transfer learning is used to solve fine-grained image recognition tasks, and promising accuracy is achieved. At the same time, compared with other attention mechanisms, it reduces the computational consumption.

The main contributions of this paper are as follows:

1) We propose a GSCAM attention module, which can capture channel and location feature information in different scales, which is better and lighter than other attention mechanisms.
2) This GSCAM module can be easily inserted into the backbone network of the mainstream classification model, which improves the network performance without changing the network structure.
3) We apply the GSCAM attention module to the backbone network of mainstream classification models. After transfer learning, it reaches promising accuracy for FGIR, and has lower training cost than other FGIR models.

The remainder of the paper is organized as follows. We first introduce the origin and overall structure of GSCAM in Sect. 3. In Sect. 4, we have carried out a large number of experimental comparisons and analysis of the results of the proposed GSCAM. Finally, we conclude in Sect. 5.

2   Related Work

Fine-grained Image Recognition: FGIR's initial purpose is to use distinguishable region borders to identify under strong supervised conditions with additional annotations [6], and later improved to use only category labels for weak supervised condition recognition [7, 8]. In the recent development, the recognition of objects is mainly realized by designing an end-to-end network model. S3NS [9] obtains the attention of distinguishable regions of local objects by extracting the local response maximum of the image.

MA-CNN [7] implicitly selects the characteristics of distinguishable regions through channel loss. DCL [8] breaks the fixed composition of different distinguishable regions by destroying reconstruction learning, and automatically detects confusing regions.

Attention Mechanism: Attention mechanism has been widely used in various computer vision tasks. The earliest model is SENet [4], which applis the attention mechanism from aspect of channels and allocates the different weights according to the contribution of each channel. In 2018, CBAM [5] combines space region attentions with feature map attentions. In the same time, Non-local/self-attention has a wide range of applications, such as NLNet [10], GCNet [11], all of which use non-local mechanisms to capture different types of spatial information and channel information, but this operation may lead to a large amount of computation.

Network Engineering: Convolution Neural Network (CNN) has developed vigorously, and a large number of advanced network structures have emerged, such as the VGG [12] network, the Inception network [13]. In 2015, ResNet [2] is proposed. Based on this network structure, there are some excellent models, such as ResNeXt [3]. In 2017, Huang [14] proposed a new network structure: DenseNet, through feature reuse and bypass setting to achieve better results and fewer parameters. In 2019, Google used NAS network parameter search, found a model scaling method that can take into account both speed and accuracy, the latest network EfficientNet [15] is proposed, which achieves the new SOTA in classification accuracy.

3   Method

In this section, we first review the classical attention module SE, CBAM, and analyze their advantages and disadvantages, then introduce the structure of our proposed Global Spatial Coordinate Attention Module (GSCAM). Next, we introduce the use of this module in the mainstream backbone network.

3.1   SE and CBAM Attention

As shown in Fig. 1, the left represents SE Attention, and the right represents CBAM. SE module, which is widely used in CNN, can explicitly construct the interdependence between feature channels, and automatically obtain the importance of each channel. Then, the useful features are upgraded, while the useless features are suppressed for the current task according to the channel importance.

   SE module [4] has been applied in various mainstream networks, which can significantly improve the performance. However, SE module only considers the internal channel information and ignore the importance of spatial location information of the target, which is very important for visual task.

   CBAM [5] represents the attention mechanism of the convolution module. It is a kind of attention mechanism module which combines spatial and channel information. It tries to introduce location information through global pooling on the channel. Compared with SE which only focuses on channel, CBAM can achieve better results.

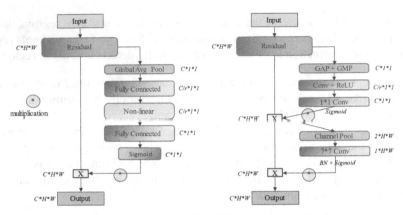

Fig. 1. The structure of SE (left) and CBAM (right)

The improvement brought by CBAM to the network is higher than that of the SE module on each benchmark network, and it takes the maximum and average value of multiple channels in each location as the weight factor. This kind of weight only considers the local spatial information, and difficult to obtain the information of long-range dependence.

3.2 (GSCAM) Global Spatial Coordinate Attention Module

We propose a novel and efficient attention mechanism called Global Spatial Coordinate Attention Module (GSCAM). By embedding location information into channel attention and paralleling a global spatial attention convergence block, our method builds multi-scale attention mechanism which combines local location information and global context information, and has a stronger ability to extract the features of regions of interest. The specific structure is shown in Fig. 2. The shadow on the left is Coordinate Attention Embedding and Generation, and the shadow on the right is Global Spatial Attention Generation.

Coordinate Attention Embedding and Generation. Inspired by coordinate attention [16], we decompose global pooling into a pair of 1D feature coding operations, that is, given an input of an intermediate convolution layer x_c, we use two horizontal and vertical spatial merge kernels to encode each channel, which are (H,1) and (1, W). The horizontal output of the cth channel is:

$$z_c^h(h) = \frac{1}{W} \sum_{0 \le i < W} x_c(h, i) \tag{1}$$

Similarly, the output of the cth channel in the vertical direction is:

$$z_c^w(w) = \frac{1}{H} \sum_{0 \le j < H} x_c(j, w) \tag{2}$$

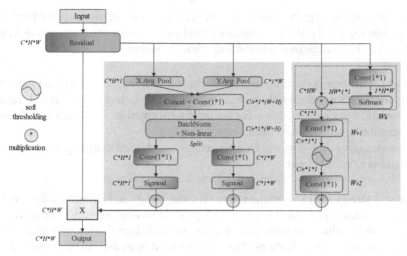

Fig. 2. The structure of GSCAM

The above two operations aggregate features along two mutually perpendicular directions, which can capture long-range dependencies in one spatial direction and retain position information in another spatial direction. According to the output of the two features obtained by this operation, we get accurate location information coding.

Then, according to the idea of coordinate attention [16], after we get the feature graph of position information, we do the join operation, and then use the 1*1 convolution transformation function F1 to get **f**:

$$\mathbf{f} = \delta\left(F_1\left(\left[\mathbf{z}^h, \mathbf{z}^w\right]\right)\right) \tag{3}$$

where $[\cdot, \cdot]$ is a join operation, δ is activation function, $f \in \mathbb{R}^{C/r \times (H+W)}$ is an intermediate feature graph encoded in two spatial directions, and r is used to control the reduction ratio of block size, similar to SE [4] blocks. Next, **f** is divided into two independent tensors, $\mathbf{f}^h \in \mathbb{R}^{C/r \times H}$ and $\mathbf{f}^w \in \mathbb{R}^{C/r \times W}$ in the spatial dimension, and then $\mathbf{f}^h$ and $\mathbf{f}^w$ are transformed into the same output as the input X by using two 1*1 convolution transformation functions F^h and F^w, and the results are obtained:

$$\mathbf{g}^h = \sigma\left(F_h\left(\mathbf{f}^h\right)\right) \tag{4}$$

$$\mathbf{g}^w = \sigma\left(F_w\left(\mathbf{f}^w\right)\right) \tag{5}$$

In order to reduce the computational cost, we use the appropriate reduction ratio r to reduce the number of channels of **f**. Finally, g^h and g^w are used for the weight of attention, and the coordinate attention output y_{ca} is expressed as

$$y_{ca} = x_c(i, j) \times g_c^h(i) \times g_c^w(j) \tag{6}$$

Global Spatial Attention Generation. Using only the location information to obtain the region of interest will lose some global semantic information. We hope to use more semantic information to guide the correctness of location information. Inspired by GCNet [11] and Non-local Net [10], we connect a global spatial information aggregation block. The block can be summarized into three operational processes:

(A) global attention collection, using 1*1 convolution W_k and Softmax functions to obtain attention weights, then obtaining context modeling global spatial features;
(B) through 1*1 convolution W_v for feature transformation, and using soft threshold operation to reduce unnecessary semantic noise;
(C) feature aggregation in global features, and using addition to aggregate global spatial features to each location.

The soft threshold [17] operation here replaces ReLU activation function, and soft threshold is usually used as a key step in signal denoising methods. Here, we adopt soft threshold to reduce the noise contained in the global spatial features and get more effective region of interest features. The soft threshold function can be expressed as:

$$S = \begin{cases} x - \tau & x > \tau \\ 0 & -\tau \leq x \leq \tau \\ x + \tau & x < -\tau \end{cases} \tag{7}$$

where x is the input feature, S is the output feature, T is the threshold and positive parameter, the soft threshold is not like setting the negative feature to zero in the ReLU activation function, but the near zero feature is set to zero, so that the useful negative feature can be retained. And the derivative value of the output of the soft threshold function to the input is either 1 or 0, which can effectively prevent the gradient from disappearing and exploding. The derivative form is as follows:

$$\frac{\partial S}{\partial x} = \begin{cases} 1 & x > \tau \\ 0 & -\tau \leq x \leq \tau \\ 1 & x < -\tau \end{cases} \tag{8}$$

The τ is expressed as follows:

$$\tau = \alpha \cdot \text{average} \left| x_{i,j,c} \right| \tag{9}$$

where α is the corresponding scaling parameter, which is denoted as follows:

$$\alpha = \frac{1}{1 + e^{-x}} \tag{10}$$

Therefore, the Global Spatial Attention output z_{gs} is expressed as:

$$z_{gs} = x_i \times W_{v2}S \left(W_{v1} \sum_{j=1}^{N_p} \frac{e^{W_k x_j}}{\sum_{m=1}^{N_p} e^{W_k x_m} x_j} \right) \tag{11}$$

where x is the input feature, i is the index of the query location, j enumerates all possible locations, W_k and W_v represent the linear transformation matrix, S is the soft threshold function and finally the coordinate attention encoded according to the location information and the global spatial information converge attention, we get the final attention output representation:

$$O(i,j) = y_{ca}(i,j) + z_{gs}(i,j) \tag{12}$$

3.3 Implementation for Commonly Used Backbone Networks

For the application of the GSCAM, we use other mainstream classification networks pre-trained by the ImageNet dataset, insert GSCAM as a network component into the backbone of the network, and then use the transfer learning method to train and identify the fine-grained image data set. Here we use the ResNet series [2, 3] as an example to illustrate where the GSCAM module is inserted, as shown in Fig. 3.

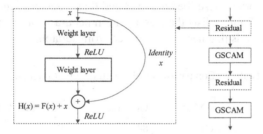

Fig. 3. The insert position of GSCAM in ResNet

4 Experiments

In this section, we used three FGIR benchmark datasets to evaluate the effectiveness of GSCAM: CUB-200–2011 (CUB) [18], Stanford Cars (CAR) [19], and FGVC-Aircraft (AIR) [20]. We first introduced the detailed setup of the experiments in Sect. 4.1 and the three datasets used in Sect. 4.2. In Sect. 4.3, we compare the classification accuracy of different methods, and also compare the number of parameters after inserting other attention modules SE, CBAM in the baseline network. Next, we carried out the ablation study of the GSCAM structure at Sect. 4.4. Finally, we studied the visualization effect of GSCAM in Sect. 4.5.

4.1 Experiment Setup

We did all experiments on RTX2080TI GPU using the PyTorch1.7. We insert the GSCAM into the widely used ResNet50_ResNeXt50 network to evaluate the performance. In the training step, only the category label of the image is used as the training label. For the training images, the image size is 550*550 as input, a then randomly cut to 448*448, and random horizontal flip is used to enhance the data. During the test, the input image is resized to 550*550, and then the center cut is to 448*448 for testing. We use SGD as the optimizer, set the initial learning rate to 0.002.

4.2 Datasets

The CUB dataset contains 11788 images of birds in 200 subclasses. The data of training set and test set are 5994 and 5794 respectively. The CAR dataset contains 196 subclasses of cars with a total of 16185 images. The training set and test set are 8144 and 8041 respectively. The AIR dataset contains 10000 images of 100 subclasses, and the segmentation ratio of the training set to the test set is 2:1.

4.3 Comparisons with Other Methods

In order to verify the performance of the GSCAM structure on FGIR tasks, we use the pre-trained ResNet50_ResNeXt50 network on ImageNet as baseline, to insert GSCAM into the ResNet network as described in Fig. 3 and then transfer to three different FGIR datasets for training. Table 1 lists the classification accuracy of our method compared with other FGIR methods that need to be trained from scratch.

Table 1. Comparison results with different methods

Method	Base Model	CUB (acc %)	CAR (acc %)	AIR (acc %)
B-CNN (ICCV15)[21]	VGG16	84.1	91.3	84.1
MA-CNN (ICCV17)[7]	VGG19	86.5	92.8	89.9
PC (ECCV18)[22]	DenseNet161	86.9	92.9	89.2
DFL (CVPR18)[23]	ResNet50	87.4	93.1	91.7
DCL (CVPR19)[8]	ResNet50	87.8	94.5	**93**
ACNet (CVPR20)[24]	ResNet50	88.1	94.6	92.4
S3N (CVPR20)[9]	ResNet50	**88.5**	**94.7**	92.8
ResNet (CVPR15)[2]	ResNet50	84.5	91.5	85.6
ResNeXt (CVPR17)[3]	ResNeXt50	85.3	92.1	86.2
ResNet + GSCAM	ResNet50	87.8	93.9	92.5
ResNeXt + GSCAM	ResNeXt50	88.3	94.2	92.9

From Table 1, we can see that with the development of time, the accuracy of FGIR models is getting higher and higher, but these network models need to be trained from scratch, requiring a lot of network structure design skills and training costs, indicating the necessity of using network transfer learning. When the ImageNet pre-trained ResNet50 and ResNeXt models are directly transferred to the FGIR task, the classification accuracy on each dataset is quite different from the most FGIR models.

When we insert the GSCAM into ResNet series network and then transfer to three FGIR datasets for training, we can see that it has obviously improved the classification accuracy in different datasets, the accuracy on ResNet50 has exceeded in most FGIR models, and the accuracy of ResNeXt50 has been closed to the SOTA level, indicating the effectiveness of the GSCAM, which can be inserted into the mainstream backbone network as an independent module to improve performance.

At the same time, we want to prove the performance of GSCAM compared with other attention, replace the position where the above ResNet network is inserted into GSCAM with SE, CBAM module, and then carry on the experiment of FGIR task on CUB dataset. Table 2 lists the classification accuracy and the number of parameters we use GSCAM, CBAM, SE and other modules respectively.

Table 2. Comparisons of different attention methods in parameter and performance

Settings	Param. (M)	M-Adds (G)	Top-1 acc (%)
ResNet50	25.56	4.14	84.5
ResNet50 + SE	25.95	4.18	85.6
ResNet50 + CBAM	25.95	4.19	86.1
ResNet50 + GSCAM	26.05	4.2	**87.8**
ResNeXt50	25.03	4.29	85.3
ResNeXt50 + SE	25.36	4.33	86.3
ResNeXt50 + CBAM	25.36	4.35	86.8
ResNeXt50 + GSCAM	25.47	4.39	**88.3**

From Table 2, we can see that compared with the widely used lightweight attention module SE, CBAM, when GSCAM is inserted to ResNet50 and ResNeXt50 network, the accuracy on CUB datasets is significantly higher than that of the other two modules. Moreover, after inserting GSCAM, the increase in the number of network parameters and computing costs is very small compared with SE and CBAM, indicating that GSCAM is also a lightweight attention module, which can significantly improve network performance while saving computing resources.

4.4 Ablation Study of GSCAM

We have studied the ablation of GSCAM structure to prove the effectiveness of this module. Here we choose CUB dataset for experiment and compare ResNet50 as baseline. On the basis of ResNet50, as shown in Fig. 3, we separately insert different components of the GSCAM to act on the input feature x, including the left shadow part CAEG (Coordinate Attention Embedding and Generation) and the right shadow part GSAG (Global Spatial Attention Generation), and finally fully insert GSCAM.

From Table 3 we can see that compared with ResNet50 baseline, adding CAEG and GSAG respectively can improve the accuracy to a certain extent, indicating that adding

Table 3. The accuracy of different GSCAM part when taking ResNet50 as baseline

Settings	Top-1 acc (%)
ResNet50	84.5
ResNet50 + CAEG (GSCAM)	86.4
ResNet50 + GSAG (GSCAM)	85.6
ResNet50 + GSCAM	87.8

attention mechanism to the original network is effective. The GSCAM effect obtained by the combination of the two is better than that of the two alone, indicating that the spatial location information plus the global context feature makes up for the lack of feature information, and achieves the best effect on the FGIR task.

4.5 Visualization Analysis

In order to demonstrate the effectiveness of GSCAM from the visual effect, we use Grad-CAM [25] to realize the visualization of convolution layer feature graph. Here we do visualization analysis on the CUB dataset, using the convolution layer of the last three stages of the baseline ResNet50 and ResNet50 + GSCAM models for visualization respectively. As shown in Fig. 4, (a)-(c) is the visualization of the convolution layer of the third to fifth stages of the ResNet50 + GSCAM model., (d)-(f) is the corresponding convolution layer visualization of ResNet50.

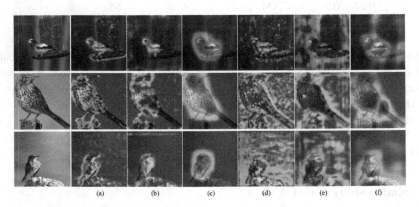

Fig. 4. The activation map of selected results

As we can see from Fig. 4, the third stage of the model focuses on the fine-grained parts of image, such as bird's eyes and feather, and the fifth stage focuses on the coarser-grained parts of image, such as bird's body. The visualization results show that the attention we get after adding GSCAM is more meaningful than the baseline model. Whether it is fine-grained feature attention or coarse-grained feature concern, our model almost covers the target object with distinguishable regions, while the baseline model does not pay enough attention to the fine-grained information of the target object, it more likely pay attention to the background information in image, and only shows correct attention in the final stage. The results show that the model with GSCAM can pay more attention to the effective attention representation of different stages and improve the accuracy of image recognition.

5 Conclusion

In this paper, we proposed a novel light-weight attention mechanism: (GSCAM) Global Spatial Coordinate Attention Module. Our GSCAM can be easily inserted into the backbone of the mainstream networks to improve performance. The experimental results show that for the FGIR task, compared with the complex network trained from scratch, the performance of SOTA can be closed by inserting our module into ResNet50 or ResNeXt50. We also prove the effectiveness of GSCAM structure through ablation experiments and visualization analysis. This module does not need to design complex network structure, and has better recognition accuracy for FGIR.

Acknowledgment. This work was supported in part by the National Natural Science Foundation of China under Grant 62071384, Key Research and Development Project of Shaanxi Province under Grant 2020ZDLGY04–09.

References

1. Du, R., et al.: Fine-grained visual classification via progressive multi-granularity training of jigsaw patches. In: European Conference on Computer Vision, pp. 153–168: Springer, Cham (2020). https://doi.org/10.1007/978-3-030-58565-5_10
2. He, K., Zhang, X., Ren, S., Sun, J.: Deep residual learning for image recognition. In: Proceedings of the IEEE Conference on Computer Vision and Pattern Recognition, pp. 770–778 (2016)
3. Xie, S., Girshick, R., Dollár, P., Tu, Z., He, K.: Aggregated residual transformations for deep neural networks. In: Proceedings of the IEEE Conference on Computer Vision and Pattern Recognition, pp. 1492–1500 (2017)
4. Hu, J., Shen, L., Sun, G.: Squeeze-and-excitation networks. In: Proceedings of the IEEE Conference on Computer Vision and Pattern Recognition, pp. 7132–7141 (2018)
5. Woo, S., Park, J., Lee, J.-Y., Kweon, I.S.: CBAM: convolutional block attention module. In: Ferrari, V., Hebert, M., Sminchisescu, C., Weiss, Y. (eds.) ECCV 2018. LNCS, vol. 11211, pp. 3–19. Springer, Cham (2018). https://doi.org/10.1007/978-3-030-01234-2_1
6. Xie, L., Tian, Q., Hong, R., Yan, S., Zhang, B.: Hierarchical part matching for fine-grained visual categorization. In: Proceedings of the IEEE International Conference on Computer Vision, pp. 1641–1648 (2013)
7. Zheng, H., Fu, J., Mei, T., Luo, J.: Learning multi-attention convolutional neural network for fine-grained image recognition. In: Proceedings of the IEEE International Conference on Computer Vision, pp. 5209–5217 (2017)
8. Chen, Y., Bai, Y., Zhang, W., Mei, T.: Destruction and construction learning for fine-grained image recognition. In: Proceedings of the IEEE/CVF Conference on Computer Vision and Pattern Recognition, pp. 5157–5166 (2019)

9. Ding, Y., Zhou, Y., Zhu, Y., Ye, Q., Jiao, J.: Selective sparse sampling for fine-grained image recognition. In: Proceedings of the IEEE/CVF International Conference on Computer Vision, pp. 6599–6608 (2019)
10. Wang, X., Girshick, R., Gupta, A., He, K.: Non-local neural networks. In: Proceedings of the IEEE Conference on Computer Vision and Pattern Recognition, pp. 7794–7803 (2018)
11. Cao, Y., Xu, J., Lin, S., Wei, F., Hu, H.: Gcnet: non-local networks meet squeeze-excitation networks and beyond. In: Proceedings of the IEEE/CVF International Conference on Computer Vision Workshops, p. 0 (2019)
12. Simonyan, K., Zisserman, A.: Very deep convolutional networks for large-scale image recognition. *arXiv preprint* arXiv:1409.1556(2014)
13. Szegedy, C., Ioffe, S., Vanhoucke, V., Alemi, A.A.: Inception-v4, inception-resnet and the impact of residual connections on learning. In: Proceedings of the AAAI Conference on Artificial Intelligence, vol. 31, no. 1 (2017)
14. Huang, G., Liu, Z., Van Der Maaten, L., Weinberger, K.Q.: Densely connected convolutional networks. In: Proceedings of the IEEE Conference on Computer Vision and Pattern Recognition, pp. 4700–4708 (2017)
15. Tan, M., Le, Q.: Efficientnet: rethinking model scaling for convolutional neural networks. In: International Conference on Machine Learning, pp. 6105–6114. PMLR (2019)
16. Hou, Q., Zhou, D., Feng, J.: Coordinate attention for efficient mobile network design. *arXiv preprint* arXiv:2103.02907 (2021)
17. Zhao, M., Zhong, S., Fu, X., Tang, B., Pecht, M.: Deep residual shrinkage networks for fault diagnosis. IEEE Trans. Industr. Inf. **16**(7), 4681–4690 (2019)
18. Wah, C., Branson, S., Welinder, P., Perona, P., Belongie, S.: The caltech-ucsd birds-200–2011 dataset (2011)
19. Krause, J., Stark, M., Deng, J., Fei-Fei, L.: 3D object representations for fine-grained categorization. In: Proceedings of the IEEE International Conference on Computer Vision Workshops, pp. 554–561 (2013)
20. Maji, S., Rahtu, E., Kannala, J., Blaschko, M., Vedaldi, A.: Fine-grained visual classification of aircraft. *arXiv preprint* arXiv:1306.5151(2013)
21. Lin, T.Y., RoyChowdhury, A., Maji, S.: Bilinear CNN models for fine-grained visual recognition. In: Proceedings of the IEEE International Conference on Computer Vision, pp. 1449–1457 (2015)
22. Dubey, A., Gupta, O., Guo, P., Raskar, R., Farrell, R., Naik, N.: Pairwise confusion for fine-grained visual classification. In: Ferrari, V., Hebert, M., Sminchisescu, C., Weiss, Y. (eds.) ECCV 2018. LNCS, vol. 11216, pp. 71–88. Springer, Cham (2018). https://doi.org/10.1007/978-3-030-01258-8_5
23. Wang, Y., Morariu, V.I., Davis, L.S.: Learning a discriminative filter bank within a CNN for fine-grained recognition. In: Proceedings of the IEEE Conference on Computer Vision and Pattern Recognition, pp. 4148–4157 (2018)
24. Ji, R., et al.: Attention convolutional binary neural tree for fine-grained visual categorization. In: Proceedings of the IEEE/CVF Conference on Computer Vision and Pattern Recognition, pp. 10468–10477 (2020)
25. Selvaraju, R.R., Cogswell, M., Das, A., Vedantam, R., Parikh, D., Batra, D.: Grad-cam: visual explanations from deep networks via gradient-based localization. In: Proceedings of the IEEE International Conference on Computer Vision, pp. 618–626 (2017)

Drill Pipe Counting Method Based on Local Dense Optical Flow Estimation

Meng Zhou, Jin Yuan, Zhuangzhuang Gao, and Zhangjin Huang[✉]

University of Science and Technology of China, Hefei, China
{menchou,yuanjin,BryantGao}@mail.ustc.edu.cn, zhuang@ustc.edu.cn

Abstract. To solve the problem of drill pipe counting in coal mines, we propose a drill pipe counting method based on local dense optical flow (LDOF) estimation. Compared to the general tracking method, we provide a new perspective for resolving the problem of drill pipe counting. Taking into account the various working conditions of the drill pipe movement and the complex lighting environment in coal mines, we leverage the local dense optical flow to obtain the movement information of the drill pipe. The model is further established through optical flow to realize the counting of drill pipe. In order to validate the proposed approach, we collect 5 videos of drill pipe movement in coal mines, which cover strong light source and occlusion situations. The experiments demonstrate that our method can realize automatic counting of drill pipe, with an average drill pipe counting accuracy of 97.92% and an average frame per second (FPS) rate of 64.2.

Keywords: Local dense optical flow · Drill pipe counting · Multi-threading · Optical flow field integral

1 Introduction

In the production process of coal mines, gas drainage technology is an effective means to solve gas explosion problem. The degree of gas drainage is determined by the depth of the borehole. In coal mines, the length of the mining drill pipe is usually used to estimate the depth of the borehole. Therefore, the accuracy of the drill pipe counting is directly related to the degree of gas drainage. It is particularly challenging owing to strong light source and occlusion.

The traditional drill pipe counting method is manual counting or monitoring video counting [9]. Both counting methods require long hours of work, which easily leads to counting errors and poses great safety hazards. Through the effective processing video of drill pipe movement, the automatic counting of drill pipe is realized. In recent years, most of the work on drill pipe counting [4,5,9,11] has been achieved mainly by tracking the drill pipe. However, the poor tracking effect will affect the counting accuracy and the speed is slow. To this end, we propose to solve the problem of drill pipe counting without tracking the drill pipe.

M. Zhou and J. Yuan—Contributed equally to this work.

Y. Peng et al. (Eds.): ICIG 2021, LNCS 12888, pp. 443–454, 2021.
https://doi.org/10.1007/978-3-030-87355-4_37

To improve the accuracy and speed of drill pipe counting, we present a drill pipe counting method based on local dense optical flow estimation. Specifically, we first leverage the local dense optical flow [6] to analyze the movement of the drill pipe. Then, the optical flow displacement is obtained by optical flow field integral. Lastly, we establish the model by judging the change of the optical flow direction, so as to realize the drill pipe counting. Furthermore, to speed up the calculation of optical flow, we utilize multi-threading to accelerate our model. The effectiveness of our method is validated on five videos for drill pipe counting task. Experimental results demonstrate that our method outperforms the prior works on drill pipe counting by a large margin, which achieves 97.92% average accuracy and 64.2 frames per second (FPS) of drill pipe counting.

2   Related Work

In this section, we briefly introduce the solutions for drill pipe counting in coal mines. It is mainly divided into traditional methods and deep learning methods.

Traditional Methods. The drill pipe counting based on the traditional method is achieved by image preprocessing, feature extraction, target detection, and target tracking. Wang [11] applied the Vibe [10] target detection algorithm and the improved Camshift algorithm [1] to realize the drill pipe counting. Dong et al. [3] combined color characteristics and motion characteristics, and used Camshift algorithm to achieve drill pipe target tracking through particle filter processing. Peng [9] utilized corner detection, combined with the pyramid optical flow method to track moving targets and established a mathematical model. The traditional counting method based on tracking has large deviations, low counting accuracy, and can not meet the requirement of real-time detection.

Deep Learning Methods. The drill pipe counting based on deep learning method is used to automatically count drill pipes by constructing a deep learning model to extract the information in the video images and track the drill pipe. Gao et al. [7] proposed a drill pipe counting method based on improved ResNet network [8] to count the number of drill pipes by establishing an image classification model. Dong et al. [5] presented a drill pipe counting method based on scale space and Siamese network [2] to achieve accurate counting of drill pipe. The deep learning counting method requires training the model in advance, which takes longer time and costs more hardware resources.

In this study, we propose a simple yet effective method to count drill pipes without tracking the drill movement. Considering the various conditions of drill pipe movement in coal mines and the high requirements for accuracy and speed, we exploit local dense optical flow to solve the problem of drill pipe counting, which can be applied in actual coal mines.

Algorithm 1: Drill Pipe Counting Method

Input: *videos*, two adjacent frames *prvs*, *next*, scaling factor β
Output: list of speed, list of distance, count result

1   *count = 0*;
2   *prvs* ← RotateAndClip(*videos[0]*);
3   **for** *i* ← 1 *to N* − 1 **do**
4   *next* ← RotateAndClip(*videos[i]*);
5   *speed*← DenseOpticalFlow(*prvs, next*);
6   *speed*← Filter(*speed*);
7   *speedlist[i]*← Mean(*speed*);
8   *distancelist[i]*← Sum(*speedlist*);
9   **if** *Mean(speed) goes from negative to positive* **then**
10   record interval position[start, end];
11   **end**
12   *heightlist*← CaculatePeaks(*distancelist[start...end]*);
13   *history* = the first height of *heightlist*;
14   **foreach** *height of heightlist* **do**
         // Filter out the smaller crests
15   **if** *height* > β * *history* **then**
16   *count* ← *count* + *1*;
         // To adjust dynamically at a certain rate
17   Update(*history*);
18   **end**
19   **end**
20   *prvs* ← *next*
21 **end**

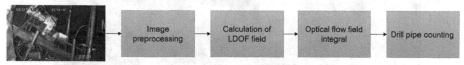

Fig. 1. Overview of our approach. Given an input video, we first process image by rotating and cropping. Then, we calculate the local dense optical flow field. The optical flow displacement is obtained by optical flow field integral. Finally, we realize the drill pipe counting by finding the interval of statistical displacement peaks and counting the number of peaks.

3 Proposed Method

Figure 1 presents the pipeline of our framework. Given a video of downhole drill pipe movement, our goal is to process the local dense optical flow (LDOF) to achieve drill pipe counting. The proposed method is summarized in Algorithm 1. This section will be organized as follows. First, image preprocessing is introduced (Sect. 3.1). Second, local dense optical flow field is calculated (Sect. 3.2). Then the optical flow displacement is obtained by optical flow field integral (Sect. 3.3). Finally, the model of drill pipe counting is described (Sect. 3.4).

3.1 Image Preprocessing

In general, the movement direction of the drill pipe is not horizontal with the video shooting direction, so we rotate the video frame to keep its movement direction horizontal. First, two points are selected on the axis of the drill pipe movement, and the slope of the drill pipe is calculated from the coordinates of these two points. Then, the angle is obtained by the inverse tangent operation, the formula is written as:

$$angle = \arctan\left(\frac{\Delta y}{\Delta x}\right)\frac{180}{\pi} \tag{1}$$

where $\frac{\Delta y}{\Delta x}$ denotes the slope of the drill pipe.

Since most areas in the video are redundant for obtaining the motion information of the drill pipe, we manually select a rectangular area containing the drill bit as the region of interest in order to reduce the computational cost. Figure 2 demonstrates the region of interest. For each frame of the video, the image is rotated, cropped to the region of interest, and then the image is converted to a grayscale image.

Fig. 2. An example region of interest for the drill pipe.

3.2 Local Dense Optical Flow Field

Optical flow is the instantaneous velocity of the pixel movement of the space moving object on the observation imaging plane. According to the velocity vector characteristics of each pixel, the image can be dynamically analyzed. Dense optical flow estimation is to compute the optical flow for all the points in the image. We use the dense optical flow algorithm proposed by Farnebäck [6].

We first utilize the region of interest to calculate the optical flow of all local pixels instead of the whole image, and normalize the optical flow velocity. We then filter the velocity. Since the velocity information in the non-moving direction is not conducive to judging the movement of the drill pipe, and there will be slight jitter during the movement of the drill pipe, only the speed of ±30° in the direction of the drill pipe movement is retained. In order to weaken the influence of workers' occlusion and light source, the local dense optical flow is averaged.

Optical Flow Magnitude Threshold. We consider that the optical flow less than 130 is basically random noise, which is filtered out in the process of calculating the optical flow. Figure 3 shows the relationship between magnitude and angle when the drill pipe stops at the highest position. As demonstrated in this figure, the value around 130 is basically evenly distributed on all the intercepted pixels.

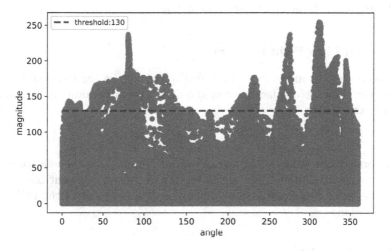

Fig. 3. Relationship between magnitude and angle when the drill pipe stops at the highest position. The horizontal red dotted line indicates magnitude threshold. (Color figure online)

Optical Flow Angle Threshold. The drill pipe will shake slightly during the movement, causing the calculated optical flow direction to shift. In order to reduce the influence of drill pipe jitter, we define the speed of the pixel point ±30° in the direction of drill pipe movement as the positive direction, the speed of 150°–210° in the direction of drill pipe movement as the negative direction, and set the speed in other directions to 0.

Figure 4 shows the relationship between the magnitude and angle of all pixels in the local area during the drill pipe movement. As illustrated in Fig. 4(a), within the range of ±30° in the horizontal direction, the magnitude is more balanced. As shown in Fig. 4(b), in the range of 150°–210° in the horizontal direction, the magnitude is relatively stable and more than 130.

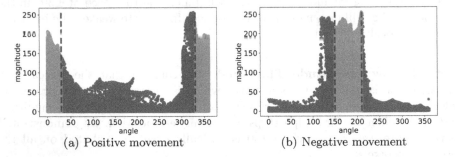

(a) Positive movement   (b) Negative movement

Fig. 4. Relationship between magnitude and angle of all pixels. The vertical red dotted line indicates angle threshold. (Color figure online)

3.3 Optical Flow Field Integral

With the continuous movement of the drill pipe, we use the integral of velocity to time to express the displacement of the drill pipe in periodic motion, and the formula is as follows:

$$S = \int_0^{T_i} V(t)\, dt \tag{2}$$

where i denotes the index of the current video frame, T_i is the i-th frame time, $V(t)$ represents the optical flow calculated for every two adjacent frames, and t denotes the time. S represents the cumulative displacement of the drill pipe in periodic motion.

3.4 Drill Pipe Counting

In coal mines, the drill pipe makes periodic motion. The counting principle is mainly to find the interval of statistical displacement peaks and count the number of peaks through positive and negative changes in the direction of the drill pipe velocity to realize the counting of drill pipe.

First, the positive and negative changes in the direction of the drill pipe velocity are judged. We find the interval of the statistical displacement crest by the positive and negative change of velocity. When the direction of the velocity changes from negative to positive, we find the end of the peak interval of the displacement calculation, and it is also the starting point of the next interval. For the last count of the drill pipe, it may happen that the speed direction of the drill pipe remains in the negative direction. In order to prevent the lack of counting, we record the interval of the current displacement peak in preparation for counting the number of peaks.

Then, we find the crest and update the crest threshold in real time, the formula is written as:

$$history = history \times (1 - \alpha) + peak \times \alpha, \quad if \ peak > \beta \times history \quad (3)$$

where *history* denotes the height of the previous wave crest, *peak* represents the height of the current wave crest, α is the weight to trade off between *history* and *peak*, and β is the scaling factor for the previous wave crest. Here, we set α to 0.6 and β to 0.3, respectively. The peak of the displacement waveform is monitored, and wave peaks with a height greater than 100 are screened out, and the peaks less than 100 are considered as noise. In the peak list, we traverse each peak and use the first peak as the historical peak, and then compare with β times the historical peak each time. If it exceeds β times the historical peak, the historical peak is updated.

Lastly, we count the number of crests for drill pipe counting:

$$count = count + 1 \ , \quad if \ peak > \beta \times history \quad (4)$$

where *count* is the number of drill pipe.

4 Experiments

4.1 Datasets and Evaluation Metrics

We collect 5 different videos of drill pipe movement in coal mines as datasets by using fixed position cameras. In different drill pipe movement videos, the angles and types of drills are not exactly the same. The video frames are 4,707, 35,609, 13,896, 8,532, and 7,536, respectively. All videos are recorded with a resolution of 1280×720 pixels. The videos include the situation of strong light source and worker occlusion.

We use drill pipe counting accuracy and speed metrics in quantitative evaluations. We define the drill pipe counting accuracy as the ratio of the number of drill pipes correctly counted by the program to the actual number of drill pipes. Speed is defined as the number of video frames processed by the program per second.

4.2 Implementation Details

In the experiment, the angle threshold is set to $\pm 30°$, the magnitude threshold is 130, the window size of the average optical flow speed is 10, the weight to trade off between *history* and *peak* is 0.6, and the scaling factor for the previous wave crest is 0.3. In order to improve the efficiency of counting drill pipes, our method leverages multi-threading to accelerate the processing of adjacent frames of video image sequences. All experiments are conducted on Intel Core i7-7700 CPU.

4.3 Experimental Validations

We perform experimental validations on the collected datasets for qualitative analysis and quantitative analysis, respectively.

Qualitative Analysis. The local dense optical flow is calculated and visualized for videos of the drill pipe movement in coal mines, as shown in Fig. 5. In Fig. 5, different colors indicate different directions of drill pipe movement. Purple shows the positive direction of the drill pipe movement, and green represents the negative direction of the drill pipe movement.

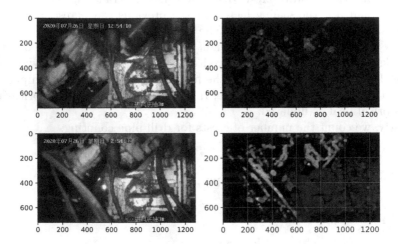

Fig. 5. Directions of drill pipe movement. Purple shows the positive direction of the drill pipe movement, and green represents the negative direction of the drill pipe movement. (Color figure online)

The speed and the cumulative displacement of the periodic motion of the drill pipe over time are shown in Fig. 6 left and right, respectively. In Fig. 6, the speed of the drill pipe movement and the cumulative displacement formed by the integral have good periodic characteristics. Under the influence of occlusion and illumination, the cumulative displacement waveform is relatively smooth.

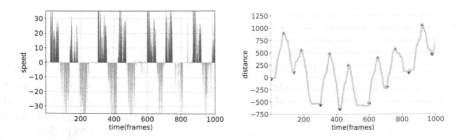

Fig. 6. Periodic motion. Left: Speed change. Green shows positive direction, red indicates negative direction Right: Distance change. Green represents wave crests and red donates wave troughs. (Color figure online)

We visualize the results of drill pipe counting, as shown in Fig. 7. It can be seen from the figure that for each drill pipe, all the counts are correct.

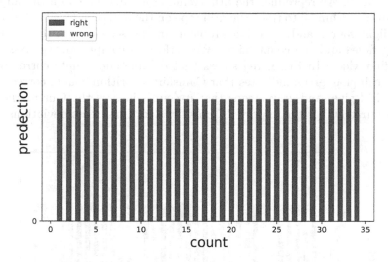

Fig. 7. Counting results of our method. The x-axis and y-axis correspond to the real counting and the predicted outputs, respectively. Red shows right counting, gray indicates wrong counting. (Color figure online)

Quantitative Analysis. The experiment is performed to show the effect of our method on the datasets. It is worth noting that the datasets contain strong light source and occlusion. It can be observed in Table 1 that with the multi-threading and local dense optical flow, our method is faster. Our method achieves 97.92% average accuracy and 64.2 frames per second (FPS) of drill pipe counting.

Table 1. Quantitative analysis. 'w/o MT' represents to leverage multi-threading, and 'Global' means to use global dense optical flow over the whole image.

Video number	#Frame	Accuracy	FPS(w/o MT)	FPS(Global)	FPS
1	4,707	100%	18.4	12.1	69.0
2	35,609	100%	18.0	11.1	63.5
3	13,896	98.67%	18.3	11.1	68.4
4	8,532	90.91%	17.7	10.6	60.6
5	7,536	100%	17.6	10.5	59.3
Average	–	97.92%	18.0	11.1	64.2

4.4   Comparisons with Existing Methods

In view of the problem of drill pipe counting, there are few related papers, such as [4,5,7,9,11]. We reproduce the drill counting method based on the improved Camshift algorithm [4] to track the drill pipe on the datasets. Due to the obvious strong light source and occlusion problems in the second to fifth videos, the tracking failed and the count failed. We perform a comprehensive comparison in the first video. In Fig. 8, red shows that our method counts correctly in a certain drill pipe, green indicates that Camshift algorithm counts correctly in a certain drill pipe, and gray means that it counts incorrectly. Our method can count accurately, but the improved Camshift algorithm exists deviations.

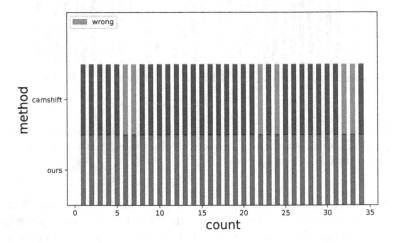

Fig. 8. Test drill pipe accuracy. The x-axis and y-axis correspond to the real counting and the predicted outputs, respectively. Red shows right counting of our method, green indicates right counting of Camshift algorithm, and gray means wrong counting. (Color figure online)

In Table 2, we compare our method with improved Camshift algorithm [4]. Our approach is five times faster than the Camshift algorithm. The counting accuracy of our method is 100%, and the counting accuracy of the Camshift algorithm is 82.35%. Our method outmatches the improved Camshift algorithm by 17.65% on counting accuracy.

Table 2. Comparison results between the improved Camshift and ours. In each column, the best number is highlighted in **bold**.

Methods	Accuracy	FPS
The improved Camshift	82.35%	12.6
Ours	**100%**	**69.0**

In Table 3, we compare our method with improved ResNet network [7] on drill pipe counting task. By contrast, our method is more robust to different videos and we achieve comparable or even better numbers of accuracy and speed. Moreover, our method does not require GPU, which takes shorter time and less hardware resources.

Table 3. Comparison results between the ResNet network and ours in terms of the accuracy and speed.

Video number	#Frame	Accuracy(Ours)	Accuracy(ResNet)	FPS(Ours)	FPS(ResNet)
1	4,707	100%	73.53%	69.0	41.0
2	35,609	100%	95.83%	63.5	44.4
3	13,896	98.67%	82.67%	68.4	43.8
4	8,532	90.91%	61.36%	60.6	50.7
5	7,536	100%	73.47%	59.3	43.8
Average	–	97.92%	77.37%	64.2	44.7

5   Conclusions and Future Work

In this work, we aim to tackle the counting problem of moving drill pipes in coal mines, and we present a drill pipe counting method based on local dense optical flow estimation. First, we preprocess the video image to facilitate the calculation of optical flow velocity. Second, the local dense optical flow is calculated and we filter the optical flow. Then, the optical flow displacement is obtained by optical flow field integral. Finally, we establish a model to count the number of drill pipes. Our method achieves better performance on drill pipe counting tasks when evaluated on datasets.

In the future, we plan to automatically detect the drill area for this task. We are also interested in extending our method to address video counting problems that include various periodic actions.

Acknowledgements. This work was supported in part by the National Key R&D Program of China (No. 2018YFC1504104), the National Natural Science Foundation of China (Nos. 71991464/71991460, and 61877056), and the Fundamental Research Funds for the Central Universities of China (Nos. WK6030000109 and WK5290000001).

References

1. Bradski, G.R.: Computer vision face tracking for use in a perceptual user interface. In: Proceedings of the Fourth IEEE Workshop on Applications of Computer Vision (WACV 1998) (1998)
2. Chopra, S., Hadsell, R., LeCun, Y.: Learning a similarity metric discriminatively, with application to face verification. In: 2005 IEEE Computer Society Conference on Computer Vision and Pattern Recognition (CVPR 2005), vol. 1, pp. 539–546, San Diego, CA, USA (2005). http://dx.doi.org/10.1109/CVPR.2005.202

3. Dong, L., He, W., She, X.: Moving drill target based on motion feature tracking method in coal mine. Coal Technol. **34**(11), 269–271 (2015)
4. Dong, L., Wang, J., She, X.: Drill counting method based on improved Camshift algorithm. Indus. Mine Autom. **41**(01), 71–76 (2015)
5. Dong, L., Wu, X., Zhang, J.: Drill pipe counting method based on scale space and Siamese network. In: 3rd International Conference on Algorithms, Computing and Artificial Intelligence (ACAI 2020), Sanya, China (2020). http://dx.doi.org/10.1145/3446132.3446179
6. Farnebäck, G.: Two-frame motion estimation based on polynomial expansion. In: Bigun, J., Gustavsson, T. (eds.) SCIA 2003. LNCS, vol. 2749, pp. 363–370. Springer, Heidelberg (2003). https://doi.org/10.1007/3-540-45103-X_50
7. Gao, R., Hao, L., Liu, B., Wen, J., Chen, Y.: Research on underground drill pipe counting method based on improved ResNet network. Indus. Mine Autom. **46**(10), 32–37 (2020)
8. He, K., Zhang, X., Ren, S., Sun, J.: Deep residual learning for image recognition. In: 2016 IEEE Conference on Computer Vision and Pattern Recognition (CVPR) (2016)
9. Peng, Y.: Research on counting method of drill pipe in coal mine. Master's thesis, Xi'an University of Science and Technology (2019)
10. Van Droogenbroeck, M., Paquot, O.: Background subtraction: experiments and improvements for vibe. In: 2012 IEEE Computer Society Conference on Computer Vision and Pattern Recognition Workshops (CVPRW 2012), pp. 32–37, Providence, RI, USA (2012). http://dx.doi.org/10.1109/CVPRW.2012.6238924
11. Wang, J.: Research and realization on the method of counting drill pipe' number based on machine vision. Master's thesis, Xi'an University of Science and Technology (2015)

Color Texture Image Segmentation Using Histogram-Based CV Model Driven by Local Contrast Pattern

Haiying Tian[1], Jianhuang Lai[2(✉)], Tie Cai[1], and Xu Chen[1]

[1] Shenzhen Institute of Information Technology, Shenzhen, China
[2] School of Computer Science and Engineering, Sun Yat-Sen University,
Guangzhou, China
stsljh@mail.sysu.edu.cn

Abstract. This paper proposes a novel texture descriptor called local contrast pattern (LCP) to drive a histogram-based Chan-Vese(CV) model for color texture image segmentation. The LCP has two features: differential contrast and orientation. The former measures the variation of local intensity and the latter extracts the texture orientation information. In order to enhance the localization, a truncated Gaussian kernel function is also incorporated that determines a positive correlation between weight and distance. Then, a novel histogram-based CV model is established which is guided by a combination of the LCP feature maps and the kernel to obtain color texture segmentation. The effectiveness of the LCP descriptor in color texture segmentation was prove to be true by many single variable validation experiments. Comparisons with many color-texture image segmentation models demonstrate that our proposed model can not only successfully partition all types of images but also bear strong robustness for illumination, noise and curve initialization.

Keywords: Color texture segmentation · Local contrast pattern (LCP) · Differential contrast · Orientation

1 Introduction

The existing active contour models can be roughly categorized into two classes: edge-based models [12,22] and region-based models [1,6,8,18]. The edge-based ones usually use a gradient-based boundary detection function to stop contours for the real edges. Many new algorithms are derived from the local region based models because they could catch more details of objects. Chunming Li et al. proposed the Local Binary Fitting (LBF) model [10,11] by generating the variances in a small local region whose size was limited by a proper kernel function. Since its locality, the model turned out to deal with intensity inhomogeneity effectively. Now many new algorithms are derived from the local region based models because they could catch more details of objects. Some researchers also combine the information of global and local regions to construct driving energy [2,7,20].

© Springer Nature Switzerland AG 2021
Y. Peng et al. (Eds.): ICIG 2021, LNCS 12888, pp. 455–466, 2021.
https://doi.org/10.1007/978-3-030-87355-4_38

Besides, They try to extract the object shape as a priori to eliminate the influence of other unwanted ones [4,13,14,19,24]. However, the methods above are invalid for color texture image segment, in addition, uneven illumination and all kinds of noises are inevitable.

In this paper, a novel histogram-based CV model driven by local contrast pattern (LCP) and restrainted by a kernel function is proposed. It aims to solve color texture image segmentation problem even in some extreme circumstances like uneven illumination, noise and multifarious initialization. There are two main contributions: firstly, the LCP descriptor is newly proposed, by calculating the local intensity changes and the gradient orientation to describe texture structure correctly. It can not only eliminate inhomogeneous intensity but also distinguish different texture types. Secondly, we incorporate the LCP descriptor into a CV model to segment color texture image by calculating statistical histograms. In order to maintain better locality, a truncated Gaussian kernel function is used to suppress undesirable clusters in global domain and smooth the curves. Experiments demonstrate the proposed scheme not only achieves effective segmentation results but also has a good robustness for illumination, noise and curve initialization on color texture image.

2   Related Works

2.1   Local Histogram-Based (LH) Model

The local histogram-based active contour model [15] can be applied to segment texture image. It make a feature transformation by calculating statistic histograms in a neighbourhood of each pixel, therefore, a histogram denotes a pixel value instead of its intensity. In fact, it is a deformation process of evolving curve by minimizing the distance between the object histogram and the average one in the CV model. Because of the statistical property of histogram, its robustness for noise and complex intensity variation is better than the traditional CV model. Though mediocre, the LH model is a powerful carrier to fusion other features to segment image.

Given a gray-scale image $I : \Omega \rightarrow [0, L]$ (L usually takes 255), Ω represents the image domain and the evolving contour C divides I into two regions denoted by $in(C)$ and $out(C)$. Let $N_{x,r}$ be a local patch centered at pixel $x \in \Omega$ with radius r, for $0 \leq \alpha \leq L$, the histogram and corresponding cumulative distribution function of x are listed below:

$$P_r^x(\alpha) = \frac{|\{z \in N_r^x \cap \Omega : I(z) = \alpha\}|}{|N_r^x \cap \Omega|}, \tag{1}$$

$$F_r^x(\alpha) = \frac{|\{z \in N_r^x \cap \Omega : I(z) \leq \alpha\}|}{|N_r^x \cap \Omega|}. \tag{2}$$

Based on the definitions above, the energy function is defined by:

$$E_{LH}(P_i, P_o, C) = \lambda_1 \int_{in(C)} W_1(P_i, P_r^x) dx$$
$$+ \lambda_2 \int_{out(C)} W_1(P_o, P_r^x) dx + \mu \int_C ds, \quad (3)$$

where λ_1, λ_2 and μ are constants, P_i^x and P_o^x are the averages of histograms at all pixels inside and outside the curve C. $\mu \int_C ds$ computes the perimeter of the curve as a constraining force to reduces redundant curves, and $W_1(\cdot)$ is the linear Wasserstein distance which compares two normalized histograms, its computation formula is shown as follows:

$$W_1(P_1, P_2) = \int_0^L |F_1(y) - F_2(y)| dy. \quad (4)$$

It is obvious that the energy function consists of two parts: a region-based fitting energy term and a length penalty term. The former term compares the histograms aiming at finding a best segmentation curve so that the pixel histogram can optimally fit the average histograms of the foreground or background. It is a crucial image force guiding the active curves to reach the real boundaries. While the latter term calculates the contour perimeter and smooths the curve. The LH model is the earliest exploration to carry histogram to generate a novel thinking on texture segmentation.

2.2   LBP-Driven Vector-Valued Chan-Vese (LBPCV) Model

The LBP-driven vector-valued Chan-Vese (LBPCV) model [17] is a histogram based vector CV model. It combines with many characteristics of the image through histogram as vector filters for texture image segmentation, like intensity, first order derivatives and especially the local binary pattern (LBP) values. From this model, one can also derive some other versions by altering the filter channels.

The LBP operator, which can extract texture features in a local region, is first proposed by Ojala et al. [16]. It has many good properties such as simplicity, illumination and rotation invariance, so it has been widely utilized in face recognition [3] and texture classification [16]. The original LBP operator is defines in a 3×3 local window centered at a pixel x (see Fig. 1), then it binarizes the intensity differences between the center pixel and its neighbors and encodes it into a binary number. Its computation formula is presented as follows:

$$LBP(x_c) = \sum_{i=0}^{p-1} s(x_i - x_c) 2^p, \quad (5)$$

where p is the total number of the neighborhood pixels, 2^p is a binomial factor for each sign $s(x_i - x_c)$, and $s(\cdot)$ is a symbolic function:

$$s(x) = \begin{cases} 1, & x \geq 0 \\ 0, & x < 0. \end{cases} \quad (6)$$

In the LBPCV model, intensity, gradient and LBP values of a pixel form a feature vector to fully describe a pixel. In the whole domain, three feature filter maps based on the original gray-scale image I can be obtained. Let x be a pixel in the derived vector-image U and U_j be the jth filter map, and then define P_{rj}^x calculating the histogram on image U_j at pixel x in a patch with radius r, P_{ij} and P_{oj} represent the corresponding averages histograms of all pixels inside and outside the curve C, so the energy function for the LBPCV model is :

$$E_{LBPCV}(\bar{P}_i, \bar{P}_o, C) = \int_{in(C)} \sum_{j=1}^{J} \lambda_{1j} W_1(P_{ij}, P_{rj}^x) dx$$
$$+ \int_{out(C)} \sum_{j=1}^{J} \lambda_{2j} W_1(P_{oj}, P_{rj}^x) dx + \mu \int_C ds, \tag{7}$$

where J is the total number of filter maps, here $J = 3$, and μ, λ_{1j}, λ_{2j} are experiential positive values, $\bar{P}_i$ and $\bar{P}_o$ are average vector histograms which are equivalent to $(P_{i1}, P_{i2}, ..., P_{iJ})$ and $(P_{o1}, P_{o2}, ..., P_{oJ})$. The LBPCV model suggests that if various features of a image be in full use, they can complement each other in an integrated vector CV segment model and finally achieve a win-win effect as a whole.

3   Proposed Method

In this section, we will creatively put forward a local contrast pattern (LCP) texture descriptor, which contains two components: differential contrast ξ and orientation θ. Next we will establish a statistical histogram-based CV model with a truncated Gaussian kernel function on LCP feature maps to segment color texture region with the capacity of anti-jamming.

3.1   Local Contrast Pattern (LCP)

Also enlightened by the Weber Local Descriptor (WLD) in extracting gradient direction, we turn to adopting the texture direction estimation by generating the local horizontal and vertical gradient. Thus, in order to fully describing texture structure, we combines the two local component, differential contrast ξ with orientation θ, as a novel local operator named local contrast pattern (LCP). A LCP value of a current pixel x_c is computed as Fig. 1 illustrated.

Differential Contrast ξ. The differential contrast ξ of the LCP descriptor highlights the differential contrast between the center pixel and points around it as the intensity variation of the current pixel. In the same 3×3 local window as LBP, ξ of the pixel x_c is computed as follows:

$$\xi(x_c) = \sum_{i=0}^{p-1} (x_i - x_c). \tag{8}$$

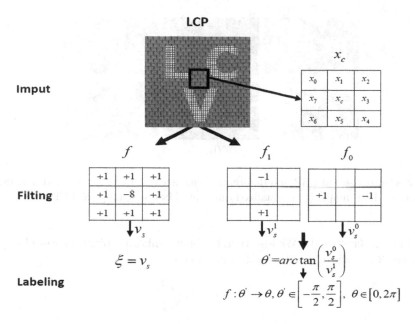

Fig. 1. Illustration of the computation of the Local Contrast Pattern (LCP) descriptor.

Unlike the LBP operator, the differential contrast ξ feature sums all the intensity differences $(x_i - x_c)$ instead of binarizing the comparison results. And it preserves the local intensity discrepancy so that it can reflect the variability of gray value effectively and further better discriminate different objects in segmentation application. To verify the performance of ξ, we test two images to compare both operators in Fig. 2. The original images are shown in (a), including synthetic and natural images, (b) and (c) are the normalized LBP maps and the normalized differential contrast maps of the LCP descriptor respectively. It is obvious that they both have the ability to describe texture, but LBP highlights the texture features of background simultaneously or even more prominent than that of the foreground, while ξ in LCP suppresses some global clusters and distinguish different image features successfully. In addition, ξ is more accurate than LBP in the extraction of texture details when referring to the head and legs of zebra image. Moreover, under the influence of light or shadow, there seems to be no serious disturbance in ξ map.

Orientation θ. The orientation θ of LCP is computed based on the gradient orientation as described in [5]. Consider the larger gradient value corresponds to the bigger significant intensity variation, we utilize vertical and horizontal templates to filter image and then combine this two gradient components to

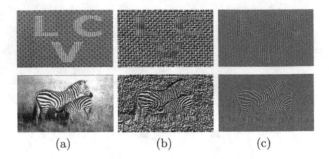

(a)   (b)   (c)

Fig. 2. Comparison of LBP and differential contrast ξ of LCP. (a) original images, (b) normalized LBP maps, (c) normalized differential contrast maps in LCP.

calculate gradient angle. We also turn to the neighboring pixels centered in pixel x_c in the 3×3 window with the formula below:

$$\theta'(x_c) = arctan(\frac{\nu_s^0}{\nu_s^1}), \tag{9}$$

where $\nu_s^0 = x_7 - x_3$, $\nu_s^1 = x_5 - x_1$, and $\theta' \in [-\pi/2, \pi/2]$. For unsigned data representation and convenient calculation, we perform a mapping $f : \theta' \to \theta$. Thus, the final orientation map θ of the LCP operator is defined as follows:

$$\theta(x_c) = arctan2(\nu_s^0, \nu_s^1) + \pi \tag{10}$$

with

$$arctan2(\nu_s^0, \nu_s^1) = \begin{cases} \theta', & \nu_s^0 > 0, \text{ and } \nu_s^1 > 0 \\ \pi + \theta', & \nu_s^0 > 0, \text{ and } \nu_s^1 < 0 \\ \theta' - \pi, & \nu_s^0 < 0, \text{ and } \nu_s^1 < 0 \\ \theta', & \nu_s^0 < 0, \text{ and } \nu_s^1 > 0 \end{cases}$$

where $\theta \in [0, 2\pi]$. The final orientation θ considers not only the value of θ' computed in Eq. 9 but also the sign of ν_s^0 and ν_s^1.

3.2   Statistical Histogram Fitting Energy Based on LCP

Consider a given gray image I whose image domain Ω can be separated into two regions Ω_i and Ω_o by a closed evolving curve C. T_ξ and T_θ are two LCP feature maps. For better localization property, we introduce a region-scalable kernel function that make the histogram of the pixel closer to the center one weight higher and decrease quickly to zero when the distance is beyond the parameter scope. So this LCP driving fitting energy based on local histogram at center pixel x of feature maps can be defined by:

$$E_x^{LCP}(P_{ki}^x, P_{ko}^x, C) = \lambda_1 \int_{in(C)} \sum_{k=1}^{2} \gamma_k K_\sigma(x-y) W_1(P_{ki}^x, P_{kr}^y) dy$$

$$+ \lambda_2 \int_{out(C)} \sum_{k=1}^{2} \gamma_k K_\sigma(x-y) W_1(P_{ko}^x, P_{kr}^y) dy, \tag{11}$$

where λ_1, λ_2 are the weighting parameters which control the image data driven force, γ_k is a choosing parameter with $\gamma_k \in \{0,1\}$, $k = 1$ represents the differential contrast map of the LCP descriptor and $k = 2$ indicates the orientation map of the LCP descriptor, and if $\gamma_k = 1$, the current kth map will be working in the energy fitting model. $W_1(\cdot)$ is the linear Wasserstein distance defined as Eq. 4, $K_\sigma(x-y)$ is the truncated Gaussian kernel. P_{kr}^y is the statistical histogram calculated in the neighborhood centered in a pixel y with radius r based on the kth LCP map, P_{ki}^x and P_{ko}^x are the averages of the statistical histograms of the pixels inside and outside curve C in a local patch whose size is defined by the distance parameter ρ of $K_\sigma(x-y)$ with a center x.

According to the level set methods, the active contour C is implicitly expressed as the zero level of a Lipschitz function $\phi : \Omega \to R$, so Eq. 11 can be rewritten as:

$$E_x^{LCP}(F_{ki}^x, F_{ko}^x, \phi) = \lambda_1 \int_\Omega H(\phi(x)) \sum_{k=1}^{2} \gamma_k K_\sigma(x-y)$$

$$\times \int_0^L |F_{ki}^x(z) - F_{kr}^y(z)| dz dy + \lambda_2 \int_\Omega (1 - H(\phi(x))) \tag{12}$$

$$\times \sum_{k=1}^{2} \gamma_k K_\sigma(x-y) \int_0^L |F_{ko}^x(z) - F_{kr}^y(z)| dz dy,$$

where $H(\cdot)$ is the Heaviside function, and the cumulative distributions $F_{ki}^x(z)$ and $F_{ko}^x(z)$ are described as follows:

$$\begin{cases} F_{ki}^x(z) = \dfrac{\int_\Omega H(\phi(x)) K_\sigma(x-y) F_{kr}^y(z) dy}{\int_\Omega H(\phi(x)) K_\sigma(x-y) dy} \\[4mm] F_{ko}^x(z) = \dfrac{\int_\Omega (1 - H(\phi(x))) K_\sigma(x-y) F_{kr}^y(z) dy}{\int_\Omega (1 - H(\phi(x))) K_\sigma(x-y) dy}. \end{cases} \tag{13}$$

For color texture image, we will embed color information into the local histograms based on the LCP texture feature maps. Given a 3-dimensional color image U for a two-phase segmentation. We first make LCP feature transform on single color component diagram U_j and get feature maps $T_{\xi j}$ and $T_{\theta j}$, so that texture information is extracted on each channel and a vector-valued feature map is obtained. Then for every pixel point, an integrated local histogram and its cumulative histogram are computed in a block contending all color channels instead of calculating in a patch of an one-dimensional image:

$$P_r^x(\alpha) = \frac{\sum_{j=1}^d |\{z \in N_r^x \cap \Omega : T_{kj}(z) = \alpha\}|}{d \times |N_r^x \cap \Omega|}, d = 3. \tag{14}$$

$$F_r^x(\alpha) = \frac{\sum_{j=1}^d |\{z \in N_r^x \cap \Omega : T_{kj}(z) \leq \alpha\}|}{d \times |N_r^x \cap \Omega|}, d = 3. \tag{15}$$

where $k - 1$ denote ξ and $k - 2$ denote θ,

Our goal is to minimize the energy for all pixels in the whole image domain. Thus, the total local histogram fitting energy based on LCP by integrating Eq. 12 in Ω is expressed as below:

$$E_{LCP}(F_{ki}^x, F_{ko}^x, \phi) = \lambda_1 \iint_\Omega H(\phi(x)) \sum_{k=1}^2 \gamma_k K_\sigma(x - y) \int_0^L |F_{ki}^x(z) - F_{kr}^y(z)| dz dy dx$$

$$+ \lambda_2 \iint_\Omega (1 - H(\phi(x))) \sum_{k=1}^2 \gamma_k K_\sigma(x - y) \int_0^L |F_{ko}^x(z) - F_{kr}^y(z)| dz dy dx. \tag{16}$$

Equation 16 is the objective function to be minimized, it is called a data fitting energy and plays a key role in driving the deforming contour C to evolute.

4   Experimental Results

In this section, we tested a number of color texture images to verify the effectiveness as well as the robustness for illumination, noise and curve initialization of the proposed model. In order to directly proof the LCP descriptor playing a key role in texture discrimination, we have done an additional set of experiments without a kernel function in our novel method. Besides, three unsupervised color-texture partitioning methods including a classical strategy called JSEG method [21], an approach by aggregating super pixels (SAS) [23] and an segmentation based on multiscale quaternion Gabor filters and splitting strategy (MQGF) [9] were used for color-texture segmentation comparison.

Color Texture Images. Figure 3 compared the results on three color texture images from "Berkeley" database listed in (a) whose target objects were obvious but background interferences were multiply. (b) and (c) were the results of our modified scheme with and without incorporating the kernel function K_σ. As we expect, the integrated histograms calculating in a vector feature image block were also valid as in single-image cases. The salient regions with inhomogeneous color and texture were captured more successfully when K_σ enhanced the effect. (d)-(f) depicted the results of three comparisons: the classical JSEG method, and the latest SAS and MQGF method. Disappointed, many unwanted contours were generated and texture details were neglected. Clearly, our model was also superior in terms of both precision and accuracy.

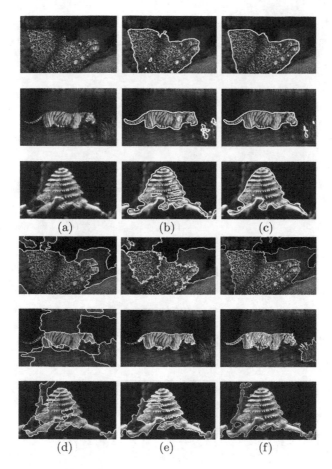

Fig. 3. Segmentation results on natural color images. (a) original images, (b) results of our method using ξ, (c) results of our method using a combination of ξ and K_σ, (d) results of the JSEG method, (e) results of the SAS method, (f) results of the MQGF method. (Color figure online)

Robustness for Illumination and Noise. In order to verify the robustness for illumination and noise still worked in color texture segmentation versions, we made some additional contrast tests in more extreme circumstances. We took three color texture images with special processing: the first one was set with a light source at the top of the object, the second one was added both uneven illumination and Gaussian white noise of variance 0.02, and the third one was polluted by a combination of Gaussian white noise of variance 0.02 and salt-and-pepper noise of density 0.05. (b) were the results of our method using ξ while (c) were the results of our method using a combination of ξ and K_σ. In spite of bad environment, the results of our strategy shown in (b) and (c) were unaffected completely, and they maintained accurate segmentations as always.

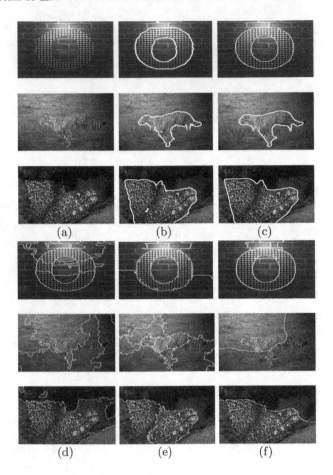

Fig. 4. Experimental results for illumination and noise. (a) original images, (b) results of our method using ξ, (c) results of our method using a combination of ξ and K_σ, (d) results of the LH model, (e) results of the LBPCV model, (f) results of the LGDF model.

(d)–(f) were the results of three contrasting approaches. Conclusion got from the distribution of cutting curves was that the bad influence of illumination to all the comparisons was very deadly, and their resistance to noise was also weaker than ours. In this experiment, we had increased the difficulty specifically, but it turns out that the robustness was still particularly evident in our novel model (Fig. 4).

5   Conclusion

In this paper, the local contrast pattern(LCP) descriptor is proposed to tackle intensity inhomogeneity and orientation information in texture image segmentation. We first use it to make image feature conversion and then we incorporate the feature maps into a histogram-based CV model with a Gaussian kernel function. The experimental results demonstrate that the proposed method can segment both gray-scale texture image and color-texture image. Furthermore, our method is proved to be very robust for image quality and curve initialization.

Acknowledgments. This project was partially supported by the Key Areas Research and Development Program of Guangdong Grant 2018B010109007.

References

1. Ding, K., Xiao, L., Weng, G.: Active contours driven by region-scalable fitting and optimized Laplacian of gaussian energy for image segmentation. Signal Process. **134**, 224–233 (2017)
2. Abdelkader Birane, L.H.: A fast level set image segmentation driven by a new region descriptor. IET Image Process. **15**, 615–623 (2021)
3. Ahonen, T., Hadid, A., Pietikäinen, M.: Face recognition with local binary patterns. In: Pajdla, T., Matas, J. (eds.) ECCV 2004. LNCS, vol. 3021, pp. 469–481. Springer, Heidelberg (2004). https://doi.org/10.1007/978-3-540-24670-1_36
4. Chan, T., Zhu, W.: Level set based shape prior segmentation. In: IEEE Computer Society Conference on Computer Vision and Pattern Recognition, CVPR 2005, vol. 2, pp. 1164–1170. IEEE (2005)
5. Chen, J., Shan, S., He, C., Zhao, G., Pietikainen, M., Chen, X., Gao, W.: WLD: a robust local image descriptor. IEEE Trans. Pattern Anal. Mach. Intell. **32**(9), 1705–1720 (2010)
6. Chunming, L., Chiu-Yen, K., Gore, J.C., Zhaohua, D.: Minimization of region-scalable fitting energy for image segmentation. IEEE Trans. Image Process. Publ. IEEE Sig. Process. Soc. **17**(10), 1940–9 (2018)
7. Fang, J., Liu, H., Zhang, L., Liu, J., Liu, H.: Fuzzy region-based active contours driven by weighting global and local fitting energy. IEEE Access **PP**(99), 1–1 (2019)
8. Han, B.: Level Sets Driven by Adaptive Hybrid Region-Based Energy for Medical Image Segmentation. Smart Multimedia (2020)
9. Li, L., Jin, L., Xu, X., Song, E.: Unsupervised color-texture segmentation based on multiscale quaternion Gabor filters and splitting strategy. Signal Process. **93**, 2559–2572 (2013)
10. Li, C., Kao, C.Y., Gore, J.C., Ding, Z.: Implicit active contours driven by local binary fitting energy. In: IEEE Conference on Computer Vision and Pattern Recognition, CVPR 2007, pp. 1–7. IEEE (2007)
11. Li, C., Kao, C.Y., Gore, J.C., Ding, Z.: Minimization of region-scalable fitting energy for image segmentation. IEEE Trans. Image Process. **17**(10), 1940–1949 (2008)
12. Li, C., Xu, C., Gui, C., Fox, M.D.: Level set evolution without re-initialization: a new variational formulation. In: IEEE Computer Society Conference on Computer Vision and Pattern Recognition, CVPR 2005, vol. 1, pp. 430–436. IEEE (2005)
13. Yang, L., et al.: Automatic liver segmentation from CT volumes based on level set and shape descriptor. Acta Automatica Sinica **47**, 327–337 (2021)
14. Luo, S., Tai, X.C., Huo, L., Wang, Y.: Convex shape prior for multi-object segmentation using a single level set function. In: 2019 IEEE/CVF International Conference on Computer Vision (ICCV) (2019)

15. Ni, K., Bresson, X., Chan, T., Esedoglu, S.: Local histogram based segmentation using the Wasserstein distance. Int. J. Comput. Vis. **84**(1), 97–111 (2009)
16. Ojala, T., Pietikainen, M., Maenpaa, T.: Multiresolution gray-scale and rotation invariant texture classification with local binary patterns. IEEE Trans. Pattern Anal. Mach. Intell. **24**(7), 971–987 (2002)
17. Wang, Y., Wang, H., Xu, Y.: Texture segmentation using vector-valued Chan-vese model driven by local histogram. Comput. Electr. Eng. **39**(5), 1506–1515 (2013)
18. XuHao Zhi, H.S.: Saliency driven region-edge-based top down level set evolution reveals the asynchronous focus in image segmentation. Pattern Recogn. **80**, 241–255 (2018)
19. Yan, S., Tai, X.C., Liu, J., Huang, H.Y.: Convexity shape prior for level set based image segmentation method. IEEE Trans. Image Process. **PP**(99), 1 (2020)
20. Yang, X., Jiang, X., Zhou, L., Wang, Y., Zhang, Y.: Active contours driven by local and global region-based information for image segmentation. IEEE Access **PP**(99), 1 (2020)
21. Yining Deng, M.B.: Unsupervised segmentation of color-texture regions in images and video. IEEE Trans. Pattern Anal. Mach. Intell. **23**(8), 800–810 (2001)
22. Zhang, K., Zhang, L., Song, H., Zhou, W.: Active contours with selective local or global segmentation: a new formulation and level set method. Image Vis. Comput. **28**(4), 668–676 (2010)
23. Li, Z., Xiao-Ming Wu, S.F.C.: Segmentation using superpixels: a bipartite graph partitioning approach. In: 2012 IEEE Conference on Computer Vision and Pattern Recognition (CVPR), pp. 789–796. IEEE (2012)
24. Zhou, X., Huang, X., Duncan, J.S., Yu, W.: Active contours with group similarity. In: 2013 IEEE Conference on Computer Vision and Pattern Recognition (CVPR), pp. 2969–2976. IEEE (2013)

A Weakly Supervised Defect Detection Based on Dual Path Networks and GMA-CAM

Huosheng Xie[✉] and ShuFeng Lin

FuZhou University, FuZhou, China
xiehs@fzu.edu.cn

Abstract. In recent research, the defect detection algorithm based on the fully-supervised object detection model has become one of the research hotspots and has achieved good results. However, fully-supervised object detection models require image-level and localization-level labels. Obtaining these labels requires a great deal of manpower. Therefore, this paper proposes a dual path defect detection network (DPNET) based on weakly supervised object detection model, which aims to identify the classification label and carry on localization for defects merely by using image-level labels. Firstly, the paper employs the deep convolutional residual network ResNet-50 as a feature classification network for defect classification. Secondly, we designed a localization network based on the global average-max pooling class activation map (GAM-CAM) and the Full Convolutional Channel Attention (FCCA) for defect localization, which can improve the defect localization accuracy. Experimental results on the DAGM dataset confirm that the proposed detection model is able to efficiently detect defects.

Keywords: Defect detection · Weakly supervised object detection · Dual Path Network · Global average-max pooling class activation map · Full Convolutional Channel Attention

1 Introduction

On the production line, the detection of defects is an irreplaceable link. However, most factories still use manual inspection [1]. Although manual inspection provides immediate correction of surface defects, manual inspection has inspection defects in aspect of accuracy, consistency and efficiency. Therefore, it has become a significant task to research an automated defect detection method.

Since 2014, Girshick et al. [2] proposed the R-CNN (Regions with CNN features) framework that embeds CNN into the object detection model, which is a landmark innovation. In the following years, Object detectors based on fully-supervised deep learning model have received great attention and research among scholars in the field of object detection. Nowadays, Existing object detectors based on fully-supervised deep learning model usually can be divided into two categories [3]. The one is two-stage detector, such as Fast R-CNN [3], Faster R-CNN [5] and Mask R-CNN [6]. The other is one-stage detector, such as You Only Look Once (YOLO) [7–10], Single Shot MultiBox Detector

Y. Peng et al. (Eds.): ICIG 2021, LNCS 12888, pp. 467–478, 2021.
https://doi.org/10.1007/978-3-030-87355-4_39

(SSD) [11] and RetinaNet [12]. The two-stage detectors generate candidate boxes with region proposal net and then further carry on classification and adjustment of the bounding box based on the previously generated candidate box, thus they have higher detection accuracy. Furthermore, the one-stage detectors directly generate predicted boxes from input images without region proposal step, so they are time efficient and can be utilized for real-time detection. Due to the ability to learn complex nonlinear input-output relationships, more and more object detection models based on CNN have been applied into the field of defect detection and have achieved remarkable results. For example, Liu et al. [12] applied the single-stage detector SSD to the field of defect detection, and added an attention mechanism module to the model structure, making the model more propitious to the detection of small defect targets. Xie et al. [14] introduced RefineDet into the field of fabric defect detection, and designed a bottom-up path enhancement structure in the head structure, which effectively enhance the accuracy of defect detection. The classification and localization accuracy of the fully-supervised deep learning model are really high, but a great many training samples with localization-level labels are required.

Owing to the high cost of the data labeling process, it is difficult for many tasks to obtain fully supervision information such as localization-level labels. Therefore, weakly supervised learning model that does not require localization-level labels information has begun to attach researchers' interest. Zhou et al. [15] creatively proposed Class Activation Mapping (CAM). CAM can visualize the localization ability of the classification network itself. However, a long-standing problems for classification network is that they often highlight the most discriminative parts rather than the integral extent of object. To overcome this limitation, many methods are proposed. Previous methods is able to be categorized into two approaches. The first approach is to erase the most discrimination parts of the object and then find new object parts, such as HAS [16], ACOL [16], ADL [18] and EIL [19]. This approach is suitable for big objects, thus it is not suitable for defect detection, which most objects belong to small objects. The second approach is to find a wide range of object parts by using spatial relationships, such as SPG [20], DANet [22] and CCAM [22]. This approach can get good results in defect localization, but the most models are too complicated and the classification ability is not as good as the original classification model. Defect detection pays more attention to the model's classification ability than localization ability, so the approach also is not suitable for defect detection.

In this paper, in order to tackle the above-mentioned problems, a simple Dual-Path Network (DPNet) is proposed for defect detection. As shown in Fig. 1, the DPNet separates classification and localization tasks into two networks. The classification network pays more attention to the classification. The localization network focus more on localization. A Fully Convolutional Channel Attention (FCCA) Block, which is an improved module in Channel Attention [23, 24], is added into the localization network to enhance the weight of the feature map channel. And we proposed a global average-max pooling class activation map (GAM-CAM) to improve the model localization ability for small objects.

The main contributions of this work are as follows:

- We propose a Dual-Path Network for defect detection, which separates classification and localization tasks into two independent sub-tasks: the object classification and the object localization.
- We propose the Fully Convolutional Channel Attention Block and the global average-max pooling class activation map to enhance the localization capability for small object defect detection.
- The experimental results show that our model achieves better defect detection results on the DAGM dataset, which shows that the proposed model can better detect defects.

The paper is organized as follows. Firstly, Sect. 2 is the detailed introduction of our defect detection method. In Sect. 3, the experimental results and analysis are described. Finally, conclusions are given in Sect. 4.

2 Methodology

2.1 The Architecture of Dual Path Network

The architecture of our network is shown in Fig. 1. The network has two parts: the classification network and the localization network. The classification network uses the traditional classification network as classifier. The location network with FCCA uses GAM-CAM to implement object location. Combining the classification of the classification network and the localization of the localization network, we can achieve object detection.

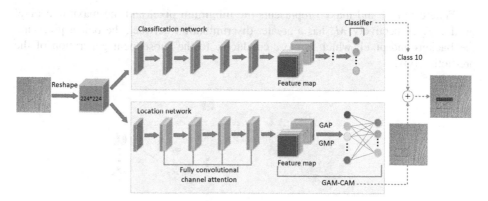

Fig. 1. The architecture of Dual Path Network

2.2 Global Average-Max Pooling Class Activation Map

Recall Class Activation Map
As mentioned above, CAM [15] can visualize the object feature information in the classification networks. As shown in Fig. 2, the main implementation principle is as follows:

1. CAM adds a global average pooling (GAP) before the fully connected layer. For each channel dimension k, GAP can calculated the average pixie value F^k by:

$$F^k = AvgPool(f_k(x, y)), \quad k = 1, 2, \ldots, n \tag{1}$$

2. Train the model. The number of input nodes of the fully connected layer is n ($F^k \in \mathbb{R}^{n \times 1}$). And the number of output nodes is C, which represents the number of C image categories. The classification result S_c ($c \in C$) can be obtained by:

$$S_c = \sum_k w_k^c \sum_{x,y} f_k(x, y) \tag{2}$$

Where w_k^c indicates the weight parameter of the fully connected layer.
3. After the model trains parameters of each layer, the weight parameter of the fully connected layer w_k^c and the last convolutional layer feature map f_k can be used to generate the score map M_c of c classes, denoted as M_c.

$$M_c(x, y) = \sum_k w_k^c f_k(x, y) \tag{3}$$

4. By using Min-Max Scaling to normalize the score map, the M_c is transformed, named as M_c'.

$$M_c' = \frac{M_c - \min(M_c)}{\max(M_c) - \min(M_c)} \tag{4}$$

Where $\min(\cdot)$ and $\max(\cdot)$ represents the minimum pixel and the maximum pixel on the M_c respectively. M_c' has a greater discrimination between the object pixel and the background pixel, which is more conducive to the subsequent generation of the prediction box.

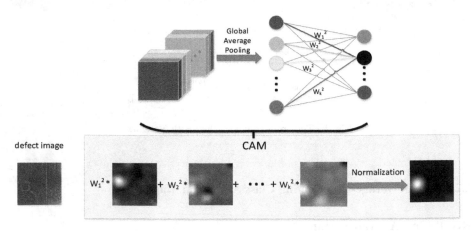

Fig. 2. CAM mechanism

Global Average-Max Pooling Class Activation Map
Given the prior work [15], we know GAP is a global average of a map, which encourages the network to find the extent of the object area as compared to GMP (Global max pooling) which is to find the maximum pixel value of a map and encourages the network to find the discriminative part. So CAM selects GAP as the bridge between the convolutional layer and the fully connected layer. We think this choice is correct. Through experiments we find GAP can really achieve better localization results than GMP on the big object. But to small object, we find that adding some the most significant area information to the global area information is able to better enhance the localization ability of the model.

Based on the discussion mentioned above, we propose the global average-max pooling class activation map (GAM-CAM). As shown in Fig. 3, GAM-CAM uses GAP and GMP to pool the last convolutional layer feature map f_k respectively. Then it mixes the two pooling information in a certain proportion to get F^k. By modifying Eq. (1), we can obtain GAM-CAM. The equation is as follows:

$$F^k = \alpha * AvgPool(f_k(x, y)) + \beta * MaxPool(f_k(x, y), \quad k = 1, 2, \ldots, n \qquad (5)$$

Where α and β are the mix ratio of GAP and GMP respectively.

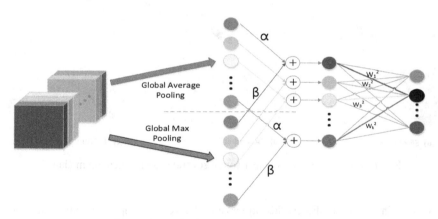

Fig. 3. Global average-max CAM mechanism

By modified the value of α and β, GAM-CAM is suitable for not only on small objects, but also on the big objects. As for how to set the suitable value of α and β, please see the experimental Sect. 3.5 to knowledge more.

2.3 Full Convolutional Channel Attention

As proved by the prior work [23, 24], the attention mechanism can improve the model's localization effect. Therefore, we add the attention mechanism to our localization model. The SE net [24] can really enhance the localization ability of the model, but the CBAM net [23] (Channel attention module + Spatial attention module) is not as good as the original model on the localization effect. In order to find the problem, we separate the channel attention module and the spatial attention module. We find that the model which add the channel attention module can get better localization result than the spatial attention module on the small object detection. Therefore, we abandon the spatial attention module and research the channel attention module.

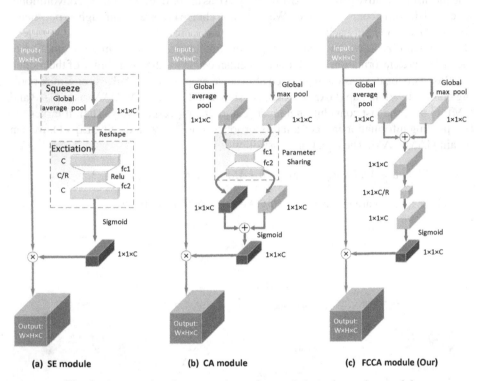

(a) SE module   (b) CA module   (c) FCCA module (Our)

Fig. 4. A comprehensive comparison of several channel attention module

As seen in Fig. 4(a), SE net adds Squeeze-and-Excitation operation after the convolution layer to determine the weight of feature map channel and increase the weight of channels that play a positive contribution to the feature map so that the training model can get better effect. Different from the SE module, the channel attention mechanism (Fig. 4(b)) uses simultaneously both GAP and GMP to obtain richer information of the feature map. On the basis of the CA and SE module, Our FCCA (Fig. 4(c)) uses the convolutional layers instead of Multilayer Perceptron (MLP) to form a fully convolutional structure, which can greatly reduce model parameters and improve detection speed.

3 Experiments

3.1 The Datasets and Evaluation Metrics

The Datasets
The experimental dataset uses the benchmark defect dataset DAGM2007. The DAGM2007 dataset contains 1046 images in the training set and 1054 images in the test set. There are totally 10 defect categories in the training set, namely Class1, Class2, ..., Class10. Due to lack of the localization label, in order to enhance the localization ability, the training set randomly selects an additional 1000 flawless images as the background class, namely Class 11. So the training set has totally 11 categories.

Evaluation Metrics
We use classification accuracy (ACC) as the experimental classification metrics and Choe et al. [25] propose the latest indicators *MaxBoxAcc2* as the experimental localization evaluation metrics. *MaxBoxAcc2* optimizes the calculation method on the basis of Cor-Loc (also known as GT-known localization accuracy). Although the weakly supervised learning model does not require localization labels in the training, the localization labels is needed when calculating the evaluation indicators. We can calculate *MaxBoxAcc2* as follows.

For a given true labeled B_i^{gt} on the test set, we calculate the box accuracy $BoxAcc2(\tau, \delta)$ under the threshold τ of the score map and the threshold δ of IoU.

$$BoxAcc2(\tau, \delta) = \frac{1}{N} \sum_i \left[IoU\left(B_i^{gt}, B_i(\tau)\right) \geq \delta \right] \tag{6}$$

Where $B_i(\tau)$ indicates the prediction box when the pixel value in the score map is bigger than the threshold τ. $IoU\left(B_i^{gt}, B_i(\tau)\right)$ calculates the intersection ratio and measured the degree of overlap between the real box and the prediction box.

The calculation method of the evaluation metrics $MaxBoxAcc2(\delta)$ of the model is as follows:

$$MaxBoxAcc2(\delta) = max_\tau (BoxAcc2(\tau, \delta)), \quad \delta \in \{0.3, 0.5, 0.7\} \tag{7}$$

The model sets different threshold τ for different methods so that $BoxAcc2(\tau, \delta)$ can get the maximum value, and then compares the performance with different methods.

3.2 Experimental Settings

The experimental backbond network for classification and localization network is ResNet-50. The epoch is 20. The number of batches is set to 16. Optimizer is stochastic gradient descent optimizer (SGD optimizer). Momentum and weight decay coefficient are 0.9 and 0.0001. The learning rate (LR) is 0.0015. The MultiStepLR is used to adjust the learning rate, which make the learning rate drop to 1/10 of the learning rate every 10 epochs.

3.3 Background vs No Background

In this section, we analyzed the role of background pictures to weakly-supervised model.

As seen from Table 1, the ACC of the model with no background data is higher than the model with background data, but the localization accuracy is extremely low. After visualize the feature map by CAM, we find the reason why causes this phenomenon. The model with no background data use the implicit features instead of defects as a classification standard. In other words, the model with no background data doesn't really learn the characteristics of defects.

Table 1. Background vs no background

Dataset	ACC (%)	Localization accuracy (%)		
		$MaxBoxAcc2_{0.3}$	$MaxBoxAcc2_{0.5}$	$MaxBoxAcc2_{0.7}$
Background	96.00	**67.19**	**39.20**	**6.18**
No background	**100.00**	18.55	11.94	2.31

To fully-supervised model, the problem does not exist because it uses the localization labels to assist the model in training. However, to weakly-supervised model, due to lack of the localization label, the dataset needs to add some background pictures to assist the model in training so that it can really learn the characteristics of defects as the classification standard.

3.4 Channel Attention

In this subsection, we compare the localization effect of three attention mechanisms.

Table 2. Localization accuracy with channel attention

Method	Localization accuracy (%)		
	$MaxBoxAcc2_{0.3}$	$MaxBoxAcc2_{0.5}$	$MaxBoxAcc2_{0.7}$
Original model	67.19	39.20	6.18
SE module	65.30	**43.60**	11.21
CA module	**72.85**	42.03	11.32
FCCA module	71.80	43.29	**12.26**

As shown in Table 2, the localization accuracy of the model with channel attention is better than the model with no channel attention. And FCCA module has higher localization effect than SE module. Although FCCA module is closed to the CA module on localization effect, FCCA module is a fully convolutional structure, which greatly reduce model parameters and improve detection speed.

3.5 Mixing Hyperparameter of GAP and GMP

As mentioned in Sect. 2.2, GAM-CAM has two hyperparameters, which is α for GAP and β for GMP. We investigate the effect of α and β on localization accuracy. In this experiment, we use the FCCA module.

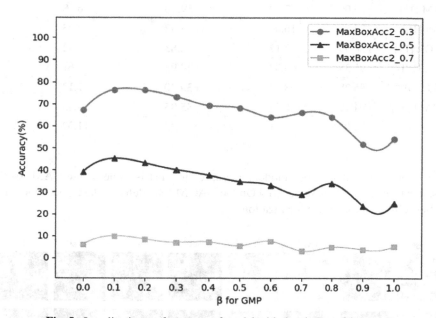

Fig. 5. Localization performance of model with the change of β ($\alpha = 1$)

From the Fig. 5, we can see the change of the localization accuracy along with β under the condition that α is 1.We find that the localization accuracy is closed to the model with GAP alone when β is 0.5 and exceed when β is 0.4. The best localization accuracy is able to be achieved when the β is 0.1.

We also conducted experiments on the CUB dataset, which the most pictures belongs to big objects. We discover that it has better result when model only uses AVG. That means the value of α and β is not absolute. They can be adjusted with the dataset.

3.6 Comparison with the Other Methods

For the purpose of showing the weakly-supervised object detection ability of the proposed method, a comparative experiment is conducted to compare our model with other weakly-supervised detection model: CAM [15], HAS [16], ACOL [16], ADL [18], SPG [20] and CCAM [22] on the DAGM2007 dataset.

Table 3. Performance comparison between the proposed method and other weakly supervised detection models

Method	ACC (%)	Localization accuracy (%)		
		$MaxBoxAcc2_{0.3}$	$MaxBoxAcc2_{0.5}$	$MaxBoxAcc2_{0.7}$
CAM [15]	96.00	67.19	39.20	6.18
HAS [16]	27.77	16.03	4.82	2.93
ACOL [17]	58.59	7.12	2.83	0.42
ADL [18]	95.38	66.03	28.93	4.61
SPG [20]	95.28	68.34	39.20	7.12
CCAM [22]	94.12	55.24	35.95	9.85
Our	**96.00**	**76.41**	**47.37**	**11.32**

As shown in Table 3, our model's classification net is same as the CAM, so the classification result is the same. And On the DAGM2007 defect dataset, our model has the best effect on the defect localization.

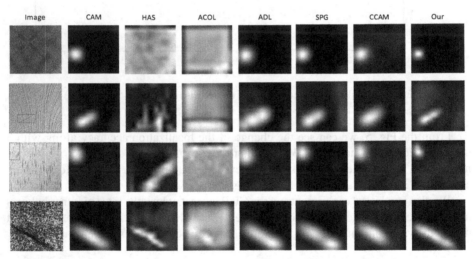

Fig. 6. The score map for proposed method and the other methods on DAGM2007

Some images also are shown in Fig. 6. It can be seen from the score map that our model can detect more detailed defect information than other models.

4 Conclusion

This paper presents a weakly-supervised Dual-Path Network based on FCCA and GAM-CAM. This method separates classification and localization tasks into two networks. The classification network concentrates on the classification. The localization network focus more on localization. FCCA and GAM-CAM is proposed to enhance the localization accuracy in the localization network. Experimental results show that the proposed model is suitable for the defect detection. And the proposed method only uses image-level labels, which greatly reduces the manual annotation cost, so this weakly-supervised defect detection model based on deep convolutional network and class activation mapping mechanism can better meet the actual industrial environment.

References

1. Czimmermann, T., Ciuti, G., Milazzo, M., et al.: Visual-based defect detection and classification approaches for industrial application. Sensors 20(5), 1459 (2020)
2. Girshick, R., Donahue, J., Darrell, T., et al.: Rich feature hierarchies for accurate object detection and semantic segmentation. In: IEEE Conference on Computer Vision and Pattern Recognition, pp. 580–587. IEEE, Columbus (2014)
3. Wu, X., Sahoo, D., Hoi, S.C.H.: Recent advances in deep learning for object detection. Neurocomputing 396, 39–64 (2020)
4. Girshick, R.: Fast r-cnn. In: IEEE International Conference on Computer Vision, pp. 1440–1448. IEEE, Santiago (2015)
5. Ren, S., He, K., Girshick, R., et al.: Faster R-CNN: towards real-time object detection with region proposal networks. IEEE Trans. Pattern Anal. Mach. Intell. 39(6), 1137–1149 (2017)
6. He, K., Gkioxari, K.G., Dollár, P.: Mask R-CNN. In: IEEE International Conference on Computer Vision, pp. 2980–2988. IEEE, Venice (2017)
7. Redmon, J., Divvala, S., Girshick, R.: You only look once: unified, real-time object detection. In: IEEE Conference on Computer Vision and Pattern Recognition, pp. 779–788. IEEE, Las Vegas (2016)
8. Redmon, J., Farhadi, A.: YOLO9000: better, faster, stronger. In: IEEE Conference on Computer Vision and Pattern Recognition, pp. 6517–6525. IEEE, Hawaii (2017)
9. Farhadi, A., Redmon, J.: Yolov3: an incremental improvement. Computer Vision and Pattern Recognition. Cite as (2018)
10. Bochkovskiy, A., Wang, C.Y., Liao, H.Y.M.: Yolov4: Optimal speed and accuracy of object detection. arXiv preprint arXiv 2004.10934 (2020)
11. Liu, W., Anguelov, D., Erhan, D., Szegedy, C., Reed, S., Fu, C.-Y., Berg, A.C.: SSD: Single shot multibox detector. In: Leibe, B., Matas, J., Sebe, N., Welling, M. (eds.) ECCV 2016. LNCS, vol. 9905, pp. 21–37. Springer, Cham (2016). https://doi.org/10.1007/978-3-319-464 48-0_2
12. Lin, T.Y., Goyal, P., Girshick, R., et al.: Focal loss for dense object detection. In: IEEE International Conference on Computer Vision, pp. 2980–2988. IEEE, Venice (2017)
13. Liu, Z., Liu, S., Li, C., et al.: Fabric defects detection based on SSD. In: The 2nd International Conference on Graphics and Signal Processing, pp. 74–78. IEEE, Taiwan (2018)
14. Xie, H., Wu, Z.: A robust fabric defect detection method based on improved RefineDet. Sensors 20(15), 4260 (2020)
15. Zhou, B., Khosla, A., Lapedriza, A., et al.: learning deep features for discriminative localization. In: IEEE Conference on Computer Vision and Pattern Recognition, pp. 2921–2929. IEEE, Las Vegas (2016)

16. Kumar Singh, K., Jae Lee, Y.: Hide-and-seek: forcing a network to be meticulous for weakly-supervised object and action localization. In: IEEE International Conference on Computer Vision, pp. 3524–3533. IEEE, Venice (2017)

17. Zhang, X., Wei, Y., Feng, J., et al.: Adversarial complementary learning for weakly supervised object localization. In: IEEE Conference on Computer Vision and Pattern Recognition, pp. 1325–1334. IEEE, Salt Lake City (2018)

18. Choe, J., Shim, H.: Attention-based dropout layer for weakly supervised object localization. In: IEEE Conference on Computer Vision and Pattern Recognition, pp. 2219–2228. IEEE, Long Beach (2019)

19. Mai, J., Yang, M., Luo, W.: Erasing integrated learning: A simple yet effective approach for weakly supervised object localization. In: IEEE Conference on Computer Vision and Pattern Recognition, pp. 8766–8775. IEEE, Seattle (2020)

20. Zhang, X., Wei, Y., Kang, G., Yang, Y., Huang, T.: Self-produced guidance for weakly-supervised object localization. In: Ferrari, V., Hebert, M., Sminchisescu, C., Weiss, Y. (eds.) ECCV 2018. LNCS, vol. 11216, pp. 610–625. Springer, Cham (2018). https://doi.org/10.1007/978-3-030-01258-8_37

21. Xue, H., Liu, C., Wan, F., et al.: Danet: Divergent activation for weakly supervised object localization. In: IEEE International Conference on Computer Vision, pp. 6589–6598. IEEE, Seoul (2019)

22. Yang, S., Kim, Y., Kim, Y., et al.: Combinational class activation maps for weakly supervised object localization. In: IEEE Winter Conference on Applications of Computer Vision, pp. 2941–2949. IEEE, Snowmass Village (2020)

23. Woo, S., Park, J., Lee, J.-Y., Kweon, I.S.: Cbam: Convolutional block attention module. In: Ferrari, V., Hebert, M., Sminchisescu, C., Weiss, Y. (eds.) ECCV 2018. LNCS, vol. 11211, pp. 3–19. Springer, Cham (2018). https://doi.org/10.1007/978-3-030-01234-2_1

24. Hu, J., Shen, L., Sun, G.: Squeeze-and-excitation networks. In: IEEE conference on computer vision and pattern recognition, pp. 7132–7141. IEEE, Salt Lake City (2018)

25. Choe, J., Oh S, J., Lee, S., et al.: Evaluating weakly supervised object localization methods right. In: IEEE Conference on Computer Vision and Pattern Recognition, pp. 3133–3142. IEEE, Seattle (2020)

Multi-Scale Spatial Transform Network for Atmospheric Polarization Prediction

Tianyi Dang[1,2(✉)], Yating Liu[3], Xinjian Gao[1], Linfang Xie[1], Yuan Yan[1,2], Qian Chen[1,2], and Jun Gao[1,2]

[1] School of Computer and Information, Hefei University of Technology, Hefei, China
{dangtianyi,xielinfang,yanyuan,chenqian}@mail.hfut.edu.cn,
{gaoxinjian,gaojun}@hfut.edu.cn
[2] Image Information Processing Laboratory, Hefei University of Technology, Hefei, China
[3] School of Data Science, University of Science and Technology of China, Hefei, China
liuyat@mail.ustc.edu.cn

Abstract. Sequential atmospheric polarization patterns can provide information for navigation when cues from a satellite source are not available. However, the real scenarios with extreme environments often cause corruption of captured atmospheric polarization data which makes the navigation unreliable. So this encourages us to focus on the atmospheric polarization patterns prediction (APP) topic. In this paper, we try to investigate and fill the gap in this task. We first propose a dataset called the Temporal Polarization 1072 (TP1072) dataset to compensate for the lack of the dataset, which makes future research more possible. And further, we propose a novel and efficient deep learning sequential prediction model named Multi-Scale Spatial Transform Network (MSST-Net) for that topic. The overall model includes a Spatial Transform decoder (STD) and an adversarial learning-based Physical Property Learning (PPL) strategy. The STD makes the model can perceive the sequential pattern easily which significantly increases prediction accuracy. And the PPL constrains the overall model to achieve more accurate physical property. The extensive experiments prove that both two modules are complement with each other and also demonstrate that our model can effectively capture the spatio-temporal cues of the atmospheric polarization mode.

Keywords: Atmospheric polarization patterns · Deep learning · Sequential data prediction

1 Introduction

As a natural attribute of the Earth, the atmospheric polarization patterns contain abundant optical information which has been widely used in many research topics such as the image defogging [6], the measurement of the distribution of airspace aerosols [21] and the aerial object detection [8]. Except that, the main

---

Supported by organization x.

Y. Peng et al. (Eds.): ICIG 2021, LNCS 12888, pp. 479–490, 2021.
https://doi.org/10.1007/978-3-030-87355-4_40

application scenario of this mode is the navigation field [5, 18, 22]. The atmospheric polarization patterns can provide stable navigation compass information because of its weather invariance and anti-interference property. Therefore, atmospheric polarization-based navigation has received more and more attention.

A real-time and accurate atmospheric polarization navigation system is highly related to the complete sequential polarization data. Recent well-designed hardware system still has various limitations such as the multi-lens channel scene error [8], CCD noise [13] and separate amplitude sensor resolution [14], when it comes to capturing polarized images. So it is difficult for the system to obtain the information of the ∞-shaped distribution continuously which is important to the polarization-based navigation, affecting the development of polarization navigation.

For solving that problem, we focus on a new task called Atmospheric Polarization Prediction (APP) which aims to predict the atmospheric polarization image at time x_{n+1} based on the previous sequential data between time x_m and x_n ($n - m + 1$ frames data). The structure of the APP task is shown in Fig. 1. It can provide a complement when the hardware does not work well. And to our knowledge, we are the first work on that topic. So we propose to treat that problem from two views: data and model.

From the data view, the main problem is that there is no dataset for that topic specifically because of the expensive costs of capturing equipment. For filling that gap, we propose a dataset called the Temporal Polarization 1072 dataset (TP1072) to cover this task. The overall dataset includes a total of 1072 frames which are organized into 563 sets of video clips. Each clip includes 5 frames of atmospheric polarization patterns data. The interval between each frame is set to 5 minutes to ensure the variance of the data. And considering different navigation application purposes, we collect data in two common scenarios in navigation, containing the sunny and the thin cloud weather. Among them, there were 34 sets under cloudy conditions and 529 sets corresponding to sunny weather. We conducted all of our experiments on that dataset, which demonstrates that the total dataset is challenging and suitable for training and evaluating deep learning prediction models.

From the model view, we aim to design a better model for the APP task. This task is essentially the video prediction task, but our initial experiments show that general deep video prediction methods [4, 10, 15] can not achieve good results on that topic. We argue the main reason is that the general models did not consider the priors of the atmospheric polarization data such as the temporal-spatial knowledge and the physical property of the polarization data. To solve the above problems well, we design a prediction model Multi-Scale Spatial Transform Network (MSST-Net) which is more competent for the APP task. The overall model includes a feature extraction backbone network, a Spatial Transform decoder (STD), and an adversarial learning-based Physical Property learning (PPL) strategy. The feature extractor can represent the previous frames better with a deep convolutional network. And then the STD introduces the temporal-spatial priors, including rotation and scale transform, to the deep model and predicts the next frame better. Finally, the PPL makes the output

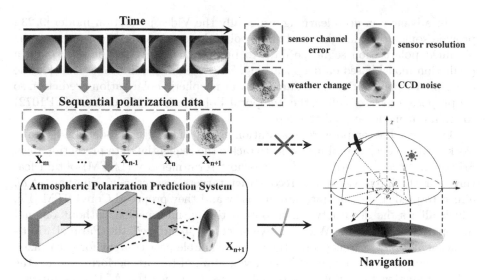

Fig. 1. The atmospheric polarization prediction task can provide a complement when the hardware does not work well.

images contain more physical properties, which are more reliable and suitable for downstream applications. Experiments on our TP1072 dataset prove the effectiveness of our model.

The main contributions of our work are as follows:

– We focus on the new atmospheric polarization prediction (APP) task and proposed the Temporal Polarization 1072 (TP1072) dataset to compensate for the gap in this field.
– We propose the Spatial Transform decoder (STD), which introduces the temporal-spatial priors of the atmospheric polarization data. The experiments show that it can bring 6.92% gains of the mean squared error metric comparing with the popular video prediction model.
– We provide an adversarial learning-based Physical Property Learning (PPL) scheme to train the overall model better. It also takes 4.49% improvements additionally.

2   Related Work

Facing to the problem of atmospheric polarization sequence data damage, the current general method modeled the atmospheric polarization patterns to replace the damaged data by simulation [3,16]. Traditional atmospheric polarization data restoration methods required accurate cloud thickness and aerosol type information to complete the modeling [2,12]. This required expensive sensors and a lot of time to collect [7], which brings limitations to further applications.

Recent advances in deep learning, especially the Video prediction model [9,23], provide some useful insights on how to solve these problems. We try to use the obtained polarization sequence data to predict the corrupted data through a prediction model based on deep learning. Since we are the first one to tackle the atmospheric polarization data damage by atmospheric polarization prediction so we propose a dataset called the Temporal Polarization 1072 dataset (TP1072) to train our model and fill the gap

Thanks to the temporal representation ability of the deep model [4,19], many works utilized deep neural networks to tackle the sequential data prediction task. Srivastava *et al.* [17] utilized two long-short term memory (LSTM) obtain features for the input video and reconstruct targets respectively. Xingjian *et al.* aimed to predict the precipitation intensity and they proposed ConvLSTM [15], which allows the deep network to obtain timing information without damaging spatial information. Wonmin Byeon *et al.* [4] utilized the Parallel Multi-Dimensional LSTM to captures the entire available past context for each pixel. These general prediction models achieved state-of-the-art performance on the video prediction task, but it is trivial to use them for the APP task directly because they did not consider the priors of the atmospheric polarization data. To solve this problem, we design a prediction model called Multi-Scale Spatial Transform Network (MSST-Net) which is more competent for the APP task.

3   Method

We propose the Multi-Scale Spatial Transform Network (MSST-Net) to tackle the atmospheric patterns prediction (APP) task likes Fig. 2 shows. The input previous frames of the atmospheric patterns data are first feed into the convolutional backbone to extract features. And then the proposed Spatial Transform decoder (STD) module predicts the next frame based on that encoded feature maps. In the training stage, the Physical Property loss is provided to achieve better physical property.

3.1   Temporal Sequential Feature Extractor

To get richer spatio-temporal relationships between polarized images, we follow ConvLSTM [15] to design a temporal sequential extractor to extract sequential temporal feature. The extractor has five cells: the memory cell i_t, the forget cell f_t, two states cell h_t, c_t and the output cell o_t. Each cell is a convolutional layer. The images in the input sequence $x_{m:n} = \{x_m, x_{m+1}, ..., x_{n-1}, x_n\}$ will enter the encoder in turn. For input x_t,The extractor will combine memory cell i_t and forget cell f_t to determine the output:

$$f_t = \sigma(W_{xf} * x_t + W_{hf} * h_{t-1} + W_{cf} \circ c_{t-1} + b_f)$$
$$i_t = \sigma(W_{xi} * x_t + W_{hi} * h_{t-1} + W_{ci} \circ c_{t-1} + b_i)$$
$$c_t = f_t \circ C_{t-1} + i_t \circ \tanh(W_{xc} * x_t + W_{hc} * h_{t-1} + b_c) \qquad (1)$$
$$o_t = \sigma(W_{xo} * x_t + W_{ho} * H_{t-1} + W_{co} \circ c_{t-1} + b_o)$$
$$h_t = o_t \circ \tanh(c_t),$$

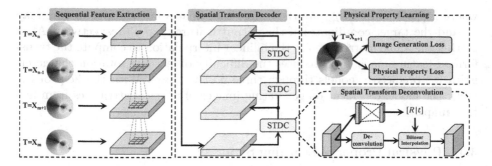

Fig. 2. Multi-Scale Spatial Transform Network (MSST-Net) includes a temporal sequential feature extractor, a Spatial Transform decoder (STD), and an adversarial learning-based Physical Property learning (PPL) strategy.

where $*$ represents convolution and $\circ$ represents the Hadamard product. W. and b. are the convolution weights and the bias parameters respectively. And we use the output cell o_t as our video representations.

3.2 Spatial Transform Decoder

The distribution of atmospheric polarization patterns is related to the real-time solar altitude angle, causing different degrees of rotation and scaling changes between the predicted results and the previous frame. And the convolutional neural network lacks the ability to model such rotation and scale variance [1]. Therefore, it is difficult for the model to predict the next frame with rotation characteristics. In order to solve this problem, we propose the Spatial Transform Decoder (STD) which consists of three Spatial Transform Deconvolution (STDC) layers likes Fig. 2 shows. These well-designed deconvolution layers combine the affine transformation and traditional deconvolution layer together to transfer the input feature maps f^s to the target one f^e, which makes the overall decoder predicts atmospheric polarization image more easily. Each STDC layer firstly regresses the affine transform matrix in an end-to-end manner based on the input feature maps f^s:

$$A_\theta = \begin{bmatrix} \theta_{11} & \theta_{12} & \theta_{13} \\ \theta_{21} & \theta_{22} & \theta_{23} \end{bmatrix} = \mathrm{FC}(f^s), \tag{2}$$

where A_θ is the output affine transformation matrix and $\mathrm{FC}(\cdot)$ means a fully-connected layer. And then we use this regressed affine transform matrix to compute coordinate relationships as follow:

$$\begin{pmatrix} x_i^s \\ y_i^s \end{pmatrix} = A_\theta \begin{pmatrix} x_i^e \\ y_i^e \\ 1 \end{pmatrix} = \begin{bmatrix} \theta_{11} & \theta_{12} & \theta_{13} \\ \theta_{21} & \theta_{22} & \theta_{23} \end{bmatrix} \begin{pmatrix} x_i^e \\ y_i^e \\ 1 \end{pmatrix}, \tag{3}$$

where (x_i^s, y_i^s) and (x_i^e, y_i^e) are the source coordinates in the input feature map f^s and the target coordinates of the output feature map f^e respectively. After getting the affine matrix, we use the bilinear interpolation to compute the transformed feature maps. STD reduces the difficulty of learning rotation characteristics for predictive models through three STDC layers. With the help of the STD, the model can focus on generating images of physical attributes from feature maps.

3.3   Physical Property Learning Strategy

Different from the RGB image, atmospheric polarization patterns have complex physical features, such as neutral points, negative polarization effect and E-vector distribution. The general loss function design does not consider the physical properties of the image. Therefore, it is difficult to generate prediction results containing physical properties by using traditional loss functions. If we use the known physical properties of polarization to design the loss function, the loss function of the model will become complicated, and the computational cost of the network will be greatly increased. To solve this problem, we design the Physical Property Learning (PPL) function. This function consists of the physical property loss and the image generation loss.

To make the output image includes more physical property as much as possible, we design an adversarial learning-based Physical Property loss. We first build a physical property discriminator D. The input of D is the ground-truth image x_{n+1}^{gt} at time $n+1$ and the prediction result $G(o_t)$, where G means our Spatial Transform Decoder, which can be interpreted as the generator in the adversarial learning framework. The D aims to classify real or fake for each input and generator is trained to fool the discriminator simultaneously. The total physical property loss $L_{physical}$ is written as:

$$\min_{G} \max_{D} V\{G, D\} = E_{x_{n+1}^{gt}} \left[\log D(x_{n+1}^{gt})]\right] + E_{o_t} \left[\log(1 - D(G(o_t)))\right]. \quad (4)$$

And except that, we also use the common used L2 loss as our image generation loss to constrain the average prediction error:

$$L_{image} = \frac{1}{HW}||x_{n+1}^{gt} - D(G(o_t))||^2, \quad (5)$$

where H and W are the height and width of the image. For training, we minimize the total following PPL object function as follow:

$$L_{PPL} = L_{image} + \lambda L_{physical}. \quad (6)$$

With the help of both image generation loss and the physical property loss, our model can learn the physical properties of atmospheric polarization patterns through iterative optimization better.

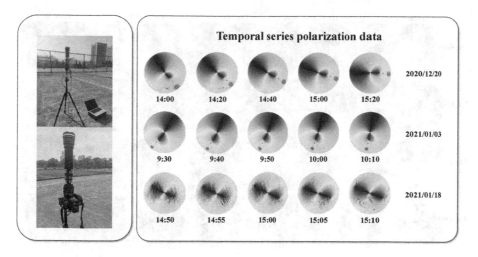

Fig. 3. Temporal Polarization 1072 dataset

4   Temporal Polarization 1072 Dataset

In order to complete the training of the time-series prediction model, we collected 43 days of atmospheric polarization patterns data and established an atmospheric polarization patterns dataset called Temporal Polarization 1072 (TP1072) dataset. Our collection equipment included a camera (D850, Nikon Corporation), a Nikon lens, and a sheye lens (Sigma 8 mmf/3.5), as well as two sets of rotating polarizers. We collected 563 series of atmospheric polarization pattern data. Each time sequence data group contains five-time sequence atmospheric polarization patterns images and the image collection interval is at least 5 min. The size of the polarization image obtained by the D850 camera is 8256 × 5504. Because the resolution is too large as the input of the network, according to the traditional processing method of atmospheric polarization modes [3], we obtained the atmospheric polarization angle (AoP) through calculation and the processing of the Stokes matrix to characterize the distribution of atmospheric polarization patterns. The size of the processed image was 256 × 256 pixels. Figure 3 shows the acquisition equipment and data of the TP1072 dataset.

5   Experiments

In this section, we first proved through experiments that the Multi-Scale Spatial Transform Network (MSST-Net) prediction model can excellently complete challenging atmospheric polarization prediction (APP) tasks. And then, we performed ablation studies to analyze the importance of each module. We also show some prediction examples at different time intervals to determine the effect of the model on different interval steps prediction tasks qualitatively. Finally, we performed a physical property evaluation, which proves that our prediction results can provide an effective supplement when the hardware equipment is not running well.

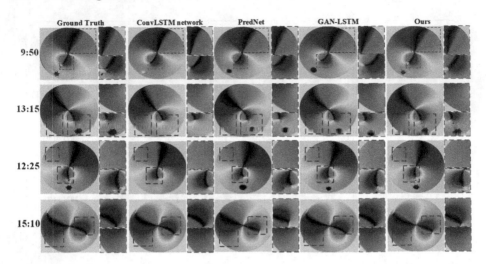

Fig. 4. Comparison of prediction results under different solar altitude angles (different times).

5.1 Quantitative Analysis of Multi-Scale Spatial Transform Network

In this part of the experiment, we demonstrate the performance of the proposed prediction model in the APP task. We compare with some widely used compute vision and traditional atmospheric polarization restoration methods [3,11,15,20]. To qualitatively evaluate the prediction results, we introduced three metrics, namely mean square error (MSE), peak signal to noise ratio (PSNR), and structural similarity index (SSIM). For the video prediction task, the higher the score of PSNR and SSIM, the lower the score of MSE represents the better performance of the model. Table 1 shows the quantitative analysis results.

Table 1. Quantitative analysis of multi-scale spatial transform network.

Method	PSNR	SSIM	MSE
ConvLSMT network [15]	27.046	0.9488	1.647
PredNet [11]	27.659	0.9382	1.543
GAN-LSTM Model [20]	27.964	0.9254	1.523
ConvLSTM+PPL	27.746	0.9480	1.573
Single-layer STDC	27.599	0.9474	1.533
Ours	29.971	0.9480	1.440

The first, second, third and sixth lines of Table 1 describe the quantitative evaluation of the proposed method and other methods on the TP1072 dataset. It can be seen that our model is superior to the other methods in PSNR and

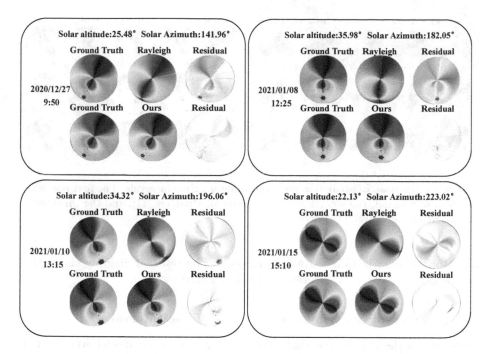

Fig. 5. Comparison results between multi-scale spatial transform network and traditional Rayleigh method [3].

MSE indexes while still ensuring SSIM. The fourth and fifth lines in Table 1 are the results of the ablation experiment. With the addition of Spatial Transform decoder (STD) module, the prediction results of the model have been significantly improved. This proves that the STD module can help the model predicts atmospheric polarization image more easily.

In Fig. 4, we show the predicted results for different solar altitude angles. The first column of Fig. 4 is ground truth, the second column is the ConvLSTM network [15] results, the third and fourth columns are the results of PredNet [11] and GAN-LSTM Model [20]. And the fifth column shows the prediction results of our model. At 9 a.m., our model can fully predict the solar morphology of overexposure points, whereas the ConvLSTM network gives fuzzy predictions near the sun. At noon, the solar overexposure point increases. Our model can still effectively deal with the cloud cover of the ∞-shaped distribution, while other models have produced fuzzy results at the solar position. At 4:10 p.m., the sun had moved out of view of the fisheye lens and a six-layer atmospheric polarization angle (AoP) isochromate appeared along the edge of the ∞-shaped distribution. Our model clearly predicts the three-layer AoP isochromate, while other models are difficult to accurately predict such distribution characteristics. It can be seen that our model effectively captures the spatiotemporal characteristics and physical distribution characteristics of atmospheric polarization patterns. Figure 5 shows the results of our model compared with the traditional

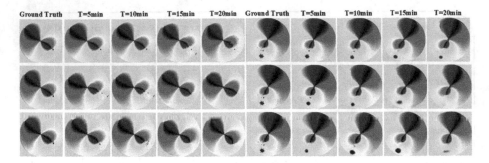

Fig. 6. Comparison of prediction results at different time intervals. The first row is the result of our model, the second row is the result of PredNet [11], and the third row is the result of the ConvLSTM network [15].

atmospheric polarization restoration method. The residual diagram shows that our method is obviously superior to the traditional method.

5.2   Prediction Experiment of Different Time Interval

This part of the experiment shows the performance of our model over different time intervals. In Fig. 6, we show the prediction results of each model under three different time intervals. When the prediction time interval is 10 min, our model can accurately predict the details of the polarization image. But other models have been wrong in predicting the details of the polarization patterns. When the input sequence interval is increased to 15 min, our model can still give clear prediction results. Other models give fuzzy predictions, and parts of the predictions change in the opposite direction to the meridian of the sun. This is not consistent with the real conditions of the polarization patterns change characteristics. When the time interval increases to 20 min, the predicted results of our model can still guarantee the symmetry of the atmospheric polarization patterns. At this time, the results of other models have shown a large degree of fuzzy prediction in the position of the sun, the AoP isochromate and the atmospheric polarization distribution shape. The experimental results show that our model can still achieve better results than other models.

5.3   Physical Property Assessment

The physical properties of atmospheric polarization patterns are varied, and there is no comprehensive measurement index for the physical properties of polarization. Therefore, the model is evaluated from the perspective of physical properties by comparing the actual course angle with the course angle calculated by the prediction results. Polarization navigation is accomplished by calculating the course angle from the solar meridian features, and we used the method proposed by Huijie Zhao *et al.* [22] to solve the course angle. The resulting course angle error is shown in Table 2. It can be seen that under different solar altitude

Table 2. The course angle error calculated from the prediction results under different solar altitude angles (different times).

Method	9:30	11:30	12:30	14:30	16:30
ConvLSMT network [15]	6.68°	7.57°	8.91°	7.87°	7.49°
PredNet [11]	6.43°	7.24°	8.39°	8.28°	7.84°
GAN-LSTM Model [20]	4.52°	5.32°	6.13°	5.78°	4.75°
Ours	3.49°	4.15°	4.08°	3.58°	3.52°

angles, the course angle error obtained by using the prediction results provided by our model is the smallest. The course angle error calculated by the prediction result of the ConvLSMT network [15] is the largest. The general prediction model only learns the color and texture transformation rules of atmospheric polarization patterns. This will leave the physical properties of the predicted results missing. The experimental results show that our model can provide a complement when the hardware does not work well.

6   Conclusion

In this paper, we focus on the new atmospheric polarization prediction (APP) task and proposed the Temporal Polarization 1072 dataset to compensate for the gap in this field. In addition, we propose an efficient deep learning sequential prediction model Multi-Scale Spatial Transform Network (MSST-Net) to solve the APP task. The overall model includes a Spatial Transform decoder (STD) and an adversarial learning-based Physical Property Learning (PPL) strategy. Through the experiment, we show that the MSST-Net can excellently complete the task of the APP.

References

1. Azulay, A., Weiss, Y.: Why do deep convolutional networks generalize so poorly to small image transformations? (2018)
2. Bréon, F.M.: Comment on Rayleigh-scattering calculations for the terrestrial atmosphere. Appl. Opt. **37**(3), 428–429 (1998)
3. Bucholtz, A.: Rayleigh-scattering calculations for the terrestrial atmosphere. Appl. Opt. **34**(15), 2765–73 (1995)
4. Byeon, W., Wang, Q., Srivastava, R.K., Koumoutsakos, P.: Contextvp: fully context-aware video prediction. In: Proceedings of the European Conference on Computer Vision (ECCV), pp. 753–769 (2018)
5. Chu, J., Zhao, K., Qiang, Z., Wang, T.: Construction and performance test of a novel polarization sensor for navigation. Sens. Actuators A Phys. **148**(1), 75–82 (2008)
6. Emberton, S., Chittka, L., Cavallaro, A.: Underwater image and video dehazing with pure haze region segmentation. Comput. Vis. Image Understand. **168**, 145–156 (2018)

7. Gruev, V., Perkins, R.: A 1 mpixel CCD image sensor with aluminum nanowire polarization filter. In: Proceedings of 2010 IEEE International Symposium on Circuits and Systems (ISCAS) (2010)

8. Horváth, G., Barta, A., Gál, J., Suhai, B., Haiman, O.: Ground-based full-sky imaging polarimetry of rapidly changing skies and its use for polarimetric cloud detection. Appl. Opt. **41**(3), 543–559 (2002)

9. Isola, P., Zhu, J.Y., Zhou, T., Efros, A.A.: Image-to-image translation with conditional adversarial networks. In: Proceedings of the IEEE Conference on Computer Vision and Pattern Recognition, pp. 1125–1134 (2017)

10. Kaneko, T., Ushiku, Y., Harada, T.: Label-noise robust generative adversarial networks. arXiv e-prints (2018)

11. Lotter, W., Kreiman, G., Cox, D.: Deep predictive coding networks for video prediction and unsupervised learning (2016)

12. Mayer, B.: Radiative transfer in the cloudy atmosphere. Eur. Phys. J. Conf. **1**, 75–99 (2009)

13. Pust, N.J., Shaw, J.A.: Dual-field imaging polarimeter using liquid crystal variable retarders. Appl. Opt. **45**, 5470 (2006)

14. Pezzaniti, J.L., Chenault, D.B.: A division of aperture MWIR imaging polarimeter. In: Proceedings of SPIE - The International Society for Optical Engineering vol. 44, no. 3, pp. 515–533 (2005)

15. Shi, X., Chen, Z., Wang, H., Yeung, D.Y., Wong, W.K., Woo, W.C.: Convolutional LSTM network: A machine learning approach for precipitation nowcasting. MIT Press (2015)

16. Siewert, C.E.: A discrete-ordinates solution for radiative-transfer models that include polarization effects. J. Quant. Spectrosc. Radiat. Transf. **64**(3), 227–254 (2000)

17. Srivastava, N., Mansimov, E., Salakhutdinov, R.: Unsupervised learning of video representations using LSTMs. JMLR.org (2015)

18. Tao, Q., et al.: Retrieving the polarization information for satellite-to-ground light communication. J. Opt. **17**(8), 085701 (2015)

19. Tulyakov, S., Liu, M.Y., Yang, X., Kautz, J.: MocoGAN: decomposing motion and content for video generation (2017)

20. Xu, Z., Du, J., Wang, J., Jiang, C., Ren, Y.: Satellite image prediction relying on GAN and LSTM neural networks. In: ICC 2019-2019 IEEE International Conference on Communications (ICC), pp. 1–6 (2019). https://doi.org/10.1109/ICC.2019.8761462

21. Schechner, Y.Y., Narasimhan, S.G., Nayar, S.K.: Polarization-based vision through haze. Appl. Opt. **42**, 511 (2003)

22. Zhao, H., Xu, W., Ying, Z., Li, X., Bo, J.: Polarization patterns under different sky conditions and a navigation method based on the symmetry of the AOP map of skylight. Opt. Express **26**(22), 28589 (2018)

23. Zhu, J.Y., Park, T., Isola, P., Efros, A.A.: Unpaired image-to-image translation using cycle-consistent adversarial networks. In: 2017 IEEE International Conference on Computer Vision (ICCV) (2017)

Dynamic Hypergraph Regularized Broad Learning System for Image Classification

Xiaoxiao Yang[1]([✉]), Yu Guo[1], Yinuo Wang[2], Peilin Jiang[1], and Fei Wang[2]

[1] School of Software Engineering, Xi'an Jiaotong University, Xi'an 710049, China
yangxiaoxiao@stu.xjtu.edu.cn, {yu.guo,pljiang}@xjtu.edu.cn
[2] Institute of Artificial Intelligence and Robotics, Xi'an Jiaotong University,
Xi'an 710049, China
wynkingdom@stu.xjtu.edu.cn, wfx@xjtu.edu.cn

Abstract. As a novel alternative to deep neural networks, the broad learning system (BLS) has exhibited outstanding performance in many machine learning tasks. The unique flat network structure enables BLS to extract the non-linear characteristics of the data. And the weights of the hidden layer are randomly generated, allowing BLS to provide rapid training for large-scale data. However, BLS focuses on approximating the target data and ignores the inherent geometric structure of the data. Graph structure can reflect the latent structure between samples of a dataset. Hypergraph learning has superior performance in modeling high-order relationships compared to simple graph-based learning methods that can only model pairwise relationships of data. In this paper, we propose a novel extension of the standard BLS. The proposed dynamic hypergraph regularized broad learning system (DHGBLS) incorporates hypergraph learning in the optimization process. And dynamic optimization is established to learn the hypergraph and the network's output weights simultaneously. In this way, the effects of various hyperedges can be automatically modulated. Experimental results on three popular datasets show the superiority of the proposed method over the standard BLS and other state-of-art classification methods.

Keywords: Broad learning system · Hypergraph regularization · Image classification

1 Introduction

Image classification aims to predict the label of an image from a set of categories. It is a fundamental research topic in the field of image processing and computer vision. The typical image classification process involves two parts: feature extraction and pattern classification [1]. With the advent of deep neural networks, computer vision, including image classification, has developed vigorously in recent years. Although deep neural networks [2] have strong learning

This work is supported by National Major Science and Technology Projects of China (No. 2019ZX01008101), Xi'an Science and Technology Innovation Program (No. 201809162CX3JC4), and Natural Science Foundation of Shaanxi Province (CN) (2021JQ-05).

Y. Peng et al. (Eds.): ICIG 2021, LNCS 12888, pp. 491–501, 2021.
https://doi.org/10.1007/978-3-030-87355-4_41

capabilities, the enormous amount of computation and a large number of hyper-parameter requirements have hindered their expansion and application in many fields. Besides, the unexplainable problem that has plagued neural networks for a long time is also one of its shortcomings.

The random vector functional link neural networks (RVFLNN) [3] propose another method to learn the parameters in neural networks, which overcomes the local minima, time consuming, and slow convergence problems caused by functional link neural networks (FLNN) [4]. Inspired by RVFLNN, Chen et al. proposed the Broad learning system (BLS) [5]. BLS eliminates the shortcomings of the application of RVFLNN in the modern big data era. The operation of BLS is as follows. The feature nodes and the enhancement nodes together form the hidden layer of BLS. The original data is transformed into sparse features through a series of feature nodes at first. Then, those sparse features are expanded at the enhancement nodes. Finally, the outputs of the feature nodes and the enhancement nodes are integrated as a state matrix. And the optimal weights are obtained by calculating the pseudo-inverse of the state matrix at the output layer. In BLS, only the weights connected to the output layer need to be calculated, while the weights of other processes are obtained through random generation. Another characteristic of BLS is its incremental learning algorithm. When the network needs to change for new inputs or new nodes, BLS can use the previous training information to quickly re-model without training the network from scratch. Based on those advantages of BLS, many extended models and applications have been derived [6–8].

In recent classification algorithms, learnings with the manifold structure of data have achieved promising performance [9–11]. They promote the performance of the algorithms by learning the underlying geometric knowledge of the data. The learning is achieved by imposing a graph constraint on the target output, where each vertex of the graph corresponds to a sample, and the similarity between samples represents the edge weight. However, traditional graphs only consider pairwise relationships and are incapable of expressing high-order relationships. Hypergraph learning [12–14] addresses the problem well. The main difference between a hypergraph and a normal graph is the number of vertices connected to them. Each hyperedge can connect any number of vertices, while each edge of traditional graphs can only connect two. But hyperedges may lead to redundancy in edges. So the construction of hypergraph is essential.

In this paper, we propose a dynamic hypergraph regularized broad learning system (DHGBLS). Our model is a novel extension of BLS incorporating graph constraints in the optimization process, which makes the learned output weights more discriminative. The dynamic learning of the hypergraph's incidence matrix and the output weights is realized through an alternate update method. Furthermore, the output weights have analytical solutions, so the optimization process of our model is efficient.

The remainder of the paper is organized as follows. We introduce the standard BLS in Sect. 2. In Sect. 3, we describe the construction of the hypergraph and the corresponding algorithms of the proposed DHGBLS are also introduced. In

Sect. 4, experiments are conducted and analyzed to verify the performance of the DHGBLS. In Sect. 5, this paper is summarized.

2 Broad Learning System

BLS is a novel alternative to deep neural networks proposed by Chen et al. [5]. Through ingenious construction in the structure of BLS, all its parameters can be obtained through random generation or calculation of pseudo-inverses. Compared with the deep learning algorithms that need to calculate numerous parameters in the filters and layers, BLS shows its unique advantages. Moreover, the incremental learning algorithm extended by BLS avoids the retraining of the entire model when new nodes or inputs are added to the network. The basic structure of BLS is shown in Fig. 1.

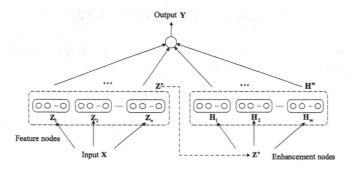

Fig. 1. The basic structure of BLS

To explain the mathematical method of BLS, a supervised learning task is considered. $\mathbf{X} = [\mathbf{x}_1, \mathbf{x}_2, \cdots, \mathbf{x}_N]^T \in \mathbb{R}^{N \times M}$ and $\mathbf{Y} = [\mathbf{y}_1, \mathbf{y}_2, \cdots, \mathbf{y}_N]^T \in \mathbb{R}^{N \times D}$ are respectively the inputs and the outputs of the training data set, where M and D represent the dimensions of the input vector and output vector. N denotes the number of the training samples.

The inputs are first transformed into k_i-dimensional features by the feature nodes. There are n groups of feature mappings, and each group contains k_i feature nodes. The mapped features of the i-th group denote as

$$\mathbf{Z}_i = \phi_i(\mathbf{X}\mathbf{W}_{ei} + \boldsymbol{\beta}_{ei}) \in \mathbb{R}^{N \times k_i}, i = 1, 2, \ldots, n, \tag{1}$$

where $\mathbf{W}_{ei} \in \mathbb{R}^{M \times k_i}$ and $\boldsymbol{\beta}_{ei} \in \mathbb{R}^{N \times k_i}$ are randomly generated, and the rows of $\boldsymbol{\beta}_{ei}$ are the same. The sparse representation of the inputs can be obtained by a sparse autoencoder. Then, the mapped features of all groups are collected as $\mathbf{Z}^n = [\mathbf{Z}_1, \mathbf{Z}_2, \cdots, \mathbf{Z}_n]$ as the input of the enhancement nodes.

Suppose that there are m groups of enhancement nodes, and each group contains p_j enhancement nodes. The activated features of the j-th group can be expressed as

$$\mathbf{H}_j = \xi_j(\mathbf{Z}^n \mathbf{W}_{hj} + \boldsymbol{\beta}_{hj}) \in \mathbb{R}^{N \times p_j}, j = 1, 2, \ldots, m, \tag{2}$$

where ξ_j is an activation function. $\mathbf{W}_{hj} \in \mathbb{R}^{(\sum_{i=1}^{n} k_i) \times p_j}$ and $\beta_{hj} \in \mathbb{R}^{N \times p_j}$ are also randomly generated, and the bias for each sample is still the same. The output of the enhancement nodes is denoted as $\mathbf{H}^m = [\mathbf{H}_1, \mathbf{H}_2, \cdots, \mathbf{H}_m]$.

Then, the output of the feature nodes and the enhancement nodes is integrated into a state matrix. The output of BLS is expressed as follows:

$$
\begin{aligned}
\hat{\mathbf{Y}} &= [\mathbf{Z}_1, \mathbf{Z}_2, \quad , \mathbf{Z}_n \mid \mathbf{H}_1, \mathbf{H}_2, \ldots, \mathbf{H}_m]\,\mathbf{W} \\
&= [\mathbf{Z}^n \mid \mathbf{H}^m]\,\mathbf{W} \\
&= \mathbf{UW}
\end{aligned}
\tag{3}
$$

where $\mathbf{U} = [\mathbf{Z}^n \mid \mathbf{H}^m] \in \mathbb{R}^{N \times (\sum_{i=1}^{n} k_i + \sum_{j=1}^{m} p_j)}$ represents the state matrix and $\mathbf{W} \in \mathbb{R}^{(\sum_{i=1}^{n} k_i + \sum_{j=1}^{m} p_j) \times D}$ denotes the weights connected to the output layer.

The optimization function is formulated by

$$
\arg \min_{\mathbf{W}} \mathcal{J}_{BLS} = \|\mathbf{Y} - \mathbf{UW}\|^2 + \lambda \|\mathbf{W}\|^2,
\tag{4}
$$

where λ is a positive constant for regularization. The weights can be obtained by calculating the ridge regression

$$
\mathbf{W} = (\mathbf{U}^T \mathbf{U} + \lambda \mathbf{I})^{-1} \mathbf{U}^T \mathbf{Y} = \mathbf{U}^\dagger \mathbf{Y},
\tag{5}
$$

where $\mathbf{U}^\dagger = \mathbf{U}^T \mathbf{U} + \lambda \mathbf{I})^{-1} \mathbf{U}^T$, $\mathbf{U}^\dagger$ is the pseudo-inverse of $\mathbf{U}$. $\mathbf{I}$ is an identity matrix.

3   The Proposed Method

Although BLS performs well in extracting information from the data itself, the underlying valuable geometric features between the data are ignored. To resolve the problem, the graph structure is used as a regularization term in the basic BLS. By preserving the local invariance of the data, the manifold structure of the data is learned. Specifically, the geometric probability distribution of the data is explored through graph constraints, i.e., adjacent points have similar conditional probabilities.

Since simple graphs can only model pairwise relations, they are incapable of more complex and multidimensional relations. Compared with simple graphs, hypergraphs can better describe the relationship between objects with multiple associations. Therefore, the hypergraph is introduced to define a broader relationship structure. The hypergraph regularized BLS (HGBLS) is proposed, and the optimization function is defined as follows:

$$
\arg \min_{\mathbf{W}} \mathcal{J}_{HGBLS} = \|\mathbf{Y} - \hat{\mathbf{Y}}\|^2 + \lambda_1 \mathbf{E}_{hg} + \lambda_2 \|\mathbf{W}\|^2,
\tag{6}
$$

where $\hat{\mathbf{Y}} = \mathbf{UW}$. $\mathbf{E}_{hg}$ is the hypergraph regularization term, which is to extract the geometric information of the data by imposing a manifold constraint on the output $\hat{\mathbf{Y}}$. λ_1 and λ_2 are regularization factors.

3.1 Hypergraph Regularized BLS

Hypergraph construction is the first step to obtain the hypergraph regularization term. In our image classification task, we regard each image in $\mathbf{X}$ as a vertex on the hypergraph. And a hypergraph $\mathcal{G} = (\mathcal{V}, \mathcal{E}, \mathbf{W}_{hg})$ can be constructed to formulate the relations among the inputs, where $\mathcal{V} = \{v_1, v_2, \ldots, v_N\}$ denotes the vertex set, $\mathcal{E} = \{e_1, e_2, \ldots, e_L\}$ is the hyperedge set, and $\mathbf{W}_{hg}$ is a diagonal matrix that denotes the hyperedge weights.

In this paper, the hyperedge generation follows a k-nn approach: a group of hyperedges is generated for each vertex depending on the neighborhood size k. And each hyperedge e_k is assigned a positive number $w(e_k)$ as the weight, which is the diagonal element of $\mathbf{W}_{hg}$. The incidence matrix $\mathbf{H} \in \mathbb{R}^{|\mathcal{V}| \times |\mathcal{E}|}$ represents $\mathcal{G}$ by defining the connection between vertices and hyperedges as

$$\mathbf{H}(v, e) = \begin{cases} \exp(-\frac{d^2}{\hat{d}^2}), & \text{if } v \in e \\ 0, & \text{if } v \notin e \end{cases}, \tag{7}$$

where d is the distance between the vertex v and the centroid vertex of the hyperedge e. $\hat{d}$ is the average distance between vertices.

Based on the $\mathbf{H}$, the diagonal matrices of vertex degrees $\mathbf{D}_v$ and hyperedge degrees $\mathbf{D}_e$ are respectively generated as

$$\mathbf{D}_v = \text{diag}(d(v)) = \text{diag}(\mathbf{H}\mathbf{W}_{hg}\mathbf{1}), \tag{8}$$

$$\mathbf{D}_e = \text{diag}(\delta(e)) = \text{diag}(\mathbf{1}^T \mathbf{H}), \tag{9}$$

where

$$d(v) = \sum_{e \in \mathcal{E}} w(e)\mathbf{H}(v, e), \tag{10}$$

$$\delta(e) = \sum_{v \in \mathcal{V}} \mathbf{H}(v, e), \tag{11}$$

and $\mathbf{1}$ is a column vector. Here, the weights of all hyperedges are set equal.

Utilizing the above information, a commonly used hypergraph regularized term [12] is obtained:

$$\begin{aligned}
\Psi(\hat{\mathbf{Y}}, \mathbf{L}_{hg}) &= \frac{1}{2} \sum_{c=1}^{n_c} \sum_{e \in \mathcal{E}} \sum_{u,v \in \mathcal{V}} \frac{\mathbf{W}_{hg}(e)\mathbf{H}(u, e)\mathbf{H}(v, e)}{\delta(e)} \left(\frac{\hat{\mathbf{Y}}(u, c)}{\sqrt{d(u)}} - \frac{\hat{\mathbf{Y}}(v, c)}{\sqrt{d(v)}} \right)^2 \\
&= \sum_{c=1}^{n_c} \sum_{u \in \mathcal{V}} \hat{\mathbf{Y}}(u, c)^2 \sum_{e \in \mathcal{E}} \frac{\mathbf{W}_{hg}(e)\mathbf{H}(u, e)}{d(u)} \sum_{v \in \mathcal{V}} \frac{\mathbf{H}(v, e)}{\delta(e)} \\
&\quad - \sum_{e \in \mathcal{E}} \sum_{u,v \in \mathcal{V}} \frac{\hat{\mathbf{Y}}(u, c)\mathbf{H}(u, e)\mathbf{W}_{hg}(e)\mathbf{H}(v, e)\hat{\mathbf{Y}}(v, c)}{\sqrt{d(u)d(v)}\delta(e)} \\
&= \hat{\mathbf{Y}}^T \mathbf{L}_{hg} \hat{\mathbf{Y}},
\end{aligned} \tag{12}$$

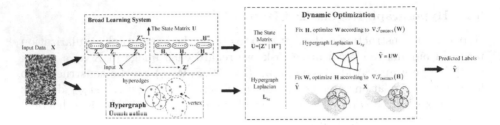

Fig. 2. The framework of the proposed Dynamic hypergraph regularized BLS

where the hypergraph Laplacian is drawn as

$$\mathbf{L}_{hg} = \mathbf{I} - \mathbf{D}_v^{-\frac{1}{2}} \mathbf{H} \mathbf{W}_{hg} \mathbf{D}_e^{-1} \mathbf{H}^T \mathbf{D}_v^{-\frac{1}{2}} \tag{13}$$

and n_c is the number of categories. This regularized term satisfies the requirement that the predicted labels $\hat{\mathbf{Y}}$ should be smooth on the graph $\mathcal{G}$. It is determined by both $\hat{\mathbf{Y}}$ and $\mathbf{L}_{hg}$.

Integrating hypergraph constraints into the optimization of BLS, we get the optimization function for hypergraph regularized BLS:

$$\arg\min_{\mathbf{W}} \mathcal{J}_{HGBLS} = \|\mathbf{Y} - \hat{\mathbf{Y}}\|^2 + \lambda_1 \operatorname{tr}\left(\hat{\mathbf{Y}}^T \mathbf{L}_{hg} \hat{\mathbf{Y}}\right) + \lambda_2 \|\mathbf{W}\|^2, \tag{14}$$

where $\hat{\mathbf{Y}} = \mathbf{UW}$. By substituting $\hat{\mathbf{Y}} = \mathbf{UW}$ into (14) and setting the gradient equal to 0, the solution of $\mathbf{W}$ can be obtained as

$$\mathbf{W} = (\mathbf{U}^T\mathbf{U} + \lambda_1 \mathbf{U}^T \mathbf{L}_{hg} \mathbf{U} + \lambda_2 \mathbf{I})^{-1} \mathbf{U}^T \mathbf{Y}. \tag{15}$$

3.2   Dynamic Hypergraph Regularized BLS

In this part, the complete DHGBLS algorithm will be introduced, and the framework of the proposed method is shown in Fig. 2. On the basis of (14), the hypergraph in our model also reflects the latent structure of the original inputs. According to (12), the constraint can be written as

$$\Omega(\mathbf{X}, \mathbf{L}_{hg}) = \operatorname{tr}(\mathbf{X}^T \mathbf{L}_{hg} \mathbf{X}). \tag{16}$$

Note that the constraint (16) only makes sense when $\mathbf{L}_{hg}$ is dynamically updated. And from the construction of the hypergraph, it can be seen that $\mathbf{L}_{hg}$ is determined by the incidence matrix $\mathbf{H}$.

Summarizing the above discussion, the cost function for dynamic hypergraph regularized BLS can be represented as a dual optimization problem as

$$\arg\min_{\mathbf{W},\mathbf{H}} \mathcal{J}_{DHGBLS} = \|\mathbf{Y} - \hat{\mathbf{Y}}\|^2 + \lambda_1 \operatorname{tr}(\mathbf{L}_{hg}((1-\beta)\hat{\mathbf{Y}}\hat{\mathbf{Y}}^T + \beta\mathbf{X}\mathbf{X}^T)) + \lambda_2 \|\mathbf{W}\|^2$$

$$= \|\mathbf{Y} - \hat{\mathbf{Y}}\|^2 + \lambda_2 \|\mathbf{W}\|^2$$

$$+ \lambda_1 \operatorname{tr}((\mathbf{I} - \mathbf{D}_v^{-\frac{1}{2}} \mathbf{H} \mathbf{W}_{hg} \mathbf{D}_e^{-1} \mathbf{H}^T \mathbf{D}_v^{-\frac{1}{2}})((1-\beta)\hat{\mathbf{Y}}\hat{\mathbf{Y}}^T + \beta\mathbf{X}\mathbf{X}^T)), \tag{17}$$

where $\hat{\mathbf{Y}} = \mathbf{UW}$. λ_1 and λ_2 are parameters for regularization. β is a trade-off parameter that balances the importance of the different components within the graph constraint.

The optimization function (17) needs to learn the weight matrix $\mathbf{W}$ and hypergraph's incidence matrix $\mathbf{H}$ simultaneously. We propose an iterative method to solve the variables alternately.

And the details of the optimization method are shown below. We first fix $\mathbf{H}$, the sub-problem boils to solving the original hypergraph regularized BLS. According to the Eq. (13) and (15), the optimal solution of $\mathbf{W}$ can be updated by iterating

$$\mathbf{W}_k = (\mathbf{U}^T\mathbf{U} + \lambda_1\mathbf{U}^T(\mathbf{I} - \mathbf{D}_{v_{k-1}}^{-\frac{1}{2}}\mathbf{H}_{k-1}\mathbf{W}_{hg}\mathbf{D}_{e_{k-1}}^{-1}\mathbf{H}_{k-1}^T\mathbf{D}_{v_{k-1}}^{-\frac{1}{2}})\mathbf{U} + \lambda_2\mathbf{I})^{-1}\mathbf{U}^T\mathbf{Y}. \tag{18}$$

Then, we fix $\mathbf{W}$ and take the derivative of Eq. (17) with respect to $\mathbf{H}$. The projected gradient method is utilized to solve the problem, and then we get [14]:

$$\nabla\mathcal{J}_{DHGBLS}(\mathbf{H}) = \mathbf{J}\left(\mathbf{I} \otimes \mathbf{H}^T\mathbf{D}_v^{-\frac{1}{2}}\mathbf{CD}_v^{-\frac{1}{2}}\mathbf{H}\right)\mathbf{WD}_e^{-2}$$
$$+ \mathbf{D}_v^{-\frac{3}{2}}\mathbf{HWD}_e^{-1}\mathbf{H}^T\mathbf{D}_v^{-\frac{1}{2}}\mathbf{CJW} \tag{19}$$
$$- 2\mathbf{D}_v^{-\frac{1}{2}}\mathbf{CD}_v^{-\frac{1}{2}}\mathbf{HWD}_e^{-1},$$

where $\mathbf{C} = (1-\beta)\mathbf{UWW}^T\mathbf{U}^T + \beta\mathbf{XX}^T$ and $\mathbf{J} = \mathbf{11}^T$. $\mathbf{H}$ is updated as

$$\mathbf{H}_k = P[\mathbf{H}_{k-1} - \alpha\nabla\mathcal{J}_{DHGBLS}(\mathbf{H}_{k-1})], \tag{20}$$

where α is the step size. The projection function P is drawn as

$$P[h_{ij}] = \begin{cases} h_{ij}, & \text{if } 0 \leq h_{ij} \leq 1 \\ 0, & \text{if } h_{ij} < 0 \\ 1, & \text{if } h_{ij} > 1 \end{cases} \tag{21}$$

Then the Laplacian matrix $\mathbf{L}_{hg}$ can be obtained with the learned $\mathbf{H}$. The process of optimization is stopped until the optimization function doesn't descend. The overall workflow of the dynamic hypergraph regularized BLS is summarized in Algorithm 1.

4   Experiments

To verify the effectiveness of the proposed method in image classification tasks, we conduct experiments on three well-known image data sets, i.e., two face image data sets: ORL [15] and UMIST [16] and a handwritten digit image data set: MNIST [17]. Example images from the above data sets are shown in Fig. 3. Table 1 summarizes these data sets, where Tn represents the number of samples randomly selected from each category for training.

We compare our proposed approach with the improved algorithm related to BLS: BLS [5], traditional graph regularized BLS, and hypergraph regularized BLS and some classic classification algorithms: SRC [18], LRC [19], SVM [20], and k-neighbor algorithm. A detailed description of settings is given below.

Algorithm 1. Dynamic Hypergraph Regularized BLS

Input: training data $\{\mathbf{X}, \mathbf{Y}\}_{i=1}^{N}$, regularization parameters (λ_1, λ_2), tradeoff parameter β, maximal iteration r, the number of feature and enhancement nodes groups (n, m), feature nodes k, enhancement nodes p

Output: output weight matrix $\mathbf{W}$

1: **Initialization:**
   Construct the initial hypergraph $\mathcal{G} = (\mathcal{V}, \mathcal{E}, \mathbf{W}_{hg})$;
   Calculate the state matrix $\mathbf{U}$ of BLS according to (3);
2: **for** iteration $t = 0$ to $r - 1$ **do**
3:    Fix $\mathbf{H}$, and update $\mathbf{W}$ according to (18)
4:    Fix $\mathbf{W}$, and update $\mathbf{H}$ according to (19)
5: **end for**

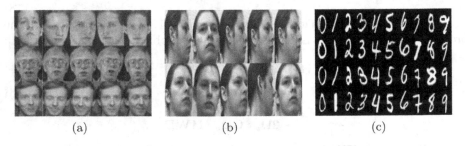

(a)   (b)   (c)

Fig. 3. Sample images from three data sets used in the experiment. Samples of subjects in (a) ORL, (b) UMIST, and (c) MNIST data sets.

4.1   Experiment Setup

The ORL Database of Faces [15] contains 10 different images of each of 40 subjects. The images are taken against a dark homogeneous background at different times with varying lighting, facial expressions, and facial details. The size of each grey-scale image is 92×112 pixels, which is cropped to 32×32 pixels in our experiment.

The UMIST Face Database [16] consists of 564 images of 20 distinct subjects. Among them, the number of images of each subject is 48 at most and 19 at least. Each image records the poses in the process of turning from profile to frontal views. The resolution of each image is 220×220, which is cropped to 56×46 here.

Table 1. Brief description of three datasets used in the experiment

Datasets	Sample size	Features	Number of classes	Tn
ORL	400	1024	40	{5, 6, 7}
UMIST	575	2576	20	{5, 10, 15}
MNIST	2000	784	10	{140}

Table 2. Average classification rates (%) of different algorithms on three databases

Databases	Tn	Settings of BLS (n, k, m, p)	Algorithms							
			LRC	SRC	KNN	SVM	BLS	GBLS	HGBLS	DHGBLS
ORL	5	(10, 25, 2, 400)	85.5	84.5	75.0	89.5	93.0	93.2	93.5	**94.2 ± 0.011**
	6	(20, 20, 2, 500)	93.1	91.3	82.5	91.1	94.4	95.6	95.6	**96.3 ± 0.015**
	7	(10, 10, 2, 500)	95.8	91.7	85.2	91.7	96.3	96.7	96.7	**97.3 ± 0.019**
UMIST	5	(20, 30, 4, 300)	75.6	77.3	60.1	71.2	84.5	86.0	85.4	**86.9 ± 0.013**
	10	(30, 25, 2, 500)	88.8	91.7	73.4	91.7	95.3	95.5	95.7	**97.1 ± 0.009**
	15	(20, 20, 2, 400)	92.0	98.2	82.4	95.3	98.2	98.5	98.9	**99.0 ± 0.011**
MNIST	140	(10, 20, 1, 500)	91.7	92.8	89.8	90.0	93.0	93.5	93.8	**94.2 ± 0.010**

The MNIST database of handwritten digits [17] has 60,000 samples for training and 10,000 samples for testing. We randomly select 2000 samples from the test set. 70% of them are used as the training set and the rest as the test set. The numbers from 0 to 9 contain 10 categories, and the original images with a resolution of 28×28 are used directly.

In our experiment, the model settings are as follows. For all BLS-related algorithms, the BLS network settings are consistent. The network settings of BLS are given in Table 2. We directly use the original training samples as the dictionary for LRC and SRC. As for SRC, the OMP [21] algorithm is applied in the solution. The hyper-parameters in the algorithms are fine tuned to achieve the best classification performance. Specifically, for the regularization parameters λ_1 and λ_2, they are searched in the range of $\{2^{-5}, 2^{-4}, \ldots, 2^4, 2^5\}$ and $\{10^{-5}, 10^{-4}, \ldots, 10^1, 10^2\}$. Experiments with different training samples are independently repeated 10 times to make the classification accuracy estimation more accurate and compelling. All the experiments are conducted on a computer with Intel Core i5-8300H CPU and 16 GB RAM.

4.2 Experimental Results

Table 2 shows the parameter settings of BLS and the average classification rates (%) of different algorithms on three databases. All results are averaged over ten repeated experiments. Besides, for the results of the proposed method, we display the standard deviation to prove the stability of the model.

Overall, among all the methods, DHGBLS achieves the best results in all classification tasks with few standard deviations. The incorporation of both graph learning and dynamic optimization admittedly enhances the performance. Although the improvement brought by dynamic optimization is not obvious sometimes, it still exists.

Compared with the typical BLS, graph regularization algorithms achieve better performance, demonstrating that learning with the manifold structure of data is effective. And the BLS-based algorithms exhibit superior performance, suggesting the powerful feature extraction ability of the BLS network. In theory, the performance of HGBLS should be better than that of GBLS, yet the results we get are sometimes inconsistent with it. The main reason is that although the number of samples corresponding to each subject in the training set is uniform, there may be differences in the test set. From the results of other comparison models, high accuracy cannot be attained when the amount of training data is small. It also confirms that the hypergraph constraints improve the learning ability of the model.

5   Conclusion

In this paper, we have proposed a dynamic hypergraph regularized broad learning system for image classification. The approach not only introduces hypergraph constraints into the optimization process but also investigates the simultaneous update of the hypergraph incidence matrix and the output weights. By alternating optimization, the optimal hypergraph structure is obtained as well as the optimal solution. Experiments have been performed on three popular datasets using randomly selected training samples. Experimental results confirm that the proposed method is superior to other improved graph-based BLS algorithms and several state-of-the-art classification methods. In the future, the application of DHGBLS to other classification and recognition tasks can be further investigated.

References

1. Cai, S., Zhang, L., Zuo, W., Feng, X.: A probabilistic collaborative representation based approach for pattern classification. In: Proceedings of the IEEE Computer Society Conference on Computer Vision and Pattern Recognition (2016). https://doi.org/10.1109/CVPR.2016.322
2. Hinton, G.E., Salakhutdinov, R.R.: Reducing the dimensionality of data with neural networks. Science (2006). https://doi.org/10.1126/science.1127647
3. Pao, Y.H., Park, G.H., Sobajic, D.J.: Learning and generalization characteristics of the random vector functional-link net. Neurocomputing (1994). https://doi.org/10.1016/0925-2312(94)90053-1
4. Klassen, M., Pao, Y.H., Chen, V.: Characteristics of the functional link net: a higher order delta rule net (1988). https://doi.org/10.1109/icnn.1988.23885
5. Chen, C.L., Liu, Z.: Broad learning system: an effective and efficient incremental learning system without the need for deep architecture. IEEE Trans. Neural Netw. Learn. Syst. **29**(1), 10–24 (2018). https://doi.org/10.1109/TNNLS.2017.2716952
6. Jin, J.W., Philip Chen, C.L.: Regularized robust Broad Learning System for uncertain data modeling. Neurocomputing **322**, 58–69 (2018). https://doi.org/10.1016/j.neucom.2018.09.028
7. Liu, B., Zeng, X., Tian, F., Zhang, S., Zhao, L.: Domain transfer broad learning system for long-term drift compensation in electronic nose systems. IEEE Access (2019). https://doi.org/10.1109/ACCESS.2019.2943188
8. Zheng, Y., Chen, B., Wang, S., Wang, W.: Broad learning system based on maximum correntropy criterion. IEEE Trans. Neural Netw. Learn. Syst. (2020). https://doi.org/10.1109/tnnls.2020.3009417

9. Song, D., Tao, D.: Biologically inspired feature manifold for scene classification. IEEE Trans. Image Process. (2010). https://doi.org/10.1109/TIP.2009.2032939

10. Li, H., Liu, D., Wang, D.: Manifold Regularized Reinforcement Learning. IEEE Trans. Neural Netw. Learn. Syst. (2018). https://doi.org/10.1109/TNNLS.2017. 2650943

11. Luo, C., Ma, L.: Manifold regularized distribution adaptation for classification of remote sensing images. IEEE Access (2018). https://doi.org/10.1109/ACCESS. 2018.2789932

12. Zhou, D., Huang, J., Schölkopf, B.: Learning with hypergraphs: clustering, classification, and embedding. Adv. Neural. Inf. Process. Syst. (2007). https://doi.org/ 10.7551/mitpress/7503.003.0205

13. Yu, J., Tao, D., Wang, M.: Adaptive hypergraph learning and its application in image classification. IEEE Trans. Image Process. (2012). https://doi.org/10.1109/ TIP.2012.2190083

14. Zhang, Z., Lin, H., Gao, Y.: Dynamic hypergraph structure learning. In: IJCAI International Joint Conference on Artificial Intelligence (2018). https://doi.org/ 10.24963/ijcai.2018/439

15. Samaria, F.S., Harter, A.C.: Parameterisation of a stochastic model for human face identification. In: IEEE Workshop on Applications of Computer Vision - Proceedings (1994). https://doi.org/10.1109/acv.1994.341300

16. Graham, D.B., Allinson, N.M.: Characterising virtual eigen signatures for general purpose face recognition. Face Recogn. (1998). https://doi.org/10.1007/978-3-642-72201-1_25

17. LeCun, Y., Bottou, L., Bengio, Y., Haffner, P.: Gradient-based learning applied to document recognition. Proc. IEEE (1998). https://doi.org/10.1109/5.726791

18. Wright, J., Yang, A.Y., Ganesh, A., Sastry, S.S., Ma, Y.: Robust face recognition via sparse representation. IEEE Trans. Pattern Anal. Mach. Intell. (2009). https:// doi.org/10.1109/TPAMI.2008.79

19. Naseem, I., Togneri, R., Bennamoun, M.: Linear regression for face recognition. IEEE Trans. Pattern Anal. Mach. Intell. (2010). https://doi.org/10.1109/TPAMI. 2010.128

20. Wu, Y., Vapnik, V.N.: Statistical learning theory. Technometrics (1999). https:// doi.org/10.2307/1271368

21. Ayach, O.E., Rajagopal, S., Abu-Surra, S., Pi, Z., Heath, R.W.: Spatially sparse precoding in millimeter wave MIMO systems. IEEE Trans. Wireless Commun. (2014). https://doi.org/10.1109/TWC.2014.011714.130846

Weighted Conditional Distribution Adaptation for Motor Imagery Classification

Rui Zhang[1,2,3(✉)], Fake Gu[1], Zheng Zou[4], Tianyou Yu[2,5], and Yuanqing Li[2,5]

[1] Dongguan University of Technology, Dongguan 523808, China
ruizhang@dgut.edu.cn
[2] Pazhou Lab, Guangzhou 510330, China
[3] Guangdong-Hong Kong-Macao Greater Bay Area Center for Brain Science and Brain-Inspired Intelligence, Guangzhou 510515, China
[4] Shenzhen Institute of Information Technology, Shenzhen 518172, China
[5] South China University of Technology, Guangzhou 510641, China

Abstract. Individual differences of electroencephalogram (EEG) signals can increase calibration difficulty, which is a major challenge in the practical application of brain computer interface (BCI). Transfer learning is an available method to predict the target subject's EEG signals by learning an effective model from other subjects' signals. This paper proposes a weight conditional distribution adaptation (WCDA) method, which can enhance feature transferability and discriminability by minimizing the conditional distribution of the same class between domains while maximizing the conditional distribution of different classes between domains. Moreover, a transferable source sample selection (TSSS) method is proposed to improve the transfer learning performance and reduce the computational cost. Experiments on two public motor imagery (MI) datasets demonstrated our approach outperforms the state of the art methods, thus providing an available way to reduce calibration effort for BCI applications.

Keywords: Transfer learning · Brain computer interface · Conditional distribution adaptation

1 Introduction

Brain computer interface (BCI) can allow the user to interact with external environment directly using brain signals. Electroencephalogram (EEG)-based BCIs have received a wide attention from both academic and practical fields, because they are safe, convenient and portable [1]. Motor Imagery (MI) is a commonly

This work was supported by the Key R&D Program of Guangdong Province Foundation under Grant No. 2018B030339001, 2018B030340001, the National Natural Science Foundation of China under Grants No. 61703101, 61876064 and the Guangdong-Hong Kong-Macao Greater Bay Area Center for Brain Science and Brain-Inspired Intelligence Foundation under Grant No. 2019015.

© Springer Nature Switzerland AG 2021
Y. Peng et al. (Eds.): ICIG 2021, LNCS 12888, pp. 502–511, 2021.
https://doi.org/10.1007/978-3-030-87355-4_42

used paradigm of EEG-based BCIs. It has been well established that MI-related sensorimotor rhythms can be detected when the user imagines the movement of his/her left-/right-hand, tongue or foot [2]. However, it is not easy to accurately recognize the sensorimotor rhythms for traditional machine learning methods. Three challenges in MI-based classification still exist: 1) large individual differences of EEG signals result in difficult obtaining the universal features of cross-time and cross-subject; 2) the signal-to-noise of EEG signals is low; 3) obtaining a large amount of subject-specific EEG data for calibration is time-consuming and may lead to fatigue of subjects [3]. These challenges greatly reduce the practicality of MI-based BCIs.

Transfer learning is an available way to address these challenges, because it can predict the information of target domain by learning an effective model from the information of source domains. Recently, several researchers have successfully applied it into the field of MI-based BCIs [4–6]. One common transfer learning method is distribution adaptation, which can minimize the discrepancy between the source and target domain distributions. For instance, Pan *et al.* proposed a transfer component analysis (TCA) method to reduce the marginal distribution differences between domains [7]. The distribution difference is measured by the method of maximum mean discrepancy (MMD) [8]. Based on the TCA, Long *et al.* proposed a joint distribution adaptation (JDA) method, which can minimize the difference of marginal distribution and conditional distribution between domains [9]. In addition, Zhang *et al.* reported an extension method of JDA, namely joint geometrical and statistical alignment (JGSA), which combined the geometrical information of features with JDA to reduce geometrical and distribution differences. Most studies only consider the discrepancies of marginal distribution or conditional distribution of the same class, without considering the discrepancies of conditional distribution between different classes. To improve the classification performance, it is essential to take into account all possible distribution differences, including marginal distribution, conditional distribution of the same class and between different classes.

In this paper, we propose a unsupervised transfer learning method, i.e., weight conditional distribution adaptation (WCDA) and apply it to MI classification. This method can not only consider the conditional distribution differences of the same class between source domain and target domain, but also take into account the distribution differences of different classes between two domains, and the importance of these two conditional distributions can be adapted via a weight parameter. In addition, we also propose a transferable source sample selection (TSSS) method and investigate the effect of source sample number on the transfer learning performance. To evaluate the WCDA and TSSS, we conduct several experiments on two public MI datasets. The experimental results verify the effectiveness of our proposed methods.

2   Methods

2.1   Transferable Source Sample Selection (TSSS)

The quantity and quality of source sample have important influence on computational cost and transfer learning performance, respectively. Therefore, it is necessary to evaluate the transferability of source sample and further select appropriate source samples before transfer. For each source domain, the feature vectors are firstly extracted from the preprocessed EEG samples by Tangent Space (TS) mapping [10]. A Support Vector Machine (SVM) classifier is trained via the obtained feature vectors, and then is employed to perform classification on each sample. Next, the predicted distance $D_{svm,(i)}$ from each sample to the SVM hyperplane can be obtained. Finally, we remove the sample where the distance is in the range of $-\delta < D_{svm,(i)} < \delta$. Here, the δ is a predefined threshold to adjust how many samples to select.

2.2   Weighted Conditional Distribution Adaptation

In this study, multiple EEG data from different subjects are given. After pre-processing, all data were divided into a source domain $D_s = (X_s, Y_s)$ with n_s labeled samples and a target domain $D_t = (X_t)$ with n_t unlabeled samples, where $X_s = [\mathbf{x}_{s,1}; \mathbf{x}_{s,2}; ...; \mathbf{x}_{s,n_s}] \in \mathbb{R}^{d \times n_s}$ and $X_t = [\mathbf{x}_{t,1}; \mathbf{x}_{t,2}; ...; \mathbf{x}_{t,n_t}] \in \mathbb{R}^{d \times n_t}$ are feature matrix, $Y_s = [y_{s,1}; y_{s,2}; ...; y_{s,n_s}] \in \mathbb{R}^{n_s \times 1}$ is the corresponding label vector of X_s, d is the number of dimensions and $y_{s,i} \in \{c1, c2\}$, respectively.

Convention distribution alignment approaches analyze the discrepancies between source and target domains via marginal and conditional distribution. This is realized by minimizing the distance:

$$D(D_s, D_t) \approx D(P(\mathbf{x}_s), P(\mathbf{x}_t)) + D(P(y_s|\mathbf{x}_s), P(y_t|\mathbf{x}_t)) \tag{1}$$

According to statistical distribution theory, if sample size is large, the conditional probability distribution $P(y|\mathbf{x})$ can be approximated by the class-conditional probability distribution $P(\mathbf{x}|y)$. Because the label y_t in target domain is unknown, we applied the base classifiers trained on the labeled source domain data to obtain the label y_t in this study.

He et al. proposed a euclidean alignment (EA) method to reduce the marginal distribution shift [5]. After EA, it is sufficient to consider the conditional distribution between domains, i.e., the second term in the formula (1). The conditional distribution distance between source domain and target domain can represent the feature transferability and discriminability. e.g., the smaller the conditional distribution distance of the same class between two domains, the more effectively transferring the learning model from the source domain to the target domain; whereas the bigger the conditional distribution distance of the different classes between two domains, the more easily discriminating the different classes by the learned classifier. In order to enhance the feature transferability and discriminability, the distribution distance between two domains in the formula (1) can be further represented by

$$\dot{D}(D_s, D_t) = \beta D^c(D_s, D_t) - (1 - \beta)D^{c1c2}(D_s, D_t) \tag{2}$$

Where the first term is the conditional probability distribution distance of the same class between domains, and the second is the conditional probability distribution distance of different classes (i.e., $c1$, $c2$) between domains. $\beta \in [0, 1]$ is the weight parameter to trade off the importance of transferability and discriminability.

In order to compute the distance between $P(\mathbf{x}_s|y_s)$ and $P(\mathbf{x}_t|y_t)$, the projected MMD was adopted. Specifically, the feature vectors $\mathbf{x}_s$ and $\mathbf{x}_t$ were firstly mapped into lower dimensional vectors $\mathbf{A}^T\mathbf{x}_s$ and $\mathbf{A}^T\mathbf{x}_t$ by a projection matrix $\mathbf{A} \in \mathbb{R}^{d \times k}$. Then, the conditional probability distribution distance of the same class was represented by

$$
\begin{aligned}
D^c(D_s, D_t) &= \sum_{c=1}^{C} D(P(\mathbf{x}_s^c|y_s^c), P(\mathbf{x}_t^c|y_t^c)) \\
&= \sum_{c=1}^{C} \| \frac{1}{n_s^c} \sum_{i=1}^{n_s^c} \mathbf{A}^T\mathbf{x}_{s,i}^c - \frac{1}{n_t^c} \sum_{j=1}^{n_t^c} \mathbf{A}^T\mathbf{x}_{t,j}^c \|^2
\end{aligned}
\tag{3}
$$

The conditional probability distribution distance between different classes can be represented by

$$
\begin{aligned}
D^{c1c2}(D_s, D_t) &= \sum_{c1=1}^{C} \sum_{\substack{c2 \neq c1 \\ c2=1}}^{C} D(P(\mathbf{x}_s^{c1}|y_s^{c1}), P(\mathbf{x}_t^{c2}|y_t^{c2})) \\
&= \sum_{c1=1}^{C} \sum_{\substack{c2 \neq c1 \\ c2=1}}^{C} \| \frac{1}{n_s^{c1}} \sum_{i=1}^{n_s^{c1}} \mathbf{A}^T\mathbf{x}_{s,i}^{c1} - \frac{1}{n_t^{c2}} \sum_{j=1}^{n_t^{c2}} \mathbf{A}^T\mathbf{x}_{t,j}^{c2} \|^2
\end{aligned}
\tag{4}
$$

Where n_s^c and n_s^{c1} represent the number of samples belonging to class c and $c1$ in the source domain, respectively, and n_t^c and n_t^{c2} are the number of samples belonging to class c and $c2$ in the target domain. $\mathbf{x}_{s,i}^c$ and $\mathbf{x}_{t,j}^c$ are the ith and the jth feature vector in the source domain and target domain, respectively, and they both belong to class c. Similarly, $\mathbf{x}_{s,i}^{c1}$ and $\mathbf{x}_{t,j}^{c2}$ are the ith and the jth feature vector in the source domain and target domain, respectively, and they belong to class $c1$ and $c2$, respectively.

In order to simultaneously enhance the feature transferability and discriminability, the Eq. (2) was required to be minimized. By incorporating Eqs. (3) and (4) into the Eq. (2), the optimization problem can be represented by

$$
\min_{\mathbf{A}} tr(\beta \sum_{c=1}^{C} \mathbf{A}^T\mathbf{X}\mathbf{M}_c\mathbf{X}^T\mathbf{A} - (1 - \beta) \sum_{c1=1}^{C} \sum_{\substack{c2 \neq c1 \\ c2=1}}^{C} \mathbf{A}^T\mathbf{X}\mathbf{M}_{c1c2}\mathbf{X}^T\mathbf{A})
\tag{5}
$$

$$+ \lambda\|\mathbf{A}\|_F^2$$

$s.t.\ \mathbf{A}^T\mathbf{X}\mathbf{H}\mathbf{X}^T\mathbf{A} = \mathbf{I}.$

Where λ is a regularization parameter, $\mathbf{X} = [X_s, X_t] \in \mathbb{R}^{d \times n} (n = n_s + n_t)$, $\mathbf{H} = \mathbf{I} - \frac{1}{n}\mathbf{1}$ is the centering matrix, $\mathbf{I}$ is a n-dimensional identity matrix, $\mathbf{M}_c$ and $\mathbf{M}_{c1c2}$ are the MMD matrix and can be computed as follows:

$$(\mathbf{M}_c)_{ij} = \begin{cases} \frac{1}{(n_s^c)^2} & \mathbf{x}_i, \mathbf{x}_j \in D_s^c, \\ \frac{1}{(n_t^c)^2} & \mathbf{x}_i, \mathbf{x}_j \in D_t^c, \\ -\frac{1}{n_s^c n_t^c} & \begin{cases} \mathbf{x}_i \in D_s^c, \mathbf{x}_j \in D_t^c \\ \mathbf{x}_i \in D_t^c, \mathbf{x}_j \in D_s^c, \end{cases} \\ 0 & otherwise. \end{cases} \tag{6}$$

$$(\mathbf{M}_{c1c2})_{ij} = \begin{cases} \frac{1}{(n_s^{c1})^2} & \mathbf{x}_i, \mathbf{x}_j \in D_s^{c1}, \\ \frac{1}{(n_t^{c2})^2} & \mathbf{x}_i, \mathbf{x}_j \in D_t^{c2}, \\ -\frac{1}{n_s^{c1} n_t^{c2}} & \begin{cases} \mathbf{x}_i \in D_s^{c1}, \mathbf{x}_j \in D_t^{c2} \\ \mathbf{x}_i \in D_t^{c2}, \mathbf{x}_j \in D_s^{c1}, \end{cases} \\ 0 & otherwise. \end{cases} \tag{7}$$

According to the constrained optimization theory, we can obtain the lagrange function for optimization problem (5) as

$$\mathbf{L} = tr(\mathbf{A}^T \mathbf{X}(\beta \sum_{c=1}^{C} \mathbf{M}_c - (1-\beta) \sum_{c1=1}^{C} \sum_{\substack{c2 \neq c1 \\ c2=1}}^{C} \mathbf{M}_{c1c2})\mathbf{X}^T \mathbf{A}) \\ + \lambda \|\mathbf{A}\|_F^2 + tr((\mathbf{I} - \mathbf{A}^T \mathbf{X} \mathbf{H} \mathbf{X}^T \mathbf{A})\eta) \tag{8}$$

Setting $\frac{\partial \mathbf{L}}{\partial \mathbf{A}} = 0$, the corresponding generalized eigen-decomposition is represented by

$$\mathbf{X}(\beta \sum_{c=1}^{C} \mathbf{M}_c - (1-\beta) \sum_{c1=1}^{C} \sum_{\substack{c2 \neq c1 \\ c2=1}}^{C} \mathbf{M}_{c1c2})\mathbf{X}^T + \lambda \mathbf{I})\mathbf{A} = \mathbf{X} \mathbf{H} \mathbf{X}^T \mathbf{A} \eta \tag{9}$$

Finally, we can obtain the optimal projecting matrix $\mathbf{A}$ consisting of k trailing eigenvectors by solving Eq. (9). A complete procedure of the proposed algorithm is summarized in Algorithm 1.

3   Experiments

In this section, several experiments are conducted with two publicly available MI datasets to verify the feasibility of the proposed methods.

3.1   Datasets and Preprocessing

1) MI 1 (Dataset 1 from BCI Competition IV). This dataset consists of left- or right-handed MI EEG data from 7 healthy subjects. Each subject was required to

---

Algorithm 1 : Weight Conditional Distribution Adaptation (WCDA)

Input: source domain data $\{(\mathbf{x}_i, y_i)\}_{i=1}^{n_s}$,
       target domain data $\{\mathbf{x}_i\}_{i=n_s+1}^{n_s+n_t}$,
       weight parameter β, regularization parameter λ,
       subspace dimension k, number of iteration T.
Output: Projection matrix $\mathbf{A}$, Classifier f.
1: Train a basic classifier f on $\{(\mathbf{x}_i, y_i)\}_{i=1}^{n_s}$ and apply it on $\{\mathbf{x}_i\}_{i=n_s+1}^{n_s+n_t}$ to obtain the
     pseudo labels $\hat{y}_t$
2: **for** $n = 1, ..., T$ **do**
3:     Construct MMD matrices $\mathbf{M}_c$ and $\mathbf{M}_{c1c2}$ via equations (6) and (7).
4:     Solve equation (9) and select k smallest eigenvectors to construct the projection
     matrix $\mathbf{A}$.
5:     Train the classifier f on $\{(A^T\mathbf{x}_i, y_i)\}_{i=1}^{n_s}$ and update the pseudo labels $\{\hat{y}_t :=$
     $f(A^T\mathbf{x}_i)\}_{i=n_s+1}^{n_s+n_t}$.
6: **end for**
7: **return** Classifier f.

---

perform 200 trials MI tasks (100 tasks per class) for 4 s during the MI experiment. Meanwhile, the EEG signals from 64 channels were collected at the sample rate 1000 Hz.

2) MI 2 (Dataset 2b from BCI Competition IV). 9 healthy subjects participated in a left- and right-handed MI experiment. For each subject, 144 trials (72 trails for each class) MI EEG signals were recorded using 22 channels with the sample rate 250 Hz. Each trial contains 4 s MI EEG signals.

For each dataset, the testing set (i.e., target domain) consisted of all trials of a subject, and the trials of the rest subjects were taken as the training set (i.e., source domain). For instance, for an evaluation on subject 1 of the dataset MI 1, 200 trials of subject 1 composed the testing set, and the remaining $6 * 120 = 1200$ trials composed the training set.

Before experiment validation, this two MI datasets were required to perform the same preprocessing process as the study [11]. First, a band-pass filter with 8–30 Hz was employed to filter out the artifacts. Then, a 0.5–3.5 s signal segment when the MI task starts was extracted for each trial. Finally, the preprocessing data without channel selection were used for the subsequent data analysis.

3.2 Feature Extraction

In recent years, spatial domain feature extraction was mainly used for MI classification. Most studies designed lots of spatial filtering algorithms to extract the discriminative features from the multichannel EEG signals. One of the most effective algorithm is common spatial pattern (CSP), which can maximize the variance difference between the two classes by the diagonalization of the spatial covariance matrices [12]. In this study, we select the upper triangular elements of spatial covariance matrices as the MI features by a tangent space mapping method, which is widely used in MI feature extraction [6,10].

3.3 Classification

In this study, a shrinkage linear discriminant analysis (sLDA) was employed as the classifier due to its simple and effective [13].

3.4 Experimental Settings

In order to verify the effectiveness of our proposed WCDA method, the following nine baseline algorithms were in comparison with our method via the above mentioned two MI datasets.

1) CSP-LDA (linear discriminant analysis) [14].
2) EA-CSP-LDA (euclidean alignment) [5].
3) RA-MDM (riemannian alignment - minimum distance to mean) [4].
4) CA (centroid alignment) [6].
5) CA-CORAL (correlation alignment) [15].
6) CA-GFK (geodesic flow kernel) [16].
7) CA-JDA (joint distribution adaptation) [9].
8) CA-JGSA (joint geometrical and statistical alignment) [17].
9) MEKT-E (manifold embedded knowledge transfer - euclidean mean) [6].

3.5 Hyperparameter Determination

In our study, we empirically set $T = 5$, $\beta = 0.9$, $\lambda = 0.1$, and $k = 35$ or 4 (for MI 1 or MI 2). The hyperparameters of the above mentioned nine baseline algorithms were set according to the corresponding publications.

4   Results and Discussion

Table 1. Mean classification performance of WCDA method and the baseline methods on the two MI datasets.

	MI1		MI2		Avg
CSP-LDA	59.71	(12.93)	67.75	(12.92)	63.73
EA-CSP-LDA	79.79	(6.57)	73.53	(15.96)	76.66
RA-MDM	73.29	(9.25)	72.07	(9.88)	72.68
CA	76.29	(9.66)	71.84	(13.89)	74.07
CA-CORAL	78.86	(8.73)	72.38	(13.38)	75.62
CA-GFK	76.79	(12.57)	72.99	(15.82)	74.89
CA-JDA	81.07	(11.19)	74.15	(15.77)	77.61
CA-JGSA	76.79	(12.35)	73.07	(16.33)	74.93
MEKT-E	81.29	(10.18)	76.00	(17.61)	78.65
WCDA	**83.79**	(8.83)	**77.39**	(14.87)	**80.59**

we compare our approach (WCDA) with the state of the arts transfer learning algorithms on two public MI datasets. Table 1 illustrates the mean classification accuracy and standard deviation in terms of each combination of source domain and target domain. From Table 1, we find that our approach achieves the highest mean accuracy consistently on both two MI datasets. For instance, the classification accuracy of WCDA on the dataset MI 1 is 83.79%, 2.5% higher than the second-best accuracy of MEKT-E. On the dataset MI 2, WCDA achieves an accuracy of 77.39% against 76% by the MEKT-E algorithm. On the two MI datasets, the average accuracy of our algorithm is 80.59%, 1.94% higher than the sencond-best accuracy.

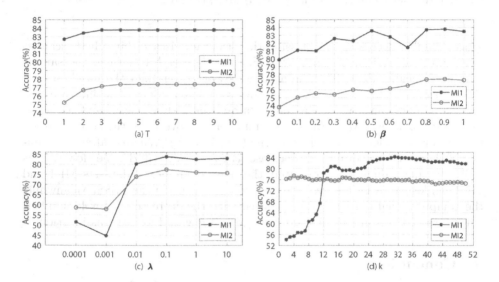

Fig. 1. Parameter sensitivity on two MI datasets: (a) the number of iterations T; (b) the weight parameter β; (c) the regularization parameter λ; (d) the subspace dimension k.

In order to investigate the effect of each hyperparameter on the our algorithm performance, we analyze the parameter sensitivity of WCDA on two MI datasets. As shown in Fig. 1, WCDA can reach a stable performance on both two datasets after only a few $T < 5$ iterations. In terms of the weight parameter β, there is a slight performance fluctuation when the β is smaller than 0.8 while the performance is steady if $\beta > 0.8$. The regularization parameter λ has a certain effect on the performance if it is lower than 0.1. As it increases, the performance becomes stable. As for the subspace dimension k, there is a little effect on the performance for the dataset MI 1 when it is bigger than 2, whereas the performance tends to stable for the dataset MI 2 when it is greater than 28. In summary, our algorithm WCDA is not sensitive to the hyperparameters T, β, λ and k.

Furthermore, we investigate the effect of the proposed transferable source sample selection (TSSS) method on the performance. As shown in Fig. 2, as the

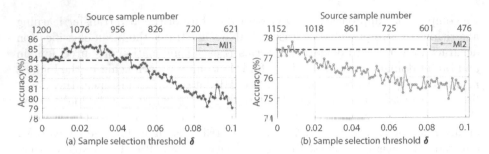

Fig. 2. Average accuracy achieved with different numbers of source sample (and sample selection thresholds) on two MI datasets: (a) MI 1; (b) MI 2.

source number decreases, the classification accuracy rises within a little scale at the beginning, and then drop slowly. For the dataset MI 1, when the sample number is nearly above 900, the accuracies are higher than the baseline (i.e., the accuracy of 83.79% in the case without sample selection). This indicates the sample number can decrease by almost a quarter without sacrificing the accuracy. For the dataset MI 2, the sample number is above 1068, the accuracies are close to or even higher than the baseline (i.e., 77.39%). Whereas after the number of the samples continues to decrease, the accuracy will decline slowly. This indicates that reducing appropriately the sample number of datasets MI 1 and MI 2 can keep or even improve the performance by using the TSSS. Meanwhile, the computational burden can be reduced with the decrease of sample number. Therefore, TSSS is an effective sample selection method for MI classification.

5   Conclusion

In this paper, we propose a unsupervised transfer learning method, i.e., weight conditional distribution adaptation (WCDA), which can minimize the conditional distribution of the same class between source domain and target domain while maximizing the conditional distribution of different classes between two domains. In addition, a transferable source sample selection (TSSS) method is proposed to improve the transfer learning performance and reduce the computational cost. The proposed WCDA method outperforms the state of the art methods by several experiments on two public MI datasets.

References

1. Curran, E.A., Stokes, M.J.: Learning to control brain activity: a review of the production and control of EEG components for driving brain-computer interface (BCI) systems. Brain Cogn. **51**(3), 326–336 (2003)
2. Pfurtscheller, G., Da Silva, F.L.: Event-related EEG/meg synchronization and desynchronization: basic principles. Clin. Neurophysiol. **110**(11), 1842–1857 (1999)

3. Arvaneh, M., Guan, C., et al.: Optimizing spatial filters by minimizing within-class dissimilarities in electroencephalogram-based brain-computer interface. IEEE Trans. Neural Netw. Learn. Syst. **24**(4), 610–619 (2013)
4. Zanini, P., Congedo, M., et al.: Transfer learning: a Riemannian geometry framework with applications to brain-computer interfaces. IEEE Trans. Biomed. Eng. **65**(5), 1107–1116 (2017)
5. He, H., Wu, D.: Transfer learning for brain-computer interfaces: a Euclidean space data alignment approach. IEEE Trans. Biomed. Eng. **67**(2), 399–410 (2019)
6. Zhang, W., Wu, D.: Manifold embedded knowledge transfer for brain-computer interfaces. IEEE Trans. Neural Syst. Rehabil. Eng. **28**(5), 1117–1127 (2020)
7. Pan, S.J., Tsang, I.W., Kwok, J.T., Yang, Q.: Domain adaptation via transfer component analysis. IEEE Trans. Neural Netw. **22**(2), 199–210 (2010)
8. Ben-David, S., Blitzer, J., Crammer, K., Pereira, F.: Analysis of representations for domain adaptation. In: Advances in neural information processing systems. pp. 137–144 (2007)
9. Long, M., Wang, J., et al.: Transfer feature learning with joint distribution adaptation. In: Proceedings of the IEEE International Conference on Computer Vision, pp. 2200–2207 (2013)
10. Barachant, A., Bonnet, S., Congedo, M., Jutten, C.: Classification of covariance matrices using a Riemannian-based kernel for BCI applications. Neurocomputing **112**, 172–178 (2013)
11. Zhang, X., Wu, D.: On the vulnerability of CNN classifiers in EEG-based BCIs. IEEE Trans. Neural Syst. Rehabil. Eng. **27**(5), 814–825 (2019)
12. Ramoser, H., Muller-Gerking, J., Pfurtscheller, G.: Optimal spatial filtering of single trial EEG during imagined hand movement. IEEE Trans. Rehabil. Eng. **8**(4), 441–446 (2000)
13. Peck, R., Van Ness, J.: The use of shrinkage estimators in linear discriminant analysis. IEEE Trans. Pattern Anal. Mach. Intell. **5**, 530–537 (1982)
14. Bishop, C.M.: Pattern Recognition and Machine Learning. Information Science and StatisticsInformation Science and Statistics, Springer, New York (2006). https://doi.org/10.1007/978-0-387-45528-0
15. Sun, B., Feng, J., Saenko, K.: Return of frustratingly easy domain adaptation. arXiv preprint arXiv:1511.05547 (2015)
16. Gong, B., Shi, Y., Sha, F., Grauman, K.: Geodesic flow kernel for unsupervised domain adaptation. In: 2012 IEEE Conference on Computer Vision and Pattern Recognition, pp. 2066–2073. IEEE (2012)
17. Zhang, J., Li, W., Ogunbona, P.: Joint geometrical and statistical alignment for visual domain adaptation. In: Proceedings of the IEEE Conference on Computer Vision and Pattern Recognition, pp. 1859–1867 (2017)

Low-Level and Physics-Based Vision

Color Multi-focus Image Fusion Using Quaternion Morphological Gradient and Improved KNN Matting

Wei Liu[1,2,3], Zhong Zheng[1], and Zengfu Wang[1,2(✉)]

[1] Institute of Intelligent Machine, Hefei Institutes of Physical Science,
Chinese Academy of Sciences, Hefei 230000, Anhui, China
[2] Department of Automation, University of Science and Technology of China,
Hefei 230000, Anhui, China
zfwang@ustc.edu.cn
[3] College of Mathematics and Computer Science,
Tongling University, Tongling 244000, Anhui, China

Abstract. Most of existing focus measures are calculated by using the luminance information of source images while the chrominance information are ignored. In this paper, we first propose a new focus measure called quaternion morphological gradient for extracting the saliency feature of color images, which is derived based on the quaternion representation of color images and a proper ranking function. Then, the quaternion morphological gradients are used to produce initial decision maps. After that, the final decision maps are estimated by using the globally optimal weight maps obtained by the improved KNN matting algorithm. Finally, a weighted-sum strategy is used to construct the fused image. To boost the robustness of matting results, the pseudo depth information of source image is added into the feature vector of KNN matting. The experimental results validate the superiority of our method compared with the state-of-the-art algorithms both in visual perception and objective metrics.

Keywords: Color multi-focus image fusion · Quaternion morphological gradient · KNN matting

1 Introduction

The MFIF has attracted increasing interest in last decades since the optical lens can only acquire images partially focused because of its limited depth of field while our human beings are not satisfied with the partially focused images in many practical applications such as digital photography and surveillance. The MFIF is an effective approach to extract the focused information from multiple partially focused images of a same scene with different focus settings and obtain an all-in-focus image [1].

To date, there are many efficient MFIF methods have been presented, they can be roughly classified into two categories, that is transform domain based methods and spatial domain based methods [1]. For the transform domain based methods, its mainly

© Springer Nature Switzerland AG 2021
Y. Peng et al. (Eds.): ICIG 2021, LNCS 12888, pp. 515–527, 2021.
https://doi.org/10.1007/978-3-030-87355-4_43

procedures usually involve three steps: firstly, the multiple input images are decomposed into a multi-scale transform domain. Then the transformed coefficients are integrated with a fusion rule. Finally, the fused image can be reconstructed by performing the inverse transform over integrated coefficients. The multi-scale transform (MST) can separate the spatially-overlapped image features in scale space effectively, which is widely applied to MFIF. The popular MST-based fusion methods consist of the wavelet-based one [2] and the multi scale geometric analysis-based one [3]. Recently, some new multiscale tools based on image filters are also applied to MFIF and achieved good results [4, 5]. Although the MST can represent underlying image salient features reasonably, the selection of an optimal transform for source images with various contexts is not a straightforward issue. Moreover, the way of separately fusion color channels may cause hue bias in the fused images.

Unlike the handling object of transform domain based methods, the spatial domain based methods select pixels with more clarity as the corresponding pixels of fused image directly. Thus, these methods have high computational efficiency and can preserve important information of source images into the fused image. The classical strategy calculating the average of source images pixel by pixel usually cause many detail loss, blurring result and high sensitivity to noise. In order to select focused pixels from source images properly, a commonly approach is to design a focus measure as the criterion to select the fused pixels. The frequently used focus measures are: spatial frequency and sum of the modified Laplacian [6]. Meanwhile, some new focus measures such as multi-scale morphological gradient [7], guided filter-based one [8], etc. are also developed to obtain high focus discrimination. Although these focus measures-based methods can perform well in rich texture regions, they will bring the misclassification results in smooth and textureless regions, which arise the spatial artifacts and discontinuity in the fused images. To mitigate spatial artifacts and provide spatial consistency, some novel MFIF methods based on advanced optimization algorithms, such as image matting [9] and lazy random walks [10], are proposed in recent years. Although these methods can precisely detect the focused regions from source images and obtain satisfactory fusion results, there still have several limitations in color MFIF. First, most of focus measures are only designed on the luminance information of source images, which lack robustness for detecting focused pixels in transition regions and smooth regions. Second, the issue of decision map misalignment with the boundaries of focused regions cannot be eliminated. Third, the boundaries of the decision map are not clear enough. Moreover, the fusion results are not good enough for source images with seriously mis-registration.

Concerning the limitations mentioned above, this paper will explore two unique characteristics of color multi-focus images, namely, the color structure information and the distances from object to focal plane (depth information), to develop an efficient fusion framework to merge multiple color images to a fully focused image. Figure 1 shows the schematic diagram of our method. To extract the quaternion morphological gradients of source image, we first encode all color channels by a quaternion matrix and then use the phase of the Clifford translation of quaternion to determine the order of two quaternions. The quaternion representation of color image can handle all color channels simultaneously, thus the way of extracting gradient can capture the color structure information fully. In the step of decision map refinement, we add the depth information of source image into the feature vector to hopefully improve the robustness of KNN matting results. Experimental results show that the proposed method is feasible and effective. This work mainly includes two contributions:

1 We design a new focus measure called quaternion morphological gradient for color images, which is derived based on the quaternion representation of color images and a proper ranking function. Different from most of existing focus measures designing on the luminance information of source images, our method fully considers the color structure information and have a reliable response to different blurred degree.
2 The pseudo depth information of each source image is incorporated into the feature vector of KNN matting to ensure an accurate and smooth result.

The remainder content is organized as follows. Section 2 introduces some background knowledge. Section 3 explains our method in detail. The experimental results are presented in Sect. 4. Finally, concluding remarks are given in Sect. 5.

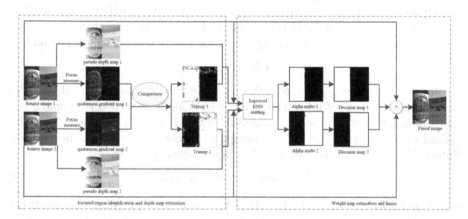

Fig. 1. Schematic diagram of the proposed fusion method.

2 Preliminary

2.1 Quaternion Algebra

In 1843, Hamilton extends the 2D complex number to 4D hypercomplex number and introduces the concept of quaternion, which has one real part and three imaginary parts [11]. A quaternion $\dot{q} \in \mathbb{H}$ is defined as follows:

$$\dot{q} = a + ib + jc + kd \tag{1}$$

where a is called the real part of $\dot{q}$, and $ib+jc+kd$ is the imaginary part, and $a, b, c, d \in \mathfrak{R}$, i, j and k are complex operators, satisfying: $i^2 = j^2 = k^2 = ijk = -1$.

Except for the algebraic form in Eq. (1), $\dot{q}$ can also be represented as:

$$\dot{q} = |\dot{q}|e^{\dot{\mu}\theta} = |\dot{q}|(\cos\theta + \dot{\mu}\sin\theta) \tag{2}$$

where $\dot{\mu} = ib + jc + kd \big/ \sqrt{b^2 + c^2 + d^2}$ and $\theta = \arctan\left(\sqrt{b^2 + c^2 + d^2}\big/a\right), 0 \leq \theta \leq \pi$. $\dot{\mu}$ and θ are referred to as the eigenaxis and phase of the quaternion $\dot{q}$, respectively.

One well-known operator of quaternion is the Clifford translation of quaternion (CTQ) [12]. Let $\dot{p}$ be a unit quaternion, the right CTQ of $\dot{q}$ is defined as:

$$CTQ_r(\dot{q}, \dot{p}) = \dot{q}\dot{p} \tag{3}$$

where p is called reference quaternion in the CTQ transform. Similarity, the left Clifford translation is $CTQ_l(\dot{q}, \dot{p}) = \dot{p}\dot{q}$. Generally, $CTQ_l(\dot{q}, \dot{p}) \neq CTQ_r(\dot{q}, \dot{p})$ but their phases are equivalent. In [13], they deeply studied the properties of CTQ and found that the phase of the CTQ result measures the similarity between $\dot{q}$ and $\dot{p}$. In next section, we will use the CTQ to derive a new focus measure for color images.

2.2 KNN Matting

As a powerful image processing technique, image matting (IM) has successfully applied in many applications [9, 14]. The IM can separate foreground region and background region from a single image accurately. This ability is very in line with the goal of MFIF. Thus, we utilize it for color MFIF task. In the model of IM, an image I can be regarded as the weighted summation of two components, the foreground F and background B.

$$I = \alpha \times F + (1 - \alpha) \times B \tag{4}$$

where $\times$ is matrix cross product, $\alpha \in [0, 1]$ is the opacity of foreground and we called it alpha matte. The goal of IM is finding the alpha matte from an observed image. It is clear that this problem have infinite solutions because it is under constrained. Usually, we need to supply some user inputs (trimaps or scribbles) so as to obtain a definite solution. Then it can be solved by the following constraint problem.

$$\alpha^* = \arg\min_{\alpha} \alpha^T L \alpha \text{ s.t. } \alpha(S) = c \tag{5}$$

where L is Laplacian matrix and $L = D - A$, A is an $M \times M$ affinity matrix, D is a diagonal matrix, M is the size of image I, S is the set of user-constrained pixels and c is the vector of constrained values. The design of affinity matrix significantly affects the performance of IM. Thus, many researchers focus on the calculation of pixel affinity [15, 16]. Among them, the KNN matting uses the nonlocal principle by using K nearest neighbors (KNN) in matching nonlocal neighborhoods to calculate the affinity between pixels, which can obtain competitive results with sparse markups [16]. Therefore, the KNN matting is suitable for refining decision maps. In the KNN matting, the computing affinity matrix A involves three steps, which are described as followed.

Firstly, for an image I, the feature vectors $FE(i)$ at a given pixel i is defined as:

$$FE(i) = (\cos(h), \sin(h), s, v, x, y)_i \tag{6}$$

where (h, s, v) are the values in HSV space and (x, y) is the spatial position of pixel i.

Secondly, we collect K matched pixels by computing KNN in the feature space. The parameter K has little effect on the results and we fixed $K = 10$ in our experiments.

Thirdly, the weight function is defined as: $k(i, j) = 1 - \|FE(i) - FE(j)\|/C$, where C is the least upper bound of $\|FE(i) - FE(j)\|$ to guarantee $k(i, j) \in [0, 1]$.

After that, the affinity matrix is $A = [k(i, j)]$, $D = diag(D_i)$ and $D_i = \sum_j k(i, j)$.

3 Proposed Method

Color MFIF is merging several partially focused color source images into a single image where each region is well focused. To extract the focused regions as much as possible, we propose a novel color MFIF based on quaternion morphological gradient and improved KNN matting. The fusion processes are explained in detail below.

3.1 Quaternion Morphological Gradient of Color Image

Usually, the image blur process will cause the loss of high frequency information, thus, many focus measures are designed by using the image gradients [6, 7, 9, 10]. As for color image, most of them are only using the luminance information while the chrominance information is ignored completely. Thus, they have limited discrimination capacity in the detection of focused regions. To improve the discrimination capacity of focus measure, we need to design a focus measure which makes full use the color structure information of source image.

Recently, the quaternion theory is introduced to solute color image processing problems and numerous quaternion representation (QR)-based methods, e.g., color image descriptor [13] and color image inpainting [17], etc. have been developed. The QR has several attractive merits, such as simultaneously handling all color channels and preserving high correlation of color channels, etc. Considering the powerful image representation ability of QR, this paper try to design a new focus measure based on QR. According to the morphology theory, it is necessary to find the local extremums when defining the corrosion and expansion operators. Unlike the morphological gradient of grayscale image that is directly calculated using pixel values, in the quaternion domain, we need to find a proper function to determine the order of two quaternions. Lexicographical ordering is a complete lattice space which can obtain unique extremum, thus, many effective color morphological methods based on lexicographical ordering have been proposed [18, 19]. However, the lexicographical ordering has several inherent problems. The first one is that it is difficult for deeper layer components to participate in extremum estimation. The second one is that the estimation result is closely related to the prioritization of components. Moreover, how to effective construct the informative components is another issue. Therefore, it is necessary to define a simple but efficient function to estimate the local extremums for color morphological gradient.

In [13], Lan et al. found that the similarity between quaternions can be measured by the phase of CTQ results. We apply CTQ to design a ranking function for estimating local extremums. Specially, for two quaternions $\dot{q}_1$ and $\dot{q}_2$, the right CTQ is first performed on them by a unit quaternion $\dot{p}$. Then, the ranking function is defined as:

$$RF(\dot{q}_1, \dot{q}_2) = \begin{cases} \dot{q}_1 > \dot{q}_2, & \text{if } \theta(\text{CTQ}_r(\dot{q}_1, \dot{p})) > \theta(\text{CTQ}_r(\dot{q}_2, \dot{p})) \\ \dot{q}_1 \leq \dot{q}_2, & \text{if } \theta(\text{CTQ}_r(\dot{q}_1, \dot{p})) \leq \theta(\text{CTQ}_r(\dot{q}_2, \dot{p})) \end{cases} \qquad (7)$$

where $\theta(\text{CTQ}_r(\dot{q}_1, \dot{p}))$ and $\theta(\text{CTQ}_r(\dot{q}_2, \dot{p}))$ are the phases of the right CTQ results of quaternions $\dot{q}_1$ and $\dot{q}_2$, respectively. Once the ranking function has been established, we calculate the quaternion morphological operators as follows.

For a color image $\mathbf{I}$, let Ω be a local region of size $w \times w$ centered on pixel x in image $\mathbf{I}$, $\dot{\mathbf{I}}$ is the QR matrix. The color erosion $\varepsilon_{\Omega,\dot{p}}(\mathbf{I})$ at region Ω is given by:

$$\varepsilon_{\Omega,\dot{p}}(\mathbf{I})(x) = \{\dot{\mathbf{I}}(y) : \dot{\mathbf{I}}(y) = \wedge_{\dot{p}}[\dot{\mathbf{I}}(t)], t \in \Omega\} \qquad (8)$$

where $\wedge_{\dot{p}}$ is the infimum according to the defined ranking function with reference quaternion $\dot{p}$. And the color dilation $\delta_{\Omega,\dot{p}}(\mathbf{I})$ is given by:

$$\delta_{\Omega,\dot{p}}(\mathbf{I})(x) = \{\dot{\mathbf{I}}(z) : \dot{\mathbf{I}}(z) = \vee_{\dot{p}}[\dot{\mathbf{I}}(t)], t \in \Omega\} \qquad (9)$$

where $\vee_{\dot{p}}$ is the supremum according to the defined ranking function with $\dot{p}$.

Now, the quaternion morphological gradient of color image $\mathbf{I}$ can be obtained as:

$$\rho_{\dot{p}}(\mathbf{I}) = \delta_{\Omega,\dot{p}}(\mathbf{I}) - \varepsilon_{\Omega,\dot{p}}(\mathbf{I}) \qquad (10)$$

From the above computation process, we can find that the estimation result is relation to the reference quaternion $\dot{p}$. Generally, we need to emphasize the image luminance feature for MFIF task, thus, the reference quaternion is set to $\dot{p} = (i + j + k)\big/\sqrt{3}$.

Figure 2 shows the quaternion morphological gradients of a pair of source images, and the size of local region is 7×7. We can find that the dilation operator shrinks the color structures which have a color close to the lower bound, whereas the erosion operator enlarges the regions which have a color close to the lower bound. Thus, these color morphological operators inherit the properties of the classic grayscale morphology. The quaternion morphological gradients can capture the edge information well and reflect the content of different regions. Therefore, it is suitable to measure the focus information of color multi-focus images.

(a1)   (b1)   (c1)   (d1)

(a2)   (b2)   (c2)   (d2)

Fig. 2. The quaternion morphological gradients of a pair of source images. (a1) and (a2) Source images; (b1) and (b2) Color erosion results of (a1) and (a2); (c1) and (c2) Color dilation results of (a1) and (a2); (d1) and (d2) The quaternion morphological gradients of (a1) and (a2).

3.2 Color MFIF based on Quaternion Morphological Gradient and Improved KNN Matting

As discussed above, the quaternion morphological gradient can measure the focus information of color image well. We will utilize this focus measure to fuse color multi-focus source images. The detailed steps are described as follows.

For source image $\mathbf{I}_n$, $n = 1, 2, \cdots N$, the quaternion morphological gradient image $\mathbf{QG}_n$ is first calculated by using Eq. (10), where N is the number of source images. In general, the pixel in focused region has higher salience value than the one in defocused region. Thus, a maximum rule is used to acquire the initial decision map $\mathbf{ID}_n$.

$$\mathbf{ID}_n(x, y) = \begin{cases} 1, & \text{if } |\mathbf{QG}_n(x, y)| > \max_{m, m \neq n} \{|\mathbf{QG}_m(x, y)|\} \& |\mathbf{QG}_n(x, y)| > T \\ 0, & \text{otherwise} \end{cases} \tag{11}$$

where T is a free parameter to ensure the focused points reliably and is set to $T = 0.5$. In Eq. (11), $\mathbf{ID}_n(x, y) = 1$ implies that the point (x, y) in $\mathbf{I}_n$ is definite focused pixel.

The obtained decision maps are quite satisfactory, but they are sparse which cannot be used in the weighted fusion step directly. Therefore, we require refining the sparse decision maps to reach the requirement of weighted fusion. The KNN matting can solve this problem because it can estimate dense and accurate result even though the user input is sparse. As an important image feature, the depth information can provide rich information on shapes of objects and 3D cues. In [20], Xiao et al. developed a robust pseudo depth measure based on semi-inverse of RGB image and proposed an RGB-'D' saliency algorithm. Experiments illustrated that the depth feature can boost the performance of RGB saliency models. Figure 3 shows the pseudo depth maps obtained by the method of [20]. We can find that the image patches within the same object have similar depth information. Thus, the risk of misclassifying focused pixels and defocused pixels in same objects will be greatly reduced, if the depth information of source image is considered in the fusion process. Moreover, duo to the clustering Laplacian of KNN matting is derived by feature vector, the selection of components in feature vector is of great significance to the matting performance. Based on these considerations, an improved KNN matting algorithm with extra depth information is proposed to estimate the final decision maps. This algorithm adds the depth information into the original color feature in Eq. (6) to form a new feature vector to construct clustering Laplacian, which greatly improves the accuracy of the correlation of adjacent pixels. The final decision map is estimated as follows.

First, for each source image, the definite focused pixels obtained by Eq. (11) are regarded as foreground $\mathbf{F}$, and the definite focused pixels of the remaining source images are all regarded as background $\mathbf{B}$. And the trimap $\mathbf{T}_n$ of source image $\mathbf{I}_n$ is:

$$\mathbf{T}_n(x, y) = \begin{cases} 1, & \text{if } \mathbf{ID}_n(x, y) = 1 \text{ and } \max_{m, m \neq n} \{\mathbf{ID}_m(x, y)\} = 0 \\ 0, & \text{if } \mathbf{ID}_n(x, y) = 0 \text{ and } \max_{m, m \neq n} \{\mathbf{ID}_m(x, y)\} = 1 \\ 0.5, & \text{otherwise} \end{cases} \tag{12}$$

In Eq. (12), $\mathbf{T}_n(x, y) = 1$ and $\mathbf{T}_n(x, y) = 0$ indicates that the point (x, y) is foreground pixel and background pixel, and $\mathbf{T}_n(x, y) = 0.5$ indicates that the point (x, y) is unknown pixel and is required to further process.

Then, we calculate the pseudo depth map $\mathbf{DP}_n$ of each source image $\mathbf{I}_n$ by the method of [20].

After the trimap $\mathbf{T}_n$ and pseudo depth map $\mathbf{DP}_n$ are obtained, we take the $\mathbf{T}_n$, $\mathbf{DP}_n$ and $\mathbf{I}_n$ as inputs to estimate alpha matte α_n by improved KNN matting:

$$\alpha_n = IKNN(\mathbf{I}_n, \mathbf{T}_n, \mathbf{DP}_n) \tag{13}$$

where $IKNN(\cdot)$ represents the improved KNN matting function. Now, the final decision map ω_n of the source image $\mathbf{I}_n$ can be obtained by:

$$\omega_n(x, y) = \begin{cases} 1, & \text{if } \alpha_n(x, y) > 0.5 \\ 0, & \text{otherwise} \end{cases} \tag{14}$$

Finally, the fused image $\mathbf{F}$ is constructed as follows:

$$\mathbf{F} = \sum_{n=1}^{N} \omega_n \mathbf{I}_n \tag{15}$$

(a)   (b)

Fig. 3. Pseudo depth maps derived from [20]. (a) Source images; (b) The corresponding depth maps of (a).

4   Experimental Results and Analysis

4.1   Experimental Settings

Experiments were conducted on 30 pairs of color multi-focus source images. 20 sets of them come from "Lytro" dataset [21] and another 10 sets are collected on the Internet. The source images with different contents stand for various cases encountered in practice well. We compare our method with five representative fusion methods, including nonsubsampled contourlet transform and sparse representation-based one (NSCTSR) [3], image matting-based one (IM) [9], boundary finding-based one (BF) [7], convolution neural network-based one (CNN) [22] and guided filter-based one (GF) [8]. We use four acknowledged metrics to evaluate the performance of different methods quantitatively. They are normalized mutual information (Q_{NMI}), image feature based metrics (Q_G), image structural similarity based metric (Q_Y) and human perception-based metric (Q_{CB}). A detailed description of these metrics can be found in [23]. For these four metrics, larger value signifies better fusion performance.

4.2 Qualitative and Quantitative Comparison

In order to exhibit the advantages of our method, three image fusion experiments are selected for comparative analysis. The fused images obtained by different methods and the close-up views are shown in Figs. 4–6.

The first experiment is conducted on "stadium" source images which are good registered but their focused objects are highly overlapping with each other. This scene is most challenging for spatial domain based methods, since the shape of the focused objects is irregular. As shown in Fig. 4(d), the IM method produces noticeable spatial artifacts around strong edges. The BF method fails to deal with this scene and all the defocused regions are selected into the fused image. The main reason is that the watershed algorithm is used to adjust the boundaries of focused regions, which is sensitive to the sharp gradients. The boundaries of steel mesh are very complex, which cause the failure of the adjustment strategy. Although the CNN and GF method can merge most of focused regions into the fused images, some small regions (the top triangular region in the red box and the right triangular region in the green box) are still blurred. Because the CNN and GF method utilize some post-processing techniques ("hole-filling" and guided filtering) to refine the decision maps, which resulting in small focused regions are lost. The NSCTSR and our method well preserve the focus information of source images and obtain satisfactory fused results.

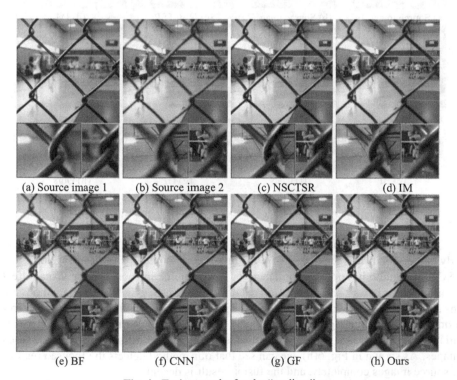

Fig. 4. Fusion results for the "stadium" set.

The second experiment is conducted on "sculpture" source images, in which the sculpture cannot be exactly registered because of the zooming in and out effect. As shown in Fig. 5(c), the fused image of the NSCTSR method appears color distortion seriously. We can see from Fig. 5(e)–(g) that the boundaries of the foreground object are blurred and partial defocused regions are also selected in the fused images (see the green boxes). The IM and our method can well extract the focused regions from source images. However, with careful observation, the IM method introduces some spatial artifacts into the boundary regions (see Fig. 5(d)), since the robust matting algorithm cannot always obtain proper weighted values for the transitional regions. By contrast, our method yields a high-quality fused image with clear boundaries.

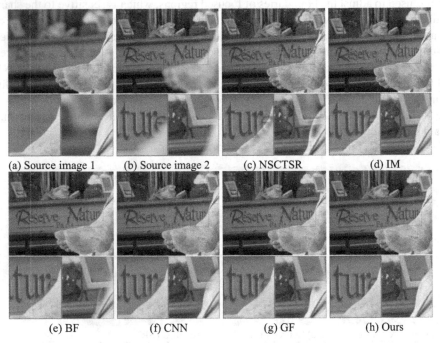

(a) Source image 1   (b) Source image 2   (c) NSCTSR   (d) IM

(e) BF   (f) CNN   (g) GF   (h) Ours

Fig. 5. Fusion results for the "sculpture" set.

The third experiment is conducted on "girl" source images which are captured at a dynamic scene. It is another reason for mis-registration. As shown in Fig. 6(c), the NSCTSR method has poor performance for "girl" source images, and the visual effect of fused image is very bad. The fusion results of the IM, BF, CNN and GF methods are unsatisfied. Due to the foreground region (e.g. girl' face) is textureless while the corresponding background region (e.g. girl' hair) possesses strong structure. These methods fail to detect the focused regions correctly, resulting in some artifacts appear in the fused images. As shown in Fig. 6(h), we can see that our method detects the focused regions of source images completely, and the fusion result is decent.

Besides the visual comparisons, it is also significant to examine the performance of different methods through quantitative comparisons, which are listed in Table 1.

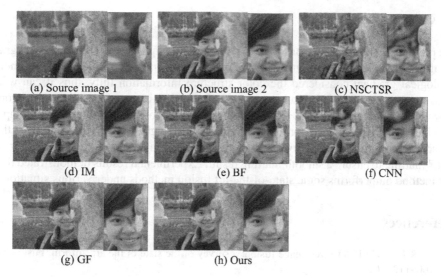

(a) Source image 1   (b) Source image 2   (c) NSCTSR

(d) IM   (e) BF   (f) CNN

(g) GF   (h) Ours

Fig. 6. Fusion results for the "girl" set.

The value of each metric is the average value over the 30 pairs of test images, and the best result of the compared methods is highlighted with bold. It can be observed from Table 1 that our method obviously outperforms the other methods in terms of the four metrics. It means that the proposed method has better performance than the other methods in fusing color multi-focus images. In addition, the average running time of different fusion methods on 20 testing images with size of 512×512 are also given in the last row of Table 1. In the experiments, all the codes are ran in the computer with Intel Processor (Intel Core i5-3470, 3.20 GHz CPU) and 8 GB RAM, and are implemented on the MATLAB R2014b software. We can find that the GF method is the most efficient method in comparison to other methods. The NSCTSR method has lowest efficiency because the performing of the nonsubsampled contourlet transform and sparse coding are both high computational cost. The CNN and our method require a lot of running time. In our method, the calculation of focus measure in quaternion domain is complex, thus the computational cost is relatively high.

Table 1. The average objective assessments of different image fusion methods

Method	NSCTSR	IM	BF	CNN	GF	Ours
Q_{NMI}	0.9165	1.1144	1.1514	1.1262	1.1389	**1.1717**
Q_G	0.6833	0.7068	0.7209	0.7198	0.7202	**0.7244**
Q_Y	0.9592	0.9731	0.9896	0.9881	0.9885	**0.9900**
Q_{CB}	0.7532	0.7817	0.8012	0.8007	0.8011	**0.8036**
Time (s)	531.39	4.76	1.85	149.31	0.32	156.32

5 Conclusions

We presented an effective color MFIF method based on quaternion morphological gradient and improved KNN matting in this paper. The computation of quaternion morphological gradient considered the color structure information fully, thus it can well measure the sharpness information of source image. To extract focused regions from source images completely, the KNN matting was used to estimate the decision maps, which makes full use of the strong correlations among neighboring pixels. Moreover, the pseudo depth information of source image was incorporated into the feature vector of KNN matting to ensure a smooth matting result. Experimental results demonstrated that our method outperforms some state-of-the-art fusion methods under various situations.

References

1. Li, S.T., et al.: Pixel-level image fusion: a survey of the state of the art. Inform. Fusion **33**, 100–112 (2017)
2. Lewis, J., et al.: Pixel- and region-based image fusion with complex wavelets. Inform. Fusion **8**(2), 119–130 (2007)
3. Liu, Y., Liu, S., Wang, Z.F.: A general framework for image fusion based on multi-scale transform and sparse representation. Inform. Fusion **24**, 147–164 (2015)
4. Jian, L.H., et al.: Multi-scale image fusion through rolling guidance filter. Futur. Gener. Comput. Syst. **83**, 310–325 (2018)
5. Liu, W., Wang, Z.F.: A novel multi-focus image fusion method using multiscale shearing non-local guided averaging filter. Signal Process. **166**, 1–24 (2020)
6. Huang, W., Jing, Z.L.: Evaluation of focus measures in multi-focus image fusion. Pattern Recogn. Lett. **28**(4), 493–500 (2007)
7. Zhang, Y., Bai, X.Z., Wang, T.: Boundary finding based multi-focus image fusion through multi-scale morphological focus-measure. Inform. Fusion **35**, 81–101 (2017)
8. Qiu, X.H., et al.: Guided filter-based multi-focus image fusion through focus region detection. Signal Process. Image Commun. **72**, 35–46 (2019)
9. Li, S.T., et al.: Image matting for fusion of multi-focus images in dynamic scenes. Inform. Fusion **14**, 147–162 (2013)
10. Liu, W., Zheng, Z., Wang, Z.F.: Robust multi-focus image fusion using lazy random walks with multiscale focus measures. Signal Process. **179**, 1–18 (2021)
11. Hamilton, W.R.: Elements of Quaternions. Longmans Green, London, UK (1866)
12. Weeks, J., Lehoucq, R., Uzan, J.-P.: Detecting topology in a nearly flat spherical universe. Class. Quantum Gravity **20**(8), 1529–1542 (2003)
13. Lan, R.S., Zhou, Y.C., Tang, Y.Y.: Quaternionic local ranking binary pattern: a local descriptor of color images. IEEE Trans. Image Process. **25**(2), 566–579 (2016)
14. Xie, W.Y., Li, Y.S., Ge, C.R.: Reconstruction of hyperspectral image using matting model for classification. Optical Engineering **55**(5), 053104 (2016)
15. Levin, A., Lischinski, D., Weiss, Y.: A closed-form solution to natural image matting. IEEE Trans. Pattern Anal. Mach. Intell. **30**(2), 228–242 (2008)
16. Chen, Q., Li, D., Tang, C.-K., Matting, K.N.N.: IEEE Conference on Computer Vision and Pattern Recognition (CVPR) **1**, 869–876 (2012)
17. Chen, Y.Y., Xiao, X.L., Zhou, Y.C.: Low-rank quaternion approximation for color image processing. IEEE Trans. Image Process. **29**, 1426–1439 (2020)

18. Angulo, J.: Geometric algebra colour image representations and derived total orderings for morphological operators-part I: colour quaternions. J. Vis. Commun. Image Represent. **21**(1), 33–48 (2010)
19. Lei, T., et al.: Multivariate mathematical morphology based on fuzzy extremum estimation. IET Image Proc. **8**(9), 548–558 (2014)
20. Xiao, X.L., Zhou, Z.C., Gong, Y.J.: RGB-'D' saliency detection with pseudo depth. IEEE Trans. Image Process. **28**(5), 2126–2139 (2019)
21. http://mansournejati.ece.iut.ac.ir/content/lytro-multi-focus-dataset
22. Liu, Y., et al.: Multi-focus image fusion with a deep convolutional neural network. Inform. Fusion **36**, 191–207 (2017)
23. Liu, Z., et al.: Objective assessment of multiresolution image fusion algorithms for context enhancement in night vision: a comparative study. IEEE Trans. Pattern Anal. Mach. Intell. **34**(1), 94–109 (2012)

Monocular Visual Analysis for Electronic Line Calling of Tennis Games

Yuanzhou Chen[1], Shaobo Cai[2(✉)], Yuxin Wang[2], and Junchi Yan[2]

[1] YK Pao School, Shanghai 200003, China
s17680@ykpaoschool.cn
[2] Shanghai Jiao Tong University, Shanghai 200240, China
{582875593,wyx-0279,yanjunchi}@sjtu.edu.cn

Abstract. Electronic Line Calling (ELC) is an auxiliary referee system used for tennis matches based on binocular vision technology. While ELC has been widely used, there are still many problems, such as complex installation and maintenance, high cost and etc. We propose a monocular vision technology based ELC method. The method has the following steps: (1) locate the tennis ball's trajectory. We propose a multistage tennis ball positioning approach combining background subtraction and color area filtering. (2) Then We propose a bouncing point prediction method by minimizing the fitting loss of the uncertain point; (3) Finally, we find out whether the bouncing point of the ball is out of bounds or not according to the relative position between the bouncing point and the court side line in the two-dimensional image.

We collected and marked 394 samples, we achieved 99.4% accuracy, and among the 11 samples with bouncing points near the line, we obtained 81.8% accuracy. The experimental results show that our method is feasible to judge if a ball is out of the court with monocular vision and significantly reduce complex installation and costs of ELC system with binocular vision.

Keywords: Hawk-eye · Electronic Line Calling (ELC) · Binocular vision · Monocular vision · Bouncing point prediction

1 Introduction

1.1 Research Background

Hawk-eye system is an instant replay system [1]. It can track and record the three-dimensional motion trajectory of the sphere through high-speed and high-quality camera and computer vision technology, predict the bouncing point according to the three-dimensional motion trajectory. It can also replay the virtual three-dimensional image in form of dynamic images and show the result to the audience and players. The hawk-eye system can display the game from multiple angles, overcome many restrictions of human judgment, and improve the accuracy of referee judgments and the fairness of the game. Furthermore, the hawk-eye system can help analyze the skills of the players, collect statistics, provide instruction for teaching ball sports. The hawk-eye system is not

© Springer Nature Switzerland AG 2021
Y. Peng et al. (Eds.): ICIG 2021, LNCS 12888, pp. 528–538, 2021.
https://doi.org/10.1007/978-3-030-87355-4_44

only used in tennis, but also in football, cricket, basketball, badminton, rugby, baseball, volleyball, billiards and other sports.

The first hawk-eye system was developed by Hawk-Eye Innovations. The system was initially implemented in 2001 and was used for TV broadcasts for cricket competitions. The hawk-eye system started to act as an auxiliary judgment in a variety of sporting competitions in a few years. In 2005, the Electronic Line Calling (ELC) technology in the Hawk-Eye system was recognized by the International Tennis League (ITF). In 2006, the US Tennis Open became the first grand slam that introduced a hawk-eye system. China Open also followed the use of ELC in the same year. In 2009, the hawk-eye system was officially introduced to cricket games. The goal-line technology used in Premier League was based on hawk-eye system. In the 2014 World Volleyball Championship, the system has also been introduced. In the U.S. Open in August last year, except Arthur Ashe and Armstrong still using the traditional manual lineup, the other 15 courts were all introduced with hawk-eye live broadcast system for the first time. There was only one referee in the competition field, which had minimized the number of staff in the court.

While the hawk-eye system is increasingly popular for sports competitions, the existing ELC systems are based on binocular vision technologies, which still have many problems. For example, the installation and maintenance process of the existing ELC systems are very complex (need to conduct court measurement, 3D modeling, and camera calibration); The costs of installation, operation and management are very high with multiple high-speed cameras and synchronization of cameras. These problems prevent the wider use of the ELC systems for sport games.

Recently in the research work of TTNet, Myint, Kotera, etc. [2–9] it was reported that monocular vision could be used to detect and track fast moving objects, which could be applied to the ELC system. We are motivated to solve the problems of ELC associated with binocular vision. With the significant advances on computer vision, we believe it is possible to develop a simple, effective and cheap ELC system with monocular vision. In this paper, we investigate the feasibility of monocular vision based ELC system, and successfully propose a monocular vision technology based ELC method. We develop and implement the ELC method, test it with custom datasets. Experiments proves the feasibility of the method, which can be used to produce effective and cheap ELC systems.

1.2 Related Works

Research on Hawk-Eye System Based on Binocular Vision: Most of the existing ELC systems are based on binocular vision technology. Paper [1, 10] describes the basic principles and key technologies of the hawk-eye system. Paper [11] is an US patent about the hawk-eye system. It also describes the process of the ELC. Paper [12] implemented a hawk-eye system based on binocular vision. Paper [13] implemented a hawk-eye system based on LabVIEW and MATLAB.

According to the above research, the hawk-eye system, based on the principles of binocular vision and camera calibration technology, predicts the bouncing point to determine whether the ball is out of bounds according to the trajectory of the ball. More details are shown in Fig. 1.

Binocular Vision. Binocular vision is the method based on the parallax (the direction difference caused by observing the same target from two different points with a certain distance) in order to obtain the three-dimensional geometric information of an object from multiple images.

Camera Calibration. In machine vision, the transformation relationship between the spatial position of an object in the world three-dimensional coordinate system and the two-dimensional position in the image coordinate system needs to be determined by the camera calibration parameters (internal and external parameters). The process of camera calibration is to solve the internal and external parameters through the relationship between 3D and 2D coordinates.

The binocular vision based hawk-eve systems have the following major processing steps: 1) Set up multiple high-speed cameras in different locations, calibrate the camera to obtain the internal and external parameters of each camera. 2) Measure the court and perform a virtual reconstruction of the court, store the relevant data of the court and rules; 3) Identify the spherical target in each frame of the picture, get the location of the ball. 4) Use the ball position information from at least two different cameras at the same time to calculate the three-dimensional world coordinates of the ball. 5) Obtain the three-dimensional motion trajectory of the ball according to the relationship of consecutive frames, predict the actual landing position. 6) Map the trajectory of the ball and the predicted bouncing point to the virtually reconstructed court to identify whether the ball is out of bounds or not.

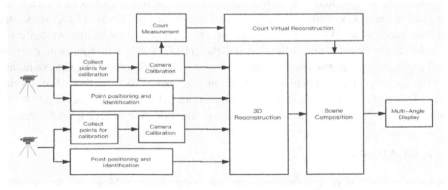

Fig. 1. The building blocks of hawk-eye system.

1.3 Our Contributions

Compared to the existing works, our work made the following major contributions.

1) We designed and implemented a ELC method for tennis based on monocular vision. According to our investigation, there are no published papers, patents or other documents applying monocular vision to tennis hawk-eye system, which shows innovation of our work

2) We designed a two-stage tennis positioning method that combines background subtraction and color area filtering, which can solve the problem of misjudgment and missing judgments in the monocular vision based ELC system.
3) We designed a bouncing point prediction method based on the minimum fitting loss of uncertain points, which can solve the problem of unobvious changing trend near the bouncing point.
4) We collected and marked 349 video samples, implemented the core algorithm and prototype system, including tennis trajectory positioning, bouncing point prediction, out-of-bounds judgment, etc. We carried out the experimental verification and analyzed the experimental results, which demonstrated the feasibility of the proposed low cost and effective ELC method.

2 Methodology

2.1 Overall Processes

In this section, we present the methodology of the proposed ELC system design. The overall process of the proposed ELC method includes the following major steps:

(1) Identify each tennis ball in each frame of the video;
(2) Fit the two curves: falling trend and rising trend;
(3) Calculate the intersection point of two curves as the prediction of the bouncing point;
(4) Determine whether the ball is out of bounds or not by comparing the relative position of the bouncing point and the court lines.

Figure 2 shows the results of our program after each step being visualized. The detailed processes of the method are shown in Fig. 3. Compared with the traditional binocular vision hawk-eye system (Fig. 1), our method does not need camera calibration and 3D coordinate reconstruction. Instead, we directly use the relative relationship of 2D coordinate to determine whether it is out of bounds or not. The following part of

Fig. 2. The yellow parts are the point of tennis balls identified, the red parts are two fitting curves (falling and rising), the blue parts are the intersection point of two curves, which is the predicted bounce point. We deterimine whether the ball is out of bound or not by the relative position of the bouncing point and the court lines. (Color figure online)

this section will focus on the tennis ball positioning method and the bouncing point prediction method.

2.2   Tennis Positioning Method

Common methods [14–18] used in detecting high-speed moving objects in video include optical flow [16], frame difference [17], and background subtraction [14, 15].

Optical Flow Method. The change of pixel intensity in time domain and the neighborhood correlation of pixels is used to determine the pixel motion, and the change of pixels between adjacent frames is compared to determine the target position and find the motion information. Optical flow method can detect moving objects without knowing any information of the scene, but noise, multiple light sources, shadows and occlusion will seriously affect the calculation results of optical flow field distribution. Moreover, the calculation of optical flow method is complex, and it is difficult to realize real-time processing.

Frame Difference Method. Frame difference method is a non parametric modeling method, which distinguishes moving foreground and background by pixel comparison. It selects the images which are continuous in time or separated by a fixed number of frames for difference. By selecting an appropriate threshold, the pixels in the difference

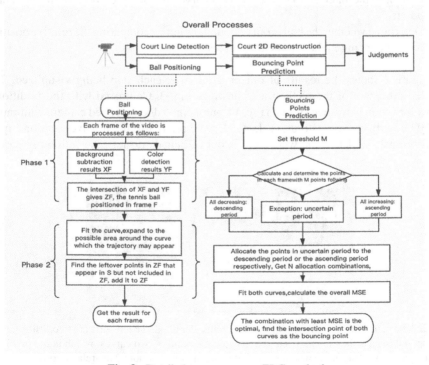

Fig. 3. Detailed process on our ELC method.

image are divided into moving foreground and background. However, the frame difference method is sensitive to environmental noise, and the selection of threshold is very important. If the threshold is too low, it is not enough to suppress the noise, and if it is too high, it is easy to ignore the changes in the image. For large and uniform color moving objects, there may be holes in the interior of the object, which can not extract the moving object completely. It can only be used when the camera is still, but there are many limitations in its application.

Background Subtraction Method. The basic idea of background subtraction is to get the approximate background image by using the background parameter model, and then compare the current frame with the approximate background image by difference. The area with larger difference is considered as the moving area, and the area with smaller difference is the background area. In this method, background modeling and updating are crucial, because the background image must be updated in real time according to the illumination and external environment changes. Aiming at the problem of scene dynamic change, researchers have proposed many modeling algorithms, such as MOG Gaussian mixture model separation algorithm [14] and KNN background separation method [15].

2.3   Tennis Bouncing Point Prediction Method

Related Works. In the hawk-eye system based on binocular vision, the prediction of bouncing point is mainly realized by the method of 3D coordinate reconstruction. The is not reported work on predicting bouncing point based on monocular vision. Bouncing point detection is based on the observed bounce of the ball. When the bouncing occurs, the ball's trajectory suddenly changes. We design an algorithm to detect the mutation to realize the bouncing point detection. TTNet treated the bounce of the ball as an event to learn, events also include service, the ball hits the net, etc. By building specific sequential events such as deep learning network, TTNet could detect different events. In paper [8], Rozumnyi et al. (2019) propopsed a method to detect trajectory mutation by using dynamic programming to find global energy minimization and the bouncing points.

Our Method. We found that there are several challenges exist in the bouncing point prediction methods: as mentioned above, the bounce of the ball is a mutation. It is relatively easy for us to distinguish the descend before bouncing and the ascend after bouncing. However, for a part of the balls appear just before or after the bouncing point, because of the speed, rotation, the change of the recording angle, the bounce of the ball trajectory mutation is not obvious. This makes it hard to distinguish between whether the ball is descending or ascending.

We propose a bouncing point prediction method based on the minimum fitting loss of an uncertain point. The process of this method is shown in Fig. 3. The general idea of this method is described as follows. Our goal is to divide the trajectory of the ball into two categories: descending phase and ascending phase. By using the least square method, both curves are fitted. The intersection point of the two curves can be regarded as the predicted bouncing point. As some of the balls are too difficult to distinguish between whether it is descending or ascending, we first mark these balls as uncertainty (as shown in Fig. 4-a), three orange points on the bottom are uncertain points), then put these uncertain points in descending phase or ascending phase respectively and get a variety of combinations. Fit both curves with the least square method, find the combination which MSE (minimum fitting error) is the smallest, that distribution of descending and ascending points is the final result. The intersection point of two curves are the final bouncing point. We use an open-source least-square curve fitting code [19] on GitHub for our work. Figure 4-b is the result of our algorithm fitting.

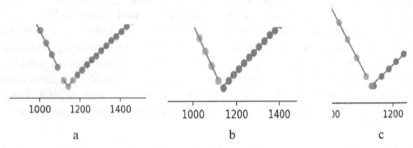

| 1000 | 1200 | 1400 | | 1000 | 1200 | 1400 | |)0 | 1200 |
| a | | | | b | | | | c | |

Fig. 4. Representative results of our fitting algorithm. a) The uncertainty point is near the falling place (three orange points on the bottom); b) The result of the optimal fitting error; c) The result of the bouncing point (intersection point) in green. (Color figure online)

3 Experiment

3.1 Datasets

In this section, we present the development of dataset for our experiments and the experiment results. In Table 1, we show our sample quantity and other added information. The datasets are already public on GitHub, but we have removed the link due to blind review.

Table 1. Sample quantity and other added information

Total number of data	349
The number of confusing data	11
Proportion of confusing data	3.2%
Average time (s)	10.0

We chose Samsung S10 mobile slow-motion (240 frames per second) to capture videos in this project. The shooting device is fixed, which can cover the service line and the baseline on one side. Figure 5 is a representative sample of the confusing data.

3.2 Results and Discussion

Results. In our experiments, we evaluate the accuracy of the judgment of balls out of bound or not in the samples. The formula of accuracy is the number of video samples judged correctly divided by total number of video samples. The judging method is calculated manually based on the relationship of location between the predicted bouncing point and the marked lines of the court.

$$L_v(M(X_v), t) = 1_{\{D(M(X_v),t)<\varepsilon\}} \tag{1}$$

$$R_{suc} = \sum_i \frac{\left\| L_v\left(M(X_{v,i}), t_i\right) \right\|}{N} \tag{2}$$

We developed and implemented the proposed ELC system. After experiments, we compute the accuracy of the method over the video samples (see Table 2).

Table 2. Accuracy of the ELC system

	Number	Success	R_{suc}
Normal	338	336	99.4%
Confusing	11	9	81.8%
Total	349	345	98.9%

One of the errors is shown in Fig. 5. The main reason is that there is strong interference and the court line is far away from the camera.

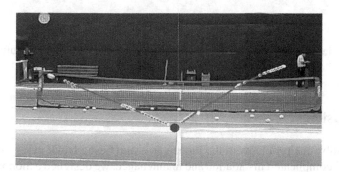

Fig. 5. A representative misjudgement on confusing segments

Influence on the Accuracy of the Camera Position. Next we evaluate the influence of camera position on the accuracy. Three images are presented in Fig. 6. It can be seen that it is relatively easy to judge image Fig. 6-a, but the other images are difficult to judge even if we watch the video for multiple times (see Fig. 6-b and -c). This may be explained by that the monocular vision method relies on the relative position rather than 3D coordinate reconstruction. Different camera positions will cause parallax, thus resulting in lower accuracy. Generally speaking, we think that four cameras should be placed on court (two cameras at each side of the court). One in between the middle of the service line and baseline, and the other is in the middle of the sideline. Finding the optimal arrangement of these cameras is left for our future work.

Fig. 6. Examples of balls with different placement. a) In the middle of the court; b) near the baseline of the court; c) near the far sideline of the court.

4 Conclusion

In order to solve the problems in the binocular vision based hawk-eye system such as high cost and complicated installation and maintenance, we designed a monocular vision based method. With this method we first identify the tennis balls in the video and predict the bounce point. Then according to the 2D image coordinates and tennis court lines we can judge whether the ball is out of line or not. In order to solve the problem of missed judgment and misjudgment in positioning, we designed a two-stage tennis positioning method that combines background subtraction and color area filtering methods. Aiming at the problem that the changing trend of the bounce point is unobvious, we designed a bouncing point prediction method based on the minimum fitting loss of the uncertainty point.

In order to verify our method, we collected and annotated 349 video samples, and implemented the core algorithm, including tennis ball trajectory positioning, bouncing point prediction, etc. We conducted expermients and the results showed that the proposed method is feasible and effective. It has an accuracy of 99.4% for the normal scenarios and an accuracy of 81.8% for challenging scenarios.

To the best of our knowledge, there is no work or attempt reported on monocular vision based ELC system for tennis games, which prove the innovation of our work. We have shared on Github [20] all the annotated samples and codes of this research work.

References

1. Liu, J.Q., Fu, P., Li, T.: On the principle of tennis "hawk-eye" system. Radio TV Broadcast Eng. **19**(10), 69–73 (2012)
2. Voeikov, R., Falaleev, N., Baikulov, R.: TTNet: real-time temporal and spatial video analysis of table tennis. In: IEEE/CVF Conference on Computer Vision and Pattern Recognition Workshops (CVPRW), IEEE, pp. 3866–3874 (2020)
3. Dung, N.M.: 2020. maudzung/TTNet-Real-time-Analysis-System-for-Table-Tennis-Pytorch. https://github.com/maudzung/TTNet-Real-time-Analysis-System-for-Table-Tennis-Pytorch (2021)
4. Myint, H., Wong, P., Dooley, L., Hopgood, A.: Tracking a table tennis ball for umpiring purposes. In: Fourteenth IAPR International Conference on Machine Vision Applications (MVA2015), IEEE, pp. 170–173 (2015)
5. Komorowski, J., Kurzejamski, G., Sarwas, G.: Deepball: deep neural-network ball detector. In: CoRR, pp. 297–304 (2019)
6. FMO: http://cmp.felk.cvut.cz/fmo/. Accessed 22 Apr 2021
7. Rozumnyi, D.: 2020. rozumden/deblatting_python. https://github.com/rozumden/deblatting_python (2021)
8. Rozumnyi, D., Kotera, J., Šroubek, F., Matas, J.: Non-causal tracking by deblatting. In: Fink, G.A., Frintrop, S., Jiang, X. (eds.) DAGM GCPR 2019. LNCS, vol. 11824, pp. 122–135. Springer, Cham (2019). https://doi.org/10.1007/978-3-030-33676-9_9
9. Kotera, J., Rozumnyi, D., Sroubek, F., et al.: Intra-frame object tracking by deblatting. In: Computer Vision and Pattern Recognition, pp. 2300–2309 (2019)
10. Owens, N., Harris, C., Stennett, C.: Hawk-eye tennis system. In: 2003 International Conference on Visual Information Engineering VIE 2003, pp. 182–185. Guildford, UK (2003). https://doi.org/10.1049/cp:20030517
11. Shlyak, Y., Komarov, V.: Method and system for real time judging boundary lines on tennis court: U.S. Patent 8,199,199. 12 June 2012
12. Ma, C.C.: Research on the Hawkeye System's Key Technology. Doctor, Xi'an University of Technology (2014)
13. Zhou, J., Meng, X.Y., Ye, M.S.: Tennis hawk-eye system based on computer vision and LabVIEW platform. Transd. Microsyst. Technol. **37**(07), 102-104+107 (2018)
14. Zivkovic, Z.: Improved adaptive Gaussian mixture model for background subtraction. In: Proceedings of the 17th International Conference on Pattern Recognition, pp. 28–31 (2004)
15. Zivkovic, Z., Der Heijden, F.V.: Efficient adaptive density estimation per image pixel for the task of background subtraction. Pattern Recogn. Lett. **27**(7), 773–780 (2006)

16. Bruhn, A., Weickert, J., Schnörr, C.: Combining the advantages of local and global optic flow methods. In: Van Gool, L. (ed.) DAGM 2002. LNCS, vol. 2449, pp. 454–462. Springer, Heidelberg (2002). https://doi.org/10.1007/3-540-45783-6_55
17. Yin, H., Chai, Y., Yang, S.X., et al.: Fast-moving target tracking based on mean shift and frame-difference methods. J. Syst. Eng. Electron. **22**(4), 587–592 (2011)
18. Wang, H.: A summary of moving target detection and tracking algorithm. Comput. Knowl. Technol. **14**(24), 194 197 (2018)
19. lmfit/lmfit-py: https://github.com/lmfit/lmfit-py. Accessed 22 Apr 2020
20. JoeyChennn/TennisPoint: https://github.com/JoeyChennn/TennisPoint. Accessed 12 Sep 2020

Multi-homography Estimation and Inference Driven by Contour Alignment

Tao Cai, Yunde Jia, Huijun Di$^{(\boxtimes)}$, and Yuwei Wu

Laboratory of Intelligent Information Technology, School of Computer Science,
Beijing Institute of Technology (BIT), Beijing 100081, China
{caitaoo,jiayunde,ajon,wuyuwei}@bit.edu.cn

Abstract. Recently, multiple homography estimation is preferable for image stitching to handle the parallax problem, by estimating homographies from the feature correspondence in each local region. However, correspondence outliers and insufficient feature coverage will lead to unreliable local homography fitting. In this paper, we propose a novel method of multi-homography estimation and inference, driven by contour alignment. Our method uses explicit structural verification through contour alignment to eliminate incorrectly fitted homographies in some regions, and to select a better homography from other regions if current homography is rejected or with worse accuracy. With the guidance of the contour alignment, dense image alignment result is obtained by further inferring the local homography per superpixel. Quantitative and qualitative comparisons demonstrate the effectiveness of our method, especially for scenes with large parallax and viewpoint changes.

Keywords: Image stitching · Image alignment · Homography estimation · Contour alignment

1 Introduction

Image stitching [28] is essential for many computer vision tasks, such as panorama making [1], virtual reality [3], video stitching [26], etc. As the first stage of image stitching, image alignment is usually performed by estimating a global transformation [1,27] between each image pair. If the camera rotates around its optical center or the scene only contains one plane, this global one is sufficient. Nevertheless, these conditions are easily violated for hand-held cameras and complex scenes, causing ghosting artifacts in the final stitched image, which is known as the parallax problem.

Existing methods in handling the parallax problem can be classified into two categories. From the perspective of seamless stitching [8,19,33], it considers that a global image alignment is unnecessary if the following seam-finding stage can find a costless seam in a locally aligned image to stitch images. In contrast, from the viewpoint of alignment quality, there are three attractive strategies to handle such parallax problem. The first one is mesh warping [4,13–17,20,22] which estimates the motion of mesh vertices and utilizes the bilinear interpolation or

© Springer Nature Switzerland AG 2021
Y. Peng et al. (Eds.): ICIG 2021, LNCS 12888, pp. 539–551, 2021.
https://doi.org/10.1007/978-3-030-87355-4_45

Fig. 1. A case of homography candidate to demonstrate the effectiveness of contours. We observed that contours enable implicit correspondence verification and feature extrapolation. The left column shows the source and target image (from *apartments* [7]) with SIFT [24] correspondences. In the right column, green points are inliers and magenta points in the sliding window are outliers based on RANSAC [6]. Contours of the source image and warped contours of the target image under this candidate are drawn in blue and red respectively. We select three regions (zoomed below) to show details.

others to obtain the full warping field. The second one is the smoothly varying warping field [7,18,21,32] which estimates a transformation for each pixel using weighted correspondences. Last one, the approximate plane based warping [12, 23,30,34] attempts to find planar regions, then to estimate a transformation for each plane. In summary, these three strategies belong to multiple transformation estimation (a.k.a. local transformation as opposed to a global transformation).

Multiple transformation estimation relies on the spatial distribution of features and the quality of feature correspondences. However, in practical situations, features may not always adequately cover all local regions and feature correspondence contains outliers. Researchers try to eliminate obvious correspondence outliers by fitting a rough global transformation [32]. But outliers cannot be completely eliminated, especially in scenes with the aforementioned challenges. Outliers and insufficient coverage will lead to unreliable transformation fitting in local regions. Therefore, a method of transformation inference is needed to eliminate incorrectly fitted transformations in some regions, and to select a better transformation from other regions if the current transformation is rejected or with worse accuracy.

In this paper, we propose a novel method of multi-homography estimation and inference for image stitching, driven by contour alignment. Our method uses explicit structural verification through contour alignment to evaluate the quality of the homography fitted in each local region. This contour alignment is an intermediate stage in the whole alignment. Not directly aligning images has at least three benefits. First, contour alignment is another form of correspondence verification, which can further eliminate the effect of correspondence outliers.

Next, If the contour is aligned, we have a much more reliable basis for the future homography inference for pixels. In other words, we mitigate the limited feature coverage. Last but not least, when an object region is textureless, there is usually contour around it. Compared to the pixel intensity, the contour can utilize more cues to decide whether they are matched by a homography for that contour is some kind of edge. Aligning this contour is like that we can sense this object. In Fig. 1, we show a case of a homography candidate to give a further concrete explanation. A good local fitting homography candidate can align its local region (the wall), yet probably misalign other very different planes (the plant), as the quality of contour alignment verifies. Moreover, regions with fewer feature points can deduce their own homographies with the help of contours (See the large white wall and the two zoomed regions of the wall which are far away from the motherland of this candidate). With the guidance of contour alignment, we can robustly infer the local homography per superpixel, thereby providing dense image alignment result.

2   Related Work

Many efforts have been devoted to remedying the limitations of the global transformation. In consideration that common scenes can be divided into a distant plane and a ground plane, Gao et al. [7] estimated a dual-homography for the alignment. At the same time, Lin et al. [21] presented a smoothly varying affine transformation to increase alignment flexibility, assuming that the scene depth varies smoothly. Scene assumption and the affine transformation have limitations. So Zaragoza et al. [32] proposed an as-projective-as-possible (APAP) method which allows local non-projective deviations for image stitching.

For complex scenes with multiple planes, feature correspondences can be in different planes even if they are spatially close to each other. By iteratively re-segmenting and re-merging to obtain approximate planes and plane fitting affine transformations, Lou et al. [23] proposed a piecewise local model for aligning images with large parallax. Xiang et al. [30] observed that many scenes have salient plane structures. So they directly detected planes from correspondences through geometric fitting and used weighted homographies for transition regions. Li et al. [13] attempted to fit planes in general scenes by leveraging triangular facets. Feature correspondences reveal the hidden planes in images. So homography candidates extracted from them also have information about those planes. Based on this, Lee et al. [12] proposed the concept of warping residual to estimate local transformations for superpixels. Differently, Zheng et al. [34] directly detected projective-consistent planes by utilizing extra scene depth.

Feature correspondences inevitably have outliers. And in textureless regions, there are probably no keypoints. In local transformations estimation, the effect of these two limitations largely increases. By introducing line segment correspondences, Li et al. [16] attempted to mitigate insufficient keypoint correspondences for a more reliable mesh warping. Observing that feature correspondences are noisy, insufficient, and less accurate, Lin et al. [20] proposed a photometric alignment method based on mesh. Differently, our proposed method neither introduces other types of correspondences nor directly builds on pixels intensity. Keypoint correspondences are more general, and using contour alignment as an intermediate stage can eliminate the effects of outliers among them. For solving the keypoint coverage problem in textureless regions, contour alignment can also take effect by extrapolating the warping field along contours

For handling the large parallax problem, seam finding is another effective way except the above multiple transformation estimation. Zhang et al. [33] proposed a stitching method that uses an inexact homography to roughly align images and depends more on a plausible seam than on the alignment. Lin et al. [19] argued that alignment should adjust accordingly for a better seam and presented a stitching method that iteratively refines alignment and seam. Herrmann et al. [8] estimated multiple registrations to represent varying transformations across different depths. The final registration decision for each pixel depends on their proposed seam finding over multiple registrations. Guided by detected objects, seam finding [9] can be in harmony with objects, and thus be more natural. Focusing on the consistency and naturality of image stitching, there are also good works, like [2, 4, 10, 15, 17, 18].

3   Methods

This section will describe our proposed method for image stitching. We focus on local transformation estimation to align images under noisy and non-uniformly distributed correspondences. There are three stages in our proposed method, the homography candidate extraction, the contour alignment, and the superpixel alignment (See the framework overview in Fig. 2).

3.1   Homography Candidate Extraction

Firstly, we will describe how to construct a set of homography candidates, covering all planar regions in the scene ideally. We denote this set as $H = \{H_1, \ldots, H_m\}$. Directly detecting planar regions is difficult, so we assume that a small local region is almost planar for simplicity. For a better local adaptation, we utilize RANSAC [6] to compute each homography candidate in a sliding window way. In the next stage, we will eliminate the side effect caused by outliers and spread those candidates along contours as an implicit extrapolation of valid feature correspondences.

3.2   Contour Alignment

Assigning homography for each contour can be seen as a labeling process and CRF [11] is suitable to model relations among labels. CRF [11] is an undirected graph model which can be denoted as $G = (V, E)$. In the graph, $V = (X, Y)$ represents all variables and X is observed variables, Y is random variables to predict. And E denotes edges in the graph, composed of edges among Y and these ones between X, Y. Those edges represent that variables connected by

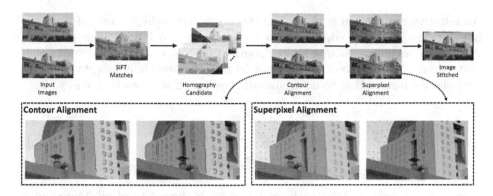

Fig. 2. An overview of our proposed contour-driven alignment for image stitching. Firstly extract homography candidates from matched points in a sliding window way. Then, split contours into units and infer their homographies to align contours. Finally, for each superpixel, we infer the homography based on contour results. To show the alignment quality, we draw only superpixel centers.

them probably appear together. To be a CRF, the random variables Y should have the Markov property, conditional on observed variables X, that is,

$$p(y_u|x, y_i, i \neq u) = p(y_u|x, y_{N(i)}), \tag{1}$$

where $N(i)$ means neighbors of the random variable y_i. The conditional probability distribution is given by

$$P(y|x) = \frac{1}{Z(x)} \prod_{ij} \Psi_{ij}(y_i, y_j, x) \prod_i \Psi_i(y_i, x), \tag{2}$$

where $Z(x)$ is the partition function for normalization, $\Psi_{ij}(y_i, y_j, x)$ is a pairwise term to represent the potential of that y_i, y_j appear together, and $\Psi_i(y_i, x)$ is a unary term, namely the potential of y_i conditioned on x. Those two potential terms are usually in exponential form, given by

$$\Psi_{ij}(y_i, y_j, x) = \exp\left\{ \sum_k \lambda_{ij}^k f_{ij}^k(y_i, y_j, x) \right\},$$
$$\Psi_i(y_i, x) = \exp\left\{ \sum_k \mu_i^k g_i^k(y_i, x) \right\}, \tag{3}$$

in which f, g are feature functions and λ, μ are learnable parameters.

Next, we will describe the graph model on contours in detail. We split all detected contours into some fixed-length units, e.g. 5 points as one unit. And each of them corresponds to a node in the CRF graph. The form of contour unit makes homography labels smooth and reduces the computational burden. For edges, we firstly use our proposed evaluation to determine whether an edge between two nodes exists. The evaluation depends on the potentials of nodes.

An intuitive explanation is that when two nodes have a high score on the same homography label, the edge between them should also have a high potential. And neighbors only exist in a limited spatial range for each node assuming that units far away from each other need not be with the same homography label. As a whole, the formulation to determine whether an edge exists is given by

$$E_{ij} = max(\sqrt{S_{ij}^a \cdot S_{ij}^r}),$$
$$S_{ij}^a = min(S_i^a, S_j^a), S_{ij}^r = min(S_i^r, S_j^r), \qquad (4)$$
$$S^r = \exp(\frac{S^a - colmax(S^a)}{\sigma}),$$

where S^a is a score matrix, each row of which is the scores of all homography candidates on a contour unit (a.k.a. the node potential). The $colmax$ is a function to calculate the maximum of each row in a matrix. Only if the scalar E_{ij} is greater than a threshold, the edge between the i-th node and the j-th node exists. Then, we evaluate the potentials of edges. Denote all contour units as $U = \{U_1, \ldots, U_u\}$, corresponding labels as $Y = \{Y_1, \ldots, Y_u\}$ and we define a cross projection distance to calculate edge potentials (a.k.a. the transition probability in CRF), that is,

$$d_{ij} = \|H_{y_i}(U_j) - H_{y_j}(U_j)\|_2^2,$$
$$\Psi_{ij}(y_i, y_j, U) = \exp(-\frac{d_{ji} + d_{ij}}{2 * \sigma_{ij}}), \qquad (5)$$

in which $i, j \in [1, u]$ and σ_{ij} is a parameter. In (5), the $H_{y_i}(U_i)$ denotes the warped one of the i-th contour unit by the homography H_{y_i}, and the others have a similar meaning. This cross projection distance Ψ_{ij} encourages that the two contour units in the same plane also have the same homography label and can spread good homographies across neighbor units.

In the remaining part of this section, we will introduce the construction of $\Psi_i(y_i, x)$ in (3). For one contour unit in the target image, we warp it to the space of the source image using a homography candidate H_{y_i}. Based on the Euclidean distance, we can find the nearest unit in the source image and think they are matched. We utilize geometric, photometric, and neighbor features to measure the similarity between matched units (a.k.a. the potential $\Psi_i(y_i, x)$). Geometric features include the tangential angle difference, the Euclidean distance, the length of matched contour segment. The angle and distance are the averages among all points on the unit. The length item refers to that a homography probably aligns this unit if it aligns most of the contour to which the unit belongs. The photometric feature is the average intensity difference on all patches centered on pixels of the contour unit. Neighbor features include the count of neighbor units, the mean of the Euclidean distance, the mean of the angle difference. The last two items are the mean among neighbor units. Neighbors comprise the units around this one in a limited range on the image space. All the above items of potentials are in exponential form finally according to the (3). At last, we use the belief propagation [5,31] to solve this inference problem and obtain homography labels for contour units.

3.3   Superpixel Alignment

We segment the whole image into edge-aware superpixels and treat each of them as a perspective consistent plane. Three characteristics of the superpixel ensure that it is suitable for the transition from contour alignment to image alignment. Firstly, compared with a large region, the superpixel is a small local region, thus having a higher probability that all pixels in each of them are perspective consistent. The second one is that treating each superpixel as a plane and choosing a corresponding homography from candidates can mitigate the parallax problem. Finally, to better utilize inference results of contour alignment, edge-aware superpixels are very suitable.

Given that around structures are usually changes of transformation, we convert regions outlined by contours to superpixels firstly. The graph on superpixels is an extension of the graph in our contour alignment stage, so here we focus on the extension part. Except for contour units, nodes in the graph also include all superpixels. The general formulation of this distribution in the graph is given by (2). In $\Psi_{ij}(y_i, y_j, x)$, edges among all superpixels and contour units include three kinds, namely unit-unit edge, superpixel-superpixel edge, unit-superpixel edge. In (4), we have shown how to determine whether a unit-unit edge exists. Similar to this, the criterion of superpixel-superpixel edges depends on scores of homography candidates on superpixels. And for a unit-superpixel edge, we mainly emphasize the neighbor relation, that is, contour units in (or around) a superpixel may have the same homography label. Those unit-superpixel edges can broadcast the accurate labels of contour units to superpixels as we expected. After we have determined those edges, we use a general form of (5) to compute potentials for them, denoted as

$$d_{ij} = \| H_{y_i}(R_j) - H_{y_j}(R_j) \|_2^2,$$
$$\Psi_{ij}(y_i, y_j, R) = \exp(-\frac{d_{ji} + d_{ij}}{2 * \sigma_{ij}}), \tag{6}$$

in which R_i, R_j are either contour units or superpixels and R is the union set of contour units and superpixels.

The next important part is the potentials of the nodes in this graph. For contour units, we utilize inference results in the contour alignment stage. For superpixels, the potentials $\Psi_i(y_i, x)$ in (2) includes the intensity error and statistical information on neighbors. The intensity error measures the quality of the alignment between a superpixel and the matched one indicated by a homography candidate. Neighbors of a superpixel include the contour units in (or close to) this superpixel. If two superpixels are close to each other based on the Euclidean distance, and their intensity errors are all smaller than a threshold, they are neighbors. The count of neighbors, the mean intensity error among neighbor superpixels, the mean count of contour units, the mean unit Euclidean distance, the mean unit angle difference, the mean unit intensity error are terms of statistical information on neighbors. The above potentials are in the exponential form as in the (3). Finally, we use the belief propagation [5] to infer the homography labels for each superpixel and achieve the target of superpixel alignment.

3.4   Image Stitching

To finally stitch the two input images, we need to extrapolate homographies in the non-overlapping region between them. We have aligned the overlapping region, so we convert this alignment to correspondences. Then, for each pixel in the non-overlapping region, we estimate a local homography according to those correspondences with a Gaussian weight about Euclidean distance. For pixels near the transition between overlapping region and non-overlapping region, we also find the homography of the nearest pixel in the overlapping region. We then calculate a weighted sum of the local homography and the nearest one to make smooth the transition from the overlapping region to the non-overlapping region. We denote the final homography of pixels in the non-overlapping region as

$$
\begin{aligned}
H_i'(P_i) &= w * H_j(P_i) + (1 - w) * H_i(P_i), \\
w &= \exp(-\|P_i - P_j\|_2)
\end{aligned}
\tag{7}
$$

where the H_j is the nearest homography, and the H_i is the local homography. The P_i, P_j are coordinates of one pixel and its nearest pixel. The $H_j(P_i)$ means the warped coordinate of P_i by the homography H_j, and $H_i(P_i)$ is similar.

4   Experiments

In this section, we will present detailed experiments about our proposed method and provide an analysis of the results. We will compare the proposed method with APAP [32], SPHP [2], ELA [14], SPW [17] which are representative methods for image stitching. We also provide results of the global homography model to reveal artifacts resulting from the parallax problem. To compare different methods objectively and fairly, the inputs are the same including a pair of images and SIFT [24] correspondences. Focusing on the quality of image alignment, we simply overlay the source image and the warped target image and treat it as the final coarse stitched image. Any other postprocessing steps are not applied.

4.1   Dataset

We build a new dataset that covers different challenging problems, such as viewpoint changes, multiple planar regions, illumination changes, textureless regions, etc. It contains 20 indoor scenes and 20 outdoor scenes, with a total of 667 pairs of images. In experiments, we reduce the resolution of input images to a quarter, that is, 480×270. We provide correspondences found by DeepMatching [25] as ground truth, relatively denser than manual labels. In the following comparisons, we can compute correspondences error to quantitatively compare methods.

4.2   Results

Quantitative Evaluation. High quality of alignment in overlapping regions is what we want. We utilize two metric to compare methods, including the EPE (Endpoint Error) and the SSIM (Structure Similarity) [29]. Correspondences

Table 1. The EPE (Endpoint Error) and the SSIM [29] over 667 pairs of images from our dataset. Our method performs best under the two criteria.

Dataset	EPE						SSIM [29]					
	Baseline	APAP	SPHP	ELA	SPW	Ours	Baseline	APAP	SPHP	ELA	SPW	Ours
forest [7]	2.188	2.126	–	2.353	2.345	**0.974**	0.701	0.709	0.669	**0.737**	0.661	0.728
apartments [7]	3.719	2.423	–	2.155	3.659	**1.337**	0.647	0.736	0.725	0.811	0.639	**0.835**
carpark [7]	3.196	1.782	–	1.763	3.127	**1.296**	0.629	0.758	0.639	0.821	0.625	**0.856**
temple [7]	3.104	1.973	–	1.661	3.020	**1.044**	0.634	0.739	0.680	0.797	0.665	**0.838**
conssite [32]	2.461	2.053	–	1.950	2.450	**1.388**	0.703	0.768	0.737	0.836	0.707	**0.858**
garden [32]	2.039	1.500	–	1.197	1.647	**1.127**	0.602	0.697	0.614	0.788	0.717	**0.794**
railtracks [32]	4.615	2.565	–	1.856	4.424	**0.852**	0.513	0.661	0.572	0.821	0.587	**0.851**
train [32]	3.822	2.865	–	2.729	4.435	**1.777**	0.560	0.632	0.569	0.690	0.547	**0.711**
chess/girl [21]	3.641	3.016	–	2.823	3.572	**2.078**	0.883	0.919	0.880	**0.937**	0.873	0.933
Our new dataset	8.080	6.523	–	7.312	7.843	**4.995**	0.647	0.703	0.724	0.766	0.680	**0.786**

found by the DeepMatching [25] are treated as ground truth. Each method outputs the homography for each pixel in the overlapping region. We compute the average Euclidean distance between source pixel coordinates and warped target pixel coordinates as the AEE. Another condition of a good alignment is that structure misalignment is small in overlapping regions. SSIM [29] is qualified to evaluate this condition. We give the quantitative comparisons in Table 1. It is obvious that a global homography is not good to handle scenes with parallax. And our proposed method has better performance, compared with others.

Qualitative Evaluation. In Fig. 3, examples from our proposed dataset are shown. All those scenes have multiple planes, depth variations, also parallax. In some regions, we can easily find outliers in correspondences, such as the red highlighted region in the images shown in the second row. The misalignment is larger near the intersection of multiple planes. The effect of correspondence extrapolation can be seen in the third-row case. The ceiling has only one valid correspondence, but in our method, it can still be aligned. In comparison, other methods have obvious artifacts around the ceiling. A similar case is present in the fourth row. A more interesting case is in the last row (the manhole cover). We can only tell two valid correspondences from the showed figure. Our method can align the manhole cover well. And we see that APAP [32] is not bad for its spatial varying homographies estimated from Gaussian weighted correspondences. It reveals that correspondences based on blob features are not very accurate, compared with pixels. To some extent, our method can handle parallax, depth variations, multiple planes in most scenes.

Baseline   APAP [32]   SPHP [2]   ELA [14]   SPW [17]   Ours

Fig. 3. Qualitative comparisons (best to zoom in) among different methods. The first three rows are nine image pairs with SIFT matches. The other rows compare the results of each method. Red rectangles and arrows highlight misalignment. An interesting result is that our method can align regions with correspondence outliers and fewer correspondences (e.g. the first three input cases). And we attribute this success to contour alignment for its correspondence verification and extrapolation characteristic. (Color figure online)

5 Conclusion

We have proposed a contour-driven method of multiple homography estimation and inference for image stitching in scenes with large parallax. We divided contours into fixed-length units and inferred a local fitting homography for each of them utilizing a conditional random field. After this step, we inferred homographies for superpixels under the guidance of previous contour alignment results and used them to complete the image warping for image stitching. Quantitative and qualitative experiments show that our method enables more accurate alignment and less ghosting caused by misalignment of contours compared with other methods.

Acknowledgment. This work was supported by the Natural Science Foundation of China (NSFC) under Grant No. 61773062.

References

1. Brown, M., Lowe, D.G.: Automatic panoramic image stitching using invariant features. Int. J. Comput. Vision **74**(1), 59–73 (2007)
2. Chang, C.H., Sato, Y., Chuang, Y.Y.: Shape-preserving half-projective warps for image stitching. In: Proceedings of the IEEE Conference on Computer Vision and Pattern Recognition, pp. 3254–3261 (2014)
3. Chen, S.E.: Quicktime vr: an image-based approach to virtual environment navigation. In: Proceedings of the 22nd Annual Conference on Computer Graphics and Interactive Techniques, pp. 29–38 (1995)
4. Chen, Y.-S., Chuang, Y.-Y.: Natural image stitching with the global similarity prior. In: Leibe, B., Matas, J., Sebe, N., Welling, M. (eds.) ECCV 2016. LNCS, vol. 9909, pp. 186–201. Springer, Cham (2016). https://doi.org/10.1007/978-3-319-46454-1_12
5. Felzenszwalb, P.F., Huttenlocher, D.P.: Efficient belief propagation for early vision. Int. J. Comput. Vision **70**(1), 41–54 (2006)
6. Fischler, M.A., Bolles, R.C.: Random sample consensus: a paradigm for model fitting with applications to image analysis and automated cartography. Commun. ACM **24**(6), 381–395 (1981)
7. Gao, J., Kim, S.J., Brown, M.S.: Constructing image panoramas using dual-homography warping. In: CVPR 2011, pp. 49–56. IEEE (2011)
8. Herrmann, C., et al.: Robust image stitching with multiple registrations. In: Proceedings of the European Conference on Computer Vision (ECCV), pp. 53–67 (2018)
9. Herrmann, C., Wang, C., Strong Bowen, R., Keyder, E., Zabih, R.: Object-centered image stitching. In: Proceedings of the European Conference on Computer Vision (ECCV), pp. 821–835 (2018)
10. Jia, J., Tang, C.K.: Image stitching using structure deformation. IEEE Trans. Pattern Anal. Mach. Intell. **30**(4), 617–631 (2008)
11. Lafferty, J.D., McCallum, A., Pereira, F.C.: Conditional random fields: probabilistic models for segmenting and labeling sequence data. In: Proceedings of the Eighteenth International Conference on Machine Learning, pp. 282–289 (2001)

12. Lee, K.Y., Sim, J.Y.: Warping residual based image stitching for large parallax. In: Proceedings of the IEEE/CVF Conference on Computer Vision and Pattern Recognition, pp. 8198–8206 (2020)

13. Li, J., Deng, B., Tang, R., Wang, Z., Yan, Y.: Local-adaptive image alignment based on triangular facet approximation. IEEE Trans. Image Process. **29**, 2356–2369 (2019)

14. Li, J., Wang, Z., Lai, S., Zhai, Y., Zhang, M.: Parallax-tolerant image stitching based on robust elastic warping. IEEE Trans. Multimedia **20**(7), 1672–1687 (2017)

15. Li, N., Xu, Y., Wang, C.: Quasi-homography warps in image stitching. IEEE Trans. Multimedia **20**(6), 1365–1375 (2017)

16. Li, S., Yuan, L., Sun, J., Quan, L.: Dual-feature warping-based motion model estimation. In: Proceedings of the IEEE International Conference on Computer Vision, pp. 4283–4291 (2015)

17. Liao, T., Li, N.: Single-perspective warps in natural image stitching. IEEE Trans. Image Process. **29**, 724–735 (2019)

18. Lin, C.C., Pankanti, S.U., Natesan Ramamurthy, K., Aravkin, A.Y.: Adaptive as-natural-as-possible image stitching. In: Proceedings of the IEEE Conference on Computer Vision and Pattern Recognition, pp. 1155–1163 (2015)

19. Lin, K., Jiang, N., Cheong, L.-F., Do, M., Lu, J.: SEAGULL: seam-guided local alignment for parallax-tolerant image stitching. In: Leibe, B., Matas, J., Sebe, N., Welling, M. (eds.) ECCV 2016. LNCS, vol. 9907, pp. 370–385. Springer, Cham (2016). https://doi.org/10.1007/978-3-319-46487-9_23

20. Lin, K., Jiang, N., Liu, S., Cheong, L.F., Do, M., Lu, J.: Direct photometric alignment by mesh deformation. In: Proceedings of the IEEE Conference on Computer Vision and Pattern Recognition, pp. 2405–2413 (2017)

21. Lin, W.Y., Liu, S., Matsushita, Y., Ng, T.T., Cheong, L.F.: Smoothly varying affine stitching. In: CVPR 2011, pp. 345–352. IEEE (2011)

22. Liu, F., Gleicher, M., Jin, H., Agarwala, A.: Content-preserving warps for 3d video stabilization. ACM Trans. Graphics (TOG) **28**(3), 1–9 (2009)

23. Lou, Z., Gevers, T.: Image alignment by piecewise planar region matching. IEEE Trans. Multimedia **16**(7), 2052–2061 (2014)

24. Lowe, D.G.: Distinctive image features from scale-invariant keypoints. Int. J. Comput. Vision **60**(2), 91–110 (2004)

25. Revaud, J., Weinzaepfel, P., Harchaoui, Z., Schmid, C.: Deepmatching: hierarchical deformable dense matching. Int. J. Comput. Vision **120**(3), 300–323 (2016)

26. Silva, R.M., Feijó, B., Gomes, P.B., Frensh, T., Monteiro, D.: Real time 360 video stitching and streaming. In: ACM SIGGRAPH 2016 Posters, pp. 1–2 (2016)

27. Szeliski, R., Shum, H.Y., Shum, H.Y., Shum, H.Y.: Creating full view panoramic image mosaics and environment maps. In: Proceedings of the 24th Annual Conference on Computer Graphics and Interactive Techniques, pp. 251–258. ACM Press/Addison-Wesley Publishing Co. (1997)

28. Szeliski, R., et al.: Image alignment and stitching: a tutorial. Found. Trends® Comput. Graph. Vis. **2**(1), 1–104 (2007)

29. Wang, Z., Bovik, A.C., Sheikh, H.R., Simoncelli, E.P.: Image quality assessment: from error visibility to structural similarity. IEEE Trans. Image Process. **13**(4), 600–612 (2004)

30. Xiang, T.-Z., Xia, G.-S., Zhang, L.: Image stitching using smoothly planar homography. In: Lai, J.-H., et al. (eds.) PRCV 2018. LNCS, vol. 11256, pp. 524–536. Springer, Cham (2018). https://doi.org/10.1007/978-3-030-03398-9_45

31. Yedidia, J.S., Freeman, W.T., Weiss, Y.: Generalized belief propagation. In: Advances in Neural Information Processing Systems, pp. 689–695 (2001)

32. Zaragoza, J., Chin, T.J., Brown, M.S., Suter, D.: As-projective-as-possible image stitching with moving dlt. In: Proceedings of the IEEE Conference on Computer Vision and Pattern Recognition, pp. 2339–2346 (2013)
33. Zhang, F., Liu, F.: Parallax-tolerant image stitching. In: Proceedings of the IEEE Conference on Computer Vision and Pattern Recognition, pp. 3262–3269 (2014)
34. Zheng, J., Wang, Y., Wang, H., Li, B., Hu, H.M.: A novel projective-consistent plane based image stitching method. IEEE Trans. Multimedia **21**(10), 2561–2575 (2019)

Scene Text Transfer for Cross-Language

Lingjun Zhang, Xinyuan Chen$^{(\boxtimes)}$, Yangchen Xie, and Yue Lu

Shanghai Key Laboratory of Multidimensional Information Processing,
East China Normal University, Shanghai 200241, China
xychen@cee.ecnu.edu.cn

Abstract. Scene text transfer for cross-language aims to erase the original scene text and generate another language text image into the original scene text image with the same style, including the style of fonts, colors, size, and background texture. Scene text transfer for cross-language is a challenging problem as the complicated background scene and a huge difference between languages, which demanding high-quality performance for both text transfer and text erasing. In this work, we propose a scene text transfer framework for cross-language which consists of three steps: regional text extraction, style transfer, and scene text combination. The regional text extraction is designed to crop the text region of a natural scene image and transform it to be a rectangle text image. In the second step, a style transfer network is proposed to retain the style of text image and transfer the text content. In the step of the scene text combination, our model combines the rendered text image with the original scene image to produce the final result. In the optimization part, we introduce a novel background consistent loss to improve the performance of background generation. Experiments demonstrate that our framework generates scene text images of higher quality than previous methods.

Keywords: Text style transfer · Generative Adversarial Networks · Dataset synthesis

1 Introduction

Scene text, which means text that appears in an image captured by a camera in an outdoor environment, *e.g.,* text in images of streets, billboards and so on, can be seen everyday and everywhere. scene text transfer for cross-language in the natural images is an essential part of many practical applications, *e.g.,* text image synthesis for scene text recognition [17] and augmented reality translation for cross-languages communication [2]. Figure 1 shows an example of translating text to different languages.

In the recent years, the development of GAN enables style transfer and scene text transfer to generate realistic synthetic images. Isola *et al.* [5] propose a

This work was partly supported by the National Key Research and Development Program of China under No. 2020AAA0107903, and the China Postdoctoral Science Foundation under No. 2020M681237.

general method based on conditional GANs [11] to generate images from one domain to another, which can be used to transfer text style. After that, Wu *et al.* [15] propose an generative network (SRNet) for text editing. Although the prior methods generate promising results for scene text transfer, the results are not satisfying especially in background in-painting. This would decease the quality especially when the length reference text is shorter than the original text, which would often happen in cross-language translation. Also, the above text transfer methods are usually focus on text image, and not designed for scene text transfer.

In this work, we present a framework for cross-language scene text transfer. The proposed method contains three steps. Firstly, the model takes in a complete real-world scene text image with label of the location of the text region. Most of the time, the text regions of the real-world images are not rectangles, so we introduce the regional text extraction step. Specifically, according to the coordinates of the text region, we calculate a perspective matrix to transform the text region to an individual rectangular image. In the step two, we propose a style transfer network for text transfer. The network takes the original text image and the content text image as input and generate the foreground text with the style of scene text image and the content of given content text image. Specifically, the network would reconstruct the background of the text region, and fuse the generated text image and background image. To make sure that the foreground text has been clearly wiped from the scene text images, we introduce a background consistent loss to minimize the distance between the background information of the output image and the input scene text image. Finally, we calculate the inverse matrix of the perspective matrix as we mentioned in the first step to put the result of text style transfer back to the original scene image to obtain our entire results.

In all, we propose a scene text transfer method which can: 1) obtain the image of the text region of a scene image, 2) edit the text region using the words of other languages without changing the text style and the background, 3) embed the result of conversion text back to original scene image.

Our model has been implemented on the experiments for English to Arabic, English to Vietnamese, and English to Thai. Experiments on both synthetic datasets and real-world datasets demonstrate the effectiveness and robustness of our method.

2   Related Works

Recently, scene text transfer for commonly used languages, such as English and Chinese, has made great progress. There are some attempts to employ style transfer methods to achieve scene text transfer. The goal of their works can be divided into two main categories: content retention [3, 5, 17] and texture retention [8, 9, 12, 15, 16].

Isola *et al.* [5] propose a general method based on cGANs to generate images from one domain to another. Gong *et al.* [3] tackle the generation task using

Fig. 1. Text transfer in different languages. From left to right are Arabic, Thai and Japanese namely.

image-to-image translation methods, and produce realistic text sequence images in the light of the semantic ones. Yang *et al.* [17] present a method to achieve artistic text stylization without supervision. They also experiment with text in various fonts and languages. Liu *et al.* [9] propose a Content Image Initialization module and an encoder-decoder network to generate natural text images with different binary text content and the arbitrary texture. Instead of using a binary text image, Li *et al.* [8] take a rendered text image as the input of the style transfer network. They propose SynthText-Transfer to generate arbitrary stylized text images with the same texture but different textual content. Whereas this pipeline involves many handcraft operations which restrict generated images' diversity, such as fixed fonts set. Wu *et al.* [15] propose an end-to-end trainable style retention network to edit text in natural images. Their method is capable of most scene images, but it may fail when the text has complex structures, especially for complex background. Wu *et al.* also make some attempts in cross-language scene text transfer *e.g.,* English to Chinese. Based on their work, Yang *et al.* [16] present a unified framework Swap-Text for scene text transfer, improving the effects on curved text. Roy *et al.* [12] design a generative network that adapts to the font features of a single character and generates other characters with the same font features.

We concluded that their methods have the following problems: 1) The poor effect of background inpainting, which is the essential part of scene text transfer. The unsatisfying results of background inpainting can lead to worse generation results, for example, although the foreground text is transferred successfully, it can be found that the adjacent areas of the original text remain in the output image. The drawbacks become very apparent especially when the words length of the content image and the style image are very different. 2) Their methods often tackle style transfer between two words in the same language. 3) The above text transfer methods are usually focused on text image, and not designed for scene text transfer.

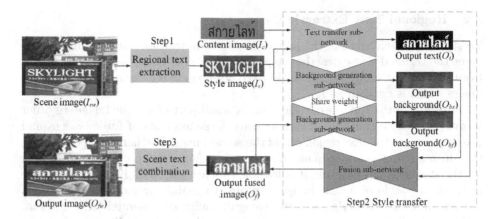

Fig. 2. Overview of the proposed framework.

3   Methods

3.1   Overview

Given a scene text image I_{s_w}, the annotations of texts location, and a content image I_c, our framework generates a synthetic image whose text region has been replaced by a new quadrilateral image with the content of I_c and text style of I_{s_w}. As illustrates in Fig. 2, our framework can be divided into three steps: **regional text extraction**, **style transfer** and **scene text combination**. **Step 1: Regional Text Extraction.** In step 1, the regional text extraction is used to extract the text image from the scene text image and transform the irregular text images into rectangle images. The transformed text image is the style reference input image for the style transfer network in step 2. **Step 2: Style Transfer.** We propose a style transfer network to learn the text style and background style of the text region and apply it to a given content image. The style transfer network takes the output of the regional text extraction step as the style input I_s, and a given content image I_c as the content input. A text transfer sub-network is used to extract the content feature of I_c and style feature of I_s, and fuse these two features to generate the foreground text O_t. At the same time, a background generation sub-network takes the style image I_s as input and outputs its background image O_{b_t}. Then, we use a fusion sub-network to fuse the background image and the transferred text image to get the final result O_f. **Step 3: Scene Text Combination.** In step 3, we embed the fusion result O_f to the scene image. The input of scene text combination step is the fusion result O_f, and the output is the final results O_{f_w} of our framework whose text region is rendered.

3.2   Regional Text Extraction

To stylize the text areas of the images in the style transfer step, we first implement the regional text extraction step. This step aims to extract the text region from a scene text image I_{s_w}. Then the extracted region is deformed to a rectangle image which is denoted as I_s.

For most of the time, text regions are a small part of a scene image. In order to avoid the style transfer network to learn large amounts of futile background features, we cut the text region out of the scene image. Furthermore, considering that in many cases, text regions of a scene image are not horizontal. Although for the style transfer network, it is feasible to learn the spatial perspective while learning the style of a text image. We aim to make our model can focus on the learning of text styles and the recognizability of generated text content, rather than distracting its attention to perspective learning. We introduce the perspective transformation to step 1. The transformation of perspective yield the following equation:

$$[x', y', w'] = [u, v, w] \times M, \tag{1}$$

$$x = x'/w', y = y'/w', \tag{2}$$

in which u, v represent the original picture coordinates, x, y indicate the picture coordinates after perspective transformation. M denotes a 3×3 transformation matrix. In our methods, the coordinates of text region in the natural scene image are denoted as u, v, and the coordinates of horizontal text image are denoted as x, y.

According to the coordinates of four corner points labeled in scene image I_{s_w} and the size of content image I_c, the perspective transformation matrix can be calculated. Afterwards, using Eq. 1, we do the same perspective transformation to each point of text region to get I_s. Through perspective transformation of extracted area, we get a rectangle text image I_s which has the same height as the given binary image I_c.

3.3   Style Transfer

Overview. We propose a style transfer network that takes I_c as the content input and I_s as the style input. The output of the network is O_f, in which the text content is the words in I_c and have the same style and background with I_s. We decompose the style transfer network into three sub-networks, namely **text transfer sub-network, fusion sub-network** and **shared background generation sub-networks**. In the **text transfer sub-network**, the texture style feature in the style image I_s and the content feature in content image I_c are extracted and concatenated to generate the desired foreground text image O_t. Background generation plays an important role in final image generation. To this end, we introduce background generation sub-networks and a background consistent loss to make sure the consistency of the final image's background and the style image's background. The **background generation sub-networks**

are used to reconstruct the background image. The inputs of the background generation sub-networks are respectively the style image I_s and the desired image of style transfer network O_f, and the outputs are namely O_{b_s} and O_{b_f}. It is worth mentioning that the two background generation sub-networks share the same parameters. The **fusion sub-network** aims to generate the fusion result of O_{b_s} and O_t to obtain the final image. Once taking in O_{b_s} and O_t, the decoding feature maps which have the same resolution are concatenated to get the final generation result O_f.

Shared Background Generation Sub-network. Background generation is a crucial part of text style transfer. The word length of two words in different languages varies enormously, so the effects of background generation largely determine the effects of the final image generation. The failed, mistaken, and incomplete erasure can lead to poor performance in image generation, for example, although the foreground text is transferred successfully, it can be found that the shadow of the original text still remains in the output image. The shadow can be more pronounced when the desired texts are much shorter than the original texts.

In order to obtain better background generation results, we present shared background generation sub-networks and a background consistent loss. The architecture of the background generation sub-network is basically an encoding-decoding structure. The sub-networks take regional text images as input, erase the texts in the image and restore the missing hole with the surrounding pixel.

We involve the background consistent loss to optimize the result of background generation, on the whole, it is an L1 loss to compare the distance between the background of I_s and the background of O_f. The loss function can be formulated as follow:

$$\mathcal{L}_{con_B} = \left\| O_{b_f} - G_b(O_f) \right\|_1 . \tag{3}$$

The O_{b_s} denotes the background of style image I_s. G_b is the background generator that is used to generate the background image of the fusion result O_f. The background consistent loss ensures the consistency of the background between the style input and the final output.

3.4 Scene Text Combination

So far, we already extracted the text region from the scene image I_{s_w}, transferred its words to other words with a different language, and got a rendered text region O_f. Our ultimate goal is to generate a complete scene text image, so we combine the text region with the original scene image by inverse perspective transformation which is introduced in this section.

To generate the final image where the style is transferred only to textual areas, we blend O_f with I_{s_w} using an inverse perspective transformation. In this step, we take in the result of style transfer network O_f and the natural scene image I_{s_w}, after fusing them together by the inverse perspective transformation we can get the desired complete scene image O_{f_w}.

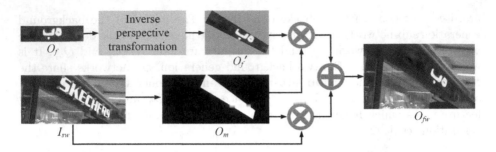

Fig. 3. An illustration for the step of scene text combination. The O_f denotes the fusion results of style transfer network, and O'_f is the result of inverse perspective transformation. I_{s_w} denotes the scene image. O_m denotes the mask generated from annotations of text region. O_{f_w} denotes the final result of our framework.

As we mentioned before, we calculate the perspective transformation matrix $M_{3\times3}$. So we utilize the inverse matrix of M to calculate the desired coordinates of text region. Once we get the inverse perspective matrix M^{-1}, we can use the variation of Eq. 1 to get the coordinates. According to these coordinates, we transform the text region image to be an arbitrary quadrangular image O'_f and get a binary mask O_m, in which the pixel value are 1 for text region and 0 for non-text region. Given the binary mask O_m, the rendered quadrangular text image O'_f, and the scene image I_{s_w}, the output image O_{f_w} can be denoted as:

$$O_{f_w} = O'_f \odot O_m + I_{s_w} \odot (1 - O_m), \tag{4}$$

in which the $\odot$ denotes the element-wise multiplication operator. After a combination of scene image and text image, we get the final output image O_{f_w}. Experimental visualized results are presented in Fig. 3.

3.5 Loss Function

Style transfer network aims to achieve cross-language style transfer for text region. To this end, besides background consistent loss we adopt the following loss functions: adversarial loss [11], L1 loss, dice loss [10], and vgg-loss [13]. Our purpose and the formulas of these loss functions are as follows.

As we mentioned before, the style transfer network is divided into three sub-networks. In the **text transfer sub-network**, we use L1 loss and dice loss to optimize the result of foreground generation. Following Wu *et al.*, we adopt a skeleton-guided learning mechanism [15] to generate the skeleton of the desired text. The loss functions are formulated as:

$$\mathcal{L}_{sk} = 1 - \frac{2\sum_{i=1}^{N}(T_{sk})_i(O_{sk})_i}{\sum_{i=1}^{N}(T_{sk})_i + \sum_{i=1}^{N}(O_{sk})_i}, \tag{5}$$

where O_{sk} and T_{sk} stand for the output and the ground truth of the texts' skeleton map respectively. L1 loss is used to minimize the pixel-wise distance between the generated text images O_t and ground-truth T_t:

$$\mathcal{L}_{text} = \alpha \mathcal{L}_{sk} + \|T_t - O_t\|_1, \tag{6}$$

where α is a hyperparameter which is set to 1.0 in our experiment.

For the **background generation sub-network** of style image background inpainting, in addition to the proposed the background consistent loss $\mathcal{L}_{con_B}$ in Sect. 3.3, we use adversarial loss and L1 loss to supervise the process of background generation. We denote the background generator and the background discriminator as G_b and D_b. The adversarial loss and L1 loss are defined as:

$$\mathcal{L}_{adv_B} = \max_{D_b} \min_{G_b} \mathbb{E}_{T_b \in P_b, I_s \in P_s} [\log D_b(T_b, I_s)] + \mathbb{E}_{I_s \in P_s} \log[1 - D_b(O_b, I_s)], \tag{7}$$

$$\mathcal{L}_{bg} = \mathcal{L}_{adv_B} + \mathcal{L}_{con_B} + \beta \|T_b - O_b\|_1. \tag{8}$$

The T_b and O_b namely denote ground truth and the output of the background image, and β is set to be 1.0 in our experiment.

In the **fusion sub-network**, L1 loss, adversarial loss and vgg-loss are employed to optimize the fusion results. We use G_f and D_f to denotes the generator and discriminator. The total loss function for fusion are as follows,

$$\mathcal{L}_{fuse} = \mathcal{L}_{adv_F} + \mathcal{L}_{vgg} + \gamma_1 \|T_f - O_f\|_1, \tag{9}$$

$$\mathcal{L}_{adv_F} = \max_{D_f} \min_{G_f} \mathbb{E}_{T_f \in P_f, O_t \in P_t} [\log D_f(T_f, O_t)] + \mathbb{E}_{O_t \in P_t} \log[1 - D_f(O_f, O_t)], \tag{10}$$

where T_f is the ground truth of generated text region, and the parameter γ_1 is set to be 10.0 in our experiment. $\mathcal{L}_{vgg}$ is consist of perceptual loss and style loss, which is formulated as:

$$\mathcal{L}_{vgg} = \gamma_2 \mathcal{L}_{per} + \gamma_3 \mathcal{L}_{style}, \tag{11}$$

$$\mathcal{L}_{per} = \mathbb{E}[\sum_{i=1}^{N} \frac{1}{M_i} \|\phi_i(T_f) - \phi_i(O_f)\|_1], \tag{12}$$

$$\mathcal{L}_{style} = \mathbb{E}_j[\left\|G_j^\phi(T_f) - G_j^\phi(O_f)\right\|_1], \tag{13}$$

where ϕ_i is the activation map from relu1_1 to relu5_1 of VGG-19 model [13]. M_i is the element size of the feature map. G is the Gram matrix. γ_2 and γ_3 are parameters which are set to 1.0 and 500.0 namely. Combining the above loss functions, the **overall loss function**:

$$\mathcal{L} = \lambda_1 \mathcal{L}_{text} + \lambda_2 \mathcal{L}_{bg} + \lambda_3 \mathcal{L}_{fuse}, \tag{14}$$

where $\lambda_1, \lambda_2, \lambda_3$ are hyperparameters to control the weight of each loss function.

4 Experiments

In this section, we introduce our works in Arabic, Thai and Vietnamese. First, we introduce the details of our experiment, including experimental settings and datasets. Then, we display the results for each step. After that, we introduce the evaluation metrics which we used to evaluate our framework. Finally, we com pare our framework to other methods to verify the advantages of the proposed framework.

4.1 Implementation Details

Experimental Settings. We select over 100 fonts and 8000 background images. The background images are from [4]. In each font, there are both minority language (we select Arabic, Thai, and Vietnamese as examples) characters and English characters. The input style images and content images are resized to $w \times 64$ and the batch size is 16, where w denotes the width depending on the length of words. As for training, learning rate is set to 1×10^{-4}, and Adam optimizer [1] is used to optimize the framework in which β_1 is set to 0.9 and β_2 is set to be 0.999. The model in style transfer network is built with Tensorflow. For each language, we use one NVIDIA 2080-TI GPU to train for about 30 h.

Datasets. Our used datasets can be divided into two parts: synthetic datasets and real-world benchmark datasets.

   Synthetic Dataset: Due to the scarcity of cross-language datasets, it is difficult to obtain paired text pictures. We synthesis minority data for model training. The core of synthesizing text image [4] is choosing fonts, color, geometric deformation for text and choosing images for background randomly, and combining them together to get style images. At the same time, minority language words are selected to generate content images. The corresponding fonts, color, geometric deformation, and background images are used to generate ground truth. we generate 100000 training images and 1000 test images for each language in Arabic, Thai and Vietnamese.

   Real-world Benchmark Dataset: To verify the feasibility of our method, we do experiment on public benchmark datasets. ICDAR-2013 [7] and ICDAR-2015 [6] are two scene images sets frequently used to evaluate the performance of models. ICDAR-2013 contains 229 training images and 233 test images. ICDAR-2015 contains 1000 training image and 500 test images. While ICDAR-2013 are mainly horizontal and focused images, ICDAR-2105 are mainly arbitrary quadrilateral text images which are shot accidentally.

4.2 Results for Each Step

As we mentioned before, our framework contains three steps: regional text extraction, style transfer, and scene text combination. The results of each step are illustrated in Fig. 4. After regional text extraction, horizontal rectangular

Fig. 4. Results of each step.

Table 1. Quantitative results on synthetic test dataset.

Method	Arabic			Thai			Vietnamese		
	MSE	PSNR	SSIM	MSE	PSNR	SSIM	MSE	PSNR	SSIM
Pix2Pix [5]	0.0981	15.32	0.4265	0.0977	15.77	0.4345	0.0965	15.84	0.4668
SRNet [15]	0.0210	18.27	0.5778	0.0203	18.72	0.6044	0.0196	18.66	0.5887
Ours	**0.0152**	**20.07**	**0.6843**	**0.0161**	**19.70**	**0.6630**	**0.0110**	**21.41**	**0.7357**

text images are extracted from the real-world scene image. Through style transfer network, we can get rendered text images with the style of style image and the content of content image. Finally, after scene text combination step, the desired rendered scene text images are generated.

Fig. 5. Comparisons to SRNet on synthetic datasets. The style images are results of regional text extraction step, and the images in the fourth column and the eighth column are results of step 2 in our framework.

4.3 Evaluation Metrics

We evaluate the generation results of synthetic test data on generally used evaluation metrics. We use the following metrics to assess the quality of generated images: MSE, which is also known as l_2; PSNR, which is peak signal to noise ratio; SSIM [14], which is used to compare the mean structural similarity index between two images. These full reference metrics need ground truth, that is why we use them to evaluate synthetic test data.

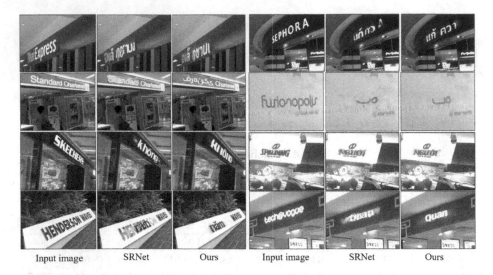

| Input image | SRNet | Ours | Input image | SRNet | Ours |

Fig. 6. Comparisons to SRNet on real-world datasets. The outputs of the overall framework. The first row displays results on Thai, the second row displays results on Arabic, and the last two rows display results on Vietnamese.

4.4   Comparison with Prior Works

In this subsection, we compare our method with SRNet [15] and Pix2Pix [5]. SRNet is a trainable style retention network which uses GAN to edit text image to another word. Pix2Pix employ conditional GANs [11] for image-to-image translation. For a fair comparison, we use the same synthetic training dataset and the same test dataset to calculate quantitative results for all compared methods. We also use trained models to apply to the real-world dataset. We train our framework, SRNet, and Pix2Pix in three languages: Arabic, Thai, Vietnamese. In order to implement SRNet on real-world dataset, we add our **regional text extraction** step and **scene text combination** step to SRNet.

Quantitative Comparison. The quantitative comparison results are shown in Table 1. We do these experiments on synthetic images, for these metrics(MSE, PSNR, SSIM) need ground truth. The smaller MSE and bigger PSNR, SSIM indicate the better generation results. We can observe that in Table 1, the results of our method outperform the compared methods. The average MSE of our method is decreased by 0.006 compared to the SRNet, the average PSNR of our method is increased by 1.6 and the average SSIM of our method is increased by 0.1. Compared to Pix2Pix, MSE is decreased by 0.08, PSNR is increased by 4.7, SSIM is increased by 0.26 in our method.

Qualitative Comparison. In order to verify that our framework can complete text transfer and background generation, we implement qualitative comparison. The visual results are shown in Fig. 5 and Fig. 6. We train our method and SRNet on both synthetic datasets and real-world datasets. As illustrates in Fig. 5 and Fig. 6, our method is more effective in background generation than SRNet, especially when the background has complicated texture and the original text are longer than the desired text. In the results of SRNet, although the desired text is generated, the shadow of the original text remains in the output image. It will be not apparent if the original text have almost the same length with the desired text. Besides, in some cases, the results of SRNet are also influenced by mistaken erasure.

5 Conclusion

In this paper, we propose a framework to achieve scene text transfer for cross-language. The framework can extract text region from real-world scene text images, transfer the text to be another word in another language, and combine the rendered text region with the original scene image. The proposed method improves the generative results in both quantitative and qualitative aspects, especially for text background generation by introducing the background consistent loss. Experiments in Arabic, Thai and Vietnamese demonstrate the effectiveness and superiority of our methods.

References

1. Da, K.: A method for stochastic optimization. arXiv preprint arXiv:1412.6980 (2014)
2. Fragoso, V., Gauglitz, S., Zamora, S., Kleban, J., Turk, M.A.: TranslatAR: a mobile augmented reality translator. In: IEEE Workshop on Applications of Computer Vision (WACV 2011), Kona, HI, USA, 5–7 January 2011, pp. 497–502. IEEE Computer Society (2011). https://doi.org/10.1109/WACV.2011.5711545
3. Gong, Y., Deng, L., Ma, Z., Xie, M.: Generating text sequence images for recognition. Neural Process. Lett. **51**(2), 1677–1688 (2020)
4. Gupta, A., Vedaldi, A., Zisserman, A.: Synthetic data for text localisation in natural images. In: Proceedings of the IEEE Conference on Computer Vision and Pattern Recognition, pp. 2315–2324 (2016)
5. Isola, P., Zhu, J.Y., Zhou, T., Efros, A.A.: Image-to-image translation with conditional adversarial networks. In: Proceedings of the IEEE Conference on Computer Vision and Pattern Recognition, pp. 1125–1134 (2017)
6. Karatzas, D., et al.: ICDAR 2015 competition on robust reading. In: 2015 13th ICDAR, pp. 1156–1160. IEEE (2015)
7. Karatzas, D., et al.: ICDAR 2013 robust reading competition. In: 2013 12th ICDAR, pp. 1484–1493. IEEE (2013)
8. Li, J., Wang, S., Wang, Y., Tang, Z.: Synthesizing data for text recognition with style transfer. Multimedia Tools Appl. **78**(20), 29183–29196 (2018). https://doi. org/10.1007/s11042-018-6656-3

9. Liu, H., Zhu, A.: Synthesizing scene text images for recognition with style transfer. In: 2019 ICDARW, vol. 5, pp. 8–13. IEEE (2019)

10. Milletari, F., Navab, N., Ahmadi, S., V-Net: fully convolutional neural networks for volumetric medical image segmentation. In: Proceedings of the 2016 Fourth International Conference on 3D Vision (3DV), pp. 565–571

11. Mirza, M., Osindero, S.: Conditional generative adversarial nets. arXiv preprint arXiv:1411.1784 (2014)

12. Roy, P., Bhattacharya, S., Ghosh, S., Pal, U.: STEFANN: scene text editor using font adaptive neural network. In: Proceedings of the IEEE/CVF Conference on Computer Vision and Pattern Recognition, pp. 13228–13237 (2020)

13. Simonyan, K., Zisserman, A.: Very deep convolutional networks for large-scale image recognition. arXiv preprint arXiv:1409.1556 (2014)

14. Wang, Z., Bovik, A.C., Sheikh, H.R., Simoncelli, E.P.: Image quality assessment: from error visibility to structural similarity. IEEE Trans. Image Process. **13**(4), 600–612 (2004)

15. Wu, L., et al.: Editing text in the wild. In: Proceedings of the 27th ACM International Conference on Multimedia, pp. 1500–1508 (2019)

16. Yang, Q., Huang, J., Lin, W.: SwapText: image based texts transfer in scenes. In: Proceedings of the IEEE/CVF Conference on Computer Vision and Pattern Recognition, pp. 14700–14709 (2020)

17. Yang, S., Liu, J., Yang, W., Guo, Z.: Context-aware unsupervised text stylization. In: 2018 ACM Multimedia Conference on Multimedia Conference, MM 2018, Seoul, Republic of Korea, 22–26 October 2018, pp. 1688–1696. ACM (2018). https://doi.org/10.1145/3240508.3240580

The Computer Measurement Method Research on Shaft's Size by the Platform of the Optoelectronic Imaging

Chang Ding[1], Xingyu Gao[1(✉)], Jun Li[2], Zeng Hu[1], Weidong Zhang[3], and Ziku Wu[4]

[1] School of Mechanical and Electrical Engineering, Guilin University of Electronic Technology, Guilin 541004, Guangxi, China
{dingchang,gxy1981}@guet.edu.cn
[2] Guilin Zhongdian Guangxin Technology Co., Ltd., Guilin 541004, Guangxi, China
[3] School of Information Science and Technology, Dalian Maritime University, Dalian 116026, Liaoning, China
[4] School of Science and Information, Qingdao Agricultural University, Qingdao 266109, Shandong, China

Abstract. The measurement of shaft's size by computer is the significant basis of the automatic industrial measurement and detection, this paper establishes the optoelectronic imaging instrument of the shaft, and the image data of shaft neck is acquired by the industrial camera. In the part of the image pre-processing, we propose the enhancement algorithm of edge line based on the binarization of the gradient operator to enhance the image's edge line. After the selection of the edge lines by the user in the local region, the paper proposes a measurement method based on the paralleled edge line's fitting and computing, which can measure the diameter of the shaft neck with the accuracy of sub-pixel. This method contains some key techniques such as the modification of the local region chosen by the user, the selection of the sample points, the fitting of the edge line, the computing method of the diameter size and so on. With the comparison of the conventional line detecting algorithm such as Hough transformation, this proposed algorithm can improve the measurement accuracy of the geometry size. In the part of the experimental results' exhibition, we use the proposed algorithm to measure another shaft neck's parameter and verify that the algorithm has the robust characteristic, with the comparison of the optoelectronic measurement result and the artificial measurement result, the reliability of the algorithm is verified.

Keywords: Optoelectronic measurement · Image processing · Extraction of edge line · Distance computation · Industrial camera

This work is supported by Innovation Driven Development Special Fund Project of Guangxi (No. AA18118002-3), Guangxi Provincial Natural Science Foundation of China (No. 2020GXNSFBA297077, No. 2018GXNSFAA294065), Key Laboratory Co-sponsored Foundation by Province and Ministry (No. CRKL200103) and the Project of Foundational Research Ability's Improvement for Young and Middle-aged Teachers of University in Guangxi (No. 2020KY05019).

Y. Peng et al. (Eds.): ICIG 2021, LNCS 12888, pp. 565–577, 2021.
https://doi.org/10.1007/978-3-030-87355-4_47

1   Introduction

Shafts are the common components in the machinery industry, of which the measurement style and precision affect the intelligent manufacture and intelligent assembly. However, the workers often measure the component by some traditional measuring tools, such as the vernier caliper, micrometer and admeasuring apparatus in the work team, which is labor-consuming and inefficient. Therefore, it is of great significance to establish the optoelectronic imaging system and study how to apply the technology of image processing to measure the multiple parameters of the shaft, which has the characteristics of time-saving and high-precision.

The measurement parameters of the precise components usually contain the distance size such as diameter, width and length. As for the optoelectronic measurement, firstly the optoelectronic instrument needs to capture the image data information and then the proposed image processing method is used to finish the computer measurement. Generally, in the pre-processing of images obtained by industrial cameras, the image's edge information needs to be enhanced before detected and measured [1, 2]. In the current study of computer measurement, the algorithm is used in the entire image instead of the image's local region and the previous research [3] does not consider the human-computer interaction. This algorithm can be used to choose the local region with two groups of edge lines in the graph and compute the diameter distance between the two paralleled edge lines. In the following, we will describe the process of image acquisition by the industrial camera. Figure 1(a) shows the shaft neck of automobile crankshaft, which is the important part for an automobile to install and assemble, and the diameter size in the fifth shaft neck needs to be computed shown as Fig. 1(a) and Fig. 1(b).

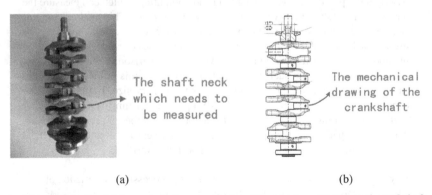

The shaft neck which needs to be measured

The mechanical drawing of the crankshaft

(a)   (b)

Fig. 1. The shaft neck which needs to be measured and its drawing. (a) The real crankshaft and its shaft neck. (b) The mechanical drawing.

The optoelectronic measurement platform is shown in Fig. 2, where the industrial camera is with the brand of MicroVision EM-200C, which can acquire the image data with the size of width and height for 1280 pixels and 960 pixels respectively. We choose the green visible light source for illumination compensation to acquire the image with high contrast. The computer has the function of real-time observation and saving image data for useful information. The visualization software provided by MicroVision company can observe the image data through the computer at the current time, so it is convenient to change the position of the light source and the shaft, which can acquire the image data by industrial camera with high quality.

The computer which is
used to acquire the
image data information

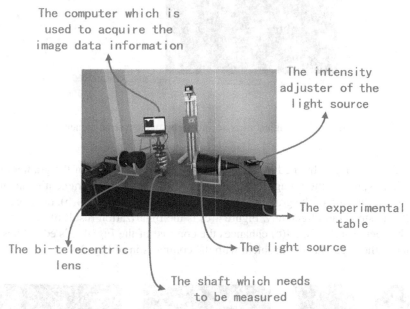

The intensity
adjuster of the
light source

The experimental
table

The bi-telecentric
lens

The light source

The shaft which needs
to be measured

Fig. 2. The optoelectronic measurement platform for the shaft

2 Image Pre-processing

The original image obtained by the industrial camera often has some diffractions and noise [4], as shown in Fig. 3. So, some effective image enhancement algorithms are proposed in this section, which mainly include image graying (Three channels of R,G and B have no use for the geometry size's measurement), image resizing (The original image is too big to show in the screen, so size compression and size expansion are required), calculation of image gradient's magnitude and the binarization of image gradient's magnitude.

Image gradient highlights [5, 6] the variation of image's gray value and reflects the edge information of image [7]. The calculation of image's gradient magnitude can be clear to present the edge line in an image, which is helpful to the edge line's display and the sample point's selection. Equation (1) shows the formula that compute the image's gradient magnitude from the image's time domain, where ∇ is the gradient operator, $\frac{\partial I}{\partial x}$ and $\frac{\partial I}{\partial y}$ represent the difference in X direction and Y direction respectively.

$$|\nabla I| = \sqrt{(\frac{\partial I}{\partial x})^2 + (\frac{\partial I}{\partial y})^2} \tag{1}$$

The upward edge line
of the shaft neck

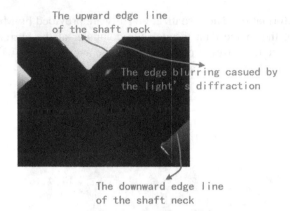

The edge blurring casued by
the light's diffraction

The downward edge line
of the shaft neck

Fig. 3. The original image acquired by the industrial camera

As for the image obtained by the industrial camera, the value of the gradient magnitude is low, this section magnify 10 times towards the original gradient's magnitude to show the function of the gradient computation, as shown in Fig. 4(b), the edge of the Fig. 4(a) is stood out effectively. Figure 4(c) is the binarization result of the Fig. 4(b), it can be seen that the Fig. 4(c) enhances the contrast of the Fig. 4(a)'s edge lines, and eliminates the edge blurring problem with the comparison of Fig. 3.

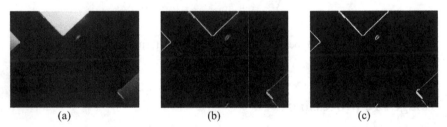

(a)   (b)   (c)

Fig. 4. The shaft neck image's magnitude and its binarization result. (a) The gray processing result. (b) The gradient magnitude after 10 times amplification. (c) The binarization of gradient magnitude with suitable threshold.

The threshold selection in the binarization process can be referred by the histogram of gradient magnitude [8], as shown in the Fig. 5, the edge lines in the Fig. 4(a) have the high gradient magnitude and low proportion and the quantile with the value of 0.99 in the Fig. 5 can be set as th in the process of gradient value's binarization, that is to say, if the gradient magnitude of the Fig. 4(a) is less than th, it is set by zero in the Fig. 4(c), and if the gradient magnitude of the Fig. 4(a) is more than th, it is set by 1 in the Fig. 4(c).

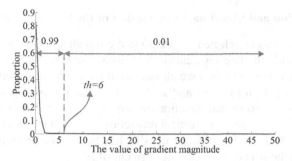

Fig. 5. The histogram of Fig. 4(a)'s gradient magnitude and the threshold selection

3   Algorithm of Distance Measurement of Paralleled Edge Lines

3.1   The Modification of the Region of the Edge Lines

In the part of size measurement, we need to modify the region of edge lines, first we ask for the user to select the region of edge line and then we modify the region with irregular shape to a rectangle region. In the common case, we ask the user to choose the four peak points of the quadrangle according to the clockwise direction, and put the edge line as the rectangle region's diagonal approximately when selecting the region. Afterwards, we can get the new rectangle region according to the four chosen peak points' coordinate and the strategy is as follows:

In the image's coordinate system, we define $A(r_A, c_A)$, $B(r_B, c_B)$, $C(r_C, c_C)$ and $D(r_D, c_D)$ as the original four peak points' coordinate, the modified coordinate of the four peak points can be defined as $A'(r_{A'}, c_{A'})$, $B'(r_{B'}, c_{B'})$, $C'(r_{C'}, c_{C'})$ and $D'(r_{D'}, c_{D'})$, from which, we can summarize the coordinate transforming formula as shown in Eq. (2).

$$\begin{cases} r_{A'} = r_{B'} = \max(r_A, r_B) \\ r_{C'} = r_{D'} = \min(r_C, r_D) \\ c_{A'} = c_{D'} = \max(c_A, c_D) \\ c_{B'} = c_{C'} = \min(c_B, c_C) \end{cases} \tag{2}$$

Now, Fig. 6 is a diagram for illustrating the process of the region modification, the blue quadrangle is the edge line's region that the user chooses and the red rectangle is the modified result.

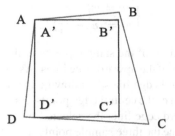

Fig. 6. The diagram of the region modification

3.2   The Selection and Coordinate Calculation of the Sample Point

The sample points can be selected according to the modified region as shown in Fig. 7. First, we can divide the line segment of A′D′ into four parts with the same distance in the vertical direction, and then we choose the three points in the middle of the line segment and name them as s_1, s_2 and s_3. Searching the left edge point and the right edge point across the horizontal direction towards s_1, s_2 and s_3, and the edge points of $p_1^1, p_1^2, p_2^1, p_2^2, p_3^1, p_3^2$ are got. The vertical projection of the sample points which locates in the middle part of the line segment of A′D′ has better measurement accuracy than which locates in the boundary of the line segment of A′D′.

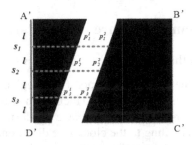

Fig. 7. The diagram of the sample points selection

In the following, we need to find the column coordinate of the left edge points and the right edge points in the image coordinate system, generally an edge line occupies multiple pixels in the image, so we need to extract the central point as the sample point from the left edge points and right edge points. We define the coordinate of the left edge point as $L(m,n)$ and define the right edge point as $R(m,n)$, the judging criteria for searching the left edge points and right edge points are shown in Eq. (3).

$$L(m, n - 1) = 0 \ and \ L(m, n) = 255, \quad R(m, n - 1) = 255 \ and \ R(m, n) = 0 \quad (3)$$

If we define the coordinate of the *ith* sample point as $p_i(m_i, n_i)$, we can get the calculating formula about $p_i(m_i, n_i)$ by using the coordinate of the left edge point and the right edge point as $p_i^1(m_i^1, n_i^1)$ and $p_i^2(m_i^2, n_i^2)$. The calculating formula is shown as Eq. (4).

$$\begin{cases} m_i = m_i^1 \\ n_i = (n_i^1 + n_i^2)/2 \end{cases} \quad (4)$$

The coordinate calculations of the sample points in the downward edge lines is the same with the sample points of the upward edge lines. As shown in Fig. 8, we can see the different width of the upward edge lines and down edge lines, which demonstrates the importance of the extraction of the central edge points. As for the selection of the central edge points in the downward edge line, the selected method is the same as the above-mentioned method, we define the three sample points' coordinate of the downward edge line as q_1, q_2, q_3.

(a)   (b)

Fig. 8. The modified region of the upward edge lines and downward edge lines. (a) The modified region of the upward edge line. (b) The modified region of the downward edge line.

In this section, we can make the interactive verification from the selection of the region of the edge lines to the illustration of the edge line's region, for example, at the beginning of the method's flow, we can initialize the zero vector with three elements to store the row coordinate of the left edge point, if we can find more than one element with the zero value in the initial vector after storing the row coordinate of the left edge point, that is to say, the selection and calculation of the coordinate of the edge line is not effective, we need to ask the user again to reselect the region of the edge line.

3.3   The Fitting of the Parallel Edge Lines

Before displaying the parallel edge lines in the space rectangular coordinate, we need to transform the coordinate point from the image's coordinate system to the rectangular coordinate system [9], the diagram of the coordinate system's transformation is shown in Fig. 9.

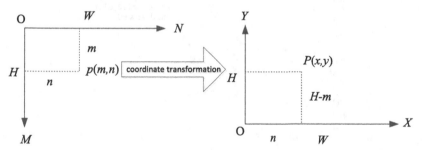

Fig. 9. The diagram of transformation from the image's coordinate system to the rectangular coordinate system

If there is a point with the coordinate of $p(m,n)$ in the image coordinate with the width of W and the height of H, after transformed, $p(m,n)$ is changed into $P(x,y)$ in the rectangular coordinate system, the transforming formula is shown in Eq. (5), where H and W represent the image's height and width respectively.

$$\begin{cases} x = n \\ y = H - m \end{cases} \tag{5}$$

According to Eq. (5), these points $p_1(m_1,n_1)$, $p_2(m_2,n_2)$, $p_3(m_3,n_3)$ and $q_1(m_4,n_4)$, $q_2(m_5,n_5)$, $q_3(m_6,n_6)$ are changed into $P_1(x_1,y_1)$, $P_2(x_2,y_2)$, $P_3(x_3,y_3)$ and $Q_1(x_4,y_4)$, $Q_2(x_5,y_5)$, $Q_3(x_6,y_6)$. In the following, we discuss the fitting method for the straight line by using the three sample points' coordinate, we take the example for fitting the upward edge lines, the fitting of downward edge lines is the same. We denote the straight line's equation for fitting the upward edge line by $y_1 = \hat{a}_1 x_1 + \hat{b}_1$, where the evaluation of $\hat{a}_1$ and b_1 can be calculated according to the coordinate of P_1, P_2 and P_3 by the least square method, the calculating formula is shown in Eq. (6), where $N = 3$, since the number of the sample points is three.

$$\begin{cases} \hat{a}_1 = \dfrac{\sum\limits_{i=1}^{N}(x_i \cdot y_i) - N\overline{xy}}{\sum\limits_{i=1}^{N}(x_i)^2 - N(\overline{x})^2} \\ \hat{b}_1 = \overline{y} - \hat{a}_1\overline{x} \end{cases} \tag{6}$$

The equation for fitting the downward edge line can be denoted as $y_2 = \hat{a}_2 x_2 + \hat{b}_2$, where $\hat{a}_2$ and $\hat{b}_2$ can be calculated by the central sample point's coordinate of Q_1, Q_2, Q_3. Since the two edge lines are paralleled in the image, the values of $\hat{a}_2$ and $\hat{b}_2$ in the fitting lines are similar. In the algorithm, we put the judging criteria as $|\hat{a}_1 - \hat{a}_2| < 0.1$ for checking the parallelism of the two straight fitting lines, if the judging criteria is false, we need to ask for the user again to reselect the region of the edge lines. Figure 10 shows the upward edge line and downward edge line in the rectangular coordinate system, which can describe the location and direction of the two paralleled edge lines in the Fig. 4(c).

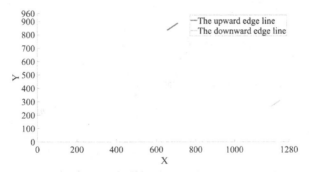

Fig. 10. The diagram of the upward edge line and the downward edge line in the rectangular coordinate system

3.4 Distance Calculation by the Parallel Edge Lines

In Ref. [10], Ge et al. proposed the size measurement by computing the distance between the intersecting points. Our proposed algorithm can measure the diameter size by the average of the six measurement results to improve the measurement accuracy. Firstly, we calculate the average distance of sample points $P_1(x_1, y_1)$, $P_2(x_2, y_2)$, $P_3(x_3, y_3)$ towards the downward edge line, with the similar principle, the average distance of sample points $Q_1(x_4, y_4)$, $Q_2(x_5, y_5)$, $Q_3(x_6, y_6)$ towards the upward edge line can be got, finally, we can average these two results and put the average of distance value as the size measurement between the two parallel edge lines. The calculating formula is shown as Eq. (7).

$$\frac{1}{2}\left[\frac{1}{3}\sum_{i=1}^{3}\frac{\left|\hat{a}_2 x_i - y_i + \hat{b}_2\right|}{\sqrt{\hat{a}_2^2 + 1}} + \frac{1}{3}\sum_{i=4}^{6}\frac{\left|\hat{a}_1 x_j - y_j + \hat{b}_1\right|}{\sqrt{\hat{a}_1^2 + 1}}\right] \qquad (7)$$

In the following, the user selects the region of edge line and measures the diameter of the shaft neck by five times, and we use the micrometer to measure the diameter of the shaft neck, through the physical measurement, we can obtain that the factual range of diameter of the shaft neck is 47.800 mm–47.850 mm, the results of five times' computer measurement for the shaft neck's diameter by the proposed optoelectronic platform are shown in Table 1, which can illustrate the effectiveness and reliability of this proposed algorithm.

Table 1. The measurement results of diameter size by the optoelectronic platform

Experimental times	1	2	3	4	5
Distance of the pixels	778.281	778.113	777.738	777.902	778.349
Measured size (mm)	47.845	47.835	47.812	47.822	47.849

Table 2 shows the comparison of the Hough transformation [11, 12] and the proposed method(1st experiment), it can be seen that the proposed method has the high performance of size measurement with the accuracy of the sub-pixel. Otherwise, the absolute difference of the slope between the two paralleled edge lines is equal to 0.0206 by our proposed method, which meets the parallelism's judging criteria as described in Sect. 3.3.

Table 2. The comparison of the Hough transformation and the proposed method

The measurement method	Hough transformation		The proposed method	
The upward edge line's equation	$y_1 = 0.94x + 215$	778 pixels	$y_1 = 0.9435x + 214.8828$	778.281 pixels
The downward edge line's equation	$y_2 = 0.92x - 832$		$y_2 = 0.9229x - 831.6074$	

4 Exhibition and Analysis of the Experimental Results

Figure 11 is the flowchart of our proposed method, which contains two feedbacks and four key techniques discussed in the Sect. 3. In the field of industrial measurement and industrial detection, the flowchart as shown in Fig. 11 can be referred.

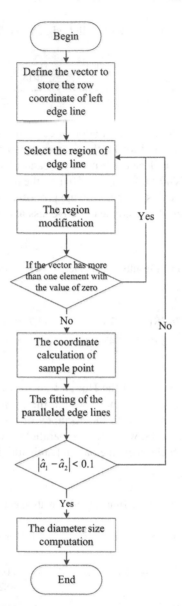

Fig. 11. The flowchart of our proposed method

In this section, we measure the industrial image (size: 1600×1200) of the shaft neck by another industrial camera with the brand of EM-500C with two diameter parameters, which can verify this algorithm's effectiveness and robustness. Figure 12(a) is the original shaft neck image with two groups of edge lines which is acquired by the optoelectronic platform shown as Fig. 2, and Fig. 12(a) has two regions of paralleled line named Shaft neck I and Shaft neck II which contain two groups of edge lines respectively. The red rectangular and the green rectangular describe the region of upward edge line and downward edge line respectively. Figure 12(b) is the enhancement result after pre-processing, it can be seen that the result reflect the edge information of the two shaft necks obviously and eliminate the problem caused by light's diffraction.

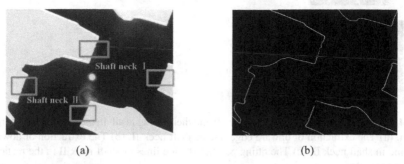

(a)   (b)

Fig. 12. The experimental industrial image and enhancement result after pre-processing. (a) The original industrial image with two shaft necks. (b) The enhancement result after pre-processing.

After the local region's selection of the two edge lines in Shaft neck I, the upward edge line and the downward edge line are shown as Fig. 13, where we can see although the upward edge line is discontinuousness, the fitting result of two parallel edge lines is effective.

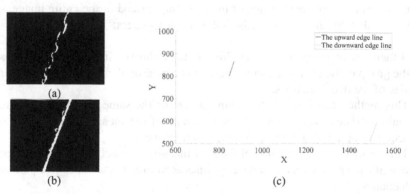

(b)   (c)

Fig. 13. The edge line's region in shaft neck I and their fitting result in the rectangular coordinate system. (a) The extraction of upward edge line in shaft neck I. (b) The extraction of downward edge line in shaft neck I. (c) The fitting paralleled edge lines of shaft neck I in the rectangular coordinate system.

Figure 14 shows the measurement result of the shaft neck II, the performance is similar with Fig. 13, and from these experimental results, the algorithm's robustness can be verified, we can utilize this proposed algorithm to measure two paralleled edge lines' distance in the two shaft neck's industrial image.

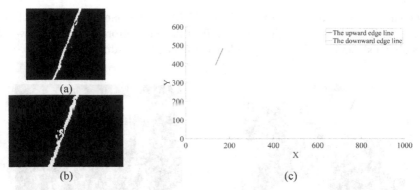

Fig. 14. The edge lines' region in shaft neck II and their fitting result in the rectangular coordinate system. (a) The extraction of upward edge line in shaft neck II. (b) The extraction of downward edge line in shaft neck II. (c) The fitting paralleled edge lines of shaft neck II in the rectangular coordinate system.

5 Conclusion

This paper discusses the size measurement algorithm based on the image's paralleled edge, and mainly describes the progress from the extraction of image's line edge to the display of the edge line's location in the rectangle coordinate system. Moreover, the local region of the edge line can be reselected and reconfirmed, the minimum processing unit of this algorithm is the local region of the edge line instead of the entire image, so we can include that this algorithm has the following advantages:

(1) If there are many groups of edge lines in the industrial image, the user can select the group of the edge lines which needs to be measured, and compute the diameter size of the two edge lines.
(2) This method can measure the diameter size of the same group of edge lines by multiple times, which can make the average of the measurement values, so the accuracy of the diameter measurement is improved.
(3) This method has the function of the man-machine interaction, we can reselect and reconfirm the local region of the edge lines according to the concerned parameters' feedback.

In the future, we can establish the optoelectronic platform with multiple industrial cameras, which can acquire the multiple images with different angles and different location of the industrial camera, and we use the multiple information to measure the complicated parameters such as the straightness and coaxiality of the shaft.

References

1. Costa, P.B., Leta, F.R., de Oliveira Baldner, F.: Computer vision measurement system for standards calibration in XY plane with sub-micrometer accuracy. Int. J. Adv. Manuf. Technol. **105**(1–4), 1531–1537 (2019). https://doi.org/10.1007/s00170-019-04297-7

2. Liu, Y., Liu, J., Ke, Y.: A detection and recognition system of pointer meters in substations based on computer vision. Measurement **152**, 107333 (2020)
3. Liu, Y., Li, G., Zhou, H., Xie, Z., Feng, F., Ge, W.: On-machine measurement method for the geometric error of shafts with a large ratio of length to diameter. Measurement **176**, 109194 (2021). https://doi.org/10.1016/j.measurement.2021.109194
4. Fan, J.F., Jing, F.S.: Dimensional inspecting system of shaft parts based on machine vision. In: 2017 Chinese Automation Congress, pp. 1708–1714. IEEE (2017)
5. Wang, H.C., et al.: Gradient adaptive image restoration and enhancement. In: International Conference on Image Processing, pp. 2893–2896. IEEE (2006)
6. Ding, C., Dong, L.L., Xu, W.H.: A fast algorithm based on image gradient field reconstructing. In: International Conference on Digital Image Processing, 100333C. SPIE (2016)
7. Zhou, C.D., et al.: Partial differential equation based image edge enhancement. In: 2016 13th International Conference on Ubiquitous Robots and Ambient Intelligence, pp. 972–978. IEEE (2016)
8. Ding, C., Dong, L.L., Xu, W.H.: Image gradient histogram's fitting and calculation. J. Eng. **2018**(1), 45–48 (2018). https://doi.org/10.1049/joe.2017.0406
9. Saini, S., Sardana, H., Pattnaik, S.: GUI for coordinate measurement of an image for the estimation of geometric distortion of an opto-electronic display system. J. Instit. Eng. (India) B **98**(3), 303–310 (2016). https://doi.org/10.1007/s40031-016-0266-0
10. Ge, J., et al: Multi-scale shaft part's image edge detection and measurement based on wavelet transform. In: 2008 IEEE Pacific-Asia Workshop on Computational Intelligence and Industrial Application, no. 1, pp. 371–375 (2008)
11. Deeptaroop, M., Rajan, Niharika, S.: Seismic data interpretation using Hough transformation technique. In: 2015 1st International Conference on Next Generation Computing Technologies (NGCT), pp. 580–583 (2015)
12. Szilvia, N., et al.: Fuzzy Hough transformation in aiding computer tomography based liver diagnosis. In: 2019 IEEE AFRICON. IEEE (2019)

Binary Multi-view Image Re-ranking

Zhijian Wu, Jun Li$^{(\boxtimes)}$, and Jianhua Xu

School of Computer and Electronic Information, Nanjing Normal University,
Nanjing 210023, Jiangsu, China
{192235022,lijuncst,xujianhua}@njnu.edu.cn

Abstract. Conventional subspace-based multi-view re-ranking methods essentially handle the Euclidean feature space transformation and tend to be inefficient when dealing with large-scale data, since the cost of computing the similarity between the query item and the database item is prohibitively high. Inspired by Hashing technique, in this paper, we propose an efficient binary multi-view image re-ranking strategy in which the original multi-view features are projected onto a compact Hamming subspace. With the intrinsic structure of the original multi-view Euclidean feature space maintained, the resulting binary codes are consistent with the original multi-view features in similarity measure. Furthermore, coupled with the discriminative learning mechanism, our method leads to compact binary codes with sufficient discriminating power for accurate image re-ranking. Experiments on public benchmarks reveal that our method achieves competitive retrieval performance comparable to the state-of-the-art and enjoys excellent scalability in large-scale scenario.

Keywords: Multi-view image re-ranking · Hamming subspace · Discriminative learning · Binary codes

1 Introduction

In visual search task, image re-ranking aims to update the query model and improve the initial retrieval accuracy by polishing the ranking list in the first place [4,15]. The core of these algorithms is to develop an accurate re-ranking model for re-evaluating the correlation between the target images and the query. Recent research suggests that subspace-based multi-view re-ranking serves as an important line of research in image re-ranking, since the traditional hand-crafted shallow features are supplementary to the deep features. Thus, the complementarity among these two heterogeneous features can be embedded within a unified multi-view learning framework for recovering a latent subspace [12,21,22].

The most representative multi-view learning framework is Canonical Correlation Analysis (CCA) [5], which is aiming at exploring the associations between two

This work was supported by the Natural Science Foundation of China (NSFC) under Grants 61703096, 61773117, 61273246 and the Natural Science Foundation of Jiangsu Province under Grant BK20170691.

Y. Peng et al. (Eds.): ICIG 2021, LNCS 12888, pp. 578–590, 2021.
https://doi.org/10.1007/978-3-030-87355-4_48

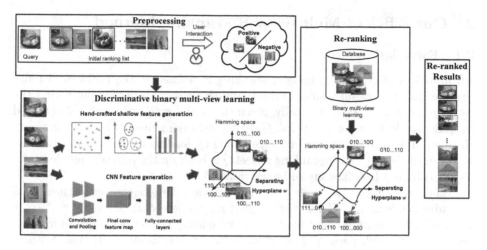

Fig. 1. The system flowchart of our BMVIR approach.

sets of variables. Besides, a wide variety of CCA variants [1,14] are developed and widely used in multi-view learning. Subsequently, multi-view re-ranking methods combining multi-view learning and image re-ranking strategy have been proposed and demonstrated their overwhelming superiority in various visual tasks [19]. In addition to CCA framework, Li et al. [10,11] develop a series of unified discriminative multi-view learning frameworks in which multi-view subspace embedding is combined with discriminative learning for accurate image re-ranking. Despite effective, these methods suffer from expensive computational cost especially in large-scale scenarios, which adversely affects real-world applications.

To address this issue, in this paper, we propose a novel binary multi-view image re-ranking method (BMVIR) for efficient and accurate image re-ranking. Inspired by image Hashing [8,20], our method attempts to recover a latent Hamming subspace from the original multi-view feature spaces, and the resulting binary codes are used for subsequent image re-ranking. More importantly, coupled with the discriminative learning mechanism, our method is capable of embedding the correlation information of the pairwise images into the generated binary codes, and thus maximally preserving the discriminating power of the compact binary codes. Benefiting from the reliable discriminant information, our method avoids the lossy coding caused by the over-dependence on the data structure for the traditional Hashing methods, and generates the similarity-preserving binary codes with sufficient discriminative power. With the help of the efficient binary codes, fast image search can be carried out via Hamming distance evaluation, which dramatically reduces the computational cost with desirable efficiency. The processing pipeline of our approach is illustrated in Fig. 1.

The rest of the paper is organized as follows. We elaborate our method in details in Sect. 2. Next, we present the experimental evaluations in Sect. 3. Finally, our work is concluded and summarized in Sect. 4.

2 Our Efficient Multi-view Re-ranking Method

2.1 Formulation

Without loss of generality, image re-ranking is defined as the problem of refining the initial retrieval results by updating the query model for improving the retrieval accuracy. Mathematically, given the initial retrieval results R obtained by query model Q, we aim to polish Q with a re-ranking model $\tilde{Q}$, and re-evaluate the query relevance of the target images using $\tilde{Q}$, leading to the re-ranked results $\tilde{R}$. More specifically, the re-ranking model $\tilde{Q}$ is built on the partially labeled samples S collected from the initial image ranks R.

When training $\tilde{Q}$, we make use of multi-view heterogeneous features of S for subspace learning. Given the original multi-view data $Z_v \in \mathbb{R}^{D_v \times n}$ ($v = 1, ..., m$), the subspace-based multi-view embedding framework seeks to uncover the underlying subspace $X \in \mathbb{R}^{d \times n}$ such that the original multi-view features can be recovered from this subspace via view-specific generation matrix $P_v \in \mathbb{R}^{D_v \times d}$ ($v = 1, ..., m$). m is the number of data views while n is the number of images. Besides, D_v indicates the view-specific feature dimensionality while d is the dimension of the latent subspace. Mathematically, the subspace recovery process is formulated as:

$$Z_v = P_v X + E_v \tag{1}$$

where $E_v \in \mathbb{R}^{D_v \times n}$ is denoted as the view-dependent reconstruction error. In general, the shared subspace is reconstructed by solving the following formulation:

$$\min_{P_v, X} \sum_{v=1}^{m} \|Z_v - P_v X\|_F^2 + c_1 \sum_{v=1}^{m} \|P_v\|_F^2 + c_2 \|X\|_F^2 \tag{2}$$

where c_1 and c_2 are the parameters controlling the tradeoff among the corresponding regularization terms which are used to prevent overfitting. Although Eq. (2) provides a general paradigm for recovering a potential subspace from multi-view features, the resulting Euclidean subspace is still prone to high similarity calculation costs. Inspired by learning to Hash, we attempt to recover a shared Hamming space directly from the original multi-view feature, yielding compact binary codes. Mathematically, encoding the Hamming subspace with binary discretization constraint is expressed as:

$$\min_{P_v, X, B, R} \sum_{v=1}^{m} \|Z_v - P_v X\|_F^2 + c_1 \sum_{v=1}^{m} \|P_v\|_F^2 + c_2 \|X\|_F^2 + c_3 \|B - X^T R\|_F^2 \tag{3}$$

$$s.t. \quad B \in \{-1, 1\}^{n \times d}, \quad R^T R = I$$

where B is the resulting d-dimensional Hamming subspace, and $R \in \mathbb{R}^{d \times d}$ is an orthogonal matrix, and c_1, c_2, c_3 are the tuning parameters controlling the tradeoff among respective regularization terms. Basically, since the binary matrix discretization constraint poses a great challenge to the optimization of the resulting Hamming space, it is not easy to generate an accurate mapping from Euclidean space to Hamming space while maximally maintaining the intrinsic correlation among multi-view data without significant loss. In our scheme, we impose the orthogonal transformation on the resulting Euclidean subspace to minimize its loss with binary code, and thus avoid the problem of direct optimization of binary matrix. The principle behind it can be explained by the invariance property of the orthogonal transformation of Euclidean space. Thus, the optimal multi-view Euclidean subspace structure is retained intact in Hamming space.

In Hashing methods, it is crucial for maintaining the discrimination capability of binary codes, whereas the correlation information contained in the inherent data structure is limited, and thus somewhat affects the performance of Hashing learning. In order to further improve the discriminating power of the binary codes, we introduce discriminative learning to minimize the similarity preserving empirical loss:

$$\min_{w} \frac{1}{2} \|w\|^2 + c_4 \|Y - w^T X\|^2 \tag{4}$$

where $w \in \mathbb{R}^{d \times 1}$ indicates the separating hyperplane in the latent subspace, whilst $Y \in \{1, -1\}^N$ is the label vector of the training samples. Accordingly, we combine Eq. (4) with Eq. (3), yielding the following binary multi-view feature learning framework:

$$\min_{P_v, X, B, R, w} \sum_{v=1}^{m} \|Z_v - P_v X\|_F^2 + c_1 \sum_{v=1}^{m} \|P_v\|_F^2 + c_2 \|X\|_F^2 + c_3 \|B - X^T R\|_F^2$$
$$+ \frac{1}{2} \|w\|^2 + c_4 \|Y - w^T X\|^2 \tag{5}$$
$$s.t. \quad B \in \{-1, 1\}^{n \times d}, \quad R^T R = I$$

As shown in Eq. (5), we incorporate Hashing learning and discriminative learning into a unified multi-view embedding framework, solving for the view-dependent generation matrices P_v, the latent representation X, the binary codes B, the decision boundary w and the orthogonal matrix R simultaneously. Thus, the re-ranking model $\tilde{Q}$ is derived. For the on-the-fly re-ranking, we first compute the binary codes $\tilde{B}$ of all the target images by optimizing the following formulation:

$$\min_{\tilde{X}, \tilde{B}} \sum_{v=1}^{m} \|\tilde{Z}_v - P_v \tilde{X}\|_F^2 + c_3 \|\tilde{B} - \tilde{X}^T R\|_F^2 \tag{6}$$

where $\tilde{Z}_v$ denotes the original multi-view features of the target images. Thus, the query relevance can be re-evaluated and re-ordered by calculating $\tilde{B} \cdot w$, leading to the re-ranked results $\tilde{R}$.

2.2 Optimization

The formulation in Eq. (5) requires simultaneous optimization of the five parameters: the view-dependent generation matrix P_v, the low-dimensional subspace embedding X, the orthogonal rotation matrix R, the binary codes B and the decision boundary w. To solve this problem, we design an iterative algorithm to alternate the optimization of the five variables for minimizing the empirical loss as in Eq. (5):

Update P_v by Fixing Others. After removing the irrelevant terms, the formulation in Eq. (5) is reduced to:

$$\min_{P_v} \|Z_v - P_v X\|_F^2 + c_1 \|P_v\|_F^2 \tag{7}$$

Let;

$$\mathcal{L} = \min_{P_v} \|Z_v - P_v X\|_F^2 + c_1 \|P_v\|_F^2 \tag{8}$$

Thus, we take the derivative of L w.r.t. P_v and set the derivative to 0, leading to the close-form solution as follows:

$$P_v = Z_v X^{\mathrm{T}} (XX^{\mathrm{T}} + c_1 I)^{-1} \tag{9}$$

Update X by Fixing Others. With the irrelevant terms discarded, the formulation in Eq. (5) is simplified as:

$$\min_{X} \|Z_v - P_v X\|_F^2 + c_2 \|X\|_F^2 + c_3 \|B - X^{\mathrm{T}} R\|_F^2 + c_4 \|Y - w^{\mathrm{T}} X\| \tag{10}$$

Analogously, we take the derivative of L w.r.t. X and set the derivative to 0 for obtaining the following close-form solution:

$$X = \left(\sum_{v=1}^{m} P_v^{\mathrm{T}} P_v + c_2 I + c_2 RR^{\mathrm{T}} + c_4 ww^{\mathrm{T}}\right)^{-1} \left(\sum_{v=1}^{m} P_v^{\mathrm{T}} Z_v + c_3 RB^{\mathrm{T}} + c_4 wY\right) \tag{11}$$

Update B by Fixing Others. While updating B, we only maintain the terms regarding B, and thus the problem is reduced to:

$$\min_{B} \|B - X^{\mathrm{T}} R\|_F^2 \quad s.t. \quad B \in \{-1, 1\}^{n \times d} \tag{12}$$

Expanding Eq. (12), we have:

$$\begin{aligned}
&\min_{B} \|B\|_F^2 + \|X^{\mathrm{T}}\|_F^2 - 2tr(BR^{\mathrm{T}} X) \\
&= \min_{B} nd + \|X^{\mathrm{T}}\|_F^2 - 2tr(BR^{\mathrm{T}} X)
\end{aligned} \tag{13}$$

Since $n \cdot d$ is constant while the projected data matrix X is fixed, minimizing Eq. (13) is equivalent to maximizing

$$tr(BR^{\mathrm{T}} X) = \sum_{i=1}^{n} \sum_{j=1}^{d} B_{ij} \tilde{X}_{ij} \tag{14}$$

where $\tilde{X}_{ij}$ denotes the elements of $\tilde{X} = X^{\mathrm{T}} R$. To maximize this formulation with respect to B, we have $B_{ij} = 1$ whenever $\tilde{X}_{ij} \geq 0$ and -1 otherwise.

Update R by Fixing Others. After removing the irrelevant variables, Eq. (5) is reduced to:

$$\min_{R} \left\| B - X^{\mathrm{T}} R \right\|_{F}^{2} \quad s.t. \quad R^{T} R = I \tag{15}$$

The objective function shown in Eq. (15) is in spirit the classic orthogonal Procrustes problem [6]. In our method, Eq. (15) is minimized by computing the SVD of the $n \times n$ matrix $B^{\mathrm{T}} X^{\mathrm{T}}$ as $S \Omega \hat{S}^{\mathrm{T}}$ and letting $R = \hat{S} S^{\mathrm{T}}$.

Update w by Fixing Others. Similar to the above-mentioned steps, we remove the irrelevant terms and rewrite Eq. (5) as follows:

$$\min_{w} \frac{1}{2} \left\| w \right\|^{2} + c_4 \left\| Y - w^{\mathrm{T}} X \right\|^{2} \tag{16}$$

we also take the derivative of L w.r.t. w and set the derivative to 0 for obtaining the following close-form solution:

$$w = (I + 2c_4 X X^{\mathrm{T}})^{-1} 2c_4 X Y^{\mathrm{T}} \tag{17}$$

We iteratively alternate the above steps until the convergence of the algorithm is reached.

Time Complexity. In our method, computing P_v requires $O(D_v \cdot n \cdot d) + O(D_v \cdot d^2) + O(d^3) + O(d^2 \cdot n)$ time cost, which can be further approximated by $O(D_v \cdot n \cdot d) + O(D_v \cdot d^2)$ because $D_v >> d$ in our case. n denotes the number of database images. In term of the time complexity of updating X, it amounts to $m \cdot (O(D_v \cdot n \cdot d) + O(D_v \cdot d^2)) + 2O(d^3) + 2O(d^2 \cdot n)$ which can be also approximated by $m \cdot O(D_v \cdot n \cdot d) + m \cdot O(D_v \cdot d^2))$. Meanwhile, optimizing w requires approximately $O(d^2 \cdot n + d^3)$ time cost. In addition, the time complexity of computing B is $O(d \cdot n)$, while optimizing R requires $O(n^3)$ time cost. Besides, the feature matching based on Hamming distance has a time complexity of $O(d \cdot n)$.

3 Experiments

In this section, we evaluate our BMVIR framework for interactive image re-ranking. We first introduce the public benchmark datasets along with the experimental setting and the evaluation protocols. Next, comprehensive quantitative analyses are carried out to illustrate the performance of our algorithm. In addition, comparative study also demonstrates the significant advantages of our algorithm over the existing image re-ranking methods.

3.1 Datasets

We evaluate our approach on two public benchmark datasets for landmark retrieval, namely Oxford5K [16] and Paris6K [17]. Both the two datasets include

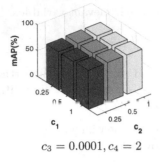 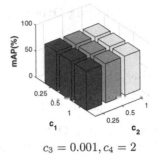

$c_3 = 0.0001, c_4 = 2$ $c_3 = 0.001, c_4 = 2$

Fig. 2. The performance of our algorithm with different parameter values $\{c_1, c_2, c_3, c_4\}$ on query "triomphe".

11 famous landmarks, each of which has five query instances, yielding a total of 55 query groups. In terms of the performance measure, we compute average precision (AP) for each query group and obtain the mean average precision (mAP) by averaging all AP scores for the overall evaluation. In addition, to assess the scalability of our algorithm in large-scale scenarios, we respectively merge Oxford5K and Paris6K with the Flickr100K [16] for large-scale evaluation. Flickr100K has a total of 100,071 images crawled from Flickr's 145 most popular tags, and is typically merged with other datasets for large-scale retrieval task.

3.2   Multi-view Features

Two heterogeneous image signatures are involved in our evaluation, namely CNN and TEDA [7]. Besides, we also make use of the VLAD+ [3] feature for the subsequent evaluation in large-scale retrieval scenario. As for the CNN feature, we directly adopt the deep model which is specifically fine-tuned for landmark retrieval and recognition task [2] and generate a 4,096-dimensional vector for feature representation. Besides, we follow [7] to compute TEDA signature which is represented by a 8,064-dimensional vector. In terms of VLAD+, we reproduce the method in [3] and also use a vocabulary of 256 visual words for producing 16,384-dimensional image feature.

3.3   Experimental Setting

As shown in Eq. (5), there are four regularization parameters c_1, c_2, c_3 and c_4 involved in the model selection. Figure 2 shows the impact of different parameters on the performance of BMVIR for query "triomphe". In implementation, we empirically set c_1 and c_2 as 0.25 and 0.5 respectively, while parameter c_3 is set to 0.001 to compromise between the multi-view reconstruction error and the binary quantization loss. In addition, c_4 is set as 2 empirically to put more weights on the similarity-preserving term for improving the discriminating power of our BMVIR model. Besides, we set the subspace dimension and the binary code length as 256 for compact representation and efficient retrieval.

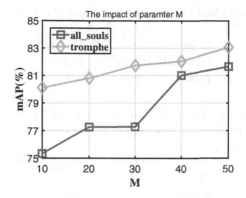

Fig. 3. The impact of the parameter M on the proposed BMVIR algorithm.

3.4 Training Samples Collection

In our method, since it is essential to indicate the query-relevance of the initial shortlisted images from scratch, we collect the query-relevant and query-irrelevant instances from the original image ranks to obtain the partial supervised information for the subspace learning. It is well known that high-ranked images are likely to be query-relevant, whereas the low-scored images are negative examples for a specific query instance in the initial retrieval results. In implementation, we use user interaction to indicate the relevance of top returned candidates in the shortlist of size M and consider the relevant images as positive training examples, whilst label L images at the bottom of the rank list as negative samples. Since our method mainly depends on the size of the shortlist M in the initial ranking list shown to the user, we discuss the influence of M in Fig. 3. It is observed that increasing M allows more positive examples involved in the training process, and thus leads to significant performance promotion. For the sake of the balance between efficiency and performance, we set M and L as 50 and 1000 respectively in practice.

3.5 Results

Baselines. We produce two separate baseline retrieval results in the first place by combining single image representation with efficient cosine similarities, which are denoted as CNN_COS, and TE_COS for short respectively. As shown in Table 1, CNN_COS consistently reports higher retrieval accuracy than TE_COS across all the performance measures, suggesting the promise of the TEDA signature and the significant heterogeneity between these two features.

Re-ranked Results by Using BMVIR. Given the initial retrieval results, we impose the proposed BMVIR on the original ranking list produced from TE_COS for accurate re-ranking. Table 2 reports the dramatic performance gains provided

Table 1. Comparison of different baselines on Oxford5K and Paris6K.

Datasets	CNN_COS	TE_COS
Oxford5K	0.6809	0.6204
Paris6K	0.7596	0.6176

Table 2. Comparison of TE_COS baseline method and TE_BMVIR re-ranking approach on some representative query groups of Paris6K.

Query	TE_COS (Baseline)	TE_BMVIR (Re-ranking)
	AP	AP
defense	0.3656	0.7233
eiffel	0.4438	0.6605
moulinrouge	0.3317	0.6532
triomphe	0.5265	0.8307
mean	0.6176	0.7731

by TE_BMVIR on the two benchmarks. It can be observed that our method significantly improves the baseline. For instance, on Paris6k, TE_BMVIR outperforms TE_COS by 35.77% on query "defense". The overall mAP score also increases from 61.76% to 77.31% accordingly. Similar advantage of TE_BMVIR is also shown on Oxford5K, indicating the mAP score is reported at 78.34% which considerably outperforms the corresponding baseline score at 62.04%. This implies that our BMVIR strategy fully explores the complementarity of heterogeneous features and combines discriminant learning to produce discriminative binary codes, and significantly improves the performance and efficiency of baselines.

Comparative Studies. To further demonstrate the advantages of our approaches, we have compared our method with other related works.

- **BMSL**: We use the recent binary multi-view fusion method BMSL [20] to produce compact binary codes from the original multi-view features. It is worth noting that this is an unsupervised multi-view learning method without discriminative learning strategy involved.
- **DMINTIR-ITQ**: In this method, we utilize the classical multi-view reranking method DMINTIR [11] to generate discriminating subspace. Next, we encode the resulting subspace representation into the binary codes by using the ITQ algorithm [6].

For the sake of consistency, we adopt the same setup of multi-view features as our method. As show in Fig. 4, our approach consistently achieves superior performance on both datasets. In particular, our method reports 78.34% mAP score on Oxford5K, and significantly exceeds the competing method BMSL reporting

Table 3. Comparison of TE_COS baseline method and TE_BMVIR re-ranking approach on some representative query groups of Oxford5K.

Query	TE_COS (Baseline)	TE_BMVIR (Re-ranking)
	AP	AP
all_souls	0.6105	0.7682
ashmolean	0.4988	0.6641
bodleian	0.3728	0.8430
hertford	0.6705	0.8755
radcliffe_camera	0.9020	0.9525
mean	0.6204	0.7834

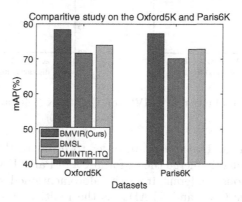

Fig. 4. Comparison of different approaches on Oxford5K and Paris6K benchmarks

score at 71.63%. This implies that the beneficial effect of the discriminative learning in our method can significantly improve the discriminant power of the generated visual representation. Meanwhile, the proposed BMVIR outperforms the DMINTIR-ITQ by 4.4% and 4.48% on respective dataset, which suggests that the unified subspace learning framework allows discriminative and compact binary representations.

In addition, we also compare our BMVIR algorithm with the state-of-the-art re-ranking methods on the two benchmarks. As presented in Table 4, the proposed approach bests all competing methods on Oxford5K including recent deep models. Surprisingly, our algorithm lags behind the state-of-the-arts on Paris6K. We argue that the disadvantage is due to the inferior performance of the original multi-view features and the insufficient complementarity between the two heterogeneous features. Since the performance of our method is achieved with very compact binary codes, this reveals the promise and the competitive performance of BMVIR along with the advantage in retrieval efficiency.

Table 4. Comparison of our method with the state-of-the-arts.

Method	Oxford5K	Paris6K
R-MAC+R+QE [18]	77.3	**86.5**
LME [13]	67.5	-
CroW+QE [9]	74.9	83.31
Ours	**78.3**	77.3

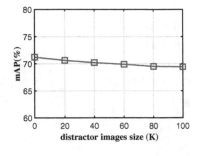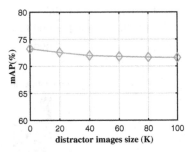

Fig. 5. Large-scale evaluation of BMVIR on Oxford5K (left) and Paris6K (right).

Scalability to Large Database. In order to evaluate the scalability of our approach, we respectively merge the Oxford5K and Paris6K with Flickr100K for large-scale evaluations. Different from the aforementioned setup of multi-view features, we use the CNN and VLAD+ as the multi-view data to explore the effect of different combinations of multiple heterogeneous features. Figure 5 illustrates the performance of our approach when the distractor images are incrementally added to Oxford5K and Paris6K. It is shown that our approach is hardly affected with the distractor images added incrementally, which substantially demonstrates the promising scalability of our approach.

Computational Cost. In implementation, training our model costs roughly 20 s, while the similarity matching takes approximately 3 ms. In contrast, the traditional retrieval scheme with cosine similarity takes about 10 ms in feature matching. This sufficiently demonstrates the real-time performance of our method using compact binary codes for instance retrieval. All the experiments are conducted under the Matlab environment using a laptop with CPU Intel Core i5-5200U 2.2 GHz and 4 GB memory.

4   Conclusions

In this paper, we have proposed a unified binary multi-view learning framework for accurate image re-ranking. In particular, we take advantage of multi-view learning paradigm to integrate the binary encoding and discriminative learning into a unified framework, resulting in compact binary codes with sufficient discriminating power for efficient and effective image re-ranking. The evaluations on the public benchmarks and large-scale scenarios reveal that our approach achieves the promising performance with desirable scalability.

References

1. Andrew, G., Arora, R., Bilmes, J., Livescu, K.: Deep canonical correlation analysis. In: ICML, pp. 1247–1255 (2013)
2. Arandjelovic, R., Gronat, P., Torii, A., Pajdla, T., Sivic, J.: NetVLAD: CNN architecture for weakly supervised place recognition. In: CVPR, pp. 5297–5307 (2016)
3. Arandjelovic, R., Zisserman, A.: All about VLAD. In: CVPR (2013)
4. Bai, S., Tang, P., Torr, P.H., Latecki, L.J.: Re-ranking via metric fusion for object retrieval and person re-identification. In: IEEE CVPR, pp. 740–749 (2019)
5. Blaschko, M.B., Lampert, C.H.: Correlational spectral clustering. In: CVPR, pp. 1–8 (2008)
6. Gong, Y., Lazebnik, S., Gordo, A., Perronnin, F.: Iterative quantization: a procrustean approach to learning binary codes for large-scale image retrieval. IEEE TPAMI **35**(12), 2916–2929 (2012)
7. Jégou, H., Zisserman, A.: Triangulation embedding and democratic aggregation for image search. In: CVPR, pp. 3310–3317 (2014)
8. Jiang, Q.Y., Li, W.J.: Scalable graph hashing with feature transformation. IJCAI. **15**, 2248–2254 (2015)
9. Kalantidis, Y., Mellina, C., Osindero, S.: Cross-dimensional weighting for aggregated deep convolutional features. In: Hua, G., Jégou, H. (eds.) ECCV 2016, Part I. LNCS, vol. 9913, pp. 685–701. Springer, Cham (2016). https://doi.org/10.1007/978-3-319-46604-0_48
10. Li, J., Xu, C., Yang, W., Sun, C., Kotagiri, R., Tao, D.: ROMIR: robust multi-view image re-ranking. IEEE TKDE **31**(12), 2393–2406 (2018)
11. Li, J., Xu, C., Yang, W., Sun, C., Tao, D.: Discriminative multi-view interactive image re-ranking. IEEE TIP **26**(7), 3113–3127 (2017)
12. Li, J., Yang, B., Yang, W., Sun, C., Zhang, H.: When deep meets shallow: subspace-based multi-view fusion for instance-level image retrieval. In: ROBIO, pp. 486–492 (2018)
13. Li, Y., Geng, B., Tao, D., Zha, Z.J., Yang, L., Xu, C.: Difficulty guided image retrieval using linear multiple feature embedding. IEEE TOM **14**(6), 1618–1630 (2012)
14. Michaeli, T., Wang, W., Livescu, K.: Nonparametric canonical correlation analysis. In: ICML, pp. 1967–1976 (2016)
15. Ouyang, J., Zhou, W., Wang, M., Tian, Q., Li, H.: Collaborative image relevance learning for visual re-ranking. IEEE TMM 1 (2020)
16. Philbin, J., Chum, O., Isard, M., Sivic, J., Zisserman, A.: Object retrieval with large vocabularies and fast spatial matching. In: CVPR, pp. 1–8. IEEE (2007)
17. Philbin, J., Chum, O., Isard, M., Sivic, J., Zisserman, A.: Lost in quantization: improving particular object retrieval in large scale image databases. In: CVPR, pp. 1–8. IEEE (2008)
18. Tolias, G., Sicre, R., Jégou, H.: Particular object retrieval with integral max-pooling of CNN activations. arXiv preprint arXiv:1511.05879 (2015)

19. Wang, L., Qian, X., Zhang, Y., Shen, J., Cao, X.: Enhancing sketch-based image retrieval by CNN semantic re-ranking. IEEE Trans. Cybern. **50**(7), 3330–3342 (2020)
20. Wu, Z., Li, J., Xu, J.: Efficient binary multi-view subspace learning for instance-level image retrieval. In: Yang, H., Pasupa, K., Leung, A.C.-S., Kwok, J.T., Chan, J.H., King, I. (eds.) ICONIP 2020, Part IV. CCIS, vol. 1332, pp. 59–68. Springer, Cham (2020). https://doi.org/10.1007/078 3 030 63020-7_7
21. Xie, Y., et al.: Joint deep multi-view learning for image clustering. IEEE TKDE 1 (2020)
22. Xu, C., Tao, D., Xu, C.: Multi-view intact space learning. IEEE TPAMI **37**(12), 2531–2544 (2015)

Identifying Abnormal Map in Crowd Scenes Using Spatio-Temporal Social Force Model

Dong Chen, Kai Fang, and Shuoyan Liu[✉]

Institute of Computer Technologies Department, China Academy of Railway Sciences, Beijing, China
061120620@bjtu.edu.cn

Abstract. Abnormal map defines the distribution of potentially dangerous in the crowd scenes. In contrast to other crowd behaviors, it has received a lot of attention among the video surveillance community to prevent abnormal situations. In this study, we conceive the abnormal map according to interaction forces of individuals. For this purpose, a grid of particles is first placed over the image and it is adverted with the space-time average of optical flow. By treating the moving particles as individuals, their change of interaction forces are then estimated using spatio-temporal Social Force Model (st-SFM). The st-SFM jointly learns and combines crowd density, intra-group stability and inter-group conflict for computing interaction forces. Finally, the abnormal map is obtained by mapping the change of interaction forces into the image plane. The experiments are conducted on a publicly available dataset from University of Minnesota for escape panic scenarios and a challenging dataset of crowd videos taken from the railway stations. The experimental results have demonstrated that such an abnormal map is not only useful but also necessary for abnormal crowd analysis and understanding.

Keywords: Video surveillance · Abnormal map · Interaction forces of individuals · Social force model

1 Introduction

Crowd behavior analysis is a challenging topic and draws increasing attention because of the large demands on crowd video surveillance, which is especially important for metropolis security [1–5]. Due to severe occlusion and perspective distortion, current works mainly focused on crowd density analysis [6–8], intra-group stability and inter-group conflict [9,10], specific crowd behaviors [11–14] and etc.

a) Crowd density estimation. This problem is mostly considered from a static perspective: approaches like [6,7] used Convolutional Neural Networks (CNN) while the approach from [8] relied on head detections to perform the density estimation.

This work was support by the fund of China Academy of Railway sciences (2019YJ114).

Y. Peng et al. (Eds.): ICIG 2021, LNCS 12888, pp. 591–600, 2021.
https://doi.org/10.1007/978-3-030-87355-4_49

b) Intra-group stability and inter-group conflict. Intra-group properties, e.g. collectiveness, stability, and uniformity, denote internal coordination among members in the same group. Whilst inter-group properties, e.g. conflict, reflect the external interaction between members in different groups [9,10].

c) Specific crowd behaviour analysis. Early works focused on a specific behaviour such as panic movement [11], wrong way displacement [12], violence, etc. More recent works [13,14] tackle the problem of characterising the motion properties of the crowd to distinguish types of crowd motion (i.e. bottleneck, laminar mainstream, etc.). However, they are not fully representative of what a crowd can look like in everyday life situations.

Different from these properties, video surveillance more concerned about whether there were the abnormal regions in the crowd scenes. However, current approaches did not take into account the abnormal factors. For example, the high density crowd moves according to certain rules, the behavior of crowd is relatively safe. However, the suddenly changed movement pattern can lead to dangerous even if the density of crowd is low. Hence, this paper proposes a concept of abnormal map, which defines the distribution of potentially dangerous in the crowd scenes. Specifically, we conceive the abnormal map according to interaction forces of individuals. Not much attention has been paid to exploiting interaction forces to analyze the abnormal crowd behavior. One effort in this direction was proposed by Mehran [11]. It uses Social Force Model (SFM) analyzes abnormal force flow in crowd scenes based on optical flow. However, discrete value of forces is not a clear evidence of abnormal behaviors. In other words, the instantaneous forces in a scene do not discriminate the abnormalities but the change of forces over a period of time does. Nevertheless, the traditional SFM is seldom considering the change of forces over time. Hence, this paper proposes the spatio-temporal Social Force Model (st-SFM), which identifies abnormal map from the perspective of time and space under the three characteristic dimensions. In addition, this method does not require training.

The contribution of this paper is threefold. First, a new concept of abnormal map is proposed to detect the abnormal region in crowd scenes. Secondly, this concept analyzes the abnormal property considering multiple factors and is robust to public scenes with variety of crowdedness. Third, st-SFM identifies abnormal map from the perspective of time and space under the three characteristic dimensions.

The rest of the paper is organized as follows: The next Section gives the proposed framework in detail. We show the performance of the proposed method on the challenging datasets in Sect. 3. Finally, Sect. 4 concludes the paper.

2   Identifying Abnormal Map in Crowd Scenes Using Spatio-Temporal Social Force Model

In this paper, we identify the abnormal map in crowd scenes using spatio-temporal Social Force Model (st-SFM), which is an extension of Social Force

Model (SFM) [11]. SFM describes the behavior of the crowd as the instantaneous interaction force of individuals. Conversely, as reported in a recent work [15], discrete value of forces is not a clear evidence of abnormal behaviors. Therefore, we modified the traditional SFM into st-SFM, which computes the change of interaction forces over time.

Figure 1 summarizes the main steps of the algorithm. In our method, we avoid tracking of objects to avert typical problems in tracking of high density crowds such as extensive clutter and dynamic occlusions. Instead, this approach incorporate a holistic approach to analyze videos of crowds using the particle advection method similar to [15]. Specifically, we first place a grid of particles over the image and move them with the underlying flow field. And then compute the social force between moving particles to extract interaction forces. Finally, we map this to image frames. In a crowd scene, the change of interaction forces in time determines the abnormal properties of the crowd. The resulting force field is denoted as abnormal map, which is used to locate the abnormal region.

Fig. 1. The summary of the proposed approach for abnormal map estimation in the crowded videos

2.1 Spatio-Temporal Social Force Model

We first describe social force model for pedestrian motion dynamics by considering personal motivations and environmental constraints. In this model, each of N pedestrians i with mass of m_i changes his/her velocity v_i as

$$m_i \frac{dv_i}{dt} = F_a = F_p + F_{\text{int}} \tag{1}$$

as a result of actual force F_a, and due to individualistic goals or environmental constraints. This force consists of two main parts: (1) personal desire force F_p, and (2) interaction force F_{int}.

People in crowds generally seek certain goals and destinations in the environment. Thus, it is reasonable to consider each pedestrian to have a desired direction and velocity v_i^p. However, the crowd limits individual movement and the actual motion of pedestrian v_i would differ from the desired velocity. Furthermore, individuals tend to approach their desired velocity v_i^p based on the personal desire force:

$$F_p = \frac{1}{\tau}(v_i^p - v_i) \tag{2}$$

where τ is the relaxation parameter.

The st-SFM model considers three characteristic of crowd surround with the individual, such as crowd density, intra-group stability and inter-group conflict. Hence, this model replaces the personal desire velocity v_i^p with

$$v_i^q = (1 - p_i)v_i^p + p_i \langle v_i^c \rangle \tag{3}$$

where p_i is the panic weight parameter and $\langle v_i^c \rangle$ is the average velocity of the neighboring pedestrians.

The pedestrian i exhibits individualistic behaviors as $p_i \to 0$ and herding behaviors as $p_i \to 1$. The st-SFM defines the p_i as collectiveness descriptors [16,17]. The collectiveness property indicates the degree of individuals acting as a union in collective motion. It is a fundamental and universal measurement for various crowd systems. The m_i defines the quality of the surrounding population, in this model it represented by the crowd density of surrounding. Overall, the interaction force is defined as

$$F_{\text{int}} = density_i \frac{dv_i}{dt} - \frac{1}{\tau}((1 - collectiveness_i)(v_i^p - v_i)) \tag{4}$$

2.2   Estimation of Abnormal Map in Crowds

In this section, we describe the process of abnormal map estimation using st-SFM. It has been observed that when people are densely packed, individual movement is restricted and members of the crowd can be considered granular particles. Thus, in the process of estimating the interaction forces, we treat the crowd as a collection of interacting particles. Similar to [15], we put a grid of particles over the image frame and move them with the flow field computed from the optical flow. To analyze the scene, we treat moving particles as the main cue instead of tracking individual objects. As the outcome, the proposed method does not depend on tracking of objects; therefore, it is effective for the high density crowd scenes as well as low density scenes. Furthermore, the particle advection captures the continuity of the crowd flow which neither optical flow nor any instantaneous measure could capture.

Particle Advection. To advect particles, we compute the average optical flow field O_{ave}, which is the average of the optical flow over a fixed window of time and as well as space. The spatial average is done by a weighted average using a gaussian kernel. To start the particle advection process, we put a grid of N particles over the image and move the particles with the corresponding flow field they overlay. The effective velocity of particles is computed using a bilinear interpolation of the neighboring flow field vectors. In the particle advection phase, the resolution of particle grid is kept at 0.25 of the number of pixels in the flow field for computational simplicity. Using the described particle advection process, particles move with the average velocity of their neighborhood. This resembles the collective velocity of a group of people in the crowd.

Computing Abnormal Map. As a tangible analogy, the particles moving by optical flow resemble the motion of the leaves over a flow of water. This notion helps in understanding the modification of social force model for the particle grid. In the case of leaves, wherever there is an obstacle, joining, or branching of the fluid, the leaves have different velocities than the average flow. By analogy, we conclude that particles are also capable of revealing divergent flows in the regions that their desired movement is different from the average flow.

We modify Eq. 4 for particle advection by defining the actual velocity of the particle v_i as:

$$v_i = O_{ave}(x_i, y_i) \tag{5}$$

where $O_{ave}(x_i, y_i)$ is the effective spatio-temporal average of optical flow for the particle i and in the coordinate (x_i, y_i).

We write the desired velocity of the particle v_i^q as

$$v_i^q = (1 - p_i)O(x_i, y_i) + p_i O_{ave}(x_i, y_i) \tag{6}$$

where $O(x_i, y_i)$ is the optical flow of particle i in the coordinate (x_i, y_i). The effective average flow field and effective optical flow of particles are computed using linear interpolation.

Using the above modification, particles move with the collective velocity of the flow of the crowd. Furthermore, each particle has a desired velocity which depends on the current optical flow. Hence, any difference between the desired velocity of the particle and its actual velocity relates to interaction of the particle with the neighboring particles or the environment. Hence, we can simply estimate interaction force, F_{int}, from Eq. 4 for every particle as

$$F_{int} = \frac{1}{\tau}(v_i^q - v_i) - \frac{dv_i}{dt} \tag{7}$$

The computed interaction forces determine the synergy between advecting particles. However, discrete value of forces is not a clear evidence of abnormal behaviors. In other words, the instantaneous forces in a scene do not discriminate the abnormalities but the change of interaction forces over a period of time does. Therefore, we define the abnormal map as following:

$$AM = \begin{pmatrix} \frac{dF_{int1,1}}{dt}, & \frac{dF_{int1,2}}{dt}, & \cdots, & \frac{dF_{int1,n}}{dt} \\ \frac{dF_{int2,1}}{dt}, & \frac{dF_{int2,2}}{dt}, & \cdots, & \frac{dF_{int2,n}}{dt} \\ \cdots & & & \\ \frac{dF_{intn,1}}{dt}, & \frac{dF_{intn,2}}{dt}, & \cdots, & \frac{dF_{intn,n}}{dt} \end{pmatrix} \tag{8}$$

In this method, we map the change of the interaction force vectors to the image plane such that for every pixel in the frame there is a corresponding abnormal map.

Algorithm 1: Abnormal map estimation by st-SFM

Input: several frames

---

1. a grid of particles is placed over the image
2. calcuate average of optical flow O_{ave}3. compute p_i
4. compute F_{int} according to Eq.7
5. estimate the abnormal map according to Eq.8

Output: abnormal map of frames

---

3   Experiments and Discussion

In this section, we experimentally evaluate the performance of the proposed method for abnormal detection task in two varied datasets: publicly available dataset of normal and abnormal crowd videos from University of Minnesota (UMN) [18] and a challenging dataset of crowd videos taken from the railway stations.

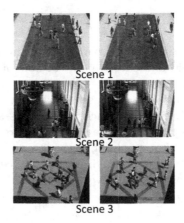

Scene 1

Scene 2

Scene 3

Fig. 2. Sample frames in three different scenes of the UMN dataset.

3.1   The UMN Dataset

We start our experiments with an in-depth analysis of our method on the UMN dataset. The dataset comprises the videos of 11 different scenarios of an escape event in 3 different indoor and outdoor scenes. Figure 2 shows sample frames of these scenes. Each video consists of an initial part of normal behavior and ends with sequences of the abnormal behavior.

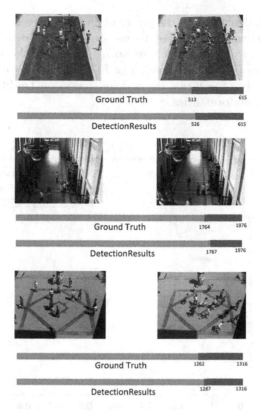

Fig. 3. The qualitative results of the abnormal behavior detection for four sample videos of UMN dataset. Each row represents the results for a video in the dataset. The ground truth bar and the detection bar represent the labels of each frame for that video. Green color represents the normal frames and red corresponds to abnormal frames. The left column shows the first frame of the video and the right column is the first frame of the detected abnormal block (Color figure online).

To evaluate the approach, 3 different video sequences of the UMN are selected. Figure 3 shows some of the qualitative results for detection of abnormal scenes. In each row, the figure depicts the first frame of the sequence on the left and a detected abnormal frame on the right. The first numbers on the horizontal bars identify the timing of the shown abnormal frames. Overall, these results show that estimated st-SFM is capable of detecting the governing dynamics of the abnormal behavior, even in the scenes that it is not trained. All videos in the dataset exhibit behavior of escape panic and the proposed approach successfully models the dynamics of the abnormal behavior regardless of the scene characteristics. Nevertheless, the detection time required by the method is shorter than that of the ground truth. The main reason is that the UMN dataset presents ground truth values for event detection, they seem to be marked a few frames early the event has occurred, as noticed in [14]. In addition, it needs some time to express the change of interaction force.

In addition, we demonstrate the power of the proposed st-SFM in capturing the abnormal behaviors in contrast to use of social force model. To compare these two models in a fair manner, we also implement the proposed method with the descriptors (i.e. optical flow). The ROC curves in Fig. 4 illustrate that the proposed model outperforms the method based on traditional social force model in detecting abnormalities.

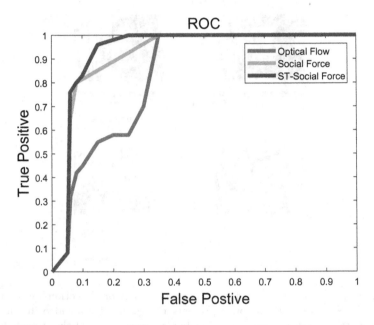

Fig. 4. The ROCs for detection of abnormal frames in the UMN dataset. Proposed method (blue) outperforms use of traditional social force model (green) (Color figure online).

3.2   The Railway Dataset

To evaluate our method in practical applications, we conduct an experiment on a challenging set of videos which has been collected from the railway stations. Detection abnormal in the railway station is of great importance to station management and public safety. Railway station situations involve several crowded scenarios. Abnormal events in the crowds may lead to a panic situation and possibly tragic consequences. Consequently, it is necessary to detect suspicious activities in a railway station scene. We mainly analyze the abnormal behavior of ticket entrance. The surveillance video is 96 min long. It shows normal events such as going through the auto-gate and entering the platform.

Figure 5 demonstrates the qualitative results of localization of abnormal behaviors in the railway station, where the abnormal individuals (walking in the wrong direction) are highlighted in a red box. The results show that st-SFM are capable of locating the abnormalities in the regions that are occupied by the crowd, while the computational cost is much lower.

Frame_1   Frame_2   Frame_3

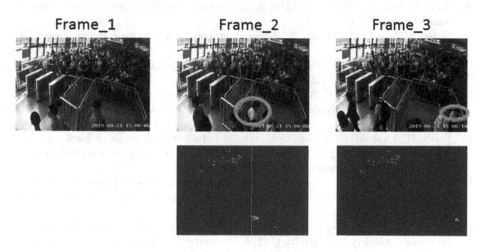

Fig. 5. Illustrates abnormal map for a sample of frames of a video stream. The abnormal location is the regions of high force flow.

4   Conclusion

We introduce the spatio-temporal Social Force Model to identify abnormal map in crowd scenes. It addresses the ability of the method to capture the dynamic of crowd behavior based on the interaction forces of individuals without the need to track objects individually or perform segmentation. The results of our method, indicate that the method is effective in detection and localization of abnormal behaviors in the crowd.

References

1. Shuai, Y., Li, H., Wang X.: Understanding pedestrian behaviors from stationary crowd groups. In: CVPR (2015)
2. Kratz, L., Nishino, K.: Anomaly detection in extremely crowded scenes using spatio-temporal motion pattern models. In: CVPR (2009)
3. Dupont, C., Tobias, L., Luvison, B.: Crowd-11: a dataset for fine grained crowd behaviour analysis. In: CVPR (2017)
4. Saligrama, V., Chen, Z.: Video anomaly detection based on local statistical aggregates. In: CVPR (2012)
5. Xian, S., Zhu, S., Wu S.: Weak supervised learning based abnormal behavior detection. In: ICPR (2018)

600   D. Chen et al.

6. Zhang, C., Li, H., Wang, X., Yang, X.: Cross-scene crowd counting via deep convolutional neural networks. In: CVPR (2015)
7. Zhang, Y., Zhou, D., Chen, S., Gao, S., Ma Y.: Single image crowd counting via multi-column convolutional neural network. In: CVPR (2016)
8. Idrees, H., Saleemi, I., Seibert, C., Shah M.: Multi-source multi-scale counting in extremely dense crowd images. In: CVPR (2013)
9. Jing, S., Kai, K., Chen, C.L.: Deeply learned attributes for crowded scene understanding. In: CVPR (2015)
10. Shao, J., Loy, C.C., Wang, X.: Scene-independent group profiling in crowd. In: CVPR (2014)
11. Mehran, R., Oyama, A., Shah, M.: Abnormal crowd behavior detection using social force model. In: CVPR (2009)
12. Luvison, B., Chateau, T., Sayd, P., Pham, Q.C., Laprest, J.: Automatic detection of unexpected events in dense areas for video surveillance applications. In: INTECH, vol. 2 (2011)
13. Fradi, H., Luvison, B., Pham, Q.C.: Crowd behavior analysis using local mid-level visual descriptors. In: TCSVT special issue on Group and Crowd Behavior Analysis for Intelligent Multi-camera Video Surveillance (2016)
14. Solmaz, B., Moore, B.E., Shah, M.: Identifying behaviors in crowd scenes using stability analysis for dynamical systems. IEEE Trans. Pattern Anal. Mach. Intell. 34(10), 2064–2070 (2012)
15. Ali, S., Shah, M.: A Lagrangian particle dynamics approach for crowd flow segmentation and stability analysis. In: CVPR, Computer Vision and Pattern Recognition (2007)
16. Zhou, B., Tang, X., Wang, X.: Measuring crowd collectiveness. In: CVPR (2013)
17. Zhou, B., Wang, X., Tang, X.: Understanding collective crowd behaviors: learning a mixture model of dynamic pedestrian-agents. In: CVPR (2012)
18. Unusual crowd activity dataset of University of Minnesota. http://mha.cs.umn.edu/movies/crowdactivity-all.avi

Robust Ellipse Fitting with an Auxiliary Normal

Zhaoxi Li[1], Cai Meng[1,2,3](✉), Dingzhe Li[1], and Limin Liu[4]

[1] Image Processing Center, Beijing University of Aeronautics and Astronautics,
Beijing 100191, China
{lizhaoxi,tsai,sy2015208}@buaa.edu.cn
[2] Beijing Advanced Innovation Center for Biomedical Engineering,
Beihang University, Beijing 100191, China
[3] Beijing Key Laboratory of Digital Media, Beihang University, Beijing, China
[4] School of Computer Science and Cyber Engineering, Guangzhou University,
Guangzhou 510000, China
2112006139@e.gzhu.edu.cn

Abstract. Ellipse fitting is a critical part of various applications. Recovering the ellipse from noisy or incomplete arcs remains challenging. In this paper, we propose an optimization method for ellipse fitting with an auxiliary normal to improve the performance. Firstly, ellipse fitting using an unerring normal is derived according to the projection from a circle in the world frame to an ellipse in the image frame. It can recover an accurate one directly from a short arc without iterative steps. Then, owing to the measurement error, an ellipse can be fitted iteratively within a tolerance range centered on the measured faulty normal. Finally, the calculation of requisite fitting matrices is simplified to speedup optimization. Each matrix can be constructed directly from a general 6-by-6 ellipse fitting matrix. Experimental results show that our method performs better than 4 state-of-the-art methods with limited tolerance.

Keywords: Ellipse fitting · Unerring normal · Faulty normal · Optimization speedup

1 Introduction

Ellipse fitting is a critical problem in computer vision. Especially, it plays an important role in ellipse detection [6,13,16]. The ellipse projected from a circle is widely used in various applications, such as UAV landing [2,11], satellite pose estimation [14], docking ring capture [24], and iris detection [15]. Owing to this projection, the closed-form solution of the normal and position of the circle can be derived by using the fitted ellipse [20]. Therefore, the ability to fit an accurate ellipse from noisy or incomplete arcs is vital to the mentioned applications. Various methods have been proposed to improve the fitting performance.

This work is supported by the National Natural Science Foundation of China under Grant 9174820.

The fitting accuracy is mainly influenced by measurement noise and elliptical incompleteness. The measurement noise originates in the pixels that cannot lie on an ellipse exactly due to the influence of light, blurring and limited resolution [15]. The incomplete ellipse indicates the scenarios that an ellipse is occluded by objects or limitation of field of camera view [24], so that partial pixels of an ellipse participate in the fitting process. Many researches have made brilliant work [1,5, 18], but the discrepancy still exists between the fitted and actual ellipses.

Note that the normal can be obtained in the specific circumstances. Dong et al. [4] use the robotic manipulator to catch cylindrical objects via tracking ellipses. As shown in Fig. 1, the planes of robot base and table are parallel, so the normals of cylindrical objects can be obtained using the robot joint angles. Furthermore, RGBD camera can be used to measure the object normal like the work [10] did. In fact, the tracking with predicted normal is more stable than that with predicted ellipse parameters. Collectively we propose an optimization method for ellipse fitting with an auxiliary normal of the circle in the camera frame to improve the fitting accuracy. Our method is robust and even can fit an accurate result from a quarter of the ellipse. The main contributions of our method are as follows:

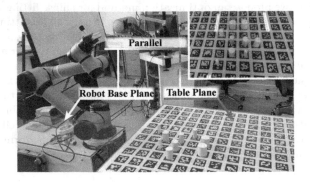

Fig. 1. An instance that the normal of cylindrical objects can be obtained by using six robot joint angles owing to the parallelism between the planes of robot base and table.

(1) The ellipse fitting method with an unerring normal is proposed. It has the ability of directly recovering an accurate ellipse from a short elliptical arc.
(2) The fitting method with a faulty normal can recover an ellipse with the minimum cost from a measured normal under a given deviation tolerance.
(3) The procedure of generating the fitting matrices with an auxiliary normal is simplified to be number-independent. Each matrix can be constructed directly from a general 6-by-6 ellipse fitting matrix instead of traversing each pixel.

The rest is organized as follows. Section 2 describes the ellipse fitting methods that use prior or non-prior knowledge. Section 3 describes our method of fitting ellipse with an unerring or faulty normal. Section 4 shows the experiments about the performance on data and tolerance analysis. Section 5 concludes our method.

2 Related Work

The common feature of ellipse fitting methods is to use a set of pixels to obtain an ellipse. From the point of whether to use prior knowledge or not, the methods are mainly divided into two categories: non-prior-knowledge (NPK) based and prior-knowledge (PK) based.

NPK based ellipse fitting is the most popular and widespread method. The methods through minimizing algebraic distance $\sum d^2(u, v; \boldsymbol{\alpha})$, where $d(u, v; \boldsymbol{\alpha}) = \alpha_1 u^2 + 2\alpha_2 uv + \alpha_3 v^2 + 2\alpha_4 u + 2\alpha_5 v + \alpha_6$ and $\boldsymbol{\alpha} = [\alpha_1, ..., \alpha_6]$, need a constraint to avoid the trivial solution. The optimal solution can be solved by considering generalized eigenvalue system [5]. Many constraints such as $||\boldsymbol{\alpha}||^2 = 1, \alpha_1 + \alpha_3 = 1, \alpha_6 = 1, \alpha_1^2 + \alpha_2^2 + \alpha_3^2 = 1$ have been proposed to improve fitting accuracy [3,7,19]. However, the estimated parameters may not satisfy $\alpha_2^2 - \alpha_1\alpha_3 < 0$ and is sensitive to noise so that they cannot result a valid ellipse. The elegant constraint $\alpha_1\alpha_3 - \alpha_2^2 = 1$ proposed by Fitzgibbon et al. [5] can ensure that the estimated parameters can form an ellipse, but the fitting ellipse is relatively flat. Halır and Flusser [8] pointed out that [5] cannot solve the problem of the singular fitting matrix. After that, two smaller interdependent matrices were used to solve this problem. Maini [12] enhanced the method of [5] by normalizing the points. Prasad et al. [18] analyzed the geometric distance and proposed the constraint $\alpha_3 = 1$ to fit ellipse. Meng et al. [13] gave a way to fit an ellipse with any constraint from a singular matrix through twice eigendecomposition. Szpak et al. [21] proposed a stable iterative method to fit a guaranteed ellipse using the Sampson distance. After that, Szpak et al. [22] further optimized the Sampson distance with the aid of a custom variant of the Levenberg–Marquardt method. Hu et al. [9] uses the maximum entropy criterion with the kernel function to formulate an optimization problem to fit ellipses.

PK based fitting methods fuse other information that can be obtained easily, such as image gradient or geometric constraints. Pătrăucean et al.[16] proved that the simultaneous usage of the positional and tangential information can improve the fitting precision. Fornaciari et al. [6] used three arcs in different quadrants to estimate ellipse center, then other parameters can be computed by two 1D accumulators. Arellano and Dahyot [1] proposed an innovative method based on the idea of point set registration to fit an ellipse, two density of parameterized ellipse and observations used the position and tangent of each pixels, than were modeled by Gaussian mixed model. Waibel et al. [23] used the constraint that the ellipse center is on a given line.

So far, none of existing fitting methods use the normal of the circle in the camera frame to fit an ellipse. Our proposed method belongs to the PK-based method. The used normal can be measured by the depth camera, robot joint angles or other sensors.

3   Methodology

3.1   Projection Formulation

In order to illustrate proposed method, it is necessary to give the transformation from the circle in the world frame $\{W\}$ to the ellipse in the image frame $\{I\}$.

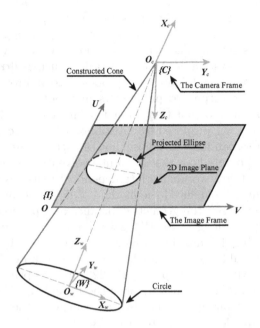

Fig. 2. Schematic representation of the circle projection from the world frame $\{W\}$ to the image frame $\{I\}$.

Figure 2 clearly shows the projection relationship between the ellipse in $\{I\}$ and the circle in $\{W\}$. The origin O_w locates at the circle center and the direction e_{wz} of Z_w axes is perpendicular to the plane of the circle. Therefore, the circle equation in $\{W\}$ is $x_w^2 + y_w^2 = r^2, z_w = 0$. Assuming that the coordinate of camera origin in $\{W\}$ is $\boldsymbol{O}_w = (x_o, y_o, z_o)$, a cone with the vertex $\boldsymbol{O}_w$ and passing through the circle can be constructed by Eq. 1, where $\tilde{\boldsymbol{p}}_w = (x_w, y_w, z_w, 1)^T$.

$$\tilde{\boldsymbol{p}}_w^T \begin{bmatrix} z_o^2 & 0 & -x_o z_o & 0 \\ 0 & z_o^2 & -y_o z_o & 0 \\ -x_o z_o & -y_o z_o & x_o^2 + y_o^2 - r^2 & r^2 z_o \\ 0 & 0 & r^2 z_o & -r^2 z_o^2 \end{bmatrix} \tilde{\boldsymbol{p}}_w = 0 \tag{1}$$

Let $\boldsymbol{R}_{wc}$ be a rotational matrix and $\boldsymbol{t}_{wc} = \boldsymbol{O}_w$ be a translation vector from $\{W\}$ to $\{C\}$. Then, Eq. 1 can be converted to $\boldsymbol{p}_c^T \cdot \boldsymbol{R}_{wc}^T \boldsymbol{U} \boldsymbol{R}_{wc} \cdot \boldsymbol{p}_c = 0$, where $\boldsymbol{p}_c = (x_c, y_c, z_c)$, $\boldsymbol{U}$ is defined as follows. Let $\tilde{\boldsymbol{p}}_I = (u, v, 1)$, then $z_c \boldsymbol{p}_I = \boldsymbol{K} \boldsymbol{p}_c$, $\boldsymbol{K}$

is the camera intrinsic matrix. Finally, Eq. 2 shows the ellipse quadratic equation in the image frame $\{I\}$.

$$\tilde{p}_I \cdot K^{-T} R_{wc}^T U R_{wc} K^{-1} \cdot \tilde{p}_I = 0, \; U = \begin{bmatrix} z_o^2 & 0 & -x_o z_o \\ 0 & z_o^2 & -y_o z_o \\ -x_o z_o & -y_o z_o & x_o^2 + y_o^2 - r^2 \end{bmatrix} \quad (2)$$

3.2 Fitting Ellipse with an Unerring Normal

In general, the ellipse is fitted only using a set of edge pixels. In our method, an additional known normal of the circle in $\{C\}$ will be provided for ellipse fitting.

Given the normal $v = (l, m, n)$ of the circle in $\{C\}$, it only can recover the yaw ψ and pitch θ but not the roll ϕ. Therefore, the rotational matrix from $\{C\}$ to $\{W\}$ can be represented by $R_{cw} = R^* \cdot R_Z$. R^* is a rotational matrix containing ψ, θ and an initial value ϕ^*. R_Z is the compensation matrix to ensure $\phi = \phi^* + \delta\phi$.

$$R^* = \begin{bmatrix} \dfrac{-m}{\sqrt{l^2 + m^2}} & \dfrac{-ln}{\sqrt{l^2 + m^2}} & l \\ \dfrac{l}{\sqrt{l^2 + m^2}} & \dfrac{-mn}{\sqrt{l^2 + m^2}} & m \\ 0 & \sqrt{l^2 + m^2} & n \end{bmatrix}, R_Z = \begin{bmatrix} cos\delta\phi & -sin\delta\phi & 0 \\ sin\delta\phi & cos\delta\phi & 0 \\ 0 & 0 & 1 \end{bmatrix} \quad (3)$$

Refer to Eq. 2, it is obvious to obtain $R_{wc} = R_{cw}^T = R_Z^T \cdot R^{*T}$. Let $U^* = R_Z U R_Z^T$. Equation 4 shows its formulation, where $u_1 = z_o^2$, $u_2 = -z_o(x_o cos\delta\phi + y_o sin\delta\phi)$, $u_3 = -z_o(y_o cos\delta\phi - x_o sin\delta\phi)$, $u_4 = x_o^2 + y_o^2 - r^2$.

$$U^* = R_Z^T U R_Z = \begin{bmatrix} u_1 & 0 & u_2 \\ 0 & u_1 & u_3 \\ u_2 & u_3 & u_4 \end{bmatrix} \quad (4)$$

Let $p = (x, y, z)^T = R^{*T} K^{-1} \cdot \tilde{p}_I$. Equation 2 can be simplified to $u_1(x^2 + y^2) + 2u_2 xz + 2u_3 yz + u_4 z^2 = 0$, only $u = [u_1, ..., u_4]$ are unknown parameters. In general, a set of edge pixels $\{(u_i, v_i)| i = 1, 2, ..., N\}$ is used to fit an ellipse. Each pixel (u_i, v_i) can be converted to $p_i = (x_i, y_i, z_i)$. Similar to [21], the fitting cost function is a variant of Sampson distance, and takes the form as follows.

$$E_v(u) = \sum_{k=1}^N \frac{u^T s_k u}{u^T \delta_k u} \approx \frac{\sum_{k=1}^N u^T s_k u}{\sum_{k=1}^N u^T \delta_k u} = \frac{u^T S u}{u^T \Delta u} \quad (5)$$

where $S = \sum s_k$, $s_k = a_k^T a_k$, $a_k = [x_i^2 + y_i^2, 2x_i z_i, 2y_i z_i, z_i^2]$, $\Delta = \sum \delta_k$, $\delta_k = \partial_p a_k^T \cdot \partial_p a_k$. Equation 6 shows the form of $\partial_p a_k$.

$$\partial_p a_k = \begin{bmatrix} 2x_k & 2z_k & 0 & 0 \\ 2y_k & 0 & 2z_k & 0 \\ 0 & 2x_k & 2y_k & 2z_k \end{bmatrix} \quad (6)$$

With above definitions in place, the fitting problem of minimizing Eq. 5 can be converted to solve $Su = \lambda \Delta u$ [5]. Both S and Δ are 4-by-4 symmetric matrices. Our previous work [13] has given a way to calculate unknown parameter u through twice eigendecomposition using Jacobi method. Then, the ellipse quadratic matrix can be obtained by combining Eq. 2, Eq. 3, Eq. 4 and fitted u. Algorithm 1 shows the process to get the fitted ellipse $\widetilde{E}$.

Algorithm 1: Fitting Ellipse with an Unerring Normal

Input: pixels $\{(u_i, v_i) | i = 1, ..., N\}$, a normal (l, m, n), the camera intrinsic K
Output: A fitted ellipse $\widetilde{E}$, fitted error ϵ

1 Construct the rotational matrix R^* by Eq. 3;
2 For each pixel, $(x_i, y_i, z_i)^T = R^{*T} K^{-1} [u_i, v_i, 1]^T$;
3 $S = \sum_{k=1}^{N} a_k^T a_k$, where $a_k = [x_i^2 + y_i^2, 2x_i z_i, 2y_i z_i, z_i^2]$;
4 $\Delta = \sum_{k=1}^{N} \partial_p a_k^T \cdot \partial_p a_k$, where $\partial_p a_k$ can be got by Eq. 6;
5 Get u, ϵ by solving $Su = \lambda \Delta u$ according to [13];
6 Get U^* by Eq. 4;
7 The ellipse quadratic matrix $E = K^{-T} R^* U^* R^{*T} K^{-1}$;
8 Obtain $\widetilde{E}$ by converting E to shape parameters;
9 Return the fitted ellipse $\widetilde{E}$ and fitted error ϵ;

3.3   Fitting Ellipse with a Faulty Normal

In practice, the normal can be measured by attitude sensors, robotic joint angles, or RGB-D cameras. Owing to the measurement error, the ellipse fitting by Algorithm 1 is not perfect. Therefore, it is necessary to optimize the fitting process by adjusting the faulty normal.

As shown in Fig. 3, e_l is the unerring normal of the circle and e_{l*} is the measured normal. Let $\delta_l = \theta_{<e_l, e_{l*}>}$ represent the normal difference and δ_{max} be the angle tolerance, i.e. $\delta_l < \delta_{max}$. Therefore, R_{cw} can be redefined as $R_{cw} = R^* \cdot R_e R_Z$, R_e is constructed by two variables $\eta \in [-\pi, \pi], \xi \in [0, \delta_{max}]$, its formulation is defined as follows.

$$R_e = \begin{bmatrix} -sin\eta & -cos\eta cos\xi & cos\eta sin\xi \\ cos\eta & -sin\eta cos\xi & sin\eta sin\xi \\ 0 & sin\xi & cos\xi \end{bmatrix} \tag{7}$$

Therefore, the optimization for ellipse fitting with a faulty normal can be converted to minimize the cost function $E(\eta, \xi)$ shown in Eq. 8. Note that $S_{\eta,\xi}, \Delta_{\eta,\xi}$ have the same definitions as S, Δ in Sect. 3.2 and are influenced by η, ξ in there.

$$(\eta^*, \xi^*) = \arg\min_{\eta_i, \xi_j} E(\eta, \xi) = \arg\min_{\eta_i, \xi_j} ln \left(\min_u \frac{u^T S_{\eta,\xi} u}{u^T \Delta_{\eta,\xi} u} + 1 \right) \tag{8}$$

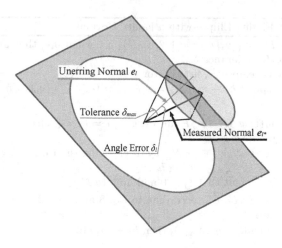

Fig. 3. The illustration of a tolerance range centered on the measured normal e_{l^*}.

A simple spatial partition based iterative method is designed to minimize the cost function $E(\eta, \xi)$. Firstly, let $E(0,0)$ be the basic cost $\hat{\epsilon}$ and $\hat{\eta} = \hat{\xi} = 0$. Then, in each iteration, the range $[\eta_{min}, \eta_{max}], [\xi_{min}, \xi_{max}]$ are discretized by search step h_η, h_ξ separately, i.e. $\eta_i = \eta_{min} + ih_\eta, \xi_j = \xi_{min} + jh_\xi, i = 0, 1, ..., N_\eta, j = 0, 1, ..., N_\xi, N_\eta = (\eta_{max} - \eta_{min})/h_\eta, N_\xi = (\xi_{max} - \xi_{min})/h_\xi$. Let ϵ^* denote the minimum cost $E(\eta^*, \xi^*)$ in these discrete data. There are two cases between $\hat{\epsilon}$ and ϵ^* that need to be discussed separately.

Case $\hat{\epsilon} < \epsilon^*$: This case only takes place when $\xi_{min} = h_\xi, \hat{\xi} = 0$, it means that h_ξ needs to be smaller. Then, the procedure sets $\xi_{min} \to 0, \xi_{min} \to h_\xi, h_\xi/10 \to h_\xi$, and continues a new iteration.

Case $\hat{\epsilon} \geqslant \epsilon^*$: it means that h_ξ, h_η can be set smaller to get more accurate results. Then, the procedure builds the new interval with η^*, ξ^* as basic center and $2h_\eta, 2h_\xi$ as its length separately. After that, the procedure set $\eta^* \to \hat{\eta}, \xi^* \to \hat{\xi}, h_\xi/10 \to h_\xi, h_\xi \to h_\eta$ and continues a new iteration.

Finally, the iterative process will be terminated if $h_\xi < 0.01°$. Algorithm 2 gives the details of overall optimization procedure.

3.4   Optimization Speedup for Fitting Ellipse

Almost all of the general ellipse fitting methods based on direct least square need to use the pixels [18] or cumulative matrices [13] to calculate a 6-by-6 fitting matrix $S_{\tilde{E}}$. However, it is time-consuming to calculate the matrices $S_{\eta,\xi}, \Delta_{\eta,\xi}$ using Eq. 5. Our method proposes a way to speedup the procedure of obtaining $S_{\eta,\xi}, \Delta_{\eta,\xi}$ only using $S_{\tilde{E}}$.

Let $Q_{\eta,\xi} = R_e^T R^{*T} K^{-1}$, q_{ij} is employed to represent the element of Q. R^* and R_e have the same definitions in Sect. 3.3. $S_{\eta,\xi}$ can be derived that $S_{\eta,\xi} = M_S^T S_{\tilde{E}} M_S$, where M_S is a 6-by-4 matrix shown as follows.

Algorithm 2: Fitting Ellipse with a Faulty Normal

Input: Pixels $P_I = \{(u_i, v_i) | i = 1, 2, ..., N\}$, a normal e_{l*}, the camera intrinsic matrix K, tolerance δ_{max}

Output: A fitted ellipse $\widetilde{E}$, fitted error ϵ

1 $h_\eta = h_\xi = 1°; \eta_{min} = h_\eta - \pi, \eta_{max} = \pi, \xi_{min} = 0, \xi_{max} = \delta_{max}; \hat{\eta} = \hat{\xi} = 0, \hat{\epsilon} = E(\hat{\eta}, \hat{\xi});$

2 Get $\widetilde{E}, \tilde{\epsilon}$ by inputting P_I, e_{l*}, K into Alg. 1, $\hat{\epsilon} = ln(\tilde{\epsilon} + 1);$

3 **while** $h_\xi \geqslant 0.01°$ **do**

4   Get $\eta_i, \xi_j, i \in [0, N_\eta], j \in [0, N_\xi]$ by discretizing the ranges $[\eta_{min}, \eta_{max}], [\xi_{min}, \xi_{max}]$ using $h_\eta, h_\xi;$

5   Remove the element that $\xi_j = 0$ and update $N_\xi;$

6   Find best $(\eta^*, \xi^*, \epsilon^*, \widetilde{E}^*)$ according to Eq. 8 and step 2;

7   **if** $\hat{\epsilon} < \epsilon^*$ **then**

8          $\xi_{max} = min(\hat{\xi} + h_\xi, \delta_{max})$, then $h_\xi \leftarrow h_\xi/10;$

9   **else**

10         $\hat{\eta} = \eta^*, \hat{\xi} = \xi^*$, than $\eta_{min} = \hat{\eta} - h_\eta, \eta_{max} = \hat{\eta} + h_\eta;$

11         $\xi_{min} = max(0, \hat{\xi} - h_\xi), \xi_{max} = min(\hat{\xi} + h_\xi, \delta_{max});$

12         $h_\eta = h_\xi \leftarrow h_\xi/10, \hat{\epsilon} = \epsilon^*, \widetilde{E} = \widetilde{E}^*;$

13 Return the fitted ellipse $\widetilde{E}$ and fitted error $\epsilon = \hat{\epsilon};$

$$M_S = \begin{bmatrix} q_{11}^2 + q_{21}^2 & 2q_{11}q_{31} & 2q_{21}q_{31} & q_{31}^2 \\ q_{11}q_{12} + q_{21}q_{22} & q_{11}q_{32} + q_{12}q_{31} & q_{21}q_{32} + q_{22}q_{31} & q_{31}q_{32} \\ q_{12}^2 + q_{22}^2 & 2q_{12}q_{32} & 2q_{22}q_{32} & q_{32}^2 \\ q_{11}q_{13} + q_{21}q_{23} & q_{11}q_{33} + q_{13}q_{31} & q_{21}q_{33} + q_{23}q_{31} & q_{31}q_{33} \\ q_{12}q_{13} + q_{22}q_{23} & q_{12}q_{33} + q_{13}q_{32} & q_{22}q_{33} + q_{23}q_{32} & q_{32}q_{33} \\ q_{13}^2 + q_{23}^2 & 2q_{13}q_{33} & 2q_{23}q_{33} & q_{33}^2 \end{bmatrix} \tag{9}$$

For $\Delta_{\eta,\xi}$, Let $L_\Delta = M_\Delta^T S_{\widetilde{E}} M_\Delta$. Equation 10 shows the definitions of $M_\Delta, \Delta_{\eta,\xi}$. Then, $\Delta_{\eta,\xi}$ can be obtained by selecting the elements from L_Δ, where l_{ij} denotes each element of L_Δ.

$$M_\Delta = \begin{bmatrix} 0_{3\times3} & Q_{\eta,\xi} \cdot \begin{bmatrix} 1 \\ 1 \\ 2 \end{bmatrix} \end{bmatrix}^T, \Delta_{\eta,\xi} = \begin{bmatrix} l_{11} + l_{22} & l_{13} & l_{23} & 0 \\ l_{31} & l_{11} + l_{33} & l_{12} & l_{13} \\ l_{32} & l_{21} & l_{22} + l_{33} & l_{23} \\ 0 & l_{31} & l_{32} & l_{33} \end{bmatrix} \tag{10}$$

4 Experiments

To verify the stability and accuracy of our method, we compare it with other state-of-the-art methods on synthetic data. Besides, we give the sensitivity analysis of measured error tolerance.

4.1   Data and Evaluation Criterion

The synthetic data contains a set of arcs extracted from the images with occluded ellipses generated by Prasad et al. [17], the major and minor axises of each ellipse are both in $\left[10, 300\sqrt{2}\right]$. The resolution of all images is (300,300). According to [20], the first solution of each ellipse is taken as the unerring normal. The synthetic intrinsic matrix contain focus length 10, and principal point (150,150).

All arcs are divided into 12 groups according to the angle subtended by the ends of an arc, the angle of each arc in i_{th} group is in $30° \cdot (i-1, i]$. The score $S_i = \frac{1}{N_i} \sum_{k=1}^{N_i} IoU(\hat{E}_{i,k}, E_{i,k}^*)$, where $\hat{E}_{i,k}, E_{i,k}^*$ are the truth and fitted ellipses of k_{th} arc in i_{th} group, the intersection over union (IoU) represents the similarity of a pair ellipses, N_i is the total number of i_{th} group.

4.2   Comparison on Synthetic Data

We analyze our method from three aspects about fitting precision, tolerance δ_{max} sensitivity and speedup performance.

Table 1. The fitting performance comparison in groups with twelve kings of angle spans. Besides, we report performance for different angle tolerances $\delta_{max} = 0°, 0.5°, 1°$.

Group	Fitzgibbon [5]	Ellifit [18]	Szpak [21]	Szpak [22]	Ours $\delta_{max} = 1°$	Ours $\delta_{max} = 0.5°$	Ours $\delta_{max} = 0°$
0–30	0.40	0.17	2.05	0.46	**21.07**	**22.88**	**23.74**
30–60	3.87	2.88	21.99	5.81	**55.34**	**62.20**	**65.95**
60–90	16.39	13.77	43.61	19.57	**67.04**	**76.27**	**85.74**
90–120	42.27	37.40	59.20	46.97	**74.91**	**81.62**	**92.12**
120–150	79.64	72.77	78.18	77.00	**84.46**	**88.39**	**96.25**
150–180	95.20	93.22	92.70	92.67	92.69	**94.81**	**98.42**
180–210	97.79	97.56	97.39	97.39	96.10	97.53	**99.02**
210–240	98.30	98.23	98.12	98.12	97.25	98.23	**99.02**
240–270	98.80	98.73	98.75	98.75	98.13	98.74	**99.20**
270–300	99.12	99.10	99.14	99.14	98.77	99.10	**99.34**
300–330	99.35	99.34	99.38	99.38	99.17	99.33	**99.49**
330–360	99.46	99.46	99.51	99.51	99.42	99.45	**99.56**

The fitting precision of our method is compared with other state-of-the-art methods. The methods of Fitzgibbon [5], Ellifit [18], and Szpak [21,22] are selected for comparison. The source code of these methods are available on-line. In order to verify the effectiveness of fitting ellipse with the unerring and faulty normals, our method is evaluated with three tolerances $\delta_{max} = 0°, 0.5°, 1°$ on 12 groups. For each tolerance $\delta_{max} > 0$, six faulty normals are generated by noising the unerring normal with six error matrices R_e mentioned in Sect. 3.3, these matrices are set to $\eta = 0°, 60°, 120°, 180°, 240°, 300°, \xi = \delta_{max} - 0.5°$. Table 1 gives the detail comparison of these methods. The examples of fitting results on

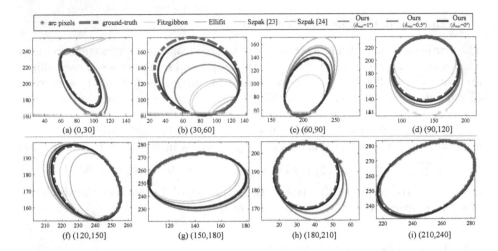

Fig. 4. Performance comparison of our method and other methods on the first 8 groups.

the first 8 groups are shown in Fig. 4. Our method has the best performance on all groups when uses an unerring normal as input, i.e. $\delta_{max} = 0°$. For ellipse fitting with a faulty normal, the precision of our method is slightly lower than that of Fitzgibbon on the arcs whose subtended angles are in $(150°, 360°]$, but is significantly higher than that of other methods on the arcs whose subtended angles are in $(0°, 150°]$.

To analyze the influence of different tolerance δ_{max} on fitting performance, the degree values at $0, 0.5, 1, 2, 3, 6, 9$ are used to get precisions on 12 groups separately. As shown in Fig. 5, an auxiliary normal obviously improves the fitting precision. An unerring normal $\delta_{max} = 0$ can reveal the best performance, then, the precision decreases gradually with the increase of δ_{max}. When $\delta_{max} > 6°$, the normal has no effect on precision improvement. Overall, we suggest $\delta_{max} \in (0, 3°)$ to get better fitting performance.

4.3   Discussion

Our method uses an auxiliary normal to enhance the ellipse fitting performance. It can obtain a more accurate ellipse from short arcs and perform best when the normal is unerring. However, there are limitations for our method:

(1) Our method is sensitive to the normal tolerance δ_{max}, and can only achieve the best performance with an accurately measured normal.
(2) For the faulty normal, our method is iterative. Therefore, it is better to refine ellipses in a region of interest to achieve real-time requirements.

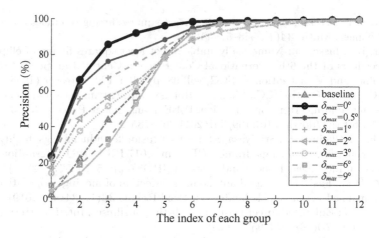

Fig. 5. The influence of different tolerance δ_{max} on fitting performance.

5   Conclusion

In this paper, we propose an optimization method for ellipse fitting with an auxiliary normal to improve the precision. The ellipse fitting with an unerring normal is fast and has best performance on synthetic arcs with various subtended angles. For the faulty normal, our method uses an iterative process to recover an ellipse by minimizing the cost function. The high parallelism of our method can reduce the time consumption. The fitting matrices fusing the normal can be computed directly from a general 6-by-6 ellipse fitting matrix. Experiments on synthetic data have validated our innovative improvements, our method performs better than other methods with limited tolerance. Meanwhile, our method has a good potentiality to be used in industrial applications, such as object catching, docking ring capture in close distance and stable ellipse tracking.

References

1. Arellano, C., Dahyot, R.: Robust ellipse detection with gaussian mixture models. Pattern Recogn. **58**, 12–26 (2016)
2. Benini, A., Rutherford, M.J., Valavanis, K.P.: Real-time, GPU-based pose estimation of a UAV for autonomous takeoff and landing. In: 2016 IEEE International Conference on Robotics and Automation (ICRA), pp. 3463–3470 (2016)
3. Bookstein, F.L.: Fitting conic sections to scattered data. Comput. Graphics Image Process. **9**(1), 56–71 (1979)
4. Dong, H., Asadi, E., Sun, G., Prasad, D.K., Chen, I.: Real-time robotic manipulation of cylindrical objects in dynamic scenarios through elliptic shape primitives. IEEE Trans. Rob. **35**(1), 95–113 (2019)
5. Fitzgibbon, A., Pilu, M., Fisher, R.B.: Direct least square fitting of ellipses. IEEE Trans. Pattern Anal. Mach. Intell. **21**, 476–480 (1999). https://doi.org/10.1109/34.765658
6. Fornaciari, M., Prati, A., Cucchiara, R.: A fast and effective ellipse detector for embedded vision applications. Pattern Recogn. **47**(11), 3693–3708 (2014)

7. Gander, W., Golub, G.H., Strebel, R.: Least-squares fitting of circles and ellipses. BIT Numer. Math. **34**(4), 558–578 (1994)
8. Halır, R., Flusser, J.: Numerically stable direct least squares fitting of ellipses. In: Proceedings of the 6th International Conference in Central Europe on Computer Graphics and Visualization. WSCG, vol. 98, pp. 125–132. Citeseer (1998)
9. Hu, C., Wang, G., Ho, K.C., Liang, J.: Robust ellipse fitting with Laplacian kernel based maximum correntropy criterion. IEEE Trans. Image Process. **30**, 3127–3141 (2021). https://doi.org/10.1109/TIP.2021.3058785
10. Jin, P., Matikainen, P., Srinivasa, S.S.: Sensor fusion for fiducial tags: highly robust pose estimation from single frame RGBD. In: 2017 IEEE/RSJ International Conference on Intelligent Robots and Systems (IROS), pp. 5770–5776 (2017)
11. Li, Z., et al.: Fast vision-based autonomous detection of moving cooperative target for unmanned aerial vehicle landing. J. Field Robot. **36**(1), 34–48 (2019)
12. Maini, E.S.: Enhanced direct least square fitting of ellipses. Int. J. Pattern Recogn. Artif. Intell. **20**(06), 939–953 (2006)
13. Meng, C., Li, Z., Bai, X., Zhou, F.: Arc adjacency matrix-based fast ellipse detection. IEEE Trans. Image Process. **29**, 4406–4420 (2020)
14. Meng, C., Li, Z., Sun, H., Yuan, D., Bai, X., Zhou, F.: Satellite pose estimation via single perspective circle and line. IEEE Trans. Aerosp. Electron. Syst. **54**(6), 3084–3095 (2018)
15. Mulleti, S., Seelamantula, C.S.: Ellipse fitting using the finite rate of innovation sampling principle. IEEE Trans. Image Process. **25**(3), 1451–1464 (2016). https://doi.org/10.1109/TIP.2015.2511580
16. Pătrăucean, V., Gurdjos, P., von Gioi, R.G.: A parameterless line segment and elliptical arc detector with enhanced ellipse fitting. In: Fitzgibbon, A., Lazebnik, S., Perona, P., Sato, Y., Schmid, C. (eds.) ECCV 2012. LNCS, vol. 7573, pp. 572–585. Springer, Heidelberg (2012). https://doi.org/10.1007/978-3-642-33709-3_41
17. Prasad, D.K., Leung, M.K.H., Cho, S.Y.: Edge curvature and convexity based ellipse detection method. Pattern Recogn. **45**(9), 3204–3221 (2012)
18. Prasad, D.K., Leung, M.K., Quek, C.: ElliFit: an unconstrained, non-iterative, least squares based geometric ellipse fitting method. Pattern Recogn. **46**(5), 1449–1465 (2013). https://doi.org/10.1016/j.patcog.2012.11.007
19. Rosin, P.L.: A note on the least squares fitting of ellipses. Pattern Recogn. Lett. **14**(10), 799–808 (1993)
20. Safaee-Rad, R., Tchoukanov, I., Smith, K.C., Benhabib, B.: Three-dimensional location estimation of circular features for machine vision. IEEE Trans. Robot. Autom. **8**(5), 624–640 (1992)
21. Szpak, Z.L., Chojnacki, W., van den Hengel, A.: Guaranteed ellipse fitting with the Sampson distance. In: Fitzgibbon, A., Lazebnik, S., Perona, P., Sato, Y., Schmid, C. (eds.) ECCV 2012. LNCS, vol. 7576, pp. 87–100. Springer, Heidelberg (2012). https://doi.org/10.1007/978-3-642-33715-4_7
22. Szpak, Z.L., Chojnacki, W., Hengel, A.V.D.: Guaranteed ellipse fitting with a confidence region and an uncertainty measure for centre, axes, and orientation. J. Math. Imaging Vis. **52**(2), 173–199 (2015)
23. Waibel, P., Matthes, J., Gröll, L.: Constrained ellipse fitting with center on a line. J. Math. Imaging Vis. **53**(3), 364–382 (2015)
24. Yang, J., Gao, X., Li, Z., Li, S., Liang, B.: Pose measurement for capture of large satellite docking ring based on double-line structured light vision. In: Proceedings of the 2017 2nd International Conference on Materials Science, Machinery and Energy Engineering (MSMEE 2017), pp. 1336–1345. Atlantis Press, May 2017

A Fast Implementation of Image Rotation with Bresenham's Line-Scanning Algorithm

Minna Xu, Yinwei Zhan$^{(\boxtimes)}$, and Yaodong Li

School of Computer Science and Technology, Guangdong University of Technology,
100 Waihuanxi Road, Higher Education Megacenter, Guangzhou 510006, China
ywzhan@gdut.edu.cn

Abstract. Image rotation is a fundamental task in image processing. It has two primary stages: rasterization of the rotated domain and evaluation of these pixel values. This paper mainly proposes a novel strategy for the first stage with Bresenham's line description, and further a natural way for the second stage. Two neighbouring sides of the boundary of the rotated image are expressed by a variation of Bresenham scanning lines, one taken as the supporting side and the other as the moving side. Then the rotated region can be expressed as stacking the copies of the moving side along the supporting side. We re-implement Bresenham's line algorithm in such a scheme that a line is expressed as successive runs of line segments, so as to rapidly realize the rasterization of the defined domain of the rotated image. At the same time, an incremental method is used to assign values to the pixels. Our method avoids lots of computation that must be conducted in previous works for determining whether a point is in the rotated domain and therefore, according to experiments, significantly decreases running time of image rotation.

Keywords: Image rotation · Bresenham's line algorithm · Image rasterization

1 Introduction

As a fundamental task in image processing, image rotation [1] is widely used in animation, geometric correction, image editing, and image understanding [2]. While image rotation seems easy as intuitively a geometric transformation, endeavors on developing better algorithms realizing image rotation has never been ended. One of the most important reasons is the pursuit of algorithm speed [3–7].

Normally, an image rotation transformation is realized via two basic operation steps. The first step is to determine the coordinate position of the rotated image's pixels and the second step is to calculate the pixel values of the rotated image via the original image. But the fact that an digital image is defined on discrete

Supported by Science and Technology Planning Projects of Guangdong Province, China, with grant numbers 2019B010150002 and 2020B0101130019.

grids makes image rotation complicated. During the process of rotation transformation, due to floating point operations and rounding operations, the transformation does not keep one-one correspondence, which implies that repeated operations may happen or holes may be generated where there are no corresponding pixels [3].

The holes happen when the transformation is conducted forward by sending pixels from the source image to the target. Instead, backward approaches by getting pixels from the source image to the target are preferred in order to avoid the holes. But one pixel in the source may be sent to two pixels in the target.

The existing algorithms for the first step of image rotation have their own advantages and disadvantages. For example, the advantage of the direct method [4] lies in its high accuracy. The obvious shortcoming is that it needs to continuously perform backward mapping and interpolation, which has a large computational complexity and an increase in processing time. Three-step method [5] successfully removes the holes, but usually involves the transformation of multiple pixel points, which is slower than the general method, so it is not suitable for processing images with large resolutions.

The increment-based image rotation method in [8] uses the idea of incremental positioning to calculate the position of the reverse mapping points, which reduces a large number of float point operations with rounding during the rotation process, and improves the speed of image rotation.

However, in the work [8] there are still some none integer operations including multiplication operations, rounding operations in line, and floating-point additions, which still cost much in running time. This means that the work in [8] didn't fully draw on Bresenham's ideas.

In this paper, we propose a fast implementation of image rotation with Bresenham's algorithm [9–11], which can rapidly rasterize the defined domain of the rotated image, and is convenient to deal with the holes. We provide a formula for counting the number of holes. It can also avoid the phenomenon that the cumulative and rounding errors caused by the general methods lead to the boundary being not strictly rectangle.

2   Related Works

2.1   Rotation

Throughout the whole context, to simplify disussion, we are mainly concerned with gray-scale images that are regarded as scalar-valued functions, for a color image can be treated as multiple gray-scale images.

Given an image

$$I : D = [0, w] \times [0, h] \to \mathbb{R}$$

of width w and height h, our objective is to investigate the rotation of I at an angle of α degree, counterclockwise. Here the rotation center is assumed to be the lower left corner $(0, 0)$ and $0 \leq \alpha \leq 45$, without loss of generality. Let $\theta = \alpha\pi/180$. Then the rotation matrix is

$$M = \begin{pmatrix} \cos\theta & -\sin\theta \\ \sin\theta & \cos\theta \end{pmatrix} \tag{1}$$

and its inverse is

$$M^{\mathrm{T}} = \begin{pmatrix} \cos\theta & \sin\theta \\ -\sin\theta & \cos\theta \end{pmatrix} \tag{2}$$

where the superscript T indicates the transpose of a matrix.

In the continuous world, the rotation of I is simply expressed as

$$I' : D' \to \mathbb{R} \tag{3}$$

where $D' = MD = \{Mx; x \in D\}$ and $I'(y) = I(M^{\mathrm{T}}y)$, for $y \in D'$.

But in the discrete world, it becomes much complicated. In the discrete situation, the domains D and D' are rasterized, approximated by grids of pixels. Assume D is rasterized as

$$G = \{0, 1, \cdots, w-1\} \times \{0, 1, \cdots h-1\} \subset \mathbb{Z}^2. \tag{4}$$

The corners of G are respectively the bottom-left $P_{\mathrm{BL}} = (0,0)^{\mathrm{T}}$, the bottom-right $P_{\mathrm{BR}} = (0, w-1)^{\mathrm{T}}$, the top-left $P_{\mathrm{TL}} = (0, h-1)^{\mathrm{T}}$, and the top-right $P_{\mathrm{TR}} = (w-1, h-1)^{\mathrm{T}}$.

After rotation, they become the corners of the rasterization G' of D', i.e.

$$\begin{aligned}
Q_{\mathrm{BL}} &= MP_{\mathrm{BL}} = (x_{\mathrm{BL}}, y_{\mathrm{BL}})^{\mathrm{T}}, \\
Q_{\mathrm{BR}} &= MP_{\mathrm{BR}} = (x_{\mathrm{BR}}, y_{\mathrm{BR}})^{\mathrm{T}}, \\
Q_{\mathrm{TL}} &= MP_{\mathrm{TL}} = (x_{\mathrm{TL}}, y_{\mathrm{BR}})^{\mathrm{T}}, \\
Q_{\mathrm{TR}} &= MP_{\mathrm{TR}} = (x_{\mathrm{TR}}, y_{\mathrm{TR}})^{\mathrm{T}}.
\end{aligned} \tag{5}$$

The objective is then to assign each pixel within G' a suitable value provided by the source image I. A diagram of rasterization and rotation of image domains is illustrated in Fig. 1.

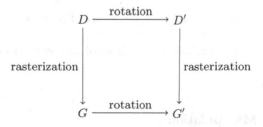

Fig. 1. A diagram of rasterization and rotation of image domains.

In practice, an image is normally held in a two-dimensional array that corresponds to a matrix. Let $X \subset \mathbb{Z}^2$ be the bounding box of G' of height h_X and width w_X determined by

$$\begin{aligned}
h_X &= y_{\mathrm{TL}} + y_{\mathrm{BR}} + 1, \\
w_X &= x_{\mathrm{BR}} - x_{\mathrm{TL}} + 1.
\end{aligned} \tag{6}$$

Therefore the image rotation problem is then to design an algorithm that realizes the rotated image $I'(y|I, \theta)$ as

$$J(y) = \begin{cases} I'(y|I, \theta), & y \in G' \\ c, & y \in B \setminus G' \end{cases} \tag{7}$$

where c is a constant for the background gray level of J, $c = 255$ in our context.

To accomplish this, in general it needs two steps: to determine the pixels occupying G' as the best approximation of D' and to calculate their values corresponding to $I : G \to \mathbb{R}$. According to Eq. (3), to implement image rotation, there are mainly two ways, forward manipulation or backward manipulation.

2.2   Forward Manipulation

As for forward manipulation, it means that, for any pixel p in G there corresponds a pixel round(Mp) in G'. But due to the rounding operation, there exist missing pixels (the so-called *holes*) in the target region G' which have no correspondence in G. See Fig. 2(a). So forward manipulation is not feasible.

(a) Forward manipulation   (b) Backward manipulation

Fig. 2. An illustration of rotations with forward and backward manipulations.

2.3   Backward Manipulation

While a forward manipulation conducts *sending* operations from G to G', a backward manipulation, for any pixel q in G', *fetches* its corresponding pixel $M^T q$ in G (followed by rounding operation), and hence avoids holes.

Backward manipulation has been a main thread in image rotation. Many works in literature contributed to faster implementation of backward mapping [3–6] and better evaluation of pixels by interpolation of neighbouring pixels [12–15].

Algorithm 1: Algorithm in [8]

Input: Image I of height h and width w; Angle θ
Output: Image J: rotation of I in θ

1 Initialization:;
2    $d_c = \cos(\theta), d_s = \sin(\theta)$;
3   Initialize the target image J of height h_X and width w_X with pixel values 255:
4    $e_x = 0$, $e_y = 0$;
5 **for** $j \leftarrow 0$ **to** $h_X - 1$ **do**
6    $\quad$ $x \leftarrow jd_s$, $y \leftarrow jd_c$;
7    $\quad$ $m = (\text{int})x$, $n = (\text{int})y$;
8    $\quad$ $e_x = x - m$, $e_y = y - n$;
9    $\quad$ **for** $i \leftarrow 0$ **to** $w_X - 1$ **do**
10   $\quad\quad$ $x_I = m, y_I = n$;
11   $\quad\quad$ **if** $e_x > 0.5$ **then**
12   $\quad\quad$ $\mid$ $m \leftarrow m + 1; e_x \leftarrow e_x - 1$;
13   $\quad\quad$ **end**
14   $\quad\quad$ **if** $e_y < -0.5$ **then**
15   $\quad\quad$ $\mid$ $n \leftarrow n - 1; e_y \leftarrow e_y + 1$;
16   $\quad\quad$ **end**
17   $\quad\quad$ $e_x \leftarrow e_x + d_c$, $e_y \leftarrow e_x - d_s$;
18   $\quad\quad$ **if** $x_I < 0$ *or* $x_I > w - 1$ *or* $y_I < 0$ *or* $y_I > h - 1$ **then**
19   $\quad\quad$ $\mid$ continue;
20   $\quad\quad$ **else**
21   $\quad\quad$ $\mid$ $J(i, j) = I(x_I, y_I)$
22   $\quad\quad$ **end**
23   $\quad$ **end**
24 **end**

2.4   Pro and Cons of a Fast Implementation

Among so many works, the one presented by Shi, S., et al. [8] is one of the most attractive implementation. The key idea in [8] is to replace multiplications with incremental additions in calculating the target pixel positions. Their approach is much faster than its previous methods.

A variation of the algorithm in [8] is shown in Algorithm 1. Here, the rotation center is set to be the left corner of the input I. We do not consider any interpolation for pixel evaluation of the output image, for the key point is at the efficiency of pixel location.

In their work [8], the authors claimed that their idea was inspired by Bresenham's line scanning algorithm.

As we all know, the Bresenham's algorithm only uses integer addition instead of multiplication and floating-point operation to achieve the optimal discretization of line segments.

Notice that in Algorithm 1, there are still some none-integer operations: multiplication operations in line 6, rounding operations in line 7 and floating-point additions in line 17.

This means that the work in [8] didn't fully draw on Bresenham's ideas.

3   A Discrete Coverage of Rotated Rectangle

In this section, we will propose a new way to discretize the rotated rectangles by taking advantage of Bresenham's line scan algorithm [9], which can result in significant savings in time cost.

3.1   Runlength Coder of Bresenham Line Scanning

Consider a coordinate system xOy with a line segment on it of end points $A(x_A, y_A)$ and $B(x_B, y_B)$ of integer coordinates. Denote $dx = x_B - x_A$ and $dy = y_B - y_A$. Suppose $x_A = 0$ and $y_A = 0$; otherwise, point A can be moved to the origin $(0, 0)$ with a translate. The rasterization of AB is then to find point sequence $(x_0, y_0) = (x_A, y_A), (x_1, y_1), \cdots, (x_n, y_n) = (x_B, y_B)$ of integer coordinates to best approximate the (theoretical) line segment AB.

Let the coordinate system xOy be split into 8 octants, each covering a conic region of $45°$, numbered successively as $\gamma = 0, 1 \cdots, 7$, starting from the positive direction of axis x counterclockwise.

Assume, without loss of generality, $x_A < x_B$, $y_A < y_B$, and the slope of AB is $0 \leq k \leq 1$. With a point on AB runs from A to B, its abscissa x_i goes from x_0 rightward to x_n with stepsize 1, and its ordinate y_i goes from y_0 upward to y_n with increment 0 or 1. This makes the rasterization of AB results in staircase-like segments of lengths $r_j \geq 1$ and height j, $j = 0, 1, \cdots, dy$, such that $\sum_{j=0}^{dy} r_j = dx + 1$. See Algorithm 2 for the realization.

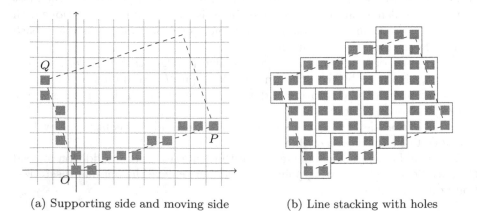

(a) Supporting side and moving side   (b) Line stacking with holes

Fig. 3. A coverage of the rotated rectangle via stacking Bresenham line scans.

In general, the rasterization of AB, i.e. the sequence (x_i, y_i), $i = 0, 1, \cdots, dx$, can be coded as

$$\langle \text{starting point: } (x_0, y_0); \text{ octant no.: } \gamma; \text{ runs: } r_j, j = 0, 1, \cdots, dy \rangle.$$

If $\gamma = 2$, the runs are counted as the point A_i moves upward along direction y in stepsize 1 while its abscissa decreases by 0 or 1. Other cases are similarly treated. For instance, in Fig. 3(a), the line OP is coded as

$$\langle \text{starting point: } (0,0); \text{ octant no.: } 0; \text{ runs: } 2, 3, 2, 3 \rangle,$$

and the line OQ is coded as

$$\langle \text{starting point: } (0,0); \text{ octant no.: } 2; \text{ runs: } 2, 3, 2 \rangle.$$

Algorithm 2: Run length coder of Bresenham line scanning

Input: (x_0, y_0) and (x_1, y_1)
Output: $\Lambda = \text{LineBres}(x_0, y_0, x_1, y_1)$; //Runs of Bresenham line scanning
1 Initialization:
2    $x \leftarrow x_0, y \leftarrow y_0$
3    $\Delta x \leftarrow x_1 - x_0, \ \Delta y \leftarrow y_1 - y_0,$
4    $e \leftarrow 2\Delta y - 2\Delta x$
5    $l = 0, \Lambda = 0, y = 1$
6 **for** $i \leftarrow x_0$ **to** x_1 **do**
7 | **if** $e > 0$ **then**
8 | | $y \leftarrow y + 1$
9 | | $p \leftarrow p + 2(\Delta y - \Delta x)$
10 | **else**
11 | | $p \leftarrow p + 2\Delta y$
12 | | $\Lambda(y) \leftarrow \Lambda(y) + 1$
13 | **end**
14 **end**

3.2 A Coverage of G'

It's clear that the definition domain G' of I' can be obtained by sweeping one side, called *moving side*, along its perpendicular side, called *supporting side*. See Fig. 3 for an illustration. Here, OP is taken as the moving side and OQ as the supporting side. With the moving edge OP marches, the point O keeps on the supporting side OQ. Then a series of copies of OP are stacked to cover a domain $\tilde{G}$ when the moving O reaches the other end Q of the supporting side. It's clear that $\tilde{G}$ is a proper subset of G' and their difference $G' \setminus \tilde{G}$ covers all the holes in G'.

Suppose the Bresenham runs of the moving side and the supporting side are respectively $\rho_{\text{supp}} = \{p_1, \cdots, p_m\}$ with total length $p = \sum_{i=1}^{m} p_i$ and $\rho_{\text{mov}} = \{q_1, \cdots, q_n\}$, with total length $q = \sum_{j=1}^{n} q_j$. Then it is clear that the number of points in $\tilde{G}$ is pq.

In another hand, during the moving side is moving, stacking holes appear between the current moving edge and the previous moving edge when the horizontal and vertical runs jump at the same time. Obviously the total number of holes is $(m-1)(n-1)$.

Therefore we have the following conclusion.

Theorem 1. *The area of the rectangle G' (i.e. the number of pixels it covers) defined by the two edges, is*

$$pq + (m-1)(n-1). \tag{8}$$

Notice that $p \approx w\cos\theta$, and $q \approx h\cos\theta$. Since rotation keeps areas, from Theorem 1, the number of holes in G' is approximately $wh - pq = wh\sin^2\theta$. With θ increases from 0 to $\pi/2$, p and q decrease while the number of holes in G' increases. When $\theta = \pi/2$, the holes amount to $wh/2$.

The sweeping technique above provides a clear interpretation of the hole phenomenon. In addition, it offers another benefit, although not conspicuous. Notice that after rounding, the corners of G' in (5) may not strictly form a rectangle. But, the sweeping technique does avoid this situation.

4   Pixel Evaluation of the Rotated Image

Now its ready to have I' evaluated on G', i.e. to determine the value of I' on G'. Suppose the current pixel is $p \in G'$. Then the next pixel to be processed along the same scanned Bresenham line is $p_1 = p + \delta$, where δ can be $(1,0)^T$ or $(1,1)^T$. Therefore their corresponding pixels in G are q_1 and q with $q_1 = M^T p_1 = M^T p + M^T \delta = q + M^T \delta$.

Denote $\delta_c = \cos\theta$ and $\delta_s = \sin\theta$. Then

$$M^T \begin{pmatrix} 0 \\ 1 \end{pmatrix} = \begin{pmatrix} \delta_c \\ -\delta_s \end{pmatrix}, \quad M^T \begin{pmatrix} 1 \\ 1 \end{pmatrix} = \begin{pmatrix} \delta_c \\ -\delta_s \end{pmatrix} + \begin{pmatrix} \delta_s \\ -\delta_c \end{pmatrix}$$

So we can simplify the calculation in such a way that substitutes the frequently manipulated matrix multiplication with incremental summation via

$$q_1 = q + \begin{pmatrix} \delta_c \\ -\delta_s \end{pmatrix}, \quad \text{or} \quad q_1 = q + \begin{pmatrix} \delta_c \\ -\delta_s \end{pmatrix} + \begin{pmatrix} \delta_s \\ -\delta_c \end{pmatrix}$$

Our proposed rotation method shows great efficiency, especially for many graphics needed to be processed in the image processing system, which usually requires high speed of image processing.

5   Experiments

To verify the effectiveness of our approach, we conduct experiments on a PC of Intel i7-7770 GPU at 3.60 GHz, with a gcc compiler of MinGW under Windows

---

Algorithm 3: Image rotation with Bresenham coder

Input: Image I of height h and width w; Angle θ
Output: Image J: rotation of I in θ

```
 1  Initialization: ;
 2      dc = cos(θ), ds = sin(θ);
 3      Initialize image J of height hX and width wX with pixel values 255:
 4      Λm = LineBres(0, 0, xr, yr); //Call Algorithm 2. ;
 5      Λs = LineBres(0, 0, xl, yl);
 6      six = siy = sjx = sjy = 0;
 7      for k ← 1 to ls do
 8          for i ← 0 to Λs(k) − 1 do
 9              jx = sjx, jy = sjy ;
10              six = 0 ;
11              px = six, py = siy ;
12              for l ← 1 to lm do
13                  for j ← 0 to Λm(l) − 1 do
14                      if px < 0 or px > w − 1 or py < 0 or py > h − 1 then
15                          continue;
16                      end
17                      ix = (px + 0.5), iy = (py + 0.5);
18                      J(jx, jy) = I(ix, iy);
19                      px += dc; py -= ds; jx++;
20                  end
21                  if lshift and l < ml.len − 1 then
22                      if px < 0 or px > w − 1 or py < 0 or py > h − 1 then
23                          continue;
24                      end
25                      ix = (px + 0.5); iy = (py + 0.5); J(jx, jy) = I(ix, iy);
26                  end
27                  jy++; px += ds; py += dc;
28              end
29              sjy++; siy += dc; if (lshift)  siy += ds; lshift = 0;
30          end
31          sjx−; lshift = 1;
32      end
```

---

10. We use a picture P0 of size 2976×3968 taken with a Huiwei P30 Pro and its lower-scaled version P1 and P2 as inputs. The sizes are 1488×1984 for P1 and 744×992 for P2.

For each picture, rotations of degrees from $5°$ to $45°$ with step size $5°$, are run under our approach Algorithm 3 together with other approaches including the forward, the backward, the backward with increments, and Shi's approach (denoted CADCD 07). Table 1 exhibits the results for picture P0; other pictures, of lower resolutions, do not reveal significant difference between our approach and Shi's. This means our approach is efficient for large images.

The data in Table 1 are also depicted in Fig. 4, in which the horizontal axis indicates rotation angle in degrees and the vertical axis indicates time cost in ms. It is seen from Fig. 4 that our approach has obvious advantages for larger angles.

In order to be clear about the cost for the coverage of rotated rectangle via Bresenham line coders, the related data are listed in the column "Stacks only" in Table 1 as well.

Table 1. Comparison of time costs running image rotations of image P0.

Degree	Forward	Backward	Backward with increments	CADCG 07	Stacks only	Ours
5	111.60	136.80	111.75	87.30	26.25	116.45
10	113.60	157.80	129.80	100.95	28.35	117.30
15	123.90	183.40	153.85	121.80	36.95	127.20
20	136.20	215.85	185.10	147.10	43.60	134.15
25	139.40	233.85	207.80	153.05	51.75	137.85
30	137.60	258.05	228.35	160.70	59.90	142.65
35	142.20	264.20	239.45	173.30	66.25	146.90
40	147.35	280.25	248.10	191.25	70.85	147.70
45	150.80	281.65	251.65	194.05	72.10	149.15

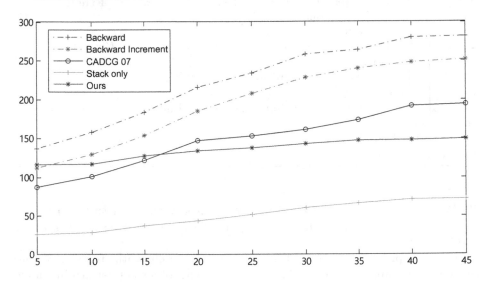

Fig. 4. Running time comparisons.

6   Conclusion

In this paper, we contributed a new idea for image rotation with a coverage strategy based on Bresenham's line expression; the boundary of the rotated image is expressed by Bresenham scanning lines. We analyzed the causes of the hole phenomenon in forward manipulation of image rotation together with the non-strict rectangle phenomenon. Our approach has obvious advantages for large images.

To improve the quality of rotated images, interpolation algorithms are commonly used, including bicubic, bilinear, midpoint, convolution-based, and nearest neighbor interpolation [12–15].

Further, we will optimize our algorithm for small size images, and incorporate suitable interpolation scheme into the fast coverage of the rotated image domain, in order to obtain high image quality besides competitive running speed.

Upon completing this manuscript, we found a work that realized fast implementation of image rotation [16]. Later we will be fed with an additional workload on the comparison with [16].

References

1. Gonzalez, R.C., Woods, R.E.: Digital Image Processing, 4th edn. Pearson/Prentice Hall, New York (2018)
2. Gidaris, S., Singh, P., Komodakis, N.: Unsupervised representation learning by predicting image rotations. In: International Conference on Learning Representations 2018 (2018). https://openreview.net/forum?id=S1v4N2l0-
3. Danielsson, P.E., Hammerin, M.: High-accuracy rotation of images. CVGIP Graph. Models Image Process. 54(4), 340–344 (1992)
4. Unser, M., Thevenaz, P., Yaroslavsky, L.: Convolution based interpolation for fast, high quality rotation of images. IEEE Trans. Image Process. 4(10), 1371–1381 (1995)
5. Chen, B., Kaufman, A.E.: Two-pass image and volume rotation. In: IEEE Workshop on Volume Graphics (2001). http://cfcs.pku.edu.cn/baoquan
6. Chien, S., Baek, Y.: A fast black run rotation algorithm for binary images. Pattern Recogn. Lett. 9(5), 455–459 (1998)
7. Watve, R.S., Shende, A.S., Kshirasagar, S.: Real time image rotation using SoC architecture. In: 8th International Symposium on Signal Processing and Its Applications, pp. 795–798. IEEE (2005)
8. Shi, S., Zhang, Y., Xi, R., Zheng, J.: A fast-high-quality image rotation approach based on Bresenham algorithm. J. Comput.-Aided Des. Comput. Graph. 19(11), 1387–1392 (2007)
9. Bresenham, J.E.: Algorithm for computer control of a digital plotter. IBM Syst. J. 4(1), 25–30 (1965)
10. Pitteway, M.L.V., Watkinson, D.J.: Bresenham's algorithm with grey scale. Commun. ACM 23(11), 625–626 (1980)
11. Reid-Green, K.S.: Three early algorithms. IEEE Ann. Hist. Comput. 24(4), 10–13 (2002)
12. Parker, J.A., Kenyon, R.V., Troxel, D.E.: Comparison of interpolating methods for image resampling. IEEE Trans. Med. Imaging 2(1), 31–39 (1983)

13. Lehmann, T.M., Gonner, C., Spitzer, K.: Survey: interpolation methods in medical image processing. IEEE Trans. Med. Imaging **18**(11), 1049–1075 (1999)
14. Keys, R.G.: Cubic convolution interpolation for digital image processing. IEEE Trans. Acoust. Speech Signal Process. **26**(6), 1153–1160 (1981)
15. Park, G., Leibon, D., Rockmore, N., Chirikjian, G.S.: Accurate image rotation using Hermite expansions. IEEE Trans. Image Process. **18**(9), 1988–2003 (2009)
16. Ashtari, A.H., Nordin, M.J., Kahaki, S.M.M.: Double line image rotation. IEEE Trans. Image Process. **24**(11), 3370–3385 (2015)

Compression, Transmission, and Retrieval

An Error-Bounded Algorithm for Streamline Compression Based on Piecewise B-Spline Curves

Donghan Liu[1], Wenke Wang[1(✉)], and Yunze Tang[2]

[1] National University of Defense Technology, Changsha 410073, China
wangwenke@nudt.edu.cn
[2] Army General Staff, Beijing 100000, China

Abstract. Streamline is one of the most commonly used visualization methods to describe flow field data. With the increase of data scale, accurate storage of streamlines needs a lot of storage space. How to store streamlines efficiently is an urgent problem to be solved. Streamline compression is an effective solution. In order to improve the compression ratio, a compression algorithm is proposed in this paper. First we use piecewise cubic B-spline curves to fit the streamlines, then a lossless compression algorithm is used to compress the fitted streamlines. The experiment illustrates that compared with the existing method, our method can achieve a higher compression ratio and strictly control the error.

Keywords: Flow visualization · Streamline compression · B-spline curve fitting · Error-bounded

1 Introduction

In many scientific fields such as aerodynamics and oceanography, it is imperative to understand the fluid's behavior. Streamline visualization is an important branch of scientific computing visualization, which plays an important role in analyzing and understanding the complex flow mechanism, insight into the flow field's physical phenomena, and discovering the scientific laws of flow [14].

With the continuous improvement of computer hardware performance, data acquisition speed and accuracy are growing rapidly. The existing large-scale flow visualization methods, such as multi-node parallel and out-of-core parallel technology [16], can improve the computing speed. However, the operations such as inter-node communication, data block I/O [6], seed point distribution calculation [3] will still take much time. Streamline data are often far larger than the original data set or exceeds the external storage capacity. Therefore, the efficient storage of streamlines is critical.

The existing lossless compression algorithms cannot achieve a high compression ratio in streamline compression. The existing streamline compression work attempts a lossless compression algorithm *gzip* for the generated streamlines and only achieves a compression ratio of 1.43 [4]. Even reduce data entropy

© Springer Nature Switzerland AG 2021
Y. Peng et al. (Eds.): ICIG 2021, LNCS 12888, pp. 627–640, 2021.
https://doi.org/10.1007/978-3-030-87355-4_52

heretofore [2], it could only obtain a compression ratio of 1.59. Lossy compression algorithms such as *fpzip* [5] can get a higher compression ratio, but also bring information loss, for it is not based on geometric information, the error is uncontrollable.

The existing streamline compression method uses cubic Bézier curve fitting and floating-point data compression to complete the compression task [4]. Compared with the traditional data compression methods, it has obtained a noticeable improvement. However, it also brings some problems: using the lossy *fpzip* algorithm cannot directly control the compression results' geometric error. To judge whether it meets the error requirements, we need to compare the decompression results after compression. As a result, this is an iterative process, and the parameters need to be adjusted manually for different data sets.

In order to solve the problems above, this paper proposes an algorithm based on cubic piecewise B-spline curves. The compression ratio of streamlines is significantly improved compared with the original algorithm. Moreover, the *fpzip* lossy compression algorithm, which is difficult to control the compression error, is abandoned. Instead, we use a lossless compression algorithm for hybrid compression to avoid adjusting the parameters iteratively.

2   Related Work

2.1   Traditional Data Compression Method

Data compression can effectively reduce the size of data, which is a crucial research field in high-performance computing and visualization [7]. Ratanaworabhan et al. [12] proposed a lossless compression method based on fast hash table lookup prediction for scientific data, which improved the compression ratio. Isenburg et al. [5] implemented the *fpzip* algorithm for lossy and lossless compression scenarios using predictive coding to compress floating-point coordinates. Lindstrom et al. [8] designed ZFP compression, which is a transform-based compressor. It transforms the original data into another space through customized orthogonal transformation, keeping the difference between the original data and the decompressed data within a given error range. Di et al. [1] proposed SZ compression, a prediction-based compressor, which fits the data by selecting the best-fit curve fitting method. These methods can compress all kinds of scientific data, but they cannot achieve a high compression ratio when compressing streamlines. Also, they cannot guarantee the effectiveness of visualization.

2.2   Streamline Compression

Different from general scientific data, streamlines also contain geometric information. The compression ratio of streamlines can be improved by making full use of geometric information. Poty et al. [9] converted and cut the wavelet's broken line points according to a specific formula and obtained different compression ratios by manually adjusting the parameters, which reduced the number of saved points. However, it was easy to produce deformation, and the error change was massive, which was difficult to control. Tao et al. [15] proposed a lossless and steady compression method for wavelets. The results have high accuracy, but the compression ratio is low, and time-consuming. An automatic curve fitting algorithm proposed by Schneider is advantageous in streamline compression field [13]. This method uses multi-segment Bézier curves recursively to fit the streamlines, which can set the upper limit of error and ensure G^0 continuity. However, frequent segmentation will increase the number of stored control points, and there is room for further improvement. Based on this work, Hong et al. [4] further explores the hybrid compression method. After using Schneider's method to fit, the lossy *fpzip* algorithm was used to compress the coordinates of the control points, further improved the compression ratio.

The *fpzip* algorithm makes the geometric error uncontrollable, and the compression error may exceed the user-specified error. To keep the error meet the requirement, the compression parameters are adjusted repeatedly.

3   Approach

Figure 1 shows the overall process of our method. For the streamlines generated by numerical integration(streamlines are formed by connecting integral points), B-spline curves are used to fit them first, and then lossless compression is performed on the fitting result. The final compression result can be decompressed for visualization.

Section 3.1 introduces the symbols and definitions used in this paper; Sect. 3.2 introduces the motivation of our algorithm; Sect. 3.3 introduces the piecewise B-spline curve fitting algorithm proposed in this paper; Sect. 3.4 presents the design of storage format suitable for our method in detail; Sect. 3.5 describes the lossless compression method selected in this paper; Sect. 3.6 introduces the decompression method.

3.1   Notations

Streamline compression based on geometric information mainly considers two metrics: compression ratio and error. In this paper, the compression ratio of streamlines ρ is defined in Eq. (1).

$$\rho = \frac{\text{Unconpressed size}}{\text{Compressed size}} \tag{1}$$

In streamline visualization, geometric errors are usually used to reflect the effect of errors on visualization. In this paper, the same method as Hong's [4] is used to calculate the maximum distance d between the streamlines and the fitting curves, which is calculated by Eq. (2). $\boldsymbol{P}_i$ is the i-th point on the streamlines, and $\boldsymbol{Q}(t_i)$ is the fitting curves sampling point when the parameter t_i is given.

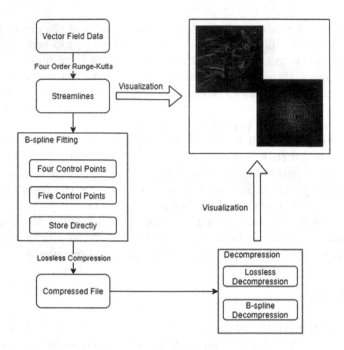

Fig. 1. Compression process.

$$d = \max_{1 \leq i \leq n} || \boldsymbol{P}_i - \boldsymbol{Q}\left(t_i\right) || \tag{2}$$

To select the error bound, it is impossible to give an appropriate measurement standard in meters or kilometers due to vector field data diversity. This paper uses the same metric as Hong's. Namely, voxel, to measure error. A voxel is a unit related to the length of the grid. For a specific data field, it is more efficient to use voxels to measure. Generally, if the error is limited to 1.0 voxel or 0.5 voxels, a better compression ratio can be obtained under acceptable error. In this paper, one voxel is defined as the grid's edge length, and the average side length is taken when the mesh size is inconsistent.

3.2   Motivation

Hong et al. uses piecewise Bézier curve to fit the streamline. In contrast, B-spline curve is a more concise and efficient form, which has the advantages of local shape adjustment and unlimited control points. Therefore, we first tried to use a single cubic B-spline curve to fit each streamline (least squares curve approximation in the NURBS book [11]). However, cubic B-spline curves have a higher C^2 continuity, while piecewise Bézier curve only keeps G^0 continuity. When the streamlines' shape is complex, cubic B-spline curves need to use more control points to maintain continuity. Therefore, this method has no obvious advantage over piecewise Bézier curve fitting, and sometimes it can get worse

Table 1. B-spline curve global fitting results

Data source	Nunmer of streamlines	Hong's fitting [4] size	B-spline curve global fitting size
Ocean current	400	96 KB	128 KB
Vec256	500	42 KB	34 KB

Table 2. Piecewise B-spline curve fitting of different number of control points

Data source	Number of streamlines	Number of control points	Fitting size
Ocean current	400	5	58 KB
Ocean current	400	6	66 KB
Ocean current	400	7	74 KB

results. We conducted two groups of comparative tests under the same error bound, as shown in Table 1.

During the experiment, we found that cubic B-spline curve fitting can obtain a better result when the number of control points is small. Therefore, we attempt to use piecewise cubic B-spline curve with a small number of control points to fit streamlines. We choose the number of control points for each B-spline curve as 5, 6, and 7 for experiments in turn. Table 2 shows a group of comparative data. It can be seen that with the increase of the number of control points, the required storage space gradually increases, so we mainly use the piecewise cubic B-spline curve of five control points to complete the fitting. Besides, if a streamline segment can be fitted by 4 control points within the error bound, the B-spline curve of 4 control points is used; if there are fewer than 4 streamline points to be fitted, the streamline coordinates are stored directly without fitting.

3.3   Fitting Algorithm Based on Piecewise B-Spline Curves

The main idea of the algorithm is as follows. For a streamline to be fitted, if one B-spline curve can be used to fit within the error bound, the result will be stored directly, otherwise it will be split where the error bound is exceeded. The fitting result of the previous segment will be stored, and the latter segment will be processed the same. The steps of the algorithm are given in Algorithm 1. In order to improve the performance of the algorithm, binary search is used to find the longest fitting subsegment in the process of piecewise fitting. The output of the algorithm is a one-dimensional array, which successively stores the coordinates and knot vector values (or streamline points) of each control point. Details of the storage format are described in Sect. 3.4.

3.4   Storage Format Design

The results of curve fitting, including control points and knot vectors, are stored in binary form. For a streamline, an integer value *length* is stored first, representing the length of the output array in Algorithm 1, and then the control points

Algorithm 1. Piecewise B-spline curve fitting algorithm

Input: Array of an integral curve, User-specified error
Output: Array of fitting result
 Step1: Determine whether the input array is empty, if so, end the algorithm.
 Step2: If the coordinates in the input array are fewer than or equal to 4, store them directely and end the algorithm.
 Step3: Fit the whole streamline with a 4 control points' B-spline curve, and if succeeded, store the result and end the algorithm.
 Step4: Fit the whole streamline with a 5 control points' B-spline curve, and if succeeded, store the result and end the algorithm.
 Step5: Using binary search to find the longest segment of the current streamline which can be fitted by one B-spline curve of 5 control points within the error bound, stogre the result and delete the fitted part in the input array. Jump to step1

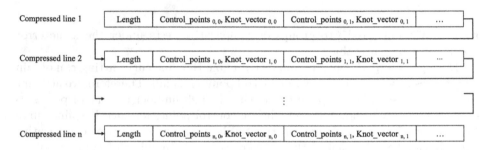

Fig. 2. Storage format in binary files

and knot vectors of each B-spline curve are stored in turn. In a two-dimensional case, each control point contains two components, and in a three-dimensional case, three components. The storage diagram is shown in Fig. 2.

 To provide the information for distinguishing when decompressing, if a streamline has one segment fitted by B-spline curves of four control points, the *length* is saved as a negative number, otherwise a positive number.

 The knot vector of cubic B-spline curves of 4 control points is always $\{0.0, 0.0, 0.0, 0.0, 1.0, 1.0, 1.0, 1.0\}$, which need not to be stored. The knot vector of cubic B-spline curves of 5 control points is formatted as $\{0.0, 0.0, 0.0, 0.0, x, 1.0, 1.0, 1.0, 1.0\}$. For each fitting result, only x changes. Therefore, only one floating-point number needs to be stored, and the rest will be filled when decompressing.

 Piecewise B-spline curve fitting needs to maintain G^0 continuity, so the first control point of the latter segment should be the same as the last one of the previous segment. That is to say, for the fitting result of each streamline, only the first B-spline curve needs to store all the control points, and the rest do not store the first control point. This can avoid information redundancy and save space.

 If the unfitted streamline points are stored in the fitting result (step2 of Algorithm 1), there are two cases.

1. The number of streamline points is smaller than or equal to 4. All the points need to be stored.
2. The rest points of one streamline, which has been fitted by one or more B-spline curves, are fewer than or equal to 4. The points except the first one need to be stored.

3.5 Lossless Compression

To solve the error uncertainty caused by floating-point compression in the hybrid compression algorithm proposed by Hong et al. [4], this paper uses a lossless compression algorithm to compress the B-spline curve fitting results without introducing additional errors.

There is still space for lossless compression in binary files compressed by the curve fitting method. In this paper, various lossless compression formats have been tried, such as rar, zip, 7z, xz. In our experiment, we found that the xz compression format obtained by LZMA algorithm [10] has the best compression effect, and the binary data of control points can be further compressed to about 55%–75% of the original. However, when using lossy compression, such as *fpzip*, the geometric error cannot be controlled, so it usually needs to adjust the parameters many times.

The main reason for lossless compression in this paper is that lossless compression will not increase any error based on curve fitting error. It can also achieve a relatively good compression effect, save the time of adjusting parameters, and has good versatility for different data sets. Lossless compression with the piecewise B-spline curve fitting algorithm proposed in this paper has achieved better results than the existing method in experiments, with a higher compression ratio, and the maximum error is strictly controlled.

3.6 Decompression Method

Decompression is divided into two steps. First, call the LZMA library function to complete the first step of decompression, and then recover streamline coordinates according to the stored information. The information needed is control points and knot vectors. The decompressed streamlines can get according to Eq. (3).

$$C(u) = \sum_{i=1}^{n} N_{i,p}(u) P_i \quad u \in [0, 1] \tag{3}$$

Following is the two-dimensional situation. The streamlines are decompressed one by one(one line in Fig. 2)

When *length* is negative, there are two cases:

1. The whole streamline is fitted by one B-spline curve with four control points. Directly decompress it according Eq. (3).

2. The whole streamline is fitted by B-spline curves of different number of control points. According to the description of Algorithm 1, in this case, the B-spline curve of four control points can only be the last segment. The last four control points are extracted from the compression result, and the remaining part is the B-spline curves of five control points. We can obtain the decompressed streamline by decompress them respectively and then splice them.

When *length* is positive, there are three cases:

1. *length* = 11. This situation shows that a streamline is fitted by a B-spline curve with five control points. *length* = 5×2+1 = 11, in which "1" represents the value need to be stored in the knot vector. Use Eq. (3) to decompress.
2. *length* < 11. In this case (step2 of Algorithm 1), only the not fitted streamline points are stored in the output array, which need not be decompressed and are directly output to the result.
3. *length* > 11. This indicate that there are several B-spline curves of 5 control points. First to calculate the number of the B-spline curves, which is 1 + (*length* − 11) //9. The "//" represents rounding division. After removing this part, if the array has any remaining, they are the streamline points. For the part of B-spline curves, since there are no duplicate control points, the last control point of the previous segment should be added from the second decompressing. For the part of streamline points, they are directly output to the decompression result.

In the three-dimensional case, the numbers 11 and 9 above are replaced with 16(5 × 3 + 1) and 13, respectively.

4   Experiment and Result

This section records the experiment and result of this paper. Section 4.1 describes the data used in the experiment; Sect. 4.2 compares the effect of our fitting method and the existing method [4]; Sect. 4.3 shows the improvement of this paper's final result compared with the existing method. Section 4.4 shows the effect of decompression.

4.1   Data Source

The streamline data used in this paper is generated based on four flow fields, including two two-dimensional flow fields and two three-dimensional flow fields. The description of flow field data is shown in Table 3.

Streamline data are generated by the fourth-order Runge Kutta method, and seed points are randomly selected. The description of streamline data is described in Table 4. It shows that the streamline data is far larger than the original flow field data.

Figure 3, 4, 5 and 6 show the visualization of the four flow fields.

Table 3. Flow field data description

Flow field data	Dimension	Grid size	Size
Ocean current	2	200×200	313 KB
Vec256	2	256×256	512 KB
Tornado	3	$200 \times 200 \times 200$	91.5 MB
Psi	3	$100 \times 100 \times 100$	11.4 MB

Table 4. Streamline data description

Flow field data	Dimension	Number of streamlines	Size
Ocean current	2	10000	30.10 MB
Vec256	2	50000	309 MB
Tornado	3	500000	2.07 GB
Psi	3	100000	107 MB

Fig. 3. Ocean current visualization

Fig. 4. Vec256 visualization

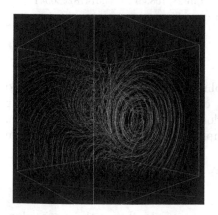

Fig. 5. Tornado visualization

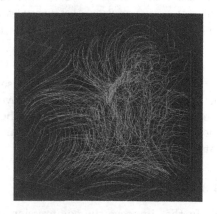

Fig. 6. Psi visualization

4.2 Fitting Comparison

Both our method and Hong's method [4] contain two parts, curve fitting and general compression. This section compares our fitting method with the fitting method used in [4]. The indexes include the fitting file size, fitting compression ratio, and the number of floating-point numbers to be stored. Four groups of streamline data are selected in the experiment, and the error bound is set to 0.5 voxels and 1.0 voxel, respectively. Table 5 and 6 show the comparison between the fitting results of [4] and that of this paper when the error bound is set to 0.5 voxels and 1.0 voxel, respectively.

Table 5. Comparison of fitting results, error bound = 0.5 voxels

Data source	Number of streamlines	Fitting size Hong's [4]/This paper	Fitting compression ratio Hong's [4]/This paper	Stored floating-point number Hong's [4]/This paper
Ocean current	10000	2135 KB/1243 KB	14.44/24.80	536408/307964
Vec256	50000	2533 KB/2056 KB	124.92/153.90	598402/476092
Tornado	500000	29.50 MB/26.50 MB	71.85/79.99	7235898/6448497
Psi	100000	17.80 MB/10.80 MB	6.01/9.91	4581543/2745106

Table 6. Comparison of fitting results, error bound = 1.0 voxel

Data source	Number of streamlines	Fitting size Hong's [4]/This paper	Fitting compression ratio Hong's [4]/This paper	Stored floating-point number Hong's [4]/This paper
Ocean current	10000	1577 KB/974 KB	19.54/31.65	393524/239214
Vec256	50000	2178 KB/1878 KB	145.28/168.49	507478/430541
Tornado	500000	27.40 MB/25.70 MB	77.36/82.48	6700749/6247055
Psi	100000	14.40 MB/9.20 MB	7.43/11.63	3682074/2312335

It can be seen that the piecewise B-spline curve fitting method proposed in this paper has an obvious improvement compared with the existing fitting method. It greatly reduces the number of floating-point numbers stored within the same error bound, thus significantly improving the streamline compression ratio.

4.3 Lossless Compression

To further improve the compression ratio, Hong et al. [4] uses the *fpzip* algorithm to compress the fitted streamlines, which changes the existing error. It needs to iteratively select the compression parameters for verification to control the error again within the error bound. Figure 7 shows this process through an experiment. Figure 7(a), (c) shows the compressed file size of two groups of data under different compression parameters of Hong's method. Figure 7(b), (d) shows the compression error of Hong's method under different compression parameters. When the precision parameter of $fpzip$ is adjusted to 28 and 30, the two groups of randomly selected data's maximum error is lower than the error bound. The file size and maximum error are marked with black arrows in Fig. 7.

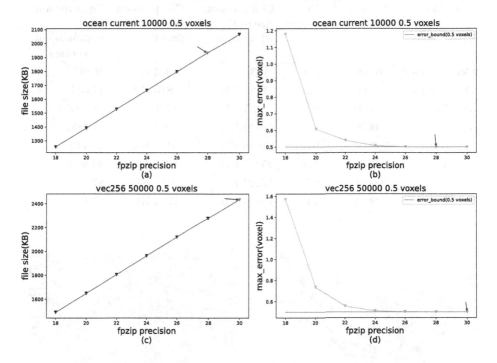

Fig. 7. Hong's compression with iteratively adjusted parameters

In this paper, the lossy compression is replaced by the lossless compression mentioned in Sect. 3.5, which can still obtain a considerable compression ratio improvement. The process of iteratively adjusting the compression parameters is avoided, making the overall algorithm process more concise and efficient. Table 7 shows the final compression ratio comparison between this method and the existing method. The $fpzip$ compression parameter in Hong's method is selected as the parameter when just not exceed the error bound. It should be noted that the lossless compression algorithm can not further compress the results obtained by using $fpzip$ compression.

4.4 Decompression

To show that our compression method can still achieve a good visualization effect after decompression, we select two groups of decompressed data for visualization display. The error bound is set to 0.5 voxels. Figure 8 and 9 show the visualization effect after decompression. Compared with the original visualization (Fig. 3 and 4), our decompression results can still describe the characteristics of the flow field well.

Table 7. Final compression results compared with Hong's Method

Data source	Number of streamlines	Error bound	Compression size of Hong's [4] method	Compression size of this paper	Compression ratio improvement percentage
Ocean current	10000	0.5	1932 KB	1034 KB	86.90%
Ocean current	10000	1.0	1439 KB	810 KB	77.64%
Vec256	50000	0.5	2435 KB	1721 KB	41.50%
Vec256	50000	1.0	2049 KB	1562 KB	31.18%
Tornado	500000	0.5	28648 KB	19170 KB	49.44%
Tornado	500000	1.0	25954 KB	18475 KB	40.49%
Psi	100000	0.5	17212 KB	9171 KB	87.60%
Psi	100000	1.0	12856 KB	7694 KB	67.14%

Fig. 8. Ocean current decompression   **Fig. 9.** Vec256 decompression

5 Conclusion

Streamline compression is an efficient method to store streamlines. The traditional compression methods have limited effect in this field. Fitting compression based on geometric information is a new idea to solve this problem. It can fully mine the compressible space and keep the acceptable loss of accuracy. In this paper, a piecewise cubic B-spline curve fitting algorithm is proposed, which greatly reduces the number of control points to be stored within the allowable error range and achieves a higher compression ratio. To avoid the uncontrollable error of the existing method, we further use a lossless compression algorithm after fitting the streamlines. This procedure will not introduce new errors and thus our method can meet the error requirement without repeatedly adjusting the compression parameters. The results demonstrate that we have achieved a higher compression ratio than the existing method.

Acknowledgments. This research was funded by the National Science Foundation of China (61972411, 61972406).

References

1. Di, S., Cappello, F.: Fast error-bounded lossy HPC data compression with SZ. In: Proceedings - 2016 IEEE 30th International Parallel and Distributed Processing Symposium, IPDPS 2016, pp. 730–739 (2016). https://doi.org/10.1109/IPDPS.2016.11

2. Ellsworth, D., Green, B., Moran, P.: Interactive terascale particle visualization. In: IEEE Visualization 2004 - Proceedings, VIS 2004, pp. 353–360, November 2004. https://doi.org/10.1109/visual.2004.55

3. Guo, Y., Wang, W., Li, S.: Feature-based adaptive block partition method for data prefetching in streamline visualization. In: Parallel and Distributed Computing, Applications and Technologies, PDCAT Proceedings 2017-Decem, pp. 510–515 (2018). https://doi.org/10.1109/PDCAT.2017.00087

4. Hong, F., Bi, C., Guo, H., Ono, K., Yuan, X.: Compression-based integral curve data reuse framework for flow visualization. J. Vis. **20**(4), 859–874 (2017). https://doi.org/10.1007/s12650-017-0428-4

5. Isenburg, M., Lindstrom, P., Snoeyink, J.: Lossless compression of predicted floating-point geometry. CAD Comput. Aided Des. **37**(8), 869–877 (2005). https://doi.org/10.1016/j.cad.2004.09.015

6. Kendall, W., Huang, J., Peterka, T., Latham, R., Ross, R.: Toward a general i/o layer for parallel-visualization applications. IEEE Comput. Graph. Appl. **31**(6), 6–10 (2012)

7. Li, S., Marsaglia, N., Garth, C., Woodring, J., Clyne, J., Childs, H.: Data reduction techniques for simulation, visualization and data analysis. Comput. Graph. Forum **37**(6), 422–447 (2018). https://doi.org/10.1111/cgf.13336

8. Lindstrom, P.: Fixed-rate compressed floating-point arrays. IEEE Trans. Visual. Comput. Graph. **20**(12), 2674–2683 (2014). https://doi.org/10.1109/TVCG.2014.2346458

9. Marion-Poty, V., Lefer, W.: A wavelet decomposition scheme and compression method for streamline-based vector field visualizations. Comput. Graph. (Pergamon) **26**(6), 899–906 (2002). https://doi.org/10.1016/S0097-8493(02)00178-4

10. Pavlov., I.: LZMA SDK (software development kit). https://www.7-zip.org/sdk.html (2021)

11. Piegl, L.A., Tiller, W.: The NURBS Book. Springer, Heidelberg (1997). https://doi.org/10.1007/978-3-642-59223-2

12. Ratanaworabhan, P., Ke, J., Burtscher, M.: Fast lossless compression of scientific floating-point data. In: Data Compression Conference Proceedings, pp. 133–142 (2006). https://doi.org/10.1109/DCC.2006.35

13. Schneider, P.J.: An Algorithm for Automatically Fitting Digitized Curves. Academic Press Inc., Boston (1990). https://doi.org/10.1016/B978-0-08-050753-8. 50132-7No. 1972
14. Sikun, L., Xun, C., Wenke, W.: Scientific Visualization of Large Scale Flow Field. National Defense Industry Press, Beijing (2013)
15. Tao, H., Moorhead, R.J.: Lossless progressive transmission of scientific data using biorthogonal wavelet transform In: Proceedings - International Conference on Image Processing, ICIP, vol. 3, issue 1, pp. 373–377 (1994). https://doi.org/10. 1109/ICIP.1994.413824
16. Ueng, S.K., Sikorski, C., Ma, K.L.: Out-of-core streamline visualization on large unstructured meshes. IEEE Trans. Visual. Comput. Graph. **3**(4), 370–380 (1997). https://doi.org/10.1109/2945.646239

Achieving Lightweight Image Steganalysis with Content-Adaptive in Spatial Domain

Junfu Chen[1], Zhangjie Fu[1,2](✉), Xingming Sun[1], and Enlu Li[1]

[1] Engineering Research Center of Digital Forensics, Ministry of Education, Nanjing University of Information Science and Technology, Nanjing 210044, China
[2] School of Computer and Software, Nanjing University of Information Science and Technology, Nanjing 210044, China
fzj@nuist.edu.cn

Abstract. Steganography is a technology that modifies complex regions of digital images to embed secret messages for the purpose of covert communication, while steganalysis is to detect whether secret messages are hidden in a digital image or not. However, the emergence of content-adaptive steganography such as S-UNIWARD prioritizes the embedding of secret messages in areas of textural complexity of images by embedding probability map guidelines. Such ways dramatically improve the security of steganography and impede the process of image steganalysis. Most of the existing steganalysis studies are aimed at improving the network structure to enhance the detection performance of the model, without considering the generation of embedding probability maps which can guide the training of the network model, eliminate some unnecessary distractions, shorten the training time and improve the final detection accuracy simultaneously. Therefore, how to obtain embedded probability maps and use them effectively becomes an important challenge in the field of steganalysis. In this paper, to solve the above problem we propose a content-adaptive lightweight network to implement an embedded probability map combined with steganalysis. Our steganalysis model includes two parts: embedding probability maps generation module and features processing module, which is trained Separately. The generation module adopts the basic framework and modifies the model to make it more suitable for steganography. In the features processing module, we adopt a pseudo-siamese architecture to manipulate two different input images. Next, we use the attention mechanism to assign weights to channel parameters. Finally, We use a simple data augmentation method to enhance our training dataset and improve final performance. Because our proposed model incorporates embedded probability maps as guidelines, experiments show that our proposed CNet has faster convergence speed, higher detection accuracy, and better robustness compared to networks such as Yedroudj-Net, SRNet, and Zhu-Net in the spatial domain.

Supported by Foundation item: National Key Research and Development Program of China (2018YFB1003205); National Natural Science Foundation of China (U1836110, U1836208); by the Jiangsu Basic Research Programs-Natural Science Foundation under grant numbers BK20200039.

© Springer Nature Switzerland AG 2021
Y. Peng et al. (Eds.): ICIG 2021, LNCS 12888, pp. 641–653, 2021.
https://doi.org/10.1007/978-3-030-87355-4_53

Keywords: Steganalysis · Content-adaptive · Attention mechanism · Embedding probability maps · Deep learning

1 Introduction

Today, the Internet and social media platforms are flooded with immeasurable amounts of digital images. People use images to share their lives and express their thoughts on social media platforms, so criminals can take advantage of the high redundancy of information in digital images to hide the messages they want to convey that are harmful to social security through steganography and spread them widely on the Internet, which poses a huge threat to social security and even national stable. With the advancement and development of steganography and steganography software, steganography not only minimizes the visualization changes caused by secret information but also avoid the discrepancies in image statistics caused by steganography, so it is increasingly difficult for people to detect the small differences between original image (Cover) and image within secret (Stego). Therefore, researchers have introduced steganalysis into the real world to counteract such discrepancies that are difficult to observe by the human eye and to reduce the harm that conveys communication can do to society and the state [4]. Therefore, lightweight steganalysis that can be deployed on mobile devices is particularly important.

In Fig. 1 are the Cover and Stego images of the 1013th image of BOSS-Base datasets [1], (a) represents the original image, (b) represents the original image corresponding to the steganographic image generated by S-UNIWARD, (c) represents the embedding probability maps of the original image obtained by S-UNIWARD, and (d) represents the pixel-by-pixel differences between (a) and (b). Both Cover and Stego are difficult to detect the differences between them by the human eye alone. (To better understanding, the carrier and change images in this article are replaced with Cover and Stego, respectively).

The dilemma of image steganalysis is that there is little information embedded in the image during the steganography operation, and the faint difference between Cover and Stego is vulnerable to content information between pixels. Content-adaptive steganography is directed by the embedding probability map generated by its distortion function when embedding secret messages. However, most of the existing research work on image steganalysis is to improve the network structure to enhance the detection performance of CNN-based steganalysis. It also leads to issues in the training process of some steganalysis models, such as the mismatch between the information contained in the images and what really needs to be focused on, and the mismatch in training effectiveness. Therefore, it is highly necessary to propose a steganalysis that allows adapting to the picture content and guiding the model to pay more attention to the features of the steganographic regions.

To solve the above dilemma, we proposed a CNN-based network to improve the final detection accuracy of differentiating steganographic images from original images in spatial domain and named CNet in this paper. CNet pruning of

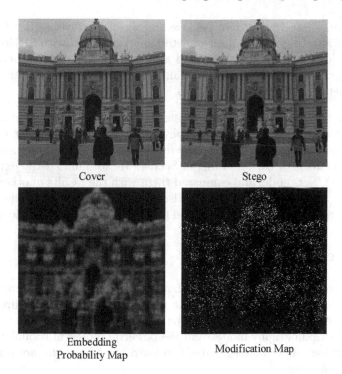

Fig. 1. An example of Cover and the corresponding Stego, Embedding probability map and the modification map.

existing saliency detection U^2-Net for generating embedding probability maps, using pseudo-siamese networks for multi-level deep integration of embedding probability maps with the pending images, amplifying steganographic noise on the pending images (if present) to reduce the potential search space of the deep network and shorten the training time. The attention mechanism is used to crop the network layer weights at training time to select more effective high-dimensional features and prevent interference caused by too many useless features in the network. Finally, the residual block is used as the base module of the classification network to effectively enhance feature recycling while strengthening the effective information in high-dimensional space. The main contributions in this paper are as follows:

(1) We have trimmed the U^2-Net model and modified its original loss function so that our generation module has priori knowledge of the steganography. The two modules learn independently and achieve the optimal learning respectively, the generated embedding probability map is used in the feature extraction process.

(2) We use a pseudo-siamese network model that leverages mid-level semantic features with embedded probability maps to integrate multi-scale information, adding attention layers to the network to manipulate the fused feature maps.

(3) The model has trimmed to achieve the most effective at the fastest rate without affecting the accuracy of detection. Compared with SRNet and Zhu-Net, CNet has less parameters and achieves better detection accuracy and faster convergence speed. Additional, the generation module can be used as a pre-network in other steganalysis.

The rest of the paper is organized as follows: in Sect. 2, we briefly review related work that including steganography and steganalysis based on CNN in the spatial domain; in Sect. 3, We describe our proposed CNet model and examine the role and effects of each module; in Sect. 4, We formulated the experimental effects of the CNet model and compared them with the results of other steganalysis models; in Sect. 5, We present a discussion and summary of the results of CNet's experiments and looking forward for steganalysis based on deep learning.

2   Related Work

Compared to dedicated steganalysis that targets a certain or a few steganography, such as [3,9], traditional generic steganalysis are more in line with the real-world environment like [6–8,11]. The emergence of deep learning substitutes the original steganography model, and the powerful representational capabilities of deep learning allow the steganalysis to learn steganography noise more intuitively and effectively.

From 2014 to 2020, there are many steganalysis based on CNN has been proposed, such as [2,12,13,15,17–20].

At the end of 2018, the Selection-Channel-Aware method was proposed to provide a new approach to the field of steganalysis. This approach assumes that the Eve can know the steganographic method and Cover in advance, but this is in a real social environment where the Eve party usually only has access to a large number of Stego images and does not know the specific steganographic algorithm at all. This also makes the method limited. CNet references the embedding probability generation method for steganographer detection to use the already trained network to modify the probability map generation to help fit faster without knowing the steganography algorithm in advance.

Until now, steganalysis that utilizes the generated embedding probability maps has never been developed. As introduced previously, content-adaptive steganography can dynamically embed secret messages based on Cover's content, so the embedding pattern varies dramatically between images. It also led to the challenging task of steganalysis, so the idea of using embedded probability maps for steganalysis was born in [5,14,16]. Although the selection channels can be directly used in steganalysis, it does not fully exert the potential of CNN (Fig. 2).

3   Proposed Method

To better combine embedded probability maps with steganalysis and to make the network lightweight. The main structure of the CNet is illustrated in Fig. 3.

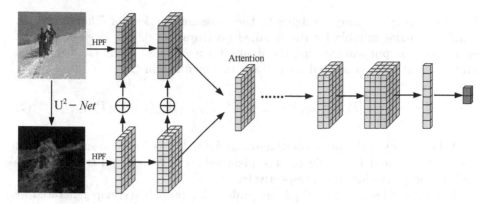

Fig. 2. Overview of the proposed CNet. It is composed of three parts: The embedding probability maps generation module, pseudo-siamese structure and the feature class module.

In detail, CNet can be roughly divided into three structures, the first one is the generation module for generating embedding probability maps, the second one is the SE-Block module for pseudo-siamese schema and attention mechanism, and the third one is the feature classification module for classifying the high-frequency features extraction obtained from the network front-end. Finally, a full-connection layer is used for making effective discrimination. Specific models for the different models are described in detail in the following sections.

3.1 Embedding Probability Maps Generation

Our generation module enables the feature map to output information with high semantic features and global statistical properties after high-level convolutional layer operationalization through the nesting of multi-layer convolutional U-Net structures. Therefore, the multi-scale deep feature fusion approach can effectively help us to obtain information fusion and generate embedding probability maps that are more suitable for real scenarios. The network structure was inspired by the saliency detection model U^2-Net, which has been applied for the first time to the information hiding domain. Compared to the original U^2-Net, we consider that the generation of embedding probability maps does not require much semantic knowledge, and we tailor the original 6-layer nested U-Net to a 4-layer nested network.

In the training process, we use deep supervision similar to U^2-Net. Our training loss is defined as:

$$L_{all} = \sum_{m=1}^{M} \frac{1}{m} \ell^m + IoU(C_j, \hat{C}_j) \tag{1}$$

Where M represent the total depth of nested U-Net architecture. Considering that the contributions of different layers to the final result are different, the invention assigns different weights to the cross-entropy loss of different layers, making it more suitable for the detailed portrayal. ℓ^m is the cross-entropy of each layers output features and the finally term. Where C_j and $\hat{C}_j$ denote the Ground Truth and generated area. For each loss function ℓ:

$$\ell = - \sum_{(r,c)}^{(H,W)} [P_{G(r,c)} \log P_{S(r,c)} + (1 - P_{G(r,c)}) \log(1 - \log \Gamma_{S(r,c)})] \tag{2}$$

Where (r,c) is the pixel coordinates and (H,W) is image size: height and width. $P_{G(r,c)}$ and $P_{S(r,c)}$ denote the pixel values of the ground truth and the embedding probability map, respectively.

In the total loss function Eq. 1, the embedding probability map generated by U^2-Net for different depth layers and the Ground Truth image are put together in the total loss by cross-entropy operation, and we multiply the generated images with different weighting factors according to the different depths. As you go deeper into the network hierarchy, the weights are reduced accordingly, and experiments have shown that information that is too high dimensional is not beneficial for generating embedding probability maps.

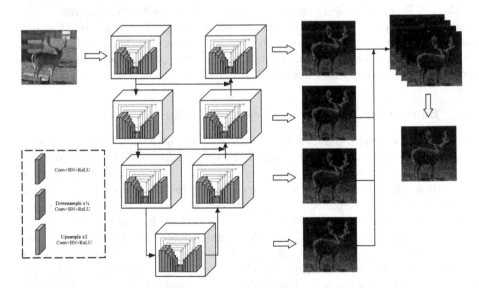

Fig. 3. The overview of the embedding probability maps generation module. We have trimmed the network architecture of U^2Net to simplify the network layers and the network structure, and the figure above shows the final module that we propose.

3.2   The Features Extraction Module

The pre-processing module of the image incorporates the image and the embedding probability map information it generates. The 30 different size-dependent high-pass filter kernels in the preprocessing layer amplify the steganographic noise in the image and are tuned along with the parameters within the network. The parameter differences between the two branches in the pseudo-siamese network also change gradually (Fig. 4).

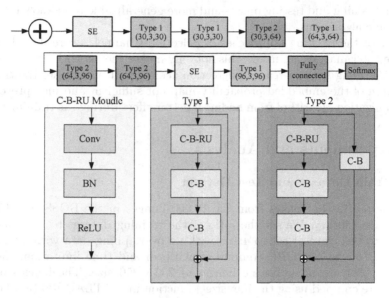

Fig. 4. The architecture after pseudo-siamese structure. The C-B-RU module is an abbreviation for the common sequence combination Conv-BN-ReLU. The C-B stands for a network structure such as Conv-BN (features map operated by convolution and batch normlization). Type1 and Type2 are the major groups of CNet, the feature extraction part are shown in the upper part of the image. For a better understanding of the internals in the network, the detailed convolution of the filter kernel size after the number of channels is labeled as such (in_channels, kernel_size, output_channels) below each Type box.

The continuous, unpooled convolutional blocks to enhance the effect of features extracting; As described in SRNet. The main discrepancy between Type 1 and Type 2 is the inclusion of a short-cut or not. In the case of deep learning, it is difficult to explain which module in the network is responsible for the decision, neither the removal of the initial preprocessing layer nor the elimination of either layer will dictate the final output of the network.

The input images are assumed to be grayscale 256×256 size. The layers apart from the pre-processing layer employ 3×3 kernels and pooling layers (both max pooling and average pooling) not be used in we proposed network. It is because the value of the signal-to-noise ratio is too small as far as the steganalysis task is concerned. Because average pooling is a low-pass filter, it enhances content but also suppresses the signal-to-noise by averaging adjacent signal; max-pooling can be thought of as a high-pass filter that makes isolated tampering points ignored, making the final decision plane decision problematic. All feature map variations in the network are due to parameter configurations in the convolutional layer.

The main gaps between our proposed model and the existing Selection-Channel-Aware deep learning steganalysis are as follows:

1) CNet does not require the involvement of embedding probability maps in both training and testing phases and more generalizable to unknown steganographic algorithms.
2) Most of the existing approaches of Selection-Channel-Aware deep learning-based steganalysis are fixed. This not only makes the network structure solidified, leading to a decrease in detection accuracy. It also makes the transformation of the embedded probability map not sufficient and may prevent the optimization algorithm from finding a better effect during the training phases.

4   Experiments and Analysis

4.1   Train Dataset and Test Dataset

We acquired Cover images from the 10,000 images in the BOSSbase1.01 Natural Image Library. We set the ratio of the training dataset to the validation dataset to test dataset set to 4:1:5, with no overlapping data within the three datasets. Due to our GPU computing platform and time limitation, the data used in CNet are all grayscale images of 256×256 size. The images in each dataset are cropped using the imresize() function in MATLAB R2018b. For better demonstrate the universal steganalysis capabilities that CNet possesses, the dataset is produced using multiple classes of adaptive steganography such as S-UNIWARD, HILL, and MiPOD. CNet's training data is primarily data that is S-UNIWARD steganography on BOSSbase. (For a more convenient representation of such datasets, we have named them BOSS_SUNI.)

During the CNNs training processing, we fixed a maximum of 400 epochs. We have found that when the network reaches a certain number of epochs, the overall result of the network does not continue to be optimized, both in terms of the loss function and in terms of the final accuracy. During our experiments, to prevent overfitting of the network, when the loss function appears stable for a while or increasing when the accuracy of the verification dataset starts to decrease, etc.

4.2   Hyper-parameters

Since our proposed CNet uses a distributed training process to getting it closer to the respective global immobility point. During the training process of the embedding probability map generation module, we mixed Cover with Stego to make the module effectively compatible with adaptive steganography with multiple classes of BPP. This prevents the network from generating different embedding probability maps based on the distribution of images, which are then learned as a target using the corresponding embedding probability maps obtained by executing the S-UNIWARD algorithm via MATLAB R2018b. The learning rate is initially set to 0.05 and then becomes 20% of the original rate every 1000 iterations until the learning rate is reduced to 0.001 and then no more changes are made to the learning rate. All training and test were run on an NVidia 2080Ti GPU card, which has 11 GB GPU memory.

In CNet, We apply a content-adaptive moment estimation max [10] (Adamax) to train our CNN. For all other parameters in Adamax, we use the default values of Adamax function in Pytorch. We did not use the dropout operation in CNet. The batch size in the training procedure is set to 32, due to GPU memory limitation (16 cover/stego pairs). During training, we set the initial learning rate to 0.01, and then the learning rate change policy was set to multiply the learning rate by 0.1 every 50 epochs until the epochs exceeded 200 with no change in the learning rate. In the preprocessing phase, whereby the weights of this layer are initialized to SRM filters (5×5 for a total of 30), but the processed of all weights of 30 different high-pass filters are learnable in the training processing.

About activations, we take the same approach, which is mimicking the truncation operation in SRM. The formula of the truncation function (TLU) is given in the following:

$$Trunc(x) = \begin{cases} -T, & x < -T, \\ x, & -T \leq x \leq T, \\ T, & x > T \end{cases} \qquad (3)$$

The use of TLU in the first layers helps to accommodate the distribution of embedding signals and forces CNN to learn high-pass filtering more efficiently and constantly updating the parameters (Table 1).

Table 1. Steganalysis Error Rates ($P_E = 1 - P_{Accuracy}$) comparison with using ReLU and TLU of a different value of T.

Activation function	ReLU	Truncated Linear Unit (TLU)				
		$T = 2$	$T = 3$	$T = 4$	$T = 5$	$T = 7$
CNet	0.1335	0.1275	0.1210	0.1360	**0.1225**	0.1320

We performed experiments comparing the different activation functions with values after preprocessing in CNet (without modifying the activation functions in the network). The performance of Different settings of the first activation function after the pre-processing layer in terms of detection error (P_E). Through experiments, we can find that the value of T has a relatively large impact on the detection accuracy, with the best effect when $T = 5$ and the second best when $T = 3$.

4.3   Experimental Results

All of the above experiments were performed on images operated by S-UNIWARD at 0.4 bpp.

According to Table 2, we found that CNN-based steganalysis requires a large dataset to assist in the training process. In our experiments, we use image flipping operations to enhance the images to increase the number of training datasets. But how to accomplish this training on a small dataset will require more in-depth research in the future. The smaller and simpler network layer of Xu-Net gives it a significant advantage in terms of parameters and convergence speed, but the final detection accuracy found to have some limitations, which proves that a deep network layer can effectively learn the high-dimensional semantic features of images. Ye-Net and Yedroudj-Net use similar operations as Xu-Net in the preprocessing layer with 30 manually designed filter kernels in the SRM, so that the three steganalysis are comparable in parameters and final detection accuracy. SRNet, Zhu-Net, and CNet are no longer limited to manually designed high-pass filter kernels, but constantly update the weights during training to take fully advantage on the potential capabilities of deep learning. So it's more both parameters and training time.

Table 2. The numbers of parameters, execution time to convergence, and Error rate comparison using Xu-Net, Ye-Net, Yedroudj-Net, SRNet, Zhu-Net and CNet.

Algorithms	The numbers of parameters ($\times 10^5$)	Execution time to convergence (hour)	Error rate
Xu-Net	**1.4**	**3.4**	0.2835
Ye-Net	10.6	3.95	0.1995
Yedroudj-Net	44.5	4.28	0.1892
SRNet	477.6	17.29	0.1523
Zhu-Net	287.1	7.36	0.1875
CNet	75.5	4.96	**0.1225**

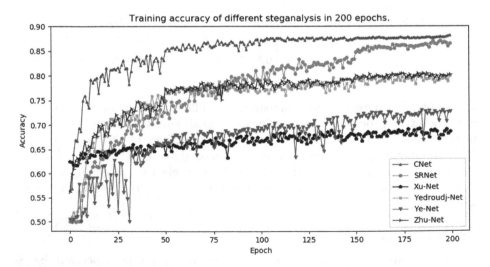

Fig. 5. The training accuracy of different steganalysis in 200 epochs comparison with CNet, SRNet, Xu-Net, Yedroudj-Net, Ye-Net and Zhu-Net.

In this part, We conducted lightweight experiments with various types of existing steganalysis, and to investigate the learning ability of each CNN-based steganalysis at a small number of training rounds, the above experiments were truncated at 200 Epochs, taking into account the overfitting problems that may occur with some of the models. Since CNet has an embedded probability map as a guide, it can have a higher classification accuracy in the first few rounds. Not only can CNet converge faster in less time, but CNet is also more accurate when it finally settles down. CNet has an acceleration of accuracy not found in other steganalysis (Table 3).

Table 3. Steganalysis Error Rates ($P_E = 1 - P_{Accuracy}$) comparison on different datasets with 0.4bpp and 0.2bpp.

	BOSS_SUNI	BOSS_WOW	BOSS_HUGO	BOSS_MiPOD
0.4 bpp				
SRNet	0.1531	0.1542	0.3194	0.2442
Zhu-Net	0.1462	0.1695	0.3168	0.2580
CNet	0.1125	0.1655	0.1572	0.1911
0.2 bpp				
SRNet	0.3077	0.3650	0.4178	0.4017
Zhu-Net	0.3145	0.3727	0.4017	0.4178
CNet	0.2726	0.3483	0.3364	0.3076

We chose the recently matured steganalysis as the control group for comparison The above experiments demonstrate that CNet not only has a low false detection rate on the BOSS_SUNI training set. And it also has some generic steganalysis capabilities on other test sets. In the 0.2 bpp experiments, the weights used were all optimal for the effect on 0.4 bpp. It has also been shown that the embedding probability maps generated through the network are also important guides. On BOSS_HUGO and BOSS_MiPOD, CNet outperforms the other two networks by a wide margin. The detection accuracy of SRNet and Zhu-Net is more closely related to their own training sets, so the detection accuracy on BOSS_HUGO is not as good as that of CNet. But on BOSS_WOW the performance of CNet is not comparable with SRNet and Zhu-Net, it may be due to the differences between WOW's steganography algorithm and others. This means that CNet is more robust. According to Fig. 5, CNet has the ability to accomplish faster learning in fewer rounds, and CNet has fewer parameters that can be deployed on lightweight devices in the future.

5   Conclusion

In this paper, we propose a lightweight content-based spatial domain steganalysis model named CNet. CNet introduces other domain knowledge into steganalysis and builds a simple and efficient network. The embedded probability maps are used in the network for guiding the network learning and reducing the potential search space. It outperforms existing CNN-Based models in terms of number of parameters, convergence time, and final detection accuracy.

The difficulty of image steganalysis lies in the fact that steganographic operations embed little information in the image, while the weak differences before and after the image are easily impressed by the content information between pixels. This indicates that introducing the embedded probability map into the steganalysis network is capable of enhancing the final detection accuracy. However, considering that the manually designed filter kernel is too relies on prior knowledge, which tends to make the network converge to a local optimal solution rather than a global optimal solution. CNet uses sophisticated filtering kernels to initialize the preprocessing layer and allows the preprocessing layer weights to participate in the backpropagation process of the network, making the final detection accuracy not limited by artificial features.

References

1. Bas, P., Filler, T., Pevný, T.: "Break our steganographic system": the ins and outs of organizing BOSS. In: Filler, T., Pevný, T., Craver, S., Ker, A. (eds.) IH 2011. LNCS, vol. 6958, pp. 59–70. Springer, Heidelberg (2011). https://doi.org/10.1007/978-3-642-24178-9_5
2. Boroumand, M., Chen, M., Fridrich, J.: Deep residual network for steganalysis of digital images. IEEE Trans. Inf. Forensics Secur. 14(5), 1181–1193 (2018)
3. Chandramouli, R., Memon, N.: Analysis of LSB based image steganography techniques. In: Proceedings 2001 International Conference on Image Processing (Cat. No. 01CH37205), vol. 3, pp. 1019–1022. IEEE (2001)
4. Chaumont, M.: Deep learning in steganography and steganalysis. In: Digital Media Steganography, pp. 321–349. Elsevier (2020)
5. Denemark, T., Fridrich, J., Comesaña-Alfaro, P.: Improving selection-channel-aware steganalysis features. Electron. Imaging 2016(8), 1–8 (2016)
6. Denemark, T., Sedighi, V., Holub, V., Cogranne, R., Fridrich, J.: Selection-channel-aware rich model for steganalysis of digital images. In: 2014 IEEE International Workshop on Information Forensics and Security (WIFS), pp. 48–53. IEEE (2014)
7. Fridrich, J., Kodovsky, J.: Rich models for steganalysis of digital images. IEEE Trans. Inf. Forensics Secur. 7(3), 868–882 (2012)
8. Goljan, M., Fridrich, J., Cogranne, R.: Rich model for steganalysis of color images. In: 2014 IEEE International Workshop on Information Forensics and Security (WIFS), pp. 185–190. IEEE (2014)
9. Ker, A.D.: Steganalysis of LSB matching in grayscale images. IEEE Signal Process. Lett. 12(6), 441–444 (2005)
10. Kingma, D.P., Ba, J.: Adam: a method for stochastic optimization. arXiv preprint arXiv:1412.6980 (2014)
11. Pevny, T., Bas, P., Fridrich, J.: Steganalysis by subtractive pixel adjacency matrix. IEEE Trans. Inf. Forensics Secur. 5(2), 215–224 (2010)
12. Qian, Y., Dong, J., Wang, W., Tan, T.: Deep learning for steganalysis via convolutional neural networks. In: Media Watermarking, Security, and Forensics 2015, vol. 9409, p. 94090J. International Society for Optics and Photonics (2015)

13. Tan, S., Li, B.: Stacked convolutional auto-encoders for steganalysis of digital images. In: Signal and Information Processing Association Annual Summit and Conference (APSIPA), 2014 Asia-Pacific. pp. 1–4. IEEE (2014)
14. Tang, W., Li, H., Luo, W., Huang, J.: Adaptive steganalysis based on embedding probabilities of pixels. IEEE Trans. Inf. Forensics Secur. **11**(4), 734–745 (2015)
15. Xu, G., Wu, H.Z., Shi, Y.Q.: Structural design of convolutional neural networks for steganalysis. IEEE Signal Process. Lett. **23**(5), 708–712 (2016)
16. Yang, J., Liu, K., Kang, X., Wong, E., Shi, Y.: Steganalysis based on awareness of selection-channel and deep learning. In: Kraetzer, C., Shi, Y.-Q., Dittmann, J., Kim, H.J. (eds.) IWDW 2017. LNCS, vol. 10431, pp. 263–272. Springer, Cham (2017). https://doi.org/10.1007/978-3-319-64185-0_20
17. Ye, J., Ni, J., Yi, Y.: Deep learning hierarchical representations for image steganalysis. IEEE Trans. Inf. Forensics Secur. **12**(11), 2545–2557 (2017)
18. Yedroudj, M., Comby, F., Chaumont, M.: Yedroudj-net: an efficient CNN for spatial steganalysis. In: 2018 IEEE International Conference on Acoustics, Speech and Signal Processing (ICASSP), pp. 2092–2096. IEEE (2018)
19. You, W., Zhang, H., Zhao, X.: A Siamese CNN for image steganalysis. IEEE Trans. Inf. Forensics Secur. **16**, 291–306 (2020)
20. Zhang, R., Zhu, F., Liu, J., Liu, G.: Depth-wise separable convolutions and multi-level pooling for an efficient spatial CNN-based steganalysis. IEEE Trans. Inf. Forensics Secur. **15**, 1138–1150 (2019)

Improving VVC Intra Coding
via Probability Estimation and Fusion
of Multiple Prediction Modes

Ziqiu Zhang, Changyue Ma, Dong Liu$^{(\boxtimes)}$, Li Li, and Feng Wu

University of Science and Technology of China, Hefei 230027, China
{ziqiu,cyma}@mail.ustc.edu.cn, {dongeliu,lil1,fengwu}@ustc.edu.cn

Abstract. The upcoming Versatile Video Coding (VVC) standard has improved the intra coding efficiency by introducing a great number of intra prediction modes. The cost on signaling the prediction modes is heavy. To reduce the mode coding overhead as well as to leverage multi-hypothesis prediction, we propose an intra coding method on top of VVC. For each block, we use a trained neural network to predict the probability distribution of all possible intra prediction modes. The predicted probabilities are used twofold. On the one hand, the probability values are used as weights to fuse the prediction signals generated by multiple modes, leading to a new prediction signal. On the other, the probability values are used by an advanced arithmetic coding instead of the context adaptive binary arithmetic coding. With the proposed method, the intra coding efficiency is improved by more than 1% averagely upon the VVC test model.

Keywords: Entropy coding · Intra coding · Multi-hypothesis prediction · Neural network · Versatile video coding

1 Introduction

The continuously increasing amount of video data raises great challenges for video storage and transmission systems, which calls for more efficient video coding technologies. Versatile Video Coding (VVC), also known as H.266, has been developed in response to the call [3]. VVC outperforms its ancestor, H.265/HEVC [8], by more than 30% bits saving under similar quality levels. Nonetheless, the development of video coding technologies beyond VVC is still necessary.

Intra picture coding, or intra coding for short, is a very important component in video coding schemes. In VVC, intra coding efficiency has been improved a lot compared to the intra coding in HEVC. Meanwhile, intra coding efficiency is still far below inter picture coding efficiency, and the gap between intra/inter coding efficiency is even larger in VVC than in HEVC [3]. Improving intra coding efficiency is then valuable for VVC and future video coding technologies.

© Springer Nature Switzerland AG 2021
Y. Peng et al. (Eds.): ICIG 2021, LNCS 12888, pp. 654–664, 2021.
https://doi.org/10.1007/978-3-030-87355-4_54

Intra prediction is a unique tool for intra coding. A lot of studies have been conducted on intra prediction in the development of HEVC and VVC. In VVC, more intra prediction modes are used than in HEVC, enhancing the flexibility to choose an appropriate prediction mode for each prediction unit. It is definitely possible to add more prediction modes in the hope of achieving more coding gain, but this is also problematic: First, if using too many modes, the signaling of the chosen modes needs more bits, incurring an overhead. Second, the decoder shall support all possible modes, more modes incur more implementation cost of the decoder, especially hardware decoder.

In this paper, we try to improve VVC intra coding not by adding more prediction modes but by addressing the above two problems. First, we want to reduce the overhead of signaling the intra prediction modes, this is accomplished by estimating the probability more accurately and by using an advanced arithmetic coding. Second, we want to further enhance the flexibility of adaptive mode selection, but do not add new prediction modules, this is achieved by multi-hypothesis prediction, i.e. fusing the prediction signals generated by multiple prediction modes.

The remainder of this paper is organized as follows. In Sect. 2, we review the existing intra prediction modes and its entropy coding process in VVC. Then, we introduce the proposed method in detail in Sect. 3. Experimental results and analyses are presented in Sect. 4. Section 5 concludes this paper.

2   Intra Prediction Modes and Related Entropy Coding in VVC

In this paper we mainly focus on the intra prediction for luma component. In HEVC, there are at most 35 intra prediction modes for luma component, including 33 directional modes, direct current (DC) mode, and planar mode. In VVC [3], the number of directional prediction modes increases to 65, and DC and planar modes are reserved, resulting in 67 normal modes. Besides, VVC has introduced several groups of new intra prediction modes. The first group is named matrix-weighted intra prediction (MIP), which consists of multiple modes and the specific number of modes depends on the prediction unit size. The second group is multiple reference lines (MRL), which uses more reference pixels to predict. MRL has two subgroups, indexed by 1 and 3 respectively. Within each subgroup there are several prediction modes. The third group is intra sub-partition (ISP), which divides the prediction unit into several sub-partitions and reconstructs the sub-partitions one by one. ISP also has multiple prediction modes.

The entropy coding of intra prediction modes in VVC is much more complex than that in HEVC. In VVC, there are a number of syntax elements for the entropy coding of intra prediction modes, including: MIP flag, MIP mode index, MRL mode index, ISP mode index, most-probable-mode (MPM) flag, planar flag, MPM index, and non-MPM mode index. The parsing of these syntax elements is as follows. For a prediction unit, the first syntax element should be MIP flag. If the MIP flag is true, then the MIP mode index should follow; otherwise,

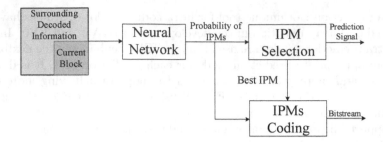

Fig. 1. The proposed neural network-based intra coding method. IPM stands for intra prediction mode.

the MRL mode index and the ISP mode index are successively parsed. Next, the MPM flag, indicating whether to use a mode in the MPM list, is parsed. If the MPM flag is true, the planar flag and MPM index are successively parsed; otherwise, the non-MPM mode index is parsed.

3   Proposed Method

In this paper, we propose a neural network-based intra coding method on top of VVC. As shown in Fig. 1, our method depends on estimating the probability distribution of all possible intra prediction modes for the current prediction unit. This probability estimation is based on the already encoded/decoded information, so that both encoder and decoder perform the identical estimation. The probability estimation is accomplished by a trained neural network. Afterwards, we use the estimated probability values in two steps: multi-hypothesis prediction, and entropy coding of the chosen prediction mode. In this section, we first discuss the details of the probability estimation, and then present the methods of multi-hypothesis prediction and entropy coding.

3.1   Neural Network-Based Probability Estimation for Intra Prediction Modes

Network Input/Output. In a previous study [7], a trained neural network was used to estimate the probability distribution of all possible intra prediction modes in HEVC. In this paper, we are considering a similar problem but in VVC. As mentioned, the intra prediction modes in VVC are much more than those in HEVC. Besides, VVC intra prediction modes consist of several groups like MIP, MRL, and ISP. It becomes quite complex if we directly estimate the probability of one group.

We propose a new notation system to uniformly represent the VVC intra modes. Figure 2 describes the proposed notation system, namely combined intra mode, for 4 × 4 blocks as an example. In short, our combined intra mode is to assign a unique mode index for each group and each mode in the VVC intra

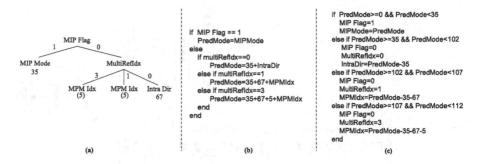

Fig. 2. The proposed combined intra mode for 4 × 4 blocks. (a) Decision tree for the VVC intra modes. (b) Combined intra mode is derived from the VVC intra mode-related syntax elements at the encoder. (c) The VVC intra mode-related syntax elements are derived from the combined intra mode at the decoder.

modes. For 4 × 4 blocks, we assign indexes 0–34 to the MIP group, indexes 35–101 to the normal intra prediction group (i.e. 67 prediction modes, non-MRL, non-ISP), indexes 102–111 to the MRL group. In total, there are 112 modes in the combined intra mode system. Note that the combined intra mode can be easily converted from/to the VVC intra modes, as shown in Fig. 2. The combined intra mode for other block sizes can be similarly derived, and omitted here.

Using the combined intra mode, the formulation of probability estimation is easier. For example, for 4 × 4 blocks, we need to predict a 112-dimensional vector that sums to 1, representing the probability values of all the combined intra modes. To fulfill the probability estimation, we note that the optimal intra mode of the current prediction unit is highly relevant to the surrounding image content, which can be characterized by the already encoded/decoded data, such as the surrounding reconstruction image, the surrounding prediction image, the surrounding residual image, the surrounding intra modes, the surrounding block partitions, and so on. These data have different formats so we process them differently in the designed neural networks.

Network Structure. The network structure for 4 × 4 block probability estimation is shown in Fig. 3(a). The surrounding reconstruction image, surrounding prediction image, and surrounding residual image are organized as three channels of a 3D tensor that is input to the convolutional branch. There are several densely connected blocks (Dense Blocks) [4] and pooling layers after the initial convolutional layer. In the other branch, the surrounding intra modes and surrounding block partitions are input, and processed by three consecutive fully-connected layers each equipped with parametric rectified linear unit (PReLU). The outputs of the aforementioned two branches are then concatenated and processed further by a fully-connected layer, followed by the softmax activation function, to give out the predicted probability values.

Figure 3(b) depicts the general network structure for blocks other than 4 × 4. In this network, the surrounding intra modes are organized into a matrix,

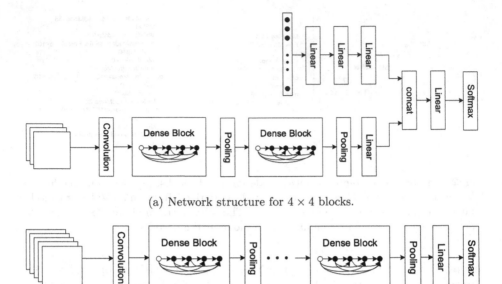

(a) Network structure for 4 × 4 blocks.

(b) Network structure for other sizes blocks.

Fig. 3. The proposed network structures.

where each block is filled with the combined intra mode index of that block; the surrounding block partitions are also organized into a matrix, where the block boundary locations are marked 1, and the other locations are marked 0. Those two matrices, together with the surrounding reconstruction image, surrounding prediction image, surrounding residual image, form five channels of a 3D tensor that is input to the network. This network has a convolutional layer, several Dense Blocks, pooling layers, and a fully-connected layer equipped with the softmax activation function for probability estimation.

Detailed configuration of network hyper-parameters is summarized in Table 1.

Network Training. The widely adopted image sets: UCID [6] and DIV2K [1], are used to generate the training data. The raw images in UCID and DIV2K are converted into YUV 4:2:0 format and then compressed by VTM, the VVC reference software. We then parse the bitstreams and extract the required data as network inputs and output labels. The networks are trained by minimizing the cross-entropy loss function:

$$L(\Theta) = -\sum_i T_i \cdot \log(Y_i(\Theta)), \tag{1}$$

where Θ is the parameter set of the neural network. T_i is the output label of the i-th training sample, which is a one-hot vector denoting the signaled mode. Y_i is the corresponding network output. $\cdot$ represents inner product.

Table 1. Network hyper-parameters

Block size $H \times W$	# Dense blocks	# Intra modes
4×4	2	112
4×8	3	230
4×16	4	222
4×32	2	211
8×4	3	230
8×8	3	230
8×16	4	222
8×32	2	222
16×4	4	222
16×8	4	222
16×16	4	222
16×32	2	222
32×4	2	211
32×8	2	222
32×16	2	222
32×32	2	222
64×64	5	222

3.2   Probability-Based Multi-hypothesis Prediction

As we have estimated the probability distribution of all possible intra modes, we propose a multi-hypothesis intra prediction method. The idea is to fuse the prediction signals generated by multiple intra modes, where the multiple intra modes already exist in VVC. Since we have the estimated probability values, we propose to use the probability values as weights when we fuse the prediction signals, i.e.

$$\bar{X}_{\text{multi-hypothesis}} = \frac{\sum_{k=1}^{n} p_k x_k}{\sum_{k=1}^{n} p_k}, \tag{2}$$

where n is the number of modes participating in the fusion. x_k is the prediction signal of the k-th mode and p_k is the corresponding probability of that mode, estimated by the trained network. Note that the probability values are estimated at decoder, instead of being pre-defined or signaled in the bitstream. In theory n can be as large as the number of all possible modes, e.g. 112 for 4×4 blocks. However, too many modes may not be helpful for the prediction accuracy, and incur heavy computational cost. In this paper, we consider using the selected high-probability modes to fuse. Specifically, after the probability estimation, we select the top-n modes with the highest probability values, and fuse their prediction signals. We empirically observed that $n = 7$ leads to a relatively high coding gain. Besides, the ISP modes in VVC are not friendly to the multi-hypothesis prediction. The ISP modes have been excluded before selecting the top-n modes.

Table 2. BD-Rate of the proposed method

Class	Sequence	BD-rate (%)		
		Y	U	V
A1 (3840 × 2160)	Tango	−1.74	−3.00	−1.51
	FoodMarket	−2.27	−2.42	−2.37
	Campfire	−0.71	0.11	1.04
Class A1 Avg.		−1.57	−1.84	−1.64
A2 (3840 × 2160)	CatRobot1	−0.81	−1.51	−0.96
	DaylightRoad	−0.84	0.31	0.13
	ParkRunning	−0.36	−0.53	−0.46
Class A2 Avg.		−0.67	−0.58	−0.43
B (1920 × 1080)	MarketPlace	−0.78	−1.39	0.09
	RitualDance	−1.42	−2.11	−1.77
	Cactus	−0.88	−0.99	−0.70
	BasketballDrive	−1.34	−0.42	−0.75
	BQTerrace	−0.75	0.36	−0.11
Class B Avg.		−1.03	−0.91	−0.65
C (832 × 480)	BasketballDrill	−0.50	0.68	0.66
	BQMall	−0.67	−1.47	−1.60
	PartyScene	−0.64	−0.12	−0.95
	RaceHorses	−1.01	−1.93	−1.35
Class C Avg.		−0.70	−0.71	−0.81
D (416 × 240)	BasketballPass	−0.58	−0.03	−1.12
	BQSquare	−0.22	−0.53	−0.89
	BlowingBubbles	−0.68	−0.15	−2.43
	RaceHorses	−1.60	−1.43	−1.92
Class D Avg.		−0.77	−0.46	−1.59
E (1280 × 720)	FourPeople	−1.69	−1.50	−1.48
	Johnny	−1.69	−1.27	−0.12
	KristenAndSara	−1.69	−1.67	−3.13
Class E Avg.		−1.69	−1.48	−1.58
Total Average		**−1.04**	**−0.95**	**−1.08**

The proposed multi-hypothesis prediction has been integrated into VVC. For each prediction unit, we now use one binary flag to indicate whether it uses the multi-hypothesis prediction or not. If using, then no further bits are required for obtaining the intra prediction signal. Otherwise, we still use the VVC intra modes. This binary flag is decided to pursue rate-distortion optimization at the encoder side. In addition, if the flag is true, we assign the one mode with the highest probability as the "intra mode" of the current prediction unit, so as to be used as the surrounding intra modes and construct the MPM list of the following blocks.

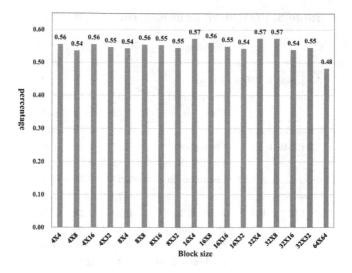

Fig. 4. Percentage of using the proposed multi-hypothesis prediction at different block sizes.

3.3 Probability-Based Advanced Arithmetic Coding

The estimated probability values are further used in the entropy coding step. For one prediction unit, if it does not use the proposed multi-hypothesis prediction, it will use one of the VVC intra modes, and the used mode shall be signaled to decoder. As we have the estimated probability values, we directly code the combined intra mode (interpreted in Fig. 2), using the multi-ary arithmetic coding engine [5] instead of CABAC. Thanks to the probability estimation accuracy, the multi-ary arithmetic coding outperforms CABAC, as observed in [7]. It is worth noting that the probability estimation is performed by a neural network that is trained with VVC coded data; the probabilities are different when we enable the proposed multi-hypothesis prediction technique. According to our experiments, we adjust the estimated probability values by decreasing the probability of the highest probability mode and increasing the probabilities of the other modes.

4 Experimental Results

The proposed method has been implemented upon the VVC reference software, VTM version 6.0. The neural network-based probability estimation is implemented with LibTorch. We follow the VVC common test conditions and choose all-intra configuration. BD-rate [2] is calculated to evaluate the coding efficiency. The overall performance of the proposed method is shown in Table 2. The average BD-rate reductions for Y, U, V channels are 1.04%, 0.95%, 1.08%. We also test the proposed multi-hypothesis prediction only, i.e., not using the advanced arithmetic coding. Results are shown in Table 3. The average BD-rate reductions for Y, U, V channels are 0.91%, 0.83%, 0.96%.

Table 3. BD-Rate of the multi-hypothesis prediction

Class	Sequence	BD-rate (%)		
		Y	U	V
A1 (3840 × 2160)	Tango	−1.53	−2.78	−1.29
	FoodMarket	−1.99	−2.13	−2.07
	Campfire	−0.78	−0.19	−1.12
Class A1 Avg.		−1.43	−1.70	−1.50
A2 (3840 × 2160)	CatRobot1	−0.77	−1.49	−0.94
	DaylightRoad	−1.13	−0.18	−0.32
	ParkRunning	−0.34	−0.51	−0.44
Class A2 Avg.		−0.75	−0.73	−0.57
B (1920 × 1080)	MarketPlace	−0.79	−1.38	0.09
	RitualDance	−1.42	−2.09	−1.76
	Cactus	−0.79	−0.89	−0.62
	BasketballDrive	−1.34	−0.41	−0.74
	BQTerrace	−0.82	0.29	−0.18
Class B Avg.		−1.03	−0.90	−0.64
C (832 × 480)	BasketballDrill	−0.65	0.53	0.51
	BQMall	−0.51	−1.29	−1.42
	PartyScene	−0.58	−0.05	−0.88
	RaceHorses	−0.77	−1.69	−1.11
Class C Avg.		−0.63	−0.63	−0.73
D (416 × 240)	BasketballPass	−0.32	0.23	−0.87
	BQSquare	0.06	−0.28	−0.62
	BlowingBubbles	−0.55	0.29	−2.29
	RaceHorses	−1.18	−1.02	−1.51
Class D Avg.		−0.50	−0.20	−1.32
E (1280 × 720)	FourPeople	−1.40	−1.18	−1.15
	Johnny	−1.30	−0.90	0.26
	KristenAndSara	−1.15	−1.14	−2.60
Class E Avg.		−1.28	−1.07	−1.16
Total Average		**−0.91**	**−0.83**	**−0.96**

In addition, we calculate the percentage of the blocks that choose the proposed multi-hypothesis prediction. Since there are different kinds of block size in VVC, we calculate the percentage for each kind of block size separately. As shown in Fig. 4, the percents for different block sizes are mostly falling into the range of 50% to 60%, except for 64 × 64 blocks where the percent is 48%. Figure 5 visualizes the block partitioning result. In terms of number, more than 50% blocks have selected the multi-hypothesis prediction in this result. All these results demonstrate that the multi-hypothesis prediction is a quite useful method for VVC intra coding.

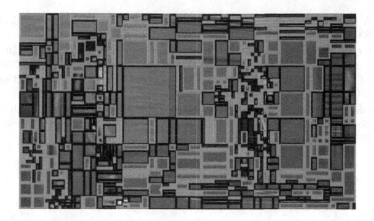

Fig. 5. Visualization of the block partitioning result (BasketballPass, 1st frame, QP = 37). Red edge indicates a block using the multi-hypothesis prediction. Black edge indicates a block using VVC intra modes. (Color figure online)

5   Conclusion

In this paper, we have proposed a neural network-based intra coding method upon VVC. Specifically, we train neural networks to predict the probability distribution over all the intra prediction modes. We then use the predicted probabilities twofold. First, we propose a multi-hypothesis prediction method by fusing the prediction signals of multiple modes and weighting by the probabilities. Second, we adopt an advanced arithmetic codec to compress the chosen intra prediction mode. Experimental results show that the proposed method achieves on average 1.04% BD-rate reduction compared to VTM.

Currently, we pursue a high compression efficiency and have used deep neural networks. In the future, we plan to simplify the neural network to reduce its computational complexity.

Acknowledgments. This work was supported by the Natural Science Foundation of China under Grants 62022075, 62036005, 62021001, and by the University Synergy Innovation Program of Anhui Province under No. GXXT-2019-025.

References

1. Agustsson, E., Timofte, R.: NTIRE 2017 challenge on single image super-resolution: Dataset and study. In: CVPR Workshops, pp. 126–135 (2017)
2. Bjontegaard, G.: Calcuation of average PSNR differences between RD-curves. Technical report. VCEG-M33, VCEG (2001)
3. Bross, B., et al.: Developments in international video coding standardization after AVC, with an overview of Versatile Video Coding (VVC). Proc. IEEE (2021). https://doi.org/10.1109/JPROC.2020.3043399
4. Huang, G., et al.: Densely connected convolutional networks. In: CVPR, pp. 4700–4708 (2017)

5. Said, A.: Introduction to arithmetic coding - theory and practice. Technical report. HPL-2004-76, Hewlett Packard Laboratories Palo Alto (2004)
6. Schaefer, G., Stich, M.: UCID: an uncompressed color image database. In: Storage and Retrieval Methods and Applications for Multimedia, pp. 472–481 (2004)
7. Song, R., et al.: Neural network-based arithmetic coding of intra prediction modes in HEVC. In: VCIP, pp. 1–4 (2017)
8. Sullivan, G.J., Ohm, J.R,, Han, W.,J,, Wiegand, T · Overview of the high efficiency video coding (HEVC) standard. IEEE Trans. Circuits Syst. Video Technol. 22(12), 1649–1668 (2012)

Initial-QP Prediction for Versatile Video Coding: A Multi-domain Feature-Driven Learning Approach

Lirong Huang⑩, Jialin Zhang⑩, and Miaohui Wang⁽✉⁾⑩

College of Electronics and Information Engineering,
Shenzhen University, Shenzhen, China

Abstract. Initial quantization parameter (Initial-QP) prediction is a key point in video compression, which directly affects the rationality of bit-rate allocation and the quality of subsequent encoded frames. However, the Initial-QP value is still determined based on some fixed parameters in the latest Versatile Video Coding (VVC) reference software, and it is difficult to reach the optimum. In this paper, we investigate the Initial-QP prediction on the VVC platform based on the Gaussian Process Regression (GPR) method. We explore the optimal relationship between Initial-QP and bit-rate under a variety of video content, and extract three different domain features to represent the complexity of video content. Moreover, we apply the proposed method for the I-frame rate control in VVC. Experimental results show that our method improves the accuracy by up to 7.69% with a slight computational complexity increase.

Keywords: Rate control · Versatile Video Coding (VVC) · Machine learning

1 Introduction

Recently, video communication has not only experienced a blowout growth in the amount of data, but also the video content has become diversified. According to the 47th "Statistical Report on China's Internet Development Status", China's online video users have reached nearly 1 billion, and the growth rate is amazing [1]. Therefore, how to balance the relationship between the overhead of video encoding and perceived quality is an important research problem. The ITU Telecommunication Standardization Sector (ITU-T) and the Moving Picture Experts Group (MPEG) have jointly established the Joint Collaborative Team on Video Coding (JCT-VC) to explore the performance improvement methods for the next generation of video encoding technology, and completed

This work was supported in part by Natural Science Foundation of Shenzhen City (No. 2021A1515011877 and No. JCYJ20180305124209486), and in part by Natural Science Foundation of Guangdong Province (No. 2019A1515010961 and No. 2021A1515011877).

© Springer Nature Switzerland AG 2021
Y. Peng et al. (Eds.): ICIG 2021, LNCS 12888, pp. 665–675, 2021.
https://doi.org/10.1007/978-3-030-87355-4_55

Versatile Video Coding(VVC) in July 2020 [2]. The VVC standard has successively added a variety of new technologies, which has significantly improved the compression efficiency. However, the rate control scheme of intra frame (I-frame) remains similar as the previous standards, and the prediction of initial quantization parameter (Initial-QP) also lacks accuracy.

The Initial-QP [8,12] refers to the initial quantization value of the first I-frame. The I-frame is a key frame that retains complete information for decoding, and it has a close quality dependency with subsequent inter prediction frames. On the one hand, if the I-frame consumes too many bits to ensure the high quality of video encoding, it will cause the subsequent video frames to lack the required number of encoding bits. On the other hand, if the I-frame with a low image quality is used as a reference video frame, the video quality of the current group of picture (GOP) will be reduced, and the channel bandwidth may be wasted.

Early in the H.264/AVC standard, the allocated target bit-rate is used as a reference to determine two sets of different QPs. Wang *et al.* used information entropy and "INTRA16 DC" mode to evaluate the complexity of video content to determine the Initial-QP value [14]. But as the video coding framework becomes increasingly complicated, this method based on the H.264/AVC can no longer take effect. In the reference software-VTM-7.0 of VVC, the sum of absolute transformed difference (SATD)-based R-λ model [3] is mainly used to determine Initial-QP, where SATD is used to reflect the frame content complexity. However, the disadvantage is that the model is obtained through a fitting method, and the Initial-QPs are fixed values obtained through statistical analysis, which cannot accurately reflect the R-D relationship of different input videos. Considering the close relationship between the Initial-QP and the content characteristics, we propose a method of using a multi-domain feature-driven approach to predict the optimal Initial-QP in the VVC platform.

The contributions of this paper are presented as follows: (1) We propose a new Initial-QP prediction model, which combines machine learning and multi-domain features for I-frame. (2) We design a new approach to express the content complexity of Initial-QP, using the features of pixel domain, coding domain and transform domain to replace the traditional representation. (3) We train a Gaussian Process Regression (GPR)-driven model to learn the prediction of the optimal Initial-QP value. (4) The proposed Initial-QP prediction model is applied for the I-frame rate control for VVC. Experimental results validate its superior performance on the VVC reference software (VTM-7.0).

The remainder of this paper is organized as follows. Section 2 demonstrates the proposed method in details. Section 3 provides the experiment setting and the comparison results on the VVC platform. Finally, Sect. 4 concludes this paper.

2   Proposed Method

In this section, we first analyze the Rate-Distortion (R-D) relationship of I-frame in VVC, and utilize multiple QPs [11] to encode I-frames to establish the optimal R-D relationship for the video sequence. We describe the details of feature extraction, and then introduce the implementation of GPR model. Figure 1 shows the structure of the proposed method.

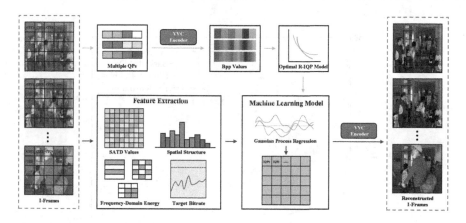

Fig. 1. The proposed multi-domain feature-driven based Initial-QP Prediction Framework. (1) Encode each CTU with multiple QP values to generate the optimal R-IQP curves. (2) Extract multi-domain features of I-frames to represent content complexity. (3) Train the machine learning model by inputting the feature vector, and finally obtain the predicted Initial-QP value.

2.1 Rate-Distortion Model Optimization of Initial-QP

VVC utilizes the R-D optimization method to select the encoding parameter of Coding Tree Unit(CTU) [4,5,9]. In the R-D optimization, QP is converted into the Lagrangian multiplier λ through the following relationship:

$$\lambda_{Mode} = c \times 2^{\frac{QP-12}{3}} \tag{1}$$

Equation (1) is used to calculate the overall RD-cost of compression, where the c value is related to the encoding structure and the position of the video frame. However, the obtained R-D relationship is not optimal [7], because it is based on statistical characteristics, and lacks the optimal choice of QP. Considering the importance of Initial-QP, the optimal R-D model requires the QP determination optimize.

In the "All-Intra" coding mode of VTM-7.0, we conduct the experiment with all the standard test video sequences of VVC, and utilize multiple QP values for encoding each CTU. We first set up 11 different Initial-QP values, and named the i-th Initial-QP as IQP_i, with values of 17, 20, 22, 25, 27, 30, 32, 35, 37, 40 and 42, respectively. Considering that traversing all QP values consumes huge computing resources, and according to experience, the best QP range is in a limited number of QP values, so the search range is only $[IQP_i - 6, IQP_i +$

6]. Then the encoder will select the QP corresponding to the minimum RD-cost as the best QP of the current CTU. In this way, it can be considered that the generated R-D curve is the best corresponding to the Initial-QP, which can be closer to the reachable R-D curve than the original method.

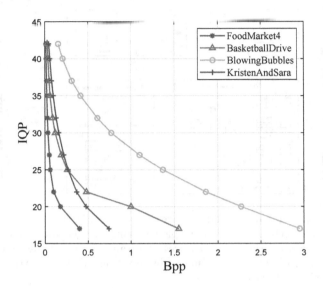

Fig. 2. Illustration of the Rate-Distortion curves.

Figure 2 shows the relationship between the optimized Initial-QP and the encoding bit-rate. We can see that different video sequences have different R-IQP relationships, and the differences mainly depend on the content characteristics of the video. According to this observation, we propose a method to predict Initial-QP based on the frame content complexity, which is to improve the rate control performance. Therefore, considering the target bit-rate of the video and the complexity of the I-frame at the same time, the Initial-QP prediction model can be expressed as:

$$IQP = \mathcal{M}(R_t, C) \tag{2}$$

where C is the feature vector of the I-frame, R_t is the target bit-rate, and M is the trained model based on the GPR method.

2.2   Multi-domain Feature Extraction

Video scenes are complex and changeable, so the content complexity of a video frame needs to be reflected from many aspects. We choose the spatial domain features to represent the spatial structure of a video frame, the frequency domain features to represent the sharpness of the pixel changes in the image gray space, and the coding features generated during the video coding process. The coding features mainly use the target bit-rate and the SATD value.

Target Bit-Rate Feature: It refers to the target bit-rate allocated to the current I-frame, denoted as R_t.

Sum of Absolute Transformed Difference Feature: SATD refers to the sum of the absolute values of transform coefficients, which is generated by the *Hadamard* transform. It is suggested in [3] as the content complexity evaluation value for the I-frame, which is adopted in HEVC and also utilized in VTM [13].

Here, the content complexity of an I-frame is defined as the sum of the SATD values of all 8 × 8 blocks in the frame. We use SATD as one of the input features, and its calculation is:

$$SATD = \sum_{i=1}^{8} \sum_{j=1}^{8} |c_{i,j}|, \tag{3}$$

where $c_{i,j}$ denotes the *Hadamard* transform coefficient.

Spatial Structure Feature: Gradient amplitude response can effectively detect most of the spatial structure information of the video frame. Some previous studies have proposed using gradient information to reflect the frame content complexity [7,8]. Therefore, the gradient feature is also considered as one of the input features. The gradient amplitude map of an I-frame can be defined as:

$$GM = \sqrt{[I \otimes h_x]^2 + [I \otimes h_y]^2}, \tag{4}$$

where I is a luminance channel of the I-frame, and $\otimes$ represents the convolution operation.

$h_d, d \in \{x, y\}$, represents the *Gaussian* partial derivative filter along the horizontal or vertical direction respectively. It is formulated as:

$$
\begin{aligned}
h_d(x, y|\sigma) &= \frac{\partial}{\partial d} g(x, y|\sigma) \\
&= -\frac{1}{2\pi\sigma^2} \frac{d}{\sigma^2} exp^{\{-\frac{x^2+y^2}{2\sigma^2}\}}
\end{aligned} \tag{5}
$$

where $g(x, y|\sigma)$ denotes the isotropic *Gaussian* function with a scale parameter of σ.

Then, the two-dimensional feature matrix GM is converted into the form of a histogram, and the feature data are divided into 10 groups to better retain the information of overall structure and local shape. The obtained feature vector is named HG.

Frequency-Domain Energy Feature: Luminance change is an important feature in expressing the frame content, and this change can be reflected more significantly in the frequency domain. We hence design a feature extraction method in the DCT transform [10]. First, the input I-frame is divided and transformed in the DCT domain with N × N blocks, and the obtained DC coefficients reflect the luminance information of the entire image. We normalize the DCT coefficient matrix by:

$$P(i,j) = \frac{C^2(i,j)}{\sum_{i=1}^{N}\sum_{j=1}^{N}C^2(i,j)}, \tag{6}$$

where $C(i,j)$ is the coefficient in the i-th row and j-th column of the DCT coefficient matrix, and i and j will not be equal to 1 at the same time so as to exclude the DC component.

Then, we calculate the information entropy for each block by

$$E_k = -\sum_{i=1}^{N}\sum_{j=1}^{N}P(i,j)log_2P(i,j), \tag{7}$$

where E_k is the number of non-overlapping N × N blocks. All blocks of the frame are arranged in descending order according to the entropy values, and then the average value of the first 40% is selected as the final frequency domain feature. Moreover, to enhance the expression characteristics of the frequency domain, we use three different $N = 4, 8, 16$ to extract the frequency domain feature, which is denoted by FDE.

Finally, the prediction model proposed in Sect. 2.1 can be reformulated as

$$IQP = \mathcal{M}(R_t, SATD, HG, FDE). \tag{8}$$

2.3   Machine Learning Implementation

We choose GPR to establish the mapping function of $\mathcal{M}(\cdot)$ in Eq. (8). GPR is a non-parametric model that performs regression analysis on prior data based on the *Gaussian* process [6,15]. The *Gaussian* process is a collection of a series of random variables that obeys the *Gaussian* distribution. The mean value function $m(z) = \mathbb{E}[gp(z)]$ and the co-variance kernel function $k(z, z')$ determine the performance of the *Gaussian* process $gp(\cdot)$ together. The kernel function we have chosen is the Matérn function. $k(z, z')$ can be expressed as Eq. (9).

$$k(z, z') = \mathbb{E}[(gp(z) - m(z))(gp(z') - m(z'))] \tag{9}$$

where z_i is the input feature vector of training data, and the data set can be expressed as $Z \triangleq \{z_i\}_{i=1}^{n}$. Its corresponding random variable is defined as the observed value, $gp_i \triangleq gp(z_i)$. Assuming z_* is arbitrary vector in Z, its corresponding observed value to be predicted can be defined as the predicted value, $gp_* \triangleq gp(z_*)$.

In addition, considering the noise in the sample data, the additive Gaussian noise is added to the observed value as $y_i = gp_i + \varepsilon_i$. The new observed values y and gp_* are still following the joint Gaussian distribution. The joint prior distribution of y and gp_* is expressed in Eq. (10):

$$\begin{bmatrix} y \\ gp_* \end{bmatrix} \sim \mathcal{N}\left(\begin{bmatrix} m_{gp} \\ m(z_*) \end{bmatrix}, \begin{bmatrix} K(Z,Z) + \sigma_n^2 I & K(Z, z_*) \\ K(z_*, Z) & K(z_*, z_*) \end{bmatrix}\right) \tag{10}$$

where $\boldsymbol{m}_{gp} = [m(\boldsymbol{z_1}), m(\boldsymbol{z_2}), ..., m(\boldsymbol{z_n}))]^T$, $\boldsymbol{y} \triangleq [y_1, y_2, ..., y_n]^T$. $K(Z, Z)$ is an symmetric positive definite co-variance matrix, and its element $k(z_i, z_j)$ is used to measure the correlation between z_i and z_j. I is the n-dimensional identity matrix. $K(Z, \boldsymbol{z_*}) = K(\boldsymbol{z_*}, Z)^T$ is the co-variance matrix between the test feature vector $\boldsymbol{z_*}$ and the training sample Z.

3   Experiment Results

3.1   Experimental Setup

In the experiment, we first evaluate the rate control accuracy of the proposed method. Then, we conduct quality performance evaluations to verify that the proposed method can effectively enhance video quality while improving the coding performance. Finally, the proposed method is compared with VTM-7.0 to demonstrate that the increased encoding complexity is affordable.

Dataset. We build two different databases, named *DatabaseA* and *DatabaseB* respectively. In *DatabaseA*, we select the 1st–20th frames of each video in the VVC standard sequences(22 in total) as the test set, and the 201st–220th frames as the training set. In *DatabaseB*, we randomly select 11 sequences from the same sequences as *DatabaseA*, the 1st–20th frames are selected as the test data. The remaining 11 sequences and some collected videos as the training data.

Training. The proposed model is implemented into the VVC reference software (VTM-7.0). The configuration mode of the encoder is "All-Intra", and the encoding parameter "TemporalSubsampling" is configured as 1. The target bit-rate of each video sequence is obtained by encoding four fixed QP values (22, 27, 32, 37) according to the default configuration. Since the experimental object is the Initial-QP, the R-D model parameters and the target bit-rate of each frame will not be updated during the encoding process.

3.2   R-D Performance Comparison

Figure 3 shows the rate control accuracy of the proposed method and VTM-7.0 based on *DatabaseA*. We select 6 classes of video sequences to make comparisons between the target bit-rates and the actual bit-rates. We can see that comparing with VTM-7.0, the average bit-rate accuracy value of the proposed method $M(R_t, C)_{GPR}$ is increased by 7.69%. At the same time, Fig. 4 shows the average bit-rate accuracy of $M(R_t, C)_{GPR}$ is increased by 7.01% on *DatabaseB*. It can be verified that the proposed method improves the rate control accuracy based on the experimental results of two data sets.

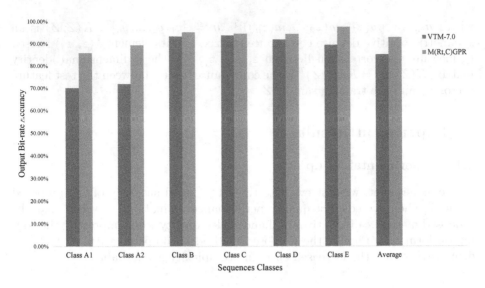

Fig. 3. Output bit-rate accuracy comparisons of GPR model and VTM-7.0 based on *DatabaseA*.

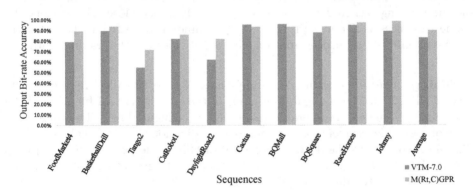

Fig. 4. Output bit-rate accuracy comparisons of GPR model and VTM-7.0 based on *DatabaseB*.

3.3   Quality Performance Evaluation

To evaluate the subjective quality of video frames, the reconstructed frames of *BasketballDrill* and *Johnny* are used as examples to demonstrate. As Fig. 5 shows, the areas marked by green rectangles demonstrate the quality differences of local edges and textures. We can find that the video frames reconstructed by the proposed model are clearer than those by VTM-7.0, which proves that our method can effectively improve the subjective quality.

Fig. 5. Comparisons of the subjective quality between the proposed method and VTM7.0. *Johnny* on the top and *BasketballDrill* on the bottom. The order from left to right is the original frame, VTM7.0, and $M(R_t, C)_{GPR}$. (Color figure online)

3.4 Ablation Experiment

In order to prove the the rationality and effectiveness of feature extraction, we conduct the ablation experiment on fusion features. The candidate features are the target bit-rate R_t, sum of the absolute values of transform coefficients $SATD$, spatial gradient histogram HG and frequency domain energy FDE. Among them, the target bit-rate must be considered. Based on the above, we set up 8 different feature sets to train the GPR model, and compare the mean-square-error (MSE) value between the obtained Initial-QP and the target one. The formulation of MSE is as Eq. 11:

$$MSE_{IQP} = \frac{1}{N} \times \sum_{i=1}^{N} (IQP - IQP_{act})^2, \tag{11}$$

where N denotes the number of sample frames, IQP is the predicted Initial-QP value, and IQP_{act} is the expected value.

Table 1 provides the test results. It can be found that the prediction effect is relatively poor when only the target bit-rate R_t is used as the input, which demonstrates that the video content is ignored. After adding the content-related features, the prediction accuracy has been improved. Among them, the MSE of selected set $FS8$ is 0.76, which is obviously the minimum of all feature sets.

3.5 Computational Complexity

We adopt VTM-7.0 and the proposed method to encode the video sequences under the same hardware condition and configuration. The average encoding time is used to represent the computational complexity. Compared with VTM-7.0, the average complexity of the proposed method is 122.89%. The increased complexity mainly comes from feature extraction and machine learning prediction.

Table 1. Ablation study on different features.

Feature set	Selected features	MSE_{IQP}
FS1	R_t	7.55
FS2	R_t, SATD	2.74
FS3	R_t, HG	3.29
FS4	R_t, FDE	3.29
FS5	R_t, SATD, HG	1.12
FS6	R_t, SATD, FDE	1.78
FS7	R_t, HG, FDE	1.23
FS8	R_t, SATD, HG, FDE	0.76

4   Conclusion

This paper introduces a new initial-QP prediction method for Versatile Video Coding based on a multi-domain feature-driven machine learning. We first utilize the multi-QP optimization method to establish the relationship between the best Initial-QP and the output bit-rate. Subsequently, we extract features from three different domains to represent the frame content complexity. Finally, we apply the proposed method for I-frame rate control. Experimental results show that the proposed method achieves more accurate rate control and less quality loss than VTM-7.0 with the tolerable complexity increase.

References

1. Cyberspace administration of China (2021). http://www.cac.gov.cn/2021-02/03/1613923423079314.htm
2. Bross, B., Chen, J., Liu, S.: Versatile video coding (draft 5). In: Joint Video Experts Team (JVET) of ITU-T SG 16 WP 3 and ISO/IEC JTC 1/SC 29/WG 11, pp. 1–394 (2019)
3. Karczewicz, M., Wang, X.: Intra frame rate control based on satd. In: Proceedings of 13th Meeting of JCTVC-M0257, ITU-T SG16 WP3 and ISO/IEC JTC1/SC29/WG11, pp. 18–26 (2013)
4. Li, B., Li, H., Li, L.: λ domain rate control algorithm for high efficiency video coding. IEEE Trans. Image Process. **23**(9), 3841–3854 (2014)
5. Li, Y., Liu, Z., Chen, Z.: Rate control for versatile video coding. In: IEEE International Conference on Image Processing (ICIP), pp. 1176–1180 (2020)
6. Quinonero-Candela, J., Rasmussen, C.E., Williams, C.K.: Approximation methods for gaussian process regression. In: Large-Scale Kernel Machines, pp. 203–223 (2007)
7. Wang, M., Ngan, K.N.: Optimal bit allocation in HEVC for real-time video communications. In: IEEE International Conference on Image Processing (ICIP), pp. 2665–2669 (2015)
8. Wang, M., Ngan, K.N., Li, H.: An efficient frame-content based intra frame rate control for high efficiency video coding. IEEE Signal Process. Lett. **22**(7), 896–900 (2014)

9. Wang, M., Ngan, K.N., Li, H.: Low-delay rate control for consistent quality using distortion-based Lagrange multiplier. IEEE Trans. Image Process. **25**(7), 2943–2955 (2016)
10. Wang, M., Ngan, K.N., Xu, L.: Efficient H. 264/AVC video coding with adaptive transforms. IEEE Trans. Multimedia **16**(4), 933–946 (2014)
11. Wang, M., Xiong, J., Xu, L., Xie, W., Ngan, K.N., Qin, J.: Rate constrained multiple-QP optimization for HEVC. IEEE Trans. Multimedia **22**(6), 1395–1406 (2019)
12. Wang, M., Yan, B.: Lagrangian multiplier based joint three-layer rate control for H. 264/AVC. IEEE Sig. Process. Lett. **16**(8), 679–682 (2009)
13. Wang, M., Zhang, J., Huang, L., Xiong, J.: Machine learning-based rate distortion modeling for VVC/H.266 intra-frame. In: IEEE International Conference on Multimedia and Expo (ICME), pp. 1–6 (2021)
14. Yan, B., Wang, M.: Adaptive distortion-based intra-rate estimation for H.264/AVC rate control. IEEE Sig. Process. Lett. **16**(3), 145–148 (2009)
15. Zhang, L., Xiu, X., Chen, J.: Adaptive color-space transform in HEVC screen content coding. IEEE J. Emerging Sel. Top. Circuits Syst. **6**(4), 446–459 (2016)

An Improved Digital Image Encryption Algorithm Based on Sine Compound Chaotic System

Jianchao Tang, Liyong Bao(✉), Hongwei Ding, Zheng Guan, and Min He

Information School, Yunnan University, Kunming 650500, China

Abstract. The rapid development of digital image transmission technology requires a more secure and effective image encryption scheme to provide the necessary security. This paper introduces an improved sine-transform-based chaotic system (ISTBCS). By linearly weighting and nonlinearly multiplying the selected classic maps, the new chaotic maps with more complex dynamics are obtained through sinusoidal transformation. Performance evaluation shows that it has chaotic characteristics such as wide range of chaos, high complexity, and strong non-periodicity. On this basis, an image encryption algorithm that uses bidirectional pixel encoding, displacement and diffusion at the same time is designed. By pixel encoding the plaintext, the small changes in the ordinary image can be propagated to all the pixels of the encrypted image, which greatly improves the ability to resist known plaintext attacks and selected plaintext attacks. Simulation results and performance analysis show that the algorithm has a large key space, strong key sensitivity, strong performance to make the structural data correlation disappear, and then can increase the entropy, has good anti attack ability, and can effectively meet the needs of image encryption.

Keywords: Multimedia security · Image encryption · Sinusoidal compound chaotic system · Complexity analysis · Anti-differential attack analysis

1 Introduction

With the rapid development of network technology, cloud computing, artificial intelligence and 5G, digital media such as images, audio and video are rapidly expanding on the information network [1]. Digital images have become one of the most popular information media among a variety of multimedia expressions due to their obvious advantages such as intuitiveness, rich content, low cost, and fast transmission speed. Because the picture information has the characteristics of large data volume, strong correlation of connected pixels and high redundancy, it is easy to copy, forge or manipulate the image by unauthorized users. In recent years, with the accidental exposure of private images and military images, image security has attracted widespread attention from the public and the government. Therefore, looking for efficient and secure image encryption methods has become a technical preface and academic research hotspot. Aiming at the problem of uneven distribution of traditional chaos, Cao et al. [2] proposed a homogenized Logistic

© Springer Nature Switzerland AG 2021
Y. Peng et al. (Eds.): ICIG 2021, LNCS 12888, pp. 676–687, 2021.
https://doi.org/10.1007/978-3-030-87355-4_56

chaotic map and applied it to image scrambling. But for the one-dimensional Logistic chaotic map, the Lyapunov exponent is low and the sequence complexity is not enough, so its security is not high enough. In [3, 4], any two kinds of classical chaotic maps are linearly coupled, and the output of them is transformed by sine and cosine. Although the improved chaotic map is in a state of complete chaos in the whole control parameter range, the chaotic sequence generated by it is unevenly distributed and the complexity is not strong enough. When it is used in image encryption, the security needs to be improved. Aiming at the problem that the security of a single chaotic image encryption algorithm is not high enough, Fang et al. [5] proposes a multiple chaotic encryption algorithm. First, hyperchaotic mapping and Logistic mapping are used to generate a cryptographic sequence, and the image is encoded with DNA. This method improves the security of the algorithm to a certain extent. But this undoubtedly increases the time of encryption and decryption, and the efficiency of the algorithm needs to be improved. Chen et al. [6] uses the method of compound chaotic mapping and deep learning compressed sensing to encrypt the image. Firstly, the image is compressed and sensed, and then it is subjected to sliding scrambling and vector decomposition. Therefore, the algorithm has a strong ability to resist plaintext attacks, and the encryption effect is significant. Behzad et al. [7] designed proposes a new one-dimensional chaotic map, called chaotic coupled Sine map (CCSM), for the scrambling and encryption processes. However, Liu [8] pointed out that reference [7] has security flaws. According to the choice of plaintext attack, only low computational complexity and data complexity are needed to achieve algorithm attack cracking. Hu et al. [9] studied the security of a composite chaotic image encryption algorithm and found that the encryption method based on simple scrambling and diffusion was not able to resist plaintext attacks and was easy to crack, and the algorithm was also completely cracked. Therefore, the literature believes that it is necessary to study new permutation cryptographic mechanisms and perform TESTU01 and NIST tests on chaotic sequences.

In view of the above research, the main reasons for the insecurity of the current chaotic image encryption algorithm. First, the security of the chaotic system used in the encryption scheme is insufficient. Related research has pointed out that the traditional chaotic mapping is not complex enough, and the generated chaotic sequence has been estimated or identify the risk. Second, the encryption algorithm structure has security flaws and cannot resist cryptanalysis algorithm attacks. For example, the generation process of chaotic key sequence has nothing to do with plaintext, which makes it vulnerable to plaintext password attacks.

In order to solve the traditional chaotic complexity, narrow chaotic interval, and insufficient security, this paper proposes an image encryption method based on improved sin-transform-based chaotic system (ISTBCS).

2 Chaos Theory

2.1 Improved Sine Chaotic System Structure

The improved sin-transform-based chaotic system (ISTBCS) proposed in this paper can use any two traditional maps as a combination of seed maps to generate a new map. The

ISTBCS can be expressed mathematically as

$$x_{i+1} = \sin(\pi((D(a, x_i) + E(b, x_i)) \times A \times \cos(\pi x_i)) + \varphi) \tag{1}$$

In the ISTBCS framework, $D(a, x_i)$ and $E(b, x_i)$ are linearly weighted first, then nonlinear cosine transformation is performed, and then sine transformation is performed after ensemble with the transfer constant φ to generate the final mapping output. In ISTBCS, usually let $A = 200$ and $\varphi = -0.5$.

2.2 Sample Chaotic Map

The traditional Logistic, Cosine and Tent maps have the characteristics of easy operation and good chaos in the variable interval. They are often used in image encryption. Now they are used as the seed map of ISTBCS to generate three sample chaotic maps. The mathematical expressions of Logistic, Cosine and Tent mapping are defined as.

Logistic mapping

$$x_{i+1} = \Gamma(\mu, x_i) = 4\mu x_i(1 - x_i) \tag{2}$$

Cosine mapping

$$x_{i+1} = \Upsilon(\mu, x_i) = \mu \cos(\pi(x_i - 0.5) \tag{3}$$

Tent mapping

$$x_{i+1} = T(\mu, x_i) = \begin{cases} 2\mu x_i & \text{if } x_i < 0.5 \\ 2\mu(1 - x_i) & \text{if } x_i \geq 0.5 \end{cases} \tag{4}$$

The variable μ is the control parameter of Logistic mapping, Cosine mapping and Tent mapping, and $\mu \in [0,1]$. According to Eq. (1), we construct the following three sample mappings.

Take Logistic mapping as $D(a, x_i)$ and Cosine mapping as $E(b, x_i)$ to get Logistic-Cosine-Sine (LCS) mapping.

$$x_{i+1} = \sin(\pi((4\mu x_i(1 - x_i) + (1 - \mu)\cos(\pi(x_i - 0.5))200\cos(\pi x_i)) - 0.5) \tag{5}$$

Take Cosine mapping as $D(a, x_i)$ and Tent mapping as $E(b, x_i)$ to get Cosine-Tent-Sine (LCS) mapping.

$$x_{i+1} = \begin{cases} \sin(\pi((\cos(\pi(x_i - 0.5) + 2(1 - \mu)x_i)200\cos(\pi x_i)) - 0.5) & x_i < 0.5 \\ \sin(\pi((\cos(\pi(x_i - 0.5) + 2(1 - \mu)(1 - x_i))200\cos(\pi x_i)) - 0.5) & x_i \geq 0.5 \end{cases} \tag{6}$$

Take Tent mapping as $D(a, x_i)$ and Logistic mapping as $E(b, x_i)$ to get Tent-Logistic-Sine (LCS) mapping.

$$x_{i+1} = \begin{cases} \sin(\pi((2\mu x_i + 4(1 - \mu)x_i(1 - x_i))200\cos(\pi x_i)) - 0.5) & x_i < 0.5 \\ \sin(\pi((2(1 - \mu)(1 - x_i) + 4(1 - \mu)x_i(1 - x_i))200\cos(\pi x_i)) - 0.5) & x_i \geq 0.5 \end{cases} \tag{7}$$

Where, $\mu \in [0, 1]$ is the control parameter.

3   Performance Evaluation of Sample Chaotic Mapping

3.1   Bifurcation Diagram

Bifurcation diagram is the most direct method to characterize whether a chaotic map enters the chaotic state. If the bifurcation diagram does not appear bifurcation in the control parameter interval, and its iteration value is all over the whole phase space in the interval, it shows that the chaotic map has strong chaos.

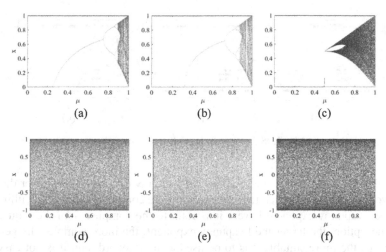

Fig. 1. Bifurcation diagrams of (a) Logistic; (b) Cosine; (c) Tent; (d) LCS; (e) CTS; (f) TLC.

Figure 1 shows the comparison of the bifurcation map between the seed map and the chaotic map transformed by ISTBCS. It can be seen from Fig. 1 that ISTBCS has good results, and its bifurcation graph is spread over the entire space, indicating that the chaos after transformation is very robust.

3.2   Lyapunov Exponent

One of the most important parameters for investigating the chaotic behavior of dynamic systems is the Lyapunov exponent (LE) [12]. The Lyapunov exponent is defined as follows

$$LE = \lim_{n \to \infty} \frac{1}{n} \sum_{k=0}^{n-1} \ln\left|f'(x_k)\right| \tag{8}$$

The Lyapunov exponent is a quantitative expression of the divergence of the chaotic map in the chaotic state. If the Lyapunov exponent is greater than 0, the system is in a chaotic state, otherwise, it is not in a chaotic state. Furthermore, if the Lyapunov exponent is larger, it indicates that the initial error of the chaotic system diverges faster. Even if the initial value is changed very small, the sequence trend is completely different in a

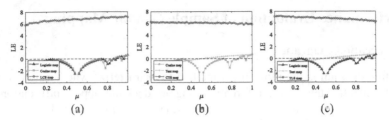

Fig. 2. LE comparison of different mappings.

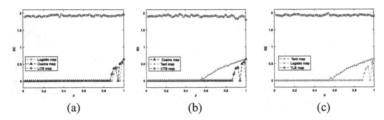

Fig. 3. SE comparison of different mappings

very small time. Conversely, the smaller the Lyapunov exponent, the slower the initial error divergence, and the generated sequence must be completely different within a long time. The Lyapunov exponent is very important to the complexity of the sequence. In image encryption, the larger the Lyapunov exponent, the more complex the generated sequence is, the more suitable it is to be used as a password, and it is not easy to be cracked. As shown in Fig. 2, the Lyapunov of the constructed chaotic map is basically greater than 5, indicating that the proposed chaotic map can produce a chaotic map with more complex chaotic behavior.

3.3 Sample Entropy

Sample entropy (SE) is used to describe the complexity of time series. The larger the SE, the lower the regularity of the time series [13]. In other words, the complexity of the corresponding dynamic system is higher. For a series $\{x_1, x_2, x_3, ..., x_N\}$, SE is defined as

$$SE(m, r, N) = -\log \frac{A}{B} \tag{9}$$

Among them, A and B are the vector numbers of $d[X_{m+1}(i), X_{m+1}(j)] < r$ and $d[X_m(i), X_m(j)] < r$, respectively. The modulus vector $X_m(i) = \{x_i, x_{i+1}, ..., x_{i+m-1}\}$, $d[X_m(i), X_m(j)]$ is the Chebyshev distance between $X_m(i)$ and $X_m(j)$. Where $r = 0.2std$ is the given distance and std is the standard deviation. It can be observed form Fig. 3 that the chaotic map constructed by ISTBCS has a larger SE than the used seed map. This shows that ISTBCS can generate chaotic maps with more complex output sequences.

3.4 NIST SP800-22 Randomness Test

For image encryption, the security of the encryption algorithm is essentially determined by the pseudo-randomness of the chaotic sequence. Therefore, we use the three sample chaotic maps generated by ISTBCS to test the randomness of NIST SP800-22. The test results are shown in the following Table 1.

Table 1. Comparison of ISTBCS generated sample mapping through NIST SP800-22.

Sub-test	LCS	CTS	TLS	Result
	P-value	P-value	P-value	(P > 0.01)
Frequency	0.088179	0.795464	0.414525	Pass
Block frequency	0.122325	0.821681	0.371101	Pass
Cumulative Sums1	0.122325	0.051001	0.199580	Pass
Cumulative Sums2	0.221786	0.350485	0.227773	Pass
Runs	0.768138	0.795464	0.714660	Pass
Longest run	0.891622	0.450564	0.663130	Pass
Rank	0.285628	0.398690	0.371101	Pass
FFT	0.944860	0.266044	0.534146	Pass
Non-overlapping	0.681642	0.350485	0.521457	Pass
Overlapping template	0.132858	0.846579	0.712394	Pass
Universal	0.386374	0.651990	0.457861	Pass
Approximate entropy	0.266044	0.739918	0.192257	Pass
Random excursions 1	0.585209	0.714660	0.800456	Pass
Random excursions 2	0.534146	0.611108	0.701253	Pass
Serial (P-value1)	0.477737	0.681642	0.321456	Pass
Serial (P-value2)	0.487086	0.651990	0.213309	Pass
Linear complexity	0.387955	0.869955	0.543217	Pass

Table 1 shows the test results of NIST SP800-22. For the three sample sequences tested, the test results are all greater than 0.01, indicating that ISTBCS has good pseudo-randomness and is especially suitable for image encryption.

4 Image Encryption Algorithm

In this section, the LCS chaotic map generated by ISTBCS will be used to design the image encryption algorithm (Image encryption algorithm based on LCS map, LCS-IEA). LCS chaotic mapping has high complexity, and can generate chaotic sequences with high security. Applying it to digital image encryption can improve the security of image encryption. The chaotic password is generated by the following Eq. (10–12), M

and N are the length and width of the plaintext image respectively, and s is the initial cipher generation sequence. Among them, $S1$, $S2$, and $S3$ are used for pixel encoding, position scrambling and gray-scale concealment, respectively.

$$S1 = floor(|s| \times 2^{14}) \mod 256 \tag{10}$$

$$S2 = floor(|s(1:MN)| \times 10^{10}) \mod MN + 1 \tag{11}$$

$$S3 = floor(|s| \times 2^{15}) \mod 256 \tag{12}$$

4.1 Image Pixel Coding

This paper first performs bidirectional prime coding on the plaintext digital image, and diffuses the correlation between the pixels of the plaintext image through coding. The specific process is as follows.

Step 1: Generate chaotic matrix $S1$.
Step 2: Input the digital image matrix $P_{M \times N}$ and turn it into $P_{1 \times MN}$.
Step 3: Forward coding $P_{1 \times MN}$, the formula is as follows

$$P'(i) = \begin{cases} P(i) + P(i_{\max}) + S1(i) \mod 256 & i = 1 \\ P(i) + P'(i-1) + S1(i) \mod 256 \ else \end{cases} \tag{13}$$

Step 4: Reverse encoding $P'_{1 \times MN}$, the formula is as follows

$$P''(i) = \begin{cases} P'(i) + P'(1) + S1(i) \mod 256 & i = i_{\max} \\ P'(i) + P''(i+1) + S1(i) \mod 256 \ else \end{cases} \tag{14}$$

4.2 Image Pixel Position Scrambling

This section uses the chaotic matrix generated by LCS to scramble the image position, break the pixel position of the image, and improve the security and effectiveness of encryption. Assuming that the chaotic matrix $S2$ and the image I to be encrypted after image pixel encoding are both matrices of size $M \times N$, the specific process of image scrambling can be expressed as follows.

Step 1: Input the image $I_{M \times N}$ after image encoding.
Step 2: Sort $S2_{1 \times MN}$ without repetition to get $S2'_{1 \times MN}$.
Step 3: Convert the image $I_{M \times N}$ into a one-dimensional matrix $I_{1 \times MN}$, and then scramble the position of $I_{1 \times MN}$ according to the order of the matrix $S2'_{1 \times MN}$.
Step 4: Recombine the matrix $I_{1 \times MN}$ to obtain a new matrix $C_{M \times N}$.

4.3 Image Grayscale Diffusion

Although the image is pixel-encoded and position scrambled, in order to strengthen the encryption effect, we further perform grayscale diffusion on the scrambled image. As shown in the following Eq. (15)

$$E(i,j) = C(i,j) \oplus S3(i,j) \tag{15}$$

Where, C is the image matrix after scrambling, and $S3$ is the chaotic matrix.

5 Safety Analysis

5.1 Histogram Analysis

The gray histogram is one of the important indicators for evaluating the effect of image encryption. You can judge whether the encryption effect is good by observing the gray histogram of the encrypted image.

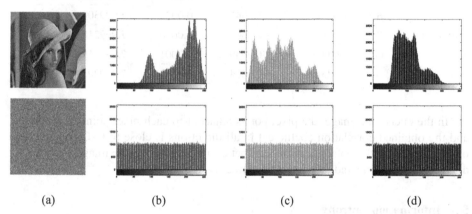

| (a) | (b) | (c) | (d) |

Fig. 4. (a) Images before and after encryption; (b) Histograms before and after R component encryption; (c) Histograms before and after G component encryption; (d) Histograms before and after B component encryption.

It can be seen from the Fig. 4 that the histogram of the image encrypted by LCS-IEA is evenly distributed, which effectively conceals the original characteristics of the pixels of the original image, which shows that the algorithm has strong interference performance and enhances the security of encryption. Prove that LCS-IEA is feasible.

5.2 Pixel Correlation Analysis

Generally speaking, the correlation coefficient between digital image pixels can be calculated as follows

$$\rho_{xy} = \frac{\frac{1}{N}\sum_{i=1}^{N}[x_i - \frac{1}{N}\sum_{i=1}^{N}x_i][y_i - \frac{1}{N}\sum_{i=1}^{N}y_i]}{\sqrt{\frac{1}{N}\sum_{i=1}^{N}[x_i - \frac{1}{N}\sum_{i=1}^{N}x_i]^2}\sqrt{\frac{1}{N}\sum_{i=1}^{N}[y_i - \frac{1}{N}\sum_{i=1}^{N}y_i]^2}} \tag{16}$$

Table 2. Comparison of the correlation coefficient of each component of Lena512 image.

		Horizontal	Vertical	Diagonal	Information entropy
Lena512 Original (this paper)	R	0.9757	0.9855	0.9663	7.253102
	G	0.9665	0.9785	0.9551	7.594038
	B	0.9441	0.9648	0.9413	6.968427
Lena512 Encrypted (this paper)	R	0.0028	0.0004	0.0012	7.999347
	G	0.0016	0.0005	0.0015	7.999208
	B	0.0113	0.0011	−0.0015	7.999404
Ref. [15]	R	0.0038	0.0094	0.0020	7.999400
	G	−0.0062	−0.0042	−0.0016	7.999200
	B	0.0109	−0.0054	−0.00695	7.999200
Ref. [16]	R	−0.0127	0.0067	0.0060	7.999100
	G	−0.0075	−0.0068	−0.0078	7.999300
	B	−0.0007	0.0042	0.0026	7.999300
Ref. [18]	R	0.0160	−0.0008	0.0020	7.999218
	G	−0.0001	−0.0039	0.0001	7.999310
	B	−0.0066	−0.0004	0.0010	7.999203

In the encrypted image, the pixel points adjacent to each pixel point are scattered, and the obtained correlation coefficient in all directions is close to 0. Compared with other algorithms, the obtained results are better, indicating that the image has a higher degree of scrambling and the encryption effect is significant.

5.3 Information Entropy

Shannon entropy is one of the criteria to evaluate whether the randomness in encrypted images is good [10]. Defined as follows

$$H(S) = -\sum_{i=1}^{n} p_i \log p_i \tag{17}$$

Table 2 shows the comparison of the information entropy data of the original image and the ciphertext image. It can be seen from Table 2 that the information entropy of the three channels of R, G, and B after encryption is very close to the maximum value of 8, indicating that the encryption algorithm has a good confidentiality effect and can resist attacks based on image information entropy.

5.4 Differential Attack

The number of pixels change rate (NPCR) and the unified average changing intensity (UACI) are defined as [14]

$$NPCR(C_1, C_2) = \sum_{i=1}^{M} \sum_{i=1}^{N} \frac{W(i,j)}{H} \times 100 \qquad (18)$$

$$UACI(C_1, C_2) = \sum_{i=1}^{M} \sum_{i=1}^{N} \frac{|C_1(i,j) - C_2(i,j)|}{H \times Q} \times 100 \qquad (19)$$

Where, Q is the maximum value of image pixels, H is the number of pixels, and W is calculated as follows

$$W(i,j) = \begin{cases} 0 \ if \ C_1(i,j) = C_2(i,j) \\ 1 \ if \ C_1(i,j) \neq C_2(i,j) \end{cases} \qquad (20)$$

Table 3. Comparison of NPCR and UACI of different components of Lena image.

Image		Lena (256 × 256 × 3)		Lena (512 × 512 × 3)	
Encryption algorithm		This paper	Ref. [17]	This paper	Ref. [17]
NPCR	R	99.6200	**99.5369**	99.6021	99.6745
	G	99.6050	**99.3215**	99.6014	99.6745
	B	99.6275	**99.2154**	99.6094	99.6029
UACI	R	33.4626	**33.1258**	33.4575	33.4457
	G	33.4876	33.3254	33.4843	33.4380
	B	33.4847	33.3514	33.4623	33.4584

Both the NPCR and UACI indicators obtained by this algorithm have passed the test, indicating that the algorithm has strong resistance to plaintext attacks and is not easy to be cracked. Compared with other algorithms, we got better results. Bold results indicate failure to pass the test (Table 3).

5.5 Noise and Data Loss Analysis

Images are subject to multiple threats during transmission. Attacks on encrypted images can cause data loss [10]. Therefore, using corrupted encrypted images in the decryption process may produce blurred or unrecognizable images. The image encryption scheme should be able to minimize the impact of data loss and noise on the restored image.

As shown in Fig. 5, the decryption result is identifiable whether it is adding salt and pepper noise or missing data. This shows that LSC-IEA has good resistance to data loss and noise.

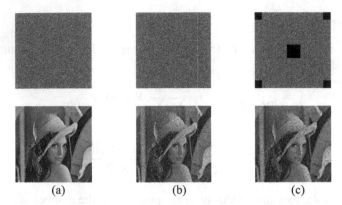

Fig. 5. (a) Normal decryption; (b) 5% salt and pepper noise; (c) 8% data loss.

6 Conclusion

This paper introduces an ISTBCS chaotic map and analyzes the system in detail. Different from traditional chaotic systems, ISTBCS provides a universal composite framework, which can use any two same or different traditional mappings to perform linear weighting and nonlinear multiplication, and then combine to obtain a sine output with complex dynamic behavior. New mapping through the analysis of bifurcation graph, Lyapunov exponent and sample entropy, it can be seen that the performance of the new map generated is completely different from that of the seed map, and the chaotic performance of the new map after effective combination is better. Next, based on LCS, we designed an image encryption law for pixel encoding, position scrambling, and gray-scale concealment. Experimental results show that LCS-IEA has high key sensitivity, low correlation, and ability to resist data loss and noise. Compared with other schemes, LCS-IEA has better randomness and ability to resist differential attacks.

Acknowledgement. This work is financially supported by National Natural Science Foundation of China (No. 61072079/61461053).

References

1. Wen, H.P.: Image encryption scheme based on quantum and spatiotemporal chaos. J. Hefei Univ. Technol. (Nat. Sci. Ed.) **43**(06), 777–783 (2020)
2. Cao, G.H.: Image scrambling method based on logistic uniform distribution. Acta Phys. Sin. **60**(11), 133–140 (2011)
3. Tian, X.P.: Sine transform chaotic system and performance analysis. J. Xi'an Univ. Posts Telecommun. **23**(06), 37–43 (2018)
4. Hua, Z.Y.: Cosine-transform-based chaotic system for image encryption. Inform. Sci. **480**, 403–419 (2019)
5. Fang, J.: An image encryption algorithm based on chaotic encryption and DNA encoding. Acta Phys. Sin.,1–22 (2021)

6. Chen, W.: General image encryption algorithm based on deep learning compressed sensing and compound chaotic system. Acta Phys. Sin. **69**(24), 99–111 (2020)
7. Yosefnezhad Irani, B., Ayubi, P., Amani Jabalkandi, F., Yousefi Valandar, M., Jafari Barani, M.: Digital image scrambling based on a new one-dimensional coupled Sine map. Nonlinear Dyn. **97**(4), 2693–2721 (2019). https://doi.org/10.1007/s11071-019-05157-5
8. Liu, Y., Qin, Z., Liao, X., Wu, J.: Cryptanalysis and enhancement of an image encryption scheme based on a 1-D coupled Sine map. Nonlinear Dyn. **100**(3), 2917–2931 (2020). https://doi.org/10.1007/s11071-020-05654-y
9. Hu, Y.C.: An image encryption algorithm security analysis based on compound chaotic sequence. Comput. Appl. Res. 1–8 (2021)
10. Zhong, Y.R.: Image encryption algorithm based on 2D Chebyshev-Sine mapping. J. Zhejiang Univ. (Sci. Ed.) 1008–9497(2019)
11. Chen, S.: Image encryption algorithm based on chaotic system and artificial neural network. Comput. Syst. Appl. **29**(08), 236–241 (2020)
12. Rosenstein, M.T.: A practical method for calculating largest Lyapunov exponents from small data sets. Phys. D **65**, 117–134 (1993)
13. Richman, J.S.: Physiological time-series analysis using approximate entropy and sample entropy. Am. J. Physiol. Heart Circ. Physiol. **278**, 2039–2049 (2000)
14. Özkaynak, F.: Role of NPCR and UACI tests in security problems of chaos based image encryption algorithms and possible solution proposals. In: 2017 International Conference on Computer Science and Engineering (UBMK), pp. 621–624. IEEE (2017)
15. Khedmati, Y.: 2D Hybrid chaos map for image security transform based on framelet and cellular automata. Inform. Sci. **512**, 855–875 (2020)
16. Wang, X.Y.: A color image encryption with heterogeneous bit-permutation and correlated chaos. Opt. Commun. **342**, 51–60 (2015)
17. Aboughalia, R.A.: Color image encryption based on chaotic block permutation and XOR operation. In: Libyan International Conference on Electrical Engineering and Technologies (LICEET) (2018)
18. Li, S., Ding, W., Yin, B., Zhang, T., Ma, Y.: A novel delay linear coupling logistics map model for color image encryption. Entropy **20**(6), 463 (2018). https://doi.org/10.3390/e20060463

Towards Binarized MobileNet via Structured Sparsity

Zhenmeng Zuo[1], Zhexin Li[1,2], Peisong Wang[2], Weihan Chen[1,2],
and Jian Cheng[1,2(✉)]

[1] University of Chinese Academy of Sciences, Beijing, China
[2] Institute of Automation, Chinese Academy of Sciences, NLPR, Beijing, China
jcheng@nlpr.ia.ac.cn

Abstract. The rising demand for deploying convolutional neural networks (CNNs) to mobile applications has promoted the booming of compact networks. Two parallel mainstream techniques include network compression and lightweight architecture design. Despite these two techniques can theoretically work together, the naive combination results in dramatic accuracy degradation. In this paper, we present Binarized MobileNet-Sp for mobile applications, by compression-architecture co-design. We first reveal the connection between MobileNets and low-rank decomposition, showing that decomposition-based architecture is not quantization friendly. Then, by adopting the view of sparsity, we propose the Binarized MobileNet-Sp, which significantly enhances the robustness to binarization. Experiments on ImageNet show that the proposed Binarized MobileNet-Sp achieves 61.2% top-1 accuracy, outperforming the naive binarization method by about 10% higher top-1 accuracy. Compared to the Bi-Real net which achieves 56.4% top-1 accuracy on the more heavy-weight and redundant ResNet-18 (which has comparable baseline accuracy with MobileNet in full-precision representation), the Binarized MobileNet-Sp achieves much higher accuracy with a significant reduction in computing complexity.

Keywords: Convolutional neural networks · MobileNet · Quantization

1 Introduction

Convolutional Neural Networks (CNNs) have been leading new state-of-the-arts in almost every computer vision tasks. One reason is the development of more advanced network architectures, like ResNet, DenseNet, etc. However, these networks are designed for higher accuracy, without optimizing the storage and computational complexity. In many real-world applications, storage consumption and latency are crucial, which on the other hand, pose great challenges to the deployment of these networks. Under this circumstance, reducing the complexity of CNNs becomes a hot topic in the computer vision field.

Z. Zuo and Z. Li—Equal contribution.

© Springer Nature Switzerland AG 2021
Y. Peng et al. (Eds.): ICIG 2021, LNCS 12888, pp. 688–699, 2021.
https://doi.org/10.1007/978-3-030-87355-4_57

To minimize the complexity of CNNs, two main directions are investigated by the community. The first straightforward way is to compress the learned models. Representative approaches include low-rank decomposition, sparsity, quantization, etc. Another parallel direction is to design efficient networks from scratch. Approaches like SqueezeNet, MobileNet, ShuffleNet fall into this direction. Theoretically, the two approaches mentioned above can work together to produce more efficient networks. However, lightweight networks tend to have limited redundancies, thus expressing more sensitivity to network compression. Previous compression methods are mainly evaluated on AlexNet, VGG and ResNet-18, which have the common characteristic of large bulk of convolutions. But the compressed models may still have higher complexity than the uncompressed efficient networks. For example, the deep compression reduced the size of AlexNet by $35\times$ from 240 MB to 6.9 MB, which is still much larger than SqueezeNet of 4.8 MB. From this point of view, the compression makes more sense when combined with lightweight networks.

In this paper, we initiate the problem of compressing lightweight architectures for extremely efficient networks, and present Binarized MobileNet-Sp. We first reveal the connection between MobileNets and low-rank decomposition, showing that decomposition-based architecture is not quantization friendly. Then from the viewpoint of sparsity, the Binarized MobileNet-Sp is proposed, which significantly enhances the robustness to binarization. Experiments on ImageNet show that the proposed Binarized MobileNet-Sp achieves 61.2% top-1 accuracy, outperforming the naive binarization method by about 10% higher top-1 accuracy. Compared to the Bi-Real net which achieves 56.4% top-1 accuracy on the more heavy-weight and redundant ResNet-18 (which has comparable baseline accuracy with MobileNet in full-precision representation), the Binarized MobileNet-Sp achieves much higher accuracy with significantly reduced complexity. Our contributions are summarized as follows:

1. We initiate the problem of compressing lightweight architectures for extremely efficient networks.
2. We reveal the connection between MobileNets and low-rank decomposition, and propose a binarization robust module from the view of sparsity.
3. The proposed Binarized MobileNet-Sp dramatically outperforms traditional binarization method, achieving the new state-of-the-art on extremely efficient networks.

2   Related Work

Convolutional neural networks often suffer from significant redundancy in parameter size and computation [3]. Consequently, a bulk of works have emerged, including but not limited to low-rank decomposition, sparsity, quantization and lightweight architecture design.

Low-Rank Decomposition: The motivation behind low-rank decomposition is to find an approximate tensor $\hat{W}$ that is close to W but facilitates more efficient computation. [4] is one of the first methods to exploit low-rank decomposition of filters by applying truncated SVD along different dimensions. By decomposing the spatial dimension $w \times h$ into $w \times 1$ and $1 \times h$, [11] achieved 4.5× speedup. [24] proposed a non-linear response reconstruction based method and [13] adopted CP decomposition to decompose a layer into five layers with 4.5× speedup for the second layer of AlexNet. Tucker decomposition was also studied in [12].

Sparsity: Pruning can remove unimportant parameters to expand the sparsity of models significantly. [6] proposed to prune the deep CNNs in an unstructured way without drops in accuracy. [5] proposed a dynamic network surgery framework which can recover the incorrectly pruned connections. [17] proposed a filter-level sparsity method which utilizing the next layer's feature map to guide filter pruning in the current layer. By adding structured sparsity regularizer, [23] proposed to reduced trivial filters, channels or even layers.

Quantization: As full-precision parameters are not required to achieve high performance, low-bit quantization has recently received increasing interest. [25] proposed incremental quantization to reduced weight precision to 2–5 bits without accuracy loss. [2,14] constrained the weights to binary(e.g. −1 or +1) or ternary(e.g. −1, 0 or +1) values to obtain acceleration in inference. Recently, several works focused on quantizing both weights and activations while minimizing performance degradation. [1] introduced Binarized Neural Networks (BNNs) with binary weights and activations, and [20] improved BNN by introducing scale factors with accuracy improvement. Multi-bit networks [15,26] are also proposed to decompose a single convolution layer into multiple binary convolution operations to achieve higher accuracy.

Lightweight Architecture Design: Some works focus on building and training lightweight networks from scratch. ResNet [7] proposed the bottleneck structure and SqueezeNet [10] replacing 3×3 convolutions with 1×1 convolutions. Based on depthwise separable convolution and linear bottlenecks, MobileNet [9] and Mobilenet V2 [21] build a lightweight model with streamlined architecture. Besides, several lightweight network [8,22] have been proposed and obtain a new state-of-the-art trade-off between accuracy and efficiency.

3   Depthwise Separable Convolution and Its Binarization

A convolutional layer maps a three-dimensional tensor $X \in \mathbb{R}^{C_{in} \times H \times W}$ to $Y \in \mathbb{R}^{C_{out} \times H \times W}$ by a four-dimensional weight tensor $W \in \mathbb{R}^{C_{out} \times C_{in} \times K \times K}$, where C_{in} and C_{out} are the numbers of input and output channels, H and W represent the spatial height and width of the input as well as the output feature maps, K denotes the kernel height and width of the weight tensor. The computational cost of standard convolution is $C_{out} \times C_{in} \times K \times K \times H \times W$, which corresponds to the kernel size times by the spatial size of the input/output feature maps. To reduce the computations, efficient representations of kernel W are designed, among which network binarization, as well as the depthwise separable convolution of MobileNets are two representative directions.

3.1 Network Binarization

In binarized neural networks, all weights and activations are constrained to be either $+1$ or -1. Specifically, we get the binarized version of weights and activations through a sign function,

$$x^b = \text{Sign}(x^r) = \begin{cases} +1 & \text{, if } x^r \geq 0 \\ -1 & \text{, otherwise} \end{cases}$$

where x^r denotes the real weights or activations. Compared to the real-valued CNN model, binarized weights obtain up to $32\times$ memory saving. Besides, most multiply-accumulate operations could be converted into 1-bit *popcnt − xnor* operations in the inference stage with binarized activations, which reduces computation requirement significantly. However, previous binarization methods are mainly evaluated on the networks which possess many redundancies such as AlexNet, VGG and ResNet. To further improve model efficiency, it's necessary to combine binary techniques with lightweight networks.

3.2 Standard Binarization of MobileNet

Table 1. Operations and parameters of depthwise and pointwise convolution.

	MAdds	Params
DW	17M	45K
DW percentage	3.1%	1.4%
PW	538M	3140K
PW percentage	96.4%	98.6%

Table 2. Baselines of MobileNet with its standard binarization accuracy.

Model	Top-1	Top-5
MobileNet	70.6%	–
Reproduced	70.1%	89.1%
Binary all layers	0.1%	0.5%
Binary 1×1	49.4%	73.3%

MobileNet is a class of streamlined and compact CNN models constructed through full utilization of depthwise separable convolutions. Briefly speaking, each depthwise separable convolution consists of two layers, i.e., depthwise convolution layer (DW) of which the number of convolution groups is equal to the number of input channels, and pointwise convolution layer (PW) with kernel size 1×1. The depthwise convolution and pointwise convolution realize intra-channel and inter-channel feature fusion, separately. Figure 1 illustrates the comparison between regular convolution and depthwise separable convolution.

(a)Regular Convolution   (b)Depthwise Sparable Convolution

Fig. 1. Illustration of regular convolution (a) and depthwise separable convolution (b). The depthwise convolution realizes the spatial feature fusion, while pointwise convolution is responsible for the cross channel feature fusion.

Theoretically, the standard network binarization method could be naturally applied to MobileNet architecture. However, as shown in Table 2, the preliminary evaluation of direct binarization of MobileNets indicates that the network could not learn anything. We argue that this is caused by the weak representational power of binarized depthwise convolution. As illustrated in the previous section, all spatial information interactions are achieved by the depthwise convolutions, which only occupy a very small proportion of the overall computations and parameters. Table 1 gives the numbers as well as the percentages of multiply-addition operations and parameters for depthwise convolutions and pointwise convolutions, respectively. From Table 1, it is worth noting that the depthwise convolutions only take 3.1% of the computations and 1.4% of the parameters. This small proportion of resources must cover all the spatial information interaction, which will go underfitting when combined with binarization.

On the other hand, the small proportion of depthwise convolutions means that we could ignore these layers during the binarization, to achieve a better trade-off between the computation and storage gain and model accuracy degradation. Thus we propose to only binarize the input feature maps and weights of 1×1 convolutions. Table 2 shows the accuracy of full-precision MobileNet, as well as network binarization results. Only binarizing the 1×1 convolutions could achieve reasonable accuracy compared with binarizing all layers.

From the last row of Table 2 we can see that the direct binarization of MobileNet results in more than 20% top-1 accuracy loss, which means more advanced binarization technique for MobileNet-like networks are needed. In the next section, we propose a compression-architecture co-design method to improve the binarization performance of MobileNet.

4   Binarized MobileNet-Sp

In this section, we introduce our method for Binarized MobileNet-Sp in detail and step by step. We notice that the depthwise separable convolution can be considered as a kind of low-rank decomposition of the original 3×3 convolutional layer regardless of the intermediate batch norm and non-linear activation layers. Empirically, this kind of cascade decomposition method is not quantization friendly. Intuitively, it results from the information bottleneck effect along with the narrower single layer which makes it difficult to propagate gradient information, especially in binarization configuration. Inspired by this point of view, we consider altering to approximate the computation-heavy layer through sparsity connections. Going along with way, we propose our Binarized MobileNet-Sp which maintains the compact architecture of the original MobileNet while making it easier to binarize.

4.1   Low-Rank Decomposition Perspective of Separable Convolution

To better understand the low-rank decomposition characteristic behind depthwise separable convolution module, we consider a standard convolution with parameter $W \in \mathbb{R}^{C_{out} \times C_{in} \times K \times K}$. In other words, W has C_{out} 3D filters, each filter is consists of C_{in} 2D kernels. We reveal that all kernels correspond to the i-th input channel lies in a rank-1 subspace. More specifically, let $W_{dw} \in \mathbb{R}^{C_{in} \times K \times K}$ and $W_{pw} \in \mathbb{R}^{C_{out} \times C_{in} \times 1 \times 1}$ represent the parameter tensor for depthwise and pointwise convolutional layers. Considering the kernels correspond to the i-th input channel, we have

$$W(o, i, :, :) \approx W_{pw}(o, i) * W_{dw}(i, :, :), o \in [1, C_{out}], \tag{1}$$

which indicates that the C_{out} elements (2D kernels) corresponds to the i-th input channel lie in a rank-1 subspace with basis $W_{dw}(i, :, :)$. Figure 2 shows an example of the low-rank decomposition view of the depthwise separable convolution.

The low-rank architecture makes MobileNets quite efficient compared to other networks like VGG. However, when combined with network binarization techniques, the intrinsic low-rank characteristic of the depthwise separable block may cause an information bottleneck effect especially in the backpropagation phase, where gradient approximation is needed due to the binarization of weights and input features. More specifically, even without binarizing depthwise convolutions, the small portion of the full-precision depthwise convolutions could not recover the information lost during the feature binarization step of 1×1 convolutions. Consequently, directly binarized MobileNet would converge to a poor local minimum.

Regular   DW   PW

Fig. 2. Illustration of the low-rank perspective of depthwise separable convolution. All kernels of the regular filters (Regular) correspond to the i-th input channel lie in a rank-1 subspace, spaned by the i-th kernel of depthwise convolution (DW).

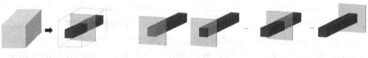

(a)Sparseness   (b)Proposed sparse connected convolutional filters

Fig. 3. Illustration of the proposed sparse connected convolutional filters. Each sparse convolution consists of a cross-spatial plane (yellow) and a cross-channel pillar (green) (Color figure online).

4.2 From Low-Rank to Sparse Connection

Through the above analysis, we know the cascade decomposition of standard convolution into depthwise separable convolution is not quantization friendly.

Instead, we consider altering to approximate the computation-heavy layer through sparse connections. Like in the low-rank approximation of the MobileNet building block, the sparse connection building block also needs to consider cross-spatial and cross-channel information fusion simultaneously. We take this property to the extreme, and propose the minimal sparse connected convolution, the process is shown in Fig. 3(a). Figure 3(b) lists some sparse convolutions, each of them has a cross-spatial plane and a cross-channel pillar, allowing both spatial and channel information fusion. Note that to make the sparse convolutional layer have a full perception of the input feature maps, the sparse convolutional filters have different sparse patterns, i.e., the cross-spatial planes are placed onto different positions of the cross-channel pillar.

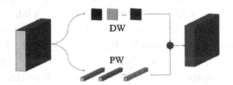

Fig. 4. Illustration of the building block for Binarized MobileNet-Sp.

Note that the sparse convolutional filter can be reformulated into the addition of two filters, i.e., the spatial filter (the plane) and the channel filter (the pillar). By collecting spatial parts and channel parts of all filters together, the sparse convolution can be reformulated into depthwise convolution and pointwise convolution, however, in a paralleled way instead of the cascade way of traditional MobileNet. Through this transformation, we get our ultimate building block for Binarized MobileNet as shown in Fig. 4. To distinguish from the traditional MobileNet, we denote our improved architecture as MobileNet-Sp, while the traditional counterpart as MobileNet-L, where "Sp" and "L" indicate the concept of sparse connection and low-rank decomposition respectively.

The sparse connection induced MobileNet-Sp and the traditional low-rank induced by MobileNet-L have several connections. (1) Both architectures use the depthwise convolution and pointwise convolution, however, the difference is that the MobileNet-L stacks these two layers while MobileNet-Sp utilizes a parallel pattern. Thus the computation and parameter size are almost the same for these two architectures. (2) When taking a global view of the whole network architectures, the MobileNet-Sp can be viewed as two twisted MobileNet-L models, with interactions across the intermediate layers.

From the above analysis, we find that like MobileNet-L, 1×1 convolution layers consume most computation and storage resources, thus we only binarize the pointwise convolution branch. More importantly, this form of network with the multi-branch structure that originates from sparsity connections could be more friendly to binarization. To be specific, the gradient backpropagation process benefits from the reserved full-precision computation and memory-efficient branch of depthwise convolution, which will be verified by detailed experiments in the following section.

5   Experiments

In this section, we thoroughly evaluate the performance of the proposed MobileNet binarization method on the ILSVRC12 ImageNet classification benchmark, as well as the properties of Binarized MobileNet-Sp through several ablation studies.

Table 3. Accuracy comparison between MobileNet-Sp and MobileNet-L.

Model	Top-1	Top-5
MobileNet (Reference)	70.6%	–
MobileNet-L	70.1%	89.1%
MobileNet-Sp	69.1%	88.6%
MobileNet-LS	70.4%	89.5%

Table 4. Accuracy comparison between binarized MobileNet-Sp and MobileNet-L.

Model	Top-1	Top-5
MobileNet (Reference)	70.6%	–
Binarized MobileNet-L	49.4%	73.3%
Binarized MobileNet-Sp	58.6%	80.9%

5.1   MobileNet-Sp vs MobileNet-L

This section compares the sparse connection based MobileNet-Sp and low-rank based MobileNet-L on the ImageNet classification task in detail. For the sake of fairness, all models for comparison are trained for 100 epochs with polynomial learning rate decay. Our results, as well as the reference MobileNet baseline, are shown in Table 3. From the results, it can be concluded that the sparse connection based MobileNet-Sp yields poorer performance than MobileNet-L, with about 1% top-1 accuracy gap. At the same time, to further compare the parallel module and the cascade module, we also report the accuracy when both the parallel and cascaded depthwise convolutions are incorporated, denoted by MobileNet-LS. The results indicate that the cascade depthwise convolution has a more powerful feature aggregation ability than parallel depthwise convolution used by MobileNet-Sp, under the circumstance of full-precision representations.

Next, we evaluate the binarization results of MobileNet-Sp and MobileNet-L. In both architectures, the depthwise convolutions, as well as the first convolution and the last fully-connected layer are not binarized. The results are shown in the last two rows of Table 4. Under the binarization setting, the behavior of these two architectures is quite different from the full-precision setting. The Binarized MobileNet-L model has a 20.7% accuracy drop than the full-precision. In contrast, the Binarized MobileNet-Sp only drops 11.5%, outperforming Binarized MobileNet-L by 9.2% top-1 accuracy, which proves our suppose.

Lightweight networks like MobileNet tend to need more training iterations to well converge. When coupled with binarization operations, it may need even more iterations. As shown in Table 5, When the training epochs doubled, i.e., from 100 epochs to 200 epochs, the top-1 accuracy improves 1.3%. There will be another 1.3% improvement when the training epochs reach 450. From the results, we can see that the binarized MobileNet-Sp can benefit from more training iterations.

Table 5. Accuracy results of Binarized MobileNet-Sp under different epochs.

Model	Epochs	Top-1	Top-5
Binarized MobileNet-Sp	100	58.6%	80.9%
Binarized MobileNet-Sp	200	59.9%	81.8%
Binarized MobileNet-Sp	450	61.2%	82.9%

Table 6. Accuracy results of different feature expanding options.

Model	Expand	Top-1	Top-5
Binarized MobileNet-Sp	Copy	57.9%	80.1%
Binarized MobileNet-Sp	CReLU	58.5%	80.6%
Binarized MobileNet-Sp	2× DW	58.6%	80.9%

5.2   Feature Expanding Options

The MobileNet architecture increases channels by 2× at each time when feature maps are reduced, which can be easily accomplished by the 1×1 convolutions. However, in our sparse connection induced MobileNet-Sp, the 1×1 convolutions need to have the same number of channels as depthwise convolutions, also the same as the number of input channels. To deal with the channel expanding problem, we propose three expanding patterns. (1) **Copy:** means to duplicate the output feature maps of the depthwise convolutions. In this pattern, no extra information and computation are produced. (2) **CReLU:** means to utilize CReLU activation function to replace ReLU function for depthwise convolutions, producing in 2× number of channels. This pattern also introduces no extra computation and parameters, however, it can utilize the negative side of features which are ignored by ReLU function. (3) **2× DW:** means to concatenate the feature maps of two distinct depthwise convolutions. In this setting, the computation and parameters are also doubled.

Table 6 illustrates the comparison results for the above three feature expanding options. It can be concluded that the naive copy pattern achieves lower performance than the other settings. The reason is that the simple copy could not introduce extra information. In contrast, the CReLU pattern achieves much better results, outperforming a simple copy pattern by 0.6% top-1 accuracy. Moreover, the 2× DW pattern brings another 0.1% top-1 improvement than using CReLU. Considering that there is only several (5 for MobileNet) expanding layers, we choose the 2× DW pattern for the following experiments.

5.3   The Effect of Feature Width and Layer Depth

The choice of layer depth and the width for each layer is a trade-off between accuracy and computing performance. Generally speaking, increasing depth and width can boost the accuracy, at the cost of increased computation and parameters. This section evaluates the trade-off performance of layer depth and width about the proposed binarized MobileNet-Sp architecture. The results are shown in Table 7.

From Table 7 it can be concluded that increasing width and depth can dramatically improve the accuracy. Another finding is that the results of doubling width or doubling depth are similar, both reach 64.8% top-1 accuracy. However, using 2× depth, the multiply-addition operations are about half of 2× width. Thus increasing depth is more efficient than increasing width.

Table 7. Accuracy of Binarized MobileNet-Sp for different width (W) and depth (D).

Model	W/D	Top-1	Top-5
Binarized MobileNet-Sp	0.5/1	51.4%	74.6%
Binarized MobileNet-Sp	0.75/1	57.4%	79.7%
Binarized MobileNet-Sp	1.0/1	61.2%	82.9%
Binarized MobileNet-Sp	2.0/1	64.8%	85.4%
Binarized MobileNet-Sp	1.0/2	64.8%	85.6%
Binarized MobileNet-Sp	0.7/2	61.9%	83.6%

Table 8. Accuracy and FLOPs comparison with other state-of-the-art binary methods.

Networks	Top-1	Top-5	FLOPs
XNOR-AlexNet [20]	44.2%	69.2%	138M
XNOR-ResNet18 [20]	51.2%	73.2%	167M
Bi-Real Net18 [16]	56.4%	79.5%	163M
MoBiNet [18]	54.4%	77.5%	52M
Binary MobileNet [19]	60.9%	82.6%	154M
Our Method	**61.2%**	**82.9%**	**52M**

5.4 Comparison with State-of-the-Art Methods

In this section, to evaluate our method, we compare our Binarized MobileNet-Sp with several recent methods. Our baseline uses 2 × DW for feature expanding and is trained for 450 epochs. As shown in the Table 8, compared with Bi-RealNet18 [16], our method improves the accuracy by 4.8% with 3× lower FLOPs. MoBiNet [18] and [19] are recent methods for binary MobileNet. Our method outperforms the MoBiNet by 6.8% with comparable speedup ratio and is more efficient than [19] with 3× lower FLOPs.

6 Conclusion

In this paper, we present Binarized MobileNet-Sp for mobile applications, by compression-architecture co-design. We first reveal the connection between MobileNets and low-rank decomposition, showing that decomposition-based architecture is not quantization friendly. Then, by adopting the view of sparsity, we propose the Binarized MobileNet-Sp, which significantly enhances the robustness to binarization. Experiments on ImageNet show that the proposed Binarized MobileNet-Sp achieves 61.2% top-1 accuracy, outperforming the naive binarization method by about 10% higher top-1 accuracy. Compared to the Bi-Real net which achieves 56.4% top-1 accuracy on the more heavy-weight and redundant ResNet-18 (which has comparable baseline accuracy with MobileNet in full-precision representation), the Binarized MobileNet-Sp achieves much higher accuracy with a significant reduction in computing complexity.

References

1. Courbariaux, M., Bengio, Y.: BinaryNet: training deep neural networks with weights and activations constrained to +1 or −1. CoRR arXiv:1602.02830 (2016)
2. Courbariaux, M., Bengio, Y., David, J.: BinaryConnect: training deep neural networks with binary weights during propagations. In: Advances in Neural Information Processing Systems 28: Annual Conference on Neural Information Processing Systems 2015, 7–12 December 2015, Montreal, Quebec, Canada, pp. 3123–3131 (2015)
3. Denil, M., Shakibi, B., Dinh, L., Ranzato, M., de Freitas, N.: Predicting parameters in deep learning. In: Advances in Neural Information Processing Systems 26: 27th Annual Conference on Neural Information Processing Systems 2013. Proceedings of a meeting held December 5–8, 2013, Lake Tahoe, Nevada, United States, pp. 2148–2156 (2013)
4. Denton, E.L., Zaremba, W., Bruna, J., LeCun, Y., Fergus, R.: Exploiting linear structure within convolutional networks for efficient evaluation. In: Advances in Neural Information Processing Systems 27: Annual Conference on Neural Information Processing Systems 2014, 8–13 December 2014, Montreal, Quebec, Canada, pp. 1269–1277 (2014)
5. Guo, Y., Yao, A., Chen, Y.: Dynamic network surgery for efficient DNNs. In: Advances in Neural Information Processing Systems 29: Annual Conference on Neural Information Processing Systems 2016, 5–10 December 2016, Barcelona, Spain, pp. 1379–1387 (2016)
6. Han, S., Pool, J., Tran, J., Dally, W.J.: Learning both weights and connections for efficient neural network. In: Advances in Neural Information Processing Systems 28: Annual Conference on Neural Information Processing Systems 2015, 7–12 December, 2015, Montreal, Quebec, Canada, pp. 1135–1143 (2015)
7. He, K., Zhang, X., Ren, S., Sun, J.: Deep residual learning for image recognition. In: 2016 IEEE Conference on Computer Vision and Pattern Recognition, CVPR 2016, Las Vegas, NV, USA, 27–30 June 2016, pp. 770–778 (2016)
8. Howard, A., et al.: Searching for MobileNetv3. CoRR arXiv:1905.02244 (2019)
9. Howard, A.G., et al.: MobileNets: efficient convolutional neural networks for mobile vision applications. arXiv:1704.04861 (2017)
10. Iandola, F.N., Moskewicz, M.W., Ashraf, K., Han, S., Dally, W.J., Keutzer, K.: SqueezeNet: Alexnet-level accuracy with 50x fewer parameters and <1 MB model size. CoRR arXiv:1602.07360 (2016)
11. Jaderberg, M., Vedaldi, A., Zisserman, A.: Speeding up convolutional neural networks with low rank expansions. CoRR arXiv:1405.3866 (2014)
12. Kim, Y., Park, E., Yoo, S., Choi, T., Yang, L., Shin, D.: Compression of deep convolutional neural networks for fast and low power mobile applications. arXiv:1511.06530 (2015)
13. Lebedev, V., Ganin, Y., Rakhuba, M., Oseledets, I.V., Lempitsky, V.S.: Speeding-up convolutional neural networks using fine-tuned CP-decomposition. In: 3rd International Conference on Learning Representations, ICLR 2015, San Diego, CA, USA, 7–9 May 2015, Conference Track Proceedings (2015)

14. Li, F., Liu, B.: Ternary weight networks. CoRR arXiv:1605.04711 (2016)
15. Lin, X., Zhao, C., Pan, W.: Towards accurate binary convolutional neural network. In: Advances in Neural Information Processing Systems 30: Annual Conference on Neural Information Processing Systems 2017, 4–9 December 2017, Long Beach, CA, USA, pp. 344–352 (2017)
16. Liu, Z., Wu, B., Luo, W., Yang, X., Liu, W., Cheng, K.-T.: Bi-real net: enhancing the performance of 1-bit CNNs with improved representational capability and advanced training algorithm. In: Ferrari, V., Hebert, M., Sminchisescu, C., Weiss, Y. (eds.) ECCV 2018. LNCS, vol. 11219, pp. 747–763. Springer, Cham (2018). https://doi.org/10.1007/978-3-030-01267-0_44
17. Luo, J., Wu, J., Lin, W.: ThiNet: a filter level pruning method for deep neural network compression. In: IEEE International Conference on Computer Vision, ICCV 2017, Venice, Italy, 22–29 October 2017, pp. 5068–5076 (2017)
18. Phan, H., He, Y., Savvides, M., Shen, Z., et al.: MobiNet: a mobile binary network for image classification. In: Proceedings of the IEEE/CVF Winter Conference on Applications of Computer Vision, pp. 3453–3462 (2020)
19. Phan, H., Liu, Z., Huynh, D., Savvides, M., Cheng, K.T., Shen, Z.: Binarizing mobileNet via evolution-based searching. In: Proceedings of the IEEE/CVF Conference on Computer Vision and Pattern Recognition, pp. 13420–13429 (2020)
20. Rastegari, M., Ordonez, V., Redmon, J., Farhadi, A.: XNOR-net: ImageNet classification using binary convolutional neural networks. In: Leibe, B., Matas, J., Sebe, N., Welling, M. (eds.) ECCV 2016. LNCS, vol. 9908, pp. 525–542. Springer, Cham (2016). https://doi.org/10.1007/978-3-319-46493-0_32
21. Sandler, M., Howard, A.G., Zhu, M., Zhmoginov, A., Chen, L.: MobileNetv 2: inverted residuals and linear bottlenecks. In: 2018 IEEE Conference on Computer Vision and Pattern Recognition, CVPR 2018, Salt Lake City, UT, USA, 18–22 June, 2018, pp. 4510–4520 (2018)
22. Tan, M., Chen, B., Pang, R., Vasudevan, V., Le, Q.V.: MnasNet: platform-aware neural architecture search for mobile. CoRR arXiv:1807.11626 (2018)
23. Wen, W., Wu, C., Wang, Y., Chen, Y., Li, H.: Learning structured sparsity in deep neural networks. In: Advances in Neural Information Processing Systems 29: Annual Conference on Neural Information Processing Systems 2016, 5–10 December, 2016, Barcelona, Spain, pp. 2074–2082 (2016)
24. Zhang, X., Zou, J., He, K., Sun, J.: Accelerating very deep convolutional networks for classification and detection. IEEE Trans. Pattern Anal. Mach. Intell. **38**(10), 1943–1955 (2016)
25. Zhou, A., Yao, A., Guo, Y., Xu, L., Chen, Y.: Incremental network quantization: towards lossless CNNs with low-precision weights. In: International Conference on Learning Representations (ICLR). arXiv:1702.03044 (2017)
26. Zhu, S., Dong, X., Su, H.: Binary ensemble neural network: more bits per network or more networks per bit? In: The IEEE Conference on Computer Vision and Pattern Recognition (CVPR), June 2019

Fast Coding Unit Partition Decision for Intra Prediction in Versatile Video Coding

Menglu Zhang[1]([✉]), Yushi Chen[1], Xin Lu[2], Hao Chen[1], and Ye Zhang[1]

[1] Department of Information Engineering, Harbin Institute of Technology, Harbin, China
19s105153@stu.hit.edu.cn, {chenyushi,hit_hao,zhye}@hit.edu.cn
[2] School of Computer Science and Informatics, De Montfort University, Leicester L1 9BH, UK
luxin5321@163.com

Abstract. In recent years, the state-of-the-art video coding standard – Versatile Video Coding (VVC) has been widely investigated. VVC achieves impressive performance by adopting more flexible partitioning method compared to its predecessor High Efficiency Video Coding (HEVC). However, the superior performance is realized at the expense of huge time consumption and increasing hardware costs, which obstructs its applications in real-time scenarios. To address this problem, we present a fast implementation for the decision process of the nested multi-type tree (QTMT) partitioning, and it significantly reduces the run-time of encoder while maintaining almost the same coding performance. Firstly, the inherent texture property of source frame is utilized to identify the prediction depth for Coding Tree Unit (CTU). Then, the spatial correlation is used to further narrow the depth range down. Finally, we skip unnecessary partition types according to the predicted Coding Unit (CU) depth, which is determined by the above predicted CTU depth and adjacent CU's depth together. Experimental results demonstrate the effectiveness of our proposed method in VVC Test Model (VTM). Compared with the original implementation of the VTM4.0 anchor, the proposed algorithm achieves an average of 49.01% encoding time savings, accompanied by only an increase of 2.18% in Bj ϕ ntegaard delta Bitrate (BDBR) and a loss of 0.138 dB in Bj ϕ ntegaard delta PSNR (BDPSNR).

Keywords: Partition decision · Spatial correlation · Texture property · Versatile Video Coding

1 Introduction

Various applications of emerging video technologies are gaining popularity today, including two-dimensional (2D), three-dimensional (3D), 360 degrees video contents with higher resolutions and frame rates. To better meet the application demands of these novel types of video, the Joint Video Experts Team (JVET) has released the next-generation video coding standard called VVC [1], which has been finalized in 2020. VVC inherits the block-based hybrid video coding framework and achieves an overall 21% bitrate savings under all intra (AI) configuration [2] compared with its predecessor HEVC. The compression efficiency is improved by adopting a series of advanced tools

© Springer Nature Switzerland AG 2021
Y. Peng et al. (Eds.): ICIG 2021, LNCS 12888, pp. 700–711, 2021.
https://doi.org/10.1007/978-3-030-87355-4_58

such as highly flexible block partition, intra prediction with 67 modes. Unfortunately, VVC acquires the superior performance whereas suffering from a huge time consumption and a significantly increase hardware costs, which affects its deployments in real-time applications. Hence, there is an urgent need to make a trade-off between coding performance and encoding complexity. Most of the computation complexity generates from the extremely flexible QTMT structure within the CU partitioning process, where the full search strategy based on recursive rate distortion cost (RDC) is implemented to choose the best coding block. This paper focuses on the great potential of speeding up the CU partitioning process.

Over the past decades, to alleviate the intra encoding complexity and accelerate the coding process, various elaborate designs have been proposed for HEVC, which provides directions for VVC. The existing fast CU partition schemes can be categorized into the following three types: statistic based methods, machine learning based methods, and deep learning based methods.

For the first type, it is mainly based on the traditional spatial-temporal correlation. In [3], Shen et al. detected the texture property and weighted average depth of the spatially adjacent coded CUs to early decide the CU size. In [4], Lei et al. classified the CUs into two categories by video contents, while neighboring CUs' depth information are used to decide CU size. In [5], Min et al. adopted a fast CU size decision algorithm utilizing the global and local edge complexities in four directions.

For the second type, it mainly models the CU partition process as a hierarchical binary classification problem. These approaches highly rely on the handcrafted features. In [6], Zhang et al. designed a three-outputs hierarchical binary classifier and derived a sophisticated RD complexity for each size of CU. In [7], Duanmu et al. used the variance and gradient kurtosis to speed up the process of both partitioning and prediction mode decision. In [8], Grellert et al. exploited features to reduce model complexity, and adopted adaptive decision scheme to enhance RD performance.

For the third type, it is mainly based on deep learning. These methods mainly relied on feeding innumerable data. In [9], Liu et al. devised the convolution neural network (CNN) based fast CU mode decision to reduce intra coding complexity to the maximum extent. In [10], Xu et al. attempted to apply CNN and long short-term memory (LSTM) network instead of full search strategy to gain optimal CU partition.

Currently, a few works on optimizing CU partition decision in VVC have been reported. Although the excellent performance of previous methods has been confirmed, it is still challenging to apply these methods in VVC due to significantly different CTU partition structure between HEVC and VVC. Actually, by considering the new characteristics of VVC, the computational complexity can be reduced, which motivates the researchers to design fast CU partition algorithms for VVC. In [11], Yang et al. modeled CTU structure decision as multi -binary- classification problems. In [12], Cui et al. presented a gradient-based early termination of CU partition algorithm via analyzing the partition characteristics and directional gradients. In [13], variance and gradient were calculated to choose the partition type.

The inspiration of this paper comes from several former HEVC works utilizing traditional methods by extracting texture property and spatial correlations. The motivations are based on the fact that the number of partition types is large and most of them can be skipped with the analysis of attributes. In short, the main contributions of this study are listed as follows: 1) A fast CU partition decision algorithm, which combined texture property and spatial correlation, is proposed for CU partition process in VVC with various partition types. 2) Instead of traverse all possible partition types to get optimal CU, this method aims to explore the relationships between partition types and CU's attributes. 3) In order to analyze the CU's property, corresponding CTU's texture property and spatial correlations are introduced. 4) To reduce the time consumption, motivated by the HEVC's method, we proposed a novel technique by skip the unnecessary split types, this method reduce the computation complexity in VVC.

The remainder is organized as follows: Sect. 2 briefly overviews the CU partitioning in VVC and the encoding complexity is analyzed as well. Section 3 illustrates the proposed fast CU partition decision method in details. The experimental results and related discussions are given in Sect. 4, followed by conclusion in Sect. 5.

2   Background Knowledge

Similar to its precursor HEVC, during the encoding process of VVC, each video picture is first cut up into several blocks, and then these blocks are predicted by either an intra or an inter way. In intra prediction, there are two important elements named CU partition decision and intra prediction mode decision. This paper focuses on the CU partition decision. In CU partition decision, VVC applies a newly-introduced QTMT to better fit the diversity of the content characteristic thus improving the coding performance. As shown in Fig. 1, a video frame is initially divided into CTU with the extended size of 128×128. Then, each CTU can be recursively split following a QTMT structure where CUs are generated. Specifically, in the first stage, CTU adopting quaternary tree (QT) is partitioned into four sub-CUs, and this stage is the same as HEVC. In the second stage, each sub-CU using QTMT structure is further recursively split into smaller CUs of different sizes to find the optimal partition mode, and it should be noted that the QT will be forbidden once the multi-type tree (MT) is adopted. From the perspective of QTMT structure, a block can be partitioned in 6 ways, including QT, horizontal binary tree (BH), vertical binary tree (BV), horizontal ternary tree (TH), vertical binary tree (TV), and non-split. BH and BV are called binary tree (BT), and the BT split a CU into two sub-CUs of equal size. Similarly, TH and TV are called ternary tree (TT), and the TT split mode generates three sub-CUs with the ratio 1:2:1 in horizontal or vertical directions. Meanwhile, the combination of BT and TT is called MT. An example of CU splitting operation is shown in Fig. 2. The solid black lines denote the QT partition, and the dotted blue lines, the orange lines indicate the BT partition and TT partition respectively.

By investigating of the CU partition process under the VVC standard, we observe that one of the factors lead to a significant increase in computational complexity is the conventional search strategy of the brute force full rate distortion optimization (RDO). Moreover, the complexity is further increased on account of additional search during mode decision loop corresponding each CU partition. The RDO process aims to choose the minimum rate distortion cost (RDC) by traversing all possible candidates one by one. The RDC and RDO are respectively defined as follows:

$$J_{RDC} = D + \lambda R \tag{1}$$

where D denotes the sum of the absolute differences between original and reconstructed samples, R represents the number of bits required to encoded the block, λ is the constant Lagrange multiplier.

$$RDO = arg\ \min_{k} J_{RDC}(k),\ k \in S_Q, S_{BH}, S_{BV}, S_{TH}, S_{TV}, S_N \qquad (2)$$

where $J_{RDC}(k)$ is the value of RDC with each partition type, S_Q, S_{BH}, S_{BV}, S_{TH}, S_{TV}, S_N signals the split type is QT, BH, BV, TH, TV, non-split, respectively.

Based on above analysis, there is an urgent need to find an efficient method to avoid unnecessary partition types because of the large number of partitioning types options. As long as the number of partition types that are needed to perform RDO is reduced, the total time spent on RDO will be decreased. To cope with this issue, this paper develops an approach which enables an early termination of traversing all possible partition types in advance based on the properties of CUs. Generally, if the CU to be encoded with smooth textures, QT partition will be directly chosen, and MT partitions are discarded in advance. On the contrary, if the CU to be encoded with uneven textures, MT partition will be directly chosen, and thus QT partitions are early terminated. The details are presented in Sect. 3.

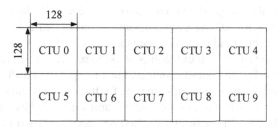

Fig. 1. The image is divided into CTU with non-overlapping.

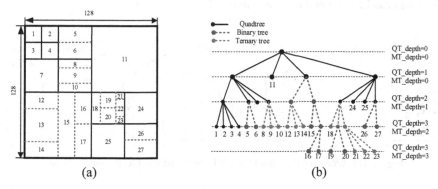

Fig. 2. Illustration of block partition in VVC: (a) CTU partition using QTMT (b) corresponding tree structure.

3 Methodology

3.1 Fast CU Partition Decision Based on Texture

Different textures within a CTU are likely to be divided into different CUs. Therefore, we take the richness of texture into account before traversing all possible split types. Generally, when a CTU has a highly complex texture, there is a tendency that the CU is likely to be coded at a deep depth which leads to a small CU size with finer partition. In contrast, a CTU owning a simple texture inclines to be coded at a shallow CU depth which brings a large CU size. Alternating current (AC) energy coefficients obtained by discrete cosine transform (DCT) is employed to evaluate the homogeneity of texture in CTU, the formula is defined as follows:

$$N_{AC} = \frac{1}{W \times H} \sum_{i=1}^{W} \sum_{j=1}^{H} (p(i,j))^2 - \left(\frac{1}{W \times H} \sum_{i=1}^{W} \sum_{j=1}^{H} p(i,j) \right)^2 \qquad (3)$$

where N_{AC} is the AC energy coefficients in CTU. W, H are the width and height, respectively. p represents the gray value and i, j are the row and column indices.

The video sequence is first divided into threshold update frames and fast CU decision frames. The proposed fast algorithm is carried out in the fast CU decision frames. When encoding these frames, the AC energy coefficients are calculated and then compared with the upper and lower threshold created in threshold update frames, and the threshold is updated in real-time to adapt various features of video sequences automatically. Figure 3 shows the frames used for threshold update and fast CU partition decision. In particular, the first frame in each frame rate groups are used for threshold update and encoded using original algorithm, yet the rest of the successive frames are coded by using the proposed algorithm. According to [14], a similar method has been proposed in H.265/HEVC to calculate the threshold, which has been verified to be reasonable. We introduced the upper and lower thresholds to take the texture of CTU into consideration. Hence, the CTU depth can be redefined as shown in Eq. 4.

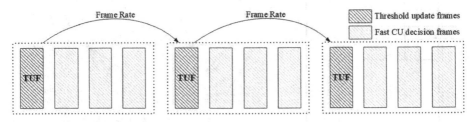

Fig. 3. Illustration of threshold update frames and fast CU decision frames.

$$DR_0 = [D_0, D_1] = \begin{cases} [D_I, D_A - 1], & N_{AC} < T_L \\ [D_I + 1, D_A], & N_{AC} > T_U \\ [D_I, D_A], & other \end{cases} \qquad (4)$$

where DR_0 is redefined CTU depth, and D_0, D_1 are the minimum and maximum of DR_0 respectively. D_I and D_A refer to borders of original CTU depth which is set in AI configuration. T_U represents the AC energy coefficients upper threshold and T_L is the lower threshold.

3.2 Fast CU Partition Decision Based on Spatial Correlation

For natural video sequences, adjacent CTUs usually contain similar texture which indicates that they may be in close depth level. In the original VVC reference software, CTU will be encoded in zig-zag order, and this means the depth information of upper and left has been extracted when encoding current CTU. This process is shown in Fig. 4. Spatial correlation between current CTU's depth and neighboring encoded CTU's depths is used to further taper the encoding depth range of CTU, which is expressed as indicated in Eq. 5.

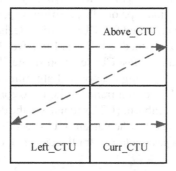

Fig. 4. Neighboring CTUs and current encoding CTU.

$$DR_1 = [D_2, D_3] = \begin{cases} [D_0, D_1 - 1], & D_{LEFT} < D_A - 1, D_{ABOVE} < D_A - 1 \\ [D_0 + 1, D_1], & D_{LEFT} > D_I + 1, D_{ABOVE} > D_I + 1 \\ [D_0, D_1], & other \end{cases} \quad (5)$$

where DR_1 is the CTU depth range. D_2, D_3 are the minimum and maximum of CTU depth respectively, D_{LEFT} and D_{ABOVE} are the encoded CTU depth of the left and above neighboring CTUs.

3.3 Integrated Fast CU Partition Decision Algorithm

The coding depth range of current CU can be predicted by exploring the CTU depth and adjacent CU together, as shown in Eq. 6. According to the predicted depth range, the unnecessary splitting types can be skipped. This relies on the fact that smaller depth range means finer partition through the MT partition type. On the contrary, the larger depth range means rough partition adopting the QT types, as shown in Eq. 7.

$$
\begin{cases}
DR_3 = DR_1 \cap DR_2 \\
DR_2 = [D_{CI}, D_{CA}] \\
D_{CI} = MAX(D_A, D_R, D_L, D_B) \\
D_{CA} = MIN(D_A, D_R, D_L, D_B)
\end{cases}
\tag{6}
$$

where DR_3 is the current CU depth range, and DR_2 is the adjacent CU depth range. D_{CI}, D_{CA} are the minimum and maximum of adjacent CU depth respectively, and D_A, D_R, D_L, D_B represents the encoded CU depth of the above, right, left and bellow neighboring CUs.

$$
DR_4 = [D_{ORG\_min}, D_{ORG\_max}] = \begin{cases}
[D_{ORG\_min} + 1, D_{ORG\_max} + 1], & D_3 \in [D_I, D_A - 2] \\
[D_{ORG\_min} - 1, D_{ORG\_max} - 1], & D_3 \in [D_I + 2, D_A] \\
[D_{ORG\_min}, D_{ORG\_max}], & other
\end{cases}
\tag{7}
$$

where DR_4 is the threshold of the VTM anchor. D_{ORG_min} and D_{ORG_max} are thresholds of directly choosing QT partition type or MT partition type, respectively.

The pseudo codes of the proposed fast CU partition decision are shown in Fig. 5. In conclusion, the algorithm is explained as follows: First, we check if the current frame is either a threshold update frame or fast CU decision frame. The thresholds are updated in each threshold update frames using the original algorithm, and the proposed method is incorporated in the fast CU decision frames. Then, we combine texture property and actual coding depths of the neighboring CTUs to narrow the depth range of current CTU. Next, the predicted depth range for the current CU is acquired. Finally, our algorithm determines which splitting types is adopted for the current CU according to its predicted depth.

Algorithm Integrated Fast CU Partition Decision Algorithm

1 **begin**
2   **for** i=0; i<the last frame; i++ **do**
3   **if** threshold update frame == false **then**
4   **initialize** the current CTU depth range
5   for each CTU:
6   compute N_{AC} and capture CTU depth of the left and above neighboring CTUs.
7   **integrate** N_{AC} and neighboring CTU's depth into the current CTU depth range DR_1.
8   for each CU:
9   **integrate** DR_1 and neighboring CU's depth into the current CU depth range DR_3.
10   predict the split types in each single CU.
11   **else**
12   carry out the original algorithm and update T_L and T_U
13   **end**
14   **end**
15 **end**

Fig. 5. Pseudo codes of the proposed algorithm.

4   Results and Discussions

The proposed algorithm is tested in the official VVC reference software VTM4.0, and the standard test sequences recommended by JVET are encoded under AI configuration and the common test conditions (CTC) [15]. The particular parameters are presented in Table 1. All the experiments are implemented with Inter Core i7-9700KF, CPU3.6GHz.

Table 1. Setting of encoding parameters.

Parament	Value
CTU size	128×128
Min QT size	8×8
Max MT size	32×32
Min MT size	4×4
Min depth	0
Max depth	5

The encoding efficiency and robustness are mainly evaluated by Bj ϕ ntegaard delta Bitrate (BDBR, %), Bj ϕ ntegaard delta PSNR (BDPSNR, dB) [16], and the coding time savings. The integral coding performance is evaluated in terms of BDBR and BDPSNR. The larger the value of increase in BDBR and the decrease in BDPSNR, the worse the coding performance. Meanwhile, time savings is applied to indicate the complexity reduction of the encoder, as defined in Eq. 8.

$$\Delta T(QP) = \frac{T_{ORG}(QP) - T_{PRO}(QP)}{T_{ORG}(QP)} \tag{8}$$

where time savings is expressed by the symbol of ΔT, T_{ORG} is the coding time of the original platform and T_{PRO} is the coding time of our proposed algorithm, quantization parameter (QP) is set as 22, 27, 32, 37, respectively.

In the evaluation, 300 frames are encoded. The comparative results between our proposed method and the original algorithm are demonstrated in Table 2. It can be seen that, compared with the original VVC encoder, our proposed algorithm can save 49.01% encoding time, on average, at the cost of the averaged 2.18% BDBR increase and 0.138 dB BDPSNR decrease. It is noteworthy that the average values in this table may differ from result of one single sequence. When observing results sequence by sequence, the more homogeneous texture distribution is, the larger number of CU skip in partition type is. For example, in Tango2 sequence, the time reduction is up to 61.31% with 2.33% BDBR increase and 0.14 dB BDPSNR decrease. In contrast, in situation of BQMall sequence which owns complex texture distribution, encoding time reduces by 30.34% and BDBR increases by 2.52%, while BDPSNR decreases by 0.14 dB.

Table 2. Comparison with the proposed and original algorithm.

Class	Sequence	BDBR (%)	BDPSNR (dB)	ΔT (%, time savings)
A1	Tango2	2.33	−0.14	61.31
	FoodMarket4	3.55	−0.22	49.29
A2	CatRobot	3.7	−0.26	42.42
	ParkRunning3	2.17	−0.13	45.08
B	BQTerrace	1.45	−0.1	33.97
	Cactus	1.7	−0.11	26.48
	MarketPlace	3.14	−0.16	59.06
	RitualDance	3.34	−0.19	64.99
C	BQMall	2.52	−0.14	30.34
	PartyScene	1.57	−0.12	44.93
	RaceHorsesC	0.84	−0.05	46.49
D	BasketballPass	−0.02	0	47.68
	BlowingBubbles	0	0	47.92
	BQSquare	−0.01	0	50.93
	RaceHorses	−0.03	0	60.97
E	FourPeople	4.63	−0.33	56.78
	KristenAndSara	6.09	−0.396	64.48
Average		**2.18**	**−0.138**	**49.01**

Figure 6 demonstrates the RD curves and time reduction curves of different sequence classes. Red RD curve and blue RD curve denote the corresponding relationship between bitrate and PSNR under different QP values (including 22, 27, 32 and 37) in the original and our proposed algorithm respectively. Obviously, the RD curves of proposed algorithm almost overlap with that of the original encoder, which indicates that the RD performance of the proposed method has almost no degradation. Namely, there is nearly no quality loss. It can be also observed from purple time reduction curves that under different QP values, we can always gain effective time savings using our proposed method. Meanwhile, in Fig. 7, we illustrate the visualization of decoded frames and CU partition comparisons of the second frame between VTM4.0 and our proposed algorithm. It is obvious that difference between decoded frames of original algorithm and ours is also scarcely observable to human eyes. As for the CU partition, for areas such as the red marked one where semantic information is more sparse, QT partitions is more suitable than MT partitions, and our proposed method can capture this property to matches reality better than the original algorithm. In a word, the robustness of proposed method can be confirmed with these experiment results under various test sequences and QP values.

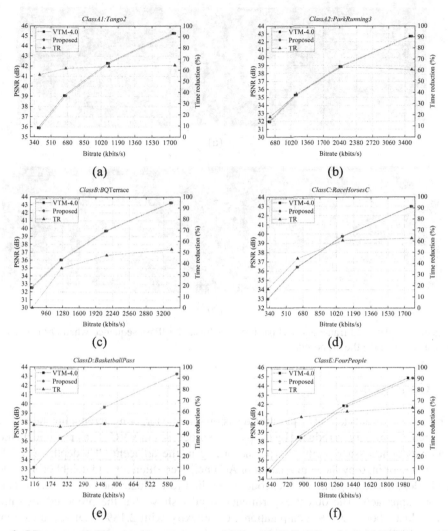

Fig. 6. RD curves of different video sequences: (a) Tango2 (b) ParkRunning3 (c) BQTerrace (d) RaceHorsesC (d) BasketballPass (e) FourPeople.

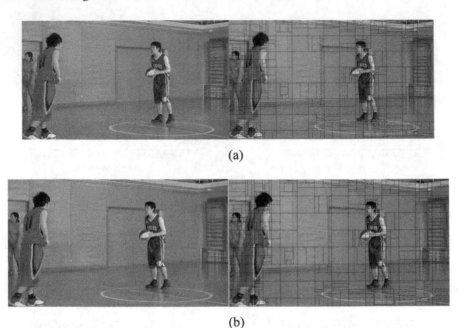

(a)

(b)

Fig. 7. The decoded frame and CU partitions of BasketballPass sequence when QP is equal to 37: (a) original (b) the proposed.

5 Conclusion

This paper presents a fast CU partition decision scheme targeting at reducing the computational complexity introduced by the partition processes in VVC. The proposed method removes unnecessary partition types according to the adjacent CUs depths and CTU depth determined by the combination of AC energy coefficients and neighboring coded CTU depth. The original VVC encoder is applied to evaluate the coding performance of our approach. The object experimental results show that the proposed algorithm can reduce about 49.01% computational complexity with 2.18% BDBR increase and 0.138 dB BDPSNR decrease. Meanwhile, subject result can also show good performance of our proposed algorithm. In summary, the proposed algorithm reveals good trade-off between coding efficiency and complexity reduction.

Acknowledgement. This work was supported in part by National Natural Science Foundation of China under Grant 61771170.

References

1. Bross, B., Chen, J., Liu, S., Wang, Y.K.: versatile video coding editorial refinements on (Draft10). Document JVET-T2001. In: Joint Video Exploration Team (JVET), Teleconference (2020)

2. Bossen, F., Li, X., Suehring, K., Norkin, A.: AHG report: test model software development (AHG3). Document JVET-N0003. In: Joint Video Exploration Team (JVET), Geneva, CH (2019)
3. Shen, L., Zhang, Z., Liu, Z.: Effective CU size decision for HEVC intracoding. IEEE Trans. Image Process. 23(10), 4232–4241 (2014)
4. Lei, J., Li, D., Pan, Z., Sun, S., Kwong, S., Hou, C.: Fast intra prediction based on content property analysis for low complexity HEVC-based screen content coding. IEEE Trans. Broad. 63(1), 48–58 (2017)
5. Min, B., Cheung, R.C.C.: A fast CU size decision algorithm for the HEVC intra encoder. IEEE Trans. Circuits Syst. Video Technol. 25(5), 892–896 (2015)
6. Zhang, Y., Kwong, S., Wang, X., Yuan, H., Pan, Z., Xu, L.: Machine learning-based coding unit depth decisions for flexible complexity allocation in high efficiency video coding. IEEE Trans. Image Process. 24(7), 2225–2238 (2015)
7. Duanmu, F., Ma, Z., Wang, Y.: Fast mode and partition decision using machine learning for intra-frame coding in HEVC screen content coding extension. IEEE J. Emerg. Sel. Top. Circuits Syst. 6(4), 517–531 (2016). https://doi.org/10.1109/JETCAS.2016.2597698
8. Grellert, M., Zatt, B., Bampi, S., da Silva Cruz, A.: Fast coding unit partition decision for HEVC using support vector machines. IEEE Trans. Circuits Syst. Video Technol. 29(6), 1741–1753 (2019)
9. Liu, Z., Yu, X., Gao, Y., Chen, S., Ji, X., Wang, D.: CU partition mode decision for HEVC hard-wired intra encoder using convolution neural network. IEEE Trans. Image Process. 25(11), 5088–5103 (2016)
10. Xu, M., Li, T., Wang, Z., Deng, X., Yang, R., Guan, Z.: Reducing complexity of HEVC: a deep learning approach. IEEE Trans. Image Process. 27(10), 5044–5059 (2018)
11. Yang, H., Shen, L., Dong, X., Ding, Q., An, P., Jiang, G.: Jiang: low-complexity CTU partition structure decision and fast intra mode decision for versatile video coding. IEEE Trans. Circuits Syst. Video Technol. 30(6), 1668–1682 (2020)
12. Cui, J., Zhang, T., Gu, C., Zhang, X., Ma, S.: Gradient-based early termination of CU partition in VVC intra coding. In: Data Compression Conference (DCC), pp. 103–112. IEEE (2020)
13. Fan, Y., Chen, J., Sun, H., Katto, J., Jing, M.: A fast QTMT partition decision strategy for VVC intra prediction. IEEE Access 8, 107900–107911 (2020)
14. Lu, X., Xiao, N., Hu, Y., Martin, G., Jin, X., Wu, Z.: A hierarchical fast coding unit depth decision algorithm for HEVC intra coding. In: Visual Communications and Image Processing (VCIP), pp. 1–4. IEEE (2016)
15. Bossen, F., Boyce, J., Suehring, K., Li, X., Seregin, V.: JVET common test conditions and software reference configurations for SDR video. Document JVET-N1010. In: Joint Video Exploration Team (JVET), Geneva, CH (2019)
16. Bjontegaard, G.: Calculation of average PSNR differences between rdcurves. Document VCEG-M33. In: ITU-T VCEG, Austin, Texas (2001)

Carrier Robust Reversible Watermark Model Based on Image Block Chain Authentication

Yating Gao[1], Ru Zhang[2], Xianxu Li[1], Jianyi Liu[2(✉)], Kaifeng Zhao[2], and Xue Cheng[2]

[1] State Grid Information and Telecommunication Branch, Beijing, China
[2] Beijing University of Posts and Telecommunications, Beijing, China
liujy@bupt.edu.cn

Abstract. Digital watermarking technology protects information security from the dimension of the existence of hidden information. At present, most watermarking algorithms only focus on the embedding and extraction of secret information, which usually brings permanent distortion to the carrier. This poses many challenges in scenarios that require high data authentication, such as medical image processing and military communications. This paper proposes a robust reversible watermarking algorithm for carriers based on block chain authentication. It is designed to mark the tampered location of the carrier with a fragile watermark, and restore the tampered information through authentication before and after, so that the peak signal-to-noise ratio of the restored carrier can be greatly improved when tampering occurs. The experimental results show that the scheme has good recovery ability in the scene of tampering with the watermark image.

Keywords: Fragile watermark · Reversible watermark · Block chain authentication

1 Introduction

With the development of increasing Internet and mobile applications, digital image media content, as one of the most important information carriers, has become the mainstream medium of information communication. Not only in personal communications and business, but also in military, political, and medical fields that require high privacy and integrity in communication, images are also one of the most important information carriers [1]. Watermarking technology protects the security of communication by "hiding the existence of secret communication". The watermarking method can not only prevent the content of communication from being intercepted, but also conceal the fact that the communication itself exists. It can provide more powerful protection for the privacy of applications in more fields, and plays an important role in the field of privacy protection.

In most of the existing watermark models that have been proposed, the original carrier usually brings irreversible distortion during the embedding stage. In some more demanding fields, such as remote sensing pictures, medical pictures, military pictures, etc., it is required that the transmission image is accurate and not damaged, and more

© Springer Nature Switzerland AG 2021
Y. Peng et al. (Eds.): ICIG 2021, LNCS 12888, pp. 712–724, 2021.
https://doi.org/10.1007/978-3-030-87355-4_59

information is retained to the greatest extent. The reversible watermarking technology is thus realized, and has received more extensive attention and rapid development. The current reversible watermarking technology, while retaining the advantages and characteristics of the information hiding algorithm, can restore the original carrier data and secret information losslessly.

In recent years, many newly proposed reversible watermarking methods try to satisfy high embedding rate and good recovery carrier quality. Xiang [2] uses self-embedding and mirroring ciphertext group strategies to embed information in encrypted images. This method provides higher security for hidden data in the encrypted domain, but its embedding rate is relatively low (less than 0.2 bpp). Qu et al. [3] introduced a pixel-based pixel value ordering (PPVO) predictor, where each pixel has two predicted values. Then, based on the pixel value of the predicted image, one of the two values will be used as the predicted value. Qu's method has been improved in [4], in which a reversible steganography scheme based on prediction error expansion (PEE) is proposed. This method is only designed for smooth images, and the prediction accuracy is unstable on large data sets, indicating that this makes this method not suitable for all images. In the article [5], a classic fragile information hiding algorithm is proposed. Through the one-way nature of the knapsack problem, combined with the hash method, the image content is converted into a watermark for self-embedding. At the same time, based on the sliding window mode, the embedding position of the watermark is selected, so that the encryption is realized in the block. Experiments show that this watermarking method has good robustness in the face of vector attacks, quantization attacks and other attack methods. And can accurately determine the location of tampering. Based on the research of the reversible watermarking framework and combining the image block chain authentication method, this paper proposes a new carrier robust reversible watermark. And on the basis of tampering with positioning, the self-recovery function is added. The reversible watermark and the fragile watermark are embedded into the image carrier in a dual mode to achieve the effects of high reversibility, high embedding rate, and robustness of the carrier against attacks in its image information hiding.

2   Related Work

2.1   Gradient Adjust Prediction

Gradient Adjust Prediction (GAP) is an edge detection algorithm in image recognition. This article is also based on this prediction method as an improvement and applied to the pixel prediction process of information hiding. The gradient prediction method uses a gradient predictor to calculate according to the seven neighbor pixels of the current predicted pixel to obtain the predicted value. The gradient adjustment algorithm is a non-linear and adaptive prediction method. It can be described as Fig. 1:

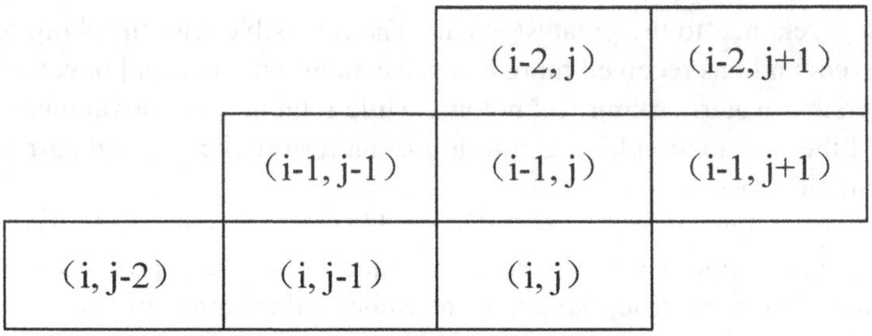

		(i-2, j)	(i-2, j+1)
	(i-1, j-1)	(i-1, j)	(i-1, j+1)
(i, j-2)	(i, j-1)	(i, j)	

Fig. 1. Neighboring pixels used in pixel prediction

Among them, taking the original image I with a given size of m × n as an example, let p(i, j) be the current pixel to be predicted. It should be noted that some pixels in the image are unpredictable because there are not enough neighbor pixels around for calculation. Therefore, it is necessary to meet the requirements of $I \leq j \leq m \leq 3$ and $j \leq n \leq n - 1$. First calculate the sum of absolute differences between the three pairs of surrounding pixels of p:

$$dh = abs(p(i, j - 1) - p(i, j - 2)) + abs(p(i - 1, j) - p(i - 1, j - 1))$$
$$+ abs(p(i - 1, j) - p(i - 1, j + 1)) \tag{1}$$

$$dv = abs(p(i, j - 1) - p(i - 1, j - 1)) + abs(p(i - 1, j) - p(i - 2, j))$$
$$+ abs(p(i - 1, j + 1) - p(i - 2, j + 1)) \tag{2}$$

Where dh and dv represent the gradient changes in the horizontal and vertical directions, respectively. Then, according to the difference range of dh and dv, the predicted value of p(i, j) can be expressed as p′(i, j):

$$p'(i,j) = \begin{cases} p(i, j-1) & d_v - d_h > 80 \\ p(i-1, j) & d_v - d_h < -80 \\ (p(i - 1, j) + p(i, j - 1))/2 + (p(i - 1, j + 1) + p(i - 1, j - 1))/4 & ELSE \end{cases} \tag{3}$$

If dv-dh > 80, then p(i, j) is classified as a sharp horizontal edge. If dv-dh < −80, then p(i, j) is classified as a sharp vertical edge. If the absolute difference between dh and dv is less than the threshold, you need to perform one more step to predict the value of p(i, j):

$$p'(i,j) = \begin{cases} (p'(i,j) + p(i, j - 1))/2 & d_v - d_h > 32 \\ (3 \times p'(i,j) + p(i, j - 1))/4 & d_v - d_h > 32 \\ (p'(i,j) + p(i - 1, j))/2 & d_v - d_h < -32 \\ (3 \times p'(i,j) + p(i - 1, j))/4 & d_v - d_h < -8 \\ p'(i,j) & ELSE \end{cases} \tag{4}$$

In this case, the pixels p(i, j) are classified into horizontal edges, weak horizontal edges, vertical edges, and weak vertical edges, respectively. The thresholds 80, 32, and 8 weights used in formula 4 are empirical constants calculated based on specific experiments.

2.2 Tampered Location and Restoration

After receiving the secret watermarked picture at the receiving end, the integrity of the picture should be authenticated before extracting the secret information. Make sure that the image has not been tampered with before extracting the watermark. The processing flow method at the receiving end is as follows.

After the image is received, the image is divided into blocks first. Taking the operation on image A as an example, first divide it into blocks in order, and divide the image into non-overlapping sub-blocks with a size of 3×3, denoted by Bi. Where i is the unique non-repeated index of sub-block B. Bi can be expressed as:

$$B_i = \begin{pmatrix} b^i_{(0,0)} & b^i_{(0,1)} & b^i_{(0,2)} \\ b^i_{(1,0)} & b^i_{(1,1)} & b^i_{(1,2)} \\ b^i_{(2,0)} & b^i_{(1,2)} & b^i_{(2,2)} \end{pmatrix} \tag{5}$$

Where b(i, j) is the pixel value at position (i, j) in the sub-block.

According to the method of formula (5), the image is divided into blocks with a size of 3×3. Obtain each non-overlapping sub-blocks $B'_1, B'_2 ... B'_n$. Since we assume that the image may change during the transmission process, in order to indicate the difference before and after the same position of the image, the symbol is used to represent the actual value of the receiving end.

In the second step, DCT changes are performed on each sub-block after block division, and the corresponding block is represented as $C'_1, C'_2 ... C'_n$.

In the third step, in each DCT sub-block, the corresponding six fragile watermarks are extracted. For example, for block C'_{i+1}, the fragile watermarks $r_{i-1}, r_{i-2}, ... r_{i-6}$ can be extracted by the following formula. That is, the fragile watermark generated from the previous sub-block information extracted from each block.

$$\begin{cases} r_{i-1} = c'^{i+1}_{(0,2)} \bmod 2 \\ r_{i-2} = c'^{i+1}_{(1,1)} \bmod 2 \\ r_{i-3} = c'^{i+1}_{(2,0)} \bmod 2 \\ r_{i-4} = c'^{i+1}_{(2,1)} \bmod 2 \\ r_{i-5} = c'^{i+1}_{(1,2)} \bmod 2 \\ r_{i-6} = c'^{i+1}_{(2,2)} \bmod 2 \end{cases} \tag{6}$$

Combining these bit planes, the intensity information R of the block is obtained.

$$R = \sum_{j=1}^{6} r_{i-j} \times 2^{j-1} \tag{7}$$

After obtaining the fragile watermark, due to the front and back dependence of the order of each sub-block of the image, we take the three sub-blocks B_h, B_i, B_j in the front and back order of h, i, j as an example, where the fragile watermark extracted from B_i is from B_h The information is generated, and the watermark extracted in B_j is generated by the information in B_i. With this rule, the method of tampering location and tampering recovery can be summarized as the following steps:

Since in the DCT transformation, the low-frequency component $c(0,0)$ of each sub-block retains most of the information of the original block B, the average intensity B_{meani} in each sub-block B_i is calculated as follows:

$$B_{meani} = c^i_{(0,0)}/3 \tag{8}$$

According to formula (8), the blocks B'_1, $B'_2...B'_n$ in the received image are generated in the same way to generate their average intensity B'_{meani}.

According to the generated average strength B'_{meani} and the strength information R_i from which the watermark is extracted, it can be determined whether the block has been tampered with and replied. The procedures for determining tampering and restoration are as follows:

1. If B'_{meani} and R_i are equal, the strength verification of the block is successful, indicating that no tampering occurred during the communication.
2. If B'_{meani} and R_i are not equal, it means that tampering may occur during the communication process, and the two situations need to be judged separately. That is, it may be that the current block of B'_{meani} has changed, or the authentication information Ri in the next block has changed.

   2.1 Judging if B'_{meani} and R_h are equal, and if B'_{meani} and R_j are not equal, it can be concluded that R_i has changed, and B'_{meani} calculated in the current block has not changed, that is, the current block B_i has not been tampered with.
   2.2 Judgment If B'_{meanh} is not equal to R_h, and B'_{meanj} is equal to R_j, it can be concluded that R_i has not changed, and B'_{meani} calculated for the current block has changed, that is, tampering has occurred in the current block B_i. At this time, the fragile watermark information R_i can be used to restore B_i. The method is to directly replace B'_{meani} with fragile watermark information.
   2.3 Judgment if B'_{meanh} and R_h are not equal, and if B'_{meanj} and R_j are not equal, it can be concluded that both the fragile watermark R_i and the B'_{meani} calculated by the current block have changed, that is, the current block B_i is tampered with. In this case, it is impossible to determine the specific tampering information. In this case, B_i can only locate the tampering and cannot be restored.
   2.4 Judging if B'_{meanh} is equal to Rh, and if B'_{meanj} is equal to R_j, it can be concluded that neither R_i nor B'_{meani} calculated by the current block has changed, that is, the current block B_i has not been tampered with. No action is required.

Follow the above steps to locate and restore the entire image, you can locate all of them and successfully restore most of the tampered information. The image is subjected to DCT inverse transformation, and the encrypted image I_w after tampering and restoration can be obtained.

3 Algorithm Design

3.1 Pixel Prediction

The Gradient Adjusted Prediction Algorithm (GAP) is an adaptive edge detection algorithm in image recognition, which is used in pixel prediction in this article. GAP operates on seven neighboring pixels of the current predicted pixel. For the predicted pixel value, since the most significant bit is the target bit, the judgment of the prediction accuracy only pays attention to the most significant bit MSB bit. Respectively, compare the prediction results with the most significant bit opposite to test the accuracy of the prediction. The pixel prediction in the algorithm and the added method of verifying the prediction accuracy are explained as follows.

Given an original image I of size m × n, let p(i, j) be the current pixel to be predicted. According to formula 9 of the gradient adjustment prediction method, the point is classified into sharp horizontal edges, sharp vertical edges, horizontal edges, weak horizontal edges, vertical edges and weak vertical edges.

$$p'(i,j) = \begin{cases} (p'(i,j) + p(i,j-1))/2 & d_v - d_h > 32 \\ (3 \times p'(i,j) + p(i,j-1))/4 & d_v - d_h > 32 \\ (p'(i,j) + p(i-1,j))/2 & d_v - d_h < -32 \\ (3 \times p'(i,j) + p(i-1,j))/4 & d_v - d_h < -8 \\ p'(i,j) & ELSE \end{cases} \qquad (9)$$

In order to check the prediction accuracy, $p'(i, j)$ needs to be compared with $p(i, j)$ and its most significant bit inverted value $p_v(i, j)$. The values of $p_v(i, j)$ and $p(i, j)$ are the same except for the MSB bit value, but the MSB value is opposite. For n-bit images, p_v can be obtained in the following way:

$$p_v = (p(i,j) + 2^{n-1}) \mod 2^n \qquad (10)$$

Denote the absolute difference between $p'(i, j)$ and $p(i, j)$ and between $p'(i, j)$ and $p_v(i, j)$ as d1 and d2, so:

$$d1 = abs(p'(i,j) - p(i,j)) \qquad (11)$$

$$d2 = abs(p'(i,j) - p_v(i,j)) \qquad (12)$$

Compared with the inverted value of p(i, j), its original value should be closer than its predicted value. Therefore, if the prediction result is correct, the value of d1 should be less than d2. If d2 is less than d1, it means that a prediction error has occurred. Store its position information i and j in the binary matrix E. For an m × n carrier image I, after the pixel prediction stage, the error bit binary matrix E is obtained, and the size is also m × n. In this article, due to the subsequent improvement of the embedding algorithm, the most significant bit matrix L is not required to participate.

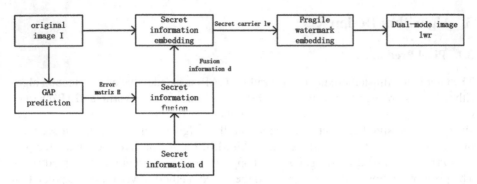

Fig. 2. Carrier embedding watermark process framework

3.2 Secret Information and Fragile Watermark Embedding

The framework of the carrier embedding watermark process used in this article is shown in Fig. 2:

The secret information embedding stage adopts the reversible watermark method in the plaintext domain, and the main process is as follows:

Use the key kw to encrypt the secret information. Subsequent use d represents encrypted information.

The error matrix E generated by the pixel prediction stage is traversed and scanned from left to right and top to bottom raster order. For the traversed pixel error bit, its position information is recorded in the one-dimensional binary array e. The length of the location information depends on the depth of the carrier picture. In order to mark the end of the error message and the beginning of the secret message, a set of flag bits f needs to be added as a mark. Use n-bit 0 to connect n-bit 1 to construct f, where n is the depth of the carrier image. For an image with 8-bit depth, f will be constructed as [0000000011111111]. Finally, the final embedded information is obtained by splicing and merging e, f, and d, and the final information to be embedded is denoted by b.

Next, scan all pixels in raster order. For the current position of the scan, if the position is an error bit in the error matrix, that is, E(i, j) is equal to 1, then the position is an unusable bit. In order to completely restore the carrier, the pixel value of each unavailable bit is left unmodified. And each available pixel (defined as a pixel that can be accurately predicted and E(i, j) is equal to 0) can be embedded in a bit b_k in the secret information b, where $0 \le k < m \times n$. For an n-bit image, the secret information can be embedded in the available pixel bits of the image I through the following formula:

$$I_w(i,j) = \begin{cases} I(i,j) & I(i,j)\bmod 2^{n-1} = 0, b_k = 0 \\ (I(i,j) + 2^{n-1}) \bmod 2^n & I(i,j)\bmod 2^{n-1} = 0, b_k = 1 \\ (I(i,j) - 2^{n-1}) \bmod 2^n & I(i,j)\bmod 2^{n-1} = 1, b_k = 0 \\ I(i,j) & I(i,j)\bmod 2^{n-1} = 1, b_k = 1 \end{cases} \quad (13)$$

Among them, I(i, j) is the pixel value of the position (i, j) in the image carrier I, I_w(i, j) is the pixel value of the point after the secret information is embedded, and b_k is the k-th position in the information to be embedded. The constant n is the image depth.

The detailed fragile watermark generation and embedding process is introduced as follows.

The image is divided into blocks. Follow the formula (5) in the previous section.

Perform DCT transformation on the sub-block B to obtain the corresponding DCT matrix sub-block C. C can be expressed by the following formula:

$$C_i = \begin{pmatrix} c^i_{(0,0)} & c^i_{(0,1)} & c^i_{(0,2)} \\ c^i_{(1,0)} & c^i_{(1,1)} & c^i_{(1,2)} \\ c^i_{(2,0)} & c^i_{(1,2)} & c^i_{(2,2)} \end{pmatrix} \tag{14}$$

Similarly, i is the unique non-repeated index of the sub-block C, and c(i, j) is the element value at the position (i, j) in the sub-block.

The average intensity is calculated as in the formula (8) in the previous section, and the average intensity $B_{\text{mean}i}$ is separated by a bit plane. The six fragile watermarks r_{i-j} of the i block are generated as follows, where the square brackets are the round-down function:

$$r_{i-j} = \left\lfloor \frac{B_{mean-i}}{2^{j-1}} \right\rfloor \bmod 2 \quad j = 1, 2, 3, 4, 5, 6 \tag{15}$$

Embed the fragile watermark into the high frequency components corresponding to the next DCT sub-block in sequence:

$$\begin{cases} c^{i+1}_{(0,2)} = \left[c^{i+1}_{(0,2)}/2 \right] \times 2 + r_{i-1} \\ c^{i+1}_{(1,1)} = \left[c^{i+1}_{(1,1)}/2 \right] \times 2 + r_{i-2} \\ c^{i+1}_{(2,0)} = \left[c^{i+1}_{(2,0)}/2 \right] \times 2 + r_{i-3} \\ c^{i+1}_{(2,1)} = \left[c^{i+1}_{(2,1)}/2 \right] \times 2 + r_{i-4} \\ c^{i+1}_{(1,2)} = \left[c^{i+1}_{(1,2)}/2 \right] \times 2 + r_{i-5} \\ c^{i+1}_{(2,2)} = \left[c^{i+1}_{(2,2)}/2 \right] \times 2 + r_{i-6} \end{cases} \tag{16}$$

Where [] is a rounding function, and each updated sub-block is subjected to inverse DCT transformation to obtain an image A_r containing a fragile watermark.

In this process, a fragile watermark is embedded in the secret image I_w with embedded secret information, and a dual-mode watermark image I_{wr} that contains both the secret information and the fragile watermark is obtained.

3.3 Secret Information Extraction and Carrier Reconstruction

The reversible recovery process framework of secret image extraction information used in this article is shown in Fig. 3:

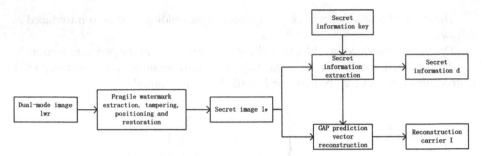

Fig. 3. Secret image extraction information reversible recovery process framework

For the information extraction stage, the tampered area was restored in the previous section. Since the most significant bit carries the most information, all MSB bit information can be restored in the tamper restoration. Since this article embeds secret information in the plaintext domain, the embedded information can be extracted directly by reading the most significant bit of each available pixel b:

$$b_k = \left\lfloor I_w(i,j)/2^{n-1} \right\rfloor \tag{17}$$

Where $0 \leq k < m \times n$. Also in the process of extracting the embedded information, there will be situations in which the wrong bit information is extracted from the unavailable bit of I_w. Therefore, it is necessary to initialize a zero matrix E as the error matrix, and for each pixel, it is necessary to compare its position with the error matrix E and determine whether it is an error bit. By continuously updating and iterating, the error bit information is continuously added to the matrix until all the error bits are restored.

For the carrier reconstruction stage, the restored prediction error pixel bit information is used, combined with prediction, in order to eliminate errors and completely reversibly restore the original carrier image, the error matrix E generated in the information extraction stage is needed. The scanned image I_w is also traversed in raster order, and the maximum effective bit of the current pixel is predicted by using the gradient adjustment method. The prediction result p′ is calculated according to Eq. (4).

Subsequently, it is assumed that the most significant bit of the pixel value of the current bit is equal to 0 and 1, respectively. After that, the absolute difference between these two values and p′(i, j) is calculated as follows:

$$d1 = abs(p'(i,j) - I_w(i,j)^{MSB=0}) \tag{18}$$

$$d2 = abs(p'(i,j) - I_w(i,j)^{MSB=1}) \tag{19}$$

Use I_r to represent the reconstructed image. For the smaller value between d1 and d2, since the smaller difference indicates that it is closer to the real pixel value of the carrier (actually it is equal to the real pixel value of the carrier), the corresponding hypothetical value is the reconstructed value $I_r(i, j)$.

$$I_r(i,j) = \begin{cases} I_w(i,j)^{MSB=0} & d1 < d2 \\ I_w(i,j)^{MSB=1} & d1 \geq d2 \end{cases} \tag{20}$$

It should be noted that in the carrier recovery stage, the information of unusable pixel bits needs to be retained, and the information at these positions has not undergone processes such as watermark embedding, and is the original carrier information. Unusable pixel bits include unpredictable pixel bits or pixel bits marked in the error matrix E, and the value $I_r(i, j)$ is consistent with $I_w(i, j)$. According to the above method, after traversing the entire image, the image receiver can restore the original carrier image to the greatest extent.

4 Experimental Results and Analysis

4.1 Summary of Experimental Results

The algorithm model proposed in this paper is applied to experiment and the results are analyzed. The standard image Lena in the standard image library is selected as the carrier image of the experiment. First of all, after applying our proposed model to the image Lena to embed secret information and fragile watermarks, without considering the tampering that occurs during the transmission process, the results obtained are shown in the Fig. 4:

(a)　　　　　(b)　　　　　(c)　　　　　(d)　　　　　(e)

Fig. 4. Lena image experiment results

In the above figure (a) is the original carrier Lena, (b) is the embedded secret information, (c) is the secret carrier image, (d) is the watermark extracted by the receiving end, and (e) is the restored carrier image. The PSNR calculation is performed on the encrypted image and the original carrier, and the result is 55dB. In the pixel prediction stage, when GAP prediction was performed on the Lena image, 8 prediction errors occurred. The actual error rate is less than 0.01%. Since the fragile watermark and the reversible watermark are embedded in different domains of the image, the redundant space used is independent of each other. In the experiment of Lena image, the actual maximum can also be embedded 258420 Bit secret information. The maximum embedding rate is about 0.986 bpp. For the reconstructed carrier, for the experimental image Lena, the PSNR of the reconstructed carrier and the original carrier is 62dB. However, subsequent experimental results show that the program still has a high degree of reversible recovery. The experimental results are better than some existing reversible watermarking algorithms.

5 Falsified Recovery Experiment Results

The test in the previous section was carried out without considering the occurrence of tampering in the insecure channel, and the effect and performance of reversible watermarking were considered. In this section, we will focus on testing the fragile watermark's tampering location ability and tampering recovery ability. Introduce the most common attack methods such as cropping and collage in tampering to verify the recovery ability of the model, the results obtained are shown in the Fig. 5:

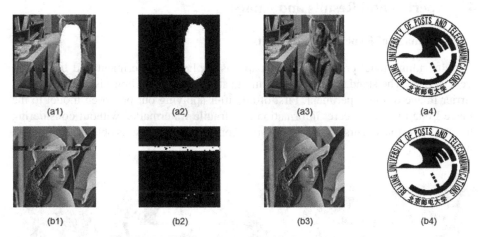

Fig. 5. Falsified location and falsified recovery results

In the above figure a1, to crop the secret image of the image barbara, the attack image obtained by the information of the human face part is erased. After receiving the attack image a1, according to the tampering positioning method in the model, the positioning and cropping information is extracted to obtain the image a2, where the black mark is the part that has not been judged to be tampered, and the white indicates that it is in the algorithm of the receiving end The part marked as tampered with, you can see that the marked area coincides with the cropped area, which proves the accuracy of the false acceptance rate in the theoretical analysis in the previous section. In image a3, the corrected image after the tampering restoration method is displayed. It can be seen that although after a large area of cropping, the plaintext image does not contain the information of Barbara's face at all, but after being tampered with and restored, most of the face's information can be restored in the correct position. From a visual point of view, the image is restored from an unusable image with most of the information destroyed to a usable image with part of the information intact. The actual peak signal-to-noise ratio (PSNR) has increased from 17.7 dB to 34.2 dB. This result also shows that the quality of the reconstructed image is greatly improved relative to the image quality at the receiving end. In a4, the watermark information extracted from the tampered image a1 can be extracted completely and correctly from the secret information shown in the figure. In addition, we also applied the experiment of collage attack. The experimental results are shown in figure b above. b1 is to cut and flip the rectangular band of the Lena image into the secret carrier image. b2 is also the tampered positioning image, in which it can be seen that the cropped rectangle is also clearly marked, and b3 is the encrypted image after the fragile watermark is restored. It can be seen that the basic information of the image has been restored. Because the low frequency part is mainly restored in the reconstruction, part of the detailed information will be missing, and some distortion can be seen in the edge part of the collage. However, the application of images has obviously better value than b1. Similarly, the secret information in b4 can be extracted correctly. This also shows that this scheme has a better recovery effect when the tampering rate of the attack is lower.

In order to compare the experimental results of the proposed method and the existing methods, we verified the method in the literature [6][7] and our method in the same picture. Table. 1 shows the comparison between the method in this paper and some existing watermark tampering restoration methods for different attack restoration degrees.

Table. 1. Comparison of tamper recovery results

Test image (512 × 512)	Degree of recovery (PSNR) (dB) Method of this article	Degree of recovery (PSNR) (dB) article [6]	Degree of recovery (PSNR) (dB) article [7]
Lena Crop 10%	50.41	49.15	44.54
Lena Crop 40%	33.02	30.14	21.51
Pepper Crop 10%	48.93	42.96	38.70
Pepper Crop 40%	34.75	29.23	24.48
Lena Collage 10%	49.12	46.79	48.82
Lena Collage 40%	32.65	27.08	22.64
Pepper Collage 10%	50.29	44.88	30.02
Pepper Collage 40%	31.60	23.47	19.33
Lena noise 10%	53.37	35.94	34.05
Lena noise 40%	33.51	25.37	22.29
Reversible average maximum tampering rate	32%	27%	24%

It can be seen from the information in the table that in our method, the image quality of tampering recovery is due to the contrast method, and our method can effectively detect the location information of random noise points, and restore these noises when recovering. However, the scheme in the comparative literature cannot detect the increased noise, and the method of tampering and recovery will not be used in the restoration. The reason for the analysis is that in our scheme, the detection accuracy used is 3×3 sub-blocks, while in the existing methods, 4×4 and 8×8 accuracy are used for detection. In terms of detection accuracy, this chapter The accuracy in the watermarking algorithm is more precise. Usually in the scenario of reversible watermarking, when the PSNR value recovered by the carrier is above 40dB, it can be considered to achieve the effect of reversible recovery. In the experimental results, the model in this paper can still achieve a reduction effect of 40.20dB when it is tampered with on average by 32%. Compared with the existing method, this result is slightly higher than the experimental effect of the existing method. It can also be proved that the proposed method has good usability in reversible watermarking.

6 Conclusion

In this paper, we propose a robust reversible watermarking model based on image block chain authentication, based on a reversible information hiding algorithm. With the dual-mode watermarking method, a fragile watermark is embedded in the DCT high-frequency component of the image. And it will not affect the embedding and extraction of existing reversible watermarks. With the help of the block chain of image block, the watermark can authenticate the front and back information after receiving the image, realize the function of locating the image information tampering and restoring the main information of the tampered area. The experimental results show that embedding the reversible watermark and the fragile watermark into the image carrier in a dual mode has good performance in anti-attack and reversible recovery.

Acknowledgement. The authors would like to thank the anonymous referees for their valuable comments and helpful suggestions. The work is supported by Science and Technology Project of the Headquarters of State Grid Corporation of China ,"The research and technology for collaborative defense and linkage disposal in network security devices" (5700-202152186A-0-0-00).

References

1. Buyya, R., Yeo, C.S., Venugopal, S., Broberg, J., Brandic, I.: Cloud computing and emerging IT platforms: vision, hype, and reality for delivering computing as the 5th utility. Future Generation Comput. Syst. **25**(6) (2008)
2. Xiang, S., Luo, X.: Reversible data hiding in homomorphic encrypted domain by mirroring ciphertext group. IEEE Trans. Circuits Syst. Video Technol. (2017)
3. Qu, X., Kim, H.J.: Pixel-based pixel value ordering predictor for high fidelity reversible data hiding. Sig. Process. **111**, 249–260 (2015)
4. Ou, B., Li, X.: Pairwise prediction error expansion for efficient reversible data hiding. IEEE Trans. Image Process. **22**(12), 5010–5021 (2013)
5. Xianhai, Z., Yongtian, Y.: Research on image authentication algorithm based on fragile watermarking. Chin. J. Electron. **01**, 36–41 (2007)
6. Kiatpapan, S., Kondo, T.: An image tamper detection and recovery method based on self-embedding dual watermarking. In: International Conference on Electrical Engineering/electronics, Computer, Telecommunications and Information Technology, pp.1–6. IEEE (2015)
7. Singh, D., Singh, S.K.: Effective self-embedding watermarking scheme for image tampered detection and localization with recovery capability **38**, 775–789

Cross-View Images Matching and Registration Technology Based on Deep Learning

Qing Zhou[1], Ronggang Zhu[2(⊠)], Yuelei Xu[1], and Zhaoxiang Zhang[1]

[1] Northwestern Polytechnical University, Xian/Shanxi, China
[2] Luoyang Institute of Electro-Optical Equipment, AVIC, Nuoyang/Henan, China

Abstract. Cross view images matching and registration is to extract the images features from different views of the same scene, and measure the similarity between features by measuring the correspondence between images, then perform pixel-level registration. Cross-view images have problems such as poor stability of feature points and big difference in scale, resulting in low efficiency of matching and registration using traditional methods. In this paper, a novel image matching method based on deep learning is adopted. Firstly, a convolutional neural network is utilized for image matching to achieve the initial selection of the target, and then the pixel level registration is carried out for the successfully matched images. Considering the problem of small samples, four feature extraction networks are used for feature extraction to achieve knowledge transfer. In the aspect of image registration, considering the difference between feature descriptors and baselines of cross view images, deep learning is introduced to improve the traditional algorithm to achieve accurate registration.

Keywords: Deep learning · Cross-perspective · Image matching · Image registration · Knowledge transfer

1 Introduction

Image matching refers to the matching of images of the same scene in different times, different shooting directions and different shooting methods (sensors). The key point is to establish the distinguishing features of the images, which are invariant to scale, translation and rotation, and keep stable under different illumination, visual angle and noise conditions. After images matching, pixel level registration of the images is carried out, and the images with the same scene are geometrically transformed and aligned, so that the aligned images share the same angle and coordinate system. Image matching and registration is a hot issue in the field of computer vision, and is widely used in three-dimensional reconstruction, stereo matching, image retrieval, image fusion and other fields.

For the target search and location with known target image template, for example, in the search task of UAV to the ground and sea target, for the given target image template, the UAV first needs to find the image matching the target template from the field of vision. If it needs to accurately locate the target, pixel-level registration of the target image and

© Springer Nature Switzerland AG 2021
Y. Peng et al. (Eds.): ICIG 2021, LNCS 12888, pp. 725–734, 2021.
https://doi.org/10.1007/978-3-030-87355-4_60

template image is also required. However, the target image template and UAV task image generally have cross-perspective issues [1, 2]. Descriptor-based feature matching method is still the mainstream method. Image pixel registration is traditionally used to achieve image matching. The traditional matching method does not consider whether the two images contain the same target. It is not reliable to judge whether the two images match indirectly by using the registration results [3, 4]. In addition, the traditional methods rely too much on the texture or gray features of the image, and the matching effect is greatly affected by the light, angle and other factors, resulting in the matching failure [5–8]. For artificial methods, it is difficult to design shared feature descriptors that represent non-linear relationships cross-view images [9].

A possible direction is to use deep learning technology to learn nonlinear similarity, which is currently in the initial exploration stage [10, 11]. In terms of registration, deep learning registration and traditional registration methods can cooperate with each other. It can not only give full play to the advantage of low error of traditional registration methods, but also improve the robustness of registration and solve the problem that the accuracy of traditional methods is easily affected by the environment [12].

Therefore, this paper introduces deep learning method to solve the problem of low robustness of existing methods [13, 14]. Firstly, the template image and task image are matched by deep learning method to achieve the initial positioning of the target image. By using the powerful feature extraction capabilities of neural networks, the high-dimensional features of the image are obtained for matching, which can effectively overcome the differences in details of images from different perspectives and greatly improve the probability of successful image matching. At the same time, it can greatly reduce the range of feature search as well as the computational pressure of the system, then, for the matched image, the pixel level registration is performed. Image registration is based on deep neural network and assisted by traditional feature point extraction algorithm. We try our best to overcome the differences of feature descriptors caused by cross perspective, fully excavate the feature similarities between cross-view images, and achieve the purpose of accurate registration. The technical idea of this paper is shown in Fig. 1.

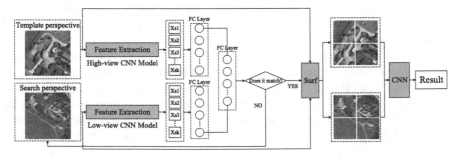

Fig. 1. Cross-view image matching and registration map.

2 Cross-View Images Matching Technology Based on Deep Learning

The training network adopts the method of knowledge transfer to reduce the difference in feature distribution between the template images and the task images. The matching network consists of feature extraction network and matching measurement network. Feature extraction network is the core of the whole image matching network, which is mainly used for image feature extraction [15]. This feature extraction network adopts RESNET network structure. RESNET is an improvement based on VGG19 network, compared with ordinary network, short circuit mechanism is added between every two layers to form residual learning [16]. RESNET is pre-trained, which can not only improve the generalization performance of the target network, but also greatly reduce the training cost [17]. The network structure is shown in Fig. 2.

In the process of network training, four images constitute a training sample, and two pairs of twin networks are trained at the same time. As shown in Fig. 2, the inputs of branch 1 and branch 2 come from different perspective images of the same scene, the inputs of branches 3 and 4 come from different perspective images of the same scene. The reason for adopting this kind of network design scheme in the feature extraction network is that through the training of the neural network, the feature distribution of images from different perspectives can be close to and aligned with each other, so as to realize the transfer learning between the source domain and the target domain [18].

In the image matching network, branch 2 and branch 3 are mainly used for cross-view images matching task. The matching probability is given through the measurement network, which includes two full connection layers FC1, FC2 and a softmax layer. Branch 2 and branch 3 extract the features of the two input images, and the subsequent measurement network learns the measurement criteria and outputs the measurement results. Finally, the softmax layer is used to evaluate the matching degree of the images in branch 2 and branch 3.

The loss function of image matching network is the sum of feature loss and matching loss, as shown in the following formula:

$$Loss = \lambda_1 d_1(D_s, D_t) + \lambda_2 d_2(D_s, D_t) + \sum_{i=1}^{n} \frac{e^{z_i}}{\sum_k e^{z_k}} \tag{1}$$

Where: d_1 function is the MMD (maximum mean diversity) distance of image features of branch 1 and branch 2; d_2 is the MMD distance of image features of branch 3 and branch 4; D_s represents the distribution of source domain data features in high-dimensional space; D_t represents the distribution of target domain data features in high-dimensional space; N is the total number of training samples; λ_1 and λ_2 is a super parameter. The empirical value of λ_1 and λ_2 is 0.1. By optimizing the two MMD distances, the distribution of the source domain and the target domain in the feature space is close; The third term of Eq. (1) is the softmax loss function, which is used to measure whether the input images of branch 2 and branch 3 match. 0 means no match, and 1 means match, where, z_i represents the input of the i-th neuron, and $\sum_k e^{z_k}$ represents the sum of the inputs of all neurons.

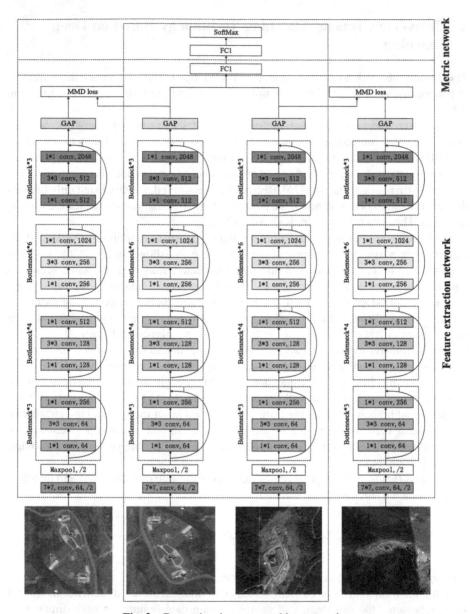

Fig. 2. Cross-view images matching network.

When the sample size is small, if the network starts to learn from zero, it is easy to over fit, so we use the pre-trained RESNET model [19]. Although there are optical differences in images from different perspectives, there are still similarities for images from the same scene [20]. Traditional transfer learning usually focuses on the domain adaptation of samples, but ignores the adaptation of features in the domain [21]. In the image collection stage, the large angle and small angle image samples are collected respectively. Compared with JDA (joint distribution adaptation) method, by iteratively setting pseudo labels on the sample categories of the target domain, the conditional distribution information of the target domain in cross-view images matching is clearer. Therefore, the conditional distribution adaptive method is used to adapt the conditional distributions $P(y_s|x_s)$ and $P(y_t|x_t)$ of the two domains to make them similar. Where, x_s is the source domain sample, and y_s is the category in the source domain image. x_t is the target domain sample, and y_t is the category in the target domain image.

3   Cross-View Images Registration Technology Based on Deep Learning

In order to ensure the generalization of deep neural network, it is necessary to add enough training samples to the network. We use translation, zoom, rotation and affine transformation to enhance data [22], and we obtain a large number of matching and unmatched image groups from the images and their transformed images, as shown in the following figure (Fig. 3).

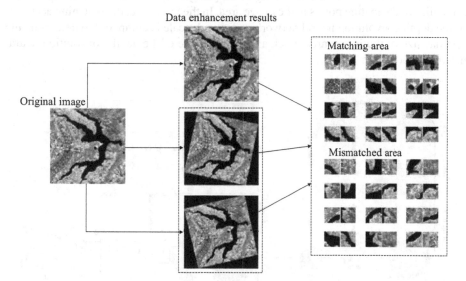

Fig. 3. Image area acquisition.

Cross-view images registration based on deep learning uses deep neural network as the main framework and traditional feature point extraction algorithm as the auxiliary method. The difference from traditional feature extraction and feature matching methods is that this method first uses the traditional feature extraction algorithm to extract the feature points of the image, and then selects the image region based on these feature points. Based on the selected image region, the depth neural network is used to pair the patches in the target image and the reference image, Learn the mapping relationship between these image regions and matching tags (matching tag is 1, mismatching tag is

730   Q. Zhou et al.

0). The depth neural network model of image region matching is obtained, and then the feature points are extracted accurately on the basis of the primary feature points. Finally, the homography matrix is obtained according to the selected feature points. The model constitutes an end-to-end architecture, which allows the whole feature mapping process to be continuously optimized through the information feedback of gradient propagation during network training.

The process is divided into two stages: mapping function learning and image registration, as shown in Fig. 4. In the mapping function learning stage, firstly, the image region is selected according to the extracted feature points and the training data is generated. These training data are obtained by extracting multi-scale patch in the way of scale increasing. The feature information and semantic information of the target are different in different sizes of image patch, such as 10×10, 20×20, 30×30 (the specific scale size is selected through experiments), the amount of feature information is different, so the matching results are also different. To solve this problem, we need to do many experiments to get the most suitable image area size, so that the neural network can get better robustness and accuracy. The output result is a probability value between 0 and 1, which is used to represent the similarity between two image regions. The larger the probability value indicates the higher the similarity of the image area block, that is, the better the reliability of the feature points in the image area. In the test phase, the matching accuracy of the depth convolution neural network under each scale is compared to determine the optimal size of the image area block and the structure of the depth convolution neural network model.

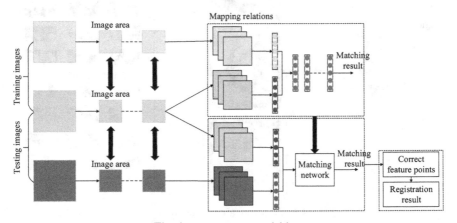

Fig. 4. Image area acquisition.

In the registration stage, the traditional feature points extraction method is used to determine the feature points of the template image and the task image, and the image patches are selected, and then the patches are input into the deep neural network model in pairs. The trained deep neural network predicts the matching label from the image region of template image and task image, sets the correct matching threshold, keeps the matching points with high reliability, and then calculates the transformation matrix of image registration according to these matching points. For the image patches, surf algorithm is used to extract local feature points [23], and then these feature points are selected as the center of the image block, the size is $S \times S$ (the area can be adjusted). Suppose that the image to be matched and the reference image are recorded as I_1 and I_2. If there are feature points in image I_1, it is recorded as $p_1 = \{p_1^1, p_1^2, p_1^3, \cdots p_1^m\}$. Similarly, if there are feature points in image I_2, it is recorded as $p_2 = \{p_2^1, p_2^2, p_2^3, \cdots p_2^n\}$. Then we can get the corresponding matching feature point pair $\left\{\left(p_1^i, p_2^j\right)\right\}$ from image I_1 and image I_2, where $i = 1,2,...,m$, $j = 1,2,...,n$. We transform these image region pairs of image 1 and image 2 into feature vectors, then input these feature vectors into two deep neural network channels, and output a matching probability between 0 and 1, which is regarded as the matching result, where 0 represents mismatching and 1 represents complete matching.

If the matching value of image region is high, the feature points of current image region are regarded as the key feature points of image registration. Finally, RANSAC algorithm is used for further registration.

4 Experimental Results

The algorithm is verified on the image matching data set of 2020 rocket army "smart arrow · fire eye" artificial intelligence challenge, consists of 1000 scenes and 3000 images, the correct matching probability is 91%. Moreover, the algorithm is verified on the self-made remote sensing data, the data set has 300 scenes and 1500 images, and the correct matching probability is up to 90%, as shown in Fig. 5, a) is a photo simulating the satellite's perspective angle, which is used as a template for the target. b) It's a mission picture that simulates the UAV's perspective. There is about 30° difference in viewing angle between template picture and task picture. c) It is a thermal graph, in which the red dot corresponds to the red dot of graph B (the lower left corner of the template image), representing the final matching output of the image matching algorithm. The results show that the matching effect is very good, and the location of the target is found accurately.

Image matching output

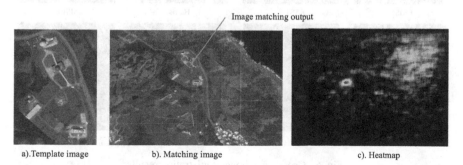

a).Template image   b). Matching image   c). Heatmap

Fig. 5. Cross-view image matching results.

After successful matching, the template image and UAV image are accurately registered to further locate the position of the target. For the image registration, we first determine the size of the image patch size. We chose 12×12, 20×20, 28×28, 36×36 four scales [24], select 20 images that have been successfully matched, the registration results are shown in Table 1, where N is the average number of feature points successfully matched and *RMS* is the average accuracy of registration. The results show that when the patch size is 28×28, the precision is the highest. So we chose 28×28.

Table 1. The registration performances of images by varying patch size.

Patch size	N	*RMS*
12×12	9	0.86
20×20	12	0.83
28×28	15	0.75
36×36	18	0.79

Since there is no mere deep learning registration algorithm at present, here, we respectively use BRISK, FAST, Harris, MSER, Surf and Our algorithm to perform image registration. The first four algorithms failed in registration. Although surf algorithm was successful, the registration accuracy was poor, and the registration error was more than 4 pixels. Our algorithm has the best registration effect (0.75pix) and achieves sub-pixel level registration, as shown in Fig. 6 and Table 2.

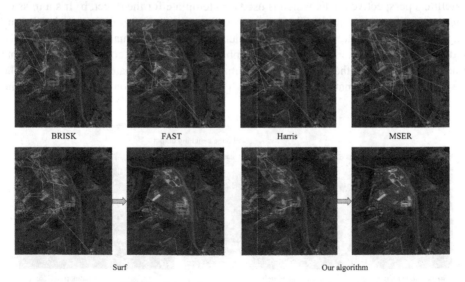

Fig. 6. Cross-view image registration results.

Table 2. Cross-view image registration accuracy.

Registration algorithm	Registration accuracy(pix)	Success (YES/NO)
BRISK	—	NO
FAST	—	NO
Harris	—	NO
MSER	—	NO
Surf	4.61	YES
Our algorithm	0.75	YES

5 Conclusion

This paper is based on the target search task of UAV in the template matching mode, integrates image matching method and image registration method, introduces deep learning algorithm, and adopts the processing idea of "match first, then register". The results show that the matching probability is 90% and the registration accuracy can reach sub-pixel. This paper uses deep learning algorithms for image matching and registration, which effectively improves the robustness and accuracy of cross-view images matching. The method proposed in this paper has been successfully implemented on the server, will be transplanted to the embedded platform in the future, and the algorithm needs to be lightened.

References

1. Tsai, C.H., Lin, Y.C.: An accelerated image matching technique for UAV orthoimage registration. ISPRS J. Photogramm. Remote. Sens. **128**, 130–145 (2017)
2. Ding, L., et al.: A practical cross-view image matching method between UAV and satellite for UAV-based geo-localization. Remote Sensing **13**(1), 47 (2020)
3. Lv, G.: Self-similarity and symmetry with SIFT for multi-modal image registration. IEEE Access **7**, 52202–52213 (2019)
4. Sreeja, G., Saraniya, O.: A comparative study on image registration techniques for SAR images. In: 2019 5th International Conference on Advanced Computing & Communication Systems (ICACCS). IEEE (2019)
5. Luo, S., Zhou, H.-M., Xu, J.-H., Zhang, S.-Y.: Matching images based on consistency graph and region adjacency graphs. SIViP **11**(3), 501–508 (2016). https://doi.org/10.1007/s11760-016-0987-1
6. Ansari, S.: A review on SIFT and SURF for underwater image feature detection and matching. In: 2019 IEEE International Conference on Electrical, Computer and Communication Technologies (ICECCT). IEEE (2019)
7. Moon, C.H., Lee, S.W.: Fast image-matching technique robust to rotation in spherical images. IEIE Trans. Smart Process. Comput. **9** (2020)
8. Zhang, B.B., Shu, H., Jiang, W.S.: Harris-SURF image matching algorithm constrained by delaunay triangulation. Geogr. Geo-Inform. Sci. (2019)
9. Zhuo, X., et al.: Automatic UAV image geo-registration by matching UAV images to georeferenced image data. Remote Sens. **9**(4) (2017)

10. Hughes, L.H., et al.: Deep Learning for SAR-Optical Image Matching. IGARSS 2019 (2019)
11. Grewal, M., et al.: An end-to-end deep learning approach for landmark detection and matching in medical images. SPIE Med. Imaging (2020)
12. Memon, M.H., et al.: Localization in images matching through region-based similarity technique for content-based image retrieval. In: 2016 13th International Computer Conference on Wavelet Active Media Technology and Information Processing (ICCWAMTIP). IEEE (2017)
13. Feng, R., et al.: Robust registration for remote sensing images by combining and localizing feature-and area-based methods. ISPRS J. Photogramm. Remote Sens. **151**, 15–26 (2019)
14. Zhou, M., et al.: Multi-sensor images registration based on SIFT and extended phase correlation. In: Twelfth International Conference on Digital Image Processing (2020)
15. Valmadre, J., et al.: End-to-end representation learning for correlation filter based tracking. IEEE (2017)
16. He, K., Zhang, X., Ren, S., Sun, J.: Deep residual learning for image recognition. In: Proceedings of the IEEE Conference on Computer Vision and Pattern Recognition, pp. 770–778 (2016)
17. Santos, Fpd, Ponti, M. A.: Features transfer learning for image and video recognition tasks. In: Conference on Graphics, Patterns and Images (2020)
18. Liu, T, et al.: Deep learning and transfer learning for optic disc laterality detection: implications for machine learning in neuro-ophthalmology. J. Neuro-Ophthalmol. **40** (2020)
19. Li, X., et al.: Small-sample image classification method of combining prototype and margin learning. In: 2019 Asia-Pacific Signal and Information Processing Association Annual Summit and Conference (APSIPA ASC). IEEE (2020)
20. Dixit, D., Tokekar, P.: Evaluation of Cross-View Matching to Improve Ground Vehicle Localization with Aerial Perception (2020)
21. Zhu, W., et al.: Investigation of transfer learning for image classification and impact on training sample size. Chemometr. Intel. Lab. Syst. **7639**, 104269 (2021)
22. Schlett, T., Rathgeb, C., Busch, C.: Deep Learning-based Single Image Face Depth Data Enhancement (2020)
23. Bay, H., Tuytelaars, T., Gool, L.: SURF: Speeded up robust features. In: Leonardis, A., Bischof, H., Pinz, A. (eds.) ECCV 2006. LNCS, vol. 3951, pp. 404–417. Springer, Heidelberg (2006). https://doi.org/10.1007/11744023_32
24. Wang, S., et al.: A deep learning framework for remote sensing image registration. ISPRS J. Photogramm. Remote Sens. **145**, 148–164 (2018)

Model-Based Rate-Distortion Optimized Video-Based Point Cloud Compression with Differential Evolution

Hui Yuan[1,2]([✉]), Raouf Hamzaoui[1], Ferrante Neri[3], and Shengxiang Yang[4]

[1] School of Engineering and Sustainable Development, De Montfort University, Leicester, UK
hui.yuan@dmu.ac.uk, huiyuan@sdu.edu.cn
[2] School of Control Science and Engineering, Shandong University, Jinan, China
[3] School of Computer Science, University of Nottingham, Nottingham, UK
[4] School of Computer Science and Informatics, De Montfort University, Leicester, UK

Abstract. The Moving Picture Experts Group (MPEG) video-based point cloud compression (V-PCC) standard encodes a dynamic point cloud by first converting it into one geometry video and one color video and then using a video coder to compress the two video sequences. We first propose analytical models for the distortion and bitrate of the V-PCC reference software, where the models' variables are the quantization step sizes used in the encoding of the geometry and color videos. Unlike previous work, our analytical models are functions of the quantization step sizes of all frames in a group of frames. Then, we use our models and an implementation of the differential evolution algorithm to efficiently minimize the distortion subject to a constraint on the bitrate. Experimental results on six dynamic point clouds show that, compared to the state-of-the-art, our method achieves an encoding with a smaller error to the target bitrate (4.65% vs. 11.94% on average) and a slightly lower rate-distortion performance (on average, the increase in Bjøntegaard delta (BD) distortion is 0.27, and the increase in BD rate is 8.40%).

Keywords: Point cloud compression · Rate-distortion optimization · Rate control · Rate and distortion models · Differential evolution

1 Introduction

A static point cloud is a representation of a three-dimensional object, where in addition to the spatial coordinates of a sample of points on the surface of the object, attributes such as color, reflectance, transparency, and normal direction may be used. A dynamic point cloud consists of several successive static point clouds. Each point cloud in the sequence is called a frame. Point clouds are receiving increased attention due to their potential for immersive video experience applications such as virtual reality, augmented reality, and immersive telepresence.

To get a high-quality representation of a three-dimensional object as a point cloud, a huge amount of data is required. To compress point clouds efficiently, the Moving Picture Experts Group (MPEG) launched in January 2017 a call for proposals for point

© Springer Nature Switzerland AG 2021
Y. Peng et al. (Eds.): ICIG 2021, LNCS 12888, pp. 735–747, 2021.
https://doi.org/10.1007/978-3-030-87355-4_61

cloud compression technology. As a result, two point cloud compression standards are
being developed: video-based point cloud compression (V-PCC) [1] for point sets with
a relatively uniform distribution of points and geometry-based point cloud compression
(G-PCC) [2] for more sparse distributions. In this paper, we focus on V-PCC for dynamic
point clouds. In V-PCC, the input point cloud is first decomposed into a set of patches,
which are independently mapped to a two-dimensional grid of uniform blocks. This
mapping is then used to store the geometry and color information as one geometry video
and one color video. Next, the generated geometry video and color video are compressed
separately with a video coder, e.g., H.265/HEVC [3]. Finally, the geometry and color
videos, together with metadata (occupancy map for the two-dimensional grid, auxiliary
patch, and block information) are multiplexed to generate the bit stream (Fig. 1 [1]). In
the video coding step, compression is achieved with quantization, which is determined
by a quantization step size or, equivalently, a quantization parameter (QP).

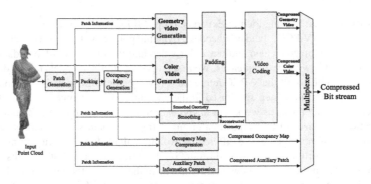

Fig. 1. V-PCC test model encoder [1].

Given a set of M quantization step sizes $\{q_0, \ldots, q_{M-1}\}$ and a dynamic point cloud
consisting of N frames, an optimal encoding can be obtained by determining for each
frame $i(i = 1, \ldots N)$ the geometry quantization step size $Q_{g,i} \in \{q_0, \ldots, q_{M-1}\}$ and
color quantization step size $Q_{c,i} \in \{q_0, \ldots, q_{M-1}\}$ that minimize the distortion subject to
a constraint R_T on the total number of bits. This can be formulated as the multi-objective
optimization problem

$$\min_{Q_g, Q_c} \left[D_g(Q_g, Q_c), D_c(Q_g, Q_c) \right] \tag{1}$$

$$s.t. \ R(Q_g, Q_c) = R_g(Q_g, Q_c) + R_c(Q_g, Q_c) \leq R_T,$$

where $Q_g = (Q_{g,1}, Q_{g,2},...,Q_{g,N})$, $Q_c = (Q_{c,1}, Q_{c,2},...,Q_{c,N})$, $D_g(Q_g, Q_c)$ is the geometry distortion, $D_c(Q_g, Q_c)$ is the color distortion, $R(Q_g, Q_c)$ is the total number of
bits, $R_g(Q_g, Q_c)$ is the number of bits for the geometry information, and $R_c(Q_g, Q_c)$ is
the number of bits for the color information. Here $D_g(Q_g, Q_c) = \frac{1}{N} \sum_{i=1}^{N} D_{g,i}(Q_g, Q_c)$
and $D_c(Q_g, Q_c) = \frac{1}{N} \sum_{i=1}^{N} D_{c,i}(Q_g, Q_c)$, where $D_{g,i}(Q_g, Q_c)$ and $D_{c,i}(Q_g, Q_c)$ are the
geometry and color distortions of the i th frame, respectively. Similarly, $R_g(Q_g, Q_c) =$

$\sum_{i=1}^{N} R_{g,i}(Q_g, Q_c)$ and $R_c(Q_g, Q_c) = \sum_{i=1}^{N} R_{c,i}(Q_g, Q_c)$, where $R_{g,i}(Q_g, Q_c)$ and $R_{c,i}(Q_g, Q_c)$ are the number of bits for the geometry and color of the i th frame, respectively. In practice, problem (1) is scalarized as follows.

$$\min_{Q_g, Q_c} [D(Q_g, Q_c) = \omega D_c(Q_g, Q_c) + (1 - \omega) D_g(Q_g, Q_c)] \tag{2}$$

$$s.t. \ R(Q_g, Q_c) \le R_T,$$

where $\omega \in [0, 1]$ is a weighting factor that sets the relative importance of the geometry and color distortions. As the number of possible solutions is M^{2N}, solving the problem with exhaustive search is not feasible when M or N is large as the computation of the distortion and the number of bits requires encoding and decoding the point cloud, which is very time consuming. In this paper, we solve the rate-distortion optimization problem (2) by first developing analytical models for the distortion and bitrate and then applying a metaheuristic based on differential evolution (DE) [4] to the analytical models. There is a need for new models as the existing ones [5–7] are not suitable for the rate-distortion optimization problem (2). Note also that the V-PCC standard does not give any solution to problem (2). In the latest MPEG V-PCC test model [8], for example, the QPs for the geometry and color are selected manually: one chooses the QPs of the first frame, and the QP values of the following frames are set according to some fixed rules (e.g., by using the same values for the low delay configuration).

2 Related Work

Only a small number of works [5–7] have proposed rate and distortion models for point cloud compression. In [5], the focus is on the point cloud library (PCL) platform [9] for the compression of static point clouds. This platform uses an octree decomposition for geometry compression and JPEG for color compression. Analytical models that describe the relationship between the encoding parameters (the maximum octree level and the JPEG quality factor) and the color distortion D_c and bitrate R are derived with statistical analysis. Let L be the maximum octree level and let J be the JPEG quality factor. The color distortion is modeled as $D_c = sJ^pL^q$, where s, p, q are model parameters. On the other hand, the bitrate is modeled as $\ln R = aLJ + bL + c$, where a, b, c are model parameters. Then, the models are used to formulate the rate-distortion optimization problem as a constrained optimization problem, and an interior point method is applied to solve it. In [6], a similar approach is applied to V-PCC for dynamic point clouds. First, distortion and rate models for the geometry information and color information are derived as follows: $D_g = \alpha_g Q_{g,1} + \delta_g, D_c = \alpha_c Q_{c,1} + \beta_c Q_{g,1} + \delta_c, R_g = \gamma_g Q_{g,1}^{\theta_g}, R_c = \gamma_c Q_{c,1}^{\theta_c}$, where $\alpha_g, \delta_g, \alpha_c, \beta_c, \delta_c, \gamma_g, \theta_g, \gamma_c, \theta_c$ are model parameters. Then, an interior point method is used to minimize the weighted sum of the distortions subject to a constraint on the total number of bits. One limitation of this work is that the distortion and rate models are functions of the quantization steps of the geometry and color information of the first frame only. Thus, these models are only suitable when the quantization steps of the following frames are set according to the default settings of the V-PCC test model and are not appropriate for the general rate-distortion optimization problem (2). In [7], a point cloud is partitioned into seven regions such that the first six regions correspond to the six patches with the largest area in the six projection planes, and the seventh region consists of all other patches. Then, the geometry and color quantization steps corresponding to each region are optimized separately using the analytical models in [6].

3 Rate and Distortion Models

In this section, we propose new analytical distortion and rate models for V-PCC. For both the geometry distortion and color distortion, we used the symmetric point-to-point distortions based on the mean squared error (MSE) [10]. Moreover, for the color information, we considered only the Y (luminance) component. To compute the actual values of the distortion and bitrate, we used the latest V-PCC test model (TMC2 v12.0) [8], where the encoder settings were modified such that the QPs of the frames can be chosen arbitrarily. Note that TMC2 v12.0 relies on the HEVC Test Model Version 16.20 (HM16.20) [11] to compress the geometry and color videos. In HEVC, the set of QP values is $\{0, \ldots, 51\}$, which corresponds to quantization step sizes $\{0.625, \ldots, 224\}$. We encoded four frames of the point cloud using the low delay configuration with group of pictures (GOP) structure IPPP.

Table 1. Dependency between the first frame and the second frame for the *basketballplayer* point cloud. Encoding is with the low delay configuration of [8].

$Q_{g,1}$	$Q_{g,2}$	$D_{g,1}$	$D_{g,2}$	$R_{g,1}$	$R_{g,2}$	$Q_{c,1}$	$Q_{c,2}$	$D_{c,1}$	$D_{c,2}$	$R_{c,1}$	$R_{c,2}$
11	11	0.306637	0.320112	126160	97880	11	11	0.000147568	0.000146696	657056	520040
14	11	0.348734	0.316439	103632	101040	14	11	0.00015884	0.0001459	490024	544440
18	11	0.418704	0.323274	92360	108104	18	11	0.000174033	0.00014684	368144	562112
22	11	0.504359	0.334045	74720	113936	22	11	0.000189179	0.000147952	280640	575800
28	11	0.620279	0.309088	64576	119544	28	11	0.000209897	0.000145801	214840	604040
18	18	0.418704	0.434988	92360	70112	18	18	0.000174033	0.000172132	368144	263520
22	18	0.504359	0.446426	74720	72096	22	18	0.000189179	0.000170755	280640	274608
28	18	0.620279	0.447552	64576	76344	28	18	0.000209897	0.000170923	214840	298392
36	18	0.824124	0.442594	53760	81296	36	18	0.00023497	0.00017086	164272	314856
44	18	1.05653	0.441371	46240	87352	44	18	0.000268242	0.000170745	127312	330416
28	28	0.620279	0.63062	64576	48088	28	28	0.000209897	0.000207024	214840	135616
36	28	0.824124	0.671394	53760	49208	36	28	0.00023497	0.000209702	164272	145872
44	28	1.05653	0.673557	46240	54880	44	28	0.000268242	0.000210265	127312	163088
56	28	1.388	0.67004	39520	59568	56	28	0.000312829	0.000210444	100992	176344
72	28	1.79778	0.647573	34480	64152	72	28	0.000366755	0.000208479	80304	188928
44	44	1.05653	1.03645	46240	31152	44	44	0.000268242	0.000269072	127312	69952
56	44	1.388	1.11769	39520	34504	56	44	0.000312829	0.000278791	100992	78960
72	44	1.79778	1.14647	34480	38784	72	44	0.000366755	0.000274503	80304	91600
88	44	2.33344	1.13333	29840	42840	88	44	0.000436296	0.000269361	64464	103600
112	44	3.21416	1.12562	26240	46504	112	44	0.000526625	0.000267529	51088	112536

3.1 Distortion Models

In [6], the geometry distortion D_g and color distortion D_c are modeled as functions of the geometry and color quantization step sizes of the first frame ($Q_{g,1}$, and $Q_{c,1}$, respectively) according to

$$\begin{cases} D_g = \alpha_g Q_{g,1} + \delta_g \\ D_c = \alpha_c Q_{c,1} + \beta_c Q_{g,1} + \delta_c, \end{cases} \tag{3}$$

where α_g, δ_g, α_c, β_c, and δ_c are model parameters. In this paper, we extend this model by including the quantization step sizes of all frames. For simplicity, we assume that the number of frames N is equal to 4. To study the effect of the quantization in the first frame on the distortion in the second frame, we fixed the quantization steps of the second frame and varied those of the first frame. Table 1 shows that the effect of the quantization step of the first frame on the distortion of the second frame is very small for both geometry and color. We observed the same phenomenon for the other frames. Consequently, we propose the following distortion models for the i th frame

$$\begin{cases} D_{g,i} = \alpha_{g,i} Q_{g,i} + \delta_{g,i} \\ D_{c,i} = \alpha_{c,i} Q_{c,i} + \beta_{c,i} Q_{g,i} + \delta_{c,i}, \end{cases} \tag{4}$$

where $\alpha_{g,i}$, $\delta_{g,i}$, $\alpha_{c,i}$, $\beta_{c,i}$, and $\delta_{c,i}$ are model parameters. The overall distortion is then modeled as.

$$D = \frac{1}{4}(\sum_{i=1}^{4} \omega D_{g,i} + (1 - \omega)D_{c,i}) \tag{5}$$

3.2 Rate Models

As the number of bits of the first frame is only determined by its own quantization steps ($Q_{g,1}$, $Q_{c,1}$), it can be modeled as in [6]

$$\begin{cases} R_{g,1} = \gamma_{g,1} Q_{g,1}^{\theta_{g,1}} \\ R_{c,1} = \gamma_{c,1} Q_{c,1}^{\theta_{c,1}} \end{cases} \tag{6}$$

where $\gamma_{g,1}$, $\gamma_{c,1}$, $\theta_{g,1}$, and $\theta_{c,1}$ are model parameters. To obtain the rate model for the second frame, we first ignore the impact of the first frame on the second frame and use the basic model

$$\begin{cases} R_{g,2} = \gamma_{g,2} Q_{g,2}^{\theta_{g,2}} \\ R_{c,2} = \gamma_{c,2} Q_{c,2}^{\theta_{c,2}} \end{cases} \tag{7}$$

where $\gamma_{g,2}$, $\gamma_{c,2}$, $\theta_{g,2}$, and $\theta_{c,2}$ are model parameters. However, Table 1 shows that the number of bits of the second frame increases when the quantization steps of the first frame increase. To take this dependency into account, we update the model as

$$\begin{cases} R_{g,2} = (\varphi_{g,(1,2)} \cdot Q_{g,1} + 1)\gamma_{g,2} Q_{g,2}^{\theta_{g,2}} \\ R_{c,2} = (\varphi_{c,(1,2)} \cdot Q_{c,1} + 1)\gamma_{c,2} Q_{c,2}^{\theta_{c,2}} \end{cases} \tag{8}$$

where $\varphi_{g,(1,2)}$ and $\varphi_{c,(1,2)}$ are the impact factors of the first frame on the second frame. Similarly, we first assume that the number of bits of the third and fourth frames are independent of the quantization steps of the other frames and model them as

$$\begin{cases} R_{g,3} = \gamma_{g,3} Q_{g,3}^{\theta_{g,3}} \\ R_{c,3} = \gamma_{c,3} Q_{c,3}^{\theta_{c,3}} \end{cases} \tag{9}$$

$$\begin{cases} R_{g,4} = \gamma_{g,4} Q_{g,4}^{\theta_{g,4}} \\ R_{c,4} = \gamma_{c,4} Q_{c,4}^{\theta_{c,4}} \end{cases} \tag{10}$$

where $\gamma_{g,3}, \gamma_{c,3}, \theta_{g,3}, \theta_{c,3}, \gamma_{g,4}, \gamma_{c,4}, \theta_{g,4},$ and $\theta_{c,4}$ are model parameters. Then we update the models as

$$\begin{cases} R_{g,3} = \prod_{i=1}^{2} (\varphi_{g,(i,i+1)} \cdot Q_{g,i} + 1)\gamma_{g,3} Q_{g,3}^{\theta_{g,3}} \\ R_{c,3} = \prod_{i=1}^{2} (\varphi_{c,(i,i+1)} \cdot Q_{c,i} + 1)\gamma_{c,3} Q_{c,3}^{\theta_{c,3}} \end{cases} \tag{11}$$

$$\begin{cases} R_{g,4} = \prod_{i=1}^{3} (\varphi_{g,(i,i+1)} \cdot Q_{g,i} + 1)\gamma_{g,4} Q_{g,4}^{\theta_{g,4}} \\ R_{c,4} = \prod_{i=1}^{3} (\varphi_{c,(i,i+1)} \cdot Q_{c,i} + 1)\gamma_{c,4} Q_{c,4}^{\theta_{c,4}} \end{cases} \tag{12}$$

where $\varphi_{g,(i,i+1)}$ and $\varphi_{c,(i,i+1)}$ $(i = 2, 3)$ are the impact factors of the i-th frame on the $(i + 1)$-th one. Finally, we use (6), (8), (11) and (12) to build the rate model as $R=\sum_{i=1}^{4} R_{g,i} + R_{c,i}$.

Model Parameters

To determine the parameters of the distortion models, we first encode the point cloud for three different sets of quantization steps (Q_g, Q_c) and compute the corresponding actual distortions and number of bits for each frame. Next, we solve the resulting system of equations to find $\alpha_{g,i}, \delta_{g,i}, \alpha_{c,i}, \beta_{c,i}, \delta_{c,i}(i = 1, \ldots, 4)$. To determine the parameters of the rate models, we encode the point cloud for eight more sets of quantization steps and use linear regression in (7), (9), and (10) to estimate the parameters $\gamma_{g,i}, \theta_{g,i}, \gamma_{c,i}, \theta_{c,i}$ $(i = 1, \ldots, 4)$. Finally, the impact factors $\varphi_{g,(1,2)}, \varphi_{g,(2,3)}, \varphi_{g,(3,4)}, \varphi_{c,(1,2)}, \varphi_{c,(2,3)},$ and $\varphi_{c,(3,4)}$, are empirically set to

$$\begin{cases} \varphi_{g,(1,2)} = \varphi_{c,(1,2)} = 0.004 \\ \varphi_{g,(2,3)} = \varphi_{c,(2,3)} = 0.0015 \\ \varphi_{g,(3,4)} = \varphi_{c,(3,4)} = 0.0010. \end{cases} \tag{13}$$

Table 2 shows the QP settings used to compute the parameters of the distortion and rate models.

Table 2. QP settings to determine the model parameters

Model parameters	$QP_{g,1}$	$QP_{g,2}$	$QP_{g,3}$	$QP_{g,4}$	$QP_{c,1}$	$QP_{c,2}$	$QP_{c,3}$	$QP_{c,4}$
$\alpha_{g,1},\delta_{g,1}; \alpha_{g,2},\delta_{g,2};$	30	30	30	30	40	40	40	40
$\alpha_{g,3},\delta_{g,3};\alpha_{g,4},\delta_{g,4}; \alpha_{c,1},$	36	36	36	36	30	30	30	30
$\beta_{c,1}, \delta_{c,1}; \alpha_{c,2}, \beta_{c,2}, \delta_{c,2};$	38	38	38	38	28	28	28	28
$\alpha_{c,3}, \beta_{c,3}, \delta_{c,3}; \alpha_{c,4},$								
$\beta_{c,4},\delta_{c,4}$								
$\gamma_{g,1},\theta_{g,1}; \gamma_{c,1},\theta_{c,1};$	30	30	30	30	40	40	40	40
$\gamma_{g,2},\theta_{g,2}; \gamma_{c,2},\theta_{c,2};$	36	36	36	36	30	30	30	30
$\gamma_{g,3},\theta_{g,3}; \gamma_{c,3},\theta_{c,3};$	38	38	38	38	28	28	28	28
$\gamma_{g,4},\theta_{g,4}; \gamma_{c,4},\theta_{c,4}$	17	25	33	41	17	25	33	41
	33	25	33	41	33	25	33	41
	17	41	33	41	17	41	33	41
	17	25	49	41	17	25	49	41
	19	24	29	34	19	24	29	34
	34	24	40	37	34	24	40	37
	27	41	37	45	27	41	37	45
	27	17	37	45	27	17	37	45

4 Optimization

To solve the rate-distortion optimization problem (2), we apply a DE variant to the analytical models derived in Sect. 3. Unlike the standard DE algorithm, this variant decreases the crossover rate with time and uses a random scaling factor. The decrease in crossover rate at runtime increases the exploitation pressure at the end of the run [12]. The randomization of the scaling factor is motivated by the experimental observation that a certain degree of randomization is beneficial [12].

The details of the implemented algorithm are as follows. A candidate solution (agent) for problem (2) is denoted by $x = (Q_g, Q_c) = (x_1, x_2, \ldots, x_{2N})$

- Choose a population size NP, an interval I for the scaling factor, and a number of iterations n.
- Build a population of NP agents $\boldsymbol{x}^{(1)},..., \boldsymbol{x}^{(NP)}$ such that each component $x_i^{(j)}, i = 1, ...,2N; j = 1, ..., NP$, is randomly chosen in the set of quantization steps $\{q_0, ..., q_{M-1}\}$ and $R(\boldsymbol{x}^{(j)}) \leq R_T$ for $j = 1, ..., NP$.
- FOR $k = 1$ to n
   - If $k < \frac{2}{3}n$, set the crossover rate to $CR = 0.9$; otherwise, set $CR = 0.1$;
      - FOR $j = 1$ to NP
      Step 1: Select randomly from the population three different agents $\boldsymbol{a}, \boldsymbol{b}, \boldsymbol{c}$ that are also different from $\boldsymbol{x}^{(j)}$
      Step 2: Select randomly an index r such that $1 \leq r \leq 2N$
      Step 3: Compute a candidate new agent $\boldsymbol{y}^{(j)}$ as follows:
         - For each $i \in \{1, ...,2N\}$, choose a random number r_i according to a uniform distribution in $(0,1)$. Choose a scaling factor w randomly in I.
         - If $r_i \leq CR$ or $i = r$, then set $y_i^{(j)} = a_i + w \times (b_i - c_i)$; otherwise, set $y_i^{(j)} = x_i^{(j)}$
         - If $y_i^{(j)} < q_0$, set $y_i^{(j)} = q_0$. If $y_i^{(j)} > q_{M-1}$, set $y_i^{(j)} = q_{M-1}$.
      Step 4: If $D(\boldsymbol{y}^{(j)}) < D(\boldsymbol{x}^{(j)})$ and $R(\boldsymbol{y}^{(j)}) \leq R_T$, note j.
      END FOR
      FOR $j = 1$ to NP, replace $\boldsymbol{x}^{(j)}$ by $\boldsymbol{y}^{(j)}$ if j was noted in Step 4.
      END FOR
   END FOR
- Select the agent from the population that gives the lowest distortion D and round the components of this agent to the nearest values in the set $\{q_0, ..., q_{M-1}\}$.

Another way of solving problem (2) is to use conventional non-evolutionary constrained nonlinear optimization algorithms. However, when the problem is not convex, such algorithms are only guaranteed to find local minima and are very sensitive to the starting point of the algorithm (see Sect. 5).

5   Experimental Results

We first study the accuracy of the proposed distortion and rate models. The bitrates and distortions were computed for the quantization steps obtained as solutions of the optimization problem (2) for a given target bitrate. In the DE algorithm, the number of iterations and the size of the population were set to 200 and 50, respectively. The interval I was $[0.1, 0.9]$. As in Sect. 3, we used the symmetric point-to-point distortions and considered only the luminance component. The weighting factor ω in (2) was set to 0.5. To compute the actual distortion and bit rates, we used TMC2 v12.0 [8] and encoded the first four frames of the point cloud for the IPPP GOP structure. Table

Table 3. Accuracy of the proposed rate and distortion models.

Point cloud	Target bitrate	Model bitrate	Model distortion	Actual bitrate	Actual distortion	SCC		RMSE	
						Rate model	Distortion model	Rate model	Distortion model
soldier	65	65.21	30.52	63.21	30.59	0.9976	0.9984	21.16	0.33
	125	125.04	18.76	123.71	18.78				
	165	171.80	15.17	172.37	15.90				
	210	205.38	13.57	224.01	13.45				
	265	263.64	11.69	293.58	11.78				
	365	355.23	9.94	393.14	10.22				
queen	65	65.04	23.17	68.32	23.68	0.9984	0.9977	5.64	0.45
	125	124.85	16.82	129.83	17.40				
	165	171.66	14.89	170.03	15.52				
	210	207.36	14.00	204.68	14.41				
	265	265.68	13.00	272.96	13.15				
	365	356.95	12.07	366.55	12.09				
loot	65	66.87	12.72	65.85	13.18	0.9967	0.9989	24.72	0.24
	125	128.59	7.67	128.69	7.78				
	165	168.82	6.37	177.53	6.55				
	210	200.39	5.70	223.29	5.72				
	265	265.51	4.81	282.94	5.01				
	365	366.18	4.05	418.73	4.28				
basketballplayer	30	30.20	12.34	27.72	12.07	0.9980	0.9988	6.27	0.13
	65	66.81	7.64	57.45	7.74				
	125	128.62	5.79	120.93	5.81				
	165	168.45	5.31	161.44	5.30				
	210	209.84	5.00	206.07	4.94				
	265	265.31	4.72	269.77	4.63				
redandblack	90	88.74	19.47	84.38	19.81	0.9844	0.9974	52.28	0.55
	180	181.99	11.06	160.63	11.30				
	270	272.13	8.70	260.27	8.41				
	360	364.78	7.55	341.36	7.19				
	480	484.93	6.70	516.77	5.96				
	640	647.51	6.08	766.76	5.14				
longdress	180	176.09	49.78	162.63	47.25	0.9980	0.9990	24.52	1.40
	270	268.93	38.66	251.10	37.42				
	360	364.74	33.00	350.09	31.96				
	480	489.00	28.85	487.61	28.03				
	640	639.86	25.83	681.42	24.62				
	840	850.50	23.33	884.63	22.60				
Average						**0.9955**	**0.9984**	**22.43**	**0.51**

3 shows the results for six dynamic point clouds (longdress, redandblack, loot, soldier, queen, basketballplayer) [13, 14]. The bitrates are expressed in kilobits per million points (kbpmp). We observe that the bitrates and distortions computed by our models have a high squared correlation coefficient (SCC) and a low root mean squared error (RMSE) with the actual values computed by encoding and decoding point clouds. This shows that our models are accurate.

Table 4. Bit allocation accuracy and BD [15] performance.

Point cloud	Target bitrate	[6]		BE	Proposed		BE	BD Distortion/ BD Color PSNR	BD bitrate/ BD Color bitrate
		Bitrate	Distortion		Bitrate	Distortion			
soldier	65	68.60	27.34	5.54%	63.21	30.59	2.75%	0.79/–0.20	21.68%/9.46%
	125	124.95	18.08	0.04%	126.51	19.12	1.21%		
	165	163.37	15.14	0.99%	174.36	15.56	5.67%		
	210	222.28	12.67	5.85%	213.68	13.69	1.75%		
	265	296.15	10.91	11.75%	275.48	11.87	3.95%		
	365	414.56	9.51	13.58%	375.18	10.20	2.79%		
queen	65	59.87	24.36	7.90%	70.16	23.66	7.93%	0.85/–0.15	7.9%/9.89%
	125	121.09	17.02	3.13%	125.39	17.59	0.32%		
	165	162.14	15.29	1.73%	172.79	15.45	4.72%		
	210	204.88	14.18	2.44%	204.68	14.41	2.54%		
	265	254.58	13.34	3.93%	267.73	13.22	1.03%		
	365	404.43	12.14	10.80%	366.50	12.09	0.41%		
loot	65	62.26	12.60	4.22%	65.26	12.95	0.41%	0.22/–0.14	9.11% 8.41%
	125	136.61	7.15	9.29%	129.43	7.81	3.54%		
	165	190.11	5.88	15.22%	177.57	6.53	7.62%		
	210	195.26	5.78	7.02%	209.90	5.80	0.05%		
	265	265.31	4.99	0.12%	283.20	5.02	6.87%		
	365	458.86	4.14	25.72%	409.71	4.32	12.25%		
basketballplayer	30	28.97	11.70	3.42%	27.72	12.07	7.61%	– 0.10/0.04	1.34%/–1.17
	65	63.53	7.34	2.26%	60.72	7.50	6.58%		
	125	149.71	5.41	19.77%	122.02	5.78	2.38%		
	165	198.11	5.03	20.07%	161.42	5.32	2.17%		
	210	276.95	4.62	31.88%	206.94	4.96	1.46%		
	265	376.71	4.39	42.15%	265.79	4.64	0.30%		
Redandblack	90	84.86	18.99	5.71%	83.85	19.83	6.83%	0.02/–0.03	11.49%/2.00%
	180	157.75	11.17	12.36%	162.06	11.24	9.97%		
	270	269.82	8.08	0.07%	253.76	8.47	6.01%		
	360	348.28	6.94	3.25%	361.63	7.02	0.45%		
	480	598.96	5.61	24.78%	520.08	5.93	8.35%		
	640	805.54	5.06	25.87%	737.76	5.19	15.28%		
longdress	180	167.65	47.05	6.86%	157.70	48.20	12.39%	– 0.19/0.03	– 1.11%/–0.41
	270	307.27	33.70	13.81%	250.05	37.46	7.39%		
	360	424.25	29.52	17.85%	348.55	31.90	3.18%		
	480	597.98	26.07	24.58%	486.96	28.07	1.45%		
	640	784.40	24.15	22.56%	665.42	24.99	3.97%		
	840	1034.7	22.79	23.18%	890.33	22.66	5.99%		
Average				**11.94%**			**4.65%**	**0.27/–0.08**	**8.40%/4.70%**

Table 4 compares the bit allocation accuracy of the proposed method to that of the method in [6]. The bit allocation accuracy is evaluated with the bitrate error (BE)

$$\text{BE} = \frac{|R_{actual} - R_{target}|}{R_{target}} \times 100\%, \tag{14}$$

where R_{actual} and R_{target} are the actual bitrate computed by the method and the target bitrate, respectively. The largest BE for the method in [6] was 42.15% (*basketballplayer*, 265 *kbpmp*), while the largest BE for the proposed method was only 15.28% (*redandblack*, 640 *kbpmp*). Moreover, the average BE for the method in [6] was 11.94%, while that of the proposed method was only 4.65%. Table 4 and Fig. 2 show that the rate-distortion performance of the proposed method is slightly lower than that of the method in [6].

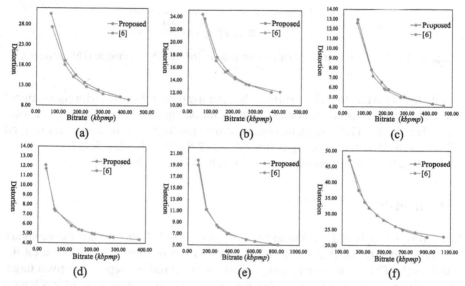

Fig. 2. Rate-distortion curves for the proposed DE-based method and the method in [6]. (a) *soldier*, (b) *queen*, (c) *loot*, (d) *basketballplayer*, (e) *redandblack*, (f) *longdress*.

Table 5 compares the time complexity of the proposed method to that of the method in [6]. The increase in the CPU time is mainly due to the pre-optimization step needed to determine the parameters of the models (11 encodings for the proposed method vs. three encodings for the method in [6]).

Table 5. CPU time on a laptop with a 2.7 GHz i7-7500U processor and 8 GB RAM.

Method	Pre-optimization (s)	Optimization (s)
[6]	3×3600	1.42
DE	11×3600	120
Full Search	0	$52^8 \times 3600$

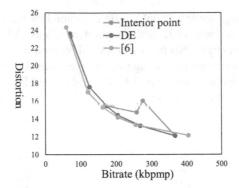

Fig. 3. Rate-distortion curves of DE, the method in [6], and the method in [16] for *queen*.

Finally, Fig. 3 illustrates how solving the optimization problem (2) with conventional non-evolutionary constrained nonlinear optimization algorithms can lead to poor solutions. Here the MATLAB implementation of the state-of-the-art interior point method in [16] was used with the starting point (2.5, 2.5, 2.5, 2.5, 2.5, 2.5, 2.5, 2.5).

The data files used in the experimental results are available in [17].

6   Conclusion

We proposed analytical distortion and rate models for V-PCC that include the geometry and color quantization steps of all frames in a group of frames. Then, we used the models and a DE variant to efficiently select the quantization steps for a given target bitrate. Experimental results show that the proposed optimization technique allows a better rate control than the state-of-the-art. Rate control is critical in applications where the bandwidth is constrained. Our optimization technique can be easily extended to the case where the point cloud consists of more than one group of frames: we first determine the model parameters of the distortion and rate models for each group separately and then use DE to minimize the overall distortion subject to the constraint on the total number of bits. As further future work, we plan to apply our technique to GOPs of more than four frames and to the V-PCC random access configuration.

Acknowledgement. This work has received funding from the European Union's Horizon 2020 research and innovation programme under the Marie Sklodowska-Curie grant agreement No. 836192 and from the Natural Science Foundation of China under grant 62172259.

References

1. MPEG-3DG. V-PCC Codec Description. ISO/IEC JTC1/SC29/WG7 N00012 (2020)
2. MPEG-3DG. G-PCC Codec Description v9. ISO/IEC JTC1/SC29/WG7 N0011 (2020)
3. Sullivan, G.J., Ohm, J., Han, W., Wiegand, T.: Overview of the high efficiency video coding (HEVC) standard. IEEE Trans. Circ. Syst. Video Technol. **22**(12), 1649–1668 (2012)

4. Price, K., Storn, R.M., Lampinen, J.A.: Differential Evolution: A Practical Approach to Global Optimization. Springer (2005). ISBN 978–3–540–20950–8

5. Liu, Q., Yuan, H., Hou, J., Liu, H., Hamzaoui, R.: Model-based encoding parameter optimization for 3D point cloud compression. In: Proceedings of APSIPA Annual Summit and Conference, pp. 1981–1986, Honolulu (2018)

6. Liu, Q., Yuan, H., Hou, J., Hamzaoui, R., Su, H.: Model-based joint bit allocation between geometry and color for video-based 3D point cloud compression. IEEE Trans. Multimed. DOI: https://doi.org/10.1109/TMM.2020.3023294.

7. Liu, Q., Yuan, H., Hamzaoui, R., Su, H.: Coarse to fine rate control for region-based 3D point cloud compression. In: Proceedings of IEEE ICME Workshops, London (2020)

8. V-PCC Test Model v12, ISO/IEC JTC 1/SC 29/WG 7 N00006

9. Point Cloud Library (PCL). http://pointclouds.org/

10. Mekuria, R., Li, Z., Tulvan, C., Chou, P.: Evaluation criteria for pcc (point cloud compression). ISO/IEC JTC1/SC29/WG11, N16332 (2016)

11. HEVC test model. https: //hevc.hhi.fraunhofer.de/svn/svn_HEVCSoftware

12. Neri, F., Tirronen, V.: Recent advances in differential evolution: a survey and experimental analysis. Artif. Intell. Rev. **33**, 61–106 (2010)

13. MPEG point cloud datasetscfp. http://mpegfs.intevry.fr/MPEG/PCC/DataSets/pointCloud /CfP/datasets

14. MPEG point cloud datasets-AnimatedPCMicrosoft. http://mpegfs.intevry.fr/MPEG/PCC/Dat aSets/AnimatedPC-Microsoft

15. Bjøntegaard, G.: Calculation of average PSNR differences between RD-curves. http://wftp3. itu.int/av-arch/videosite/0104-Aus/VCEG-M33.doc

16. Byrd, R.H., Hribar, M.E., Nocedal, J.: An interior point algorithm for large-scale nonlinear programming. SIAM J. Optim. **9**(4), 877–900 (2006)

17. Yuan, H., Hamzaoui, R., Neri, F., Yang, S.: Data files for ICIG 2021 paper (Version 1.0), Zenodo (2021). https://doi.org/10.5281/zenodo.5034575

Adaptive Quantization for Predicting Transform-Based Point Cloud Compression

Xiaohui Wang[1], Guoxia Sun[1(✉)], Hui Yuan[2,3], Raouf Hamzaoui[2], and Lu Wang[1]

[1] School of Information Science and Engineering, Shandong University, Qingdao, China
`sun_guoxia@sdu.edu.cn`
[2] School of Engineering and Sustainable Development, De Montfort University, Leicester, UK
[3] School of Control Science and Engineering, Shandong University, Jinan, China

Abstract. The representation of three-dimensional objects with point clouds is attracting increasing interest from researchers and practitioners. Since this representation requires a huge data volume, effective point cloud compression techniques are required. One of the most powerful solutions is the Moving Picture Experts Group geometry-based point cloud compression (G-PCC) emerging standard. In the G-PCC lifting transform coding technique, an adaptive quantization method is used to improve the coding efficiency. Instead of assigning the same quantization step size to all points, the quantization step size is increased according to level of detail traversal order. In this way, the attributes of more important points receive a finer quantization and have a smaller quantization error than the attributes of less important ones. In this paper, we adapt this approach to the G-PCC predicting transform and propose a hardware-friendly weighting method for the adaptive quantization. Experimental results show that compared to the current G-PCC test model, the proposed method can achieve an average Bjøntegaard delta rate of -6.7%, -14.7%, -15.4%, and -10.0% for the luma, chroma Cb, chroma Cr, and reflectance components, respectively on the MPEG Cat1-A, Cat1-B, Cat3-fused and Cat3-frame datasets.

Keywords: Point cloud compression · G-PCC · Predicting transform · Adaptive quantization

1 Introduction

With the development of 3D scanning technology, point clouds are becoming more and more popular to represent the surface of 3D objects and scenes. Point clouds contain geometry and attribute information. The geometry information is represented by a list of 3D coordinates, while the attribute information may include color, reflectance, normal direction, etc. Point clouds are used in various applications such as gaming, autonomous navigation, virtual reality, cultural heritage, and so on. A point cloud usually contains millions of points, resulting in a huge amount of data. For efficient storage and transmission, point cloud compression [1] is required.

© Springer Nature Switzerland AG 2021
Y. Peng et al. (Eds.): ICIG 2021, LNCS 12888, pp. 748–758, 2021.
https://doi.org/10.1007/978-3-030-87355-4_62

Many point cloud attribute compression methods have been proposed [2]. In this paper, we focus on the Moving Picture Experts Group (MPEG) G-PCC. G-PCC can be divided into geometry and attribute compression. Geometry compression usually uses an octree to voxelize the original point cloud. In attribute compression, the redundancy is removed by inter-point or inter-block prediction, followed by efficient transform of the prediction residuals, under the guidance of geometry information. Next, quantization is applied to compress the residuals. Generally, the quantization step size is uniform for each coding unit (point or block). The larger the quantization step size, the lower the bitrate (and the greater the reconstruction error), and vice versa. Thus, the quantization step size plays a vital role in compression performance and reconstruction quality [3].

However, a uniform quantization step size only considers the global information and lacks flexibility. For example, because of the inter-point dependency, a smaller quantization step size should be applied to the residual values of the important points as they will affect the reconstruction of their successors in the coding order.

G-PCC offers three solutions for attribute coding: region-adaptive hierarchical transform (RAHT) [4], predicting transform (PT) [5] and lifting transform (LT) [6]. Both PT and LT are LoD-based methods. To improve the coding efficiency of PT, we apply the adaptive quantization method used in LT to PT and propose a hardware-friendly weighting method for the adaptive quantization. Given a voxelized point cloud, assume that the geometry information has been encoded and the LoDs have already been generated. We traverse all points in reverse LoD-based coding order to generate quantization weights for the nearest neighbors of the current point. Points that are more frequently used to predict subsequent points are considered to be more important, and their quantization weights are set to be larger. Then, the prediction residuals are quantized by multiplying them by the ratio of the quantization weight to the quantization step size. Experimental results demonstrate that the proposed method can achieve better compression performance than the latest G-PCC test model [7].

The remainder of the paper is organized as follows. In Sect. 2, related work is briefly presented. Section 3 describes the details of the proposed adaptive quantization method. Experimental results and conclusions are given in Sect. 4 and Sect. 5, respectively.

2   Related Work

Figure 1 shows the encoder architecture of G-PCC. Using the reconstructed geometry information, the points are recolored by the attribute transfer module. The recolored points are then predicted and transformed by RAHT, PT or LT. Finally, the attribute residuals are quantized and entropy coded by the quantization and arithmetic encoder modules, respectively. Tabatabai *et al.* [8] proposed a conversion method between the quantization parameter (QP) and the quantization step size. Iguchi *et al.* [9] proposed a pre-defined QP table to determine the quantization step size and reduce the conversion processing time. Dean and Iguchi [10] and Dean [11] proposed a quantization control method based on LoDs and used different quantization step sizes for different LoD layers. All these previous quantization methods use a fixed quantization step size for all points in the same LoD layer or in a group of LoD layers. Mammou *et al.* [6] note that the LoD-based prediction strategy makes points in lower LoDs more influential since they are used more often for prediction and propose to use influence weights computed during the transform process in order to guide the quantization process of LT attribute coding. In this paper, we adapt this approach for PT attribute coding and propose a hardware friendly weighting method for the adaptive quantization. Extensive experimental results show that our method can improve the coding efficiency of PT attribute coding in G-PCC.

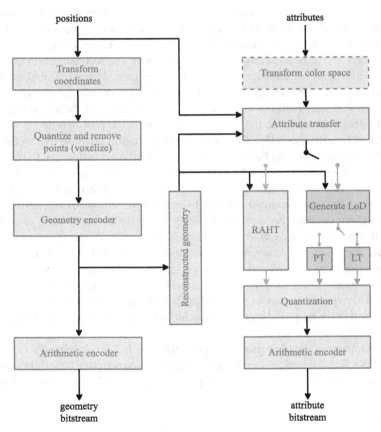

Fig. 1. G-PCC encoder architecture [12]

3   Proposed Method

We first start by explaining how the LoDs are formed. Let L be the number of LoDs and let $(d_l)_{l=1...L-1}$ be a set of user-defined thresholds which satisfy $d_l < d_{l-1}$ and $d_{L-1} = 0$. Then, a point cloud can be partitioned into a set of disjoint subsets called refinement levels $(R_l)_{l=0...L-1}$ as follows [12, 13]. First, add all the points in the point cloud to the set of non-visited points NV and set the set of visited points V to the empty set. At iteration $l = 0$, remove the first point in NV and add it to both R_0 and V. Next, at each iteration $l \geq 1$, generate a refinement level R_l as follows: iterate over all the points in set NV and compute the minimum distance D of the current point to the set V. If D is greater than or equal to d_l, then the current point is removed from NV and added to both R_l and V; otherwise skip this point. The level of detail LoD_l is obtained by taking the union of the refinement levels $R_0, R_1, \ldots, R_l$. Figure 2 shows an example with $L = 4$.

3.1 PT in G-PCC

For PT, the attribute values are encoded/decoded by following the coding order defined in the LoD generation process, i.e., the LoD-based coding order (see the example in Fig. 2). Specifically, the attribute value of each point in $R_j (j > 0)$ is predicted from the attribute values of its three nearest neighbors in LoD_{j-1} where only the already encoded/decoded points are considered for prediction. In the example of Fig. 2, suppose that P_7 in R_2 is the point to be encoded. Then the already encoded points P_0, P_1, and P_{11} in LoD_1 will be used for the prediction. After prediction, the prediction residuals (i.e., the difference between original and predicted attribute values) are quantized and entropy coded by an arithmetic encoder. Finally, from the inverse quantized residuals and the predicted values, the attribute information of a point can be reconstructed. This LoD-based prediction strategy makes the points in lower LoD layers more important than those in higher layers since they are used more often for prediction.

G-PCC uses a fixed quantization step size to quantize the prediction residuals of all points. But quantization usually causes distortion, i.e., the reconstructed attributes are not equal to the original ones. Since the distortion of points in lower LoD layers will directly affect the prediction accuracy of the subsequent points, it is beneficial to use a different quantization step size for points with different importance.

3.2 Proposed Adaptive Quantization Method

To apply different quantization steps to points with different importance, we introduce a quantization weight that measures the importance of each point. Let $w(P)$ be the quantization weight of point P. We compute $w(P)$ by applying the following traversal procedure:

Step 1: Set the initial weight of all points to 256.
Step 2: Traverse the points according to the inverse LoD-based coding order (i.e., the order determined by increasing the distance (e.g., Manhattan or Euclidean) to the origin point).
Step 3: For the current point P_i in R_j, update the quantization weights of its three nearest neighbors $(P_{i,k})_{k=1,2,3}$ in LoD_{j-1} as follows:

$$w(P_{i,k}) \leftarrow w(P_{i,k}) + ((\alpha(P_{i,k}) \times w(P_i)) \gg 8), \qquad (1)$$

where $P_{i,k}$ is the k-th nearest neighbor of P_i in LoD_{j-1}, and

$$\alpha(P_{i,k}) = 2^{6-k}, \qquad (2)$$

Figure 3 illustrates the computation process of the quantization weights. Since the quantization weights are completely determined by the reconstructed geometry, they do not need to be encoded into the bitstream. Also, since the computation of the quantization weight is achieved by arithmetic shift and integer multiplication, the proposed method is hardware-friendly.

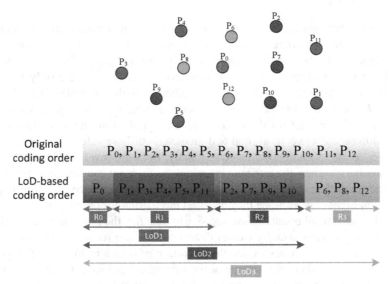

Fig. 2. LoD generation procedure. In the LoD-based coding order, the points are ordered according to decreasing distance (e.g., Manhattan or Euclidean distance) to the origin point (P_0).

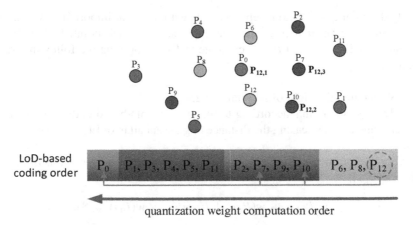

Fig. 3. Quantization weight computation process. The quantization weights of P_0, P_7, and P_{10} are computed first.

After updating the quantization weight, the residual of each point is quantized as follows. Let a be the original attribute value of point P_i and $\hat{a}$ be the predicted attribute value. The prediction residual r is given by

$$r = a - \hat{a} \tag{3}$$

If Q_{step} is the quantization step for P_i, then the quantized residual can be written as

$$\bar{r} = \left\lfloor \frac{a - \hat{a}}{Q_{step}} \right\rfloor = \left\lfloor \frac{r}{Q_{step}} \right\rfloor, \tag{4}$$

where $\lfloor x \rfloor$ is the greatest integer smaller than or equal to x. At the encoder side, the prediction residual associated with P_i is multiplied by the quantization weight $w(P_i)$. Thus, the adaptive quantized residual of P_i can be written as

$$\bar{r}' = \left\lfloor \frac{r \times w(p_i)}{Q_{step}} \right\rfloor = \left\lfloor \frac{r}{Q_{step}/w(p_i)} \right\rfloor, \tag{5}$$

where the actual quantization step of point P_i can be seen as $Q_{step}/w(P_i)$. To make sure that the actual quantization step is greater than or equal to one, we replace (5) by

$$\bar{r}' = \left\lfloor \frac{r}{Q_{step}/\min\left(Q_{step}, w(p_i)\right)} \right\rfloor. \tag{6}$$

The proposed adaptive quantization method improves the reconstruction quality of the important points in lower LoD layers by applying different quantization steps for points with different importance. In this way, the overall prediction accuracy of the point cloud and the coding efficiency can be enhanced.

4 Experimental Results

We implemented the proposed method in the latest G-PCC reference software (TMC13 version 12.0 [7]) and conducted experiments under the CY condition (lossless geometry, near-lossless attribute) of the Common Test Conditions (CTC) [14] using the MPEG Category 1-A, Category 1-B, Category 3-fused, and Category 3-frame datasets. The G-PCC CTC consist of four test conditions: C1, C2, CW, and CY. C1 is for lossless geometry and lossy attributes applications. C2 is for lossy geometry and lossy attributes applications. CW is for lossless geometry and lossless attributes applications. CY is for lossless geometry and near-lossless attributes applications. The first two test conditions (C1 and C2) adopt LT or RAHT for attribute compression, while the last two (CW and CY) adopt PT for attribute compression. Category 1-A and Category 1-B include static objects and scenes with position and color information. Category 3-fused includes dynamically acquired point clouds of a single frame with position, color and reflectance information. Category 3-frame includes dynamically acquired point clouds with position and reflectance information. Figure 4 shows an example from each category.

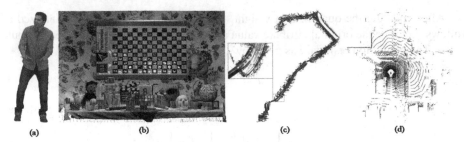

(a)   (b)   (c)   (d)

Fig. 4. Point clouds from four categories. (a) loot_viewdep_vox12 form Cat1-A (b) ulb_unicorn_hires_vox15 from Cat1-B (c) citytunnel_q1mm from Cat3-fused (d) Ford_01_vox1mm-100 from Cat3-frame

The computer used for conducting the experiments has a 3.70 GHz Intel Core i7–7700 processor and 32 GB RAM. To evaluate the rate-distortion performance, we computed the distortion at five bitrates obtained by varying the quantization parameters. The distortion was computed with the point-to-point peak signal-to-noise ratio (PSNR) metric proposed by MPEG [15]. Full details of the coding configurations can be found in [7].

Table 1 shows the experimental results. In the table, Bjøntegaard delta rate (BD-rate) (%) [16] represents the average attribute rate increment of the proposed method compared to TMC13 at the same PSNR, while Complexity Ratio (%) is the ratio of the encoding time (resp. decoding time) between the proposed method and TMC13. We can see that an average −6.5%, −14.5%, −15.2% and −0.1% BD-rate for Luma, Chroma Cb, Chroma Cr and Reflectance can be achieved, respectively. We can also see that the encoding complexity and decoding complexity of the proposed method are increased only slightly. Figure 5 compares the rate-PSNR curves of TMC13 and the proposed method. We can see that the proposed method can achieve better rate-distortion performance than TMC13, especially at low bitrates.

Table 1. Average BD-rate for attributes and complexity ratio on CY

Dataset category	BD-rate (%)				Complexity ratio (%)	
	Luma	Cb	Cr	Reflectance	Encoding	Decoding
Cat1-A	−10.6	−21.1	−22.0	NA	102	103
Cat1-B	−3.6	−10.4	−10.8	NA	101	102
Cat3-fused	−0.3	−0.2	−0.2	−0.1	102	102
Cat3-frame	NA	NA	NA	−0.2	102	102
Overall	**−6.5**	**−14.5**	**−15.2**	**−0.1**	**102**	**102**

Table 2 shows the detailed BD-rate of each sequence. By analyzing the results, we can see that the average gain for Cat1 is larger than that for Cat3. This is because Cat3 consists of only one LoD layer, and the proposed method is not suitable when the points have similar importance.

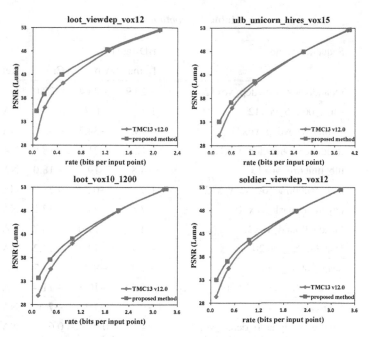

Fig. 5. Rate-PSNR curves. The PSNR is computed for the Luma component and the rate is computed for three color components.

Therefore, we forced the number of LoD layers in Cat3 to be equal to 12. Table 3 shows that an average -6.7%, -14.7%, -15.4%, and -10% BD-rate reduction can be achieved by the proposed method.

Table 2. BD-rate of each sequence for attributes on CY.

Dataset category	Sequence name	BD-rate (%)			
		Luma	Cb	Cr	Reflectance
Cat1-A	basketball_player_vox11_00000200	-22.9	-25.7	-40.3	NA
	boxer_viewdep_vox12	-24.6	-46.2	-47.4	NA
	dancer_vox11_00000001	-18.2	-23.7	-36.6	NA
	egyptian_mask_vox12	-7.6	-23.9	-12.4	NA
	facade_00064_vox11	-4.1	-10.2	-16.4	NA
	frog_00067_vox12	-6.1	-13.0	-14.5	NA
	longdress_viewdep_vox12	-4.5	-12.9	-10.3	NA
	loot_viewdep_vox12	-28.4	-56.2	-54.0	NA
	queen_0200	-12.5	-28.8	-26.2	NA

(continued)

Table 2. (*continued*)

Dataset category	Sequence name	BD-rate (%)			
		Luma	Cb	Cr	Reflectance
	redandblack_viewdep_vox12	−20.9	−25.4	−22.0	NA
	shiva_00035_vox12	1.3	−0.7	−1.0	NA
	soldier_viewdep_vox12	−15.5	−34.2	−40.6	NA
	thaidancer_viewdep_vox12	−12.2	−21.5	−18.5	NA
	ulb_unicorn_vox13	−8.8	−19.1	−18.0	NA
Cat1-B	arco_valentino_dense_vox12	1.3	−0.2	0.2	NA
	egyptian_mask_vox20	−7.5	−24.5	−12.2	NA
	facade_00064_vox20	−4.3	−11.0	−18.7	NA
	frog_00067_vox20	−5.7	−12.5	−14.2	NA
	head_00039_vox20	−2.4	−9.7	−14.7	NA
	house_without_roof_00057_vox20	−5.4	−10.3	−11.4	NA
	landscape_00014_vox20	−0.1	−7.3	−7.5	NA
	palazzo_carignano_dense_vox20	1.4	0.0	0.6	NA
	stanford_area_2_vox20	−8.1	−13.6	−15.8	NA
	staue_klimt_vox20	0.2	−2.9	−3.2	NA
	ulb_unicorn_hires_vox20	−10.5	−29.4	−26.8	NA
	ulb_unicorn_vox20	−9.3	−18.9	−18.3	NA
Cat3-fused	citytunnel_q1mm	−0.3	−0.2	−0.2	−0.3
	overpass_q1mm	−0.1	−0.1	−0.1	0.0
	tollbooth_q1mm	−0.5	−0.3	−0.2	0.0
Cat3-frame	ford_01_q1mm	NA	NA	NA	0.0
	ford_02_q1mm	NA	NA	NA	0.0
	ford_03_q1mm	NA	NA	NA	0.0
	qnxadas-junction-approach	NA	NA	NA	−0.3
	qnxadas-junction-exit	NA	NA	NA	−0.1
	qnxadas-motorway-join	NA	NA	NA	−0.3
	qnxadas-navigating-bends	NA	NA	NA	−0.5

Table 3. Average BD-rate for attributes and complexity ratio on CY. The number of LoD layers was changed to 12 for the Cat3 dataset.

Dataset category	BD-rate (%)				Complexity ratio (%)	
	Luma	Cb	Cr	Reflectance	Encoding	Decoding
Cat1-A	−10.6	−21.1	−22.0	NA	102	103
Cat1-B	−3.6	−10.4	−10.8	NA	101	102
Cat3-fused	**−2.6**	**−3.3**	**−3.2**	**−1.8**	102	102
Cat3-frame	NA	NA	NA	**−13.6**	102	102
Overall	**−6.7**	**−14.7**	**−15.4**	**−10.0**	**102**	**102**

5 Conclusion

To improve the coding efficiency of PT in G-PCC, we adapted the adaptive quantization method used in LT to PT. To take into account the relative importance of the points, we introduced a hardware-friendly quantization weighting method by analyzing the LoD structure. Experimental results show that the proposed method outperforms PT attribute coding with the latest G-PCC test model [7].

Acknowledgement. This work has received funding from the National Natural Science Foundation of China under Grant 62172259 and 61871342, and the OPPO Research Fund.

References

1. Schwarz, S., Preda, M., Baroncini, V., et al.: Emerging MPEG standards for point cloud compression. IEEE J. Emerg. Sel. Topics Circ. Syst. **9**(1), 133–148 (2019)
2. Liu, H., Yuan, H., Liu, Q., et al.: A comprehensive study and comparison of core technologies for MPEG 3-D point cloud compression. IEEE Trans. Broadcast. **66**(3), 701–717 (2020)
3. Chen, T., Long, C., Su, H., et al.: Layered projection-based quality assessment of 3D point clouds. IEEE Access **9**, 88108–88120 (2021)
4. de Queiroz, R.L., Chou, P.A.: Compression of 3D point clouds using a region-adaptive hierarchical transform. IEEE Trans. Image Process. **25**(8), 3947–3956 (2016)
5. Mammou, K..: PCC test model category 3 v0. In: 120th MPEG meeting, document N17249, ISO/IEC JTC1/SC29/WG11, China (2017)
6. Mammou, K., Tourapis, A., Kim, J., et al.: Lifting scheme for lossy attribute encoding in TMC1. In: 122th MPEG Meeting, Document m42640, ISO/IEC JTC1/SC29/WG11, US (2018)
7. G-PCC Test Model v12 user manual. In: 132th MPEG Meeting, Document N00005, ISO/IEC JTC1/SC29/WG7, Online (2020)
8. Tabatabai, A., Graziosi, D., Zaghetto, A.: New contribution on quantization parameter definition. In: 126th MPEG Meeting, Document m47507, ISO/IEC JTC1/SC29/WG11, CH (2019)
9. Iguchi, N., Dean, H. C.: Quantization parameter table in attribute coding. In: 126th MPEG Meeting, Document m47401, ISO/IEC JTC1/SC29/WG11, CH (2019)

10. Dean, H. C., Iguchi, N.: Delta QP for layer of lifting/predicting transform and RAHT. In: 126th MPEG meeting, Document m47834, ISO/IEC JTC1/SC29/WG11, CH (2019)
11. Dean, H. C.: CE13.16 report on Slice-based quantization control. In: 126th MPEG Meeting, Document m47399, ISO/IEC JTC1/SC29/WG11, CH (2019)
12. G-PCC codec description. In: 132th MPEG Meeting, Document N00011, ISO/IEC JTC1/SC29/WG7, Online (2020)
13. Kathariya, B., Zakharchenko, V., Chen, J., et al.: Binary tree based Level-of-Details Generation for Attributes Coding in G-PCC. In: 124th MPEG Meeting, Document m44940, ISO/IEC JTC1/SC29/WG11, China (2018)
14. Common test conditions for G-PCC. In: 132th MPEG Meeting, Document N00032, ISO/IEC JTC1/SC29/WG7, Online (2020).
15. Mekuria, R., Li, Z., Tulvan, C., Chou P. A.: Evaluation criteria for PCC (Point Cloud Compression). In: 115th MPEG Meeting, Document N16332, ISO/IEC JTC1/SC29/WG11, CH (2016)
16. Bjontegaard, G.: Improvements of the BD-PSNR model. In: 35th ITU Meeting, Document VCEG-AI11, ITU-T SG16 Q.6, Germany (2008)

Anti-forensics for Double JPEG Compression Based on Generative Adversarial Network

Dequ Huang[1], Weixuan Tang[2], and Bin Li[1,3(✉)]

[1] Guangdong Key Laboratory of Intelligent Information Processing and Shenzhen Key Laboratory of Media Security, Shenzhen University, Shenzhen 518060, China
`huangdequ2019@email.szu.edu.cn, libin@szu.edu.cn`
[2] Institute of Artificial Intelligence and Blockchain, Guangzhou University, Guangzhou 510006, Guangdong, China
`tweix@gzhu.edu.cn`
[3] Shenzhen Institute of Artificial Intelligence and Robotics for Society, Shenzhen 518129, China

Abstract. The JPEG standard is one of the most widely used image formats. If a JPEG image is tampered and saved in JPEG format again, it would lead to double JPEG compression (DJPEG). Therefore, DJPEG detection is a research hotspot in image forensics. On the other side, tamperer would try to perform anti-forensics operation on DJPEG image to avoid detection, but there are few related reports so far. In this paper, we propose a DJPEG anti-forensics method based on a generative adversarial network called AFDJ-GAN (Anti-Forensics for Double JPEG Compression with Generative Adversarial Network). On behalf of the anti-forensics side, the generator takes the double JPEG compressed image as input, and obtains the reconstructed image removed from compression artifacts, and uses simulated JPEG compression to convert it into generated simulated Single JPEG compressed (SJPEG) image. On behalf of the forensics side, the discriminator tries to distinguish between real SJPEG image and generated simulated SJPEG image by the feature extracted by the simulated histogram layer. Via alternant updating these two networks, the generator can learn to erase the DJPEG traces. The experimental results show that the proposed method has achieved state-of-the-art anti-forensics performance against different DJPEG detectors, and outperformed existing methods with regards to image quality.

Keywords: Double JPEG compression · Anti-forensics · GAN

This work was supported in part by NSFC (Grant 61872244, 62002075) and in part by Guangdong Basic and Applied Basic Research Foundation (Grant 2019B151502001) in part by the Guangdong R&D Program in Key Areas under Grant 2019B010139003 and Shenzhen R&D Program (Grant JCYJ20200109105008228).
D. Huang and W. Tang—Contributed equally to this work.

Y. Peng et al. (Eds.): ICIG 2021, LNCS 12888, pp. 759–771, 2021.
https://doi.org/10.1007/978-3-030-87355-4_63

1   Introduction

JPEG compression is one of the most widely used image formats. When the JPEG compressed images are tampered by operations such as copy-move, stitching, and erasing, they would usually JPEG compressed afterwards and would undergo double JPEG compression (DJPEG) [2,3,21]. Therefore, on the side of image forensics, there is great demand to develop the technique of double JPEG compression detection, which aims to distinguish between single-compressed JPEG image and double-compressed image [2,3,13,14,17,21–23,27,28,30].

On the other hand, a wise tamperer will perform specific post-processing on the double-compressed image to deceive the forensics detectors. This is called anti-forensics technology. By studying anti-forensics technology, we can expose the shortcomings of current forensics methods and enhance the robustness and reliability of the forensics system. However, there are few reports on existing DJPEG anti-forensics methods [15,20,26]. Some methods are designed for specific DJPEG detectors, and the anti-forensics performance on other DJPEG detectors is unknown. More severely, some methods will introduce artifacts in the pixel domain or lower the visual quality of the image.

To overcome the above difficulties, we propose AFDJ-GAN (Anti-Forensics for Double JPEG Compression with Generative Adversarial Network). It simulates the game between the forensics side and the anti-forensics side, wherein the latter utilizes the generator to erase the traces of DJPEG and generate the simulated single JPEG compression (SJPEG) images that can deceive the forensics detector, while the former utilizes the discriminator to distinguish the simulated SJPEG image from the real SJPEG image. The experimental results show that the proposed AFDJ-GAN can effectively degrade the detection performance of most DJPEG forensics methods, and maintain high image visual quality.

Our main contributions are highlighted as follows.

- We propose AFDJ-GAN to simulate the rivalry between anti-forensics and forensics on DJPEG issue, wherein the generator transforms the double-compressed image into the simulated generated SJPEG image, and the discriminator tries to distinguish between the simulated generated SJPEG image and real SJPEG image. Via alternately updating these two networks, AFDJ-GAN can learn to erase DJPEG artifacts.
- We design a delicate network structure for AFDJ-GAN. As for the generator, the first part extracts multi-scale features. The second part obtains reconstructed image. And finally the simulated JPEG compression layer outputs simulated SJPEG image. As for the discriminator, the features extracted by the simulated histogram layer are classified by a CNN-based classifier.
- We conduct extensive experiments to evaluate AFDJ-GAN from different aspects. Experimental results show that AFDJ-GAN can achieve the state-of-the-art anti-forensics performance against different advanced forensics detectors. Besides, according to objective and subjective evaluation, AFDJ-GAN can maintain high image visual quality.

2   Related Works

Most DJPEG detection methods rely on the features of discrete cosine transform (DCT) coefficients, as double compression leaves detectable traces in the DCT domain [17]. Li et al. [13] modeled the distribution of the first digits for different AC modes. Shang et al. [23] calculated DCT difference matrix for texture areas which are impacted by JPEG compression. With the development of deep learning technique, several methods based on convolution neural network (CNN) have been proposed recently. Barni et al. [3] proposed a CNN that can capture DJPEG traces from DCT histogram features or spatial images. Park et al. [21] analyzed the diversity of 1120 compressed quantization tables and proposes a CNN wherein quantization table information is fed into the fully connected layer. Amerini et al. [2] and Zeng et al. [30] proposed CNNs consisting of a DCT domain branch and a spatial domain branch.

On the other side, the goal of JPEG compression anti-forensics is to eliminate the artifacts introduced by JPEG compression. Stamm et al. [25] first proposed an anti-forensics method that adds noise to the DCT coefficients in the JPEG image to deceive the JPEG detector. Fan et al. [8] proposed a JPEG deblocking method based on total variation minimization to smooth the block boundary and DCT histogram distribution. Luo et al. [18] proposed a method based on generative adversarial network, where the generator learns how to hide JPEG compression traces via competing against the discriminator. Another similar research field is JPEG compression artifact removal, such as [5,7,9–12,16,19]. They aim to erase JPEG compression artifacts for improving the visual quality instead of deceiving the forensics detector. As for DJPEG anti-forensics, Sutthiwan et al. [26] proposed a method that shrinks and zooms a double-compressed images to destroy the JPEG grid and erase the trace of DJPEG, however it would smooth the image and has poor undetectability. Li et al. [15] proposed a method which adaptively adds dithering noise to DCT coefficients to hide the trace of DJPEG, but it works under the situation that same quantization table is used in two compressions. Milani et al. [20] proposed a method that modifies the first digits of DCT coefficients, which makes the distribution of first digits similar to SJPEG. However, it will introduce obvious artifacts of modification.

3   Proposed Method

3.1   Notations

In the remaining of this paper, images represented in spatial domain and images represented in DCT domain are denoted as $\mathbf{S}^{H \times W \times C}$ and $\mathbf{D}^{H \times W \times C}$, respectively, where H, W, and C are the height, width, and channel number of the image. The elements in $\mathbf{S}^{H \times W \times C}$ are spatial pixels, while the elements in $\mathbf{D}^{H \times W \times C}$ are DCT coefficients. Specifically, the double-compressed images, uncompressed images, reconstructed images, which are represented in spatial domain, are denoted as $\mathbf{S}_{dc}^{H \times W \times C}$, $\mathbf{S}_{uc}^{H \times W \times C}$, and $\mathbf{S}_{rc}^{H \times W \times C}$, respectively. The generated simulated SJPEG images and real SJPEG images, which are represented in DCT domain, are denoted as $\mathbf{D}_{g\_sc}^{H \times W \times C}$ and $\mathbf{D}_{r\_sc}^{H \times W \times C}$.

3.2   Overview

In this paper, we propose the AFDJ-GAN (Anti-Forensics for Double JPEG Compression with Generative Adversarial Network) to simulate the competition between forensics and anti-forensics on the issue of double JPEG compression, as shown in Fig. 1. In general, the generator is on behalf of the anti-forensics side, which takes the DJPEG image represented in spatial domain as input and obtains the reconstructed image that has removed all compression traces in spatial domain, and outputs the generated simulated SJPEG image represented in DCT domain. On the other hand, the discriminator represents the forensics side, and tries to distinguish between the generated SJPEG image and the real SJPEG image. It takes both images represented in DCT domain as input, and then performs simulated histogram layer on them for classification. In training stage, the generator is trained with the discriminator by iteratively generating simulated SJPEG images via simulated JPEG compression layer. In testing stage, the well-trained generator is used to produce reconstructed image, and standard JPEG compression can be applied in practical anti-forensics situations.

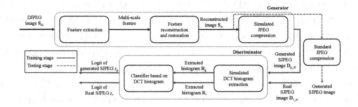

Fig. 1. The framework of the proposed AFDJ-GAN.

3.3   Generator

The structure of the generator is composed of three parts, wherein the first part destroys the JPEG grid, the second part obtains a reconstructed image that has removed any compression artifacts, and the third part generates a simulated SJPEG image for the reconstructed image, as shown in Fig. 2.

The first part is incorporated with [26] for feature extraction. It takes the DJPEG image $S_{dc}^{H \times W \times C}$ as input, shrinks it with a scaling factor s, and then rescales it to the original size. We set s as 0.7 and 1.2 for more abundant information. This operation can destroy the JPEG grid and eliminate the DJPEG artifacts in spatial domain. However, it would also lead to smoothing, so the rescaled images are concatenated with the DJPEG image to preserve the texture details. Then it uses a standard convolutional layer and two dilated convolutional layers with dilation rate 2 and 4 to extract features in different scales.

The second part firstly utilizes a convolutional layer followed by a leaky rectified linear unit (LeakyReLU) and then 4 Residual in Residual Dense Blocks (RRDB) are applied to reconstruct the extracted feature. The structure of RRDB is the same as described in [29]. It then utilizes several convolutional layers to

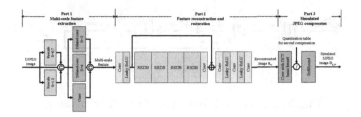

Fig. 2. The network structure of the generator.

restore features in spatial domain. Within all convolutional layers, the kernel size is 3×3. The channel number is 64 for the first two layers and is C for the last layer. It finally outputs the reconstructed image $\mathbf{S}_{rc}^{H \times W \times C}$.

The third part is a simulated JPEG compression layer. It firstly performs convolution with 8×8 DCT basis kernels on the reconstructed image, and divides it by quantization table. Since the rounding operation is non-differentiable, it uses the SoftRound operation as in [24] to approximate the rounding operation and ensure gradients propagation. The SoftRound operation can be expressed as $y = [x] + (x - [x])^3$, where $[\cdot]$ is the rounding operation. Finally, it outputs the simulated SJPEG image represented in DCT domain as $\mathbf{D}_{g\_sc}^{H \times W \times C}$.

Since the goal of the generator is to remove all DJPEG traces, and ensure that the reconstructed image can deceive the discriminator after undergoing a JPEG compression, its loss function is designed from two aspects. To guide the generator to remove DJPEG traces and maintain the visual quality, we design a reconstructed loss L_{re}, which is calculated as the L_1 distance between the reconstructed image $\mathbf{S}_{rc}^{H \times W \times C}$ and the corresponding uncompressed image $\mathbf{S}_{uc}^{H \times W \times C}$, as shown in Eq. (1). To make the generator deceive the discriminator and obtain better anti-forensics performance, we design the adversarial loss L_{adv}. We input the $\mathbf{D}_{g\_sc}^{H \times W \times C}$ into the discriminator and get its logit z_g, i.e., the probability to be classified as the generated image, then calculate the negative logarithmic likelihood function, as shown in Eq. (2). The overall loss for the generator L_G is the weighted sum of L_{re} and L_{adv}, as shown in Eq. (3), where λ is a hyper-parameter to balance the two loss.

$$L_{re} = \left| S_{uc}^{H \times W \times C} - S_{rc}^{H \times W \times C} \right| \tag{1}$$

$$L_{adv} = -log(1 - z_g) \tag{2}$$

$$L_G = \lambda L_{re} + L_{adv} \tag{3}$$

3.4 Discriminator

The structure of the discriminator consists of two parts, as shown in Fig. 3. The first part extracts histogram for AC coefficients in generated or real SJPEG image via simulated histogram layer, and then the second part distinguishes the extracted histogram via a CNN-based classifier.

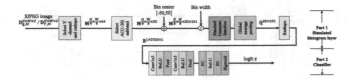

Fig. 3. The network structure of the discriminator.

In the first part, we use the simulated histogram layer to make statistics for DCT coefficients within images, and the detailed steps are as follows.

1. We input a SJPEG image represented in DCT domain, such as $\mathbf{D}_{r\_sc}^{H\times W\times 1}$ and $\mathbf{D}_{g\_sc}^{H\times W\times 1}$. The elements within these images are DCT coefficients.
2. We reshape the image into matrix $\mathbf{M}^{H/8\times W/8\times 64}$ wherein $m_{h,w,c}$ is the DCT coefficient at the (h,w)-th DCT block and c-th DCT subband. In this way, each channel corresponds to a specific DCT subband.
3. We select 20 subbands in zigzag order, wherein each subband would be extracted with a histogram, as shown in Step 4 and 5. Within each histogram, the range of bins is set as $[-50, 50]$, and thus the number of bins are 101.
4. We simulate the process of making statistics for the k-th bin in the histogram with respect to DCT coefficient $m_{h,w,c}$ as

$$p(h,w,c,k) = e^{-\frac{(m(h,w,c)-b_k)^2}{\sigma^2}} \tag{4}$$

wherein $1 \leq h \leq H/8, 1 \leq w \leq W/8, 1 \leq c \leq 20, -50 \leq k \leq 50$, b_k is the center of for the k-th bin in the histogram and σ is the bin width. Note that $m(h,w,c)$ close to b_k corresponds to a large output, indicating that $m(h,w,c)$ is counted in the this bin.
5. We simulate the process of making statistics for the k-th bin in the histogram with respect to c-th subband as

$$q(c,k) = \frac{64}{H\times W} \sum_{h}^{H/8} \sum_{w}^{W/8} p(h,w,c,k) \tag{5}$$

wherein $1 \leq c \leq 20, -50 \leq k \leq 50$.
6. All $q(c,k)(1 \leq c \leq 20, -50 \leq k \leq 50)$ can form a matrix $\mathbf{Q}^{20\times 101}$. Such a matrix can be reshaped into $\mathbf{R}^{1\times 2020\times 1}$ for subsequent classification.

The second part is used to distinguish between simulated generated SJPEG image and the real SJPEG image according to histogram features $\mathbf{R}^{1\times 2020\times 1}$. We use the CNN architecture, which consists of two convolutional layers and two pooling layers. Then two fully-connected layers and a sigmoid activation function are deployed to output the softmax logits.

As the counterpart of the generator, the discriminator tries to distinguish the generated simulated images from the real SJPEG images, so we use the cross-entropy function for binary classification. The loss function of the discriminator is shown in Eq. 6, where z_r and z_g are the softmax logits for $\mathbf{D}_{r\_sc}^{H \times W \times C}$ and $\mathbf{D}_{g\_sc}^{H \times W \times C}$, z_r' and z_g' are the labels for $\mathbf{D}_{r\_sc}^{H \times W \times C}$ and $\mathbf{D}_{g\_sc}^{H \times W \times C}$, respectively.

$$L_D = -z_r' log(z_r) - z_g' log(z_g) \tag{6}$$

4   Experiments

4.1   Experimental Settings

Datasets. Because forensics side and anti-forensics side usually perform training on their own datasets and compete on another unknown dataset, we use three datasets, wherein 64×64 *BOSS* is used to train the anti-forensics methods, 64×64 *RAISE4K* is used to train the forensics methods, and $64 \times 64/256 \times 256$ *DIV2k* are used for testing.

- 64×64 *BOSS*: The original *BOSS* [4] consists of 10,000 RGB images with size 512×512. We select 8,695 images for training and 870 images for validation. Then we non-overlap crop each image to 64 images with size 64×64 and compress them as 64×64 *BOSS*, which consist of a training set of 556,480 images and a validation set of 55,680 images.
- 64×64 *RAISE4K*: The original *RAISE4K* [6] contains 4,000 raw images with size 4288×2848. We select 3,600 images for training and 400 images for validation. We randomly crop each image into 150 images with size 64×64, and compress them as 64×64 *RAISE4K*, which consists of a training set of 540,000 images and a testing set of 60,000 images.
- $64 \times 64/256 \times 256$ *DIV2k*: The original *DIV2k* [1] contains 800 high quality RGB images with 2K resolution. We randomly crop them into 50,000 64×64 and 3,000 256×256 images, and compress them as 64×64 *DIV2k* and 256×256 *DIV2K*, respectively.

We use the PIL library for JPEG compression as follows. To create the SJPEG versions of the three datasets, we compress the images with $QF = 75, 85, 95$, respectively. To create the DJPEG versions for 64×64 *BOSS*, we select the quality factor of the second compression, i.e., QF_2, from [75, 85, 95], and randomly select the quality factor of the first compression, i.e., QF_1, from [50, 55, 60, 65, 70, 75, 80, 85, 90, 95, 98] without the selected QF_2. Therefore, there are three DJPEG versions for this dataset, and each is first compressed with mixed QF_1 and then compressed again with a specific QF_2. To create the DJPEG versions for 64×64 *RAISE4K*, 64×64 *DIV2k* and 256×256 *DIV2k*, we select QF_2 from [75, 85, 95] and QF_1 from [50, 60, 70, 80, 90]. Therefore, there are 15 DJPEG versions for each dataset corresponding to different (QF_1, QF_2) pairs.

DJPEG Detector. Four DJPEG forensics methods are used in our experiments. Method based on DCT domain proposed in [3] is denoted as $\mathcal{D}_b^{hist}$. Method based on pixel domain proposed in [3] is denoted as $\mathcal{D}_b^{pix}$. Method proposed in [2] is denoted as $\mathcal{D}_a$. Method proposed in [21] is denoted as $\mathcal{D}_p$. $\mathcal{D}_b^{hist}$,

$\mathcal{D}_b^{pix}$, and $\mathcal{D}_a$ are trained on 64×64 *RAISE4K* and test on 64×64 *DIV2k*. As for $\mathcal{D}_p$, the pre-trained model in [21] is used and is tested on 256×256 *DIV2k*.

DJPEG Anti-forensics Methods. Five methods were tested in our experiments. Method proposed in [11, 20, 26] and [12] are denoted as $\mathcal{AF}_1$, $\mathcal{AF}_2$, $\mathcal{AF}_3$ and $\mathcal{AF}_4$. Our proposed AFDJ-GAN is denoted as $\mathcal{AF}$. The model is trained for 20 epochs and the batchsize is 64. Adam optimizer is used, and the initial learning rate is set as 2e−4, and is halved in every 5 epochs. Hyper-parameter λ is set as 0.005. In the testing stage, standard JPEG compression is applied to generate anti-forensics image. We use the PyTorch framework for training with 4 GPUs of Nvidia Tesla P100. Note that we train the models in [11] and [12] to remove the DJPEG traces and then perform standard JPEG compression to obtain anti-forensics images.

4.2 Performance of Anti-forensics

In this part, we compare the performance of our proposed AFDJ-GAN $\mathcal{AF}$ with $\mathcal{AF}_1$ [26], $\mathcal{AF}_2$ [20], $\mathcal{AF}_3$ [11], $\mathcal{AF}_4$ [12]. The evaluation metric is the true positive (TP) rate, where DJPEG images and SJPEG images are considered as positive instances and negative instances, respectively. The experimental results are shown in Table 1, and the following observations can be made.

Table 1. The detection rate of DJPEG detectors $\mathcal{D}_b^{hist}$ [3], $\mathcal{D}_b^{pix}$ [3], $\mathcal{D}_a$ [2] and $\mathcal{D}_p$ [21] for DJPEG images $\mathcal{J}$ and anti-forensics images generated by $\mathcal{AF}_1$ [26], $\mathcal{AF}_2$ [20], $\mathcal{AF}_3$ [11], $\mathcal{AF}_4$ [12] and our AFDJ-GAN $\mathcal{AF}$.

QFs	QF2	75					85					95				
	QF1	50	60	70	80	90	50	60	70	80	90	50	60	70	80	90
$\mathcal{D}_b^{hist}$	$\mathcal{J}$	0.997	0.990	0.909	0.927	0.873	0.996	0.996	0.998	0.983	0.969	1.000	0.998	0.997	0.998	0.998
	$\mathcal{AF}_1$	0.520	0.587	0.418	0.449	0.445	0.620	0.645	0.354	0.314	0.503	0.782	0.761	0.655	0.527	0.090
	$\mathcal{AF}_2$	0.052	0.056	**0.116**	0.260	0.609	0.692	0.861	0.044	**0.085**	0.418	0.381	0.443	0.144	0.031	0.022
	$\mathcal{AF}_3$	0.773	0.725	0.537	0.856	0.502	0.855	0.877	0.837	0.873	0.937	0.799	0.783	0.780	0.825	0.827
	$\mathcal{AF}_4$	0.488	0.661	0.867	0.843	0.822	0.560	0.687	0.590	0.764	0.869	0.212	0.288	0.562	0.632	0.758
	$\mathcal{AF}$	**0.003**	**0.042**	0.246	**0.229**	**0.289**	**0.042**	**0.172**	**0.004**	0.119	**0.146**	**0.012**	**0.009**	**0.011**	**0.003**	**0.002**
$\mathcal{D}_b^{pix}$	$\mathcal{J}$	0.956	0.966	0.859	0.848	0.826	0.966	0.985	0.970	0.962	0.952	0.868	0.871	0.901	0.905	0.956
	$\mathcal{AF}_1$	0.426	0.362	0.214	0.879	0.204	0.489	0.400	0.351	0.179	0.741	0.366	0.349	0.370	0.389	0.281
	$\mathcal{AF}_2$	0.983	0.971	0.936	0.889	0.988	0.991	0.994	0.955	0.845	0.616	0.896	0.888	0.948	0.961	0.975
	$\mathcal{AF}_3$	0.849	0.874	0.871	0.869	0.793	0.762	0.764	0.708	0.524	0.832	0.223	0.295	0.390	0.544	0.701
	$\mathcal{AF}_4$	0.339	0.478	0.496	0.672	0.519	0.327	0.334	0.337	0.533	0.669	0.107	0.163	0.312	0.592	0.662
	$\mathcal{AF}$	**0.058**	**0.117**	**0.104**	**0.525**	**0.194**	**0.046**	**0.064**	**0.135**	**0.126**	**0.257**	**0.017**	**0.048**	**0.078**	**0.215**	**0.187**
$\mathcal{D}_a$	$\mathcal{J}$	0.996	0.986	0.889	0.874	0.823	0.983	0.989	0.987	0.979	0.814	0.995	0.996	0.971	0.956	0.776
	$\mathcal{AF}_1$	0.535	0.611	0.369	0.551	0.531	0.480	0.440	0.401	0.459	0.466	0.698	0.664	0.181	0.145	0.119
	$\mathcal{AF}_2$	0.153	0.133	0.444	0.166	**0.325**	0.119	0.002	**0.001**	0.496	0.531	0.584	0.442	0.151	0.566	0.310
	$\mathcal{AF}_3$	0.907	0.878	0.866	0.850	0.812	0.885	0.863	0.876	0.919	0.751	0.922	0.894	0.714	0.517	0.219
	$\mathcal{AF}_4$	0.522	0.559	0.585	0.740	0.776	0.557	0.512	0.547	0.453	0.635	0.736	0.718	0.598	0.519	0.363
	$\mathcal{AF}$	**0.004**	**0.003**	0.149	0.113	0.427	**0.018**	**0.001**	0.002	0.124	0.122	0.054	0.033	0.007	0.032	0.069
$\mathcal{D}_p$	$\mathcal{J}$	0.996	0.993	0.880	0.911	0.669	1.000	0.998	0.952	0.956	0.910	1.000	1.000	1.000	0.998	0.947
	$\mathcal{AF}_1$	0.378	0.607	0.132	0.331	0.067	0.556	0.504	0.184	0.022	0.065	0.289	0.256	0.209	0.117	**0.002**
	$\mathcal{AF}_2$	0.993	0.988	0.900	0.999	0.999	1.000	0.999	0.955	1.000	1.000	1.000	1.000	0.985	0.980	0.935
	$\mathcal{AF}_3$	0.966	0.979	0.857	0.891	0.634	0.914	0.887	0.776	0.769	0.773	0.970	0.955	0.850	0.538	0.085
	$\mathcal{AF}_4$	0.762	0.746	0.766	0.799	0.570	0.653	0.726	0.560	0.676	0.672	0.878	0.775	0.810	0.554	0.143
	$\mathcal{AF}$	**0.008**	**0.013**	**0.008**	**0.006**	**0.004**	**0.066**	**0.014**	**0.005**	**0.006**	**0.002**	**0.202**	**0.112**	**0.093**	**0.042**	**0.009**

- It can be observed that $\mathcal{AF}_1$, $\mathcal{AF}_2$, $\mathcal{AF}_3$ and $\mathcal{AF}_4$ cannot achieve satisfied anti-forensics performance. For example, $\mathcal{AF}_2$ is almost ineffective against $\mathcal{D}_b^{pix}$ and $\mathcal{D}_p$ as it cannot lower the detection accuracy of these two detectors. Although $\mathcal{AF}_1$ outperforms $\mathcal{AF}_2$ against $\mathcal{D}_b^{pix}$ and $\mathcal{D}_p$ by 0.522 and 0.721, respectively, its performance is not satisfied in the situation of low QF_1 and QF_2. $\mathcal{AF}_3$ has the worst overall performance, and the average detection accuracy for $\mathcal{AF}_3$ is quite high. $\mathcal{AF}_4$ performs worse in the situation of high QF_1 while its overall performance is also worse.
- Our proposed AFDJ-GAN can outperform the existing methods against different forensics detectors. Please note that $\mathcal{AF}_1$ performed the best in previous anti-forensics methods. Our proposed AFDJ-GAN, i.e., $\mathcal{AF}$, outperforms $\mathcal{AF}_1$ against $\mathcal{D}_b^{hist}$, $\mathcal{D}_b^{pix}$, $\mathcal{D}_a$ by 0.517, 0.368, 0.535 in the case of $(QF_1, QF_2) = (50, 75)$, and 0.088, 0.094, 0.050 in the case of $(QF_1, QF_2) = (90, 95)$, respectively. These results indicate that our method is suitable to process images with different QF pairs.
- Although our proposed AFDJ-GAN, i.e., $\mathcal{AF}$, is trained on 64×64 *BOSS*, it can be used to generate images with size 256×256 to fool $\mathcal{D}_p$. On 15 QF pairs, the average improvement of $\mathcal{AF}$ over $\mathcal{AF}_1$ is 0.209. The results indicate that our proposed AFDJ-GAN has great migration performance across different image sizes.

Table 2. PSNR and SSIM value of DJPEG images $\mathcal{J}$ and anti-forensics images generated by $\mathcal{AF}_1$ [26], $\mathcal{AF}_2$ [20], $\mathcal{AF}_3$ [11], $\mathcal{AF}_4$ [12] and our method $\mathcal{AF}$.

QFs		Methods					
QF2	QF1	$\mathcal{J}$	$\mathcal{AF}_1$	$\mathcal{AF}_2$	$\mathcal{AF}_3$	$\mathcal{AF}_4$	$\mathcal{AF}$
QF2 = 75	50	33.97\0.907	32.41\0.893	33.30\0.906	**34.37\0.920**	34.34\0.914	34.14\0.905
	60	34.28\0.915	32.79\0.904	33.35\0.918	34.70**0.921**	34.68\0.918	**34.72**\0.918
	70	**37.90\0.961**	33.46\0.913	32.03\0.904	34.57\0.914	35.50\0.933	35.09\0.917
	80	**36.46\0.946**	33.40\0.912	29.70\0.841	34.94\0.923	35.40\0.928	35.62\0.929
	90	**39.43\0.971**	34.08\0.920	31.55\0.892	35.15\0.928	35.62\0.925	35.70\0.926
QF2 = 85	50	34.29\0.910	32.49\0.892	34.02\0.914	**35.11\0.921**	34.69\0.914	34.60\0.912
	60	34.57\0.915	32.78\0.899	33.99\0.916	**36.95\0.954**	35.91\0.929	35.04\0.920
	70	35.49\0.927	33.12\0.904	34.57\0.923	**35.66\0.929**	35.59\0.926	35.52\0.926
	80	**37.91\0.957**	33.62\0.911	33.90\0.928	35.75\0.930	35.68\0.929	36.16\0.932
	90	35.84\0.931	33.48\0.909	29.58\0.826	36.31\0.934	36.38\0.936	**36.47\0.938**
QF2 = 95	50	33.75\0.897	32.39\0.888	28.45\0.820	**36.90\0.949**	36.51\0.939	34.18\0.898
	60	34.39\0.908	32.67\0.895	30.69\0.865	**36.46\0.938**	36.11\0.937	34.76\0.909
	70	35.30\0.922	33.06\0.902	34.98\0.928	**37.80\0.961**	36.91\0.941	35.51\0.921
	80	**36.48\0.937**	33.46\0.910	35.35\0.936	35.74\0.928	35.94\0.930	36.41\0.935
	90	**38.34\0.955**	33.89\0.918	36.05\0.947	37.34\0.948	37.46\0.951	37.61\0.950

(a)   (b)   (c)   (d)   (e)   (f)   (g)

Fig. 4. Qualitative results of the proposed method in the case of $(QF_1, QF_2) = (60, 95)$. (a) is DJPEG image (b)–(f) are anti-forensics image generated by [11,12,20,26], and our proposed method, (g) is SJPEG image.

4.3 Visual Quality

In this part, we evaluate the visual quality of anti-forensics images from two aspects, including objective evaluation and subjective evaluation.

Objective Evaluation. For objective evaluation, we evaluated the visual quality by peak-signal-to-noise-ratio (PSNR) and structural similarity (SSIM) between SJPEG images and anti-forensics images. The results are shown in Table 2. The average PSNR and SSIM of our AFDJ-GAN (35.44 and 0.922) are comparable to the results of $\mathcal{AF}_3$ (35.85 and 0.933) and $\mathcal{AF}_4$ (35.78 and 0.930). Note that $\mathcal{AF}_3$ and $\mathcal{AF}_4$ only focus on the visual quality and thus its PSNR and SSIM are quite high. However, its anti-forensics performance is far from satisfaction, as shown in Table 2. The average PSNR and SSIM of our AFDJ-GAN are obviously higher than that of $\mathcal{AF}_1$ (33.14 and 0.905), $\mathcal{AF}_2$ (32.77 and 0.898).

Subjective Evaluation. For subjective evaluation, we compare the details of images. The results are shown in Fig. 4. It can be observed that $\mathcal{AF}_2$ [20] introduces obvious block artifacts, as shown in Fig. 4(b). The reason is that this method modifies the first digits of the AC coefficients, which leads to discontinuity among adjacent blocks. $\mathcal{AF}_1$ [26] is similar to low-pass filtering, which will loss the high-frequency details, as shown in Fig. 4(c). In contrast, our proposed AFDJ-GAN, $\mathcal{AF}_3$ [11] and $\mathcal{AF}_4$ [12] do not introduce unnatural artifacts, and maintains richer textures and sharper edges similar to SJPEG images.

4.4 Ablation Study

In this part, we conduct ablation studies on the network architecture of AFDJ-GAN. We regard AFDJ-GAN as baseline and design several variants with different network structure. In variant I, we remove the first part, i.e., the feature extraction part with rescaling operation, from the generator. In variant II, we remove the discriminator, and only use the first and second parts of the generator to minimize reconstructed loss L_{re}. In variant III, we replace the adversarial loss L_{adv} with histogram loss L_{hist}, which is calculated as the mean square error between the histogram features of generated and real single-compressed image. We compare the anti-forensics performance and visual quality of these variants in Table 3. Results of Variant I indicate that rescaling operation would slightly reduce the image quality, but it can significantly improve the anti-forensics performance. Results of Variant II indicate that only using reconstruction loss can improve the visual quality but degrade the anti-forensics performance against DJPEG detectors. Results of Variant III indicate that L_{hist} has its limitation, and optimizing over L_{hist} cannot bring satisfied performance against DJPEG detectors. Therefore, considering both anti-forensics performance and visual quality, the original AFDJ-GAN is the best choice.

Table 3. Anti-forensics performance and visual quality for different variants.

Method	Anti-forensics performance				Visual quality	
	$\mathcal{D}_b^{pix}$	$\mathcal{D}_b^{hist}$	$\mathcal{D}_a$	$\mathcal{D}_p$	PSNR	SSIM
Variant I	0.238	0.110	0.086	0.346	35.64	0.931
Variant II	0.636	0.582	0.433	0.899	**36.11**	**0.939**
Variant III	0.501	0.498	0.390	0.752	35.99	0.935
AFDJ-GAN	**0.145**	**0.089**	**0.077**	**0.039**	35.44	0.922

5   Conclusion

In this paper we propose a DJPEG anti-forensics method based on generative adversarial network called AFDJ-GAN, which consists of a generator that removes DJPEG traces and performs simulated JPEG compression, and a discriminator that extracts histogram and distinguishes between the generated simulated SJPEG image and real SJPEG image. Delicate network structure is designed, especially the simulated JPEG compression layer and simulated histogram layer that enable gradient propagation in training process. The experimental results show that AFDJ-GAN can achieve the state-of-the-art performance against different DJPEG detectors, and maintains satisfied visual quality. Ablation experiments demonstrate the effectiveness of the network structure. In the future, we hope to extend our GAN-based method to more general anti-forensics scenarios.

References

1. Agustsson, E., Timofte, R.: NTIRE 2017 challenge on single image super-resolution: dataset and study. In: Proceedings of the IEEE Conference on Computer Vision and Pattern Recognition Workshops, pp. 126–135 (2017)

2. Amerini, I., Uricchio, T., Ballan, L., Caldelli, R.: Localization of JPEG double compression through multi-domain convolutional neural networks. In: IEEE Conference on Computer Vision and Pattern Recognition Workshops, pp. 1865–1871. IEEE (2017)
3. Barni, M., et al.: Aligned and non-aligned double JPEG detection using convolutional neural networks. J Vis Commun. Image Represent. **49**, 153–163 (2017)
4. Bas, P., Filler, T., Pevný, T.: "Break our steganographic system": the ins and outs of organizing BOSS. In: Filler, T., Pevný, T., Craver, S., Ker, A. (eds.) IH 2011. LNCS, vol. 6958, pp. 59–70. Springer, Heidelberg (2011). https://doi.org/10.1007/978-3-642-24178-9_5
5. Cavigelli, L., Hager, P., Benini, L.: CAS-CNN: a deep convolutional neural network for image compression artifact suppression. In: International Joint Conference on Neural Networks, pp. 752–759. IEEE (2017)
6. Dang-Nguyen, D.T., Pasquini, C., Conotter, V., Boato, G.: RAISE: a raw images dataset for digital image forensics. In: Proceedings of the 6th ACM Multimedia Systems Conference, pp. 219–224 (2015)
7. Dong, C., Deng, Y., Loy, C.C., Tang, X.: Compression artifacts reduction by a deep convolutional network. In: Proceedings of the IEEE International Conference on Computer Vision, pp. 576–584 (2015)
8. Fan, W., Wang, K., Cayre, F., Xiong, Z.: JPEG anti-forensics with improved trade-off between forensic undetectability and image quality. IEEE Trans. Inf. Forensics Secur. **9**(8), 1211–1226 (2014)
9. Galteri, L., Seidenari, L., Bertini, M., Del Bimbo, A.: Deep universal generative adversarial compression artifact removal. IEEE Trans. Multimed. **21**(8), 2131–2145 (2019)
10. Guo, J., Chao, H.: Building dual-domain representations for compression artifacts reduction. In: Leibe, B., Matas, J., Sebe, N., Welling, M. (eds.) ECCV 2016. LNCS, vol. 9905, pp. 628–644. Springer, Cham (2016). https://doi.org/10.1007/978-3-319-46448-0_38
11. Kim, T., Lee, H., Son, H., Lee, S.: SF-CNN: a fast compression artifacts removal via spatial-to-frequency convolutional neural networks. In: IEEE International Conference on Image Processing, pp. 3606–3610. IEEE (2019)
12. Kim, Y., Soh, J.W., Cho, N.I.: AGARNet: adaptively gated JPEG compression artifacts removal network for a wide range quality factor. IEEE Access **8**, 20160–20170 (2020)
13. Li, B., Shi, Y.Q., Huang, J.: Detecting doubly compressed JPEG images by using mode based first digit features. In: IEEE 10th Workshop on Multimedia Signal Processing, pp. 730–735. IEEE (2008)
14. Li, B., Zhang, H., Luo, H., Tan, S.: Detecting double JPEG compression and its related anti-forensic operations with CNN. Multimed. Tools Appl. **78**(7), 8577–8601 (2019). https://doi.org/10.1007/s11042-018-7073-3
15. Li, H., Luo, W., Huang, J.: Anti-forensics of double JPEG compression with the same quantization matrix. Multimed. Tools Appl. **74**(17), 6729–6744 (2015). https://doi.org/10.1007/s11042-014-1927-0
16. Lin, M.H., Yeh, C.H., Lin, C.H., Huang, C.H., Kang, L.W.: Deep multi-scale residual learning-based blocking artifacts reduction for compressed images, pp. 18–19 (2019)
17. Lukáš, J., Fridrich, J.: Estimation of primary quantization matrix in double compressed JPEG images, pp. 5–8 (2003)

18. Luo, Y., Zi, H., Zhang, Q., Kang, X.: Anti-forensics of JPEG compression using generative adversarial networks. In: 26th European Signal Processing Conference, pp. 952–956. IEEE (2018)
19. Maleki, D., Nadalian, S., Mahdi Derakhshani, M., Amin Sadeghi, M.: BlockCNN: a deep network for artifact removal and image compression. In: Proceedings of the IEEE Conference on Computer Vision and Pattern Recognition Workshops, pp. 2555–2558 (2018)
20. Milani, S., Tagliasacchi, M., Tubaro, S.: Antiforensics attacks to Benford's law for the detection of double compressed images. In: IEEE International Conference on Acoustics, Speech and Signal Processing, pp. 3053–3057. IEEE (2013)
21. Park, J., Cho, D., Ahn, W., Lee, H.-K.: Double JPEG detection in mixed JPEG quality factors using deep convolutional neural network. In: Ferrari, V., Hebert, M., Sminchisescu, C., Weiss, Y. (eds.) ECCV 2018. LNCS, vol. 11209, pp. 656–672. Springer, Cham (2018). https://doi.org/10.1007/978-3-030-01228-1_39
22. Pevny, T., Fridrich, J.: Detection of double-compression in JPEG images for applications in steganography. IEEE Trans. Inf. Forensics Secur. 3(2), 247–258 (2008)
23. Shang, S., Zhao, Y., Ni, R.: Double JPEG detection using high order statistic features. In: IEEE International Conference on Digital Signal Processing, pp. 550–554. IEEE (2016)
24. Shin, R., Song, D.: JPEG-resistant adversarial images. In: NIPS 2017 Workshop on Machine Learning and Computer Security, vol. 1 (2017)
25. Stamm, M.C., Tjoa, S.K., Lin, W.S., Liu, K.R.: Anti-forensics of JPEG compression. In: IEEE International Conference on Acoustics, Speech and Signal Processing, pp. 1694–1697. IEEE (2010)
26. Sutthiwan, P., Shi, Y.Q.: Anti-forensics of double JPEG compression detection. In: Shi, Y.Q., Kim, H.-J., Perez-Gonzalez, F. (eds.) IWDW 2011. LNCS, vol. 7128, pp. 411–424. Springer, Heidelberg (2012). https://doi.org/10.1007/978-3-642-32205-1_33
27. Wang, J., Wang, H., Li, J., Luo, X., Shi, Y.Q., Jha, S.K.: Detecting double JPEG compressed color images with the same quantization matrix in spherical coordinates. IEEE Trans. Circ. Syst. Video Technol. 30(8), 2736–2749 (2019)
28. Wang, Q., Zhang, R.: Double JPEG compression forensics based on a convolutional neural network. EURASIP J. Inf. Secur. 2016(1), 1–12 (2016)
29. Wang, X., et al.: ESRGAN: enhanced super-resolution generative adversarial networks. In: Leal-Taixé, L., Roth, S. (eds.) ECCV 2018. LNCS, vol. 11133, pp. 63–79. Springer, Cham (2019). https://doi.org/10.1007/978-3-030-11021-5_5
30. Zeng, X., Feng, G., Zhang, X.: Detection of double JPEG compression using modified DenseNet model. Multimed. Tools Appl. 78(7), 8183–8196 (2019). https://doi.org/10.1007/s11042-018-6737-3

Exponential Hashing with Different Penalty for Hamming Space Retrieval

Lifang Wu, Yukun Chen, Wenjin Hu, and Ge Shi[⊠]

Faculty of Information Technology, Beijing University of Technology, Beijing, China

Abstract. Hamming space retrieval enables efficient constant-time search through hash table lookups constructed by hash codes, where in response to each query, all data points within a small given Hamming radius are returned as relevant data. However, in Hamming space retrieval, the search performance of the existed hashing schemes based on linear scan dropped when the length of the hash codes increases. The reason is that the Hamming space becomes very sparse and it is difficult to pull the similar data into the Hamming ball and to push the dissimilar data outside the ball. Currently, the existing deep hashing methods based on hash table lookups pay too much attention to similar samples outside the ball and ignore the learning of dissimilar samples inside the ball, leading to a biased model. In this paper, we introduce discriminatory penalty into the exponential loss functions to optimize the Hamming space, leading to Exponential Hashing with Discriminatory Penalty (EHDP), which discriminately penalizes similar/dissimilar data inside and outside the Hamming ball. Technically, EHDP capitalizes on exponential function to discriminatively encourage similar/dissimilar data approaching/away and to up-weight/down-weight the dissimilar data inside/outside the ball. Extensive experiments demonstrate that the proposed EHDP obtains superior results on three benchmark datasets.

Keywords: Image retrieval · Deep hashing · Hamming space retrieval

1 Introduction

With the rapid development of multimedia technology, massive high-dimensional multimedia information floods the Internet, causing a burden on search engines [6,19,23]. To ensure the efficiency of storage and retrieval of multimedia data, approximate nearest neighbour (ANN) search has been concerned by researchers. As one of the solutions of ANN search, hashing has attracted attention in recent years because of its small storage space and fast matching speed.

With the development of deep neural networks, deep supervised hashing [3,5,16,20] has received continuous attention from academia and industry, which benefits from end-to-end representation learning and hash coding with nonlinear hash functions. With compact hash codes, Hamming space retrieval returns data points whose distance from the query point is less than or equal to

© Springer Nature Switzerland AG 2021
Y. Peng et al. (Eds.): ICIG 2021, LNCS 12888, pp. 772–784, 2021.
https://doi.org/10.1007/978-3-030-87355-4_64

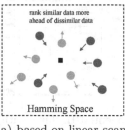
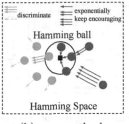

(a) based on linear scan   (b) our method

Fig. 1. Comparison between hashing methods based on linear scan and our method.

the Hamming radius 2 by hash table lookups for constant-time retrieval [2]. The core problem is how to pull more similar samples inside the Hamming ball and to push dissimilar samples outside the ball. In recent years, many hashing methods based on linear scan have achieved excellent performance [3,25]. Their goal is to rank similar data more ahead of dissimilar data, as shown in Fig. 1(a). However, in Hamming space retrieval, the retrieval performance of these methods dropped seriously as the length of the hash codes increases. The reason is that the data distribution becomes sparser [10,21,22], and treating the similar/dissimilar data points equally in the optimization will result in sub-optimal solutions. In other words, it is more difficult to pull similar data into the given Hamming ball and to push dissimilar data outside the ball. To tackle this problem, one natural idea is to penalize samples discriminatively, as shown in Fig. 1(b). On the one hand, discriminate dissimilar samples inside and outside the Hamming ball. On the other hand, keep focusing and concentrating on similar samples so that more similar data can enter into the Hamming ball in high-dimensional space.

Motivated by the above, a novel supervised hash architecture Exponential Hashing with Different Penalty (EHDP) is proposed in this paper as shown in Fig. 2. The penalty with different weights are given to the similar/dissimilar pairs with different hamming distances. More specifically, the similarity-preserving loss function is designed based on the exponential function to penalize for discriminatively encouraging similar(dissimilar) data approaching inside(departing away from) the Hamming ball and exponentially up-weighting/down-weighting the dissimilar data inside/outside the Hamming ball. With the idea of different penalty, EHDP can pay more attention to similar data while keeping dissimilar data away from the ball. The main contributions of this paper are as follows:

1) A novel loss function based on exponential function is designed to optimize Hamming space.

2) The discriminative penalty is proposed to explore how to distinguish similar/dissimilar data for optimizing Hamming space and how to maintain the above two with different priorities in Hamming space optimization.

3) Extensive experiments demonstrate that the proposed EHDP can improve effectiveness of Hamming space retrieval and obtains superior results on three benchmark datasets, MS-COCO, NUS-WIDE and ImageNet.

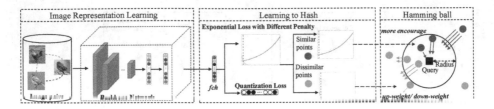

Fig. 2. The architecture of the proposed Exponential Hashing with Discriminatory Penalty (EHDP), which is comprised of two key components: (1) a convolutional neural network for learning high-dimensional representation of each image, (2) the different penalty that discriminatively penalizes similar/dissimilar data inside and outside the Hamming ball, and an l_2 loss for controlling the quantization errors.

2 Related Work

Many deep hashing methods have been proposed over the years. A comprehensive survey can be referred in [17]. We only review some of the methods that are more relevant to this paper.

Deep hashing has received continuous attention from academia and industry due to the excellent performance. DHN [25] jointly preserved the pairwise similarity and reduced quantization errors based on end-to-end framework. Hash-Net [3] improved DHN by up-weighting similar training pairs and actualized low quantization error by using continuation. Benefit from the idea of classification, GreedyHash [16] and CSQ [24] made loss functions to optimize easier and achieve superior performance.

In addition to the above methods designed for linear scan, there are a number of other hash methods used by hash table lookups. DCH [2] proposed a pairwise cross-entropy loss based on Cauchy distribution, which focuses on pulling similar pairs inside the ball but lacks enough push on dissimilar pairs, therefore, the model is biased. MMHH [8] explicitly characterizes the Hamming ball by max-margin t-distribution to focus on the data outside, but neglects the data inside, which limits the retrieval performance. Different from the above previous works, this work capitalizes on exponential function to discriminatively encourage similar/dissimilar data approaching/away and to up-weight/down-weight the dissimilar data inside/outside the ball.

3 Methodology

In this section, we introduce the problem definition. Then, the backbone network and hash layer are presented, followed by our design of Exponential Hashing with Different Penalty. Finally, we summarize the overall objective function.

3.1 Problem Definition

In the image retrieval implementation, we suppose that there are N points $\mathbf{X} = \{\mathbf{x}_i\}_{i=1}^N$ in a training set, where the pairs of x_i and x_j are provided with similarity

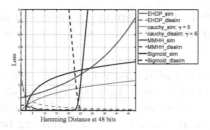

Fig. 3. Loss function compared at 48 bits.

label informations s_{ij} ($s_{ij} = 1$ if x_i and x_j are similar while $s_{ij} = 0$ if they are dissimilar). Deep supervised hashing is to encode data points into compact K-bit binary codes by learning a non-linear hash function $h(x_i) \in \{-1, 1\}^K$ via deep neural networks, so that the binary codes can preserve the similarity information according to the pairwise label matrix $S = \{s_{ij}\}$.

The key challenge of Hamming space retrieval is effectively concentrating similar data points to the Hamming radius $H \leq 2$ while excluding the dissimilar ones from the ball to facilitate pruning. We present EHDP towards this challenge.

3.2 Deep Architecture

The architecture of EHDP is shown as Fig. 2. Like the previous work [8], we replace the classification layer of AlexNet with a fully connected hash layer *fch* of K-dimensional units, which maps the feature representation to K-dimensional continuous value for each image x_i. We acquire binary hash codes by the sign function $b_i = \text{sgn}(u_i)$. Note that we do not add the tanh activation function [7, 14] behind the hash layer due to its saturated region. A novel EHDP model is designed for learning compact and concentrated binary hash codes.

3.3 Exponential Hashing with Different Penalty

As shown in Fig. 3, the hashing method based on the sigmoid function probability with linear scan cannot concentrate enough similar data points within Hamming distance 2, because it is only significantly sensitive at distance $K/2$. As for the Cauchy distribution, its dissimilarity loss exists an infinite point at Hamming distance 0, and its similarity loss accounts for a higher proportion of the total loss at a small distance, which is not conducive to pruning. The max-margin t distribution focuses more on the data pairs outside the Hamming radius 2. However it severely neglects the data inside the margin, which affects the model performance. Moreover, with the increase of training iterations, there will be more similar data points accumulated within the Hamming ball of radius 2. The above methods which encourage small distances for similar pairs with up-weighting, interfere the learning of dissimilar data pairs in Hamming space optimization. This may result in a biased model for Hamming space retrieval.

To address these problems, we propose a novel and simple exponential loss function based on the metric structure with the following properties, which defined as Eq. (1):

- Distinguish the learning of similar and dissimilar data, which means that similarity and dissimilarity losses have different penalty ranges.
- Distinguish different priorities of similar and dissimilar data in Hamming space optimization inside and outside the Hamming ball.

$$
\begin{aligned}
L = \sum_{s_{ij} \in S} & \left(s_{ij} \exp\left(\gamma d\left(b_i, b_j\right)/K \right) \right) + \\
& \sum_{s_{ij} \in S} \left((1 - s_{ij}) \exp\left((H - d\left(b_i, b_j\right))/H \right) \right),
\end{aligned}
\tag{1}
$$

where $H = 2$ is the specified radius of the Hamming ball in Hamming space retrieval, $d\left(b_i, b_j\right)$ is the Hamming distance of a pair of hash codes, K is the length of the hash codes, and γ is the hyper-parameter for controlling the measurement ranges of similarity loss.

We will further explain the loss of design from the following two aspects: the exponential loss function, hyper-parameter γ.

The Exponential Loss Function. The loss function we proposed is based on the exponential function, stemming from the fact that the trend of the exponential loss is more in line with our requirements. As shown in Fig. 3, the similarity loss highly penalizes similar data far from the Hamming radius, while the dissimilarity loss highly penalizes dissimilar data for small distances. Our loss function can pay more attention to difficult samples [6]. In addition, the exponential curve has a certain distinction. For dissimilar curves, our loss function can down-weight/up-weight the inside and outside of the Hamming ball, which is beneficial to the attention of the ball. It should be noted that, unlike the dissimilarity loss, the similarity loss is positive throughout the Hamming space. With the learning of the hash function, more similar data are concentrated inside the Hamming ball. The similarity loss encourages positive and smaller gradients in favor of making the similar data as concentrated as possible, which is conducive to the stability of recall in high dimensional space.

Hyper-Parameter γ. As for the similarity loss, exponential function will increase uncontrollably with the increase of distance. So we adjust the measurement range of similarity loss by using the discrimination factor γ to differentially focus on Hamming space optimization.

3.4   Objective Function

Since the minimization of Equation (1) is a discrete optimization, it is a standard NP-hard problem [6,11]. This kind of problem is usually solved by employing the continuous relaxation $u_i \in \mathbb{R}^{K \times 1}$ instead of b_i. Hence, we need to leverage an approximate distance to replace Hamming distance. Since the cosine distance measures each pair of continuous values on a unit sphere and the discrete Hamming distance $d(b_i, b_j)$ measures each pair of hash codes on a unit hypercube, the cosine distance on continuous value is always the upper bound of the discrete Hamming distance on the hash codes [2]. Therefore, in this paper, the cosine distance is used to approximate this relationship.

$$d(b_i, b_j) = \frac{K}{2}\left(1 - \cos(u_i, u_j)\right), \tag{2}$$

where u_i is the continuous value of each image x_i. To control the quantization error caused by continuous relaxation, we use the l_2 regularization function to control the quantization loss like [1,10,18]:

$$Q = \sum_{i=1}^{n} \|u_i - b_i\|_2^2. \tag{3}$$

According to Eq. (1) and (3), we obtain the objective function of the proposed EHDP as:

$$\min_{\Theta} L + \alpha Q, \tag{4}$$

where Θ represents the network parameter set to be back-propagated, and α is a hyper-parameter to balance between L and Q.

For a query image x_i, we can obtain its hash code directly through forward-propagation by the EHDP model, as follows:

$$b_i = \text{sgn}(u_i). \tag{5}$$

4 Experiments

The proposed EHDP is evaluated on three widely used benchmark datasets: MS-COCO, NUS-WIDE and ImageNet.

4.1 Datasets and Settings

MS-COCO [12] is a multi-label dataset containing 122,218 images, where each image is labeled by several of the 80 semantic concepts. We randomly sample 5,000 images as query set and take the remaining images as the database, from which we randomly sample 10,000 images as the training set.

NUS-WISE [4] is also a multi-label image dataset containing 269, 648 images from the web with the 81 categories. We randomly sample the same size of query and training set as MS-COCO.

ImageNet [15] is a large single-label dataset, containing over 1.2M images in the training set and 50K images in the validation set with 1000 categories. We randomly select 100 categories in the training set for retrieval database and in the validation set as query, like the setting in [2,8]. What's more, 130 images from each category in the database are randomly sampled for the training.

The proposed EHDP is compared with five state-of-the-art deep supervised hashing methods: DHN [25], DSH [13], HashNet [3], DCH [2], CSQ [24]. According to the evaluation protocol [2,8], we evaluate the performance of pruning by Recall and Precision within Hamming radius 2 ($R@H \leq 2$, $P@H \leq 2$). In order to evaluate the performance of Hamming space retrieval in a balanced way, we use F1 score to measure the retrieval performance. We also adopt the widely used mean average precision (mAP) to measure the accuracy of our method and other competitors.

The scheme is implemented based on the **PyTorch** framework and the AlexNet architecture [9] is adopted as the backbone for all comparison methods. The learning rate of the hash layer fch is set to 10 times over that of the other layers'. We set the mini-batch size as 128 and use Root Mean Square prop (RMSprop) as the optimizer with a weight decay of 0.00001. We select the hyper-parameters of our EHDP $\gamma = 4$ and $\alpha = 0.01$ by grid search. In addition, all experiments are conducted five times using different random seeds and the mean value is reported.

4.2   Result

Result on Multi-label Datasets

Precision and Recall. We provide $R@H \leq 2$ and $P@H \leq 2$ of EHDP and compared methods in Fig. 4 to evaluate the performance of Hamming space retrieval. As shown in Fig. 4, DHN and HashNet with the sigmoid function have $R@H \leq 2$ drop rapidly when the hash code length increases to 32 bits or more. This indicates that they cannot effectively aggregate similar data in the Hamming ball, and the sigmoid function may not be suitable for Hamming space retrieval. Thanks to the classification idea, CSQ has high $P@H \leq 2$. However the $R@H \leq 2$ is low on the multi-label datasets, which may be related to the determination method of CSQ's hash center on the multi-label datasets. The performance of EHDP is significantly higher than all competitors, especially the $R@H \leq 2$ in the high-dimensional Hamming space. This is due to the positive similarity loss throughout the Hamming space and the effect of γ.

F1 Score. For Hamming space retrieval, $R@H \leq 2$ and $P@H \leq 2$ are equally important. In order to compare the retrieval performance of different methods in a balanced way, we use the F1 score, as shown in Table 1. The F1 scores of our method are significantly higher than those of other methods in all datasets. It shows that EHDP can discriminately encourage similar/dissimilar data concentrating/away and exponentially up-weight/down-weight the dissimilar data inside/outside the Hamming ball. This further illustrates that it is effective to use the exponential function to focus on similar data using hyper-parameter γ and distinguish dissimilar data inside and outside the Hamming radius 2.

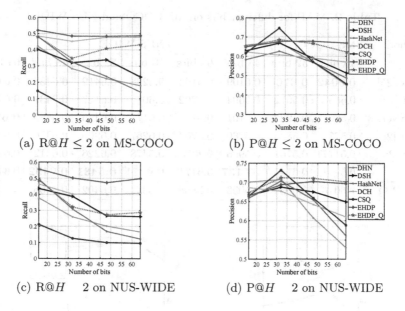

(a) R@$H \leq 2$ on MS-COCO

(b) P@$H \leq 2$ on MS-COCO

(c) R@H 2 on NUS-WIDE

(d) P@H 2 on NUS-WIDE

Fig. 4. R@$H \leq 2$ and P@$H \leq 2$ with different bits on MS-COCO and NUS-WIDE.

Table 1. F1 score for different bits on MS-COCO and NUS-WIDE.

Method	MS-COCO				NUS-WIDE			
	16 bits	32 bits	48 bits	64 bits	16 bits	32 bits	48 bits	64 bits
DHN [25]	0.4659	0.3414	0.2812	0.2350	0.4441	0.3270	0.2541	0.2101
DSH [13]	0.4347	0.3604	0.3665	0.2846	0.4816	0.4299	0.3361	0.3245
HashNet [3]	0.4714	0.3711	0.2879	0.1953	0.5182	0.3726	0.2287	0.1658
DCH [2]	0.4883	0.4483	0.4593	0.4553	0.5175	0.4539	0.4525	0.4542
CSQ [24]	0.1998	0.0517	0.0413	0.0363	0.2633	0.1575	0.1251	0.1188
EHDP	**0.5216**	**0.4871**	**0.4813**	**0.4830**	**0.5673**	**0.5306**	**0.5123**	**0.5303**
EHDP-Q	0.4963	0.3821	0.4255	0.4408	0.5249	0.3961	0.3456	0.3566

MAP. The mAP results of all methods are listed in Table 2. Compared with other methods, EHDP can achieve close or even higher accuracy, especially on the imbalanced dataset ImageNet. Please note that our EHDP is used for Hamming space retrieval. It indicates that the proposed method does not reduce the accuracy and the sorting ability of the whole space. This is attributed to the exponential function of the curve against a harder sample with a higher gradient.

Result on Imbalanced Dataset

Precision and Recall. As shown in Fig. 5, we provide R@$H \leq 2$ and P@$H \leq 2$ of all methods on ImageNet, a single-label and imbalanced dataset. The recall

Table 2. MAP for different bits on MS-COCO and NUS-WIDE.

Method	MS-COCO				NUS-WIDE			
	16 bits	32 bits	48 bits	64 bits	16 bits	32 bits	48 bits	64 bits
DHN [25]	**0.6042**	**0.6765**	0.6109	0.6104	0.6228	0.6412	0.6458	0.6468
DSH [13]	0.5651	0.5672	0.5694	0.5792	0.6075	0.6177	0.6431	0.6421
HashNet [3]	0.5607	0.5922	0.6101	0.6119	0.6171	0.6426	0.6485	**0.6735**
DCH [2]	0.5774	0.5836	0.5760	0.5704	0.6261	0.6300	0.6376	0.6395
CSQ [24]	0.5177	0.5761	0.5995	**0.6278**	0.5478	0.6226	0.6312	0.6554
EHDP	0.5981	0.6145	**0.6137**	0.6171	**0.6371**	**0.6431**	**0.6492**	0.6433
EHDP-Q	0.6016	0.6039	0.6053	0.5858	0.6337	0.6402	0.6406	0.6362

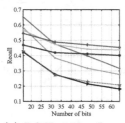

(a) R@$H \leq 2$ on ImageNet

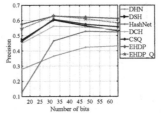

(b) P@$H \leq 2$ on ImageNet

Fig. 5. R@$H \leq 2$ and P@$H \leq 2$ with different bits on ImageNet.

Table 3. F1 score and mAP for different bits on ImageNet.

Method	F1 score				mAP			
	16 bits	32 bits	48 bits	64 bits	16 bits	32 bits	48 bits	64 bits
DHN [25]	0.3519	0.3085	0.3095	0.2966	0.3431	0.3198	0.3740	0.4216
DSH [13]	0.4349	0.3402	0.2719	0.2359	0.4277	0.5234	0.5377	0.5522
HashNet [3]	0.1705	0.4302	0.4174	0.3627	0.2730	0.4817	0.5563	0.5780
DCH [2]	0.4828	0.4827	0.4598	0.4523	0.5178	0.5595	0.5547	0.5549
CSQ [24]	0.4509	0.4729	0.4596	0.4559	0.4699	0.5533	0.5744	**0.6008**
EHDP	**0.5511**	**0.5310**	**0.5143**	**0.4983**	**0.5470**	**0.6034**	**0.5986**	0.6005
EHDP-Q	0.4666	0.3386	0.2930	0.2664	0.4658	0.5588	0.5799	0.5706

of EHDP is slightly ahead of its competitors in high-dimensional space, and its precision outperforms DCH by 8.3% on average. Please note that we do not use the imbalanced parameter w_{ij}. The above experimental results indicate that our hyper-parameter γ and positive similarity loss can play a role in the extremely imbalanced dataset, ensuring that the recall is higher than the other methods and greatly improving the precision.

F1 Score and MAP. Table 3 shows the excellent F1 score and mAP results of our EHDP on ImageNet. This indicates that EHDP achieves higher comprehensive retrieval performance in Hamming space retrieval on ImageNet. In addition, compared to CSQ, the mAP performance of EHDP achieves absolute increases of 3.8% on average across all four bits. This proves that the proposed exponential loss against a hard sample with a high gradient can further improve the accuracy and the sorting ability of the whole space.

Table 4. The ratios of returning **zero** images for all methods in different datasets with 64 bits.

dataset	DHN [25]	DSH [13]	HashNet [3]	DCH [2]	CSQ [24]	EHDP	EHDP_Q
MS-COCO	53.1%	40.2%	48.7%	18.3%	51.7%	**2.9%**	10.6%
NUS-WIDE	40.9%	21.8%	36.7%	21.3%	32.2%	**1.6%**	5.8%
ImageNet	35.4%	34.1%	33.1%	18.0%	33.5%	**11.2%**	28.9%

Effectiveness of Hamming Space Retrieval. In Hamming space retrieval, it is possible to retrieve zero images for many queries especially when the length of the hash codes increases. As shown in Table 4, we provide the ratios of returning **zero** images for all methods in different datasets with 64 bits. Compared with DCH, according to Fig. 4(a), 4(c), 5(a) and Table 4, EHDP achieves higher recalls and only 2.9%,1.6%,11.2% queries return zero images on MS-COCO, NUS-WIDE and ImageNet, which proves that EHDP is more effective than DCH.

4.3 Ablation Study

EHDP-Q is the EHDP variant without using the l_2 loss (Equation (4)), i.e., $\alpha = 0$. From Fig. 4, Table 1, Table 2 and Table 3, EHDP outperforms EHDP-Q by huge margins of 5.7%, 12.9% and 18.2% in average F1 score on MS-COCO, NUS-WIDE and ImageNet, respectively. EHDP-Q incurs the ratios of returning **zero** images increases of 7.7%, 4.2% and 17.7% on three datasets with 64 bits. This result verifies that the l_2 loss can aggregate relevant data effectively into Hamming ball and testifies the necessity of controlling the quantization error.

4.4 Sensitivity to Hyper-Parameter

We conduct experiments to test the sensitivity of the α parameter and γ parameter towards search performance. Figure 6 compares the F1 score and mAP for EHDP with different α and γ using 16 bits and 64 bits on ImageNet.

With the increase of α, both the F1 score and mAP increase at first and then drop rapidly. When the length of the hash codes is 16 bits, the F1 score and mAP also increase first and then decrease as γ increases. While using 64 bits hash code, the best results of which γ equals 4, 6, and 8 are close. To these points, we select $\gamma = 4$ and $\alpha = 0.01$.

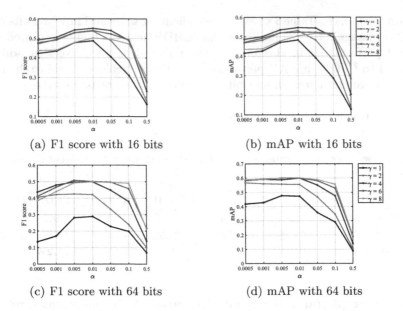

(a) F1 score with 16 bits   (b) mAP with 16 bits

(c) F1 score with 64 bits   (d) mAP with 64 bits

Fig. 6. Sensitivity study for EHDP using 16 bits and 64 bits on ImageNet.

5   Conclusion

We presented Exponential Hashing with Different Penalty (EHDP), which is able to obtain effective hash codes for Hamming space retrieval. This is thanks to the exponential functions designed to penalize for discriminatively encouraging similar (dissimilar) data approaching inside (departing away from) the Hamming ball and the exponentially up-weighting/down-weighting the dissimilar data inside/outside the Hamming ball. Extensive experiments conducted on three benchmark datasets demonstrate that the proposed EHDP with Different Penalty could partially resolve the problem of data sparse.

In the future, we will explore how to more fully express complex semantic information by one hash code on multi-label datasets. Besides, we will study to experiment with the impact of noisy datasets.

Acknowledgments. This work was supported in part by Beijing Municipal Education Committee Science Foundation (KM201910005024), Beijing Postdoctoral Research Fundation (Q6042001202101).

References

1. Cao, Y., Liu, B., Long, M., Wang, J.: Cross-modal hamming hashing. In: ECCV, pp. 202–218 (2018)
2. Cao, Y., Long, M., Liu, B., Wang, J.: Deep Cauchy hashing for hamming space retrieval. In: CVPR, pp. 1229–1237 (2018)

3. Cao, Z., Long, M., Wang, J., Yu, P.S.: HashNet: deep learning to hash by continuation. In: ICCV, pp. 5608–5617 (2017)
4. Chua, T.S., Tang, J., Hong, R., Li, H., Luo, Z., Zheng, Y.: Nus-wide: a real-world web image database from national university of Singapore. In: ICMR, pp. 1–9 (2009)
5. Fu, H., Li, Y., Zhang, H., Liu, J., Yao, T.: Rank-embedded hashing for large-scale image retrieval. In: ICMR, pp. 563–570 (2020)
6. Hu, W., Wu, L., Jian, M., Chen, Y., Yu, H.: Cosine metric supervised deep hashing with balanced similarity. Neurocomputing **448**, 94–105 (2021)
7. Jiang, Q.Y., Li, W.J.: Asymmetric deep supervised hashing. In: AAAI, vol. 32 (2018)
8. Kang, R., Cao, Y., Long, M., Wang, J., Yu, P.S.: Maximum-margin hamming hashing. In: ICCV, pp. 8252–8261 (2019)
9. Krizhevsky, A., Sutskever, I., Hinton, G.E.: ImageNet classification with deep convolutional neural networks. In: NeurIPS, pp. 1097–1105 (2012)
10. Li, Q., Sun, Z., He, R., Tan, T.: Deep supervised discrete hashing. In: NeurIPS, pp. 2482–2491 (2017)
11. Lin, M., Ji, R., Liu, H., Sun, X., Wu, Y., Wu, Y.: Towards optimal discrete online hashing with balanced similarity. In: AAAI, vol. 33, pp. 8722–8729 (2019)
12. Lin, T.-Y., et al.: Microsoft COCO: common objects in context. In: Fleet, D., Pajdla, T., Schiele, B., Tuytelaars, T. (eds.) ECCV 2014. LNCS, vol. 8693, pp. 740–755. Springer, Cham (2014). https://doi.org/10.1007/978-3-319-10602-1_48
13. Liu, H., Wang, R., Shan, S., Chen, X.: Deep supervised hashing for fast image retrieval. In: CVPR, pp. 2064–2072 (2016)
14. Liu, H., Wang, R., Shan, S., Chen, X.: Learning multifunctional binary codes for both category and attribute oriented retrieval tasks. In: CVPR, pp. 3901–3910 (2017)
15. Russakovsky, O., et al.: ImageNet large scale visual recognition challenge. IJCV **115**(3), 211–252 (2015)
16. Su, S., Zhang, C., Han, K., Tian, Y.: Greedy hash: towards fast optimization for accurate hash coding in CNN. In: NeurIPS, pp. 798–807 (2018)
17. Wang, J., Zhang, T., Sebe, N., Shen, H.T., et al.: A survey on learning to hash. TPAMI **40**(4), 769–790 (2017)
18. Wang, W., Shen, Y., Zhang, H., Yao, Y., Liu, L.: Set and rebase: determining the semantic graph connectivity for unsupervised cross modal hashing. In: IJCAI, pp. 853–859 (2020)
19. Wang, Y., Sun, Z.: Towards joint multiply semantics hashing for visual search. In: Zhao, Y., Barnes, N., Chen, B., Westermann, R., Kong, X., Lin, C. (eds.) ICIG 2019. LNCS, vol. 11903, pp. 47–58. Springer, Cham (2019). https://doi.org/10.1007/978-3-030-34113-8_5
20. Weng, Z., Zhu, Y.: Online hashing with efficient updating of binary codes. In: AAAI, vol. 34, pp. 12354–12361 (2020)
21. Xie, Y., Liu, Y., Wang, Y., Gao, L., Wang, P., Zhou, K.: Label-attended hashing for multi-label image retrieval. In: IJCAI, pp. 955–962 (2020)
22. Yan, C., Pang, G., Bai, X., Shen, C., Zhou, J., Hancock, E.: Deep hashing by discriminating hard examples. In: MM, pp. 1535–1542. ACM (2019)
23. Yang, G., Miao, H., Tang, J., Liang, D., Wang, N.: Multi-kernel hashing with semantic correlation maximization for cross-modal retrieval. In: Zhao, Y., Kong, X., Taubman, D. (eds.) ICIG 2017. LNCS, vol. 10666, pp. 23–34. Springer, Cham (2017). https://doi.org/10.1007/978-3-319-71607-7_3

24. Yuan, L., et al.: Central similarity quantization for efficient image and video retrieval. In: CVPR, pp. 3083–3092 (2020)
25. Zhu, H., Long, M., Wang, J., Cao, Y.: Deep hashing network for efficient similarity retrieval. In: AAAI, vol. 30 (2016)

A Controllable Image Steganography with Chaos and User Key

Jianyi Liu, Yuhan Wang, Zhen Yang$^{(\boxtimes)}$, Ruifan Zhang, and Ru Zhang

School of Cyber Space Security,
Beijing University of Posts and Telecommunications, Beijing 100876, China
yangzhenyz@bupt.edu.cn

Abstract. In recent years, the steganography of images has been greatly developed. In the existing image steganography algorithms, users cannot participate in the encryption process and cannot fully trust the steganography process. Therefore, this paper hopes to increase the importance of user roles in the steganography process so that it can control the hiding process. This paper is based on the classic F5 algorithm to improve, to achieve user participation, so that users can control the embedding position of secret information. At the same time, in response to the traditional methods of cracking the F5 algorithm and steganographic keys, chaos technology is incorporated on the basis of the original algorithm to jointly improve the overall security of the algorithm. This paper can effectively solve the problem of lack of user participation and security guarantee in existing steganography algorithms. This has important theoretical and practical significance for the application of steganography technology.

Keywords: Image steganography · Chaos technology · Key control · F5 algorithm

1 Introduction

Steganography is a key branch of information hiding technology. In the Fig. 1, the prisoners Alice and Bob, who are being held in two different cells, want to discuss the escape through information exchange under the continuous supervision of the guard Wendy. In order to successfully complete the escape, it is necessary to communicate without attracting the attention and suspicion of the guardian Wendy. Therefore, Alice and Bob came up with a way to hide secret information in irrelevant information, and then transmit it through open channels to achieve covert communication and exchange useful information. During this period, Wendy can see the content of the interactive information, but if the hiding effect is good, Wendy will only think that the information is normal, and will not find the hidden content. This is the meaning of the "prisoner model".

© Springer Nature Switzerland AG 2021
Y. Peng et al. (Eds.): ICIG 2021, LNCS 12888, pp. 785–797, 2021.
https://doi.org/10.1007/978-3-030-87355-4_65

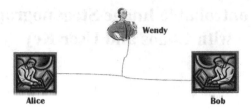

Fig. 1. Prisoner model

The specific realization of steganography is shown in Fig. 2, which constitutes the model of steganography as a whole. The model is mainly composed of two parts: the embedding and extraction of secret information. The whole model can perfectly realize the covert communication of secret information. Theoretically, any carrier with redundant information space can be used to hide secret information inside, such as image [1, 2], audio [3, 4], text [5, 6]and so on [7, 8]. Images are also one of the most commonly used and most important information carriers in human life.

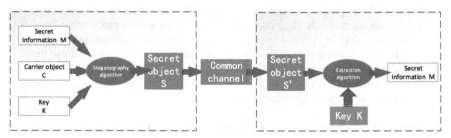

Fig. 2. The process of covert communication is that the sender inputs the selected carrier object C, secret information M and the key K previously negotiated with the receiver into the steganographic algorithm system, and embedding the secret information into the carrier by some steganographic method. Output the secret object S containing secret information, and put the secret object S into the public channel for transmission. During this time, S is visible to all, may undergo steganographic analysis. Natural effects cause distortion or data loss, so the encrypted object received by the receiver is represented here as S'. The receiver inputs S' and key K into the extraction algorithm. After the extraction process, the output secret information M can be obtained, so as to complete the covert communication.

There have been many research results on the steganography of images. This paper optimizes and improves the F5 algorithm in the frequency domain steganography algorithm. Combined with the purpose of increasing user participation in the steganography process and improving the security of the steganography algorithm itself, it designs and implements a method that can be used by users. Controlled, security-enhanced image information hiding algorithm to complete the work of embedding the secret information of each carrier image. This paper is conducive to solving the key issues in batch steganography and user-controllable steganography algorithms, and provides a certain theoretical basis and practical significance for the application of this idea in more fields in life, society and so on.

2 Related Work

To design a secure controllable steganography algorithm, we need to know corresponding research about controllable steganography for user participation control and chaos technology for secure information hiding.

2.1 Controllable Steganography

There are few research materials on information hiding systems that users can participate in. Qu [9] propose CFRQI is able to effectively help the sender control the whole process of information transmission for better information security. Yuwei [10] proposes a QR code security authentication technology combining information hiding and visual secret sharing, which can be applied to user information transmission and identity authentication. Yang [11] proposes to build an adaptive multi-modal information hiding system. The input of the system adds the concept of "secret level". For input control, the system adaptively selects a suitable one from the algorithm library containing five known steganographic algorithms based on the secret level represented by the number entered by the user and the length of the secret information and other related information under the action of the selection function. Algorithm, and then embed secret information. So as to achieve the purpose of users participating in the information hiding process.

The existing literature only added the user's control to the choice of the final steganography algorithm, and did not make the user really participate in the specific information embedding part. Therefore, in order to give users more security in the information hiding process and truly increase their participation in embedding, it is more necessary to design and research an information hiding algorithm that allows users to control the embedding position of secret information.

2.2 Chaos Technology

As early as 1954, the former Soviet Union's A.N. Kolmogorov mathematician, in the study of the origin of probability, first described the KAM theory, and clearly proposed that in addition to the dissipative system can produce chaos, conservative systems can also produce chaos [12]. With the deepening of research, researchers have been able to reasonably explain the phenomenon of chaos, and have found effective means to control chaotic dynamic system and make use of chaotic characteristics.

The chaotic system contains a variety of chaotic maps. One-dimensional Logistic chaotic mapping is widely used because of its good performance and simple structure. It has the advantages of good ergodicity and high sensitivity to initial values [13].The mathematical expression used to describe the Logistic mapping can be represented as follows:

$$x_{n+1} = \mu x_n (1 - x_n) \tag{1}$$

When the value of μ is 4, the logistic equation is:

$$x_{n+1} = 4x_n (1 - x_n) \tag{2}$$

At this time, the Logistic mapping can reach the surjective state, that is, the independent variable and the variable are both in the interval (0,1). Moreover, an approximate
uniform pseudo-random distribution characteristic can be presented in this interval,
which means that the distribution of the chaotic sequence generated by the Logistic
mapping has better ergodicity. The probability density function at this time is:

$$\rho(x) = \begin{cases} \frac{1}{\pi\sqrt{x(1-x)}}, & 0 < x < 1 \\ 0, & other \end{cases} \tag{3}$$

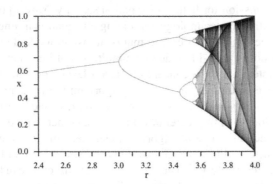

Fig. 3. Logistic map bifurcation diagram.

As shown in the Fig. 3, when $\mu \in (3.56994567, 4]$, the generated sequence is a chaotic
sequence, which can be used in pseudo-random number generation, image encryption,
etc. In order for Logistic mapping to be applied more securely, two limitations should
be noted condition:

The inverted branch phenomenon occurs when μ is in the interval of [3.56994567,
3.678573). Although the sequence generated by the Logistic mapping at this time is in
a chaotic state, it does not have better randomness. Therefore, the value of the system
parameter μ falls within the interval of [3.678573, 4] to have a better effect.

If the initial value of the system x_0 is set to 0, 1, $1/\mu$, $1-1/\mu$, the subsequent logistic
sequence will also only change from 0, 1, $1/\mu$, $1-1/$ These values are composed of μ, so
the initial value x_0 of the Logistic chaotic system cannot be these four values.

2.3 DCT Coefficient Scrambling Method

In the F5 algorithm, the DCT coefficients need to be scrambled before the secret information is embedded. The scrambling method uses the user's input as a seed, inputs
it into the pseudo-random number generator to generate a pseudo-random sequence,
and then generates a pseudo-random sequence according to the label Perform position
replacement of DCT coefficients. After research, it is found that most of the existing F5
algorithms use statistical pseudo-random number generators, and most of them are linear
and cycle dependent on the initial value. Although such methods are easy to implement

and fast, the output results are relatively easy to predict. Other pseudo-random sequence generation methods take a long time to initialize. After three tests, the average value is 466 s, which affects the entire steganography time to a certain extent. Therefore, on this basis, in order to improve the security of the scrambling and ensure the uniformity of the scrambling, a chaotic scrambling method is introduced to replace the original scrambling method.

This paper refers to the position scrambling in chaos scrambling, and uses the popular Logistic mapping method to generate pseudo-random number sequences, thereby scrambling DCT coefficients. However, this paper does not directly use the original Logistic mapping method. This is because its probability density function does not obey a uniform distribution, so the generated chaotic sequence is also not uniform, so it is impossible to guarantee that all DCT coefficients can wait for possible positions. Replacement, so that the purpose of uniform distribution of secret information cannot be achieved. Therefore, first homogenize the Logistic mapping.

From the previous introduction, we know that in logistic mapping, when the system parameter μ belongs to $3.56994567 < \mu \leq 4$. In this range, a state of chaos is reached. And when $\mu = 4$, the probability density of logistic mapping is (3). If the random variable x is transformed into a random variable y:

$$y = \frac{2}{\pi}\arcsin\sqrt{x} \qquad (4)$$

At this time, the random variable y is uniformly distributed on (0,1). Therefore, the random variables in the chaotic sequence are processed and transformed according to (4) to generate a sequence of y, which is a uniformly distributed random sequence. The effect of homogenization is shown in the Fig. 4.

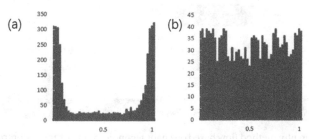

Fig. 4. Frequency map before and after logistic mapping homogenization. (a) is the frequency map before homogenization. (b) is the frequency map after homogenization

It can be seen that the homogenization effect is better. Next, we discusses the specific scrambling implementation process. Assuming that the size of the image is M × N, first multiply all the values of the y sequence by the size of the image to enlarge and round to generate a random sequence with an interval of [1, M × N], generate a chaotic pseudo-random sequence, and replace it accordingly The location of the DCT coefficients (Fig. 5).

Fig. 5. The recovery effect of reverse scrambling after chaotic scrambling of DCT coefficients. The image effect after reverse scrambling is shown in (a). In the case of floating-point number type conversion and rounding, repeated integers appear in the final sequence, which increases the judgment conditions. The improved effect is shown in (b). Because many values have no control boundary during iteration, they exceed [1, M × N], resulting in invalid replacement. After controlling the boundary, it is embedded and restored after scrambling, as shown in (c).

3   User-Controllable Steganography

In the existing information hiding process, users hardly participate, so ordinary users cannot confirm the security of the hiding technology. This article intends to hide information under the control of the user. The information hiding method adopted is a matrix embedding method, which is based on the improvement and expansion of the F5 algorithm. The first thing to do is to replace the original scrambling method with chaotic scrambling to improve security, and then introduce user control into the core part of the secret information embedded in the steganography algorithm, so that the user can control the embedding position of the secret information in the carrier. Figure 6 shows the flow of the steganography algorithm based on chaos technology and user key control.

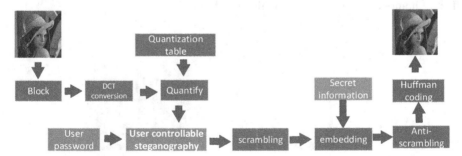

Fig. 6. Steganography method flow based on chaos technology and user key control and extraction methods are reciprocal

3.1   Embedding Algorithm

In the F5 algorithm, the values of k and n used for matrix coding can be calculated according to the length of the secret information and the steganographic capacity of the carrier, thereby generating the embedded matrix$H_{k \times n}$. Among them, according to the hash function of F5, it can be found that when the values of k and n are fixed, the composition of the matrix $H_{k \times n}$ is determined and unique. The form of this matrix is:

each column is composed of unique The composition of 0 and 1 is completely arranged (except for all zeros) and arranged in ascending order. For example, when $k = 2$ and $n = 3$, the only certain form of the embedding matrix is: $\begin{pmatrix} 0 & 1 & 1 \\ 1 & 0 & 1 \end{pmatrix}$. Multiply this matrix by the carrier sequence to the left, and then XOR with the secret information to calculate a position (or none) in the carrier that needs to be modified. Then make changes. Since the embedding position is calculated by the matrix, if you use different matrices to calculate the results will be different, so the embedding position may not be the only fixed, increasing the difficulty of the attacker to crack, so think of the matrix exchange Way to generate a new matrix, which can achieve the goal and ensure the calculation efficiency. After that, the subsequent steps are continued to complete the embedding work, and the generation of the new matrix forms a mapping relationship with the user key, so that the user can control the steganography.

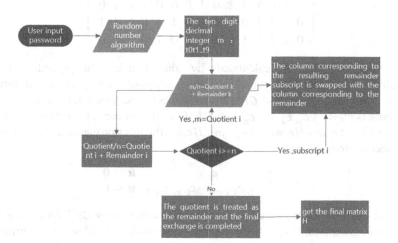

Fig. 7. Steganographic matrix generation algorithm. The process of generating a unique corresponding matrix H applied to the embedding of secret information according to the password input by the user.

The specific matrix generation algorithm is shown in Fig. 7. As can be seen from Fig. 7, the process of generating a unique corresponding matrix H applied to the embedding of secret information according to the password entered by the user. Specifically, the user password is input into the random number algorithm to generate a ten-digit decimal integer $T(t_0 t_1 \ldots t_9)$, k/n obtains the quotient 0 and Remainder 0. For the remainder, subscript the obtained remainder The corresponding column is exchanged with the column corresponding to the remainder. For quotient, when quotient > n, continue to use quotient/n, and get the remainder and repeat the above operation. Until the quotient result < n, treat the quotient as the remainder before, and complete the last column transformation. Get the final embedding matrix H, and participate in the subsequent embedding work. Take the example of $k = 3$ to observe the change of the matrix:

$$
\begin{pmatrix} 0 & 0 & 0 & 1 & 1 & 1 & 1 \\ 0 & 1 & 1 & 0 & 0 & 1 & 1 \\ 1 & 0 & 1 & 0 & 1 & 0 & 1 \end{pmatrix} \rightarrow \begin{pmatrix} 0 & 0 & 0 & 1 & 1 & 1 & 1 \\ 1 & 1 & 0 & 0 & 0 & 1 & 1 \\ 1 & 0 & 1 & 0 & 1 & 0 & 1 \end{pmatrix}
$$

The matrix on the left in (4–2) represents the matrix used by the F5 algorithm, and the matrix on the right represents the embedded matrix generated by the simulation user through random selection of the key, and the different colors represent the two columns where the user key control changes.

This part is extracted from the entire steganography algorithm for effect display, taking k = 4, assuming that the input key is a 32-digit number: 32145687845612312345678876 543211, the corresponding large integer is 2065750248, and the user control matrix generation algorithm is used to obtain The subsequent matrix used for embedding is specifically:

$$
\begin{pmatrix} 0 & 0 & 0 & 1 & 0 & 0 & 0 & 1 & 1 & 1 & 1 & 1 & 1 & 1 & 0 \\ 1 & 1 & 0 & 1 & 1 & 1 & 0 & 1 & 0 & 0 & 0 & 1 & 0 & 1 & 0 \\ 0 & 1 & 1 & 1 & 0 & 1 & 0 & 0 & 0 & 1 & 1 & 0 & 0 & 1 & 1 \\ 0 & 1 & 1 & 1 & 1 & 0 & 1 & 1 & 1 & 0 & 1 & 0 & 0 & 0 & 0 \end{pmatrix}
$$

According to the H calculated by the matrix, the specific way of embedding the secret information is: suppose the secret information is: $m^T = (m_1, m_2, \ldots m_k) \in GF^k(2)$, The lowest bit sequence of the available n DCT coefficients is $c^T = (c_1, c_2, \ldots c_n) \in GF^n(2)$, that is the carrier. First, the bitwise XOR operation of m and Hc, we get $u = m \oplus Hc, u$ is the location that needs to be modified, and the secret information is:

$$
c' = \begin{cases} c, & u = 0 \\ (c_1, c_2, \ldots, \neg c_i, \ldots c_n), & u = i \end{cases}
$$

For the modified encrypted data, it is judged whether a new DCT coefficient with a value of 0 is generated. If not, repeat the previous steps until all secret information is embedded. If so, the embedding operation is invalid. Reselect n available (non-zero AC) DCT coefficients (including a new available AC coefficient and n-1 AC coefficients that have not changed in the previous embedding), and embed again.

Integrating the above embedding methods, summarizing the overall process of the steganography algorithm proposed in this paper, it can be summarized as follows:

1) Block the digital image into multiple non-overlapping 8*8-pixel blocks
2) Perform DCT transformation on each pixel in each block
3) Use the standard quantization table for quantization to obtain DCT quantization coefficients
4) According to the password input by the user, initialize the logistic sequence and perform operations such as homogenization, and then realize the position scrambling of the DCT quantization coefficients.
5) According to the length of the secret information to be embedded and the steganographic capacity of the carrier, the parameter k is calculated, and then the code word length $n = 2^k - 1$.

6) According to the values of k and n, an initial matrix $H_{k \times n}$ is generated, and then according to the above-mentioned user control strategy, a uniquely determined true embedding matrix is generated according to the user's password.
7) For the scrambled DCT coefficients, a user-controllable matrix coding method is used to embed secret information.
8) Inverse scrambling and inverse chaos deduce the order of DCT coefficients.
9) Continue to perform Huffman encoding to obtain a JPEG file, and output the encrypted image.

3.2 Extraction Algorithm

The extraction algorithm and the embedding algorithm exist as a pair, which is a process of inverse operation. When extracting, the secret information can be obtained by left multiplying the secret sequence c' with the embedded matrix H, which is consistent with the basic F5 algorithm. This is because, in this algorithm, the new matrix used in the embedding part is obtained by multiple column exchanges based on the check matrix in F5, which is equivalent to the ascending matrix with the same number of rows and columns used in the F5 algorithm Right multiplied by multiple elementary matrices (consisting of 0, 1), That is $H_{new} = H_{F5}M$. According to the associative law, M is the 0, 1 matrix of rank n obtained by multiplying multiple elementary matrices. In the embedding process, $H_{new}c$ is equivalent to multiplying H_{F5} with a sequence of carrier sequence rearrangement (Mc). Therefore, the embedding method is essentially the same as F5. When extracting, it is equivalent to scrambling the carrier sequence first, and then extracting the secret information with the original matrix of the F5 algorithm. So Hc' can get the secret information by inverse operation.

4 Experiment

4.1 Performance Analysis of Steganography Method Based on Chaos Technology and User Key Control

The algorithm proposed in this paper only transforms the columns of the embedded matrix in the F5 algorithm multiple times, and the corresponding only is that the calculated position where the secret information needs to be embedded is different from F5, so the embedding efficiency of the two algorithms is the same. In this paper, five images are used to embed secret information using the F5 algorithm and the algorithm

Table 1. Comparison of embedding efficiency

Algorithm	Image				
	a	b	c	d	e
F5	1	2	2	1	1
Ours	1	2	2	1	1

proposed in this paper. The quality factor of control compression is 80, and the size of the secret information is 6KB of the same content. In general, the larger k is, the higher the embedding efficiency is, and the same k represents the same embedding efficiency. The experimental results are shown in Table 1. This experiment randomly selects five images from the BOSSbase_1.01 data set for performance test experiments.

In order to achieve the embedding effect, this paper chooses the peak signal-to-noise ratio of the images before and after the steganography of the two algorithms for comparison. The experiment still uses the same test picture, and the secret information and other settings are also consistent with the embedding efficiency experiment. The experimental results are shown in Table 2.

Specifically, it can be seen from Table 2 and Fig. 8 that after the two algorithms are steganographic under the same conditions, there is little difference in the value of the peak signal-to-noise ratio, indicating that the algorithm proposed in this paper has a similar effect on image distortion as F5.

Table 2. Embedding effect (PSNR) comparison

Algorithm	Image				
	a	b	c	d	e
F5	42.0504	44.7973	36.8378	43.0897	41.0311
Ours	42.2951	43.8326	38.0522	44.6390	42.0024

In summary, by comparing the experimental data, it can be shown that the experiment in this paper has little effect on the embedding efficiency, embedding effect and running time of the F5 algorithm. The analysis in the following two subsections can prove that the algorithm proposed in this paper is better than the F5 algorithm in other aspects. Significantly improved, without affecting the performance of the other, so it can reflect the advantages of the algorithm in this paper.

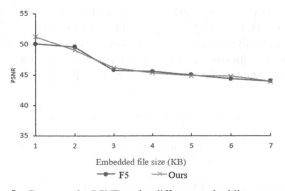

Fig. 8. Compare the PSNR under different embedding amounts

4.2 Security Analysis of Key and Key Space

The key is used both in the chaotic scrambling of DCT coefficients and in the controlling the embedding position of secret information by the user. For the chaotic scrambling part, we uses logistic mapping, and the initial conditions in logistic can be set as the key. Our key consists of 16 or 32 characters or numbers, each of them can be represent by a 8-bit binary number. The initial value x_0 is calculated as follows:

$$x_0 = \sum_{i=1}^{16 or 32} \sum_{j=0}^{8} k_{ij} \times 2^{j-1} \Big/ 2^{256} mod\ 1 \qquad (6)$$

Among them, k_{ij} represents j-th bit number or character of the i-th key.

Therefore, the key is 128-bit or 256-bit, that is, the key space of the algorithm in this paper is 2^{128} or 2^{256}, which is much larger than 2^{100}, so the key space is large enough to effectively resist exhaustive attacks and is safe.

Regarding the sensitivity analysis of the key, for the same image $test.jpg$ (512×512), the same secret information and the same quality factor (80) are specified. This paper does an experiment, input the key twice separately to ensure that the values mapped to the (0,1) interval are 0.351236591 and 0.351236592, and the accuracy difference is 10^{-9}. The effect of intercepting DCT coefficient scrambling for the same area is shown in Fig. 9.

In order to observe the sensitivity of the key more intuitively, the DCT coefficient position sequence generated by the scrambling corresponding to the two keys is made difference, and the position deviation caused by the two keys is observed. In order to show the effect, this paper only selects the first 300 positions. The position sequence number difference corresponding to the DCT coefficient of is displayed in Fig. 10.

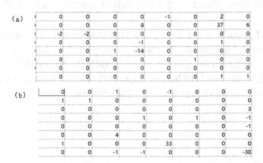

Fig. 9. Comparison of scrambling situation.(a) is the scrambling effect of DCT coefficients generated by the key 0.351236591 corresponding to a certain area. (b) is the scrambling effect of DCT coefficients generated by the key 0.351236592 corresponding to the same area.

It can be observed from Fig. 10 that the key is only modified by 1×10^{-9}, but the resulting positional scrambling sequence changes are very huge and very obvious.

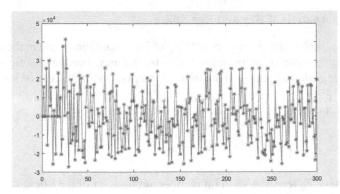

Fig. 10. The deviation of the DCT coefficient position sequence corresponding to the two keys

5 Conclusion

To strengthen users' participation in information hiding and improve the security of the existing classic F5 algorithm, we propose a controllable steganography algorithm based on chaos and user key. The DCT coefficient scrambling part of the F5 algorithm is replaced with a more secure and uniform chaotic scrambling. Then, the uniquely determined embedding matrix form used in the F5 algorithm is diversified to form a mapping with the user key, which satisfies not only the user's participation in the hiding process but also the improvement of the security of the steganography algorithm.

User-controllable steganography is specifically embodied in the control of the embedding position of secret information in this paper. Based on this, the scope of user control can be increased, such as controlling the selection of carrier sets, specific steganography algorithms, etc., to a greater extent User engagement.

Acknowledgement. The authors are deeply indebted to anonymous reviewers for their constructive suggestions and helpful comments. The work is supported by the National Key Research and Development Program of China (No. 2019YFB1406504), the National Natural Science Foundation of China (No. U1836108, No. U1936216, No. 62002197, No. 62001038) and the Fundamental Research Funds for the Central Universities (No.2021RC30).

References

1. Wang, Y., Zhang, W., Li, W., Yu, X., Yu, N.: Non-additive cost functions for color image steganography based on inter-channel correlations and differences. IEEE Trans. Inf. Forens. Secur. **15**, 2081–2095 (2020)
2. Yang, Z., Wang, K., Ma, S., Huang, Y., Kang, X., Zhao, X.: IStego100K: large-scale image steganalysis dataset. In: Wang, H., Zhao, X., Shi, Y., Kim, H.J., Piva, A. (eds.) Digital Forensics and Watermarking, pp. 352–364. Springer, Switzerland, Cham (2020)
3. Yang, Z., Peng, X., Huang, Y.: A Sudoku Matrix-Based Method of Pitch Period Steganography in Low-Rate Speech Coding. In: Lin, X., Ghorbani, A., Ren, K., Zhu, S., Zhang, A. (eds.) SecureComm 2017. LNICSSITE, vol. 238, pp. 752–762. Springer, Cham (2018). https://doi.org/10.1007/978-3-319-78813-5_40

4. Zhongliang, Y., Xueshun, P., Yongfeng, H., Chin-Chen, C.: A novel method of speech information hiding based on 3D-magic matrix. J. Internet Technol. **20**(4), 1167–1175 (2019)

5. Couchot, J.-F., Couturier, R., Guyeux, C.: STABYLO: steganography with adaptive, BBS, and binary embedding at low cost. Ann. Telecommun. Annales des Télécommun. **70**(9–10), 441–449 (2015)

6. Yang, Z., Wei, N., Liu, Q., Huang, Y., Zhang, Y.: GAN-TStega: Text Steganography Based on Generative Adversarial Networks. In: Wang, H., Zhao, X., Shi, Y., Kim, H.J., Piva, A. (eds.) IWDW 2019. LNCS, vol. 12022, pp. 18–31. Springer, Cham (2020). https://doi.org/10.1007/978-3-030-43575-2_2

7. Boukis, A.C., Reiter, K., Frölich, M., Hofheinz, D., Meier, M.A.R.: Multicomponent reactions provide key molecules for secret communication. Nat. Commun. **9**(1), 1439 (2018)

8. Sarkar, T., Selvakumar, K., Motiei, L., Margulies, D.: Message in a molecule. Nat. Commun. **7**(1), 11374 (2016)

9. Qu, Z., Chen, S., Wang, X.: A secure controlled quantum image steganography algorithm. Quantum Inf. Process. **19**(10), 1–25 (2020). https://doi.org/10.1007/s11128-020-02882-4

10. Yuwei, Y., Su, Y.: Research on security and authentication technology of two-dimensional code based on steganography and visual secret sharing. Intell. Comput. Appl. **10**(08), 14–18 (2020)

11. Yang, Z.: Research on an adaptive multi-modal information hiding system. Central China Normal University (2020)

12. Kolmogorov, A.: On conservation of conditionally periodic motions under small perturbations of the Hamiltonian. Dokl Akad Nauk SSSR **98**, 527–530 (1954)

13. Liu, W., Liu Yipei, Y.: Image encryption algorithm based on Logistic chaotic scrambling. Sci. Technol. Innov. **2020**(36), 125–126 (2020)

Author Index

Printed in the United States
by Baker & Taylor Publisher Services